CW01091607

1 MONTH OF
FREE
READING

at

www.ForgottenBooks.com

By purchasing this book you are eligible for one month membership to ForgottenBooks.com, giving you unlimited access to our entire collection of over 1,000,000 titles via our web site and mobile apps.

To claim your free month visit:

www.forgottenbooks.com/free646345

ISBN 978-0-656-24087-6
PIBN 10646345

This book is a reproduction of an important historical work. Forgotten Books uses
state-of-the-art technology to digitally reconstruct the work, preserving the original format
whilst repairing imperfections present in the aged copy. In rare cases, an imperfection in
the original, such as a blemish or missing page, may be replicated in our edition. We do,
however, repair the vast majority of imperfections successfully; any imperfections that
remain are intentionally left to preserve the state of such historical works.

The Victoria History of the
Counties of England
EDITED BY WILLIAM PAGE, F.S.A.

A HISTORY OF

SURREY

VOLUME III

OF THE COUNTIES
OF ENGLAND

SURREY

CONSTABLE AND COMPANY LIMITED

This History is issued to Subscribers only
By Constable & Company Limited
and printed by Eyre & Spottiswoode Limited
H.M. Printers of London

INSCRIBED
TO THE MEMORY OF
HER LATE MAJESTY
QUEEN VICTORIA
WHO GRACIOUSLY GAVE
THE TITLE TO AND
ACCEPTED THE
DEDICATION OF
THIS HISTORY

The Thames at Runnymede

HISTORY
COUNTY OF

EDITED BY

H. E. MALDEN, M A

(Hon. Fellow of Trinity Hall)

VOLUME THREE

)N)(

AND **COMPANY** LIMITED

911

THE
VICTORIA HISTORY
OF THE COUNTY OF

EDITED BY

H. E. MALDEN, M.A.

(Hon. Fellow of Trinity Hall)

VOLUME THREE

CONSTABLE AND COMPANY LIMITED
1911

CONTENTS OF VOLUME THREE

CONTENTS OF VOLUME THREE

CONTENTS OF VOLUME THREE

LIST OF ILLUSTRATIONS

LIST OF ILLUSTRATIONS

LIST OF ILLUSTRATIONS

LIST OF ILLUSTRATIONS

LIST OF ILLUSTRATIONS

LIST OF MAPS

EDITORIAL NOTE

THE Editor wishes to thank all those who have kindly assisted him by reading the proofs of this volume and have otherwise helped in passing the pages through the Press, particularly Mr. A. R. Bax, F.S.A.; the Rev. T. S. Cooper, M.A., F.S.A.; Mr. Julian S. Corbett, LL.M., F.S.A.; Mr. E. Gardner, M.B.; Mr. W. Edgar Horne; Miss Keate; Col. F. A. H. Lambert, F.S.A.; Mr. H. Lambert; and Mr. Percy Woods, C.B.

The Editor desires further to acknowledge the courtesy he has invariably received from all those to whom he has applied for information. He would more especially mention in this respect, His Grace the Lord Archbishop of Canterbury; the Rt. Hon. the Earl of Onslow, G.C.M.G.; the Rt. Hon. the Lord Hylton, F.S.A.; the Rt. Hon. the Lord Ashcombe; Sir Henry D. Le Marchant, Bart.; Lieut.-Colonel H. Godwin-Austen; Mr. F. W. Smallpeice; the late Rev. T. R. O'Fflahertie; and the Clerk of the Surrey County Council. He is also indebted in a like manner to His Grace the Duke of Norfolk, K.G.; His Grace the Duke of Northumberland, K.G.; the Lady Henry Somerset; the Rt. Rev. H. E. Ryle, D.D., Dean of Westminster; the Hon. Sir Charles Swinfen-Eady; the late Rev. Sir Edward G. Moon, Bart.; Sir John Watney, F.S.A.; the Rev. W. H. Ady, M.A.; the Rev. Edward Atkinson, D.D.; Mr. H. Cosmo O. Bonsor, D.L., J.P.; Miss Broadwood; Mr. H. Chancellor; the late Rev. J. R. Charlesworth; Mr. J. Collyer; Mr. W. Cunliffe, M.A.; Mr. F. B. Eastwood; the late Mr. W. J. Evelyn; Dr. W. E. St. Lawrence Finny; the Rev. J. K. Floyer, M.A., F.S.A.; the late Mr. G. Leveson-Gower; Mr. J. Henderson; the late Major Heales; Mr. Gordon Home; Miss Jackson; the Rev. A. H. Johnson, M.A.; Mr. A. H. Lloyd; Mr. F. Mount; the Rev. W. H. Oxley, M.A.; Mr. W. P. D. Stebbing; Mr. H. A. Style; Mr. F. Turner; Miss Ethel Lega-Weekes; the Rev. S. Wetherfield, M.A.; Miss Wheeler; and the late Mr. S. Woods.

Thanks are also tendered to Lord Northcliffe, Mr. Herbert O. Ellis, Mr. J. H. C. Evelyn, the Kingston Corporation, the Surrey Archaeological Society, and Mr. G. West, for the loan of pictures and plans for reproduction.

A HISTORY OF
SURREY

TOPOGRAPHY

THE HUNDRED OF GODALMING

CONTAINING THE PARISHES OF

ARTINGTON [1]	HAMBLEDON	PUTTENHAM
CHIDDINGFOLD	HASLEMERE	THURSLEY
COMPTON	PEPER HAROW	WITLEY
GODALMING		

The history of the hundred is generally coincident with that of the manor. The earliest definite reference to the hundred is the confirmation of Artington Manor, and possibly Godalming also, to Stephen de Turnham, in 1206.[2] In 1221 the king directed the Sheriff of Surrey to give full seisin of the manor of Godalming, the hundred, and the market (town) of Haslemere to Richard, Bishop of Salisbury, which manor, &c., were belonging to Edelina de Broc, *salvo iure nostro et heredium ipsius Edeline.*[3]

On 24 May 1224, Thomas de Bauelingham and Mabel his wife, eldest daughter and co-heir of Stephen de Turnham, levied a fine, and for 35 marks of silver gave to the Bishop and church of Salisbury, the bishop holding the hundred, all their rights in the hundred of Godalming, and in the manor of Godalming, saving to Thomas and Mabel the tenement which they held in Artington and Catteshull.[4]

It does not appear therefore that the bishop obtained full possession of the hundred till the reign of Henry III, and subsequently Witley, in the hundred, remained a royal manor of ancient demesne, having no connexion with the courts of the hundred, except in suits for the recovery of land and debts ; neither is Puttenham represented in the courts.

The hundred remained in the hands of the bishop till 1541. In that year it was conveyed, under an Act of Parliament, to Thomas Paston, and by him to the Crown, 20 April 1542.[5] Elizabeth granted the manor and hundred, 3 November 1601, to Sir George More of Loseley for £1,341 8s. 2¾d.[6]

---

[1] Including Littleton and Loseley, i.e. that part of the parish of St. Nicholas, Guildford, which lay outside the borough boundaries as they were in 1831. For the sake of convenience the account of the whole parish has been included in the hundred of Godalming. The extent of the hundred is taken from *Pop. Ret.* 1831, p. 632.

[2] *Rot. de Oblat. et Fin.* (Rec. Com.), 339. Compare the accounts of Artington and Godalming.

[3] *Rot. Lit. Claus.* (Rec. Com.), i, 455.

[4] Lib. Evident. B. no. 363, Salisbury.   [5] Aug. Off. Hen. VIII, Box C, 12.

[6] The original grant is at Loseley. It is copied by Symmes (Town Clerk of Guildford, temp. Chas. II), B.M. Add. MS. 6167. It contains a grant of the 'bondmen, bondwomen, villeins, and their sequele,' but this is probably only a customary form and does not mean that there were any then.

A HISTORY OF SURREY

The lordship of the hundred continued in the family of More and More-Molyneux of Loseley till 1871, when it was conveyed with the manor to Mr. James Stewart Hodgson. The lordship of the hundred was by this time meaningless. The courts of the hundred had become at an early period indistinguishable from those of the manor. There are at Loseley a large number of Hundred Court Rolls, views of frankpledge, and views of frankpledge on the rectory manor, from the time of Edward III downwards. Courts were held at three weeks' intervals for ' playnts and accions,' dealing with tenants of all the manors in the hundred except the royal manors of Witley and Puttenham. Two ' lawdays,' or leets, were held at Hocktide and Michaelmas, except for the town of Godalming, for which a ' lawday ' was held on St. Matthew's Day ; this was called Enton lawday. These included in their business the view of frankpledge, the *Visus Personatus*, election of tithing-men, of ale-taster, a reeve (*prepositus*) for Godalming by the customary tenants, and of a bedell, and the receiving of the burgage rents of Haslemere. There were also yearly leets at Catteshull, Hambledon, Loseley, Artington, Farncombe, and Compton. The hundred and three-weekly courts and Enton court were held, latterly at least, in the old town hall of Godalming, where the market house now stands.[7] Fines levied in the hundred court were accounted for to the More-Molyneux family as lords of the hundred up to at least 1790.[8]

[7] Rolls at Loseley, *passim*, and Misc. Bks. Exch. L.T.R. vol. 169 ; Godalming Hundred, 1–3 Edw. VI.
[8] Accts. at Loseley.

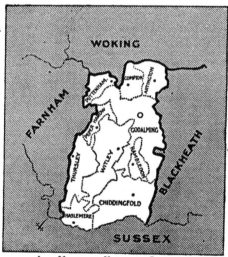

Index Map to the Hundred of Godalming

ARTINGTON

(IN THE PARISH OF ST. NICHOLAS, GUILDFORD)

Ertindun (xiii cent.)

The parish of St. Nicholas, Guildford, contains 2,693 acres. It is for the greater part of its eastern side bounded by the Wey, on the left bank of which it lies. A great part of the parish is in the borough of Guildford, and part has always been in the borough, so far as is known. But the rural part of the parish has always been in Godalming Hundred, and the parish, 3 miles north to south, 2 or 1½ miles east to west, was originally a rural parish. The idea suggested in old histories that Guildford was once in this parish on the left bank of the Wey is baseless. The name 'Bury Fields,' in St. Nicholas parish, refers of course to the town fields, not to the town. Neither have draining or building revealed any old foundations on the left bank. The Guildford Cemetery is in the parish of St. Nicholas, in the part included in the borough since 1904. It is under a joint committee on which the rural parish is represented.

The main part of the parish is on the Green Sand, with an outcrop of the Atherfield and of the Wealden Clay in the middle of it. But the northern part crosses the chalk ridge of the Hog's Back and reaches on to the Woolwich Beds and London Clay beyond.

Guildford station is in the parish, and of late years, in the neighbourhood of the station and on the Hog's Back, building has much increased. The Portsmouth road also traverses the parish, and houses extend along it for a mile, connecting Guildford with the hamlet of St. Catherine's. The old Portsmouth road came past St. Nicholas's Church, along Bury Fields, and up what was called the Little Mount into the line of the present road. The old Farnham road came along the ridge of the Hog's Back and down the Great Mount by a very steep descent.[1] The Act of Parliament for making the new Farnham road was passed in 1796, but the road was not begun till some years later. A parcel of land south of the Great Mount is in Farnham Manor, and was the site probably of a lodging of the Bishop of Winchester when he was travelling on the road. The end of the Hog's Back is known as Guildown, and this old Farnham road is the *Strata de Geldedone* referred to in the Pipe Rolls of 1189 as the southern boundary of the purlieu of Windsor Forest.

In the south of the parish part of the common called Peasemarsh is included. Great part of this was inclosed in 1803. It is very poor soil. In the old river gravel on it some palaeolithic flints have been found.

The northern part of the parish beyond the Hog's Back is called Guildford Park. This was the site of the old royal park of Guildford. Much of the history of the park is involved in that of the forest of Windsor, the Surrey bailiwick of which extended over the whole county north of the Hog's Back and

west of the Wey. It would appear that Henry II inclosed the park at the beginning of his reign.[2] The custody of the park often went with the office of constable of the castle and steward of the king's manor, for Guildford was a royal manor and castle from before the Conquest. There was a manor-house in the park, but it was quite a small place. The residence of the kings, who were frequently in Guildford, was in the castle. It was here that the extensive buildings and decorations of Henry III were executed, not at the park manor-house, for they involved buying of land for the extension of the building, an impossibility at the latter place, which lay in the middle of the park surrounded by the king's land on every side. In 1299 the park was assigned to Margaret, second wife of Edward I,[3] but reverted to the Crown under Edward II. When Edward III granted the royal manor in fee-farm to the good men (*probi homines*) of Guildford the park and castle were reserved. Helming Leggette was given the custody of the park for life in 1370.[4] On the decease of Sir Hugh Waterton it was granted to Sir John Stanley for life in 1409–10.[5] In 1444 it was granted to John Genyu and Richard Ludlow, serjeants of the king's cellar, and to Richard's heirs.[6] But in 1463 Edward IV granted it to Thomas St. Leger, who married his sister Anne, widow of the Duke of Exeter, and gave him the further charge of certain enlargements of the park made before 1475–6.[7] St. Leger received the herbage and pannage of the park, without rendering account, and £10 a year for the maintenance of the deer in winter.[8] The manor of Cleygate in Ash was granted to St. Leger in 1475,[9] for the further maintenance of the game. He was attainted for rebellion against Richard III, when the custody of the park was perhaps given to William Mistelbroke, who received Cleygate.[10] In 1488 Sir Reginald Bray received the custody of the park, and Cleygate.[11] Sir Michael Stanhope was the next holder.[12] When Guildford Grammar School was re-founded by Edward VI, the Marquis of Northampton held it.[13] Under Elizabeth Lord Montague was keeper, and had much anxiety with poachers of deer and snarers of rabbits and pheasants.[14] He died 1592, and Sir Thomas Gorges, who had married Northampton's widow, was perhaps the next keeper. In his time Norden's survey was executed. He describes the park as of 6¼ miles' circuit with 7½ miles of pales. Part of the southern side was inclosed and cultivated. It contained 1,620 acres by estimation, and was 'meanely timbered,' not enough to repair the pales. There were about 600 fallow deer, but 'not above 30 bucks,' i.e. males of two years old and upwards. The manor-house was 'puled down and defaced.' This stood, by his plan, where the farm called Manor Farm is now. There were three other lodges. The chief lodge was by the bank of the river, and is partly

---

[1] Long poles used to be put through the hind wheels of the coaches coming down this hill.
[2] Close, 9 Hen. III, m. 6.
[3] Pat. 27 Edw. I, m. 4.
[4] Pat. 43 Edw. III, pt. i, m. 33.

[5] Pat. 10 Hen. IV, pt. ii, m. 13.
[6] Pat. 22 Hen. VI, pt. ii, m. 2.
[7] Exch. Accts. bdle. 516, no. 11.
[8] Pat. 2 Edw. IV, pt. ii, m. 14.
[9] Pat. 15 Edw. IV, pt. ii, m. 4.
[10] Pat. 1 Ric. III, pt. iv, m. 12.

[11] MS. of Mr. Anstis, quoted by Manning and Bray, *Hist. of Surr.* i, 514.
[12] Mr. Anstis' MS., Manning and Bray *Surr.* i, 25.
[13] Chart. of the school.
[14] Loseley MSS. *passim.*

3

standing now as a farm-house at the end of Walnut Tree Close, between the railway and the river. The 'Deer Leap,' or place for taking deer alive, was by the side of the Great Mount, where a path now leads from the mount to the new Farnham road.[15] Mr. Carter was then under-keeper. He was the Mr. John Carter who later received a grant of Guildford Castle. Gorges died in 1610, and John Murray, afterwards Earl of Annandale, succeeded. In 1631 Charles I granted it to him in fee-simple, to be held as for a quarter of a knight's fee, and by his heirs for ever.[16] His son, the second earl, died childless, and the Guildford Park Estate was ultimately sold in 1709 to the Hon. Thomas Onslow, afterwards Lord Onslow, and the park was disparked before 1717. The park extended from the road on the Hog's Back to the road between Woodbridge and Worplesdon, and from close to the river to a line of hedges and a green lane east of a small stream and west of Strawberry Grove, which exactly corresponds to the boundary on John Norden's plan.

West of St. Catherine's Hill stand St. Catherine's House, in which the late Mr. W. More-Molyneux lived, and Mount Browne, the residence of the Dowager Marchioness of Sligo. Littleton School was built by Mr. James More-Molyneux of Loseley in 1843. It has been recently enlarged, and a service is celebrated there on Sundays by a curate of St. Nicholas. It was let to the County Council in 1903. A new school is in course of erection.

ARTINGTON MANOR was originally MANORS a part of Godalming, from which it was separated by Henry II, who, about the year 1171, bestowed it on Master David of London, an ambassador at Rome.[17] This Master David granted it in fee farm to Ralph de Broc for £15, with whose daughter Stephen de Turnham had it in marriage.[18] In 1191 and again in 1205 Stephen obtained royal confirmations of his right to the manor.[19] In 1220, shortly after Stephen's death, his widow Edelina, daughter of Ralph de Broc, put forward her claim to certain rents in Artington against Stephen's five co-heiresses, Mabel wife of Thomas de Bauelingham, Alice wife of Adam de Bendeng, Eleanor wife of Roger de Layburn, Eleanor wife of Ralph son of Bernard, and Beatrice wife of Ralph de Fay.[20] Edelina entered into the land, but probably only for life. The manor was divided into four portions, of which Mabel de Bauelingham obtained one, the manor of Artington; Beatrice de Fay a second; a third portion, which was Alice de Bendeng's, afterwards formed part or the whole of the manor of Braboeuf; and a fourth became the manor of Piccard's.

Artington Manor, i.e. the portion of the original manor which was assigned to Mabel de Bauelingham, descended with her manor of Catteshull[21] till William Weston and his wife Joan sold the latter in 1384–5, but retained Artington.[22] A rent roll of William Weston's lands in Artington, dated 3 November 1394, is among the Loseley Manuscripts.[23] John Weston of Weston died seised of Artington 17 November 1440, leaving three married daughters, Agnes wife of John atte Hull, Joan wife of John Skynet, and Anne wife of Thomas Slifield.[24] Of these we find that Agnes atte Hull died in widowhood in the year 1488 seised of the manor of Artington, Henry atte Hull being her grandson and heir.[25] The overlordship was conveyed to Sir George More of Godalming, 3 November 1601, and the manor of Artington has since been in the family of More of Loseley. Artington Manor Farm was the manor house.

BRABOEUF MANOR, which extends very widely about St. Catherine's Hill and towards Godalming, includes that portion of Stephen de Turnham's manor which was assigned to his daughter Alice de Bendeng, for she granted her portion of Artington to Geoffrey of Braboeuf in 1232,[26] and he had confirmation of the grant in 1251.[27] He had other lands in Artington and Guildford, and in 1257, together with Richard Testard, obtained a royal grant of the sites of old mills in Guildford which they had recently sold to the king, and also of new mills which they were to remove to the site of the old ones.[28] Cicely 'la Braboeuf' held a quarter of the manor at 'Artington next Braboeuf' at her death in 1347,[29] probably as dower. John Braboeuf witnessed deeds of Artington in 1337 and again in 1350.[30] Andrew Braboeuf, son of Andrew and Cecily de Braboeuf, died seised of one quarter of Artington in 1361–2, leaving a daughter Agnes,[31] who married first Robert Danhurst, and secondly, Robert Loxley. At her death her grandson Robert Danhurst inherited her lands. He died s.p.m. in 1481–2, having settled Braboeuf on Bernard Jenyn and his wife Elizabeth, who was niece of Agnes Braboeuf's second husband Robert Loxley.[32] Bernard Jenyn settled the manor on his second son Thomas,[33] who died in March 1508–9.[34] Sir John Jenyn, kt., son of Thomas Jenyn, died holding Braboeuf in 1545, leaving a son Edward aged five,[35] who died a minor and was succeeded by his aunt Joan, wife of Robert Kemp.[36] Agnes, wife of John Wight of Wimbledon, and daughter of Joan Kemp, was in possession of Braboeuf in 1559,[37] and was succeeded by her son Rice (Riceus) Wight, who died at Artington 31 October 1602. His son John was born in 1674 and died in 1656, his son John did

---

[15] Norden's Surv. 1606; Harl. MSS. 3749.   [16] Cart. Chas. I, R. 8, m. 2.
[17] Pipe R. 17 Hen. II (Pipe R. Soc.), 144 et seq.
[18] Testa de Nevill (Rec. Com.), 225. It seems probable therefore that Master David only had a life interest in Artington, and that after his death Stephen de Turnham held it of the gift of Henry II.
[19] Pipe R. 3 Ric. I, m. 3; Rot. Cart. (Rec. Com.), 160.
[20] Maitland, Bracton's Note Bk. 1410; Excerpta e Rot. Fin. (Rec. Com.), ii, 25. There was apparently another daughter Clemency, see Piccard's Manor.

[21] Vide infra.
[22] Feet of F. Surr. 8 Ric. II, 73, 75.
[23] Hist. MSS. Com. Rep. vii, App. pt. i, 599.
[24] Chan. Inq. p.m. 19 Hen. VI, no. 5.
[25] Ibid. (Ser. 2), iv, 14.
[26] Cal. Chart. R. (Rec. Com.), i, 366. It seems probable that he already possessed a tenement called Braboeuf in Artington. Indeed, in 1496 it was declared that 'the manor of Braboeuf and the manor of Artington are not one, nor was any part of it ever part of Artington.' Memo. R. Exch. L.T.R. Trin. 11 Hen. VII, m. xvi. It seems, however, that the lords of Braboeuf also possessed a part of the original manor of Artington.

[27] Add. Chart. 24582, 24583, 24584.
[28] Cal. Chart. R. (Rec. Com.), i, 456.
[29] Chan. Inq. p.m. 22 Edw. III (1st nos.), no. 20.
[30] Montagu Burrows, The Family of Brocas, 430–2.
[31] Chan. Inq. p.m. 35 Edw. III (1st nos.), no. 21.
[32] Memo. R. (Exch. L.T.R.), Trin. 11 Hen. VII, m. 16, 'Recorda'; Feet of F. Surr. 42 Edw. III, 1; 10 Ric. II, 23.
[33] Chan. Inq. p.m. (Ser. 2), lxxxiii, 20.
[34] Ibid. xxv, 48.   [35] Ibid. lxxii, 96.
[36] Ibid. cxiii, 46.
[37] Feet of F. Surr. Trin. 1 Eliz.

1707 and was succeeded by his eldest surviving son William, who died in 1722, and his son Tempest Wight died 1768.   John Wight, his son, died 1817, his son Arthur Wight died 1847, having married Jane More-Molyneux of Loseley. His son Albert Wight died in 1905, and his widow, *née* Mary Anne Boulderson, is lady of the manor.[88]

Braboeuf Manor House is now occupied by Mr. J. A. C. Younger. It has been much modernized, but retains much of its original 16th-century work. It was evidently a half-timber house consisting of a main body facing east, as at present, with projecting wings at either end ; the north wing has disappeared, but the south wing still stands with the main portion. To the south of this old building are a modern dining-room and conservatory, and a modern wing extending to the west.

The walls are now of modern stone, with mullioned windows. The ground floor of the main (former) central body contains the hall, entered directly by the main entrance close to the south wing ; the library, at the north end of the hall, and doubtless once a part of it ; and the stair hall and other rooms to the west, behind the hall, &c. The south wing contains chiefly the billiard-room. Over the hall is the drawing-room, with a fine fireplace (dated 1586), and bedrooms, &c., and on the second floor are attic bedrooms.

The entrance doorway—now within a modern porch—has an old oak moulded frame. The hall has a good late 16th-century ceiling, with heavy beams running east and west, and a shallower one running lengthwise (north and south), and upon the latter and the walls are the joists, also running east and west ; all the beams and joists have moulded soffits. The fireplace on the west side of the hall contains some 17th-century carving, made up with later work ; the walls of the hall are lined with late 16th or early 17th-century panelling ; some of it is set in an irregular fashion. Doorways at the ends give access to the library and billiard-room, and an archway opposite the entrance doorway open on to the stair hall. The thin wall dividing the hall from the library is evidently a later insertion, but it is covered with the old panelling on the hall side. The library has a plain plaster ceiling, which probably conceals some moulded woodwork as in the hall, and a heavy encased wood girder close to the partition would, no doubt, prove to be similar to the others. In the library is a large cupboard front containing some of the original carved late 16th-century oak work in its cornice, &c., made up with more modern woodwork ; it stood formerly against the partition at the south end of the hall. The staircase is late 17th-century work ; it has turned balusters, and heavy panelled square newels with shaped heads, and very heavy moulded handrail, 8 in. by 7 in.

The drawing-room on the first floor has a good stone fireplace and chimneypiece in its outer or east wall between the two windows. The opening has a flat, four-centred arch, enriched with leaf and rose ornament ; above this is a fluted frieze with roses and portcullises. The rest of the space above this is divided by pilasters into two bays, the lower parts treated as panels with a moulded cornice, and containing leaf designs ; the upper parts filled with a large Tudor rose and a portcullis carved in high relief; each is surmounted by a small crown. At the top, close to the ceiling, is carved the date 1586. The whole of the fireplace is decorated with paint, most of it modern, but said to be a restoration of the original colour. The room has modern oak wall lining, and an enriched plaster ceiling of four bays divided by moulded wood beams. In some of the bedrooms on this floor are some 17th-century panelling and plain old beams, and one of the attic bedrooms also has some similar panelling below its window.

Over the porch entrance outside is set a small old stone, carved with a representation of a phoenix, perhaps the mark of an insurance company.

The grounds and park contain nothing of note. There appears to have been no formal garden about the house, or it has long since disappeared, as also has the ancient dovecot which is mentioned in various old records.

Beatrice de Fay's portion of Artington consisted of 20*s.* rent and a quarter of a mill. These she granted to the abbey of Wherwell, co. Hants, towards the maintenance of a chaplain to celebrate in the chapel of St. Mary in the little meadow called St. Mary's Garden.[39] In 1241-2 the abbess sued her tenants in Artington for rent.[40] At the time of the surrender of the abbey in November 1539 lands and rent in Artington were still amongst its possessions.[41] These were leased out by the Crown from time to time, the lessee in 1567 being Michael Kettelwell,[42] and in 1595 Sir John Wolley, kt.[43] At this date the lands included 'Millmeade' in Guildford. Sir John's son Francis Wolley possibly obtained a grant in perpetuity, for he bequeathed his lands in Artington to ' the maiden child christened by his wife and Mrs. Bridget Weston in Pirford Church by name of Mary Wolley,' with remainder to Sir Arthur Mainwaring.[44] The latter was disputing lands called the ' Holy Lands' in Artington in 1628 ; they had lately been the property of Wherwell Abbey, and were claimed by a certain Thomas Tuesley. At this date they included ' an ancient dwelling-house'[45] near St. Catherine's Hill, various fields at Artington, and one-sixth of Millmead.[46] The estates have since been broken up, and part has been bought by the Wight family.

LITTLETON near Loseley Park is a hamlet of Artington, and now consists of Orange Court, Orange Court Farm, and a few cottages. Littleton is mentioned in the Domesday Survey as being held by Wulwi the huntsman, who had been in possession of it before the Conquest.[47] Under Edward the Confessor it was assessed for 2 hides and paid no geld, but in 1086 it was only assessed for 1 virgate. In 1218-19

88 Parish Reg. of St. Nicholas, Guildford.
89 Probably the chapel of the Blessed Virgin, with which the Abbess Euphemia inclosed a large space 'which was adorned on the north side with pleasant Vines and trees.' V.C.H. Hants, ii, 133. Egerton MS. 2104 (A), no. 254.

40 Feet of F. Surr. 26 Hen. III, 273, 274, 279.
41 Misc. Bks. Aug. Off. ccccxiv, 17-21.
42 Enr. of Leases (Aug. Off.), 9 Eliz. R. 4, no. 3.
43 Partic. for Leases, Surr. 37 Eliz. R. 2, no. 23.
44 Chan. Inq. p.m. (Ser. 2), cccxxxiv, 60. See under Burpham in Worplesdon.

45 Possibly the house now called the Priory, some of which is very old.
46 Exch. Spec. Com. 6 Chas. I, no. 5666 ; 5 Chas. I, no. 5665 ; Exch. Dep. Mich. 4 Chas. I, 21.
47 V.C.H. Surr. i, 328b.

William le Gras of Littleton granted 2 acres in a field called la Hulle and other land on 'Lidhe' and Guildown to Robert son of William of Littleton for a yearly rent.[48] In 1285 Nicholas le Gras, who was Sheriff of Surrey, obtained a grant of free warren in his demesne lands of Littleton and Artington.[49] He died before December 1293,[50] and seems to have been succeeded by Ralph le Gras,[51] whose brother and heir was Roger. Roger le Gras died seised of the manor of Littleton on 28 November 1303, having been murdered in Essex.[52] His heir was his brother Nicholas, aged twenty-two.[53] It then included a capital messuage and three free tenants and an annual rent held of John of Cobham by service of entertaining him in food and drink for two nights yearly.[54] Nicholas le Gras, brother to Roger, was in possession of it in 1323-4.[55] The manor included much more than the present hamlet and ran up to the road (via regia) on the Hog's Back.[56] It is interesting to see that these old manors, Loseley and Littleton, were, like the old parishes generally,[57] bounded by the ridge of the chalk downs. John le Em of Compton had lands and rent there in 1325,[58] and William Shepherd and his wife Margaret sold 60 acres of land and 2s. 6d. rent in Littleton to Arnold Brocas in 1394 (vide Loseley), probably for the use of William Sidney, with whose half of Loseley it seems to have since descended. It is now held with Loseley.

In 1406-7 a Richard atte Park held land in Littleton.[60] A house called 'Hamptons' was sold with land in Littleton in 1630,[61] while Orange Court Farm was purchased circa 1750 by Sir William More-Molyneux of Loseley. John Orange is among Artington tenants in a 14th-century roll; and in 1464 Robert Bussebrigge left in perpetuity lands in St. Nicholas, Guildford, called Orenges to Thomas Costyn, and in 1481 Henry Costyn succeeded.[62]

LOSELEY MANOR (Losele xi cent., Lousle xiii cent., Loseley xvi cent. et seq.), which was held before the Conquest by Osmund the thegn, was assessed at 2 hides in 1086, and was at that time in possession of Earl Roger of Shrewsbury, who had also obtained Osmund's manor of Eaton Mewsey in Wiltshire. Loseley was held of Earl Roger by Turold,[63] who, with his successors, continued to hold it of the various lords of Eaton Mewsey.[64] Among the under-tenants, successors of Turold, was Richard de Dol, one of the supporters of the barons in their struggle against John.[65] He held 2 hides in Loseley to Hugh de Dol in January 1204-5.[66] Loseley descended to Robert son of Hugh de Dol, whose widow Eleanor obtained from the overlord the custody of the manor during the minority of Robert's son and heir, also named Robert. She pledged it in 1285

to Henry Gerard of Guildford for six years.[67] In 1316-17 'Elbrede atte Park de Lousle in viduitate mea' granted land in Loseley to Robert and his wife Isabella. This was the northern part of the manor, bounded by the 'via regia de Guldedone,' i.e. the Hog's Back road.[68] It shows that the whole had not been acquired in 1204-5. This Robert was commissioner of array for Surrey in 1324,[69] and made an agreement four years before his death by which his daughter Joan had for life the whole of the profits of the manor, together with Loseley Hall, while he himself only retained the solar or upper room to the east of Loseley Hall and an annual rent of 20 marks.[70] He died 22 March 1355-6, leaving as heirs the same daughter Joan de Bures, then a widow aged sixty, and John de Norton, grandson and heir of his second daughter Margaret. The solar and rent were divided between them in 1357,[71] and the custody of John de Norton's lands was granted to John de Tye.[72] After the death of Joan de Bures in March 1371-2 one moiety of Loseley descended to her son William de Bures, on whom she had entailed it, while the other moiety was inherited by John Norton, great-grandson of her sister Margaret.[73] This second moiety was committed to the custody of William de Brantingham during the minority of John Norton.[74] In 1395 John Crosse conveyed lands in Loseley to Master Arnold Brocas and others, evidently trustees.[75] One moiety of the manor, probably the Norton moiety,[76] was eventually obtained by William Sidney. He was the William Sidney to whom Margaret, then wife of Robert Danhurst, released lands in Artington in 1426-7.[77] William Sidney died 1449, and his elder son William acknowledged the right of his mother, Thomasine, to half Loseley Manor in dower in 1452,[78] and died seised of the reversion, as was said, in October 1463.[79]

This William Sidney, described as of Stoke D'Abernon and of Baynards, left two daughters, Elizabeth and Anne, subsequently married to John Hampden and William Uvedale. But he had a younger brother, also named William Sidney, of 'Kyngsham' (Sussex), whose son Humphrey successfully claimed the moiety of Loseley under the will of William Sidney, his grandfather, after the death of Thomasine his grandmother, who survived both her sons William and died in January 1498. This claim was made in 1508. There is a large parchment roll at Loseley of an Inspeximus of the Record of Proceedings before the barons of the Exchequer enrolled Michaelmas term 23 Henry VII (1508). The unsuccessful parties were the widow and daughters of William. Humphrey Sidney's attorney was Christopher More, and the suit is evidently connected with the acquisition

48 Feet of F. Surr. 3 Hen. III, 20.
49 Chart. R. 13 Edw. I, m. 4.
50 Cal. Close, 1288-96, p. 339.
51 Ibid. 444.
52 Cal. Pat. 1301-7, pp. 272, 459.
53 Chan. Inq. p.m. 32 Edw. I, no. 47.
54 Ibid.
55 Pipe R. 17 Edw. II, 'De Ob. Sust.'
56 D. of 8 Hen. IV, referred to below.
57 V.C.H. Surr. ii, 6.
58 Feet of F. Surr. 18 Edw. II, 83.
59 Ibid. 18 Ric. II, 55.
60 D. at Loseley—compare 'Elbrede atte Park de Lousle,' below.

61 Com. Pleas D. Enr. East. 6 Chas. I, m. 17.
62 D. at Loseley.
63 V.C.H. Surr. i, 314a.
64 De Banco R. 60, m. 83; Chan. Inq. p.m. 30 Edw. III, 45; ibid. 8 Edw. II, 68.
65 Rot. Lit. Claus. i, 285, 307.
66 Feet of F. Surr. 6 John, file 3, no. 17.
67 Wrottesley, Pedigrees from the Plea R. 433; De Banco R. 60, m. 83.
68 D. at Loseley.
69 Parl. Writs (Rec. Com.), ii (2), 666, (21).
70 Chan. Inq. p.m. 30 Edw. III, no. 45.

71 Abbrev. Rot. Orig. (Rec. Com.), ii, 241.
72 Ibid. ii, 252.
73 Chan. Inq. p.m. 45 Edw. III (1st nos.), no. 4.
74 Fine R. 1 Ric. II, pt. i, m. 21.
75 Close, 19 Ric. II, m. 29 d.
76 Vide infra.
77 Feet of F. Surr. 5 Hen. VI, 20. A year later William Sidney and John Strode held one fee in Loseley; Lay Subs. R. bdle. 184, no. 75.
78 Harl. Chart. 56, B. 25; and Loseley R. below.
79 Exch. Inq. p.m. (Ser. 1), file 1805, no. 2.

by More of the Sidney moiety, which he after-wards held. In 1515–16 Sir Christopher More acquired the rights of John Twistleton, goldsmith, of London, probably a mortgagee ; and before 1532–3 he had evidently purchased this moiety in addi-tion to the other (*vide infra*), for William son of Humphrey Sidney then released all his rights to him.[80]

The other moiety was in the hands of a John Strode and Katherine his wife in 1429, and of Katherine widow of John and John her son in 1435, and of a Robert Strode in 1454–5.[81] They, in granting a lease of land bounded by William Sidney's land, spoke of 'nostra pars de manerio de Losele,' and gave the grant at Loseley. This moiety there-fore may possibly have included the manor-house, and may have been the Bures moiety. Robert Strode, heir of Thomas Strode, conveyed to trustees, 8 October 1476,[82] and by this means no doubt the moiety was acquired by John Westbroke, for John Westbroke held his first court at Loseley in 1481.[83] John Westbroke was summoned to warrant the manor of Loseley to Gilbert Stoughton and Thomas Purvoche in 1500,[84] and on 31 October 1508 John Westbroke of Godalming sold to Christopher More, gentleman, all his moiety of Loseley Manor, reserv-ing an annuity to himself and his wife Elizabeth for life.[85] Christopher More held his first court at Loseley 11 January 1508–9.[86] In 1530 he had licence to inclose 12 acres of land and a grant of free warren and free fishery within the park, of which this may have been the nucleus.[87] Sir Christopher More died 1549. His son William be-gan to build the present house, which was completed in 1569.[88] William, who was knighted in 1576, was the

More of Loseley. A-zure a cross argent with five martlets sable thereon.

most trusted agent of Elizabeth's Government in Surrey, and a special favourite of the queen. The lords lieutenant, the two Lords Howard of Effing-ham, and the Council, seem to have remitted all business to him. He also acquired much property in the county and elsewhere. In 1570 the Earl of Southampton was removed to his custody and remained at Loseley for three years.[89] Queen Elizabeth visited the house three times, in 1576, 1583, and again in 1591.[90] Sir William's son and heir, Sir George More, kt., who succeeded to the estate in 1600,[91] was Lieutenant of the Tower, and represented both Guildford and Surrey county in Parliament, as his father had done before him.[92] He was twice visited by James I at Loseley.[93] He died and was buried in the Loseley Chapel, St. Nicholas,

Guildford, in 1632, his heir being Poynings, son of his eldest son Sir Robert More, kt., who had predeceased his father.[94] Loseley remained the pro-perty of his heirs male till 1689, when at the death of Robert More, the then holder, his sister and sole surviving heiress, Margaret wife of Sir Thomas Molyneux,[95] inherited the manor. Their eldest son, Sir William More-Molyneux, died 1760. His eldest son James had died the year before. His son Thomas More-Molyneux died unmarried in 1776, and left the property to his sisters in succession, and then to James Freeman *alias* Molyneux, son of Jane Freeman, who was afterwards the wife of Samuel Hill of Duke Street, gentleman. James, son of Thomas, became owner in 1802, as James More-Molyneux, and died 1823. His son James died 1874. William More-Molyneux, son of James,[95a] died 1907. The present owner is Mrs. More-Molyneux McCowan, daughter of his brother, Admiral Sir Robert More-Molyneux.

View of frankpledge was held at Loseley by the Bishop of Salisbury as lord of Godalming ;[96] and thus when the Mores of Loseley obtained Godalm-ing they also obtained the right of view of frankpledge on their manor of Loseley. There was an oratory in this manor from the end of the 14th century, when Robert de Dol had licence to hear mass there.[97] Sir George More enlarged the new house and. added a chapel where he held licence for services in 1605.[98] But this extension became ruinous, and was pulled down by the late Mr. James More-Molyneux about 1835.

Loseley lies about 2 miles to the south-west of Guild-ford. There was certainly a moated house near this site at a much earlier date, but the present mansion was built from the ground between 1563 and 1569, by Sir William More. Sir Christopher More, who came out of Derbyshire, must have occupied from about 1515 an older house which probably stood on the site of the lawn to the south of the present house, and he obtained in 1530 a licence to empark. The 'park' still remains, and forms—with its green turf, flower-gardens, and trees, gathering on the west into a great avenue which is perhaps more like a forest ride—a worthy setting for the fine old house.

As originally planned, the house of 1563 was to have occupied three sides of a square, a central gate-house and flanking walls, with perhaps minor offices, forming the fourth side, thus leaving a great open quadrangle in the middle. In conformity with this clinging to earlier traditions in planning is the style of architecture in which the house is built, which leans to the older Gothic in all its forms, rather than to the Renaissance.

The original plan was never fully carried out, but was confined in execution to the main block of the south side of the square, thus giving the principal

[80] Copy of Inq. p.m. and deeds at Loseley.
[81] Deeds at Loseley.
[82] Ibid.
[83] Fragment of roll there.
[84] Feet of F. Surr. Trin. 15 Hen. VII, 13 ; De Banco R. 15 Hen. VII, m. 21.
[85] Add. Chart. 13557. More was, as we have seen, simultaneously acquiring the Sidney moiety.
[86] Loseley MSS.
[87] Pat. 22 Hen. VIII, pt ii, m. 3.

The present park is much more than 12 acres.
[88] See *Arch.* xxxvi, 294, where there is printed an account of the expenses of building Loseley House, and also an inventory of the goods of William More in 1556.
[89] Kempe, *Loseley MSS.* 229 et seq.
[90] *Hist. MSS. Com. Rep.* vii, App. 629, 638, 649.
[91] Chan. Inq. p.m. (Ser. 2), cclxiv, 179.
[92] *Return of Members of Parl.* pt. i.

[93] *Dict. Nat. Biog.* xxxviii, 414.
[94] Chan. Inq. p.m. (Ser. 2), ccccxxxvii, 106.
[95] Inscription in church of St. Nicholas, Guildford.
[95a] The writer desires to acknowledge his obligations to this gentleman for the free use of his MSS.
[96] *Hist. MSS. Com. Rep.* vii, App. 599, 600, &c.
[97] Egerton MS. 2033, fol. 53b.
[98] Licence at Loseley.

front to the north—a fact that, with the sombre colour of the stonework, and the stone roofs, accounts for the somewhat gloomy aspect of the house. Early in the 17th century, however, a considerable addition was made by Sir George More, the son of the founder, in the shape of a western wing, which included a gallery 121 ft. long by 18 ft. wide, and a chapel. This wing, said to have been designed by the famous John Thorpe, was entirely removed about 1835, but more recently a low range of offices has been erected in the rear of the house. Built of Bargate stone rubble, with dressings of firestone or clunch, the main front consists of a series of gables and interspaces backed by the long line of the main roof and planned with a pleasing irregularity, to which the numerous stacks of brick chimneys contribute. The pedimental doorway is of classical design and of 17th-century date, but in all other respects the front exhibits its original features, most noticeable of which are the long ranges of mullioned windows, in groups of two, three, four, and six lights. The early character of the work is evidenced in these, which have elliptical heads to the lights and a hood-mould with returned ends, such as might have been employed in work fifty years older in date. The great window of the hall bay is very tall and of three tiers of eight lights, including those in the return walls. Among the other coats and badges preserved in its glazing are the arms of the More family, with the date 1563.

The rear of the house is not so imposing. At the south-east angle is a large projecting group of gables, and a garden porch of later character occupies the centre of the recessed portion, with smaller gables to the right and dormers in the roof over.

In the interior the drawing-room is remarkable for its elaborate frieze, on which appears the rebus of the More family, a mulberry-tree intertwined with the motto, Morus tarde Moriens—Morum cito Moriturum. The room is panelled from floor to ceiling, and the latter is a fine specimen of plaster rib-work with pendants and devices framed in the geometrical patterns, among them being the cockatrice (which occurs in other rooms also), a bearing of the Mudge family, to which Sir William More's mother belonged. The great window of this room is of six lights, three on either side of a broad pier, which in the interior is finished as a carved console.

The stately mantelpiece, a masterpiece of delicate carving in hard chalk, may without exaggeration be placed among the finest things of its kind in England. The fireplace opening is spanned by a flat arch, with rusticated keystones, and flanked by caryatides and coupled Corinthian columns, which stand upon pedestals bearing swags of fruit. Above is a frieze of arabesque or strap pattern, surmounted by a modillion cornice : and the overmantel is formed of six panels enriched with scrolled cartouches, bearing coats of arms, and framed in by male and female caryatides holding up the carved frieze and cornice under the ceiling.[98a]

Many of the other rooms have panelling, ceilings, and other features of interest, and the character of the house has been admirably kept up by the successive generations of its owners.

In some of the upper rooms are fine tapestries, including a good specimen of the Mortlake Tapestry. There was at one time a collection of armour and weapons which were mostly exhibited in the great hall, but these have been removed, and their place is now taken by pictures, many of which are of great interest, such as those of James I and Anne of Denmark, painted in celebration of their visit to Sir George More in 1603 ; and the large painting of Sir William More-Molyneux with his wife Cassandra and all their children. Besides these there are in other parts of the house many portraits of the More and Molyneux families ; and, among royal and eminent personages, Edward VI, presented by Henry VIII to Sir Christopher More; Anne Boleyn; Queen Elizabeth, presented by herself to Sir William More ; and Sir Thomas More, who was, however, no connexion of this More family.

The finest collection of manuscripts of family, local, and public interest, which is preserved in any private house in Surrey, is at Loseley. Sir Christopher, Sir William, and Sir George More, the three generations of owners whose lives covered the time from the beginning of the 16th century till the early part of the reign of Charles I, were continually employed in the public service. The first was King's Remembrancer in the Exchequer, Sheriff and member for the county ; Sir William was at different times or simultaneously Sheriff, Deputy-Lieutenant, and member for the county or for Guildford, and Vice-Admiral of Sussex ; Sir George was Sheriff, Deputy-Lieutenant, member of Parliament, and also Lieutenant of the Tower, Chancellor of the Garter, and Treasurer to the Prince of Wales ; Sir William was also executor to Sir Thomas Cawarden, who was Master of the Revels from Henry VIII to the first year of Elizabeth, and kept his papers. They were also stewards of manors, constables of the castle, and keepers of the chase at Farnham, and all of them active justices of the peace. In these various capacities they received a vast quantity of official correspondence, besides private letters from many persons of importance. The bulk of these letters is preserved in twelve volumes, but over and above there is a great mass of letters, accounts, memoranda, Hundred Rolls and Court Rolls of Godalming Hundred and of many manors, deeds and printed pamphlets. The greater number belong to the Tudor reigns and the time of James I, but they extend earlier and later. Among them are letters and papers of Dr. John Donne (1573–1631), poet and Dean of St. Paul's, who was imprisoned in the Marshalsea for clandestinely marrying Anne daughter of Sir George More. Later papers of much interest are memorials of a tour in Spain in the 18th century. Mr. A. J. Kempe printed a small selection of papers in extenso in 1835.[99] William Bray, the historian of Surrey, had previously had access to the papers. They have been catalogued, very incompletely, for the Historical MSS. Commission.[99a] Recently the whole has been deposited on loan at the Public

[98a] The effect of this chimneypiece and of the room generally is admirably rendered in Plate LXXI of Nash's Mansions of Engl. in the Olden Times. It is a point in common between Loseley and Wakehurst in Sussex that the latter also boasts a chalk mantelpiece. A good example of a small chalk chimneypiece is preserved in the old house which now forms the museum of the Surrey Archaeological Society in Guildford. The panels in the great hall bear the badges of Henry VIII and Catherine Parr, and are said to have been brought from Nonsuch Palace.

[99] Kempe, Loseley MSS.

[99a] Hist. MSS. Com. Rep. vii.

ARTINGTON : LOSELEY HOUSE, PRINCIPAL FRONT VIEW

ARTINGTON : LOSELEY HOUSE, CHALK MANTELPIECE IN DRAWING-ROOM

Record Office. The present writer acknowledges with gratitude the kindness of the owner, who has given him free access to such a collection, interesting to the historian generally and invaluable to the historian of Surrey in particular. It is not too much to say that the history of the administration of a county under Elizabeth could be compiled from these sources alone.

PICCARDS MANOR seems to have formed a part of Stephen de Turnham's manor of Artington, for it appears in 1279 in the possession of Joan wife of William Branche and descendant of Clemency, one of Stephen de Turnham's daughters.[100] Joan and William were granted free warren in Artington by Henry III.[101] It passed with their manor of Peper Harow to Henry of Guildford, who died seised of land and rent in Artington together with pleas of court there early in the 14th century.[102] His kinsman and heir, John son of Gilbert the Marshal of Guildford, paid relief for the manor in 1319–20 [103] and granted it to John Piccard of Guildford and his wife Margaret in 1323.[104] It is evidently from this family that the manor obtained its name of Piccards. In 1350 John son of John Piccard and his mother Margaret conveyed all their lands in Artington to Master Bernard Brocas, clerk, in exchange for lands called Heysull in Chiddingfold.[105] From this date Piccards descended with Peper Harow (q.v.) till the death of Sir Richard Pexall, c. 1571.[106] He bequeathed it to Pexall Brocas the elder son of his daughter Anne, who had married Bernard Brocas of Horton.[107] In 1586 Pexall Brocas sold ten-twelfths of the manor to Sir William More of Loseley,[108] who evidently bought up the remaining two-twelfths, for he died seised of the whole in July 1600.[109] Since then the descent of the manor has been coincident with that of Loseley (q.v.).

For an account of the church of *CHURCH ST. NICHOLAS*, see the history of Guildford, within the boundaries of which it is situated.

The ruins of *ST. CATHERINE'S CHAPEL* stand on St. Catherine's or Drake Hill,[110] about a mile south of Guildford Bridge. The building was a plain parallelogram of 45 ft. 6 in. by 20 ft. 6 in., inside measurement. The walls are mainly of sandstone, 3 ft. thick, the windows, doors, and buttresses faced with chalk. At the north-west corner is a turret, with vice, leading perhaps to a priest's room, as the top of the turret does not seem like a belfry. The buttresses between the three windows on each side and at the angles ran up into pinnacles. There were large east and west windows, and west and also north and south doors. The side windows over the north and south doors were at some period converted into doorways, approached by outside steps and probably connected by a gallery or bridge across the chapel. The northern door opened inwards, the southern outwards. The only possible use was to allow a great number of

people to pass through the chapel, by the upper and lower doors simultaneously, to venerate relics. The present building is mainly early 14th-century. In the Pipe Roll 14 Henry III (1230) 50s. was allowed to the sheriff for his disbursement of so much to the priest of St. Catherine's Chapel, by which it would seem that the chapel, in the old royal manor of Godalming, was still in the king's hands. The subordinate manor of Artington was then held by the co-heiresses of Stephen Turnham.

In 1317 Richard de Wauncey, rector of St. Nicholas, had rebuilt the chapel and received licence for its consecration after rebuilding.[111] He had bought it and the neighbouring ground from the holders of the manor of Artington before 1301. Andrew Braboeuf granted by charter to Richard de Wauncey, rector of St. Nicholas, and his successors, all his rights on Drake Hill and in the chapel of St. Catherine.[112] But in 1317 the king appointed Robert de Kyrkeby to the chapel of Artington, belonging to the king because the lands of John the Marshal were in the king's hands. The rector's grant had been annulled, and in 1318 the chapel was granted to Richard le Constable, chaplain to the king and rector of St. Mary's, Guildford.[113] But in 1328 Bernard Brocas, rector of St. Nicholas, received a grant of the chapel,[114] and the apparently delayed consecration was carried out [114] in spite of the remonstrance of Constable. The chapel was valuable because attached to it was the right of holding a fair on St. Matthew's Day, and receiving the tolls. The lord of the manor of Godalming, the Bishop of Salisbury, had, however, certain dues from the fair. In the Godalming Hundred Rolls [116] the steward accounted to the lord for 3s. 4d., perquisites from the fair *pro agro, picagio, stallagio, et diversis occupationibus.* On 22 September 1453 the tithing-man of Artington presented one absentee and nine persons for breaking the assize of ale at the fair. This probably comprised all the inhabitants. At least a century later there were only eleven men, for in 1546 the court presented that all the inhabitants of Artington were sellers of beer at the time of the fair, and paid according to ancient custom 1d. each, hence the sum of 11d. was due, and paid. At this time the manor was in the king's hands, and these dues were going to him and not to the rector of St. Nicholas. The episcopal registers are silent as to appointments to the chaplaincy, and it may be that the rectors failed to provide payment for a separate priest. The chapel itself therefore may have become disused. It does not appear among the chapels or chantries suppressed under Edward VI. In 1653 John Manship, presented to St. Nicholas by the Parliament, sold his rights in the fair to Mr. Wight, lord of the manor of Braboeuf; and Sir William More, lord of the manor of Godalming, failed to recover the tolls in a Chancery suit.[117] Mr. Wight's representatives have since enjoyed the tolls of the fair, which are

[100] See below under Peper Harow. It is also called 'one quarter of Artington manor.'
[101] *Plac. de Quo War.* (Rec. Com.), 741.
[102] Chan. Inq. p.m. 6 Edw. II, no. 57.
[103] Pipe R. 13 Edw. II. 'Sussex Oblata.'
[104] *Cal. Pat.* 1321–4, p. 295.
[105] Inq. a.q.d. cccxcviii, 7; Montagu Burrows, *Hist. of Family of Brocas,* 432, 434.

[106] The records of two leases, one in 1500, the other in 1503, are among the deeds of the Brocas family; ibid. 436.
[107] P.C.C. Will 1571, 46 Holney.
[108] Close, 28 Eliz. pt. xviii.
[109] Chan. Inq. p.m. (Ser. 2), cclxiv, 179.
[110] Winton Epis. Reg. Stratford, fol. 43b.
[111] Winton Epis. Reg. Sandal, pt. 2, fol. 12b.
[112] Charter among Loseley MSS.

[113] Chart. 18 Edw. II; cf. *Parl. R.* (Rec. Com.), ii, 378.
[114] Pat. 2 Edw. III, pt. ii, m. 9.
[115] Winton Epis. Reg. Stratford, fol. 43b.
[116] Loseley MSS. Godalming Hundred Court, 21 Sept. 1377.
[117] The Chancery reference cannot be found; the fact is alluded to in Loseley letters, and was vouched for by Manning and Bray. A copy of the pleadings is at Loseley.

now insignificant. At the change of style it was brought on to 2 October. Within the memory of the last generation universal selling of beer by the inhabitants continued, and the fair was of real commercial importance. Turner drew the chapel in *Liber Studiorum*. The old Portsmouth road went over the hill, near the chapel, and a cross-way led to the ferry, which is probably on the site of the ford for the Pilgrims' way. The fair was at the crossways.

CHARITIES   Caleb Lovejoy in 1677 left property in Southwark for the teaching and apprenticing of boys in the parish, the preaching of a sermon, and the providing of a dinner, on the anniversary of his death. The surplus was to go to the foundation of almshouses for poor women. In fact the property was insufficient, and the almshouses were not built till 1841. They hold four women. They are nearly on the site of the house of Caleb Lovejoy's father, which can be fixed from an agreement recorded in the Parish Register.

George Benbrick in 1682 gave sums charged on land at Alton and at Shalford for poor freemen (of the borough) or their widows residing in St. Nicholas.

CHIDDINGFOLD

Chedelingefelt (xii cent.) ; Chidingefalde (xiii cent.) ; Chudyngfold (xiv cent.). Twenty-eight different spellings are found.

The parish of Chiddingfold lies between Haslemere and Witley on the west, Godalming and Hambledon on the north, Dunsfold on the east, and Sussex on the south. Part of the parish was transferred to the ecclesiastical parish of Grayswood in 1900. The village is 7 miles south of Godalming. The area is 7,036 acres of land, and 7 of water. The soil is the Wealden Clay, very deep and tenacious in wet weather, but not unfertile. The parish is well wooded. The oak flourishes as usual upon this soil, and the ash is grown commercially for the making of walking-sticks and umbrellas. There are tile and brick works.

Formerly glass-making was largely carried on. The industry was curiously persistent, though not probably continuous, in the neighbourhood. Much Roman glass, some of it now in the museum of the Surrey Archaeological Society at Guildford, has been found in Chiddingfold. Remains of a Roman villa exist, but the glass is more abundant than would necessarily be the case were it merely the rubbish from one house, and probably glass was made here. In the 13th century (c. 1225–30) Simon de Stokas granted land in Chiddingfold, at Dyer's Cross, to Laurence the Glass-maker.[1] The history of the industry in the 14th century, and under Elizabeth, is dealt with in an earlier volume of this history.[2] On Thursday after Michaelmas, 1440, John Courtemulle of Chiddingfold was presented and fined for leather-dressing outside a market town. These country industries are continually noted, the same people being fined again and again.

The Godalming Hundred Rolls show that the parish was divided into two tithings of Chiddingfold Magna and Chiddingfold Parva in 1538. Earlier there had been three, Chiddingfold Magna to the west, Pokeford or Chiddingfold Parva to the east, Sittinghurst in the middle, afterwards merged in Chiddingfold Parva. The rolls show[3] that there were at least eight bridges, Southbrugge or Stonebridge, Middilbrugge, Pokeford Bridge, Bothedenesbrigge, Hazelbridge, Godleybridge, Jayesbridge, and Denebrugge, reparable by the *Villa de Chudyngfold,* and complaints were constant of the bad state of repair or the flooding of the *via regia,* the road, no doubt, which runs from Godalming through Hambledon and Chiddingfold into Sussex, which was reparable by certain tenants in Chiddingfold, and easily became impassable on the heavy clay. It was continually *submersa,* or *profunda,* or *noxia.* There are traces of another old road in the parish, running north-eastward towards Dunsfold. The common over which this road goes is always High Street Common on old maps and deeds. Rye Street is parallel to it on the north. There were two mills at Sittinghurst and le Estmull. But the most remarkable presentment to be made at a Hundred Court is that on 29 September 1483, when Richard Skynner of Chiddingfold 'non venit ad missam in festialibus diebus sed vivit suspiciose'; was a Lollard, in short. The lord of the hundred was a bishop, we may remember.

There are no references to common fields in the rolls in Chiddingfold, though they are frequent in Godalming proper. There seem never to have been common fields in the Weald, which was scarcely inhabited, or thinly inhabited only, in 1086 and before then. Nevertheless the common lands of the manor of Godalming within Chiddingfold were inclosed under an award dated 1811, now in the custody of the clerk of the peace.

There is a Congregational chapel, built in 1871, and a small Particular Baptist chapel at Ramsnest Common.

Schools were built at private expense in 1868, and in 1872 at Anstead Brook.

Chiddingfold and its neighbourhood abound in ancient farm-houses and cottages, prominent among which may be mentioned Lythe Hill Farm, with half-timber work of two periods, the richer and later being a gabled wing with square and circle patterns in the timber framing, probably c. 1580 ; but the main body of the house is at least half a century earlier. The wing is panelled, and has a good mantelpiece of c. 1700. It was owned by the Quenell, Queuel, or Quyneld family, to which, as the name is uncommon, the Quynolds who held land at Ware, Hertfordshire, in the 14th century, may have belonged. They were in Chiddingfold in the 14th and 15th centuries. Peter Quenell, of Lythe Hill, died in 1559,

QUENELL of Chiddingfold. *Azure a cross argent between two roses or in the chief and two fleurs-de-lis argent in the foot.*

[1] D. in Surr. Arch. Society's Museum.   [2] *V.C.H. Surr.* ii, 295.   [3] Hund. Ct. 27 Apr. 1357, *inter alia.*

and was buried at Chiddingfold. His father was John Quenell, as was shown by a monument formerly at Haslemere. Peter's eldest son Thomas died in 1571; he married Agnes Ireland.[4] His brother Robert Quenell succeeded to Lythe Hill. He became owner of the Imbhams iron furnace in Chiddingfold (the works probably reached into Haslemere) after 1574.[5] Robert died in 1612.[6] His wife was Elizabeth Hall, heiress of George Hall of Field, Compton, whence the Quenells came to Field.[5a] Their son Peter, who was born in 1580 and died in 1650, was a gentleman of coat armour at the Heralds' Visitation in 1623. He made guns for the king when the Civil War was breaking out, and his son Peter tried to raise a Royalist company in 1642, but it was soon disarmed.[7] Peter married his cousin Alice Cranley. Their son Peter, born in 1605, served in the king's army, and was nominated as one of the intended knights of the Royal Oak. He died in 1666, and was buried at Compton. His son Peter sold Imbhams to William Golden,[8] and perhaps also sold Lythe Hill.

Hallands is another well-preserved timber house, of the 16th century, smaller, and of a plain oblong plan, with a lean-to against one of the long sides, a great chimney in the centre, having two large open fireplaces, back to back, in the kitchen and parlour on the ground floor, and sleeping apartments on the floor over, the upper story being bracketed out on three sides and the gable ends further projected. The brackets are of a classical scroll pattern.

The Crown Inn, opposite the church, retains a fine 14th-century king-post roof, over what was originally the open hall. A curious feature of the exterior is the canted wing in the rear, the angle of which has been planned askew to conform to the line of an ancient passage way. This wing, which is of massive timber framing, has an overhanging upper story, showing the projecting ends of the floor joists, stiffened with occasional brackets. There is a fine example of the corner-post at the angle of the main front, the bracket of which has been hewn out of the solid butt of a tree. Besides some excellent examples of oak-joisted ceilings and panelling, the interior contains two or three ancient fireplaces, one of which, on the ground floor, has a massive moulded and arched beam over the wide opening. Two of the adjacent cottages show ancient features, such as four-centred arches of brick to first-floor fireplaces, and half-timber walls.

MANORS   The manorial rights have always belonged to the lords of Godalming. Chiddingfold was a tithing of Godalming Hundred.[10] Three tithing-men reported for it in Godalming courts. No separate court was ever held for Chiddingfold as a manor, although Edward I in 1300 granted a fair to the Bishop of Salisbury at his 'manor of Chiddingfold.'[11] The fair was to be held yearly on the eve, day, and morrow of the Nativity of St. Mary (7–9 September). At the same time the bishop had a grant of a weekly market on Tuesday, but both have long ceased to be held. As living in the royal demesne the tenants were free from tolls elsewhere.[12] The rents from tenants at Chiddingfold formed a considerable item in the profits of Godalming Manor. The latter included in 1543 the holders of Killinghurst, 'le Crown,' and Pockford,[13] and in 1601 the rent of assize from free tenants in Chiddingfold amounted to £9 6s. 8¼d.[14]

ASHURST or *FRIDINGHURST* (Ayshurst, xiii cent. ; Fridinghurst or Ashurst, xvi cent. et seq.). The site of Fridinghurst manor-house is in Prillinghurst Copse; the Court House is now attached to a labourer's cottage. The existing Court Rolls commence in 1550. The manor contains 1,134 acres, chiefly in Chiddingfold, but also in Thursley (anciently Witley), Shalford, and Hascombe, with reputed members in Witley.

A Stephen de Hassehurst in the 13th century, and Margaret atte Assch and Richard Asshehurst, both holding Frithinghurst Mead at Pockford in the 14th century, are known to have existed.[15]

There was an ancient manor of Ashurst in Witley which included in 1369 a fishery in Frithinghurst and a meadow called Frithinghurstmead.[16] Frithinghurstmead was afterwards part of the Fridinghurst property,[17] but not properly belonging to the manor. It seems that the manor of Ashurst in Witley, with members in Chiddingfold, drops out of sight, while the manor of Fridinghurst, with members in Witley, appears. The history of Ashurst in Witley is as follows :—

Henry of Guildford held land of Queen Margaret, including what was afterwards parcel of Fridinghurst Manor.[18]

The separate existence of Ashurst Park probably dates from the grant of free warren to Henry of Guildford in his demesne lands of Chiddingfold.[19] This took place in 1303, and in 1312 Henry of Guildford was returned as holding tenements called Ashurst and Bovelythe (in Thursley) of the Witley manor.[20]

The park of Ashurst came into the king's possession, but was not always in the same custody as that of Witley until near the end of the 16th century.[21] In 1363 the farmer of Witley Manor stated in his account that the rent of 16s. 8d. due from the tenant of Ashurst had not been paid for more than eight years because it was held by the king.[22] Later the manor and park were granted to Adam Pinkhurst, one of the archers of Edward III ;[23] but six months afterwards, in June 1378, Philip Walwayn the elder had a grant of the manor and

---

[4] Will printed in *Surr. Arch. Coll.* vol. xv.

[5] *V.C.H. Surr.* ii, 271.

[6] *Chiddingfold Reg.*

[5a] Hundred Court 1357, Subsidy R. 1487.

[7] Loseley MSS. 1 Aug. 1642.

[8] *Vide infra.*

[9] See Ralph Nevill, F.S.A., *Old Cottage and Domestic Archit. South-west Surr.* (2nd edit.), 59. The Rev. T. S. Cooper has copied ancient deeds which make mention of a building on this site in 1383, the 'aula' spoken of being in all likelihood the shell of the existing building with its fine roof. Under the date 1548 a later deed refers to some additions lately made to 'le Croune'—perhaps the canted wing above described.

[10] *Parl. Writs* (Rec. Com.), ii (3), 338 ; Exch. Mins.Accts. Surr. 34 & 35 Hen. VII, Div. Co. R. 64, m. 21.

[11] Chart. R. 28 Edw. I, m. 6, no. 24 ; Cart. Antiq. H.H. 21.

[12] Add. MS. (B.M.) 19572.

[13] Exch. Mins.Accts.34 & 35 Hen.VIII, Div. Co. R. 64, m. 21.

[14] Pat. 43 Eliz. pt. xvi.

[14a] Deeds in hands of Mr. James Sadler of Chiddingfold.

[15] Mins. Accts. bdle. 1010, no. 5.

[16] Ibid.

[17] Chan. Inq. p.m. 6 Edw. II, no. 57.

[18] Chart. R. 31 Edw. I, m. 2. But Ashurst Park was probably partly at least in Witley.

[19] Chan. Inq. p.m. 6 Edw. II, no. 57.

[20] Mins. Accts. bdle. 1010, no. 5 ; ibid. no. 7.

[21] Ibid. bdle. 1015, no. 9.

[22] *Cal. Pat.* 1377–81, p. 104.

park for life in lieu of an annuity of £10.[34] In April 1379 a commission was issued for inquiry touching the persons who, 'in no small number both of horse and foot,' broke into the park, killed and carried away the deer, and intimidated the parker in his lodge.[35] It is a significant fact that in October of the same year masons, carpenters, and other workmen were repairing Ashurst manor-house.[36] The house was still under repair in 1385, when Philip Walwayn and William Taillard were given power to take sufficient carpenters and labourers for the work, and to 'imprison the disobedient.'[37] Walter Bedell had a grant of the manor and park in 1438.[38] In 1445 the sheriff accounted for Ashurst Park and Manor.[39] They were granted for life in 1464 to George, Duke of Clarence, who conveyed them, with other lands, to trustees on 'going across the sea in the King's service' in 1475.[40] In 1479, a year after the attainder of the Duke of Clarence, the same custodian, Thomas Wintershull, held both Witley and Ashurst, described in the singular as 'the manor.'[31]

Ashurst, in Witley, as a separate manor from Witley, now drops out of sight. Ashurst Park was probably united with Witley Park, to which it seems to have been adjacent (in the hollow to the east of the top of Hindhead). Fridinghurst was probably carved out of members of Ashurst and Chiddingfold by a successful intrusion of the Husseys of Hascombe. For, referring back to 1438, we find Walter Bedell, then appointed custodian, engaged in a suit against Henry Hussey for usurping rents of Ashurst.[31]

The manor of Ashurst and Fridinghurst came later into the possession of the Forde family. Edmund Forde, who acquired it from Henry Windsor and Eleanor his wife in 1549,[32] held the first court of which record remains in 1550, and in 1560 Thomas Rythe and Constance his wife and john Hussey further confirmed it to Forde.[34] It passed from Forde to Blackwell. In 1567 Thomas Blackwell held his first court, in 1583 Margaret Blackwell his widow, in 1586 William Blackwell, in 1608 Henry Blackwell. In 1610 Henry and William Blackwell, brothers, sold the manor to John Middleton of Horsham and Thomas Burdett of Abinger for £1,100.[35] They held their first court in 1611, and conveyed the manor in 1622 to Peter Quenell of Chiddingfold and Thomas Payne of Pitfold.[36] But in 1625 Henry Hooke of Bramshott held his first court ; in May 1679 john Hooke his son, and in 1685 john and his wife Griselda, and their son Henry and Elizabeth his wife conveyed the manor to William

Hooke of Bramshott.
Quarterly sable and argent a cross quarterly between four scallops all countercoloured.

Salmon,[37] who held his first court in 1687. It passed to Salmon's daughter, who married William Bishop. In 1717 William Bishop held his first court, with Elizabeth his wife. In 1725 George Bishop, their son, held his first court ; in 1733 William Bishop held a court ; and courts were held in this name up to 1778, probably by father and son: In 1783 the court was held in the name of William Bishop, a minor ; in 1804 by W. Bishop ; in 1835 by his widow and john Cuming Bishop, a minor ; in 1877 by Henry Parlett Bishop.

The manor and certain outlying portions bought at various times by the lord are distinguished in conveyances.

GOSTRODE reputed *MANOR* was held of Poyle in Guildford. Edward of Gostrode held 10 acres of land in Chiddingfold in 1254-5, which he had inherited from his father Alwin of Gostrode, who had it of the grant of Nigel of Littleton.[38] Later in the same century William of Gostrode was one of the tenants of Poyle for a house and 40 acres of land, not a manor.[39] His son Thurstan paid relief for a messuage and 52 acres of land in Chiddingfold in 1302-3.[40] john of Gostrode was the Bishop of Salisbury's bailiff in Godalming about the year 1320.[41]

Poyle. Argent a saltire gules in a border sable besanty.

In May 1325 another William of Gostrode was pardoned for acquiring 7s. rent in Chiddingfold from John de la Poyle without licence.[42] William died c. 1328, and was succeeded by his son William,[43] who held of the king because of the minority of John de la Poyle. He was probably the one free tenant who held at Chiddingfold of John de la Poyle in 1332.[44]

After the death of William about twenty years later his son Thurstan of Gostrode inherited tenements in Chiddingfold which were part of Henry de la Foyle's serjeanty in Guildford and Stoke,[45] and consisted of a messuage, 40 acres of land, and 12 acres of wood.[46] This Thurstan was still living in 1372.[47] William Novelt of Gostrode held Dyers in Chiddingfold before William Hammond, who was the tenant in 1547.[48] The Peytoes preceded the Chalcrofts till 1659. Gostrode was in the possession of john Chalcroft in the 18th century, and passed at his death to one of his sisters, Hannah widow of Richard Hughes.[49]

Gostrode is now a farm in the south of Chiddingfold belonging to Mr. Luttmare-Johnson.

COMBE BRABIS was held of the manor of Braboeuf in Artington by a rent of 2s. and services, and therefore was separated before the statute of

[34] *Cal. Pat.* 1377-81, p. 257.
[35] Ibid. 361.   [36] Ibid. 398.
[37] *Feet of F. Surr. East.* 8 Jas. I.
[39] *Pat.* 16 Hen. VI, pt. i, m. 25.
[39] Foreign Accts. 23 Hen. VI, no. 79, m. 1.
[40] *Cal. Pat.* 1461-7, p. 328 ; ibid. 1467-77, pp. 457, 829.
[41] Ibid. 87, 381.
[32] Exch. R. 18 Hen. VI, m. 45.
[33] Feet of F. Surr. Mich. 3 Edw. VI; Recov. R. Hil. 3 Edw. VI, rot. 349.
[34] Feet of F. Mich. 2 & 3 Eliz. Misc. Co.

[35] Close, 7 Jas. I, pt. xlv ; Feet of F. Surr. East. 8 Jas. I.
[36] Close, 20 Jas. I, pt. xxiv, no. 15.
[37] Feet of F. Surr. East. 1 Jas. II.
[38] Assize R.872, m. 8. This land was ancient demesne, as part of Godalming Manor.
[39] Chan. Inq. p.m. 27 Edw. I, no. 44.
[40] *Abbrev. Rot. Orig.* i, 244.
[41] *Parl. Writs* (Rec. Com.), ii (2), 217, 939. In 1337, and again in 1343, John Gostrode witnessed conveyances dated at Artington ; Montagu Burrows, *Hist. of the Brocas Family*, 430-1.

[43] *Cal. Pat.* 1324-7, p. 120.
[42] Chan. Inq. p.m. 2 Edw. III (1st nos.), no. 43.
[44] Ibid. 6 Edw. III (1st nos.), no. 24.
[45] Ibid. 28 Edw. III (1st nos.), no. 34.
[46] *Abbrev. Rot. Orig.* (Rec. Com.), ii, 244.
[47] He witnessed a grant at Chiddingfold dated Sunday after St. Andrew, 1372 ; Add. Chart. 24654.
[48] Misc. Bks. (Land Rev.), vol. 190, fol. 230.
[49] Manning and Bray, *Hist. Surr.* i, 650.

CHIDDINGFOLD : THE CROWN INN

CHIDDINGFOLD CHURCH : NAVE AND CHANCEL IN 1868, BEFORE RESTORATION

Quia Emptores. It was held by the Purvoch family, and a rental of Thomas Purvoch of 1507 is in evidence.[50] Laurence Rawsterne, husband of Anne daughter of Thomas Purvoch, Jun., son of the above-mentioned Thomas, sold Combe in 1546 to William Hammond,[51] who had other lands in Chiddingfold which passed to Henry Hooke,[52] clothier, of Godalming. The latter held his first court in 1560, and his son John held a court at Combe in 1571–2 and 1577–8 ; he sold the manor in 1592 to William Peyto, a yeoman.[53] John Peyto of Pound, son of William, died seised of the manor of Combe Brabis in 1616.[54]

John Peyto left two daughters, Anise and Eliza-beth. Anise married John Courtneshe of Chidding-fold, yeoman, in 1630, who in 1632 bought Eliza-beth's share of the manor.[55] He held his last court in 1676, and died 1681.[56] William his son held a court in 1694, and in 1711 conveyed the manor to Henry Welland of Witley, yeoman.[57] Henry Welland died 1739,[58] leaving a son Thomas, who held his first court in 1745, and died 1749 ; his son Tho-mas died unmarried 1758.

The manor went to Thomas's three cousins Anne, Jenny, and Mar-garet. Their trustees con-veyed two-thirds to Mr. John Leech, of Alton, co. Hants, surgeon, in 1764, and the remainder in 1768. Mr. Leech died in 1778. His son John died intestate 1786. Mr. Leech, his son, by agree-ment dated 22 Septem-ber 1803, released to the tenants of the manor all heriots, fines, reliefs, ser-vices, &c., and put an end to the manor's ex-istence, they on their part surrendering their com-mon rights in the waste.[59]

Combe Court was built by Mr. John Storer about fifty years after this.

PRESTWICK, otherwise *HIGH PRESTWICK,* and *OKELANDS,* otherwise *ROOKELAND* or *NOOKELAND,* were dependencies of Catteshull in Godalming.[60] High Prestwick and Prestwick are tenements which were of some importance in the early history of Chiddingfold.[61] Robert of Prestwick and William Prestwick witnessed deeds at Chidding-fold in the 14th century.[62] A little later Sir Thomas Fleming was possessed of a tenement called Prestwick, which included land extending from Fridinghurst to the land of Robert of Prestwick and from Prestwick Hatch to Shoelands.[63]

But this (Great) Prestwick to the west of Chidding-fold, to which the family of the same name belonged, was not part of the lands of the manor, which was at High Prestwick, and should probably be rightly called Oke or Okelands. A Richard de Oke, or del Hoc, witnessed local deeds in the 13th century. In 1316 Richard Lawrens conveyed land out of the tenement called 'del Ok' to William Frensh. Richard Frensh, heir of William, in 1327 granted to Robert de Prestwick money to be paid out of tenements held of Oke. This brings the Prestwicks first into con-nexion with Oke, afterwards High Prestwick, to which, perhaps, they gave the name. In 1434 a Robert Prestwick had a life interest in a moiety of the manor.[64] In 1581 the demesne lands were divided between Thomas Hull and Thomas Ropley.[64a] The farm and land called 'High Prestwick formed part of the estate settled by Sir William Elliott on his wife Joan in February 1620–1.[65]

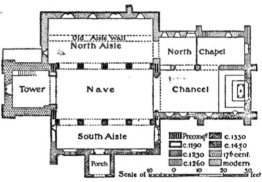

Old Aisle Wall
North Aisle

North Chapel

Tower

Nave

Chancel

South Aisle

Porch

Precong | c.1330
c.1190 | c.1450
c.1230 | 17th cent.
c.1260 | modern

Scale of 10 0 10 20 50 feet

PLAN OF CHIDDINGFOLD CHURCH

The existing Court Rolls date from 1649, after the manor had been divided. Courts were held between 1649 and 1676 by Richard Baker and Robert Elliott, in 1697 and 1711 by Henry Baker and Thomas Elliott. In 1723 Henry Holloway, husband of Elizabeth, only surviving child of Henry Baker, and Richard Elliott held a court. Henry Holloway died in 1755, leaving his property to his daughter's son Stephen Mills. Stephen Mills and Richard Elliott held a court in 1762. Stephen Mills died in 1772. His heir was his sister Mary the wife of William Sadler of Chiddingfold, yeoman.

[50] Information kindly supplied by Mr. Percy Woods of Guildford.

[51] Feet of F. Surr. 37 Hen. VIII. He held courts there in 1550 ; Add. MS. (B.M.) 6167, fol. 107.

[52] Misc. Bks. (Land. Rev.), cxc, 230.

[53] As early as 1559 Thomas Peyto, father of William, had bequeathed land at Combe to his wife Agnes ; Chan. Proc. (Ser. 2), bdle. 10, no. 101.

[54] Chan. Inq. p.m. (Ser. 2), ccclxxviii, 139.

[55] Deeds *penes* Rev. T. S. Cooper.

[56] Par. Reg.

[57] Ct. R. ; cf. Manning and Bray, *Hist. Surr.* i, 651.

[58] Par. Reg. Witley.

[59] Deeds of Mr. James Sadler, Chid-dingfold.   [60] Deed, ibid.

[61] Manning and Bray (*Hist. Surr.* i, 652) state that Prestwick was a manor, the demesne lands of which were divided into moieties in 1580 (correctly 1581), one moiety being in the tenure of Thomas Hull and the other in that of Thomas Ropley ; that Hull's moiety eventually came to

Nicholas Elliott and Ropley's to Richard Baker ; and that Elliott's moiety eventually descended to Thomas Smyth, and Baker's to William Sadler. The Ropleys of Rod-gate held various lands in the parish up to 1621, including Magwicks.

[62] Add. Chart. 24654, 26628.

[63] Rentals and Surv. (P.R.O.), R. 628.

[64] Deeds in possession of Mr. James Sadler of Chiddingfold.

[64a] Abstract of deed *penes* Rev. T. S. Cooper.

[65] Harl. Chart. 57, H. 43.

Richard Elliott died in 1785, leaving his moiety to his nephew Thomas Smyth of Burgate. It came eventually to his six daughters in 1837, and they sold in 1838 to Mr. James Sadler, son of William Sadler above. Mr. James Sadler of Cherfold, his descendant, is now, therefore, lord of the whole manor.

There are certain scattered lands in Chiddingfold known as College Lands, which were granted by Sir Thomas St. Leger, brother-in-law of Edward IV, for the formation of his chantry in St. George's Chapel, Windsor, 30 March 1481.[61a] They were in the hands of the chapter of Windsor and then of the Ecclesiastical Commissioners, and were eventually sold to Mr. Sadler, lord of Prestwick Manor.

The church of *ST. MARY*, on slightly **CHURCH** rising ground in the centre of the village, stands in a beautifully shaded churchyard, entered through a modern lich-gate. The ivy, with which the whole church is overgrown, conceals many features of archaeological interest. A few of the old wooden 'bed-heads' are still to be seen in the churchyard.

The church is built of Bargate stone rubble, with external dressings of the same stone, but the internal masonry is chiefly in clunch and firestone. In Cracklow's view (1823) and in pre-restoration photographs the outside face is shown as covered with a thin coat of plaster, which has been removed, together with most of the 'healing' of Horsham slabs which then covered the greater part of the roofs, an edging only being left at the eaves.

In plan the building consists of nave 39 ft. by 19 ft. 9 in., having aisles 9 ft. 6 in. wide before the restoration, but that on the north has been widened to 17 ft. 9 in., and lengthened a few feet to the west; a wide and shallow south porch, 8 ft. 6 in. by 8 ft.; chancel 34 ft. 3 in. by 16 ft., chapel on the north of the same length, and 11 ft. wide; and west tower about 15 ft. square internally, with a modern heating chamber on the north. Originally the nave and its aisles (as at Alfold) made almost a square.

Between the nave and its aisles are exceptionally lofty arcades of four narrow arches. The chapel originally opened into the chancel by two arches, and by a half arch into the nave; a third, with the intervening pillar, was added to the west in 1870 in the course of a 'restoration' of an exceptionally destructive character. A great deal of the external stonework seems to have been renewed or re-tooled; the chancel arch, an interesting early 13th-century example, was taken down and rebuilt with heightened piers, being made central with the nave, instead of with the chancel, as before. The north aisle was rebuilt on a much extended plan, the windows in the north wall of the chapel were renewed to a different design and shifted. The ancient east windows in the chancel and chapel and those in the south aisle—exceptionally valuable examples of early tracery—were largely renewed in Bath stone, the former being shortened; and the quaint and characteristic 17th-century tower was raised some 14 ft., the whole being dressed up to imitate 13th-century workwhole

There is some possibility that the nave occupies the same area as a pre-Conquest original, and that

portions of its quoins remain in the piers at the angles. This would account for the extraordinary loftiness of the arcade walls—which are no less than 23 ft. in height, the measurement to the top of the capitals of the octagonal pillars being about 14 ft. 8 in. These pillars, which are 1 ft. 10 in. in diameter, have an unpleasantly drawn-out appearance, resembling in this the somewhat similar late nave arcades of Oxted Church. They have octagonal capitals and bases, flatly moulded, and the arches of two orders, a hollow and a chamfer, are slightly four-centred. There is reason to believe that they are as late as the end of the 15th or the beginning of the 16th century, and that they superseded much earlier arcades of normal proportions, with, perhaps, a row of clearstory windows over them, which would be very necessary for the lighting of the nave under the older arrangement. Most probably, with the rebuilding of the arcades, dormer windows were introduced in the nave roof. It seems clear that the southern arcade was shifted 2 ft. to the southward in rebuilding.[66]

The early church would appear to have remained till the end of the 12th century, when aisles were added to the nave, and the forerunners of the present arcades were pierced through the older walls. These had pillars spaced as the later ones, and probably circular. The old stones—greenish firestone—were reworked and used again with the clunch employed for the new work, and the keel-moulding between quirked hollows that formed the outer order of the first arcades was re-used in part in the northern arches. Part of what may have been one of the earlier capitals was lying loose in the tower some years ago. It was decorated with foliage.

The aisles were probably quite narrow as first built —not more than about 6 ft. 6 in. in width. The west window of the south aisle remains in its original position, and is a narrow lancet only 7 in. wide. In the early part of the 14th century the outer walls were rebuilt so as to add another 3 ft. to the width, the inner and outer doorways of the porch being moved outwards and rebuilt in the new work. The outer doorway has a pointed arch, with hood-moulding, and shafts having moulded capitals, the abacus of which is prolonged.

Before restoration the porch retained a foliated barge-board and a string-course of 14th-century date. The inner doorway is of plainer character, and a small holy-water stoup of 14th- or 15th-century date is in the angle adjoining. To the eastward in the south wall is a square-headed three-light window, which, together with one to the west of the porch, and that in the east end of this aisle, dates from the reconstruction of the aisle in about 1330; the last two, however, had been deprived of their tracery, which has been restored. In the three-light window this was of a net pattern, which is somewhat unusual in conjunction with a square head.[67] Two shallow tomb-recesses remain in the outer face of the eastern part of this wall. They have segmental-arched heads with mouldings of 14th-century character.

The chancel in its rebuilding, about 1230, was probably greatly extended. It is spacious and lofty, with a stately row of five lancets and a priest's door in

[61a] *Cal. Pat.* 1476–85, p. 269.
[66] This would give a width of 17 ft. 9 in. for the original nave.

[67] These early examples of the square head in tracery windows are exceptionally numerous in Surrey and Sussex. Bisley, Wanborough, St. Mary's Guildford, Ock-

ham, Fetcham, Cobham, Dorking (before rebuilding), and Godalming are other instances in Surrey where this type of window occurs.

14

CHIDDINGFOLD CHURCH FROM THE SOUTH-EAST IN 1868, BEFORE RESTORATION

CHIDDINGFOLD CHURCH FROM THE SOUTH-WEST IN 1868, BEFORE RESTORATION

the southern wall. The western lancet has a sill-transom, below which is a low side window, at present glazed, but the rebate and hooks for the shutter remain. In the same wall, to the east, are a good trefoil-headed piscina of c. 1260, and the original piscina with oak credence shelf, nearer to the altar, which has been turned into an aumbry. This wall and the east wall have a chamfered plinth and the original buttresses, with their stone water-tables, in good preservation.

The work to the chancel was either altered soon after its erection, or, more probably, resumed after suspension for lack of funds or some other reason. Then, in about 1260, the north chapel was built, and the present east window put in the chancel. It will be noted that the wall between the chancel and chapel is thinner than the outer walls, which seems to indicate that the two had been planned at the same time, although built with an interval. The eastern part of the partition wall is blank; the western has two pointed arches of two orders—a chamfer and a hollow —resting upon an octagonal column and semi-octagonal responds, only the column having a capital and base of plain section. The space to the west-ward was pierced in 1870 with another smaller arch, thus making a second column in place of the respond. The windows of this chapel are practically new, except that in the east wall, which has been renewed upon the old lines. It is of two trefoiled lights with a quatre-foil in the head. The east window of the chancel, very gracefully proportioned, of three trefoiled lights with three trefoiled circles over, within an inclosing arch and hood-moulding, is a most valuable example of its period, c. 1260. In 1870, very reprehensibly, its lights were shortened about 18 in. There was a circular gable-light in the east wall before 1870, of which a modern copy, as an unpierced panel, has been preserved.

The chancel arch had originally low responds, which were raised about 3 ft. when the whole arch was shifted and reconstructed in 1870. The arch itself, which is of two orders, with bold roll and hollow mouldings on its western and chamfers on the eastern face, has been rebuilt on the original lines. The outer order of the jambs has a roll moulding with good stops, and the capitals, of a fine bold section, have their abacus continued as an impost to the outer order of the arch.[68]

If it is somewhat difficult to fix a date for the tower before the alterations of 1870 masked its character, but the 17th century may be hazarded approximately, as its windows before they were altered had segmental-arched heads, and there was a parapet with obelisks at the angles, resembling that at the neighbouring church of Witley. It may have superseded an earlier stone tower, or perhaps one of timber.

The north aisle in its present form is entirely new, save for the lancet of c. 1200 rebuilt in its west wall, and is of discordant character—especially a wheel window in its east gable. Originally this aisle had a lean-to roof like that of the north chapel.

The roof over the chancel is in the main that of the 13th century, and still retains its richly-moulded

cambered tie-beams and king-posts. The nave roof, also with moulded tie-beams and wall-plates, is perhaps as old, but owing to the great height it is difficult to speak with certainty. The aisle and chapel roofs appear to have been renewed in 1870.

At this time also the seating and fittings generally were renewed, but a few old seats, perhaps as old as the 17th century, were worked in; and in the vestry is preserved one of much older date, with scrolled tops to the ends, resembling in design the remarkable late 13th-century nave seats at Dunsfold hard by. A Jacobean communion-table now stands in the vestry. There is a 13th-century font, disused, besides the modern one.

The church contains few ancient monuments, but in the churchyard is the grave of the mother of Dr. Young, the author of *Night Thoughts*.

The registers date from 1563.

Among the church plate are a cup and paten of 1661 (probably a thank-offering by Dr. Layfield on his reinstatement in the rectory after a long persecution by the Puritans), and a handsome silver flagon of tankard shape, bearing the hall-marks of 1747.

Of the eight bells one is probably of the second half of the 15th century, and is inscribed in black letter :—

Sancts. Trinitas Ora Pro Nobis

The second is by Richard Eldridge, 1622; the third by Bryan Eldridge, 1656; the fourth by Samuel Knight, 1699; and the tenor by William Eldridge, undated. Of the three modern bells one is by Mears & Stainbank, 1870; two by Warner & Sons, 1894.

ADVOWSON   The church is not mentioned in the Domesday Survey. Chiddingfold was then parochially part of Godalming, of which it was later a chapelry. It was in existence late in the 12th century, for circa 1180 Ralph de Lechlade granted the church of Chiddingfold with the chapel of Piperham (i.e. Haslemere) to his clerk, Geoffrey de Lechlade, to hold for an annual pension of 1 lb. of wax; and a vicar was instituted in 1185.[69] Again, a few years later, Savaric, Archdeacon of Northampton, bestowed the church and chapel upon Richard son of Richard for a similar rent to Ralph de Lechlade.[70] A pension of 2 marks was conveyed, after the death of Ralph, to Thomas de Chebeham by Philip, Canon of Heytesbury, of which prebend Godalming was a member.[71] In a survey of Godalming Rectory taken in 1220 Chiddingfold is still called a chapel, the chaplain being appointed by the rector of Godalming, to whom he paid 100s. yearly, while the pound of wax was still due to Godalming Church.[72] In 1291 however, the *church* of Chiddingfold with its chapel was assessed at £20.[73] The right of presentation rested with the Deans of Salisbury, until it was transferred to the Bishop of Winchester when the Ecclesiastical Commissioners acquired Godalming Rectory in 1846 (q.v.).

In 1852 the advowson was transferred from the Bishop of Winchester to the Bishop of Lichfield,[74] and, finally, in May 1872, was exchanged with the Crown, in whom the right of presentation is now vested.[75]

[68] The work recalls that of the chancel arch of the same date in Clymping Church, Sussex.

[69] *Reg. of St. Osmund* (Rolls Ser.), i,

268, 301–3; Winton Epis. Reg. Woodlock, fol. 11, 12.

[70] Ibid. 301.

[71] Ibid. 297.

[72] Ibid.

[73] *Pope Nich. Tax.* (Rec. Com.), 208.

[74] *Lond. Gaz.* 4 June 1852, p. 1578.

[75] Ibid. 5 May 1873, p. 2265.

CHARITIES Henry Smith's Charity applies to this parish, and was augmented by an annuity of 10s., paid by the parish officers since the sale of Poors' Land for the benefit of the new workhouse *circa* 1794, but this has not been paid for many years. Ballard's (before 1850) and Callingham's (1898) charities are for the repair of graves, the residue distributed to the poor, &c.

COMPTON

Contone (xi cent.).

Compton parish, 2 miles north-west of Godalming, 4 miles west by south of Guildford, is about 2½ miles from north to south, 1½ miles from east to west, and contains 1,995 acres. The northern part of the parish extends over the narrow chalk ridge of the Hog's Back, the main part is in the Green Sand, with a considerable outcrop of the Atherfield Clay in the eastern part. On the west the land rises towards the high ground about Puttenham Heath. Compton Common lies east of the village. North-east of the village, south of the Hog's Back, are two eminences in the sand, one Budburrow Hill, now crowned by the mortuary chapel, the other Rowbury Hill, near the house of the late Mr. G. F. Watts, R.A., called Limnerslease. These are apparently referred to by Aubrey (1673) and Coxe (*circa* 1726) as Robin Hood's Butts, and connected with an apocry-

phal story of a French invasion, and defeat of the invaders. The time indicated is that of the invasion of Louis of France in 1216, but there was no battle at Compton, and the hills are natural. It is said that skeletons were found here, but if so they were only interments of probably Anglo-Saxon date. Neolithic flint implements and flakes are not uncommon on the north side of the parish.

In the wood to the north-west of the village, at the foot of the Hog's Back, are very extensive caves, excavated in the Green Sand. Within the memory of the last generation sand was brought from them for sale to builders in Guildford, and they were probably excavated for the sand ; but local tradition also connects them with the smuggling trade, and calls them Smugglers' Store-houses. It is not impossible that they were used for such a purpose, as the extensive cellars under several old farm-houses and cottages below the chalk ridge in Surrey pretty certainly were used.

The parish is wholly agricultural, except for one recently introduced industry. The late Mr. G. F. Watts, R.A., who resided at Limnerslease, to the north of the parish church, and Mrs. Watts started a pottery and terracotta-making school, which continues. The pupils trained at it were employed in the decoration of the mortuary chapel in the cemetery, which Mr. Watts built. This is in brick and terracotta, from his own designs, on the side of the hill, about half a mile from the church. The style is a sort of neo-Byzantine.

There are one or two ancient timber houses of some interest in the village, which chiefly consists of a winding street straggling away to the south of the church. One of these, formerly the inn, a good deal 'restored,' stands on a raised bank, so high above the road that a basement story stone is entered by a door on the street, the ground floor being approached by another door on the bank above. The first floor and

COMPTON : OLD INN

attic stories have a considerable projection, and the whole of the three upper stories are of timber framing, the corbelled corner-posts being cut out of solid butts. The doors have flat arched heads ; and the date of the whole house appears to be about the second quarter of the 16th century. Several of the other cottages in the village are highly picturesque, and many date back at least to the 16th century. They are of timber construction, with tile-hanging over the upper stories, and high-pitched tiled roofs, those of a farm-house at Compton being hipped over the wings of the front in a somewhat unusual manner. Some good chimneys occur. The coffee tavern is ancient and picturesque. Not far from it the manor pound still survives. There is a nursery garden in connexion with the Guildford Hardy Plant Nursery.

Polsted Manor is a modern house, but behind it stands the old manor-house, a small 16th-century timber-framed building.

Eastbury Manor, Monk's Hatch, Brook House, Sunny Down, now occupied as a school, and Prior's Wood Lodge are modern houses.

The original manor of COMPTON, MANORS which afterwards divided to form Compton Westbury and Eastbury, was held by Brixi in the time of Edward the Confessor.[1] At the time of the Domesday Survey it was held of the king by Walter son of Other, founder of the De Windsor family, of whose manor of Stanwell it continued to be held[2] until 1541, when Lord Windsor exchanged the overlordship with the king for other lands in Surrey and Sussex.[3] The tenants of Compton held it by knight's service, which was rendered after the division by the lord of Eastbury only.[4]

No record of the under-tenants can be found until 1201 when Cecily of Compton was holding a knight's fee and a half in Surrey, which evidently included the manor of Compton.[5] John de Gatesden held half a knight's fee of William de Windsor in Compton, circa 1212.[6] He or another John granted a life-interest in Compton Manor to Nicholas Malemeins for a yearly rent of 10s. in 1249.[7] In 1260 a settlement[8] of Compton was made on John de Gatesden and his wife Hawise de Nevill, daughter of Robert de Courtenay, and widow of John de Nevill.[8a] Hawise survived her husband, who died shortly before 1262,[9] leaving a young daughter, probably Margaret, the wife first of Sir John de Camoys, whom she deserted for Sir William Paynele or Pagenal, whom she ultimately married.[10] Margaret owed money to the Crown in 1291,[11] whence perhaps a part of Compton, since known as COMPTON WESTBURY, was granted to Henry of Guildford for life only with reversion to

the grantors and to the heirs of Margaret. He was a tenant among several in 1291.[12]

In 1303 Henry of Guildford received a grant of free warren in his demesne lands of Compton,[13] and in 1308 obtained a release of land in Compton from Sir William Paynel and Margaret daughter of John de Gatesden.[14] Henry of Guildford was the chief benefactor of Dureford Abbey in Sussex, to which he bequeathed a large sum of money for the maintenance of two chaplains.[15] After his death his heir, john the Marshal of Guildford, held Westbury,[16] and received from the Abbot of Dureford a corrody of bread and ale, a yearly pension, and a messuage within the abbey, and four ' Paris candles whereof sixteen make the pound ' nightly.[17] The abbey bought many lands for the support of Henry of Guildford's chaplains, and amongst them in 1330 the manor of Westbury, then in the possession of John of Brideford.[18] The abbot retained the court and customary dues of Westbury, but leased the land to a tenant, who undertook to supply the abbot's officers with ' horsemeate and manesmeate ' when they held their yearly court at Compton.[19] In 1532 one William Wynter obtained such a lease of the land for fifty-six years, but at the time of the Dissolution it was taken into the king's hands, together with the abbey's other possessions.[20] In October 1537 the king granted all the possessions of Dureford Abbey in Compton to Sir William Fitz William, K.G., whom he created Earl of Southampton in that same year.[21] He held his first court 8 june 1541. He died in 1542 without heirs male,[22] so that as Westbury had been granted to him in tail male, it then reverted to the king, by whom it was sold in 1545 to Sir Christopher More,[23] who in January 1535 had a lease of it in perpetuity from the abbot.[24] After this grant the history of the manor was coincident with that of the Mores' manor of Loseley (q.v.).

Mr. James More-Molyneux of Loseley sold a small part, including the manor-house, to Mr. George Best, owner of Eastbury, shortly before 1842. The manor-house is now the cottage of the gardener of Eastbury Manor.

COMPTON EASTBURY, the eastern moiety of the original manor of Compton, was not included in the grant to Henry of Guildford,[25] but was held by Sir William Paynel in right of Margaret, daughter of John de Gatesden. John Paynel, William's brother, succeeded to the manor, which he granted to John of Brideford,[26] who retained it when he sold Compton Westbury to Dureford.[26] John of Brideford obtained a release from Eva St. John, widow, formerly second wife of Sir William Paynel,[27] of her right to dower in East-

[1] P.C.H. Surr. i, 322b.
[2] Testa de Nevill (Rec. Com.), 220 ; Chan. Inq. p.m. 10 Ric. II, no. 46 ; ibid. 6 Hen. V, no. 46 ; Cal. Inq. p.m. Hen. VII, i, 19.
[3] Deeds of Purchase and Exchange, Hen. VIII, C. 22.
[4] Chan. Inq. p.m. 6 Edw. II, no. 57.
[5] Red Bk. of Exch. (Rolls Ser.), i, 148.
[6] Testa de Nevill (Rec. Com.), 220.
[7] Feet of F. Surr. 33 Hen. III, 1.
[8] Ibid. 44 Hen. III, 4.
[8a] Cott. MS. viii, 22 (12 Aug. 1253).
[9] Excerpta e Rot. Fin. ii, 384.
[10] Exch. K.R. Proc. bdle. 14f, file 301. And see the story quoted by Camden, Brit. p. 172 (ed. Gibson), from Rolls of Parl. 30 Edw. I, of John de Camoys' conveyance

of his wife Margaret to William Pagenal. There was, however, another Margaret, daughter of another John de Gatesden ' the younger,' who died in 1258 leaving a widow Margery ; Excerpta e Rot. Fin. ii, 316, 326 ; Cal. Chan. Inq. p.m. Hen. III, 454.
[11] Ibid.
[12] Ibid.
[13] Chart. R. 31 Edw. I, no. 29.
[14] Feet of F. Surr. 2 Edw. II, 26.
[15] Dugdale, Mon. vii, 936 ; Cal. Pat. 1317-21, p. 246.
[16] Parl. Writs (Rec. Com.), ii (3), 338 (13).
[17] Cott. MS. Vesp. E. xxiii, fol. 106a.
[18] Cal. Pat. 1327-30, p. 505. He was one of the executors of Henry of Guildford.

[19] Decrees of Ct. of Aug. E. 35 Hen. VIII, xiv, 12.
[20] Dugdale, Mon. vii, 936 ; Valor Eccl. (Rec. Com.), i, 321.
[21] L. and P. Hen. VIII, xii (2), 1008 (19).
[22] Dict. Nat. Biog. xix, 232.
[23] Partic. for Grants (Aug. Off.), Hen. VIII, 411.
[24] Close, 37 Hen. VIII, pt. iii, no. 26. Chan. Inq. p.m. 6 Edw. II, no. 57 ; ibid. 10 Edw. II, no. 61.
[25] Parl. Writs. (Rec. Com.), ii (3), 338 (13).
[26] De Banco R. Trin. 12 Edw. II, m. 234.
[27] Inq. a.q.d. ccix, 21.
[28] Cal. Pat. 1313-17, p. 646.

bury in 1321.[30] He was assessed in Compton for a subsidy in 1332, but died very shortly after. Eastbury passed to William Cook of Brideford and William Wreyford. In 1333 William Cook granted a lease for eight years of a moiety of a third part of the (original undivided ?) manor of Compton to Richard de Windsor the overlord ;[31] and in the same year William Wreyford conveyed a moiety of Eastbury, together with the reversion of the dower of Rose widow of john of Brideford, and a messuage and rent which the Abbot of Dureford held during the life of joan wife of Robert Gerneys, to Richard atte Welle.[32] In 1343, the lease being just expired, Richard de Windsor brought a suit[33] against Richard atte Welle and William Cook of Brideford concerning one-third of the manor, Richard atte Welle appearing as William's bailiff. The action was probably collusive to settle the title. The result is not on record, but Windsor apparently lost ; for William Cook of Brideford in 1343 granted by deed to Richard atte Welle and Sybil his wife all his rights in Eastbury.[34] Further, in 1349 Richard atte Welle, by deed dated at Compton, enfeoffed John de Shackleford, John de Walton, and Richard Pruwet, of his manor in the parish of Compton and in Tunshamstede or Unstead in Shalford, with certain reservations,[35] in trust for his wife Sybil and his children and his brother, with reversion. Sybil afterwards married William Seward and had a daughter Maud, wife of Thomas Swanton.

In 1387 William Seward and his wife Sybil were holding the whole of Eastbury for the life of Sybil,[36] as the inquisition of Miles de Windsor says, but the trial referred to says that Richard atte Welle son of Sybil's former husband had granted it to William Seward for life with remainder to Richard's heirs. This Richard died without heirs.

In 1397 William Wallyng and his wife Isabella claimed the manor from William Seward after Sybil's death. Isabella was daughter of Christina, sister of Richard atte Welle the elder. They were successful ; but meanwhile, William Seward had probably conveyed to john Guvynes, who is said to be have held the manor in 1398.[37] In 1398 William and Isabella Wallyng acknowledged the right of one Elias Beare to the manor, but the proceedings did not terminate till 1410.[38] Clemence Wallyng daughter of Isabella married a Thomas Beare.

The Seward family afterwards claimed again, and in 1422 the manor was restored to Maud, widow of Thomas Swanton and daughter of the above Sybil, wife of Richard atte Welle and afterwards of William Seward.[39]

In 1428 Maud Brocas was charged for a quarter part of a knight's fee in Compton which Richard atte Welle formerly held of Richard Windsor. She was possibly Maud Swanton remarried to a Brocas, whence the manor came into this family.[40] Thomas Brocas, who represented Guild-ford in Parliament, had been a tenant in Compton in 1398.

Arnold Brocas, who was knight of the shire for Surrey in 1441-2, was in possession of Eastbury in 1451[41] and was succeeded by Benedict Brocas, who was holding it in 1485,[42] and is said to have died in 1488. His son and heir Richard was holding Eastbury in 1504,[43] when he was at law with William Lussher, lessee of Westbury. In 1515 he made a grant to Gilbert Stoughton.[44] The grant did not alienate Compton from the Brocas family. One

Brocas. *Sable a leo-pard rampant or.*

COMPTON : THE COFFEE TAVERN

[30] Feet of F. Surr. 14 Edw. II, 28.
[31] Assize R. 1431, m. 65 d.
[32] Feet of F. Surr. 14 Edw. III, 25.
[33] Assize R. 1431, m. 65 d.
[34] Referred to in 1397, Coram Rege R. Mich. 21 Ric. II, m. 70 &c. [35] Ibid.
[36] Chan. Inq. p.m. 10 Ric. II, no. 46.

[37] Chan. Inq. p.m. 22 Ric. II, no. 52.
[38] Feet of F. Surr. 11 Hen. IV, 82.
[39] Coram Rege R. 645, m. 59.
[40] She was known as Maud Brocas in 1427, when she was said to be holding the manor of Eastbury of Richard Windsor. Chan. Inq. p.m. 6 Hen. VI, 46.

[41] Chan. Inq. p.m. 30 Hen. VI, no. 11.
[42] Cal. of Inq. p.m. Hen. VII, i, 19.
[43] Com. Pleas D. Enr. East. 20 Hen. VII, m. 155.
[44] Com. Pleas D. Enr. Hil. 6 Hen. VIII.

consideration had been a perpetual payment to the Black Friars of Guildford for masses for Richard, and perhaps this was not paid. At any rate the next holder to be found is Lawrence Rasterne who married Anne daughter of Thomas Purvoch and Joan Brocas.[45] Their son was William Rasterne,[46] who died 1562. His only surviving child Martha married John Lussher. She was involved in an action in the Court of Requests 1574–5 with her mother's second husband William Grey.[47] John Lussher died before October 1603, when Martha his widow held a court.[48] Her son John Lussher mortgaged the manor to Richard Carrill 10 November 1630,[49] and in December 1631 Lussher and Carrill conveyed the manor to trustees for John Kempsall of St. Clement Danes.[50] John Kempsall had a son Edward, married again and had a son John, and died 1659.[51] Edward the elder son had only an annuity out of the manor, which had been leased to a Dr. Tichborne and settled on the elder John's second wife and their children.[52] John the younger sold to Dr. Edward Fulham in 1662, who in 1667 further secured himself against the claim of John's mother and her second husband Thomas Weston.[53]

LUSSHER. *Gules three martlets or and a chief or with three molets azure therein.*

The estate remained in the Fulham family, for the Rev. Edward Fulham held it at his death in 1832.[54] It was purchased by Charles Devon,[55] who sold the manor and manor-house to George Best, who resided there c. 1848. Mr. Best died 1870. His widow died 1873, when the manor was sold to Colonel McC. Hagart, C.B. His sister, Mrs. Ellice, is now owner.

DOWN PLACE, the manor which includes the northern part of Compton parish, was a part of the main manor of Compton at the time of the Domesday Survey. Gregory de la Dune held half a knight's fee there of William de Windsor c. 1212.[56] It was held with Compton of the manor of Stanwell until the sale of the overlordship by Lord Windsor to Henry VIII.[57]

In 1386 Elizabeth Stonhurst was holding the manor of Miles Windsor,[58] and a few years later she paid poll tax for herself and four servants in Compton in 1381.[59] She is probably identical with Elizabeth de Doune who appears in the Godalming Hundred Court Rolls, the Artington and the Catteshull courts,

1382–5, as holding land in Compton, Artington, and Cherfold in Chiddingfold; perhaps Downland in Chiddingfold was so named from her holding it. Down was subsequently in the hands of Robert Hull.[60] In 1427 Margery Knollis was in possession,[61] but by 1451 it had again changed hands and was held by George Daniell.[62] William Brocas in 1452 held 'le Doune' in Artington.[63] That this was part of Down in Compton appears likely from his son holding the manor of Down in 1485. If so, it had been confiscated before by Edward IV and given to his brother-in-law Sir Thomas St. Leger, who held it towards the end of the 15th century. He was the chief instigator of the rising in Surrey in 1483.[64] After his attainder and execution Down Place was forfeit to the king, who granted it to his servant William Mistelbroke in tail male,[65] but William Brocas was holding Down soon afterwards, see above.[65] The attainder of Sir Thomas St. Leger having been reversed at the accession of Henry VII,[67] his heiress Anne, wife of George Lord Roos, entered upon the manor,[68] but seems to have alienated it, for under Henry VIII William FitzWilliam, Earl of Southampton, was in possession, and settled it on his wife, Mabel, and his heirs by her. He died in 1542 without issue, and the manor descended, in accordance with the terms of the settlement, to his half-brother Sir Anthony Browne, kt., father to the first Lord Montague.[69]

ST. LEGER. *Azure fretty argent a chief or.*

Down Place under Guildown was among lands granted in 1592 to William Tipper, a fishing grantee.[70] However, the rightful owners succeeded in recovering their lands, for in 1610 Anthony Viscount Montague, a descendant of Sir Anthony Browne, sold the manor to Richard Coldham.[71] From him it descended to his son Richard.[72] In 1668 Richard Coldham and George Coldham the younger were dealing with it.[73] Richard Coldham conveyed it in 1688 to the trustees of the estates of Gerard Gore, deceased,[74] whose daughter Sarah married Sir Edward Turnor, Speaker of the House of Commons in 1661.[75] Arthur

COLDHAM. *Azure a molet argent pierced gules.*

45 Catteshull Manor R. 12 June 23 Hen. VIII, and brass of Thomas and Joan Purvoch in Godalming Church. They had a son Thomas who married Jane. The wife of the father or the son might be Joan Brocas.
46 Ct. of Req. bdle. 39, no. 91, 17 Eliz.
47 Ibid.
48 Close, 7 Chas. I, pt. xxvi, no. 28.
49 P.C.C. will proved 27 Jan. 1659.
50 Close, 11 Chas. I, pt. xxv, no. 25.
51 Feet of F. Surr. East. 14 Chas. II;
Trin. 19 Chas. II.
52 Coll. Topog. et Gen. i, 17.
53 Brayley, Hist. of Surr. v, 225.
54 Testa de Nevill (Rec. Com.), 220.
55 Deeds of Purchase and Exchange (Aug. Off.), Hen. VIII, C. 22.

48 Chan. Inq. p.m. 10 Ric. II, 46.
49 Exch. Lay Subs. bdle. 184, no. 29, m. 1.
50 Chan. Inq. p.m. 22 Ric. II, no. 52. Robert Hull and his wife Elisora (?) appear in the protracted lawsuit of 1398–1410 owing homage to Eastbury. The question arises whether 'Elisora' could have been 'Elizabeth' Stonhurst.
51 Ibid. 6 Hen. VI, 46. She also held Cherfold, vide supra, Catteshull R. 7 Hen. VI.
52 Chan. Inq. p.m. 30 Hen. VI, no. 11.
53 Godalming Hund. R. 1452.
54 V.C.H. Surr. i, 365; Chan. Inq. p.m. V.O. Ric. III, no. 18.
55 Cal. Pat. 1476–85, p. 529.
56 Cal. of Inq. p.m. Hen. VII, i, 19.

47 Rolls of Parl. (Rec. Com.), vi, 273.
60 Feet of F. Surr. East. 4–5 Hen. VI.II.
61 Chan. Inq. p.m. (Ser. 2), lxxxix, 1 43·
70 That is, one of a class of professional informants who made it their business to report to the Crown questionable titles o. landowners. In many cases the lands were thereupon resumed by the Crown, and regranted to the informants, and the original owner had to pay highly in order to recover them; Pat. R. 34 Eliz. pt. vii.
71 Feet of F. Surr. Trin. 8 Jas. I;
Recov. R. Mich. 9 Jas. I.
72 Add. MS. (B.M.), 6171.
73 Feet of F. Surr. Mich. 20 Chas. II.
74 Close, 4 Jas. II, pt. i, no. 17.
75 Dict. Nat. Biog. lvii, 373.

Turnor succeeded, and, dying in or before 1724, left his son Edward heir. Edward by his will (proved 1 July 1736) left his estates to his cousin Sarah, daughter of his father's elder brother Sir Edward,[76] and wife of Francis Gee, whose daughter, also named Sarah, married Joseph Garth. Their son Edward, first Earl Winterton,[77] thus inherited Down, and his son, Edward, second Earl Winterton, was in possession in 1808.[78] Between 1831 and 1838 the third earl sold it to Mr. James Mangles, M.P. for Guildford in 1831, 1832, and 1835.[79] Mr. Mangles died in 1838. The property was set-

TURNOUR. *Nine pieces erminees and argent with four mill-stone turners sable in the argent.*

tled for life on Mrs. Mangles. Mr. Frederick Mangles his son lived there. About 1859 it was sold to Mr. Faviell, who rebuilt the house. Mr. Bett bought it in 1890, and Mrs. Bett now lives there.

FIELD PLACE was parcel of the possessions of Henry of Guildford,[80] who held a part of it of Walter of Wintershull in 1312. It was occupied by a Matilda atte Felde apparently in 1343 ;[81] and by Bernard Brocas in 1349.[82] He was rector of St. Nicholas Guildford.

Later it is named amongst the lands forfeited by Sir Thomas St. Leger,[83] after which it was, like Down, granted to William Mistelbroke,[84] but afterwards reverted to St. Leger's daughter Anne wife of George Manners, Lord Roos.[85] His sons, Thomas, Earl of Rutland, and Sir Richard Manners, kt., sold Field Place to Thomas Hall and his wife Joan in 1542.[86] After her husband's death Joan married James Rokley, who held the manor in her right.[87] It descended to her son, George Hall.[88] His widow Juliana married a Thomas Washington about 1569–72, and George's only child Elizabeth Hall married Robert Quenell before 1580.[89] The Washingtons and Quenells of Chiddingfold were jointly interested in the manor in 1585.[90]

MANNERS, Lord Roos. *Or two bars azure and a chief gules.*

Robert and Elizabeth Quenell had a son Peter who resided at Lythe Hill, Haslemere.[91] Robert died in 1612. Peter Quenell the son, who held his first court in 1615, had a son Peter born in 1603,[92] who married in 1628 Elizabeth Grey, and resided at Field Place, holding a court in 1635, though his father the older Peter did not die till 1650.[93] Peter the younger was already owner.[94] He died in 1666 and was buried at Compton. His will was proved by his widow Elizabeth,[95] who was assessed for hearth tax at Compton *circa* 1675.[96] His son Peter died in 1684,[97] leaving two daughters, minors : Elizabeth subsequently wife of Robert Beare and Joan subsequently wife of John Waight, to whom Field Place descended in moieties.[98]

In 1709 John and Joan Waight, Nathan and Elizabeth Hickman, and sundry mortgagees joined in a conveyance of the whole manor to Samuel Manship.[99] His widow Anne held a court in 1726. Their son John Manship held a court in 1738 and died in 1751. His son John did not come into possession till his mother's death in 1788, and was holding still in 1808.[100] Soon after this the manor was purchased by George Smallpeice,[101] who died in 1853. After his widow's death in 1869 it passed to his nephew Job Smallpeice. He sold it to Mr. John King before 21 May 1875. Mr. John King died 15 May 1893. Mrs. King his widow died 16 August 1902, after which date the estate was sold to Colonel Annand.

POLSTED, the most easterly part of the parish, was distinguished from the main manor of Compton[102] early in the reign of Richard I, for in 1196 Walter de Windsor warranted it to Hugh of Polsted and his wife Cecily to hold by knight's service,[103] while in 1199 mention is made of a house which had belonged to Gerard of Polsted and to the land of Richard the Reeve (*prepositus*) of Polsted.[104] At the time of the confirmation to Hugh of Polsted William de Astinges was laying claim to the service from the manor, but apparently failed to prove his right to it, for in 1219 Michael of Polsted, probably a son of Hugh, obtained confirmation of his land in Polsted from William de Windsor.[105] In 1261 a second Hugh of Polsted conveyed the manor to Simon Passelew and his heirs.[106] About ten years later John de Middleton conveyed the manor to William of Wintershull,[107] on whose younger son Walter it was settled, together with Bramley (q.v.).[108] In 1308–9 John de Polsted

[76] See Priv. Act 2 Geo. III, cap. 52.
[77] *Dict. Nat. Biog.* lvii, 373 ; Berry, *Suss. Gen.* 368.
[78] Manning and Bray, *Surr.* ii, 7.
[79] *Ret. of Memb. of Parl.* ii, 333.
[80] Chan. Inq. p.m. 6 Edw. II, no. 57.
[81] Godalming Hund. Ct 31 July, 21 Aug. 11 Sept. 1343.
[82] In lawsuit of 1397, *vide* Eastbury.
[83] Chan. Inq. p.m. Ric. III, V.O. no. 18.
[84] *Cal. Pat.* 1476–85, p. 529.
[85] Feet of F. Surr. 226, 4 & 5 Hen. VIII.
[86] Feet. of F. Surr. Mich. 34 Hen. VIII. See Exch. P.M. Wards and Liveries, 1 Edw. VI, vol. 3, p. 26, on Thomas Hall.
[87] Misc. Bks. (Exch. T. R.), vol. 169, fol. 109*b*.
[88] Chan. Inq. p.m. (Ser. 2), lxxxv, 54.
[89] Inq. p.m. Wards and Liveries, 15 Eliz. bdle. 100, no. 30.
[90] Feet of F. Surr. Hil. 28 Eliz.
[91] Haslemere Reg.
[92] Ibid.

[93] P.C.C. Will 1650. Pembroke 57.
[94] Feet of F. Surr. Mich. 1650.
[95] Archd. Ct Surr. 3 Oct. 1666.
[96] Lay Subs. R. bdle. 188, no. 504.
[97] P.C.C. Adm. 29 Aug. 1684. Hare 124.
[98] Feet of F. Surr. 3 Anne ; Mich. 3 Anne ; Trin. 6 Anne.
[99] Close, 8 Anne, new no. 4999.
[100] Manning and Bray, *Hist. of Surr.* ii, 70.
[101] Brayley, *Hist. of Surr.* v, 226, and private information.
[102] Cecily de Compton held three half-knights' fees, c. 1201 (*Red Bk. Exch.* Rolls Ser. i, 148). Possibly, therefore, her holding included Polsted and Down as well as Compton, but the three were held separately until the De Windsors a few years afterwards (*Testa de Nevill* [Rec. Com.], 230).
[103] Feet of F. Surr. 7 Ric. I, 4. The name of the Surrey manor is Polsted, though it is evidently derived from 'Pol-

stead' in Suffolk, from which the family took their name.
[104] Feet of F. Surr. 10 Ric. I, 41. An agreement between Akina widow of Philip Blund and her son Philip and certain women, Juliane, Ernhina, Emma, Alice, and Rose, as to land and a mill in Polsted, including 2 acres in Westden and Goster, a meadow in Bromhell, and land in Estdon and Molherst.
[105] Pipe R. 3 Hen. III, m. 16 d.
[106] Feet of F. Surr. 45 Hen. III, 30. Hugh and his heirs were to receive a yearly rent of 1*d.*, but quitclaimed their right to ward, marriage and relief of the tenants. About 1275 William le Hare and his wife Joan granted one quarter of a messuage and carucate of land in Polsted to Hugh de Oyldebof to hold of the heirs of Juliane ; ibid. 3 Edw. I, 16.
[107] Ibid. 56 Hen. III, 8.
[108] De Banco R. 724 (Hil. 20 Hen. VI), m. 477. *Hist. MSS. Com. Rep.* vii, App. 599.

granted land to Thomas his son ; Richard de Polsted was a witness.[109] They were perhaps then tenants of the Wintershulls. In 1424 Joan then wife of William Catton and Agnes Basset, sisters and co-heirs of Thomas Wintershull, to whom Walter Wintershull's estates had descended, sued John Loxley for the manor,[110] and again in 1441 Agnes Bassett and John Weston son of Joan Catton disputed it against John Jenyn. The latter claimed to be enfeoffed of it, jointly with Bernard Jenyn of Brabœuf, who is said to have married Elizabeth daughter of John Loxley, son of Robert Loxley, half-brother of Thomas Win-

tershull.[111] The Jenyns seem to have made good their claim to the manors, for Thomas Jenyn, son of Bernard, held it at his death in March 1508–9.[112] He left an infant son John, afterwards knighted, who died in 1545.[113] His widow married Stephen Adams, who was holding the manor in her right a few years after Sir John's death.[114] It was

JENYN.   *Argent a fesse gules with three besants thereon.*

ultimately inherited by Agnes, or Anne, niece of Sir John and wife of John Wight (or Weight),[115] who sold it to Sir William More of Loseley in 1558,[116] from which time its history has been coincident with that of Loseley.

Court baron was attached to Westbury, Eastbury, Field Place, and Polsted,[117] but there seems to be no record of courts held for Down, which was not called a manor till 1386.[118] The court of Polsted was held during the 17th century in a meadow under a walnut tree.[119] In 1249 the tenant of Compton had estovers in the wood of Compton towards the repair of the ' house of the court of Compton.'[120]

In the Godalming Hundred Rolls,[121] it appears that in the 14th, 15th, and 16th centuries the tithing-man and tithings of Compton attended at the hundred courts at Godalming. But a view of frankpledge was held regularly at Compton on the Thursday after St. Matthew's Day, when the tithings of Eastbury, Westbury, and Polsted and of part of Hurtmore in Compton were represented. On 22 September 1453, no one attended from Polsted ' eo quod nullus est residens neque inhabitans super eandem decenam,' and the same is recorded of Hurtmore in Godalming the same year. But on 18 September 1483 the tenant of Polsted paid 8d. at the Godalming court, *pro sua secta relaxanda,* and the tithing of Hurtmore appears later, but no tithing-man for Polsted. The inhabitants of the manors,

which were also tithings in Compton, owed suit to the court at Godalming (q.v.), when the Bishop of Salisbury, lord of the manor as well as of the hundred, held courts which from an early period combined the functions of a court baron and a hundred court.

In 1547 it was stated that the lords of Down had failed to pay suit to Godalming for many years.[122]

The church of *ST. NICHOLAS* is built on a spur of sand hill rising out of the valley in which the village stands. The east end of the building is approached from the road by the steep path overshadowed with cypresses and other trees, and the churchyard, which is very picturesque and well-wooded, shares in the undulating nature of the site. Behind the church to the west are some fine cedars and other trees. The church, which is one of the most interesting in the county, is built of Bargate stone, flints, and chalk, with Bath stone used in the modern work. A good deal of the exterior is covered with a brownish plaster ; the roofs are tiled and the spire of the western tower is shingled. Nearly all the internal dressings are in clunch or hard chalk.

The church was restored in 1843, under Mr. H. Woodyer, and further works were carried out in 1869 and 1906. It consists of a western tower about 10 ft. square internally ; nave 47 ft. 6 in. long by 18 ft. at its western end and 16 ft. 6 in. at the eastern ; north and south aisles, of the same length, 7 ft. 3 in. wide, south porch, and chancel 27 ft. (originally 28 ft.), by 13 ft. at its western end. The eastern part of the chancel is vaulted and separated from the western by a low arch. It is of two stories, the upper forming a chapel over the sanctuary, a very rare feature in this country. On the north is a

COMPTON CHURCH FROM THE SOUTH-EAST

[109] Deed at Loseley.

[110] De Banco R. 655 (Mich. 3 Hen. VI), m. 123.

[111] Ibid. 724, m. 477. It is possible that John Loxley claimed it as a descendant of Alice, widow of Thomas Wintershull and wife of Henry Loxley ; if so ere must have been some definite settlement on Alice by the Wintershulls, and is seems unlikely since Polsted is not

mentioned in the inquisition taken upon her death. Chan. Inq. p.m. 8 Ric. II, 24.

[112] Chan. Inq. p.m. (Ser. 2), xxv, 48.

[113] Ibid. lxxii, 96.

[114] Misc.Bks. (Exch. T.R.), clxix, 109b.

[115] See under Brabœuf in Artington.

[116] Feet of F. Surr. East. 4 & 5 Phil. and Mary.

[117] Chan. Inq. p.m. 6 Edw. II, 57 ; Add. MS. (B.M.) 6171.

[118] Chan. Inq. p.m. 10 Ric. II, 46.

[119] Add. MS. (B.M.), 6171.

[120] Feet of F. Surr. 33 Hen. III, 1.

[121] Loseley MSS.

[122] Misc. Bks. (Exch. L.T.R.), clxix, 113b.

modern vestry and on the south a small projecting building, originally of two stories, which may have served for an anchorite's cell or for viewing relics. There is a modern coal shed on the north of the tower.

The tower has no buttresses, and is of very rude construction, built entirely of rag rubble, without any ashlar dressings to quoins and windows, the latter being narrow round-headed slits in the rubble-work ; a modern window of very incongruous design has been pierced in the west. It has no staircase, and its whole appearance suggests a date prior to the Norman Conquest. The rag-work quoins of the early nave are still visible and of the same character. The timber spire, which is fairly lofty, is probably of 14th-century date. The tower arch, plain pointed, on square piers, dates from about 1160 and replaces an earlier and smaller opening. A peculiarity of the plan is that the nave contracts in width towards the east, being 18 in. narrower at its eastern end than at the west. Its floor is said to have been higher than that of the chancel previous to the restoration of 1843, a fact borne out by the stilted

square at the top with the angles canted off to a circular necking. This rests upon a short circular stem and base, and the whole upon a square table and chamfered plinth. The north aisle retains its low pitch and one of its original windows, but the walls of the south aisle were raised about 3 ft. in the 15th century ; one of its original windows remains in the south wall, but blocked on the inside, and another in the west wall ; the remainder are of 14th and 15th-century dates. In the north aisle are two shallow tomb-recesses, with depressed cusped arches, of 14th-century date. A blocked rood-loft door appears at the back of the eastern respond in this aisle. The chancel arch is of two orders, the outer circular in form, the inner obtusely pointed. These are nook-shafted with volute capitals to the outer order.

The shell of the chancel walls is perhaps of late 11th-century date, though heightened and otherwise altered in subsequent periods ; three of its windows can be traced, one in each wall. The bowl of a pillar-piscina of this period has lately been found plastered up in the wall of the upper chapel, to which

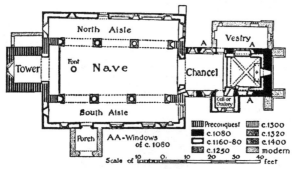

PLAN OF COMPTON CHURCH

bases of the arcade-piers. These arcades, which with the aisles and the chancel arch date from about 1160, are of three arches on each side, and with their columns are entirely worked in hard chalk. The arches are very slightly pointed, square-edged and of one order, with a flat moulded label, a rare and note-worthy feature being the coeval treatment of the thin coat of plaster on their soffits, which is cut into patterns (scallop, zigzag, and nebule) at the edges, as at Godalming and the crypt of St. James's Clerkenwell. The capitals have square abaci and are carved with varieties of the scallop, volute, and different types of foliage, those on the south being peculiarly rich. The columns and responds are circular, with round bases on square plinths. The north and south doors, which have circular heads, are both of this period, the former having a plain roll-moulding and the latter an outer order of zigzag, with a hood. In the centre of the nave at its western end is the large font of late 12th-century date. The design is peculiar, and looks like a rude imitation of a Vene-tian well-head, the bowl being shaped as a capital,

it had evidently been removed when that chapel was formed. The basin has two drain-holes—an earlier and a later—a circular-headed niche being made to fit the older drain. Clear proof was found during the underpinning of the chancel in 1906 that when the two-storied sanctuary was formed in its eastern half, in about 1180, the older walls were merely thickened by the addition of an independent 'skin,' about 1 ft. thick, on the inside, to serve as an extra abutment for the vault. The original plastering still remains on the older face, now hidden. This vault is of very low pitch, with segmental ribs, clumsily constructed, springing from a string-course, with corbels in the eastern angles. It is inclosed by a low and wide segmental arch, beautifully moulded, with nook-shafts having foliate capitals and chamfered imposts, all in chalk. The arch has a hood-moulding enriched with the dog-tooth ornament, and two orders, both moulded, the outer having a cusped or horse-shoe border in relief over a deep hollow, which gives a very rich effect. In the south wall are a piscina and aumbry of the same period, and in the

Compton Church : Chancel and Sanctuary Arches showing
12-century Balustrade in Upper Chapel

Compton Church : The Tower, showing Straight
Joint of Pre-Conquest Nave Quoin

western part of the chancel proper are windows, one in either wall, of like date, within plainly splayed pointed heads. That on the south has, however, been altered externally in the 13th century, so that it is now a low side window of two lights. Hard by a very carefully finished squint (c. 1160) pierces the chancel arch pier. Its other end is blocked by the pulpit. In either wall to the east is a small doorway with a pointed head. The western jamb of the south door stands on an early base. That on the north now gives access to the modern vestry, but no doubt originally opened to a stair which led to the upper chapel, a purpose at present served by a modern staircase placed within the small building on the opposite side, which is entered by the other door. A wide lancet, of date about 1250, is found on either side of the chancel, westward of these doors, and a two-light window of about the same date remains in the south wall of the lower sanctuary.

The anchorite's cell, or watching-place, whichever it be, on the south side of the chancel has several interesting features : a tiny round-headed window apparently of 12th-century date ; a door opening outwards suggesting that there was a porch or out-building of timber attached to the southern side ; and a squint with a peculiar cross-shaped opening to the chancel. This squint, which would command a view of the altar, is high enough for a person to kneel within it on the cell side, and the oak board on its sill shows a depression worn by constant use. The squint also looks towards a nameless tomb, quatrefoil panelled, of 15th-century date, beneath a window of the same period in the north wall of the sanctuary, which probably served as an Easter Sepulchre. In the recent underpinning of the chancel walls several male skeletons (one having abundant bright red hair on the skull), buried one above another, were found beneath this tomb, and it has been suggested that these were successive occupants of the anchorite's cell.

The present east window of the upper chapel is modern, and replaces one of three lights with four-centred or elliptical heads, probably of late 16th-century date. Standing upon a beam above the low arch which forms the entrance to the lower sanctuary is the unique piece of early wooden screen-work or balustrading, placed here when the vaulting was constructed, about 1180.[123] It consists of nine semicircular arches, cut out of a single plank, resting upon octagonal shafts, having foliate capitals and moulded bases. A modern deal capping now crowns the top. The chancel roof is covered with modern boarding on the inside. In the nave and north aisle the roof timbers are ancient, perhaps of the 12th century : the south aisle roof has been largely renewed. Few churches possess such interesting early 17th-century fittings as the communion-table, rail and gates, with pierced scroll-carving, newels and balusters, the pulpit and sounding-board, also elaborately carved, and the chancel screen, now placed at the west end, and also enriched with pierced scroll-work and circular arches on baluster shafts. The seats in the chancel and body of the church are all modern.

In the southern window of the sanctuary is a beautiful fragment of early 13th-century glass representing the Blessed Virgin and Child. Other ancient fragments of grisaille or pattern-work have disappeared within living memory. The glass now in the west window of the south aisle, but originally made for the east window of the sanctuary, appears to be of 17th or 18th-century date, and its subject is the Baptism of our Lord.

The chancel walls have been re-plastered, but there may be ancient paintings under the whitewash in the nave.

Resting within the blocked north doorway, outside, is part of a late 12th-century coffin lid, bearing a floriated cross.

In the centre passage of the nave is a slab bearing the brasses of a civilian and his wife, dated 1508. The man wears a long fur-lined coat, with a girdle, from which hangs a *gypcière*. His hair is long and he has square-toed shoes. The lady is attired in a pedimental head dress and a tight-fitting gown with fur cuffs of a somewhat unusual shape, her waist being confined by a long ornamented girdle reaching to the feet. Beneath the husband are the figures of two sons, and one of a daughter, as appears by the indent, was originally below the wife's effigy. The inscription reads :—

'Pray for the sowllis of Thomas Geñyu and
    Margaret hys wyfe,
the whych decesyd the yere of our Lord MCCCCC
    and VIII, on whos sowllis Ihu have marcy. Amen.'

Above the figures was a shield, now gone, but which, according to Manning, bore—Argent on a fesse gules three bezants, for Jennings, quartering Gules a bull's head cabossed argent armed or.

From Manning we learn that a marble stone bore the following inscription, lost at the time when he wrote :—

'Hic jacet Robertus Soule et Margareta uxor ejus,
    quorum
animabus propicietur Deus. Amen.'

Besides these, there are several slabs and monuments of the 17th and 18th centuries, including a stone at the east end of the nave inscribed to 'Elizabeth wife of Peter Quynell, Esq., daughter and sole heiress to Edmund Grey, Rector of Woolbeding, 1684.'

Her husband, according to an entry in the register, was buried at Compton on 7 May 1666.

On a tablet in the south aisle are inscriptions to members of the Fulham family, 17th and 18th centuries. In the churchyard is the fragment of a coped coffin-slab bearing a cross, of 12th or 13th-century date.

On a jamb-stone of the small blocked window in the south aisle is an incised sundial.

A rare detail is some ancient ridge- or crest-tiles on the nave roof. The registers date from 1639. The churchwardens' accounts begin 1570, and the book is bound up with part of an old processional belonging originally to the Abbey of Hyde, near Winchester.

The plate includes a fine communion cup and cover or paten, of 1569, with a somewhat unusual form of ornament on the paten ; another paten and a flagon of 1683 and 1687, given to the church by Dr. Edward

Fulham, Canon of Windsor, who died 1694, aged 90, and was buried at Compton.

Of the bells, the treble is by Brian Eldridge, 1634, and the second by the same founder, 1660. The tenor is by Mears, 1845.

ADVOWSON   The church was mentioned in the Domesday Survey of Compton.[124]

The advowson seems to have been in dispute early in the 14th century between the lords of Polsted and Compton Westbury, for, though Hugh of Polsted granted the advowson with Polsted to Simon Passelew,[125] Henry of Guildford, lord of Westbury, died seised of it ; his successor, john the Marshal, disputed the presentation, and finally john of Brideford presented a rector.[126] Thenceforward the history of the advowson was coincident with that of Compton Westbury, saving that during the 17th and 18th centuries the Mores and their descendants sold the right of presentation for several turns to members of the Fulham family.[127] It is now in the hands of the owner of Loseley and Westbury.

CHARITIES   The charities are Smith's Charity, on the usual terms for the relief of deserving poor, charged on the Warbleton estate, Sussex ; a bequest by Richard Wyatt, in his will, 20 March 1618, for the maintenance of one poor man, with 1s. 9d. a week and clothes once a year, in the almshouses at Godalming—trustees, the Carpenters' Company ; 50s., charged on land in Compton, in bread and money to the poor and clothes to two aged persons, by john Thompsall, first distributed in 1674, in the hands of the churchwardens and overseers ; a gown yearly to one poor woman, and the overplus bread, by Mrs. Jane Aburne, by will 19 May 1708.

A convalescent home for four inmates was founded in 1884 by Miss Hagart, and is supported by Mrs. Ellice of Eastbury.

GODALMING

Godelminge (xi cent.) ; Godhalminges and Godeliming (xiii cent.) ; Godlyman (xvii cent.).[1]

The town of Godalming is 32 miles from London, and 4 from Guildford. The parish is of an extremely irregular shape, the extreme measurements being 6 miles north and south, 4 miles east and west. The area is 6,980 acres of land, and 59 of water.

The parish is entirely upon the Lower Green Sand, with the exception of alluvium in the valley of the Wey. The town lies in the valley, but its outskirts extend on to the hill to the south, called Holloway Hill, and to the north near Hurtmore, where the Charterhouse School stands. The most extensive open ground is Highden Heath to the south, near Hambledon. High Down is a corruption ; it was Hyddenesheth in 1453,[2] and Hyde Stile is near it. Hyden Ball rises to 592 ft. above the sea. Chauncey Hare Townshend, a poet of some celebrity, born at Busbridge in Godalming, 1798, celebrated the view from it. Burghgate, or Burgate Farm, where a road comes up the declivity of the sand from the Weald, perhaps gives its name to Bargate stone, a well-known building stone. But Topley[3] says that though the stone occurs freely in the parish, it does not occur here.

Manning and Bray suggest that this was the entrance to Godalming Common Park, which stretched over the waste land hence to the common fields on Holloway Hill and near Busbridge, south of the town. The tenants by copy of court roll had to repair the park palings.[4] The park is marked with no inclosure in Rocque's map ; but, from absence of any early reference to it, the probability is that 'park,' in the sense of 'a pound,' is here intended. The meadows to the west up the Wey, are called Salgasson. In the 14th century this was spelt Chelnersgarston. The meadows by the river, north of the town, were lammas lands, common pasture for the parish, under regulations as to the number of beasts allowed to townsmen. Westmede was old common pasture closed from Lady Day to St. Peter ad Vincula.[5] The common fields had been partly alienated to private use in Elizabeth's time. In Court Rolls of 23 September 1591 it appears that Arnold Champion had alienated to john Westbroke 6 acres by estimation, lately parcels of the field called 'Godalmyng field,' and four closes of 16 acres lately parcel of the field called 'Ashtedfielde' in Godalming. The fields in Shackleford were called Estfield, Southfield, and Buryland.

Shackleford inclosure had begun earlier. On 5 October 1503 Robert Bedon had inclosed 'land called Andyelle,' 'Rydys and Wodecrofte, that was never before inclosed.' The final Inclosure Act for Godalming and Catteshull was passed in 1803,[6] and Peasemarsh, partly in Godalming, Compton, and Artington, was inclosed by an Act of the same year.[7]

The three ancient mills of the Domesday Survey were at Catteshull (mentioned 22 September 1453), Westbrook (mentioned 21 September 1441), and Eashing ; and there was a mill called Southmill at Lalleborne[8] (Laborne).

The road from Guildford to Portsmouth passes through the parish, and also the South Western Railway (Portsmouth line), opened through in 1859. In 1849 however, the line had been taken from Guildford to Godalming old station, now used for goods only as a siding. Farncombe station was opened when old Godalming station was disused in 1898. The Wey Navigation was extended from Guildford to Godalming in 1760, with four locks.

The old bridge of Godalming was owned by the lords of the manor and hundred. It was only open

124 *V.C.H. Surr.* i, 322b.

125 Feet of F. Surr. 45 Hen. III, 30. It is also mentioned in the conveyance of Polsted by John de Middleton.

126 Egerton MSS. 2031, 2034.

127 Inst. Bks. P.R.O.

1 In 1647 it was spelt God Almaigne. The pronunciation of that time is illustrated by the following 17th-century proverb :—

'He that shall say well, do well, and think well in mind,
Shall as soon come to heaven, as they that dwell at Godalming.'

(Add. MS. (B.M.), 6167, fol. 167).

2 Ct. R.   3 *Geol. of the Weald,* 123.
4 Ct. R. 2 Chas. I, Monday after St. Matt.   5 Ct. R. Aug. 2, 1453.
6 43 Geo. III, cap. 99. The award was dated 1811.
7 43 Geo. III, cap. 94.
8 Thursday after Michaelmas 1,108 ; Ct. R.

to the public in times of flood, when the ford was dangerous. This is the bridge at the east end of the town; it was first improved when the Portsmouth road was made, or improved, in 1749.[9] It was taken over by the county 5 April 1782, and the first stone of the new bridge was laid by Lord Grantley 23 July 1782.[10] The bridge near the church was made where a ford existed, about 1870. Bolden Bridge, just above it, was formerly repaired by the lord of the manor.[11]

Broadwater, in the Portsmouth road, is the seat of Mr. E. G. Price. Munstead Hall, picturesquely situated in the woods on what used to be called Munstead Heath, on the hills north-east of the town, is the seat of Sir Henry Jekyll, K.C.M.G. Applegarth, on Charterhouse Hill, is the seat of Sir John Jardine, K.C.S.I., M.P.

The situation of the town is very pleasant, as it lies in a great valley of green meadows, with the Wey winding in and out, and with wooded hills rising all around, on the spurs of which the outlying parts of the town are scattered. There is a modern Godalming, consisting of red-brick streets and trim villas, well surrounded with trees, lying to the north of the old town and around the railway station: but the old town follows the Portsmouth road, with streets right and left. At the junction of the principal of these — Church Street with the High Street— is placed the town hall or market-house, the successor of an older one, dating from 1814. With its small tower and cupola, polygonal end on open arches, and general irregularity, it groups well with its surroundings. For use it is superseded by new municipal buildings in Bridge Street, completed in 1908.

Both the High Street and the cross streets abound with old houses, some of timber and plaster, some tile-hung, and others with 18th and 19th-century brick fronts. In the outskirts of the town, on the south-west side, the houses are built on high banks above the road, with raised footways. Other specially picturesque parts are in Wharf Street, by the water-mill, and in Church Street, where are some ancient timber houses with projecting upper stories. Owton or Hart Lane, now called Mint Street, has some ancient half-timber work. The White Hart Inn, in the High Street, near the Market house, is another good example of a timber house with two overhanging stories having nicely carved brackets; and the adjoining shop has a

projecting gable-end quite in keeping. The Angel Hotel, on the other side of the High Street, though its front has been modernized, has some interesting old timber work in the rear; and the 'King's Arms,' where Peter the Great and his suite of twenty-one lodged on the way from Portsmouth to London in 1698, is another hostelry. Among other ancient timber houses in the High Street is one which has the Westbrook arms on a pane of glass; but it was not their home. They lived at Westbrook, where the last of them died, 1537. It is now cut up into a bank and a shop, but retains its projecting gables, with richly carved barge-boards, and a hint of timber framing, concealed by stucco. Its date appears to be about the middle of the 16th century. But more interesting architecturally than any of these is a house with an overhanging upper story at the corner of Church Street and High Street. It is probably a house called ' at Pleystow,' belonging to the Croftes family in the 16th century. The upper story, like many of its neighbours, had been coated with plaster, but in the course of repairs a piece of this fell off, and disclosed some timber framing of unusual character. The whole front was then stripped, with the result that a very rich design of timber pargeting,

GODALMING : OLD TIMBER-FRAMED HOUSE

[9] 21 Geo. II, cap. 36.   [10] MS. at Loseley; 22 Geo. III, cap. 17.   [11] Loseley MSS.

3   25   4

consisting of interlaced squares and circles, has been brought to view. The narrow, winding street, the irregular roof-lines and overhanging stories, with this beautiful piece of detail in the foreground, make the whole corner a delightful study.

Very different in character, but equally valuable to the lover of old domestic architecture, are the elaborately ornamented brick fronts of 17th-century date in the High Street. As Mr. Ralph Nevill, F.S.A., observes,—'They are good examples of how to treat rough stone with brick dressings, and are of a more graceful and fanciful character than the later work when affected by the intrusion of Dutch taste under William III.'[12] One of these has, in an oval panel, the date 1663, and very elaborate cornices of cut brick. This retains also its mullioned windows, with ornamental casement glazing. Another, also of local stone, with cut brick dressings and brick panel-work, has good curved and pedimental gables.

Besides these specially valuable examples there are numerous specimens of the sober brick houses of the 18th century, with excellent plain details both inside and out.

On the high ground to the north-west of the town stand the buildings of Charterhouse School, which was moved here from its old home in London in 1872. The main block, designed by Hardwick, is built round three sides of a great court open to the west, called Founder's Court, with the chapel on the south, the head master's house, 'Saunderites,' on the north, and a tall tower with a spire, Founder's Tower, on the east, flanked on the north by the school museum and part of the old foundation scholars' house, 'Gownboys,' and on the south by the other part of the same house. An archway under Founder's Tower opens to the south walk of an arcaded cloister, Scholars' Court, leading directly to the west door of the school library, a fine room flanked by classrooms on the north and south, and opening on the east to a great hall, also flanked by classrooms, built in 1885 from the designs of Sir A. Blomfield. The cloister walk already mentioned is crossed at right angles by two other walks, one running at the back of the east block of the great court, and leading northwards to 'Saunderites,' and southwards through 'Gownboys,' to another passage which ends in a lobby east of the chapel, and a second walk near the west end of the library, leading to a block of classrooms on the north, and to the east end of the passage just mentioned on the south. South of this passage is a third house, 'Verites,' forming the south front of the group of buildings, which are collectively known as 'Block.' To the west and south of 'Block' lie the cricket and football grounds, with 'Crown,' the school pavilion, on the east, and the fives and tennis courts on the west. From Founder's Court a road leads westward down the hill past the rifle range to the racket courts and swimming baths, and beyond them to the River Wey, and the school bathing-place. The main

CHARTERHOUSE SCHOOL.
Or a cheveron between three rings gules with three crescents argent on the cheveron, which are the arms of Sutton, the founder.

approach to the school from Godalming is by a road running up the valley between Frith Hill on the east and Charterhouse Hill on the west, which turning on itself passes westward over a bridge and reaches the level top of the hill on which 'Block' stands just to the south-east of the great Hall. To the north is one of the outhouses—as distinguished from those in 'Block'—'Girdlestoneites,' with a group of classrooms and workrooms near it on the north-west, and to the south of the road is another house, 'Weekites.' The remaining houses of the school lie to the east and south, standing picturesquely among their trees and gardens on the slopes of the hill.

A few relics from the old buildings in London were transplanted to Godalming in 1872, notably the arch of entrance to the old schoolrooms, carved all over with names of bygone Carthusians, which being placed in the lobby east of the chapel, together with a number of other similarly adorned stones, has caused a continuance of the custom of name cutting, and all the walls of the lobby are covered with names, singly or in groups, of those who from time to time have made their mark in the school.

The general arrangement of the various houses is fairly uniform, consisting of a 'hall' for the use of the upper boys, and a 'long room,' in 'Gownboys,' called 'writing school,' for the Juniors, separate studies for the upper boys, and long dormitories with cubicles. In the halls are panels with the names of monitors and those who have represented the school in cricket, football, &c.

The chapel is a simple rectangle in plan, with a central passage and rows of seats facing towards it on the north and south, a south aisle at a higher level than the chapel proper, a west organ gallery and lobby, with canopied stalls on the east, and a south-west tower, under which is the main entrance. A cloister has lately been added on the south in memory of Dr. W. Haig-Brown, for many years head master, and is now filled with brass tablets and other memorials.

The library, originally a big schoolroom, contains a valuable collection of books, drawings, and pictures, and there are a number of pictures in the Great Hall, and the 'Orator' and 'Gold Medallist' boards from Old Charterhouse. The uses of 'Hall,' which is separated from 'Library' by a movable wooden partition, are many and various, such as concerts, rifle corps drill, examinations, prize-givings, 'call over,' and the like.

Of late years, a new museum, surrounded by classrooms, and new science classrooms have been built, and a wooden building with a central hall and classrooms at either end, familiarly called 'Barn,' has been taken down and set up again on a new site, to be used as a music-room. To former generations of Carthusians it chiefly recalls memories of a dreary ceremony known as 'extra school.'

The playing fields have been greatly extended in the last twenty years. 'Green,' south of the main buildings of the school, is devoted to school matches and first eleven cricket, while 'Big Ground,' west of the chapel, holds the same position in regard to football. On 'Under Green' are eight cricket grounds, rather close together, and on 'Lessington' are five football grounds. And there are a number of other grounds besides.

---

[12] Ralph Nevill, F.S.A., F.R.I.B.A., *Cottage and Domestic Architecture of South-west Surr.* (ed. 2), 47.

GODALMING : EASHING BRIDGE

The hamlet of Eashing contains many old cottages of architectural interest, and an ancient bridge over the Wey. One of the cottages is on the river close to the bridge. It is largely of timber framing. The other cottages at Lower Eashing form a highly picturesque group, with high-pitched roofs, hipped gables, and dormers of half-timbered construction, with a specially fine and lofty group of chimneys, connected with the main roof by a sort of lean-to. An ivy-clad stone wall to the fore-court heightens the artistic effect, and within the court is an ancient well-house, retaining its old wheel and bucket.[13] Another cottage in this neighbourhood has a fine crow-stepped chimney. Near Eashing House is a brick and timber building, with circle work in the gable. Eashing House itself was built by Ezra Gill in 1729–36 on the site of the house called Jordans.

Eashing Bridge, of three low stone-built round arches, with breakwaters between them, is probably of early 13th-century date. It has lately been acquired by 'The National Trust for the Preservation of Places of Natural Beauty and Historical Associations.' It was formerly repaired by the lord of the manor. In 1568 it is presented in the Hundred Court as *valde ruinosa*, the obligation of repair being on the queen. But in 1588 it was *ruinosa* still.[14]

The name Eashing is of great antiquity. It is mentioned in Alfred's will, where it was left to his nephew Ædhelm. In the Burghal Hidage, a document attributed by Professor Maitland to the 10th century,[15] it appears as a site of a fortified place, where

the expression *myd Æscingum* shows that it was a tribal name. The burh is not likely to have been here. There are two tithings of Godalming, Lower Eashing where are the hamlets of Lower and Upper Eashing, as here described, and Upper Eashing Tithing, quite separate from it. The latter is 'High Tithing' of the Hundred Rolls, about Busbridge, which name has superseded it as the name of a hamlet. Busbridge seems to have been named from a family who came from Kent, in 1384 spelt 'Burssabrugge' and 'Burrshebrugge' (Hundred Rolls). There was other land called Bushbridges the possession of the same family in the Godalming common fields. James de Bushbridge sold Bushbridge or Busbridge to John Eliot of Godalming under Henry VIII.[16] His grandson Laurence Eliot sailed with Drake round the world. His son William, born 1587,[17] was knighted 1620. He built the old house of Busbridge, to judge from the features of the building, and formed the park, having a grant of free warren in his lands of 500 acres in 1637,[18] and died 1650. His son William, born 1624, died 1697, leaving a son William, born 1671, who died 1708. His brother Laurence sold the property in 1710. It passed through the hands of various owners. Among these was Philip Carteret Webb, F.R.S., born 1700,

ELIOT of Godalming.
Azure a fesse or.

---

13 These cottages are illustrated in Mr. Nevill's *Old Cottage and Domestic Architecture of South-west Surr.* (ed. 2), 65 1 and in *Old Cottages and Farmhouses in Surr.* by W. Galsworthy Davie, and

W. Curtis Green, pl. 22, 23, 24, and 29.
14 Loseley R.
15 Maitland, *Dom. Bk. and Beyond*, 502 et seq.

16 *Survey of Godalming*, 1, 2, 3, Edw. VI.
17 Godalming Registers.
18 Pat. R. 13 Chas. I, pt. xxvii.

solicitor to the Treasury 1756–65, M.P. for Haslemere 1754–67. He was a distinguished lawyer,
antiquary, and collector. He died at Busbridge in
1770. Chauncey Hare Townshend the poet was
born here in 1798, when his father owned the property, which he bought in 1796. It now belongs to
Mr. P. Graham. The house was pulled down in
1906, and a new one is being erected on a new site.

The hamlet of Shackleford contains some old cottages and farm buildings and many new houses in very
beautiful scenery. Hall Place, the house of Richard
Wyatt, who built the Mead Row Almshouses, was
pulled down. The offices were made an inn, called
Cyder House. The inn was acquired by Mr. William
Edgar Horne, who turned it into a modern mansion.
The panelling and overmantel of the dining-room came
from the Cock Tavern in Fleet Street, London, whilst
the gallery railings in the hall came from the old
Banqueting Hall at Whitehall.

Neolithic implements found upon Charterhouse
Hill and the school cricket ground are now in the
school museum.

King Edward's school is in the Laborne tithing of
Godalming parish, close to Witley Station. It is a
school for destitute boys who have never been convicted of crime, who are trained for the Army, Navy,
or industrial life, and is under the control of the
Governors of Bridewell and Bethlehem Hospital. The

SHACKLEFORD: OLD CIDER PRESS HOUSE AT
HALL PLACE

corresponding girls' school is in Southwark. This
building was erected in 1867, and enlarged in 1882
and 1887, and will hold 240 boys. It is in the
Italian Renaissance style in brick. There is a chapel
for the joint use of this school and the Convalescent
Home for women and children in Witley.

The Technical Institute and School of Science and
Art in Bridge Road was built in 1896 in the Renaissance style from designs by Mr. S. Welman.

A cemetery was opened in 1857. The present
cemetery was opened in 1899. It serves both the
civil parishes, the town and Godalming Rural, and is
under joint management.

A Roman Catholic chapel used to exist, but had no
resident priest. The new Roman Catholic Church of
St. Edmund King and Martyr is in Croft Road. It

was consecrated in 1906. It consists of a plain nave
and chancel divided by a pointed arch. It is of local
stone with a tiled roof. On the north is a low tower.

The Unitarian chapel in Mead Row was built
before 1809, when worship is first recorded there in
the church books, in accordance with a resolution
passed as far back as 1788, for a Baptist congregation
which had met at Worplesdon, and which admitted
another body of Unitarian Baptists who met at
Crownpits, Godalming, in 1814. In 1818 the
Baptist qualification was dropped, and the meeting
became Unitarian as the older members died.

A Congregational chapel was opened in 1730 in
Hart Lane. The building has been replaced since.
Under Charles II the population of Godalming had
been very largely nonconformist ; 700 or 800 people
met in a conventicle every Sunday, and 400 or 500
monthly in a Quaker's house, out of a population of
under 3,000.[19] In 1725 there was no meeting house,
but ' several kinds of Protestant Dissenters of no great
consideration as to numbers or quality.'[20] The congregation may be considered however the lineal representative of the conventicle of the reign of Charles II,
organized in 1730. There is now a Wesleyan chapel,
a Friends' meeting house, and a small Baptist chapel,
opened in 1903.

The parish is divided into two civil parishes,
Godalming Urban and Godalming Rural.[21] The
former includes the borough of 897 acres.

There were anciently nine tithings, for which tithingmen were chosen : Godalming Enton (the town),
Binscombe, Catteshull, Eashing, Farncombe, Hurtmore,
Laborne, Shackleford, Tuesley. Tithingmen also
attended the Godalming Hundred Court from Shackleford, Artington and Littleton (in St. Nicholas Guildford), Compton, Peper Harow, Chiddingfold Magna,
Chiddingfold Parva, and Haslemere. But the names
of the tithings vary from time to time, nor are they
all constantly represented in the extant rolls. High
Tithing, from which tithingmen also came, is the
same as Upper Eashing, answering nearly to Busbridge. To the Godalming Enton Court Vann,
Haslemere, Chiddingfold, Shackleford, Eashing, and
Godalming constantly sent tithingmen. All these were
originally in the manor and were perhaps in the parish.
There were parish churches at Compton, Chiddingfold, and Haslemere, and churches at Tuesley, Hurtmore, Catteshull, Artington (St. Catherine) ; there
are modern churches at Farncombe, Shackleford, and
Busbridge.

In Domesday in the manor held by Ranulf Flambard, which was afterwards known as the Rectory
Manor, there are twelve cotarii mentioned. In the
king's manor of Godalming there were no cotarii,
but in Tuesley, held by Flambard, were six cotarii.
Tuesley was afterwards included in the Rectory
Manor. In the rolls preserved at Loseley there
are fourteen, and in the survey of 1 Edward VI,
eighteen cotholders, on the king's manor. They
are described as libere tenentes[22] or ' free tenants,' but their services seem to have been similar
to the ordinary villein services in kind, though
different in particulars. They all paid small money
rents. They got in the lord's hay ;[24] and did suit at
the courts.[25] They paid heriots on succession, and

[19] V.C.H. Surr. ii, 39, 40.
[20] Bishop Willis' Visitation, 1724–5.
[21] 56 & 57 Vict. cap. 73.
[22] See below.
[23] Mins. Accts. Misc. Co. 33, 34
Hen. VIII, no. 12.
[24] Ct. R. 24 Aug. 31 Edw III.
[25] Ct. R. 23 Aug. 31 Hen. VI, &c.

fines, and were admitted, like other tenants of the manor, at the courts which did common service as both hundred and manorial courts. For instance, on 15 June 19 Henry VI (1441) Juliana wife of john Savage was admitted 'ad unam parcellam terrae unius cotlonde vocatam Hykemannes,' as heiress of Christiana wife of john Peck, and paid a fine of two shillings, doing fealty. Only six weeks after this, on 27 July 1441, Juliana who was the wife of John Savage was deceased. There was no heriot, because juliana had no beast. John her husband was admitted as tenant for life of the 'cotlond,' paying a fine of one shilling and four-pence.[16] The cotholders had perhaps a share in the common fields : on 16 March 8 Richard II (1385) john Farnham claimed, as heir, Edward Waterman's land. Ed-ward Waterman was a cotholder, and some of his land lay *in campo* and some *in communi campo.* But it is possible that this may have been apart from his cotholding. One of the services of the cot-holders was to convey prisoners to the county gaol at Guildford Castle. This service was due from Waterman's land, and fur-ther he was hangman ap-parently, for after the conveyance of prisoners the words are added *et eos suspendet.* The convey-ance of prisoners led on one occasion to a mis-adventure which illustrates the lawless action possi-ble in the 14th century, though the perpetrator was a Frenchman of Ca-lais, before Calais belonged to England, in the service of Margaret, the second wife of Edward I. Richard atte Watere of Godalming came to the king's court in 1317 or 1318, and complained that his tenure obliged him to convey prisoners to Guildford Castle from the court at Godalming, and that Andrew de Caleys, constable of the castle of Queen Margaret at Guild-ford, took Richard *vi et armis*, and shut him up with his prisoners for three months and more, and only let him go on payment of a heavy ransom. It was ordered that the sheriff should produce Andrew to answer to this on the morrow of St. Martin.[17]

The obligation to convey prisoners, at their own proper charges, lay in the cotholders as late as 1670.

There was no chance then of the guard and prisoners being locked up together, but the county gaol was in Southwark, and the obligation much more burdensome than when it was at Guildford.[18] The question was raised at the same court whether the cotholders were bound to repair the fence of the common pound of Godalming. This seems to differentiate them from the other customary

GODALMING : 'THE WHITE HART' (*see p. 25*)

tenants ; for there was no question that the latter had to repair it. The obligation occurs frequently, and had been affirmed so lately as by the court held on the Monday after St. Matthew 1626.[19] They certainly repaired the fence of the lord's pound or pinfold.[20]

Queen Elizabeth incorporated the BOROUGH town by a charter dated 25 January 1574–5,[21] when the cloth trade was flourishing there.[22] The corporate body was to con-sist of the warden (*gardianus*) and inhabitants, who were to have the usual right of impleading, and also a common seal. At the same time the queen granted

[16] Loseley R. of dates cited.
[17] De Banco R. Trin. 11 Edw. II, m. 162.
[18] Ct. R. 14 Oct. 22 Chas II.
[19] R. in steward's hands.
[20] R. *passim*; Exch. Mins. Accts. 34 & 35 Hen. VIII, Div. Co. R. 64, m. 22.
[21] Pat. 17 Elis. pt. vii, no. 4.
[22] Though the inhabitants complained of their great poverty ; possibly only for the sake of rhetoric.

the town a weekly market on Wednesdays,[32] thus forgoing her own right as lady of the manor to the market granted by Edward I. She also granted them an annual fair to last three days, beginning on the eve of Candlemas Day, which did not interfere, however, with her own manorial fair held in June.[34] The warden was to collect the tolls of market and fair for the maintenance of the town. The queen herself appointed the first warden, John Perrior,[35] to hold office till the following Michaelmas, at which time a warden was to be nominated by the chief inhabitants of the town in the presence of the other inhabitants, and then elected by the majority. In the following reign ordinances were drawn up 'for the better order and government of the town,'[36] directing that there should be eight assistants chosen from such inhabitants as had borne office as bailiff, constable, or tithingman, to be elected for life by the warden and inhabitants, a warden chosen by the majority of the assistants from their own number, and a bailiff elected yearly from those who were capable of being constable or tithingman. The warden and assistants had power to levy assessments on the householders, more especially for the repair of the town clock, and opposition to them might be punished by disfranchisement.

The present extent of the borough of Godalming dates from November 1894.[37]

Before its incorporation by Elizabeth there were no traces of any institutions which might indicate the existence of a borough. During the lordship of the Bishops of Salisbury, Godalming was merely a market town with an annual fair held by the bishop under a royal grant of 1300.[38] In the *Nomina Villarum* of 1315 it is not distinguished as a borough. Constantly in the Hundred Rolls persons are presented for carrying on trades outside Godalming because in so doing they are *extra villam mercatoriam*. They seem to have been content with fines time after time, especially for the privilege of dressing leather where they pleased. In 1563 Godalming was constituted a market town by statute.[39]

The great industry in the 16th century was in woollen stuffs. The trade was in decay in the 17th century.[40] Shortly after the ordinances of James I the townspeople were in great distress, for in 1630 they were suffering from want of a market for their manufactures, chiefly Hampshire kerseys,[41] whilst a few years before they had been obliged to postpone their fair for fear of the plague,[42] but were nevertheless visited by the dread sickness in 1636-7.[43] The present industries are tanning (Westbrook) and paper-making (Catteshull). There are also flour-mills.

GODALMING : OLD BRICK HOUSES (*see* p. 26)

[32] In 1674 the day of the market was changed from Wednesday to Friday, but had returned to Wednesday by the 19th century. *Cal. S.P. Dom.* 1673-5, p. 95.

[34] See Chart R. 28 Edw. I, m. 6; Add. MS. 6167, fol. 167; *Parl. Papers,* 1835, xxiv, 735 et seq.

[35] See *V.C.H. Surr.* ii, 346-7, and *Surr. Arch. Coll.* xix.

[36] See *Parl. Papers,* 1835, xxiv, 735.

[37] Under Loc. Govt. Bd. Orders Confirm. Act (No. 11), 9 Nov. 1892.

[38] Chart. R. 28 Edw I, m. 6, no. 24. It may be this grant which gave rise to the tradition that the town had a royal charter in 1300 ; cf. *Parl. Papers,* 1835, xxiv, 735. The market-day recited was Monday, and the fair was held on the eve, day, and morrow of St. Peter and St. Paul.

[39] 5 Eliz. cap. 4, sec. 44.

[40] *V.C.H. Surr.* ii, 342.

[41] *Cal. S.P. Dom.* 1629-31, p. 391.

[42] Ibid. 1625-6, p. 45.

[43] Ibid. 1636-7, p. 353.

and timber-yards.[44] In 1666 Elizabeth's charter was confirmed by Charles II.[45]

In 1825 an Act was passed for paving, lighting, and otherwise improving the town of Godalming,[46] which, till then, had been ill-lighted with oil, and guarded only by a bellman or watch supported by arbitrary assessments levied by the warden and his assistants.[47] The first attempt to pave the town had been made in 1528.

In 1484 the lord of the manor had received 4s. profit from the watch of Godalming.[48] It is stated in a Parliamentary account of the borough drawn up in 1835[49] that the greater part of its bye-laws appeared to be illegal ; that the town was governed neither according to the charter of Elizabeth nor the institutions of James I ; that the choice of warden was always so arranged as to ensure the election of a nominee three years after his nomination ; that the number of assistants had diminished, and that the bailiff, who had then been in office twenty years, had succeeded his father. At this time the chief duty of the warden was to take the lead in all public meetings, to advise the constables, who were appointed at the court leet held by the lord of Godalming, and to defray the surplus expenditure, which was considerable, owing to the lack of any town property ; while the assistants aided the warden, and the bailiff collected the tolls of the fair. The corporation was reconstituted by the Municipal Corporation Act of 1835,[50] under which the title of 'warden' was changed to that of 'mayor,' whilst four aldermen and twelve councillors took the place of the former 'assistants.'

The town has never had any property of importance. The tolls of the market and fair it possessed by Queen Elizabeth's charter of incorporation. They were levied in kind until 1825, when the tolls of market were for the sake of the town's prosperity forgone by the warden and assistants. The only other source of income was the Market House, which was leased from time to time, though still used for town purposes.[51] The old market house was pulled down in 1814 and a poor building erected in its place. The old house had been also the Hundred House, where the hundred court was held. It was from its appearance of a date not later than the 15th century. In 1616 it was in need of repair, as appears from the will of John Purchase, dyer, of Godalming. It is referred to as the 'Hundred House' in a deed of 1532. A court of pie powder was held there on market-days.

GODALMING MANOR was a posses- MANORS sion of King Alfred, who bequeathed it to his nephew Ethelwald.[52] The latter doubtless forfeited it to the Crown, for he rebelled

against Edward the Elder in 905 and died in arms.[53] Edward the Confessor held Godalming,which remained an appurtenance of the Crown till Stephen's son, William Earl de Warrenne, obtained a grant of it,[54] but probably resigned it with his other lands before 1159. It seems that Henry II granted it to Stephen de Turnham,[55] for in 1206 he obtained a confirmation of Artington, and with it the hundred and all other appurtenances which he had of the gift of Henry II.[56] In 1221 a mandate was issued to the Sheriff of Surrey to deliver to the Bishop of Salisbury seisin of the manor and hundred of Godalming, which had been held by Edelina de Broc, Stephen's widow.[57] Mabel de Bavelingham, one of Stephen and Edelina's five co-heiresses, released the manor and hundred to the Bishop of Salisbury in 1224,[58] while ten years afterwards three of the remaining co-heiresses sued Robert Bishop of Salisbury for the manor,[59] but were evidently unsuccessful, for it remained the property of that see till 1541–2.[60] In 1294 the king granted the bishop free warren in his demesne lands in Godalming.[61] In 1541 the Bishop of Salisbury exchanged Godalming Manor and Hundred for the prebend of Bluebery, then held by Thomas Paston, one of the gentlemen of the Privy Chamber,[62] and evidently an agent for the king, to whom he immediately gave Godalming in exchange for other estates.[63] In 1595 Anthony Viscount Montague was appointed steward of the manor,[64] and in 1601 Queen Elizabeth sold it to Sir George More of Loseley,[65] in whose family it remained for more than two and a half centuries.[66]

Mr. James More-Molyneux sold it about 1865–70 to Mr. James Stewart Hodgson, who died in 1899. It is now in the possession of Mr. F. A. Crisp of Hurtmore, who bought it in 1909.

There were court baron and court leet in connexion with Godalming Manor.[67] The lord of Godalming also had relief and heriot.[68] In 1394 Richard II granted to John Waltham, Bishop of Salisbury, all the amercements of the tenants and residents in his fee and in that of the dean and chapter, together with assize of all victuals, waifs and strays, and freedom from purveyance.[69] These liberties were claimed by Sir George More in 1605–6.[70] The fishing and fowling rights throughout the hundred were leased to Richard Bedon while the manor was in the king's

SEE OF SALISBURY. *Azure Our Lady standing with the Child in her arms or.*

[44] *V.C.H. Surr.* ii, 340.
[45] No enrolment of the charter has been found ; *Parl. Papers,* 1835, xxiv, 735.
[46] 6 Geo. IV, cap. 177.
[47] *Parl. Papers,* 1835, xxiv, 735 et seq.
[48] Add. R. 26892.
[49] *Parl. Papers,* 1835, xxiv, 735.
[50] 5 & 6 Will. IV, cap. 76, schedule B.
[51] *Parl. Papers,* 1835, xxiv, 735 et seq.
[52] Birch, *Cart. Sax.* ii, 178 ; i, 178 et seq.
[53] *Angl.-Sax. Chron.* (Rolls Ser.), i, 181–2.
[54] *V. C. H. Surr.* i, 298b ; *Red. Bk. of Exch.* ii, 654 ; *Pipe R.* 2 *Hen. II* (Rec. Com.), 10.
[55] Manning and Bray state that the land which Henry II exchanged with Salisbury

Cathedral was the manor of Godalming. In the deed of exchange, however, mention is only made of Godalming Church with its appurtenances, i. e. the rectory manor. *Sarum Chart. and Doc.* (Rolls Ser.), 29–30 ; Cart. Antiq. C. C. 9.
[56] *Rot. de Oblatis et Fin.* (Rec. Com.), 339. The history of the manor and that of the hundred are elsewhere coincident.
[57] *Rot. Lit. Claus.* (Rec. Com.), i, 455.
[58] Feet of F. Surr. 8 Hen. III, 23 ; *Sarum Chart. and Doc.* (Rolls Ser.), 165.
[59] Maitland, *Bracton's Note Bk.* 800.
[60] See below.
[61] Chart. R. 22 Edw. I, m. 3.
[62] *L. and P. Hen. VIII.* xvii, 14.
[63] Pat. 34 Hen. VIII, pt. iii, m. 23 ;

Feet of F. Div. Co. Trin. 34 Hen. VIII ; ibid. Hil. 35 Hen. VIII. There is a very full and interesting survey of the manor taken early in the reign of Edward VI. Misc. Bks. (Land Rev.), vol. 190, fol. 223 et seq. and Misc. Bks. (Exch. T. R.), vols. 168–9.
[64] *Hist. MSS. Com. Rep.* vii, App. 654.
[65] Pat. 43 Eliz. pt. xvi.
[66] For an account of the family see under Loseley.
[67] See the account of the hundred.
[68] Misc. Bks. (Land Rev.), vol. 190, fol. 237.
[69] Mem. R. (Exch. K. R.) East. 17 Ric. II, 'Records,' m. 6 (not marked).
[70] Pipe R. 3 Jas. I under 'Sussex resid.'

hands.[71] Early in the 17th century a dispute arose between Sir George More and Mr. Castillion, farmer of the rectory manor, as to the fishing rights belonging to the latter.[72]

CATTESHULL (Chatishull, Cateshull, xii cent. ; Catteshull, xiii-xiv cent. ; Catteshill, xviii cent.) is a manor and tithing in the north-east of Godalming, and included lands in Chiddingfold.[72a] Its separate existence seems to date from the reign of Henry I, who gave Catteshull to Dyvus Purcell.[73] Geoffrey Purcell, the king's usher (hostiarius), son of Dyvus, held it free of toll as it had been in his father's time,[74] and gave it to Reading Abbey on becoming a monk there.[75] This gift was confirmed both by the Empress Maud[76] and by her opponent Stephen, the latter stipulating in his grant that Ralph Purcell should hold 20s. of land in Windsor of the monks.[77] No mention is made of Catteshull in the confirmatory grants of Henry II to Reading Abbey,[78] and he seems to have regranted it to Ralph de Broc, son of Dyvus Purcell (identical with Ralph Purcell), to hold by the service of usher of the king's chamber.[79] This service or serjeanty by which the manor was held was variously stated as 'the keeping of the linen'[80] and being 'usher of the laundresses.'[81] Ralph de Broc's daughter Edelina having married Stephen de Turnham,[82] the manor passed to one of his (Stephen's) five heiresses, viz. Mabel wife of Thomas de Bavelingham,[83] who was also known as Mabel de Gatton. In 1224 she established her claim against the Bishop of Salisbury, lord of Godalming, in Artington and Catteshull.[84] She conveyed the manor to her son-in-law Robert de Manekesey in 1234, but the sale was opposed by John Hamo de Gatton, whom Edelina de Broc had empowered to perform the service due.[85] Mabel was given the option of buying back the manor,[86] but does not seem to have done so, for in November 1234 the king confirmed the grant to Robert de Manekesey.[87] In 1254-5 Robert de Gatton was in possession of Catteshull.[88] He died c. 1264, leaving a son Hamo,[89] that was succeeded by his son Hamo de Gatton,[90] who dowered his wife Margery with Catteshull at the church door.[91] Their son, Edmund de Gatton, was an infant at his father's death, and died a minor. He had two sisters and co-heirs, Elizabeth wife of William de Dene, and Margaret wife of Simon de Northwood.[92] Of these

Margaret obtained her purparty of her brother's lands in 1315,[93] although Guy de Ferre, custodian of Edmund's lands during his minority,[94] accounted for the manor in February 1319-20.[95] Margaret's portion evidently included the whole of Catteshull. Her son Sir Robert de Northwood, kt., inherited it and made good his claim to it against Robert de Dol of Loseley, who asserted that Robert de Manekesey had granted it to his grandfather Hugh de Dol and his wife Sibyl.[96] Sir Robert was in possession of Catteshull at his death in 1360,[97] and was succeeded by his son Thomas, who only survived his father a year.[98] One of his sisters and heirs, joan wife of John Levyndale, was apportioned certain rents in Catteshull, while his other sister, Agnes, afterwards wife of William Beaufoy, received the rest of the manor,[99] and conveyed it to John Legg, or Leigh, serjeant-at-arms, who is said to have been her second husband, William Brantingham, and john West.[100] During the lifetime of John Legg land in Catteshull was leased to Elizabeth widow of Peter Stonhurst.[101] William Brantingham held a court there 25 July 1383, but almost immediately conveyed the manor to Thomas Holland, Earl of Kent, and others, probably trustees, for William Brantingham obtained in 1384 a quitclaim of the rights of Joan Weston, wife of William Weston, daughter of Agnes and heiress of John Legg or Leigh.[102]

William Brantingham was in possession in 1407 when he granted the manor to trustees, evidently for the purpose of a conveyance to his kinsman John Brantingham, which was completed in 1413.[103] John was still holding in 1421, but in 1428 Richard Brantingham was assessed in a feudal aid for the manor. In 1430 John Brantingham sold it to Thomas Wintershull senior, and others, to the use of Robert, father of Thomas,[104] who was lord of Wintershull in Bramley (q.v.). In his family it remained[105] till 1565, when John Wintershull sold it to William More of Loseley.[106] His direct descendants retained it till 1836,[107] at which date james More-Molyneux sold it to George Marshall.[108] Mr. Marshall died in 1853, having bequeathed his estate to his wife, who died 1874, leaving it to her daughter Mrs. Fairclough.

When the lord of Godalming held his yearly view of frankpledge at Catteshull the lords of that

[71] Misc. Bks. (Land Rev.), vol. 190, fol. 237.
[72] Hist. MSS. Com. Rep. vii, App. 660.
[72a] Court Rolls passim.
[73] Testa de Nevill (Rec. Com.), 223.
[74] Add. Chart. (B.M.), 19572.
[75] Ibid. 19576.
[76] Ibid. The date of her confirmation was probably May 1141, in which month she visited Reading. See Arch. Journ. xx, 284-96.
[77] Add. Chart. (B.M.), 19584.
[78] Harl. MS. 1708, fol. 21 et seq.
[79] Testa de Nevill (Rec. Com.), 223, 227.
[80] Red Bk. of the Exch. 561, 1013. In Inq. p.m. of Robert de Gatton, 48 Hen.III, 90, he is 'marescallus meretricum,' and the Red Book of the Exchequer leaves no doubt whatever that the literal meaning is correct. See also Chan. Inq. p.m. 20 Edw. I, no. 25.
[81] Assize R. 80, m. 3 d. See Blount, Jocular Tenures (ed. W. C. Hazlitt), 126.

[82] Testa de Nevill, 223 ; Red Bk. of Exch. 561 ; ibid. 1013, where it appears that the heirs of Ralph de Broc's second daughter, Juliane, had no share in Catteshull.
[83] Fine R. 3 Hen. III, m. 9.
[84] Feet of F. Surr. 8 Hen. III, 65.
[85] Bracton's Note Bk. 1171 ; Assize R. 80, m. 3 d. Robert de Manekesey married Mabel's daughter Isabel ; Assize R. 867, m. 18 d.
[86] Maitland, Bracton's Note Bk. 1171.
[87] Cal. of Chart. R. i, 188.
[88] Assize R. 872, m. 23. He may have been either the above-mentioned Robert de Manekesey or his son.
[89] Chan. Inq. p.m. 48 Hen. III, no. 20.
[90] Ibid. 20 Edw. I, no. 25.
[91] Ibid. 29 Edw. I, no. 58.
[92] Abbrev. Plac. (Rec. Com.), 318.
[93] Cal. Close, 1313-18, p. 237.
[94] Cal. Pat. 1292-1301, p. 570.
[95] Pipe R. 13 Edw. II.
[96] De Banco R. 331, m. 311. Roger son and heir of Thomas Lewkenor released

all his right in the manor to Sir Robert de Northwood in 1344 (Loseley D.).
[97] Chan. Inq. p.m. 34 Edw. III (1st nos.), no. 72.
[98] Ibid. 35 Edw. III, pt. 2 (1st nos.), no. 13.
[99] Close, 37 Edw. III, m. 38.
[100] Feet of F. Surr. 48 Edw. III, 2 ; Fine R. 3 Ric. II, m. 3 ; Loseley D. 3 Ric. II.
[101] Chan. Inq. p.m. 5 Ric. II, no. 34.
[102] Feet of F. Surr. 8 Ric. II, 73.
[103] Loseley D.
[104] Ibid. and Chan.Inq. p.m.17 Edw.IV, no. 48.
[105] Cal. Pat. 1476-85, p. 499 ; Exch. Inq. p.m. mlix, 2 ; Feet of F. Mich. 33 Hen. VIII.
[106] Recov. R. Mich. 7 & 8 Eliz. m. cccxii ; Pat. 7 Eliz. pt. i ; Deed at Loseley.
[107] Feet of F. Trin. 7 Jas. I ; East. 32 Chas. II ; Chan. Inq. p.m. (Ser. 2), ccccxxxvii, 106.
[108] Brayley, op. cit. v, 215.

manor were wont to have the amercements.[109] They also had court baron, heriot, and relief.[110]

The chapel of St. Nicholas at Catteshull is mentioned in the Dean of Salisbury's survey of Godalming in 1220. The lady of the manor claimed suit of court from its tenants, but the chaplain and vicar were strictly prohibited from paying it.[111] The chapel was near the present manor-house, on the right-hand side of the road from Catteshull to Munstead.

FARNCOMBE MANOR was held by Ansgot under Edward the Confessor, and became demesne land of Odo, Bishop of Bayeux, after the Conquest. He added it to the land which he had out in farm at Bramley ('convertit ad firmam de Bronlei'). One of the king's reeves, Lofns, claimed the manor in 1086, asserting that he had held it when the king was in Wales (i.e. in 1081), and had kept it till the bishop took his journey into Kent (i.e. in 1082).[112] It was probably granted out to tenants by the Crown after the forfeiture of Bishop Odo's lands, for in 1280 Reginald of Imworth and his wife Matilda held the manor in her right[113] and granted it to John son of john Adryan, to hold of Matilda and her heirs.[114]

The manor passed to the Ashursts of East Betchworth in the latter part of the 14th century. In 1371 William Prestwyke and others in Farncombe paid fine for leave of absence from the hundred court.[115] There are similar payments by the lord of Farncombe, not named, in 1377 and 1384. In 1382 William Ashurst paid a fine of the same amount, xiid.[116] The Ashursts held High Ashurst in Mickleham and other land in that neighbourhood, and probably had acquired Farncombe about 1382, and did not find it convenient to attend Godalming Hundred Court. Ashursts paid for non-attendance in 1412, 1440, and 1447. In 1413 Margaret Ashurst conveyed Farncombe Manor to her son William.[117]

In 1452 the death of William Ashurst, the holder of land in Farncombe, is mentioned.[118]

In 1503-4 John Ashurst of Farncombe paid 19s. 9d. towards an aid,[119] and he died seised of the manor in February 1506-7, leaving a brother and heir William.[120] He is said to have sold the manor, 12 January, to john Skinner, who had married john Ashurst's widow.[121] James Skinner sold it to John

Mellersh in 1552,[122] and John Mellersh, clothier, died 1567 holding the manor of Farncombe, which he entailed on his son John and heirs.[123] john cut off the entail by recovery 1573,[124] but died seised in 1623 leaving a daughter and heir Juliane who married John Launder.[125] In 1675 John Launder senior, his grandson, and the latter's son John Launder junior, conveyed the manor to Thomas Mathew and others,[126] probably as trustees to sell, for five years later Robert Pratt sold it to Anne Duncombe of Albury,[127] who, with her second husband, Timothy Wilson, conveyed it to trustees in 1685.[128] After the death of Anne's granddaughter, Mary wife of Charles Eversfield, the manor, which had been divided among her four daughters, was sold by them, 1733-4, to Henry Page,[129] who left it by will to his nephew John Skeet,[130] after his widow's death. She died 1784, and John Skeet was in possession in the same year.[131]

His widow died in 1800, having bequeathed Farncombe in moieties to her two daughters, Sarah Hall and Elizabeth Geering Lane. The former's infant

SHACKLEFORD : THE OLD GARDEN, HALL PLACE

daughters Eliza and Sarah inherited her moiety.[132] In 1841 the manor was the property of William Saunders Robinson and others.[133] The British Freehold Land Society bought the land c. 1850-5 and pulled down the Manor House, which stood at the angle between Manor Road and Farncombe Street. The manor was advertised for sale in 1859, with 76 heriots and £2 a year quit-rents.[134] It was bought by Mrs. Marshall, and belongs now to Mr. George Marshall, her grandson.

In the road near Farncombe, besides several

[109] Chan. Inq. p.m. 20 Edw. I, no. 25.

[110] *Plac. de Quo Warr.* (Rec. Com.), 743 ; Misc. Bks. (L.T.R.), clxix, 114.

[111] *Reg. of St. Osmund* (Rolls Ser.), i, 297. The chapel is said to be 'in curia quae fuit Stephani de Thurneham.'

[112] *V.C.H. Surr.* i, 302a.

[113] Reginald died c. 1280, leaving an infant son John ; Chan. Inq. p.m. 8 Edw. I, file 25, no. 8.

[114] Feet of F. Surr. 8 Edw. I, 7.

[115] Godalming Hund. Ct. 2 Oct. 45 Edw. III.

[116] Ibid. 29 Oct. 1 Ric. II ; Oct. 8 Ric. II ; 6 Ric. II.

[117] B.M. Add. MS. 6167, fol. 182 ; Hund. Ct. R.

[118] 12 Oct. 31 Hen. VI.

[119] Add. R. (B.M.), 1355.

[120] Chan. Inq. p.m. (Ser. 2), xx, 24.

[121] Deeds quoted by Symmes. Add. MS. (B.M.), 6167, fol. 182.

[122] Feet of F. Surr. Mich. 6 Edw. VI.

[123] P.C.C. Will proved 7 Feb. 1568.

[124] Recov. R. Hil. 16 Eliz.

[125] Chan. Inq. p.m. (Ser. 2), ccccv, 151.

[126] Feet of F. Surr. 27 Chas. II. Symmes quotes a conveyance by John Launder to Thomas Mathew and Robert Pratt. Add. MS. (B.M.), 6167, fol. 182.

[137] Close, 32 Chas. II, pt. iii, no. 28.

[138] Feet of F. Surr. East. 1 Jas. II.

[139] Feet of F. Surr. Hil. 6 Anne ; Close, 7 Geo. II, pt. iv, no. 5.

[130] Manning and Bray, op. cit. i, 624.

[131] Recov. R. East. 24 Geo. III, m. 241.

[132] Manning and Bray, op. cit. i, 624.

[133] Brayley, op. cit. v, 219.

[134] *W. Surr. Times*, 27 Aug. 1859.

3

5

picturesque half-timber cottages and other ancient houses, there is a charming block of red-brick almshouses in Mead Row, founded in 1622 by Richard Wyatt, citizen of London, and owner of Hall Place, Shackleford. This has a wonderful row of chimneys, very irregular in outline, at the back, and in the centre is the chapel, in which are some curious details.[135]

A small stone and brick cottage on the road leading to Binscombe[135a] has a good chimney and a brick hood-moulding over its windows.

HURTMORE (Hormera, xi cent.; Hertmere, xiii cent.; Hurtmere, xiv cent.), also a tithing in Godalming, was held before the Conquest by Alwin. In

1086 Tezelin held it of Walter Fitz Other, founder of the Windsor family,[136] in which the overlordship was still vested in 1541.[137] The under tenant in 1166 was Philip of Hurtmore,[135] and in january 1199–1200 William of Hurtmore released his claim in land in Hurtmore to Thomas son of Philip in consideration of a life annuity.[138] Thomas of Hurtmore held a fee in Hurtmore.[140] A Thomas of Hurtmore granted the manor to the Priory of Newark, Surrey, in 1259,[141] and about twenty years afterwards the prior granted to Mary Norries and her grandson Robert common of pasture in 'Quachet' and land called 'Lyth,' formerly the demesne of Thomas of Hurtmore.[142]

GODALMING CHURCH FROM THE EAST

The prior leased the manor from time to time, for in 1527 Henry Tanner obtained a lease of it for forty years,[143] and in 1535 the farm of the manor was £4 13s. 4d.[144] On the surrender of the priory in 1538 Hurtmore was taken into the hands of the king, who in April 1542 gave it with other lands to Andrew Lord Windsor in part exchange for the manor of Stanwell.[145] The latter's son William succeeded to his estates in the following March,[146] and his son and heir Edward Lord Windsor sold the manor to Eustace Moone of Farnham in 1564–5.[147] Edmund Moone, son of Eustace, sold Hurtmore to Francis Clarke in 1590.[148] He was resident in 1592.[149] In 1595 he conveyed it to his son john Clarke and his wife Mary. Their children were baptized at Godalming 1596–1601.

In 1606 john Clarke sold it to Sir Edward More of Odiham.[150] For some reason he obtained a grant of it from the Crown in 1615,[151] probably on account of recusancy. By his will he directed that his daughter and her husband Sir William Staunton, recusant convict,[152] should have the house free of rent for life. He died in 1623, having settled Hurtmore on his infant grandson Edward More.[153] The latter was dealing with Hurtmore

---

[135] There are excellent photographs of the front and back in *Old Cottages and Farmhouses in Surr.*, B. T. Batsford, 1908. The will of Richard Wyatt and other ancient documents relating to the almshouses are printed in *Surr. Arch. Coll.* iii, 277.

[135a] Illustrated in Mr. Ralph Nevill's *Old Cottage and Domestic Architecture of South-west Surrey.*

[136] *V.C.H. Surr.*, i, 323a.

[137] When they exchanged it with the king, in whom the overlordship was afterwards Vested; see below. Chan. Inq. p.m. 10 Ric. II, no. 46; ibid. 22 Ric. II, no. 52; ibid. 9 Hen. V, no. 45; ibid. 17 Hen. VI, no. 36.

[138] *Red Bk. of Exch.* 315.

[139] Feet of F. Surr. 1 John, 6; Pipe R. 2 John, m. 15 d.

[140] *Testa de Nevill* (Rec. Com.), 221.

[141] Feet of F. Surr. 43 Hen. III, 28. For an *inspeximus* of this gift see Dugdale, *Mon.* vi, 384.

[142] *Cal. of Anct. D.* iii, 284. Thomas of Hurtmore had granted Robert Norries land in Southcroft in Hurtmore; ibid. iii, 279, 283.

[143] Mins. Accts. Surr. 31 & 32 Hen. VIII, no. 146.

[144] *Valor Eccl.* (Rec. Com.), ii, 33.

[145] D. of Purchase and Exchange (Aug. Off.), 33 Hen. VIII, C. 22. Strangely enough Stanwell was the *caput* of the barony of Windsor of which Hurtmore was held. The exchange is said to have been forced upon Lord Windsor by Henry VIII. See Dugdale, *Baronage*, ii, 307–8. In 1651 the fee-farm rent due from the manor to the Crown was sold by the trustees of the Crown lands to John Johns, a merchant of London; Close, 1651, pt. ix, no. 23.

[146] Chan. Inq. p.m. (Ser. 2), lxviii, 28.

[147] Pat. 7 Eliz. pt. i; Chan. Inq. p.m. (Ser. 2), ccxiv, 236.

[148] Feet of F. Surr. East. 32 Eliz.; Recov. R. Trin. 32 Eliz.

[149] Godalming Ct. R. (view of frankpledge), 11 Oct. 34 Eliz.

[150] Close, 4 Jas. I, pt. xxxiii, modern ref. no. 1870.

[151] Pat. 13 Jas. I, pt. xv, no. 2.

[152] Subs. R. 4 Chas. I, bdle. 186, no. 439.

[153] Chan. Inq. p.m. (Ser. 2), cccxcix, 155.

in 1643,[154] and again in 1657.[155] His two children died in infancy.[156] In 1679 Isabel More, spinster, was in possession of the manor and sold it to Ralph Lee, executor to Simon Bennett of Calverton,[157] whose daughters, Frances wife of James fourth Earl of Salisbury[158] and Grace wife of John Bennett, held it in moiety. The fifth Earl of Salisbury had the remainder of Grace Bennett's share.[159]

James first Marquis of Salisbury sold Hurtmore in 1786 to John Richardson of Shackleford,[160] whose heir, John Aldborough Richardson, was in possession in 1804.[161]

In 1814 he and his wife sold Hurtmore to William Keen. William Keen sold in 1828 to James Henry Frankland and Mary his wife of Eashing. Mr. Frankland died in 1859. His son Major Frankland took the name of Gill, and died unmarried in 1866. Hurtmore passed to his sister, Mrs. Sumner, and from her to her niece, Miss Kerr.[162]

Though the conveyance of Hurtmore in 1598 ascribes a court leet to it,[163] and though it is spoken of as a manor, it is doubtful if it really was such. No court baron can be traced, and the assertion about view of frankpledge in a court leet is untrue. The Hurtmore people answered at the Godalming hundred court for view of frankpledge except a few who appeared at Compton. Trespasses, &c., in Hurtmore are continually noticed in the Godalming courts.

One mill is mentioned in the Domesday Survey of the manor,[164] and mention is made of mills in Thomas of Hurtmore's grant to Newark Priory.[165]

TAYLORS was held by Nicholas Taillard in 1486-7.[166] He conveyed it to Polsted and others, trustees, who enfeoffed Tho-mas Purvoch. His son Tho-mas Purvoch enfeoffed Arnold Champion as purchaser or trustee.[167] Thomas Purvoch junior had a daughter Anne who married Lawrence Raw-sterne. It passed from him to Richard Compton,[168] who had married Agnes daughter of Arnold Champion.[169] Richard's son Thomas brought a suit in 1574 against Henry Hooke, who, having married Agnes widow of Richard Compton, entered upon the 'manor of Taylors,' which was settled on her for life, and spoiled the woods and suffered the manor-house to decay.[170] Thomas Compton left it to his nephew John Compton in 1606.[171] This Sir John Compton died seised in 1653. His grandson and heir was Comp-

TAILLARD. *Quarterly argent and sable a cross paty counterchanged.*

ton Tichborne.[172] He died and left it to his cousin Sir Henry Tichborne, bart., who held it in 1658,[173] and Sir Henry Joseph Tichborne was in possession in 1695.[174]

In 1696 it was conveyed to John Yalden.[175] Edmund Yalden his grandson died in 1814 (aged 89)

COMPTON of Godal-ming. *Ermine a bend sable with three helms or thereon.*

TICHBORNE. *Vair a chief or.*

holding Taylors,[176] and left it to Edmund Woods his sister's son.[177] He died 1833 and it passed to his daughter Katherine. It was sold to the Marshall family, to whom it still belongs.

VANN (Fenne, xii and xiii cents.; Fanne, xiv and xv cents.), on the borders of Hambledon and Chiddingfold, was really a tithing,[178] but was called a manor later. It is mentioned in a conveyance of 1198-9, when Emma, widow of William of Vann, released land there to William of Vann.[179] In 1232 Walter of Vann witnessed a grant of land in Arting-ton,[180] while Laurence of Yately and his wife Isabel granted lands in Godalming and Vann to Thomas of Vann in 1279.[181] Thomas atte Vann conveyed Vann to Robert atte Vann and his brother Walter in con-sideration of a life-rent in 1324.[182] It was held of William atte Vann in 1332, Henry Hussey being the tenant.[183] Tenants and tithingmen at Vann occur often in the Godalming Hundred Court. In 1371 Walter Webbele surrendered the tenement of William Piperham to Walter atte Vann and his heir. This was Piperham in Haslemere, which subsequently was conveyed as a separate parcel, with the manor of Vann.[184]

Walter atte Vann was subsequently in debt. In 1412 John Loxley for 'le Fanne' and Thomas atte Vann pay 6d. for leave of absence from the hundred court.[185] In 1448 Bernard Jenyn or Jenings was summoned to the court[186] to do fealty, probably for Vann, for in 1476 John Hill and John Mellersh, probably trustees, enfeoffed Bernard Jenings of 'land in the manor of Vann' in tail male. John son of Bernard succeeded to it at his father's death,[187] and his son

154 Recov. R. Mich. 19 Chas. I, m. 9.
155 *Notes of F.* Surr. Trin. 1657.
156 Godalming Par. Reg.
157 Feet of F. Div. Co. Trin. 31 Chas. II ; and will of Simon Bennett, Cottle, 127. He left each of his daughters £20,000. Hurtmore is not mentioned.
158 Close, 31 Geo. III, pt. iii, no. 7.
159 Deed of 23 Nov. 1725, produced in sale of 1828.
160 Close, 27 Geo. III, pt. i, no. 18.
161 Manning and Bray, op. cit. i, 626.
162 Private and local inform.
163 Close, 38 Eliz. pt. v ; Recov. R. Mich. 22 Geo. III, m. 418.
164 *V.C.H.* Surr. i, 323a.

165 Feet of F. Surr. 43 Hen. III, 28.
166 Godalming Rental at Loseley.
166 Esch. Inq. p.m. 67 Hen. VIII, file 1070.
168 Misc. Bks. (Land Rev.), vol. 190, fol. 223.
169 Berry, *Hants Gen.* 328.
170 Chan. Proc. C.c 15 Eliz. 51.
171 P.C.C. Will (Stafforde, 33).
172 Godalming court baron 30 Sept. 1653.
173 Recov. R. Mich. 1658, m. 108.
174 Close, 7 Will. III, pt. iv, no. 10.
175 Feet of F. Surr. Mich. 8 Will. III.
176 Godalming Ct. R. 26 Oct. 1814.
177 Ibid.

178 Godalming view of frankpledge, 17 Edw. III, &c.
179 Feet of F. Surr. 10 Ric. I, 39.
180 *Cal. of Chart.* R. i, 366.
181 Feet of F. Surr. 7 Edw. I, 17. They were to be held of Isabel and her heirs.
182 Feet of F. Surr. 18 Edw. II, 14.
183 Chan. Inq. p.m. 6 Edw. III (1st nos.), no. 66. See also ibid. 23 Edw. III, pt. i, 77.
184 Godalming Hund. Ct. 2 Oct. 45 Edw. III.   185 Ibid. 10 Nov. 1412.
186 Ibid. 18 Apr. 26 Hen. VI. He married Elizabeth daughter of John Loxley (see Braboeuf).
187 Chan. Proc. Ser. 2), lxxxiii, 20.

Nicholas is said to have settled the manor on his wife Margaret for life, with remainder to their son Bernard.

Margaret's third husband, Henry Mannock, held in right of his wife in 1548.[188] He died in 1563, having quarrelled with his wife, to whom he left nothing in his will.[189]

In 1564 Margaret brought a suit against Ralph, great-nephew of john Jenings, who had entered upon the manor after the death of Bernard.[190] Ralph Jenings held it,[191] and was succeeded by his son Thomas, who sold it to Thomas Cowper in 1590.[192] Thomas Cowper's brother and heir Martin sued for the lands as part of his inheritance,[193] and released his claim to John Hollinshed and Richard Sheppard in 1597.[194]

In 1608 they conveyed it to the Vintners' Company for the use of Mary Clarke wife of John Clarke of Battle in Sussex, and her son Francis and her other sons in succession.[195]

John Clarke, the third son, parted with it to William Byerley in 1635,[196] but apparently the purchase money was not all paid,[197] and it reverted to his son Mark, and afterwards to his son Antony, who was in possession in 1665,[198] and in 1689 sold to John Childe[199] the manor of Vann and a parcel of land called Pepperhams. John Childe died 1701, and was succeeded by his son John.[200] He sold to John Greenhill in 1722.[201] In 1734 it was entailed on Peter, son of Sir Peter and Sarah Anna Myers, and Sarah his wife, daughter of john Curryer. The latter in her widowhood settled it[202] in 1758-9 on her daughter Sarah, wife of Thomas Geldart, but her son Peter Myers was treated as tenant in a court of 1762 as a defaulter. The Geldarts are said in a court of 1789 to have obtained Vann from Peter Myers. In 1822 Richard Smyth of Burgate died holding the manor,[203] and it was in the Smyth family for some time later. There is no record of any court in the reputed manor.

The reputed manor of *WESTBROOK* lies to the west of the town. From an undated customary of Godalming of the early part of the reign of Edward III, of which a 16th or 17th-century copy exists at Loseley, it appears that there was a Richard de Westbrook holding land in Godalming; by the marginal notes on the copy this seems to be the same land that was afterwards held by Thomas Hull, owner of Westbrook. The conditions of tenure are plainly servile in origin, including carriage of harvest and serving as reeve with food allowance. In 1334 a Robert Westbrook and his wife Bona were enfeoffed of land in Godalming,[204]

but whether of what was afterwards called Westbrook is not clear. Westbrooks occur frequently in the Godalming courts. They held Prestwick in Chiddingfold soon after 1327,[205] and Asshtede,[206] which afterwards both belonged to the Westbrooks of Westbrook, but there is no evidence of their holding Westbrook. It was probably a holding in Godalming named from them. The original ' Westbroke ' was perhaps that in Hampshire. There were members of the family about the neighbourhood, and they were rising in the world. A John Westbrook acquired the Strode moiety of Loseley in or before 1481.

According to Symmes, William Westbrook was buried at Godalming in 1437, and Thomas Westbrook in 1493; both holders of the manor.[207] It appears from a rental at Loseley that John Westbrook held Westbrook in 1486. john Westbrook sold his moiety of Loseley Manor in 1508.[208] He died in 1513-14 and was buried in Godalming Church.[209] William Westbrook died in 1537. His widow Margaret resided at Westbrook, and after her death the manor descended to the heirs of his sisters Florence Scarlet and Elizabeth Hull.[210]

Thomas Hull and John Scarlet a minor were holding Westbrook in moieties in 1547.[211] john Scarlet's portion seems to have passed to William Morgan, who sold it to Thomas Hull about the year 1576.[212] He was thus seised of the whole of Westbrook. A Thomas Hull and his wife Florence were dealing with it in 1600, and again in 1622.[213] Their son Thomas Hull was an ardent Royalist,[214] who suffered sequestration in April 1649 for lending money to maintain the war against Parliament.[215] He was obliged to compound, and in 1656 sold Westbrook to john Platt, clerk of West Horsley,[216] who afterwards held weekly conventicles at his house in Godalming,[217] and died in 1670. His son John, who was knighted in 1672, was raising money on the manor in 1674,[218] and is said to have built Westbrook Place.[219] In 1688 the manor was sold to Sir Theophilus Oglethorpe, kt.,[220] who sat in Parliament for Haslemere from 1698 till 1701.[221] His eldest son Louis was killed at Schellenberg in 1704. The next son, Theophilus, who also represented

[188] Survey of manor of Godalming, 1-3 Edw. VI; Land. Rev. Misc. Surv. vol. 190, p. 248, &c.

[189] P.C.C. Wills (Stephenson, 47).

[190] Chan. Proc. (Ser. 2), lxxxiii, 20.

[191] Chan. Inq. p.m. (Ser. 2), clxii, 146.

[192] Feet of F. Surr. Trin. 32 Eliz.; Recov. R. Trin. 32 Eliz. m. 22.

[193] Chan. Proc. Eliz. C.c. xiii, 59; ibid. C.c. xiv, 41.

[194] Com. Pleas D. Enr. Trin. 39 Eliz. m. 9.

[195] Close, 6 Jas. I, pt. xi, no. 11.

[196] Close, 12 Chas. I, pt. xxvi, 25; 13 Chas. I, xxv, 8.

[197] Will of John Clarke, P.C.C. 2 June 1637 (Goare, 99).

[198] B.M. Add. MS. 6167, fol. 168.

[199] Feet of F. Surr. Mich. 1 Will. and Mary.

[200] Godalming Ct. R. 17 Oct. 1701.

[201] Recov. R. Hil. 9 Geo. I, Vann, Winterhull and High Loxley.

[202] Close, 32 Geo. II, pt. i, no. 8; cf. Feet of F. Surr. East. 32 Geo. II.

[203] Will.

[204] Feet of F. Surr. 7 Edw. III, 29. It consisted of a messuage, a carucate of land, and 13s. 8d. rent.

[205] Deed Rev. T. S. Cooper.

[206] Godalming R. 1384.

[207] Inscriptions quoted by Symmes, Add. MS. (B.M.), 6167, fol. 167. It is probable that Symmes confused 1437 and 1537; the date of Thomas Westbrook is doubtful.

[208] Add. Chart. (B.M.), 13557.

[209] Where there is an altar-tomb in his memory. See Surr. Arch. Soc. Proc. vii, 279. Ralph Nevill, F.S.A., Notes on the Restoration of Godalming Ch.

[210] See V.C.H. Surr. ii, 592, under Compton Hall.

[211] Misc. Bks. (Exch. T.R.), clxix, 223.

[212] Close, 20 Eliz. pt. xx; Feet of F. Sutt. Mich. 18-19 Eliz.

[213] Feet of F. Surt. East. 42 Eliz.; ibid. Trin. 20 Jas. I.

[214] He had an elder brother Humphrey who died without issue.

[215] Cal. of Com. for Compounding, iii, 2018.

[216] Close, 1656, pt. xxxi, no. 20.

[217] A. R. Bax, 'Conventicles in Surr.' Surr. Arch. Coll. xiii, 159.

[218] Feet of F. Surr. East. 26 Chas. II.

[219] Aubrey, Nat. Hist. and Antiq. of Surr. iv, 17.

[220] Before 1690, for in March of that year Lady Oglethorpe had a pass to go to her house near Godalming; Cal. S.P. Dom. 1689-90, p. 512.

[221] Dict. Nat. Biog. xlii, 50.

Haslemere, and died at the Jacobite court of St. Germains about 1728, was dealing with the manor in 1727.[222] His younger brother, General James Edward Oglethorpe, the great philanthropist and founder of Georgia, next came into possession. In spite of his frequent absences from England, he was five times elected member of parliament for Haslemere. After his final return from Georgia he was made a general in the English army and served under the Duke of Cumberland in the rebellion of 1745. He died in 1785, having left the manor by will to his widow, who devised it to be sold for the general's great-nephew, the Marquis of Bellegarde.[223] It was bought in 1788 by Christopher Hodges, who sold it in 1790 to Nathaniel Godbold, a quack doctor.[224] The latter's son of the same name was living there in 1824 and died 1834.[225] In 1844 part of the estate was sold to the Direct London and Portsmouth Railway Company ;[226] and the house, after being occupied only for short terms, became the Meath Home for Epileptics in 1892. Mr. G. J. Hull bought the house, part of the estate, and the manor. The manor is now held by Mr. H. Thackeray Turner.

A quit-rent of 10s. 6d. was payable from Westbrook to the lord of Godalming manor, of whom it was held.

OGLETHORPE. *Argent a fesse dancetty between three boars' heads sable.*

Near Westbrook are the town mill and a tanning mill.

In the roll of a leet-court held at Godalming in 1483 mention is made of 'Westbrokesmyll.'[227] Two fulling mills were sold with the manor in 1624, 1647, and 1727.[228]

Binscombe, about 1½ miles from Westbrook, seems to have been closely connected with that manor. 'Bedelescombe' and Farncombe sometimes sent two tithingmen between them, sometimes one each separately, to the hundred court of Godalming.[229] A list of tenants of Westbrook Manor at Loseley (circa 1670) contains some names in Binscombe, and it is called sometimes a manor, but always in connexion with Westbrook. The existing houses are the property of Mrs. More-Molyneux McCowan, owner of Loseley. There is a Friends' burial ground dating from the 17th century. This is now no longer used.

CHURCHES The church of ST. PETER AND ST. PAUL is charmingly situated in the meadows close to the River Wey, set in a large and prettily kept churchyard.

It is built of Bargate stone rubble, originally of a bright yellow colour, and of hard texture. The dressings in the earliest periods were executed in the same stone, but from the end of the 12th century clunch or hard chalk was employed for wrought ware in the successive enlargements, Bath stone being used in the 19th-century additions. The roofs are tiled and the lofty spire is covered with lead—a valuable example of this treatment.

In its present form the church has been considerably

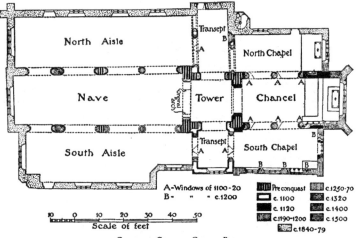

A—Windows of 1100-20   B— " " c.1200

Pre conquest   c.1250-70
c.1100   c.1320
c.1120   c.1400
c.1190-1200   c.1500
c.1840-79

10   0   10   20   30   40   50
Scale of feet

GODALMING CHURCH : GROUND PLAN

[222] Recov. R. Trin. 13 Geo. I, m. 271.
[223] Gent. Mag. lvii, 1025.
[224] Manning and Bray, op. cit. i, 611.

[225] Gent. Mag. xciv, 120 ; Feet of F. Surr. East. 57 Geo. III.
[226] Brayley, op. cit. v, 214.
[227] Add. R. (B.M.), 26892.
[228] Recov. R. Trin. 22 Jas. I, m. 35 ;

ibid. Mich. 23 Chas. I, m. 46 ; ibid. Trin. 13 Geo. I, m. 261.
[229] Add. R. (B.M.), 26892 ; ibid. 1355 ; and Rolls at Loseley, passim.

extended laterally and to the westward, the north transept has been prolonged, and the north chancel rebuilt on a larger plan, all within the 19th century—in 1840 and 1879. It consists therefore now of nave, 68 ft. 9 in. by 20 ft. 6 in. at the east end and 19 ft. 5 in. at the west end ; aisles of different lengths, 20 ft. wide ; transepts about 12 ft. 3 in. wide and originally 14 ft. 9 in. long ; central tower 16 ft. 6 in. square ; chancel 40 ft. 5 in. long by 17 ft. 3 m. ; and north and south chancel aisles, respectively 35 ft. 6 in. by 14 ft. 9 in. and 34 ft. 6 in. by 16 ft.

We owe it to Mr. Ralph Nevill, F.S.A.[280] (who, with the late Sir Gilbert Scott, carried out the last enlargements), and later to the painstaking and acute observation of Mr. S. Welman,[281] that a very complete architectural history of the building can be put together. Probably there are at least twelve periods of work to be traced in the walls of the present church. The nucleus around which it has grown lies in the centre, the eastern half of the nave representing the simple aisleless nave of the pre-Conquest church, and the central tower its short, square chancel. This would give a nave of about 32 ft. by 20 ft. ; the chancel, which had an inclination towards the north, being 16 ft. 6 in. wide and in length originally about a foot longer. This Saxon church had walls averaging 3 ft. in thickness, and disproportionately lofty—about 25 ft.—as was commonly the case in work of this period. Until 1879 the original chancel arch, a plain circular-headed opening about 10 ft. wide, of one order, with plain chamfered imposts, remained as the western arch of the present central tower; but, against the wish of Mr. Nevill, this interesting feature was then removed, and a wide and lofty pointed opening put in its place. The outline of the gable wall above this arch (upon which the west wall of the tower had been subsequently raised), together with the drip-stone or weathering of the pre-Conquest chancel which abutted against its eastern face, was noted by Mr. Nevill, and their true relationship to the earliest structure finally established by Mr. Welman's subsequent discovery of two curious eyelet holes in the apex of this eastern gable of the nave. These are double-splayed, their narrowest diameter being in the heart of the wall, but the internal splay was protracted downward on the western face to throw the light in that direction. Doubtless they lit a roof-chamber over the nave.

About the year 1100 the primitive church received its first enlargement, in the form of a long chancel (about 33 ft. 3 in. by 17 ft. 3in.), a low tower being raised upon the gabled walls of the original chancel, and the eastern wall thickened by about a foot on the western side, an arch of two plain orders, with chamfered imposts, being pierced through it. This arch still exists, but in 1879 it was lifted up on higher piers, the old imposts being left in position and new added to mark the increased height. Earlier alterations had brought to light the remains of six of

the windows of this period, three in either side wall of the chancel (lettered A on the plan), and the base and part of the jamb of a priest's door at the west end of the south wall : the east wall of this chancel no longer exists, having been pulled down and rebuilt farther eastward in the 14th century.[282] There are traces of flat pilaster buttresses having been added to strengthen the junction between the first and second period work. This chancel also inclines to the north.

About 1120 (third period) narrow transepts were added, some of the windows of which can also be traced, arches were pierced in the hitherto solid north and south walls of what had been the first chancel—now the central tower—and the latter was heightened by an additional stage, which still retains in each face the two round-headed openings that were then formed, with a string-course of rounded section below them. A small door of this period has been preserved in the rebuilt end of the north transept.

In the last ten years of the 12th century, but perhaps not quite at one and the same time, aisles were added to the nave, two lofty pointed arches being pierced in either wall, and smaller ones in the west walls of the transepts. This may be called the fourth period. At about the same date, but perhaps slightly earlier, the arches to the transepts from the central tower were altered to a pointed form, and perhaps widened.

In the fifth period, c. 1200, the chancel aisles, or north and south chancels, were thrown out, their arcades being pierced through the second-period walls, leaving the original windows largely intact, but blocked up. These chapels were lit by tall narrow lancets, the south chapel having five in its southern wall and three in its eastern, parts of which still remain (lettered B on plan), although displaced by later insertions.[283]

For some reason this displacement began very soon, for in about 1250 the curious grouped lancets, with acutely pointed heads and inner-plane arcade, in the south wall, took the place of two of the single lancets : and in 1270 an early essay in bar tracery was inserted in the east wall of the chancel. This is of five lights, the central wider and taller than the others, with three circles above, having cinquefoil cusping on a recessed plane, and the whole united by a pointed inclosing arch and hood moulding. At some time between 1200 and 1300 the first spire, lower than the present, and covered with oak shingles, replaced the original squat cap of the 12th century.[284]

Period eight—the 14th century—produced further changes, in the shape of the blocking up of the plain lancets in the western part of this south chapel, and the insertion of square-headed three-light windows with cusped ogee tracery, this type of window being inserted also in the transepts and nave aisles, and probably in the north chancel aisle. At the same time the chancel was extended about 4 ft. eastward, a large five-light window and diagonal

[280] Vide Mr. Ralph Nevill's account of discoveries made in 1879, in Surr. Arch. Coll. vii, 277.

[281] S. Welman, The Parish and Church of Godalming.

[282] The angle stone of the original foundation of the earliest east wall may be seen outside, where the south chantry abuts on the chancel.

[283] Mr. Welman points out that Richard de Chiddingfold, vicar, instituted by Savaric Archdeacon of Northampton and Treasurer of Salisbury, in or about 1200, probably engineered the work of this period. The sections of mouldings closely correspond to those of the same date at Chiddingfold Church.

[284] It is not easy to determine the date of the parapet which at one time crowned the tower and inclosed the base of the spire. Its corbels, which alone remain, are of various patterns and of more than one date : and such parapets on corbeltables were not uncommon in 12th-century towers, as at Witley, hard by, and at Clymping and Yapton, Sussex. Most probably this parapet dates from the erection of the first spire.

buttresses accompanying the rebuilding. In this period the first timber spire probably gave place to the much loftier one of oak covered with lead, which remains substantially as then reconstructed, save for the later addition of broaches at the angles when the parapet wall was removed.

To the ninth period—the 15th century—belong the extension westward of one bay of the nave and aisles, a window in the north wall of the north transept, a corresponding one in the south transept, and others which have been destroyed or shifted within recent times.

In the end of the 15th or beginning of the 16th century the roof of the nave was ceiled with panelling, the south chapel roof reconstructed, and a large doorway, having a four-centred arch within a square frame, was inserted in the west end of the church. This in 1840 was removed to its present position beneath the tracery window in the east wall of the south chapel. During the 17th and 18th centuries a western gallery and other galleries were erected; the south aisle walls were raised to provide the necessary height, and re-roofed with a span roof. Wooden frame windows were inserted in several places, and dormers made to light the north aisle.

In 1840, after the church had passed through the usual stages of neglect, disfigurement, and mutilation that characterized the 17th, 18th, and early 19th centuries, a severe 'restoration' swept away not only abuses, but many valuable ancient features. Most of the work of 1879 was of the nature of a true archaeological restoration, in which much of the bad work

of 1840 was undone and many valuable ancient features were brought to light.

The windows and doors of the nave and aisles and north chantry belong for the most part to 1840 and 1879, including that in the east wall of the north chantry, but the east window dates from 1859. The stair turret on the north side is also modern.

Some points of detail in the interior of the church have now to be considered.

On the window sills of the south chapel are carved fragments, in a very hard shelly limestone, of pre-Conquest date. Two seem to have formed the rims of a circular basin or basins, but they are hardly large enough to have served for a font, as has been suggested, nor does the shape at all suggest such a use. The total diameter of the two halves is only 1 ft. $7\frac{1}{2}$ in. by $6\frac{3}{4}$ in. in height and $3\frac{3}{4}$ in. thickness. The upright face is ornamented with four horses' heads, separating alternate designs of interlaced work and a running scroll, such as are found in the pre-Conquest arch at Britford Church, near Salisbury. A third fragment, with a basket-work pattern, may have been part of the block on which this basin stood; and two others with a scroll-pattern and figures, much defaced, suggest the stem of a churchyard cross. Some of these were found built into the walls, notably in the west arch of the tower, i.e. the chancel arch of the pre-Conquest church, suggesting that they had formed part of some building of even older date.

Next in interest and date to these are the remains of the priest's door and six windows of c. 1100 in the chancel walls. The windows have splays running

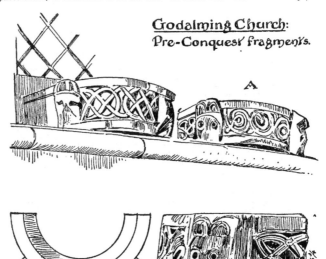

Godalming Church:
Pre-Conquest fragments.

A

Plan of A.   R: End of A.   P.M.Johnston del.

39

out to a narrow chamfered edge, without rebate or groove for glazing. The rough plaster of the splays is cut into patterns round the circular internal head, such as zigzag, fret, and saw-tooth ; [235] and both on the plastering and stonework are painted well-preserved coeval patterns in red and white. The somewhat later transept windows are not so ornamented. In the south wall of the south transept is a 12th-century piscina and the remains of what may have been sedilia.

In the west wall of the south transept is the arch of 1190, with characteristic mouldings and a slightly

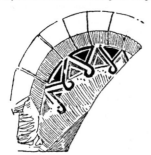

PAINTED DECORATION IN GODALMING CHURCH

incised cheveron ornament on the bell of one of its capitals. The two eastern arches of the north and south nave arcades are set upon unusually lofty piers, those on the south being circular, while the north are octagonal, an alteration of later date. The north and south arches of the tower are perfectly plain, and possibly a little earlier.

The nave roof is ancient—the eastern part perhaps even of 13th-century date—but the flat panelled ceiling added in the reign of Henry VII was in 1840 turned into one of canted shape ; the old painted shields, bearing local and other coats of arms, which were fixed at the intersection of the ribs of the panelling, were preserved and re-used in the new work. Similar wooden shields, displaying general and local heraldry, initials of benefactors, &c., existed up to the same date in the south chantry and the adjoining transept. In both transepts, in the south chapel, and in the main chancel, are ancient roofs, parts of which may be as old as the 12th or 13th century, but with considerable reconstruction at different dates. The south chapel roof has somewhat elaborate mouldings on many of its timbers, of very much later date. This roof was always a span roof ; but that of the north chapel, prior to 1840, when the extension took place, was a lean-to, as was also that of the north aisle of the nave.

Among smaller features may be noted the early 14th-century sedilia, piscina, and aumbry in the south wall of the chancel ; the early 13th-century piscina and aumbry in the north chancel ; and the unusually large double piscina, with two aumbries over, in the south chapel of the same date. The two piscinae are divided by a small octagonal shaft with cap and base. Beneath these is an altar-tomb of marble on chalk and brick base,[236] and a disused font also of late character and quite plain.

In the same south chapel, on the partly unblocked splays of the destroyed lancets, are some very valuable and well-preserved fragments of painting, coeval with the lancets themselves (c. 1200). These, which are somewhat elaborately executed in several colours, show figures of about life-size within trefoil-headed canopies. On the east splay of the easternmost lancet on the south side St. John the Baptist is shown, with hairy mantle, and bearing a disc on which is the Agnus Dei. Having been covered up from about half a century after the date of execution until 1879, these paintings are exceptionally well preserved. It is said that in 1840 many others, on the general wall surfaces, were uncovered only to be destroyed.

Aubrey mentions one or two coats of arms in the glazing of the chancel and south chantry windows, including those of England and France, but these no longer exist. There is a part of a lion, or, in the east window of the south chancel, and a rose with diamond quarters in the north transept.

A very large and solid oak chest, of the same date as the chantry, 5 ft. 7 in. by 1 ft. 9¼ in. and 2 ft. 4 in. high, has lately been placed here. It belongs to the pin-hinge group of the 13th century, and has a pierced quadrant to the standards, and a money-hutch inside with a secret well below.[237] A good oak railing, which formerly fenced three sides of the sacrarium, was removed in 1867, and parts of it used as stair balusters in a house known as the 'Square.'

The pulpit is Elizabethan. There are two communion tables ; one of Elizabethan or Jacobean date, which formerly had extending leaves, now stands in the north chancel, cruelly mangled to suit modern taste, and concealed by upholstery ; the other, a good but more modern table, has now been placed in the vestry.

Besides the altar tomb above mentioned, there are no monuments of importance,[237a] and, what is rather surprising in a church of this size and antiquity, practically none of pre-Reformation date. In the chancel are brasses to Thomas Purvoch and wife, 1509, and John Barker, 1595, in armour; and there are slabs, some with brass plates, escutcheons, and carved armorial bearings. The inscriptions to Thomas and Isabella Westbrook no longer exist, but the old family of the Eliots of Busbridge are largely represented : and on the south side of the chancel is an alabaster and black marble tablet, with a kneeling figure, to Judith Eliot, wife of William Eliot, 1615. The inscription is of

---

[235] Similar to the cut plaster edges at Compton Church in this neighbourhood.

[236] To John Westbrook 'Squyer' and Elizabeth his wife, as recorded in Manning and Bray's Surrey : the brass inscription strip and coats of arms are now missing, as is also a monument to William Westbrook

of the same family (to whom the south chantry belonged), dated 1437, according to Symmes's MS. The inscription, quoted in Mr. Welman's book, reads like one of a century later, and describes the deceased as 'Catholike of Faith.' Vide supra, note 207.

[237] This chest closely resembles others

of the same date and class at Rogate and Bosham churches, Sussex ; all described and illustrated in the Arch. Journ. lxiv, 243-306, and in Surr. Arch. Coll. xx, 68-89.

[237a] This is owing to the fact that the lords of the hundred and manor were absentees.

the quaintly laudatory style so often met with in monuments of this period.

In the south transept is a tablet to the Rev. Owen Manning, Canon of Lincoln, rector of Peper Harow and vicar of Godalming for thirty-seven years, joint author of Manning and Bray's *History of Surrey*, who died in 1801. He is buried in the churchyard.

The Registers of Godalming, edited by Mr. H. E. Malden, have been published by the Surrey Parish Register Society (vol. ii), and extracts from them in a paper on the church by the late Major Heales, F.S.A.[227b] They commence in 1582, but copies of earlier entries are to be found in Symmes's MS. in the British Museum, among which is :—

'1541, July 7, Sir James Wall, Soul Priest of Godalming, was buried.'[228]

The famous Nicholas Andrews, 'Vic. de Godalmyn,' has signed each page of vol ii, from March 1636 to 1642. In the plague-year, 1666, there are many entries of deaths due to 'ye great sickness,' which, no doubt owing to the proximity of the Portsmouth road, must have spread from London with fatal effect.

Besides more modern pieces, there are patens of 1685 and 1722 among the church plate, and a fine silver alms basin of 1632.

The bells have all been recast in the 18th and 19th centuries. Prior to 1849 or 1850 there was a unique survival (so far as Surrey is concerned) of a sanctus bell, hung externally at the base of the south-east side of the spire. This now does duty at the cemetery chapel. It was cast by Richard Phelps in 1724.

The church of St. John the Baptist, Busbridge, is of Bargate stone with chalk quoins and windows in 13th-century style. There is a central tower. It was consecrated in 1867.

The church of St. John the Evangelist, Farncombe, is of Bargate stone, with a bell-turret but no tower or spire, in 13th-century style. It was consecrated in 1849. The Rev. Charles C. R. Dallas, rector 1859–80, was as an ensign in the 32nd Foot wounded at Quatre Bras. The church was built upon land given by the late James More Molyneux which had escheated to him as lord of the manor owing to the tenant having committed murder.

The church of St. Mary the Virgin, Shackleford, is of Bargate stone in a good 13th-century style, built by Sir Gilbert Scott. It is cruciform, with north and south aisles divided from the nave by arcades of four arches. A central tower and spire were built in 1865.

The ancient site of the parish church was Minster Field at Tuesley. A chapel dedicated in honour of the Virgin Mary was still standing in a ruinous state there in 1220, and its memory was preserved by celebrations on the Purification, the Vigil of the Assumption, and the Nativity of the Virgin. There was also a burying-ground there.[229] After the dis-

solution of free chapels under Edward VI, the chapel in Godalming called Oldminster, with a cemetery round it, was leased to Laurence Eliot.[240] The foundations of this chapel, which have been uncovered in recent years, prove it to have been stone-built, with a nave 21 ft. by 14 ft., and a chancel 11 ft. long, of the same width as the nave, and separated from it by a wall with an arch or door in it. The nave itself was divided up the centre longitudinally by a wall or foundation, and many ancient interments were found within this area, the skeletons being disposed from east to west. The close called 'Chapel Fields' is mentioned with the Eliots' manor of Busbridge in May 1622 ;[241] it is close to Minster Field. A fair was held on Lady Day at the Old Minster as late as the 16th century.

GODALMING RECTORY was a separate fee in the time of Edward the Confessor, when Ulmaer held it of the king. In 1086 it consisted of a church and three hides, and was held of Godalming Manor by Ranulph Flambard, who became chief adviser of William II :[242] he also held the church at Tuesley,[243] and Tuesley was parcel of the rectory manor.[244] Ranulph fled from Henry I to Duke Robert of Normandy ; and though he was pardoned by Henry in 1106,[244] he does not appear to have regained entire possession of his lands, for a few years later[244] the king granted Ranulph's fee in Godalming, Tuesley, Enton, and Guildford, together with Heytesbury co. Wilts, to the church of St. Mary, Salisbury, as a prebend on condition that Ranulph should hold the churches for life as a canon of Salisbury.[246] It was known as the prebend of Heytesbury, and, Ranulph Flambard having died in 1128,[247] the prebend was annexed to the possessions of the Deans of Salisbury.[241] The cathedral obtained a confirmation of Godalming Church and a grant of 30 librates of land in Godalming in 1157 in return for the castle of Devizes.[249] The rectory was impropriate to the dean by 1285. In a visitation of the manor dated 1220 it is stated that there had been a vicar there for a long time, but he had never been residentiary.[250]

The estate and the advowson were leased frequently. In a dispute between the lessee (Mr. Castillion) and the vicar in 1578 some curious evidence was given of the former state kept by the dean when he visited the rectory house, then ruined, north of the church. He spent '30 hogsheads of drink at Christmas.'[251] A picturesque old house which stood here till about 1860 must have been a successor to the one described. The dispute continued till 1628. The final decree in Chancery preserves the survey of the rectory manor made in 1622.[252]

The manor remained the property of the successive Deans of Salisbury till the Act of 1649 abolishing deans and chapters. Whilst it belonged to the State a survey of the rectory manor was taken.[253] It included, besides the right of presentation and tithes, the

[227b] *Surr. Arch. Coll.* iv, 205.

[228] Add. MS. 6167 ; being part of 'Collections for a History of Surrey' made by Mr. Symmes, an attorney of Guildford, in about the year 1670.

[229] *Reg. of St. Osmund* (Rolls Ser.), i, 297.

[240] *Misc. Bks.* (Land Rev.), vol. 190, fol. 237.

[241] Harl. Chart. 57 H. 43.

[242] *V.C.H. Surr.* i, 298b.

[243] Reg. of St. Osmund, fol. 42.

[244] *Dict. Nat. Biog.* xix, 237.

[244] Between 1109 and 1117.

[244] *Sarum Chart. and Doc.* (Rolls Ser.), 3.

[247] *Dict. Nat. Biog.* xix, 237.

[248] *Sarum Chart. and Doc.* (Rolls Ser.), 358.

[249] Ibid. 29. Manning and Bray state that this grant referred to the manor of Godalming, but mention is only made of the church with its appurtenances. The deed is clearly one of restoration, an amicable settlement of the late disputes as to

the cathedral's property. See ibid. 22 ; *Pipe R.* 1 Ric. I (Rec. Com.), 216 ; 2 Hen. II, 10 ; 4 Hen. II, 161 ; ibid. (Pipe R. Soc.), i, 55 ; iv, 42 et seq. ; *Testa de Nevill* (Rec. Com.), 225.

[250] *Reg. of St. Osmund* (Rolls Ser.), i, 297.

[251] Loseley MSS. ii, 31 ; ix, 55, and a loose paper.

[252] Chan. Decrees, 3 Chas. I, No. 247/4. The survey is quoted by Manning and Bray, *Hist. of Surr.* i, 644.

[253] *Proc. of the Surr. Arch. Soc.* vii, 50.

3
41
6

parsonage or rectory, glebe and 'sanctuary lands,' and the profits of court leet where 'one constable for the Deanes' was sworn. The lease by a former dean to Valentine Castillion was confirmed, but the manor was sold to George Peryer.[254] The dean and chapter were reinstated after the Restoration,[255] and the successive deans continued in possession till 22 May 1846, when the manor was transferred to the Ecclesiastical Commissioners.[256] The rectory manor was sold with the land about 1860 to Mr. John Simmonds, whose son, Mr. J. Whateley Simmonds, is now owner. The Commissioners retained the great tithes, and the advowson was vested in the Bishop of Winchester.

The early history of the advowson
ADVOWSONS of the parish church is coincident with that of the rectory manor. After the deprivation of Dr. Andrews, whose Calvinistic parishioners petitioned against him in 1640,[257] the king presented Isaac Fortrey. The Crown again presented in 1660,[258] but withdrew the presentation at the petition of the dean and chapter.[259]

The parsonage or rectory, now demolished, was directly north of the church. Parts of the vicarage house are of great antiquity.

The ecclesiastical parish of St. John the Baptist, Busbridge, was formed in 1865.[260] The advowson was then vested in Emma Susan, wife of Mr. John C. Ramsden of Busbridge Hall.[261]

Farncombe was formed into an ecclesiastical parish in 1849 ; [262] the living is in the gift of the Bishop of Winchester.

Shackleford parish was formed in 1866.[263] The living is also in the patronage of the bishop. These three are rectories, endowed by the Commissioners out of the great tithes.

There were also churches or chapels at Catteshull and Hurtmore, now lost. Traces of the Catteshull Chapel remained near the manor house when Manning wrote.

The wooden chapel of All Saints, Hurtmore, was held in 1220 by Nicholas, apparitor of the Chapter of Guildford, for half a mark, who had it from Thomas of Hurtmore. The latter had made a composition for it with the Chancellor of Salisbury.[264] In 1260 the Prior of Newark, then lord of Hurtmore, pleaded that he had been permitted to present to Hurtmore 'Church.'[265] It has long disappeared, but its site was south-west of the Charterhouse Hill towards Eashing.

Wyatt's Almshouses were founded
CHARITIES in 1619 by Richard Wyatt, of London, carpenter. The management is vested in the Carpenters' Company. They stand in Mead Row, Farncombe.

Smith's Charity exists in Godalming as in other Surrey parishes ; it is distributed here in money, not in bread. Richard Champion in 1622 left a house and land in Crayford, now represented by £1,138 consols, which is administered as Smith's Charity.

The Meath Home for Epileptic Women and Girls was founded by the Countess of Meath, who in 1892 bought for the purpose the manor house of Westbrook, near Godalming station. A new wing was added in 1896. It accommodates seventy-four patients.

HAMBLEDON

Hameledune (xi cent.), Hameledon (xiii cent.), Hameldon (xiv cent.).

Hambledon is a small parish inclosed on the north, east, and west by Godalming, bounded on the south by Chiddingfold. It is about 3 miles from north to south, rather over 1 mile wide in the south, but tapering to the north. It contains 2,721 acres. The village is 4 miles from Godalming town. The northern part of the parish is on the Green Sand, which rises into a considerable elevation towards Highden Heath (Hyddenesheth in 1453). Hyde Stile is near it ; High. Down is a probable corruption. The clay in the south of the parish is very thickly wooded, chiefly with oak ; and Hambledon Hurst, an oak wood, through which a clay track runs, the old highway from Godalming to Chiddingfold and beyond, is, when passable in dry weather, one of the most picturesque woodland walks in Surrey. This highway was continually being presented as out of· repair in the Godalming Hundred Courts in the 14th, 15th, and 16th centuries.[1] It is crossed more than once by a stream, which ultimately joins the Arun. On 21 September 1340, Thomas le Beel,

rector of Hambledon, was presented for having dug a ditch in the highway.

Brick-making is carried on in the clay soil. Iron also occurs in considerable quantities in the same soil; Lord Montague claimed an iron mine at Hambledon,[2] and Mine Pits Copse no doubt preserves the name of it, though the part of the wood now so named is over the Godalming border. On 20 February 1570 Lord Montague had had trouble with the commoners who resented his cutting wood for his ironworks, perhaps in Hambledon Hurst.[3]

The school (under the National Society) was enlarged in 1874.

The Union Workhouse for the Hambledon Union is in the parish. It was originally built as a parish workhouse in 1786, but has been much enlarged.

A small outlying portion of Hambledon, an *enclave* of Godalming and Hascombe, was transferred to Hascombe by the Local Government Board in 1884. It included Lambert's Farm on the road through Hascombe highway.

Within the bounds of the parish are several old houses and·cottages, as well as a number of good

[254] Close, 1651, pt. xiv, no. 4.
[255] See Cal. S.P. Dom. 1663–4, pp. 169, 191.
[256] Parl. Papers, 1847–8, xlix, 167.
[257] V.C.H. Surr. ii, 33 ; Inst. Bks. (P.R.O.).
[258] Inst. Bks. (P.R.O.)

[259] Cal. S.P. Dom. 1663–4, pp. 169, 191.
[260] Lond. Gaz. 30 June 1865, p. 3283.
[261] Ibid.
[262] Pop. Ret. Surr. 1901, p. 5.
[263] Ibid. p. 6.

[264] Reg. of St. Osmund (Rolls Ser.), i, 297.
[265] Curia Regis R. 166, m. 21d.
[1] See 21 Sept. 1377, and other places.
[2] Loseley MSS. June 10 1595, x, 116.
[3] Loseley MSS. x, 28.

modern houses. The old manor-house close to the churchyard is one of the best of the old buildings.

HAMBLEDON MANOR included lands MANOR in Chiddingfold, Godalming, and Witley.

In the time of Edward the Confessor, Azor held Hambledon.[4] After the Conquest it was held in chief by Edward of Salisbury, ancestor of the first Earl of Salisbury, and remained for some time a member of the honour of Salisbury.[5]

The immediate tenant in 1086 was Randulf. His successors in the 13th century took their name from Hambledon. In consideration of a grant to William de Brademer of certain land in Fetcham and Letherhead in 1207, Robert of Hambledon obtained a release of William's claim to a hide of land in Hambledon in favour of his own son, Richard of Hambledon.[6] This hide had formerly been held by Robert de Smallbrede, and may therefore have been identical with the lands called Great and Lesser Smallbredes, which were attached to the manor in 1621.[7] In 1251 free warren in Hambledon and Prestwick was granted to Robert Norris, but there is no proof that he held the manor.[8] Richard of Hambledon, the son of Henry of Hambledon, was lord of the manor later in the same century.[9] His successor in 1316 was Walter of Hambledon;[10] he apparently died leaving heirs who were minors, for in 1321 the king granted Hambledon to John de Toucester during his pleasure.[11] Before 1324 it appears to have been acquired by Robert Fleming and Alice his wife, for in that year they had licence for a chapel in their manor of Hambledon.[12] A 14th-century extent of the purparty of a certain inheritance assigned to Thomas Fleming includes a hall at Smallbredes with a solar and kitchen and a chapel.[13] The history of the manor during the next century is obscure. It would appear from the patronage of the church, which both before and after this period belonged to the lords of the manor, that it changed hands several times, for the advowson was successively in the possession of Edward the Black Prince, John de Bursebrigg, Richard Earl of Arundel, John Ryouns, William Petworth, Robert Payn, John Wintershull and Henry Payn, Robert Marshall and Richard Payn, Richard Monsted and Edmund Sumner, and Robert atte Mille and John Busbridge and others.[14] It is directly stated that Richard Earl of Arundel held the lordship of Hambledon by reason of the custody of the heir, a woman; it is therefore possible that the above-mentioned patrons of the church were also holding the manor either as guardians or feoffees to the use of the heir of the

at Hyls or Hulls. In 1350 Thomas at Hyl was lord of the manor and Maud was his wife.[15] She was clearly seised of the manor and is said to have been Maud of Hambledon.

At his death in 1489 John Hull was lord of Hambledon.[16] Probably he was a descendant of Maud wife of Thomas Hull whose death was presented at Godalming Court, October 1410.[17] The sons of John Hull were Richard and Edward.

In 1538 John Hull of Hambledon died. John Hull of full age was his heir.[18] He held in 1547–9[19] and Giles Hull in 1567 and 1572. Giles Hull was father to Samuel and Joseph who sold in 1606 to Lawrence Stoughton.[20] In 1613 he sold to Laurence Eliot of Busbridge,[21] a yearly rent being reserved to Samuel Hull during his life.[22] Laurence Eliot who held a court in 1614 died holding the manor in 1619,[23] and left a son Sir William Eliot who settled the manor on himself and his wife Joan in tail male.[24] He died in 1650. His son Sir William with his wife and son William barred the entail in 1692.[25] William the son died 1707. The manor was mortgaged and in 1710 was sold to John Walter[26] except the next presentation to the church, which William had already granted to his brother, Laurence Eliot. John Walter settled the manor on his son Abel's wife Anne Nevill in 1729, and they conveyed it in 1737 to James Jolliffe and others,[27] possibly trustees for Hitch Young.[28] In 1759 it passed to the latter's grand-nephew the Hon. William Bouverie, created Earl of Radnor 1761. His son Viscount Folkestone was in possession in 1770.[29] In 1800 his son Jacob Pleydell Bouverie sold it to Henry Hare Townsend of Busbridge.[30] Mr. Thomas Mellersh of Godalming purchased it from him in 1823, and it has since remained in the Mellersh family.

HULL of Hambledon. Argent a cheveron azure between three demi-lions passant gules with three bezants on the cheveron and a chief sable with two piles argent therein.

BOUVERIE, Earl of Radnor. Party fessewise or and argent an eagle sable with two heads having on his breast a scutcheon gules with a bend vair.

[4] V.C.H. Surr. i, 325a.

[5] Testa de Nevill (Rec. Com.), 220, 221b.

[6] Feet of F. Surr. 9 John, 30.

[7] Harl. Chart. 57, H. 43.

[8] Chart. R. 35 Hen. III, m. 3. There is, however, a possibility that Robert of Hambledon was 'Robert Norris of Hambledon.'

[9] Testa de Nevill (Rec. Com.), 221; Anct. D., B. 4012.

[10] Parl. Writs (Rec. Com.), ii (3), 338 (13).

[11] Abbrev. Rot. Orig. (Rec. Com.), i, 263. There are numerous records of members of the Hambledon family in Surrey during the 13th century, and as late as 1342 John of Hambledon owed suit to Godalming Hundred Court (Ct. R. 24 Oct. 17 Edw. III).

[12] Winton Epis. Reg. Stratford, fol. 6a.

It is worthy of note that the Flemings were connected with the Norris family, for in 1319–20 a release was granted to Robert son of William Fleming from a warranty of dower, claimed by Lucy late wife of Robert Norris of Fordham in Essex (Anct. D. [P.R.O.] B. 3625).

[13] Rentals and Surv. P.R.O., no. 628.

[14] Egerton MS. 2033, fol. 17, 58, 88.

[15] Lay Subs. R. bdle. 184, no. 29.

[16] P.C.C. Will proved 23 Oct. 1489; Miller 39.

[17] Thomas Hull held land at Heydon in Godalming close to Hambledon. John Hull was in possession of Heydon in 1428–9 (Catteshull Customary, 7 Hen. VI.)

[18] Catteshull Court, 23 Sept. 30 Hen. VIII.

[19] In a survey of Godalming (Misc. Bks. Exch. L.T.R. vol. clxix, fol. 109b) John Hull senior is mentioned as owing

suit at Godalming Hundred Court for the manor in 1549, and a marginal note says that Giles Hull held it later.

[20] Feet of F. Surr. Hil. 4 Jas. I; Mich. 6 Jas. I.

[21] Close, 11 Jas. I, pt. xxxv, no. 23.

[22] Harl. Chart. 57, H. 43, 44.

[23] Chan. Inq. p.m. (Ser. 2), ccclxxx, 127.

[24] Harl. Chart. 57, H. 43, 44.

[25] Feet of F. Surr. Mich. 4 Will. and Mary.

[26] See Close, 7 Geo. II, pt. vi, no. 1.

[27] Feet of F. Surr. Mich. 12 Geo. II; Release Enr. in Chan. 1733, pt. B. 6, no. 9.

[28] Manning and Bray say that Hitch Young bought it c. 1737; Hist. of Surr. ii, 56.

[29] Com. Pleas Recov. R. Trin. 11 Geo. III, m. 104.

[30] Manning and Bray, Hist. of Surr. ii, 56.

The old manor house is at the west end of the church. It is now called Court Farm from the court baron having been held there.

The lands of Great and Lesser Smallbrede, Shadwells and Durcombes are mentioned in another deed of 1622–3.[31] In 1707 Shadwell Field and Upper, Lower, and Little Darkham were included in Hyde Style Farm in the northern part of Hambledon, and Shadwell is an existing name north-west of the farm-house. These seem to be the latter two. Smallbrede was probably adjoining them, and perhaps Great Smallbrede is preserved in what is called the Great House on the right-hand side of the road from Hambledon to Godalming, south of Hyde Style Farm. Smallbrede was on the road, for the Hundred Roll of the Court of 21 September 1340 refers to injury to the *via regia* at Smallbrede.

The lord of Hambledon Manor had court baron, and in Manning and Bray's time court leet in 'High Hambledon.'[32] View of frankpledge and assize of bread and ale were claimed by Robert parson of Hambledon in 1278–9. He failed to appear and justify his claim, whereupon the Bishop of Salisbury was allowed those liberties as pertaining to his hundred of Godalming.[33] As late as 1808 the lord of Godalming Hundred was paid 2s. when a court leet was held at Hambledon.[34] The steward of the bishop regularly held a view of frankpledge at Hambledon on St. Matthew's Day, and tried cases of trespass, assault, failure to maintain highways and bridges, breaking of the assize of bread and ale, &c.[35]

The church of *ST. PETER* is a small CHURCH building almost entirely rebuilt in 1846, consisting of nave, with small north aisle and vestry, south porch, and chancel. There is a bell-turret at the west end. It is most picturesquely situated, with very fine views from the churchyard, in which are two splendid yews; the trunk of the larger, which must be of an immense age, measures about 30 ft. in circumference and is hollow. The smaller one measures 17 ft. at 5 ft. from the ground.

Cracklow (1824) describes the old church as consisting of a nave and chancel, 'of rough materials, covered partly with tiles, and partly with stone slates,' with 'a small open chapel on the north belonging to the manor, with a gallery on the north sides and another at the west end. The floor of the church is paved with bricks, and the entrance is by a path at the west end; there is a wooden turret, rising through the roof near the middle of the nave, containing one bell, and surmounted by a small spire covered with shingles. The basin of the font is cut out of a solid block of stone. The style of the architecture affords but few data on which to form any idea of the period of its foundation. The Royal Arms are painted on the shell of a turtle placed over the pulpit, which was presented by the Earl of Radnor, patron of the church. Among the monuments

are some for the family of Hull, of the early date of 1489.'

Cracklow's view, taken from the south-west, shows a porch of timber at the west end, a somewhat lofty nave, with its modern bell-turret nearly central (as in the neighbouring church of Hascombe, before rebuilding), a square-headed blocked doorway in the south wall, and eastward of it a two-light window, apparently of 13th-century date, beyond which again are two two-light windows, square-headed and probably 'churchwarden' insertions: one is quite low down in the wall. In the south wall of the chancel is a lancet of 13th-century character, probably a low side window.

The approximate dimensions of the old church were: nave 30 ft. by 16 ft., chancel 16 ft. by 13 ft., and north chapel 16 ft. by 7 ft., and the new church is of about the same size. As might be expected from the date of the rebuilding, the present church has not much to recommend it, but the design is pretty good in parts, and there is a profusion of carving, quite excellent for the period, especially a cornice on the outside of the south wall of the chancel, with minute heads and paterae by the same hand as the restored heads in the wall-arcade of 'the Round' at the Temple Church, London.

A good deal of chalk has been used in the interior, especially in the arcade of three arches to the north aisle, and in the chancel arch. The font, octagonal and modern, is a copy of that in Bosham Church, Sussex. The original font appears to have been of 11th or 12th-century date and to have resembled in design that in the neighbouring church of Alfold. The roofs are modern.

The 17th-century altar-table is now in the vestry, in which also is a deal chest of about the same date.

The registers date from 1617.

When the church was rebuilt in 1846, the then rector, the Rev. E. Bullock, gave a cup, paten, and flagon. The only ancient communion vessel is a small paten with the London hall-marks of 1691.

There is one bell by William Eldridge, 1705.

There is no mention of a church ADVOWSON at Hambledon in the Domesday Survey. A church existed in 1291.[36] The lords of the manor presented to it in the 14th century, and the advowson of the church remained in their possession[37] till the last William Eliot (who sold the manor to John Walter) granted the presentation to his brother Laurence Eliot.[38] His son Francis Eliot sold it to Lord Folkestone in 1761.[39] It is now in the hands of Lord Radnor, his descendant.

Henry Smith's Charity (1627) for CHARITIES the relief of deserving poor exists as in most Surrey parishes.

Richard Wyatt (1618) left money for the maintenance of one poor man of the parish in the Carpenters' Almshouse at Godalming.

---

[31] Harl. Chart. 57, H. 44.
[32] Hist. of Surr. ii, 55.
[33] Plac. de Quo Warr. (Rec. Com.), 38.
[34] Manning and Bray, Surr. ii, 55.

[35] Hund. R. passim, preserved at Loseley.
[36] Pope Nich. Tax. (Rec. Com.), 208.
[37] William More of Loseley presented in 1568; he probably had a lease of the

advowson. Hist. MSS. Com. Rep. vii, App. 620.
[38] Close, 7 Geo. II, pt. vi, no. 1.
[39] Close, 1 Geo. III, no. 6077, sub. no. 5.

HASLEMERE

Hasulmore (xiv cent.) ; Haselmere (xvi cent.).

Haslemere is a market town and a small parish 9 miles south-west of Godalming, of irregular form about 2 miles in breadth at the south end, and nearly 2 miles at the greatest measurement from north to south. The soil is mainly the Lower Green Sand, but the parish also extends over some of the Atherfield Clay and the Wealden Clay. It includes part of Weydown Common, and Grayshott Common to the north, and open land about East (or Haste) Hill to the east, and other open land ; but is mostly agricultural land or woodland. The parish is traversed by the Portsmouth line of the London and South Western Railway, and by the road from Guildford to Midhurst. It contains 2,253 acres. A part of the town was in the parish of Thursley, but has been transferred to Haslemere by the Local Government Act of 1894. The house called Weycombe was transferred from Chiddingfold to Haslemere by order of the Local Government Board, 1884.[1]

The woollen industry existed here as elsewhere in West Surrey, and the iron works at Imbhams and in Witley gave employment to charcoal burners, called colliers as elsewhere in Surrey, in Haslemere parish. The names of Foundry Road and Hammer Lane imply ironworks in the parish.

The present industries include brick and tile works, and several handicrafts introduced of late years by artistic and benevolent residents or neighbours, such as the linen, silk, and cotton weaving in Foundry Road, introduced by Mr. and Mrs. King of Witley *circa* 1895 ; tapestry, by Mr. and Mrs. Blunt ; silk weaving, by Mr. Hooper ; artist's wood and cabinet works, by Mr. Romney Green ; faience and mosaic works by Mr. Radley Young, in Hammer Lane ; weaving of ecclesiastical vestments, etc., by Mr. Hunter, on College Hill. The local museum and library, very far superior in plan and arrangement to the ordinary local museum, is connected with these local industries, as part of a general scheme to revive artistic taste and intellectual interests in a country place. But though Haslemere is a centre for a residential district, which since Professor Tyndall first built a house upon Hindhead has housed a remarkable body of literary, artistic, scientific, and otherwise distinguished residents, from Professor Tyndall and Lord Tennyson downwards, the greater part of the residential district is outside the parish of Haslemere, though a considerable number of houses have been built, or old houses adapted, in the place itself.

The tradition preserved by Aubrey[2] that Haslemere was a place of ancient importance, once possessing seven churches, but destroyed by the Danes, is of no value. It is unsupported by a scrap of documentary evidence, and is contrary to probability, as the place, unnamed in Domesday, was on the confines of the Wealden Forest, in a generally thinly inhabited country and was neither an ancient parish nor an ancient manor. It was a chapelry of the parish of Chiddingfold and was part of the first royal and then episcopal manor of Godalming. Old Haslemere, on

East Hill, also called Haste Hill in deeds, south-east of the town, was merely a tenement in the 14th century,[3] but the name 'Churchliten field' there[4] and 'Old church-yard' of Haslemere are suggestive of a church having been on the spot. The place where the present church stands, upon the opposite side of the town, was called Piperham.[5]

The boundaries of Surrey and Sussex have perhaps been slightly altered here to the loss of Surrey. On 6 September 1616 some forty inhabitants of Haslemere and the neighbourhood sent a letter to Sir George More, lord of the hundred and manor of Godalming, complaining that some two years back John Misselbroke had altered the course of the stream called Houndley's Water, near Carpenter's Heath, where it formed the county boundary, and that Richard Boxell of Linchmere in Sussex had kept up the diversion.[6] Carpenter's Heath was the name of the land about Shottermill, on the borders of Godalming and Farnham Manors and Hundreds. Though the diversions deprived Sir George of land, no further action appears to have taken place.

Cinerary urns, made on a wheel, with calcined bones in them, and some flints about them, but no bronze or iron, were found in Mr. Rollason's meadow, called Beeches, between Haslemere and Grayshott, and were presented to the local museum in 1902. Close by was the floor of a kiln, with tesserae and burnt stones and charcoal. Neolithic flint implements are fairly common in the neighbourhood.

There are Congregational and Particular Baptist chapels in Haslemere.

The town is beautifully placed on the slope of a gentle hill—Black Down ridge—its church lying away from the town on a high spur. There is a market-house, placed in the middle of the wide street on the site of the Town Hall. It is not in itself of any great antiquity or beauty, but it harmonizes with its surroundings. For grouping, colouring, and the artistic setting of trees, creepers, and lovely backgrounds the streets of Haslemere are justly renowned ; and the new houses blend on the whole very happily with the old : but considered individually for antiquity or architectural merit they cannot compare with the houses of Godalming. Tile-hanging is the characteristic feature of the houses, which are mostly gabled and of brick or timber and plaster construction, with, in many cases, fine brick chimney stacks, and tiled roofs. Besides the High Street, which contains many picturesque examples of low-pitched gabled houses, there are interesting old houses in Shepherd's Hill (half timber and tile-hanging, to upper story, with plastered cove below) and East Street, which latter has a good moulded brick cornice. Most of these appear to date from early in the 17th century, but there are a few perhaps of earlier date, and a number belonging to the 18th century.

BOROUGH   Haslemere, which was originally only a tithing of Godalming, seems to have first gained importance through its market, which was especially mentioned with the manor

---

[1] Loc. Govt. Bd. Order 16532.
[2] *Hist. of Surr.* (ed. 1718), iv, 28.
[3] Godalming Hundred Rolls, Loseley MSS. *passim.* The rent of Old Haslemere was 6d. *per acre* to the lord.
[4] *Gent. Mag.* 1802, pt. ii, p. 817.
[5] See below, under the account of the church.
[6] Loseley MS. date cited.

A HISTORY OF SURREY

of Godalming in 1221,[7] nearly eighty years before the lords of Salisbury had a weekly market in Godalming itself. In point of population it does not seem to have even approached the neighbouring[8] parishes of Witley and Chiddingfold. Although it was not expressly called a borough in the return of 1315,[9] it is called 'burgus' in 1377.[10] In 1394 John Waltham, Bishop of Salisbury, had licence to grant a charter to Haslemere, giving the town a market on Wednesdays and an annual fair on the eve and day of the Holy Cross, and three succeeding days.[11]

In an account of rents received in Godalming Manor, dated 1543, the 'burgesses' of the 'borough' of Haslemere are said to owe 12s. 2d. rent for certain lands there,[12] which rent is evidently identical with 12s. 1d. called 'le Burgage Rent' paid to the lord of Godalming by the tenants called the burgage holders in Haslemere.[13] The inhabitants held by burgage tenure in the 14th century when the Court Rolls of Godalming Manor and Hundred begin.

The tenants of the tithing owed suit to the Hundred Court of Godalming, but a view of frankpledge was held at Hocktide at Haslemere, and a court leet with it, in the 17th century, for the borough.[14] The town was considered a separate manor from Godalming, after the charter of 1596 at least.[15] Separate Court Rolls exist for it.

The burgage-rent was collected annually by the bailiff of the borough, who seems to have been the only officer, for in 1596, at the time when the Crown was still holding Godalming Manor, Queen Elizabeth addressed a re-grant of the market and fairs to the bailiff and inhabitants of the borough.[16] In the preamble to this grant she asserted that the town had sent two burgesses to Parliament from time immemorial, and confirmed their right to do so in the future. She further recited the charter of Richard II, and as the markets and fair had fallen into disuse, restored to them the market on Tuesdays, the fair, now twice a year on St. Philip and St. James's and Holy Cross Day. Tolls were to be levied, a court of pie powder held, and the tolls to be applied by the bailiff and others to the relief of the poor inhabitants.[17] The original grantees having all died, John Billinghurst of Coldwaltham, co. Sussex, claimed the right to gather the tolls as heir of John Steede, the last surviving grantee. He was accused of misemploying the profits of the fair and market, which seem at that time to have amounted to about £7 yearly, and a decree was issued in 1662 vesting the trust in the lords of the manor of Godalming for the relief of the poor of Haslemere, an account being given at the court leet of the borough.[18] According to the inscription on

the almshouses on the common near Lythe Hill, James Gresham, who represented Haslemere in the Parliament of 1678–9, by his 'care and oversight' caused the almshouses, then called the Toll House, to be built in 1676, for the habitation of decayed inhabitants of the borough, out of the profits of the market.[19] However, after the death of Sir William More, lord of Godalming, John Billinghurst again tried to make good his claim to the tolls, and obtained a reversal of the former decree,[20] but in 1691 the grant was found to be in favour of the poor of the borough.[21] Thomas Molyneux, then lord of Haslemere Manor, the minister of Haslemere, and others, were appointed trustees,[22] and John Billinghurst ordered to restore £42 11s. which he had collected.[23] The market produced little, being in the centre of a poor country. The view of frankpledge and court baron, held together in this case as at Godalming, give a few interesting glimpses of town management. So anxious were the burgesses to keep down the poor-rate that they decreed at the court of 4 May 1627 that no one in this leet shall let, devise, grant, &c., any messuage, &c., or room, to any 'forriner,' unless he and they can satisfy the bailiff and overseers that he can maintain himself and family—penalty £10. This was repeated 7 May 1628. Under Charles I the records of the court were kept in Latin. One result of the Commonwealth is that English was used, as was also the case in Guildford. On 30 April 1652 Puritan opinion forbade any person to set up a game called 'nine holes' in this borough—penalty 5s. But cleanliness was some way off godliness, for on 10 April 1654 it was ordered that no one was to leave a dunghill standing in the borough above a month—penalty 12d. On 22 April 1658 the Market House, the Fish Cross, and the Butter Cross, were reported to be very ruinous. Robert Cobden and William Shudd were bound to repair them, under penalty of £10, to be done before the feast of St. Michael the Archangel. This feast survives in all its full sanctity as a date in spite of the opinions then prevailing. After the Restoration Mr. Richard Symmes, the steward of Godalming, had the record of the court kept again in Latin. It is interesting to find that in 1678 among the 'foreign' tradesmen who set up stalls at the market, but who were fined 11s. for doing so without the bailiff's leave, was Robert Smyth of Farnham, bookseller. The old Crosses and Town Hall, ruinous in 1658, were pulled down, the two former after 1735. The Town Hall was not pulled down till 1814, when the present hall was built by the two members. For this date there is a plan of the town, a copy of which is preserved in the present Town Hall.

[7] Rot. Lit. Claus. (Rec. Com.), i, 455.
[8] In the earlier Subsidy Rolls Haslemere is not even mentioned. Probably it was included in Godalming at that time. In the returns for the poll tax of 1380, 62 names are given under Haslemere, whereas 238 were returned under Godalming, 233 under Witley, and 176 under Chiddingfold (Lay Subs. R. bdle. 184, no. 29). Nor does it ever seem to have been very extensive, for the hearth-tax return of 1674 only accounts for 61 households (ibid. bdle. 188, no. 496).
[9] Parl. Writs (Rec. Com.), ii (3), 338. The vill of Haslemere is there set down as a possession of the Bishop of Salisbury.

[10] Mins. Accts. bdle. 1010, no. 7. An account of the manor of Ashurst, wherein one item is given as 30s. rent in the hamlet of Chiddingfold and 'in burgo de Haselmere.'
[11] Chart. R. 15–17 Ric. II, no. 6.
[12] Exch. Mins. Accts. 34–5 Hen. VIII, Div. Co. R. 64, m. 20.
[13] Godalming R. passim and Misc. Bks. (Land Rev.), cxc, 235.
[14] Godalming R. Loseley MSS.
[15] Vide infra.
[16] Petty Bag Char. Inq. xxvi, 18.
[17] Writs of Privy Seal, May, 38 Eliz.
[18] Petty Bag Char. Inq. xxvi, 18; Hist. MSS. Com. Rep. vii, App. 679.
[19] See Char. Com. Rep. iii; Parl. Papers, 1824, xiv, 635. It was this James Gresham

who persuaded the bailiff to substitute his name for that of Denzil Onslow in the return of burgesses for 1679. See also Loseley MSS. i, 132.
[20] Proc. as to Charitable Uses, Confirmations, &c. 2 Jas. II, 25. On the ground that Elizabeth had intended the profits of the market and fair for the public benefit of the borough and not for the poor only, so that the matter did not come within the cognizance of the Charity Commissioners who had issued the decree.
[21] Chan. Decrees and Orders, Mich. 1691, A 425.
[22] Ibid. Hil. 1692, A 232.
[23] Chan. Rep. 1693, A–D, Chan. Orders and Decrees, Hil. 1693–4, A. 365b.

46

Haslemere ceased to be a borough after the Municipal Reform Act of 1835.[34]

Although the charter of 1596 asserts that Haslemere sent two burgesses to Parliament from time immemorial,[35] the first extant return of burgesses for the town dates from 1584, only twelve years before.[36] It is evident, therefore, that Haslemere was one of the towns which Elizabeth caused to return members in order to increase her influence in the House, a supposition strengthened by her own statement that she granted the market and fairs in the hope that if the inhabitants of the town should thereby enjoy greater prosperity they would feel themselves the more bound to do all possible service to her and her successors.

The electors were inhabitant freeholders, whether paying rent to the lord of the manor or not, the burgage holders in fact.[37] Tenants of land which had been part of the waste of the manor, or of houses upon it, could not vote from such qualification only. The number of such burgage holders varied considerably, because as different owners represented different interests the burgages were deliberately divided into small parts to multiply votes. Haslemere was a rotten borough in the sense of being thoroughly penetrated with corruption, and was the scene of very violent electoral contests,[38] till in 1784 Sir James Lowther, afterwards Earl of Lonsdale, bought the manor and many freeholds in it, and made it a close borough, though a rival interest, that of the Burrell family, existed. The second Earl of Lonsdale in fact abolished many of the freeholds, creating them only for the purpose of an election, when the burgages required are said to have been conveyed to the charcoal-burners and others of the neighbourhood, or to servants of his friends, with the understanding that they should be surrendered for a consideration when the need was over. But there were a few distinguished members for Haslemere. Carew Raleigh, son of Sir Walter, was elected to fill the vacancy in the Long Parliament caused by the death of Sir Poynings More in 1649, and the famous General Oglethorpe sat from 1722 to 1754. The Rt. Hon. Sir John Beckett was one of the last two members. It was among the forty-six boroughs whose population stood lowest at the time of the Reform Bill of 1832, and accordingly was then disfranchised.[39]

The manor of MANORS HASLEMERE descended with the hundred and manor of Godalming till 1784, when the sisters of Thomas More-Molyneux and their trustees sold to Sir James Lowther under a private Act.[30] Sir James was created Earl of Lonsdale the same year, and died in 1802. to his cousin Sir William Lowther, who inherited the

LOWTHER, Earl of Lonsdale. Or six rings sable.

title of Viscount Lowther, and was created Earl of Lonsdale in 1807. He died in 1844. The manor was purchased from his heirs by James Stewart Hodgson of Lythe Hill, Haslemere, in 1870. His widow held it, and died 1907. Mr. J. Whateley Simmonds, J.P. has lately bought the manor. A description of the manor in 1814 says that 'the manor was held by burgage tenure, the Burgesses paying for their several tenements a burgage rent of 12s. 1d. to the lord of Godalming. The Borough and Manor are not co-extensive, as some of the lands in the borough are in the manor of Godalming. Officers are elected at a Court Leet in April or May, a Bailiff, a Constable, Searchers and Sealers of Leather and and an Ale taster. No Court Baron has been held since 1694.'

The court leet was held up to 1839, when the practice was discontinued.[31]

The manor of IMBHAMS (Imbeham xiii–xv cents.; Imbhams and Embornes, xvi cent.) was parcel of Loseley Manor, held of the honour of Gloucester, but adjacent land bearing the same name was held of the Bishop of Salisbury's manor of Godalming.

In 1285 Eleanor widow of Robert de Dol, late lord of Loseley, had dower in Imbhams,[32] and recovered land in Chiddingfold from various tenants including Alan of Imbhams.[33] From her time the manor descended with Loseley to her son Robert, at whose death in March 1356–7 it was found that he held two holdings of the name. The one was held of the Earl of Gloucester, and the other of the Bishop of Salisbury for 18s. 8d. and suit of court at Godalming. The manor-house was in that part of Imbhams which was held of the earl. None of the arable land seems to have been profitable, since it lay in the Weald, and the pasture was of no value on account of the great size of the trees.[34] Imbhams was not included in Robert de Dol's agreement with his daughter Joan de Bures,[35] but was assigned immediately after his death to his heirs, the same Joan and John Norton.[36]

Joan died in 1371, her heir being her son William Bures,[37] who succeeded to the moiety of Loseley, including presumably a moiety of Imbhams, which she held in her own right. The other moiety, afterwards known as NORTH IMBHAMS, passed to John Norton, descended from her sister Margaret,[38] who must have died almost immediately after her, for in 1375 he had been dead about four years, having been seised of a moiety of a piece of land called 'Imbeham,' held of the king in chief, owing to the vacancy of the see of Salisbury, but formerly held of the bishop at a rent of 6s.[39] His heir John Norton was under age. This was parcel of the manor of Loseley. It was the portion in Haslemere, and by an unknown process passed to the Coverts. It did not pass first to the Sidneys, to whom the Norton moiety of Loseley proper came, for in the proceedings by which Humphrey Sidney established his claim to the inheritance in 1508,[40] though land in Chiddingfold (which then of course included Haslemere) is mentioned, this land was held of the manor of Bramley.[41] The Norton portion was already

34 5 & 6 Will. IV, cap. 76.
35 Writs of Privy Seal, May 38 Eliz.
36 Ret. of Memb. of Parl. i. The first members recorded as representing Haslemere were Christopher Rythe of Lincoln's Inn, and Miles Rythe of the same.
37 Journ. of the House of Commons, 20 May 1661, p. 253.
38 Ibid. xxxii, 49; xxxv, 361; Mere-

wether and Stephens, Hist. of Boroughs, ii, 1380.
39 Parl. Papers, 1831–2, xxxvi, 3, 5, 41.
30 20 Geo. III, cap. 45.
31 Privately communicated.
32 De Banco R. 60 (Mich. 13–14 Edw. I), m. 83.
33 Close, 15 Edw. I, m. 1 d.

34 Chan. Inq. p.m. 30 Edw. III, no. 45.
35 See under Loseley.
36 Abbrev. Rot. Orig. (Rec. Com.), ii, 241.
37 Chan. Inq. p.m. 45 Edw. III, no. 4.
38 See Loseley.
39 Chan. Inq. p.m. 49 Edw. III, no. 18.
40 See under Loseley.
41 Inform. Rev. T. S. Cooper.

in the hands of William Covert of Slaugham and Harlcombe, who died in 1494. In 1504 his son John Covert died seised of the manor of Imbhams in Haslemere, Chiddingfold and Alfold, held of the Bishop of Salisbury.[42] His heir was his cousin Richard, from whom it went to John's nephew Giles, who held at the time of the survey of Godalming made by Edward VI, and died in 1557,[43] holding of the Crown, which then held the bishop's manor of Godalming. He was succeeded by his brother Richard. He was father of Antony Covert, father of John and Antony, all of whom held it.[44] John conveyed to Antony in 1625, the conveyance including the pond which supplied the water for the Quenells' iron furnace called Imbhams.[45] The Coverts sold to Peter Quenell the elder in 1627.[46]

Quenell had already acquired SOUTH IMBHAMS, the other moiety, which went with the Bures portion of Loseley, probably to the Strodes, who had land in Chiddingfold,[47] and so to the Westbrooks. John Westbrook was lord of the manor of Imbhams alias Southymbhams, in 1492, and granted land which had escheated to him as lord. When he sold Loseley to Sir Christopher More he did not convey the manor of South Imbhams[48] specifically, and it continued in his family. He died in 1513, and his son William in 1537. His heirs were his sister Florence Scarlett, widow, and Elizabeth wife of Edward Hull. John, grandson of the former, sold his moiety of South Imbhams to Thomas Quenell in 1568.[49] Thomas left it, subject to his wife's life interest, to his brother Robert Quenell in 1571, and Scarlett levied a fine to Robert Quenell in 1576.[50]

Thomas Hull, son of Elizabeth Hull, had sold his share to the same Robert Quenell in 1574.[51] This Robert was father to Peter, who acquired the other part of Imbhams, vide supra, in 1626. The Quenells were ironmasters, and Peter, a Royalist, cast guns for the king at Imbhams as long as he was allowed.[52] He died in 1649. His son Peter served in the king's army, and also borrowed money. He died in 1666. Peter Quenell his son held a court in 1669, but under an arrangement to satisfy his father's debts sold with his mother's concurrence in 1677 to Thomas Newton and William Yalden.[53] The latter took the manor and held a court in 1679. He died in 1740, aged 91. His son William died in 1742, leaving a son William who died in 1796. He had a daughter Elizabeth, wife of Ralph Bennet, and two other daughters. The trustees of the estate sold it to George Oliver of Brentford in 1797. His son George died at a great age after 1870, and the manor was sold to the late Mr. James Stewart Hodgson of Lythe Hill, Haslemere, whose widow died in 1907.

William Yalden the younger was of 'the Newhouse,' since known as the Manor House. The old manor house is a moated farm of the 16th century.

The church of ST. BARTHOLO-CHURCH MEW is embowered in trees, among which the grey stone tower with stone-

slated roof has a more venerable aspect than is warranted by its actual age. The churchyard, which is extremely pretty and well kept, abounds in choice shrubs and trees, and has a great number of old and new monuments. Professor Tyndall lies here, but under a gorse and heather-covered mound, without stone or other memorial.

The church was originally only a chapel-of-ease to Chiddingfold. The tower at the west end is practically all that remains of ancient date, and there is reason to suppose that this goes no further back than the middle of the 17th century. The nave, north aisle, and chancel, after having been greatly altered about 1837, were partly rebuilt in 1870–1, a south aisle being added at the same time. The style in which the new work was designed is that of the middle of the 13th century. When the rebuilding took place a number of the older gravestones were built into the walls inside and out. There is a good deal of modern glass of varying merit, including a two-light window designed by the late Sir Edward Burne-Jones to the memory of the poet Tennyson, its subject being Sir Galahad and the Holy Grail. Some old glass said to have been brought out of Kent by the Rev. M. Sanderson at the end of the 17th century has been redistributed, part being in the west window of the tower, and the rest in the west window of the north aisle ; originally the whole was in the east window of the chancel. A writer in the *Gentleman's Magazine* for 1801 gives the subjects as follows :—

' 1. St. Matthew. 2. Our Saviour's Ascension. 3. St. Mark. 4. Adam and Eve in Paradise. 5. The Nativity. 6. Noah going into the Ark. 7. St. Luke. 8. Saul thrown from his horse, and his attendants offering him assistance : " Savl, Savl, qvid persecv'is me ?" 9. Offering of the Wise Men. Among the numerous presents, I distinguished some fine hams, poultry and mutton. 10. St. John.'

The same writer describes the nave as ' separated from the transept [i.e. aisle] by four pointed arches resting on low round pillars, part of a wooden screen remaining under the chancel arch. The font is a large octagonal stone supported on a pillar corresponding with it. On one of the bells is inscribed, " Peace and good neighbourhood." '

Another writer says[54] of the arcade between the nave and north aisle, 'the pillars that support the arches are of oak, and of large dimensions.' Mr. J. W. Penfold, an old resident, in giving his recollections of the church as he remembers it ' in the early days of William IV,' says ; 'The north aisle was separated from the nave by huge oak pillars, with heavy carved ribs or struts forming arches to support the low roof, and much obscuring the view into the nave. . . . About 1837 the oak pillars were removed, and neat fluted iron columns were substituted.'[55]

From Cracklow's view of 1823 it would seem probable that the old nave and chancel retained features of 13th-century date, but that the building had been greatly altered in the 16th and following centuries.

[42] Chan. Inq. p.m. (Ser. 2), xxxi, 263.
[43] Ibid. cxiv, 42.
[44] Feet of F. Surr. Hil. 14 Jas. I; Chan. Proc. Eliz. H.h. vi, 60.
[45] Feet of F. Surr. Hil. 22 Jas. I.
[46] Ibid. East. 2 Chas. I, and East. 4 Chas. I.
[47] Strode Deeds at Loseley, q.v.
[48] Add. Chart. 13557. See Loseley. Imbhams was included in the marriage

settlement of William More in 1551 (Feet of F. Surr. Mich. 5 Edw. VI). It was probably an overlordship attaching to Loseley, merged in the general overlordship acquired by the Mores in the whole hundred and manor of Godalming by grant in 1601.
[49] Com. Pleas D. Enr. East. 18 Eliz. m. 43.
[50] Feet of F. Surr. East. 18 Eliz.

[51] Ibid. Hil. 17 Eliz.
[52] For an account of the Quenell family see Surr. Arch. Coll. xv, 40.
[53] Chan. Decree, 3 July 27 Chas. II, 790, no. 13.
[54] Gent. Mag. 1802, pt. ii, 817, 818.
[55] Preface to Haslemere and Hindhead, in the 'Homeland Handbooks' series. This timber arcade was the only one of ancient date in Surrey.

The registers date from 1572.

The church plate includes a cup and paten cover of 1669, a credence paten of 1672, a paten of 1718, a cup of 1730, and a flagon of 1793—all of silver.

The place where the present church stands upon the side of the town opposite to 'Old Haslemere' (*vide supra*) was called Piperham, and the church here is the 'capella de Piperham' which with Chiddingfold is mentioned in 1180 and 1185 in the Salisbury Registers.[56] A deed of 1486 in the possession of Mr. J. W. Penfold shows that the road from the upper end of Haslemere Street leading to the present church then led to Piperham Church. A fragment of a Court Roll at Loseley of 6 & 7 James I mentions the road as out of order leading from 'Pepperham's church in Haslemere by Pilemarsh.' Pilemarsh is between the present church and Haslemere Station. There probably was another church, now gone, on East Hill, whence the tradition of seven churches. Also in 1458 John Piperham leased to John Boxfold of Haslemere his tenement called Piperhammes next the church in Haslemere on the understanding that Boxfold should perform all services due to the king, the lord of the fee, and to the church.[57] There was also a tenement called Howndleswater, otherwise Peperham in Haslemere, of which John Bridger was possessed when he died in February 1580-1.[58]

The parish was a chapelry in the parish of Chiddingfold, but in 1363 Bishop Edyngton of Winchester granted licence for the consecration of a long-existing chapel and burial-ground at Haslemere in place of the old churchyard near the old church.[59] The district possessed parish officers and registers of its own, and though a rector was usually, till recently, instituted to the rectory of Chiddingfold with Haslemere, a separate curate was often in residence. It has been in all respects a separate parish since 1869.

ADVOWSON The history of the advowson is coincident with that of the mother-church of Chiddingfold till 1868. In that year a rector was instituted to the churches of Chiddingfold and Haslemere on the understanding that he should resign the latter when called upon to do so. This he did in 1869, when Haslemere became a separate rectory.

Smith's Charity is distributed as in other Surrey parishes.

CHARITIES James Bicknell by will 27 November 1633 left the produce of certain land, of about 13s. 4d. a year, to the churchwardens for the poor. James Gresham, lessee of the tolls of the market, left the tolls and an almshouse in 1676. The almshouse exists, but is now unendowed. In 1816 Mr. Shudd, a solicitor of the town, left £350 to the poor.

There is a cottage hospital founded by John Penfold, opened in 1898, in commemoration of the Diamond Jubilee of the late Queen Victoria; a convalescent home, founded and maintained by Jonathan Hutchinson; and a holiday home at East Hill, established by Mrs. Stewart Hodgson in 1884, for the reception of poor girls from London.

PEPER HAROW

Pipereherge (xi cent.); Piperinges (xiii cent.); Pyperhaghe (xiv cent.).

Peper Harow is a small parish lying west of Godalming town. It measures about 4 miles from north to south, about 2 miles in breadth in the northern and under a mile in the southern part. The soil is exclusively the Lower Green Sand, except for alluvium in the valley of the Wey, which runs in a winding course across the parish from west to east. The southern part of the parish includes Ockley Common and Pudmoor, extensive heathlands connected with Thursley Common and Elstead Heath. In the northern part of it is Peper Harow Park, the seat of Viscount Midleton, extending to both sides of the Wey, and reaching on the southern bank into Witley parish. The area is 1,301 acres of land and 19 of water. The road from Farnham to Godalming crosses the parish from west to east. The population is over 200.

The charter of Edward of Wessex to the church of Winchester, c. 909,[1] gives the boundary of Elstead and of Peper Harow as it now exists in part: 'Aerest aet vii dican to Ottanforda, swa to Sumaeres forda, (now Somerset Bridge), ðouan to Ocanlea (Ockley Common).'

The park and grounds at Peper Harow contain some fine timber, notably some cedars of Lebanon, which were put in as seedlings from pots in 1735.[2]

In the park are the remains of Oxenford Grange, a grange of Waverley Abbey. The fifth Viscount Midleton employed Mr. Pugin to build an imitation 13th-century farm here, and a gatehouse to the park in the same style in 1844, and in 1843 Mr. Pugin built an arch of similar design over the Bonfield Spring in the neighbourhood—a medicinal spring of local repute, said by Aubrey to be good for all eyesores and ulcers. This land of Oxenford is now counted in Witley parish.[3]

A conveyance to Sir Walter Covert in 1605 speaks of the land in the 'Parish and Field' of Peper Harow. But the end of 'the Field' is not known. There was no Inclosure Act.

PEPER HAROW MANOR *PEPER HAROW* was held by Alward under Edward the Confessor, and after the Conquest came into the possession of Walter, Governor of Windsor Castle, son of Other, ancestor of the Windsors,[4] to whose honour of Windsor the overlordship of the manor belonged.[5] The actual tenant of Peper Harow in 1086 was a certain Girard,[6] one of whose successors, Osbert of Peper Harow, sold Peper Harow to Ralph de Broc. His son-in-law Stephen de Turnham received a confirmation of the

56 *Reg. of St. Osmund* (Rolls Ser.), i, 268, 301, 303. 57 Add. Chart. 27757. 58 Exch. Mins. Accts. 34-5 Hen. VIII, Div. Co. R. 64, m. 19; Chan. Inq. p.m. (Ser. 2), cxcvii, 64. 59 Winton Epis. Reg. Edyngton, ii, 46a. This would be the present, i.e. Piperham, church.
1 Kemble, Codex Dipl. 1093, v, 176.
2 MS. at Peper Harow.
3 For a further account of it see under Witley.

4 *V.C.H. Surr.* i, 323a.
5 *Testa de Nevill* (Rec. Com.), 220; Chan. Inq. p.m. 27 Edw. III (1st nos.), no. 61; ibid. 1 Ric. III, 23; ibid. (Ser. 2), 12, 97.
6 *V.C.H. Surr.* i, 323a.

sale from King John in 1205.[7] Stephen's daughter Clemency received Peper Harow as her portion on her marriage with her first husband Alan de Plugenhay ;[8] she afterwards married Wandrith de Corcell, and her third husband, Henry Braybrok, who evidently survived her, sued Ralph son of Bernard and his wife Eleanor, daughter of Clemency by Wandrith de Corcell,[9] for Peper Harow as having been settled on him at his marriage with Clemency.[10] Clearly the suit was decided in favour of Ralph and Eleanor,[11] for William Braunch, husband of their daughter Joan, held a fee in 'Piperinges' of the honour of Windsor.[12] William and Joan settled a rent of 2 marks from the manor on Giffard, Abbot of Waverley, and his successors in 1246,[13] and Joan was still in possession of Peper Harow in 1279, when she claimed free warren there under a charter of Henry III, her right being disputed on the ground of the previous disafforestation of the whole county.[14] A fresh grant of free warren in Peper Harow was issued to Henry of Guildford in 1303, when he was lord of the manor.[15] Joan Braunch died before 21 December 1279, leaving a son and heir Nicholas,[16] who suffered a recovery to Henry of Guildford, marshal of the king's household 1297-8, and gave him a release. Henry died 1312 holding the manor,[17] and among the executors of his will was Hervey (or Henry) de Stanton,[18] who obtained a release of the manor from Henry de Stoughton.[19] Henry de Stoughton was assessed for feudal aid in Peper Harow in 1316.[20] He is said to have obtained it from Henry of Guildford 1312-13 and to have conveyed it to Henry de Stanton c. 1360-2, from whom it descended to Hervey de Stanton.[21] He held the

STOUGHTON. *Azure a cross engrailed ermine.*

manor for some time.[22] The Stoughtons recovered their estate, though by illegal means, for in 1343 Henry de Stoughton was fined for persuading Walter de St. Neot to come to Bagshot calling himself Master Hervey de Stanton, and in that name to make quitclaim of Peper Harow to John son of Henry de Stoughton.[23] In the same year Sir Andrew Braunch, son of Nicholas,[24] purchased Henry Stoughton's rights in Peper Harow for £100.[25] He was succeeded by a young son and heir Thomas, who died in the wardship of the king in 1360, leaving, though he was only eleven years of age, a widow Mary,[26] to whom dower was assigned in the manor.[27] Stephen de Wydeslade, Andrew

Braunch's nephew by his sister Eleanor, heir to Thomas, seems to have sold the manor, for in 1368 it appears in the possession of John Chapman and Geoffrey Edyth, evidently trustees, who conveyed it early in 1368 to Bernard Brocas, clerk, for life, with remainder to Sir Bernard Brocas of Beaurepaire and his wife Mary in tail.[28] The latter's son and heir, Sir Bernard, succeeded to Peper Harow at his father's death in 1395,[29] but forfeited it by his share in the conspiracy to restore Richard II.[30] His son William, however, was restored to his father's estates in the following year,[31] and died in 1456.[32] His son William, sheriff of Berkshire and Oxfordshire in 1459, held the manor,[33] as is recorded by his wife's inscription in Peper Harow Church. It had been seized by Edward IV and granted in 1477 to his servant John Smyth,[34] but it was clearly recovered by Brocas. His son John followed, and was succeeded by William Brocas, also of Beaurepaire.

His two daughters and heirs, Anne and Edith, were aged respectively twelve and nine at their father's death in July 1506.[35] Edith, who was ultimately her sister's heir, married Ralph Pexsall,[36] during whose tenure the house and demesne lands, except the rights of fishing, were leased for ten years to John Moth of Sherborne.[37] Ralph's son, Mr. Richard Pexsall, afterwards knighted, was holding in the survey of the manor of Godalming in 1547.[38] He was once attacked at Peper Harow by a certain 'Bedon,' who with his friends had entered upon lands belonging to the Parsonage.[39] Sir Richard's daughter Anne having married Bernard Brocas of Horton, a descendant of Sir Bernard, the supporter of Richard II, most of the Pexsall lands were settled

PEXSALL. *Argent a flowered cross engrailed sable between four birds azure having beaks and legs gules and collars argent with a scallop argent in the cross.*

BROCAS. *Sable a leopard rampant or.*

on her son Pexsall Brocas,[40] and among them a considerable portion of Peper Harow. In 1585 he sold

[7] *Rot. Chart.* (Rec. Com.), i, 160b.
[8] Maitland, *Bracton's Note Bk.* 116.
[9] *Curia Regis R.* no. 162 (Hil. 43 Hen. III), m. 21.
[10] *Bracton's Note Bk.* 116.
[11] It turned upon the point whether, after the death of Wandrith de Corcell, Edelina, Stephen's widow, had any right to re-enfeoff Clemency and Henry de Braybrok.
[12] *Testa de Nevill* (Rec. Com.), 220, 221; *Curia Regis R.* 87, m. 7.
[13] Feet of F. Surr. 31 Hen. III, 313.
[14] *Plac. de Quo Warr.* (Rec. Com.), 74.
[15] *Chart. R.* 31 Edw. I (no. 96), m. 2.
[16] Chan. Inq. p.m. 8 Edw. I, no. 1.
[17] Ibid. 6 Edw. II, no. 57.
[18] *Cal. Close* (Rec. Com.), 1307-13, p. 474.

[18] Add. MS. (B.M.), 5846, fol. 78.
[20] *Parl. Writs* (Rec. Com.), ii (3), 338.
[21] Stoughton MSS. quoted by Manning and Bray.
[22] Add. MS. (B.M.), 5846, fol. 78.
[23] *Cal. Pat.* 1343-5, p. 150.
[24] Feet of F. Surr. 17 Edw. III, 37.
[25] Chan. Inq. p.m. 27 Edw. III (1st nos.), no. 61; ibid. 34 Edw. III (1st nos.), no. 58.
[26] Close, 34 Edw. III, m. 22.
[27] Feet of F. Surr. 42 Edw. III, 12. It is worthy of notice that John Brocas mainprised that Henry Stoughton would pay the fine due for his share in the Bagshot conspiracy. See *Cal. Pat.* 1343-5, p. 150. See also Loseley MSS.

[29] Chan. Inq. p.m. 19 Ric. II, no. 3.
[30] Ibid. 1 Hen. IV, pt. ii, no. 2. For an account of the family see Burrows, *Brocas of Beaurepaire.*
[31] Pat. 2 Hen. IV, pt. i, m. 19.
[32] Chan. Inq. p.m. 34 Hen. VI, no. 9.
[33] He died in 1484; Chan. Inq. p.m. 1 Ric. III, no. 23.
[34] *Cal. Pat.* 1476-85, p. 43.
[35] Ibid. (Ser. 2), xx, 97.
[36] Pat. 4 Hen. VIII, pt. i, m. 21.
[37] Burrows, *Brocas of Beaurepaire,* 441.
[38] He also held Piccards in Artington.
[39] See a letter by Sir Richard quoted in *Brocas of Beaurepaire,* 197.
[40] Will of Sir Richard, 1571, P.C.C. 6 Holney.

ten-twelfths of the manor and the advowson to Henry Smythe,[41] the remaining two-twelfths of the manor being in possession of Pexsall's aunt Margery Cotton, and of Edward Savage, son of Sir John Savage, second husband of Eleanor widow of Sir Richard Pexsall.[42] The former conveyed her share to Henry Smythe in 1594,[43] while Edward Savage sold his to Sir Walter Covert, kt.,[44] who in 1605 bought the other eleven parts from Henry Smythe.[45] Sir Walter died 22 January 1631–2,[46] the manor being settled on his widow Joan for life, with remainder to John Covert, son of Sir Walter Covert of
Maidstone, who in June 1655 sold the reversion at Joan's death to the Hon. Denzil Holles of Damerham, afterwards Lord Holles, who died 1680.[47] The manor descended to his son, Francis, Lord Holles.[48] At the death of his son Denzil (who had no issue) in 1694, the manor reverted to John, Duke of Newcastle, male heir of the elder branch

HOLLES, Lord Holles. *Ermine two piles sable.*

of the family.[49] He sold it in February 1699–1700 to Philip Frowde,[50] who in 1713 sold it to Alan Brodrick, afterwards Viscount Midleton.

In 1725 Viscount Midleton was 'expected to reside shortly,' and was patron.[51] He died 1728. His son Alan, second viscount, died 1747. In his time his first cousin Vice-Admiral Thomas Brodrick was residing at Peper Harow.[52] George, the third viscount, son of Alan the second, died 1765. He was succeeded by his son George, created Baron Brodrick of Peper Harow in the peerage of the United Kingdom. He died 1836. His son George Alan was succeeded in 1848 by his cousin Charles, grandson of the third viscount, who died in 1863. The

BRODRICK, Viscount Midleton. *Argent a chief vert and therein two spear-heads argent having drops of blood upon them.*

manor passed to his brother the Very Rev. William John Brodrick, who dying in 1870 was succeeded by his son William, the late Lord Lieutenant of Surrey. Viscount Midleton died in 1907, and was succeeded by his eldest son, the present viscount.

There is mention in 1353 of a manor-house[53] at Peper Harow. It formed for a time the residence of William Brocas and his widow Joan, who was buried in the church in 1487.[54] The third viscount pulled down the old house, but at his death in 1765 the new house, which was being built from designs by Sir William Chambers, was not completed. It was finished by his son when he came of age ten years later, and afterwards added to, under the advice of Wyatt. It is a plain Italian building, in brick and stucco.

RIEHULL (or Royal *hodie*) in Peper Harow was a very early grant to Waverley Abbey by Ralph the sheriff, confirmed by the pope in 1147.[55] It is presumably part of the land in Peper Harow of which the Earl of Southampton, the grantee of Waverley, died seised in 1542. In 1602 Henry Smith, who owned Peper Harow,[56] settled 'Ryalls' on his son William on his marriage.[57]

The property continued with the Smiths till about 1837, when it passed to Mr. Fielder King, son of George and Elizabeth King, under the will of — Smith, brother of the latter. The King family sold the property to Lord Midleton.[58]

Besides the liberty of warren claimed by Joan Braunch and granted to Henry of Guildford, the lords of Peper Harow had free fishery, which last was reserved by Ralph Brocas in granting a lease of the manor. He also claimed hospitality from his tenant when he came to the manor to hold his courts. There is mention in the survey of 1086 of a mill at Peper Harow; this had fallen into ruins before 1353.[59]

The church of *ST. NICHOLAS* is
CHURCH situated in the park. The churchyard, which is beautifully kept, is surrounded by trees. The ancient parts of the church are built of local sandstone rubble, with dressings of clunch, covered with rough plaster; the modern work is in local stone rubble with Caen stone dressings, except the tower, which is coursed stone. The roofs are tiled.

The church consists of a nave about 35 ft. by 20 ft., and a chancel 18 ft. long by 20 ft. wide. These represent the extent of the mediaeval building. To them in 1826 a western tower was added, replacing the wooden bell-turret with shingled spire shown in Cracklow's view. A north aisle was added to the nave and a mortuary chapel opening out of it to the chancel by the then Viscount Midleton in 1847, from the designs of the late A. W. Pugin, while in 1877 the nave was reroofed and reseated, and a new porch added on the south side, to replace one built in 1826. There is a vestry on the north of the aisle. These successive works have considerably changed the ancient aspect of the building; but even so they have stopped short of what was proposed to be done, judging by the plate published in Brayley's *Surrey.*

The nave is entered through the south porch by an ancient round-headed doorway of two plain orders, with a hood-mould and impost simply chamfered. The only other ancient features in this wall are the external south-east quoins of chalk and a single-light window low down in the wall close adjoining, with an ogee trefoiled head, evidently inserted to light the south nave altar, and dating from about 1330; it is set in a recess going down to the floor on the inside. The two windows to the westward are quite modern. In the south wall of the chancel, near to its western end, is a low side window renewed in modern stone. All the other windows and external features in the chancel, chapel, north aisle, and tower are modern.

41 Close, 27 Eliz. pt. xv; Feet of F. Surr. Hil. 35 Eliz.
42 Chan. Proc. Eliz. S.s. 15.
43 Feet of F. Surr. Hil. 36 Eliz.
44 Ibid. Trin. 3 Jas. I.
45 Ibid. Mich. 3 Jas. I; Close, 3 Jas. I, no. 1809.
46 Chan. Inq. p.m. (Ser. 2), ccclxvii, 187.   47 Close, 1655, pt. xxxvii.
48 Chan. Decrees Enr. (1313), vi, fol.

100. He was sued by the administrator of the estate of his stepmother Hester, for money due for a release of her life interest in Peper Harow.
49 Feet of F. Surr. Hil. 11 Will. III; Luttrell, *Brief Historical Relation of State Affairs,* ii, 496.
50 Close, 11 Will. III, pt. iv, no. 5.
51 Bishop Willis's Visit. at Farnham.
52 Registers.

53 Chan. Inq. p.m. 27 Edw. III (1st nos.), no. 61.
54 Major Heales, 'The Brasses in Peper Harow Church,' *Surr. Arch. Coll.* vii, 34.
55 B.M. Lansd. MS. 27.
56 Harl. MS. 1561, fol. 190–1.
57 Chart. at Peper Harow.
58 Local information.
59 Chan. Inq. p.m. 27 Edw. III (1st nos.), no. 61.

In the interior the most striking features are the much-restored chancel arch and its flanking recesses—that to the south pierced with a squint—dating from the middle of the 12th century. But though parts of the works are old, particularly in the recesses, the whole has been so much renewed, with the addition of carved shafts and elaborate mouldings, that it possesses little interest for archaeologists. The arcade to the new aisle, also a very elaborate piece of work, has been built to accord with the chancel arch, the materials used being chalk and Caen stone, with shafts of Irish marble from Lord Midleton's estates in that country.

Within the chancel practically all is new, including the sedilia in the south wall, but the piscina is said to be a copy of that formerly in existence. The chancel and chapel windows, which are entirely modern, are designed in the style of the early part of the 14th century, and there are also some image niches and other features in the new work with much carving about them. The roofs, fittings, and glass are also modern.

The chancel roof is panelled and covered with sacred emblems. That of the chapel has quatrefoiled bosses, with painting and gilding in the panels. The reredos, of Caen stone, has five canopied compartments, the middle one containing a cross supported by angels, and the other four cherubim standing on their wheels.

Besides the monuments to Lord Midleton's family in the chapel there are some brasses of ancient date, one on the north wall of the chancel to Joan Adderley, bearing date 1487. It is fixed in a slab of Sussex marble, and represents her in widow's dress kneeling at a prayer-desk before a representation of the Blessed Trinity with labels inscribed, 'Ihu Mercy—Lady helpe' and the inscription in black letter :—

Ex vestra caritate orate *pro anima* Johane Adderley *quondam uxoris* Johanis Adderley *quondam* Majoris Civitatis London', et *nuper uxoris Willelmi* Brokes, armigeri, Patroni istius *ecclesie*, *que quidem* Johana obiit xviij die *Novembris* 2° *Domini* mccccccclxxxvij ; *cujus anime* propicietur Deus. Amen.

In front of the altar rails is another slab bearing a brass cross which formerly marked the actual place of her burial.

Among the church plate is a paten of 1717 and a chalice and paten of peculiar design and uncertain date, made at Danzig, Germany.

There are three bells, all of 17th-century date.

The registers of baptisms begin in 1697, of burials in 1698, of marriages in 1699. There is a note at the beginning that the old registers were destroyed when the rectory house was burnt 'in Dr. Mead's time.' He was rector 1661 to 1687.

ADVOWSON The church is not mentioned in the Domesday Survey of Peper Harow, but it was assessed at £5 in 1291.[60] The advowson was an appurtenance of the manor, with which it has descended till the present day.

CHARITIES The charities are a rent-change on an estate at Shelley in Essex, for the use of poor persons, amounting to 30s., left by Nicholas Wallis, rector in 1606 ; and Smith's Charity for the relief of aged and infirm persons of good character, apprenticing children, portioning maids, &c., payable out of the Warbleton estate, Sussex, and amounting to about £3 a year or under.

PUTTENHAM

Potenham and Putenham (xiii cent.).

Puttenham is a village on the south side of the Hog's Back, 4½ miles west of Guildford, 5½ miles east of Farnham. The parish is roughly triangular. The base from north-east to south-west is nearly 3 miles long; the line from the apex to the middle of the base, north-west to south-east, is under 2 miles. The west side is longer than the northern side. It contains 1,931 acres of land and 29 acres of water. The village lies in the north-east angle of the parish. The northern part of the parish is on the chalk of the Hog's Back ridge, though, as is almost invariably the case, the village is not on the chalk. The rest of the parish is Upper Green Sand, Gault, and Lower Green Sand, which is the predominating soil.

The views from the upper ground are extremely picturesque, embracing the Hindhead and Blackdown ranges, and extending over Sussex to the South Downs, while the foreground is broken and diversified with woods and heaths. Puttenham Heath, close to the east of the parish, is mostly covered with turf, and a nine-hole golf course has been made on it, with a club-house opened in 1897. Puttenham Common, to the south-west, is a true heath, covered with heather, fern, and furze, and rising to over 300 ft. above the sea, with a deep depression between it and the chalk to the northward.

The parish is purely agricultural. Chalk was dug on the Hog's Back. The district of the famous Farnham hops extends into Puttenham. The northern boundary of the parish is the road along the ridge of the Hog's Back. One sign of the antiquity of the road is the frequency with which it forms the old parish boundaries. Captain James, R.E., traced the so-called Pilgrims' Way through the parish below the chalk. It went on as a lane to Seale, and has been converted since 1903 into a good road.

On Puttenham Heath is a fairly large tumulus called Frowsbury, which has never been explored. Neolithic flints are not uncommon near it. On Puttenham Common is a considerable entrenchment, with one bank and ditch. It is of about 530 ft. on the south, east, and west sides, but the north-east angle is slightly obtuse, the south-west angle slightly acute, so that the east and west sides are not parallel, and the north side is shorter than the other. On the west there is no distinct bank, and no ditch, but the hill falls sharply to a stream in the grounds of Hampton Lodge, and has been perhaps artificially scarped. The water below is within missile range of the entrenchment. Romano-British pottery and a rude pavement were found near this, to the north-east, in 1870. Many neolithic flints have been found on the borders of the parish, near Shoelands, a little further north.

There is a cemetery with a chapel on Puttenham

Heath, opened in 1882. The schools were built in 1850.

MANORS There are four manors or reputed manors in Puttenham; Puttenham Bury and Puttenham Priory—moieties of one manor, Rodsell and Shoelands. Of these Rodsell alone is mentioned in the Domesday Survey.

The main manor of PUTTENHAM was a member of the manor of Bramley in Blackheath Hundred.[1] It is uncertain whether it was included with Rodsell in 1086 or whether the 'two manors' of Wanborough recorded in Domesday were Wanborough and Puttenham, or whether it was included in Bramley. It seems to have followed the history of Bramley, for it was in the king's hands in the 12th century, since, c. 1199, Geoffrey Bocumton exchanged 15 librates of land, which he had had in Puttenham by the king's gift, for 12 librates of land in Stoke by Guildford.[2] The lands of Ralph de Fay, lord of Bramley under Henry II, were in 1203 granted to Robert de Barevill.[3] Robert was sued for land in Puttenham by Geoffrey de Roinges before the time of this grant,[4] and evidently established his rights, for in 1221 the king gave Robert de Barevill ten oaks towards the mending and rebuilding of his houses in Puttenham.[5] Ralph de Fay's lands were restored and descended to his son Ralph,[6] who was succeeded by John de Fay, his son, in 1223.[7] At John's death his lands were divided between his two sisters, Maud wife of Roger de Clere and Philippa Neville.[8] Puttenham, however, had been assigned to Ralph de Fay's widow Beatrice, in dower. It was seized in 1241 owing to her excommunication, but restored in 1242. It was again taken into the king's hands in 1246.[9] Puttenham was then divided between the two sisters, Philippa and Maud. Philippa's moiety was afterwards called Puttenham Bury, while her sister's portion became the manor of Puttenham Priory.

Philippa Neville gave PUTTENHAM BURY with Bramley in free marriage with her daughter Beatrice to William of Wintershull.[10] For the next 300 years Puttenham Bury and Bramley followed the descent which is given under Bramley.[11] In 1541 Edmund Pope, a lineal descendant of William of Wintershull and his wife Beatrice, sold both manors.[12] Bury was purchased in 1541 by Robert Lusher of Cheam and his wife Elizabeth, who also bought Puttenham Priory in 1544.[13] His father Thomas was holding Shoelands, but Robert predeceased him, dying in 1545.[14] His widow Elizabeth, aunt of Sir Olliph Leigh (see below), married George Beaumont,[15] and retained for life an allowance out of Puttenham Bury Manor,[16] and the whole of Puttenham Priory,[17] which she leased to her son Thomas Beaumont in 1587.[18] Robert's son, Nicholas Lusher, died 26 May 1566, leaving an infant son Nicholas.[19] His lands were therefore taken into the queen's hands during the minority of the heir. She leased the demesne lands of Puttenham Bury and Shoelands to Mary, Nicholas Lusher's widow.[20] In 1610 Nicholas, son and heir of Nicholas Lusher, and his son Richard sold the two manors of Puttenham and the manor of Shoelands to Sir Olliph Leigh of Addington and his brother Sir John Leigh.[21] Sir Olliph died 1612.

PUTTENHAM COMMON, LOOKING TO HINDHEAD

His son Sir Francis and the latter's uncle Sir John held the estates in coparceny, and demised a part of Shoelands to one Nicholas Harding. They then divided them, Sir John taking the two Puttenhams, and Sir Francis Shoelands. On Sir John's death in 1624, Sir Francis took the whole.[22] Sir Francis Leigh, who had married Elizabeth daughter and heir of William Minterne of Thorpe, conveyed the manor of Puttenham Bury in 1625 to his father-in-law for life, with reversion to his younger son Francis Leigh, and failing his male issue to his elder son Wolley Leigh, later an ardent Royalist. William Minterne

1 Chan. Inq. p.m. 15 Edw. I, no. 15; bid. (Ser. 2), ii, 7.
2 Rot. de Oblat. et Fin. (Rec. Com.), John, p. 41.
3 Liberate R. 4 John, m. 6.
4 Rot. Cur. Regis (Rec. Com.), ii, 79; Feet of F. Surr. 1 John, 19.
5 Rot. Lit. Claus. (Rec. Com.), i, 469.
6 Testa de Nevill (Rec. Com.), 225; Red Bk. of Exch. ii, 560.
7 Excerpta e Rot. Fin. (Rec. Com.), i, 102.
8 Ibid. 346, 354.
9 Ibid. 355, 448; and Close R. 26 Hen. III, m. 10.
10 Feet of F. Surr. 33 Hen. III, 23.
11 See under Bramley in Blackheath Hund.
12 Feet of F. Surr. Trin. 33 Hen. VIII; ibid. Hil. 33 Hen. VIII.
13 Chan. Inq. p.m. (Ser. 2), cxliii, 32.
14 Exch. Inq. p.m. (Ser. 2), bdle. 1094, no. 15.
15 Surr. Visit. (Harl. Soc.), xliii, 14.
16 Harl. Chart. 111, E. 25.
17 Feet of F. Surr. Trin. 29 Eliz.
18 Ibid.
19 Chan. Inq. p.m. (Ser. 2), cxliii, 32.
20 Harl. Chart. 111, E. 25.
21 Feet of F. Surr. Hil. 7 Jas. I; ibid. East. 11 Jas. I.
22 Feet of F. Surr. Mich. 13 Jas. I; deed of 26 Jan. 1615–16; P.C.C. will, proved 25 Sept. 1624.

died in 1627, and bequeathed all his lands, with the exception of one-half of Shoelands, to Wolley Leigh.[30] Francis Leigh having died without children in 1637,[34] Wolley should have succeeded to all the manors. But some rearrangement of trusts must have been made. Sir Francis Leigh the father was still alive, and it is he who held a court in 1643.[35] Sir Francis died 1645, and Wolley Leigh very soon after him. In 1645 the estate was conveyed by Thomas Leigh, Wolley's half-brother, or son, to William Leigh, another half-brother,[36] whose widow, Lydia Leigh, was lady of the manor as early as 1661, and held courts up to 1711, when she was buried at Puttenham.

In 1728 Jasper Jones and his wife Frances were in possession of the two manors.[37] Frances was only daughter and heir of Francis Leigh of the Middle Temple, son of the said William and Lydia. She

and her husband sold the manors in 1744 with Bury Farm to Brigadier-General James Edward Oglethorpe, founder of the colony of Georgia.[38] He sold the manors in 1761 to Thomas Parker,[39] who rebuilt the Manor House, since called the Priory ; but parts of an older house of Elizabethan or Jacobean date, including a shaped gable of Bargate stone and brick, remain at the back. In 1775 he sold the whole property. Admiral Cornish bought the Manor House and some other property, and after his death in 1816 it was sold to his wife's nephew Richard Sumner, who died in 1870. His son Mr. Morton Cornish Sumner owned it, and died before 1880. His widow died recently, and the owner now is Mr. Ferdinand F. Smallpeice. The manors were bought by Mr. Nathaniel Snell, from whom they were bought by Mr. E. B. Long with Hampton Lodge in 1799. He was succeeded by Mr. H. L. Long and by Mr. Mowbray Howard of Hampton Lodge, *vide infra*. Mr. F. F. Smallpeice has since bought the manors.

PUTTENHAM PRIORY or *PRIOR* was the moiety of the original manor of Puttenham which Maud de Fay, one of the sisters of John de Fay, inherited. She granted it in 1248 to the Priory of Newark by Guildford.[30] In 1279 the prior claimed assize of bread and ale and view of frankpledge in his manor of Puttenham.[31]

At the time of the surrender of the priory in 1538 the farm of the manor of Puttenham was £6.[32] The king thus being in possession of the manor as part of the lands late of Newark Priory, granted it to Edward Elrington and Humphrey Metcalfe in exchange for other lands in various counties.[33] On the sites of Puttenham and other manors granted at the same time there grew two hundred oaks and elms, 'part timber and most part usually croppyd and shrude of sixty and eighty years growthe,' of which a great many were reserved ' by

PUTTENHAM

[30] Chan. Inq. p.m. (Ser. 2), ccccxxxviii, 125. Bridget wife of William Minterne was also to have a life interest in half of Shoelands.

[34] *Surr. Arch. Coll.* vii, pt. i, p. 111.

[35] Manning and Bray, op. cit. ii, 17, think that it was Francis son of Wolley's

half-brother Thomas, but this is incorrect.

[36] Feet of F. Surr. Mich. 21 Chas. I ; Recov. R. East 24 Chas. I.

[37] Feet of F. Surr. Mich. 2 Geo. II.

[38] Close, 19 Geo. II, pt. i, no. 26.

[39] Feet of F. Surr. Mich. 2 Geo. III.

[30] Feet of F. Surr. 32 Hen. III, 35.

[31] *Plac. de Quo Warr.* (Rec. Com.), 747.

[32] Dugdale, *Mon.* vi, 384.

[33] L. and P. Hen. VIII, xix (1), 442 (16).

custome of olde tyme' to the farmer for the repair of the houses on the manors [34] (for which compare the grant by Henry III to Robert de Barevill, above). In 1544 Edward Elrington and Humphrey Metcalfe sold the manor to Robert and Elizabeth Lusher, then owners of Puttenham Bury. Thenceforward the two manors generally follow the same descent.

The lords of Puttenham Priory seem to have had view of frankpledge and assize of bread and ale in their manor.[35] William of Wintershull and his wife Beatrice also had view of frankpledge in Puttenham.[36] Both Puttenham Bury and Priory had courts baron.[37]

RODSELL lies to the south of the parish between Shackleford in Godalming and Cut Mill. Under Edward the Confessor Tovi held it. Bishop Odo of Bayeux held it in demesne after the Conquest,[38] and added it to the land which he held out in farm at Bramley.[39] The bishop's lands fell to the Crown at his final exile, and with them Bramley. The history of the holding from this time is obscure. In 1273 William Palmer of Rodsell obtained from John son of William a lease for life of a messuage and half a virgate of land in Puttenham.[40] In 1508 William Lusher held the manor of 'Redsale' (evidently Rodsell by the context).[41] In 1568 William Lusher, son and heir of George Lusher, had a rent-charge on lands in Rodsell and Puttenham.[42] Richard Wyatt purchased lands in Puttenham from Sir John and Sir Francis Leigh, who were connected by marriage with the Lushers,[43] and Richard's son Francis Wyatt died in 1634 holding the manor and farm of Rodsell,[44] which he had settled on his wife Timothea in April 1621.[45] He also held the wood called Prior's Wood in Puttenham and Compton. His son Richard entered upon the manor after his mother's death.[46] He died in June 1645, leaving a younger brother Francis, who was his heir.[47] Francis died in 1673. His son Francis died in 1723, having survived his son, also Francis, who died in 1713, aged twenty-six. The latter's elder son Richard married Susan daughter of Sir Thomas Molyneux of Loseley, and died s.p. in 1753. His younger brother William died in 1775, and his son Richard in 1784. Richard son of Richard died unmarried in 1816. His heir, another Richard, of Horsted Keynes, sold Rodsell in 1819 to Edward Beeston Long, who was followed by his son Henry Lawes Long of Hampton Lodge.[48] It is now the property of Mr. Mowbray Howard of Hampton Lodge.

SHOELANDS (Sholaund, xiii cent.; Sheweland,

Lusher. Gules three martlets or and a chief or with three molets azure therein.

xvi cent.; Sholand and Shoeland, xvii and xviii cents.) was probably a sub-manor of Burgham, for its tenants paid rent to the lord of Burgham.[49] In 1235 Ralph Attewood granted to John de Fay land in Shoelands.[50] The lords of Burgham in 1251 were William of Wintershull and Beatrice his wife,[51] and when, at that date, Peter de Ryvall granted a carucate of land and 5s. rent in Shoelands and Puttenham to the Prior and church of Selborne, co. Hants, for ever, William of Wintershull and his wife confirmed the land to the priory to be held of them and their heirs by rent of a gilded spur yearly within a week of the Nativity of John the Baptist (June 24).[52] The rent of the gilded spur is mentioned in an extent of the Wintershulls' lands dated 1287. The men of the priory in Shoelands and Puttenham were to be free from view of frankpledge. At the same time William and Beatrice released to the prior all their claim to the road which led from a certain close (hega) at 'Otteford,' before the prior's gate at Shoelands as far as the house of Ralph Du Bois.[53] This was probably a right of way to the main road in the Down, up the existing steep and certainly ancient lane.

For some time the priory remained in possession of Shoelands, paying an annual rent of 6d.,[54] probably in lieu of the gilded spurs. In 1338 Ralph Poynaunt incurred the greater excommunication for stealing an ox from the manor of the Prior and convent of Selborne at 'Schoulonde.'[55] The priory was suppressed owing to its poverty, and by Waynflete's influence added to the foundation of Magdalen College in 1484.[56] Thomas Lusher was tenant of some Hampshire lands under the priory, 1462, and just before the foundation of Magdalen Shoelands had been granted for life to Richard Lusher.[57] Apparently it was somehow retained, for it never belonged to Magdalen, and William Lusher was seised of it late in the 15th century. From him it descended to his son Thomas. Thomas's son Robert, the purchaser of the Puttenham manors, predeceased his father in 1545, leaving a son Nicholas aged ten.[58] After Thomas's death his grandson Nicholas entered upon the manor, and in 1561 was sued by his uncle William for a rent from the manor, which he claimed as bequeathed him by Robert.[59] After the death of Nicholas Lusher in 1566 Shoelands was taken into the queen's hands, the demesne lands being leased with those of Puttenham Bury to Mary Lusher,[60] Nicholas's widow. Their son Nicholas was knighted after 1580, and his son Richard Lusher of Shoelands was admitted as a student at the Inner Temple in 1602. Shoelands seems to have been sold with Puttenham Bury and Priory to Sir Olliph and Sir John Leigh. Sir Francis, the son of the former (see Puttenham Bury), conveyed a moiety of it in February 1615–16 to William Minterne to the use of his wife Bridget Minterne, with remainder to Francis Leigh and

[34] Partic. of Grants, Aug. Off. Hen. VIII, no. 411, E. 6.
[35] Plac. de Quo Warr. (Rec. Com.), 747.
[36] Feet of F. Surr. 35 Hen. III, 24.
[37] Harl. Chart. 111, E. 25.
[38] V.C.H. Surr. i, 301b.
[39] Ibid. 302a.
[40] Feet of F. Surr. 2 Edw. I, 14.
[41] De Banco R. East. 23 Hen. VII.
[42] Feet of F. Surr. Hil. 11 Eliz.
[43] Will of Francis Wyatt, proved Lond. 10 Feb. 1635.

[44] Chan. Inq. p.m. (Ser. 2), ccclxxiii, 90.
[45] Ibid.
[46] Ibid. mxxxvii, 12.
[47] Ibid. mxxiv, 34.
[48] Brayley, Hist. of Surr. v, 239.
[49] Chart. of Selborne Priory (Hants Rec. Soc.), 1891, p. 117.
[50] Plac. de Jur. and Assiz. 19–20 Hen. III, Calendar 21 (xlix), 85.
[51] Chan. Inq. p.m. 15 Edw. I, 15.
[52] Feet of F. Surr. 35 Hen. III, no. 23, 24.

[53] Ibid. In 1198–9 Thurbert Du Bois leased a virgate of land in Puttenham to a certain Richard le Curt; ibid. 10 Ric. I, 34.
[54] Chart. of Selborne Priory (Hants Rec. Soc.), 1891, p. 117.
[55] Ibid. 89.
[56] See V.C.H. Hants, ii, 179.
[57] Doc. of Selborne at Magdalen College, Oxford.
[58] Chan. Inq. p.m. (Ser. 2), lxxxv, 55.
[59] Chan. Proc. (Ser. 2), cx, 13.
[60] Harl. Chart. 111, E. 25.

contingent remainder to Wolley Leigh.[61] Wolley Leigh died seised of the reversion of this portion of the manor,[62] his grandmother Bridget Minterne and his father Sir Francis Leigh being still alive, and of the other half on his father's death.

Sir Thomas Leigh, Wolley Leigh's son apparently, dealt with one moiety only in 1661,[63] and again in 1665.[64] Sir Thomas Leigh died in 1677, leaving a son Sir John Leigh, bart. He was succeeded about 1692 by his son Sir John Leigh, born 1681, married 1700, and in 1703 a recovery was suffered by Sir John to Sir Stephen Lennard, father of his son's wife.[65] He died in 1737. The recovery probably barred the entail, and Shoelands is not specifically mentioned in the last Sir John's will.

LEIGH. *Or a cheveron sable with three lions argent thereon.*

The other moiety was apparently sold to John Caryll of Tangley, whose son-in-law Henry Ludlow was in possession in 1695.[66] It descended in his family till 1767, when the whole manor apparently was part of the property assigned to Giles Strangways.[67] He sold it to the tenant, Francis Simmonds, whose grandson Thomas, a yeoman farmer, was the owner in 1806.[68] In 1823 he sold to Mr. E. H. Long, and the property has passed, as Puttenham, to Mr. Mowbray Howard. Thomas Packington, who has been described as an owner, was merely a tenant about 1623.[69]

Shoelands House bears the date 1616 or 1618 over the porch. The date has been replaced after removal. The house was therefore partly built by William Minterne or his son-in-law Sir Francis Leigh, or by Thomas Packington (of Shoelands in Visitation of 1623). It has a fine mullioned window, blocked now, to the south, an old chimney-stack on the same date, and a Jacobean staircase with good carving of about the same date. This work probably marks a rebuilding of an older house, when the staircase was put in to reach rooms built over an old high hall the rafters of which are visible in one place in the wall of an upper room.

There are no mills given in the survey of Rodsell [70] in 1086, though there are five given under Bramley.[71] In 1587 there were no fewer than four mills in Puttenham Priory,[72] and about the same time there was one water-mill in Puttenham Bury Manor.[73] This may have been Cutt Mill, which was afterwards in the possession of Francis and Richard Wyatt.[74]

The family of Frollebury seems to have been of some importance in Puttenham during the 13th and 14th centuries. In 1296 William Frollebury and his wife Joan had two messuages and land there, which they held of Thomas son of William Frollebury.[75] Stephen Frollebury and his wife Katharine held the same land in 1340.[76] Frollesbury is an existing house in Puttenham.

CHURCH

The church of ST. JOHN THE BAPTIST stands high above the road, the ground rising in steep banks round it on the south and east. The churchyard, which is bordered on the south by a low wall and the grounds of the manor-house (commonly called Puttenham Priory) has some fine trees and shrubs, and is carefully kept.

The building is of local sandstone rubble with dressings of hard chalk, mostly replaced on the outside by Bath stone; parts of the north aisle and the chancel are plastered, and the roofs are tiled. In plan the church consists of a long and very narrow nave 52 ft. 3 in. by 16 ft. 9 in., and chancel 29 ft. 2 in. by 12 ft. 6 in.; these probably represent the extent of the early church.[76a] On the north of the nave is an aisle about 7 ft. wide, opening to the nave by an arcade of four arches, representing the first extension in the latter part of the 12th century : and on the north of the chancel is a chapel 29 ft. 7 in. by 13 ft. 8 in., partly opened to the chancel by a pair of small arches—an addition of about 1200.

At the eastern end of the south side of the nave is a transeptal chapel, 12 ft. square, added about 1330 ; and the west tower, very large and massive in proportion to the church, dates from the early part of the 15th century. The south porch in its present form is modern, dating from the general restoration of the building in 1861. The north chapel seems to have been largely rebuilt at the beginning of the 19th century.

Judging by the different levels of the arcade bases, which increase in height from west to east, the ancient floor of the nave must have been laid on an inclined

PUTTENHAM : SHOELANDS MANOR HOUSE

61 Chan. Inq. p.m. (Ser. 2), ccccxxxviii, 125.   62 Ibid. mxxiv, 1.
63 Feet of F. Div. Co. East. 13 Chas. II.
64 Ibid. Trin. 17 Chas. II.
65 Recov. R. Hil. 2 Anne.
66 Feet of F. Surr. East. 7 Will. III.
67 For detailed descent see under Bramley.

68 Manning and Bray, *Hist. of Surr.* ii, 19.
69 Chan. Proc. 1621-5 (Ser. 2), bdle. 364, no. 16.
70 *V.C.H. Surr.* i, 301*b*.
71 Ibid. 301*a*.
73 Feet of F. Surr. Trin. 29 Eliz. Not necessarily separate buildings, but possibly four separate mill-stones.

73 Harl. Chart. 111, E. 25.
74 Chan. Inq. p.m. (Ser. 2), ccccixxiii, 90 ; mxxiv, 34.
75 Feet of F. Surr. 24 Edw. I, 3.
76 Ibid. 13 Edw. III, 16.
76a Cf. the plan of the neighbouring church of Compton, where the nucleus of a pre-Conquest plan has survived through later alterations.

plane, following the natural slope of the ground, and there is reason to believe that this sloping floor remained till 1861.

The church is entered from the south by a round-headed doorway built of clunch, very much retooled. It is of two moulded orders, the outer standing upon a shaft with square abacus and scalloped capital of unusual design. The abacus is continued as an impost moulding across the inner order of jamb and arch, which are plain except for a quirked bead on the angle. A round-headed window to the west appears to be modern, but may be a copy of one found at the restoration ; and the traceried windows to the east of the porch are quite modern. The north arcade, in chalk or clunch, is of four semicircular arches of a single square order without a label, an unusual number, necessitated by the lowness of the wall through which they were pierced : a diminutive arch has been pierced through the east respond at the restoration. The piers are circular and their bases have square sub-bases with angle spurs and chamfered plinths. The capitals are square, with chamfered abaci and somewhat irregular scalloping of the common pattern, the capital of the west respond only differing from the others in having the scalloping concave with a small round-topped

touched up. The last-named seems to have been rebated for a shutter. The thinness of the transept walls (1 ft. 10 in.) is exceptional.

The date of the chancel arch is if anything somewhat earlier than that of the chancel, which may be placed at about 1200. It is pointed, of two orders chamfered like the jambs, which have no shafts, but only an impost moulding at the springing. Its setting out on plan shows some irregularity. A string-course of a round section remains within the chancel, and on the north side are the two arches to the chapel. These are of one pointed order, with narrow chamfers, and the central column has a circular moulded capital and base. The east window and the buttresses flanking it are modern, but the two eastern windows in the south wall are apparently restorations, and follow the lines of the east window of the transept. An 18th-century engraving shows three-light windows in the east walls of the chancel and north chapel, both apparently of early 14th-century character. The two eastern windows in the south wall of the chancel, now restored in stone, are shown as plain wooden frames in this old view. The piscina is also restored. The window in the western part of the south wall of the chancel is ancient, built of chalk, and dates

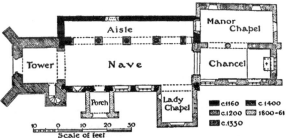

PUTTENHAM CHURCH : GROUND PLAN

cresting Just above the necking.[7b] The modern plastering is cut with scalloped edging round the arches —an ancient feature found at Compton, but here probably only borrowed. There are no ancient windows in the aisle, which is lit by dormers of modern date, and the door in the north wall is modern.

The west tower wears a somewhat battered appearance from the friable nature of the sandstone of which it is built, and most of the windows and other dressings inside and out, including the lofty arch to the nave, have been renewed in Bath stone. It has a large square stair-turret on the south side, and is finished by a plain parapet of modern date.

The transept chapel, which is shown in Cracklow's view (c. 1824) as having a large square window with a wooden frame in its south wall, now has a poor three-light traceried opening of discordant character in its place ; but the three-light window in its east wall and the small single-light opening to the west are original early 14th-century features, though a good deal

from about 1400. It is of three lights with six small lights over, under a square hood-moulding, which terminates on one side in the bust of an angel and on the other in that of a mitred bishop or abbot. The westernmost of the three lights has its sill lowered in a very peculiar manner to serve as a low side window—a feature very noticeable in Cracklow's view. This light alone retains the original iron stanchions and cross-bars, and the lower part has the mullions rebated for a shutter.

The windows in the north wall and the door in the east wall of the north chapel are insertions of the early part of the 19th century, the former probably replacing lancets. A blocked recess with an oak lintel in its west wall seems to have been a door of communication between the chapel and the aisle. The floor of the chapel is raised above that of the chancel, and there is a platform or altar-pace at the east end. The roof is ceiled.

Both the nave and the chancel roofs are ancient and

[7b] One of the capitals at Compton is precisely similar, and there are others very like it at Rustington and Sompting, Sussex.   The same masons must have worked in and out of the two counties, as at Alfold and other Surrey churches there is a   striking resemblance to features in the sister county.

of massive oak timbers. The chancel roof, of rafters, collars and struts, has large moulded plates and tie-beams excessively cambered, and is perhaps of 14th-century date.

The font, seating, quire stalls, and other fittings are all modern, and a very large organ, bracketed out overhead, blocks up the narrow chancel.[77] The altar is well raised, as, owing to the site, there are four steps between the sacrarium and the nave.

In the chancel is the small brass of a priest in mass vestments inscribed : ' Hic jacet dñs Edward' Cranford' quonda' Rector isti' Eccl̃e. qui objt viij° die mens' Augusti Anno dm̃ Millo. cccc°. xxxj° cui' al̃e p'piciet' deus. Amen.'

In the north chapel is a small stone with indents of man and wife and the brass inscription below ; the date may be about 1504 [77a] :—' Hic Jacent Ricardus Lussher et Etheldreda uxor ejus quorum animabus propicietur Deus.'

Also a large slab of Sussex marble bearing in Roman capitals the inscription : ' Hic jacet sepult̃ corpus dominæ Dorotheæ unius filiarum John̄ Hunt de lindon in Com̃. Rutland armigeri nup' uxoris charis-simac Nicholai Lussher militis cui quatuor pẽp'it filios totidemque puellas nempe Ricard̄, Gulielm̃ Nichos Iañ, Mariam et Ann̄ adhuc superstites Johañem Janīm et Johānam, in cunabilis defunctos, et de hac vita decessit 18 Feb : 1604 orans ut ignoscat ei peccata sua Omnipotens et Misericors Dominus.'

Aubrey gives another inscription as existing in his day on a slab in the north chapel to Nicholas Lusher of Shoeland, esq., son and heir of Robert Lusher, who died in 1566.

There is also a small brass, with the arms of Wyatt impaling Burrell, to Francis Wyatt, 1634, now set in a marble slab on the chancel wall ; it came from a stone in the middle of the north chapel, which formed the burial spot of the Wyatts of Rodsell.

Fixed to the sill of the westernmost window of the chancel is an oblong brass plate, with an inscription to the memory of Henry Beedell and his son Henry, both rectors of Puttenham, who died respectively in 1636 and 1692. Besides these there are one or two ledgers bearing heraldry and some marble tablets of more recent dates.

The registers date from 1562.

The only ancient pieces of church plate—a silver cup and paten, dated respectively 1636 and 1674, are of interest from their association with the Beedells, father and son. The paten is known to have been given by the son, ' who gave back to the church the alienated or chantry lands which his father, the pre-ceding rector, had purchased. Perhaps he also gave the cup.'[77b]

The bells are all modern.

ADVOWSON There was no church here at the time of the Domesday Survey so far as is known. The advowson probably be-longed subsequently to the lord of the manor. The king seems to have possessed it before 1305, when he granted it with Shalford, Wonersh, and Dunsfold churches to the Hospital of St. Mary without Bishops-gate.[78] In 1342 the prior and brethren of the hospital had licence to appropriate the churches of Puttenham and Dunsfold,[79] but apparently the appropriation was never carried out, for the living was a rectory in 1535. The annual pension due from the rectory at this time was 20*s*.[80] In 1537 Thomas Elliott obtained a lease of this pension together with Shalford rectory for ninety-nine years.[81] St. Mary without Bishopsgate was taken into the king's hand at the time of the Dis-solution, but when Queen Elizabeth granted Shalford Rectory to John Wolley[82] she retained the advowson of Puttenham, which has ever since belonged to the Crown. In 1694 Thomas Swift, Jonathan Swift's ' little parson cousin,' became rector.

Richard Lusher presented the parsonage to the church. His gift consisted of a house, garden, and croft lying on 'Gildowne,' and half an acre of land at Rods-mill (Rodsell) in a field called the 'Pece.' They were given to the parson on condition that he should sing or say thirty masses yearly in the parish church, and also a Placebo and Dirige on Thursday before the Nativity of the Virgin Mary (September 8).[83] After the sup-pression of chantries by Edward VI these premises were leased by the king to Henry Polsted and William More. No provision seems to have been made for the parsonage till Henry Beedell, rector early in the 17th century, bought back the parsonage, which his son Henry, who succeeded his father as rector, gave to the parish,[84] confirming the gift in his will.[85] The two Henry Beedells, father and son, held the living from 1598 to 1692.

Manning and Bray quote a will in the Archdeacon's office, by which a certain Stephen Burdon, an inn-keeper of Southwark in 1503, directed 6*s*. 8*d*. to be paid for an image of St. Roke to be given to Putten-ham Church.[86]

In 1725 the return was that there was no chapel, no lecturer, no curate, no Papist, one Quaker, no gentleman, ' nor any school but what teaches children to read and write.'[86a]

CHARITIES The charities are Smith's Charity, founded 1627 for the relief of the deserving poor, and a small sum em-ployed in the same way from the rent of the golf-links.

Mr. Richard Wyatt, 1619, left two nominations to the Carpenters' Company's Almshouses at Godalming to this parish.

Mr. Robert Avenell, 1733, left money with a trus-tee for the relief of the deserving poor, but this seems to have disappeared.

In 1725, in answer to Bishop Willis's Visitation, the churchwardens returned that there were rents of about £4 from lands called the Church Lands applied to the relief of the poor.

---

[77] The present font is the successor of that described in Manning and Bray's *Surr.* as ' of a square form, of free-stone.'

[77a] Richard Lusher's will was proved 1504 ; P.C.C. Holgrave, 18.

[77b] Rev. T. S. Cooper, in *Surr. Arch. Coll.* x, 343.

[78] Chart. R. 33 Edw. I, m. 49.

[79] *Cal. Pat.* 1340–3, p. 410.

[80] *Valor Eccl.* (Rec. Com.), ii, 28.

[81] Misc. Bks.(Land Rev.), vol. 190, p.168.

[82] Pat. 32 Eliz. pt. 17.

[83] Partic. of Sales of Colleges, Misc. Bks. (Aug. Off.), vol. 68, p. 56.

[84] Monumental inscription in Putten-ham Church.

[85] Proved 20 July 1693.

[86] *Hist. of Surr.* ii, 20

[86a] Willis' Visitation.

THURSLEY

Thoreseley (xiv cent.).

Thursley was originally a part of the parish of Witley. The length of the old parish was about 6 miles from north to south, about 2 miles wide in the northern part, tapering to the south and inclosing the town of Haslemere in an elbow at the extreme south. The boundary was here altered in 1902, by order of the Local Government Board, 7 March 1902, part of Thursley, covering 392 acres, which had been much built over by the extension of Haslemere, being transferred to Haslemere parish.

The area of the parish is now 3,986 acres, 1,202 of which are heath land, and 29 water. The parish is traversed throughout its length by the London and Portsmouth road, which rises in easy slopes for over 2 miles from Thursley Common to the top of Hindhead, 903 ft., or by another survey 895 ft., above the sea.

The road winds below the top of the hill along the edge of the great hollow called vulgarly the Devil's Punch Bowl. The old name was Haccombe, i.e. Highcombe, Bottom. The old road was higher up the slope near the top ; it can still easily be seen. The stone marking the site of the murder of a sailor of name unknown, by three fellow travellers in September 1786, is now by the side of the new road. But the crime was committed upon the old road, which was diverted in 1826. The murder is further commemorated by a tombstone, with a bas-relief of the act, in Thursley Churchyard. The perpetrators were hung in chains on a gibbet by the side of the road, pictures of which exist. The whole district was formerly extremely wild and dangerous. Pepys travelling in Surrey in 1668 engaged a guide to conduct him over the road from Guildford to Petersfield. This was a mere track. A properly metalled road was made first in accordance with an Act of Parliament of 1749 for completing the road from Kingston to Petersfield. The road which branches off from Hindhead to Haslemere and into Sussex, to Midhurst, was made at the same time. The view from Hindhead challenges comparison with any in the south of England. Though not so extensive as that from Leith Hill, which including the Tower is 60 ft. higher, the foreground is more broken and diversified. The whole western half of the South Downs lies in front to the south, the Hampshire chalk hills to the west, the whole country to the Thames Valley is overlooked northwards. The advanced position of the hill, jutting out southward from the Green Sand range of Surrey, yields a view eastward along the middle of the Weald, with the Leith Hill range on one hand, the South Downs on the other, and Crowborough Beacon, in Sussex, appearing in the blue distance beyond. Till some forty years ago the spot was still desolate. The 'Royal Huts,' the old inn, was the only house except two or three cottages which stood near it. Since then, Professor Tyndall having led the way, many houses have been built, but not on the top of the hill, and not generally in Thursley parish. The summit, and all the beautiful open common to the north, has been preserved as open space, by

the purchase of this part of the waste of the manor of Witley, from the representatives of the late Mr. Whitaker Wright, by subscribers for the Commons Preservation Society (1905). Thursley is still a purely rural parish ; there is a small village near the church, and a small collection of houses at Bowlhead Green, where a Congregational chapel was built in 1865. The picturesqueness of the parish is not exhausted with Hindhead. The view from the churchyard westward is very fine, and the valley of Cosford is very beautiful.

The soil is the Lower Green Sand almost entirely ; the parish merely touches the Atherfield and Wealden clays on part of its south-east border. The Hammer Ponds, which formerly worked iron forges and a furnace owned by the Smiths of Rake, Witley, are partly in the parish. On the common, but in Frensham parish, are the curious conical sand-hills called the Devil's Jumps. They are natural, not, as has been supposed, barrows. Neolithic implements have been found, an axe-head by Mr. Iolo Williams, now in the Charterhouse Museum, some arrow-heads and flakes, also in the Charterhouse Museum. The farm near the church seems to belong to the 16th century in the back part and interior. The principal landowners are Mr. R. W. Webb of Milford House, Witley ; the Earl of Derby, Captain Rushbrooke of Cosford, Mr. Yalden H. Knowles, and Mrs. Gooch.

There has never been a separate manor of Thursley, but the manor of Witley extends over the parish. In the 16th century tenants of Witley Manor were holding lands at Jordans, Robyns, Bagleys, and elsewhere in the 'hamlet' of Thursley.[1]

The church of ST. MICHAEL, CHURCH THURSLEY, was originally a chapel-of-ease to Witley. The mother church is mentioned in Domesday, but this is not, making it a matter of doubt whether there was a chapel on the site prior to about 1100, which is the approximate date of the earliest features in the existing building. There are a number of 18th and 19th-century monuments in the churchyard, among which is the famous 'sailor's tomb,' mentioned above.

The church is constructed of Bargate stone rubble with Bargate stone and chalk dressings in the old parts. The same rubble, with dressings of Bath stone

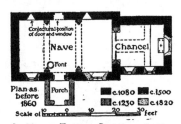

Plan as before 1860

Porch

Conjectural position of door and window

Nave

Font

Chancel

■ c.1080 ■ c.1500
▨ c.1230 ▧ c.1820

Scale of 10 0 10 20 30 feet

St. Michael, Thursley : Plan as before the Enlargements of 1860, etc.

[1] Misc. Bks. (Land Rev.), vol. 290, fol. 129.

and some red brick, is employed for the new work. Before enlargement there was a nave 38 ft. 3 in. by 21 ft., and a chancel 18 ft. by 16 ft. 9 in., separated by an arch, and with a porch on the south of the nave. Rising out of the centre of the nave, was—and happily still is—a slender timber bell-turret, with graceful shingled spire standing upon four enormous baulks of moulded timber, which rest upon the nave floor, and are tied together with braces. The whole turret closely resembles that of the west end of Alfold Church in this neighbourhood, and the two were doubtless erected, about 1500, by the same hands.

Until about the year 1860 the proportions of the simple early building of about 1100 remained unaltered, save for the addition of this timber turret and spire (which, however, made no alteration in the area occupied by the nave and chancel) ; at that time the church received its first enlargement by the addition of a short aisle and a vestry on the north of the nave ; new windows were inserted in the west and east walls and on the south of the nave, and the church was reseated, a gallery being retained at the west end. In 1883–4 the nave was lengthened westwards, and a transept, baptistery, and porch added on the south of the nave, the additions involving the removal of the old west wall and part of the south wall. The accompanying plan, drawn with the help of one taken before the 1860 alterations, shows some of the ancient features that still remain, as well as those that have been removed in the successive enlargements.

The turret and its spire are shingled, and on the south side of the former is a large old sundial, in place of a clock, bearing the inscription, ' Hora pars vitae.' The body of the turret has been heightened 3 ft. Its timbers are remarkably massive as seen from within the nave. Four huge uprights, worked with a series of hollow chamfers, and measuring on the square about 2 ft. 6 in., rise from the nave floor, and great arches of oak spring from them and span the nave. These arches, which are four-centred or elliptical in outline, have a hollow chamfer on the edges, and between them are two other arches of similar shape, but rising from a beam on either side (north and south), carried by a low four-centred arch.

The nave retains only one of its original windows, a small round-headed opening, somewhat widely splayed, in the eastern part of the north wall. It was preserved when the church was enlarged, and now looks into the aisle. Originally there was a similar window to the westward and a small door between in this wall, probably matched by others in the opposite wall ; and in the west end the outline of a round-headed opening was noticeable until the last extension. The south wall seems to have been altered about the middle of the 13th century, when a lancet and doorway took the place of the earlier features. Later still, perhaps in the 15th century, a two-light opening was inserted in the eastern part of the south wall, destroying another early window, and this and a similar insertion in the east wall of the chancel seem to have been fitted with wooden frames in place of the stone tracery early in the 19th century.

The chancel arch, built of hard chalk, is of mid-13th-century date. Its piers are square to a height of 4 or 5 ft. from the floor, and then rise in two chamfered orders, with pyramidal stops at the base, the chamfers continuing without any break round the arch. This arrangement suggests that there was originally a low screen standing in the opening. There are at present the lower parts of a 15th-century screen, which has been deprived of its traceried upper half. The arch should be compared with one of similar date and character in West Clandon Church, near Guildford. In the north-east angle of the nave is a moulded bracket of black marble which looks as if it had carried the beam for the rood, independently of the low screen. The north wall of the chancel is strangely devoid of features, there being no window, door, or aumbry therein. There is a break in the wall horizontally near the top, which is much thinner. In the south wall are two lancets of about 1250, the openings of which appear to have been widened at some time, and the western, which was a low side window and has

CHANCEL ARCH, THURSLEY (FURNITURE OMITTED)

had its head raised since Cracklow's view of 1823 was taken. In the eastern part of the same wall is a small piscina of 1250.

Both in the nave and chancel the roofs are mostly ancient, the timbers of black oak, very massive and in good preservation; some of the beams are of unusual size for so small a building. There are some slight remains of plain 15th-century seats, worked in with new material, in the chancel.

The font is the original, a large circular tub-shaped block of hard Bargate stone, brownish-orange in colour, and quite plain save for a band of cheveron or arrow-head ornament incised round the rim, and a little lower down a projecting moulding of circular section, which may have served the practical purpose of giving a grip to the chain or rope by which this huge block was hoisted about between the quarry and the church. This font appears to belong to an early group in Surrey and Sussex, in which are comprised Tangmere (with a circular moulding), Alfold, Yapton and Walberton, the last two showing similar incised ornamentation to the rims.

Of the three bells one is mediaeval, with an undecipherable black-letter inscription, the others are modern.

Among the church plate is a cup of 1662 and an old pewter plate.

The registers date from 1613, which leads to the inference that it was a separate parish in fact; it had churchwardens of its own, but up to the middle of the 19th century it was usually held with Witley.[3]

ADVOWSON

A chapel at Thursley was taxed with Witley in 1291.[4] It is said to have been erected into a separate parish in

THE FONT, THURSLEY

1838,[5] and the benefice is still in the gift of the vicar of Witley.

CHARITIES

Henry Smith's Charity applies to Thursley. Moon's Money, a charity of unknown origin, was applied to the maintenance of the workhouse.

WITLEY

Witlei (xi cent.); Whitle or Witle (xiii cent. onwards).

Witley is bounded on the west by Thursley, formerly a chapelry of the parish. It is rather over 6 miles from north to south, and 2 miles from east to west, tapering somewhat towards the south. It contains 7,210 acres of land, and 40 of water. The soil of most of the parish is Lower Green Sand; the south-eastern part is on the Atherfield and Wealden Clays. On the west side of the parish Witley Common is an extensive waste of heather, connected with Thursley Common and the waste land running thence up to Hindhead, all included in the manor of Witley. The escarpment of the Green Sand to the south is abrupt, affording fine views southward and eastward, and the central part of the parish are 300 ft. above the sea. The parish was divided into four tithings. Milford to the north, containing the hamlets of Milford and Mousehill, and now a separate ecclesiastical parish, Ley or Lea in the centre, containing the hamlet of Wheeler Street; Stoatley; and Birtley, which includes Witley Street and all the parish to the south. Witley Park was in the last.

The parish is intersected from north to south by the London and Portsmouth road, and in the same direction by the London and South Western Railway

to Portsmouth. Milford station is in Witley, but Witley station is in Godalming parish.

Pinewood is the seat of Viscount Knutsford; Rake of Archdeacon Potter; Lea Park was the home of the late Mr. Whitaker Wright. At the sale of this property in 1905, the manorial rights over part of the waste of Witley, including Thursley and part of Hindhead, were acquired by trustees for the Commons Preservation Society. The principal landowners are Mr. Webb, Mrs. Francis E. Eastwood of Enton, Mr. E. A. Chandler, the Earl of Derby, and the various purchasers of the Lea estate.

The soil of Witley Common contains a considerable percentage of ferruginous sand. There were ironworks in the parish on Witley and Thursley Heaths, but the more important part of them was probably in the Thursley chapelry, now a separate parish. But iron was found also in Witley Park, in the clay. These ironworks seem to have been among the last which were kept open in Surrey.[1] They were working in 1767.

The social troubles of the year 1549 led to riots in Witley among other places, dignified by an old inhabitant as 'the general rebellion in these parts,' when the pale of Witley Park was demolished. The rebellion was largely against inclosing of lands.[2]

3 Inst. Bks. (P.R.O.).
4 *Pope Nich. Tax.* (Rec. Com.), 208.
5 Sumner, *Conspectus of Dioc. of Winton,* 116.

1 See *V.C.H. Surr.* ii, 273, and Topley, *Geol. of the Weald,* 134, for the valuable ferruginous sand in Witley.
2 Mr. M. S. Giuseppi, in *Surr. Arch.*

Coll. xviii, 17, quoting Exch. K.R. Spec. Com. 2244. The same insurrection is referred to in a paper among the Loseley MSS. now at P.R.O.

Witley Park was in the hollow, east of Hindhead and south of the road called Park Lane. The whole property is still called Witley Park.[3]

The ancient cottages near the church are very picturesque. The White Hart Inn may be of 16th-century date, though it has been restored externally. In Milford and in Brook there are also old cottages. Near Stroud are the remains of a moat, where possibly the lodge of Witley or Ashurst Park once stood. Leman Lane, an old road on the eastern boundary of Lea Park, possibly is a very old right of way, retaining its characteristic name, and nature, of the muddy way.

The Witley Institute was built by Mr. John Foster in 1883. It contains a good reference library of 240 volumes, and a lending library of over 700 volumes.

On Witley Common is a moated barrow of considerable size, apparently undisturbed.[4] Other barrows are said to have existed, and to have been opened, but no record is known of their contents.

Neolithic implements and flakes are fairly common. An Anglo-Saxon gold ring of curious make has been found at Witley.[5]

The ecclesiastical parish of Milford was separated from Witley in 1844. The village is about a mile and a half south of Godalming. The parish is traversed by the London and Portsmouth road and by the Portsmouth line of the London and South Western Railway, which has a station there.

Milford House, the seat of Mr. R. W. Webb, J.P., is a substantial brick house of the style of Queen Anne's reign. It was built by Thomas Smith, who succeeded to the property in 1705. His daughter Mary married Philip Carteret Webb, from whom Mr. R. W. Webb is descended.

In and around the hamlet of Milford are a number of old houses and cottages. One, a farm-house, with a fine old yew tree in front, has a large roof of steep pitch over the centre, which covered the hall, and a gabled wing of slight projection at either end, in which both the upper story and the gable-end overhung. Its timber-framed construction is now hidden by plaster, and the barge boards of the gables are plain. The arms of Paine quartered with an unknown coat are in a window. The window-frames appear to be 17th-century insertions in some cases, but one at least of the chimneys is original. The general date of this house may be about 1500.

At Mousehill, to the west of Milford, is a fine old brick manor-house of 17th-century date, with a large chimney at either end having crow-stepped set-offs, and there is some curious panelled work in brick, the window heads with shouldered-arches under a string-course being very unusual.

At Milford is a small Congregational Chapel opened in 1902.

WITLEY MANOR was a possession of MANORS Earl Godwin, and after the Conquest was among the lands of Gilbert son of Richer (Richerius) de Aquila,[6] whose grandfather Engenulf de Aquila had accompanied William the Conqueror and fell at the battle of Hastings.[7] Gilbert's son Richer demanded his father's lands in England; these were at first refused him, but were temporarily restored upon his invoking French aid. For his complicity in

WITLEY : COTTAGES SOUTH-EAST OF THE CHURCH

[3] *Vide infra.*
[4] *Surr. Arch. Coll.* xviii, p. xix.
[5] *V.C.H. Surr.* i, 271.
[6] *V.C.H. Surr.* i, 323b.
[7] Ordericus Vitalis, *Hist. Eccl.* (Duchesne), 501.

WITLEY: THE WHITE HART

the rebellion of William Clito his whole honour of Aquila escheated to the Crown, and was only fully re-granted in 1154.[8] He died in 1176 and was succeeded by a son of the same name.[9] The latter's son Gilbert went away into Normandy shortly before 1200, at which date the sheriff accounted for his lands at Witley.[10] The custody of this manor was given first to Stephen de Turnham, and afterwards, in 1204–5, to William, Earl de Warenne, Gilbert's brother-in-law,[11] who obtained the grant on behalf of his sister.[12] The lands had probably been restored to Gilbert before 6 April 1226, when he had licence to cross to Normandy,[13] but they were again taken into the king's hands in September of the same year,[14] perhaps as a pledge for his loyalty to Henry III, for they were restored in the following spring on payment of a fine.[15] Gilbert de Aquila was dead before January 1231–2,[16] and his lands escheated to the king,[17] probably owing to his or his heir's adherence to French interests,[18] for in 1232 Henry III granted his barony to Peter de Rivaulx, the Poitevin favourite, promising that, if he should restore it to Gilbert's heirs by a peace or of his own free will, Peter should not be dispossessed without compensation.[19] Peter de Rivaulx, however, seems to have lost the lands at the time of his deprivation in 1234, for in December of that year the king granted them with a similar promise to Gilbert Marshal, Earl of Pembroke.[20] He exchanged them almost immediately with the king's brother Richard,[21] but temporarily only, for he surrendered them to the Crown in June 1240.[22] In the year following Henry granted the honour of Aquila to Peter of Savoy, uncle of Queen Eleanor,[23] and entailed it on his heirs in 1246.[24] It was doubtless the general dislike of foreigners which caused the ill-feeling that arose between Peter of Savoy and his tenants at Witley. They roused his anger by neglecting the homage due to him, and he in revenge increased their rents.[25] On the baronial victory in 1264, Peter of Savoy having fled from the country, Witley was granted to the custody of Gilbert de Clare, Earl of Gloucester.[26] But after Evesham, Peter's lands were restored, and on his death in 1268 Queen Eleanor received Witley in accordance with a settlement made by Peter her uncle.[27] The king and queen granted the manor to their son

Edward, who surrendered it to his mother for her life.[28]

She granted the tenants a release from the oppressive exactions of her predecessor on condition that they should cause a yearly service to be held in Witley Church for the souls of her husband and of Peter of Savoy.[29] In 1275 she gave the manor for life to her steward Guy Ferre,[30] who surrendered it to the Crown c. 1279.[31] In 1283 Queen Eleanor was again in possession, for she then had a grant of a weekly market on Fridays at her manor of Witley,[32] and her charter to Guy Ferre was confirmed in 1289.[33] She died in 1291.

Edward I visited Witley in June 1294,[34] and in 1299 assigned the honour of Aquila, and possibly Witley also, but there is no definite proof that Witley was parcel of the honour, in dower to Queen Margaret,[35] who was in actual possession of Witley in 1313,[36] and possibly earlier, for Guy de Ferre the former tenant for life had died before 1303.[37] Witley seems to have been assigned with the honour to the next queen, Isabella, who was in possession in 1329.[38] Queen Isabella surrendered it with her other lands in 1330,[39] and it formed part of Philippa of Hainault's dower in January 1330–1.[40] During the latter's life Andrew Tyndale held the manor in lease, and after her death, in 1369, the lease was renewed for twenty years.[41] He died c. 1377,[42] and the manor was thereupon granted by Richard II to his nurse Mundina Danos for life, the grant being afterwards extended to her and her husband Walter Rauf, the king's tailor, in survivorship.[43] They seem to have renewed the exactions of Peter of Savoy, whereupon the tenants of the manor raised a subscription among themselves and brought a plea against Mundina and her husband,[44] and though they were not at the time successful they were able in the next reign to obtain an exemplification of the Domesday entry relating to Witley,[45] and a confirmation of Queen Eleanor's charter.[46] Walter Rauf died 12 June 1421,[47] but Mundina survived him, at any rate till 1423, when she had confirmation of the former grants of Witley.[48] The reversion of Witley Manor was given to John Feriby, king's clerk, for life, in 1422 ;[49] Henry VI also granted a life-interest in the

---

[8] Dugdale, *Baronage*, i, 497. That he retained some lands, possibly including Witley, is inferred from his grant of Oxenford in 1147.

[9] *Chronica Roberti de Torigneio* (Rolls Ser.), 270.

[10] Pipe R. 2 John, m. 15 d. ; *Testa de Nevill* (Rec. Com.), 225 ; *Cal. Doc. France*, 225–6. [11] Close, 6 John, m. 14.

[12] *Testa de Nevill* (Rec. Com.), 225.

[13] *Cal. Pat.* 1225–32, p. 26.

[14] *Excerpta e Rot. Fin.* (Rec. Com.), i, 147.

[15] Fine R. 11 Hen. III, pt. i, m. 12.

[16] *Cal. Pat.* 1225–32, p. 458.

[17] *Excerpta e Rot. Fin.* (Rec. Com.), i, 119.

[18] It is most likely that it was the heir who sacrificed his English order to retain his French lands, for Gilbert's widow had dower in his English lands, which were nevertheless accounted for among the 'Terrae Normannorum.'

[19] *Cal. Chart. R.* i, 162. It is interesting, in face of Peter de Rivaulx's deprivation, to note that Hubert de Burgh pledged himself to resist any possible attempt of

the king to violate the charters granted to the Poitevin (ibid. i, 165).

[20] Ibid. i, 190.

[21] Ibid. i, 191 ; *Red Bk. of Exch.* (Rolls Ser.), 803.

[22] *Cal. Chart. R.* 252.

[23] Rymer, *Foedera*, i, 399.

[24] *Cal. Chart. R.* i, 293, 296.

[25] Assize R. no. 873 (43 Hen. III), m. 6.

[26] Pat. 48 Hen. III, m. 8.

[27] Feet of F. Div. Co. Mich. 44 Hen. III.

[28] Pat. 53 Hen. III, m. 24 and 21.

[29] Pat. 7 Hen. IV, pt. i, m. 29.

[30] *Cal. Pat.* 1272–81, p. 125.

[31] Ibid. 355.

[32] Close, 11 Edw. I, m. 7.

[33] *Cal. Pat.* 1281–92, p. 329.

[34] Letters close and patent are dated thence by the king 25 June 1294.

[35] *Cal. Pat.* 1292–1301, pp. 76, 79, 102.

[36] Close, 6 Edw. II, m. 14, 15.

[37] Mins. Accts. (Gen. Ser.), bdle. 1015, no. 8. Mention is made of his executors in this account. Edward II visited Witley

in 1324 (*Cal. Close*, 1323–7, pp. 203, 205).

[38] Pat. 3 Edw. III, pt. ii, m. 19 d.

[39] Rymer, *Foedera*, ii, 835, 893.

[40] *Cal. Pat.* 1330–4, p. 55.

[41] *Abbrev. Rot. Orig.* (Rec. Com.), ii, 304. At first he paid £20 yearly, from which the parker's wages of 2d. daily were deducted : after 1369 he paid £30 yearly, which seems to have been about the value of the manor. Queen Philippa granted £30 from it to Gilbert of Imworth (*Cal. Pat.* 1343–5, p. 380). See also the first grant to Mundina Danos (ibid. 1377–81, p. 120), and Andrew Tyndale's account (Mins. Accts. [Gen. Ser.], bdle. 1015, no. 9).

[42] *Cal. Pat.* 1377–81, p. 21.

[43] Ibid. 120, 159, 609.

[44] Coram Rege R. no. 511 (Hil. 12 Ric. II), m. 17.

[45] *Cal. Pat.* 1399–1401, p. 502.

[46] Pat. 7 Hen. IV, pt. i, m. 29.

[47] Esch. Inq. p.m. (Ser. 1), file 1427, no. 1.

[48] *Cal. Pat.* 1422–9, p. 87.

[49] Ibid. 16.

manor to Sir Bryan Stapilton, kt., with remainder after his death to James Fiennes, afterwards Lord Say,[40] who was in possession of it in 1450, when he was executed by Cade's mob.[61] His lands fell to the king, who bestowed Witley on his brother Jasper Tudor, Earl of Pembroke, in 1453.[62] On the accession of Edward IV, the Earl of Pembroke was attainted and forfeited his lands to the king,[63] who granted Witley to the Earl of Kent in tail male,[64] and at the earl's death without heirs male in January 1462–3 to George, Duke of Clarence,[65] his ill-fated brother.[66] On the duke's execution Witley was again seized by the Crown, the stewardship of the manor being granted in 1478 to Sir George Brown, kt., for life.[67] Jasper Tudor's attainder was reversed in 1485 ; probably he regained Witley. At his death in 1495 Henry VII was his heir. Again in 1511 the stewardship of the manor was given to William Fitz William and William Cope, and in 1527 to Sir William Fitz William and Sir Anthony Browne.[68] The demesne lands were held in 1547–9 by Thomas Jones,[69] son of Thomas, Server of the Chamber to Henry VIII (buried in the church), the manorial rights being reserved to the Crown.[60]

In 1551 the manorial rights and the park were given in exchange for other lands to Edward Fiennes, Lord Clinton and Say,[61] who almost immediately conveyed them to Sir Richard Sackville, Chancellor of the Court of Augmentations.[62] The latter conferred the stewardship on William More of Loseley.[63] Queen Mary evidently resumed the manor. In 1599 Queen Elizabeth sold the whole manor and park together with courts leet and baron to trustees for Elizabeth Egerton, widow of Sir John Wolley and sister of Sir George More,[65] her favourite maid of honour. Her son Sir Francis Wolley sold it in 1605 to Sir George More his uncle,[66] who in 1613 sold the park to his brother-in-law Sir Edward More,[67] and the manor to Henry Bell of Rake.[68] It was settled on his great-nephew Anthony Smith the younger.[69] It descended in the Smith family till it passed by the marriage of Philip Carteret Webb in 1763 with Mary Smith[70] to his family. Mr. Robert William Webb of Milford House sold the manor to Mr. Whitaker

Wright of Lea Park. Since his death part of the waste has been acquired by trustees, to preserve the open ground for public enjoyment,[71] and other parts separately sold. Mr. G. H. Pinckard of Combe Court bought the quit-rents of the manor.

The lords of Witley seem to have had a PARK park there early in the 13th century,[72] but it is not specially mentioned in the grants of the manor till after April 1247, when Peter of Savoy obtained free warren in his demesne lands of Witley.[73] In 1303 the profits of the park amounted to 33s. 5d.,[74] and ten years later Queen Margaret sent five oaks from her park at Witley for making shingles to cover the king's great hall at Westminster.[75] Early in the following year Queen Margaret made complaints against certain persons who had broken several of her parks, including Witley,[76] and a similar petition was made by Queen Isabella in 1329.[77] In the grant to Mundina Danos in 1378 vert and venison in the park were reserved to the king, while the grantee undertook to pay the parker his wages of 2d. a day.[78] Amongst the charges brought against the tenants of the manor by Mundina Danos and her husband was that of breaking into their warren,[79] while they claimed free warren in the lands of bond-tenants as well as in their demesne lands.[80] Frequent appointments to the office of keeper occur in the Patent Rolls, sometimes in conjunction with that of Ashurst Park. In 1514 Thomas Jones (Johns) and his son Robert had a grant of the office of keeper in survivorship.[81] Sir William Fitz William and Sir Anthony Browne were made masters of the hunt at Witley when they obtained the stewardship of the manor,[82] but in the survey of Witley Manor dated 1547 Thomas Jones was said to be custodian of the park, which was 6 miles in circuit.[83] It was not always included in the leases of the demesne lands, but in May 1596 was granted in farm to Elizabeth Wolley, Francis her son, and George More her brother,[84] and finally sold to Elizabeth Wolley with the manor, with which it descended till 1613. Sir George More then sold to his brother-in-law, Sir Edward, grounds called Witley Park, which he had

---

[60] Pat. 21 Hen. VI, pt. i, m. 18.
[61] Chan. Inq. p.m. 29 Hen. VI, no. 11.
[62] Pat. 31 Hen. VI, pt. ii, m. 26. The manor was first granted to Edmund, Earl of Richmond, and the Earl of Pembroke for twelve years, and a few months afterwards the former grant was cancelled and the manor settled on Pembroke in tail male.
[63] R. of Parl. (Rec. Com.), vi, 278.
[54] Cal. Pat. 1461–7, p. 225.
[55] Ibid. 226, 227. It seems probable, however, that William son and heir of Lord Say was still occupying the manor in conjunction with his mother Emeline; ibid. 1467–8, p. 116.
[56] To whom there is a tablet dated 1468 on the north wall of the church, erected in his lifetime.
[57] Cal. Pat. 1476–85, p. 92. It is said that Sir Reginald Bray held the manor for life under Henry VII. B.M. Add. MS. 6167. Perhaps the stewardship is meant.
[58] L. and P. Hen. VIII, iv, 1385. In May 1513 William Fitz William granted the sub-stewardship to Christopher More ; Loseley MSS. Hist. MSS. Com. Rep. vii, App. 600a.
[59] Misc. Bks. (Land Rev.), vol. 190, fol. 129 et seq.
[60] Jones's first lease was for 21 years

(Pat. 1 Mary, pt. xiii). In 1553 Sir John Gage obtained a lease to date from the expiration of Jones's lease, nevertheless the latter and his nephew William Stoughton obtained renewals of his lease in 1568 and 1588 (Pat. 10 Eliz. pt. iii, no. 3 ; 29 Eliz. pt. iv, no. 5 ; 37 Eliz. pt. ii, no. 1).
[61] Pat. 5 Edw. VI, pt. vii, no. 14.
[62] Close, 5 Edw. VI, pt. v, no. 1.
[63] Loseley MS. ix, 10.
[64] Possibly the object of the transaction with Lord Clinton and Say was to ensure the Crown against any claim he might bring to the manor. The manorial rights seem to have been included in the grant to Sir John Gage.
[65] Feet of F. Surr. Hil. 2 Jas. I.
[66] Close, 11 Jas. I, pt. xxxvi, no. 3.
[67] Ibid. 12 Jas. I, pt. xxv, no. 23.
[68] Chan. Inq. p.m. (Ser. 2), mxxvi, 54 ; Surr. Arch. Coll. xviii, 29.
[70] She was great-granddaughter of Thomas brother and heir of the younger Anthony Smith. See an interesting account of the manor by Mr. E. Foster, Surr. Arch. Coll. xviii, 79.
[71] See account of parish. Certain parts

of the waste were, however, reserved by Mr. Webb, and certain quit-rents were separately sold.
[72] In the charter of Gilbert de Aquila, confirming Oxenford to the abbey of Waverley, the following clause occurs : 'et claudent tantum de parco quantum pertinet ad predictum tenementum de Oxenford cum toto exitu suo et non pluta sicut ceteri homines mei de H. Witley' ; Pat. 11 Edw. II, pt. ii, m. 36.
[74] Mins. Accts. (Gen. Ser.), bdle. 1015, no. 8.
[75] Cal. Close (Rec. Com.), 1307–13, p. 507.
[76] Cal. Pat. 1313–17, pp. 135, 137 228.
[77] Ibid. 1327–30, p. 476.
[78] Ibid. 1377–81, p. 159.
[79] Coram Rege R. no. 511 (Hil. 12 Ric. II), m. 17.
[80] Free warren had been granted to Peter of Savoy in his demesne lands in Witley ; Cal. Chart. R. i, 315.
[81] L. and P. Hen. VIII, i, 886.
[82] Ibid. iv, 1385.
[83] Misc. Bks. (Land Rev.), vol. 190, fol. 134.
[84] Pat. 38 Eliz. pt. xii.

previously held on lease.[85] In 1656 Edward More, grandson of Sir Edward, sold it to Thomas Russell[86]; it was probably already broken up into farms. Russell was possibly trustee for Simon Bennett, whose daughter Frances carried a moiety of the park in marriage to James fourth Earl of Salisbury. Her sister Grace died in 1730 without issue, and her moiety also passed to James, the sixth Earl. His son the first Marquess of Salisbury sold it to William Smith of Godalming in 1791.[87] William Smith bequeathed the estate to his brother, Richard Smith of Burgate, whose niece Mary, widow of George Chandler, inherited it in 1838, and held it with remainder to her son Allen.[88] Mr. Allen Chandler sold it to the Earl of Derby, in 1876.

In the 15th century the lords of Witley Manor had both court baron and view of frankpledge together with the chattels of fugitives and outlaws;[89] they also had a right to heriot and relief from certain of their tenants,[90] and claimed a custom called 'grasaves,' or 'Grayside,' which was valued at 5s. 4d. yearly.[91] From time to time their tenants claimed various privileges, asserting that Witley was ancient demesne. On this ground in 1380, and again in 1401, they were exempted from paying the expenses of knights to Parliament.[92] On the other hand, in the suit brought against Peter of Savoy by the men of Witley, the jurors allowed the exactions of Peter of Savoy, but denied that Witley was ancient demesne of the Crown.[93] In 1389 the tenants, with a few exceptions,[94] were said to be villeins and bond-tenants, and were bound to act as reeve of the lord's manor, and to perform certain other services.[95]

They obtained a recognition of their position as tenants in ancient demesne in the proceedings in 1401, including right of exemption from Juries.[96] This privilege, with the exemption from contribution to expenses of knights of the shire, was confirmed 20 June 1574.[97]

Free fishery was recounted among the appurtenances of the manor in 1443.[98]

WYTLEY CHESBERIES alias WYTLEY CHEAS-BURIES is a small reputed manor. It is near Wheeler Street. In 1310 William de Chussebury de Muleford was husband of Dionisia, co-heiress of Stephen de Asshurst.[99] They levied a fine of land in Witley, Godalming, &c. The name Cheshury appears in subsidies in 1332 and 1381. In 1566 there was an inquiry in the Catteshull court as to whether Henry

Chittie, tenant of Chesberies, was or was not subject to the court's jurisdiction.[100] In 1575 Henry Chittie *alias* Bocher parted with the manor of Chesberies to Laurence Stoughton, parson of Witley.[101] In 1580 Laurence sold to George Weller.[102] In 1605 Weller parted with the manor of Chesberies to Thomas Compton,[103] doubtless the owner of Taylors, Godalming.[104] It afterwards went to the Duncombes. In 1726 John Duncombe sold to John Marche, yeoman. It descended to Richard Marche, and through the Winkworth and Sparkes families from him to Mrs. Eastwood, who lately sold it to Mr. Heatley.

OXENFORD GRANGE, within Peper Harrow Park, but in the parish of Witley, was a part of the manor of Witley until Richer de Aquila granted it to the abbey of Waverley early in the 12th century.[105] His gift is mentioned in the bull of Pope Eugenius III, dated 1147, confirming to the abbey all its property,[106] and the grange of Oxenford with land at Ribella was included in the lands confirmed to the abbey by Richard I.[107] Richer's grandson, Gilbert de Aquila, in confirming his grandfather's gift, mentioned the right of the abbot to inclose so much of Witley Park as belonged to Oxenford.[108] In the 'Taxatio' of 1291 Oxenford was rated at £1,[109] and the abbot seems to have objected to paying the tenth for it,[110] but his claim to exemption was disallowed.[111] The grange remained among the possessions of the abbey till the Dissolution, at which time it was valued at £4 13s. 4d.[112]

It was included in the grant of the site of Waverley to Sir William Fitz William,[113] with which it descended to Anthony, first Viscount Montague,[114] who died seised of a messuage called Oxenford, 9 October 1592.[115]

His son by his second wife, Sir Henry Browne, sold to Sir George More of Loseley in 1609.[116] Sir George, his son Sir Robert, and their respective wives, levied a fine to John Hone in 1613,[117] and Bartholomew Hone his son, of Oxenford, and others conveyed to John Chesterton of St. Giles in the Fields in 1619.[118] After his death in February 1624-5, it was held by his wife Anne for life, who survived her two sons, Walter, who died in 1638,[119] and John.[120] The reversion became divided among the three sisters of John and their representatives, namely, Mary wife of Henry Fox, Jane wife of John Smith of Richull, and Martha wife of Antony Covert. On 8 February 1667 Antony Covert and his son conveyed their third to John Platt of Westbrook and his heirs,[121] and in 1676 his son Sir John Platt, and John Smith son

[85] Close, 11 Jas. I, pt. xxxvi, no. 3.
[86] Feet of F. Surr. Mich. 1656, pt. 1.
[87] Close, 31 Geo. III, pt. iii, no. 7.
[88] Brayley, *Hist. of Surr.* v, 254.
[89] Pat. 21 Hen. VI, pt. i, no. 18.
[90] Misc. Bks. (Land Rev.), vol. 190, fol. 134; Mins. Accts. (Gen. Ser.), bdle. 1015, no. 8.
[91] Partic. of Grants (Aug. Off.), 6 Edw. VI, 1515.
[92] Add. Chart. 27744-7.
[93] Assize R. 873, m. 6 (1259). Peter brought forward as evidence against them the entry under the barony of Aquila in Domesday Book, which, strangely enough, was employed by the tenants themselves in asserting their privileges two centuries later.
[94] Viz. the tenants of Bouelith, Winkesworth, Balham, Dene, Writrowe, Stutley, High Ashurst, and Oxenford.
[95] Coram Rege R. 511 (Hil. 12 Ric. II), 17.

[96] B.M. Add. Chart. 27444-5; *Cal. Pat.* 1399-1401, p. 502. On the ground that the manor was entered under the barony of Aquila in Domesday Book. Perhaps it was understood that the manor had pertained to the Crown before 1086, and that it had passed from Earl Godwin to Earl Harold, and thus to William I, and had been held by him as ancient demesne before the grant to Aquila.
[97] Pat. 16 Eliz.
[98] Pat. 21 Hen. VI, pt. i, m. 18.
[99] De Banco R. Hil. 3 Edw. II, m. 180.
[100] View of Frankpledge, 27 Sept. 8 Eliz.
[101] Feet of F. Surr. Hil. 17 Eliz.
[102] Ibid. Trin. 22 Eliz.
[103] Ibid. Mich. 3 Jas. I.
[104] Private information.
[105] The abbey was founded in 1128. The grant must therefore have been made between that date and the confirmatory

charter of Pope Eugenius, which was given in 1147.
[106] Lansd. Chart. 27.
[107] Cart. Antiq. S. 20.
[108] Pat. 11 Edw. II, pt. ii, m. 36.
[109] *Pope Nich. Tax.* (Rec. Com.), 206.
[110] Ibid. 209b.
[111] *Cal. Pat.* 1340-3, p. 128.
[112] *Valor Eccl.* (Rec. Com.), ii, 34.
[113] *L. and P. Hen. VIII,* xi, 88.
[114] See *V.C.H. Surr.* ii, 624.
[115] Chan. Inq. p.m. (Ser. 2), ccxxxv, 110.
[116] Close, 8 Jas. I, Modern Ref. no. 2027.
[117] Feet of F. Surr. East. 11 Jas. I.
[118] Close, 17 Jas. I, pt. xiv, no. 55.
[119] Chan. Inq. p.m. (Ser. 2), cccxix, 31.
[120] Ibid. vol. ccccxxxvi, 100.
[121] Feet of F. Surr. Trin. 19 Chas. II.; Close, 18 Chas. II, pt. iv, no. 1.

of John and Jane, conveyed two-thirds to Denzil, Lord Holles,[132] from whom it passed as Peper Harow (q.v.). This portion included the grange itself.

Chesterton Fox, son of Henry Fox and Mary, was possessed of the other third in 1680,[133] and in 1705 it was sold by Mary Horish and Anne Fox, daughters of Chesterton Fox, to Edmund Stillwell of Thursley.[134] His descendants sold to Viscount Midleton c. 1822.

The remains of the Grange are now included in Peper Harow Park. They consist of only part of a cottage, the rest having been pulled down in 1775 when the present mansion-house at Peper Harow was approaching completion. The fifth Viscount Midleton employed Mr. Pugin to build an imitation 13th-century farm here. The land of Oxenford is counted now in Witley parish. It was apparently, when in the hands of Waverley, extra-parochial, and is tithe-free. In 1802 and 1803 the inhabitants successfully resisted an inclusion for rateable purposes in Witley.[135]

MOUSEHILL (Mushulle, xiv cent. ; Moussulle, xv cent.) is a hamlet of Milford. The family of Court were the chief landowners there in the 14th century. In 1335-6 Cecily widow of Richard le Court leased land at Mousehill to Thomas atte Dene and Robert son of John le Court.[136] Robert Court is said to have held court baron for the manor of Mousehill early in the reign of Henry V.[137]

Robert Court conveyed all his lands in Witley to his son Thomas Court in 1426.[138] Thomas is said to have had a daughter Julia who married John Hedger. His granddaughter Marion married Richard Shudd.[139] From the Courts the estate became known as Court Thorn in Mousehill.[140] In 1548 the manor of Court was held by Richard Shudd,[131] son of Richard and Marion, who was succeeded by John Shudd. He conveyed in 1611 to his son Richard. In 1614 Richard bequeathed Court Thorn in Mousehill to his brother Thomas, together with Court Hall in Mousehill, which he had purchased from John Fludder,[133] subject to the condition that Thomas granted his right in other property to a third brother John. This arrangement was carried out in 1615,[133] John Stillwell (vide infra) being an executor. Thomas Shudd entered upon his bequest in 1614. He died in 1649[134] holding Court Hall and Mousehill, and his son Thomas was in possession of them c. 1618, and died in 1699.[135] They passed, through the marriage of his sister Joan to John Stillwell of Lower House in Thursley, to the Stillwell family.[136]

The 'manor of Court Thorn or Mousehill' remained in the possession of John Stillwell's descendants till about 1822, when it was purchased by Viscount Midleton.[137] A court baron existed as late as 1701.

RAKE in Milford is an Elizabethan house near the

watercourse which runs from Witley to Milford. The owner of the estate had a mill near his house, the whole being described c. 1548 as a tenement and 26 acres of land and a fulling-mill.[138] Robert Mellersh, who was then the owner, was succeeded by his widow Joan, after whom their son John held Rake.[139] He was involved in a suit with the tenant of Witley. Thomas Jones, concerning the damage caused to the demesne lands of Witley by the overflow of water from the pond at Rake, and a right of way claimed by Mellersh through the lands of Witley Manor.[140] In 1592 he sold a messuage and mill in Witley to Henry Bell. There seems no doubt that this sale referred to Rake,[141] for Henry Bell was possessed of 'Rake farm' at his death.[142] It passed to his nephew Antony Smith, who settled it upon his great-nephew Antony Smith Meale; it descended to the latter's grand-daughter Anne, the wife (1748) of Thomas Woods of Godalming, whose grandson Thomas Woods sold the house and mill in 1836 to Thomas Durrant. He died in 1879 ; the property was sold to the trustees of the Busbridge estate, and the late owner was the Hon. Violet Monckton, but it has been sold again recently to Archdeacon Potter.[143]

Rake House, built by Henry Bell in 1602, is one of the best examples of the half-timber manor-house remaining in Surrey.[144] Its timber framework, filled with bricks laid herring-bone fashion, the many original windows, and a large and finely proportioned chimney-stack rising from the ground on the west side are noteworthy features. The plan is important, as typical of the smaller gentleman's house of the beginning of the 17th century. It is L shaped, with the staircase carried up in a gabled excrescence built in the inner angle of the L (a feature occurring in a house of similar plan at Shottermill). The hall or kitchen occupies roughly the middle of the long stroke of the L, having the great open fireplace at one end and a screen along one side. Two kitchen offices filled the top of the L, and two parlours, separated by a large chimney-block, the short stroke. The annexe containing the staircase served also as an entrance porch, and there was a second doorway opposite to it in the rear of the hall. The parlour filling the outer angle of the L is approached by a third outer door, which opens into the lobby formed by the thickness of the chimney between the two parlours ; and in the other parlour is an oak mantelpiece, very delicately carved with arabesque and foliage patterns, caryatides, and arches, bearing the date 1602 and the initials H. B.

ROAKE or ROKELAND was held in 1548 by Walter son of John Roke,[146] who was doubtless a descendant of Richard atte Roke, one of the tenants who protested against the exactions of Mundina Danos in 1389.[146] Walter's granddaughters, Alice Clarke

[132] Feet of F. Surr. Trin. 28 Chas. II.
[133] Recov. R. Trin. 31 Chas. II, rot. 56.
[134] Close, 4 Anne, pt. ii, no. 9.
[135] Manning and Bray, Hist. of Surr. ii, 47.
[136] Add. Chart. (B.M.), 27741.
[137] Manning and Bray, ii, 46, quoting from the court rolls.
[138] Add. Chart. (B.M.), 27748.
[139] From an old pedigree communicated.
[130] Chan. Inq. p.m. (Ser. 2), cccii, 123.
[141] Misc. Bks. (Land. Rev.), vol. 190, fol. 132.

[132] Chan. Inq. p.m. (Ser. 2), cccii, 213.
[133] Feet of F. Surr. Trin. 13 Jas. I.
[134] Witley Ct. R. 5 Apr. 1649.
[135] Deeds communicated by Mr. Woods.
[136] Feet of F. Surr. Trin. 30 Chas. II.
[137] Brayley, Hist. of Surr. iv, 312. James Stillwell conveyed them to John Stillwell in 1785 ; Feet of F. Surr. Trin. 25 Geo. III.
[138] Misc. Bks. (Exch. L.T.R.), 168, fol. 79 et seq.
[139] Misc. Bks. (Land Rev.), vol. 190, fol. 132.
[140] For a full account of the proceedings

see Mr. Giuseppi, 'Rake in Witley,' Surr. Arch. Coll., xviii, 11-60.
[141] Ibid.
[142] Chan. Inq. p.m. (Ser. 2), vol. dxxvi, 54.
[143] Misc. Bks. (Land Rev.), vol. 190, fol. 129 (Surv. of Witley Manor).
[144] Surr. Arch. Coll. xviii, 56, &c. ; and private information.
[144] Surr. Arch. Coll. xviii, 61.
[145] Misc. Bks. (Land Rev.), vol. 190, fol. 129 (Surv. of Witley Manor).
[146] Coram Rege R. Hil. 12 Ric. II, m. 17. In 1327 a Thomas of Roke and his wife Joan appeared at Godalming Hundred Court, Joan being executrix of Henry Lanewey ; Add. R. 26892.

and Jane Payne, inherited Rokeland, which ultimately passed to Thomas Clarke,[147] who sold 'the manor of Rokeland' and a house called Rokehouse to Thomas Carrill in 1585.[148] Six years later the Carrills alienated Rokeland to John Westbrook,[149] whose descendants held it for nearly a century.[150] In 1674 Richard and William Westbrook sold it to Thomas Smith of Witley,[151] with which manor it has since descended.

CHURCHES The church of *ALL SAINTS* stands upon a gentle slope on one side of the village. The churchyard is beautiful and has some fine trees; and the cottages at the south-eastern angle, with the church stile, combine to make a most picturesque and oft-painted group, the square tower and slender spire of the church appearing behind. There are many 17th and 18th-century gravestones in the churchyard.

The church is built of local sandstone rubble, with dressings of the same or Bargate stone ; brick and Bath stone have been partly used for modern additions. Horsham slabs still remain upon the roofs, together with ordinary tiles, and the spire is covered with oak shingles.

The church consists of nave, 44 ft. 6 in. by 18 ft. 6 in. with north and south transepts (the south, which is ancient, being 13 ft. 9 in. by 15 ft. 6 in.), central tower (about 14 ft. square) and spire, chancel, 26 ft. 6 in. long, by 15 ft. 2 in., and north chapel known as the Witley Manor Chapel, originally 27 ft. by 15 ft. The nave is the oldest part of the building, and probably the plan and main structure of this date from the last quarter of the 11th century. The central tower, transepts, and chancel belong to the next period, 1190, while the north chapel was added and other alterations made in the first half of the 14th century. There is a porch on the south of the nave, patched work of 19th-century date, and another giving access to the north transept of more recent date. This transept has been thrown out on an enlarged scale, and a short aisle and vestry built in 1890 on the north of the nave. Before these extensions the insertion of 'churchwarden' windows, &c., in the early part of the 19th century, and a severe 'restoration' in 1844 had robbed the church of some of its interest.

Externally, the most ancient feature is the south doorway within the porch, which preserves its jambs and their plain heavy nook-shafts, with cushion capitals, of date c. 1080. Part of the abacus is plain except for a small moulding, but the rest, of a slightly later date, has been carved with another moulding and the star-pattern.[152] The original semicircular arch has been replaced by a rude pointed one, apparently of early 19th-century date. The substance of the nave walls, which are unusually lofty for a church of

this size, is of the latter part of the 11th century, but no windows of this period are now visible, they having been replaced by large two-light openings of 'churchwarden' character. The west window and the doorway below are apparently of 15th-century date. On the gable of the south porch, which is a modern antique, is an ancient oak barge-board, perhaps as old as the latter part of the 14th century, but belonging originally to a demolished house in the village.

The south window of the south transept is a 'churchwarden' insertion, but in the west and east walls are small narrow lancets, dating from about 1190. The eastern is set with a pointed-arched recess on the inside, indicating the position of the chapel altar. This transept retains its original roof of somewhat acute pitch.

Above the crossing rises the tower, of solid dignified square form, in two stages, without buttresses. It is built like the rest of the church of local rubble, with Bargate stone quoins and other dressings. At the south-east angle is a circular stair-turret of modern

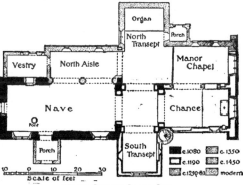

WITLEY CHURCH : GROUND PLAN

(plan labels: Organ; North Transept; Porch; Vestry; North Aisle; Manor Chapel; Nave; Font; Chancel; South Transept; Porch; Scale of feet 0 10 20 30; legend: c.1080, c.1190, c.1250-80, c.1350, c.1450, modern)

date, and in the lower stage are lancet windows with pointed heads. A string-course of half-round section separates the stages, and upon this stand, in each face, two round-headed openings divided by a broad mullion : these are chamfered and rebated. The tower is crowned by a coped parapet resting upon a corbel, and at the angles are small obelisks or pinnacles, evidently 17th-century additions ; the corbels of the parapet being variously moulded and coeval with the tower.

The shingled spire is of 14th or 15th-century date. Altogether this tower is one of the most interesting studies in early masonry in Surrey. Within it rests upon plain pointed arches, worked in clunch, and having steeply chamfered imposts and narrow chamfers to the piers.

In the south wall of the chancel, at its western end, is a trefoiled lancet, which old photographs show to

---

[147] In the above-mentioned survey Thomas Clarke's name is inserted in the margin as heir of Richard son of Walter Roke.

[148] Close, 27 Eliz. pt. viii.
[149] Feet of F. Surr. Hil. 33 Eliz.
[150] Chan. Inq. p.m. (Ser. 2), ccclxxxii, 448.

[151] Feet of F. Surr. Trin. 26 Chas. II.
[152] Illustrated in *V.C.H. Surr.* ii, 448.

74.

have been a low side window : its sill has been lately raised. Further east is a wide lancet with pointed head, and at the angle a good example of a late 12th-century buttress with a string-course of semi-octagon shape, which also appears beneath the east window. The latter, which has replaced the original early lancets, is an interesting design in flowing tracery of three lights, worked in clunch.[153] The gable has a moulded barge-board. The east window of the Witley Manor Chapel, also of three lights, is a restoration on the old lines of a reticulated pattern tracery. The windows in the north wall are also new, but perhaps restorations, and the north transept, porch, aisle, and vestry are modern.

Coming to the interior, we find few features of antiquity in the nave, which has a new oak-panelled roof and seating. The internal opening of the south doorway has been enlarged and otherwise altered. The character of the tower arches and the south transept has been noted above. In the chancel are handsome modern alabaster sedilia and other fittings, but the curious piscina with thirteen foliations to the drain and the aumbry above it are of about 1350. The face of the latter is sloped back, so as to keep the door automatically closed ; adjacent to this are the remains of the earlier semi-octagonal string found also on the outside.

The arches between the two chancels appear to have been pierced at a later date than that of either chancel, and originally there was probably a wall between the two with a door in it. The western arch is wide, of two plain chamfered orders, and the other quite narrow, of 15th-century date, with a plain tomb standing in it which was used as an Easter sepulchre. Eastward of this, on the chapel side under a pointed arch and credence shelf, is a piscina in Sussex marble, bearing curious ornamentation of wavy lines. This bowl was probably transferred here from the main chancel when the later piscina there was made and the chapel built.

The original oak roof (c. 1190) remains over the south transept. It is of braced collar-beam construction, with fine massive timbers. The corresponding north transept roof was preserved when the walls supporting it were removed to extend the area, and a noteworthy detail of this is the billet ornament upon the wall plates, a feature rarely found in woodwork.[154]

The handsome screen between this transept and the north chapel is of the 15th century. On the south wall of the nave, high up, is a painting of 12th-century date in two tiers. It measures about 16 ft. in length, by about 9 ft. in height, but is obviously a fragment of a scheme which probably covered the entire nave ; the colours used are red, pink, yellow, and white, and the whole composition and treatment recall the early Lewes school as represented in Hardham, Clayton, and other Sussex churches. The subjects are uncertain, but the upper tier seems to contain scenes connected with the Nativity, and the lower legendary incidents in the lives of saints. One nimbed figure in the lower tier bears a T-headed staff. In the background is some architecture of arcaded towers and domed roofs with scale-shaped tiles. On the east wall of the south

transept and elsewhere are further slight remains of colour decoration, chiefly in red.

Some good 15th-century heraldic glass (among which are the arms of France and England quarterly, and France impaling France and England) remains in the windows of the Witley Manor Chapel, but it has been shifted and releaded within the last century, and not all of it is ancient. One fragment on which was depicted the hawthorn bush and crown, with the initials H. E. in black letter beneath it, formerly marked the connexion of the manor with Henry VII. It and the remaining old glass are conjectured to have been placed in the windows by Sir Reginald Bray (temp. Henry VII). The font dates from about 1250. Its octagonal bowl, which has been renewed or recut, rests upon a central drum and eight small shafts with moulded bases, standing upon a circular plinth.

Some ancient seats belonging to the first half of the 14th century, which may have originally stood in the nave, have been placed in the same chapel. The sanctuary is bordered with a dado of modern marble.

A fragmentary inscription in black letter, cut in a piece of stone let into the north wall of the chancel, bears the date 1468, and records the fact that the manor of Witley was held by the ill-fated Duke of Clarence, brother of Edward IV. It reads :— 'Georgii Ducis Clarence et Dñs (sic) de Wytle, ac fratris Edwardi quarti, regis Anglie et Franc . . .' This accounts, probably, for the heraldic glass in the windows.

The Easter sepulchre contains a brass to Thomas Jones, Jane his wife, and their six children, 'which Thom's was one of the Servers of the Chamber to our Souverayne lorde Kinge Henry VIII.'

A brass in the north wall of the manorial chapel bears the date 1634, and commemorates Henry Bell, 'Clarke Controwler of the Household to our late Soveraigne Lord King James of Blessed Memorie.'

There are also tablets in the chancel and north chapel to the wife of a 17th-century vicar of Witley (in which her virtues are likened to those of Sarah, Rebecca, Rachel, and Ruth) ; and to Anthony Smith, 'Pentioner' to Charles I and II, with a curious Latin couplet containing allusions to his gift of a bell to the church, and his benefactions to the poor of Witley.

An ancient almsbox of enamelled iron, with 14th or 15th-century tracery on the front, stands by the south door. Although an undoubted antiquity, it has been presented to the church in recent years.

The registers date from 1558.

There are eight bells in the tower, the treble and third by Bryan Eldridge, 1648 ; the second bears Richard Eldridge's initials and the legend, ' Our Lord our hope, 1604.' The fourth is by William Eldridge, 1670.

Among the church plate are chalices of the years 1638 and 1639, the second being an ancient piece imported from Yorkshire, the gift of Mr. John Harrison Foster, of Witley. There is also a paten of the date 1717, and an old pewter tankard of a poor type.

The church of St. John the Evangelist, Milford, was built in 1844. It is of Bargate stone, which is found in the neighbourhood, in 14th-century

---

[153] Illustrated in *V.C.H. Surr.* ii, 456 ; cf. the east windows of Woking, Dorking, and Mickleham — the last two destroyed.

[154] A 12th-century beam in the nave of Old Shoreham Church, Sussex, is one of the few instances of its occurrence.

style, with a bell turret. The north aisle was added in 1894.

The church of All Saints, Grayswood, was built in 1900–1 and consecrated in 1902.

ADVOWSONS

A church is mentioned in the Domesday Survey of Witley.[155]

The advowson of Witley Church was appurtenant to the manor until Gilbert Marshal, Earl of Pembroke, gave it to the Abbey of St. Mary de Gloria, Anagni, to which Pope Gregory IX granted an indult to enter in possession in September 1238, a vicar's portion being reserved.[156] This appropriation does not seem to have been carried into effect, and the advowson itself was evidently restored to the lords of the manor before 1289,[157] when it was included in the confirmatory grant to Guy Ferre.[158]

In 1321 Queen Isabella presented a rector to Witley Church.[159] In 1342 Edward III gave the advowson to Dartford Priory,[160] to which the church was appropriated c. 1368,[161] but the prioress, doubting the validity of the former appropriation and 'being in no small need,' obtained a fresh licence from the pope in October 1395.[162] In 1544, after the suppression of the priory, the king sold the rectory and advowson of Witley as a manor to Thomas Jones, 'his servant,'[163] who sold them in 1571 to Thomas Smith, controller of the queen's household.[164] In 1642 a Thomas Smith his grandson presented to the vicarage, and left the manor in his will for sale.[164a] In 1670 George Smith his son [165] presented. From him the rectory manor descended in moieties to Susan Smith and Sarah wife of Michael Purefoy.[166] Susan Smith either inherited or purchased the second moiety, for she was possessed of the whole rectory and advowson in 1715,[167] and alienated them to the use of William Myers.[168] He died in 1739. His son William Myers made a settlement of Witley rectory on his marriage in 1743.[169] In 1775 William Myers his son sold the rectory, advowson, and great tithes of Witley (but not of Thursley) to John Leech, Ph.D., of Alton and John Chandler of Witley.[170] The former took the rectory, manor-house, and part of the land, the latter the advowson of Witley and Thursley, the vicarage house, and other lands.

This Mr. Chandler's grandson was patron and vicar in 1837. The present patron is Mr. E. A. Chandler. The rectory manor passed ultimately to Mr. John Leech, of Lea, M.P. for West Surrey, son of Dr. Leech, who died in 1847. His widow Mary married William Wight, and died 1878. The manor was then sold to W. H. Stone, whence it probably passed with Lea, where Dr. Leech and Mr. Stone had lived, to Whitaker Wright, and was seemingly lost sight of as a manor.

There were manorial rights attached to the rectory as well as court leet.[171] With regard to the latter, the parson of Witley claimed view of frankpledge and assize of bread and ale in 1279, but the king recovered seisin of them through his default.[172] Apparently, however, the rectors had regained view of frankpledge before the Dissolution, and the rector had both court baron and court leet late in the 17th century.[173]

Milford was formed into a separate ecclesiastical parish in 1844. The vicar of Witley is patron of the living.[174]

Grayswood was formed into a separate ecclesiastical parish from Chiddingfold, Haslemere, Thursley, and Witley in 1900. The Bishop of Winchester is patron [175] of the living, which is a vicarage.

---

155 *V.C.H. Surr.* i, 323.

156 *Cal. of Papal Letters,* i, 164, 176. The gift was made before 26 Oct. 1237.

157 It is doubtful whether the Earl Marshal had any right to alienate the advowson of which he had only the custody; the church is expressly excepted, however, in Queen Eleanor's first grant of the manor to Guy Ferre.

158 *Cal. Pat.* 1272–81, p. 125; ibid. 1281–92, p. 329.

159 *Epis. Reg. Winton* (Hants Rec. Soc.), 446.

160 Pat. 31 Edw. III, pt. ii, no. 12. It appears therefore that Philippa of Hainault

did not have it in dower with Witley Manor, for we infer from the wording of Edward's grant that it referred to the advowson itself and not the reversion.

161 *Wykeham's Reg.* (Hants Rec. Soc.), ii, 23.

162 *Cal. of Papal Letters* (Rec. Com.), iv, 517.

163 *L. and P. Hen. VIII,* xix, i, 374; Aug. Off. Partic. of Grants, 650. He was son of the Thomas Jones, server of the chamber to Henry VIII, to whom there is a brass in the church.

164 Close, 14 Eliz. pt. 27.

164a Will proved Lond. 7 Mar. 1658 (Pell 152).

165 Inst. Bks. P.R.O.

166 Feet of F. Surr. Hil. 1689–94 (year not given); ibid. Hil. 2 Will. and Mary.

167 Recov. R. East. 1 Geo. I, m. 57, 67.

168 Feet of F. Surr. Trin. 1 Geo. I.

169 Recov. R. East. 16 Geo. II, rot. 24.

170 Close, 17 Geo. III, pt. v, no. 7.

171 Partic. for Grants (Aug. Off.), 650.

172 *Plac. de Quo Warr.* (Rec. Com.), 738.

173 Add. MS. 6167.

174 *Pop. Ret.* 1891, i, 350.

175 Ibid. 1901, p. 5.

THE HUNDRED OF BLACKHEATH

The hundred of Blackheath (Blackfelde, x cent.; Blacheatfeld, xi cent.; Blakehethfeld, xiii and xiv cent.) is bounded on the north by Woking, on the west by Godalming, on the east by Wotton. and on the south by the county of Sussex.

Tyting, in St. Martha's parish, was in Woking Hundred in 1086 and subsequently,[2] but is now counted as in Blackheath. In 1086 three virgates (rated) of Gomshall were in Wotton Hundred, not in Blackheath, but as Gomshall was ancient demesne, and the tenants were quit of all sheriffs' courts, it made little difference.

Blackheath is a high, heathy common, chiefly in the parishes of Albury and Wonersh ; but much of the adjacent country, which is partly inclosed and partly open heath or planted with conifers, equally deserves the name. The population must always have been chiefly round about this country, and the place of meeting of the hundred court might have been expected to be upon it, as at Farnham ; but in 1377[3] it was held at La Perie, which is also referred to in the Godalming Rolls as the place of holding. This would seem to be near Perry Bridge in Shalford parish, over the Wey, on the road from Godalming to Bramley, on the extreme verge of the hundred.

The jurisdiction of the sheriff's court was practically much curtailed by private rights. In Domesday Odo of Bayeux held Bramley, which included a great deal of the then inhabited part of the hundred. This no doubt explains the low assessment at 6½ hides, against 97 under Edward the Confessor, and was perhaps the origin of the separate court leet of Bramley. The lords of Shalford, Wintershull, and Gomshall, and the rectors of Shalford and Cranleigh also had courts leet, and the lord of Albury view of frankpledge, but the latter gave the profits to the Crown.[4] The lord of Shere claimed view of frankpledge previous to 1238,[5] the lord of Albury claimed the same, and it was granted to Bramley by charter of Henry III.[6] But all these townships paid an annual fine to the sheriff. In 1671 Shere paid 20s., Gomshall 12s., Albury 13s. 8d., Shalford 6s. 8d.[7] The royal rights, such as

---

[1] The extent of the hundred at the time of the *Population Returns* of 1831.
[2] Close, 23 Chas. II, pt. ix, no. 24.   [3] Manning and Bray, *Hist. of Surr.* ii, 99.
[4] Assize R. 895.   [5] Viz. 1226-7 and 1236-8 ; *Plac. de Quo Warr.* (Rec. Com.), 742.
[6] Ibid. 743.   [7] Pat. 23 Chas. II. pt. ix, m. 23.

70

they were, were granted by James I in 1620 to Sir Edward Zouche of Woking, and to the heirs male of Sir Alan his uncle, together with Woking Hundred and Manor and other lands, to be held by the service of bringing in the first dish to the king's table on St. James's Day and paying annually £100. All feudal incidents were expressly abrogated.[8]

Charles II granted this rent and the reversion of the hundred for 1,000 years to Viscount Grandison, Henry Howard, and Edward Villiers, in trust for the Duchess of Cleveland.[9] In 1708 James Zouche, younger son of Sir Edward, the last of the male heirs, died. The Duchess of Cleveland succeeded, but died on 9 October 1709. Her trustees in 1715 sold the rights in this hundred, as well as in Woking, to John Walter of Busbridge House, Godalming, whose son sold them to Lord Onslow in 1752, having obtained by Act of Parliament in 1748 a grant of the fee simple after the expiration of the 1,000 years.[10] The interest of the present Earl of Onslow in the hundred, if it continues, is purely nominal.

There was 'a Hundred Hedge' bounding Blackheath Hundred towards Godalming, referred to in rolls of Catteshull Manor at Loseley.

[8] Pat. 18 Jas. I, pt. vi, m. 1.   [9] Ibid. 23 Chas. II, pt. ix, m. 24.
[10] Ibid. 22 Geo II, pt. ii, m. 14 ; *Com. Journ.* xxv, 601.

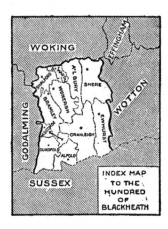

ALBURY

Eldeberie (xi cent.), Aldebur (xiii. cent.), Aldebury (xiv cent.), Aldbury (sometimes in xviii cent.).

Albury is a parish 5 miles east of Guildford and 7
miles west of Dorking. The parish is bounded on the
north by Merrow and West Clandon, on the west by
St. Martha's and Wonersh, on the south by Cranleigh,
on the east by Shere. A detached portion, the manor
of Wildwood, used to lie in Alfold to the south, and
detached portions of Cranleigh, Shere, and Wonersh
lay in Albury. These were transferred to the parishes
surrounding them respectively in 1882. The existing parish contains 4,405 acres of land and 14 of
water. It is 6 miles from north to south, and nowhere more than 2 miles from east to west. It is of
the typical form and soils of the parishes to the south
of the chalk ridge. The northern boundary is on the
crest of the chalk, the village is in the valley upon the
sand south of the chalk hill, but close to it, and the parish
extends across the sand on to the Atherfield clay and
Wealden clay for a short distance, to the south. There
is open common on the chalk. Southwards the extensive heaths of Blackheath and Farley Heath are
partly or wholly in the parish. The continuation of
the high ridge of Greensand, of which Leith Hill, Holmbury, and Ewhurst Hills are part, further eastward,
reaches across the southern end of the parish, but
falls away into the valley through which the Guildford and Horsham line runs, bending northward to
form its eastern side. The views here across the
Weald, and westward to Hascombe Hill and Hindhead beyond, are very beautiful. Below the escarpment of these hills part of Smithwood Common is in
Albury. But it is to the north, on the chalk, at Newlands Corner, where the old road from Shere to Guildford runs up the down, and where Albury Downs reach
600 ft. above the sea, that the most famous view in
the parish is to be seen. Its beauty consists not in
extent merely, but in the broken foreground, east and
west along the valley between the chalk and the sand.
Some very ancient yew trees mark the line of the old
road, commonly called Pilgrims' Way, along the slopes
of the downs. The ancient bridle-way over St. Martha's
Hill comes down into Albury through a deep lane.
The modern road from Guildford to Dorking traverses
the parish, and also the Redhill and Reading branch
of the South Eastern Railway. Chilworth and Albury
station is just outside the parish.

The Tillingbourne stream runs through the parish
from east to west, working two mills. It is augmented
by the water from the deep springs in the chalk which
form the Shireburn Ponds, deep pools at the foot of
the slope of the down surrounded by trees. The
upper and more picturesque is usually called the
Silent Pool. The springs which supply them are
supposed to have connexion with those which break
out on the other side of the chalk, due north, in
Clandon Park. The operations of the Woking Water
Company, who have tapped the chalk between them,
have undoubtedly led to a diminution of the supply in
the Shireburn Ponds.

Albury parish is somewhat rich in antiquities. At

Newlands Corner is a large barrow, not marked on the
Ordnance map, and neolithic flints are fairly numerous on and below the hills. The name Harrowshill
borne by part of the down may indicate an Anglo-
Saxon holy place. But the most considerable antiquity
of the parish is on Farley Heath, near the road from
Albury to Cranleigh. The banks, with a very slight
exterior ditch forming three sides of a quadrangular
inclosure, are fairly well marked, especially to the
west. The east bank is not now visible. The inclosure is not exactly rectangular, but the north-west
angle is slightly acute, the south-west slightly obtuse.
The sides are 220 yds., and the interior space must
consequently have been 10 acres. In the middle of
this was a smaller quadrangular inclosure which Manning and Bray describe as of 22 yds. each way. This
is now not to be traced, but stone foundations are
visible where it was, and a great abundance of Roman
tiles and some pottery are easily found in the whole
inclosure. Many Roman coins were found by excavations conducted in 1839 and 1840 by the late Mr. Martin Tupper, and it is said British coins also.[1] A gold
coin of Verica found here is in private hands.

When Aubrey wrote he saw, or imagined, the ruins
of a Roman temple on the spot, and the bases of the
two pillars in the south arcade of old Albury Church
are reputed to have been brought from this place.
Further inclosing banks to the east are said to have
formerly existed. Some of the coins found here
by Mr. Tupper, and some found afterwards by
Mr. Lovell, the schoolmaster of Albury, were sent
to the British Museum. A systematic exploration,
and a classification of remains, and pending this
a cessation of the practice of taking road metal from
the surface of the common, are much to be desired.
The Roman road traced in Ewhurst parish would, if
continued, have come close by here, and went on no
doubt either to Newlands Corner or to the gap in the
hills at Guildford. This is the Old Bury which gave
its name to the parish.

The old village of Albury had grown up by the
banks of the Tillingbourne, and partly within what is
now Albury Park, around the village green, which
adjoined the churchyard ; but Mr. Drummond, in
1842, finally removed it bodily half a mile to the
westward, leaving the ancient church intact, and built
a new parish church in the new village that grew up
at what formerly had been known as the hamlet of
Weston Street.

Albury Park also used to extend on to the chalk
hill above Shireburn Lane, over what is now farming
land. The road up the hill was called Old Park Pales
Lane.[2] Early in the 19th century a Maypole still
stood at the corner where Blackheath Lane joins the
west end of Weston Street.

Albury Park, the Surrey seat of the Duke of Northumberland, K.G., is famed both for the sylvan beauty
of its park and for its gardens. The magnificent trees—
especially a noble avenue of old beeches, some huge
walnut trees and clumps of hawthorns—the irregular
levels of velvety turf across which stretch long vistas,

---

[1] It is unknown exactly what coins were
found by Mr. Tupper, but they are supposed
to have extended from Domitian to Mag-
nentius.

[2] Manning and Bray, op. cit. ii, 126.

including peeps of the little Tillingbourne stream and of the lake before the house, with its swans; the half-ruined ancient church, almost hidden by its stately cedars, and the house—make this park, though its area is but small, one of the loveliest in Surrey. The gardens also merit the praise bestowed on them by William Cobbett: 'Take it altogether,' he says, ' this certainly is the prettiest garden I ever beheld. There was taste and sound judgment at every step in the laying out of this place.' The famous John Evelyn, in 1667, at the request of Thomas Howard, Earl of Arundel and Duke of Norfolk, 'designed the plot of the canal and garden, with a crypt through the hill.' Although the canal has been drained, a terrace of beautiful green sward, about a quarter of a mile in length, remains, together with the 'crypt,' and a wonderful yew hedge, 'or rather,' as Cobbett writes, ' a row of small yew trees, the trunks of which are bare for about 8 or 10 ft. high, and the tops of which form one solid head of about 10 ft. high, while the bottom branches come out on each side of the row about 8 ft. horizontally. This hedge or row,' he adds, 'is a quarter of a mile long. There is a nice, hard sand road under this species of umbrella; and summer and winter, here is a most delightful walk.'[3]

The Catholic Apostolic Church, close to Albury Park, is a cruciform building, with a western tower and an octagonal chapter-house, designed in a starved imitation of late 15th-century architecture, and built about 1840 by Mr. Drummond. Immediately opposite, on the south side, is a fine old timber-framed house, with square and circle patterns in its main gable, moulded barge-boards, projecting upper stories and mullioned windows, recalling the design of Great Tangley, in Wonersh parish, a few miles to the west. This was no doubt an important house at one time. In and around Albury are many half-timber cottages and houses, as at Madgehole, Jelleys, Colman's Hollow, Mayor House Farm, and Shophouse Farm.[4] Pit House is another ancient house with an old roof not far from the site of a Roman settlement. Many years ago there was in Albury village an important house called Weston House after the ancient family of that name, who held the manor for centuries. Its staircase, of Spanish mahogany, was re-erected in the County Club at Guildford. This was at the west end of Weston Street, and is not to be confused with Weston House, still standing, at the east end.

Weston House, in Weston Street, is the seat of Mr. W. W. Wright; Weston Lodge, of Colonel Martindale; Dalton Hill, of Colonel Malthus.

Albury has had several distinguished residents. William Oughtred, the famous mathematician of his day, was rector from 1610 to 1660, holding the preferment through the Civil War time till he died in

possession a month after the Restoration. Samuel Horsley, afterwards Bishop of Rochester and of St. Asaph, was rector 1774–80. The Rev. Edward Irving resided a good deal in the parish when the Catholic Apostolic Church was being founded. Mr. Martin Tupper was a resident till a few years before his death, and composed his once-famous *Proverbial Philosophy* here. The scene of his romance, *Stephen Langton*, is laid in the neighbourhood, but embodies no real local history.

The history of *ALBURY MANOR* before the Conquest is obscure. It is quite uncertain whether the two 'mansæ' in Albury, held by Chertsey at the Conquest, and attributed (falsely) to the grant of Frithwald of the 7th century,[5] were part of their East Clandon Manor reaching into this parish or at one of the two other places in Surrey called 'Aldeberie.'

In Domesday it appears that Azor held it of the Confessor, and it was granted after the Conquest to Richard de Clares, ancestor of the de Clares and their descendants,[6] in whom the overlordship was vested till it lapsed in the 16th century.[7] Roger D'Abernon was tenant under Richard,[8] and his descendants were lords of the manor for more than five centuries.[9] In the 13th century[10] it formed the dower of Joan widow of Ingram D'Abernon. John D'Abernon obtained a grant of free warren here in 1253.[11] The manor passed with Elizabeth daughter and co-heir of William D'Abernon, who died in 1359, to the Croyser family,[12] and through Elizabeth's granddaughter Anne to Henry Norbury.[13] From them it descended to Joan wife of Sir Urian Brereton,[14] who conveyed it in 1550–1 to Henry

D'ABERNON. *Azure a chevron or.*

Polsted and his wife Alice in consideration of an annuity to Joan and her heirs.[15] The manor was so settled that after the death of Alice, who survived her husband, it remained to Vincent, son and heir of Edward Randall.[16] His estates descended to Sir Edward Randall of Edlesborough, Buckinghamshire,[17] who sold the manor in 1633–4 to John Gresham of Fulham.[18] In 1638 John Gresham and George Duncombe conveyed it to the trustees of Thomas, Earl of Arundel.[19] After some delay, owing to the sequestration of the earl's estates,[20] during which time George Duncombe resumed possession and held courts, Mr. Henry Howard paid the purchase money to the Duncombes before 1655,[21] and acquired Albury. He was grandson to the Earl of Arundel, and later succeeded as Duke of Norfolk. He conveyed it to trustees for sale in 1680.[22] It was purchased by

[3] Cobbett, *Rural Walks and Rides.*
[4] *Old Cottages and Domestic Architecture in South-west Surr.* (2nd ed.), 91.
[5] Birch, *Cart. Sax.* i, 39.
[6] *V.C.H. Surr.* i, 319a.
[7] *Excerpta e Rot. Fin.* (Rec. Com.), i, 272; Chan. Inq. p.m. 8 Edw. II, no. 68; ibid. 3 Hen. V, no. 37; ibid. (Ser. 2), cclxxiii, 99.
[8] *V.C.H. Surr.* i, 319a.
[9] The detailed history is coincident with that of Stoke D'Abernon (q.v.).
[10] Add. Chart. (B.M.), 5562.
[11] *Cal. of Chart. R.* i, 435.

[12] Chan. Inq. p.m. 18 Ric. II, no. 108.
[13] Feet of F. Div. Co. 14 Hen. VI, 184; Add. Chart. (B.M.), 5618.
[14] See account of the family under Stoke D'Abernon.
[15] Feet of F. Div. Co. Mich. 3 Edw. VI. The annuity descended to Joan's daughters, Mary wife of Sir Robert Peckham, and Anne wife of Sir George Cobham. The latter's son, Sir John Cobham, forfeited his share to the Crown. James I granted it to Sir Edward Randall, then lord of Albury, and to others; Chan. Inq. p.m. (Ser. 2), clxix, 40; Pat. 3 Jas. I, pt. xxv.

[16] Chan. Inq. p.m. (Ser. 2), cxci, 78; Chan. Proc. Eliz. R 1, x, 54.
[17] Chan. Inq. p.m. (Ser. 2), cclxxiii, 99.
[18] Close, 9 Chas. I, pt. xli, no. 118. Gresham mortgaged it immediately to George Duncombe of Albury; Close, 10 Chas. I, pt. xxviii, m. 33.
[19] Feet of F. Surr. Hil. 13 Chas. I.
[20] *Cal. of Com. for Compounding,* iv, 2471.
[21] Evelyn's *Diary,* 10 Aug. 1655; cf. 19 June 1662.
[22] Close, 32 Chas. II, pt. xiv, no. 10.

Heneage Finch, first Earl of Aylesford, Solicitor-General to Charles II, who presented to the church in 1691,[32] and was in possession of the manor in the latter part of the 17th century.[33] His son the second earl lived at Albury. The fourth earl sold the manor to his brother, Captain William Clement Finch,[35] of whom Samuel Thornton, Governor of the Bank of England, bought it in 1800. He made it his residence.[36] In 1811 John Thornton and his wife Eliza sold the rent from the manor to Charles Wall,[37] who

FINCH, Earl of Aylesford. *Argent a cheveron between three griffons passant sable.*

appears to have sold in 1819 to Henry Drummond, M.P. for West Surrey from 1847 to 1860, an enthusiastic supporter of Irving. The 'little prophetic parliament' which originated the Catholic Apostolic Church met at his house at Albury, and at a later date he built a church for the community near his park.[38] From Henry Drummond the manor descended through his daughter Louisa to her son the present Duke of Northumberland.[39]

An engraving of 1645 gives a clear idea of the ancient house that then stood upon the site of the present building. This shows an irregular elevation of half-timber gables, backed by a long ridge of roof with many chimneys, and flanked by a square-topped wing on the right, the whole inclosed within a walled courtyard, in which is an arched gateway. This picturesque and rambling structure, which must have had many points of resemblance to the old house of the Evelyns at Wotton, judging by John Evelyn's drawing of the latter, was burnt down in Queen Anne's reign and rebuilt by the Earl of Aylesford. Mr. Samuel Thornton, M.P., owner from 1800 to 1811, altered it again. It was remodelled in red brick and stone by Pugin during Mr. Drummond's ownership. Perhaps the most interesting of its treasures is the fine collection of old paintings formed here by Mr. Drummond, which include a portrait of Melanchthon by Holbein, Cornelius Schall's 'Four Doctors,' and portraits of many royal and noble personages connected with the Northumberland family.

WESTON MANOR, known in the 17th and 18th centuries as Weston Gomshall, possibly to distinguish it from the second Weston, is situated about the village now called Albury, but formerly known as Weston Street. It gave its name to an ancient Surrey family who occur as lords of many manors, and now hold West Horsley. Early in the 13th century David son of Nicholas was dealing with land in Weston.[50] In 1254-5 John of Weston granted a messuage, mill, and a carucate of land in Weston to Thomas of Weston to hold

of him and his heirs.[51] Early in the next century John D'Abernon unjustly dispossessed Thomas of Weston of his common of pasture in Albury.[52] He seems to have been succeeded by William of Weston, who obtained licence to hear service in the chapels of his manors of Weston and West Clandon.[53] In 1335 this William of Weston was in possession. The manor was to revert at his death to his grandson William.[54] Margery widow of the William Weston of Weston and Clandon died seised of a tenement in Albury

WESTON of Weston. *Sable a cheveron or between three lions' heads razed argent.*

called Weston in 1361 ;[55] and John Weston of Weston died in 1440, leaving a son who died without issue and three daughters, of whom the one, Anne, married Thomas Slyfield ;[56] another, Joan, Thomas Pope; and the third, Margaret, William Wells.

Thomas Slyfield and his son John granted the manor to Richard Eliot,[57] whose son Richard mortgaged and finally sold it to George Holman of London.[58] He conveyed to George Duncombe of Shalford in 1610–11.[59] Sir Richard Onslow and his son Arthur seem to have had some claim on the manor from 1644 to 1677,[40] but it remained in the possession of the Duncombe family, for in 1693 George Duncombe was dealing with it,[41] and his daughters Hester Woodroffe and Anne Sturt sold it in 1724 to Abel Alleyne,[42] after whose death it was sold to Sir Robert Godschall. He died in 1742, and it descended to Nicholas Godschall.[43] His only daughter and heiress Sarah married William Man, F.R.S.,[44] who

DUNCOMBE. *Party cheveronwise and engrailed gules and argent three talbots' heads razed countercoloured.*

took the name of Godschall and lived at Weston.[45] His son, the Rev. Samuel Man Godschall, succeeded. After his death it was sold to Henry Drummond, then lord of Albury,[46] since when its history has been coincident with that of Albury.

There was a second Weston Manor near the parsonage house of Albury, but lying in a detached part of Shere parish, and called Weston in Shere.[47]

Alderbrook, the seat of Mr. Pandeli Ralli, is possibly the site of 'Aldrebrook,' granted in 1374-5 by Roger Libbesofte and Joan his wife to Robert Brown.[48]

CHURCHES The old church of *ST. PETER* and *ST. PAUL* lies close to the stream, and within a short distance of the

32 Inst. Bks. (P.R.O.), B. 6.
34 Aubrey, *Nat. Hist. and Antiq. of Surr.* iv, 65.
35 *Gent. Mag.* liii, 576.
36 Manning and Bray, *Hist. of Surr.* ii, 125.
37 Add. Chart. (B.M.) 40623. Mrs. Wall lived there in 1816 (old print).
38 *Dict. Nat. Biog.* xvi, 29.
39 *Gent. Mag.* (new ser.), viii, 413.
30 Feet of F. Surr. 13 Hen. III, 23
31 Ibid. 38 & 39 Hen. III, 17.
32 Assize quoted by Symmes ; Add. MS. (B.M.), 6167, fol. 24.
33 Egerton MS. 2031, fol. 113 ; 2032, fol.

90. The first grant was between 1305 and 1316, the second between 1333 and 1345.
84 Feet of F. Surr. 9 Edw. III, 9.
86 Chan. Inq. p.m. 36 Edw. III, pt. ii (1st nos.), no. 75.
56 Chan. Inq. p.m. 19 Hen. VI, no. 5.
87 Chan. Proc. (Ser. 2), bdle. 41, no. 12, where it is thus stated, but Manning and Bray (op. cit. ii, 126) quote an enfeoffment of Henry Slyfield son of Thomas, and say that he joined in a sale of the manor to Richard Eliot in 1521.
88 Close, 42 Eliz. pt. viii ; ibid. 42 Eliz. pt. xxiv.

89 Close, 8 Jas. I, pt. viii.
40 Recov. R. Mich. 29 Chas. I, m. 240; ibid. Mich. 1650, m. 19 ; ibid. Hil. 28 & 29 Chas. II, m. 57.
41 Feet of F. Surr. Hil. 4 & 5 Will. and Mary.
42 Ibid. Hil. 10 Geo. I.
43 Feet of F. Surr. Hil. 16 Geo. II.
44 *Gent. Mag.* xxii, 432.
45 Ibid. lxxii, 1169.
46 Brayley, *Topog. Hist. of Surr.* v, 160.
47 For its history see under Shere.
48 Feet of F. Surr. 48 Edw. III, 115.

house of Albury Park. It is a most picturesque build_ing, containing features of great archaeological interest. The chancel has for many years been roofless, and the whole building is covered with masses of ivy, which is slowly but surely disintegrating the walls.

The church is constructed of ironstone and sand_stone rubble, with dressings of Bargate stone, clunch, and firestone, chiefly plastered. The nave roof is partly covered with Horsham slabs, the aisle and porch with tiles, the transept with slates, and the tower has a domed covering of shingles and lead.

The plan is unusual in several respects, consisting of a nave 30 ft. 9 in. by 19 ft. 4 in. with north porch, a south aisle 13 ft. 1 in. wide and 32 ft. 6 in. long, a tower to the east of the nave 15 ft. 6 in. by 14 ft. 2 in., a south transept opening out of the aisle and tower 20 ft. by 15 ft. 10 in., and a chancel 26 ft. 3 in. by 14 ft. 4 in.

In origin the nave is that of the pre-Conquest church, or at least of that mentioned in Domesday. The character of the north-east quoin and the lofty walls rather favours the former date, but all the original windows and other features have been replaced by later insertions, so that the evidence is meagre. The tower, between the nave and the chancel, either stands upon the site, or incorporates part of the walls, of the original chancel; probably the internal area is that of the latter, and its walls have been thickened in an outward direction to 3 ft. 10 in., the two upper stages being decreased in thickness. There is no staircase, and the tower is now open to the roof. The walls are plastered externally. The ground story is lighted only by a small round-headed window on the north side, 6 in. wide, splaying out, without a rebate, to 2 ft. on the inside. In the next stage is a very interesting two-light opening in the north wall, under a semicircular arch, having a central shaft with scalloped capital and base, recalling those in the tower of Cobham Church in this county.[49] This and other features suggest a date of about 1140-50. On the east and south sides of the middle stage are other coupled lights, but with plain piers of masonry instead of the little column. Above these again, in the topmost stage (which was crowned with brick battlements about 1820), are two separate openings on each face, large, with square heads, on the west, and small and round-headed on the other sides. The round-headed arches towards the nave and chancel are in firestone, on square jambs, with chamfered and hollow-chamfered imposts, each about 9 ft. wide, and high in proportion. The eastern has a quirked roll on the angle, with a chamfered hood-moulding having a plain sunk zigzag or hatched pattern on its outer face. The western arch has a similar roll-moulding with a hollow cut set on the angle, and above it a shallow ornament

like a circular cusping, with balls at the points of the cusps.[50] The arch to the transept from the tower is of late 13th-century character, but it has been much modernized.

Of the 12th-century chancel no trace remains, and the walls of the present chancel are apparently a good deal later. They incline markedly to the north on plan, and the partly-destroyed windows in the north and south walls and the gutted opening of a late tracery window in the east wall give no certain clue to the date, while no piscina or aumbry is now visible. Probably the 13th-century chancel was re-modelled in the 16th century.

A spacious south aisle was added to the nave about 1280, with an arcade of three pointed arches of two chamfered orders, on octagonal columns with moulded capitals, the eastern and western arches having a corbel of similar section in place of a respond.[51] The bases of the columns are evidently spoil from some more ancient building, being circular capitals in Sussex marble, turned upside down and mutilated to fit their new position. These are mounted upon rough circular

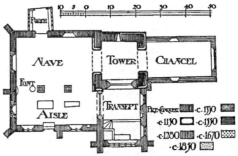

PLAN OF ALBURY CHURCH

plinths of Bargate stone, which may be older than the bases themselves, the mouldings of which indicate work of about 1200. Upon the western face of both columns is a small shallow square-headed niche. All the windows of the nave and aisle have been robbed of their tracery, so that they present a very forlorn and gaping appearance. This is the more to be regretted, as, from the delicacy of the mouldings, they must have been very graceful examples of early bar tracery when perfect. They are built of a curious mixture of chalk, or clunch, and dark red-brown iron-stone. The window in the west wall of the aisle has been altered in the 17th century, its head being made circular. That in the west wall of the nave was of three lights, and above it in the apex of the gable is a plain circular opening, also devoid of tracery; another smaller one is in the corresponding gable-end of the aisle. The buttresses of the west and south walls, and the wide south doorway, appear to be all of

49 The tower of the neighbouring church of Shere has a similar two-light opening in its second stage, but with a square pier between the lights.

50 As in the doorway to the chapter-house, Oxford Cathedral, and New Romney, Kent. Something like it is found in the cusped ornament round the chancel arch at Eastbourne, and the arch to the inner chancel at Compton, Surrey.

51 Almost exactly the same as a corbel in the south aisle of Cranleigh Church, a few miles to the south-west.

the 1280 period. Owing to the rise in the ground outside, there are now three steps down into the aisle. In the eastern part of this south wall there are indications of a blocked piscina.

The transeptal chapel, which opens by a modern or greatly modernized arch, with a screen in it, into the aisle, is apparently only a little later than the aisle. It has two buttresses at either angle, and the setting of a large ancient window filled with modern tracery, and in its east wall are two windows of two lights worked in chalk, which appear to be ancient ; the sub-arches are simply pointed, and there is no cusping in the head. Under the southern of these is an ancient piscina. This transept, which has been incongruously roofed with slate, was restored and richly decorated in colour, from the designs of Mr. Pugin, as a mortuary chapel for the Drummond

ALBURY OLD CHURCH : THE PORCH

family, whose motto, 'Gang warily,' with the initial D, is powdered on the walls, roof, and screens inside. All the windows are filled with stained glass. Between the two eastern windows is a modern niche, containing a carving of the Crucifixion, with our Lady and St. John ; and against the south wall, on a raised platform, is an altar-tomb to Mr. Drummond, members of whose family are commemorated by slabs with brass crosses in the floor below.

The roofs over the nave and aisle, much patched, and covered with lath and plaster, are ancient. The

floors are paved with old stone slabs, and some ancient tiles remain in the aisle.

One of the most interesting features of the building is the beautiful timber porch on the north side of the nave. The north doorway, to which it conducts (which retains its original oak door and strap-hinges, oak lock-case, and a key over a foot long), is a century and a half earlier (c. 1330), the porch dating from about 1480. A curious point is that it is nearly a foot longer on its eastern side (9 ft. 6 in.) than on its western. The openings in the sides are square-headed and delicately moulded,[52] with a moulded cornice on the inside and a richly traceried and carved barge-board, in which are pierced quatrefoils with rosettes in their centres. The wide outer opening has a flat four-centred head, with roses in the spandrels.

This porch door—the principal entrance from the old village—commands a view of a remarkable painting of St. Christopher, over the opposite door in the south wall of the aisle, which was brought to light during some repairs a few years ago. The details (such as the pleated shirt worn by the saint) fix the date of the painting at about 1480, the same as the porch. On the east wall of the aisle is a fragment of earlier painting, probably nearly two centuries older, and there are traces of colour on the columns and elsewhere. Probably the nave and arcade walls would yield other subjects if carefully searched.

The early font has been carried off to the new parish church, but its base block, a great circular drum of Bargate stone, remains close to the western column of the arcade.

In the floor of the aisle is a slab of blue marble, slightly tapering, 6 ft. 3 in. long by 2 ft. 1 in. at the head, with a very worn inscription, which appears to read as follows :—

WILLEMVM : TERNVM : DE : WESTONE : SVSCIPE : CIST (for CHRISTE) : LVMEN : ETERNVM : QVEM : DEPRIMIT : HIC : LAPIS : ISTE :

From the character of the lettering, which appears to have been filled with a black substance, this may be the tomb slab of the founder of the western aisle or chantry towards the end of the 13th century.

Westward of this is another marble slab in the pavement, bearing the brass of John Weston of Weston, who died in 1440. He is represented in complete plate armour. Above the head is the matrix of a shield, set diagonally, and over it there may have been a helm and crest. It is somewhat singular that, point for point, down to the minutest detail, this brass agrees with that of Sir John Throckmorton, dated 1445, in Fladbury Church, Worcestershire. Each shows a small spring pin passing through a ring, or staple, on the left side of the breastplate, and another on the left elbow-piece—both connected with extra defences to the left, or bridle, arm.[53] The ground on which the feet stand is covered with flowers. Beneath is the inscription :—Hic jacet Johis Westoñ de Westoñ Armiger qui objit xxiiiⁿ die :

[52] The mouldings and plain square-headed openings are exactly like those of the chapel screen of Croydon Palace, and also a parclose screen in Wonersh Church, near Albury.

[53] Although this type of military brass is a fairly common one, the detail referred to is very seldom met with. It occurs also on the brass of a knight of the De

Cuttles family, in Arkesden Church, Essex, c. 1440. These three brasses may well have been executed by the same engraver in London.

ALBURY OLD CHURCH FROM THE SOUTH-EAST IN 1875, BEFORE THE CHANCEL WAS UNROOFED

DUNSFOLD CHURCH: 13TH-CENTURY PEWS

Novembris · Anno dm̄ Millm̄o CCCC° xl ' cuiŏ
aiē p̄p̄īciet' de' amē :

There is also a small brass on the north wall, framed
into a tablet, commemorating Henry Wicks, a servant
of Queen Elizabeth, King James, and King Charles
(1657) ; and monuments to Elizabeth Merrye, 1652,
Edith Duncombe, daughter of John Carrill, late of
Tangley, 1628 (south wall), and others to the Duncombe, Risbridger, and other local families of the
17th and 18th centuries. These are all of good
design, according to their periods, and of rich materials ; alabaster and black and white marble being
employed, and the heraldry coloured and gilt.

Of the new church all that need be said is that it is
in brick, and modelled upon the church of Than,
near Caen, in Normandy, that it is transeptal, with
an apsidal chapel, added by the late Duke of Northumberland, and has a tower at the north-west angle.
There is much stained glass, including a memorial
window to Mr. Drummond, painted by Lady Gage ;
and the font, probably of early 12th-century date,
was removed here from the old church.

The registers date from 1559.

The plate includes a silver cup, paten cover, flagon,
and silver alms-bason, of 1714, the last-named inscribed :—' The gift of Heneage, Lord Guernsey
[Master of the Jewell House] to the Parish of Albury
the place of his birth, 1714.'

The bells, brought from the old church, are six in
number, and, with the exception of the treble, which
was added in 1841, they date from 1695, and bear
the name of William Eldridge.

Albury Church is mentioned in
ADVOWSON the Domesday Survey of the manor.

The advowson was and is vested in
the lord of Albury Manor. The living was valued
at £12 in 1291,[54] and at £18 in 1535.[55]

The charities are numerous ; in
CHARITIES addition to the usual Smith's Charity,
an annuity of £1 12s., charged on
land, was left by Alice Polsted in 1586 for distribution
among the poor ; the interest on £400 was left by
William Risbridger in 1754 to put poor children to
school, to be given in bread, and to provide a sermon,
with a gratuity for the poor who listened to it. The
Duncombe Charity, for the poor generally, was left in
1705 and 1712 by Olive daughter of John Child of
Guildford and widow of Henry Duncombe of Weston,
Albury, who died 1688. This was invested in land
and produces £200 a year.[56]

ALFOLD

Alfaude (xiii cent.) ; Aldfold, Awfold (xvii cent.).

Alfold is a rural parish on the borders of Surrey
and Sussex, bounded on the north by Hascombe and
Cranleigh, on the east by Cranleigh, on the south by
Rudgwick, Wisborough Green, and Kirdford (all in
Sussex), on the west by Dunsfold. It measures
roughly 2½ miles north to south, a little over a mile
east to west. It now contains 2,974 acres. The
parish formerly extended into Sussex, and inclosed an
outlying piece of Albury. In 1880 the Albury part
was added to Alfold,[1] and in 1884 the Sussex portion was transferred to parishes in the county.[2]
About 150 acres, with ten to fifteen inhabitants
only, were added to Sussex, and about 50 acres taken
from Albury. The soil is Wealden clay, and grows
nothing much except forest trees and oats. There
are no wastes in the parish, and the roadside grass is
not above 20 acres in all. A great part of the parish
is wooded, and it was all formerly in the Wealden
Forest ; 917 acres are tithe-free, as ' woodland in
the Weald of Surrey and Sussex.'[3]

In Sydney Wood were glass-houses, of which the
only relic is the name Glass House Fields. A glass-
house is marked in Speed's map. Aubrey (17th century) saw the graves of French glass-makers in the
churchyard, but the industry was extinct in his time,
so the French were not refugees after the Revocation
of the Edict of Nantes, as stated by Brayley. Charcoal was extensively burnt in the parish for gunpowder works in Dunsfold, Cranleigh, and Sussex.

A road from Guildford to Arundel, made in 1809,[4]
traverses the village. Before this time there was
no made road in the parish, and fifty years ago there
was no other. The disused Wey and Arun Canal
passes through the parish.

Alfold Park, which belonged to the manor of
Shalford, contained 300 acres. It had ceased to be
a park when Speed's map was made, and was not
mentioned among twenty-one Surrey parks of the
compass of a mile in the proceedings under the Act
for the Increase of Horses.[5] It is unknown when it
was disparked. The house is, though partly modernized, a good specimen of an old timbered house,
formerly with a hall with a louvre over, the chimney
being a Tudor addition. There are the remains of
a moat round it. The house is now known as
Alfold Park Farm. There are also the remains of
a moat at Wildwood Farm. The parish was rich
in timbered farms and cottages, some of them being
now altered, some pulled down.

A Baptist chapel was erected in 1883, and an elementary school in 1876. Sydney Manor is the residence of Mr. George Wyatt, Sachel Court of
Mr. Thomas Wharrie.

In the lane leading up to the church, and close to
the churchyard gate, the village stocks are still preserved ; a shed-roof has lately been erected over them.

Besides the ancient tile-hung cottages grouped
round this lane, a notable example of the half-timber
house, originally built by a substantial yeoman in
the early years of the 16th century, remains in
Alfold House at the entrance to the village. This
was originally constructed entirely from the foundation of timber framework, filled with wattle and
daub. In plan it was of ⌐-shape with hall (about
23 ft. by 19 ft.) between offices and living rooms.

---

[54] *Pope Nich. Tax.* (Rec. Com.), 208.
[55] *Valor Eccl.* (Rec. Com.), ii, 29.
[56] *Return to Parl.* 1786 and present Information.

[1] By Loc. Govt. Bd. Order 10910, 2 Dec.
[2] Dec.
[3] Loc. Govt. Bd. Order 16533, 24 Mar.

[1] Cf. *V.C.H. Surr.* ii, 613.
[4] Stat. 49 Geo. III, cap. 12.
[6] 27 Hen. VIII, cap. 6.

In late years it has been a good deal injured by the insertion of modern windows in place of the ancient mullioned openings filled with lead lights, but it still retains its arched doorway and a projecting gable, carried on a moulded bressummer and brackets and having a foliated barge-board.[6]

WILDWOOD,[7] now represented by *MANORS* Great and Little Wildwood Farms and Wildwood Copse and Moat, was formerly possessed by the lords of Albury and Stoke D'Abernon, the D'Abernons and their successors.[8] In the 13th century the D'Abernon family had land in Alfold,[9] and in a deed of 1313 John D'Abernon's wood called 'le Wylwode' is mentioned. This was probably the wood of 40 acres of oaks, possibly the

ALFOLD : OLD HOUSE

'Wealden' Wood named in the inquisition on the Albury Manor.[10] In 1391 Elizabeth Grey, lady of Stoke D'Abernon, widow of Sir William Croyser,

granted the soil and wood of Wildwood except the moat, grange, and manorial rights[11] to John, Duke of Lancaster, and others.[12] The descent of Wildwood followed that of Albury till 1626, when Sir Edward Randyll alienated it to Elizabeth Onslow, widow, and Sir Richard Onslow,[13] from whom it seems to have passed to the Duncombes of Weston.[14] With Weston it descended to Nathaniel Sturt, who is said to have sold it in 1736 to either Richard or Francis Dorrington, from whom it was purchased by Henry Page. He bequeathed it to his cousin Richard Skeet of Effingham, whose son Richard succeeded him as owner.[16]

MARKWICK and *MONKENHOOK* were among the possessions of Waverley Abbey,[16] but Markwick only was assessed as the property of the abbey in 1534–5.[17] The 'manors of Markwick and Monken hook' were included within the grant of the site of the abbey to Sir William Fitz William, at whose death they appear under the name of the manor of Alfold,[18] and descended to Anthony, second Viscount Montagu,[19] who alienated the estate *circa* 1623,[20] evidently to agents in a sale to Simon Carrill of Tangley, for it appears afterwards in the possession of the three daughters of John Carrill,[21] and descended with that part of his estate which was assigned to Henry Ludlow and his wife Margaret.[22] Giles son of Thomas Strangways sold them in 1784 to Thomas Boehm, the owner in 1808.[23] The Earl of Onslow is now lord of the manor.

It was said in the 17th century that the lord of Markwick had both court baron and court leet, while the lord of Monkenhook had court baron.[24] The courts were held at Rickhurst and Hook Street.

The reputed manor of *SYDNEY alias HEDGECOURT* or *RICKHURST* lies partly in Dunsfold. The family of Sydney can be traced in the surrounding parishes from the 14th century, while John at Sydney witnessed a deed concerning lands in Alfold in 1313.[25] In 1413 the lord of the manor of Shalford Bradestan is said to have granted Rickhurst and other land in Alfold to William Sydney and his wife Agnes.[26]

In 1595–6 Richard Ireland died possessed of a house called 'Sydneys,' which was held of the lord of

[6] Resembling one in a house at Shamley Green and another in the rear of West Horsley Place, Surrey.
[7] Formerly an outlying part of Albury parish.
[8] See the account of Stoke D'Abernon.
[9] *Surr. Arch. Coll.* xviii, 222.
[10] *Chan. Inq. p.m.* 1 Edw. III, no. 53.
[11] The manorial rights probably appertained to Albury Manor, for Wildwood itself never seems to have been a separate manor.
[12] *Close,* 14 Ric. II, m. 8 d.
[13] *Feet of F. Surr.* Mich. 2 Chas. I.
[14] See Albury.
[15] Manning and Bray, op. cit. ii, 7.

[16] In 1346 the Abbot of Waverley proved his claim to view of frankpledge in his 'manor of Bramley.' *Cal. Pat.* 1345–8, p. 220. This may possibly refer to Markwick and Monkenhook, which appear to be the only lands in or near Bramley held by the abbey. In a bill of sale in 1784 they include land in Dunsfold and Bramley.
[17] *Valor Eccl.* (Rec. Com.), ii, 34. Probably it included Monkenhook.
[18] *Chan. Inq. p.m.* (Ser. 2), lxx, 29.
[19] See *V.C.H. Surr.* ii, 624.
[20] *Recov. R.* East. 20 Jas. I, m. 51 and 14.
[21] *Feet of F. Surr.* Hil. 23–4 Chas. II;

Hil. 25–6 Chas. II; Hil. 26–7 Chas. II; Mich. 30 Chas. II. Symmes, writing later in the same century, says that their uncle, Simon Carrill, was the purchaser; Add. MS. 6167, fol. 135.
[22] *Exch. Spec. Com.* 6485. See under Bramley.
[23] Manning and Bray, op. cit. ii, 70; and Bill of Sale, in which the manor includes Graffham and Burningfold, that is probably some land of the latter.
[24] Add. MS. (B.M.) 6167, fol. 135.
[25] Add. Chart. 5585. See also *Cal. Feet of F. Surr.*; *Surr. Arch. Coll. passim.*
[26] Manning and Bray, *Surr.* ii, 64.

Pollingfold.[27] He left a sister and heir Elizabeth, a minor at the time of his death, and it was probably from her that it passed ultimately to the Dorrington family, who held it during the 17th and following centuries.[28] Sydney Wood was purchased by Sir John Frederick, lord of Hascombe, with which manor it descended till the 19th century.[29] It was in 1903 the property of Mr. George Wyatt, but has since been bought by Messrs. J. E. Sparkes and H. Mellersh.

The church of *ST. NICHOLAS CHURCH* stands upon a knoll of rising ground in the centre of the village, flanked by a cluster of charming old tile-hung cottages. The churchyard is prettily surrounded by trees, and contains several larches and one or two yews of some antiquity.[30] Dotted about among the graves is a number of cypresses and other evergreens, and in early spring the grass is thick with crocuses and daffodils. The churchyard has been extended considerably beyond its ancient boundaries.

The building in itself and with its surroundings is delightfully picturesque, especially as viewed from the south-east.

Bargate stone rubble, plastered outside and in, has been employed for the walls, with dressings of the same stone ; but internally the hard chalk, or clunch, also quarried locally, has been used in the south arcade, the chancel arch, and the 15th-century features of the chancel. The chancel roof and the roofs over the aisles and porches are still 'healed' with Horsham slabs ; the bell-turret and its spire are covered with oak shingles, and the porches are of oak.

In plan the church consists of a nave, 36 ft. 4 in. by 21 ft. 2 in., north and south aisles, about 7 ft. 5 in. wide (the south aisle is slightly longer than the nave) ; chancel, 17 ft. 5 in. wide by 16 ft. 5 in. long ; north and south porches, and a vestry lately erected on the north of the chancel. The simple outlines of nave and chancel give the plan of the primitive church, erected perhaps about 1100, of which the only visible relic besides plain walling is the remarkable font.

The south aisle was added about 1190, the old walls being pierced with three plain, square-edged, obtusely pointed arches, unrelieved by moulding, chamfer, or label, and springing from columns and responds circular in plan, on square plinths, and having capitals of an early circular form, simply moulded.[31] The western respond only has a circular moulded base with angle-spurs. The church must have remained with one aisle till about 1290, when that on the north was thrown out. Its three arches were discovered blocked up in the north wall of the nave at the restoration of 1845 ; they were then opened and the aisle rebuilt on its old foundations. The

arches, in rough Bargate stone, are moulded in three orders (a hollow between two wave-mouldings), and these spring direct from octagonal piers, without capitals, which have chamfered plinths instead of bases.[32] The chancel arch is of somewhat similar design, but in a firestone, or clunch, and springing from plain square piers. The mouldings indicate a slightly later date—c. 1320—to which period may be referred the south aisle windows, with ogee and reticulated tracery, and the outline at least of the east window of the chancel. The windows of the north aisle appear to be entirely modern, and are copies of those on the other side, but its doorway (c. 1290) has been replaced from the old north wall and retains the original oak door with very elaborate diagonally-braced framework on the back, a massive oak lock-case, and some good wrought-iron hinges and straps, partly ancient. The south door, less elaborate, is perhaps of the same date.

The two-light window and piscina in the south wall of the chancel, and the splayed opening with

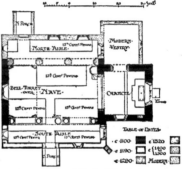

PLAN OF ALFOLD CHURCH

four-centred arch in the wall opposite, are of 15th-century date, the piscina being a restoration.[33] The splayed opening now communicates with a modern vestry, but it is probable that it was originally an arch over a tomb or Easter sepulchre in the thickness of the wall, and the splays repeated on the outer face suggest that there was at one time a small chapel or vestry abutting upon the north wall of the chancel into which this arch opened. There is a small buttress at the south-east angle of the south aisle and a low one beneath the east window of the chancel, both perhaps dating from about 1320. Parts of the picturesque oak porches may belong to the same early

[27] Chan. Inq. p.m. (Ser. 2), ccxlvii, 30. The Sydneys had held Baynards in Pollingfold (Inq. of 4 Edw. IV preserved at Loseley).

[28] Aubrey (*Hist. and Antiq. of Surr.* iv, 92) says that it was in the possession of Captain Dorrington in 1673. There is a memorial to Francis Dorrington in Alfold Church. He died 1693, aged 75. The monument was erected by his grandson Edward Dorrington.

[29] Manning and Bray, op. cit. ii, 69.

[30] The largest measures about 23 ft. in circumference at 4 ft. from the ground.

[31] The general character of this arcade resembles the south arcade of Rustington Church, Sussex, while the curious features of the north arcade are exactly reproduced in the north arcade of that church. In each case these arcades correspond closely in date. The font, strangely enough, is very like that in Yapton Church, Sussex, within a few miles of Rustington.

[32] Besides the north arcade of Rustington Church, which so exactly resembles this, there are other arcades without capitals at Fetcham, Surrey, and Slindon and Coldwaltham, Sussex.

[33] Cracklow's View of 1824 shows that the two-light window has been shifted to the eastward and raised in the wall at the 1845 restoration, being possibly shortened at the same time.

date, but they have been much restored and are largely of new material. That on the south side appears in Cracklow's view very much as at present.

The timber bell-tower, standing on huge oak posts worked into a series of hollow mouldings, rises from the floor of the nave at its western end and occupies the western bay of the arcades, its width across the nave (20 ft. 6 in.) being considerably greater than from west to east (11 ft. 6 in.). It is spanned both ways by arched braces, those on the sides being much lower and forming complete four-centred arches. The framework of the bell-chamber above and of the spire is ancient, and the whole forms a most interesting piece of mediaeval carpentry, the date of which may be placed at about 1500.[34] The bell-cage is coeval.

The present west window of the nave, a disproportionately large one of five lights, replaces a simple two-light opening, having been inserted, together with its glass, quite lately as a memorial.

All the roofs of nave, south aisle, and chancel are of massive oak timbers, the spaces between the rafters being plastered. Such roofs are difficult to date precisely, but these may well be as old as the beginning of the 14th century.

The chancel screen is a restoration, incorporating parts of one of 15th-century date, and great part of the oak seating is of the same period, the bench-ends being of a plain square shape, with a moulded capping. The pulpit is an interesting example of Jacobean date, retaining its sound-board, suspended by a scrolled iron rod.

No ancient paintings are now visible, but in the works of 1845, on removing the whitewash, traces of a Crucifixion were found over the east window of the chancel, and a diaper of flower pots with lilies and roses on the north side of the nave. These were unfortunately covered up again, and in recent years the chancel walls have been elaborately painted with diaper patterns and figures. All the glass now in the church is modern.

The altar is raised on three steps above the chancel, the latter, however, being on the same level as the nave.

Few churches in Surrey have such an interesting font. It is in Bargate stone, tub-shaped, with a broad shallow base of recessed section round which winds a cable-moulding, the upper part of the bowl having an arcade of eight circular-headed arches on square piers with small square imposts—incised in a very shallow fashion. Within each arch is a Maltese cross on a long stem. A similar ornament was added to the ancient font in St. Martha's Chapel (q.v.) in 1849 by Mr. Woodyer. The date of the font is about 1100, and its design in the matter of the arcade and crosses is remarkably like that of the early font in Yapton Church, Sussex.

The most ancient monument within or without the church is to a yeoman family, the Didelsfolds, dating from 1670. The monument of Francis Dorrington is of 1693. In the churchyard is a slab said to cover the grave of the last of the glass manufacturers. A few incised marks may be found on the pillars of the south arcade and on one of the splays of the opening in the north wall of the chancel. The parish chest is of 1687.

The registers of burials date from 1658, of baptisms from 1661, and among other items of interest contain several certificates for touching for the king's evil.

Besides three pieces of 1819, 1820, and 1821, there are a silver chalice and paten-cover of 1570, and a pewter tankard-shaped flagon dated 1664. A curious pewter almsdish and a pewter plate have been lost between 1839 and 1876.

Of the three bells the treble and tenor are by Bryan Eldridge of 1631 and 1625, and the second is by William Eldridge, 1714.

The advowson belonged to the *ADVOWSON* lords of Shalford Manor, and is mentioned in the grant of that manor to John son of Geoffrey.[35] Richard son of John inherited the advowson, which formed a part of his widow's dower, and at her death descended to the successive Earls of Ormond, lords of Shiere Vachery,[36] till early in the 16th century, when Edmund Bray presented to Alfold.[37] Either he or his descendants seem to have sold it, and it afterwards continually changed hands. In 1681 Elizabeth Holt, and in 1694 Christopher Coles, presented, and in 1711 it was in the gift of Jacob Whitehead. William Elliott presented in 1801, and the Rev. William Elliott in 1817. The present patron is Sir Henry Harben of Warnham.

BRAMLEY

Bronlei, Brunlei, Brunlege, Brolege (xi cent.), Bromlegh, Bromley, Bromle, (xiii cent.).

Bramley was originally a part of the ecclesiastical parish of Shalford, with a separate chapel since probably the 11th century at least, for there may be work of that or the 12th century in the church, and it would seem to be one of the three churches in Bramley Manor in 1086. It was a distinct civil parish from Shalford before it was ecclesiastically separated in 1844. The parish lies south-east of Guildford, about 3 miles. It is about 5 miles north to south, and 2 miles from east to west, but tapers towards the south. It contains 4,510 acres of land, and 34 of water. It is bounded on the north by Shalford, on the east by Wonersh and Cranleigh, on the south by Hascombe and Dunsfold, on the west by Godalming and an outlying part of Dunsfold. The soil is the Lower Greensand over the great part of the parish, this soil rising into hills of some elevation on the borders of Godalming parish to the west. Southwards occurs a rather wider outcrop of Atherfield clay than is usually seen in the neighbourhood, but the Wealden clay is in the south-east.

[34] The timber towers of Dunsfold and Thursley (q.v.) in Surrey, of the same date and character, should be compared with this; probably they are all the work of the same gild.

[35] See under Shalford.

[36] Egerton MSS. 2032, fol. 131 ; 2033, fol. 72 ; 2034, fol. 72, 113 ; Feet of F. Surr. 10 Hen. VII, 31.

[37] Egerton MS. 2034, fol. 159.

The country is well wooded. There are extensive roadside wastes, but no large commons. The land is agricultural. There is a water-mill, Bramley Mill, or Snowdenham Mill, worked by a tributary of the Wey, which flows from Hascombe into Bramley village, where it joins another stream which falls into the Wey below the railway bridge of the Brighton line. The mouth of this stream was utilized for the old Wey and Arun Canal, which here left the former river, and passed along the eastern verge of Bramley parish. This canal was virtually disused when the railway was opened in 1865, and was barely passable for a small boat above Bramley village in 1872, and is now quite blocked and dry in places. There is a station at Bramley on the Brighton line from Guildford to Horsham, opened in 1865.

A road from Guildford to Horsham passes through Bramley. A branch leads from the village to Hascombe and Dunsfold and Alfold.

Historically it is remarkable that Bramley, which

Hooper, Woodrough of the Hon. E. P. Thesiger, Bramley Grange of Colonel Fox Webster, Nore of Colonel Godwin Austen, and Unstead Park of Mr. L. C. W. Phillips. Lord John Russell had a lease of the last named during Sir Robert Peel's ministry, when the Whigs were out of office.

The Parish Schools were built by Mrs. Sutherland in 1850, and enlarged in 1874, 1894, and 1901.

St. Catherine's School for Girls (Church of England middle class school) was built by subscription in 1885, and incorporated by charter with Cranleigh Boys' School in 1898. There is a handsome red-brick chapel in 13th-century style containing good painted glass, showing English and other female saints on opposite sides of the chapel.

In 1884 Brookwell and Graffham were transferred from Dunsfold civil parish to Bramley, being before isolated parts of Dunsfold, and High Billinghurst was transferred from Bramley to Dunsfold.[1]

The parish abounds in ancient houses. Bramley

BRAMLEY : OLD HOUSES

gave its name to the very extensive possessions of the Bishop of Bayeux in the neighbourhood, so that the manor of Bramley intruded into several neighbouring parishes of later date, was not itself a parish. Whatever the enumeration of population in Domesday may mean, Bramley is the third in order in the county, coming after only Southwark and Guildford. As is the case all over the dry soils of Surrey, a great many neolithic flint implements and flakes have been found. Some are in the Surrey Archaeological Society's museum at Guildford, some in the Charterhouse Museum.

The cemetery was made in 1851 by the late Mrs. Sutherland, and enlarged by the late Mr. Percy Ricardo in 1890. The Constitutional Hall, which includes a Conservative Working Men's Club, was opened in 1888. Thorncombe is the residence of Captain Fisher Rowe, Bramley Park of Colonel Ricardo, Snowdenham Hall of Mr. John Kinnersley

East was the name both of a house and a manor ; the house is a three-gabled brick and stone building, nicely proportioned. Opposite to it is a far more interesting half-timber house, the details of which recall Great Tangley manor-house, in the adjoining parish of Wonersh. Tangley Manor was rebuilt by Mr. Carrill in Elizabeth's reign. He was also lord of Bramley East. The date of the latter may be about 1560. The most valuable feature is a two-storied gabled staircase wing resembling those at Rake House and Shottermill, in which the timber framework is designed in squares, four quadrants of a circle being placed back to back within each square, the total effect being a pattern of intersecting squares and circles. The grouping of roofs and crow-stepped chimneys in this building is very picturesque.

At Nursecombe, an outlying hamlet, is an interesting old timber-framed house of the 16th century—

1 By Loc. Govt. Bd. Order, 16532, dated 24 Mar.

3   81   11

probably of two dates—with projecting upper stories, ornamental barge-boards to the gables and a delightful jumble of tiled roofs. There is a picturesque porch to the front, having an oak doorway with four-centred arch and carved spandrels. Among other interesting details are the moulded joist-boards and brackets, the barge-boards of two patterns, and pendants to the barge-boards and wall plates. There is a good gable of timber pattern-work at the back, retaining its barge-board.

Another old house, at Snowdenham, although marked by later alterations, exhibits internally some door-posts of perhaps 15th-century work. A stable belonging to this house is in a very perfect condition and apparently of early 17th-century date.

Thorncombe Street, a straggling hamlet to the south of Nursecombe, contains a number of old timber-framed cottages. One of these, T-shaped in plan, has some very solid half-timber work, and the original windows with lead lights. An old farmhouse called Slades, in the same hamlet, has a good staircase and other woodwork of 18th-century date.

MANORS At the time of the Domesday Survey the manor of *BRAMLEY* covered apparently the inhabited parts of the county from near Shalford Church southwards to the Sussex border. All the manors of the parishes of Wonersh, Cranleigh, Hascombe, Dunsfold, and Alfold, and part of Shalford seem to have been formed out of it. Alnod Cild held it in the time of Edward the Confessor. After the Conquest it became the holding of Odo of Bayeux, who found various pretexts for annexing to it land in Clandon and Gomshall, the manors of Chilworth and Sutton, and lands elsewhere.[2] It is recorded in Domesday that the manor paid no geld since Odo held it. After the forfeiture of the Bishop of Bayeux it escheated with his other lands to the Crown. Under Henry I Eustace de Brutvile held it for a short time.[3] Henry II gave the manor to Ralph de Fay, who was, however, dispossessed during the war between the king and his son, the young King Henry.[4] Bramley paid tallage as king's demesne in 1187.[5] It was afterwards held for a short time by Baldwin de Bethune,[6] but in 1196 £46 is given as the ferm of Bramley for half a year before it was given to John Count of Mortain.[7] After his accession John granted the manor to Ralph de Fay, son of the former tenant.[8] His son John de Fay had seisin of his father's lands in 1223,[9] and after his death in 1241 the manor was divided between his two sisters, Maud de Clerc and Philippa de Fay.[10] They each held a moiety by service of half a knight's fee, the two portions being afterwards accounted

separate manors. Maud de Clere's portion was again divided into three in the 17th century, but Philippa's remained entire, and is now known as the manor of Bramley.

Philippa married a William Neville[11] and enfeoffed her only daughter Beatrice, who married William of Wintershull, lord of the manor of Wintershull in Bramley, of her portion of the manor of Bramley.[12] Beatrice survived her husband[13] and entailed the manor on their younger son Walter,[14] whose son Thomas succeeded him,[15] and married Alice[16] afterwards wife of Henry de Loxley, who held with Alice, or was at all events answerable for dues from the manor.[17] Thomas died on Good Friday 1339,[18] holding half the manor of Bramley of John de Hadresham as of his manor of Combe Neville.[19] He left a son and heir William,[20] who died in 1361. He was succeeded by his brother,[21] Thomas Wintershull, from whom the manor descended to his son Thomas.[22] The latter died in January 1414–15, leaving a son, also Thomas, whose proof of age was taken in 1418.[23] He died in 1420, his heirs being his sisters, Joan wife of William Weston of Sussex, and Agnes wife of William Basset.[24] Joan married a second husband, William Catton.[25] No more is known of Agnes Basset ;[26] in 1485, after the death without issue of William Weston, Joan's only son, the manor was divided between Margaret Appesley, Joan's daughter, and John Pope, son of Thomas Pope and Joan, another of her daughters.[27] Margaret Appesley died 27 August 1516, leaving a son and heir, John Welles, by her first husband William Welles.[28] In January 1534–5 John Welles died possessed of half the manor of Bramley, and was succeeded by his son Thomas Welles,[29] who, with his wife Cecily, joined with Edmund Pope (probably a descendant of John Pope and as such seised of the other half of the manor) in a sale of the whole manor to William Harding of Knowle in Cranleigh, citizen and mercer of London, and his wife Cecily.[30] After William Harding's death in September 1549[31] the manor was divided between his daughters Helen and Catherine. Catherine married in 1559 Richard Onslow,[32] who became Speaker of the House of Commons and Solicitor-General.[33] Helen in 1561 sold her share to her brother-in-law Onslow.[34] From him the manor descended to his son Sir Edward, whom Queen

HARDING of Knowle.
Argent a bend azure with three martlets or thereon.

[2] *V.C.H. Surr.* i, 295*b*, 296*a*, 298*a*, 301, 302*a*, 305*b*.
[3] *Testa de Nevill* (Rec. Com.), 225.
[4] Ibid.
[5] Pipe R. 33 Hen. II, m. 15 d.
[6] Exch. K.R. Misc. Bks. vol. 6, fol. 73. In the printed *Testa de Nevill* the name is given 'Becchōū.'
[7] Pipe R. 8 Ric. I, m. 17 d.
[8] *Cal. Rot. Chart.* (Rec. Com.), 33. He confirmed at the same time a tithe of the manor to the monks of Lyre.
[9] *Excerpta e Rot. Fin.* (Rec. Com.), i, 102.
[10] Ibid. i, 346, 352.
[11] Wintershull Chart. quoted by Manning and Bray, op. cit. ii, 28. By the In-

quisition below it would seem that William and Philippa had a son of whom the manor was held.
[12] Feet of F. Div. Co. 33 Hen. III.
[13] Chan. Inq. p.m. 15 Edw. I, no. 15.
[14] Ibid. 5 Hen. V, no. 52.
[15] Ibid. 20 Edw. III (1st nos.), no. 46.
[16] Ibid. 8 Ric. II, no. 24.
[17] Pipe R. 26 Edw. III, m. 30.
[18] Chan. Inq. p.m. 20 Edw. III (1st nos.), no. 46.
[19] Ibid. 14 Edw. III, no. 7.
[20] Ibid. 11 Edw. III, pt. 2 (1st nos.), no. 82.
[21] Ibid.
[22] Ibid. 5 Hen. V, no. 52.
[23] Ibid. 6 Hen. V, no. 53.

[24] Ibid. 8 Hen. V, no. 86 ; Feet of F. Div. Co. Hil. 9 Hen. VI.
[25] *Surr. Visit.* 216 ; and Feet of F. Div. Co. Hil. 9 Hen. VI.
[26] Manning and Bray quote a deed dated 2 Ric. III, by which William Swan, a trustee, conveyed Bramley to William Weston, son of William and Joan Weston.
[27] Chan. Inq. p.m. (Ser. 2), xxvii, 61.
[28] Ibid.
[29] Exch. Inq. p.m. file 1085, no. 1.
[30] Feet of F. Surr. Hil. 33 Hen. VIII.
[31] Chan. Inq. p.m. (Ser. 2), lxxxix, 136.
[32] Feet of F. Div. Co. Hil. 3 Eliz.
[33] *Hist. MSS. Com. Rep.* xiv, App. pt. ix, 475.
[34] Lord Onslow's D.

Elizabeth had knighted.[35] The manor was settled on
Sir Edward's son Thomas at his marriage with Mary
Lennard in 1616.[36] He died in the same year and
was succeeded by his brother Sir Richard Onslow,
knight of the shire for Surrey from 1627 to 1658.[37]
Bramley descended to his son Arthur,[38] whose son
Richard was created Baron Onslow in 1716.[39]
George, first Earl Onslow, grand-nephew of Richard
first Baron Onslow, sold Bramley to William Lord
Grantley in 1805.[40] He also owned the whole of
the other moiety, thus uniting the portions which
had been separate for nearly six centuries. He was
succeeded by his nephew Fletcher Norton, third Lord
Grantley, in 1822.[41] The Grantley property was sold
in 1886, and Captain W. H. Waud is now lord of
the manor.

The second moiety, which was assigned to Maud
de Clere, descended at her death in 1250 to Alice
daughter of Maud's daughter Agatha and William
de Ros, who afterwards married Richard Longespee.[42] Her daughter Alice, wife of Richard Breus,[43]
granted it in 1266 to Maud Longespee to hold for
life.[44] In 1271 Richard and Alice Breus conveyed
the manor to William Breus and his wife Mary in
exchange for Akenham Manor, co. Suffolk.[45]
In 1293 Mary Breus obtained licence to grant
Bramley in fee simple to Walter de Gedding for his
good services to her.[46] Evidently this grant was only
for life, for Mary Breus was holding it at her death in
May 1326.[47] She was succeeded by her grandson Sir
Thomas Breus,[48] whose widow Beatrice held Bramley
for life.[49] Sir Thomas Breus, kt., died seised of it in
1395,[50] leaving two children who died within a week
of their father. The manor of Bramley, however,
after being for a time in the hands of trustees,[51] instead of passing to his niece and heir Elizabeth, wife
of William Heron, descended in tail male to George
de Breus son of John brother of Thomas de Breus the
elder.[52] This George died seised of it in 1418.[53]
Dower was assigned out of the manor to his widow
Elizabeth, afterwards wife of Thomas Slyfeld.[54] She held
it of the inheritance of Sir Hugh Cokesey, kt., great-
grandson of Agnes sister of George de Breus.[55] After
Hugh's death in February 1445–6 [56] Bramley remained
with his widow Alice in accordance with the terms of
a previous settlement,[57] but at her death descended to
his sister Joyce Beauchamp, then wife of Leonard
Stepelton.[58] Her son Sir John Greville, kt., succeeded her as lord of the manor [59] and died seised of

it in 1480, leaving a son Thomas who assumed the
name of Cokesey.[60] At his death there was a partition
of the family estates, and the Surrey part, including
Bramley, passed to the Earl of Surrey.[61]

The manor of Bramley is mentioned as a possession
of his son Thomas Duke of Norfolk, in 1545.[62] His
widow, Agnes, Duchess of Norfolk, held it for life with
reversion to the king by reason of her husband's attainder.[63] Her grandson and
heir, being restored to the
dukedom, sold Bramley to
Richard Carrill (or Caryl) in
1559.[64] Richard Carrill died
in February 1575–6 [65] and
was succeeded by his son John
Carrill, attorney of the Duchy
of Lancaster. His kinsman
and heir, John Carrill, proved
himself of age in 1578,[66]
and died seised of the
manor of Bramley in 1612,
leaving a son Simon,[67] on
whom he had settled it at
the time of his marriage with Elizabeth daughter
of Sir Francis Aungier.[68] Elizabeth survived her
husband, and Bramley ultimately passed to her son
John Carrill, who in 1649 granted it,[69] as a security
probably, to a relative, George Duncombe, for life, at
the yearly rent of one peppercorn.[70] John Carrill
mortgaged all his property heavily. His widow,
Hester, married Sir Francis Duncombe, who
complained that he had to abandon his profession as
barrister-at-law in order to give proper attention to
the estates of his stepchildren. These were Lettice,
Elizabeth, and Margaret, daughters of John Carrill.
At the age of sixteen Lettice Carrill married John
Ramsden,[71] and joined with her husband in a suit
against her stepfather for ill-treatment of herself and
her sisters and mismanagement of their estates.[72]
Bramley was divided among the three sisters, Lettice
Ramsden's portion of the estate being known as the
'manor of EAST BRAMLEY or Great Tangley.' [73]
In 1673 she conveyed it to John Child.[72] His grand-
son Charles Child left it to his nephew Charles Searle,
who conveyed it in 1759 to Fletcher Norton, first
Lord Grantley,[74] in whose family it descended together with the first moiety of the manor.

John Carrill's second daughter Elizabeth, wife of
Peter Fermor, conveyed her third of the estate in

CARRILL of Bramley.
*Argent three bars sable
with three martlets sable
in the chief.*

[35] *Hist. MSS. Com. Rep.* xiv, App. pt. ix,
476.

[36] Com. Pleas D. Enr. Mich. 14 Jas. I,
m. 33.

[37] Chan. Inq. p.m. (Ser. 2), cclxv, 105.

[38] Feet of F. Surr. Hil. 22 Chas. I ;
ibid. Div. Co. Mich. 1649.

[39] *Hist. MSS. Com. Rep.* xiv, App. pt. ix,
489.

[40] Manning and Bray, *Hist. of Surr.* ii,
79 ; Recov. R. Trin. 10 Geo. III, m. 195.

[41] Brayley, *Topog. Hist. of Surr.* v, 121.

[42] Chan. Inq. p.m. 46 Hen. III, no. 1.

[43] Coram Rege R. 58, m. 5.

[44] Feet of F. Div. Co. 51 Hen. III, 9.

[45] Feet of F. Div. Co. 56 Hen. III, no.
73. Bramley was to be held of Richard and
Alice by William and Mary, and after the
death of Alice's son, Giles Breus, the
manor was said to be held of his heirs
(Chan. Inq. p.m. 19 Edw. II, no. 90), but
in all subsequent documents the successors

of William and Mary are said to have
held it in chief. See Chan. Inq. p.m. 29
Edw. I, no. 52 ; ibid. 4 Edw. II, no. 40 ;
Cal. Pat. 1324–7, p. 262.

[46] *Cal. Pat.* 1292–1301, p. 79.

[47] Chan. Inq. p.m. 19 Edw. II, no. 90 ;
Esch. Enr. Accts. i, 25.

[48] Feet of F. Div. Co. 11 Edw. III,
22 ; Chan. Inq. p.m. 35 Edw. III, pt. i,
no. 39.

[49] Pat. 46 Edw. III, pt. ii, m. 6.

[50] Chan. Inq. p.m. 19 Ric. II, no. 7.

[51] Close, 3 Hen. IV, pt. i, m. 24.

[52] Wrottesley, *Pedigrees from the Plea
R.* 230.

[53] Chan. Inq. p.m. 6 Hen. V, no. 48.

[54] Ibid. 10 Hen. V, no. 33.

[55] Ibid. 12 Hen. VI, no. 4.

[56] Ibid. 24 Hen. VI, no. 36.

[57] Ibid. 38–9 Hen. VI, no. 49.

[58] Ibid. 24 Hen. VI, no. 36.

[59] Ibid. 13 Edw. IV, no. 32.   [60] Ibid.

[61] He was descendant of William Breus,
elder brother of Peter father of Sir Thomas
Breus, who succeeded to the manor in
1326. William Breus' daughter Alina
married John, Lord Mowbray ; *Cal. Close,*
1330–3, pp. 259, 479 ; *Cal. Pat.* 1330–4,
p. 128.

[62] Chan. Inq. p.m. (Ser. 2), lxxii, 26.

[63] Ibid. lxix, 189.

[64] Feet of F. Surr. Trin. 1 Eliz.

[65] Chan. Inq. p.m. (Ser. 2), clxxv, 74.

[66] Ibid. clxxxiii, 65. By *Visit. of Surrey*
(Harl. Soc.), 89, the first John was brother
of Richard, the second John Richard's son
of W. and L. Inq. p.m. xlvi, 9.

[67] W. and L. Inq. p.m. xlvi, 9.

[68] Ibid. xxix, 155.

[69] Com. Pleas D. Enr. East. 1649, m. 16.

[70] *Visit. of Surr.* (Harl. Soc.), 89.

[71] Exch. Dep. Hil. 21 & 22 Chas. II, 26.

[72] Exch. Spec. Com. 6484, 6485.

[73] Feet of F. Surr. Hil. 25–6 Chas. II.

[74] Manning and Bray, op. cit. ii, 83.

1674 to Ambrose Holbech and Lawrence Lord,[75] probably as trustees to sell to Richard Gwynn, clothworker of London,[76] whose niece and heiress Susan Clifton had a daughter Trehane, who married Sir William Chapple, justice of the King's Bench. His daughter Grace married Sir Fletcher Norton, first Lord Grantley,[77] who thus obtained another third of this manor.

John Carrill's third daughter married Henry Ludlow, and their share of the estate was known as *WEST BRAMLEY.*[78] Henry Ludlow, by will in 1724 (proved P.C. Cant. 15 October 1730), devised the manors of West Bramley, Markwick, Monkenhook, and Shoelands in Puttenham to his daughter Elizabeth. She became insane, and on her death her next heirs were found to be her father's first cousin's sons Captain Harcourt Masters and Mr. Giles Strangways. By a deed of partition in 1750 West Bramley fell to Captain Harcourt Masters. He sold West Bramley to William Hammond, who was already tenant of the manor-house.[79] William Hammond sold it to John Shurlock and Richard Elliott. John Shurlock's grandson John conveyed his interest to Thomas Smyth, nephew of Richard Elliott, who thus owned the whole of West Bramley.[80] He sold it to William Lord Grantley,[81] who already owned the rest of the original manor, with which it has since descended.

William de Breus and William Wintershull with their wives, lords of the divided manor of Bramley in the time of Edward I, made good their claim to view of frankpledge, assize of bread and ale and liberties of pillory and cucking-stool according to a charter of Henry III.[81a] The lord of Bramley used also to hold pleas for merchants attending Shalford fair, and to take the stakes set up in his fee.[82]

View of frankpledge was held by William, grandson of Walter Wintershull, on Wednesday in Whitsun week.[83] He also had a rent called 'worksilver' from his free tenants in Bramley.[84] The view of frankpledge was sold with the manor to William Harding in 1542.

Of the liberties peculiar to the de Breus' half of the manor of Bramley free warren was granted to Walter de Gedding in 1304.[85] Among items given in the account of Robert the Tailor, 'bedell' of Sir Thomas de Breus in 1354 and the following years, are a rent called 'Toppingselver' from Clandon and 'Workselver' from various tenants.[86]

THORNCOMBE STREET or *MARSHALS* was that land of 'Torncumba' of which Stephen de Turnham the king's marshal was enfeoffed by William and Roger de Paceys, and which he was holding in 1205 in accordance with a charter of Ralph de Fay.[86] It probably returned to the de Fay family through Beatrice daughter and co-heiress of Stephen de Turnham and wife of Ralph de Fay.[87] It afterwards formed part of lands granted to John of Wintershull by Maud de Fay.[88] No documentary evidence concerning Thorncombe during the next three centuries has been found.

In 1502 John Mellersh recovered the manor of Thorncombe, &c., from Robert Marshall.[88]

In 1505 John Onley and others acquired the manor of Thorncombe *alias* Marshall from John Apryze, Robert Marshall and Elizabeth his wife being called to warrant.[89]

In 1510 Onley conveyed to William Lusher.[90] George Lusher settled it on his son William on his marriage (1564–5); and subsequently, in 1593, his son's first wife being dead, was trying to recover possession against John Comber, to whom William had conveyed it in 1583,[91] presumably on a second marriage with a daughter of Comber. In 1596 Comber and William Lusher were able to convey it to Henry Mellersh, at whose death it seems to have been split up into fifths, which descended respectively to Martha wife of Robert Roydon, Anne wife of John Wight, Eleanor wife of William Skynner, James and Christopher Hobson, and Margaret wife of John Scales,[91a] which last sold her fifth to Francis Aungier in 1604.[92]

The portions of the manor often reappear, and 'Marshall or Marshalls' kept its name as a farm. It was owned by Budds and Balchins, and conveyed by George Chandler's trustees to Mr. Richard Gates, in 1839. He sold it to Mr. Fisher in 1849, and it is now, as Thorncombe, the property of Captain Fisher-Rowe.

The manor of *WINTERSHULL* seems to have been separated from Bramley Manor soon after the death of Ralph de Fay the younger, for in 1227 a royal confirmation was made to Henry Wintershull of 'all the land of Wintersell and all service of the land saving the king's service only,' which he had of the gift of John de Fay.[93] Ralph de Fay's widow, Beatrice, had also granted land in Bramley to Henry Wintershull.[93a] The manor remained in the Wintershull family, though not in that branch which held Bramley halfmanor. It was held of Bramley by the service of a knife for cutting bread yearly.[94] In 1279 John Wintershull proved his claim to view of frankpledge in the manor.[95] In 1327–8 Francis Wintershull

WINTERSHULL. Or two bars gules and a label sable.

75 Feet of F. Surr. Hil. 26 & 27 Chas. II.
76 Close, 30 Chas. II, pt. vi, no. 30.
77 Dict. Nat. Biog. xli, 211; x, 62.
78 Feet of F. Surr. East. 31 Chas. II.
79 Close, 25 Geo. II, pt. i, no. 5.
80 Manning and Bray, op. cit. ii, 83, 112; Brayley, op. cit. v, 121.
81 Brayley, op. cit. v, 120.
81a Plac. de Quo Warr. (Rec. Com.), 743.
82 Chan. Inq. p.m. 15 Edw. I, no. 69.
83 Chan. Inq. p.m. 11 Edw. III (pt. 2, 1st nos.), no. 82.
84 Feet of F. Surr. Hil. 33 Hen. VIII.
85 Chart. R. 33 Edw. I, no. 98.
85a Mins. Accts. bdle. 1010, no. 23.

86 Cal. Rot. Chart. (Rec. Com.), i, 160. Stephen was confirmed at the same time in the possession of lands which had been his father-in-law's, Ralph de Broc.
87 See the account of Artington.
88 Deed quoted by Manning and Bray, op. cit. ii, 85. The rent due from the tenement of Geoffrey 'de Torcumba' in Bramley had been granted by John de Fay to the Prioress of Amesbury; Curia Regis R. 108, m. 9.
88a De Banco R. East. 17 Hen. VII, m. 146 d. [Recovery]. It is probably from this family that it took the name of Marshals.
89 De Banco R. Hil. 20 Hen. VII, m. 360.

90 Ct. R. of Selhurst Manor. Feast of St. Edmund, 2 Hen. VIII.
91 Chan. Proc. Eliz. Ll, i, 34.
91a Feet of F. Surr. East. 5 Jas. I; East. 7 Jas. I. Henry Mellersh's will (1597) names his four daughters, of whom one is Martha, who married Robert Roydon, but the other names are not those of these co-heiresses. His only son died young, and there were only four daughters.
92 Ibid. Hil. 1 Jas. I.
93 Cal. Rot. Chart. (Rec. Com.), i, 48.
93a Maitland, Bracton's Note Bk. 679.
94 Chan. Inq. p.m. (Ser. 2), lxxxix, 133.
95 Plac. de Quo Warr. (Rec. Com.), 747.

witnessed a conveyance of land in Bramley.[96] John Wintershull was lord in 1340.[97] In 1362 John vested the manor in trustees for himself, his son John and his heirs, and other children and their heirs in succession.[98] John the younger made his will in 1396, mentioning his children, Thomas, John, and Joan.[98a] John had a son Robert,[99] whose son Thomas died seised of the manor in 1476–7.[100] Robert, son of Thomas, petitioned for the manorial records to be delivered to him by Elizabeth Wintershull.[101] Robert died in 1487,[102] leaving a son Robert, then eight years old,[103] who died in 1549, and was succeeded by his son John. John, son of John Wintershull,[104] made proof of his age in 1565, but died in 1571.[105] He left an infant son William, who afterwards, in 1601, conveyed Selhurst or Wintershull to George Austen,[106] probably for the purpose of a settlement, as Austen was not in possession a few years later.

William Wintershull was probably a recusant. He was connected with the Lumleys, recusants, to whom he let the manor-house; and he ultimately conveyed the reversion of the manor to trustees for their benefit. Henry Lumley parted with his interest, and by a series of conveyances the manor passed to George Chandler, who in 1655 conveyed one moiety in possession and one in reversion to his brother Richard.[107] Richard Chandler held a court in 1663. Thomas Chandler his son held a court in 1667, and made a conveyance of the manor in 1671[108] to John Child, who held a court in 1672. His grandson Charles Child is said to have sold the manor after 1723 to Mr. Barrett, father of George Barrett, the owner in 1808,[109] and it is now in the possession of Mr. George W. Barrett.

HAM was held by Henry de Guldeford, when he died in 1312–13, of the Prior and convent of Sandleford.[110] Ham was connected with the manor and park of Ashurst (see Witley). The keeper of these was accountable for rent of land called 'Hamme,' circa 1369–71.[111] The rent occurs again in 1374–5,[112] and in 1439–40 Walter Bedall, keeper of Ashunt Manor and park, took proceedings against Sir Henry Hussey for usurping the profits of Ham.[113] Ashunt and Frydynghurst seem to be the same estate. The Windsor family bought land in them, and the Fordes from them.[114] Thomas Mellersh was dealing with Hamland in 1574,[115] and is said to have owned Nore and Ham Manor,[116] and to have bought the latter from Forde, of Harting, Sussex.[117]

NORE, which with Ham is called a manor, was acquired by George Austen of Shalford, by marriage with Anne, daughter and co-heiress of Thomas Mellersh of Nore. The Mellersh family had held it for some time. George Austen died holding the capital messuage of Nore in 1611, together with Hameland and Unstead Manors.[118] It is still the

property of the family, and the residence of Colonel Godwin Austen, owner of Shalford Park.

Rushett Farm was called Marhoks before the Durgats held it in the 16th century,[119] and was afterwards in the possession of Joshua Mellersh.[120] Birtley House was perhaps originally Berkeley, for in 1604 Brian Annesley held 'Burtley,' otherwise Burkeley.[121] It was held by Henry Polsted, to whose fam.ly it had passed from Thomas Elliott of Yateley. Ralph de Fay, when lord of Bramley, had granted 10s. rent from the tenement of William 'of Berkele in Bromlegh' to the priory of Amesbury.[122] 'Bromley House in Bromley Street' was the residence of Dame Joan Pole in 1548.[123] The house was afterwards claimed by Lawrence Stoughton, to whom it descended by various enfeoffments from Drew, brother and heir of Charles Barentyne, son of Dame Joan.[124]

The church of the HOLY TRINITY, CHURCH originally a chapel attached to Shalford, has been grievously injured by several restorations and enlargements. It stands towards the north of the village street, near the corner at the cross roads. The site is level, and the churchyard is prettily planted with trees and shrubs, there being a fine old yew on the north side. It is built of Bargate stone rubble, with dressings of hard chalk in the older parts and of Bath stone in the new. The squat spire is shingled, and the chancel has been re-roofed in slates with very inharmonious effect.

Until 1850 the plan was cruciform, and consisted of a nave, about 57 ft. by 21 ft., chancel 31 ft. 6 in. by 21 ft., south transept (or Ludlow chapel) about 17 ft. square, and low tower and spire on the north forming a north transept of about the same dimensions. At the west end was a porch, within which was a plain doorway of mid-12th-century date, to which period the nave seems to have belonged. The head of this doorway, with zigzag moulding, has been rebuilt on modern jambs. The chancel and tower, which still remain, were evidently added in about 1210, and the south transept, roofed, with its gable parallel to that of the chancel, in about the middle of the 13th century. Both tower and chancel have been much modernized within, but externally, save for the slated roof of the chancel and some modern outbuildings and buttresses, they have been little altered. The chancel has a slight inclination to the north on plan.

There are three long lancets in the east wall ; the middle one slightly higher, and three in each of the side walls, worked in hard chalk, their internal splays radiating round the head, without scoinson arches—a mark of early date in the period. Under the easternmost lancet on the south side of the chancel is a piscina with a pointed arch, upon the apex of which a fleur-de-lys is carved in relief—an ornament of not

96 Add. Chart. (B.M.), 24839.
97 Ct. R. quoted by Manning and Bray, op. cit. ii, 86.
98 Deed quoted by Manning and Bray, op. cit. ii, 86.
98a Ibid.
99 See Frenches in Worplesdon.
100 Chan. Inq. p.m. 17 Edw. IV, no. 48.
101 Early Chan. Proc. lxvii, 239. It appears from the petition that Robert the elder had two sons named Thomas, and that Elizabeth was widow of the younger Thomas.
102 Will. P.C.C. proved 23 Nov. 1487.
103 Exch. Inq. p.m. 3 & 4 Hen. VII, 1059, no. 2.
104 Chan. Inq. p.m. (Ser. 2), lxxv, 53 ;
lxxxix, 133.
105 Ibid. 15 Eliz. clxv, 176.
106 Feet of F. Surr. East. 1 Jas. I ; Hil. 1 Jas. I.
107 Feet of F. Surr. East. 1655.
108 Ibid. Mich. 1671.
109 Manning and Bray, op. cit. ii, 87.
110 Chan. Inq. p.m. 6 Edw. II, no. 43.
111 Mins. Accts. bdle. 1010, no. 5.
112 Ibid. bdle. 1010, no. 6, 7.
113 Pat. 17 Hen. VI, pt. i, m. 13 d.
114 Feet of F. Surr. Mich. 34 Hen. VIII; Mich. 3 Edw. VI ; Mich. 2 & 3 Eliz.
115 Ibid. Trin. 16 Eliz.
116 Manning and Bray, op. cit. ii, 87.
117 Private inform.
118 Chan. Inq. p.m. (Ser. 2), cccxcvii, 90.
119 Misc. Bks. (Exch. L.T.R.), 168.
120 Chan. Inq. p.m. (Ser. 2), ccclxii, 52.
121 Ibid. cccvi, 149.
122 Maitland, Bracton's Note Bk. 553.
123 Star Chamb. Proc. Edw. VI, i, 82.
124 Chan. Proc. (Ser. 2), bdle. 170, no. 91.

very common occurrence in the beginning of the 13th century. The chancel arch is lofty, pointed, of two chamfered orders upon stop-chamfered jambs, having square-edged moulded imposts at the springing. On the south side of this arch are traces of a squint, which formerly opened into the south transept. The door to the vestry on the north of the chancel is modern, and it does not appear that there was ever a priest's door. The roofs of both chancel and nave are ancient, of collar-beam construction, with braces and struts, and of somewhat flat pitch—that of the former being only 45 degrees.

The destroyed transeptal chapel on the south had a single lancet in each wall, and on either side of the nave before its enlargement was a plain blocked doorway of later date than the 12th-century door in the west wall.

In 1850 the north aisle was added in the style of the early 14th century, and in 1875 the south aisle followed, being prolonged into what had been the transeptal chapel, which was rebuilt, and vestries were built to the east of the tower. The west front, with its 'Norman' windows, is modern. The present font is modern, as is also the chancel screen.

In the chancel windows is some heraldic and pattern glass, noticed by Cracklow in 1824, parts of which are ancient.

There are many monuments of late 17th and 18th-century date to the Ludlow family.

There are a silver paten of 1592 and a cup and paten-cover of 1664, besides more modern pieces, among the church plate.

There are six bells.

The registers of baptisms and marriages date from 1566, with three baptisms, entered later, in 1563, 1564, and 1565 respectively. In 1676 Bishop Morley for the first time licensed a burial-ground round the chapel of Bramley.[125] The register of burials begins from that year.

The parish church was probably ADVOWSON one of the three churches contained in Bishop Odo's fee in 1086.[126] Until 1844 Bramley was a chapelry of Shalford, but in that year it was constituted a separate parish under Sir Robert Peel's Act for establishing parishes.

In Thorncombe Street were five CHARITIES cottages built and owned by the parish. They are described by one who remembers them as disgracefully bad. They were sold by the parish in 1837.

Mrs. Finchett in 1815 left £100 stock to trustees to provide a dole of bread yearly for the poor.

Smith's Charity exists as in other Surrey parishes. About £22 10s. in all is distributed in bread and clothing.

CRANLEIGH

Cranlygh, Cranleigh, Cranlegh, Cranle (xiii cent.).[1] Cranley till recently. Cranleigh of late years to avoid confusion in post and railway with Crawley.

Cranleigh, a parish 8 miles south-west of Guildford, bounded on the north by Shere, Albury, and Wonersh, on the west by Alford and Hascombe, on the east by Ewhurst, on the south by the county of Sussex, contains 7,697 acres of land and 61 of water. It measures rather under 6 miles from north to south, just under 4 from east to west.

The northern part of the parish rises to about 700 ft. above the sea in Winterfold Hill, part of the great stretch of the heath and fir upland called Hurt Wood adjoining Blackheath to the north, and eastward rising still higher in Ewhurst, Holmbury, and Leith Hills, in Ewhurst, Ockley, and Wotton respectively. This part of the parish is Greensand. From the base of the hills to the Sussex border the soil is Wealden Clay, with superficial patches of sand and gravel. The village is on the latter, on Cranleigh Common, part of which is one of the best cricket pitches in Surrey. Smithwood Common is to the north-west of the village. Small detached parts of Cranleigh were added to Albury and Wonersh, and part of the border at Moxley was added to Shere 24 March 1884.[2]

The village is traversed by the road from Guildford to Horsham. The London, Brighton and South Coast Railway line from Guildford to Horsham, opened in 1865, passes through the parish, which contains two stations, Cranleigh and Baynards. The disused Wey and Arun Canal runs through the parish. On the clay are extensive brick and tile works. Formerly Cranleigh was a great seat of the iron industry.[3] The oak timber of Vachery was a valuable property sold to London merchants in the 15th century.[4] Vachery Pond, an artificially-made lake covering 61 acres, was used as a reservoir for the Wey and Arun Canal, and was probably enlarged for that purpose. But it is marked on the map before the canal existed, and was certainly made as a forge or hammer pond. Hammer Farm is on the stream, which is dammed up to make it, a little lower down. A fish-pond is mentioned at Vachery in the 13th century,[5] but it need not have been so extensive, probably was not, as the subsequent reservoir, even if it is included in this.

A Baptist chapel was built in 1889, and there is a small Wesleyan mission chapel on the common.

A few old-fashioned gabled and tile-hung houses remain near the church, including the post office, and another with a half-timber wing. Ancient houses of important families, now represented by farm-houses, also existed at Vachery (near Baynards in Ewhurst) and Knowle, and the north and south transeptal chapels in the church are still known respectively as the Vachery and Knoll (or Knowle) chapels. A house called Sansoms has some old panelling and other features of interest internally, although the exterior has been modernized.

There is a very picturesque 16th-century cottage at the south end of the village, but the houses have mostly

125 The licence is in the parish chest.
126 V.C.H. Surr. i, 301.
1 Add. MS. (B.M.), 7606.
2 Loc. Govt. Bd. Order 16532.
3 V.C.H. Surr. ii, 272.
4 Anct. D. (P.R.O.), C. 242.
5 Chan. Inq. p.m. 25 Edw. I, no. 50.

been rebuilt in a substantial but unpicturesque manner. The rectory is on the site of an old house surrounded by a moat now drained. Winterfold, on the hills, is the modern residence of Lord Alverstone, Lord Chief Justice, Nanhurst of Lady Carbutt, Barrihurst of Colonel W. A. Browne. Wyphurst is an old farm converted into a large modern house, the seat of Mr. Chadwyck Healey, C.B., K.C. It has been enlarged from designs by R. Blomfield, R.A., F.R.I.B.A. The other large houses of the parish are on the site of old manor-houses, and fall under the manorial description.

Part of the Roman road, which runs through the parish, and which probably went from near Shoreham to Staines, can be traced in Cranleigh parish.[6]

The Peek Institute was founded by the late Sir H. W. Peek, in memory of Lady Peek. It includes a club, with reading and billiard rooms, and a library.

Cranleigh School was opened 12 October 1865, and largely added to in 1869, when the chapel was built by the late Sir H. W. Peek at a cost of £6,500. Further additions have been made subsequently. The style is Early English, in brick, with stone wings. The school was originally called the Surrey County School, and special advantages were offered to Surrey boys. It is now equally open to boys from any place. The object of the school is to afford a public-school education on moderate terms, and the religious teaching is distinctively Church of England.[7] The whole of the original cost was borne by subscribers, and Sir H. W. Peek, Lord Ashcombe, Sir Walter Farquhar, Mr. Douglas D. Heath, and Archdeacon Sapte, rector of Cranleigh, were among the most prominent of the early supporters and governors of the school. The Rev. J. Merriman, D.D., St. John's College, Cambridge, was the first head master. The late head master was the Rev. G. C. Allen, M.A., St. John's College, Cambridge.[8] Mr. C. H. Tyler, M.A., was appointed 1909.

A reputed native of Cranleigh was Thomas de Cranleigh, Fellow of Merton, 1366, first Warden of Winchester, 1382, Warden of New College, 1389, Chancellor of the University of Oxford, 1390, Archbishop of Dublin, 1397, Chancellor of Ireland 1397 to 1400; he died in 1417, aged about eighty.

Cranleigh seems at the time of the Domesday Survey to have formed part of the vills of Shiere, Gomshall, and Bramley. The parish of Cranleigh contains Vachery, part of Pollingfold, Holdhurst, Knowle, Utworth, and Redinghurst, the first three of which were members of Shiere or Gomshall, and the last two of Bramley.[9]

VACHERY in Cranleigh parish was
MANORS a member of the manor of Shiere Vachery. The lords of Shiere kept it in

their own hands. The name itself (*vaccaria*, or dairy) gives sufficient reason for this. Henry III granted bucks to John son of Geoffrey to stock his park of Vachery.[10] His son John obtained a grant of a weekly market and an annual fair at Cranleigh, on the eve, feast, and morrow of Lammas Day,[11] and appropriated to himself free warren there.[12] There was a manor-house in Vachery in 1296;[13] at present there is a farm-house and the remains of a moat. The Earls of Ormond resided either at Shiere or Vachery.[14] The farm-house was sold by Earl Onslow in 1783.[15] Nanhurst Farm cum Treewell, part of Vachery, was sold by Lord Onslow in 1815.[16]

In 1820 Vachery was the property of Thomas Lowndes.[17]

HOLDHURST Manor (Holehurst, xiv cent.) was an outlying portion of the manor of Shiere, which was called 'Sutton or Holhurst at Downe.'[1] The lands belonging to it in Shiere and Abinger are no doubt the lands which it appears from Domesday were seized by the Bishop of Bayeux, and added to his manor of Bramley.[18] These are treated under Shiere. Later, Holdhurst in Cranleigh and Holdhurst in Shiere became separate estates.

The history of the property, before its division, seems to be as follows :—

In 1297 Walter of Holdhurst conveyed land in Bramley and Shiere to his son John.[19] There was a Walter of Holdhurst living at Cranleigh in the early years of the reign of Edward III.[20] In May 1368-9 Thomas of Holdhurst and his wife, Alice, were in possession of the manor;[21] possibly incorrectly so-called, for the Court Rolls of Gomshall Towerhill of 1367 say that Thomas Holdhurst held a yard-land in Cranleigh. It continued in his family till the reign of Henry VIII, when, on the death of Thomas of Holdhurst, John Wood and Arnold Champion succeeded in 1532.[22] Arnold Champion died seised of a moiety of the manor in 1546.[23] According to Manning and Bray it was afterwards the property of Richard Wood (possibly son of the above John) and of John his son. His sister and heir, Agnes wife of Richard Welles, conveyed it to Richard Onslow of Knowle, 31 December 1568[24]; and in 1584 James Hobson and his wife Anne conveyed a moiety of the manor to Richard Browne and Edward Onslow.[25]

Meanwhile Sutton in Shere was now separated from Holdhurst in Cranleigh and the connexion forgotten. Edmund Hill was in possession of the whole of 'Sutton *alias* Holhurst *alias* Halhurst at Downe,' meaning Sutton in Shere, in 1554;[26] but this had no connexion with the land in Cranleigh.[27] Sir Edward Onslow, son of Thomas, was in possession at his death in 1615[28] of the Cranleigh land.

[6] *Surr. Arch. Coll.* vi, 1, and private information to the writer from the late Mr. James Park Harrison, who traced the road.

[7] See also *V.C.H. Surr.* ii, 221.

[8] Mr. Allen was instituted to the living of Send, Oct. 1908.

[9] Vachery was a member of Shiere Manor (Chan. Inq. p.m. 25 Edw. I, 50; Fine R. 27 Edw. I, m. 1). Pollingfold and Holdhurst were held of Gomshall Towerhill; Chan. Inq. p.m. (Ser. 2), ccxlvii, 72; Ct. R. quoted by Manning and Bray, op. cit. i, 539. Utworth was a member of Bramley, and Redinghurst broke off from Utworth; Feet of F. Surr.

[10] 19 Hen. III, 16; Add. Chart. (B.M.), 17606.

[11] Close, 29 Hen. III. m. 15.

[11] Chart. R. 56 Hen. III, m. 2.

[12] *Plac. de Quo Warr.* (Rec. Com.), 742*b*.

[13] Chan. Inq. p.m. 25 Edw. I, no. 50.

[14] See Mins. Accts. bdle. 1250, no. 4, where under the heading Shere and Vachery the accountant states that there was no return from the 'said house' since it was assigned as the lord's 'hospicium.'

[15] Egerton MS. 2651, fol. 213.

[16] Deeds *penes* Messrs. Whateley & Barlow, Godalming.

[17] Egerton MS. 2651, fol. 215.

[18] *V.C.H. Surr.* i, 305*b*.

[19] Feet of F. Surr. 26 Edw. I, 85.

[20] Add. Chart. (B.M.), 7610, 5940, 7628; and Ct. R. of Gomshall Towerhill.

[21] Anct. D. (P.R.O.), B. 3942.

[22] Ct. R. quoted by Manning and Bray, op. cit. i, 539.

[23] Chan. Inq. p.m. (Ser. 2), lxxxv, 71.

[24] Manning and Bray, op. cit. iii, 539. Cf. Feet of F. Surr. Hil. 11 Eliz.

[25] Ibid. Mich. 26 & 27 Eliz.

[26] Misc. Bks. Exch. L.T.R. clxix, 211; clxviii, 69.

[27] See below, Shere, for Sutton descent.

[28] Chan. Inq. p.m. (Ser. 2), cccli, 105. Cf. Feet of F. Surr. East. 4 Jas. I.

On 10 September 1616 Elizabeth Onslow, widow, and her son Thomas Onslow made a settlement of 'all and every the manors of Cranley *alias* Cranleigh, Knowle, Holehurst, and Utworth in the parishes and hamlets of Bramley, Shalford, Wonersh, Guildford, Hascombe, and Cranley,' on the intended marriage of Thomas with Mary daughter of Sir Samuel Lennard. Thomas died the following December, perhaps before the marriage could take place. Richard his brother succeeded him.[79] This shows that Holdhurst in Cranleigh was united in the hands of the Onslows, and that Sutton in Shere (q.v.) was not then considered part of it. The manors are described as 'late of Sir Richard Onslow, Thomas' grandfather,' who died in 1571.

Holdhurst continued in the Onslow family till 1818, when it was alienated to Thomas Puttock.[80] In 1823 Mr. Walter Hanham bought it. About 1839 it came into the possession of Mr. John Bradshaw,[81] and in 1878 the present owner, Sir George Francis Bonham, bart., H.M. representative at Berne, bought it from Mr. Bradshaw's heir.

The early history of *KNOWLE* Manor (Knolle, xiii to xviii cent.) is somewhat obscure.[82] Robert, William, and Henry at Knowle witnessed deeds at Cranleigh in 1303–4.[83] Peter at Knowle granted a house and lands in Shere to Bartholomew of Shere in 1308–9,[84] and a few years afterwards Bartholomew released land in Shere to Henry at Knowle and his wife Cassandra.[85] In 1336 Henry and Cassandra granted Cravenhurst out in farm.[86] Walter at Knowle witnessed deeds at Cranleigh in 1360, 1404, and 1411.[87] In 1481–2 the trustees of Thomas Slyfield of Great Bookham conveyed Knowle to Robert Harding, afterwards master of the Goldsmiths' Company.[88] He bequeathed it to his nephew Thomas Harding.[89] Robert Harding left two crofts and a cottage towards the maintenance of the aisle called Our Lady Aisle in Cranleigh Church.[90] In 1549 William Harding of London, mercer, died seised of Knowle, which he had bequeathed to his daughter Catherine,[41] with whom it went in marriage to Richard Onslow.[42] The manor henceforward remained in the Onslow family. At one time they resided there,[43] and Arthur Onslow, the Speaker, took from it his title of Viscount Cranley, since merged in the earldom of Onslow. It was for sale with the rest of the Onslow estates in Cranleigh in 1815, and passed ultimately with Holdhurst to Mr. Hanham and Mr. Bradshaw and to Sir George F. Bonham, bart.

REDINGHURST (Redinghers, xiii cent.; Riding-

hersh, xiv cent.). This manor was originally a member of Utworth. A deed of the latter end of the 13th century records the quitclaim to Robert of Redinghurst of the service which he owed to Thomas of Utworth for Redinghurst, except one penny yearly.[44] In 1331 John son of Robert of Redinghurst was enfeoffed of his father's lands in Cranleigh.[45] His son John was still living in September 1364,[46] and seems to have been succeeded by Walter Redinghurst.[47] In 1494 the manor was conveyed by the trustees of John Redinghurst to John Bysshe of Burstow,[48] whose grandson William settled it on his son John in 1544.[49] John Bysshe bequeathed it to his wife Mary.[50] In 1635 it was the property of Edward Bysshe.[51] His son, Sir Edward, Garter and Clarencieux King of Arms, was dealing with it in 1654,[52] and later conveyed it to John Hill.[53]

BYSSHE. *Or a cheveron between three roses gules.*

William Chennell and his wife Mary conveyed it to Henry Chennell in 1780.[54] It passed soon after to Mrs. Ayling, and from her to Henry Streater Gill, who sold it to Mr. Evershed, owner in 1804.[55]

UTWORTH Manor, which extends into Wonersh and Dunsfold parishes,[56] was held of Bramley. In 1234 John de Fay, lord of Bramley, granted the Abbess of Fontevraud 2 marks rent from Utworth in exchange for an annuity due to her.[57] Other rents were due from the manor to Beatrice, mother of John de Fay.[58] Roger de Clare confirmed the grant of a rent from Walter of Utworth to the Abbess of Wherwell towards the support of a chaplain in the chapel of the Garden of St. Mary.[59] Walter son of Elias of Utworth laid claim to Chilworth Church in 1224,[60] and was probably the Walter of Utworth who conveyed the manor to his son Thomas in return for a life annuity in 1247–8.[51] There is a late 13th-century agreement between Edmund and Lawrence of Utworth as to land in Bramley.[52] · They seem to have been succeeded by Thomas of Utworth, who witnessed many charters at Cranleigh.[53] In 1394–5 Walter Utworth witnessed a grant to John Redinghurst.[54] William Utworth was living in 1462.[55] In 1580 William Morgan, who is said to have been a descendant of William Utworth's granddaughter Catherine, held the manor,[56] which he settled on his son John, after-

79 Com. Pleas D. Enr. 14 Jas. I, m. 33.
80 Ct R.
81 Brayley, *Hist. of Surr.* v, 172.
82 Manning and Bray (*Hist. of Surr.* i, 536) state that Robert at Knoll possessed it temp. Edw. I, and that a settlement was made on his son William in 1315–16.
83 Add. Chart. 5939, 7613.
84 Feet of F. Surr. 2 Edw. II, 28.
85 Ibid. 7 Edw. II, 6.
86 Add. Chart. 17304.
87 Ibid. 7631, 7616, 17337.
88 Close, 21 Edw. IV, m. 9; Manning and Bray, op. cit. i, 537.
89 *Surr. Arch. Coll.* vi, 38.
40 Ibid. 41. He died Feb. 1503–4.
41 Chan. Inq. p.m. (Ser. 2), lxxxviii, 78.
42 Feet of F. Div. Co. Hil. 3 Eliz.
43 *Hist. MSS. Com. Rep.* xiv, App. pt. ix, 476.
44 Add. Chart. 7606.

44 Ibid. 7610.
46 Close, 38 Edw. III, m. 7 d.
47 Add. Chart. 7603.
48 It was granted him by the trustees of a certain John Redinghurst, decd.; Add. Chart. 7626, 7597, 7638, 7622; Manning and Bray (op. cit. i, 540) state that Joan, one of the daughters and co-heirs of John Redinghurst, married John Bysshe.
49 Add. Chart. 7641.
50 Chan. Inq. p.m. (Ser. 2), cxlviii, 23.
51 Feet of F. Surr. Mich. 11 Chas. I.
52 Ibid. Mich. 1654; Trin. 1655.
53 Ibid. East. 13 Chas. III.
54 Ibid. East. 20 Geo. III.
55 Manning and Bray, *Hist. of Surr.* i, 540.
54 Lease in 1821 of part of the waste of Utworth manor near Dunsfold Church.
57 Feet of F. Surr. 19 Hen. III, 16. Thomas of Utworth bought a release

from this rent in 1260–1; Feet of F. Surr. 45 Hen. III, 24.
58 Ibid. 25 Hen. III, 20.
59 See Artington; Chartulary of Whetwell Abbey; Egerton, MS. 2104, A. fol. 105b.
60 Maitland, *Bracton's Note Bk.* 928.
51 Feet of F. Surr. 32 Hen. III, 28 and 37.
52 Ibid. 12 Edw. I, 17. This Edmund was juror in a perambulation of Windsor Forest in 1300. Select Pleas of the Forest (Selden Soc., xiii), 117.
53 Add. Chart. 7609, 7610, 7623, 7631.
54 Ibid. 7604.
55 Cal. Pat. 1461–7, p. 201.
56 According to *Visit. of Surr.* (Harl. Soc. xliii, 23), Catherine daughter of William Utworth married John Gunter, and their daughter Catherine married Henry Morgan. They had a grandson William Morgan.

wards Sir John Morgan.[67] He sold it m 1614 to Sir Edward Onslow,[68] in whose family it remained till 1815, when it was sold to Mrs. Sarah Shurlock of Bramley. She died before 1821, and her daughter and heiress married Mr. Charles Hemming of Dorsetshire.[69] Mr. Walter Hemming sold Utworth in 1889 to the late Sir Edward Carbutt. The house is now inhabited by the bailiff of Lady Carbutt's estate at Nanhurst.

RYE FARM, if we may conclude that it was the tenement known as 'la Ree,' was released in 1394 by John grandson of Walter at Ree to John Redinghurst.[70] In 1406-7 it was the dower of Tiffania widow of John Redinghurst.[71] It was conveyed to Robert Harding with Knowle Manor.[71]

NANHURST (Knauenhurst, xiv cent.), part of Vachery,[72] was rented by Edmund Constantin of Robert Redinghurst in 1303.[74] It belonged at one time to Lord Onslow, but was for sale in 1778. It

gate of stone erected as a memorial in 1880. The boundaries of the churchyard have been greatly extended within the last half-century, to meet the growth in population.

The church is built of ironstone rubble and conglomerate, with a little Bargate rubble, and with dressings of Bargate stone and clunch, the modern portions being in the same stone with Bath stone dressings. A good deal of the old walling is plastered externally. The roofs are still in part covered with Horsham slabs, and the quaint conical roof of the tower, with a gablet at the apex from which rises the weathercock, is shingled. The nave roof is old and of oak, but the roofs of the aisles, transepts, vestry, and chancel, are modern, and chiefly of stained deal, those of the aisles being of wretched and flimsy construction. The modern porch (1862) is of oak. Few Surrey churches have suffered more barbarous illtreatment under the name of 'restoration' than this.

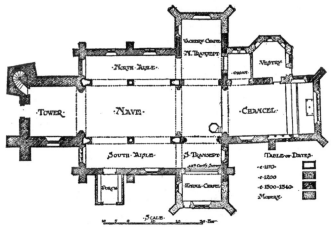

PLAN OF CRANLEIGH CHURCH

was part of the estate of the late Sir Edward Carbutt, bart. The tenement called Furshulle, or Freeswell (xix cent.), also part of Vachery, granted to Walter at How and William Clynon in 1303,[75] was settled by the latter on his son Henry,[76] while Henry at How granted to Walter at How two crofts and a messuage in Furshullshamme in 1337.[77]

The church of *ST. NICHOLAS* stands
CHURCH picturesquely on rising ground, backed by beautiful old trees. The well-kept churchyard has an exceptionally fine cedar and other trees, besides two yews, one near the chancel, of great antiquity, and is approached through a modern lych-

Very few are built on such spacious lines. The tower is unusually large, almost a square of 20 ft. internally, with walls 3 ft. 9 in. thick, and very massive buttresses ; the nave is slightly wider, and 36 ft. in length ; the transepts are about 16 ft. in width (they have been lengthened in modern times), and the chancel is about 34 ft. long by 20 ft. wide. Its axis inclines about 5 degrees to the north of east. Both nave and chancel are exceptionally lofty, the walls of the former being about 30 ft. in height. The present timber south porch is modern—a memorial to Jacob Ellery—and the vestry and organ-chamber on the north side of the chancel are also modern,

[67] Chan. Inq. p.m.(Ser. 2), cclxxxi, 85.
[68] Feet of F. Surr. Hil. 11 Jas. I.
[69] Deeds *penes* Messrs. Whateley & Barlow, Godalming.
[70] Add. Chart. 7604 ; see also Add.

Chart. 7631, in which William at Ree is stated to have land called 'Church land' in Cranleigh.
[71] Ibid. 7603.
[72] Close, 21 Edw. IV, m. 9.

[73] Onslow Deeds.
[74] Add. Chart. 7613.
[75] Ibid. 5939.
[76] Ibid. 5940.
[77] Ibid. 7602.

by Butterfield, under whom the restoration of the church, in 1845 and subsequently, was carried out. The north and south transepts originally had lean-to roofs, a continuation of those over the aisles, and only projected about 5 ft. beyond the aisles. The northern was known as the Vachery Chapel, the southern as the Knowle or Knoll Chapel. There seems to have been another chapel in the south aisle and probably in the north aisle also.

There is evidence of the existence of a church here in 1244, and the short nave preserves the dimensions of an early aisleless nave, which no doubt had a short chancel occupying the area of the central part of the crossing. This would give an internal dimension of about 36 ft. in length by 20 ft. in width, and these sizes and proportions coincide with those of the original church of Alfold. As early as the last quarter of the 12th century, this church of Cranleigh must have needed additional space. Aisles were therefore thrown out on both sides in about 1170, of which the round columns and responds, or half-piers, remain with characteristic mouldings and angle-spurs to their bases, all executed in clunch. Also there has been built into the pier of the arch from the north aisle to the transept one of the peculiar cat's-head corbels which were a common feature in the period. It was a bold idea of the 12th-century architect to divide the nave space into two arches, with a central column and such short responds ; probably he was led to it by the necessity of economizing the scarce building materials at his disposal. But anyway, the result seems to have been that the arches and capitals of the arcades were crushed by the weight of wall above them, being provided also with insufficient abutment, so that before a century and a half had expired it was found necessary when widening the first aisles to renew the capitals of the columns and responds, and to put new arches upon them. The capitals are of an octagonal form, moulded in accordance with their date, c. 1325. The first aisles were probably not much more than 7 ft. wide. In about 1200–10 chapels were thrown out on either side of the new chancel, the arches of which remain. In the subsequent widening of the aisles, the arches leading from them into the transepts were rebuilt. That in the south aisle has a corbel closely resembling one in Albury Old Church, of about the same date.

The main arch of the north transept is of two orders with moulded imposts, of a section common in the south of Sussex ; that to the south transept has shafts of trefoil section under a capital with a circular abacus. These are in chalk, and are exactly like the shafts to an arch in the north transept at Godalming. The wide and plain south doorway, approached through a modern porch, and the windows and buttresses of this aisle are all of about 1300, though so much re-tooled that they might be taken for modern work. The two windows in the opposite wall, made in clunch, are good examples of the plain square-headed openings found in the aisles of this period. They are of two lights, those in the eastern window being much wider than those in the western, with ogee trefoiled heads to the lights and cusping in the spaces over. Internally they have oak lintels. The three-light window in the west end of the north aisle is modern, and a copy of that in the corresponding position in the south aisle, the heads being filled with reticulated tracery.

A puzzling feature is the pair of piers, now carrying nothing but image niches of doubtful antiquity with modern statues, at the east end of what was the original nave. There can be little doubt that they were built as chancel-arch piers in about 1300, on the site of the original but much narrower chancel arch, and that when the work had got so far, the present extended chancel was decided upon and the piers left as built. The capitals are of the same section as those put upon the older nave piers. The present chancel arch and the chancel must have been built immediately after, and may be dated at about 1300 by the fine triple sedilia in the south wall. These have moulded arches with a trefoiled inner order like those at Dunsfold, but the shafts, with their capitals and bases, are modern. The existing east window is modern, having been refashioned on a larger scale by Butterfield, who designed the elaborate reredos and tabernacle work ; the side windows are modern and very bad, dating from 1845 or before. The piscina and all other features in the chancel are modern or modernized.

The western tower has been practically left untouched by the mischievous 'restorations' that have so greatly injured the rest of the church. It dates from about 1300, but the two windows in the ground story would appear to be insertions of slightly later date, the west window exhibiting flowing tracery of about 1340, in clunch, bearing such a strong resemblance to that of the east window in Witley Church, that they must have been executed by the same masons. Both are of three lights, with a cinquefoil figure of flowing tracery in the head, the tracery-plane at Cranleigh, and in the window of the south wall also, being recessed by a hood and outer arch, as well as by a deep hollow, which gives a rich effect of shadow. The windows of the upper stories are short lancets, single in the intermediate stage and coupled in the bell-chamber. The original floor, of massive timbers, remains above the ground story. The tower arch, in clunch, has recessed chamfered orders with a scroll-moulding for the hood. The west doorway, which has continuous mouldings, a chamfer and a wave moulding, with a scroll section for the hood, retains its original oak door, hinges, and closing-ring. The newel-stair is contained in an enormous buttress-like projection, of curiously irregular plan, at the north-west angle.

The modern work of 1845 and 1862 is inharmonious in character, and the extension of the transepts, with high-pitched compass roofs and coped gables, has quite altered the original aspect of this part of the church and confused its architectural history.

Of the roofs, that of the nave only is old, probably dating from about 1300. It is quite plain in character, and the present skimpy tie-beams are modern. The chancel roof is a pretentious hammer-beam construction in stained deal, and the aisle roofs are of the meanest description. One of the parclose screens remains, now spanning the archway of the Knowle Chapel, but formerly in the main arch of the south transept. It is heavily-built, and, of course, of late design, having fourteen openings with ogee-cinquefoiled heads, and dates from the middle of the 15th century. The pulpit of the 1845 restoration, was made out of the rich traceried panels, cornice, and pinnacles of another ancient screen dating from about the same period. On the chancel arch are the marks of the rood screen, but no trace of the stair-turret, if any ever existed, remains. A plain old lectern, after a period of banishment to the belfry, has now disappeared altogether.

The church, in 1845, was found to have been extensively decorated with wall paintings, which were unhappily swept away to give place to raw modern plaster. These occurred over the chancel arch and in the spandrels of the nave arcades, but no records have been preserved as to the dates and subjects.

Until the beginning of the 19th century there was an exceptional quantity of ancient stained glass of very fine design remaining. A Jesse-tree was almost complete in the window of the Knowle Chapel in 1798, but within a few years some fragments only were left, including, in the centre, a headless seated figure holding a rose, a Crucifixion in the upper part, and, in Lombardic lettering, the names Josaphat, Ashur, Salomon, Ezechial, and Joathan. In 1841 scarcely anything of this remained, and some fragments had probably been removed by Lord Onslow to West Clandon Church, but, if so, they no longer exist there. When Manning and Bray published their *History of Surrey* in 1808–14 there also remained in the Vachery Chapel on the north side effigies of our Lord and the Blessed Virgin seated, and two angels censing.[78] The figure of the Blessed Virgin has disappeared, but those of our Lord and the two angels, together with some good pattern-work, have been worked up into the reticulated tracery of the modern east window of the chancel. Our Lord, seated on the throne in a green tunic and yellow mantle, has the right hand raised in benediction, while with the left He holds the cross and orb. The background is ruby, with a white border. Some of the pattern-work in the other quatrefoil figures of this window, consisting of crosses with fleur-de-lys ends, in white on red and gold on red, is also ancient, the date of the whole being c. 1340.

The font, standing to the west of the first pillar in the north nave arcade, is of doubtful antiquity ; if not new, severe re-tooling has robbed it of all appearance of age. The bowl is octagonal and quite plain, standing upon a large central drum and eight small shafts without capitals, having a cable-moulding twined in and out round them, for a base.

Outside, beneath the east window, is an early 14th-century coffin-lid, with a cross within a circle on a long stem carved in low relief. Manning and Bray and Brayley mention a slab in the nave floor, with the legend in Gothic capitals :—

WALTER KNOLL GIST YCY . DIEV DE S'ALME
EIT MERCI

Also a brass plate, formerly existing in the chancel, to William Sydney, esq., who died 8 October 1449. Both these seem to have disappeared early in the 19th century.

Within the chancel rails on the south side is a brass half-figure of a priest[79] in mass vestments, with scrolls proceeding from his mouth, bearing the words :—

ESTO MIHI PECCATORI : SANA ANIMĀ MEĀ QUIA
PECCAVI TIBI

Up to the restoration of 1845 a good specimen of the combined altar-tomb and Easter sepulchre, in Sussex marble, remained against the north wall of the chancel. Most improperly, it was then demolished, and the brasses upon and over it were permitted to disappear. It bore the effigies of a man and woman with a child between them, all kneeling, each having inscriptions issuing from the mouth, the man's having the words : ' Have m'cy Jhesu in honour of thy gloriovs resvrreccion ' ; the woman's : ' And grant vs the merite of thy bytter Passion ' ; and the child's : ' Accipe parentes, et infantem, bone X͞pe.'

Fortunately a facsimile of the plate on the wall behind is preserved in an engraving, probably of the size of the original, in Hussey's *Churches of Kent, Sussex, and Surrey*. This, as is often the case in Easter sepulchres, was a representation of the Resurrection of our Lord, Who is stepping out of the tomb bearing the cross and pennon and displaying the bleeding wounds, while guarding the tomb are four soldiers. Detached from the tomb, on the other side of the chancel, was a shield bearing a merchant's mark and the initials R. H. ; and on the tomb itself, beneath the figures, was the imperfect inscription, which when complete read : ' Of your Charite pray for the soulys of Robert Hardyng late Alderman & Goldsmith of London and Agas his Wyffe whos body here lyeth heryed, And departyd this present lyfe the XVIII day of Febrvar͞y in the yere of ovre Lord God MCCCCC and III for whos Sowlys and all x͞pen we pray you say Paternoster and Ave.' Above the man's figure were the arms of Harding, which were : Argent a bend sable with three martlets or thereon.

Among the stones cast out of the church in 1845 were three inscribed :—

' 1664. May 19ᵗʰ Sir Richard Onslow, Bart., aged 63.'
' 1679. Aug͡t 27ᵗʰ Dame Elizabeth Onslow his widow, aged 78.'
' 1688. July 21ˢᵗ Sir Arthur Onslow, Bart., aged 67.'

On the outside of the south wall of the south aisle is a tablet of Sussex marble, very weather-worn, bearing the date 1630. A few others of no great age or importance have been re-fixed on the aisle side of the north arcade.

The bells are six in number, the oldest with the inscription : PRAIS GOD 1599 A W, and a coin. Two others have : 1638 BRYAN ELDRIDGE ; another is by Bryan Eldridge, 1660 ; the treble by William Eldridge, 1709 ; and the third, re-cast in 1862, used to have the inscription : OUR HOPE IS IN THE LORD R.E. 1605.

With the exception of a silver paten of 1789 the church plate is modern and uninteresting.

The registers commence in 1566 and have been somewhat irregularly kept. As might be expected, they contain numerous entries relating to the Onslow family.

The modern chapel of ease of St. Andrew, on the Common, was dedicated in 1900.

ADVOWSON The origins of Cranleigh as a parish are unknown. In Domesday it is not recognized. It belonged to the extensive manors of Shiere and Gomshall, and when Shiere was divided in 1299, the greater part of it was included in the manor called Shiere Vachery or

[78] Manning and Bray, op. cit. i, 540. The late Major Heales, F.S.A., in his paper on this church in *Surr. Arch. Coll.* vi, 30, in recording the general disappearance of the old glass, omits to note that parts of these Vachery Chapel fragments still survive.

[79] Perhaps commemorating Richard Caryngton, rector, who died in 1507.

Shiere cum Vachery and Cranleigh. It is recognized as a parish in the Taxation of Pope Nicholas, 1291. The advowson of the rectory was granted in 1244 by Roger de Clare, lord of Shiere, to John Fitz Geoffrey.[79] Robert Montalt, who had married Emma, widow of Richard son of john, presented to the church after the latter's death.[81] Two of the coheirs of Richard son of john, viz. Matilda Beauchamp and Robert Clifford, had possession of the advowson. The successive representatives of their families presented to the church[83] in alternation till the attainders of john, Lord Clifford, 1461, and Richard Earl of Warwick, 1471, after which the advowson was escheat to the Crown.[83] Henry VIII granted it to Sir Edward Bray,[84] who sold it to Walter Cresswell,[85] to whose son William it descended.[86] At his death one-third descended to his granddaughter Elizabeth, the other two-thirds to his son Christopher,[87] who ultimately inherited his niece's portion.[88] He sold it to Michael Pyke in 1640.[89] From this time it frequently changed hands. In 1691 Ralph Drake and his wife Mary and Anne Glyd conveyed it to Henry Cheynell.[90] The Rev. james Fielding inherited it at his father's death late in the 18th

century.[91] In 1806 the Rev. John Wolfe was patron.[92] It is now in the gift of Sir W. Peek, bart. The chapel at La Vacherie, to which chaplains were appointed in 1302 and subsequently,[93] was only the north transept of the parish church of St. Nicholas, dedicated in honour of the Trinity.

There was an anniversary in Cranleigh Church maintained from lands in the parish. Edward VI granted these to Henry Polsted.[94]

PEEK, Baronet. *Azure a star argent with three crescents argent in the chief.*

Cranleigh Cottage Hospital, founded in 1859, is said to have been the first of the kind set up in England. It is partly self-supporting, patients paying on a varied scale according to position, and partly supported by subscriptions.

CHARITIES

Smith's Charity is distributed in Cranleigh, as in other Surrey parishes, to the value of £23 18s. 8d., charged on the Warbleton Estate, Sussex.

DUNSFOLD

Duntesfaud and Dunterfeld (xiii cent.) ; Dunttesfold (xiv cent.).

Dunsfold is a small parish bounded on the west by Chiddingfold and Godalming, on the north by Hascombe and Bramley, on the east by Hascombe and Alfold, on the south by the county of Sussex. It contains 4,028 acres of land and 11 of water. The parish is roughly a parallelogram of 3 miles from north to south and 2 miles from east to west. An outlying portion to the north, between the parishes of Bramley and Wonersh, is now the ecclesiastical parish of Graffham, and is included in the civil parish of Bramley, to which it was transferred with Brookwell in 1884 ; at the same time High Billinghurst was transferred from Bramley to Dunsfold. The parishes hereabouts were formerly very much intermixed, portions of various manors being included parochially in the parish where the *caput manerii* lay. Dunsfold, not named in Domesday, was probably in 1086 uninhabited woodland belonging to the manor of Bramley. It is mentioned in the Taxation of Pope Nicholas, 1291, but is not separately assessed in the early Subsidy Rolls of Edward III.[1]

Dunsfold is still one of the most completely rural and sequestered parishes of the county. The northern part of the consolidated parish just touches the Atherfield Clay at the foot of the escarpment of the Green-

sand hills, but the main part of it is on the Wealden Clay. There is a patch of sand and gravel on Dunsfold Common. The parish is still thickly wooded, and the oak trees are very numerous. There were iron forges, or furnaces, in the 16th century in the parish. Thomas Gratwyck and Richard March owned three in Dunsfold, and Thomas Glyde one at Durfold, which is in the parish.[2]

In 1653 the Dunsfold forges were still at work,[3] and as late as 1758 in a list of militia William Gardiner, 'furnaceman' of Dunsfold appears.[4] Burningfold[5] Wood and Furnace Bridge preserve the names of places of charcoal-burning and iron-founding. Norden's *Surveyor* says that the woods at Burningfold were destroyed by the ironworks ; but in the 18th century charcoal was being made for the government gunpowder mills Just over the Sussex border close to Burningfold, and the woods exist still. Bricks and tiles are now made in the parish. The disused Wey and Arun Canal skirts the eastern side of the parish.

Dunsfold village consists chiefly of small houses and cottages scattered round a very large green. The cottages are highly picturesque and a feature is the number of well-designed chimneys. One of these cottages has an unglazed window with wooden stanchions and shutter, such as were the rule in houses before glass came into general use. Mr.

[79] Feet of F. Div. Co. 28 Hen. III, 199.

[81] Egerton MS. 2032, fol. 11, 50.

[83] Egerton MS. 2032, fol. 11 ; 2034, fol. 38 ; *Wykeham's Reg.* (Hants Rec. Soc.), i, 76, 106, 117, 124 ; De Banco R. 749, m. 339.

[83] Chan. Inq. p.m. 4 Edw. IV, 52.

[84] L. and P. Hen. VIII, xiv (2), 780 (33).

[85] Feet of F. Surr. Hil. 22 Eliz.

[86] Ibid. Trin. 2 Jas. I.

[87] Chan. Inq. p.m. (Ser. 2), cccxcvii, 93.

[92] Ibid. ccccxxxvi, 20 ; William Holt presented to the living in 1632. See Inst. Bks. (P.R.O.).

[89] Feet of F. Surr. Hil. 16 Chas. I.

[90] Ibid. Trin. 3 Will. and Mary.

[91] Manning and Bray, *Hist. of Surr.* i, 546.

[92] Brayley, *Hist. of Surr.* v, 173.

[93] Winton Epis. Reg. Beaufort, fol. 55a.

[94] Pat. 2 Edw. VI, pt. i, m. 14.

[1] *V.C.H. Surr.* i, 441.

[2] S.P. Dom. Eliz. xcv, 20, 61 ; xcvi, 199. See Loseley MSS. Letter of 31 Oct. 1588.

[3] *V.C.H. Surr.* ii, 273.

[4] List of militia of the three southwest hundreds of Surrey, at Loseley.

[5] Burningfold however may be a name connected with a kindred, the Burnings, like Burningham in Norfolk. There was a Burningfold in Haslemere (rentals of 1517 and 1653), a small tenement, perhaps Buringfold's originally.

Ralph Nevill[1a] notes the common occurrence of slabs of Sussex or Petworth marble for steps and paving-stones, and occasionally in mantel-pieces, in these cottages and houses—a fact due to its having been dug in the neighbourhood of the church until within the memory of persons now living.[4]

At Burningfold is a fine old house of timber framework. The two gables of the front are covered with tile-hanging, but in the central space on ground and first floors the original construction is exposed and exhibits some square and circle patterns in the framing, bearing considerable resemblance to the work at Great Tangley. There are some good mullioned windows with lead glazing, and the interior retains a little oak panelling.

The Baptist chapel was erected in 1883, and the elementary school in 1839.

BURNINGFOLD Manor seems origi-
MANORS nally to have been a member of Bramley.[7]

There is record of Stephen 'de Brunfeld' in a suit against the Abbot of Westminster in 1199.[8] In 1233–4 John de Fay, lord of Bramley, sued Richard of Burningfold for customary service in Bramley.[9] In 1229 John de Fay gave to Roger de Bydon land in the woods of Burningfold and Witherfold;[10] and in 1235–6 Roger granted the land to Sandon Hospital to be held of him.[11] The Witherfold lands reverted to the Crown and were granted to Ralph Camoys of Wotton.[12]

Richard of Burningfold and his wife Isabel were dealing with land in Dunsfold in 1271–2,[13] and he was one of the tenants who in 1280 paid rent due from Bramley Manor to the Prior of Carisbrook in accordance with a grant of Ralph de Fay.[14] In 1386–7 Robert Adam and his wife Elizabeth sold to Robert March certain lands in Dunsfold with the reversion of one-third of a quarter of a house which Joan widow of John of Burningfold was holding in dower.[15] Two centuries later Burningfold was in the possession of William March and of John his son,[16] and in 1569 of John's son Richard March,[17] who was succeeded in 1584 by his son William.[18] In 1604 William March sold the manor, all manorial rights, and the ironworks there[18a] to George Duncombe for £886.[18b] But John Middleton, Richard Wyatt of Hall Place, Shackleford, and Thomas Burdett, also had claims on the estate,[19] and Duncombe sold his rights to the other three in 1608.[20]

Middleton seems to have purchased those of Burdett, for in 1619 Henry Wyatt inherited one-third of the manor at his father's death,[21] John Middleton conveyed two-thirds to Arthur Middleton in 1622,[22] and finally Henry Wyatt sold his rights in the manor to Arthur Middleton,[23] whose two youngest sons succeeded to the manor.[24] They sold it in 1657 to Henry, afterwards Sir Henry Goring, bart., whose direct descendant, Sir Harry Goring of Horsham, conveyed the manor to John Tanner in 1722.[25] He died in 1751, and his executors sold it about 1756 to Viscount Montagu (who died in 1767),[26] and Manning and Bray incorrectly state that his son Anthony Joseph sold it by auction to Edmund Woods in 1768;[27] but Montagu mortgaged the estate to Robert and Henry Drummond,[28] of Drummond's Bank, in 1781, and his son sold it to Edmund Woods jun. in 1790.[29]

GORING, Baronet. *Argent a cheveron between three rings gules.*

Mr. Woods died in 1833,[30] his daughter Katherine succeeded. She was succeeded by her sister Charlotte Woods, who built and endowed the school on the Green in 1850.[31]

It now belongs to Mr. Samuel Barrow.

FIELD PLACE, a farm in the south of the parish, is a reputed manor.[32] In the 15th century it was the property of William Cranley and his wife Margaret.[33] It descended to their son William and from him to his son Henry.[34] Henry Cranley leased the manor to his younger son John for forty years after his own death with remainder to his eldest son Emery.[35] From him it descended in moieties to his daughters, Alice wife of Peter Quenell,[36] and Jane wife of George Stoughton.[37] The whole manor descended to Peter Quenell, son of Alice and Peter.[38] He sold it to William Yalden in 1651.[39] In 1677 William Yalden and Mary Yalden, widow, conveyed the manor to William Sadler.[40] In 1808 it was the property of William, nephew of Thomas Sadler,[41] and in 1850 of James Sadler of Chiddingfold.[42] Land in Chiddingfold, of this manor, was held by Giles Covert, who died in 1556, holding of the Dean and Chapter of Windsor.[43]

[1a] *Old Cottage and Domestic Architecture in South-west Surr.* (2nd ed.), 87.

[4] Large *Paludina* marble, Topley, *Geol. of the Weald*, 105.

[7] In 1583–4, however, Richard March is said to have held it of Viscount Montagu as of his manor of Shalford Bradestan; Chan. Inq. p.m. (Ser. 2), cciv, 97.

[8] *Rot. Cur. Regis* (Rec. Com), ii, 60.

[9] *Close*, 18 Hen. III, m. 27 d.

[10] *Chart.* quoted by Manning and Bray, ii, 60.

[11] Feet of F. Surr. 19 Hen. III, 177.

[12] *Cal. Pat.* 1317–21, p. 565.

[13] Feet of F. Surr. 56 Hen. III, 27.

[14] Exch. K.R. Transcripts of Charters, bdle. 2.

[15] Feet of F. Surr. 10 Ric. II, 9. The lands were the right of Elizabeth, who was evidently an heiress of John of Burningfold; see also ibid. 2 Hen. IV, 4, which seems to refer to the same lands.

[16] Surv. of Bramley, Edw. VI.

[17] Feet of F. Surr. Hil. 12 Eliz.

[18] Chan. Inq. p.m. (Ser. 2), cciv, 97.

[18a] See *V.C.H. Surr.* ii, 273.

[18b] Close, 2 Jas. I, pt. xx.

[19] Ibid. 6 Jas. I, pt. ii, no. 29.

[20] Ibid. ; Feet of F. Surr. Hil. 5 Jas. I.

[21] Chan. Inq. p.m. (Ser. 2), ccclxxx, 132. Wyatt left by his will, 12 Mar. 1618, one-third of his share to his third son Francis, who died 1634, and does not refer to this property in his will. Henry borrowing money on the land refers to it as his by right of descent, and his mother's will in 1632, printed in *Surr. Arch. Coll.* iii, speaks of his having acquired an estate from his brothers and sisters against the intention of his father.

[22] Feet of F. Surr. Mich. 20 Jas. I.

[23] Ibid. Trin. 14 Chas. I. Arthur Middleton is said to have died just afterwards seised of two-thirds of the manor only. The title to the Wyatt third was probably in doubt.

[24] Chan. Inq. p.m. (Ser. 2), ccclxxxvi, 124.

[25] Feet of F. Surr. Hil. 8 Geo. I.

[26] Haslemere Registers ; Private Deeds.

[27] Manning and Bray, *Hist. of Surr.* ii, 61.

[28] Com. Pleas D. Enr. Trin. 30 Geo. III, m. 257.

[29] Ibid. and see Land Tax Assessments.

[30] Private information.

[31] Brayley, *Topog. Hist. of Surr.* v, 125.

[32] In 1347 Richard *de Feld* was an agent in a conveyance of land in Dunsfold; Feet of F. Surr. 21 Edw. III, 3.

[33] Chan. Proc. (Ser. 2), bdle. 48, no. 8.

[34] Feet of F. Div. Co. Mich. 37 Hen. VIII.

[35] Chan. Proc. (Ser. 2), bdle. 48, no. 8.

[36] *Visit. of Surr.* (Harl. Soc.), pp. 162 and 86.

[37] Feet of F. Div. Co. Hil. 5 Jas. I ; Ibid. East. 6 Jas. I.

[38] Feet of F. Surr. East. 1650.

[39] Ibid. Mich. 1651.

[40] Ibid. Hil. 28 & 29 Chas. II.

[41] Manning and Bray, *Hist. of Surr.* ii, 60.

[42] Brayley, *Topog. Hist. of Surr.* v, 125.

[43] Harl. MS. 756, fol. 309.

Field Place, a small manor-house, shows a most delightful collection of roofs of all sorts of pitches and dispositions, and two good chimneys, one of which has crow-steps to the breast below. Part of the house is built of brick and stone.

GRAFFHAM GRANGE was an old house held by the abbey of Waverley of Roger de Clare, c. 1238, and inhabited by a family who took their name from it. About that year Walter Giffard, Abbot of Waverley, (1236–51), granted all the rights of the abbey in Graffham to Walter de Graffham for a rent of 16*s.* a year, still paid to Markwick, a former possession of the abbey, in 1808.[44]

Elias of Graffham owned a mill in Shalford in the 13th century.[45] About 1325 Eleanor widow of John of Graffham signed a bond at Graffham.[46] In 1367 John of Graffham resigned Graffham to his son Hugh.[47] Thomas of Graffham, 10 July 1445, granted all his land in Dunsfold and elsewhere to John Provys and Thomas George.[48] John Elliot died seised of a messuage called 'Graffam' in 1640.[49] It passed from the Elliots to the Mellersh family, from whom Mr. Richard Eager bought it in 1803. He sold it to Mr. James Stedman of Guildford in 1832. Mr. J. C. McAndrew was the later owner, and it now belongs to Mr. F. A. Shepherd.

HIGH LOXLEY, a farm near Park Hatch, in Hascombe, was in the possession of the Hull family in the 16th and 17th centuries.[50] Thomas Hull conveyed it to John

Machell, who sold it in 1682 to John Child;[51] his grandson Charles Child is said to have succeeded to it and to have left it to his niece Martha Searle (see Tangley, in Wonersh). It was purchased in 1770 by Peter Flutter, whose daughter carried it in marriage to John Martyr.[52]

HULL. *Argent a cheveron azure between three demi-lions passant gules with three benants on the chevron and a chief sable with two piles argent therein.*

SMITHBROOK Manor was a possession of the Knights of St. John,[53] and was an appurtenance of their preceptory of Poling, co. Sussex.[54] Queen Elizabeth granted the manor to Edward Wymarke,[55] who appears to have sold it to George Austen of Shalford.[56] George Austen died seised of it in 1621.[57] From that time it descended with the rectory manor of Shalford (q.v.).

The church of *ST. MARY AND CHURCHES ALL SAINTS* stands remote from the village on a hillock well elevated above the surrounding country. To the east of the church is the rectory-house, a picturesque gabled and tile-hung structure, probably dating from the 15th century.

The churchyard, approached from the east, is large,

and has been extended down the slope of the hill to the south during recent years. Besides other trees it contains two yews, one of which, with a hollow trunk, close by the south porch, is probably one of the most ancient trees·in the county.

The walls are constructed of Bargate stone rubble, of a bright yellow colour in places, with dressings of the same stone, and the mortar joints of the walling are galleted with chips of ironstone in parts ; but this, although an ancient local fashion, may only date from recent restorations, when large parts of the walls were re-faced or re-pointed and some rebuilt. In Cracklow's view they appear as plastered externally. A border of Horsham slabs, with which the entire church was roofed originally, remains on the nave and north transept roofs, but they have mostly been replaced by tiles. The timber bell-turret, at the west end, and its square spire, are covered with oak shingles.

Its cruciform plan follows a favourite local type, Cranley, Ewhurst, Witley, Godalming, and St. Martha's chapel being neighbouring examples of cross churches. But in these cases the plan seems to have grown to the cruciform shape, whereas here it would appear to have been designed from the first. The nave is 47 ft. long by 20 ft. 9 in., the chancel (the axis of which inclines to the north) 31 ft. 6 in. by 16 ft. 3 in., and the transepts, which vary in width between 12 ft. 2 in. and 12 ft. 10 in., have the shallow projection of 8 ft. internally. There is a spacious porch on the south of the nave coeval with the church ; and on the north of the chancel vestries and an organ-chamber have been built in modern times. There are original buttresses, two at each angle, except on the east side of the transepts. The west respond of the south transept arch is an entire octagonal column, the obvious assumption being that the intention of the builders—abandoned during the progress of the work—was to build an aisle on this side instead of a transept. The timber turret at the west end is carried on four huge oak baulks with arched braces, and is probably a 15th-century addition.

The date of the entire church is between 1270 and 1290, and it is remarkable for being practically all in the one style. If there were an earlier building —the place itself is not named in Domesday—no trace of it remains in the stonework. About 1304 the advowson, which was (as it now is) in the hands of the Crown, was given by Edward I to the hospital of St. Mary at Spital without Bishopsgate, and to this circumstance is doubtless due the erection of the church, and the exceptional beauty and regularity of the work.[58]

The chancel is of two bays, each with a two-light window, in which the lights have trefoiled cusping with a circle over containing a pointed trefoil ; the whole within a pointed inclosing arch, and worked with mouldings on three planes, some parts being exceptionally delicate and rich for country work. This

[44] Deeds formerly in possession of Mr. Mellersh of Godalming, quoted by Manning and Bray, op. cit. ii, 59. Possibly the rent was included in the advowsons, &c. in Dunsfold belonging to the abbey at the Dissolution. The advowson did not belong to it.

[45] Feet of F. Surr. 32 Hen. III, 53.

[46] Deeds quoted by Manning and Bray, op. cit. ii, 59.

[47] Ibid.

[48] Ibid.

[49] Chan. Inq. p.m. (Ser. 2), mcci, 147.

[50] Feet of F. Surr. Trin. 20 Jas. I ; Com. Pleas D. Enr. Mich. 23 Chas. I.

[51] Recov. R. Trin. 14 Chas. II, m. 137; R. of West Bramley quoted by Manning and Bray.

[52] According to Manning and Bray, *Hist. of Surr.* ii, 60.

[53] Cott. MS. Claud. E. 6, fol. 143.

[54] Ibid. fol. 281.

[55] Pat. 30 Eliz. pt. vii, m. 1.

[56] See Manning and Bray, op. cit. ii, 59.

[57] Chan. Inq. p.m. (Ser. 2), cccxcvii, 90.

[58] There are points of resemblance between this work and that in Trotton Church, Sussex, and in the transepts of North Stoke Church in the same county, both somewhat elaborate work of about the same date.

design is repeated in the two remaining windows in the side walls of the nave (there were two others in the western bay, filled up when the timber tower was built), and in the opposite walls of the transepts, the only variation in the design being that the two western windows of the chancel were prolonged downwards, after the manner of a certain class of low side windows. The east window of each transept is of a different design, smaller and plainer, consisting of two trefoiled lights with a quatrefoil over, the whole worked on one plane, with chamfers instead of mouldings, and without an inclosing arch. The east window of the chancel is large and of three trefoiled lights, with three cinquefoiled circles above within a moulded inclosing arch, but without a hood. There is a quatrefoil panel in the apex of the gable, originally an opening pierced for ventilation, but reproduced in this meaningless form at the 1882 restoration, when

its place. The rafters and boarding of the roof still retain scroll patterns painted c. 1280.

Besides the priest's door in the south wall of the chancel, there is a small doorway in the north wall of the north transept and the usual south door in the nave, all having engaged shafts with capitals and bases, delicate hollow stop-chamfers to the jambs, and moulded arches and labels. The nave doorway retains its original oak door, with coeval wrought-iron hinges, strap-work, closing ring, scutcheon, and a large solid oak lock-case. This doorway has a pointed segmental head on the inside, moulded and having a moulded hood which is made to die into the string-course of plain circular section which runs almost entirely round the church on the inside.

The chancel and transept arches are doubly hollow chamfered, and the former has no capitals. Those of the transept arches are boldly moulded, of differing

DUNSFOLD CHURCH FROM THE SOUTH-EAST

also the east window was raised in the wall and a transom with blank panels inserted beneath it—a very unwarrantable tampering with the fine design. The west window of the nave has interlacing tracery in three lights, the centre cinquefoiled and the others trefoiled, with pointed trefoils and quatrefoils in the spaces above. This window has a hood-mould—the only one used externally—and its mouldings and character are so far different from the others as to suggest that it is an insertion of slightly later date (c. 1300).

The south porch is remarkable for its exceptional antiquity, the main timbers, including the trefoiled bargeboard (which has a curious ' halved ' joint at the apex) being coeval with the church. Early in the 16th century, however, the original doorway was removed and the present one, with four-centred head and Tudor roses in the spandrels, put in

sections, corresponding to those in the door-shafts. The chancel arch was, most reprehensibly, heightened and widened, a hood-moulding being added in the restoration of 1882, and in this way a squint and image-niche on the northern side of the arch were displaced. Both transepts retain their piscinae, that in the south transept having grooves for the oak shelf. The northern one is in the north wall, i.e. on the gospel side of the altar, a somewhat unusual position. Part of what may have been a piscina belonging to one of the nave altars is preserved in the vestry. The triple sedilia and piscina in the chancel are a most beautiful composition, the four arches having undercut hood-mouldings dying into the circular string-course over them. The arches have a wave-moulding as the outer order, as in the windows and doors, and a hollow for the inner, which is worked into a light and graceful trefoil. The mouldings of the capitals and bases of the sedilia are also peculiarly good, and the two centre ones are of Sussex marble, together with their shafts. The seat levels are stepped up, and the piscina has a credence shelf and an elegantly moulded bowl with two circular basins.[59]

Ancient roofs, no doubt coeval with the walls, remain in the nave and transepts, but that of the chancel is of modern deal. Perhaps the most interesting feature in the church is the 13th-century seating in the nave, in an almost perfect state. The design of the standards, which is nearly alike in the dozen or so ancient benches, is quaint—resembling a pair of cows'-horns with balls on the tips ; and round the edges is worked a hollow chamfer. These benches had a narrow plank for seat—lately widened—and a thick rail to rest the back against, the space between it and the seat being filled with a thin plank. They stood upon a continuous oak plate or curb, which has lately been done away with, and a separate block put under each standard.[60] In the vestry is preserved part of the very graceful fleur-de-lys termination of the quire stalls of the same date—the only fragment

round the whole of the nave under the string-course.'[61] On the east wall of the nave and transepts the remains of a hunting-scene, with a hare and stag, suggested the mediaeval allegory of The Three Dead and the Three Living—of which subject there is a painting in existence at Charlwood Church, Surrey.[62] St. Christopher and St. George appear to have been painted on the north wall of the nave, probably in the 15th century, and an undecipherable painting of this later period still remains within the space occupied by the timber tower, on the south wall of the nave.

Some grisaille quarries, coeval with the windows, still remain in the chancel, and the bordering of the modern glass in the east window is copied from the old. The font with small circular bowl in Sussex marble is of uncertain date, but probably late 13th-century, although some authorities have placed it as late as the latter part of the 17th century. The only mediaeval monument now visible is a stone slab dug up in the nave and now placed in the south transept, which has moulded edges, and probably once bore a cross. It is a monumental slab and not a coffin-lid.

Aubrey mentions a gravestone in the chancel to ' John Shipsay, Dr. of Divinity, Rector of the Parsonage of Dunsfold,' who was 'chaplayn to King Charles the First,' and died in 1665, but this is no longer to be seen.

The registers commence in 1628. The first volume, which ends in 1653, is partly transcribed in volume two, which contains baptisms to 1810, burials to 1812, marriages to 1752. The registers of baptisms and marriages are completed in volumes three and four. They contain, among other items of interest, a record that Sarah Pick, on 18 March 1665, 'did penance in a white sheet,' with the remarkable addendum that ' She was excommunicated eode die': and another notice of the penance in private of one ' J. Bames and An his wife ' in 1667.

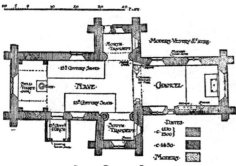

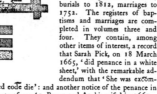

PLAN OF DUNSFOLD CHURCH

remaining. It resembles others of like pattern at Merrow, Effingham, and Great Bookham in this county. An Elizabethan or Jacobean altar-table is also preserved in the vestry.

The walls of the church appear to have been painted at about the time of the completion of the work with a series of very small subjects, of which copies made at the time they were discovered have been framed and hung up in the nave. They seem to have been executed chiefly in red outline, and on the south wall of the nave, immediately westward of the transept arch, ' the scheme of human redemption was probably set forth, commencing with the Fall of Man, and ending with the Coronation of the Blessed Virgin'—the last within a quatrefoil . . . A band of interlacing, or chain-work, is said to have run

There is a silver cup of 1566 and a ewer of 1578 among the church plate ; also an old pewter tankard-shaped flagon, no longer used.

Of the six bells three are modern, added in 1892. One, recast in 1893, was by William Knight of Reading, 1583, inscribed *multis annis resonet campana Johannis*. Another bears the date 1621, and the inscription ' Our hope is in the Lorde ' : and a third of 1649 is by Bryan Eldridge.

ADVOWSONS   The advowson of the parish church was at first in the hands of the king, who granted it with that of Shalford to St. Mary Spital without Bishopsgate in 1304-5 ;[63] it followed the history of Shalford

[59] The range of sedilia and piscina at Preston, Sussex, is a coarse edition of these. Trotton, Lynchmere, and Sompting, Sussex, have very similar piscinae.

[60] Burstow, Chiddingfold and Witley, in Surrey, have one or two seats of somewhat similar character and date. Didling, Sussex, Minstead in the New Forest, Winchfield, Hants, Clapton in Gordano, Somerset, and Churchdown, Gloucestershire, are other examples of nave seating of the late 13th or early 14th century.

[61] J. L. André, F.S.A., *Surr. Arch. Coll.* xiii, 9.

[62] Another was found at Fetcham in this county, and the same subject was formerly to be seen over the chancel arch at Battle, Sussex.

[63] Chart. R. 33 Edw. I, no. 49.

Rectory until the suppression of the priory, from which time the church has been in the gift of the Crown.[64]

The church of St. Andrew Graffham, built in 1861 of the local sandstone, is in 14th-century style, with a bell-turret containing two bells surmounted by a spire.

The ecclesiastical district of Grafham or Graffham was formed in 1863 out of the civil parishes of Bramley and Dunsfold. The living is in the gift of the vicar.

CHARITIES The parish benefits from Henry Smith's charity and from Wyatt's Hospital in Godalming.

EWHURST

Yweherst and Uhurst (xiii cent.) ; Iwehurst (xiv cent.) ; Ewehurst (xv cent.).

Ewhurst is a parish bounded on the north by Shere, on the east by Ockley (formerly detached, now added to Abinger) and Abinger, on the west by Cranleigh, on the south by the county of Sussex. It is 5 miles from north to south, and a mile and a half from east to west, of a fairly regular form. It contains 5,417 acres. The village is 12 miles south-east of Guildford, and 11 miles south-west of Dorking.

The northern part of the parish is on the Greensand hills—Ewhurst Hill, Pitch Hill, and Coneyhurst Hill ; but the greater part of it is upon the Wealden Clay, in the ancient forest. It is still well wooded, and the oak grows with great vigour in the soil. It has no large open spaces, except upon the hills to the north ; and these have been much inclosed and planted during the last twenty years. A road from Rudgwick in Sussex, whence are branches to Horsham and Pulborough, runs through the village to Shere. By the side of this road, where it crosses the summit of the hill, stood Ewhurst Mill, which for many years was a conspicuous landmark visible for many miles. Of late years it has been disused as a mill, the sails are taken down, and the greater growth of trees has helped to make it less easily seen.

Till the 19th century had advanced some way there was no properly made road in Ewhurst parish. A Roman road existed, which was carefully traced by the late Mr. James Park Harrison,[1] and is laid down on the 6-in. Ordnance map as running west of the village. When King John was at Guildford and Knepp Castle in Sussex on the same day, 21 January 1215, in winter-time when unmade ways were foul, he very probably used this road. Nothing shows the backwardness of the Weald more than the absolute disuse and forgetting of these lines of through communication. Ewhurst is not named in Domesday. It was part of the great royal manor of Gomshall, but was probably sparsely inhabited. That there was some population soon afterwards is implied by Norman work in the church. But it was a chapel to Shere still, the earliest evidence of it as a parish being in 1291.

The schools were built in 1840. In 1870 another school was built at the hamlet of Ellen's Green, in the extreme south of the parish.

The house of Baynards Park is in Ewhurst parish, though most of the park is in Cranleigh. It is now the seat of Mr. T. J. Waller.

Among modern houses in Ewhurst parish are Coverwood, the seat of Mr. H. F. Locke-King ; Ewhurst Place, the seat of Col. Thomas Warne Lemmon ; Woolpits, high up Coneyhurst Hill, the seat of Mr. H. L. Doulton.

The Ewhurst Institute and Reading Room was built by subscription in 1901.

SOMERSBURY Manor, which includes the central portion of Ewhurst *MANORS* parish, was originally a member of Gomshall.[2] It was separated from the main manor in the 12th century, when Henry II retained it at the time of his grant of Gomshall to William Malveisin and Ingram Wells.[3]

The first indication of a tenant occurs in 1272, when Herbert of Somersbury obtained from the parson of Ewhurst a quitclaim of a house and land in Ewhurst.[4] He was still living in 1276,[5] but seems to have been succeeded by Henry of Somersbury, probably his son, who was holding land of the manor of Gomshall in 1298–9.[6] Early in the next century Richard and Henry of Somersbury were buying land in the neighbouring parish of Cranleigh.[7] About the year 1317–18 Henry of Somersbury died holding Somersbury, which then consisted of a house and half a carucate of land in Gomshall.[8] He was succeeded by his son Henry, who obtained licence to hear divine service in the oratory of Ewhurst.[9] At his death the manor descended to his son Richard,[10] who enfeoffed Eleanor, Countess of Ormond,[11] probably in order to secure himself against any claim she might make on the manor as a member of Shiere Vachery, for in 1344–5 she re-enfeoffed Richard of Somersbury of it.[12] He then alienated it to a certain Agnes, afterwards wife of Walter of Hamme,[13] who conveyed it in 1364–5 to John Busbridge on consideration of a life-rent to Walter and Agnes.[14] John Busbridge was succeeded by his son Robert,[15] who died holding the manor in 1416, leaving a son and heir Thomas.[16] In September 1455 John Busbridge, who was then holding Somersbury, died leaving a brother Robert, during whose minority the king granted the custody of Somersbury to Richard Langport, clerk.[17] The heir had already alienated it to a certain Thomas Playstow,[18] so

[64] Inst. Bks. P.R.O.
[1] Surr. Arch. Coll. vi, 1.
[2] Testa de Nevill (Rec. Com.), 225.
[3] See the account of Gomshall in Shere.
[4] Feet of F. Surr. 56 Hen. III, 3.
[5] Chan. Inq. p.m. 4 Edw. I, 47, where he appears as a juror in an inquisition touching Gomshall.
[6] Add. Chart. (B.M.), 5578 ; Chan. Inq. p.m. 27 Edw. I, no. 45.
[7] Feet of F. Surr. 32 Edw. I, 17 ; 34 Edw. I, 9.
[8] Chan. Inq. p.m. 11 Edw. II, no. 50.
[9] Egerton MS. 2032, fol. 60b.
[10] Feet of F. Surr. 6 Edw. III, 36.
[11] Chan. Inq. a.q.d. ccclvii, 1.
[12] Feet of F. Surr. 18 Edw. III, 8.

She held Shiere Vachery for life. The original connexion with Gomshall had been perhaps forgotten.
[13] Chan. Inq. a.q.d. ccclxvii, 1.
[14] Feet of F. Surr. 38 Edw. III, 42.
[15] Chan. Inq. p.m. 6 Hen. IV, no. 46.
[16] Ibid. 4 Hen. V, no. 23.
[17] Cal. Pat. 1461–7, p. 179.
[18] Ibid.

that it seems probable that on that account it was forfeited to the Crown. It was granted with Shiere to John, Lord Audley, and forfeited by his son James after the insurrection at Blackheath.[19] It was then farmed by a certain William Cokys,[20] and in October 1511, Henry VIII granted it with other lands in Ewhurst to Thomas Salter, Sewer of the Chamber, to hold for the annual rent of a red rose.[21] The manor seems, however, to have been restored to John, Lord Audley, for he conveyed it in 1532 to Thomas Wolley the younger.[22] In 1549 Ambrose Wolley sold the manor to Robert Whitfeld,[23] who held it till 1576, when he sold it to Nicholas Dendy[24] and his son John, who were also holding Breach.[25] Nicholas died at Ewhurst in October 1587 and was succeeded by John Dendy,[26] who conveyed the manor to Edward Dendy in 1621.[27] In 1640 Henry Ockley and his wife Beatrice were in possession, and sold the reversion to John Clifton of Worplesdon.[28]

In 1648 these three conveyed it to Richard Evelyn of Baynards.[29] John Dendy was farming it at the time of the Commonwealth.[30] It descended from Richard Evelyn to his daughter Ann, wife of William Montague, who conveyed it to William Freeman in 1674.[31] In 1680 William Montague, junior, ' seised in fee in reversion,' surrendered all his rights to William Freeman. The latter in 1700 granted a lease for a year to Sir Richard Onslow ' to test the possession,' and his son, Thomas Onslow, afterwards the second Lord Onslow, mortgaged the property in 1714,[32] as owner. It continued in Lord Onslow's family till about 1863, when it was bought

ONSLOW, Earl Onslow. *Azure a fesse gules between six Cornish choughs.*

SCARLETT, Lord Abinger. *Checky or and gules a lion ermine and a quarter azure with a castle argent therein.*

by the late William Lord Abinger, in whose heir it now remains.

It seems possible that the manor of *BAYNARDS*, which lies on the boundary between Ewhurst and Cranleigh, was originally a part of Pollingfold (q.v.), and never a separate manor, though so called, for tenants of the Baynards estate appear in the court rolls of Pollingfold (extant between 1772 and 1883). In 1447 William Sydney the younger obtained a licence to impark 800 acres of land appertaining to

his ' manor ' of Baynards.[33] According to a monumental inscription in Cranleigh Church, quoted by Aubrey in the 17th century, William Sydney died in 1449.[34] He was succeeded by a son William, whose widow Elizabeth obtained the custody of his lands during the minority of his daughters Elizabeth and Anne.[35] Baynards Manor appears to have been the portion of Anne, who married William (afterwards Sir William) Uvedale.[36] According to his will[37] a rent was to be paid to his eldest son and the residue of the profits divided between his younger son John and his brother Thomas. The manor was conveyed to Reginald Bray or his brother John. Edmund Lord Bray, son of the latter, sold it in 1535 to his brother Sir Edward Bray. Sir Edward Bray died in 1558. His son Sir Edward mortgaged Baynards, 2 November 1580, to John Reade of Sterborough,[38] to whom he sold Pollingfold 3 December, a month later. On 29 October 1587 John Reade released his rights in Baynards to George More of Loseley, afterwards knighted, and a fine was levied in 1588 confirming the conveyance. Baynards was bought by More with his wife's money, she being a wealthy heiress.[39] He probably rebuilt the house with the great hall, which now exists, for his home while his father Sir William was alive.[40] In 1604, after the death of the latter, Sir George, his wife Constantia, and his son Sir Robert, conveyed Baynards to Sir Francis Woolley of Pirford, Sir George More's nephew, for a sum of money and the manor of Witley in exchange.

MORE of Loseley. *Azure a cross argent with five martlets sable thereon.*

On 6 March 4 James (1607) Sir Francis Woolley sold Baynards for £4,400 to Edward Bayninge, gentleman, of London. He presumably died, leaving an heir Andrew Bayninge, who sold it 15 February 1608-9 to Isaac Woder of Plumstead in Kent. Woder, who also had acquired Knowle in Cranleigh, described as ' a manor in Surrey and Sussex,' in the same year, sold Baynards 28 February 1609-10 to Robert Jossey. His son James Jossey *alias* Hay mortgaged his property, and was clearly in considerable difficulties, for on 23 January 1628-9 his mother Margaret surrendered to him all her jointure, Pollingfold Manor, Coneyhurst Hill, and two rooms over ' the great dining chamber ' at Baynards. The mortgage changed hands, and finally Richard Gurnard, citizen and clothworker, conveyed his rights under it to Richard Evelyn, father of the diarist, 13 November 1629. On 30 August 1630 Jossey released all his rights in Baynards and Pollingfold to Richard Evelyn, and in 1631 a lessee of Mrs. Jossey's jointure surrendered his lease to Evelyn.[41]

[19] Pat. 7 Edw. IV, pt. i, m. 6.
[20] Rentals and Surv. (P.R.O.), xviii, 51.
[21] L. and P. Hen. VIII, i, 1916.
[22] Feet of F. Surr. East. 23 Hen. VIII.
[23] Ibid. Mich. 3 Edw. VI.
[24] Ibid. Mich. 18 & 19 Eliz.
[25] Ibid.
[26] Chan. Inq. p.m. (Ser. 2), ccix, 118.
[27] Feet of F. Surr. Hil. 18 Jas. I; Recov. R. East. 19 Jas. I, rot. 59.
[28] Deed of Lord Onslow.

[29] Ibid.; Close, 22 Chas. I, pt. ii, no. 5.
[30] Surr. Arch. Coll. xvii, 88.
[31] Feet of F. Surr. East. 26 Chas. II.
[32] Deeds of Lord Onslow.
[33] Chart. R. 25 & 26 Hen. VI, no. 12.
[34] Antiq. of Surr. (ed. 1718), iv, 85.
[35] Cal. Pat. 1461-7, p. 273.
[36] Till 1487 it was held in dower by Elizabeth their mother, who had remarried Sir Thomas Uvedale. See Cal. Inq. p.m. Hen. VII, i, 170, 171.

[37] See Surr. Arch. Coll. iii, 171.
[38] Cf. Feet of F. Surr. Trin. 22 Eliz.; a conveyance to Sir Thomas Cotton, probably for the purposes of the mortgage.
[39] Settlement at Loseley.
[40] John Evelyn in his letter to Aubrey prefixed to Aubrey's Hist. and Antiq. of Surr. says that More built the house. Some of it, however, is probably older.
[41] Deeds of Lord Onslow.

He settled the manor on his youngest son Richard,[42] who in 1648 acquired Somersbury (see above), and the entire property descended to the Onslow family as already stated.[43] A distinction of Baynards is that it has belonged at various times to the four leading families in Surrey since the year 1500, namely Bray, More, Evelyn, and Onslow. The second Sir Edward Bray who held it married Elizabeth Roper, granddaughter of Sir Thomas More, whence the fact or legend that Sir Thomas More's skull was preserved at Baynards.

John Evelyn visiting it in 1657 describes the house as 'a very fair noble residence having one of the goodliest avenues of oaks up to it that ever I saw.'[44]

Later, however, the house ceased to be used as a gentleman's house, Arthur Onslow the Speaker, Lord Cranley, resided at Knowle, and Baynards was merely a farm-house. In 1818 Lord Onslow sold Pollingfold and Baynards to John Smallpeice of Guildford. In 1824 Pollingfold was sold to Richard Gates, and in 1832 the estate was reunited by the Rev. Thomas Thurlow, son of the Bishop of Durham and nephew to the Lord Chancellor Thurlow. He added to and restored or rebuilt the house, under the direction of Sir Matthew Digby Wyatt, and made a fine collection of paintings, armour, furniture and tapestry, which remain in the house. He raised the roof of the original hall, turning one of the rooms over it into the present gallery at the end, and altered the entrance. Mr. Thurlow died in 1874, and was succeeded by his son Mr. Thomas Lyon Thurlow, who in 1889 sold Baynards and the manor of Pollingfold to Mr. T. J. Waller, the present owner. The house is mainly of brick, but the foundations are of Sussex marble and the roof of Horsham slates, both found in the neighbourhood. The house is very handsome, with an air of antiquity about it, and the grounds are picturesque. An avenue of Wellingtonias leads from the station towards the house.

The reputed manor of BREACH was probably a member of Gomshall Netley.[45] In the 16th century it was the property of John Agmondesham.[46] He mortgaged the manor to William Atlee and Nicholas Dendy, who disputed the division of the estates. Nicholas Dendy died during the dispute, but it was settled by compromise that his son John should have the northern half of the lands, i.e. North Breach.[47] Finally, in 1594, William Atlee conveyed all his right to Ralph Dendy, probably the heir of John Dendy.[48]

In 1630 Edward Dendy sold the manor to Walter Longhurst,[49] whose descendants remained in possession for nearly a century and a half. Ralph Longhurst and Richard Stening[50] were holding South Breach at the time of the Commonwealth. In 1768-9 Richard Longhurst and his wife Anne sold the manor to John Vincent of Stoke by Guildford.[51] His grandson and heir died leaving an only daughter,[52] probably the Mary Hone, who joined with her husband, William Smith, in a sale of the manor, under the name of North Breach, to Samuel John Symons Trickey in 1803.[53] It afterwards belonged to a family named Donithorne, from whom it was bought by Mrs. Fletcher Bennett about 1877. It is now in the hands of the Bennett trustees.

CONEYHURST is situated on the rising ground north of the village and was in the possession of Ambrose Wolley in 1553, and probably formed a part of his manor of Somersbury. It was then sold by him to Sir Edward Bray,[54] who bequeathed it in 1558 to his son Edward on condition of paying off a mortgage.[55] In 1593 it was in the possession of a certain Ralph Dalton,[56] to whose son, Richard, it descended in November 1601,[57] and from him it passed in 1615 to his two daughters, Joan and Elizabeth, who were then both minors.[58] Joan married Richard Bridger, and Elizabeth, Henry Matchwick.[59] In 1676 the whole manor was settled on Joan,[60] and descended from her to her nephew Henry Bridger. Henry died in 1695, and his cousin Richard covenanted with Edward Wood, who had married Elizabeth daughter to Henry, to levy a fine.[61] In 1776 it was the property of Thomas Wood,[62] who died in 1779 leaving a son and heir Thomas,[63] in whose family it continued.

POLLINGFOLD in Ewhurst extended into Cranleigh parish and into Sussex. It was held of the lords of Gomshall,[64] and the first under-tenant of whom record has been found is John of Pollingfold, who lived in the time of Edward I.[65] From him the manor passed to Lettice wife of William Man,[66] who sold it in 1334 to a certain Robert,[67] who was perhaps a trustee for the Brocas family, for in 1345 Sir John Brocas had a grant of free warren there.[68] The manor was released by his widow to his son Sir Bernard with remainder to Sir Bernard's half-brother John, but, John having died, his brother Oliver succeeded to Pollingfold, where he took up his residence.[69] He granted it in 1397 to Sir Bernard's son Bernard,

---

[42] It was settled on him in tail male, but by a subsequent deed was entailed on him and his heirs.

[43] In 1648 Baynards, Somersbury, and Ewhurst Mill were settled on Mrs. Elizabeth Evelyn, wife of Richard. She kept an interest till her death, 1692, and held a court in 1690, as lady of the manor of Pollingfold.

[44] Evelyn's Diary (ed. W. Bray), 305.

[45] Manning and Bray quote Ct. R. of Gomshall Netley, in which this manor is stated to be the property of John Amersham, and late of John of Breach (Hist. of Surr. i, 503).

[46] Feet of F. Surr. Trin. 29 Eliz. In August 1462 William Agmondesham had granted to Thomas Smallpeice the rents and service of lands called Hakkers in Ewhurst in the vill of Gomshall; See Surr. Arch. Coll. xviii, 224.

[47] Chan. Proc. (Eliz.) Aa, ix, 43; Dd,

v, 53. John also claimed certain quit-rents in the whole manor.

[48] Feet of F. Surr. Trin. 36 Eliz.

[49] Ibid. Surr. Trin. 6 Chas. I.

[50] Surr. Arch. Coll. xvii, 88. Parliamentary Survey of Church Lands.

[51] Feet of F. Surr. Mich. 9 Geo. III. The manor here seems to have included both North and South Breach, while the later deeds possibly also refer to both moieties under the name of North Breach.

[52] Feet of F. Surr. Mich. 3 Geo. III.

[53] Manning and Bray, Hist. of Surr. i, 503.

[54] Feet of F. Surr. Mich. 1 Mary.

[55] P.C.C. 47 Welles.

[56] Chan. Inq. p.m. (Ser. 2), ccxl, 9.

[57] Ibid. cclxx, 144. [58] Ibid. ccclv, 87.

[59] See Feet of F. Surr. East. 13 Chas. I; East. 14 Chas. I.

[60] Ibid. Hil. 28 & 29 Chas. II.

[61] Ibid. 9 Will. and Mary; and deeds of the Wood family.

[62] Ibid. Trin. 16 Geo. III.

[63] Manning and Bray, op. cit. i, 503.

[64] After its division into East and West Pollingfold the former was held of Gomshall Netley and the latter of Gomshall Towerhill; Chan. Inq. p.m. (Ser. 2), ccxlvii, 72, and Ct. R. quoted by Manning and Bray, i, 501.

[65] Plac. Abbrev. (Rec. Com.), 262.

[66] Chan. Inq. p.m. 27 Edw. I, 45; John's grandson Robert of Pollingfold sued Lettice for the manor, but was unsuccessful as he had described it as lying entirely in Surrey, whereas 100 acres of land and 20s. rent were in Sussex (De Banco R. 281, m. 78).

[67] Feet of F. Surr. 8 Edw. III, 3. The surname of the purchaser is torn away in the conveyance. The initial letter appears to be a T.

[68] Chart. R. 19 Edw. III, m. 8.

[69] Close, 4 Edw. III, 21; Burrows, Family of Brocas, 425 et seq.

whose son and heir William entered upon it in 1405–6, and died in 1456,[70] before which date he is said to have sold it to William Sydney of Loseley.[71] It was evidently divided between the two daughters of William son of William Sydney ; of these, the one, Anne, married William Uvedale, and the other, Elizabeth, married John Hampden.[72] The manor was divided in moieties, whence doubtless arose the names *EAST* and *WEST POLLINGFOLD*. The Uvedale moiety, East Pollingfold, chiefly in Ewhurst, was alienated by Anne[73] to Sir Edward Bray and others in 1528.[74] He had already purchased Elizabeth Hampden's moiety, or West Pollingfold, and Baynards from his brother Edmund Lord Bray,[75] whose uncle Reginald, to whom Edmund was heir, or whose father, John, had apparently purchased it from Michael Dormer, to whom Sir John Hampden had conveyed it in 1520,[76] and thus the manor was reunited, but not for long. In 1581 Sir Edward sold the manor of Pollingfold with 40 acres of land and 30s. rent in Sussex to John Rede,[77] who conveyed it to Edward Tanworth seven years later.[78] The latter sold it in 1595 to George, afterwards Sir George More,[79] of Baynards, with which it has since descended (q.v.).

EAST POLLINGFOLD apparently was again separated from the main manor before 1560, and in October 1606 Sir Thomas Leedes, son of John Leedes of Wapingthorne, Sussex, sold it to John Hill of Ewhurst.[80] Some years after the latter's death it was assigned to one of his daughters, Sarah, wife of John Stevens.[81] A John Stevens was in possession in 1690,[82] but in 1695 Robert Gardiner and his wife Mary held it,[83] probably in her right, and conveyed it in 1701 to George Mabank,[84] evidently as a marriage portion, for in 1790 George Mabank Gardiner sold it to John Crouze.[85]

The remains of a moated inclosure called the Site of Pollingfold Manor House are just outside Baynards Park, in Cranleigh parish. This house was presumably pulled down by Sir George More when he rebuilt Baynards close by. But there is some doubt whether it was really the old manor-house, for the court baron was recently held at Moated Farm, an old moated house now also pulled down, in Ewhurst parish.[86] If Baynards had taken the place of the old manor house the courts would have been held there.

MAYBANKES, in the south of the parish, was occupied in 1503 by William Edsalle,[87] and was granted with Somersbury Manor, Saltland, and Slehurst in Ewhurst to Thomas Salter in 1511.[88] About the same time Rumbemyr in Ewhurst was occupied by Richard Astret, and Marschall by Thomas Edsalle.[89] Lands called Mascalls Pipers and Potfelds were sold by Robert Browning to Nicholas Dendy in the 16th century.[90] At the same time Moon Hall was held (of Coneyhurst Manor) by William Ticknor,[91] and land called Sprout or Prout was the subject of a dispute

between Agnes Hill and her uncle, Richard Hill.[92] Thomas Hill sold it in 1608 to Sir Francis Wolley.[93]

The church of *ST. PETER AND CHURCH ST. PAUL* consists of a chancel 24 ft. 9 in. by 15 ft. 9 in. ; a central tower 17 ft. 10 in. by 15 ft. 3 in. ; a north transept 21 ft. 5 in. by 19 ft. 2 in. ; a south transept 23 ft. by 18 ft. 3 in. ; a nave 34 ft. 5 in. by 19 ft. 5 in. The whole structure was almost completely rebuilt in 1838–9, for during the progress of some repairs the central tower collapsed and brought down much of the chancel in its fall. The nave would appear to have been less altered than the rest, and is of 12th-century date. Alterations were evidently made, however, late in the 15th century, and a century or so later the nave at least was a good deal altered as regards its windows. But in view of the devastating repairs of 1838 the early history of the church must remain a matter of uncertainty, for they included a skin of plaster which hides all evidence possibly contained in the walling. The present church, however, is probably on the foundations of the old one.

The windows of the chancel all date from 1838, that to the east being of three cinquefoiled lights and 'perpendicular' design. To north and south are plain rather wide single lancets. To the south is also a plain pointed door of the same date as the windows. Externally the chancel appears entirely modern, and the walls are of rubble plastered with sham joints representing masonry.

The tower rests upon four two-centred arches, all of two continuous chamfered orders, heavily plastered and probably completely modern. Above these the tower rises in two stages. The second one, containing the ringing chamber, is quite plain. The belfry stage however, is of 12th-century design with round-headed shafted openings, pilaster buttresses, and a crowning corbel table with plain corbels and small round connecting arches ; above this is a tiled broach spire of a somewhat obtuse type. The whole of this part of the tower is completely modern, as are also the diagonal buttresses set in the angles of the chancel and transepts and the nave and transepts. The ringing chamber is reached by a wooden stair in one flight in the north transept.

The north transept appears to have been wholly rebuilt in 1838. It is lit on the north by three wide grouped lancet lights with wide chamfered pilastered external jambs, and (over these) a trefoil light. To east and west are two single lancet lights, and on the west is also a small pointed door, all of which date from the rebuilding. The south transept is similar in every way, but lacks the door, and retains an old window of late 15th-century date. This is of two rather wide trefoiled lights with submullions over and a square main head. It has been a good deal disfigured in the resetting and restoration.

[70] Close, 7 Hen. IV, m. 29.
[71] *Hist. MSS. Com. Rep.* ix, App. i, 39a.
[72] *Cal. Inq. p.m. Hen. VII,* i, 170.
[73] Evidently she married Henry Roberts as her second husband.
[74] Feet of F. Div. Co. Hil. 19 Hen. VII.
[75] Chan. Inq. p.m. (Ser. ii), ccxlvii, 72.
[76] Close, 12 Hen. VIII, pt. xxiii.
[77] Feet of F. Div. Co. Trin. 23 Eliz.
[78] Ibid. Surr. East. 30 Eliz.
[79] Ibid. Hil. 37 Eliz.

[80] Com. Pleas D. Enr. Mich. 4 Jas. I, m. 7 ; Manning and Bray quote a court roll recording the death of John Leedes, seised of Pollingfold in 1560. He was succeeded by a son John, evidently father of Sir Thomas.
[81] Deeds quoted in Manning and Bray, op. cit. i, 502.
[82] Feet of F. Surr. Trin. 1 Will. and Mary.
[83] Ibid. East. 7 Will. III.
[84] Ibid. Trin. 13 Will. III.

[85] Ibid. Hil. 30 Geo. III.
[86] Information from Mr. Waller of Baynards.
[87] Rentals and Surv. (P.R.O.), portf. xviii, no. 51.
[88] L. and P. Hen. VIII, i, 1916.
[89] Rentals and Surv. P.R.O. portf. xviii, 51.
[90] Chan. Inq. p.m. (Ser. 2), ccix, 118.
[91] Ibid. ccxi, 9.
[92] Chan. Proc. (Ser. 2), bdle. 97, no. 37.
[93] Close, 5 Jas. I, pt. xxv.

EWHURST CHURCH : WEST PORCH

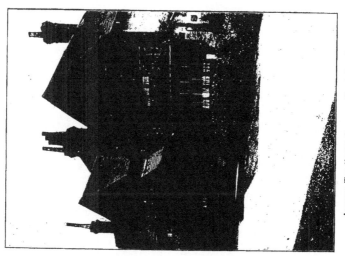

ALBURY : THE GRANGE (FORMERLY COOK'S PLACE)

The nave is lit on the north by three windows, all of two rounded lights. The first and third are very rough and probably very late. The middle one is of better workmanship, has spandrel sinkages, and is of 16th-century date. It is placed higher in the wall than the others in what is apparently the round-headed internal reveal of a 12th-century window which has been partly cut away to allow for this. The heavy coats of plaster, both inside and out, however, make this a little uncertain. On the south is a window of late 15th-century date of two wide trefoiled lights with sub-mullions over and a segmental main head, and of the same character as the east window of the south transept. West of this is the south door. This is of 12th-century date, though somewhat restored. It is of rather rough workmanship, with a semicircular head of two non-concentric orders, the inner, which is square, being a little below the outer, which is rather awkwardly worked with a pair of rolls and a chamfer. The jambs have circular shafts with plain cushion capitals and cone bases. The west window of the nave is of 15th-century date and has three cinquefoiled lights with sub-mullions over and a two-centred main head. Under the window is the west door, which is of the same date. It has a two-centred head and a continuous hollow chamfer, and is of chalk, almost the only use in the church of this material. In the south jamb are the remains of a holy-water stoup. Covering this door is an open timber porch of late 15th-century date, with a scalloped barge-board and a rounded arch of entrance, but otherwise of the plainest design. The nave walls are of rubble, plastered and ruled with sham jointing to represent 12th-century masonry.

The roofs of the chancel and the north transept are quite modern, and that of the north transept is partly modern, but also retains some moulded beams of late 16th-century date. The nave has its late 16th-century roof complete. It is ceiled with a plaster barrel vault and has moulded tie-beams and wall plates and strutted king-posts.

The font has been very much restored with roman cement, but the square bowl appears to be of 12th-century date and is of very crude design. The flat faces are ornamented with saltire ornaments of clumsy rolls. The four supporting columns are modern.

The pulpit is a fair example of early 17th-century work. It is octagonal with two stages of panelling in each face, the lower forming an arcade of enriched arches and the upper carved with arabesques in flat bands. The altar-table is of late 17th-century date with fluted legs, an inlaid top and a carved rail decorated with cherub-heads. The altar-rails are a good example of early 18th-century church fitting. They are returned on the flanks to form three sides of a square with rounded and mitred corners. The handrail is broad and moulded and is carried on panelled posts and twisted balusters. In the chancel are a pair

of handsome carved chairs of late 17th-century date, and, possibly, foreign workmanship. In the nave are four painted tablets of the commandments and texts. These are inclosed in handsomely carved frames of late 17th-century design. These and the altar rails were brought from Baynards in 1879 and were the gift of Mr. T. L. Thurlow. The font cover is from the same donor and is partly made up of some 17th-century consoles.

At the north-west of the nave is a small vestry cut off from the rest of the nave by a screen in part made from the 17th-century clerk's desk. There are no monuments.

In the east window of the chancel are three shields of arms. The first of these is the arms of Rev. Thomas Thurlow of Baynards—Argent a cheveron between couplecloses sable with three portcullises argent on the cheveron, impaling Argent a lion in a double tressure counter-flowered azure, for Lyon. Above is the crest of Hovell—A golden greyhound lying down with collar and line sable. The second shield is Onslow quartered with Harding of Knowle—Argent a bend azure with three martlets or thereon. The third shield is : Or a fesse checky azure and argent and a bend engrailed gules all within a double tressure counter-flowered gules, for Stewart, with a scutcheon of pretence—Azure a bend between six scallops argent, for Freshfield.

The tower contains a clock and six bells. The treble and second were cast by Mears of London in 1839. The third is inscribed 'Sancte Petre Or' in black-letter smalls and capitals and bears the leopard's face, cross flory and coins of John Saunders. The fourth has the same marks and is inscribed 'Sancte Johannis Ora Pro Nobis.' The fifth and tenor were cast by William Eldridge in 1671.

The first book of the registers contains all entries from 1614 to 1719. The second contains all entries from 1720, baptisms and burials running to 1803 and 1810, and marriages to 1773. The latter, after 1754, are entered in manuscript, but in the form of the printed book. A third book, a printed one, continues the marriages to 1812, and a fourth book carries the baptisms and burials to 1812.

ADVOWSON The advowson belonged in 1206 to Merton Priory.[93] At that date William Brews disputed the presentation, but Judgement was given for the priory. The latter retained the advowson until its dissolution.[94] The living was not appropriated, but paid a pension to the priory. This pension was granted in 1541 to the Dean and Chapter of Canterbury,[97] while the king retained the right of presentation. The advowson remained thenceforward with the Crown.[98]

CHARITIES Smith's Charity is distributed as in other Surrey parishes. A Mr. Worsfold gave, at an unknown date, a rent-charge of £1 2s. 8d. for teaching poor children.

---

93 Curia Regis R. 42, m. 17.
96 Winton Epis. Reg. ; Egerton MS. 2032, fol. 60 ; 2033, fol. 20, 91, &c.

97 L. and P. Hen. VIII, xvi, 878 (59).
98 Inst. Bks. (P.R.O.) A. 79 ; B. 197 ;
C. 347.

HASCOMBE

Hascumbe (xiv cent.).

Hascombe parish, about 12 miles south of Guildford, contains 1,587 acres. It is in two portions, one nearly three-quarters of a mile from north to south and half a mile from east to west ; the other half a mile each way, with tongues of the parishes of Bramley and Dunsfold separating them. Of these two portions the north-western is rather larger than the south-eastern. The whole is bounded by Godalming and Bramley on the north, by Godalming on the west, by Dunsfold and Alfold on the south, and by Bramley and Cranleigh on the east. The north-western portion is almost entirely on the Greensand and Atherfield Clay, and contains Hascombe Hill, formerly, from a large beech tree, known as Hascombe High Beech, which is 624 ft. above the sea. A telegraphic semaphore formerly stood here. The south-eastern portion is on the Wealden Clay. Hascombe village and church lie in a valley north of Hascombe Hill. The school was opened in 1867.

Park Hatch, the seat of Mr. Joseph Godman, is on the southern slope of Hascombe Hill, in a deer park of about 200 acres. Hall Place, the seat of Mr. E. L. Rowcliffe, is in the south-eastern detached portion of the parish. The old disused Wey and Arun Canal skirts this part of the parish. In 1884 Lambert's Farm, which abuts on the village street, was transferred from Hambledon to Hascombe.

There are no old houses or cottages of special architectural interest in the village, but many are to be found in the surrounding hamlets and lanes of a highly picturesque character.

Mr. Ralph Nevill notes that ' Hoe Farm is a timber house, rudely framed with great curved struts, and has . . . a look as if it might be of unusual age. Such framing is often shown in manuscripts.'

On Hascombe Hill, at the western end, is an ancient camp. It is roughly rectangular, following the slope of the hill, and from the curiously regular form of the ground it makes a sort of square of 200 yds. Water was procurable a little way down the hill. Lieut.-Colonel Godwin Austen has found sling stones on the hill, rounded flint pebbles, where no such should be geologically, and Mr. Godman found a good flint arrow-head lower down the southern slope.

HASCOMBE was held of the joint MANORS lords of Bramley.[1] Richard and John of Hascombe were tenants of Bramley in 1241–2,[2] but Hascombe probably did not separate from Bramley till early in the next century.[3] In 1306–7 Henry Hussey bought the reversion of the

manor of Hascombe from Henry Sturmy, to whom it should have descended at the death of Joan wife of John of Wintershull, who had already obtained a release of other lands in Bramley and Hascombe.[4] This Joan was probably the wife of Walter of Huntingfield, of whose grant the manor is said to have come to Henry Hussey in the inquisition of 1349.

In 1307 Henry Hussey obtained a grant of free warren in Danhurst and Hascombe.[5] In 1331 he was succeeded by his son Henry, afterwards Sir Henry Hussey, kt.,[6] who died seised of Hascombe in 1349, his heir being his grandson Henry, son of his son Mark, aged six years.[7] This Henry Hussey, or his cousin of the same name,[7a] died seised in 1409, and was succeeded by his son Henry,[8] who held for life with remainder to his son Nicholas for life and reversion to Henry elder brother of Nicholas.[9] Henry was outlawed and forfeited his rights in 1454.[10] Nicholas was sheriff of Surrey and Sussex, victualler of Calais, and Lieutenant of Guisnes Castle under Henry VI. Edward IV seized Hascombe, alleging that Nicholas had refused to render account since the change of dynasty,[11] but pardoned him in 1467.[12] Nicholas Hussey left two daughters, Catherine wife of Reginald Bray, and Alice or Constance, wife of Henry Lovel.[13] Probably the co-heiresses sold Hascombe to the Coverts, for William

Hussey. *Barry ermine and gules.*   Covert. *Gules a fesse ermine between three martlets or.*

Covert died seised of it in 1494.[14] His son John, who died in 1503, bequeathed his lands, failing his heirs male, to his cousin Richard Covert.[15] Giles Covert[15a] was in possession of the manor in 1547,[16] died in 1556, and was succeeded by his brother Anthony.[17] The manor was then successively owned by Anthony, who died in 1631, John, and Anthony Covert.[18] The last lived at Hascombe about 1654,[19] and was succeeded by John Covert,[20] whose son Anthony sold the reversion to John Fawkes of Guildford.[21] His son John

[1] Chan. Inq. p.m. 23 Edw. III, pt. i, no. 77 ; ibid. 10 Hen. IV, 17 ; ibid. (Ser. 2), cxiv, 42.
[2] Assize R. 37, m. 21 d.
[3] Feet of F. Surr. 1 Edw. II, 11.
[4] Ibid. 34 Edw. I, 3 and 12.
[5] Charter R. 35 Edw. I, m. 16.
[6] Chan. Inq. p.m. 6 Edw. III (1st nos.), no. 66.
[7] Ibid. 23 Edw. III, pt. i, no. 77.
[7a] Compare manor of Freefolk (*V.C.H. Hants*, iv), and see De Banco R. Hil. 2

Hen. VII, m. 430 ; Mich. 3 Hen. VII, m. 154.
[8] Chan. Inq. p.m. 10 Hen. IV, no. 17.
[9] Add. Chart. 18726.
[10] Esch. Inq. p.m. (Ser. 1), 32–3 Hen. VI, file 1801, no. 2. He had previously conveyed the manor to Richard Bitterley and John Hole. Anct. D., B 4199.
[11] Exr. Accts. (Foreign), 5 Edw. IV, no. 99 P.
[12] Cal. Pat. 1467–77, p. 20.
[13] Winton Epis. Reg. Fox, i, fol. 3a.

[14] Chan. Inq. p.m. (Ser. 2), x, 38.
[15] Ibid. xxiii, 263.
[15a] Son of Giles, nephew of John, Harl. Soc. Publ. xliii, 39.
[16] Misc. Bks.(Ld. Rev.),vol.190,fol.143.
[17] Chan. Inq. p.m. (Ser. 2), cxiv, 42.
[18] Feet of F. (Surr.), Hil. 31 Eliz.; Hil. 14 Jas. I ; Hil. 1654.
[19] Add. MS. 6167, fol. 252.
[20] Feet of F. Surr. Mich. 34 Chas. II.
[21] Aubrey, Nat. Hist. and Antiq. of Surr. iv, 93.

sold the manor In 1723 to Leonora Frederick and her son John Frederick who was created baronet in

FREDERICK, Baronet. *Or a chief azure with three doves argent therein.*

THISTLEWAITE. *Or a bend azure with three pheons or therein.*

the same year.[28] Early in the 19th century Hascombe became the property of Robert Thistlewaite through marriage with Selina Frederick,[29] daughter of Sir John's younger son Thomas, who succeeded his brother in the baronetcy. Sir Henry Edmund Austen of Shalford bought it of their son and sold it in 1841 to Joseph Godman of Park Hatch, grandfather of the present lord of the manor.

GODMAN of Park Hatch. *Party ermine and ermines a chief indented or and therein a lion passant vert.*

The old manor-house was at Place Farm, south-east of the church and north of Hascombe Hill.

CHURCH The church (not mentioned in Domesday) of *ST. PETER*[34] is situated in the midst of lovely wooded scenery in the fork between two roads near a cluster of houses. The churchyard is planted with fine trees and shrubs, and is approached through a modern lychgate.

The church was entirely rebuilt in 13th-century style in 1864 from designs by Mr. H. Woodyer, in Bargate stone, with Bath stone dressings. It is small, but very thoroughly finished in every detail, and consists of a nave, a small western tower, with shingled spire, a chancel with a polygonal apse, a south chapel and a south porch. Almost the only relic of the old church is the 15th-century chancel screen, which has, however, been elaborately decorated in colour. The narrow lancet windows are filled with glass by Hardman, and on the walls of the apse are carved the angels of the seven churches, each holding a stone candlestick. There are an alabaster reredos and sedilia, a credencetable, and a squint from the south chapel, which contains the squire's pew and is screened off from the nave. The stone pulpit has a carved figure of St. Peter. The font of Sussex marble has a small square bowl on a square-banded pedestal and plinth, and bears the inscription on its western face, 'The gift of Richard Holland, rector, 1690.' It somewhat resembles in form two Sussex fonts not far away, at Lurgashall and North Chapel, also of Sussex marble, and bearing date 1661. In 1890 the nave was

decorated in colour, the subject being the Miraculous Draught of Fishes.

The old church must have been a curious and singularly attractive little building, judging by the drawing preserved in Cracklow's *Churches of Surrey* (1824). The late Mr. J. L. André has also left a careful sketch of the church taken from the southeast, Cracklow's view being from the north-west, accompanied by a small block plan to scale, from which its dimensions can be approximately recovered.

It was built of Bargate rubble, and the walls were plastered externally. It consisted of nave, about 40 ft. by 20 ft. internally, and short chancel with a semicircular apse about 15 ft. in length and 17 ft. in width. On the north of the nave, somewhat unusually, was the principal entrance, protected by a timber-framed porch with arched opening and foliated barge-board of 14th-century character. A little to the west of the middle of the nave roof (which was covered with Horsham slabs) rose a timber bell-turret with shingled spirelet, containing two bells (re-cast at the re-building), this turret being described by Cracklow as 'a loft of timber,' viewed from within the nave. At the west end there was a gallery erected in 1784. The south door was a plain round-headed opening of mid 12th-century date, and two very perfect little windows of the same date remained, one in either wall, in the eastern part of the nave. (In Mr. André's sketch the stove pipe is seen projecting through that on the south.) In the apse were two lancets of early 13th-century character, while to the west of that on the south side was a two-light tracery window of the first half of the 14th century, and another of similar date and style in the eastern part of the nave beyond the apse. A plain opening filled with a wooden frame had been pierced in the west wall about 1800, and another in the western part of the south wall, high up, to light the gallery.

The earliest monuments are to Richard Holland, rector, and to his wife, who died respectively in 1694 and 1664. The ancient family of Didelsfold is represented by later memorials.

All the church plate is of 19th-century date, one chalice being engraved with seven kneeling angels and the Agnus Dei, the River of Life, the Holy City, the twelve angels and the names of the tribes of Israel and of the twelve Apostles of the Lamb, &c. No less than 300 precious stones (including those mentioned in the Apocalypse) have been employed in the jewelling of this remarkable cup, which was the work of Mr. J. A. Pippet, of the firm of Messrs. J. Hardman & Co., Birmingham, who also executed the wall-paintings in the church. Underneath the foot is 'Vernon Musgrave Rector of Hascombe A.D. 1889.'

The bells are all modern.

The registers of baptisms date from 1646, of marriages from 1658, of burials from 1659.

ADVOWSON No church is mentioned in the *Taxatio* of 1291, but Henry Hussey died seised of the advowson in 1305.[36] It belonged to the successive lords of Hascombe till early in the 19th century, when Algernon

[28] Feet of F. Surr. Hil. 9 Geo. I; Recov. R. East. 9 Geo. I, m. 13, 16.
[29] Brayley, *Hist. of Surr.* v, 127; Recov. R. East. 1 Geo. IV, m. 6.
[34] Commonly so called. Salmon, *Antiquities of Surr.* (ed. 1735), called it St. John's. In 1535 Arnold Mellersh desired by will to be buried before the high altar in the church of St. Michael, Hascombe.
[36] Harl. MS. 5193, fol. 26.

Wallington appears to have purchased it.[56] In 1835 Alan Mackenzie presented to the church.[57] In 1841 the advowson was the property of Mrs. T. C. Stone,[58] and in 1906 of the trustees of Mr. E. Thompson.

Dr. Conyers Middleton, author of *The History of the Life of Cicero*, was presented to the living in March 1746–7,[59] but did not apparently reside.

CHARITY.—Smith's Charity is distributed in money and clothing.

ST. MARTHA'S OR CHILWORTH

St. Martha's (1291) ;[1] St. Martha and All Holy Martyrs, and Martyr's Hill (1464) ; Martha Hill (1468) ; Marters Hill (1538) ; St. Martha on the Hill (1589).

St. Martha's is a small parish, now ecclesiastically merged in Albury, 2 miles south-east of Guildford, bounded on the north by Stoke and Merrow, on the west by Shalford, on the south by Wonersh, on the east by Albury. It contains 1,060 acres. Its greatest length north to south is under 2 miles, its greatest breadth on the northern border is under a mile and a half. The soil is chalk in the north, on the downs, but most of it is on the Greensand, which rises in St. Martha's Hill to 570 ft. above the sea. The hill, crowned by what is now called the chapel of St. Martha, is abrupt and isolated, forming a more conspicuous object than the height, which is surpassed by the hills to the south of it, would indicate. It is higher than the chalk down to the north of it, and the views from it south-west towards Hindhead, and eastward along the valley to Albury and Shere, are among the most picturesque in the county.

The valley to the south of the hill, through which the Tillingbourne flows, has for long been the seat of industries dependent upon the good water-power supplied by the stream. There was a mill in Domesday, a corn-mill and a fulling-mill in 1589,[2] and from before that date gunpowder mills, which still continue.[3] There was a paper-mill which was burnt down in 1896 and has never been rebuilt. Cobbett, in his *Rural Rides*, has a remark, often quoted, upon the extreme beauty of this valley as God made it, and its pollution by the two worst inventions of the Devil, gunpowder and bank-notes being manufactured in it.

Postford Mill is on the boundary of this parish and of Albury. The road from Guildford to Dorking and the Reading branch of the South Eastern Railway traverse the southern end of the parish ; Chilworth and Albury station, opened 1849, is just inside it.

An ancient bridle way from the ferry over the Wey at St. Catherine's Hill, through the Chantry Woods, and over St. Martha's Hill, close by the church, and so down to Albury, has been generally identified with the Pilgrims' Way. The line, straight over the top of a steep isolated hill which might have been easily turned upon either side, does seem to indicate some ancient route to some object of interest upon the hill. If to the church, the Holy Martyr, St. Thomas of Canterbury, one of the patrons of Newark Priory, to which the church was appropriated, whose shrine at Canterbury travellers here might be seeking, may have superseded St.

Martha in popular language as the patron of the hill.

Neolithic flint implements and flakes are of more than usually abundant occurrence on this road, on the hill and in the fields to the north of it. On the hill, near the top and towards the southern side, were several curious earth-circles about 28 to 30 yds. in diameter marked by a slight mound and ditch. The best was destroyed a few years ago by the Hambledon District Council, who made a reservoir on the hill to which water is pumped to supply houses on Blackheath. The persons responsible for the work made no effort to observe or record any discoveries. The next best marked lies nearly due south of the church. To the south-west is another, fairly well marked, but much overgrown by heather, ferns, and fir trees. The fourth, nearly obliterated, is south-east of the church. South-west of the church marks in the ground visible in a dry season may indicate nearly obliterated hut-circles. Small flint implements are to be found in them scratched out by rabbits. At the western corner of the hill, near the road opposite Tyting, is a large barrow with trees upon it, which has, apparently, never been disturbed. On the north side of St. Martha's Hill lies the old farm-house of Tyting, which from the period of the Domesday Survey belonged to the Bishops of Exeter. It stands in a quaint old-world herb-garden, and still retains a small oratory with a group of three lancets in chalk, probably of early 13th-century date.

Chilworth is an erroneous name for the parish. It is an ancient manor, and the few houses usually called Chilworth are partly in St. Martha's and partly in Shalford parishes. Of modern houses Lockner Holt and Brantyngeshay in the part of the parish which reaches Blackheath to the south are the residences of Mrs. Sellar and Mr. H. W. Prescott, respectively. The elementary school was opened in 1873. There are one or two old houses in the hamlet of Chilworth. Some of these are probably due to the settlement here in Elizabeth's reign of workmen employed under Sir Polycarp Wharton in the manufacture of gunpowder.

MANORS There are two reputed manors in St. Martha—Chilworth, to the south, and Tyting, to the north, of St. Martha's Hill.

CHILWORTH (Celeorde, xi cent. ; Cheleworth, xiii and xiv cents.) was held by Alwin under Edward the Confessor, and after the Conquest came with Bramley, in which it lay, into the hands of Odo, Bishop of Bayeux.[4] It was afterwards held of the lords of Bramley by the tenants of Utworth Manor[5] (q.v.), with which it descended till 1614, at which date Sir John Morgan, who was knighted at Cadiz in 1596,[6] sold

[56] Inst. Bks. (P.R.O.).
[57] Ibid.
[58] Brayley, *Hist. of Surr.* v, 127.
[59] *Dict. Nat. Biog.* xxxvii, 346.
[1] 'Taxatio Ecclesiastica,' Cott. MS. Ti-
berius C. x. which is nearly contemporary with 1291.
[2] Settlement on the marriage of John Morgan of Chilworth.
[3] *V.C.H. Surr.* ii, 301.
[4] Ibid. i, 301.
[5] It is first recorded as being in their possession in 1240–1 ; Feet of F. Surr. 25 Hen. III, 7.
[6] S.P. Dom. Eliz. cclix, 84.

Utworth but retained Chilworth.[7] Sir John's daughter Anne married Sir Edward Randyll,[8] whose son Sir Morgan Randyll, kt., was seised of the manor in 1640–1, when he was proved insane.[9] His brother, Vincent Randyll, succeeded him.[10] His son Morgan Randyll, who was for some years member of Parliament for Guildford, sold the manor in 1720 to Richard Houlditch, a director of the South Sea Company.[11] After the company's failure the directors' lands were sold to indemnify its victims. The estates of Richard Houlditch were purchased by Sarah, Dowager Duchess of Marlborough, who bequeathed them to her grandson John, Earl Spencer,[12] who was succeeded in 1746 by his son John, afterwards Viscount Althorp.[13] His son sold the manor in 1796 to Edmund Hill,[14] from whom it passed to William Tinkler, whose son William owned it in 1841.[15] It was sold in 1845, together with Weston in Albury, to Mr. Henry Drummond, and is now in the possession of the Duke of Northumberland.[16]

SPENCER, Earl Spencer. *Argent quartered with gules fretty or over all a bend sable with three scallops argent thereon.*

On the south side of St. Martha's Hill stands the manor-house of Chilworth, which has an ornamental brick gable and porch. On the site of this was a cell belonging to the priory of Newark, and St. Martha's was probably always served by a canon resident here. Their large walled and terraced gardens and stewponds for fish still remain.

TYTING (Tetinges, xi cent ; Titing, xiii cent.) was held by Elmer the Huntsman before the Conquest, and afterwards became a possession of Bishop Osbern of Exeter, who had been chaplain to Edward the Confessor.[17] It was held by the successive Bishops of Exeter till 1548. In 1234–5 John le Chanu and his wife Katherine quit-claimed to William Bishop of Exeter Katherine's rights in Tyting.[18] From time to time this manor was assessed among the Bishop's temporalities.[19] In August 1549 John Veysey, then Bishop of Exeter, sold the freehold to Thomas Fisher.[20] He shortly afterwards conveyed it to Henry Polsted,[21] whose son Richard, together with

SEE OF EXETER. *Gules St. Paul's sword erect surmounted by St. Peter's keys crossed saltirewise.*

William Morgan, was in possession in 1571.[22] He married Elizabeth, daughter of Sir William More of Loseley, and had from him an assignment of a ninety-nine years' lease which Sir William and Henry Weston are said to have acquired in February 1566–7.[23] Richard Folsted died in 1576,[24] and in the next year Francis Polsted alienated Tyting to Sir William More, probably as trustee for Elizabeth (Polsted),[25] but William Morgan's interest still continued, for in 1602 he died seised of lands and tenements called 'Titing.'[26]

Early in the same century both Sir George More, son of Sir William More, and Ann Randyll, granddaughter of William Morgan, joined with George Duncombe in a conveyance of the manor to John Astrete or Street,[27] who is said to have been holding the estate in 1602.[28] He was succeeded by his son John.[29] John Street and George Duncombe conveyed to Francis Williamson in 1637. He sold to Vincent Rundyn, and the latter to George Duncombe of Albury, who by his will of 1672 left in it trust for his family, Richard Symmes being one of the trustees.[30] Manning and Bray say that it was conveyed in 1710 to Abraham Woods, from the trustees of whose sons William it came to Philip Carteret Webb in 1747. From Mr. Webb it descended to his son, John Smith Webb,[31] who sold it to Robert Austen of Shalford,[32] in whose family it still remains.

ST. MARTHA'S Chapel,[33] a well-known landmark for all the country side, stands upon the summit of a ridge of Greensand, about 570 ft. above the sea. Although called a chapel, it seems always to have possessed the rights of a parish church ; and it is probably to be identified with one of the three churches mentioned in Domesday as standing on the manor of Bramley, then held by Bishop Odo of Bayeux, who may well have built the original of the present building. The site itself is an extremely ancient one, and several circular earthworks still remain on St. Martha's Hill.

CHURCH

The building as we now see it is largely of modern date, an object-lesson of the mischievous results of fanciful restoration, the nave, which had long lain in ruins, being rebuilt in a pseudo-'Norman' style, and the chancel and transept largely reconstructed in 1848. The chancel and transepts had remained intact until about 1846, although the nave was a roofless ruin, and only fragments of the large west tower existed ; but in that year part of the roof fell in and services were suspended. The then Lord Loraine co-operated with two other neighbouring county gentlemen, Mr. H. Currie, of West Horsley, and Mr. R. A. C. Godwin Austen, of Shalford, to rebuild the ruined nave and restore the eastern limb, the last fragments of the western tower being at the

[7] Feet of F. Surr. Hil. 11 Jas. I.
[8] Chan. Inq. p.m. (Ser. 2), ccccxxxvii, 72.
[9] Ibid. ccccxcii, 15.
[10] Feet of F. Surr. Hil. 1649.
[11] Ibid. Mich. 7 Geo. I.
[12] *True Copy of the Last Will and Testament of Sarah, late Duchess Dowager of Marlborough* (ed. 1744), 2 et seq.
[13] Collins, *Peerage* (ed. 1779), i, 340.
[14] Manning and Bray, op. cit. ii, 118.
[15] Brayley, *Topog. Hist. of Surr.* v, 131.
[16] See account of Albury.
[17] *V.C.H. Surr.* i, 300a. In the Domesday Survey Tyting is accounted for in Woking Hundred. In Speed's

map of Surrey, 1676, Tyting is just within the boundary of Woking Hundred.
[18] Feet of F. Surr. 19 Hen. III, 19.
[19] *Pope Nich. Tax.* (Rec. Com.), 207 ; Esch. Inq. (Ser. 1), file 1760, no. 1.
[20] Pat. 3 Edw. VI, pt. vi, m. 16 et seq.
[21] Feet of F. Surr. East. 5 Edw. VI.
[22] Loseley MS. x, 59.
[23] Manning and Bray, op. cit. ii, 119. The lease had been granted by Veysey to Sir Edmund Walsingham in 2 Edw. VI (1548). Elizabeth Polsted paid money to Henry Weston shortly after 1576 (Loseley MS. ix, 36).

[24] Loseley MS. x, 59.
[25] Feet of F. Surr. Mich. 19 & 20 Eliz.
[26] Chan. Inq. p.m. (Ser. 2), cclxxxi, 85.
[27] Feet of F. Surr. East. 6 Jas. I ; Hil. 19 Jas. I.
[28] Manning and Bray, op. cit. ii, 119.
[29] W. and L. Inq. p.m. xxxix, 94.
[30] Manning and Bray, op. cit. ii, 119, from Symmes Add. MS. 6167. From Symmes' position as trustee the account is probably correct.
[31] Recov. R. Trin. 25 Geo. III.
[32] Manning and Bray, op. cit. ii, 119.
[33] 'Saynt Marter' is the title given in the inventory of church goods taken in the reign of Edward VI.

same time removed. This tower, which seems to have been very massive and large, is shown in ruins in the engraving published in Grose's *Antiquities*, from a sketch taken in 1763,[84] it having been thrown down by a severe explosion at the Chilworth gunpowder factories in that year. This view shows part of the vault (apparently a plain quadripartite one without ribs) as then existing, and beneath is a circular squared-edged arch opening into the nave. The simple character of this arch, which was devoid of ornament except for a chamfered impost at the springing, suggests that it may have been part of Bishop Odo's work of the last decades of the 11th century; and a small round-headed window in the south wall of the nave, shown in Cracklow's view of 1824, coincides very well with this date. There seems to have been a plain early doorway in the north and south walls, features that together with the windows have been reproduced in some sort in the new work. The nave, built on the old foundations, measures 45 ft. in length by 15 ft. 1 in. at the west, and 16 ft. at the east; the central crossing, 12 ft. 6 in. by 13 ft. 6 in. wide; the north transept, 11 ft. 8 in. by 12 ft., and the south transept, 12 ft. 8 in. by 12 ft.; while the chancel is 23 ft.

were dug up, and now lie on the floor of the chancel. Two buttresses against the south wall of the chancel are probably not mediaeval, but a sort of buttress projection in the angle between that wall and the east wall of the south transept was possibly made to allow of a squint being pierced from the transept to command the high altar.

There is reason to believe that the barrel-shaped font, of sandstone, is the one described by Manning and Bray as at Elstead Church, whence it had disappeared before 1845. The St. Martha's font was brought 'from another church,' where it had been thrown out into the churchyard in 1849, and the carving added on the spot. The original was early Norman, like that at Thursley.[85]

The silver cup and paten bear the London hall-marks of 1780.

The bells are all modern.

An iron church in Chilworth hamlet was built in 1896 and is served from Shalford.

ADVOWSON   St. Martha's was probably one of the three churches appurtenant to Bramley in 1087,[85a] and the advowson alienated by the lord of Bramley, at the time when Chilworth was granted out to the lords of Utworth, for Elias of Utworth[86] owned late in the 12th century, and granted it to the Priory of St. Thomas the Martyr at Aldebury.[87] The priory retained the advowson until its surrender in 1538.[88] In the episcopal registers of 1463 record is kept of an indulgence granted to pilgrims to, or benefactors of, the church of St. Martha and All Holy Martyrs.[89] After the surrender of the priory the advowson seems to have become the property of the lords of Chilworth Manor, with which it has since descended.

SCALE OF FEET

NORTH TRANSEPT

NAVE

FONT

CHANCEL

SOUTH TRANSEPT

c. 1190   13th Cent.   c. 1230   c. 1340

PLAN OF ST. MARTHA'S OR CHILWORTH CHURCH

long by 16 ft. 8 in. The thickness of the present west wall (3 ft. 6 in.) represents that of the walls of the destroyed western tower. The transept and crossing walls are 2 ft. 3 in. on an average.

The authority for the present central tower is very questionable, and in any case its 'Norman' style is out of keeping with the plain early pointed arches on which it stands, parts of which are original work of *circa* 1190.

Probably the first chancel was apsidal, and this square space represented the quire.

There is no window in the west wall of the north transept or the north wall of the chancel, and all the other windows are restorations. It is on record that foundations were discovered in the ground to the east of the transepts, probably those of chapels, perhaps apsidal. Three aumbries were found in the chancel, and two stone coffin-lids, with floriated crosses, much worn,

The church in 1291 is called *ecclesia* not *capella*, and the canons of Newark were endowed with all the usual parochial revenues in 1262.[40] They presented a vicar previous to 1330,[41] and as late as 1412.[42] Latterly it was a donative, probably from the time of the Dissolution, and an annuity was paid to a curate by the patron. The duty was usually done by the incumbent of some neighbouring parish or his curate. The registers are in consequence imperfect, entries being in existence in Wonersh, Albury, and elsewhere referring to St. Martha's; but there is a register with some entries of baptisms and burials from 1779, and of marriages from 1794. Since 1849 it has been attached to Albury, and the rector of Albury, the Rev. H. E. Crossley, was instituted by the Bishop of Winchester as rector of Albury and vicar of St. Martha's in 1904.

[84] In an engraving by Hill, probably made between 1740 and 1750, published in the *Eccl. Topog. of Surr.*, all four walls of the tower are shown as standing. Russel, *Hist. of Guildford*, mentions that there were three bells in the tower, and that most of the materials were carried off by Lord Spencer's steward 'to mend the roads.'

[85] Information of the late Rev. J. R. Charlsworth and of the late Mr. H. Woodyer.
[85a] *V.C.H. Surr.* i, 301*a*.
[86] See under Utworth.
[87] i.e. the priory of Newark; Maitland, *Bracton's Note Bk.* 928.

[88] See *V.C.H. Surr.* ii, 104.
[89] Bishop Waynflete's Register, quoted by Manning and Bray, op. cit. ii, 119.
[40] Winton Epis. Reg. Waynflete i (2), fol. 83.
[41] Ibid. Stratford, fol. 120*a*.
[42] Ibid. Beaufort Inst. fol. 92*a*.

VIEW SHOWING ST. MARTHA'S HILL

ST. MARTHA'S CHAPEL FROM THE SOUTH-WEST

·SHALFORD

Scaldefor (xi cent.) ; Scaudeford (xiii cent.) ; Shaldeford (xiv cent.) ; Shalforde (xvi cent.).

The parish of Shalford lies south-east of Guildford. It is intersected by the River Wey from south to north, and the Tillingbourne running east and west joins the Wey close to the village. It is bounded on the north by St. Mary's and Holy Trinity parishes, Guildford, and by Stoke ; on the east by Chilworth ; on the south-east by Wonersh ; on the south by Bramley ; on the south-west by Godalming ; on the west by St. Nicholas Guildford. The parish contains about 2,560 acres. It is 6 miles long from north to south, 2 miles broad, generally, with a narrow tongue running out further to the west.

The soil is chiefly the Lower Greensand, with an outcrop of Gault, and also of Wealden Clay at Shalford Park. But like all the parishes on the southern side of the chalk range the northern boundary extends on to the chalk down, where a suburb of Guildford, called Warwick's Bench, is in Shalford parish, not included in Guildford Borough.

Shalford Common is a stretch of open grass extending from near Tangley Manor in Wonersh to the Wey. Trunley Common and Gosden Common are almost touching it to the south-west of the parish, and part of Peasemarsh Common is in Shalford to the west. From near Shalford village towards St. Martha's Hill, the Chantry Woods, so named from part of them having formed the endowment of the Norbrigge Chantry in Trinity Church, Guildford, are a wooded ridge on the highest part of the Greensand. Half the parish is open common or wood.

The old Common Fields, finally inclosed in 1803, lay between Shalford village and Guildford, on the east side of the road. On the west side is Shalford Park. This road intersects the parish, and divides to Shalford Common, leading south to Horsham, east to Dorking.

The parish is also intersected by the Red Hill and Reading Branch of the South Eastern Railway. Shalford Station was opened in 1849. The London Brighton and South Coast and London and South Western Railways intersect the parish, but there are no stations upon them. The canal, made in 1813, connecting the Wey and the Arun, left the former river in Shalford parish. It became unnavigable about 1870, and is now quite abandoned.

There is a brewery at Broadford on the Wey. At Summersbury there is a tannery, which has been established over a century.[1] Cloth-making was carried on at Shalford in the 17th century.[2] There are chalk pits and lime kilns on the slope of the downs, in the northern part of the parish.

In 1086 there were three mills at Shalford.[3] One water-mill only is mentioned in an extent of East Shalford in 1332.[4] When the manor was divided the lords of each moiety had half the mill. In 1547 Christopher More of Loseley held the mill, which had recently belonged to Robert Wintershull.[5] This

is Pratt's mill now existing on the Tillingbourne. The other two mills seem to have been upon the River Wey, near Unstead, and near the weir above St. Catherine's lock [6] respectively, being referred to in a lawsuit in 1379 between the inhabitants of Shalford and Robert de Chisenhale, &c.[7]

A cottage near the old way from St. Catherine's Ferry to St. Martha's Hill, isolated from the village by the old Common Fields, is traditionally called the Pest House. It is usually known now as Cyder House Cottage. In the last house of the parish on the left-hand side of Quarry Hill on the road into Guildford, John Bunyan is said to have held a meeting.

Neolithic implements and a few Roman coins have been found near East Shalford Manor House,[8] and palaeolithic implements have been found between the Chantry Woods and the chalk down.

Opposite the church is an old house called Dibnersh, the residence of the Misses · Morris. It formerly belonged to the Duncombe family (see Albury and Ockley), and was sold to Mr. Robert Austen in 1755.

Bradstone Brook is the seat of Mr. J. H. Renton ; it was built in 1791 by Mr. Thomas Gibson. Gosden House, the property of Mr. F. E. Eastwood, is the residence of Mr. S. Christopherson. A considerable number of small gentlemen's houses have been built in the parish, and a large residential suburb of Guildford is springing up about Pewley Hill in Shalford.

There is a Wesleyan chapel on Shalford Common, originally established in 1843. A new building was erected in 1895. Near the eastern border of the parish is a small iron church where services are held, and another on the borders of Peasemarsh.

The cemetery was opened in 1886. The Village Hall, presented by Mr. Edward Ellis of Summersbury in 1886, is near the station. It contains a refreshment room, meeting room, and reading room.

The school was built as a Church of England school in 1855. In 1881 it was transferred to a school board, and the buildings were enlarged in 1882.

Shalford is one of the prettiest and most charmingly situated villages in Surrey, lying as it does in the midst of water meadows, with tall poplars and other fine trees, between the River Wey and its tributary the Tillingbourne. The village consists of a winding street of picturesque old cottages, with a few others straggling up side lanes and down to the water. The Seahorse Inn is a pleasant old-world hostelry with square-leaded panes to the windows. Many of the cottages appear to have been smartened up as to their fronts in the beginning of the 19th century, but the backs and interiors show them to be really old. A short lane leads down to the little water-mill, tile-hung almost to the ground, and having a large projecting upper story carried on wooden pillars.

It is probable that its proximity to Guild-

1 *V.C.H. Surr.* ii, 341.
2 Ibid. ii, 344.
3 Ibid. i, 319a.

4 Chan. Inq. p.m. 6 Edw. III (2nd nos.) no. 84.
5 Misc. Bks. (Exch. L.T.R.), vol. 168, p. 72.

6 Estate map 1617 *penes* Col. Godwin-Austen.
7 Manning and Bray, op. cit. ii, 99.
8 *V.C.H. Surr.* i, 253.

ford made Shalford a favourite country retreat, and that this accounts for there being several houses of some pretension. Among others, near to the mill, is one which as it does not face the road is easily overlooked. It has a gable of stone with very ornamental brick dressings, and this and the other gables, which are curved and pedimental, bear a close resemblance to the early examples of brickwork in Godalming, Guildford, Farnham, &c., and both inside and out it has many points in common with the old manor-house of Slyfield, in Great Bookham parish.

This house, called Old House, but formerly Mill House, has some good mullioned windows with lead glazing, in square and diamond panes, and a good door-head. It is panelled in nearly all the rooms, and there is a particularly fine staircase, very like that at Slyfield, with rusticated newels, and instead of balusters pierced arabesque scroll-work cut out of the solid.

As a relic of the past, the stocks and whipping-post, shaded by the yew tree under the churchyard wall, are of interest.

The manor of SHALFORD or EAST SHALFORD[9] was held jointly by two brothers in the time of Edward the Confessor.[10] In 1087 it was held by Robert (possibly de Wateville) of Richard de Tonbridge.[11] The latter was the ancestor of the de Clares, and the manor continued to be held of the honour of Clare.[12] It is probable that the de Watevilles were the under-tenants until the reign of Henry II, when Robert de Wateville is said to have sold the manor to Robert de Dunstanville.[13] Walter de Dunstanville gave the manor with his sister Alice in marriage, but repossessed himself of it, whereupon Gilbert Bassett, son of Alice, obtained a confirmation of his rights from King John.[14] Richard de Camvill and his wife Eustacea (daughter and heiress of Gilbert Bassett) are said to have had the custody of Shalford during the minority of the heir of Walter de Dunstanville.[15] Richard's daughter Idonea married William Longespée son of the Earl of Salisbury,[16] and with him seems to have retained the manor[17] in spite of continued suits by a certain Sibyl.[18] Finally, William Longespée granted the manor to John son of Geoffrey, Earl of Essex.[19] His son John died seised of it, leaving a brother and heir Richard,[20] whose widow Emma, afterwards wife of

CLARE. *Or three che-verons gules.*

Robert de Montalt,[21] held it in dower.[22] She conveyed her right in it to Hugh le Despenser the younger, to whom Idonea Crumbwell, one of the heirs of Isabel

LONGESPÉE. *Azure six lioncels or.*

DESPENSER. *Argent quartered with gules fretty or with a bend sable over all.*

sister and co-heir of Richard son of John,[23] also released her claim in that moiety of the manor which should have descended to her at the death of Emma de Montalt,[24] this conveyance being forced on her against her will.[25] Robert, Lord Clifford, the other co-heir of Isabel,[26] made no quitclaim to the Despensers. Therefore when, at the forfeiture of the latter's estates, Shalford was taken into the king's hands,[27] this moiety remained with Robert Clifford and became the manor of Shalford Clifford.[28]

SHALFORD CLIFFORD was settled by Robert, Lord Clifford, on his youngest son Thomas for life.[29] In 1373 Sir Roger Clifford, kt., second son, but ultimately heir, of Robert, conveyed the reversion at his brother's death to his own son Thomas and his wife Elizabeth,[30] who survived her husband.[31] Their grandson and heir, Thomas, Lord Clifford, was killed at St. Albans in 1455, leaving a son and heir John, Lord Clifford, who was killed at

CLIFFORD, Earl of Cumberland. *Checky or and azure a fesse gules.*

BROWNE, Viscount Montagu. *Sable three lions passant bendways between double cotises argent.*

[9] In contra-distinction to the rectory manor of West Shalford ; Early Chan. Proc. liii, 119.

[10] V.C.H. Surr. i, 319a. They are said to have lived ' in una curia.'

[11] Ibid.

[12] Testa de Nevill (Rec. Com.), 219 ; Chan. Inq. p.m. 25 Edw. I, 50; ibid. 18 Edw. III (1st nos.), no. 50 ; ibid. (Ser. 2), x, 164.

[13] Manning and Bray, op. cit. ii, 59. Quoting 'Plac. de Banco, East. 14 Hen. III, in pell. scacc. reg. reman. rot. 19,' but this reference cannot be verified.

[14] Cal. Rot. Chart. (Rec. Com.), i, 41.

[15] Abbrev. Plac. (Rec. Com.), 47.

[16] Rot. Lit. Pat. (Rec. Com.), i, 178b ; Rot. Lit. Claus. (Rec. Com.), ii, 123, 138.

[17] Testa de Nevill (Rec. Com.), 219.

[18] She is said to have been the second wife of Walter de Dunstanville. She appears first as Sibyl wife of Ingram de Pratellis and afterwards as Sibyl Ferrars ; Close, 10 Hen. III, m. 5 ; ibid. 12 Hen. III, m. 13 d, 3 d.

[19] Deed then in possession of Sir John Nicholas quoted by Symmes ; Add. MS. 6167, fol. 370.

[20] Chan. Inq. p.m. 4 Edw. I, no. 47.

[21] Pat. 29 Edw. I, m. 32.

[22] Chan. Inq. p.m. 6 Edw. III (2nd nos.), no. 61.

[23] Chan. Inq. p.m. 25 Edw. I, no. 50.

[24] Feet of F. Surr. 17 Edw. II; Cal. Pat. 1313–17, p. 402.

[25] Cal. of Pat. 1330–4, p. 440. Apparently restitution was not made to Idonea.

[26] Pat. 7 Edw. III, pt. i, m. 27 ; Chan. Inq. p.m. 25 Edw. I, no. 50. Robert was brother and heir of Roger son of Isabel ; Chan. Inq. p.m. 6 Edw. III (2nd nos.), no. 61. Roger forfeited his lands before his death in 1344, and with them the reversion of Shalford ; Pat. 15 Edw. II, m. 7.

[27] Esch. Accts. 5–8 Edw. III, ii, 54, m. 11 ; Chan. Inq. p.m. 6 Edw. III (2nd nos.), no. 61.

[28] The temporary custody of the other half was granted to William Hatton ; Esch. Accts. 5–8 Edw. III, ii, 54, m. 11.

[29] Chan. Inq. p.m. 18 Edw. III (1st nos.), no. 50.

[30] Feet of F. Surr. 2 Ric. II, 15. The conveyance was not complete till 1379.

[31] Chan. Inq. p.m. 13 Hen. VI, no. 42.

Ferrybridge and attainted in 1461.[32] His lands were granted to an usher of Edward IV, Nicholas Gaynesford,[33] who was himself attainted at the accession of Richard III.[34] The manor was granted by that king to Sir John Neville.[35] On the accession of Henry VII it was restored to Henry, Lord Clifford, 'the shepherd lord,' with the other possessions of his father, John, Lord Clifford.[36] His grandson Henry, second Earl of Cumberland, sold Shalford to Sir Anthony Browne in January 1543–4.[37] Sir Anthony had inherited Shalford Bradestan, the other moiety of the original manor. Thus the two moieties were re-united and descended to Sir Anthony's son, who was created Viscount Montagu in 1554.[38] Francis, third viscount, sold the manor to Sir John Nicholas in 1677.[39] In 1733 the executors of Edward Nicholas, his son, who died in 1726, sold the manor to Thomas, Lord Onslow,[40] in whose family it has since remained, the present owner being William Hillier, Earl of Onslow.

When the manor was taken into the king's hands in 1333 (vide supra) the custody of SHALFORD BRADESTAN, the second moiety of Shalford, was granted successively to William Hatton, Henry Hussey, and Thomas de Ponings.[41] The last held it for life. At his death it was granted in tail to Sir Thomas de Bradestan, from whom it obtained the name of Shalford Bradestan. He was succeeded in 1360 by his grandson and heir Thomas,[42] who died a minor in 1374, leaving an infant daughter Elizabeth,[43] who married Walter de la Pole.[44] He died seised of Shalford Bradestan in right of his wife in 1434.[45] Their grandson Sir Edmund Ingaldesthorp, kt., inherited the manor.[46] At his death in 1456 his widow Joan held the manor in dower, her husband's heirs being the children of his daughter Isabel, Marchioness Montagu. One of these, Lucy Fitz William, inherited Shalford Bradestan at Joan's death in 1494,[47] and bequeathed it to her son William Fitz William and his wife Mabel[48] for life, with reversion to her son Sir Anthony Browne, who had purchased the other part of Shalford Clifford (vide supra), so that the whole was reunited and descended as above. The demesne of the whole manor called East Shalford Manor was purchased in 1779 by Robert Austen,

BRADESTAN. Argent a quarter gules with a rose or therein.

and is the property of Colonel Godwin Austen, his descendant.

There was a custom that the lord of Shalford might tally his bond-tenants 100s. yearly.[49] In the 13th century John son of Geoffrey, lord of Shiere, unjustly appropriated view of frankpledge to himself there.[50] The right of free warren was appurtenant to the manor.[51] In the 14th century the lords of Shalford Clifford and Bradestan paid Romscot to the vicar of Shalford.[52]

AUSTEN OF SHALFORD. Azure a cheveron argent between three choughs or.

The early history of the reputed manor of UNSTEAD (Townhampstead, Ownstead, or Unsted, xvi cent.) is obscure. In 1256–7 William de Wintershull acquired land in Dunsfold, Hascombe, Bramley, and 'Tunchamstede,' from Geoffrey de Braboeuf.[53] Late in the 13th century William son of Eustace of East Catteshull granted lands in East Catteshull in Bramley to John son of Ralph de Tonhamstede, in exchange for land there called Pinnokesland.[54]

In 1385 William Wehbe complained at the Godalming Hundred Court of trespass upon his land at 'Tunhamstede.'[55] Later in the 15th century Henry Stoughton was seised of Unstead, and his son Thomas was in possession in 1459–90.

Thomas had a son Gilbert, and in 1517 Gilbert Stoughton died seised of Unstead, held of the manor of Selhurst (or Wintershull), his son Laurence being his heir.[56]

In 1547 Laurence Stoughton conveyed it to John Parvish, jun., in exchange for lands in Stoke.[57] John Parvish of Unstead was buried in 1583.[58] His nephew Thomas Parvish sold the manor in 1588 to his cousin Henry Parvish, citizen and haberdasher of London, who died 4 August 1593, having settled his estate on his sons and their heirs female.[59]

The capital messuage was bought in 1608 by Sir George More of Loseley from Gabriel Parvish, son of Henry,[60] and he in 1609 conveyed to George Austen,[61] who died seised of it in 1621, and was succeeded by his son John.[62] He sold it in 1626 to the trustees of Henry Smith's Charity in Godalming,[63] and they conveyed it to the Corporation of Godalming for a sewage farm in 1894.

The reputed manor was apparently divided among the Parvish family, and Unstead Manor Farm was a possession of the Onslow family during the 17th

[32] Chan. Inq. p.m. 4 Edw. IV, no. 52.
[33] Pat. 5 Edw. IV, pt. ii, m. 5; 1 Edw. IV, pt. iii, m. 7.
[34] Harl. MS. 433, fol. 145.
[35] Ibid. fol. 168.
[36] Materials for Hist. of Hen. VII (Rolls Ser.), i, 117.
[37] L. and P. Hen. VIII, xix (1), 80 (64). Cal. S.P. Dom. 1547–80, p. 63. Sir Anthony Browne's widow married Lord Clinton, Lord High Admiral, who in 1558 speaks of his manor of Shalford Clifford; Hist. MSS. Com. Rep. vii, App. 614. The queen granted 'all lands and tenements by name of Shalford or Shalford Clifford to Thomas Butler as "concealed lands" (Pat. 33 Eliz. pt. v, m. 1 et seq.), but Vicount Montagu probably made his claim good, and remained in possession.
[38] Recov. R. Mich. 29 Chas. II, m. 56.

[40] Close, 7 Geo. II, pt. vii, m. 46.
[41] Esch. Accts. 5–8 Edw. III, ii, 54, m. 64 et seq.
[42] Chan. Inq. p.m. 34 Edw. III (1st nos.), no. 61.
[43] Ibid. 48 Edw. III (1st nos.), no. 10.
[44] Pat. 19 Ric. II, pt. ii, m. 17.
[45] Chan. Inq. p.m. 12 Hen. VI, no. 33.
[46] Cal. Inq. p.m. Hen. VII, i, 96. He was son and heir of Margaret, daughter of Elizabeth and Walter de la Pole. Margaret had married Thomas Ingaldesthorp.
[47] Ibid. 483; Chan. Inq. p.m. 35 Hen. VI, no. 20.
[48] Sir William Fitz William, created Earl of Southampton, died 1542. His widow Mabel, Countess of Southampton, was holding in 1546. See Losterford in Wonersh.
[49] Chan. Inq. p.m. 6 Edw. III (2nd nos.), no. 84.

[50] Plac. de Quo War. (Rec. Com.), 742.
[51] Feet of F. Surr. Trin. 26 Eliz.
[52] Chan. Inq. p.m. 48 Edw. III (1st nos.), no. 10.
[53] Feet of F. Surr. 50 Hen. III, 193.
[54] Add. Chart. 17279.
[55] Godalming Hund.R.1 June, 8 Ric. II.
[56] Ct. R. of Selhurst at Loseley, Feast of St. Edward the King, 8 Hen. VIII, and deeds quoted by Manning and Bray, op. cit. ii, 99. But part of Unstead was held of the manor of Stonebridge in Shalford.
[57] Feet of F. Surr. Hil. 1 & 2 Edw. VI.
[58] Parish Registers.
[59] Chan. Inq. p.m. (Ser. 2), ccxxxvi, 74.
[60] Close, 6 Jas. I, pt. i, no. 7.
[61] Ibid. 7 Jas. I.
[62] Chan. Inq. p.m. (Ser. 2), cccxcvii, 90.
[63] Com. Pleas D. Enr. Trin. 4 Chas. I, m. 23.

and 18th centuries.[64] It was exchanged by George, first Earl of Onslow, with John Sparkes, from whom it eventually came to Captain Albemarle Bertie,[65] who sold it in 1800 to Captain William Pierrepont.[66] He conveyed it to Mr. H. Trowers. It is now part of the property of Mr. L. Phillips. The farm is on the right-hand side of the road leading from the Portsmouth road to Bramley, formerly called Trowers.

SHALFORD RECTORY MANOR. King John granted to John of Guildford, parson of Shalford, a yearly fair to be held in the church and church-yard on the vigil, day, and morrow of the Assumption. The parson took no toll, but claimed the stakes fixed in the cemetery and his fee outside, and held pleas for merchants staying in his fee. When the fair grew so large that it extended into Bramley Manor, the lords of Bramley took the stakes of merchants in their fee, and also held courts for them.[67] In 1304-5 Ed-ward I granted two messuages and land with the services of free tenants in Shalford and the advowson of Shalford to the Hospital of St. Mary Without Bishopsgate.[68] The prior evidently leased the rec-tory from time to time. Roger Elliot, who had obtained such a lease in 1475-6, complained that the prior forced him, be-ing ' a stranger not acqueynted in the Cite of London and ferr from his frendes and wife,' to pay his rent a second time.[69]

HOSPITAL OF ST. MARY WITHOUT BISHOPSGATE. *Party argent and sable a mill-rind cross counter-coloured with a martlet gules in the quarter.*

After the Dissolution Queen Elizabeth granted the rectory of Shalford with court leet, view of frank-pledge, law-days, and assize of bread and ale, to her secretary John Wolley.[70] She sold it in 1590 to his brother-in-law, George More,[71] afterwards Sir George More, from whom it was purchased in 1599 by John Austen,[72] who built Shalford House on a place called the Timber Yard, on the rectory manor, 1608-10.[73] The rectory still remains in the possession of his descendants. George Austen died at Shalford in 1621, leaving a son John, who inherited the rectory manor.[74] Robert Austen and his mother Elizabeth were in possession in 1714, at which date Robert Austen was living in the ' Parsonage House.' [75] The present owner is Lieut.-Colonel Henry Haversham Godwin Austen, of Nore, Bramley.

The house of Shalford Park is said to be close to the site of the old rectory manor-house, but the actual site was called the Timber Yard. In 1609 Sir George More conveyed the manor of Unstead to George Aus-ten, subject to redemption on the payment of £800 in 1611, in the tenement of the said Austen, ' now in building upon a parcel of land called the Tymber Yarde parcel of the ·parsonage of Shulforde in the Parish of Shulforde.' [76] Colonel Godwin Austen, lord of the manor, has the building accounts from 1608 to 1610, showing that it was built in stone and brick.

The house was much altered, and a top story added by Sir Henry Edmund Austen, who succeeded, as a minor, in 1797. The front part of the house, now quite modernized in appearance, is internally of the original date ; but the carved wooden mantelpiece in the room to the left of the front door, bearing the date 1631, was brought from elsewhere. The oak room, on the right hand of the front door, has good panel-ling, mantelpiece, and ceiling of the later 17th cen-tury. The carved mantelpiece bears the curious motto *Heyme incalesco, aestate refrigero*—which, as Mr. Ralph Nevill remarks, is ' a proof that our ancestors were sufficiently alive to the advantages of open fire-places.' The library was originally the kitchen. The mantelpiece bears the date 1681, and the iron fire-back has the royal arms of Charles II. The dining-room was built by the late owner in 1875. The mantelpiece, chalk, with the date 1609, was brought from Tyting Farm.[77] There was a fine gallery of pictures, some of which are still in the house, which is at present let as a private hotel.

The church of *ST. MARY* is the **CHURCH** third that has stood on the present site since 1789, in which year the mediaeval building, possibly retaining parts of that mentioned in Domesday, was rebuilt. A view of the church from the south-east, as it appeared in 1780, shows a picturesque irregular building of cruci-form plan, having a short and rather high nave with a south porch, a central tower, and shingled spire, apparently of 12th or 13th-century date, beneath which is a transept, or rather two transeptal chapels, conjoined, and having a double-gabled roof, with 15th-century windows, and a longish chancel with a priest's door and a three-light east window of 15th-century date.

In 1789 the church was rebuilt in local stone rubble with brick dressings—a very ugly, heavy structure—having a squat tower with domed roof of copper, surmounted by a cupola. There was no chancel, only an alcove or shallow apse, projecting from the east end of the nave. Cracklow's view of 1824 pre-serves the memory of this building, which, in 1847, was in its turn entirely demolished to make way for the present structure, an ambitious but unsatisfactory example of the 13th-century style. This consists of nave, aisles, transepts, and chancel, with south porch and tower with shingled spire at the north-west angle. The whole building is excessively high in proportion to its length, and the detail is starved and bad.

There are no monuments of any interest except some tablets to the Austens and to the local family of the Eliots, of 17th and 18th-century dates.

The old font is at present turned upside down, and placed as a mounting block outside the vicarage. · It may shortly be restored to the church. There are two pieces of old glass, preserved from the original church, showing the arms of Canterbury and Winchester.

The church plate is of the 18th century, and of no great interest.

[64] Feet of F. Div. Co. Hil. 22 Chas. I ; ibid. Mich. 1649 ; ibid. Mich. 28 Chas. I.

[65] Manning and Bray, op. cit. ii, 99.

[66] Feet of F. Surr. East. 41 Geo. III.

[67] Chan. Inq. p.m. 15 Edw. I, no. 69.

[68] Chart. R. 33 Edw. I, 49. The ad-vowson is mentioned in the conveyance of Shalford Bradestan to Hugh le De-spenser by Idonea de Crumbwell, but the lords of Shalford Bradestan never pre-sented.

[69] Early Chan. Proc. liii, 119.

[70] Pat. 32 Eliz. pt. xvii.

[71] Feet of F. Surr. Mich. 32 & 33 Eliz.

[72] Ibid. Hil. 41 Eliz.

[73] Accounts *penes* Col. Godwin Austen, and a deed at Loseley.

[74] Chan. Inq. p.m. (Ser. 2), cccxcvii, 90.

[75] Exch. Dep. Mich. 9 Anne, 3 ; ibid. Mich. 1 Geo. I, 5.

[76] Close, 7 Jas. I, no. 1981.

[77] Information of Col. Godwin Austen.

There are five bells of 1789, and one of 1866, all by the firm of Warner. When the six were complete they each bore a part of the verse :—

'Thy glory Lord we will resound | to all the listening nations round | and with our tongues | our voices raise | to Thee O God | in songs of praise.'

Before 1789, four, dated 1613, by Robert Eldridge, bore the verse :—

'Lord plead my cause against my foes | Confound their force and might | Fight on my part against my foes | That seek with me to fight.'

In the Edwardian inventory eight bells and a 'sawnce' bell are mentioned.

The registers begin in 1564, but there are no marriages till 1581. There is a gap between 1651 and 1653, and the marriages are lost from 1754 to 1782.

The church is mentioned in the *ADVOWSON* Domesday Survey.[78] In 1224 it was stated that the king's ancestors had always presented to Shalford and its chapelries, but

that Ralph de Fay, lord of Shalford, last presented in the time of the war.[79]

It was granted with the rectory to the Hospital of St. Mary Without Bishopsgate in 1304–5. After the Dissolution it passed into the possession of various persons.[80] Towards the close of the 17th century the Crown presented and continues to do so.[81]

There seems to have been a chapel attached to the manor of Shalford Bradestan, for in 1374–5 Ellen, mother of Sir Robert Bradestan, held in dower the chancel of the chapel there.[82]

CHARITIES
Smith's Charity is distributed as in other Surrey parishes. Many small rents and payments were due to the church.[83]

In 1715 Dr. Shortrudge, Sir Francis Vincent, and others settled the residue of the profits on estates in Hertfordshire on the vicars of Shalford, Great Bookham, Effingham, and Letherhead, on condition of their reading prayers in church on Wednesdays and Fridays, and preaching appropriate sermons on 30 January and on Good Friday. (See Great Bookham.)

SHERE

Essira (xi cent.); Sire, Schyre (xiii cent.); Shire and Shyre (xiv cent.); Shire (xv cent.); Shire and Shiere (xviii cent.); Shere (xix cent.).

The parish of Shere is midway between Guildford and Dorking. The village is 6 miles east of the former, and 6 miles west of the latter. The parish is bounded on the north by East Clandon and West Horsley, on the east by Abinger, on the south by Ewhurst and Cranleigh, on the west by Albury. It is about 4½ miles from north to south, and from 2 to 2½ miles from east to west, and contains 6,400 acres of land and 12 of water. The Tillingbourne stream runs from east to west through the northern part of it. The soil exhibits the usual characteristics of a parish south of the Chalk. The northern part is Chalk, on the downs, and the parish extends southward over the Upper Greensand and Gault, and the Lower Greensand, which forms the largest portion; but it does not quite reach the Atherfield and Wealden Clays. Ewhurst and Cranleigh on the Clay, parishes of a later date,[1] were no doubt partly in the original parish of Shere. There is an ancient and picturesque mill at Shere, and in the hamlet of Gomshall a tannery and a brewery. Iron was once worked in Shere.[2] The parish is now, however, essentially agricultural, the land in the valley between the chalk downs and the sand hills being fertile. The only special industry is the raising of watercresses in ponds fed from the Tillingbourne. Great quantities of this are grown, and sometimes sent away to great distances. The downs to the north are mostly open grass, or wooded, and rise to 600 or 700 ft. above the sea, while to the south are great expanses of open heather and firwoods on the sandhills, Hurtwood Common, and parts of Holmbury and Ewhurst Hills, at an elevation of more than 700 ft. in their highest points. Part of Albury Park is in

the parish. The road from Guildford to Dorking goes through the northern part of the parish; the Redhill and Reading branch of the South Eastern Railway runs nearly parallel to it. Gomshall and Shere station was opened in 1849. In Gomshall is a Congregational chapel, founded in 1825.

No important discoveries of prehistoric remains seem to have been made in the parish. Neolithic flint implements, however, occur near Holmbury Hill, but five parishes were formerly so closely intermixed here that it is difficult to assign the discoveries to any one.

Shere has often been called one of the most beautiful villages in England; certainly few can surpass it in Surrey for a combination of those qualities that go to make up the ideal village. It lies in the valley of the Tillingbourne, immediately beneath the Albury Downs, sheltered from the north by the hills, and bounded on the west by the beautiful domain of Albury Park. Happily the presence of the Duke of Northumberland's seat at Albury Park, and the wise action of other local landowners, have operated to keep the speculating builder at arm's length, and such additions as have been made to the old village in recent years have not seriously detracted from its charm. Shere is, therefore, the haunt of painters, many of them residents in and around, and samples of their handiwork may be inspected in the ancient Black Horse Inn, the building itself being partly of 16th-century date, with a great open fireplace under an arched beam, and other ancient features. In front of this inn are two old elms, and the view looking past them to the church, with its tall timber spire and lych-gate, is far-famed.

Aubrey mentions 'the extraordinary good parsonage house,' which still remains at the western end of the village, near the stream, although no longer used as

78 *V.C.H. Surr.* i, 319a.
79 Maitland, *Bracton's Note Bk.* 913. Ralph was lord of Bramley, with land in Shalford.
80 Winton Epis. Reg. quoted by Manning and Bray, op. cit. ii, 107. Amongst the

patrons was George Austen, who died seised of the advowson, and whose son John presented to the church in 1622; Chan. Inq. p.m. (Ser. 2), cccxcvii, 90; Feet of F. Surr. Mich. 20 Jas. I.
81 Inst. Bks. (P.R.O.).

82 Chan. Inq. p.m. 48 Edw. III, Add. no. 42.
83 Churchwardens' Bks. quoted by Manning and Bray, *Hist. of Surr.* ii, 103.
1 In *V.C.H. Surr.* ii, 8, 9.
2 Ibid. 270.

the rectory. It is an ancient timber-framed building, as to which Aubrey repeats a tradition that it was built upon woolpacks, 'in the same manner as our Lady's Church at Salisbury was;'[3] and in his day the house was 'encompassed about with a large and deep moat, which is full of fish.'

When every other house or cottage is old and interesting it is difficult to mention all, but a few may be singled out as presenting specially noteworthy features, or as typical of the others. The large number of ancient cottages is perhaps accounted for by the statement that Aubrey makes, that there was here a very ancient manufacture of fustian. Another cause certainly was that such important families as the Butlers, Earls of Ormond, the Audleys, and the Brays, had their mansions in Shere, and gave employment to lesser folk in their neighbourhood.

One or two of the houses in the village retain their ancient bargeboards to the gables. These are

massive stack of fines having a diagonal member on each face of the square, with a good head and base mould. The half-timber front is now hidden by rough-cast. Another old house on the road to Gomshall is noteworthy for an overhanging gable, and for the fact that the spaces between the timbers are filled with flints, instead of plaster or bricks. Most of the other old houses in the village are covered with rough-cast, which is coloured locally in a pleasant shade of buff.[4]

Wolven's Farm, which lies some miles to the east of Albury village, is a fine example of the 17th-century brick house, with panelled chimneys, mullioned windows with leaded lights, and a double-storied porch with a brick pediment to its upper window. In this and other details the house closely resembles Crossways Farm, Abinger, about 2 miles distant.

Local tradition says that Hound House, in the royal manor of Gomshall in Shere, was named from

SHERE VILLAGE

variously treated : one, which might well be of 15th-century date, or even older, being pierced with trefoils ; another is foliated, with the points of the cusping rounded so as to give a continuous wavy line. In Shere itself a very old cottage in Lower Lane shows a joist-board (i.e. a moulded board covering the projecting ends of the joists carrying the upper story) of late 15th-century character. There is also an old house, long and low, with an overhanging gabled wing on the right, and a hipped-roof wing to the left end, on which side is a particularly fine chimney, with crow-stepped base and a

the keeping of the king's hounds there, but there is no record of it apparently. It is, however, known that hounds were kept here about 1800, and some old stone kennel troughs have been found.

The village is historically interesting as the seat of the Bray family (*vide infra*).

It seems strange that Gomshall, which has always been a place of considerable population and importance, should never have had a church of its own.

Holmbury St. Mary is the name now given to the two hamlets of Felday in Shere, and Pitland Street in Shere and Abinger, which were erected into an eccle-

---

[3] This tradition is so constantly met with that there can be no doubt it is another way of saying that the house, or church, or bridge, was erected from the proceeds of a tax on wool ; or else (which in this case at least, as in that of London

Bridge, would appear to be more probable) that the foundations of the structure were actually laid on wool-sacks filled with concrete, a method of construction still frequently employed in watery sites.

[4] This buff-coloured plastering is very characteristic of Western Surrey. Other examples may be noted in Godalming, Ockley, Guildford, Chobham, Woking, and Letherhead.

siastical parish, made up from portions of Shere, Ockley, Abinger, Ewhurst, Cranleigh, and Ockham, 28 September 1878. The schools (Church of England) were built in 1860 and enlarged in 1900. There is a Congregational chapel.

This neighbourhood was formerly one of the wildest in Surrey. Sheep-stealers, smugglers, and poachers found a refuge in these remote hills. Some of the cottages have, still existing, very large cellars (excavated easily in the sandy hill), which are far too large for any honest purpose, and were no doubt made for storing smuggled goods till they could be conveniently taken on to London. Of late years the picturesque neighbourhood has attracted many visitors, who have built large houses. Joldwyns is the seat of Sir William Paget Bowman, bart., Holmbury of Mr. W. Joynson Hicks, Holmdale of Mr. Barlow Webb, Aldermoor of Mr. H. T. Willis, R.A., Hurtwood Cottage of Mr. Frank Walton, R.I., A.R.A. These houses are all included in the modern extension of Abinger, but belong to this district, the church of which is in Shere.

Peaslake is a hamlet of Shere, lying at the bend of the valley between Holmbury and Ewhurst Hills, which shared formerly the inaccessibility of Felday and its wild character. It has been more recently brought into the circle of civilization, and a road from Ewhurst, practicable for wheels, has been brought into it since district councils were instituted. It was formerly accessible from the north, but was on the edge of the accessible country with no real road beyond. A Working Men's Club was erected in 1891 by the Misses Spottiswoode of Drydown, in many other ways benefactors to the neighbourhood. Of late years several new houses have been built. Peaslake School was founded by Lord Ashcombe, Mr. Justice Bray, the Misses Spottiswoode, and others in 1870.

At Shere the principal residents, besides those already named, are : at Burrows Lea, Sir Herbert Barnard ; at Ridgeway, Lady Arthur Russell ; at Hurstcote, Mr. Somerset Beaumont ; at Shere Lodge, Miss Locke King ; at Hazel Hatch, The Hon. Emily Lawless; and at Burrows Cross, Mr. Benjamin W. Leader, R.A.

The parish hall was built by subscription to commemorate the Diamond Jubilee of 1897.

It is not right to dismiss the parish of Shere without mentioning that it was the birthplace, ultimate home, and deathplace of William Bray, the county historian, who was born here 1736, and died 1832. He completed and supplemented the already voluminous labours of Manning, and if slips and omissions do occur in their work it is difficult to over-estimate their industry and care, and their general accuracy is wonderful, considering especially the absence of those catalogues, indexes, and printed calendars which aid the modern topographer and genealogist.

MANORS — There are four manors in the parish of Shere or Shiere, viz., Shiere Vachery,[5] Shiere Ebor, Gomshall Netley, and

Towerhill. The two former are moieties of the original manor of SHIERE, which, under Edward the Confessor, had belonged to his queen, Edith. She held it till her death, when William I appropriated it, together with all her lands.[6] In 1086 the king held it in demesne, but William Rufus granted it to William de Warenne when he endowed him with the earldom of Surrey.[7] The overlordship continued with the successive Earls of Surrey, of whom the manor was held as of Reigate Castle.[8]

WARENNE, Earl of Surrey. *Checky or and azure.*

The actual tenant early in the 13th century was Roger de Clare.[9] In 1243–4 he conveyed the manor to John son of Geoffrey, a younger son of Geoffrey Fitz Peter, Earl of Essex, in return for a life-rent paid at Shere Church.[10] In 1246 John de Gatesden, who had apparently acquired this rent at the same time as the manor of Lasham,[11] remitted it to John son of Geoffrey.[12] The manor, having passed from John to his son and grandsons,[13] was divided into moieties at the death of Richard son of John.[14] The one moiety, Shiere Vachery, was assigned to his sister Joan Butler ; the other, afterwards known as Shiere Eboracum or Ebor, to his nephew Richard de Burgh, Earl of Ulster.[15]

SHIERE VACHERY descended at Joan Butler's death to her son Edmund Butler,[16] who was succeeded by his son James, first Earl of Ormond, and his wife Eleanor.[17] Their son James, Earl of Ormond, inherited Shiere, which descended from him to his son James.[18] The latter's son, the 'White Earl,'[19] granted it to his son James,[20] whom Henry VI created Earl of Wiltshire in 1449 in reward for his fidelity to the interests of the house of Lancaster. He succeeded his father as Earl of Ormond, and was beheaded after Towton in 1461. Shiere, being thus forfeited to the king, was granted by him to John, Lord Audley in 1467,[21] in tail male. Nevertheless, John, brother of the late earl, was restored as Earl of Ormond, although apparently not to his estates. He died in 1478. His brother Thomas, also attainted after Towton, was restored in blood by the first Parliament of Henry VII, and in 1486 granted the manor to Sir Reginald Bray, kt., reserving to himself the right of easement when staying within the lordship of Shiere.[22]

Sir Reginald Bray, statesman of the reign of Henry VII, was Lord Treasurer of England, director of the king's great building operations at St. George's

BUTLER, Earl of Ormond. *Or a chief indented azure.*

---

5 So called since it included the hamlet of Vachery in Cranleigh.
6 *V.C.H. Surr.* i, 279, 298a.
7 Ibid. i, 340. His original Surrey endowment consisted of the lands of Queen Edith.
8 Chan. Inq. p.m. 4 Edw. I, no. 47 ; 31 Edw. I, no. 32 ; 6 Ric. II, no. 15 ; 31 Hen. VI, no. 11.
9 *Testa de Nevill* (Rec. Com.), 120, 221A.

10 Feet of F. Div. Co. 28 Hen. III, 199.
11 See Lasham in Odiham Hundred (*V.C.H. Hants* iv).
12 Feet of F. Div. Co. 30 Hen. III, 62.
13 For an account of John son of Geoffrey and his descendants, see East Shalford.
14 Chan. Inq. p.m. 25 Edw. I, no. 50a.
15 Fine R. 27 Edw. I, m. 1.

16 Chan. Inq. p.m. 31 Edw. I, no. 32 ; Inq. a.q.d. clv, 7.
17 Chan. Inq. p.m. 1 Edw. III (1st nos.), no. 8 ; Feet of F. Div. Co. 3 Edw. III, 51.
18 Chan. Inq. p.m. 6 Ric. II, no. 15.
19 Ibid. 7 Hen. V, no. 49.
20 Ibid. 31 Hen. VI, no. 11.
21 Pat. 7 Edw. IV, pt i, m. 6.
22 Anct. D. (P.R.O.), C, 3273.

3

15

Chapel, Windsor, and at Westminster, but especially notable as being, with Cardinal Morton, probably the true author of Henry's successful policy. Lord Audley was, however, in actual posses-sion of Shiere Vachery, and gave compensation to Sir Regi-nald Bray in the form of an annual rent of £10.[17] He died in 1491, and was buried in Shere Church, and his son James, Lord Audley, received the profits of the manor in 1497, whilst encamped with the Cornish rebels at Black-heath.[18]

BRAY, of Shire. *Ar-gent a cheveron between three eagles' legs razed sable.*

He was leader of the rebellion, and must have marched through Shere on his way with the insurgents from Guildford to Kent. Consequently the manor was again forfeit to the Crown, but seems to have been restored to Sir Reginald, who had perhaps a lawful claim from the Earl of Ormond's grant, and was Henry's chief supporter, and most trusted ser-vant. He had no children, and left this manor, among others, by will, in 1503, to his nephew Edmund Bray,[19] summoned to Parliament as Lord Bray in 1529. From him Shiere Vachery passed by sale, in 1535, to his brother Sir Edward Bray.[20] He died in 1558, and his son Edward in 1581. Reginald, son of Edward, was baptized in 1555, and his eldest son Edward, baptized in 1580,[27] died seised of Shiere in 1635.[28] His son Edward was dealing with it seven years later,[29] and in 1676 Edward Bray, his wife Susan, and their son Edward were in posses-sion.[30] Edward Bray the elder was buried at Shere in 1679. Edward the son was also buried there in 1714. In 1723 Edward and Benjamin Bray his surviving sons were owners of the manor.[31] Benjamin died un-married. Edward had an elder son George in holy orders, who was succeeded in 1803 by his brother William, the historian of Surrey. His great-grandson, Sir Reginald More Bray, Judge of the High Court, is now owner.

The manor-house, certain lands, and the advowson of the church at Cranleigh were sold owing to a family quarrel between Sir Edward (who died in 1581) and his stepmother, Jane daughter of Sir Matthew Brown. Sir Edward resided at Baynards (q.v.).

At the time of the partition of the lands of Richard son of John, his nephew Richard de Burgh, Earl of Ulster, received a moiety of Shiere,[32] which ultimately became the manor of *SHIERE EBOR* or *EBORA-CUM*. This descended to William, Earl of Ulster, whose daughter Elizabeth married the son of Edward III, Lionel, Duke of Clarence,[33] and then, through the marriage of their daughter Philippa with Edmund Mortimer, Earl of March, to Roger, Earl of March,

who was declared heir to the throne in 1385.[34] The moiety passed to his daughter Anne, to whose son Richard, Duke of York, it owes the name of ' Ebor.' The Duke of York seems to have held this manor jointly with his wife Cecily, and with her conveyed it to Sir Thomas Brown and other trustees in 1448-9,[35] perhaps in trust for some of his very numerous family. However, after the death of Richard and the accession of his son to the throne as Edward IV, Sir George Brown, son of the original trustee, released all right in the manor to Cecily,[36] who continued to hold it till her death in 1495,[37] when it descended to Henry VII as heir of Edward IV.[38] During the reign of Henry VIII, Shiere formed part of the dower of his successive queens,[39] until, after the execution of Katharine Howard, he granted it with other lands to John Cokk of Broxbourne.[40] The latter conveyed it in 1544 to William Fitz William and his wife Joan,[41] who alienated it to Sir Edward Bray in 1548.[42] Thus for a

MORTIMER. *Barry or and azure a chief or with two pales between two gyrons azure and a scut-cheon argent over all.*

RICHARD, Duke of York. *France quartered with England with the difference of a label argent having three roundels gules on each point.*

short time the manors of Shiere Vachery and Ebor were owned by one lord, who also possessed Gomshall Netley and Towerhill. He bequeathed Shiere Ebor to his fourth wife Mary,[43] who married Edmund Tilney, Mas-ter of the Revels to Queen Elizabeth.[44] After her death the manor passed to Edward Bray, grandson and heir of Sir Edward,[45] who sold it in 1609 to William Risbridger, perhaps a descendant of the William Risbridger who under Henry VIII had held demesne lands of Shiere in lease.[46] John Risbridger died holding the manor of Shiere Ebor and a tenement called Shiere Farm in 1631.[47] The manor remained in this family till 1754, when William Risbridger sold to William Wakeford. In 1761 it was conveyed to Thomas Page,[48] who sold it in 1771 to William Bray,[49] who subsequently succeeded to Shiere Vachery. Since then the two manors have followed the same descent. The land is still called ' The Queen's Hold.'

About 1276 the original manor of Shiere had appur-tenant to it six and a half fees. Of these fees there were some at a distance (e.g. Benetfield, co. Sussex, and Lasham, co. Hants[50]). View of frankpledge was a

[23] Rentals and Surv. R. 828.
[24] Ibid.
[25] P.C.C. 26 Blamys.
[26] Chan. Proc. (Eliz.), G g, X, 44.
[27] Wonersh Par. Reg.
[28] Chan. Inq. p.m. (Ser. 2), ccclxxv, 44.
[29] Feet of F. Surr. Mich. 18 Chas. I.
[30] Ibid. Hil. 28 & 29 Chas. II.
[31] Feet of F. Surr. Trin. 20 Geo. I.
[32] Fine R. 27 Edw. I, m. 1.
[33] Cal. Pat. 1340-3, p. 187.

[34] Chan. Inq. p.m. 5 Ric. II, no. 43; 22 Ric. II, no. 34.
[35] See Feet. of F. Div. Co. 27 Hen. VI, 343.
[36] Close, 12 Edw. IV, m. 21 d.
[37] Mins. Accts. bdle. 1114, no. 15.
[38] Ibid.(Hen. VII), bdles. 1423 to 1447.
[39] L. and P. Hen. VIII, i, 155; vii, 352; xv, 144 (2); xvii, 1154 (33).
[40] Ibid. xix (1), 80 (48).
[41] Ibid. 278 (76).
[42] Feet of F. Surr. Hil. 2 & 3 Edw. VI.

[43] P.C.C. 22 Darcy.
[44] Chan. Proc. Eliz. B b, xiv, 54.
[45] Feet of F. Surr. Mich. 7 Jas. I.
[46] L. and P. Hen. VIII, xvii, 1154 (33).
[47] Chan. Inq. p.m. (Ser. 2), ccclxii, 17.
[48] The conveyance was made by Morgan Morse, probably as agent for William Wakeford; see Feet of F. Surr. Mich. 2 Geo. III.
[49] Manning and Bray, op. cit. i, 523.
[50] Chan. Inq. p.m. 7 Edw. III, no. 39; 7 Edw. III (additional), no. 89.

privilege claimed by John son of Geoffrey,[51] and at the division of the manor was assigned to the Butlers, who held it once a year.[52] Both Shiere Vachery and Ebor had court baron,[53] and the lords of Shiere Vachery were granted a market on Tuesdays and an annual fair in 1309,[54] and free warren in 1330.[55]

The manor of GOMSHALL lies on the Tilling-bourne to the east of Shere village. In early times it was royal demesne. Earl Harold had it, and after the Conquest King William held it in demesne. Odo, Bishop of Bayeux, wrongfully annexed half a hide which had belonged to this manor to his manor of Bramley.[56] It is mentioned with lands granted to the Earl of Warenne in 1154 and 1155-6.[57] He probably resigned Gomshall with his other English lands to Henry II,[58] who granted it in moieties to Robert de Wendenale and to William de Clere.[59] Under Richard I William Malveisin's lands in Gomshall were escheat to the Crown,[60] and they or others appear to have been given to the Dapifer of Ponthieu,[61] Ingram de Fontains, who held one moiety of the manor, while William Malveisin had the other.[62] Ingram's lands were escheat to the Crown in or before 1194.[63] Richard I granted the manor in moieties to William de Es and Alan Trenchmere.[64] The moiety of William de Es became the manor of Gomshall Netley, and the other was known later as Gomshall Towerhill.[65]

GOMSHALL NETLEY, the moiety of Gomshall granted by King Richard to William de Es,[66] was held in 1217 by Eustace de Es,[67] and in 1233 passed from him to Sir Matthias Besille, kt,[68] who granted it to the abbey of Netley, co. Hants.[69] Thus it came to be called Gomshall Netley. In the Taxation of 1291 £10 is returned as the abbey's annual income from 'Gomshall Grange.'[70] In 1332 the Abbot of Netley's tenants in Gomshall complained that he had exacted other services from them than he ought, since they were tenants in ancient demesne.[71] After the suppression of the abbey Henry VIII granted to Sir Edward Bray the reversion of Gomshall Netley at the termination of a seventy years' lease, which John Redforde and his wife Thomasina had obtained from the abbey in 1502.[72] Since this time it has descended in the same family with Shiere Vachery, and is now in the possession of Mr. Justice Bray.

The old manor-house was separated from the manor about 1640. It is a farm, usually called John John's Lodge, and stands opposite to the modern house of Netley. It is largely of 16th-century date, and possibly occupies the site of the Saxon aula.

This house has a fine chimney, rising from the ground with a stack of diagonally-placed flues on its flint and rubble base. At either end of the front is a projecting gabled wing, that on the left having some good square and circle pattern-work in its timber construction, resembling that at Great Tangley in Wonersh parish. The upright timbering of the main portion between these wings seems to indicate a date early in the 16th, or possibly late in the 15th century, the pattern-work in the wing being nearly a hundred years later. Modern windows and other injudicious alterations have somewhat altered the ancient character of this house, but the old door, with a flat-arched head, still remains in the left wing.

The present Netley House was built by Mr. Edmund Shallet Lomax about, or shortly before, 1800, and is now the residence of Col. Fraser.

GOMSHALL TOWERHILL. Alan Trenchmere possibly held his moiety for life only,[72] for by 1205 he was succeeded by William de Braose, who had a grant of it in tail.[74] William's family was starved to death, and he himself driven into exile by John; he died abroad, and John evidently gave his moiety of Gomshall to Peter de Maulay.[75] William's son, the Bishop of Hereford, took part in the civil war against John, and extorted the restoration of the family estates to himself in trust for his nephew.[76] After his death this manor was granted to Rowland de Bloet.[77]

In 1218 Reginald Braose, the bishop's younger brother, had the manor,[78] from which his widow claimed dower in 1230,[79] and William Braose was holding it in 1281,[80] and conveyed it to a sub-tenant, John Savage. William Braose was still living in 1311, when John Savage died, leaving a young son, Roger,[81] who, having been imprisoned for felony in Newgate, broke prison and forfeited his estates.[82] In 1332 the king committed the custody of the manor to John Pulteney, Lord Mayor of London, who did the customary service for it to John de Ifield.[83] A year having elapsed, the manor was restored to the overlord, John de Ifield.[84] At John's death the king granted this manor for life to Eleanor, Countess of Ormond,[85] then lady of Shiere, and obtained from John of Ifield's heirs a release of their rights in it.[86] At her death Edward III granted the custody of the

BRAOSE. *Azure crusily and a lion or.*

51 Close, 38 Hen. III, m. 13 d.
52 Chan. Inq. p.m. 12 Edw. III (1st nos.), no. 40.
53 Ibid. 7 Edw. III, no. 39 ; 31 Edw. I, no. 82.
54 Chart. R. 3 Edw. II, m. 7, no. 19.
55 Ibid. 3 Edw. III, m. 5, no. 13.
56 V.C.H. Surr. i, 298a.
57 Red Bk. of the Exch. (Rolls Ser.), 654, 666.
58 See V.C.H. Surr. i, 342.
59 Testa de Nevill (Rec. Com.), 225.
60 Pipe R. 1 Ric. I (Rec. Com.), 11, 217.
61 Ibid. 216.
62 Testa de Nevill (Rec. Com.), 225.
63 Pipe R. 6 Ric. I, m. 1.
64 Testa de Nevill (Rec. Com.), 325,

says that King Richard gave it to William de Es and Alan Trenchmere, and that after Alan's death John gave his share first to William de Braose and afterwards to Peter Maulay.
65 Curia Regis R. 113, m. 27 d.
66 Rot. Canc. 3 John (Rec. Com.), 28.
67 Cal. Pat. 1216-25, p. 53.
68 Cal. Chart. R. i, 174.
69 Anct. D. (P.R.O.), D. 131,200.
70 Pope Nich. Tax. (Rec. Com.), 214.
71 De Banco R. 290, m. 276.
72 L. and P. Hen. VIII, xiii, (1). 646 (39).
73 Rot. Canc. 3 John (Rec. Com.), 28 ; Pipe R. 2 John, m. 15 d.
74 Rot. Chart. (Rec. Com.), i, 134b.
75 Testa de Nevill (Rec. Com.), 225.

76 Rot. Lit. Claus. (Rec. Com.), i, 232b.
77 Ibid. 238b.
78 Ibid. 348.
79 Cal. Close, 1227-31, p. 389.
80 Chart. R. 9 Edw. I, no. 24.
81 Cal. Close, 1307-13, p. 430.
82 Abbrev. Rot. Orig. (Rec. Com.), ii, 59.
83 Ibid. ii, 56 ; Cal. Close, 1330-3, p. 436. John of Ifield appears to have succeeded William de Braose in the overlordship.
84 Cal. Close, 1330-3, p. 515.
85 Abbrev. Rot. Orig. (Rec. Com.), ii, 159.
86 Anct. D. (P.R.O.), A. 3974, 3975, 3976.

manor to Peter Atwood for life,[87] and, subsequently, to Thomas Stowes.[88] In founding the abbey of St. Mary Graces near the Tower of London in 1376 the king endowed it with the reversion of this moiety of Gomshall. Hence it obtained the name of Gomshall Towerhill.[89]

In 1539, after the dissolution of the abbey, the king granted Gomshall Towerhill to Sir Edward Walsingham,[90] who conveyed it to Sir Edward Bray in 1550.[91] In 1589 it was granted as 'concealed lands' to Walter Coppinger and others.[92] It was, however, restored to its former owners, for Sir Edward Bray conveyed it to trustees for the use of his wife Mary for life, with final reversion to his grandson and heir Edward in tail male,[93] and since that time it has remained, with Shiere Vachery, in the Bray family. Towerhill is an old and picturesque farmhouse close to the station.

In 1086, when Gomshall was royal demesne, the villeins there were exempt from the sheriff's jurisdiction.[94] Both Netley and Towerhill had court baron.[95] Eleanor Countess of Ormond had view of frankpledge in Gomshall Towerhill.[96] In 1281 William Braose was granted free warren there.[97]

SUTTON was in 1086 in Wotton Hundred. It is a hamlet now chiefly in Shere parish, but with a few cottages in Abinger parish and Wotton Hundred.

It is apparently that in Wotton called 'Sudtone' which the Bishop of Bayeux had rated in his manor of Bramley.[98] It was subsequently associated with Holehurst or Holdhurst, in Cranleigh, a parish non-existent in 1086 (Holdhurst Manor extends beyond Cranleigh parish), and Sutton was called Holdhurst at Down, or the manor of Downe, to distinguish it from the rest of Holdhurst in the Weald.[99] It may once have been held with the rest of Holdhurst (see under Cranleigh), but Richard Hill died holding Downe in 1551, and his son Edmund Hill was in possession in 1554.[100] He was alive in 1582, and Richard Hill his son, who married Elizabeth daughter of the first Sir Richard Onslow of the family in Surrey, was in possession c. 1586.[101] Richard conveyed it in 1595 to Ralph Hill.[102] He conveyed it to Edward Allford, who sold it to William Leigh of Abinger and Thames Ditton in 1609.[103] From this family it was conveyed, c. 1620, to Oliver Huntley, who sold it in the following year to Richard Holman. The latter conveyed it to Henry Hilton in 1636.[104] The Hussey family seem to have acquired an interest in Sutton as early as 1646, when Sir William Smyth, bart., and his wife Mary, whose interests were possibly derived

from Henry Hilton, transferred their rights in one-third of the manor to Peter Hussey.[105] Thomas Hussey of London, who is said to have acquired the whole manor, was buried at Shere in 1655. He left a son Peter, who was visited at Sutton by John Evelyn, August 1681.[106] He died 1684, and his son Peter (who died in 1724[107]) left a daughter Mary, who in 1720 married Edward Bngden. Before 1728 Sutton was sold to Edward Pike Heath. His niece Frances married the Hon. Henry Knight, and they sold it to Mr. Edmund Shallet between 1750 and 1761.[108] Mr. Shallet was sheriff of the county in 1758. His daughter married Caleb Lomax. For the later descent see under Wotton.

There was a house at Sutton of considerable size, which was pulled down by Mr. Edmund Shallet Lomax, son of Mr. Shallet's daughter and heir, when he built Netley (see above), but the remains of the walled garden and some other fragments are conspicuous upon the left-hand side of the road leading from Gomshall station towards Holmbury St. Mary.

There was a second WESTON Manor, to be distinguished from that in Albury, near the parsonage house of Albury, but lying in a detached part of Shere parish, and called Weston in Shere. In the Weston genealogy taken, it is said, from the College of Arms,[109] a Thomas de Weston, living c. 1305, and his son Thomas are described as lords of the manor of 'Weston in Shire.' It would seem that the family must have been early divided, for others are described as of 'Weston in Albury.'[110] William Weston held it of the abbey of Netley at his death in 1483.[111] Edmund Pope, a descendant, no doubt, of Joan wife of Thomas Pope,[112] sold it in 1540 to John Risbridger of Albury,[113] whose son John sold it the same year to Thomas Baker.[114]

In 1621 it formed part of the portion of Mary daughter of George Hyer on her marriage with Robert Boothby.[115] In 1709 William Boothby conveyed it to George Wheeler.[116] Dr. William Shaw purchased a moiety from Bridges Baldwin and his wife Frances in 1746.[117] Dr. Shaw's son sold the manor in 1804 to the Hon. Robert Clive, a younger son of the first Lord Clive (who died in 1833), who improved the house.[118] The house was at one time the residence of Elias Ashmole the antiquary. The manor seems to be non-existent, and the house is pulled down.

In the Domesday Survey two mills are mentioned at Shere.[119] In the 13th century there was still a water-mill there.[120] It formed part of the rents granted to Richard, Earl of Ulster, being held by

---

[87] *Abbrev. Rot. Orig.* (Rec. Com.), ii, 288.

[88] Pat. R. 12 Ric. II, pt. i, m. 1.

[89] Dugdale, *Mon.* v, 718 ; *Cal. Pat.* 1385-9, p. 539.

[90] *L. and P. Hen. VIII*, xiv (1), 1354 (50).

[91] Chan. Inq. p.m. ccxlvii, 72.

[92] Pat. 31 Eliz. pt. vii, m. 31.

[93] Chan. Proc. (Eliz.), Bb xiv, 54.

[94] *V.C.H. Surr.* i, 298a.

[95] The Court Rolls for 1481 and 1504 are at the Public Record Office ; Gen. Ser. cciv, 50, 51.

[96] *Abbrev. Rot. Orig.* (Rec. Com.), ii, 159.

[97] Chart. 9 Edw. I, no. 24.

[98] *V.C.H. Surr.* i, 305b.

[99] See Harl. Chart. 78 G. 53 ; 79 F. 38a, b ; 75 H. 41.

[100] Misc. Bks. (L.T.R.), vol. 168, fol. 69.

[101] Harl. Chart. 78 G. 53.

[102] Ibid. 79 F. 38a, b.

[103] Ibid. 75 H. 41 ; see under Abinger. These transactions had only to do with Sutton *alias* Holdhurst at Down in Shere, Abinger, and Ewhurst, not with Holdhurst in Cranleigh (q.v.).

[104] Feet of F. Surr. East. 18 Jas. I ; Mich. 19 Jas. I ; Trin. 12 Chas. I.

[105] Ibid. Hil. 21 Chas. I. It is said, however, that it was Thomas Hussey who purchased the whole manor ; Manning and Bray, op. cit. i, 497.

[106] *Diary*, 30 Aug. 1681.

[107] For Hussey pedigree see the parish registers and monuments in Shere Church.

[108] Manning and Bray, op. cit. iii, 497-8.

[109] Printed in Brayley, op. cit. ii, 81, &c.

[110] Ibid.

[111] *Cal. Inq. p.m. Hen. VII*, i, 162.

[112] See under Weston in Albury.

[113] Feet of F. Surr. Trin. 32 Hen. VIII.

[114] Add. Chart. (B.M.), 28236.

[115] Feet of F. Div. Co. Mich. 20 Jas. I ; Close, 19 Jas. I, pt. xiii, no. 7.

[116] Ibid. Surr. Mich. 8 Anne.

[117] Recov. R. Mich. 20 Geo. II, m. 38. Dr. Shaw is said to have obtained the manor from a niece of a former proprietor ; Manning and Bray, *Hist. of Surr.* ii, 127.

[118] Ibid. ii, 188 ; Brayley, op. cit. v, 160.

[119] *V.C.H. Surr.* i, 298a.

[120] Chan. Inq. p.m. 25 Edw. I, no. 50a.

William, Earl of Ulster, in 1334, when it is described as 'two watermills under one roof.'[121] It is mentioned again in 1382.[122]

One mill is mentioned in Gomshall in 1086. It was probably on the site of Netley Mill. In the 13th century there was a water-mill belonging to 'Estcourt' in Gomshall.[123]

CHURCHES The church of *ST. JAMES* lies somewhat to the east of the village street. It is mentioned in the Domesday Survey.[124]

The church is second to none in Surrey for beauty and antiquarian interest. Its situation, on a bank above the stream, which flows on its northern side, with a screen of tall young elms between, and a background of more ancient trees, and the wooded hillside, is very lovely ; and the churchyard, not too trim or level, with a number of ancient monumental stones and a few wooden 'bed-heads,' bounded by a low stone wall, with a modern but picturesque lych-gate on the west, makes a charming setting.

The church is built of Bargate rubble, with ironstone rubble, flints, and miscellaneous materials, some probably derived from Roman buildings on Farley Heath, the dressings being of Bargate stone, firestone and clunch, and the south and west porches are of brick and timber. The modern vestries on the north of the nave are built of stone and brick. The roofs are tiled, except that of the south aisle, which is roofed with Horsham slabs, and the spire is covered with oak shingles.[125] A good deal of the original thin coat of yellow plaster remains on the walls. Few churches in Surrey have survived the era of destructive restoration with such small loss to their antiquity as Shere ; indeed, what mischief has been done is traceable to the 'churchwarden' period or even earlier ; the exception to this observation is the incongruous group of vestries built against a blank, and probably very early, wall on the north of the nave.

The plan offers many interesting problems. It consists of a nave, 40 ft. 9 in. long, and 18 ft. 6 in. wide at the west, widening out to 19 ft. 6 in. at the east ; a broad south aisle, 45 ft. 9 in. by 16 ft. 3 in. ; a central tower, with floor-space of about 15 ft. square ; a chancel, 32 ft. long by 19 ft. 2 in. ; a south chancel, opening out of the chancel, tower and south aisle, 36 ft. long by 16 ft. 9 in. ; a shallow transeptal recess on the north of the tower in place of the original transept ; and west and south porches, with the modern vestries, before alluded to, on the north of the nave. In addition, there would appear to have been in the mediaeval period an anchorite's cell on the north side of the chancel.

The oldest part of the church is the north wall of the nave, but whatever original features, in the shape of windows or door, it may have possessed, have been obliterated, and therefore its date is somewhat a matter of speculation. If not earlier, it may date from the last quarter of the 11th century. To this nave a tower was added, probably on the site of the earlier chancel—as at Albury, hard by—in about 1150. The internal square of this is almost exactly the same as at Albury, and it has on its north side, in the middle stage, a very similar round-arched window,

with two sub-lights, originally divided by a small column, as in that tower. On the south side is a single-light opening of the same date. Three unusually wide and long round-headed openings occur above a string-course, or set-off, in each face of the bell-chamber, and over these there was, perhaps, in the first instance, a low parapet, corbelled out, inclosing a squat, pyramidal roof, both features giving place at a later period to the timber spire. Parts of one of the first tower arches can be traced on the south side. Owing to the failure of the crossing arches because of the weight of the top story, these arches, early in the 14th century, were replaced by wide and lofty pointed ones on the east and west, and by smaller ones on the other sides. The first arches were circular and probably of two orders, with a hood-moulding. The great thickness of these tower walls—4 ft. on the ground—is noteworthy.

The circular stair at the south-west angle of the tower, originally external, is now, of course, within the aisle. It retains two loopholes for lighting, and a small door with a pointed arch. On the southern side the head of one of the original flat buttresses appears above the roof, beneath the string that runs below the bell-chamber. The whole tower was probably completed soon after 1150.

The 12th-century transepts may have been roofed with span roofs at right angles to those of nave and chancel (before the aisle was thrown out) ; or, which seems on the whole the more probable, with span roofs set parallel to the axis of nave and chancel, as at St. Mary's, Guildford. In either case there would appear to have been apsidal ends to these chapels as at Guildford, and there may have been an apse to the chancel itself. Certain ashlaring with a curved face, built in as old material into the 14th-century chancel, may well have formed part of the destroyed apses. Among the few relics externally of this 12th-century work, besides the tower, are the bases of the two flat and narrow pilaster buttresses, on the south side, the western at what would have been the west end of these transepts or chancel aisles, and the eastern at the chord of the apse. These are composed of different kinds of stone—clunch or firestone, and Bargate stone—as though they had been altered and perhaps heightened at a later date. Another very remarkable survival consists of the curiously-shaped rafter-ends—a roll set within a broad hollow—almost unique in their way, in the piece of roof over this portion : this roof being in itself evidence for the second theory as to the original form taken by these chancel aisles. The fine marble font and south doorway are also of this period, but perhaps of slightly later date, c. 1170. This doorway, the most beautiful of its period in Surrey,[126] must have been originally placed in the unpierced south wall of the nave, and shifted out to its present position, when the aisle was built, in about 1200. It shows very few traces of having been moved, and all the stones appear to have been correctly rebuilt. The doorway is extremely elegant in proportions and detail, and consists of a circular arch of two orders, with a hood-moulding, the outer order resting upon a Sussex marble shaft with abacus, capital, and base of the same material, the abacus being carried round the inner order, as an

121 Chan. Inq. p.m. 7 Edw. III, no. 39.
122 Ibid. 5 Ric. II, no. 43.
123 Egerton MS. 2033, fol. 63.
124 V.C.H. Surr. i, 298a.
125 In Cracklow's view the roofs are

all covered with Horsham slabs ; see post.
126 Illustrated in V.C.H. Surr. ii, 433.

impost, and the capitals carved with early stiff-leaf foliage. All the remainder is delicately wrought in clunch, both orders of the arch displaying an enriched cheveron on the face, with a roll moulding on the angle, and a plain cheveron on the soffits. The enriched cheverons have foliage patterns within them. The hood-moulding has a small half-moon sinking carried as a pattern round its outer member, and at the top a head, now defaced, is inserted. The masonry is fine-jointed and fine-axed, both marks of the date. The dials and other scratchings on the stonework are noted later. On the inside is a plain circular arch, much loftier than that of the outer opening. There must have been a doorway or an arch of this same enriched cheveron pattern at Merstham Church, about 15 miles to the eastward along the same road, judging from the voussoirs now lying loose in the north chapel.[137]

The next period is that of about 1200, when the aisle was thrown out on the south of the nave, and an arch pierced in what had been the west wall of the south transept or chancel aisle. The three flat buttresses, of three stages, at the west end of the aisle, belong to this date. The west doorway of the nave is of the same period, and has a richly-moulded arch of two orders, acutely pointed, with Sussex or Purbeck marble capitals and shafts to the outer order. The inner order of the jambs is square on plan, with a square capital, this and the other having square abaci and crochet foliage. The arch at the east end of the aisle has two orders, richly moulded, and similar capitals, and among the mouldings of both is the keel-shaped moulding. The jambs, with their delicate shafts, bases, and capitals, are entirely of marble, four shafts to each side. The light and fragile character of this arch gives a clue to the entire disappearance of the corresponding arcade, which has been replaced by the three existing ugly pointed arches on octagonal piers. They are cased all over in plaster, both piers and arches (as was also the arch at the end of the aisle), and possibly the remains of the original work are still in existence beneath the plaster. Three of the lancets of this date remain, two in the aisle and one in the west wall of the nave. They are in Bargate stone, with broad chamfers to the outside opening. A lancet and a curious pointed arched recess[138] in the north wall of the nave, at its eastern end, are of about the same date. A pair of lancets in the western bay of the chancel aisle, broad openings with flat internal arches, would appear to be later—c. 1250.

At the eastern end of the south chancel south wall is a two-light tracery window of plain and somewhat unusual design. It is of two trefoiled lights, with a small trefoil in the head, the tracery and arch being worked on three distinct planes: externally there is a hood-moulding of scroll and bead section. The east window of the south chancel is of similar character and has three trefoil-headed lights, the central wider than the others, the spaces over

being occupied by two irregular trefoils and four small quatrefoils within a large circle. There are two coeval buttresses at the south-east angle of the rectangular east end of the chapel, which is referred to in wills as the Lady Chapel, superseded the apse about 1300, at which date it became necessary to rebuild the tower arches, an additional archway being pierced between the new square-ended chapel and the chancel. The lofty octagonal timber spire—57 ft. in height from the nave floor—a magnificent piece of mediaeval carpentry, was also probably added then or soon afterwards. It would appear to have been covered with lead originally, and retained a part of the ancient lead work until the middle of the last century, together with oak shingles.

These extensive alterations were probably undertaken at the instance of the rich abbey of Netley, to whom the advowson of Shere was sold by Roger de Clare in 1243. To Netley Abbey, therefore, is probably due the rebuilding of the chancel in its present form, with its beautiful tracery windows executed in hard chalk, between 1300 and 1320.[139] The details of the work show that it was begun shortly after the square east end of the Lady Chapel, and the new windows of the chancel were made to harmonize with the recently completed tracery windows of the chapel. This is very noticeable in the case of the great east window, which, with minor variations, is almost a *replica* of that in the east wall of the Lady Chapel. Its central light is of ogee form, cinquefoiled, and the side lights have rather ugly flat trefoiled heads with a cinquefoiled figure above, but the same circle, filled with four quatrefoils, which is the chief feature in the other, appears in this window also. The diagonal buttresses of the east wall and the buttress on the north side are of this date. The side windows, of two lights, have tracery of the ordinary net type. A piscina of this date, with ogee trefoiled head and credence shelf, remains in the south wall. In the western bay of the north wall are two curious squints, one with a quatrefoil aperture and the other, close by to the eastward, a square opening. Both communicated with an anchorite's cell, or a sacristy, whichever it may have been, which stood on this side, and was probably built at the same time as the chancel. Its roof was a lean-to, but its area is uncertain.[140] The oblique squint with the square head must have been used, in any case, for commanding a view of the high altar; while the quatrefoil may have served the purpose of communicating the recluse.

Slightly later again, in c. 1330, the north transept was shortened and brought to its present form of a mere recess between the enlarged buttresses of the tower, which at this time superseded the flat buttresses of c. 1150. The beautiful four-light window, of flowing tracery, executed in hard chalk, which has weathered admirably, has no hood-moulding externally, unlike the others, and bears other traces of

[137] As at Canterbury Cathedral (the *Aquae Castellum* of the monastery), the arched recesses in the east wall of the nave at Barfreston Church, and the chapel in Dover Castle. In the last-named the same stiff-leaf capitals, of somewhat French character, occur. Cf. also the capitals in the wooden screen at Compton Church, Surrey.

[138] This recess and its little window were probably made for the double purpose of inclosing a tomb and giving space for an altar flanking the earlier west arch of the tower.

[139] It is possible, however, that the chancel had been rebuilt in the 13th century, and that the monks of Netley

only remodelled it and put in tracery windows.

[140] Other possible anchorites' cells, which may have been either sacristies or chambers for the display of relics to the Canterbury pilgrims in some cases, existed, or can be traced, at Blechingley, Chessington, Compton, and Letherhead.

118

Ground Plan

HASCOMBE CHURCH FROM THE NORTH-WEST BEFORE RE-BUILDING

(From Cracklow's View, 1824)

SHERE CHURCH : TOWER AND CHANCEL LOOKING EAST

different handiwork, although the design has been kept in harmony with the chancel windows.

The church of the middle of the 14th century remains substantially unaltered, save for the insertion of windows in the west wall and the rebuilding of the porches. A three-light window, in the west wall of the aisle, of handsome character, with a deep hollow and recessed tracery, dates from the last quarter of the 14th century. Another, of two lights, with a square head, in the west gable of the nave is of an ordinary 15th-century type ; and a third, in the south wall of the aisle, of three lights, with an ugly flat segmental head, is dated by the inscription on a brass remaining in the south aisle : ' Pray for the soullis of Olever Sandes and Ione his wife, ye which made this wyndow and this auter, which Olev' dyed ye VII. day of Novēber, ye yer of Our Lord MVXII, on whos soll Jhū have m'cy.' There was another window, of later date, high up in the north wall of the nave, near its eastern end, but this has been renewed in a quasi-13th-century style in recent years. The window in the south aisle to the east of that of 1512 is a two-light nondescript opening, originally a lancet, with a square mullion and jambs, probably of 18th-century date, to which period the quaint external door to the gallery with its flight of steps, to the east of the south porch, also belongs.

From the churchwardens' accounts [131] we learn that, in 1547, the porch—probably that at the west end—was renewed, and in spite of modern patchings the substance of this remains. The fine panelled door of the inner doorway, well studded with nails, and having a good key-plate, bears in the upper part a small shield of arms—two bends and a canton, impaling a bend—with the date 1626. At the north-west angle of the nave is a huge tapering brick buttress, erected in the 18th century.

The south porch, although its roof appears to be of old timber, is of comparatively modern brickwork. The door of the inner doorway, rough oak-boarding nail-studded, is possibly of 12th-century date.

The ancient oak roofs, of plain character, remain throughout. Those of the chancel and Lady Chapel are of trussed collar construction. The interesting detail of the rafter ends of 12th-century date on the south side has been above noticed. In the tower is a fine bell-cage, probably as old as the 14th century, although altered in 1895 to admit two new bells. The doorway to the tower stairs has a door made up of the carved rails of some 17th-century pews. Of the chancel screen, concerning which we have the testimony in the churchwardens' accounts that it was made in the eighteenth year of Henry VII, there are no remains, but in Brandon's *Parish Churches* [131a] it is described as then (1848) in existence—' a plain Perpendicular rood-screen with its doors.' No other ancient woodwork or mediaeval fittings remain, except the very interesting chest now in the south porch.[132] It bears a general resemblance to the one

at Godalming, especially in the stop-chamfered framed ends, and the lid works with a pin-hinge. There is an elaborate locking arrangement, and inside are remains of two hutches for money and valuables. The date is about 1200, and it belongs to a group of early 13th-century chests that were probably made in obedience to the command of Pope Innocent III, to collect alms for the help of poor Crusaders.

The oak gallery at the west end is of 18th-century date.

The church must have been at one time rich in colour, judging from the fragments of wall-painting that remain. Practically all has been destroyed except a very graceful spray of vine pattern, painted in dark red on the soffit of the arch to the chancel east window.

In several windows there are remains of ancient glass, of 13th, 14th, and 15th-century dates. In the south aisle one of the lancets has some good square quarries of green glass, with a rose or cinquefoil within border-lines, coeval with, or only slightly later than, the early 13th-century opening. Another variety is diamond-shaped, with grisaille foliage patterns. In the quatrefoils and interspaces of the Lady Chapel and chancel east windows are the evangelistic symbols, the arms of England, Butler, Warenne, and Clare, and other ornaments contemporary with the early 14th-century stonework. These are some of the best of the little ancient glass left in Surrey. Other windows retain red roses, the Lancastrian badge, probably placed here by James, the second Earl of Ormond, in whose family the manor of Shiere was vested in the 15th century. The device of the Brays, who afterwards succeeded to the estates—the bray, or flax-crusher—appears on the quarries of another window.[133] In the great east window the lower lights are filled with good modern glass.

The ancient floor levels appear to have been preserved, together with a good deal of old stone-paving. There are two steps at the eastern tower arch, another at the access to the sanctuary, and two to the altar platform in the Lady Chapel. From the churchwardens' accounts we know that besides this altar and that of the high chancel there was an altar to St. Nicholas (perhaps that in the south aisle), and images of St. Anthony, St. Roche, St. John the Baptist, and our Lady of Pity.

Close to the west respond of the aisle arcade stands the beautiful font of Purbeck marble, mounted on a stone base-block and step. Its date may be either that of the south doorway—c. 1170—or of the aisle —c. 1200—probably the former. The upper part of the bowl is square with three scallopings, beneath which it changes into a circular form of a bold round section, and the parts left at the angles are carved into the foliated capitals of the four corner-shafts, which, with a stout central drum, support the bowl. These rest upon a continuous base-moulding, which

131 Itm payed for the carryeng of tymbre to the Pytt and for ij. sawyers that dyd helpe lade yt for the new porch, ij*s*.
Itm payed to the sawyer for the sawyng of tymber for the porche, iiij*s*. viij*d*.
Itm payed for the sawying of the porche at another tyme, iiij*s*. iiij*d*.
Itm payed for nayles for the selles of the kastors of the porche, iij*d*.
Itm payed for the naylies for to tacte on the bordes, iiij*d*.

Itm for iij. lode of tymber for the porche, xij*s*.
Itm for the carryeng of the same tymber to the churche, x*d*.
Itm for expences in meatt and drynke when the old porche was taken downe and the settyng of the new porche up, xij*d*.
Itm payed to John Fraunces for the workyng and framyng of the porch, xxx*s*.
Itm for iiij. lytell bordes whyche was

framyd in the porche, and for the tymber of the box, iiij*d*.
The last item refers to the 'poore men's boxe,' which was made in the same year, at a cost of vj. xj*d*.
131a Op. cit. 98.
132 Described and illustrated in *Arch. Journ.* lxiv, 272, 273.
133 Similar quarries, painted with the device of the Brays, are to be found at Stoke D'Abernon.

has a deep hollow between two round members, and is carried separately round the shafts and drum.[134]

The oldest monument is a small brass to Robert Scarclyff, rector, 1412, in mass vestments. In his lengthy will, preserved at Lambeth, he directs that his body be buried in the chancel of 'Schire' Church, to the south-west of the tomb of Master John Walter.[135] He leaves special vestments to this church, and a picture, with a representation of the Trinity, the Blessed Mary, and St. Christopher in four divisions, to stand at the Lady altar. There are also bequests of various kinds to the poorer parishioners and others, and the residue of his effects were to be divided among poor couples of Shere, and in marriage portions for poor maidens of the parish.

Until 1747, when it was taken down and the brass effigy laid on the chancel floor, there was on the south side of the chancel an altar tomb to John Touchet, Lord Audley, who died 20 September 1491. The upper half of the brass, 19½ in. long, showing a man in plate armour, alone remains, together with part of the inscription. At the east end of the Lady Chapel is a small brass to the wife of John Redfford; and one to Oliver Sandes is fixed to the window-sill of the north transept.[136]

Besides these there is an early 17th-century tablet, with a pediment over it, to the right of the great east window; and in the chancel and Lady Chapel are a few others of no great age or importance. Among these are some monuments to the Brays and Duncombs. Against the south wall of the chancel is a tablet to the memory of William Bray, joint author of Manning and Bray's *History of Surrey*, who died in 1832, at the great age of ninety-seven.

There are two small dial-marks, 5½ in. in diameter, on the lower stones of the eastern of the two pilaster buttresses on the south chancel wall; and on one of the stones, which is a piece of Reigate or firestone, is a mason's mark, the letter R upside down. On the south doorway, also of the 12th century, are five or six dial-marks, two being very regularly scratched on the stone, and of the same size as those on the buttress. There are also a number of small crosses cut in the jambs of this doorway. The toolmarks on this door are very well preserved.

The only ancient articles of church plate are the very graceful silver cup and paten-cover of 1569, now in use at the daughter church of Peaslake.

All the six mediaeval bells mentioned in the inventory of Edward VI's commissioners were recast in 1590, but so badly that, according to the churchwardens' accounts, a suit was instituted against the founder. They were recast by Richard Phelps in 1712, and two new ones have lately been added to the ring.

The registers now extant date from 1591. A volume from 1545 to 1590 has perished in the last hundred years.

Curious churchwardens' accounts are preserved,

dating from 1500. Copious extracts have been printed from them by Manning and Bray.[137] The most curious thing recorded in them is the possession by the parish of two bows, which were hired out for the benefit of the rood light. The common idea that every peasant possessed a war bow, and could use it, is untrue. A load of wood was cut, at Vachery, for remaking the rood-loft, in 1506. One entry states that the entire church was re-roofed with 'shingles' in about 1500. By 'shingles' in this instance stone slabs are undoubtedly intended.

The accounts show that there were lights before the rood, St. John, and St. Nicholas, besides the sepulchre light. Church ales were held at Whitsuntide, and in 1504 £1 8s. 8d. was taken for drinking at the feast from visitors from Ewhurst, Wotton, Abinger, and Albury.

The church of *ST. MARY* at Felday is in the old Shere parish. It was built of local stone and Sussex marble in 1879, at the expense and from the designs of the late Mr. Street, R.A. The style is 13th century. It consists of a nave, side aisles separated from the nave by arcades of three pointed arches, a chancel, and raised north annexe to the chancel. There is a screen at the west end, and a chancel screen of oak. The interior is highly decorated, and there are nine windows of stained glass. There is a turret at the west end, and six bells. The church stands upon a steep declivity, and the fall of the ground has been utilized to introduce two vestries and a sexton's room under the east end. The vestries communicate with the chancel, and the raised north annexe is above them. In the churchyard is a finely-sculptured churchyard cross.

The church of *ST. MARK* Peaslake was opened as a chapel of ease to Shere in 1889. It is of Weald stone, and has a nave and chancel with apsidal end, a bell-turret of wood, and three bells.

ADVOWSONS The advowson of the original parish church was in dispute between the Abbots of Netley and the lords of Shiere Vachery from the 13th till the 16th century. Roger de Clare sold it to the abbey in 1243.[138] In 1244 the abbot had licence to appropriate the church,[139] and the king confirmed the advowson to the abbey in 1250–1;[140] but the appropriation was not carried into effect.[141] In 1253 the abbey is said to hold the patronage 'at the king's request.'[142] In 1258–9 John son of John, lord of Shiere Vachery, proved his claim to present as lord of the manor, but allowed the abbey to present for one turn. Consequently, in 1277–8, the abbot again brought forward his claim, but failed to prove it;[143] and for some years the lords of Shiere Vachery continued to present;[144] but between 1346 and 1366 the abbot presented twice,[145] after which James, Earl of Ormond, disputed his claim,[146] but without success, for the abbey presented in 1379–80,[147] and again in 1390,[148] and continued to do so till John Lord Audley

---

[134] This font is illustrated by a good steel engraving in Hussey, *Churches of Kent, Suss. and Surr.* 341.

[135] This John Walter, the immediate predecessor of Robert Scarclyff, willed to be buried in the chancel before the image of St. James, and bequeathed all his blocks of hewn stones lying about the manse of his rectory to the repair of the steps before the high altar of the church, and all his planks, or *Estriches bordes*, at his rectory

to the repair of the ceiling of the high chancel of the church. *Estriches bordes* means deal boards imported from eastern countries.

[136] In the British Museum (Add. MSS. 32490, D. 9; K. 33; QQ. 22, 31) are preserved rubbings of the brasses before they were mutilated.

[137] Op. cit. i, 529, &c.

[138] *V.C.H. Surr.* ii, 146; Feet of F. Surr. 29 Hen. III, 23.

[139] *Cal. of Papal Letters,* i, 211.

[140] Cart. Antiq. L. 26.

[141] *Cal. of Papal Letters,* i, 283.

[142] Ibid.

[143] De Banco R. 19, m. 61.

[144] Egerton MS. 2032, fol. 286, 74a.

[145] Ibid. 2033, fol. 30a.

[146] *Wykeham's Reg.* (Hants Rec. Soc.), i, 61; ii, 600.

[147] Ibid. i, 105.

[148] Ibid. i, 176.

again claimed the right.[149] The dispute was only settled when Sir Edmund Bray presented in 1518. Before the next presentation came the abbey was dissolved. The advowson descended with Shiere Vachery till Morgan Randyll bought it in 1677 [150] for Thomas Duncomb,[150a] who was then rector. It was leased or sold for occasions by the Duncomb family, but remained with them till Thomas Duncomb sold it to John Smallpeice in 1831 [151] for the Rev. D. C. Delasfone, rector, with which the former sale may be compared. Mr. Justice Bray is the present patron.

There was a chantry of our Lady in Shere Church. In the 14th century the rector was responsible for finding a chaplain at the altar of St. Mary in his church.[152] The chantry was maintained from the profits of the 'Chantry House,' which was granted after the suppression of chantries to Henry Polsted.[153] It descended with his manor of Albury (q.v.).[154]

Early in the 14th century Christine daughter of William 'called the Carpenter' had licence to dwell in Shere Churchyard as an anchoress.[155]

The living of St. Mary Felday is in the gift of the bishop

CHARITIES Mr. Thomas Gatton left £400 in 1758 to educate poor children. In 1842 Mr. Lomax added to the endowment, and a school was established on the scheme of the National Society. The present buildings date from 1877, and were enlarged in 1898.

Smith's Charity exists as in other Surrey parishes.

In 1657 Mr. Maybank left £26 for the poor of Shere, which was invested in land in Cranleigh.

At some date unknown, but probably before 1714,[156] Mrs. Charity Duncomb left money invested in land in Cranleigh, bringing in £1 6s. per annum, to provide bread weekly for poor widows.

In 1746 the Rev. George Duncomb left £6 a year out of his freehold in Shere, £1 4s. to buy bread for the poor of Shere, £1 16s. for the poor of Albury, £2 13s. for teaching children, 7s. for the parish clerk.

In 1784 Francis Haybitle, farm labourer of Peaslake, left a rent-charge of 15s. a year on a cottage in Shere to provide bread for the poor.

In 1818 Charles Hammond gave £100 to be invested in the Funds, and the interest applied to the improvement of the psalmody in Shere Church.

WONERSH

Wonherche (xiv cent.); Ognersh and Ignersh (xvi and xvii cents.).

Wonersh is a village about 3½ miles south by east of Guildford. The parish is bounded on the north by Shalford and St. Martha's, on the east by Albury, on the south by Cranleigh, on the west by Bramley and the ecclesiastical parish of Graffham, formed from Bramley and an outlying part of Dunsfold. It measures rather over 5 miles from north-west to south-east, and at the widest part a little over 2 miles from east to west; it tapers towards the south. The northern part of the parish is upon the Greensand, with an outcrop of Atherfield Clay at its base. The southern part reaches on to the Wealden Clay. About the village itself, however, the soil is sand and gravel washed down by a tributary of the Wey, which, rising in Cranleigh parish, traverses Wonersh and falls into the Wey in Shalford. The road from Guildford to Cranleigh and Horsham traverses the parish, and the disused Wey and Arun Canal also. The London, Brighton and South Coast line from Guildford to Horsham cuts the southern part of it. Bramley station on this line is close to the village of Wonersh, though in Bramley parish. The two villages are curiously close to each other. The parish is agricultural, and there is a good deal of waste land. Part of the heath-covered high ground of Blackheath is included in Wonersh, also part of Shalford Common, Shamley Green, once spelt Shamble Lea, and part of Smith-wood Common in the south end of it. Along the road to Guildford is a great extent of roadside waste.

Wonersh was one of the flourishing seats of the clothing trade in West Surrey. The special manufacture was blue cloth, dyed, no doubt, with woad, licence to grow which was asked in the neighbourhood in the 16th century.[1] Her Majesty objected to the too free growth of woad as prejudicial to her customs.[2] The blue cloth of Wonersh commanded a sale in the Canary Islands, among other places. Aubrey [3] tells the story of how the market was lost by the dishonesty of the makers in stretching their webs. But the clothing trade was dwindling in the whole neighbourhood in the 17th century,[4] and Wonersh only shared in the general decay.

Prehistoric remains are rather abundant. Numerous palaeolithic flints have been found in the drift gravel near the stream, neolithic implements and flakes are abundant, especially on Blackheath and near Chinthurst Hill. In 1900 a small round barrow was opened on Blackheath. It had contained a cinerary urn, broken to pieces when found, in which were burnt bones. The urn had been inclosed by flat slabs of ironstone. In the barrow were two neolithic flints, a round disc, and an axe-head or hammer of rude make.[5]

There is a Congregational chapel in Wonersh. St. John's Seminary, built as a place of education for Roman Catholic clergy for the diocese of Southwark, was opened in 1891. It stands near the road to

149 Egerton MS. 2034, fol. 88a.
150 Recov. R. Hil. 28 & 29 Chas. II, m. 150.
150a See Manning and Bray, op. cit. i, 529.
151 Feet of F. Surf. East. 1 & 2 Will. IV.
152 Egerton MS. 2033, fol. 63.
153 Chan. Inq. p.m. (Ser. 2), cvi, 56; cclxxiii, 99.

154 Close, 10 Chas. I, pt. xxviii, m. 33; 32 Chas. II, pt. xiv, no. 10.
155 Egerton MS. 2032, fol. 74.—Compare the account of the cell adjoining the north wall of the church.
156 Before 1714, for in 1786 Thomas Duncomb, rector, did not know when she died. His father, grandfather, and great-grandfather had been rectors before him,

dying in 1764, 1746, and 1714 respectively, and none of them left widows.
1 At Unstead; Loseley MSS. (1 Apr. 1586), vii, 29 B.
2 See Loseley MSS. (10 Apr. 1585), xii, 60. A letter from the council on the subject.
3 Nat. Hist. and Antiq. of Surr. (ed. 1718), iv, 97.
4 See V.C.H. Surr. ii, 344-8.
5 Surr. Arch. Coll. xv, 156.

Cranleigh between Wonersh and Shamley Green. It is built in the Italian Renaissance style, and will accommodate over one hundred students as well as the teaching staff.

On Blackheath is a Franciscan monastery with accommodation for students, built in 1892; this is

WONERSH : THE POST-OFFICE, SHAMLEY GREEN

a handsome building with a chapel of stone in the Renaissance style.

The churchyard is closed to interments. The cemetery, between the village and Blackheath, was given by Mrs. Sudbury of Wonersh Park in 1900. Burials previously took place in the new churchyard at Shamley Green.

There is a Liberal club in the village.

Among the many interesting old cottages and houses in the village are two or three with very perfect half-timber fronts, having projecting upper stories showing the ends of the floor-joists, with boldly-curved brackets, or jutty-pieces, at intervals, ogee-curved braces, and in one case a recessed centre flanked by projecting wings, of which one has been removed recently. Several good chimneys of various patterns are noteworthy. On the eastern side of the village is a good example of early 18th-century architecture with hipped roof and sash windows.

Shamley Green, an outlying hamlet, contains a most interesting collection of old houses and cottages, some of which have evidently seen better days. The post-office [6] presents a charming study in roof-lines,

and has a fine pair of chimneys and a timber-framed gable of very sharp pitch, filled in with brick. This gable possesses a good foliated barge-board of early character, very like one in the rear of West Horsley Place and another at Alfold. At the top of the Green is another good timber house with a projecting gable with a moulded bressummer on brackets and a barge-board of tracery work in the form of small quatrefoils pierced through the solid board. There is a good chimney, rising from the ground, with moulded brick bases to the shafts of the flues. More interesting still is a house with a half-timber front, a good projecting window, and a fine chimney. On the left side of the front is a wing of rubble and brick with tile-hung gable; the centre braces and a gable on the right are framed in squares, with braces cut into ogee curves.[7] The gable is framed on a bressummer, and has a bold projection on spurs or brackets, the soffit being coved in plaster with moulded wooden ribs. The curved braces occur in the gable-end also, and the gable is framed with a rich barge-board of pierced quatrefoils set in moulded circles, resembling that in the before-mentioned example. In the apex of both gables is a clever arrangement for concealing the junction of the two sides of the barge-board. The story beneath this gable rests upon an elaborately moulded joist-board or bressummer. The ground story has been built out in brickwork. This house may date from about 1500.[8]

Wonersh Park is a beautifully-timbered park through which runs a small stream. It formerly belonged to Richard Gwynn, who died in 1701, aged seventy-two.[9] His heiress was Susan Clifton, whose daughter and heiress Trehane married in 1710 Sir William Chapple, serjeant-at-law in 1723, who became a Judge of the King's Bench in 1737 and died in 1745. He probably rebuilt the house. Sir William's eldest son, William, is said[10] to have been unmarried. In the Wonersh Registers his marriage is entered, but is erased with such success that though his name and parentage are legible that of the lady is entirely gone, and the details of the probable *mésalliance* are consequently lost. All Sir William's sons died without issue, except one, whose two daughters predeceased him. His surviving daughter Grace therefore became his heiress, and married in 1741 Fletcher Norton of Grantley in Yorkshire, who was Attorney-General in 1763, Speaker of the House of Commons 1770, being then M.P. for Guildford, and was

NORTON, Lord Grantley. *Azure a sleeve ermine with a bend gules over all.*

⁶ Illustrated by Mr. Nevill in his *Old Cottage and Domestic Architecture in South-west Surr.*

⁷ A common fashion in half-timber houses, as e.g. in a small house at Linsted, Kent ; at East Mascalls, Sussex ; and in cottages in Wonersh, West Horsley, and East Clandon, Surrey.

⁸ *Old Cottages and Farmhouses in Surr.* by Davie and Green, has good photographs of this house.   ⁹ Parish Registers.

¹⁰ Manning and Bray, op. cit. ii, 112.

WONERSH VILLAGE

WONERSH : OLD HOUSES, SHAMLEY GREEN

created Lord Grantley in 1782. His family held Wonersh Park till 1884, when it was sold to Mr. Sudbury, husband of Mrs. Sudbury, the present owner. The house contains some pictures of note, and is a good example of early 17th-century architecture, inclosing the remains of a much older house. On the floor above the state rooms is a long gallery, and the staircase is so placed as to suggest its being part of the original plan. The western wing contains a fine suite of reception-rooms. Sir Fletcher Norton added a library and billiard-room of noble proportions, and further additions in the shape of an eastern wing were made about 1836.

The 'Grantley Arms' public-house is a fine old timbered house, with curiously arched wooden heads to the gable windows. It may be of 15th-century date in part. Plunks, another early house, has a double-gabled front, dating from the end of the 15th or the beginning of the 16th century. There is a quatrefoil barge-board here also, and doubtless good half-timber work is behind the present plaster face. The joist-board, of good section, is also a noticeable feature. The rear of the house is of more ordinary character, but a picturesque medley of roofs, gables, and chimneys.

Other old cottages and houses lie scattered around the lanes and hamlets in Wonersh parish, including good old cottages at Blackheath; a long timber farmhouse at Halldish, or Aveldersh; Northcote Farm, Hull Hatch, an old timber-framed house, and Reel Hall.

The schools (National) at Norley Common were built in 1840 and enlarged in 1884. The infant school at Lawns Mead was opened in 1890, that at Blackheath in 1892.

The ecclesiastical parish of Shamley Green was separated from Wonersh in 1881. A Congregational chapel was built there in 1870.

Wood Hill, in the same parish district, is the residence of Captain Sparkes, R.N., C.M.G., J.P., one of the principal landowners in the whole parish. Longacre is the residence of Sir Charles Crosthwaite, K.C.S.I.; Willinghurst of Captain Ramsden, D.L., J.P.

The original Wonersh Schools, built in 1840, are in this part of the parish.

Wonersh is not named in Domesday. All the subsequent manors were included in the manors of Bramley and Shalford.

TANGLEY or GREAT TANGLEY (Tangeley, xiii cent.) was originally parcel of the manor of Bramley.[11] In 1238-9 Walter of Tangley and his wife Maud were dealing with land in Worplesdon.[12] In the same years Ernald son of Richard of Tangley was proved to be nephew and heir of John of Burningfold.[13] This Ernald held a messuage and a virgate of land in Bramley of William Brokere and his wife Edith.[14] About 1315-16 Sir Robert Fitz

Pain held ' a tenement called Tangelee ' by lease from Roland Vaux, who held it for life by right of his wife, then deceased.[15] Tangley then came into the possession of the Burley family. John Burley and his wife Agatha were dealing with land in Wonersh, and the service of Richard Tigenor, William Loxley, and others in 1367-8.[16] In 1542 another John Burley and his wife Katherine were seised of Tangley.[17] In 1545 John Burley entailed the reversion of it, after the death of himself and his wife Sybil, on Richard Carrill of Bramley.[18] John son of Richard

BURLEY. Sable a chief argent three tilting spears palewise counter-coloured.

Carrill inherited the manor after the death of Sybil, who survived her husband.[19] Thenceforward its descent is identical with that of the Carrills' manor of Bramley till 1677, when, at the partition of John Carrill's estates, it was assigned to his daughter Lettice, wife of John Ramsden.[20] In 1693-4 they sold it to John and Leonard Child.[21] In 1759 John's great-grandson Charles Searle sold the manor to Sir Fletcher Norton,[22] with whose estates it has since descended.[23]

In 1808 court leet and court baron are mentioned as appurtenant to the manor.[24]

The manor-house, where Hester wife of John Carrill lived during her widowhood,[25] is very ancient. It lies in the northern part of the parish, and has been made the subject of innumerable paintings, and has also been well described and illustrated.[26] The moat by which the present house is surrounded would appear to have been intended for purposes of defence as well as to drain away the water from the house, which lies somewhat low. Remains of stone buildings have been discovered. Within late years the house has twice been enlarged, having been rescued by its late owner, Mr. Wickham Flower, from the somewhat neglected state into which it had sunk as a mere farm-house, and surrounded by flower-gardens and covered walks. The south front, built in 1582 by John Carrill, can challenge comparison with any ancient house of its class in Surrey. This is not, however, the earliest part of the house: although subdivided into three floors in 1582, the hall, of the middle of the 15th century, with its original open roof, remains. It was of four unequally spaced bays, and the framed principals of the roof can be seen in the bedrooms. They consist of heavily-cambered tie-beams, 1 ft. 8 in. deep in the centre by 10 in., having under them a four-centred arch of solid timber, 4 in. thick, serving as braces to the massive story-posts, 10 in. by 9 in., on which the beams rest. A short king-post, with an arched brace 3 in. thick from each face, rises from the centre of the beam to support the collar and leon beams. The width of this hall was 20 ft., and its

11 Chan. Inq. p.m. 9 Edw. II, 63, where Tangley is said to be ' in eadem tenura de Bromlegh.'
12 Feet of F. Surr. 23 Henry III.
13 Chan. Inq. p.m. 23 Hen. III, no. 77.
14 Feet of F. Surr. I Edw. I, 12. Everard son of Richard Tangley is said to have been the heir of John of Bromfeld, 1288-9, Chancellors' R. 17 Edw. I, 20.
15 Chan. Inq. p.m. 9 Edw. II, no. 63.

16 Feet of F. Div. Co. 41 Edw. III, 676.
17 Feet of F. Surr. Hil. 33 Hen. VIII.
18 Chan. Inq. p.m. (Ser. 2), clxxv, 74.
19 W. and L. Inq. p.m. 10 Jas. I, xlvi, 9.
20 Exch. Spec. Com. 6485.
21 Feet of F. Surr. Hil. 4 & 5 Will. and Mary.
22 Manning and Bray, op. cit. ii, 110.
23 See under Bramley.
24 Manning and Bray, op. cit. ii, 110.

25 It was said to be much decayed in 1670-1. Exch. Dep. Hil. 21-22 Chas. II, 26.
26 By the late Mr. Charles Bailey (Surr. Arch. Coll. iv, 278); Mr. Ralph Nevill, F.S.A. (Old Cottage and Domestic Architecture in South-west Surr. 82, &c.); Messrs. Davie and Green (Old Cottages and Farmhouses in Surr.); and in Country Life (21 Jan. 1905).

length, including the musicians' gallery, which was built out as an upper floor over the entry or vestibule, 29 ft. This hall, as was commonly the case, must have had a central hearth, the smoke from the wood fires finding its way out at the upper windows, or through a louvred turret in the roof. The original front door still remains. Doubtless there were various outbuildings and offices, beside double-storied wings with parlours and sleeping apartments, which have been either removed to make way for the later additions, or so masked as to be indistinguishable from them. The new front of 1582 was built on in advance of the old hall. It is of two stories, and its elevation consists of two gables of unequal size with a smaller gable between, below which is the porch entered by a wide doorway, having a four-centred arch. The most interesting features of this front are the barge-boards with moulded hip-knobs, or pendants, at the apex ; the overhanging upper stories; the mullioned and transomed oriels and other windows, some on carved brackets ; and the ' square and circle ' patterns of the timber framework. The latter is in some cases enriched with shallow carving of fleurs-de-lys—a very rare feature in half-timber treatment. Many other details worth notice might be cited, such as a doorway in the garden wall, chimneys (one with a crow-stepped base), panelling, doors, and internal fittings. It is now the property of Colonel Kennard.

LITTLE TANGLEY was assigned to Elizabeth Ludlow at the partition of John Carrill's estates.[27] After her daughter Elizabeth's death it was sold to William Hammond of Bramley.[28] It is now the residence of Mr. Cowley Lambert, F.R.G.S.

The reputed manor of CHINTHURST (Chilthurst xvi cent.) formed, together with a moiety of Loseley, the dower assigned to Thomasine widow of William Sidney by his son William in 1452.[29] It had then lately been held by John Hover. It passed with Loseley to Sir Christopher More in 1532, and descended to his son[30] William More of Loseley, who exchanged it in 1557 for Polsted Manor in Compton with John Wight and his wife Agnes.[31] John Wight, a descendant of this John (see Artington), sold the manor to John Sparkes of Gosden in 1791.[32] The manor was then held successively by his son and grandson, both being his namesakes.[33] It is now the seat of Mr. W. V. Cooper.

HALLDISH is a small farm in Shamley Green. In the 14th century indulgence was granted to Bartholomew of 'Haveldersh' and his wife Joan, who were buried in Wonersh churchyard.[34] In the 17th century it was in the possession of the Duncombe family, and descended with Weston in Albury to Nathaniel Sturt and his wife Anne.[35] Their grandson, the Rev. George Chatfield, was owner in 1808.[36] It was purchased before 1841 by Henry Drummond of Albury,[37] and belongs to the Duke of Northumberland his grandson.

Green Place, the present residence of Mrs. Leighton,

was reported in the 17th century to have been ' sometime a fair and large house now ruinated,' and formerly the property of Baron Roos.[38] It was the property of the Elyots, afterwards of Busbridge, in the 15th century.[39] Thomas and Henry Elyot have brasses in Wonersh Church.

LOSTERFORD in Wonersh is called a manor in the 16th century. In 1547 John Scarlet died seised (inter alia) of the manor of Losterford, held of the Countess of Southampton (Fitz William) as of the manor of Shalford Bradestan.[40] He left a son John aged seven years and upwards. In 1576 Thomas Paston bought a moiety of the manor of Losterford and Wykes of John Scarlet.[41]

In 1579 William Tycknor bought the manor of Losterforde alias Lastarforde of Nicholas and Thomas Parson, no doubt the same as Paston above.[42] Losterford House is now the residence of Colonel Cust.

ROWLEYS, another reputed manor, was bought by Robert Harding, goldsmith, in 1508, of Humphrey Sydney. Robert's son William had a daughter Catherine (see Bramley), who married Richard Onslow, in whose family Rowleys descended,[43] till in 1806 the Earl of Onslow sold it to Richard Sparkes,[44] who was succeeded by his son John Sparkes.[45]

CHURCHES

The church of ST. JOHN THE BAPTIST is approached by a short lane from the village street, through iron gates in the lofty inclosing wall of Wonersh Park, its churchyard adjoining the park. The churchyard is surrounded by noble old trees and is beautifully kept.

The old parts of the church are built of ironstone rubble, conglomerate, chalk rag, Bargate rubble and other materials, with hard chalk or clunch for the dressings and a good deal of what seems to be Caen stone in the inside of the chancel and north chapel. The roofs are tiled. The nave and south aisle (thrown into one area and under one roof) and the transeptal chapel on the south were largely rebuilt in 1793 by the then Lord Grantley—it is said from plans by his butler—in red brick and in the plainest sort of meeting-house style.

In the alterations of 1793, the end of the chancel was cut off so as to make it coterminous with the transeptal chapels, a small alcove being built out to contain the altar. In the recent restoration(1901–2) some of the worst of these mutilations were undone, the chancel being extended to what was probably its original length, and the north chapel or chancel aisle, which had also been reduced in length, prolonged eastward on the old foundations.

The present dimensions therefore are :—nave 39 ft. 6 in. by 20 ft., or, with the space that originally formed an aisle on the south, 30 ft. 6 in. in width ; chancel, 32 ft. 5 in. by 20 ft. 3in. ; north chapel, 21 ft. 5 in. by 14 ft. 5 in. ; tower, on the north of the nave, opening into it and into the chapel, 13 ft. 9 in. by 13 ft. 5 in. ; and south chapel (now used as organ-chamber and vestry), 21 ft. 3 in. by 18 ft.

The tower, somewhat unusually placed on the north

[27] Exch. Spec. Com. 6485.
[28] Close, 25 Geo. II, pt. i, no. 5.
[30] Harl. Chart. 56 B 25.
[30] See under Loseley ; also Chan. Inq. p.m. (Ser. 2), lxxxix, 134. Feet of F. Surr. Mich. 5 Edw. VI.
[31] Com. Pleas D. Enr. East. 4 & 5 Phil. and Mary, m. 367.
[32] Feet of F. Surr. Mich. 31 Geo. III.

[33] Manning and Bray, op. cit. ii, 111 ; Brayley, Topog. Hist. of Surr. v, 148.
[34] Index to Epis. Reg. of Winchester ; Egerton MS. 2032, fol. 128.
[35] Feet of F. Surr. East. 10 Geo. I.
[36] Manning and Bray, op. cit. ii, 108.
[37] Brayley, Topog. Hist. of Surr. v, 148.
[38] Add. MS. (B.M.), 6167, fol. 467.
[39] Harl. MS. 1561, fol. 216.

[40] Inq. p.m. Wards and Liveries, 1 Edw. VI, iii, 11.
[41] Feet of F. Surr. Trin. 18 Eliz.
[42] Ibid. Hil. 21 Eliz.
[43] Chan. Inq. p.m. (Ser. 2), ccclv, 96 ; and Manning and Bray, op. cit. ii, 110.
[44] Manning and Bray, op. cit. ii, 111 ; Recov. R. East. 44 Geo. III, m. 231.
[44] Brayley, Topog. Hist. of Surr. v, 148.

side of the nave at its eastern end,[44] and with its western wall askew, is in three stages, the topmost, which is embattled and contains the bells, being an addition of 1751, and taking the place of a shingled spire. The upper stage is of brick and rubble, with broad brick string-courses and wide, round-headed, louvred openings. A peculiarity of the lower stages is that there are no dressed stone quoins to the angles, which are formed of thin layers of ironstone rubble, the construction resembling that of the late 12th-century church at Wisley. As however, all the openings are later insertions, it is difficult to pronounce with certainty as to its date : but it seems to have been built up against a nave of pre-Conquest date, in which traces of round-headed windows finished in plaster were discovered in 1901. This nave was probably that of the chapel built in pre-Conquest times, or at any rate before the close of the 11th century. The early windows were not preserved at the restoration. Until the early years of the 13th century this tower was detached on three sides. It opens into the nave by a plain square-edged pointed arch, having chamfered abaci, and this may date from about 1180. Early in the 13th century the chancel was also rebuilt, on a much wider and larger plan. The fine lofty chancel arch, of unusually bold span, shows by its mouldings that it was executed about 1220, and there are the outlines of three blocked lancets in each of the side walls of the chancel, a piece of string-course on its north wall, and remains of a low side window or priest's door on the south, which agree with that date. At about the same time the lancet that lights the ground story of the tower was inserted, replacing perhaps a smaller and earlier opening.

Towards the close of the 13th century a chapel was thrown out on the south of the chancel, and as evidence of this the arch of communication between the two, with characteristically moulded capitals, remains. The piers and arch are of the same section, of two orders with narrow chamfers, and the capital is really no more than an impost moulding breaking their junction. Nothing but this arch remains of the chapel, which was rebuilt in brick in 1793.

In about 1400—perhaps slightly earlier—a corresponding chapel was made on the north side, opening to the chancel and tower by somewhat elaborately moulded arches, of two orders, with shafts having moulded capitals and bases. A good image-niche of this period, with ogee cinquefoiled head and carved brackets, remains high up in the south wall of this chapel, and hard by is a roughly formed squint having a piscina in its sill ; while eastward of both on the chancel side is a door, low in the wall, with a flight of steps leading to what was perhaps a charnel behind the altar, paved with tiles of various dates. This is

shown in an 18th-century engraving as having a low lean-to roof of stone, just above the ground, with two small lancet slits under gablets abutting against the east wall of the chapel. This curious and rare roofing was destroyed in 1793. Another curious doorway, also of this period, now blocked, is set beneath the lancet window in the north wall of the tower. It also is very low down in the wall and is planned to open outwards : the head is pointed within a square, with a shield and foliage in one spandrel : its presence here is hard to explain, but probably it was merely inserted in the 18th century, being brought from elsewhere in the church, as Cracklow's view shows a small porch, now no longer

WONERSH CHURCH FROM THE NORTH

existing, against this wall of the tower. The door to the rood-loft, also of 15th-century date, is visible, its sill being at a height of some 8 ft. from the floor, in the south wall of the tower, close to the west face of the chancel arch ; and on the opposite side, against the east wall of the nave, is some wrought clunch, which has formed the jamb of an opening at the corresponding level through the south wall of the nave. This wall, with its arcade to the aisle, was removed when the nave was gutted in 1793. A lancet to the west of the tower in the north wall appears to be modern, and the only ancient feature

<hr />

[44] The neighbouring church of Bramley has a tower similarly placed and other examples of northern towers occur at West Clandon and (originally) Tooting : while towers on the south of the nave are found at Fetcham, Godstone, and Lingfield.

in this wall is a large embattled corbel, set at some height above the floor towards the western end. The soffit of the chancel arch retains a groove for a boarded tympanum, which originally formed a background for the rood and attendant images.

The modern extensions of the chancel and north chapel are in excellent taste and in general conformity with the old work : they include a fine east window, piscina, and sedilia, new windows in the chancel and north chapel, and a door in the latter.

In 1793 the nave and the space formerly occupied by the aisle were re-roofed under one span, with great queen-post trusses, and the whole ceiled. The ceiling has now been removed, exposing the somewhat naked constructional timbers. The roofs of the chancel and north chapel are modern (except for a moulded beam, of 15th-century date, in the former, which, however, appears to have crowned a screen or rood gallery), and are elaborately ornamented with bosses, on which are carved sacred emblems, shields of arms, &c., the whole

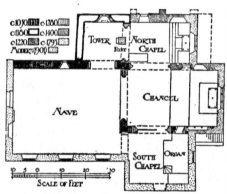

PLAN OF WONERSH CHURCH

being coloured and gilt. The painted glass is all modern and exceptionally good, especially that in the east window of the north chapel, with figures of St. George and St. Alban. A few slight traces of mediaeval colour decoration remain, as on the voussoirs of the chancel arch. The altar-pace in the north chapel is paved with old tiles dating from the 13th to the 15th centuries. The chancel is paved in black and white marble, laid in squares and patterns, and the sanctuary is raised three steps above the nave. The chapel altar is brought forward to allow of the passage way behind it. Both the chancel and chapel altars have stone slabs, incised with the five crosses, on wooden framework, that of the high altar being handsomely carved in several woods. The chancel seats are elaborately carved in oak, with figures of saints as finials to the stall-ends, and the nave and tower are seated with benches in elm, very beautifully figured. There are one or two pieces of old oak beams lying in the 'crypt' passage behind the chapel altar, and within the arch to the south chapel is a good plain oak screen of 15th-century date, having moulded work, but no

tracery. This has been copied in a modern screen in the opposite arch. There is a fine old Flemish chandelier hanging in the centre of the chancel, and in the north chapel is a pair of Georgian altar-candlesticks.

The font, of cup-shaped bowl, stem and base, is a restoration in sandstone, incorporating a curious band of ribbed work in a coarse grit-stone below the bowl, which, from its archaic character, may be of pre-Conquest date. This font was found buried beneath the floor at the restoration.

In the nave, aisle, and chapels are a few old slabs and ledgers, some with armorial panels. There is a large Purbeck marble altar-tomb in the north chapel, of 15th-century date, probably that of the founder of the chapel, but without name or inscription of any kind. Its sides are ornamented with quatrefoiled tracery panelling and shields, originally filled with coats-of-arms in latten, but these have all disappeared. An earthenware jar, now in the vestry, was found under the floor near this tomb. It is said that the person interred in the tomb was embalmed, as the cassia used in the embalming still exudes from the tomb in damp weather. In the south chapel, now the vestry, is another altar-tomb with a marble slab to the memory of Robert Gwynn, a 'Filezar of London,' with a fine heraldic panel and the date 1701. Built into the west wall of the nave are the fragments of a fine Elizabethan mural monument, with cornice pilasters and a foliaged scroll-work panel of good design : the inscription is missing. One of the grave-slabs, now missing, recorded the death of one of the Carills of Tangley, and the rhyming epitaph ended with the line, 'Caryll sings carols in the heavenly quire.'

On the floor of the chancel is a brass with figures of a civilian and wife and an imperfect inscription to 'Thomas Elyot de Wonersh' and his wife Alicia, dated 146—. Another, with figures of a civilian and lady and groups of twelve sons and eleven daughters, bearing date 1503, is to Henry Elyot and Johanna his wife. Within the chancel rails are two small brass inscriptions, to Elizabeth, one of the daughters of Thomas Blennerhayset, 1513 ; and to Elizabeth, daughter of Henry Bosseville : 'who died the 9 daye of February 1578, beinge 27 dayes olde.''

Some of the tool marks on the 12th and 13th century arches are very well preserved, and on the arch between the tower and the nave is a dial, or incised circle.

The bells are modern.

Among the church plate are a silver cup and cover, with the usual band of arabesque foliage round the bowl of the latter, and the date 1569, with the corresponding hall-marks. Another silver paten bears the hall-marks of 1811, with the inscription—noteworthy for the date :—' Ut dignius celebretur Eucharistia in Eccl. par. de Wonersh in Com̃. Surriensi, haec Patina Deo dicata est A.D. 1812. Gulᵐᵒ H. Cole Vicario. J. Sparkes et E. Chitty Sacrorum Custodibus.'

The registers date from 1539.

Christ Church Shamley Green was built in 1864 as a chapel of ease to Wonersh. It is in the 13th-century style, of sandstone with a west turret and spire.

On Blackheath is a chapel of ease to the parish church. It is built of stone in Italian Gothic or Romanesque style.

ADVOWSONS The church of Wonersh was formerly a chapel of Shalford, and as such was in the presentation of the king.[47] In 1304–5 Edward I granted it to the Hospital of St. Mary without Bishopsgate and called it a church in his charter.[48] The Prior of St. Mary held the advowson till the Dissolution, when it came into the hands of the Crown.[49] In 1590 Queen Elizabeth granted it with Shalford rectory to her secretary Sir John Wolley.[50] His son and heir Sir Francis Wolley died holding the advowson in 1609.[51] George Duncombe was dealing with it in 1650, Roger Duncombe in 1677, and George Duncombe in 1693.[52] In 1765 George Duncombe sold it to Sir Fletcher Norton, whose son, William Lord Grantley, held it in 1808.[53] It was acquired by Lord Ashcombe after the sale of the Grantley estates, and presented by him to Selwyn College, Cambridge.

Shamley Green was formed into a parish from Wonersh in 1881.[54] The living is in the gift of Lord Ashcombe.

CHARITIES Smith's charity is distributed as in other Surrey parishes. Mr. John Austen of Shalford left money for poor relief in 1620. Mr. Henry Chennell of Wonersh left land, the produce to be devoted to putting six poor boys to school, in 1672. Mr. Gwynne of London gave land and bank stock, in 1698, to put four poor boys to school and to distribute bread to fifteen poor persons every Sunday after service.

The charities are now (1908) being amalgamated under a scheme by the Charity Commissioners.

[47] Maitland, *Bracton's Note Bk.* 913 ; *Cal. Pat.* 1216–25, p. 497.
[48] Chart. R. 33 Edw. I, no. 49.
[49] Egerton MS. 2031, fol. 118 ; ibid. 2033, fol. 42 ; ibid. 2034, fol. 176.
[50] Pat. 32 Eliz. pt. xvii.
[51] Chan. Inq. p.m. (Ser. 2), ccxlix, 74 ; ccciv, 60.
[52] Feet of F. Surr. Mich. 1650 ; Mich. 29 Chas. II ; Hil. 4 & 5 Will. and Mary.
[53] Manning and Bray, op. cit. ii, 113.
[54] Census 1891. *Administrative and Ancient Co.* i, 350.

THE HUNDRED OF WOTTON

CONTAINING THE PARISHES OF

ABINGER	DORKING	WOTTON [1]
CAPEL	OCKLEY	

Wotton Hundred [2] (Odeton, xi cent. ; Wodetone, until xvi cent.) was found by the Domesday Commissioners to include Dorking, Sutton in Shiere, part of Compton in Sussex, Burgham, Wyke, Worplesdon, Betchworth, Milton, Anstie Farm, Abinger, and Paddington. Of these, Sutton in Shiere was shortly

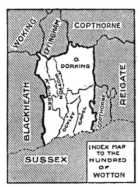

INDEX MAP TO THE HUNDRED OF WOTTON

afterwards attached by the Bishop of Bayeux to his manor of Bramley in Blackheath Hundred, [3] while Compton, as the county borders became more settled, was presumably included in Sussex with the other lands of Roger de Montgomery, who held it at the time of the Survey. It has been suggested that Burgham, Wyke, and Worplesdon owed their inclusion in Wotton Hundred [4] to a clerical error, and it was possibly due to the same cause that Ockley at the time of the Survey was placed in Woking. It seems probable that ' Becheworth' refers to East Betchworth, now in Reigate Hundred : Milton and Anstie Farm are both in Dorking parish.

The sheriff's courts were held in Dorking, whence the usual later name. The hundred does not appear to have been alienated from the Crown until it was granted by James I to Sir Edward Zouche, 1620, at the same time and in the same manner as the hundreds of Blackheath and Woking (see under Blackheath Hundred), and likewise descended to Earl Onslow.

[1] *Population Returns*, 1831, ii, 636.
[2] The hundred appears as Dorking Hundred in Norden's Map of Surrey (1610), given in *V.C.H. Surr.* i, while the name Wotton is alternative to Blackheath, by a mere error of Norden's.
[3] *V.C.H. Surr.* i, 305b.　　　　[4] Ibid. 313b.

ABINGER

Abinceborne (xi cent.) ; Abinworth, Abyngworth (xiii cent.) ; Abyngeworth (xv cent.).

Abinger is a parish bounded on the north by West Horsley and Effingham, on the east by Wotton and Ockley, on the south by the county of Sussex, on the west by Ewhurst and Shiere. It is 9 miles from north to south, and varies from 1½ to ¾ mile from east to west. It contains 7,560 acres. The church is 8 miles south-west of Dorking. Abinger, Wotton, and Ockley were formerly much intermixed, but on 5 December 1879[1] a long outlying strip of Ockley between Abinger and Ewhurst, and two smaller portions of Ockley isolated in Abinger, were added to Abinger ; at the same date[2] a part of Wotton on the Sussex border was added to Abinger. On 25 March 1883[3] a very small curiously outlying piece of Ockham and two very small portions of Cranleigh and Ewhurst, near the eastern slope of Holmbury Hill, were added to Abinger. The northern portion of the parish is on the chalk downs, nearly 700 ft. above the sea. It runs southward over the narrow Upper Green Sand and Gault, and on the western side of Leith Hill on the Lower Green Sand rises to over 800 ft. on High Ashes Hill. Abinger Church is 550 ft. above the sea, and is the highest old parish church in Surrey, except Tatsfield. The southern part of the parish sinks rapidly down to the Wealden Clay. The streams which rise in the parish flow to the Tillingbourne, which runs from Leith Hill to join the Wey at Shalford, and in the other direction to the head waters of the Arun. The parish is agricultural ; but at Abinger Hammer, on the Tillingbourne, was an iron forge.[4] The South Eastern Railway, Redhill and Reading branch, and the road from Dorking to Guildford traverse the northern part of the parish.

The ancient remains in Abinger, since the extension of the parish in 1879–83, are extensive and interesting. Neolithic flints, including a fine axe-head in private possession, have been found about Holmbury Hill. In a field near Abinger Hall a small Roman villa was found in 1877, with some coins of Constantine the Great and his family. The remains were left open, and Dr. Darwin used the Roman mosaic floors *in situ* for observations upon the work of earthworms, aided in his investigation by his niece, Miss Wedgwood of Leith Hill Place. The remains mostly perished from exposure, or were removed, and the remainder is now covered up again. It appeared to be a small country house, of no great pretensions.

On Holmbury Hill—now in Abinger, but in Ockley when the old Surrey histories were written—is a considerable earthwork, covering almost exactly 10 acres, 857 ft. above the sea. The four sides are nearly opposite the cardinal points. The western, northern, and eastern ditches make nearly three sides of a square, but the southern side follows the irregular contour of the steep slope of the hill. There are double banks and ditches on the north and west, where the ground outside is nearly as high as the inside, and double, or treble, scarped banks on the south, obscured by diggings for sand. On the east, where the ground falls more rapidly, is a bank and ditch, with a low outside bank to it, but no ditch visible beyond. There is a poor water supply inside.

ABINGER : CROSSWAYS FARM HOUSE

near the east side, and an abundant supply a little way down the hill. The entrance was at the north-west corner, by a causeway across the ditches, the banks being raised slightly to command it on either side.[5] The arrangement of the old parishes about it was curious, and can scarcely be fortuitous. The work was in Ockley, which was also outside it to the south-east. Ewhurst was bounded by the works on the south-west. Shiere enveloped it to the north-west, north, and east, bounded by its ditches. But across a strip of 200 yds. of Shiere on the east were three patches of Ewhurst, Cranleigh, and the far-distant Ockham, and just outside these the old parish of Abinger. An archer on the banks in Ockley parish could have shot into four other parishes with ease, and nearly into Abinger. The bits of Ewhurst, Cranleigh, and Ockham were on habitable ground, with wood and water.

The visitor to Holmbury Hill is not usually interested in the banks and ditches as his first object. It commands what may fairly challenge the place of the finest view in Surrey. The whole expanse of the Weald, with the South Downs as a background, from Portsdown Hill to Lewes ; the adjacent range of sand hills, with Leith Hill forming a half distance on the one hand and Pitch Hill on the other ; the Hindhead range, with Hampshire behind it, crossing the western distance ; the chalk hills to the north and the country beyond them—offer a panoramic view only surpassed by that from Leith Hill, which, 100 ft. higher, here cuts off the country to the east. But the growth of trees on the back of Leith Hill intercepts the sight northward, except from the top of the tower. The immediate foreground to Holmbury Hill is more broken and picturesque. The Pilgrims' Way from Winchester to Canterbury passes north of the parish at the foot of the North Downs.

Close to the west end of Abinger Church, by the farm which was the old manor-house of Abinger, is a mound which seems to have been raised from a ditch round it, part of which remains as a pond. It is marked on the Ordnance map (6-in.) as a barrow ; but it is large for a barrow, and perhaps not too small for a fortress—a *mota*, standing, as often happened, close by the church. It has never been explored.

At Abinger Cross Ways is a fine old brick house, dating from the latter half of the 17th century. Abinger Hatch, the well-known inn, has ancient features, and there are many picturesque farms and cottages, especially to the south, in the Weald.

Abinger Hall, under the chalk down in the north of the parish, has succeeded a small house called Daniells belonging to a family named Dibble, many of whom occur in the Parish Registers. It was bought by the Dowager Countess of Donegal after the death of her husband in the War of the Spanish Succession, 1706, and she resided here 'during her son's minority,'[6] which terminated in 1716. It was in the hands of her grandson, John Chichester, whose heir was his elder brother Arthur, first Marquis and fifth Earl of Donegal, who about 1783 sold it with 16 acres of land to Captain Pitts of the Engineers, who had previously bought other land in the neighbourhood.[7] He rebuilt the house, then called Paddington House,

on the site of the present cricket ground. This house was built in 1783.[8] Captain Pitts sold it in 1797 to Commodore Robinson of the H.E.I.C. Marine Service, who died in 1803.[9] His executors sold it to Mr. Shardon, who died in 1810.[10] In 1814 it was bought by Sir James Scarlett, who became chief baron of the Exchequer, was created Lord Abinger, and died 1844. The third Lord Abinger sold it in 1867 to Mr. Gwynne, who sold it to Thomas Farrer, subsequently Lord Farrer, in 1869. He built the present Abinger Hall in 1872. The second Lord Farrer now resides there.

At the north-eastern edge of Pasture Wood, adjoining the Common, is a house called Parkhurst, which in 1766 belonged to John Spence, "formerly of Wandsworth, Dyer," who sold it in that year to Richard Durnford, of Gracechurch Street, pin-maker. He in the year 1799 sold the property to Charles Lynd, of Berners Street, from whom it passed to his nephew and heir, Charles Lynd, of Belfast, and was by him conveyed in 1786 to the Right Honourable George Lord Macartney, whose greatest service was that of going on the first embassy to China in 1792. In 1795 he sold Parkhurst to William Philip Perrin, who partly rebuilt and enlarged the house, and with great public spirit made good the road hereabout at his expense.[11] On Mr. Perrin's death in 1820 he left Parkhurst to his nephew, Sir Henry FitzHerbert, by whom in 1838 it was sold to Mr. Edmund Lomax, of Netley Park, Shiere, who had resided at Parkhurst since before 1827. Mr. Lomax died in 1847, leaving the estate to his daughter, Mrs. Peter Scarlett, from whom it passed to her son, Colonel Leopold Scarlett. He in 1884 sold the property to Colonel T. H. Lewin, its present owner, who considerably enlarged the house and gardens. There is a priest's hiding-place in the north-west corner of the older portion of the house.

Parkhurst is remarkable for possessing the first larch trees introduced into the south of England. Tradition has it that the seedlings were sent to Lord Macartney, the then owner of Parkhurst, by John, Duke of Atholl, in 1780. The trees stand in the Long Meadow, on the east side of the park. The largest is 10 ft. 6 in. in circumference, and 118 ft. high. The park contains remarkably fine timber.

In all the earlier documents relating to Parkhurst prior to 1814 it is described as 'a tenement and farm,' but after that year it takes the style of 'mansion.'

The celebrated scene in Bulwer Lytton's novel, *My Novel*, where Riccabocca is put in the stocks, is laid at Abinger Church, near Parkhurst, where the stocks are to be seen to this day. During Mr. Spence's tenure of Parkhurst he was visited there by the French philosopher, Jean Jacques Rousseau, who stayed with him some days, but being haunted by fear of spies fled in terror, having accidentally met the curate of Abinger, who he was persuaded was an emissary of the Government.[12] Mr. William Bray, the distinguished historian of Surrey, left some diaries which have been privately printed, in which the following entry occurs :—' July 23, 1759. To the "Hatch" to dinner, Mr. Evelyn, Mr. Godschal, Mr. Bridges, Mr. Steere, Mr. Spence," Mr. Cour-

[5] *Surr. Arch. Coll.* xvii, 72.
[6] Manning and Bray, *Hist. of Surr.* ii, 136.
[7] Inform. from Lord Farrer.

[8] Leaden tablet found in the foundations inscribed *Henry Pledge November* 18, 1783. *This House was bilt.*
[9] Monument in church.
[10] Ibid.

[11] Manning and Bray, *Surr.* ii, 136.
[12] 'Of Parkhurst, where Rousseau was his guest for some time.' This note is in Mr. Bray's handwriting.

tenay, and Mr. Walsh there ; left at 7 ; paid for dinner and wine, 4s. 6d.'[13]

The house called Pasture Wood, built fifteen years since, is the seat of Mr. F. J. Mirrielees. Feldemore is the seat of Mr. Edwin Waterhouse. High Ashes is the seat of Lord Justice Vaughan-Williams ; it was a small farm-house, which he has improved.

The schools (National) were built in 1863, and the school at Abinger Hammer in 1873.

MANORS   At the time of the Domesday Survey *ABINGER* was held by William Fitz Ansculf, who also held the honour of Dudley. In the time of King Edward a huscarle had held it of the king.[14] From Fitz Ansculf the overlordship evidently passed with Dudley through the Pagenels to the Somery family, who held it at least as late as the 13th century. The lord of Abinger owed suit to their court at Bradfield.[15]

Early in the 13th century Gilbert de Abingworth (Abinger) held one knight's fee in Surrey ;[16] his name is also found in a list of the jurors in a suit concerning land in Titings.[17] Possibly he was connected with the family of Jarpenvill, who appear about this time in the history of Abinger. Geoffrey de Jarpenvill shortly afterwards held a knight's fee in Abinger;[18] and in 1273 David de Jarpenvill was holding Abinger Manor.[19] At David's death, 1293, the manor, which should have passed to his daughters, fell into the hands of his brother Thomas, who in 1295 settled it on himself, with remainder to his son Roger and Nora his wife.[20] Evidently Roger succeeded his father before 1316, for about that date he was concerned in a dispute touching the church of Abinger,[21] and in 1322 he was holding the manor.[22] Ten years later he made a settlement on his son Thomas and Avice his wife, daughter of William de Latimer. The effect of this settlement, however, was nullified by a suit brought against Thomas de Jarpenvill in 1348 by Margaret wife of Henry de la Marlere, and Margery wife of William de Harpesbourne, the daughters of Joan daughter of David de Jarpenvill, who had married Geoffrey Fitz Waryn.[23] Also in 1360 Sir John de Aylesbury, knight, the great-grandson of Margaret, another daughter of David de Jarpenvill, asserted his claim against Thomas and Avice.[24] The plaintiffs apparently succeeded in ousting Thomas de Jarpenvill, for some years later Hugh son of Margaret de la Marlere released his right in Abinger Manor to Sir John de Aylesbury,[25] a course which was also followed by Margery Franklin, formerly the wife of William de Harpesbourne.[26] Sir John de Aylesbury, who filled the office of high sheriff for the county of Buckingham,[27] died in 1409 seised of the manor of

Abinger,[28] and was succeeded by his son Thomas, who held until his death in 1418.[29] John son and heir of Thomas, who was a minor at the time of his father's death, died in 1422,[30] leaving Hugh his son and heir, an infant, who survived his father only about a year.[31] The heirs of Hugh were his father's two sisters, Isabel wife of Sir Thomas Chaworth, knight, and Eleanor Aylesbury. Evidently in some ensuing division of the property[32] Abinger fell to the share of Eleanor, and through her marriage with Sir Humphrey Stafford passed into his family.[33] Eleanor's son Humphrey,

AYLESBURY. *Azure*   STAFFORD. *Or a che-*
a cross argent.   *veron gules.*

who had been one of the leaders in Lord Lovel's Worcestershire rising, was attainted and executed at Tyburn in 1486 ;[34] his lands, including the manor of Abinger, were granted to Sir John Guldeford, knight,[35] who, however, does not seem to have retained them long, for in 1511 another grant was made, to Sir Richard Jermigan.[36] Before 1546, however, Abinger passed again into the possession of the Staffords ; in that year Humphrey, presumably the son of that Humphrey who was attainted under Henry VII, having been restored to his father's lands died in possession,[37] leaving Humphrey his son and heir, whose death took place two years later.[38] In 1551 Sir William Stafford and his wife Dorothy, and Sir Humphrey Stafford (presumably son and heir of the last-named Humphrey) and his wife Elizabeth sold the manor to Thomas and Edward Elrington. Thomas Elrington held a court in 1563.[39] In 1578 and 1580 Thomas and Edward alienated in two moieties[40] to Richard Brown of Cranleigh, trustee for Richard Hill, and William Morgan of Chilworth. Hill and Morgan held a court as joint lords in 1586, and in 1589 William Morgan settled his moiety on his son John,[41] who settled it on his daughter Anne on her marriage with Edward Randyll of Chilworth 1602.[42] He was knighted, and in 1622 conveyed his moiety to Richard Evelyn.[43] The other moiety, which was sold in 1580 by the Elringtons to Richard Browne[44] in trust for Edmund Hill of Sutton in Shiere, was conveyed by his son Richard in 1595 to Sir Oliph

13 Inform kindly supplied by Lieut.-Col. T. H. Lewin of Parkhurst.
14 V.C.H. Surr. i, 322a.
15 Chan. Inq. p.m. 1 Edw. I, no. 15.
16 Red Bk. of Exch. (Rolls Ser.), ii, 560.
17 Rot. Cur. Reg. (Rec. Com.), i, 140.
18 Testa de Nevill (Rec. Com.), 220.
19 Chan. Inq. p.m. 1 Edw. I, no. 15.
20 Feet of F. Surr. 23 Edw. I, no. 44.
21 Egerton MSS. 2031, fol. 46.
22 Feet of F. Surr. 6 Edw. III, no. 13.
23 Parl. R. (Rec. Com.), vi, 191.
24 De Banco R. 421, m. 265 d.
25 Close, 30 Edw. III, pt. i, m. 9 d.
26 Close, 1 Ric. II, m. 16 d. Manning and Bray (Surr. ii, 137) say that Thomas de Jarpenvill conveyed the manor

to Sir John Aylesbury by charter, 44 Edw. III. This may have been by way of an agreement after the suit.
27 Cal. Pat. 1381–5, p. 481.
28 Chan. Inq. p.m. 11 Hen. IV, no. 9.
29 Ibid. 6 Hen. V, no. 35.
30 Ibid. 10 Hen. V, no. 3.
31 Ibid. 2 Hen. VI, no. 21.
32 Fine R. 2 Hen. VI, m. 1.
33 Although no actual record of this marriage has been found, the circumstantial evidence seems fairly conclusive ; Humphrey Stafford left a widow Eleanor, and her son Humphrey inherited Abinger ; Cal. Pat. 1476–85, p. 11.
34 See Bacon, Hist. of Hen. VII (ed. 1878), 333.
34a Pat. 2 Hen. VII, pt. i, m. 18.

35 L. and P. Hen. VIII, i, 214.
36 Exch. Inq. p.m. (Ser. 2), bdle. 1093, no. 1.
37 Chan. Inq. p.m. (Ser. 2), lxxxvii, 77.
38 Feet of F. Surr. East. 5 Edw. VI.
39 Pat. 21 Eliz. pt. vi ; Feet of F. Surr. Hil. 22 Eliz.
40 A settlement on John's marriage with Anne Lumsford, widow, daughter of John Love of Winchelsea ; Chan. Inq. p.m. (Ser. 2), cclxxxi, 85.
41 Ibid. ccccxxxvii, 72.
42 Deeds in possession of the late Mr. W. J. Evelyn. Despite the inquisitions of 1603 George Evelyn was then possessed of only the other moiety.
43 Feet of F. Surr. Hil. 22 Eliz. ; Trin. 23 Eliz.

Leigh of Addington,[45] to avoid making sale ' of any lands of his more ancient inheritance.' This conveyance was probably in trust, for in the same year it was acquired by George Evelyn of Wotton.[46] The whole manor is still in the possession of the Evelyn family.[47]

The Domesday entry for *PADDINGTON* (Patisdene, Patinden, xii cent. ; Padyngden, xvi cent.), afterwards known as *PADDINGTON PEMBROKE*, states that William Fitz-Ansculf then held it, and that a huscarle had held it of King Edward.[48] The overlordship passed, as in the case of Abinger, with the honour of Dudley.[49]

The first notice of immediate lords of the manor occurs in 1188, when William Buffere[50] paid seven pounds fourteen shillings towards the ferm of Paddington. William Buffere gave shelter to a certain outlaw named Avice Wylekin, which occasioned the forfeiture of his lands to the Crown.[51] A grant was then made to Alan Trencherman, lord of Gomshall, who is described as holding the ' vill' of Paddington ;[52] his tenure marks the beginning of a close connexion which apparently existed between a portion of Paddington and the manor of Gomshall. At Alan's death Paddington reverted to the Crown, and was then granted to William de Braose,[53] who fell under King John's displeasure, and had to flee from England. He died

abroad, and his wife and son were put to death by order of King John.[54] Paddington meanwhile was granted to Peter de Maulay,[55] but afterwards Giles, Bishop of Hereford, a younger son of William de Braose, succeeded in recovering it.[56] Reginald, brother of Giles, was the next lord ; he was succeeded by his son William,[57] who met his death in the Welsh wars. Paddington then passed to Eva, daughter of William de Braose, who had married William de Cantlow,[58] and on the death of her son George without issue the manor passed to John, son of his sister Joan by Henry de Hastings.[59] John de Hastings died seised in 1325, leaving a son and heir Lawrence.[60]

HASTINGS, Earl of Pembroke. *Or a sleeve gules.*

Part of the manor seems to have been leased by Lawrence to his nephew, William de Hastings, whose tenure was probably, by the date of his death, ended by the Black Death of 1349. The inquisition on his death is among the many evidences of the severity of the visitation, for it records that almost all the tenants were then dead.[61] John son and heir of Lawrence committed Paddington to the charge of trustees, who apparently held it for

ABINGER : MILL HOUSE

[45] Feet of F. Surr. Hil. 37 Eliz. ; Close, 37 Eliz. pt. vi.
[46] W. j. Evelyn, esq., Deeds.
[47] For an account of the family, see under Wotton.
[48] *V.C.H. Surr.* i, 322a.
[49] Chan. Inq. p.m. 19 Edw. I, no. 14.

[50] Pipe R. 34 Hen. III, m. 2 d.
[51] *Testa de Nevill* (Rec. Com.), 224.
[52] Pipe R. 2 John, m. 15 d.
[53] *Rot. Cart.* (Rec. Com.), i, 134b.
[54] Matt. Paris, *Chron. Maj.* (Rolls Ser.), 523, 531-2.
[55] *Testa de Nevill* (Rec. Com.), 224.

[56] *Cal. Pat.* 1225-32, pp. 194, 205 ; *Rot. Lit. Claus.* i, 238b.
[57] Pat. 32 Hen. III, m. 10.   [58] Ibid.
[59] Exch. Inq. (Ser. 1), file 2, no. 7.
[60] Chan. Inq. p.m. 18 Edw. II, no. 83, m. 6-7.
[61] Ibid. 23 Edw. III (2nd pt. 1st nos.), 37.

his heirs.[62] His widow Anne was holding part of Paddington in dower at her death in 1384 ; she left a son and heir John, who was then fifteen years of age.[63] John married Philippa, daughter of the Earl of March,[64] but had no issue ; and after his death in 1590 Philippa became the wife of Richard, Earl of Arundel, and held Paddington in dower.[65] After the death of Richard,[66] who held the manor for life, the trustees enfeoffed by John de Hastings the elder released the manor to William de Beauchamp, his kinsman, on condition of his assuming the title of Earl of Pembroke,[67] from which title it took the name of Paddington Pembroke. After the death of William his wife Joan held Paddington in dower,[68] and at her death it passed to the family of Nevill by the marriage of Edward Nevill with Elizabeth daughter of Richard Beauchamp, the son of William and Joan.[69] Edward Nevill died seised in 1476,[70] leaving George Nevill his son and heir, then aged thirty-six. Probably the manor remained in the hands of the Nevills from this time until it passed to the Evelyns, since George Nevill, lord of Abergavenny, was holding it in the time of Elizabeth,[71] and it formed part of the possessions of the Edward Nevill who died in 1623.[72] Six years later Henry Nevill, lord of Abergavenny, conveyed the manor to Richard Evelyn,[73] from whom it descended with Wotton to the present owner.

NEVILL. *Gules a saltire argent with a rose gules thereon.*

The manor of *PADDINGTON BRAY*, which still retains a separate identity, may perhaps be identified with the three hides which were held of Paddington Manor by a certain Hugh, a homager, in 1086. Later they seem to have been held in demesne by William and Eva de Cantlow, who, in 1250, sub-enfeoffed Adam de Gurdon of the 'manor' of Paddington.[74] Adam de Gurdon died in 1305,[75] leaving a daughter and heir Joan, aged '40 and more.' No record of Joan's death has been found, but in 1337 Agnes de Gurdon, presumably a kinswoman, died seised, leaving as her heir Thomas son of Thomas de Syndlesham.[76] He was followed by his son Thomas,[77] who died in 1361, and his kinsman Robert de Lenham is named as his heir in the inquisition taken after their death.[78] There is, however, record of a conveyance by Thomas de Syndlesham of his share in the manor during his lifetime to one John Kingesfold, who afterwards alienated to William Rykhill.[79] The next lord of whom there is record, after William Rykhill, is a certain Robert White, who was holding about 1475.[80] His daughter Alice, by her marriage with Sir John Yonge, brought her share in Paddington to his family, and it was inherited

by her son John Yonge, who in 1492 conveyed it to John Leigh.[81]

After the death of John Leigh in 1524[82] his nephew and heir of the same name ceded his Surrey property to the king in return for lands in other counties ;[83] and the king soon after granted Paddington to Sir William Roche,[84] from whom it ultimately passed to the family of Bray, and thus obtained its name of Paddington Bray. In 1556 Owen Bray alienated to Owen Elrington,[85] with whom he was connected by marriage.[86] Edward Elrington alienated the manor in two moieties as in the case of Abinger, and here also one moiety passed to William Morgan.[87] John Morgan, the son of William, sold his share in Paddington to Sir Christopher Parkins,[88] whose widow Anne transferred it to Richard Evelyn in 1624.[89] The other moiety passed with the second moiety of Abinger to the Evelyn family through the hands of Richard Browne, Richard Hill, and Oliph Leigh.

BRAY. *Argent a chevron between three eagles' legs torn off at the thigh sable.*

Some land in Paddington belonged to the monastery of St. Mary Graces on Tower Hill,[90] and was after the Dissolution granted to John Leigh under the title of 'Paddington Manor.'[91] It seems possible that this land was identical with the hide of land in Gomshall which was said in 1086 to be in the hundred of Wotton.[92]

There was a water-mill at Paddington which is first mentioned in Domesday as worth 6s., and again in the inquisition taken after the death of Adam de Gurdon as worth 10s. 3d. Possibly it stood on the site of the existing mill on the Tillingbourne just above Abinger Hammer.

CHURCHES The church of *ST. JAMES* consists of a chancel 29 ft. 7 in. long and 18 ft. wide, a large north chapel with arcade of three bays 38 ft. 4 in. long and 17 ft. 9 in. wide, a south vestry and organ bay, a nave 47 ft. 9 in. long and 18 ft. wide, a south porch and western bell-turret. The roofs are covered with Horsham slates.

The present nave is that of an early 12th-century church which had a chancel smaller than the present one. About 1220 this chancel was rebuilt and made equal in width to the nave, and a north chapel was added at the same time or very soon after. From that date the building remained little altered to modern times, when a south vestry and organ bay were added and a south porch built (1857). The bell-turret is old, but of uncertain date. The east window of the chancel consists of three modern lancets. Below the sill is a moulded string-course with bosses which

62 Chan. Inq. p.m. 49 Edw. III, no. 70.
63 Ibid. 7 Ric. II, no. 67.
64 Placita in Cancellaria, 270.
65 Close, 21 Ric. II, pt. 1, m. 6, 7.
66 Chan. Inq. p.m. 21 Ric. II, no. 2.
67 Cal. Pat. 1399-1401, p. 444. He never was Earl of Pembroke.
68 Chan. Inq. p.m. 14 Hen. VI, no. 35.
69 Ibid. 12 Hen. IV, no. 34.
70 Ibid. 16 Edw. IV, no. 66.
71 Exch. Dep. Trin. 28 Eliz. no. 14.
72 Chan. Inq. p.m. (Ser. 2), ccclix, 157.
73 Close, 5 Chas. I, pt. xxvi, no. 11.

74 Feet of F. Surr. 34 Hen. III, 10.
75 Chan. Inq. p.m. 33 Edw. I, no. 25.
76 Chan. Inq. p.m. 11 Edw. III (1st nos.), no. 35.
77 Chan. Inq. p.m. 23 Edw. III (2nd part, 1st nos.), no. 137.
78 Chan. Inq. p.m. 36 Edw. III (pt. 2, 1st nos.), no. 37.
79 De Banco R. no. 574, m. 379 d.
80 Early Chan. Proc. bdle. 52, no. 44.
81 Feet of F. Surr. 5 Hen. VII, no. 25.
82 Chan. Inq. p.m. (Ser. 2), xl, 12.
83 L. and P. Hen. VIII, xix (1), g. 80 (20).

84 Ibid. xix (2), g. 166 (53).
85 Pat. 3 & 4 Phil. and Mary, pt. vi. m. 11.
86 L. and P. Hen. VIII, xvii, 1154 ; Harl. Soc. Publ. xliii, 178.
87 Pat. 21 Eliz. pt. vi ; Feet of F. Surr. Hil. 22 Eliz.
88 Feet of F. Surr. Mich. 15 Jas. I.
89 Ibid. East. 22 Jas. I.
90 Partic. for Grants (Aug. Off.), 708.
91 Ibid.
92 V.C.H. Surr. i, 298a.

runs round the south wall as far as the vestry, breaking up to form labels over a trefoiled piscina and a
single chamfered sedile, both being modern. Above
is a single trefoiled window in new stone. The
arcade to the chapel is of three bays with pointed
arches of two chamfered orders with hollow labels,
and has been reworked and in part rebuilt. The
pillars are round, with moulded capitals and bases.
In the east wall of the chapel are three 13th-century
lancets with chamfered rear arches, and in the north
wall three similar lancets, but with external rebates.
At the west end of the north wall is a small modern
porch over a doorway which has a pointed arch of
two orders with a label, the inner order having a raised
zigzag moulding. The outer order has jamb-shafts
with foliate capitals and shafts, one capital and perhaps a little of the label being late 12th-century
work, but all the rest is modern or reworked. It is
clearly not in its original position. In the west wall
of the chapel is a lancet with an external rebate like
those on the north.

There is no chancel arch. On the south side the
nave wall sets back a few inches at the east, but a few
feet down the nave regains its original 12th-century
thickness, though setting back here and on the north
side a little below the windows. Of these there
are three in the north and south walls, short and
narrow round-headed lights set high in the wall.
They date from the beginning of the 12th century,
but have been a good deal repaired. The south wall
has at the east a late 15th-century square-headed window of three trefoiled lights, inserted to light an altar,
and the south door is in modern 13th-century style.
There is a blocked round-headed west doorway showing internally only, and above it a modern three-light
window of 14th-century style.

The organ chamber on the south side of the chancel
has an arcade of one sub-divided bay. In the south
wall are two modern lancets; the vestry adjoining it
has an outer doorway, a modern lancet opening from
the chancel, and another on the external wall. The
chancel and north chapel roofs are modern, but that
of the nave is old, with canted sides, boarded, and
with simple beaded fillets, perhaps of 17th-century
date. The font at the west of the nave is modern,
in 13th-century style; and the fittings are all modern
except the altar table, which has some carving apparently of 18th-century date.

There are three bells; two bear the inscription
'William Eldridge made mee, 1674'; the third

was recast by Mears and Stainbank in 1880, but
was probably originally of the same date as the
others.

The plate consists of a silver cup, with cover paten,
a plate, and a flagon, all with the London hall-mark of
1736. They are inscribed, 'The gift of the Countess
of Dongall and the Earl her son.' There is a brass
almsdish presented in 1880 by Miss M. A. Roe.

The Registers date from 1599.

At Forest Green, a common with scattered houses
about it, in this district, 3 miles to the south, formerly an outlying part of Ockley, is a small church
consisting of a nave and chancel, in brick with stone
dressings, built by Mr. Ernest Hensley, of Sprat-
ham on the borders of Wotton and Abinger, in 1897,
in memory of his son who died by an accident.

ADVOWSONS There is no mention in Domesday Book of a church in Abinger;
no record of it has been found until
a presentation by Adam de Gurdon at some date between
1282 and 1304.[93] In the 14th century the church
appears as the parish church of Abinger *alias* the
parish church of Paddington;[94] and the fact that it
served the spiritual needs of both manors probably
accounts for alternate presentation by either lord.
Accordingly, between 1305 and 1316, Thomas de
Jarpenvill presented to the church;[95] and about the
same time his son Roger occasioned grave scandal by
laying violent hands upon the rector. The next presentation was made by one Henry de Somerburie;
the living, however, once more fell vacant before
1316, and presentation was then made by Roger de
Jarpenvill.[96] It is possible that the more intricate
succession to the manor of Paddington may account
for the tenants' apparent carelessness in taking their
turn at nominating; at any rate, the next presentation was again made by a member of the Jarpenvill
family. Some time before 1366 Thomas de Syndlesham, the Paddington tenant, took advantage of his
turn, and shortly afterwards Thomas de Jarpenvill
presented.[97] About this date we find a pronounce-
ment of the union of the two halves,[98] and from that
time the advowson, with an occasional variation,
remained in the hands of the lords of Abinger, and
is now in the gift of Mr. Evelyn. The exceptions to
be noted are a presentation by the Crown in 1638;
by one Henry Herbert in 1683; and by Joseph Offley
in 1685.[99]

CHARITY Smith's Charity is distributed as in
other Surrey parishes.

CAPEL

The parish of Capel is bounded on the north by
Dorking, of which it was formerly a part, on the east
by Leigh and Newdigate, on the south by the county
of Sussex, on the west by Wotton and Ockley. A
part of Capel lying across the north of Ockley separates that parish from Dorking. The body of Capel
parish is 4 miles from north to south and 1½ miles
east to west, but this projecting tongue makes the
breadth at the north end 3 miles. It contains
5,680 acres of land and 15 of water. The soil of

the greater part is Wealden Clay, but the north-west
part abuts upon the high Green Sands of Leith Hill
and Coldharbour Common, rising to 900 ft. above
the sea. In this part of the parish there was a landslip in the reign of Elizabeth, recorded by Camden
and Aubrey, when the sand slipped upon the under-
lying clay and made a precipitous scar in the side of
the hill, even now visible for many miles from the
southward. The place was called Constable's Mosses;
Constable resided at a farm still called Mosses. The

93 Egerton MS. 2031, fol. 1.   95 Ibid. m. 46.   97 Ibid.
94 De Banco R. 574, m. 379 d.   96 Egerton MS. 2033, fol. 1.   98 Ibid.   99 Inst. Bks. (P.R.O.).

ABINGER : PARKHURST

ABINGER CHURCH : NAVE LOOKING EAST

road running under or across this landslip from Cold-harbour to Leith Hill—since 1896 a public road, before that date private (though a public footpath existed and a public bridle-track crossed it)—is called Cockshott's Road, from a farm at the end of it ; and may fairly claim to be among the most picturesque roads in the south of England. The road slipped again badly about 1866. Capel parish is traversed by the main road from Dorking to Horsham, made in 1755, and the northern part by the old road from London to Arundel through Coldharbour, diverted since 1896 in its course from Coldharbour Common towards Ockley as a part of the transactions for open-ing Cockshott's Road. The London, Brighton, and South Coast Railway line to Portsmouth passes through the parish, in which lies Holmwood Station, opened in 1867. The parish is agricultural except for small brick and tile works. There are open commons at Beare Green, Misbrook's Green, Clark's Green, and Cold-harbour Common or Mosses' Hill, so called from the farm mentioned above. Many small pieces of waste were brought into cultivation early in the 19th century.

There is one conspicuous work of antiquity in the parish now. On the hill called Anstiebury, formerly Hanstiebury, above Coldharbour, 800 ft. above the sea—taken from Dorking and added to Capel by the Local Government Act of 1894—is a fine prehistoric fortification. A nearly circular top of a hill has been surrounded by banks and ditches, triple upon the most exposed sides, but probably never more than single and now completely obliterated for a short space on the south, where the slope is nearly perpen-dicular, and where some old digging for sandstone seems to have gone on. The space inside the inner bank is about 11 acres, the shape an ellipse, roughly speaking. The hill is thickly planted. Mr. Walters, of Bury Hill, Dorking, owned it and began the planting which makes the shape of the works harder to see, in summer time especially. There is a damp spot inside where a water supply might have been found, and a good water supply in a shallow well in a cottage garden close outside it. The entrance to the north-east, where a grass road comes through the banks, is not the original entrance, but was made when part of the interior was cultivated, after Mr. Walters' time, for access by carts. The entrance was more probably on the north side, nearly opposite the gate which leads into the wood from Anstie Lane. A path here crosses the banks diagonally, flanked in its course by the innermost bank, here higher than elsewhere. Flint arrow-heads are said to have been found in or near the works, and also coins near it, but exact records are lacking.

The work is the largest of its kind in Surrey, next to the inclosure on St. George's Hill.

Anstie Farm, north-east of the hill on the high ground,[1] still held of the manor of Milton, is no doubt *Hanstega*, held of that manor in 1086, but it is in Dorking parish, not Capel. The land reached down to the Roman road eastward, and to the old road from Dorking westward. Either might be the ' highway ' which probably named the place: The Stone Street enters Capel close by Bucking-hill Farm and leaves it close to Anstie Grange Farm. It has been traced for the entire length in the parish,

and excavated by the writer. Two or three feet of the centre of the causeway were found intact in the ground, made of flints set in cement, as hard as a wall. It is unused now throughout, except for a very few yards near Beare, where it coincides with a private road. In the field opposite Beare its course is very visible. It goes up the hill in the copse called Round Woods in a slight cutting ; it leaves the new house called Minnick Fold on the right and Minnick Wood Farm on the left. It was excavated in Perry Field, the field beyond, which was not cultivated until after 1824.

Capel was the old Waldeburgh or Waleburgh borough of Dorking ; the borough or tithing in the Weald. It was a chapelry of Dorking till late 13th or early 14th century.[2]

The (National) school was built in 1826 and enlarged in 1872.

There is a Wesleyan chapel, and a Friends' meet-ing house.

The Society of Friends was early established, and is still well represented in Capel. The Bax family, who lived at Pleystowe and Kitlands at opposite ends of the parish, were among Fox's earliest converts, and are often mentioned in his Journal. The Steeres and Constables were other families of Friends. At Pley-stowe a meeting was held which was as old as any in the county ; a burying-ground was made on Richard Bax's ground there in 1672. The meeting house in Capel was built in 1725.[3]

There are a number of important old houses in and around the parish. One of these is still called Temple Elfande, or Elfold. The name belonged to a manor of the Templars transferred to the Hospitallers which had no preceptory attached.[4] The name Tour-nament Field, and other such names occurring in the 18th-century leases, are most likely an invention of the Cowpers in the 17th century. For tournaments, always forbidden by law, would not have been habitually held at a small preceptory, had there been one here, of which there is no evidence. The present house is in substance of mid-16th-century date, and was built by Sir Richard Cowper. It is built of narrow red bricks and half-timber work, chiefly covered with tile-hanging, and with stone slabs on the roofs, and was evidently much larger at one time, as, besides an entire wing, now long since pulled down, foundations of out-buildings and of garden and courtyard walls are met with in digging. A curious feature outside is a cross-shaped loophole over the front entrance. Some excellent and rare encaustic tiles, 5⅝ in. square, have been dug up lately on the site, the patterns of which help to give the date of the house as not long after 1541. The character of the older chalk fireplaces inside con-firms this date. There are also the usual farm-house fireplace, with a great beam over the opening, of great width and depth, several large carved oak brackets supporting the beam-ends of the upper stories, the pilasters of a stone doorway, and many original doors of good design, besides panelling of several dates. The loftiness of some of the rooms on the first floor is noteworthy, as are the coved or cradled plaster ceilings of the upper passages. It had for long sunk to the position of a mere farm-house

---

[1] Manning and Bray, *Surr.* i, 570, curi-ously misdescribed Anstie Farm as ' at the foot of the hill southward,' confusing it with Kitlands.

[2] See the account of the advowson.

[3] Books lately in custody of Mr. Marsh of Dorking.

[4] See Lewes MS. 200, fol. 6*b*.

before passing into the hands of the present tenant, Captain Harrison, R.N.

Aldhurst Farm, rather nearer to the village, is another ancient house, although of less consideration. It has evidently been extended and partially rebuilt more than once, but the nucleus is still that of an early 16th-century timber house, with very low ceilings and stone-slab roof. Inside, an old staircase and some good doors are to be seen. In the wooded bottom to the south-west several fine footprints of the iguanodon were found in grubbing up trees some years ago, and are now preserved here.

Taylor's is a picturesque house still retaining as a nucleus the timber open-roofed hall of mid-14th-century date, and also an oak screen of roughly gouged-out timbers and moulded beams of the same exceptionally early date. There are good panelled rooms of later date, and the 15th, 16th, and 17th-century additions all present interesting features. Externally most of the timber construction is masked by modern tile hanging.

Greenes is another ancient house, once much larger, and still showing a timber hall about 18 ft. wide internally, divided up at a later date into floors, but still boasting some fine massive oak trusses and story-posts, with moulded arched braces and king-posts over. A smaller hall, about 15 ft. wide, detached from the other, and now used as a stable, appears to be but a fragment of a range of timber buildings. It also has a series of huge roof-trusses of king-post construction and arched braces of four-centred shape. These two halls appear to be of late 14th-century and early 15th-century date respectively.

Osbrooks, formerly Holbrooks and Upbrooks, after passing through the farm-house stage, has of late years been carefully restored, and now presents a most interesting example of the country gentleman's house of the end of the 16th or an early part of the 17th century. It is mostly of timber framing, filled in with herring-bone brickwork. Its tiled roofs and good groups of chimneys, the many gables with their barge-boards, projecting with brackets over the ground and first floors. These show timber framing, with an oriel window, stone-slab roofs, leaded glazing, and two exceptionally good brick chimneys.

Bonet's or Bonnet's Farm is another ancient house of quite exceptional beauty and interest, although shorn of its ancient proportions. The present front has been modernized, but in the rear are two fine gables, projecting with brackets over the ground and first floor. These show timber framing, with an oriel window, stone-slab roofs, leaded glazing, and two exceptionally good brick chimneys.

Other old farm-houses and cottages in the parish, such as Pleystowe and Ridge, are well worthy of examination for the features of antiquity to be found in them ; and in Capel village a picturesque piece of half-timber work, with a good chimney and roof, may be noted among others. There are now two old inns—the Crown Inn, originally a farm-house, adjoining the churchyard on the south, and the 'King's Head.' The former has half-timber gables, with pendants at the apex of the barge-boards, on one of which is carved 'W S. 1687.' Broomells is now a new house. The name, as Brome, occurs in a charter of the 13th century.[44]

It is not to be confounded with Broome Hall, the seat of Sir A. Hargreaves Brown, bart. The latter large house, in a commanding situation under Leith Hill, was mainly built by Mr. Andrew Spottiswoode, the king's printer, circa 1830. It was afterwards the seat of Mr. Labouchere, and then of Mr. Pennington, M.P. for Stockport. Sir A. Hargreaves Brown made extensive additions to it. It used to be called Lower House, but it is mentioned by Aubrey as Broomhall.

Kitlands, the property of Mr. A. R. Heath, is on the site of a farm which is mentioned in the Court Rolls in 1437. The house was reconstructed by degrees by Mr. Serjeant Heath, who bought it in 1824, and by Mr. D. D. Heath, his son, uncle to the present owner. But part of the interior is the old timber building of circa 1500. The place was held by the Bax family from 1622 to 1824, a very unusually long tenure of the same farm by a yeoman family, notwithstanding many vague statements of other immemorial holdings.

Arnolds, formerly called Arnold's Beare, was rebuilt by Mr. Bayley in 1885. Mrs. Bayley, his widow, has recently sold it. The Arnolds were also landholders in Betchworth. Beare, now called Bearehurst, the seat of Mr. Longman, and Beare Green, near Holmwood Station, show that the name Beare, which occurs in the Court Rolls of the 14th century, was widely spread. A Walter de la Bere had land in Ewekene (Capel) in 1263.[5]

Lyne House, the seat of Mr. Evelyn Broadwood, is a property bought by Mr. James Tschudi Broadwood circa 1792.

On the border, within a few yards of Sussex, is Shiremark Mill, built in 1774 out of the materials of the old Manor Mill at Mill House on Clark's Farm.[6]

Coldharbour is an ecclesiastical district formed in 1850. The church and the principal cluster of cottages stand in Capel parish. The body of the village is still called The Harbour, but Crocker's Farm and the cottages opposite used to be called Little Anstie, as opposed to Anstie Farm (vide supra).

The church is higher above the sea than any other in Surrey—over 800 ft.—and the sea is visible from the churchyard, through Shoreham Gap. The old road from London to Arundel ran through Coldharbour. The original line below the church was in the ravine at the lower side of the common, quite impassable for wheels. In the old title deeds it is referred to as the King's High Way. The village is as picturesque as any in England. On a stone in a cottage wall, in Rowmount, are the initials ' J. C. (John Constable) 1562.' The stone has been placed in a later wall. Constable's Farm was the house on the road a few yards higher up the hill, which may very well date from before that time.

The endowed school was founded by Mr. Robert Barclay of Bury Hill before 1819, with £50 a year from Government stock. It was further supported by subscriptions, and enlarged in 1846, 1851, 1860, and 1888. It was a free school from the beginning, but the endowment used to provide not only pay for the teacher, but a gown and bonnet for the girls, and smock-frock and boots for the boys annually. The infant school was built by Mr. John Labouchere in 1851. It was endowed by his family after his death

---

[44] Brayley, *Hist. Surr.* v, 73. [5] Assize R. 47 Hen. III, Surr. R. [6] Deeds in possession of late Rev. T. R.
13.   O'Fflahertie of Capel.

136

CAPEL: BONET'S FARM

in 1862. It is now brought under one management with the endowed school.

MANORS — CAPEL was, and is, for the most part, in the manor of Dorking, though it also extends into Milton Manor. Parochially it was all included in Dorking.

From a suit in 1279 it appears that in the reign of Henry III John de Elefold had granted lands in Capel to the Master of the Templars in England, and his son Thomas in that year withdrew from an attempt to recover them.[7] In 1308, when the Templars' lands were seized, Temple Elfold was among them.[8] The land was known later as the manor of *TEMPLE ELFANDE*. With the rest of the Templars' lands it passed to the Knights of St. John of Jerusalem, in accordance with a suggestion made by Pope John XXII.[9] The Chartulary of St. John of Jerusalem[10] describes it in 1308

KNIGHTS OF ST. JOHN. *Gules a cross argent.*

as held of the Earl of Warenne, but no service was done and no ecclesiastical benefice was supported by it. There was a house, and the total value was £4 11s. 2d. a year. It remained with the Knights of St. John till the dissolution of the order, 1539, when it appears as Temple Elphaud, in Surrey.[11]

After the Dissolution it was granted to John Williams and Antony Stringer, who conveyed it immediately to William Cowper[12] of London, who also held land at Horley and in Charlwood, Surrey.

The Cowper, or (more usually) Cooper, family continued to hold for nearly two centuries. In March 1590–1 John Cowper, serjeant-at-law, the son of William Cowper, died, seised of a capital messuage in Capel called Temple Elephant.[13] In the next year John's brother Richard, who had the reversion of the estate after the death of John's widow Julian, who survived Richard,[14] also died, leaving Richard his son and heir, who was then aged eighteen.[15] The younger Richard,

COWPER of Temple Elfande. *Argent a bend engrailed between two lions sable with three roundels argent on the bend.*

afterwards knighted,[16] married, first, Elizabeth Young, to whose father Richard the elder had mortgaged Temple Elfold, and secondly, Elizabeth daughter of Sir Thomas Gresham. He died seised in 1625.[17]

His son Richard Cowper or Cooper settled Temple Elfold on Barbara Miller his wife, on his marriage in 1646. She died without issue the same year, and Richard resettled the estate on his second wife Sarah

Knightley, in 1647. His son and heir by her, John, settled it on his marriage with Elizabeth Lewin in 1671.[18] Their son John sold it to Ezra Gill of Eashing in 1728.[19] Ezra Gill settled the manor, manor-house, and park of 144 acres, on 16 April 1729, in anticipation of his marriage with Mary Woods,[20] who died 1767, when the estate passed to her son William Gill. He died in 1815, and was succeeded by his brother Henry Streeter Gill, who died in 1818.[21] His daughter married J. H. Frankland, who assumed the name of Gill. They sold Temple Elfold in 1833 to Mr. James Tschudi Broadwood of Lyne Capel, whose great-grandson is the present owner.

BROADWOOD of Capel. *Ermine two pales vairy or and gules and a chief vert with a ring between two fir trees torn up by the roots or therein.*

The reputed manor of *HENFOLD* in Capel appears first in the reign of Henry VIII. In 1511 and 1512 the manor of Aglondes More and Henfold, in East Betchworth, Buckland, and Capel, was conveyed by Robert Gaynsford to Sir Henry Wyatt.[22] This was Sir Henry Wyatt, father to Sir Thomas Wyatt the poet, who in 1540 conveyed it to Robert Young.[23] Robert died seised of it in 1548, leaving his grandson John, then nine years old, to succeed him.[24] John died in 1629, leaving a son and heir William,[25] who succeeded him. Henfold, however, was probably not a real manor. In 1776 in a court roll of the manor of West Betchworth, and again in 1823, Henfold is mentioned as in the manor, being broken up into several holdings. The name Aglondes More has disappeared. The house called Henfold, which is the seat of Mrs. Farnell Watson, and is in the manor of West Betchworth.[26]

CHURCHES — The church of St. John the Baptist (until the early part of the 16th century dedicated in honour of St. Lawrence) stands on the west of the main road that runs north and south through the village, and opposite to the road that forks off to the east in the direction of Temple Elfold. It is on somewhat elevated ground, although the surrounding country is flat, and commands pretty and extensive views of wooded and pastoral scenery. The churchyard, bounded on the east and south by a stone wall, is entered through a modern lych-gate, and also by a stone stile, ancient at least in idea. A great slab near it bears the ripple-marks which are often met with in this locality. The path to the south door is of stone flags. There is a fine old yew, and also a number of cypresses, and among the gravestones are many of the 17th and 18th centuries.

Until its enlargement in 1865 the church presented

[7] Assize R. no. 879, m. 14.

[8] Dugdale, *Mon.* vi (2), 833.

[9] 7. Delaville le Roulx, *Doc. concernant les Templiers*, p. 50, no. xxxviii.

[10] Cotton MS. *Nero*, E. vi, fol. 141.

[11] Exch. Mins. Accts. 31 & 32 Hen. VIII, no. 114, Midd.

[12] L. *and P. Hen. VIII*, xviii (1), g. 346 (3), and g. 226 (79.)

[13] Chan. Inq. p.m. (Ser. 2), ccxxviii, 64.

[14] Deed of 1601 in possession of the late Rev. T. R. O'Fflahertie of Capel. Richard

the elder had mortgaged his reversion and Richard the younger reclaimed it.

[15] Chan. Inq. p.m. (Ser. 2), ccxxxiii, 104.

[16] The name 'Lady Cooper,' no doubt Elizabeth Gresham, is scratched with a diamond upon an existing window at Temple Elfold.

[17] Chan. Inq. p.m. (Ser. 2), ccccxix, 30.

[18] Deeds copied by the late Rev. T. R. O'Fflahertie of Capel.

[19] Deeds quoted by Manning and Bray, *Hist. of Surr.* iii, 597.

[20] Deed communicated by Mr. Percy Woods, C.B.

[21] *V.C.H. Surr.* ii, 611 ; Feet of F. Surr. Trin. 55 Geo. III.

[22] Feet of F. Surr. Trin. 3 Hen. VIII ; East. 4 & 5 Hen. VIII.

[23] Ibid. Trin. 32 Hen. VIII.

[24] Chan. Inq. p.m. (Ser. 2), lxxxvii, 64.

[25] Ibid. ccclxxv, 97.

[26] Rolls copied by the Rev. T. R. O'Fflahertie of Capel.

3

18

a very good example of the hamlet-chapel of the late 12th or early 13th century.[27] Even now, in spite of a new aisle, vestries, and organ-chamber on the north side, and other modern alterations, its ancient proportions and character can be made out without much difficulty. It consisted originally of a nave, 42 ft. 3 in. long by 22 ft. 9 in. broad, with a western porch, and a chancel 25 ft. long by 15 ft. 9 in. in width, with roofs of comparatively low pitch on account of the exceptional breadth of the nave, and a timber-framed bell-turret at the west end, terminating in a short oak-shingled spire. The roofs were covered with Horsham slabs, and the walls were built of local hard sandstone rubble, plastered, with dressings of hard chalk and fire-stone from the neighbouring hills. Cracklow's view of 1824 shows the church in this state, with the three lancet windows in the south wall of the chancel and the curious diagonal buttresses at the angles of the nave. The chancel had a wooden-framed east window under a circular head ; there was no porch to the south door (which was the same as the present), the spire of the bell-turret was not so tapering as now, and a curious late vestry is shown attached to the south side of the west porch. As to the nave windows, what appears to be the base of an original lancet is shown to the west of the old south door, and above it a wooden three-light opening, evidently made to light the western gallery, while to the east of the doorway is another three-light window, with a square hood moulding, which looks like a 16th-century insertion.

With regard to the north and west sides of the building, not shown in Cracklow's view, it is not difficult to reconstruct the plan on paper with the aid of the features still remaining in the actual church. The massive west wall, no less than 4 ft. thick, remains much as it was erected about 1190. The other walls of the nave are 3 ft. in thickness, and those of the chancel 2 ft. 9 in., both dimensions being exceptional for a comparatively small aisleless church. Originally the church had no buttresses, and it seems probable that it was lighted by three lancet windows on the north side of the nave and two on its southern side, of which now no trace remains, the present windows being all modern. The west and south doorways are original features, and most interesting. We cannot now say if there was the usual north doorway in the nave, as the aisle of 1865 has made a clean sweep of any such ancient features, but it seems improbable that there would be three doors in such a comparatively small building. The two that remain are interesting, the western being slightly the narrower—3 ft. 6 in. wide, while the southern measures 3 ft. 10½ in. The height of the internal opening of the western, which has a semicircular head, is altogether exceptional, nearly 12 ft. The external arch is set much lower, with that peculiar tympanum between the two heads so often met with, and the reason for which is one of the minor problems of ecclesiology. Sometimes, as at Trotton Church, Sussex, a consecration cross has been found painted in this blank space. These doorways also have the additional peculiarity that the two apex stones of the

external arches are left as projecting blocks on the inside, as though meant to be carved. This is found also in the south doorway of Wanborough Chapel, in the west of the county.[28] Both the west and south doorways are in hard clunch, or fire-stone, somewhat sharply pointed, and of one order. They have hood-mouldings, without stops or return ends at the springings, of three sides of an octagon in section, the inner side being embellished with a continuous border of dog-tooth ornament. The original tooling, where left, shows somewhat coarse vertical and diagonal lines, done with the broad chisel and axe. The effect of these severely simple but well-proportioned doorways is enhanced by their retaining their original wrought-iron strap-hinges, both lower and upper hinges having two small ornamental straps with curled ends on either side of them. The hinge-straps themselves terminate in similar scrolls. The latch and drop-ring handle of the western door appears to be old also, and are perhaps original. Although the boarding on which this ironwork is mounted is modern, the plain ledges across the backs appear to be old. There are three steps down into the church at the west end and two at the south door ; the latter is set to the east of the centre of the nave, instead of to the west.

The original chancel arch has disappeared, and its place has been taken by a wider one of early 14th-century design in fire-stone, which appears to be modern. We may surmise that the ancient arch had square jambs, and resembled in design the two doorways. The present tracery window in the east wall is also entirely modern, and replaces the wood-framed opening of the churchwarden era, shown in Cracklow's view, which latter, in all probability, displaced two lancet openings of the same character as those in the side walls. There were probably three of these in either wall, but those on the north side have been destroyed in making the organ chamber and vestries. The three lancets in the south wall of the chancel are the only original windows left in the church. They are very interesting examples of their period (c. 1190), and have happily passed unscathed through the ordeal of restoration. Like the rest of the original ashlaring, their dressings are worked in clunch and firestone. They have sharply-pointed heads to the external openings, the curves being so slight as almost to present the appearance of straight lines,[29] and are rebated both inside and out, which implies that the glazing was originally placed against the outer rebate (instead of, as now, in a groove), and that the inner rebate was occupied by a shutter. It is not often that this double rebate is found. The internal heads are splayed equally with the jambs and are almost semicircular in outline, the point of the arch being so slight as to be unnoticeable.

Beneath the easternmost lancet is a pretty little piscina of the same period. It has a segmental head beneath a blind trefoil arch of horse-shoe outline, The drain has a small circular dishing. The aumbry, of similar form, in the opposite wall is modern. In about 1300 diagonal buttresses with gabled capping-stones were added to the angles of the nave. To the

[27] The chapel mentioned in the confirmation of Henry of Blois (see advowson) must have been a timber building, erected perhaps earlier in the 12th century, and probably it would be much smaller than the stone chapel that succeeded it.

[28] Possibly the projecting stones were left to prevent the door being lifted bodily off its hinges.

[29] In this they recall the lancets of the chancel at Chipstead, where the internal heads are gabled or triangular in form.

same period belongs the western porch, so far as its walls are concerned. The doorway, with its pointed segmental head, and the square loophole in the northern wall, are of this date, but the remarkable roof is a survival of the original timber porch, the walls being built anew, probably because of the exposed situation. Each separate rafter is shaped as a bold horseshoe trefoil, as though built for a barge board. There is something very suggestive of Saracenic art in the whole look of this roof.

Of the original font, the Sussex marble base alone remains, being built in against the nave wall, west of the south porch. It shows the common arrangement of four angle shafts and a central drum, through which the drain was pierced, the latter making a large hole in the base. Doubtless the bowl was of square form, with perhaps a shallow arcade cut round the sides, according to the common type, of which so many examples remain in the home counties.[30] The modern font is made of serpentine, with some little carving and gilding.

The roofs of the chancel and nave are both ancient, and possibly coeval with the original building. They are of trussed collar construction, with massive tie-beams and wall plates, the latter being of enormous scantling, and worked with double hollows in the chancel, exactly the same as at West Clandon chancel. The posts and beams of the timber bell-turret, and its carved braces, appear to have been partially renewed. The copings to the gables are modern.

In pre-Reformation wills an altar of our Lady and an image of the same are specified. This altar was probably on the south of the chancel arch on the nave side. An image of St. Lawrence (and probably an altar) stood in the chancel.

To the south wall of the chancel are affixed two monuments of some interest, the eastern being that of John Cowper and his wife, date 1590. It is composed of alabaster, with panels of black marble, on which is cut the inscription, the whole retaining the original colouring in a very perfect state. At the apex, within a circular disc, is a shield of Cowper impaling argent a fesse between three trefoils sable, which are the arms of Blackdenn. This shield is festooned with twisted red ribbons, and stands within a broken pediment, beneath which and an entablature bordered by black marble columns is a circular arch. Within this are the kneeling figures of John Cowper and his wife, facing each other at a fald-stool of graceful design, on which are prayer-books. The husband is represented in the scarlet robe of a serjeant-at-law, with a coif and a cloak over his shoulder. The wife's figure, kneeling on a cushion, in the ruff, stomacher, and fardingale of the period, is uncoloured—probably an indication that the monument was put up during her widowhood, and that thus the effigy was not completed as to colouring by her descendants. The inscription in the two panels reads :—

HEARE LYETH BVRYED NEER TO THIS MONVMENT IOHN COWPER LATE SERIEANT AT LAWE DECEASED WHO WAS BORNE AT HORLYE IN Y^E COVNTY OF SVRREY IN AO DO : 1539. & AT HIS AGE OF 26 YEARS TOKE TO WIEFE IVLYAN THE DAVGTER OF CVTHBERT BLACKDENN

ESQUIOR AND THEN BEGAN TO STVDDY THE COMON LAWE IN THE INNER TEMPLE AND THER CŌTINVED 24 YEARES WHICH TIME HE SPENT IN THIS MANNER · 8 · YEARES VNDER THE BARR · 8 · YEARS AT THE BARR · AND · 8 · YEARS AT THE BENCHE AND THEN WAS CALLED TO BE SERIEANT AT THE LAWE IN W^{CH} DEGREE HE CONTYNVED ONE YEARE AND A HAVLFE AND THEN ENDE^D HIS LIEFE THE 15 DAYE OF MARCHE A° 1590, BEING THEN OF THE AGE OF · 51 · YEARS.

NEC PRIMVS NEC VLTIMVS MVLTI
ANTECESSERVNT ET OMNES SEQVENTVR.

Below the inscription panels is an apron of scroll-work in alabaster.

The other monument, to the westward, is also finely designed, according to its period, and is in Sicilian marble, with Corinthian columns and pediment, having at top a cartouche, bearing the family arms, and over it the crest of a black lion holding a silver tilting-spear. The inscription is as follows :—

" Underneath lyeth the body of ROB^T COWPER late of *London*, Gent. a younger son of RICHARD COWPER late of *Temple Elfont*, Esqr (by SARAH Eldest daughter of W^M KNIGHTLEY late of *Kingston* Esqr.) who was Son & Heir of s^r RICHARD COWPER Kn^t, by Dame ELIZ. 2^d Daughter of s^r THOMAS GRESHAM K^{NT} He Dyed ye 23^d of May 1720, In the 65th year of his Age. To whose Memory this Monum^t was Erected by his 3 Neices, the Daughters & Coheirs of RICHARD COWPER late of *London* Gent. Viz^t Sarah the Eldest Daughter Wife of John Vincent of *Hampstead* in the County of Midd^x Brewer, Mary ye 2^d Daughter, wife of *Henry Ashton* of *Hackney* in ye same County of *Midd*. Gent. and *Hannah* the youngest Daughter wife of RICHARD DAWSON of *Lambeth* in the County of *Surry* Glass maker."

In addition to these monuments, Manning and Bray give the following :—

' On a brass plate in capitals' :—

' HERE LYETH THE BODY OF DAME ELIZABETH, THE SECOND DAUGHTER OF SIR THOMAS GRESHAM OF LYMS-FEILD IN THE COUNTY OF SURREY, KNT., AND WIFE OF SIR RICHARD COWPER OF CAPEL IN THE SAID COUNTY, KNT. SHEE DECEASED THE XXTH OF AUGUST ANNO DOMINI 1633.'

' On a brass plate, on a gravestone, in capitals' :—

' HERE LYETH INTERRED THE BODY OF SARAH COWPER, WIFE OF RICHARD COWPER, OF TEMPLE ELFANT IN SURREY, ESQ., ELDEST DAUGHTER OF WILLIAM KNIGHTLEY OF KINGSTONE-UPON-THAMES, ESQ., HAVING HAD ISSUE SEAVEN SONNES & ONE DAUGHTER, AND DECEASED THE 3^D DAY OF NOVEMBER IN THE 38TH YEAR OF HER AGE, ANNO DOMINI 1662.'

' On a black marble grave-stone in the chancel in capitals, is this inscription' : —

' SARAH, DAUGHTER OF JOHN COWPER ESQ., AGED 9 MONTHS. DIED THE 22^D AUGUST 1676.'

' On the floor' :—

' WILLIAM HEWITT, 1760.'

---

[30] As at Beddington, Great Bookham, West Clandon, Surrey; and many others in Kent, Sussex, Middlesex, &c. Frensham, Merstham, Mickleham, Seale, and Worplesdon in

There are no remains of ancient wall paintings or glass, but in the nave, chancel, and north aisle are many modern stained glass windows, by Clayton & Bell and other firms, some very good (as in the aisle and the side windows of the chancel), others of poor quality. The seating, pulpit, reredos, and other fittings are all also modern, but in the vestry are preserved a number of carved pew doors, of 17th-century date, worked up into a cupboard ; also a wrought iron hour-glass stand.

The registers date from 1653.

Among the plate is a two-handled cup, of date about 1655, evidently a porringer, and very similar in design and size to one in use as a communion cup at Winterborne Whitchurch, Dorset, which is dated 1653. There is some repoussé ornamentation in circles on the bowl, with traces of gilding, and the handles are S-shaped. Beneath the foot is engraved a Tudor rose within a beaded circle. The bowl has at some time been soldered to the foot, which was probably higher originally. There are patens of 1781 and 1786, some modern pieces ; and a pewter plate bearing (1) the name RICHARD KING, and devices of two bears or badgers flanked by fluted columns ; (2) a crowned rose, with a word beginning ' GRA . . ' ; and (3), S over RE.

Of the six bells two are 19th century, two are by Thomas Mears, and dated 1797, and no. 4 and 5 bear the following inscriptions respectively :—

' OUR HOPE IS IN THE LORD R.E. 1605,' and ' OMNIA HABENT FINEM R.E. 1593,'

the initials in both cases being those of Richard Eldridge, a well-known Surrey founder.

CHRIST CHURCH, COLDHARBOUR, was built in 1848 at the expense of Mr. Labouchere, of Broome Hall. The Duke of Norfolk gave the ground in the waste of the manor. It has a plain nave and chancel in 13th-century style, with rather a fine pointed arch between them. The church is of local stone, with chalk dressings. There is a stone bell-turret on the west end. It was refitted, and an organ chamber added in 1904 by Sir A. Hargreaves Brown in memory of his mother. The heads on the corbels at the spring of the arch over the east window outside are portraits of Mr. John Labouchere the founder and of Mrs. Labouchere.

ADVOWSONS Capel was originally a chapelry of Dorking. The chapel, which gives its name to the parish, seems first mentioned in a confirmation by Henry de Blois, Bishop of Winchester 1129–71, of the grants of churches, &c., given to the Priory of Lewes by the Earls of Warenne. He confirms to them ' Ecclesiam de Dorking cum Capella de la Wachna.' The charter is witnessed by Robert, Archdeacon of Surrey, who witnessed the charter of Henry to Waverley in 1130.[81] This seems to be Capel ; for in 1361 Adam atte Plesshette granted land which had been held by Edith Pipestre of the grant of Maurice de Ewekne

lying in the parish ' Capelle de Ewekene,' along with land in Ockley at Henhurst which is on the border of Capel.[82] In Pope Nicholas's taxation of 1291 ' Dorking cum Capella ' is the style of Dorking parish ; so that it would appear that Capel became first called a separate parish between 1291 and 1361. This was possibly about 1334–7, when the church of Dorking with Capel was transferred from Lewes Priory to Reigate Priory, just founded by the last Earl of Warenne and Surrey.[83] The tithes of Capel were let immediately afterwards ;[84] and the whole revenue was entirely at the disposal of the priory, and was granted to Lord William Howard with Reigate Priory at the Dissolution. The lay impropriator henceforth paid what he chose to the curate-in-charge of Capel. This state of things existed until 1868, when an endowment was raised by neighbouring landowners.

Charles Lord Howard of Effingham, son of Lord William Howard, leased the rectory, as it was called, and possibly the advowson also, to John Cowper, 28 May 1587. Julian Cowper, John's widow, conveyed to Richard Cowper, John's nephew and eventual heir, in 1603.[85] The Cowpers of Temple Elfold in Capel conveyed the lease to other persons for terms of years only, and in 1644 Mr. Richard Cowper had the advowson, and engaged in a lively controversy with the Committee of Plundered Ministers, declining to pay anybody else than the Rev. John Allen, whom they had removed.[86] He carried his point, and though the committee kept the man of their choice, they had to pay him out of the estates of the Chapter of Winchester.[87] But for an interval, while the controversy was proceeding, Capel baptisms and burials were performed at Newdigate, there being no parson in Capel. In 1660 the Cowper leases expired, and the rectory of Capel was, with others, confirmed to the Earl of Peterborough, as heir of Lord William Howard.[88] His daughter Mary sold in 1677 to Sir John Parsons. The widow of his son Humphrey settled it on her daughter Anne, wife of Sir John Hynde Cotton. In 1766 they sold to John Rogers for £5,700, subject to the payment of £20 a year to the curate. He died 1778, leaving it to his wife, who married secondly William Chivers, to whom it was conveyed. William Chivers died 1805, when it descended to his nephew Noah Chivers, who conveyed in 1812 to the Duke of Norfolk. His heir sold in 1844 to Charles Webb, who died 1869, leaving his property in trust ; and the advowson and rectory are now in the hands of his trustees.[89]

Coldharbour is an ecclesiastical district formed in 1850 under 7 & 8 Vict. cap. 94, from portions of the parishes of Capel, Dorking, Wotton, and Ockley.

The living is in the gift of the trustees of Mr. John Labouchere.

CHARITIES Smith's Charity is distributed as in other Surrey parishes.

Capel Cottage Hospital was built by the widow of the Rev. John Broadwood in 1864. It is maintained chiefly by public subscription.

---

81 Exch. T.R. B ⅔ fol. 49. The volume is also lettered Cartae Antiquae de Prioratu de Lewes.

82 Charter in possession of the late Rev. T. R. O'Fflahertie, Vicar of Capel. Compare Manning and Bray, Surr. iii, App. cxxx ; 'land in the parishes of Dorking and Ewekenes' in a charter of 1481. 'Ewekenes,' now usually spelt

Eutons, is a farm in Capel ; there are remains of a moat near it.

83 Winton Epis. Reg. Orlton, i, fol. 57 d. But in 1508 it was still called a chapel of Dorking.

84 Winton Epis.Reg.Edendon,ii,fol.41-2.

85 Deed at Loseley reciting the former lease to John Cowper.

86 Add. MS. (B.M.), 1566, fol. 11.

87 Bodl. MSS. 323, p. 271 ; 325, p. 223 ; 327, p. 508.

88 Pat. 12 Chas. II, pt. xviii, no. 16. Pro concessione Johanni Vicecomiti Mordaunt, in trust for his elder brother the earl's daughter Mary. (See above.)

89 Abstract of title to rectory and glebe of Capel. Sold in 1910 to Mr. Crisp of Godalming.

In 1871 Mr. Charles Webb of Clapham was commemorated by his family in the building of almshouses for six aged couples.

Mr. Thomas Summers, of Horsham, left £100 in 1807, which was invested in 3 per cent. consols. The income provides bread for the poor (see Droking also). The vicar and churchwardens of Capel, who were trustees of Smith's and Summers' Charity, obtained leave from the Charity Commissioners to devote the funds to a more useful purpose, the bread having been distributed among a large number of people quite well able to provide for themselves, or given to the poor in such quantities that they could not consume it while it was good. All the bakers in the parish had to be employed, and the baker in Coldharbour (q.v.) sent bread three miles and a half to Capel, which was given to the Coldharbour people who had walked the same distance to receive it, and who carried it back to a hundred yards from where it was baked. The Parish Council, however, on becoming manager of parochial charities restored the bread dole.

DORKING

Dorchinges (xi cent.) ; Dorkinges (xiii cent.) ; Dorking (xviii cent.).

Dorking is a market town 23½ miles south-west of London, 12 miles east of Guildford. The market was claimed by the Earl of Warenne and Surrey in 1278 as of immemorial antiquity.[1] The parish is bounded on the north by the two Bookhams and Mickleham, on the east by Betchworth, on the south by Capel, on the west by Wotton. It contains 1,329 acres of land and 10 of water, and is about 5 miles from north to south and 4 from east to west, but is slightly narrower towards the south. Capel, which lies south of it, was anciently part of the parish, and for the most part of the manor. The parish extends over the usual succession of soils in this part of Surrey. The northern part is on the chalk downs, partly capped by gravel and sand. The town and church are on the sand, the southern part is on the Wealden clay.

From the high chalk down about Denbies, and from Ranmore Common on the north-west border of the parish, the views are beautiful and extensive. Between the spectator and the steep side of Box Hill, immediately to the east, the transverse valley of the Mole runs through the chalk range. Southward lies Dorking in the valley between the chalk and the well-wooded sand hills, which rise to the fir-tree clad heights of Redlands Wood, and to Anstiebury and Leith Hill beyond. The lower ground of the Weald, thickly wooded, extends south-eastwards, and the horizon is marked by the South Downs near Lewes. The boundary of the sand and the clay runs north and south for some way on the southern side of Dorking. The Redlands Woods are a steep sand ridge of north and south direction covered with fir trees, with a silver fir,[1a] probably the tallest tree in the county, standing up above them all, while east of it extends the Holmwood Common, a high open common on the clay, thickly studded with hollies and furze bushes, with occasional houses dotted about it. The Glory Woods, a favourite resort of Dorking people, are on the sand hills nearer to the town. There is a small common close to the town called Cotmandene, formerly famous as the cricket ground where the great Dorking players, who did so much for the Surrey eleven, were trained. Caffyn, who first taught scientific cricket to the Australians, was one of them, and Jupp and the two Humphreys were among the last. Milton Heath is another common west of Dorking. Towards the high ground of the Leith Hill range parts of Broad Moor, Coldharbour Common, and the plantation called the Warren are in Dorking parish.

Dorking town consisted till recently of one long street, High Street, which bifurcated at the south-west end into West Street and South Street, the road to Guildford passing out of the former, that to Horsham out of the latter. In the last thirty or forty years a good deal of building has broadened out the town, as well as extended it at both ends.

The parish was divided into six tithings called Boroughs ; namely, East Borough, including West Betchworth, at the east end of the town ; Chipping Borough, the body of the town, a name which justifies the Earl of Warenne's claim to an ancient market; Milton Borough, lying west ; Westcote Borough, still farther west and south-west ; Holmwood Borough, to the south ; and Walde or Wold or Wale Borough, farther south still, but now known as Capel parish, and distinct from Dorking.[2] But in the 14th and 15th centuries, when Milton and Westcote were separate manors, both the views of frankpledge held in Dorking recognized the Chipping Borough, East Borough, Waldeborough, and Forreyn Borough only as tithings.[3] The names are the same in the view of frankpledge of 7 October 1597, but on 27 September 1598 the names are changed to Chipping Borough, East Borough, Capel and Homewood Borough. The last therefore answers to Forreyn Borough, as also appears by local names in the latter tithing.

The town is administered as an urban district under the Local Government Act of 1894, which superseded a local board established in 1881. The Act of 1894 separated the urban district from Dorking rural parish, which is administered by a rural parish council.

The parish is almost entirely residential and agricultural. But there are lime works on the chalk, though not so extensive as those in neighbouring parishes, a little brick-making, water-mills (corn) at Pixham Mill, and timber and saw-mills.

Poultry rearing is an ancient pursuit of the neighbourhood, and the Dorking fowls with an extra claw are a well-known breed, which it is not necessary to derive from Roman introduction.

Sand of fine texture and often in veins of pink colour is also dug about Dorking, and some exten-

---

[1] Plac. de Quo War. (Rec. Com.), 145.   [1a] Dead in 1909.
[2] Dorking Manorial Rolls, 14th, 15th, and 16th centuries passim. The first five boroughs were confirmed and defined by a County Council order, 26 July 1894, under the provisions of the Loc. Govt. Act, 56 & 57 Vict. cap. 73.

[3] e.g. View of frankpledge, 7 Oct. 16 Hen. VI, in Dorking Manorial Rolls.

sive caverns were formerly excavated for this purpose under parts of the present town.

The road from London to Horsham passes through Dorking, and continues over the Holmwood Common. This is the turnpike which was made in 1755 [4] in response to the astounding statement of the people of Horsham that if they wanted to drive to London they were compelled to go round to Canterbury. Arthur Young justly described it as the worst instance of the want of communication which he had heard of in England.[5] The Act was for the making of a road from Epsom, through Letherhead, Dorking, and Capel, with a branch to Ockley. The old road from Dorking into Sussex went up Boar Hill to Cold-harbour, and down to Ockley.[6] This road was impassable for wheeled traffic as late as the earlier part of the 19th century, when it was such a narrow ravine that bearers carrying a coffin had to walk in single file with the coffin slung on a pole. It was repaired about 1830, chiefly at the instance of Mr. Serjeant Heath of Kitlands, Capel, who threatened to prosecute the parish. The road from Reigate to Guildford passes through Dorking from east to west.

The South Eastern Railway, Redhill and Reading branch, has two stations in Dorking, Box Hill and Dorking, opened in 1849. In 1867 the London Brighton and South Coast Railway, Portsmouth branch, was brought through Dorking, where there is a station near the Box Hill station of the South Eastern Railway.

The ancient road called Stone Street (see in Ockley on the name) ran through Dorking. It is to be traced in much of its course by flint pavement which is found in draining and field work. It is laid down fairly correctly upon the Ordnance Map. It enters Dorking parish close to Anstie Grange Home Farm (not to be confounded with Anstie Farm), and runs along the side of the hill under the Redlands Woods, and above the Holmwood Common. Folly Farm lies just west of it. Near Dorking it has not been accurately observed, but it has no relation to the direction of the streets. Drainage operations show that it left South Street to the east, and crossed West Street just opposite the yard occupied by Messrs. Stone & Turner; a foot passage opposite their premises is just on the line. It continued in a straight line for Pebble Lane, where there is little doubt that it mounted to the old bridle way over Mickleham Downs to Epsom race-course; it must have left Dorking Church to the south-east. Manning and Bray [7] say that the flints were found north-east of the church in a nursery garden, and sold to the road surveyor. But the description is vague and not incompatible with its having passed the church as described. It has not been traced in the north part of Dorking parish.

The prehistoric fortified hill of Anstiebury, formerly in Dorking parish, was included in Capel by the Local Government Act of 1894, and has been described under Capel.

There is a barrow, unopened apparently, on Milton Heath, north of the road. Camden says that Roman coins were found in Dorking churchyard, and others

have been mentioned. In 1817 a find of 700 Anglo-Saxon coins was made in Winterfold Hanger, on Lower Merriden Farm, west of Redlands Wood.[8]

The town of Dorking used to consist of many houses of respectable antiquity, but has been much modernized of late. The 'Old King's Head' is a fine brick Jacobean building, standing at the west end of the High Street, on the north side. It used to be called the 'Chequers,' and received its latter name in 1660. The licence was withdrawn about 1800, renewed about 1850, and is now again withdrawn. It is usually said to be the original of Dickens' 'Marquis of Granby,' but at the time when the *Pickwick Papers* were written it was not an inn at all. Opposite the 'Old King's Head,' just before High Street divides into West Street and South Street, was the old 'Bull Ring.'

A few old houses are to be found in the High Street and side streets, but most of them have been re-fronted or otherwise modernized, and a comparison with the sister towns of Letherhead, Guildford, and Godalming, is in this respect very disappointing. In the town itself perhaps the most interesting old houses are the White Horse Inn—anciently the 'Cross House,' from its sign, the cross of the Knights of St. John,' a quaint, low structure largely of timber and plaster, with three gables, and a large courtyard opening from the High Street, probably on a very ancient site, and as it stands perhaps 400 years old. The town abounds in ancient hostelries of lesser size, such as the 'Red Lion' (originally 'The Cardinal's Cap ') and the 'Black Horse,' and in the side streets are one or two small half-timber houses with overhanging upper stories.

The gallows used to stand on a hill called Gallows Hill on the left-hand side of the road going towards Coldharbour by way of Boar Hill. A house now occupies the spot. It is marked in the map of Ogilvy's *Book of Roads*. The parish registers of 1625 to 1669 record at intervals the burial of persons hanged there when the Assizes were held in the town.

The old market-house stood in the street opposite the 'Red Lion.' Pictures show a gabled, probably 16th-century building, of the same type as the Farnham market-house, but the original wooden supports had been changed for brick arches at the west end; they remained under the east end. It was demolished in 1813.

The market on Thursdays, claimed by John de Warenne in 1278, is still held on the spot in the street. There is a fair, also existing in 1278, on Ascension Day. Down to ten years ago the practice of Shrove Tuesday football continued in the streets of Dorking. Shop windows were barricaded, all business suspended, and the town given over to a very tumultuous game. When the practice became known through the papers as a curiosity surviving here, idle people came from a distance to assist. The nuisance, always great, was intolerable, and it was suppressed with some difficulty by the police. But the year 1907 is said to have been the first in which no attempt was made to continue it. In 1830 there was a very serious riot in Dorking during the Swing Riots.[10]

[4] Act 28 Geo. II, cap. 45.
[5] In 1622 Sir Robert More wrote to his father, Sir George, that he could not drive from beyond Horsham to Loseley as he had intended, because it had rained, but that he hoped to find a way round by East Grinstead, Godstone, and Reigate (Loseley MSS. vol. i, p. 149). It would seem that the clay roads had become worse by 1750.
[6] Ogilvy, *Bk. of Roads*; Burton, *Iter Surriense*, &c.
[7] *Hist. of Surr.* iii, App. xlvi.
[8] *V.C.H. Surr.* i, 272.
[9] It was held of the manor of St. John of Jerusalem, Clerkenwell.
[10] *V.C.H. Surr.* i, 429.

St. Joseph's Roman Catholic Church was rebuilt in 1895 chiefly at the expense of the Duke of Norfolk. The original temporary building had been erected by the Duchess of Norfolk in 1872. There is a Congregational chapel in West Street, representing an ancient congregation formed in 1662 under the Rev. James Fisher, the ejected minister of Fetcham, at whose house a small body of Nonconformists met in 1669, but the minister who was licensed in 1672 under the Indulgence was Mr. Feake, a Fifth Monarchy man, who had been imprisoned under the Protectorate. There was a congregation of Presbyterians under the Rev. John Wood, late rector of North Chapel in Sussex, meeting at his house.[11] This Presbyterian body does not seem to have survived,[12] but after the death of Mr. Wood at an advanced age in 1693, became merged in the Congregational body. A chapel was built in 1719. In 1834 this was pulled down and rebuilt, and much improved and altered in 1874.[13]

Congregational schools were built in 1858.

There is a Baptist chapel, built in 1869; and a Wesleyan chapel, built in 1850. Wesley made the first of ten visits here in 1764, and in 1772 opened a chapel in Church Street, now converted into cottages.

The Society of Friends were strong in the Dorking neighbourhood about the time of their foundation. Possibly the first meetings of the Friends in Surrey were held at the house of Thomas Bax, in Capel, near Dorking. There had been a Friends' meeting at Bax's house for upwards of twenty years in 1677.[13a] Fox, however, records in his Journal a meeting at Reigate in 1655, which may precede this. The Old Friends' Meeting House in West Street, Dorking, bore the date 1709. The present meeting house near Rose Hill was built in 1846.

There was a meeting of Plymouth Brethren in a chapel in Hampstead Road, opened in 1863.

The cemetery was opened in 1856.

The Public Hall in West Street was built by a company for meetings and entertainments in 1872.

Denbies is the residence of the Hon. Henry Cubitt, the lord-lieutenant. It stands upon the brow of the chalk down, close to Ranmore Common and church. The church, however, is in Great Bookham parish (q.v.). Denbies com-

CUBITT. *Checkered or and gules a pile argent with a lion's head razed sable thereon.*

mands fine views over the weald which faces it from across the Mole Valley. Ashcombe, from which the peerage of Ashcombe is named, was a piece of land lying close to it, and Ashcombe Hill was the old name of the brow. Denby was probably a farmer who lived there. The farmhouse was bought in 1754 by Mr. Jonathan Tyers, the founder of Vauxhall Gardens, who laid out the grounds in what was intended to be a style appealing to serious reflections, with a temple, two skulls, in-

scriptions and verses of the tombstone kind, much admired then and very absurd, a sort of Lenten Vauxhall. Mr. Tyers died in 1767, and the estate was sold to the Hon. Peter King. His son Lord King sold it in 1781 to Mr. James White, who sold it in 1787 to Mr. Denison, whose son William Joseph Denison was M.P. for West Surrey. After Mr. Denison's death in 1849 it was bought by Mr. Thomas Cubitt, who built the present house. He was father to Lord Ashcombe, the father of the present owner.

Bury Hill (in Westcote borough) is the seat of Mr. Robert Barclay, representative of the ancient Scottish house of Barclay of Urie. The name is as old as the 14th century,[14] but no trace or record of a fortification can now be found.[14a] The ground was part of the waste of the manor of Milton. Mr. James Walter was buying land in Milton Manor in 1753,[15] and he built the house then and planted the grounds. Mr. Walter died

BARCLAY. *Azure a cheveron argent with three crosses formy argent in the chief.*

in 1780, when Viscount Grimston, his daughter's husband, succeeded him here. In 1812 he sold it to Mr. Robert Barclay, great-grandfather of the present owner. The Nower, a favourite walk for Dorking people, is a hill adjoining this property.

The Rookery, the property of Mr. Brooke, is the seat of Mr. Lionel Bulteel. An estate here was bought in 1759 by Mr. David Malthus, who built the house and laid out the grounds with the ponds and waterfalls, which make it a picturesque place. The Rev. Thomas Malthus, the economist, his son, was born here in 1766. In 1768 it was bought by Mr. Richard Fuller, banker, of London, of the family of the Fullers of Tandridge, Surrey (q.v.), and was sold by the executors of his great-grandson, Mr. George Fuller, in 1893. The old name of the valley where the Rookery stands was Chartgate, or Chartfield.

Milton Heath (in Milton borough), the seat of Mr. J. Carr Saunders, was built by the late Mr. James Powell, of the Whitefriars Glass Works.

Deepdene (in Holmwood borough), lately the seat of Lilian, Duchess of Marlborough, was originally built by the Hon. Charles Howard, after coming into possession of a part of the manor in 1652. In 1655 Evelyn visited him, and admired the gardens which he had already begun to lay out in the deep valley which gives the place its name. It is probable that there was already a small house on the spot. Some thirty years later Aubrey saw and admired the landscape gardening, then evidently far more advanced. Mr. Howard died in 1713 (he was buried at Dorking, according to the inscription at Deepdene, in 1714); his son Henry Charles Howard died in 1720. His second son Charles succeeded as Duke of Norfolk in 1777 and rebuilt the house. His son Charles, eleventh duke, sold it in 1791 to Sir William Burrell, bart., whose son Sir Charles sold it in 1806 to Mr. Thomas Hope. Mr. Hope largely altered the house, and

---

11 *V.C.H. Surr.* ii, 40.
12 They are not recorded in Bishop Willis' Visitation, 1724–5.

13 Information from the late Rev. J. S. Bright, Congregational minister, Dorking.
13a Papers formerly in possession of Mr. March of Dorking.

14 Dorking Court Rolls, *passim.*
14a A Roman station has been gratuitously supposed to be here; *Gent. Mag.* Apr. 1844.
15 Court Rolls, Milton Manor.

began the great collection of paintings and statuary carried on by his son, the late Mr. Beresford Hope, who also added to the house and built the Italian south-western front.

Charte Park, formerly called the Vineyard, was the property of the Sondes or Sonds family, after they had parted with Sondes Place.[16] The late Mr. Beresford Hope bought Charte Park, and threw it into the grounds of Deepdene, pulling down the house.

Westcott, also spelt Westcote, and erroneously Westgate, is one of the Dorking boroughs (*vide supra*), and with Milton was made into an ecclesiastical parish in 1852 (*vide infra*). A considerable village existed before then, and many houses have since been built.

In Squire's Wood, south of Westcote, is Mag's Well, one of the sources of Pip Brook, which runs through Dorking to the Mole. It was formerly of some repute as a medicinal spring, and is strongly impregnated with iron. A building, now gone to ruin, existed over it, and within the writer's memory children still bathed in it.

Holmwood Borough was the ancient division of Dorking, to the south of the town. The ancient spelling in the Court Rolls is invariably Homewood, the numerous hollies have led to the change in the name. But as far back as 1329 the reeves' accounts include carriage of firewood from 'Dorkynge Ywode vel Homewode' to Kingston, where the distinction between the 'High Wood,' the skirts of the big forest of the Weald, and the 'Home Wood,' sufficiently explains the name. In 1562 Kingston still depended upon this neighbourhood for firewood.[17] Manning and Bray state, however, that Dorking was supplied lately with coal from Kingston; showing a curious reversal of former relations.

The Holmwood Common is a large high-lying common thickly covered with furze bushes and hollies, about 600 acres in extent. Defoe states that it was as lately as the time of James II the haunt of wild deer. Agricultural writers of a hundred years ago marked it down as good cornland wasted.

The school of the parish of St. Mary Magdalen, Holmwood, was built in 1844, and enlarged in 1870 and 1884. That now in the parish of St. John the Evangelist was built in 1849 and enlarged in 1875 and 1883.

A great number of gentlemen's houses surround the Holmwood Common, and some standing upon it represent the original intrusions of squatters upon the waste of the manor—confirmed by lapse of time. Holmwood Park was the seat of the late Mrs. Gough Nichols, widow of the celebrated antiquary. Francis Larpent, Judge Advocate-General to Wellington's army in Spain and the South of France, formerly lived here. Oakdale is the seat of Lady Laura Hampton; Oakdene of Mr. Augustus Perkins; Redlands of Colonel Helsham Jones; Anstie Grange of Mr. Cuthbert E. Heath; Moorhurst, an ancient farm on the border of the old parishes of Dorking and Capel, of the Hon. W. Gibson, who has opened a small Roman Catholic chapel there. It is the property of Mr. Cuthbert E. Heath, of Anstie Grange.

The present condition of the Holmwood is in curious contrast with what was its state not more than 100 years ago, when the road to Horsham running over the desolate common was a frequent scene of highway robbery, and was openly used by smugglers. William Dudley, of Coldharbour, who died in 1902, aged nearly 101, told the writer that a man with whom he worked had been a witness when the turnpike keeper boldly refused to open his gate at night to a body of smugglers with kegs of brandy on their horses.

In the Domesday Survey *DORKING MANORS* was in the hands of the king. Milton and Westcote were even then separate manors. It had been held by Edith, widow of the Confessor, and like the other holdings of the late queen in Surrey, was granted to William de Warenne I, when he was created Earl of Surrey.[18] His original Surrey endowment consisted of the manors which had been Edith's,—Dorking, Reigate, Shiere, Fetcham. But one Edric had held Dorking, or part of it, at some previous time, and had given two hides out of it to his daughters. In 1086 Richard of Tonbridge held one of these hides—no doubt Hamsted Manor, which belonged subsequently to the Clares. The other hide was probably Bradley Manor, the lands of which lie in Holmwood tithing and Mickleham.

Richard I appears to have confirmed the grant of Edith's lands to the Earls of Surrey,[19] and in 1237 William de Warenne is recorded as holding Dorking.[20] John de Warenne claimed it in 1278 as held by his ancestors from before legal memory.[21] In 1347 John de Warenne died seised of the manor.[22]

WARENNE, Earl of Surrey. *Checkered or and azure.*

FITZ ALAN, Earl of Arundel. *Gules a lion or.*

He was succeeded by his nephew Richard, Earl of Arundel, who died in 1376,[23] leaving another Richard as his son and heir. About this time the Arundel lands began to pass through a period of vicissitude. Richard, Earl of Arundel, was attainted in 1397 and beheaded, after a long series of open altercations with the king,[24] and Dorking was granted to Thomas Mowbray, Earl of Nottingham,[25] afterwards Duke of Norfolk, his son-in-law. He was banished in 1398 and died in exile in 1400. On the accession of Henry IV, Thomas, son of the unfortunate Richard, was restored. He died on 13 October 1415, leaving three sisters as co-heirs:[26] first Elizabeth, the second wife of Thomas Mowbray, first Duke of Norfolk, whose share in the property descended in moieties to her son John, second Duke of Norfolk, and to Joan, her daughter by a second husband, Sir Robert Gonshill.

---

[16] In 1515–16 John Sondes of Charte alienated Sondes Place to John Caryll; and in 1594 Michael Sondes was heir to the copyhold of Sir Thomas Sondes of Charte; Dorking Ct. R.
[17] *V.C.H. Surr.* ii, 264.

[18] Ibid. i, 298.
[19] Cart. Antiq. x, 29.
[20] Feet of F. Div. Co. [21] Hen. III, no. 236.
[21] *Plac. de Quo War.* (Rec. Com.), 175.

[22] Chan. Inq.p.m. 21 Edw. III (1st nos.) no. 23.
[23] G.E.C. *Complete Peerage.*
[24] *Dict. Nat. Biog.* xix, 98.
[25] Pat. 21 Ric. II, pt. i, m. 5.
[26] Chan. Inq. p.m. 4 Hen. V, no. 54.

This Joan became the ancestress of the Earls of Derby by her marriage with Sir Thomas Stanley.[17]

MOWBRAY, Duke of Norfolk. *England with a label argent.*

STANLEY, Earl of Derby. *Argent a bend azure with three harts' heads caboissed or thereon.*

The second co-heir of Thomas, Earl of Arundel, was Joan Beauchamp, Lady Abergavenny; her share descended to her granddaughter Elizabeth, afterwards the wife of George Nevill, who thus gained the lands and title of Abergavenny. Margaret, wife of Sir Roland Lenthale, was the third heir, but her claim to part of the inheritance lapsed at the death of her son Edmund, who died without issue[28] before July 1447.[29]

The history of the manor is obscure, even with the aid of the Court Rolls placed at the service of investigators by the courtesy of successive Dukes of Norfolk. For the rolls are far from continuous, and generally lack the name of the lord or lords whose courts are held. It is obvious, however, that on the death of Thomas, Earl of Arundel, in 1415, his widow, Beatrix of Portugal, held the manor as dower.[30] The courts were held for a *Domina* (feminine) from 1413 to 1431, when there is a break of five years. In 1435 and 1438 *Dominus*, in the masculine singular is used, probably Roland Lenthale, for his son Edmund. In 1444 *Domini* begins, the Bishop of Bath and Wells and others,[31] feoffees of Edmund Lenthale.[32] This trust seems to have expired between 26 March 1450 and 21 July 1450, for *Domini* is used in the former, *Dominus* in the latter. The singular is used till 15 February 1451, after which the manor was divided, courts being henceforth held for *Domini* when the number is distinguished at all. In 1528 the question was raised in the court baron (17 September 1528) 'whether Edmund Lenthale deceased was while alive sole holder of the manor of Dorking or holder with others.' Unfortunately it was not answered in the extant records, but it would seem likely that he was sole holder, and that after his death the manor went to John Mowbray, third Duke of Norfolk. The inquisition taken after the latter's death in 1461 is unfortunately now missing,[33] and the entry in the calendar is insufficient. In 1468[34] John, Duke of Norfolk, and his wife Elizabeth had a grant of certain privileges, including return of writs, within their manor of Dorking.[35]

This Duke of Norfolk died in 1475,[36] leaving an only child Anne, who was for some years betrothed to Richard, Duke of York, who perished in the Tower. She died unmarried in 1480,[37] and members of the Nevill and Stanley families, as well as descendants of Margaret and Isabel, daughters of the first duke, appear as her co-heirs. A partition of Dorking was probably then made.[38]

In a document of 1531 George Nevill, Lord Abergavenny, is mentioned[39] as being one of the joint holders of the manor of Dorking. Again, later in the 16th century, Henry Nevill was in possession of part of the manor,[40] and on 1 August 1587[41] Edward Nevill, Lord Abergavenny, held his first court, with no indication of being only a joint holder, and in 1623 died seised[42] of the manor of 'Dorking Capel,' not that he was concerned only with the part of the manor in Capel, for the court chose bedells for Dorking and for Capel, and tenants from both attended. Edward Nevill's son Henry seems to have conveyed his share of the manor to the Howard family.[43]

The family of Stanley, Earls of Derby, in like manner again became involved in the history of Dorking at the death of Anne Mowbray. In 1622 Thomas, Earl of Derby, died seised of a moiety,[44] which apparently consisted of two quarter parts. In order to explain his possession of more than one quarter it is necessary to consider the third co-heir of Anne Mowbray, namely, William, Lord Berkeley. This William was the son of Isabel daughter of the first Mowbray, Duke of Norfolk,[45] and although there seems no actual record of his own connexion with Dorking Manor, his son Maurice was seised of a fourth part in 1504.[46] It seems as though he must have shortly afterwards conveyed his portion to the Earls of Derby, first because, as stated above, they were afterwards seised of two quarter parts; secondly, because the Berkeleys are not again found in possession; and thirdly, because lands did undoubtedly pass from the one family to the other.[47]

However, that may have been, it seems that two quarter parts were in the possession of the Earls of Derby. In 1586 Henry, Earl of Derby, conveyed one quarter to Sir Thomas Browne,[48] and in 1594 Henry's son Ferdinand died seised of the other quarter.[49] The portion which remained in the Derby family was

[27] *Dict. Nat. Biog.* liv, 75.
[28] Chan. Inq. p.m. 29 Hen. VI, no. 27.
[29] Aug. Off. Anct. Chart. i, 24.
' [30] She died in 1439 seised of Dorking; Chan. Inq. p.m. 18 June 1440 (copy). Perhaps even then there was a division.
[31] 18 July 1447, a tripartite indenture was made between Lenthale's trustees, the Duke of Norfolk and Lord Abergavenny, giving the profits of the manor to the trustees till such time as Lenthale's debts were paid by them, and providing for masses for his soul. The inquisition p.m. was apparently postponed till, as we should say, the estate was wound up; D. in Aug. Off. Anct. Chart. i, 234.
[32] Ct. R. 14 Dec. 23 Hen. VI.
[33] *Cal. of Chan. Inq. p.m.* (Rec. Com.), iv, 316.

[34] Chart. R. 8–10 Edw. IV, m. 14.
[35] The Roll of 14 Sept. 1468 ends up with some accounts and ' To my lorde of Norfolk ye Audytores.' The plural still used in the Court Rolls may refer to him and his wife.
[36] Chan. Inq. p.m. 17 Edw. IV, no. 58.
[37] G.E.C. *Complete Peerage.*
[38] The Nevills were descended from Joan sister of the Earl of Arundel, who died 1416, the Stanleys from Elizabeth daughter of his sister Elizabeth. The partition did not apparently extend to an actual apportionment of the holdings. Tenants admitted to the manor do fealty 'to the lords' collectively, one court baron was held for the whole, and one view of frankpledge, and the dues were probably divided.

[39] Chan. Inq. p.m. (Ser. 2), li, 48.
[40] Chan. Proc. (Ser. 2), bdle. 159, no. 11.
[41] This was after Philip, Earl of Arundel (heir to the Duke of Norfolk), was thrown into the Tower, but before he was attainted (1589).
[42] Chan. Inq. p.m. (Ser. 2), cccxcix, 157.
[43] They were in possession in 1652; H. K. S. Causton, *Howard Papers,* 365.
[44] Chan. Inq. p.m. (Ser. 2), xxxix, 110.
[45] *Dict. Nat. Biog.* xxxix, 225.
[46] Feet of F. Div. Co. Trin. 19 Hen. VII.
[47] *Dict. Nat. Biog.* liv, 78.
[48] Feet of F. Surr. Trin. 28 Eliz.
[49] Chan. Inq. p.m. (Ser. 2), ccxlii, 88.

apparently conveyed to the Howards some time during the 17th century,[50] since the Browne moiety was the only one which did not belong to them in the time of George II.[51]

Sir Thomas Browne died in 1597 seised of one portion of the manor, which passed to his son Matthew.[52] It appears at intervals in the possession of the Browne family, and finally, about 1690, on the death of Sir Adam Browne, without male issue, passed from his family by the marriage of his daughter Margaret with William Fenwick.[53] At her death, according to Manning and Bray,[54] this part of the manor passed by sale to Abraham Tucker, and from him, by the marriage of one of his daughters, to his grandson Sir Henry St. John Mildmay, who sold it in 1797 to the Duke of Norfolk.[55]

The remaining portion of the manor passed at the death of Anne Mowbray into the family of Howard. Margaret daughter of the first Mowbray duke, and sister of that Isabel who married into the Berkeley family, became the wife of Sir Robert Howard, and to her son John her share in the Dorking manor now passed.[56] John was a keen partisan of Richard III, who in 1483 revived the title of Duke of Norfolk in his favour.[57] He met his death at the battle of Bosworth Field, and his lands, by an Act of attainder in the first Parliament of Henry VII, lapsed to the Crown.[58] His son Thomas, also attainted then, was restored in blood in 1488, and to the earldom and his estates in 1489. In 1514 he was created Duke of Norfolk. His son Thomas, third Duke of Norfolk in the Howard line, was attainted under Henry VIII, and only escaped execution by the timely death of the king; his lands, however, were forfeited, and his portion in Dorking Manor was granted by Edward VI to Henry Duke of Suffolk.[59] Under Queen Mary the duke was restored to his possessions. From that time this portion seems to have remained in the family of Howard; the other portions were gradually joined to it until, in 1797, the whole manor was in the possession of the Duke of Norfolk, with whose descendants it has since remained.

The earls had a manor-house in Dorking; but though Aubrey mentions traces of a castle, there are neither records nor visible remains. The Town Fields were on the south side of the town, towards the direction of the modern workhouse. The common meadow and pasture was on the north by the Pip Brook; but it is worthy of notice that as early as the 14th and 15th centuries the manorial rolls tell us that the villeins of the manor held land in severalty, this custom being specially noticeable in Waldeborough, where there seem to have been no common fields. The rights

HOWARD, Duke of Norfolk. *Gules a bend between six crosslets fitchy argent.*

of the lord over a villein tenantry, chivage, marriage, and so on, were then in full force. In 1442–3 the homage are bidden to produce a fugitive female villein. It is needless to say that there is no evidence of the outrageous *droit de seigneur* mentioned by Aubrey. In the court held 30 December, 5 Henry VI (1426), Johanna Brekspere paid 6s. 8d. for licence to marry whom she would. But as early as the accounts rendered for 1329–30, customary services, carrying, reaping, &c., and *xxii plena opera* appear commuted for money payments. The custom of the manor was Borough English, and daughters were co-heiresses. A court baron was held every three weeks, and a court leet and a view of frankpledge twice a year.

In 1278 John de Warenne claimed and was allowed free warren in all his demesne lands in Dorking. The lord had, however, an inclosed warren, which was often mentioned in the Court Rolls owing to the inhabitants stealing rabbits from it. Under Henry V and Henry VI the warren was let out at farm. Possibly the lord had an inclosed park, for in the courts of 8 February and 16 August 1283 persons are accused of breaking the earl's park; but in the first instance the fine *pro fractura parci* is only 6d., in the second 20s., so *parcus* may only be the pound, or some small inclosure. No record of imparking or disimparking seems to exist. If there was a park it must have been near Charte Park of later times, where Park Copse, Park Farm, and Park Pale Farm, all to the east of Charte Park, may show that this is only part of a formerly more extensive inclosure.

BRADLEY was a small reputed manor held by service of half a knight's fee of the manor of Reigate.[61] A Thomas de Bradley appears in a dispute in the court of Dorking of 1283. Mr. Bray had deeds in his possession showing a settlement, by John de Bradley and Maud his wife, on William son of Richard Bradley in 1340, and another settlement of land in Bradley 1389–90, by Nicholas Slyfield, on John Penros.[62] It passed to the Sondes of Sondes Place, Dorking, and appears as a manor in the time of Edward IV,[63] and is also mentioned in an inquisition taken after the death of Robert Sondes in 1530.[64] It seems to have remained in the Sondes family until the middle of the 17th century, when Sir George Sondes conveyed it to William Delawne,[65] but perhaps by way of mortgage only, for Lewis, created Lord Sondes 1760, seems to have sold it rather later than that to Henry Talbot. He sold it to Mr. Walter, M.P., who was buying much land in the district.[66] It was certainly possessed by Mr. Walter of Bury Hill and his son-in-law Viscount Grimston, who sold it to Mr. Denison of Denbies, in which estate it remains. It has had no courts held within the memory of man. It is now the property of the Hon. Henry Cubitt of Denbies, the lord-lieutenant.[67]

There seems to have been a small manor called *HAMSTED* in Dorking. In Domesday Richard of Tonbridge held one hide which had been detached from

[50] H. K. S. Causton (*Howard Papers*, 365) states that Charles Howard in 1652 found himself heir to three fourth parts of the manor of Dorking, two of which had been purchased by his grandfather Thomas, Earl of Arundel.
[51] Recov. R. Mich. 14 Geo. II, rot. 211.
[52] Chan. Inq. p.m. (Ser. 2), ccliii, 88.

[53] Feet of F. Surr. Hil. 4 & 5 Will. and Mary.
[54] *Hist. Surr.* i, 558.
[55] Ibid.
[56] *Dict. Nat. Biog.* xxviii, 42.
[57] Ibid.
[58] *Parl. R.* (Rec. Com.), vi, 410.
[59] Pat. 6 Edw. VI, pt. ii.
[60] Assize R. *apud* Guildford, 7 Edw. I, rot. 28.

[61] Survey of manor of Reigate taken 1 Apr. 1623, 21 Jas. I.
[62] Manning and Bray, *Hist. of Surr.* i, 563.
[63] Feet of F. Div. Co. file 74, no. 64.
[64] Chan. Inq. p.m. (Ser. 2), ii, 48.
[65] Feet of F. Surr. Trin. 1654.
[66] Manning and Bray, *Hist. of Surr.* i, 564.
[67] Inform. from Lord Ashcombe.

146

Dorking : Old Market House, pulled down in 1813

Dorking : Milton Court, c. 1845

Dorking : Milton Court, Staircase, c. 1845

Dorking.[68] In 1262 Hawisia widow of John de Gatesden, the name of a Clare tenant,[69] sued Robert Basset for a third part of a mill and 40 acres of land as her dower in Hamsted and Dorking.[70] In 1314 Gilbert de Clare, killed at Bannockburn, was seised of Hamsted, held of him by Agnes de Badeshull.[71] Hugh le Despenser, sister's son to Gilbert, died seised of it in 1350, when it was held by John de Warblyngton of the honour of Clare.[72] In 1560–1 John Caryll sold land in Hamsted to Sir Thomas Browne of Betchworth.[73] The description places it at the west end of Dorking, where Hamsted Lane, an old name, preserves its memory.

The manor of *MILTON* (xi et seq. cent. Middleton) was held of William Fitz Ansculf by a certain Baldwin at the time of the Domesday Survey ; Uluric held it of King Edward.[74] It passed with the honour of Dudley from William Fitz Ansculf to the family of Somery ; early in the 13th century one Simon Fitz Giles owed one knight's service for Milton to the honour of Dudley.[75]

The manor was possibly granted to the nuns of Kilburn by Roger de Somery,[76] for their prioress was found to hold lands of him at his death ; there is, however, reason to suppose that they had gained possession of it somewhat earlier, since Margery, Prioress of Kilburn, was seised of a knight's fee in Milton in 1232.[77] Again, in 1269, Matilda, a prioress whom Dugdale omits from her list,[78] had transactions touching the moiety of a virgate of land in Milton.[79]

The manor remained with the nuns until the dissolution of the monasteries, when they exchanged it for other Surrey lands with John Carleton of Walton on Thames, and Joyce his wife.[80] From John Carleton the manor passed to Richard Thomas, who was holding it in 1552.[81] Richard Thomas continued to hold under Philip and Mary ;[82] his tenure was not, however, popular among his tenants, who were indignant at his having inclosed lands on Milton Common otherwise known as Anstey Heath, where the aforesaid tenants had had common of pasture from time immemorial. Waterden Wood is also mentioned. Anstey Farm and Waterden lie on the two sides of the road in Milton Manor near Coldharbour. Milton Gore, close by, is the only part of the heath in question now uninclosed.

It is probable that the grant to Richard Thomas was only for a period of years, for at the death of his widow Katharine, who had subsequently become the wife of Saunders Wright, it reverted to the Crown.[83] Queen Elizabeth in 1599 gave it to Ralph Lathom.[84] The grant, however, was cancelled before it took effect, and the next year the manor passed from the Crown to George Evelyn[85] in consideration of some £700. From that time it descended with Wotton in the Evelyn family.

Milton Court, the seat of the late Mr. L. M.

Rate (ob. 1907), is the old manor-house of Milton. It is a fine Jacobean house, mostly of brick, with wings projecting in front and behind and a projecting portico in front, showing five gables to the front, over the wings and portico ; and between these, to the back, there are three gables, the chimneys occupying the intermediate spaces on this side. The gables are all of the rounded pattern common in Kent and the Netherlands. The house was rebuilt by Richard Evelyn, and completed in 1611 (accounts in possession of Mr. Rate). There was no high hall, but a gallery ran along the front of the house with a projecting bay over the porch. This has been altered into a drawing-room and other rooms. The staircase in the east wing is a very fine specimen of Jacobean woodwork. Mr. Rate bought the house in 1864, and it was restored under the direction of late C. Burgess.

The manor of *WEST BETCHWORTH* was held by Richard de Tonbridge at the time of the Domesday Survey, and the overlordship appears to have remained with the honour of Clare.[86] In the 13th century John de Wauton held half a knight's fee in Betchworth of that honour ;[87] he subsequently forfeited his lands to the king, who in 1291 made a grant of them to John de Berewyk.[88] At John's death in 1313 his heir was found to be his grandson Roger Husee, then a minor.[89] Roger died seised in 1362,[90] and was succeeded by his brother John, who died a few years later leaving his son John as his heir.[91] This John conveyed the manor to Richard Earl of Arundel.[92] It remained in the Arundel family until 1487, when it was sold to Thomas Browne.[93] It was still in the possession of the Brownes in the time of Elizabeth,[94] and from that date appears to have descended with the portion of Dorking Manor which was in their hands.

Betchworth Castle, now only a picturesque ruin, perched on a bank above the Mole, and almost concealed by trees and creepers, was built, or, more probably, rebuilt, by Sir Thomas Browne. Judging by the print in Watson's 'Memoirs,' the mansion which, in the middle of the 15th century, replaced an earlier fortified house or castle, must have been extremely picturesque with its battlemented gables, clustered chimneys and oriel windows, standing among lawns and gardens descending to the Mole. The ivy is disintegrating the walls, and almost the only architectural feature is the arch of a fireplace. A remarkably fine avenue of lime trees leads to the ruin.

The Domesday Survey records that Abbot Æthelrige had held *WESTCOTE* of King Edward ; also that Ralph de Fougeres then held it.[95]

In the 13th century Westcote (*villa de Westcote*) was *terra Normannorum* held by Gilbert de Aquila and taken into the hands of King Henry III. The Earl of Warenne and Surrey had paid a fine and held it

[68] *V.C.H. Surr.* i, 298.
[69] *Testa de Nevill* (Rec. Com.), 219. John de Gatesden also had lands in Hamsted (Feet of F. Surr. 33 Hen. III, 379).
[70] Assize R. 47 Hen. III, Surr. m. 4.
[71] Chan. Inq. p.m. 8 Edw. II, 68, m. 63.
[72] Ibid. 23 Edw. III (2nd pt. 1st nos.), no. 169.
[73] Manning and Bray, *Hist. Surr.* i, 566.
[74] *V.C.H. Surr.* i, 322a.
[75] Ibid.
[76] Chan. Inq. p.m. 1 Edw. I, no. 15.

[77] Feet of F. Surr. Trin. 32 Hen. III, no. 49.
[78] *Mon. Angl.* iii, 424.
[79] Feet of F. Surr. Hil. 53 Hen. III, no. 25.
[80] L. and P. Hen. VIII, xv, g. 733 (48).
[81] Feet of F. Surr. Trin. 6 Edw. VI.
[82] Star. Chamb. Proc. Phil. and Mary, bdle. 6, no. 45.
[83] Pat. 41 Eliz. pt. x, m. 25.
[84] Ibid.
[85] Pat. 42 Eliz. pt. xvi, m. 1.

[86] *V.C.H. Surr.* i, 319b.
[87] *Testa de Nevill* (Rec. Com.), 221.
[88] Chart. R. 19 Edw. I, m. 84.
[89] Chan. Inq. p.m. 6 Edw. II, no. 43.
[90] Ibid. 35 Edw. III, pt. i, no. 98.
[91] Ibid. 44 Edw. III (1st nos.), no. 33.
[92] Close, 47 Edw. III, m. 16.
[93] Feet of F. Surr. 15 Hen. VI, no. 8.
[94] Chan. Inq. p.m. (Ser. 2), ccliii, 88.
[95] *V.C.H. Surr.* i, 326b.

for his sister the wife of Gilbert.[95] Later John de Gatesden (see Hamsted Manor) held it.[97] He died in 1269 or before, when a survey of the manor was taken, late in his hands.[98] His daughter Margaret married Sir William Pagenel, but it would seem that the Latimer family had some previous claim upon Westcote, for in 1306 Alice widow of William le Latimer sued William Pagenel and Margaret his wife for dower in Westcote Manor, which had been granted by Latimer to Pagenel and his wife. Pagenel acknowledged her claim and granted her lands in Leicestershire to the required amount.[99] In 1317 William Pagenel died seised of the manor, leaving John his brother and heir, then fifty years of age.[100]

In 1355 Eva widow of Edward St. John, and formerly wife of William Pagenel, who was probably the son of John Pagenel, died seised of one-third of Westcote Manor which she held in dower. Her heir was Laurence de Hastings, lord of Paddington Pembroke (q.v.), with which Westcote descended from that time.[101]

There was a mill at Westcote at the time of the Domesday Survey; it is also mentioned in the inquisition taken at the death of Laurence de Hastings in 1348, when it was stated to be a water-mill.[102]

At the time of Alice le Latimer's suit (q.v.) the manor was valued at forty pounds odd.

George I granted to John Evelyn the privilege of holding two annual fairs in his manor of Westcote, on 15 April and 28 October.[103]

Westcote retains many picturesque old houses of the 16th, 17th, and 18th centuries, including some with gables of Bargate stone rubble and ornamental brick; and a farm-house with fine brick chimneys dating from about 1670.

SONDES PLACE, in Milton borough, the vicarage house since 1839, belonged to a family of Sondes, who migrated to Surrey in the 15th century, and who were ancestors of the present Lord Sondes. In 1590 John Carill, of Warnham, conveyed Sondes Place for £1,000 to John Cowper of Capel, Serjeant-at-Law.[104] Cowper possibly sold it to Christopher Gardiner, who died about 1597, and is described as of Dorking,[105] and whose son Christopher, baptized 1595,[106] resided at Sondes Place. The latter married Elizabeth daughter of Sir Edward Onslow of Knowle in Cranleigh.[107] William Gardiner of Croydon, by deed of 1678, granted the manor or lordship of Sondes Place to Francis Brockett.[108]

The parish church is approached by CHURCHES a little stone-flagged alley from the High Street, and stands in the midst of a large and prettily kept churchyard, no longer used for burials, in which are numerous gravestones and railed tombs, some of 17th and 18th-century dates.

It is dedicated to ST. MARTIN, and is, as it stands, absolutely modern, having been rebuilt in 1835-7 (the chancel excepted), and the nave, till then an unsightly structure of brick and compo, with slender iron columns and many galleries, again rebuilt in 1873 from the designs of Mr. H. Woodyer, who in 1866

had rebuilt the ancient chancel. In 1835-7 the central tower had been rebuilt, or remodelled, and crowned with a lofty spire, which it had not before possessed, and these features, which were not reproduced in the original position in the later re-edification, were replaced by a lofty western tower and spire, erected to the memory of Dr. Samuel Wilberforce, Bishop of Oxford, and then of Winchester, who was killed by a fall from his horse near Dorking in 1873. The present church, which is constructed of black flints and Bath stone, is a handsome and spacious edifice in a somewhat mixed style of 13th and 14th-century Gothic architecture, consisting of a lofty clearstoried nave, with western tower and spire, porches, transepts, chancel and vestries. Nearly all the windows are filled with stained glass of varying merit, and there are many elaborate fittings, including altar and reredos, pulpit, lectern and choir stalls, font and chancel screen of oak, in commemoration of Wm. Henry Joyce, M.A., vicar, 1850-70, beneath which is a brass to his memory.

The floor and lower parts of the walls of the old church remain in vaults under the present church. It was a large and picturesque structure, occupying much the same area as the present, cruciform, with a central tower, north and south aisles to the nave, under lean-to roofs, and a south porch, built of local rubble and flints plastered externally, with dressings of firestone, and having the old Horsham slate on all the roofs, except the chancel and north transept. The nave was about 65 ft. by 30 ft., its aisles being between 12 and 14 ft. long, the north transept about 27 ft. by 23 ft. wide, the south transept 26 ft. by 23 ft., the central tower about 27 ft. square, and the chancel 40 ft. by 22 ft. Probably little or nothing remained of the building recorded in Domesday, except as old material worked up on the walls; but the chancel seems to have retained to the last at the angles of the east and four flat pilaster buttresses of mid-12th-century character. To a date towards the close of the same century the lower part of the central tower and the remarkable north transept appear to have belonged. The latter is well shown in a carefully accurate steel engraving forming the frontispiece to Hussey's Churches of Kent, Surrey, and Sussex.[109] The design of this transept end consisted of a lofty gable with a small lancet in the upper part, below which was a pilaster buttress with steeply sloped weathering, this buttress being pierced at about half its height with a longer lancet,[110] and similar lancets flanking it right and left, while at the angles were other pilaster buttresses. In the eastern wall of the same transept there were three lancets of like proportions and a pilaster buttress. There appears to have been some early work in the south transept also, but masked by alterations made in the repairs of 1674 and 1762, when a large circular-headed window was inserted in the gable end, a huge, unsightly buttress erected against the south-east angle of the tower, and the upper part of the central tower was altered. Evidence is scanty as to other work of the earlier periods, especially as to

94 Testa de Nevill (Rec. Com.), 225.
97 Ibid. 229.
98 Chan. Inq. p.m. 53 Hen. III, no. 19.
99 De Banco R. 161, m. 145.
100 Chan. Inq. p.m. 10 Edw. II, no. 61.
101 In William Pagenel's inquisition, the Hastings family are mentioned as being overlords, so that the manor probably reverted to them on the failure of heirs in the Pagenel family.
102 Chan. Inq. p.m. 22 Edw. III (1st nos.), no. 47.
103 Pat. 12 Geo. I, pt. ii.
104 Close, 32 Eliz. pt. vi.   105 Will.
106 Dorking Reg.   107 Ibid.
108 Com. Pleas D. Enr. 30 Chas. II), m. 5. The present Sondes Place is another house.
109 Corroborated by old pen drawings in the writer's possession.
110 Cf. the tower buttresses at Clymping, Sussex, similarly pierced with early lancets, in work of c. 1170.

ABINGER CHURCH FROM THE SOUTH-EAST, c. 1845

DORKING: ST. MARTIN'S CHURCH, CHOIR, c. 1845

DORKING: ST. MARTIN'S CHURCH, CHANCEL, c. 1845

the nave arcades and crossing arches, but they were probably of late 12th or early 13th-century date. In the first half of the 14th century considerable alterations were effected. A clearstory of coupled lights having ogee, trefoiled, and cinquefoiled heads was formed on both sides of the nave, and other windows inserted, in about 1340. The chancel at this time received a fine large east window of five lights, the central higher than the others, with flowing tracery in the head resembling that of the east window in Witley Church.[111] The windows in the south wall, of three and two lights, with square heads, may have belonged to the same or a slightly later date. The upper story of the tower, although its parapet had been made plain in 1762, retained two-light windows with pointed heads of 15th-century character, and in the east wall of the south transept, the south wall of the south aisle, with its porch, and the west wall of the nave, were other windows of the 15th century. If it seems hard to forgive the 1835 rebuilding of the nave, it is almost impossible to excuse the destruction of the ancient chancel, with its fine east window, in 1866. The north aisle had no windows in its wall, but was lit by wooden dormers in the roof.

The monuments in the old church prior to its demolition do not appear to have been of great importance. Aubrey records many tombstones as existing on the floor of the church in his time (1673, &c.), some of which bore the indents of brasses. These have all disappeared. The following mural monuments have been preserved and set up in the new church :—(1) The Howard monument, to the memory of Charles Howard of Greystoke Castle and of Deepdene,[112] fourth son of Henry Frederick, Earl of Arundel (died 31 March 1713), and Mary his wife (died 7 November 1695); of Henry Charles Howard, his son and heir (died 10 June 1720), and Mary his wife (died 7 October 1747); and of Mary Anne Howard, the late wife of Charles Howard, jun. (died 28 May 1768). (2) A monument, removed from a mausoleum formerly in the churchyard, to the second wife of Henry Talbot, son of a Bishop of Durham, who purchased Charte Park in 1746 and died in 1784. (3) To Abraham Tucker, author of *A Picture of Artless Love* and *The Light of Nature Pursued*, who lived at his estate of Betchworth Castle till his death in 1774. (4) A brass plate to Jeremiah Markland (1693–1776), the classical scholar, who lived at Milton Court.

The registers date from 1538.

The church plate is all modern, presented recently by the Rt. Hon. George Cubitt, M.P., of Denbies, now Lord Ashcombe. There is a ring of eight bells, of which no. 2, 3 and 4 are dated 1709 and bear the names of William Fenwicke, Mrs. Margaret Fenwicke, John Hollier and John Pinny, 'benefactors'; while no. 5 has the inscription, 'JOHN WILNER MADE ME 1626.' The others are modern. The 'pancake' bell used to be rung between 11 o'clock and noon on Shrove Tuesday down to the early part of the 19th century.

ST. PAUL'S CHURCH was built in 1857 in a new district on the south side of the town. It is a

stone building, consisting of a nave and chancel, in quasi 14th-century style, with a small bell-turret at the west end.

ST. MARY MAGDALENE'S CHURCH, HOLMWOOD, was built in 1838. It was successively enlarged in 1842, 1846, 1848, and 1863. Mr. James Park Harrison was the original architect, and the church is a successful imitation of 13th-century style, built in sandstone, with a tower to the south-west. The sites for church, parsonage, and school were given by the Duke of Norfolk.

The church of *ST. JOHN THE EVANGELIST, NORTH HOLMWOOD*, was built, in 1875, of stone in an intended 12th-century style, with a tower and spire.

The church of *HOLY TRINITY, WESTCOTE*, was consecrated in 1852. It was built by Sir Gilbert Scott in 14th-century style. It is of stone, with a small western turret. Mr. Charles Barclay gave £1,000 to the building, and Lady Mary Leslie £1,000 endowment. The clock was put up to commemorate the Jubilee of 1887. The parsonage house was built at the sole expense of the late Mr. Charles Barclay, of Bury Hill; the Westcote Schools (National) by subscription in 1854 ; an infant school by subscription in 1882. St. John's Chapel, the Countess of Huntingdon's Connexion, was built by Mr. John Worsfold in 1840, and endowed with £40 a year, a house, small glebe, and a benefaction for charities.

ADVOWSON The advowson of the church of Dorking was attached first to the Priory of Lewes,[113] and then, in 1334, to the Priory of Holy Cross at Reigate until the dissolution of the monasteries.[114] It was then granted to Lord William Howard,[115] created Lord Howard of Effingham. Charles second Lord Howard of Effingham, created Earl of Nottingham, inherited from his father. His eldest son William having died in his lifetime, his daughter Elizabeth, by marriage the Countess of Peterborough, inherited,[116] and conveyed it in 1657 to her son, John Mordaunt,[117] an ardent Royalist, to whom Charles II shortly afterwards granted the titles of Baron Mordaunt of Reigate and Viscount Mordaunt of Avalon, as a reward for his many services.[118]

In 1660 Dorking with Capel (q.v.) and other churches was confirmed to John Mordaunt in trust for Mary daughter of his brother the Earl of Peterborough.[119] Mary sold it in 1677 to Sir John Parsons. The widow of his son Humphrey settled it on her daughter Anne, wife of Sir John Hynde Cotton, who conveyed it to him. He sold it in 1766 to Mr. Edward Walter of Bury Hill. At his death in 1780 it descended to his daughter and her husband Viscount Grimston. The latter sold it in 1789 to the Duke of Norfolk.[120] The rectorial tithes were bought by various people in lots, among whom were the late Mr. Rate of Milton Court and Mr. Williamson of Guildford. The advowson to the vicarage remained with the Dukes of Norfolk till the Right Hon. G. Cubitt, M.P., now Lord Ashcombe, bought it about 1865, and it remains in his hands. The vicarage of St. Paul is in the gift of trustees.

111 Illustrated by the late J. L. André, F.S.A. in *Surr. Arch. Coll.* xiv, 1. For Witley see *V.C.H. Surr.* ii, 456. The east window of Mickleham Church, prior to 1872, exhibited a similar design, and the west window of the tower at Cranleigh belongs to the same group.

112 See *ante* under Deepdene.
113 Cott. MS. Vesp. F, xv, fol. 18b.
114 Pat. 8 Edw. III, pt. ii, m. 34 ; and Winton Epis. Reg. Orleton, i, fol. 57 d.
115 *L. and P. Hen. VIII*, xvi, g. 947 (12) ; xvii, g. 443 (5). [67.
116 Chan. Inq. p.m. (Ser. 2), ccclxxxii,

117 Feet of F. Surr. East. 1657.
118 G.E.C. *Complete Peerage*, v, 368.
119 Pat. 12 Chas. II, pt. xviii, m. 16.
120 Abstract of title to Capel Rectory till 1766 ; Manning and Bray, *Hist. Surr.* iii, 593 ; private information.

The district of St. Mary, Holmwood, was taken out of Dorking and Capel parishes and erected into a separate parish in 1838. The living is in the gift of the Bishop of Winchester.

The parish of St. John, North Holmwood, was formed in 1874 from the northern part of the parish of St. Mary. The Bishop of Winchester is patron of this living also.

The parish of Holy Trinity, Westcote, was formed with Milton, in 1852. The living is in the gift of Mr. Robert Barclay of Bury Hill.

CHARITIES Smith's charity exists, but unlike the usual practice in the other Surrey parishes is administered by the parish, not by the trustees. The Rev. Samuel Cozens, Presbyterian minister in Dorking 1656–9, who probably resigned before 1662, left land at Chislet in Kent which was added to Smith's land.

Cotmandene Almshouses for eighteen poor persons were erected on land given to the vicar and churchwardens by the Hon. Charles Howard of Deepdene and Sir Adam Browne of Betchworth Castle in 1677, and were endowed by Mrs. Susannah Smith. A decree in Chancery established the legacy in 1718. Mr. William Ansell left £200 consols in 1830. Mr. Richard Lowndes of Rose Hill left £320 consols in 1831.

Messrs. Joseph and John Sanders gave £700 consols in 1839 to the same object.

In 1706 Mr. William Hutton left 6s. a year accruing out of a copyhold in Brockham for bread to the poor on Good Friday.

In 1725 Mrs. Margaret Fenwick left by will £800 which was laid out in the purchase of a farm called Fordland in Albury, for the apprenticing of poor children, providing a marriage portion for maid-servants who had lived blamelessly in the same family for seven years, and the residue to the poor in alms.

Summers' Charity was founded in 1807 by Mr. Thomas Summers, a hatter of Horsham, who used to travel between Horsham and Dorking. He left £100 each to Horsham, Dorking, and Capel. The money was laid out in buying £134 3 per cent. consols. and the income is devoted to buying bread for the poor.

An annuity of 20s. for forty poor widows is charged upon a piece of land called Poor Folks' Close in Dorking, but the benefactor is unknown.

Dorking Cottage Hospital, containing seventeen beds and three cots for children, was built in 1871 on land given at a nominal rent by Mrs. Hope of Deepdene. It is supported by voluntary contributions and payment of patients. The Right Hon. G. Cubitt, M.P. (Lord Ashcombe), gave £1,000 towards the building.

OCKLEY

Aclea (x cent.), Hoclei (xi cent.), Okeley (xiii cent.), Occle, Ockel (xiv cent.), Okkeleghe, Hocklegh (xv cent.), Okeleigh, Okeley (xii cent.), and many other variations.

Ockley is 7 miles south-west of Dorking. It has been bounded since 1879, when the outlying portions were consolidated with neighbouring parishes, by Abinger and Wotton on the west, by Capel on the north and east, and by the county of Sussex on the south. In 1901[1] a further rectification of the boundary with Wotton and Abinger was made. The parish contains 2,992 acres, and measures about 4 miles from north-east to south-west, and about 1½ miles from west to east. Since the outlying portions on Holmbury and Leith Hills have been separated the parish is entirely on the Wealden Clay, but in the northern part considerable beds of *paludinae*, forming the conglomerate called Sussex marble, occur.

The parish is agricultural, except for a little brick and tile making.

The Portsmouth line of the London, Brighton, and South Coast Railway passes through its eastern side. Ockley and Capel Station, in Ockley, was opened in 1867. Through the whole length of the parish the Roman road from London to Chichester, called the Stone Street, runs. For a considerable distance it is still used, but at both extremities of the parish the modern roads turn off abruptly from it, though the old line has been traced through the fields and copses. Ockley Church, Ockley Court, the remains of a fortified place to be noted presently, and probably the original Ockley village, lay a little

distance off the road to the east. Along the line of what is called in the manorial rolls Stone Street Causeway, and all round Ockley Green, a large stretch of open common lying along the west side of the road, cottages and houses sprang up. These are now known as Ockley village, but were formerly called Stone Street.[2] There is no doubt that near here was fought the great battle in which Ethelwulf and Ethelbald defeated the Danes, probably in 851. It was at Aclea, among the Suthrige, according to the Anglo-Saxon Chronicle, and the existence of the road explains the movements of the armies.[3] The discovery of human remains on Etherley Farm in 1882 may place the actual scene of conflict on the dry hillside north-west of Ockley Green.[4] Ockley in Surrey does not seem, however, to be the scene of the Synod of the 8th century; the circumstances of which point to a place in the north of England.

On the far side of the field north of Ockley Church, among some trees, is an earthwork. It was apparently a pear-shaped inclosure with the broader end to the east. The length is nearly 300 ft. At the eastern end is a broad mound with an extension thrown back at a right angle to face north. Outside this north-eastern angle is a ravelin or platform with traces of a ditch round it. The southern side is bounded by a stream than an artificially-straightened ravine. The eastern front may have been covered with an inundation. On the northern side only the traces of a ditch remain, but in the angle where this joins the stream, to the west, are traces of a small mound. West of this angle again are traces of an

[1] By Local Govt. Bd. Order, no. 42600.

[2] As e.g. in Burton, *Iter Surriense*, 1751, Rocque's map, 1770, and the map in Gibson's Camden, 1695. N.B.—The modern spelling Stane Street is an affectation. The natives call it Staan Street, as they call Dorking Darking, but the old spelling is Stone, and the local family name derived from it is Stonestreet.

[3] *V.C.H. Surr.* i, 331, 332.

[4] Ibid. The remains were in Wotton parish, but Ockley is very much nearer to the site than Wotton.

OCKLEY GREEN, WELL, c. 1845

DORKING CHURCH, BEFORE 1835

artificial bank, perhaps to make another inundation. Aubrey in the 17th century recognized the 'mole and mote' of a castle, and a small castle of the De Clares, built in Stephen's time and dismantled by Henry II, is not impossible. It is a likely spot, near a main road, which was then no doubt in use for its whole length.

Aubrey has preserved a tradition, repeated and ridiculed by later writers, that there was a castle here destroyed by the Danes, who placed battering engines on Bury Hill. All who notice the story take Bury Hill to be Anstiebury Camp, 2 miles or more away. But where the road ascends from Ockley towards Dorking, just before the branch to Coldharbour goes off on the left, the hill was called Bury Hill.[4a] It is very much nearer, under half a mile away instead of over two, and although too far for a catapult to act, it is not an impossible camp for some force attacking a strong place near Ockley Church. Danes may be, of course, any enemy, described by that name from confusion of traditions.

In the southern part of the parish, near Oakdale Farm, is a considerable moated inclosure with a double moat on two sides. The lane near it is called Smugglers' Lane. It is a way out of Sussex which avoids the high road.

Dotted about on the village green are several houses and cottages embowered in trees; and some of the trees along the main road are also of great size and beauty. Opposite to the turning that leads to the church is a picturesque old cottage with rough-cast walls and stone-slab roof, and several others in the village street are evidently of some antiquity. But it is the group of exceptionally fine old farm-houses within the borders of the parish which specially demand attention.

The finest of these is King's Farm, in the south-west of the parish, a large rambling structure, chiefly of half-timber, but largely covered with weather tiling, with overhanging stories, projecting oriel bay windows, having moulded bressummers and shaped brackets and tall chimney stacks—the shafts of the chimneys set diamond-wise upon square bases. Almost equally interesting are Boswell's or Bosell Farm, close to King's Farm, and Buckinghill Farm, in the north of the parish, both having overhanging timber-framed gables and stone-slab roofs. Holbrooks is another ancient farm-house. All have great open fireplaces and other characteristics of a past age, and their remoteness from railways and main roads has aided to preserve their primitive character. One called Trouts, though close to the railway line, is not easily accessible. It used to be known as Farley lands.[5] On a beam in the kitchen was lately a carved inscription :—

'LOOK WELL TO THY HOUSE IN EVERY DEGREE
AND AS THY MEANS ARE SO LET THY SPENDINGS BE
15 · .'

Eversheds is an old farm-house and reputed manor, in the eastern part of the parish. It was the property of an old yeoman family named Evershed. Mr. John Evershed bought the manor of Ockley, as noted below, in 1634, and Eversheds was sold with the manor in

1717. Its claim to be a manor rests only upon a mistaken identification with the *Arsette* of Domesday. Evershed is a place-name which gives its name to a family. Eversheds is the house of an Evershed. *Arsette* is possibly Hartshurst, a farm in Wotton under Leith Hill.

Vann is the seat of Mrs. Campbell. It was held of Ockley Manor by a family named Margesson in the 17th century. Vann Pond is an extensive sheet of water, made by damming a stream in a narrow valley, with a view to providing water-power for a linen mill in the 18th century; but the mill was never built.

Elderslie, on Ockley Green, is the seat of Mr. J. W. Arbuthnot. Mr. George Arbuthnot, grandfather of the present owner, resided there and died in 1843. The fountain on the green was built by Miss Jane Scott, governess in the Elderslie family, in 1841.

The present Rectory House, by the side of the Stone Street Causeway, was built at his own expense by the Rev. Thomas Woodrooffe shortly after he was instituted as rector in 1784. The older rectory was 1 mile further south, 2 miles from the church. This was not the original rectory, but was a farm-house on the glebe.

The Domesday Survey [4a] records that MANOR OCKLEY (Ockley, Okeleigh, Ocklie, Hokeleye, Okkle, Ockele, &c.) was held by Ralph of Richard of Tonbridge, and that Almar held it of King Edward; also that Richard himself held half a hide in this manor. The manor is here put under the heading of Woking Hundred. This may probably be merely a mistake; but it is worth notice that Manning and Bray record that there was land in Ockley held of East Horsley Manor, in Woking Hundred,[6] and there was an isolated bit of Ockham parish inclosed in Ockley, Ockham being also in Woking and a manor of Richard of Tonbridge. This may be Richard's half-hide, valueless because it was on the barren slope of Holmbury Hill.

In the early 13th century Alice daughter of Odo de Dammartin held *inter alia* one knight's fee in Ockley of the honour of Clare.[7] She held Tandridge also, and her lands passed to the Warblington family.[8] It seems probable that one of Alice's predecessors enfeoffed the Malemayns family with Ockley, to be held by one knight's fee of their manor of Tandridge,[9] for they seem to have been already established in Ockley, as well as elsewhere in Surrey. In 1213 Walter, Prior of Merton, made an exchange with Nicholas Malemayns of land in Ockley.[10] In 1241 John de Plessets paid 100 marks for the custody of the land and heirs of Nicholas Malemayns.[11] Nicholas Malemayns in 1278 claimed to have a park in Ockley in his manor.[12] In 1293 the king presented to the living of Ockley on the grounds of his custody of the lands and heirs of Nicholas

MALEMAYNS. *Gules three right hands or.*

[4a] Local information.
[5] Westcote Ct. R. 5 Nov. 1736.
[4a] V.C.H. Surr. i, 320b.
[6] Hist. of Surr. ii, 162.

[7] Testa de Nevill (Rec. Com.), 219.
[8] John de Warbleton had a wife Alice; Vriothesley, Pedigrees from Plea R. 285.
[9] Chan. Inq. p.m. 33 Edw. III, no. 41.

[10] Feet of F. Surr. 14 John, no. 42.
[11] Fine R. 25 Hen. III, m. 16; but this was not only in Ockley.
[12] Plac. de Quo War. (Rec. Com.), 744.

A HISTORY OF SURREY

Malemayns, 'tenant in chief.'[13] The reason why he is called tenant-in-chief may be explained by a possible minority of the Warblington heir and also by the fact that in 1289–90, when the Earl of Gloucester married Joan of Acre, daughter of Edward I, he surrendered all his lands to his royal father-in-law. He received a grant back of most of them, but not all, the same year. The king clearly reserved some manors in his own hands till his daughter's son should be of age ; when the earl died in 1295 Ockley does not appear in his *Inquisitio* as part of his lands. When, however, the son of his royal marriage, the young earl, was killed at Bannockburn, 1314, Ockley was one of his fees,[14] together with several other Surrey manors which are not mentioned in connexion with his father. Edward I is said to have presented the manor by patent[15] to Nicholas Malemayns. No such entry is in the Patent Rolls, but in a Charter Roll of 20 January 1296 it appears that Nicholas Malemayns surrendered Ockley to the Crown, and that the king, after holding it for some time, re-granted it to him and his heirs by his wife Alice. In 1300 a grant was made to Nicholas Malemayns of the assize of bread and ale and view of frankpledge in his manor of Ockley, as his ancestors had them,[16] and in 1302 he received a grant of free warren, a weekly market on Tuesdays, and a fair on the feast of St. Margaret (the patron saint of the church).[17] Nicholas died at an unknown date. Another Nicholas died in 1350. This Nicholas Malemayns married Alice and left three daughters : Beatrice, who married Otho de Graunson ; Catherine, who married Sir Henry Newdigate ; Parnel, who married Sir Thomas Sentomer. The manor was divided between them. When Sir Otho de Graunson died in 1359, seised of one-third of the manor, it was said to be held of the manor of Tandridge, in spite of Nicholas Malemayns having been called tenant-in-chief. The succession to the various parts is very uncertain ; but Beatrice the widow of Sir Otho de Graunson, the Newdigates, the descendants of Sir Thomas Sentomer, and in 1450 Richard Wakehurst, presented to the living. The heirs of the Graunsons do not appear again ; but they may be represented by Margaret, wife of John de Gaston (or Garton), who in 1368 conveyed one-ninth of the manor to William Newdigate.[18] The Newdigates continued to present to the living at intervals till 1407. Meanwhile Parnel Malemayns and Sir Thomas Sentomer had two daughters, Alice and Elizabeth. The latter disappears ; Alice married Sir William Hoo. His son Thomas granted Ockley to his brother John and John Glemham. Glemham, the survivor, or his heir, enfeoffed Sir Thomas Hoo, Lord Hoo and Hastings, who died 1481. He left four daughters, but by a previous arrangement the manor passed to Richard Culpepper. Whether he represented any of the other branches or not is unknown. Probably the rights of the others, much

broken up, had been conveyed to the Hoos,[19] or forgotten.

Ockley remained in the possession of the Culpepper family until the time of Charles I, when it was sold to George Duncombe, of Weston,[20] who held his first court in 1638. He died in 1646, and was succeeded by his grandson George, son of his elder son John, deceased. This George held his first court in 1648, but on his death soon afterwards, childless, the estate went to his uncle George of Shalford, who held his first court in 1654. He in his lifetime conveyed it to his second

CULPEPPER. *Argent a bend engrailed gules.*

son, Francis, who held his first court 22 March 1658–9. Francis was created a baronet in 1662. He died before his father, in 1670 ; his widow Hester and her second husband, Thomas Smyth, held a court October 1671. Sir William Duncombe, her son, succeeded in 1675, and in 1694 sold the manor to Edward Bax of Capel. Bax retained the manor-house and a little land round it, which was now separated from the manor, and in 1695 sold the manor to John Evershed, of an old yeoman family, which appears, in different holdings, in the rolls and parish books.[21]

John Evershed received from Queen Anne a grant of three fairs yearly at Stonestead Causeway, 6 October, 10 May, and 3 June.[22] Evershed in 1717 conveyed to John Young,[23] who in the same year released to Thomas Moore or More.[24] Thomas More held courts till 1734. His nephew William[25] held courts till 1745, and died in 1746. He left the manor in trust for Frederick son of Lord North of Guildford (who held courts 1746–9), but the estate was sold under a private Act in 1751[26] to Frank Nicholls, Ph.D., who had some lively controversy with the tenants on the subject of heriots.[27] Dr. Nicholls died in 1778, and was succeeded by his son John. He sold in 1784 to Lee Steere of Jays in Wotton, who died before the conveyance was completed, leaving his interest in the estate to his grandson Lee Steere Witts, who took the name of Steere. His great-great-grandson (Mr. H. C. Lee Steere) is the present owner.[28]

Ockley Court, the residence of Mrs. Calvert, widow of Colonel Calvert, is the old manor-house of Ockley. In 1744 Nathaniel, son of Edward Bax, sold it to Mr. Thomas Tash, who died in 1770. His son William married a Miss Calvert, and having no children left the property to his wife. She left it to her relative (? nephew) Charles Calvert of Kneller Hall, Middlesex, M.P. for Southwark. He died in 1833. His son Charles William succeeded, and was followed by his brother Colonel A. M. Calvert. His son Mr. W. A. Calvert lived recently at Broomells in Capel.

[13] *Cal. Pat.* 1292–1301, p. 33.
[14] Chan. Inq. p.m. 8 Edw. II, no. 68. Ockley is here said to be held by Thomas de Warblington, of whom Malemayns was evidently holding as sub-tenant.
[15] Inq. Misc. Chan. file 329, 20 Edw. IV, no. 103.
[16] *Cal. Pat.* 1292–1301, p. 535.
[17] Charter R. 30 Edw. I, no. 15.
[18] Feet of F. Surr. 42 Edw. III, no. 14.

[19] See Inq. of 20 Edw. IV, no. 103, for descent to Lord Hoo.
[20] Feet of F. Surr. Mich. 13 Chas. I.
[21] From Ct. R. See History of the Bax family and Edward Bax's account book furnished by Mr. A. R. Bax.
[22] Rot. Orig. 2 Anne, pt. i, m. 1.
[23] Feet of F. Surr. East. 3 Geo. I.
[24] Ibid. Mich. 4 Geo. I.
[25] Manning and Bray, *Surr.* ii, 163.
[26] Ibid.

[27] On the usual point, whether the tenant holding more than one copyhold owed a separate heriot on each or one for the whole.
[28] Mr. Richard Symmes, whose MSS. (B.M. Add. MSS. no. 6167) were used by Manning and Bray, was steward of the manor 1662–82, and Mr. Bray was steward under Dr. Nicholls up to 1788. All the existing Court Rolls have been examined.

OCKLEY CHURCH : SOUTH PORCH

OCKLEY CHURCH : SOUTH WALL OF NAVE

Holebrook is a farm in Ockley. William le Latimer (*vide* Wotton), who died in 1327, held Holebrook in Ockley of Nicholas Malemayns by payment of 40*d.* a year.[29]

CHURCHES   *ST. MARGARET* is prettily situated in a well-kept churchyard abutting upon the high road, and surrounded by some exceptionally fine trees. The site is level and low-lying, at some distance from the present village, and close to a patch of woodland. It must originally have been surrounded by woods.

The building is of sandstone and rubble, dug from the neighbouring hills, with a small admixture of clunch, or hard chalk. Before 1873 it consisted only of a nave about 40 ft. by 22 ft., and a short chancel 22 ft. wide by 19 ft. long, with a large tower, about 17 ft. square internally, and a porch on the south of the nave; but in that year it was enlarged by the addition of a spacious north aisle, with an arcade of pointed arches, and an organ-chamber and vestries on the north of the chancel, while the chancel itself was nearly doubled in length.

There is no trace in the walls of work earlier than the beginning of the 14th century, to which date the nave and chancel both originally belonged.

There are two windows at present in the south wall of the chancel, one of which, to the west, is partly ancient and indicates a date of about 1300. It is of two lights, cinquefoiled, and has a trefoiled spherical triangle, inclosing a trefoil, in the head. In the eastern window, which may have been removed from the north wall at the enlargement, the latter figure has six foliations. The roof and all other features in the chancel are modern.

The south wall of the nave appears to be slightly later—*circa* 1320—and has two good buttresses and two well-proportioned traceried windows, each of two lights. The eastern of these retains the original net tracery, executed in local sandstone, but that to the west has been restored. Next to it eastward is the south entrance doorway, which is a plain example of the same date. It is approached through a most picturesque porch of open oak framework on a base of herringbone brick and timber. This has an arched opening to the front and two others on the sides, with arched braces inside, and the sides are partly filled in with a rail and turned balusters. The foliated bargeboard is a restoration of that shown in Cracklow's view. Although probably not earlier than the first half of the 17th century, this porch retains all the spirit of the mediaeval carpentry in design and execution. The framework is put together with projecting oak pins, and the roof, of somewhat flat pitch, retains its heavy stone healing.

The massive western tower is another instance of the clinging to a traditional style. It is rude Gothic of 1700 — that being the date, with the name WILLIAM BVTLER SEN, inscribed on the slope of a buttress on the west wall. William Butler was a leading parishioner, perhaps churchwarden, in 1700. The builder was Edward Lucas. The parish account books give the date as 1699, when the contract for building was signed. The heads of the twin openings in the upper stage and of those below are elliptical or obtusely pointed, while in the interior the arch of the nave and the blind arches in the other walls are pointed, but with classical mouldings and imposts. The present battlements were heightened at the restoration of 1873.

There is a curious square-headed two-light window of diminutive proportions next to the buttresses at the south-east end of the nave. Its openings, though only 8 in. wide, are further protected by stanchions and cross-bars. Its height from the floor removes it from the class known as low side-windows, but it corresponds very curiously with similar openings at Send and Woking churches in Surrey, which also occur in the eastern part of the nave and in the neighbourhood of an altar. All are of late date (c. 1480 to 1520).

The nave roof is of early 14th-century date and retains its original moulded tie-beams and plates. That of the chancel is modern, but both are 'healed' with Horsham slabs.

In the eastern window of c. 1320 in the south wall of the nave is preserved some good glass with crocketed canopy-work, borders, and grisaille quarries of coeval date. There are no old wall-paintings.

One or two ledgers with heraldry and some tablets of late 17th and early 18th-century dates remain in the tower, but with these exceptions the church is remarkably destitute of ancient monuments.

The registers date from 1539. They and the parish account books (which commence in 1683) are very full, and contain many curious entries.

Besides modern pieces, the church plate includes a silver cup and paten of 1614 and a paten of 1716.

There are six bells, all dated 1701, hung in a good solid cage, which is of the same date.

St. John's Church on Ockley Green was consecrated 5 December 1872 by Bishop Wilberforce. It is a plain building of stone, with pointed windows and a bell-turret.

ADVOWSON   The first reference to the church of Ockley is in the *Taxatio* of Pope Nicholas, 1291.

In 1293 the king presented to it on behalf of Nicholas Malemayns his ward.[30] The advowson remained with the manor until 1694 when Sir William Duncombe, at the same time that he sold the manor, sold the advowson to John Constable of Ockley. Edward Bax, who bought the manor (q.v.), was a Quaker, and would not buy the advowson. Constable sold it in 1711 to Edward Bingdon of Dorking, who left it in 1719 in trust for his sons James and Edward. It was sold in 1724 for £1,000 to Clare Hall, Cambridge.[31] The College

CLARE COLLEGE, CAMBRIDGE. CLARE impaling DE BURGH *all in a border sable with drops or.*

probably then knew nothing of the ancient ownership of Richard de Tonbridge, ancestor of their foundress.

CHARITIES   Smith's Charity is distributed as in other Surrey parishes.

In 1624 Mr. Henry Spooner left a rent-charge of 10*s.* a year to the poor of the parish.

In 1731 Mrs. Elizabeth Evershed left £100 to be invested in land to provide education 'according to the canons of the Church of England' for poor children of the parish. With other benefactions of the late Mr. George Arbuthnot and the late Mr. Lee Steere, this provides an endowment of about £43 a year for the schools.

[29] Chan. Inq. p.m. 1 Edw. III, no. 56.   [30] Cal. Pat. 1292–1301, p. 33.   [31] College Bks., communicated by the Master.

WOTTON

Odetone and Wodeton (xi cent.) ; Wodetone, Wodinton and Woditon (xiii cent.) ; Wodeton (xv cent.) ; Wodyngton, Wootton, and Wotton (xvi cent. and onwards).

Wotton parish is bounded on the north by Effingham and Little Bookham, on the east by Dorking, Capel, and Ockley, on the south and west by Abinger. It formerly had a detached portion on the Sussex border, now attached to Abinger (see Abinger parish). The parish is still over 6 miles long from north to south, and never more than a little over a mile broad, and in places less. It contains 3,782 acres of land and 14 of water. The church is 3 miles west-by-south of Dorking, and 9 miles east-by-south of Guildford. The Redhill and Reading branch of the South Eastern Railway and the road from Dorking to Guildford pass through the north of it. Two branches of the Tillingbourne rise in the northern slopes of Leith Hill, and run first from south to north and then east to west towards the Wey, uniting at Wotton House. The streams on the other slope of Leith Hill run to the Arun. The parish has the usual apportionment of soil in this part of Surrey. The northern boundary is on the summit of the chalk, here 577 ft. above the sea, the parish then crosses the Upper Green Sand and Gault ; the church, manor-house, and such compact village as exists are on the Lower Green Sand, and it reaches across this soil on to the Wealden Clay. It is now purely agricultural and residential, but iron mills, a wire mill, and perhaps gunpowder mills formerly existed in it.[1]

The most striking feature of the parish now is undoubtedly the natural beauty which makes it the favourite resort of all lovers of the picturesque near London. The traveller, on foot or horseback (the road is not one for wheels), passing from the chalk country sees in front of him an ascending mass of broken chalk and hills, thickly planted with conifers and other trees upon their northern side. Leaving Wotton House on the right a bridle road leads through a forest of beeches alongside a succession of troutpools, up the valley where John Evelyn first began the ornamental planting of his brother's grounds. Friday Street Pond, an old millpond with a cluster of cottages by it, is a Swiss lake in miniature. Passing on by another hamlet, King George's Hill, so named from a now extinct public-house, the path leads out on to the heather-covered common of Leith Hill. A view opens gradually to the west, as the ground ascends, but it is not till the traveller reaches the southern brow of the hill that the panorama bursts suddenly upon him. The summit of Leith Hill is the highest spot in the south-east of England, 967 ft. above the sea. The tower, which is not on exactly the highest point, but somewhat south of it, was intended to bring the height up to 1,000 ft., and has more than done so. It was built by Mr. Richard Hull of Leith Hill Place, in or before 1765, who acquired from Sir John Evelyn of Wotton the top of the hill, part of the waste of the

manor of Wotton.[2] Two rooms were fitted up in it by Mr. Hull, and a staircase led to the upper room. Mr. Hull, dying in 1772, was buried under the lower room, by his own direction. A stone in the wall of the tower used to record the fact. After his death the tower was uncared for and became ruinous and a haunt for disorderly characters. In 1796 Mr. Philip Henry Perrin of Leith Hill Place repaired it and raised it a few feet, adding a coping, but built up the door, filled up the interior for half the height with earth and stones, and left the upper part a mere shell. In 1864 Mr. W. Evelyn of Wotton again repaired it, built the upper room, added a battlement, and made the top accessible, first, by means of a turret and staircase, then, when that was closed for a time, by an outside wooden staircase, and then by the turret stair again. The view from the top of the tower is more comprehensive than that from the hill, looking over the trees to the north, which obstruct the latter. The ground falls very abruptly to the south, giving a peculiar impression of height above the Weald below. The greater part of the county of Sussex, much of Kent as far as Ashford, Essex, the Laindon Hills, Middlesex, St. Paul's Cathedral, Highgate, Hampstead, and Harrow, Hertfordshire, Dunstable Down in Bedfordshire, the Chilterns in Buckinghamshire, Nettlebed in Oxfordshire, Berkshire, Hampshire, Inkpen in Wiltshire, and the sea through Shoreham Gap, are visible in clear weather.[3] But though the view from the tower is necessarily the most extensive in Surrey, those from the western parts of Leith Hill are more picturesque, looking as they do over the more broken foreground afforded by Holmbury Hill. The small ditches round the tower, sometimes ignorantly mistaken for an ancient encampment, were made by the Royal Engineers, who were encamped here in 1844, correcting the Ordnance Survey. The cottages near the foot of the hill are collectively known in the neighbourhood as The Camp.

In addition to the ground near the top of the hill, there is a very large extent of open country, covered with heather and conifers, in Wotton parish. The part on the east side of the parish is called Broadmoor.

A fine polished neolithic flint found near the tower is preserved at Leith Hill Place. The present writer has found a very considerable number of flint flakes and a few implements not very far from the tower. In Deer Leap Wood, to the north of Wotton House, in what was part of the park attached to it, is a mound with traces of a double ditch round it. The mound is about 12 to 14 ft. high, and about 90 yds. in circumference. It seems to have been dug into, but no record of exploration is to be found. It is marked as a barrow on the 6-in. Ordnance map.

At the southern foot of Leith Hill, a jar containing about thirty gold coins of Henry VIII, Edward VI, and Elizabeth was found in 1837. The coins are at Wotton House.

Tillingbourne, or Lonesome, as it used to be called, or earlier still Filbrook Lodge, is the property of the

[1] *V.C.H. Surr.* ii, 236, 312, &c., and Evelyn's Letter to Aubrey—vol. i of Aubrey's *Surr.*

[2] Mr. Hull bought the land on which the Tower stands. It remained part of his estate, Leith Hill Place, q.v., under successive changes of ownership till Mr. Wedgwood sold it to Mr. Evelyn in the last century. The inscription on the Tower gives the date 1766, but the 66 is an evident restoration, and the Court Rolls of the manor speak of the tower as existing in 1765.

[3] Copy of the bearings of various points taken by the Royal Engineers in 1844, in the possession of Mr. Malden.

Duke of Norfolk. The present occupier is Mr. Sidney Ricardo. The original house was built by the side of the valley, which runs northward from near the tower towards Wotton Hatch, in 1740, by Theodore Jacobsen, a Dutch merchant resident in England. A stream was artificially diverted to form what is now a picturesque waterfall, and a fountain and other ornamental waterworks were made in front of the house. These, with part of the garden, mark its former site. The original house was neglected, and by 1845 had become ruinous. It was pulled down before 1855, but a steward's house on the estate, lying a little farther north, was let as a gentleman's house, and has been enlarged to form the present Tillingbourne House.

Tanhurst, on the south-western slope of Leith Hill, late the residence of Mrs. Cazalet, formerly of Greenhurst, Capel, is the property of Lady Vaughan Williams, wife of Lord Justice Williams and daughter of the late Mr. Edmund Lomax. Before 1795 it was bought by Mr. William Philip Perrin, owner also of Parkhurst (see Abinger) and Leith Hill Place. The next owner was Sir H. Fitzherbert, during whose ownership the eminent Sir Samuel Romilly rented the house up to the time of his death in 1818. It was bought by Mr. E. Lomax (see Shiere) in 1827.[4] Mr. Lomax, who was twice married, died in 1839, and left Netley in Shiere to Mrs. Fraser, Parkhurst in Abinger to Mrs. Scarlett, children of his first wife, and Tanhurst to Lady Vaughan Williams, daughter of his second wife. Lord Justice and Lady Vaughan Williams reside at High Ashes on the same property.

Jayes Park, close to Ockley Green, is the seat of Mr. Henry Lee Steere, lord of the manor of Ockley, but this house is in Wotton. Jayes was the seat of the Steere family for many generations. Mr. Lee Steere, who died in 1784, left it to the son of his daughter and of Mr. Richard Witts, Lee Steere Witts. On reaching his majority in 1795 he assumed the name of Steere, and the family have resided ever since at Jayes. The schools were built in 1852, rebuilt in 1874, and enlarged in 1885.

The ecclesiastical parish of Okewood formed from Wotton, Ockley, and Abinger in 1853 is a district formerly very difficult of access owing to the clay lanes. In addition to the parish church there is a Congregational chapel and a national school built in 1873.

Hale House, containing some old parts, is the property of Mr. H. Lee Steere of Ockley, and the residence of Mr. Henry P. Powell. This is no doubt the place belonging to Edward de la Hale (died 1431), who

restored Okewood Chapel (*vide infra*). In the Ockley Court Rolls, 1648, it appears that a Mr. Steere had lately built a good house at Hale, of which part remains in the present house.

Redford is the seat of Lady Abinger. Leith Vale was the seat of the late Miss Cooper Brown (ob. 1907), who was for many years churchwarden of Okewood.

According to Domesday, Harold held *MANOR WOTTON* T.R.E., and at the time of the Survey Oswald, an Englishman, held it.[5] It is noteworthy that in 1086 Richard de Tonbridge, the ancestor of the Clares, Earls of

WOTTON CHURCH : THE WEST TOWER FROM THE SOUTH

Gloucester, who afterwards held Wotton in chief, was already holding there one hide of Oswald.[6] Richard is known to have gained possession of other parts of Oswald's land, and he even sublet some of Oswald's former possessions at Mickleham to him.[7] The overlordship of Wotton seems to have always afterwards been with the honour of Clare.[8]

The first immediate lord of whom there is mention is Ralph de Camoys, who owed one knight's service

4 Bill of sale.   6 Ibid.   8 Chan. Inq. p.m. 43 Hen. III, no. 28;
5 *V.C.H. Surr.* i, 328a.   7 Ibid. 283 and 317a.   ibid. 49 Edw. III (1st pt. 2nd nos.), no. 46.

for Wotton to the honour of Clare,[9] and in 1235 made a grant of land in Wotton,[10] while in 1241 he was definitely reported to be seised of the manor.[11] It is known, however, that in the reign of King John one Ralph de Camoys claimed that part of the vill of Tansor (Northants) had been granted to his grandfather by Roger de Clare[12] and it is possible that Wotton may have been granted at the same time. In 1259 Ralph died, leaving Ralph his son and heir aged forty.[13] The younger Ralph was succeeded some twenty years later by his son John,[14] from whom Wotton apparently passed to the family of Fancourt. Probably by sale, since the impoverishment of the Camoys family at that date is a matter of common knowledge.[15] Walter de Fancourt was seised of the manor in 1280,[16] and presented a priest to Okewood Chapel in 1290.[17] In 1306 Matilda his widow, who had married one Henry le Perkes,[18] claimed dower in the manor of Wotton from William le Latimer, into whose hands it had by that time passed.[19]

William le Latimer died in 1327,[20] leaving William his son and heir, aged twenty-six.[21] This William survived his father only eight years,[22] and during the minority of his son, another William, the manor seems to have been in the custody of Thomas Latimer,[23] who was probably his uncle and the heir. Thomas, possibly in return for his custodianship, retained the manor during the term of his life ; at his death in 1356 it passed into the possession of William,[24] who was then twenty-six years old. William conveyed it to trustees in 1377. At his death in 1381[25] he left Wotton by will to his cousin, Thomas de Camoys,[26] who presented to the living in 1382.[27] Thomas

LATIMER. *Gules a cross paty or.*

CAMOYS. *Argent a chief gules with three roundels argent therein.*

enfeoffed certain trustees of the manor, who curiously enough bore the same surnames as those to whom William Latimer had released in 1377.[28]

Thomas de Camoys died seised in March 1422,[29] and Hugh his grandson and next heir survived him

only five years.[30] Wotton, however, is not mentioned among Hugh's possessions at his death. Roger lord of Camoys, probably a younger son of Thomas, was in possession shortly after the death of Hugh,[31] and in 1429 he released all his rights in the manor to Thomas Morestede.[32] The dispersion of the Camoys' lands after the death of Thomas de Camoys is well known,[33] and its occurrence immediately before the Civil War, which wrought so much confusion in landed property, increases the difficulty of tracing them.

According to Manning and Bray,[34] who give a contemporary court roll as their authority, Wotton was held by Sir William Estfield in 1444. In 1479 Stephen Middleton was in possession, and some five years later it was held by Humphrey de Bohun.[35] Sir David Owen, a natural son of Owen Tudor, married as his first wife the heiress of the Bohuns of Midhurst,[36] and Wotton perhaps passed to him with his wife or was bought by him, for it became his property, and he left it to Henry son of his third wife Anne Devereux,[37] and after him to his son John by the same wife. Sir Owen died in 1542. John held courts from 1548 to 1553.[38] His son Henry held courts in 1568 and 1579, when he and Elizabeth his wife conveyed the estate to George Evelyn of Long Ditton,[39] in whose family it has since remained.

Wotton House, the home and birthplace of the famous John Evelyn, is built, like so many old houses, in a hollow. There is nothing visible in the present rambling and irregular building of older date than the close of the 16th century, and even such parts of this date as remain are so surrounded by later additions as to be distinguished only with difficulty.

EVELYN of Wotton. *Azure a griffon passant and a chief or.*

Besides rebuildings and extensions of the 17th and 18th centuries, the east wing, which had been destroyed, was added on an enlarged plan by Mr. W. J. Evelyn in 1864. Thus, although the core of the house is ancient, but little remains visible externally of the house in which John Evelyn lived, and which he helped to render famous by the beautiful gardens, largely of his own creation. These in part remain, although greatly altered in later times. Fortunately two drawings, still at Wotton, from John Evelyn's own hand, give a minute record of the house, with its moat and artificial waters, as they appeared in the middle of the 17th century.[40] In

---

[9] *Testa de Nevill* (Rec. Com.), 219.
[10] Feet of F. Surr. 19 Hen. III, no. 20.
[11] Ibid. Div. Co. 25 Hen. III, no. 170.
[12] *Plac. Abbrev.* (Rec. Com.), 82.
[13] Chan. Inq. p.m. 43 Hen. III, no. 28.
[14] Ibid. 5 Edw. I, no. 1.
[15] *Cal. Close*, 1279–88, pp. 52–4, &c.
[16] Feet of F. Surr. 8 Edw. I, no. 10.
[17] Wykeham's Register.
[18] De Banco R. 161, m. 183.
[19] Ibid.
[20] Chan. Inq. p.m. 1 Edw. III (1st nos.), no. 56.
[21] Ibid.
[22] Ibid. 9 Edw. III (1st nos.), no. 51.
[23] Feet of F. Surr. 26 Edw. III, no. 7.
[24] Chan. Inq. p.m. 29 Edw. III (1st nos.), no. 30.
[25] Exch. Inq. p.m. (Ser.1), file 457, no. 1.

[26] Harl. MS. 6148, fol. 139.
[27] *Wykeham's Register* (Hants Rec. Soc.), i, 132.
[28] Close, 13 Ric. II, pt. i, m. 12 d.
[29] Chan. Inq. p.m. 9 Hen. V, no. 29.
[30] Ibid. 5 Hen. VI, no. 26.
[31] Close, 7 Hen. VI, m. 7 d.
[32] Ibid ; see also Feet of F. Surr. 11 Hen. VI, no. 20.
[33] The difficulty of tracing the direct Camoys line was experienced at the time of the revival of the Camoys barony in 1838.
[34] *Hist. of Surr.* ii, under Wotton. Bray was steward of Wotton.
[35] Chan. Inq. p.m. 1 Ric. III, no. 26. Possibly some light may be thrown on these changes of ownership by the fact that in 1465 (Close, 4 Edw. IV, m. 11 d.)

one Thomas Middleton being enfeoffed to the use of William Estfield, kt., demised property in Middlesex to Humphrey Bohun. This entry seems at any rate to prove the existence of some relationship between those three persons which may explain their having been connected with the manor in turn.
[36] *Suss. Arch. Soc. Coll.* vii, 25.
[37] See Sir David's will, printed in *Suss. Arch. Coll.* vii, 38. [38] Ct. Rolls.
[39] *Cat. Anct. D.* iii, 75 (A 4510).
[40] *Surr. Arch. Coll.* xvii, 70. One bears the title, in John Evelyn's writing, ' The prospect of the old house at Wotton, 1640 ' ; the other ' A Rude draght of Wotton Garden before my Bro : altered it & as it was 1640 ; South.'

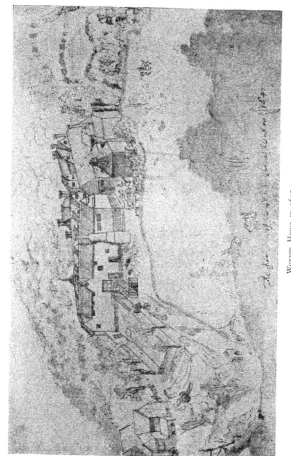

WOTTON HOUSE IN 1640

(*From a Drawing by John Evelyn*)

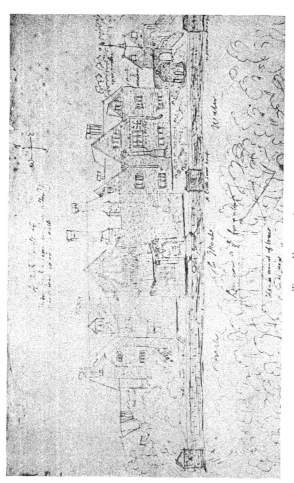

WOTTON HOUSE IN 1640

(From a Drawing by John Evelyn)

Abbot's Hospital, Guildford, is a poor oil painting of Wotton House from the north of about the same date. The Elizabethan house, apparently, was of brick, with tiled roofs—pantiles in some cases—mullioned windows, and tall stacks of chimneys. It was built in a rambling fashion with long ranges of stabling and outbuildings, including a dovecote. It was surrounded by a moat which was enlarged into a swan pool in the rear of the house, and the view of the garden front shows a low terrace wall following the moat, with some little summer-houses, a rustic temple, and a formal flower garden. There is also a large oriel window with a high leaded roof projecting over a stone entrance doorway, marked on the drawing, 'Hall dore to the Garden.' Among the many treasures in the present house is the Prayer Book used by Charles I on the scaffold. There are also the MSS. of John Evelyn and a Bible of three volumes filled with notes. In the library his large and curious collection of books remains, many of the bindings displaying his device of intertwined palm, olive, and oak branches, with the motto, 'Omnia explorate, meliora retinete.' Kneller's fine half-length portrait of John Evelyn is in the drawing-room, together with his son and Mrs. Godolphin, his 'deare friend,' whose worthy life' he has 'consecrated to posterity.'

There are several ancient houses of minor importance in the parish; one with gables and stone-mullioned windows, set in an old-world garden at a corner of the high road, is specially noteworthy.

There was a mill at Wotton in the time of Domesday, which reappeared among the possessions of William le Latimer in 1337. It does not seem to occur elsewhere. It was possibly on the site of the old disused mill-dam at Friday Street, or on the stream higher up, where an old dam, now cut, and former pond are visible. The mill (this or both these) at Wotton was afterwards used for manufacturing purposes of different kinds.

The manor of GOSTERWOOD (Gostrode, xiv cent.) in Wotton should probably be identified with the hide of land in Wotton which was held by Corbelin of Richard de Tonbridge at the time of the Domesday Survey.[41] In 1280 Nicholas Malemayns acquitted Henry de Somerbury of services which were exacted from him in connexion with his free tenement in Wotton.[42] Henry died seised of this tenement in 1317, and it is recorded that he did suit for it at Nicholas Malemayn's court at Ockley.[43] In 1337 another Henry de Somerbury, who died in that year, had this holding in his possession; it then appears as 'Gostrode in the vill of Wotton.'[44]

From that time the material for the history of Gosterwood is scanty. In 1527 Robert Draper and Elizabeth his wife conveyed it to Henry Wyatt and others, and it is here for the first time called a manor.[45] Richard Hill died seised of it[46] in 1550, leaving it to his son Edmund, who was still holding it in 1574,[47] when he settled it on his wife Catherine Brown. This son Richard conveyed it in

1593 to George Evelyn, in whose descendants it has remained.

LEITH HILL PLACE is in the outlying part of Ockley, which was inclosed in Wotton and added to this parish in 1879. It is traditionally the head of a manor, but this is erroneous. It stands in the manor of Wotton, and not in the manor of Ockley, as other outlying parts of the parish were.

The house was a gentleman's house of very considerable antiquity, to judge from the sketch of its old state furnished by Mr. Perrin to Manning and Bray's history. The sketch was dated 1700, and shows a 16th-century front upon probably an older house. There was a secret chamber in the wall, usually called a priest's hole, only accessible by a trap-door, but this has now been opened into the adjoining room.

The builder is unknown. The site of the house was originally called Welland, but Leith is mentioned among the properties which fenced Ockley churchyard in 1628. In 1664 Mrs. Mary Millett, widow, of Harrow, Middlesex, settled Leith Hill Place on herself for life, with remainder to Henry Best of Gray's Inn. Katherine daughter and heir of Henry Best married Henry Goddard of Richmond, co. York. In 1706 they sold to John Worsfold of Ockley, who sold it to Colonel Folliott,[48] afterwards General Folliott, who was a justice of the peace resident in Ockley parish as early as 1728.[49] He altered the house of Leith Hill Place to its present form. His admission as a tenant of Wotton Manor is not on record, as the court rolls are not complete so early. Two acres of the waste were granted to him in 1742. He died in 1748, his only child Susanna having died in 1743.[50] In 1760 John Folliott, his heir, alienated Welland to Richard Hull, who built Leith Hill Tower in 1765, receiving a grant of the Tower and 4 acres of waste.[51] In 1777 Richard Hull alienated to Harry Thompson.[52] In 1788 Thompson's heirs alienated to Philip W. Perrin, owner and resident at Parkhurst. During his ownership the house was let as a school. Mr. Perrin died in 1824, and his heir was Sir Henry Fitzherbert, who sold in 1829 to John Smallpeice, who conveyed it in 1847 to Josiah Wedgwood, a descendant of the great Wedgwood and cousin and brother-in-law to Charles Darwin. His daughters Miss Wedgwood and Mrs. Vaughan Williams reside there now.

The reputed manor of ROOKHAM (Rokenham, xiv cent.) in the parishes of Ockley and Wotton may be connected with the grant of two crofts made by Thomas de Rokenham to his son John in 1314.[53] These lands evidently passed to the Newtimber family in the same century, for in 1399 Robert Newtimber conveyed to trustees a messuage and two curtilages, with other lands and tenements at Rookham, which were said to have formerly belonged to John de Rokenham.[54] In 1418 the trustees of Thomas de Pinkhurst, whose family had held property in Rookham for some years,[55] released his lands to Robert Newtimber.[56]

41 V.C.H. Surr. i, 328a.
42 Feet of F. Surr. 8 Edw. I, no. 10.
43 Chan. Inq. p.m. 11 Edw. II, no. 50.
44 Ibid. 11 Edw. III (1st nos.), no. 39.
45 Feet of F. Surr. Hil. 18 Hen. VIII.
46 Chan. Inq. p.m. (Ser. 2), xcii, 79.
47 Recov. R. Hil. 17 Eliz.
48 Manning and Bray, Hist. of Surr. iii, App. clvi.

49 Ockley Parish Bks.
50 Family tomb of General Folliott in Ockley churchyard and registers.
51 The inscription on the tower says 1766, but the grant of the tower is 1765.
52 Richard Hull died 1772, aged eighty-three (inscription formerly visible in the tower), so this Richard was his heir. Manning and Bray (loc. cit.) say that

General Folliott's widow and Mary Harloe his niece sold to Richard Hull in 1754, and that Hull's heirs sold to Thompson in 1773. This is not compatible with the court roll, unless the site of the house had been separated from the manor. It is supposed now to be in the manor.
53 Add. Chart. 9021.   54 Ibid. 18687.
55 Ibid. 18654.   56 Ibid. 18702.

Apparently Rookham passed from the Newtimbers to the family of Hale,[57] since in 1537 Thomas Bourgh, grandson of Elizabeth sister of Henry at Hale, granted out rent from lands called Rookham and Newtimber in Ockley and Wotton.[58] From him the estate passed to John Caryll, who in 1560 made a settlement of the ' manor of Rookham ' on his son Thomas.[59] It seems probable that the manor soon afterwards ceased to exist as a separate entity ; for in 1610 a certain John Hayne died seised of 'lands called Frenches, late parcel of the tenement called Rookham in Wotton.' These lands are stated to have comprised 18 acres in extent.[60] Hayne also held lands in Ockley called Millmeades, alias Ruckingham meades, but in the Ockley Court Rolls of 1648 William Hayne holds these of Ockley Manor, while Rookham in Wotton is unmentioned ; they were not therefore part of this manor and are still included in Ockley Manor.

his death (1558), being the jointure of his widow Jane. Their son Sir Edward, his son Reginald, and Lady Bray conveyed the reversion to Thomas Godman of Letherhead. In 1601 he conveyed it to John Aleyn, whose son Henry conveyed to George Evelyn of Wotton.[64]

The church of *ST. JOHN THE CHURCHES EVANGELIST* is not mentioned in Domesday, but from certain evidence in the existing structure it was probably standing in the 11th century. It is most beautifully situated on the summit of a steep ridge, its east and south sides overlooking a beautiful green valley and the hillside opposite, which has all the appearance of the wild down-land country of Sussex or Dorset, with patches of bracken and blackberry bushes and clumps of fine park-like trees, many, no doubt, of John Evelyn's own planting. In the hollow behind this hill, to the south

CHAPEL OF ST. JOHN THE BAPTIST, OKEWOOD, FROM THE SOUTH-WEST

Rookham is a farm south of Okewood Hill, just north of the Sussex border, upon the edge of the detached part of Wotton parish now added to Abinger, east of Ockley. Rucknam Mead and the old Ruckenham contributed to the repair of Ockley churchyard fence in 1628.[61]

WESTLAND was in Wotton, Abinger, Cranleigh, Albury, Ewhurst, and Wonersh. The courts were held at Okewood Hill in Wotton. In 1424–5 John Newdigate was owner, and granted a lease of it.[62]

In 1494 John Newdigate conveyed it to Ralph Leigh of Paddington in Abinger,[63] with which it passed to Sir Edward Bray. It was separated after

east, lies Wotton House. The churchyard is surrounded by noble trees—here, again, in some cases, of Evelyn's planting. Two grand old beeches, with wide-spreading boughs, that formed a conspicuous feature, immediately to the north-east of the church, have unhappily been cut down within recent years ; other fine beeches are to be seen to the west of the church, and there is a very beautiful avenue of limes and horse-chestnuts leading to the south porch. The churchyard contains a number of old wooden ' bedheads,' and a number of curiously-carved 18th-century head-stones, some table-tombs and other memorials ancient and modern, among the latter being many

---

[57] Probably Edward de la Hale, the benefactor of Okewood Chapel (q.v.), was a member of this family, as the places are all close together.
[58] Add. Chart. 18792.

[59] Ibid. 18846.
[60] W. & L. Inq. p.m. bdle. 36, no. 163.
[61] Ockley Parish Bks.
[62] Manning and Bray, *Hist. of Surr.* ii, 153.

[63] Feet of F. Surr. 9 Hen. VII, 33.
[64] Manning and Bray, *Hist. of Surr.* ii, 152. (Bray was steward of the manor.) From Ct. R. and deeds of Mr. Evelyn.

158

stones to the family of the late Sir Edward Vaughan-Williams. The most interesting of the older monuments is a beautifully-carved urn, of white marble, bearing cherubs' heads, which marks the grave of William Glanville nephew of John Evelyn, on the north side of the churchyard.

The church is largely covered with ivy, especially the tower; and however picturesque the covering, it is much to be regretted, as causing slow but sure injury to the fabric, and hiding interesting features and marks of age. The walls are for the most part constructed of hard yellow Bargate stone rubble, still covered generally with a thin coat of ancient plaster or mortar, with dressings of Bargate stone and firestone. The modern parts are faced with the same rubble and with dressings of a ruddy sandstone and Bath stone, the vestry on the north being of old red brickwork. The roofs are still covered with Horsham slabs, except the porch and vestries, which are tiled. From the flat conical roof of the tower rises a picturesque square wooden superstructure, also covered with a flat-pitched conical roof.

In plan the church consists of a western tower, 11 ft. from east to west internally, by 15 ft. from north to south; nave, 33 ft. long by 18 ft. wide; chancel, 19 ft. long by 15 ft. wide; a short aisle opening by a single arch from the north side of the nave at its eastern end, 17 ft. 6 in. long by 13 ft. 6 in. wide, and communicating with the Evelyn Chapel, on the north side of the chancel, 19 ft. long by 14 ft. 6 in. wide. From this again a comparatively modern door opens into a second mortuary chapel recently turned into a parish room for vestry meetings. On the south side of the tower is an exceptionally roomy porch, rebuilt, but upon old foundations, and a modern vestry on the south side of the chancel. With all these alterations and additions, the plan of the simple tower, nave, and chancel of the early church remains.

The walls of the nave are of exceptional height (over 18 ft.), and they and the lower part of the tower are in all probability of pre-Conquest date; other indications of this period being the huge stones of which the quoin on the north-west of the nave and the piers of the tower arch are constructed. The plain, rude arch itself, of exceptional height and of flattened horseshoe outline, springing from a point about 6 in. within the line of the jambs, with rudely-chamfered imposts, returned at the ends, is quite consistent with this early date. Both arch and piers are square-edged. The comparative thinness of the east and west walls of the tower (2 ft. 4 in.), taken with their height, and the piers and arch being built of through stones—all tooled with the pick, instead of the axe or chisel—are other indications of the early date claimed, which may well be about 1050. The upper courses of stones in the piers are in Bargate

stone, all the rest being in firestone.[46] In the south wall of the tower, to the west of the later doorway, is a small early window, now blocked, unfortunately invisible on the outside owing to the ivy. The north and south walls of the tower are considerably thicker than the east and west walls—over 3 ft. on the north and 3 ft. on the south—and there is a set-back of a few inches at a height of about 8 ft. from the floor. As usual in early towers, there is no staircase. The upper windows are plain, square-headed openings, much hidden by the ivy, but perhaps of 13th-century date.

A peculiar and very puzzling feature is the blocked arch in the west wall of the tower, corresponding to that in the east wall. It is a few inches north of the centre of the tower, and while the piers have chamfered imposts similar to those of the eastern archway, the arch itself is obtusely pointed. This, however, may be due to its crown having been reset at the time when it was blocked up and the early 13th-century window inserted within it. The puzzle is into what this arch originally opened; and as all traces above ground of the building have vanished, the suggestion can only be offered tentatively that a *por-*

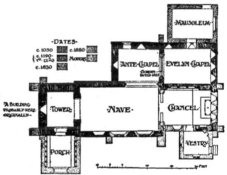

PLAN OF WOTTON CHURCH

ticus, such as has been found in this position at St. Peter's, Barton-on-Humber, and other pre-Conquest churches, may have stood here on the western side of the tower. A little excavation would throw light on the nature of this annexe.

The two buttresses at either disengaged angle of the tower appear to be ancient features modernized, excepting, possibly, that on the south face, which may be original, but here again the ivy prevents any examination. The north wall of the nave is blank for more than half its length, but a careful search might disclose an original window behind the plaster.

The south porch, which is built against the wall of the tower, is modern in its present form, but is upon the lines of an older structure. The well-known reference in Evelyn's *Diary* to his having been in-

[46] The masonry of the piers has something of the appearance of 'long and short' work, a well-known characteristic of pre-Conquest building. Some of the 'long' stones are over 2 ft. in height, the 'short' ones being less than half that dimension. There is a close resemblance between this arch and the early chancel arches, of horse-shoe shape (both pre-Conquest or late 11th century) at Elsted and Chithurst, Sussex.

structed in the rudiments of learning from the age of four years by one Frier by name in the porch of Wotton Church, applies in 'ali likelihood, not to the predecessor of this porch, but to the tower, which is spacious, and forms a sort of *porticus*, or lobby, to the nave.

In the south wall of the tower, within the porch, is a very remarkable doorway. It is wide, with a pointed head of somewhat distorted shape, and of two orders with a hood-moulding and shafts to the jambs. The hood-moulding has a member of pear-shaped section, and there is another such member in the outer order, flanked by quirked hollows. The inner order has a chamfer on the edge, but projecting from its angle, worked on the face of the chamfer are a series of minutely-carved little busts, each only about 3 in. in height, representing laymen and ecclesiastics, four on either side of the arch. The bottom one on each side is a modern restoration; the others appear to represent a pope (with the tall extinguisher-shaped head-dress of the period), a king, a priest, a nobleman, a queen (with crown and wimple), and a pilgrim. The voussoirs on which these are carved are of green firestone, and the alternate voussoirs are chalk, the sandstones alternating in the outer order. The impost moulding is carried round the chamfer, and forms the abacus of the shaft capital. This is circular with moulded upper part and necking, the intervening space being filled with vertical concave flutings, in this detail and the alternation of the arch stones recalling the south arcade of the nave at Aldingbourne Church, Sussex—work of the same date c. 1190–1210. The shafts have moulded annulets and bases.[66] The inner jambs and arch of the doorway appear to have belonged to an earlier opening, the arch being semicircular and a good deal worn, but it is possibly of the same date as the outer arch. A hideous cast-iron gate, apparently put here at the restoration of 1858, disfigures this curious and beautiful doorway, and every time it is opened cuts into its arch-stones.

Of the original chancel arch, destroyed in the same disastrous period to make way for the present wide and lofty arch, no very full information is attainable, but it would appear to have been a narrow, square-edged opening, perhaps not more than 6 ft. in width, and, flanking it on either side, tall pointed-arched altar recesses were found, of which the outline of half of the arches can still be seen. They were then blocked up so that the original depth, which was probably not more than a foot, can only be guessed.

The church seems to have been largely remodelled, the chancel practically rebuilt, and the aisle with its chancel or chapel added on the north side about 1210. The existing triplet of lancets in the east wall of the chancel is entirely modern, replacing a three-light probably of the 14th or 15th century and portions of the original group of three lancets that preceded this were found in the wall at the 1858 restoration. In the south wall of the chancel is a small sedile under a plain, pointed arm, and in the southern part of the east wall a simple piscina, both of c. 1210. Above the sedile is a two-light window, a pair of lancets, under one arch internally, worked

in firestone, and now opening into the modern vestry. These are shown in an old engraving of the church prior to 1858. Beyond them, to the west, is a single lancet, shown in the same engraving, beneath which, and divided from it by a sill transom, is a wider square or oblong opening rebated for a shutter, which is one of the best instances in Surrey of the low side window. Unfortunately the firestone of this and the lancet window over it was exchanged for Bath stone at the 'restoration,' at which time the low side window was brought to light and unblocked.[67] There is now no iron grate in the opening, and the present shutter is modern and fanciful in design.

The chancel of c. 1210 opened to the north chapel by a wide pointed arch, which, since about the beginning of the 17th century, has been blocked up and used as a screen for displaying the monuments of the Evelyn family within the chapel. This arch is of two orders, with narrow chamfers to arch and piers, and with an impost moulding of very peculiar section carried round the chamfers, the piers standing upon a moulded plinth similarly treated. In the restoration of 1858 the blank wall within the arch was filled with tracery in stone and marbles of very inappropriate character. The arch that opens from the nave into the aisle is of the same date and character, and its imposts are of the same section. There was a third arch of this period between the aisle and the eastern chapel of which the outlines are still traceable in the wall. Possibly it showed signs of failure or was inconveniently large, for at about the same time that the arch in the chancel was blocked up this was partly filled in, and a small arch, preserving something of the character of the original, but clumsily imitated, was inserted within it, the older imposts redressed, or copies of them, being used.

The chapel beyond this has two blocked lancets in its northern wall and three in the east, all of c. 1210, and the latter are particularly good and well-preserved examples of the period. They are rebated externally for a wooden frame, and have obtusely pointed external heads, with the internal splays radiating equally round the jambs and heads—a mark of early date. The central lancet is slightly higher than the others. In the western part of the north wall of this chapel is a small square recess, perhaps an aumbry, but it is simply chamfered without any rebate. There is above this, and beneath the sill of the lancets, a string-course of semicircular section, which is also carried along the walls of the aisle. Instead of being mitred where it jumps to a higher level here, the horizontal portion of the string-course is butted up against the vertical strip in a very unusual manner. In both the north and west walls of this aisle is a lancet of similar character to the foregoing, and, in the western part of the north wall, a nicely-proportioned doorway of two chamfered orders. All the masonry in this chapel and aisle is in the original firestone, delicately tooled with a broad chisel, and with extremely fine joints.

The nave, prior to 1858, had in its south wall a window of two lancets under one pointed internal arch, which still remains, towards the western end. Eastward of this was a three-light opening of 15th or

[66] For an illustration of this doorway see *V.C.H. Surr.* ii, 432. The resemblance to the work at Aldingbourne is so marked, even to the use of firestone and chalk in the alternate voussoirs, that the same masons must have been employed.

[67] See a contemporary woodcut and account of the church in the *Illus. Lond. News* for 1858. For a drawing of the low side window, see *Surr. Arch. Coll.* xiv, 96.

WOTTON CHURCH FROM THE SOUTH-EAST, C. 1845

WOTTON HOUSE

(From Brayley's 'History of Surrey')

16th-century date, with a square head and hood-moulding ; and beyond this to the east was another three-light window, transomed, under a segmental arch, and apparently of late 17th-century date. The two large windows of 13th-century design in the eastern part of the south wall replace those last described.

To the end of the 17th century belongs the brick vestry, or mortuary chapel of the Evelyn family, on the north of the chapel proper. It is of thin bricks, and has a circular window in its east gable, and a door between it and the chapel, a modern doorway, lately inserted, being pierced in its northern wall.

The roofs of the nave and chancel are modern and incongruous. The seating, pulpit, font, and all other fittings are also modern, with the sole exception of an interesting oak screen, with bannisters, and iron spikes or prickets for candles at the top, separating the chapel from the aisle. This bears the date 1632, and is almost the only bit of screenwork of its period remaining in Surrey. Within the chapel is preserved a font of white marble, with circular fluted basin on a tall baluster stem of about the same date, but possibly as old as the date of John Evelyn's birth in 1620. Cracklow records that 'in one of the south windows was formerly this fragment in black letter, "Orate pro anima Johannis de la Hale."'

John Evelyn's tomb in the north chapel is coffin-shaped and quite plain, about 3 ft. from the floor in the eastern part of the chapel, and his wife's, of the same plain design, is to the westward and close to the south wall. Their coffins are said to be inclosed in these tombs above ground. He died on 27 February in 1705-6, in his eighty-sixth year, and his wife Mary, daughter of Sir Richard Browne, ambassador of Charles I at Paris, on 9 February 1708-9. The inscriptions are upon the white marble covering slabs, and that on John Evelyn's runs thus :—' Here lies the body of John Evelyn, Esq., of this place . . . Living in an age of extraordinary events and revolutions, he learnt, as himself asserted, this truth, which pursuant to his intention is here declared : that all is vanity which is not honest, and that there is no solid wisdom but in real piety.' Evelyn's own desire was to be buried ' within the oval circle of the laurel grove planted by me at Wotton,' or, if this were not possible, in this chapel, where his ancestors lay : ' but by no means in the new vault lately Joining to it.'

Besides these there are several inscribed ledgers upon the floor with heraldic panels, one, in brass, near the east end, bearing the griffon and chief of Evelyn and the bars and martlets of Ailward with a fine piece of mantling. On the south wall, near its west end, is the beautiful monument of George Evelyn, the purchaser of Wotton, who died in 1603, aged seventy-seven. It is of alabaster, with panels of black slate or 'touch,' on which are the inscriptions, now hardly decipherable, and is divided into three compartments. In the centre, high up, under a circular arch, is the kneeling figure in armour of George Evelyn. Above the cornice is a medallion bearing his coat-of-arms, and a helm and mantling, and the crest of a griffon passant. On the rounded pediments of the side compartments (within which are skulls) are draped urns, and within the recesses below, under heavy entablatures and circular arches, are the figures of his two wives kneeling and facing towards him. Rose, the first, bore him ten sons and six daughters,

and Joan, the second, six sons and two daughters. Beneath each figure is an inscription panel, and below is a long panel on which the twenty-four children are carved in low relief, all kneeling ; a narrow inscription panel and some carved scrolls and consoles completing the design. The whole monument, an excellent example of the taste of its time, retains the original colouring and gilding.

Adjoining this, to the east, is the very fine monument (alabaster, coloured, with slate panels) of Richard Evelyn, fourth son of George Evelyn, high sheriff of Surrey and Sussex in 1634, and his wife Eleanor Stansfield, with their five children. Richard, the father of the celebrated diarist, died in 1640. Fat nude boys in contemplation support the upper pedimented entablature over the principal cornice, and in the centre at the summit is a draped female figure, blindfolded ; other ' virtues' in attitudes of grief flank the boys. Two large and beautiful draped angels, one holding a flaming heart and the other an open book, are drawing back the curtains to display the kneeling figures of Richard Evelyn and his wife. He is habited in the doublet, trunk-hose, and heavy cloak of his time, with his hair falling in curls over a deep collar. He kneels on a cushion with hands joined in prayer before a draped prayer-desk, facing his wife, whose flowing head-dress, falling in ' long folds behind, and gracefully-gathered gown, are charming examples of the lady's dress of the period. Their three sons and two daughters, in the panel below, kneel on cushions before another desk, the centre figure of the boys being the celebrated John. All the heraldry—which includes a very fine coat with mantling and a helm bearing the griffon crest in the panel at the top—and the smaller architectural ornaments, such as the consoles and scroll-work at the bottom, are models of delicate and spirited carving, and the figures of the angels and the husband and wife are among the best of that age. The original colouring is very perfect.

Opposite to these is the monument of Elizabeth Darcy, daughter of Richard Evelyn, who died in 1634. It is in the same taste as the foregoing, and probably by the same sculptor, who may well have been the celebrated Nicholas Stone. The bust of the lady, weeping, looks out from a curtained recess, and below her is the recumbent figure of her dead babe in its cot.

On the south side of the chancel is a tablet to Dr. Bohun, 1716, presented to the living in 1701 by John Evelyn. The inscription tells us that he left the sum of £20 for the poor of Wotton, and a similar sum for the decoration of the altar. He is described by Evelyn as ' a learned person, and excel·ent preacher.' Elsewhere in the chancel and nave are a number of later 18th and 19th-century monuments, and in the brick mortuary chapel of the Evelyns is a large white marble monument, by Westmacott, to the memory of Captain Evelyn, who died in 1829, bearing a striking inscription by Dr. Thomas Arnold of Rugby.

On the Jambs of the door in the north aisle are a few early marks, such as a small cross.

The registers of baptisms and burials date from 1596, and of marriages from 1603.

The communion plate is chiefly of 17th and 18th-century dates. The oldest piece is a silver paten of 1685, bearing the arms of Evelyn impaling Browne.

These were the arms of the celebrated John Evelyn and his wife. He was not then the owner of Wotton House, as he did not succeed his elder brother George till 1699. Another paten, inscribed : 'The gift of Lee Steere Steere, Esq'. To the Parish of Wootton,' is probably of the date 1724. A third dates from 1857. There is a cup of 1753, and a handsome silver flagon of 1706, tankard-shaped, with a high lid, and bearing the arms of Evelyn and Browne as on the paten of 1685, encircled by stiff feathering, with the inscription : 'The Gift of Mary Evelin, widdow of John Evelin Late of Wootton Esq.' It was presented in memory of her husband, who died in 1705.

The pierced cast-bronze plate, now used as an almsdish or collection-plate, is a beautiful but very unsuitable ornament of the church, being adorned with figures of nude gods and goddesses riding on dolphins and sea-monsters. It is a recent gift to the church.

The bells are three in number, the first inscribed :— ✠ ORA MENTE PIA PRO NOBIS VIRGO MARIA. The second has : ✠ ✠ ✠ O ✠ ✠ IOHANNES CHRISTI

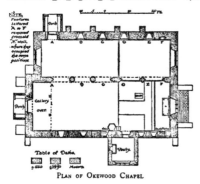

PLAN OF OKEWOOD CHAPEL

CARE MONARE PRO NOBIS ORARE. Both are of the latter part of the 14th century, and Mr. Stahlschmidt considers that they were cast by a Reading or London founder. The third bell, by Richard Eldridge, bears the inscription : OUR HOPE IS IN THE LORD 1602 RE.'

The ancient *CHAPEL of ST. JOHN THE BAPTIST, OKEWOOD*, is practically shut in by a small oak wood, except on the south side. It is perched upon the top of a hillock, round which winds a tiny stream, and is approached on one side by a rustic bridge. The churchyard is very picturesque, and contains many old trees, and some cypresses of more recent growth. There are a few wooden 'bed-heads' and a number of 18th-century headstones and table-tombs. The chapel itself is most picturesque, especially as viewed from the south-west or south-east, and is built of local sandstone rubble, plastered with the original coat of yellow-coloured mortar, the windows and other dressings in the old part being in hard chalk and firestone, the roofs covered with Horsham slabs, diminishing in size towards the ridge,

and the wooden bell-turret at the west end being of oak boarding, crowned by a squat spirelet of oak shingles. The modern parts are quite in keeping with the old.

The plan, as originally built in about 1220, was a simple parallelogram, of nave and chancel, under one roof, without structural division, 56 ft. 6 in. long by 20 ft. wide internally, the side walls being 2 ft. 6 in. and the east and west 3 ft. in thickness. There were, till the modern alterations, a door on the north and four lancet windows, the same number and a priest's door on the south, while in the west wall were a door and window of three lights, and in the east wall another three-light window of 15th-century date. In the western part of the south wall is a rudely-formed window of 18th-century date.[68] The original roof, with massive tie-beams and wall-plates, still remaining, is probably of the later period ; the popular tradition being that Edward de la Hale, whose brass remains in the chancel, in thankfulness for the escape of his son, who, while hunting in the forest, was attacked by a wild boar and nearly killed, founded the existing chapel on the site of the averted tragedy. This, however, is an incorrect version, as there is a record of the presentation of Sir Walter de Fancourt to the chapel in 1290, and there can be no doubt that the little chapel had then been standing for some seventy years. What is fairly certain is that Edward de la Hale endowed the chapel with lands, re-roofed and repaired it, and put the windows and a door-way in the end walls. In the early years of the 18th century, about 1709, the chapel is recorded to have fallen into a condition of dilapidation, when it was repaired, and a number of rough buttresses added (some of which still remain), by the care of two neighbouring yeomen, Mr. Goffe and Mr. Haynes, who sold three of the bells to help the work. John Evelyn is stated to have had a hand in an earlier reparation.[69] His representative, the late Mr. W. J. Evelyn, restored the building in 1867, and it was further restored and enlarged at his cost by the addition of a north aisle and a vestry in 1879. Although this extension was necessary, and was carried out with unusual respect for the ancient windows, door, &c., which were rebuilt in the same relative positions in the new wall, it is to be regretted for the unavoidable destruction of some very interesting early wall-paintings found on the walls and window-splays.

The south wall shows the original work, particularly in a pair of well-preserved lancet windows in the chancel. Beneath these on the inside, and apparently originally round the entire chapel, is a string-course of keel or pear-shape section. The windows have peculiar heads internally, i.e. straight-sided, or triangular, instead of arched, as in the chancel of Chipstead Church, Surrey, of slightly earlier date. They are rebated externally to receive the glass. There is a good piscina near to these with a credence shelf over, beneath a trefoiled head. It has two drains, dished in a square form. The opening is bordered by a bold bowtel moulding between two hollows, and is 1 ft. 8 in. wide, while that of the credence niche over it, which is simply chamfered on the edges, is

[68] Probably made in 1709. [69] In Evelyn's *Diary* is the entry, under 14 July 1701 : 'I subscrib'd towards re-building Oakwood Chapel, now after 200 years almost fallen down.'

162

only 1 ft. 5½ in. in width. There is also a small plain piscina of the first period in the south wall of the nave, beneath a lancet window and a square aumbry, of like date, originally in the north wall of the chancel, and now in the north aisle.

The ancient doorway and lancet windows of c. 1220, re-set in the rebuilt north wall, are good examples of their period. The north doorway, which retains its ancient oak door, and the priest's door on the south, now opening into the vestry, are plain to the point of rudeness. The western doorway, of c. 1430, within a modern porch, is wide and low, with a four-centred arch, which, with the jambs, is simply moulded. The door, of wide oak boards, with plain strap-hinges, is coeval, and the east and west windows, with cinquefoil-headed lights under square heads, also of the later date, are of the plainest character. In the flooring of the chancel and modern north chapel are a number of stone 'sets,' alternately white and yellow, apparently part of an ancient floor.

The arcade, of three arches in the nave and of two in the chancel, with a wide pier marking the junction, is, of course, modern, as are also the east and west windows of the aisle. The large raking buttresses on the south, east, and west sides date from the 18th century; and between the two on the east wall a sexton's shed has been inserted. There is a small modern gallery at the west end, and above this rises the bell-turret, also of modern date, which, with its silvery oak shingles, makes a very pleasing feature.

The main roof, as before mentioned, is ancient, that of the aisle being, of course, new; the seating and all other furniture being likewise modern.

In the last restoration the walls and window-splays were found to be covered with ancient paintings— figure subjects and scroll-work patterns of unusual excellence—chiefly of the early part of the 13th century, but some of 14th and 15th-century dates. As most of these occurred upon the north wall, they were unhappily destroyed when it was pulled down, but tracings were made which are said to be still in existence. On the north wall were two pairs of large figures, and on the east wall two single figures, two others, with ornamental patterns, being painted over the south door of the chancel. St. George and the dragon, on the south wall, near the west end, of 15th-century date, is mentioned among the destroyed subjects,[69a] and on the eastern part of the south wall of the chancel is still preserved the Visitation, the figures of St. Mary and St. Elizabeth being drawn in coarse red outline, about life-size, with red drapery. At the west end, on the north, west, and south walls, 'numerous small figures, parts of a large subject,' said to have been of 15th-century date, were uncovered, but were not preserved.

In the two lancets on the south side of the chancel are preserved some rare and beautiful fragments of ancient glass. That in the eastern of the two is of early 13th-century date, coeval with the window in which it stands. It is grisaille pattern work, the design being in large diamonds, almost the width of the opening, inclosed in white borders. Sprays of stiff-leaf foliage, with bunches of fruit, fill the diamond spaces, which are a deep, rich grey-green in places. In the western are fragments of two dates, including some very elegant natural leafage of early 14th-century character, and a flaming sun, a rose, and some flowered quarries of the 15th century.

A good late-17th-century chest is preserved in the church.

There are no monuments of special interest or antiquity with the exception of the interesting brass to Edward de la Hale, 1431, which lies in the chancel floor, and is now covered by a trap-door. The figure is unusually small, only 1 ft. 5½ in. in height, and has been very delicately engraved. It shows him in plate-armour, with his gauntleted hands joined in prayer, a helm of pointed oval shape, a collar of SS, roundels at the armpits, skirt of taces, and long-toed sollerets, with one rowelled spur. A long sword against his left side is slung from the right hip, and a dagger is suspended on the right side; his feet rest upon a lion. Above the head is a curved scroll bearing the words, IHŪ MERCY, and at the foot is an inscription plate now set upside down—

HIC IACET EDWARDUS DE LA HALE ARMIG' DE COM SURR'

QUI OBIIT VIII°. DIE MENSIS SEPTEMBR' ANNO DŇI MILLŌ.

CCCC°. XXXI°. CUIUS ANIME P'PICIETUR DEUS AMEN.

The registers date only from 1670.

Of the plate in use at the chapel, the oldest piece, a silver cup, with a disproportionately large and deep bowl, dates from 1794. It bears the usual star ornament, and on the other side are the arms of the Evelyns of Wotton, with the inscription: 'The Gift of Mr. and Mrs. Evelyn of Wotton to Oakwood Church, Surrey, 6 January 1878.' The other pieces are dated 1837 and 1844, with similar ornament, arms and inscription; there is also a brass almsdish.

In the library at Wotton House are preserved some other pieces, replaced by the foregoing, viz.: a plated cup, and a cup, paten, plate and flagon of pewter, the plate bearing the date 1692, which appears from the marks to be that of the other pewter pieces. There is little doubt that they were all provided at the time of the repair of the chapel in 1701.

The one bell is modern.

ADVOWSONS Wotton Church is mentioned in the Taxation of Pope Nicholas, 1291. William Latimer presented in 1304,[70] and again in 1305.[71] In 1306 divers malicious persons broke into the parson's house, and even carried their atrocities to the length of killing one of his servants.[72] From this time onwards the advowson appears to have followed the descent of the manor. Queen Philippa, to whom the custody of William Latimer had apparently been granted, presented in 1345:[73] the advowson was granted with the manor to Thomas Morstede in 1429,[74] belonged afterwards to the Owens,[75] and passed with the manor to the Evelyn family.

The presentation of the chapel of Okewood [77] went with that of Wotton.[78]

69a Traces of this have lately been found by Mrs. Shearme, wife of the vicar.
70 Winton Epis. Reg. Pontoise, fol. 41a.
71 Ibid. Woodlock, fol. 3b.
72 Cal. Pat. 1301–7, p. 479.
73 Ibid. 1345–8, p. 250.

74 Close, 7 Hen. VI, no. 7 d.
75 Feet of F. Hil. 14 Eliz.
76 Ibid. Surr. Trin. 21 Eliz.
77 Okewood is no doubt the correct spelling. A small stream which rises in Ockley and Wotton, and flows past the chapel, is called the Oke. Compare Okehampton on the Oke in Devonshire. It joins the Arun.
78 Close, 9 Hen. V, m. 17; 7 Hen. VI, m. 7.

Edward de la Hale endowed the chapel with lands which in 1547–8 were valued at 120s. 6d. a year. The chapel was suppressed in 1547,[79] and the lands, chapel and chapel-house granted to Henry Polstede and William More.[80] The materials of the chapel were valued for sale. A pension of 100s. was granted to the 'chantry priest,' Hamlet Slynn.[81] The inhabitants petitioned against the destruction of the chapel, and obtained its restoration to them for use as a church.[82] In 1560–1 a petition to the same effect was presented, reciting the former facts, and adding that the former priest was not then there. Elizabeth granted a perpetual payment of £3 6s. 8d. from the Exchequer to the priest officiating at Okewood, which is still received.[83]

In 1723 Sir John Evelyn, the patron, and Richard Miller, esq., gave £200 in aid of the endowment. In 1725 Dr. Godolphin, Dean of St. Paul's, and Sir William Perkins of Chertsey, gave £100 each, and in 1741 Mr. Offley, rector of Abinger, left two farms to trustees for the repair of the building, the surplus to go to the curate in charge, provided that he held two services every Sunday.[84] The conditions were not fulfilled in the latter part of the 18th century, when the services were very irregularly performed. A cottage near the chapel, called Chapel House, is the traditional home of the priest. But there was no later parsonage house till 1884, when the present vicarage was built by Lord Ashcombe. The ecclesiastical parish of Okewood was formed in 1853 of parts of the old parishes of Wotton, Abinger, and Ockley, upon the Sussex border. The chapel was in the outlying part of Wotton, which was united to Abinger civil parish in 1879.

CHARITIES

In 1717 William Glanville, nephew to John Evelyn, left by will a rent-charge on a farm near Pulborough to provide 40s. each for five poor boys who, on the anniversary of his death, should attend at his tombstone in Wotton churchyard and repeat from memory the Creed, the Lord's Prayer, and the Ten Commandments, read 1 Cor. xv., and write two verses of the same chapter. The two best performers receive in addition £10 each to apprentice them to some trade. Wotton boys under 16 years old have the first chance, but failing suitable claimants from Wotton, Shiere, Abinger, Cheam, Epsom, and Ashtead parishes, and the tithing of Westcote, Dorking have the next right of competing.

Smith's Charity is distributed as in other Surrey parishes.

---

[79] By Act of 1 Edw. VI, cap. 14.
[80] By Act of Pat. 2 Edw.VI, pt. i, m. 32.
[81] Exch. Anct. Misc. no. 82, m. 3, 2 Edw. VI.
[82] Aug. Decrees, Misc. Bks. vol. 105, fol. 231.
[83] Exch. Memo. R. East. 3 Elis. rot. 116.
[84] Papers preserved at Okewood Vicarage, formerly at Wotton House.

THE HUNDRED OF REIGATE

This hundred was known as the hundred of Cherchefelle at the time of the Domesday Survey and afterwards. The name Reigate occurs in 1199.[2] In 1086 Buckland, Chipstead, Gatton, Merstham, Nutfield, and .Reigate (Cherchefelle) were placed in this hundred, which also included Orde, which has been identified with the parish of Worth in Sussex;[3] possibly, however, it represents North and South Worth in Merstham (see under that parish). Charlwood was probably included in Merstham, of which manor it was a member (see account of Charlwood). The chief manor in Leigh (q.v.) appears, shortly after the Survey, as a member of Ewell, and was probably so regarded in 1086 also. Burstow and Horley (q.v.) were in Wimbledon and Banstead. Part of Betchworth appears in Wotton Hundred,[4] but was included in Reigate Hundred before 1279.[5]

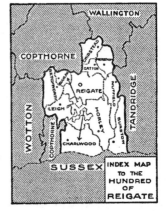

INDEX MAP TO THE HUNDRED OF REIGATE

The hundred seems to have always been a royal one.[6] A grant of the office of bailiff of this hundred with that of Tandridge was made in 1485 to Thomas Body.[7] To a lay subsidy levied in 1546 the hundreds of Tandridge and Reigate contributed together £420 10s. 8d., of which £235 5s. 8d. was raised in Reigate Hundred.[8] A lease of the farm of the two hundreds for twenty-one years was made in 1617 to Thomas Hunt.[9] A Parliamentary Survey [10] made in 1651 shows that the certainty money due from both hundreds annually amounted to £4 14s. 6d., whilst profits of court, amercements, and other perquisites were valued annually at £8 13s. 4d. The courts leet for both hundreds were kept at Under-

[1] The parish of Newdigate, which is partly in this hundred, is treated under Copthorne Hundred.
[2] V.C.H. Surr. i, 297, note 4.
[3] Assize R. 877, m. 56.
[7] Mat. for Hist. of Hen. VII (Rolls Ser.), i, 256.
[9] Pat. 15 Jas. I, pt. xxxi, no. 44.
[5] Ibid. i, 316a.   [4] Ibid. i, 321a.
[6] Ibid. 878, m. 34.
[8] Lay Subsidies, Surr. bdle. 185, no. 220.
[10] Parl. Surv. Surr. no. 3.

snowe,[11] and were held by the sheriff of the county, who received the profits and accounted for them to the public exchequer ; the lord might also call and keep a court leet in any of the townships or tithings in the hundreds which paid a common fine. The surveyors stated that they could not discover that a three-weekly court had ever been held for the hundreds, although they believed the lord thereof might hold 'one if he pleased.

BETCHWORTH

Becesworde (xi cent.), Beceswrde (xii cent.), Bechesworth (xiii cent.).

Betchworth is a parish midway between Dorking and Reigate, about 3 miles from each, 26 miles from London. It is bounded on the north by Mickleham, Headley, and Walton on the Hill, on the east by Buckland and Reigate, on the south by Leigh, on the west by Dorking. It measures 4 miles from north to south, and 2 miles from east to west, and contains 3,713 acres of land and 30 of water. It is traversed by the River Mole, which runs in a circuitous course from south-east to north-west ; and the Gadbrook, a tributary of the Mole, forms part of the southern boundary. It is, characteristically of all the parishes on the southern escarpment of the chalk, placed on the three soils, the northern part being on the summit and slope of the chalk downs, the central part with the old village and church being on the sands, and the southern part on the Wealden Clay. The chalk furnishes the chief industry. Chalkpits and limeworks have existed for time out of mind, and the very extensive works of the Dorking Grey Stone and Lime Company are in the parish, where lime is burnt and cement manufactured on a large scale. There are also brickyards in the parish, which is, however, mostly agricultural and residential. Gadbrook Common is to the south of the parish, and there is open down-land to the north, interspersed with plantations, Betchworth Clump, a group of beeches, standing up conspicuously on the crest of the chalk hill. The Duke's Grove is a fir plantation below Brockham Warren, planted by a Duke of Norfolk. The road from Dorking to Reigate passes through the parish. A line of yew trees on the side of the chalk has been taken to mark an ancient way leading from the ford of the Mole along the downs, but if such existed the continuity has been interrupted by the chalkpits and limeworks. A lane coming from the south, and leading to a formerly existing wooden bridge over the Mole in Wonham Park, is called Pray Lane.

The Redhill and Reigate branch of the South Eastern Railway cuts the parish from east to west, and there is a station at Betchworth, opened in 1849.

There seem to be no records of prehistoric remains in Betchworth. A palimpsest brass, with the arms of the Fitz Adrians, under-tenants of Brockham, on the reverse, was found in the church, and is now in the British Museum. Historically the manors have been transferred from one hundred to another. In Domesday part of Betchworth was held with Thorncroft and counted with that manor in Copthorne. This is probably West Betchworth, now in Dorking parish and Wotton Hundred. Another manor, East Betchworth, with a church, was counted in Wotton Hundred. The transference of East Betchworth to Reigate before 1279 [1] may be connected with its acquisition by the de Warennes, lords of Reigate. The tenants did villein service in Reigate, mowing a meadow called Friday's Mead.

The parish of Betchworth has become a favourite residential neighbourhood. Broome Park, south of the railway, is the property of Lady Louisa Fielding. The park comprises about 80 acres. It was formerly the residence of Sir Benjamin Brodie, the eminent doctor. The second baronet removed to Brockham Warren, formerly the seat of Mr. Mackley Brown. Broome Park was sold to General the Hon. Sir Percy R. B. Fielding after 1891. On the site was an old house, now absorbed in or superseded by later buildings. There was also a small house on another site called the Temple, now pulled down. A mantelpiece in the house is said to have been brought from it, and has the crest of Briscoe, a greyhound seizing a hare, upon it. The Old House, an 18th-century house on the east of the village street, is the seat of the Rev. Walter Earle. Captain Morris, of the Life Guards, well known in the latter part of the 18th and earlier 19th century as a writer of convivial songs, lived in Betchworth.

The inclosure award for Betchworth Common fields and waste is dated 30 April 1815, pursuant to the Act 52 Geo. III, cap. 60. The fields which lie north of the church and west of the village are still in fact open fields.

The inclosure award of Shellwood Manor [2] included waste in Betchworth parish, that is about Gadbrook Common. A conveyance of Wonham Manor, 1689, naming the Upper and Lower Great Field of 25 acres, and the Great South Field, 11 acres, seems to show open fields also in that manor, but when they were inclosed is unknown.

There was a parish school which was enlarged in 1850,[3] but existed before that date, supported partly by endowments from a Mr. Reynolds and the Duke of Norfolk. The present provided school was built in 1871 and enlarged in 1885.

Brockham Green is a district formed from Betchworth, and made into an ecclesiastical parish in 1848. The village, clustered round the green, about 1½ miles

---

[11] Undersnowe was a place between Godstone, Oxted, and Tandridge, where three ways meet, near the south-east corner of Rooksnest Park, in Tandridge Hundred.

[1] Assize R. 877, m. 56.

[2] 12 Jan. 1854. See Blue Bk. Incl. Awards.

[3] Return at Farnham.

west of Betchworth village, is picturesque and flourishing. The church, built on land given by Mr. Hope of Deepdene, is of 13th-century style, of stone, with a central tower and spire.

Brockham Warren is the residence of Sir Benjamin Brodie, bart. ; Brockham Park of Mr. Robert Gordon, J.P. ; Brockham Court of Mrs. Davidson ; Brockham House of Mr. Henry Foley. Brockham Court was built by a former Duke of Norfolk on the site of the old manor-house,[4] having been separated from the manor. Brockham Bridge over the Mole is repaired by the county to the value of two-thirds, and the remaining third by the district council, Brockham being a contributory area. Brockham Home and Industrial School was established in 1859 by Mrs. Way of Wonham Manor, Betchworth, for orphan girls from eleven to sixteen, who are trained for domestic service and afforded a home later when out of place. An Infants' Home was added by Miss Way in 1872. The two are under the management of the same committee of ladies.

There is a Particular Baptist Chapel in Brockham. A school was built in 1830, and rebuilt in 1840.[6] After the passing of the Education Act of 1870 a School Board was formed for Betchworth, and the present provided school at Brockham was built in 1879 and enlarged in 1901.

At the time of the Domesday Survey, MANORS Becesworde, which is probably EAST BETCHWORTH, was stated to be in the hundred of Wotton ;[6] 'Richard de Tonbridge, lord of Clare, himself held 'Becesworde' in demesne.[7] It was assessed for 2 hides and valued at £8. In King Edward's time it had been held by Cola, when it was assessed at 6 hides and worth £9.[8] It subsequently passed to the de Warennes, probably before 1199, as Earl Hamelin de Warenne and his wife held the church in East Betchworth (q.v.) before that date. It is possible that the manor had passed from Richard de Tonbridge to William de Warenne when the latter was created first Earl of Surrey by William II in 1088. It is afterwards described as being, with the castle and town of Reigate and manor of Dorking, 'parcel of the county of Surrey,'[9] and Dorking at least (q.v.) probably formed part of the original endowment made at the creation of the earldom of Surrey.[10] Betchworth was held with Reigate by succeeding Earls of Warenne and Surrey.[11] The surrender of those manors to the king in 1316 by John de Warenne, Earl of Surrey, their re-grant to the earl with remainder to his illegitimate sons, and their final inheritance by Richard Earl of Arundel, nephew and legitimate heir of john de Warenne, is fully dealt with under Reigate (q.v.). John de Warenne died in 1347,[12] but it was not until the death in 1361 of his widow, the Dowager Countess of Surrey, that the Earl of Arundel succeeded to his uncle's earldom.[13]

A settlement between the sons of Richard was made in 1366,[14] and on his death his eldest son Richard

succeeded to the manor and was seised of it at the time of his disgrace and death in 1397, when his estates became forfeit to the Crown.[16] His eldest son Thomas, to whom his father's title and estates were restored in 1400,[16] died without issue in 1415, and his lands were divided among his three sisters and co-heirs, Elizabeth Duchess of Norfolk, then wife of Sir Gerrard Osflete or Ufflete, kt., joan de Beauchamp, Lady Abergavenny, and Margaret wife of Sir Roland Leynthale, kt.[17] The manor of East Betchworth appears to have been assigned to his second sister, Joan wife of William Lord Abergavenny. She died in 1434, and was succeeded by her son Richard, whose daughter and heir Elizabeth married Edward Nevill, son of Ralph, Earl of Westmorland.[18] Nevill received the lands of his wife's inheritance, and afterwards took the title of Lord Abergavenny.[19] He died seised of the manor of East Betchworth in 1466, leaving his son George as heir.[20] The manor remained in possession of this family throughout the next century. In the reign of Henry VIII, when a muster was made of able men who, with weapons and harness, were meet to serve the king, it was stated that Betchworth with Brockham could contribute thirty-seven men.[21] In 1629 Henry, ninth Lord Abergavenny,[22] conveyed the manor for £1,080 to Sir Ralph Freeman,[23] Master of Requests. Freeman also held other offices under the Crown, being in 1629 Auditor of the Imprests and afterwards Master-Worker of the Mint.[24] He married Catherine Bret.[25] Of his two sons, George died in 1678, and Ralph held the manor in 1684.[26] The latter's sons Francis and George held courts in 1707 and 1715 respectively, but died without issue. Elizabeth daughter and eventually sole heir to Ralph Freeman carried the manor to the family of Bouverie

NEVILL, Lord Abergavenny. *Gules a saltire argent with a rose gules thereon.*

FREEMAN. *Azure three lozenges argent.*

BOUVERIE. *Party fessewise or and argent an eagle sable with two heads and on his breast a scutcheon gules with a bend vair.*

by her marriage with Christopher, younger son of Sir Edward Des Bouverie.[27] Christopher Bouverie, after-

[4] Local information from Mr. J. R. Corbett.
[5] Return at Farnham.
[6] Vide supra.
[7] V.C.H. Surr. i, 321.
[8] Ibid. i, 321 and note.
[9] Cal. Close, 1348–9, p. 316.
[10] V.C.H. Surr. i, 298, note 2.
[11] Red Bk. of Exch. (Rolls Ser.), 561 ; Cal. Pat. 1301–7, p. 95 ; 1307–13, p. 531.

[12] Chan. Inq. p.m. 21 Edw. III (1st nos.), no. 58.
[13] G.E.C. Peerage, &c.; see under Surrey.
[14] Feet of F.Div.Co. 40 Edw. III, no.17.
[15] Chan. Inq. p.m. 21 Ric. II, no. 137, m. 11; Dict. Nat. Biog.
[16] Dict. Nat. Biog.
[17] Chan. Inq. p.m. 4 Hen. V, no. 54.
[18] G.E.C. Peerage.
[19] Ibid.

[20] Chan. Inq. p.m. 16 Edw. IV, no. 65.
[21] L. and P. Hen. VIII, xiv (1), 294.
[22] Chan. Inq. p.m. (Ser. 2), cccxcii, 112 ; cccxcix, 157.
[23] Close, 5 Chas. I, pt. xxvi, m. 12.
[24] Dict.Nat.Biog.; Harl.Soc.Publ. xv,295.
[25] Ibid. ; Feet of F. Surr. Mich. 1652.
[26] Harl. Soc. Publ. xv, 295 ; Feet of F. Surr. East. 36 Chas. II.
[27] Wotton, English Bar, iv, 150.

wards knighted by Queen Anne, died in 1732–3 ; his eldest son Freeman died unmarried in 1734, when his second son John inherited the property.[28] John died in 1750 while 'on his travels in Turkey.'[29] His sisters, Anne wife of John Hervey and Elizabeth Bouverie,[30] held the manor in 1752,[31] when according to Manning the manor was limited to the Herveys. Christopher, last surviving son of John Hervey and Anne, died without issue in 1786,[32] having devised the manor to his aunt, Elizabeth Bouverie, who in turn devised the manor and mansion-house at Betchworth to a distant cousin, the Hon. William Henry Bouverie,[33] who belonged to the elder branch of this family, and whose son Charles succeeded to the manor in 1806.[34] It was still in the latter's possession in 1816,[35] but was sold in the following year, according to Brayley, to the Rt. Hon. Henry Goulburn,[36] in whose family it has since remained, Major Henry Goulburn, grandson of the above-mentioned Henry, being present lord of the manor.[37]

John de Warenne, Earl of Surrey, seems to have had free warren in his demesne lands at Betchworth,[38] as three times during the early 14th century he made complaint of the trespasses committed in his free warren there.[39] The Domesday Survey records the existence of a mill at Betchworth which was valued at 10s.[40] In 1287–8 William de Aguillon granted to Ralph de Hengham and his heirs a mill which was to be held for the annual rent of one rose.[41] No further trace of this mill is apparent ; it is possible that it was situated on the land called Aglonds (vide Aglonds More), of which mention occurs in the 15th century, and to which de Aguillon possibly gave his name.

The manor-house of East Betchworth was built by Sir Ralph Freeman in the reign of Charles I. It was called Betchworth Place, and therefore probably superseded an older manor-house on another site. It is a fine 17th-century mansion of red brick, and contains some antiquities brought from Italy by Mr. John Hervey in the 18th century.

In 1409 a conveyance was made by Stephen Hervey and his wife Agnes to William Asshurst, junior, of a messuage, 20 acres of land, and 20d. rent in East Betchworth.[42] This probably represents the reputed manor of LE MORE, of which John son of William Asshurst died seised, together with land called Aglonds, in 1507, his father having held the lands before him.[43] In 1499 Le More, afterwards known as Aglonds More, or More Place, had been settled on Agnes wife of John Asshurst, the reversion being to his brother and heir William.[44] Agnes apparently married John Skinner, senior, as her second husband, as in 1512 the

manor was stated to belong to John Skinner and Agnes for the life of Agnes,[45] and seems to have been conveyed from the trustees of Agnes's marriage settlement to Sir Henry Wyatt and Sir John Leigh and John Skinner for 200 marks of silver.[46] The next record of Aglonds More shows that in 1547 John Woodman of Colley died seised of the manor, which he held of the Earl of Arundel as of the manor of Colley.[47] He left as heir his son Richard, who married Julia Huntley of Woodmansterne,[48] and was in turn succeeded by his son and grandson, both called William.[49] The grandson married Winifred Balam, and was succeeded by his second son Richard.[50] In 1650 a warrant was issued for the Council of State and Admiralty Committee to apprehend Richard Woodman, described as of More Place in the parish of Betchworth, on the grounds that he and John White, a weaver, had harboured a stranger from Germany, supposed to be a Papist, who was also to be arrested and brought with the other two before the Council. Search was to be made for arms and ammunition, and all books and papers were to be seized.[51] In 1706–7 Richard Woodman, probably the son of the man referred to above, was holding the manor,[52] and in 1739 a conveyance was made to the trustees of John Bouverie, then a minor,[53] who also held the manor of East Betchworth (q.v.). Bouverie's sister Elizabeth held both manors in 1752,[54] after her brother's death, and Aglonds More has since that time descended with the manor of East Betchworth,[55] Major Goulburn being now lord of the manor. More Place has been occupied for fifty years by Mr. J. R. Corbett, well known as a breeder of Jersey cattle.

The house was one of the old timber-framed houses with very massive oak beams, probably dating from the time of Henry VI. On the north side was a lofty hall, broken up as far back as the 17th century into rooms. The tie-beams of the hall roof are still visible in the attics. At the same date probably the house had a southern side built on to it. The timbers in the ceilings of this are Spanish chestnut. There is a good Jacobean mantelpiece. The octagonal turret to the south was added more recently.

At the beginning of the 13th century BROCKHAM was in the possession of the de Warenne family, as between the years 1219 and 1225 William de Warenne enfeoffed Thomas son of Ralph Niger of the land of Brockham, to be held for the rent of 60s. sterling, together with a virgate of land in East Betchworth, lately in the tenure of Adam son of John le Brabazun, for which a rent of 40d. or a pair of gloves furred with grey was to be given yearly.[56] The manor was held of the heirs of the Earl of Warenne and Surrey as late as 1609 for the same annual payment

[28] Wotton, English Bar, iv, 150 ; Gent. Mag. 1733, p. 46 ; Lond. Mag. 1734, p. 566.
[29] Gent. Mag. 1750, p. 525.
[30] Wotton, English Bar, iv, 150.
[31] Feet of F. Div. Co. Mich. 26 Geo. II.
[32] Manning and Bray, Hist. of Surr. i, 206.
[33] P.C.C. 635 Walpole (will of Eliz. Bouverie).
[34] Manning and Bray, Hist. of Surr. ii, 206.
[35] Feet of F. Surr. Mich. 57 Geo. III.
[36] E. W. Brayley, Topog. Hist of Surr. iv, 250.
[37] Burke, Landed Gentry.
[38] Cal. Pat. 1301–7, p. 95 ; 1307–13, p. 531 ; 1321–4, p. 448.

[39] Ibid.
[40] V.C.H. Surr. i, 321.
[41] Feet of F. Surr. Trin. 15 Edw. I.
[42] Ibid. East. 10 Hen. IV.
[43] Chan. Inq. p.m. (Ser. 2), xx, 24.
[44] Ibid.
[45] Feet of F. Surr. Trin. 3 Hen. VIII ; East. 4 Hen. VIII.
[46] Feet of F. Surr. East. 4 Hen. VIII (See Asshurst in Mickleham).
[47] Chan. Inq. p.m. (Ser. 2), lxxxvii, 75.
[48] Ibid. ; Surr. Arch. Coll. vii, 330 ; Harl. Soc. Publ. xliii, 108.
[49] Harl. Soc. Publ. xliii, 108.
[50] Ibid.
[51] Cal. S.P. Dom. 1650, p. 530. Thomas Woodman, of Betchworth, gentleman, was

a suspected person in 1655 ; B.M. Add. MS. 34013.
[52] Recov. R. East. 5 Anne, rot. 159.
[53] Close, 13 Geo. II, pt. xix, no. 16. The deed states that the conveyance was from Anthony Wibard ; he was probably a trustee for Woodman, as according to Manning the transfer in 1739 was from Woodman himself, and there is moreover no evidence of a sale from Woodman to Wibard between the years 1707 and 1739.
[54] Feet of F. Div. Co. Mich. 26 Geo. II.
[55] Manning and Bray, Hist. of Surr. ii, 209; Feet of F. Surr. Mich. 57 Geo. III.
[56] Manning and Bray, Hist. of Surr. ii, 209 (quoting from deed in private hands).

of 60s.[57] It passed from Thomas Niger to Giles Niger or le Neyr.[58] Apparently Thomas Niger left a widow, Agnes, who married John son of Adrian, as in 1242–3 John Adrian and Agnes his wife were holding a third of the manor as Agnes's dower.[59] At the same date William de Fakeham, who had evidently been enfeoffed by Giles le Neyr, granted the other two-thirds to John Adrian, a right of dower being however reserved to Julia wife of Giles le Neyr.[60] Three years afterwards Giles le Neyr quitclaimed all right in the manor to Adrian.[61] Confirmation of this transfer was made to Adrian and his heirs by John son of William de Warenne in 1254.[62] John

ADRIAN. *Argent two bars wavy gules and a chief checky or and azure.*   FROWYK. *Azure a cheveron between three leopards' heads or.*

grandson of John Adrian seems to have married Margaret daughter of Henry Frowyk,[63] and in 1348 a settlement was made by which the manor, failing other heirs, was to revert to Henry Frowyk and his heirs.[64] John Adrian held the manor until after 1356, in which year he received licence from the bishop to celebrate mass in his house at Brockham.[65] He apparently died without issue, as by 1377 the manor had come into the possession of Henry de Frowyk, who shortly before his death in 1378 made a settlement by which the reversion was granted to Henry son of Thomas de Frowyk in fee.[66] This second Henry was evidently the grandson of the first, whose son Thomas predeceased his father.[67] Henry the grandson died in 1386, leaving two sons, the elder of whom, Thomas, continued the senior branch of the family, holding Oldford in Middlesex, land in Hertfordshire, and then or later South Mimms, while from the younger descended the Frowyks of Gunnersbury.[68] The manor of Brockham remained in the elder branch of the family, as the will of the elder son Thomas, proved in 1448, states that the manors of Oldford and Brockham were to remain in the hands of feoffees for a year, his debts being paid from the issues therefrom, after which Brockham was to

remain to his wife Elizabeth for her life, reverting to his son Henry and his issue.[69] Henry was succeeded by his son Thomas, and the latter by his son Henry, who married Ann Knolles and died in 1527, leaving as sole heir his daughter Elizabeth, wife of John Coningsby, who was holding it with her husband in 1530.[70] In 1547 Elizabeth settled an annuity of £27 on Mary, widow of her brother Thomas, who had predeceased his father.[71] Elizabeth Coningsby married William Dodd as her second husband, but at her death was succeeded in the lordship of Brockham by Henry Coningsby, her son by her first husband, who was knighted in 1585.[72] Sir Henry died in 1590 and was succeeded by his eldest son Ralph,[73] who held until 1606,[74] in which year he joined with his brothers Philip and Henry in conveying the manor to Thomas Wight,[75] who died seised of it in 1609.[76] His son, Gabriel Wight, succeeded him,[77] and the manor remained in this family, passing from father to son, until the end of the 18th century.[78] In 1793 Henry Wight, the last surviving son of William Wight, died without issue.[79] He devised his Surrey estate to his sister, Lady Elizabeth Harington, for her life. After her death one-half was to remain successively to Elizabeth White, a kinswoman, and to John Wight of Braboeuf (Artington), q.v., for their lives, remainder to right heirs of testator. The other half was devised to William Martin and his heirs or, failing them, was to descend with the first half. The whereabouts of Martin being unknown, advertisement for him was to be made in the *London Gazette*.[80] This was done[81] after the death, in 1794, of Elizabeth Harington, who had married the Rev. John Chaundler as her second husband[82] and had held Brockham after her brother's death.[83] John Wight inherited a moiety in 1794, and, according to Manning, the other moiety was claimed shortly afterwards by the two daughters of William Martin, Elizabeth and Sarah wife of William Hibbet, and they, with John Wight, held the manor in 1808.[84] Elizabeth appears to have given up her share soon after, as in 1809 William Hibbet and Sarah were in full possession of a moiety of the manor, the other moiety being still held by John Wight.[85] The entire manor afterwards became the property by purchase of Henry T. Hope of Deepdene, who held it in 1844.[86] In 1878,

HOPE OF DEEPDENE. *Azure a cheveron or between three bezants.*

---

[57] Chan. Inq. p.m. (Ser. 2), ccix, 189.

[58] Feet of F. Surr. 27 Hen. III, no. 11.

[59] Ibid.   [60] Ibid.

[61] Ibid. 30 Hen. III, no. 32.

[62] Add. Chart. 24551, 24552.

[63] Manning and Bray, *Hist. of Surr.* ii, 209.

[64] Feet of F. Surr. Mich. 22 Edw. III.

[65] Egerton MS. 2033, fol. 47; Manning and Bray, *Hist. of Surr.* ii, 209.

[66] Ibid. quoting from private deeds.

[67] F. C. Cass, 'South Mimms,' *Lond. and Midd. Arch. Soc.* 70; Harl. MS. 1546, fol. 57b.

[68] F. C. Cass. 'South Mimms,' *Lond. and Midd. Arch. Soc.* 70; Harl. MS. 1546, fol. 57b; Manning and Bray, *Hist. of Surr.* ii, 209; Chauncey, *Hist. of Herts.*

[69] Will of Thomas Frowyk, P.C.C. Bk. Rowse, 13.

[70] F. C. Cass, 'South Mimms,' *Lond. and Midd. Arch. Soc.* 70; Recov. R. Hil. 22 Hen. VIII; P.C.C. Porch, 28 (will of H. Frowyk, 1527). Manning says that by 1515 the manor of Brockham had passed to the younger branch of the family, that is, to the Frowyks of Gunnersbury, and that Elizabeth Coningsby was the heiress of this branch. This, however, from the relationships mentioned in the wills, etc. referred to above, would seem to be impossible.

[71] Feet of F. Surr. Hil. 1 Edw. VI; Manning and Bray, *Hist. of Surr.* ii, 209.

[72] Berry, *Herts. Gen.* 163; Harl. Soc. Publ. xxii, 45; Shaw, *Knights of Engl.* ii, 83.

[73] Chan. Inq. p.m. (Ser. 2), ccxxiii, 51.

[74] Feet of F. Surr. Hil. 39 Eliz.; Mich. 44 & 45 Eliz.

[75] Ibid. East. 4 Jas. I.

[76] Chan. Inq. p.m. (Ser. 2.), ccix, 189

[77] Ibid.

[78] *Visit. of Surr.* (Harl. Soc. xliii), 81 Feet of F. Surr. Trin. 14 Chas. II; Manning and Bray, *Hist. of Surr.* ii, 211; Recov. R. East. 6 Geo. III; Baker, *Hist. of Northants,* ii, 23.

[79] Baker, loc. cit.

[80] P.C.C. Dodwell, 534.

[81] Lond. Gaz. 1795, 1796.

[82] See note 80.

[83] Feet of F. Surr. Trin. 34 Geo. III.

[84] Manning and Bray, *Hist. of Surr.* ii, 211.

[85] Feet of F. Surr. Trin. 49 Geo. III; Recov. R. Trin. 49 Geo. III, rot. 305, 17.

[86] E. W. Brayley, *Hist. of Surr.* iv, 251.

after his decease, it was in the hands of his trustees,[87] and is now held by his grandson Lord Henry Francis Pelham-Clinton-Hope.

In 1199 William de Wonham received a grant from Walter de Lingfield of half a virgate of land, afterwards included in the manor of *WON-HAM* in Betchworth, to hold for the annual rent of 4s.[88] The name of Wonham also occurs as that of witness to a deed early in the 13th century.[89] It is probable that this family therefore held land in Betchworth for several centuries. Manning states that a William Wonham held manorial courts in 1533 and in 1552.[90] In 1622 a William Wonham died seised of the ' manor, capital messuage and farm of Wonham,' and was succeeded by his grandson,[91] who held the manor until 1646, in which year he conveyed it to Andrew Cade.[92] The deed of conveyance records the name of the manor as ' Wonham *alias* the borough of Wonham,' by which title it is afterwards known. In 1678 the manor was held by Andrew Cade and Mary his wife.[93] He was, according to Manning, the cousin and heir of the first Andrew. The second Andrew Cade seems to have left a daughter and heir Anne, who married Henry Royall, and later, with his wife, quitclaimed the manor in 1687 from themselves and the heirs of Anne to John Coldham,[94] who was presumably a trustee.[95]

It would seem that Henry Royall and Anne left three daughters and co-heirs, of whom Ann wife of Darby Daniell and Rebecca wife of Daniel Cox conveyed their shares to Richard Hutchinson in 1690 and 1694.[96] in trust. Richard Broomhall, second husband of Rebecca Cox, held a court in 1696.

In 1711 Richard Hutchinson joined with Rebecca Broomhall, widow of Daniel Cox, and Frances Evelyn, the third heiress, widow, in a sale to William Arnold.[97] The manor passed soon after to John Taylor, who held his first court in 1721, from whom it descended to his son, also called John.[98] In 1751 it was conveyed by the latter's widow Dorothy, then wife of John Rapley, to John Luxford, the sale including ' the capital messuage or tenement wherein Rebecca Broomhall formerly dwelt' and appurtenances, including the names of the Hop Ground Moors and Pight Lake.[99] Luxford by will (proved 13 June 1775) devised his houses and lands in East Betchworth and elsewhere to his sister Jane and her husband Abraham Langham, in trust for his nieces and heirs Elizabeth Langham and Ann, Mary, Harriet, and Elizabeth Luxford, with remainder to his nephew James Luxford.[100] In 1788 all these parties conveyed to the Hon. Charles Marsham.[101] Brayley states that Mr. Marsham, afterwards Earl of Romney, sold the estate in 1793 to John Stables, who lived at More Place, and from whom it was purchased in 1804 by J. H. Upton, Viscount Templetown.[102]

In 1840 Wonham Manor was bought by Mr. Albert Way, F.S.A., who married Emmeline daughter of Lord Stanley of Alderley. Their only daughter,

Alithea, married her cousin Mr. Albert Way, who died in 1884, leaving a son of the same name. The Hon. Mrs. Way, who survived till 1906, was lady of the manor. It is still (1910) in the hands of her trustees for sale.[103] The manor-house is old, but much modernized.

A water-mill called Wonham's is mentioned at the beginning of the 14th century. In 1328 Edward III granted a confirmation in mortmain to the priory of Reigate of divers grants, including that of the ' water-mill at Wonham with pond, water-courses, &c., in East Betchworth, formerly in the tenure of William de London and Roger de London, and of 26s. 8d. yearly rent there granted them by Roger son of Roger de London of Reygate.'[104] At the surrender of Reigate Priory Wonham's water-mill and lands there, which had been demised to farm to William Hevyr, were valued at 53s. 4d.[105] The water-mill does not appear to have passed to the owner of the manor of Wonham at once,[106] but was included among the appurtenances by 1678[107] and has since passed with the manor.

CHURCH
The church of *ST. MICHAEL* is set among charming surroundings, the large and pretty churchyard being bordered on the south and west by lofty elms and other trees. It is approached from the north by a village street of picturesque old cottages, some of which are half-timbered. There are a good many ancient head-stones among the monuments, and besides other notabilities lies buried here Captain Morris, who died in 1838, aged 93, famous in his day as a song-writer, and particularly as the author of the well-known lines in which ' the sweet shady side of Pall Mall ' is preferred to all the charms of the country-side, including the oaks, beeches, and chestnuts of Betchworth. There is a modern lych-gate on the north. The church is built of chalk rubble, quarried from the neighbouring hills, with dressings of clunch and firestone, which have stood very well on the north side, but have weathered badly, especially in the modern work, on the south and west. Bath stone has been used for most of the modern dressings. The roofs are still covered entirely with the ancient Horsham stone slabs.

As now standing the building consists of nave, 60 ft. 3 in. by 21 ft. 9 in., with north and south aisles, 7 ft. 8 in. and 8 ft. 8 in. wide respectively, and south and west porches, a chancel 33 ft. 4 in. by 17 ft. 6 in., with a large south chapel co-terminous, 13 ft. 4 in. at its widest, a tower between the chapel and the south aisle of the nave about 14 ft. 6 in. square, and modern vestry and transept on the north of nave and chancel. This plan, in which there are many puzzling irregularities, was brought to its present form in the restoration of about 1850, prior to which the tower was central between the nave and chancel. It was then removed bodily to its present position, much to the bewilderment of students of archaeology, who without knowledge of what was done must find the plan a very difficult one to decipher.

[87] E. W. Brayley, *Hist. of Surr.* iv, 251 (ed. E. Walford, 1878).
[88] Feet of F. Surr. file 1, no. 36, 10 Ric. I.
[88] Add. Chart. 24586.
[90] Manning and Bray, *Hist. of Surr.* ii, 212.
[91] Chan. Inq. p.m. (Ser. 2), cccxciv, 48.
[92] Feet of F. Surr. Mich. 22 Chas. I.
[93] Ibid. East. 30 Chas. II.
[94] Ibid. Hil. 2 & 3 Jas. II.
[95] *Vide infra.*
[96] Feet of F. Surr. Mich. 2 Will. and Mary ; Mich. 6 Will. and Mary.
[97] Ibid. 10 Anne.
[98] Close, 25 Geo. II, pt. iii, m. 20.
[99] Ibid.
[100] P.C.C. Alexander, 237.
[101] Feet of F. Surr. Mich. 28 Geo. III.
[102] Brayley, *Hist. of Surr.* iv, 251.
[103] Local information.
[104] *Cal. Pat.* 1327–30, p. 326.
[105] *Valor Eccl.* (Rec. Com.), ii, 63 ; Dugdale, *Mon. Angl.* vi, 519.
[106] Feet of F. Surr. Mich. 22 Chas. I.
[107] Ibid. East. 30 Chas. II.

From the fact that a church is mentioned in Domesday and that a capital or base of a pre-Conquest shaft is to be seen built into a modern window,[108] it is practically certain that there was a Saxon church, and that of stone. It probably had a fairly large nave and a short, narrow chancel, which, as in the case of Godalming, was, after the Conquest, transformed into a low tower, with a new chancel built out to the eastward. One of the arches of this tower, with two square orders and cushion capitals having chamfered abaci, was rebuilt when the tower was shifted, and now opens from the tower into the south aisle of the nave. Its character suggests the date of c. 1080. Early in the 13th century the church was greatly enlarged. The nave received first a south aisle of c. 1200, and perhaps slightly later one on the north side. A clearstory was added on both sides, with irregular circular windows,[109] the chancel was rebuilt or extended eastwards, an aisle or Lady chapel being added on the south, all within the first quarter of the 13th century, to which date the three lancet windows in the north wall of the chancel and the arches opening to the south chapel belong. They are pointed, of two orders, the outer square-edged, and the inner chamfered, on octagonal and circular capitals and heavy round columns with shallow octagonal responds. The present chancel arch is of this date, but would appear to have been rebuilt higher and wider at the restoration of 1850; the arches immediately adjoining it in the nave were made at this latter date, to give access to the transept and the rebuilt tower. Piers and arches are of three recessed chamfered orders, the moulded imposts, of a characteristic section, which take the place of capitals, being returned round the chamfers, as at Wotton and elsewhere. The chancel has a slight inclination in the axis of its plan towards the north, and its walls diverge as they go eastward to the extent of 1 ft. The present east window of geometrical tracery is modern, and replaces one of 15th-century date shown in Cracklow's view; and similarly the east window of the Lady chapel, also of 15th-century date, was in 1850 exchanged for one with net tracery. This change, though ill-judged, may have been in the nature of a restoration, as one at least of the three windows in the south wall of the chapel retains ancient tracery of this character (c. 1320). Its companions, right and left, do not appear in Cracklow's view, but may have been blocked up at that date, 1824.

The nave arcades are of about 1200, with circular and octagonal piers and responds, having moulded capitals and bases of varying sections, supporting pointed arches of two orders with narrow chamfers. The aisles are narrow in proportion to the wide nave, and were perhaps even narrower originally, as all the windows in their walls are of later date. Probably they were at first mere passages, 6 ft. or so in width, and were widened to the extent of about 2 ft. (as a break in the west wall of the south aisle seems to indicate) early in the 14th century, when the Lady chapel windows were inserted. The newer windows, which no doubt replaced early lancets, were not all made at the same time : those in the south wall of the south aisle are two-light tre-

foil-headed openings, with a cusped vesica-shaped quatrefoil over, under a plain hood-moulding (c. 1320) ; while the single-light windows in the west wall of both aisles, and two similar openings in the north wall of the north aisle, having cusped ogee heads, are slightly later, c. 1330, and a remarkably beautiful two-light window in the eastern part of the same wall, having net tracery and a scroll section hood moulding, is of the same date. Another two-light opening to the westward between the two single-light windows, also an admirable example of its period, dates from about 1390. It has cinquefoiled heads under a pointed segmental arch, and the terminals of the hood-moulding are carved into heads, which appear to represent cowled canons—perhaps in reference to the connexion of the church with the priory of St. Mary Overy, Southwark.

The western porch is modern, and contains nothing worthy of remark : that on the south side is also modern, replacing one of brick. Most of the features of the tower, externally and internally, date only from its rebuilding, in a new position, in 1850; but, owing to the poor quality of the stone used, the tower has already assumed a deceptive appearance of antiquity. Its belfry lights in Cracklow's view are apparently of 15th-century date, while the present are of early 13th-century design.

The roofs appear to be modern throughout, but the timber ceiling over the tower, with heavily-moulded beams, is of 15th-century date, and appears to have been shifted with the tower. In the chancel are the remains of a piscina : there must have been three or four more in pre-Reformation times. A holy-water stoup of 14th-century character is to be seen near the south doorway. The pulpit of marbles and glass mosaic, needless to say, is new, so also are the font, the chancel stalls, the lectern and stone reredos sculptured with the Last Supper. Into the modern seating of the nave are worked some panels carved with the linen-fold pattern, of early 16th-century date. In the vestry is preserved a remarkable chest, hewn out of an oak trunk of great size, roughly squared, and bound round with seven massive iron straps. It bears a general resemblance to the similarly fashioned chests at Newdigate and Burstow in this part of Surrey ; and while there is no reason why they should not be of very early date, yet they may equally be quite late.

There are no old wall-paintings or glass, but nearly all the windows are filled with modern stained glass of varying merit. The chancel has recently been panelled in oak.

On the north wall of the chancel has been placed the brass, originally in the floor, to Thomas Wardysworth, vicar, dated 1533. In style it closely resembles the palimpsest fragment of a priest's brass at Cobham, Surrey.[110] The figure is in Mass vestments, and holds a chalice, in which is the Host, inscribed in Roman letters IHC. The inscription, which is in black letter, reads—

HIC IACET DÑS WILLMUS WARDYSWORTH QUONDAM
VICARIUS HUI' ECCLĪE QUI OBIIT V DIE JANUARII ANNO
DÑI MCCCCCXXXIII. CUIUS ANIMÆ P'PICIETUR DEUS. AMEN

108 Illustrated in *V.C.H. Surr.* ii. It consists of a series of square-edged bands or fillets, one above another.

109 Resembling the early 13th-century clearstory lights in the neighbouring churches of Merstham and Chipstead. Cf. also Rustington, Lancing, and Ifield, Sussex.

110 Dated c. 1510 by Mr. Mill Stephenson, *Surr. Arch. Coll.* xv, 34, but perhaps twenty years later.

In the part of the Lady chapel now used as a vestry are three small brass plates, also mural, one of which bears the inscription—

HIC JACET THOMAS MORSTED ET ALEANORA UX' EI'. Q'OR' A'I'AB' P'PICIETUR DE'. AME'.

. The others are to the memory of Mrs. Bridgett Browne, 1627, and to Peter Gade, 1679· In the other part of the chapel (south wall) is a monument to Gabriel Wight, of Brockham, 1621 ; another to Stephen Harvey, 1618 ; and in the nave is a tablet to Sir Benjamin Collins Brodie, bart., the famous surgeon, 1862.

The six bells were recast in 1876, before which date there seem to have been five, one bearing the inscription, SIT NOMEN DOMINI BENEDICTUM ; another ROBERTUS MOT ME FECIT 1590 ; and the others of 1667, 1721, and 1750.

Among the plate is a cup of 1639 and another of about the same date with an inscription round the upper part : 'This belongeth to the Parish of St. Bridgett,' i.e. St. Bride, in the City of London. There are two silver flagons of 1639 and pieces of 1715 and 1776, besides a few pieces of modern plate, given by the same donor who presented the cup formerly belonging to St. Bride's, Fleet Street.

The registers date from 1558, with certain gaps and damaged portions. They contain an explanatory note to the effect that about this time (in the early 18th century) the register was damaged owing to the vicar's greyhound bitch rearing a litter in the parish chest.

The Domesday Survey records the *ADVOWSON* existence of a church at Betchworth (which must be East Betchworth), held at that time by Richard de Tonbridge, lord of Clare.[111] It afterwards passed to the family of de Warenne. Earl Hamelin and his wife Isabella, daughter and heir of the third Earl of Warenne, gave the church of East Betchworth to the priory of St. Mary Overy, Southwark, before 1199 ;[112] confirmation of this and . divers other grants to the priory was made during the 14th and 15th centuries.[113]

A vicarage was ordained before 1377, as in that year an inquiry concerning the vicar of Betchworth was held by an official of the Bishop of Winchester. The inquiry was directed at the instance of the parishioners themselves, who alleged that the vicar did not proceed in orders, wasted the goods of the vicarage, suffered the house of residence to go to ruin, kept a mistress, revealed the secrets of the confessional, and left the church unserved.[114] The vicar seems to have resigned in consequence, as in the June following the inquiry, which was held in February, William Spencer was

PRIORY OF ST. MARY OVERY. *Argent a cross indented gules with a lozenge gules in the quarter.*

instituted vicar, owing to the resignation of John de Westone.[115]

The convent of St. Mary Overy retained possession of the advowson until the Dissolution.[116]

In 1545 Henry VIII made a grant in fee to Thomas Burnell and William his son of the rectory, late in the tenure of Sir Nicholas Carew, knight, deceased, and of the advowson, to be held of the king by the service of one fortieth part of a knight's fee, and for the year.'y rent of 19s.[117] The king in the following year granted this yearly rent to Roland Hill and his heirs.[118] Both these grants, however, appear to have been annulled, or else surrender was made to the Crown, as Edward VI, in the first year of his reign, granted both rectory and church to William Franklin, Dean of the King's Free Chapel of St. George the Martyr in Windsor Castle, and the chapter of the same and their successors.[119]

DEAN AND CANONS OF ST. GEORGE, WINDSOR. *Argent a cross gules.*

The presentation to the church has remained with the Dean and Chapter of Windsor until the present day.[120]

In 1634 or 1635, when a certain Robert Tourney was vicar, the rectory being demised to one Daniel Leare, the parishioners of Betchworth petitioned for the augmentation of the vicarage out of the impropriate parsonage ; the vicarage, formerly worth £30, having been decreased to £10 by the augmentation of the parsonage.[121] On 10 May 1637, when the case was heard, the Dean and Chapter of Windsor offered an annual sum of £5 for the augmentation of the vicarage, a like offer being made by Leare, and it was therefore ordered that the said £10 should be duly assured to the vicar and his successors.[122]

The Parliamentary Report of 1658 says that the Poor Knights of Windsor were patrons.[123] This is either a confusion, or the patronage of the abolished chapter had been conveyed to them.

In 1715 Hugh Griffiths, vicar, rebuilt the vicarage.

Smith's Charity is distributed as in *CHARITIES* other Surrey parishes.

In 1660 Mr. Richard Arnold by will left the rent of land at Steyning in Sussex to provide clothing for ten poor people not given to drunkenness. This land has been sold.

In 1662 Mr. Andrew Cade left £100 by will to provide bread for the poor.

In 1662 Mr. Richard Arnold's daughter Mary gave 30s. a year charged on land at Medley Bottom in Betchworth to provide bread.

In 1706 Mr. Richard Hutton left the rent of a cottage to provide bread—distributed on Good Friday. In 1725 the return to Bishop Willis's visitation calls the cottage john Parkhurst's house.

In 1725 Mrs. Margaret Fenwicke of Betchworth Castle left £200 to buy lands, to provide for appren-

111 *V.C.H. Surr.* i, 321.
112 Ibid. note ; Pat. 3 Edw. IV, pt. iii, m. 21.
113 *Cal. Pat.* 1388–92, p. 111 ; 1461–7, p. 307.
114 *Wykeham's Reg.* (Hants Rec. Soc.), ii, 266.
115 Ibid. i, 86.

116 Egerton MSS. 2031–4 ; *Wykeham's Reg.* (Hants Rec. Soc.), i, 86, 101, 132, 240 ; *Valor Eccl.* (Rec. Com.), ii, 62.
117 L. and P. *Hen. VIII*, xx (1), 620 ; Pat. 36 Hen. VIII, pt. xx. From the terms of the grant it seems probable that Carew had a lease of the rectory only ; he never held the advowson.

118 Pat. 38 Hen. VIII, pt. ix, m. 39.
119 Pat. 1 Edw. VI, pt. v, m. 27.
120 Inst. Bks. (P.R.O.), 1614–1835 ; *Clergy Lists.*
121 *Cal. S.P. Dom.* 1634–5, p. 422 ; 1636–7, p. 241.
122 Ibid. 1637, p. 95.
123 Lambeth Registers, vol. 21, no. 5.

ticing children, and for marrying maidservants born in Betchworth and living seven years in the same employment, the surplus, If any, to go to the poor. A house and certain parcels of the Common Fields of Letherhead were bought for the purpose. The house was allowed to fall into ruins, and the land was sold at the inclosure of the Letherhead Fields.

In 1777 Mr. John Turner left money and a house in Nassau Street, Westminster, to relieve the poor not in receipt of parish relief, to provide clothing, and to put children to school. These benefactions are recorded in the church, and in spite of waste and neglect produce about £180 a year.

The vicar, Hugh Griffiths, who rebuilt the vicarage, reported to Bishop Willis in 1725 that Mr. Cade had left £20 as a stock to be employed in setting the poor to work, but that it was all spent in 1669. Also Mr. Arnold left £40 to buy 2 acres of land next the vicarage, the profits to go to the vicarage ; but this had never yet been done, nor the money received. But this is perhaps the £40 which Mr. Griffiths records in the registers that he obtained from the parish to help in rebuilding the vicarage, done otherwise at his own expense. He records the rebuilding in the parish register, with the subscription *Laus soli Deo—Not to ye Parish.*

BUCKLAND

Bocland (*Testa de Nevill*), Bukelonde (xiii cent.) ; Bokelond (xiv cent.).

Buckland is a small parish and village 2 miles west of Reigate. It is bounded on the north by Walton-on-the-Hill, on the east and south-east by Reigate, on the west and south-west by Betchworth. It contains 1,866 acres of land and 10 of water. It covers the three soils, as usual, the northern boundary being on the summit of the chalk hills, and the parish extending across the sand on to the Wealden Clay. The village and church here, as elsewhere, are situated on the sand. It measures about 1½ miles from east to west, and barely 2 miles from north to south. A small detached portion inclosed by Reigate was added to that parish under the Divided Parishes Act of 1882. Part of the south of Buckland has been added to the ecclesiastical parish of Sidlow Bridge, formed in 1862. The parish is purely rural.

Buckland is traversed by the road from Dorking to Reigate and by the Redhill and Reading branch of the South Eastern Railway. No prehistoric antiquities are recorded.

The rector in 1725 returned to Bishop Willis that there was no chapel, no lecturer, no curate, no Papist, no Nonconformists, no school. The history of the parish seems as uneventful as might be expected, before and since. A succeeding rector, the Rev. Oliph Leigh Spencer (1783–96), was author of a life of Archbishop Chicheley, founder of All Souls College, Oxford, the patrons of the living, and supported his brother by arguments in a rather famous lawsuit when the latter, Mr. Woolley Leigh Spencer, claimed a fellowship at All Souls as being of founder's kin. The claim was successful, 1762. Mr. Oliph Leigh Spencer was himself a fellow.[1]

There is no record of inclosure.

Buckland Court, the seat of Major F. M. Beaumont, is near the church. Mr. F. H. Beaumont, J.P., lord of the manor, resides at The Cottage. Shagbrook

was the seat of the late Sir George Thomas Livesey ; Broom Perrow of Mr. J. H. Bovill.

A national school was built in 1822.[2] It was rebuilt in 1862, and enlarged in 1886. It is subsidized from Johnson's Charity, given in 1857, which produces £11 5s. a year. The National Society are trustees.

At the time of the Domesday Survey *MANORS BUCKLAND*, assessed for 2 hides, was held by 'John' of Richard de Tonbridge,[3] lord of Clare.[3] The manor remained part of the honour of Clare,[4] and was held of the Earls of Gloucester,[5] descendants of Richard de Tonbridge.

In the first half of the 13th century Buckland was held as one knight's fee by Alicia de Dammartin.[6] She was the daughter of Odo de Dammartin and Margery his wife ; before 1231 she was married to John de Wanton,[7] who thus became possessed of Buckland. In 1293 the manor and church of Buckland were conveyed to Guy Ferre, Junior, by John Wauton,[8] a settlement being made in 1302 on Guy and his heirs, with remainder in default of issue to Sir John Claron and his issue, afterwards to the right heirs of Guy.[9] Guy Ferre[10] was in the suite of Eleanor Countess of Bar, daughter of Edward I, whom he constantly accompanied abroad ;[11] after her death he probably continued in the service of her daughter Joan.[12] He died childless in 1322–3, and his lands at Buckland therefore passed to Claron.[13] Eleanor widow of Guy Ferre retained a third of the manor as dower,[14] as she presented to the church which belonged to the manor after 1346.[15] Sir John Claron died in or before the year 1342,[16] but it is not apparent who his heirs were. The next record of the manor shows that two-thirds of it were held by John de Warenne, Earl of Surrey, at his death in 1347, and that he held in the right of his wife Joan, daughter of Eleanor Countess of Bar.[17]

John de Warenne, Earl of Surrey, died without male issue, his next heir being Richard, Earl of

[1] *Notes of Opinions and Judgements of the late Sir John Eardley Wilmot, Ch. Justice of the Common Pleas,* by John Wilmot (1802).
[2] Returns at Farnham.
[3] *V.C.H. Surr.* i, 316.
[4] *Testa de Nevill* (Rec. Com.), 219, 220b.
[5] Chan. Inq. p.m. 16 Edw. II, no. 66 ; 21 Edw. III (1st nos.), no. 58 ; 9 Hen. V, no. 51.

[6] *Testa de Nevill* (Rec. Com.), 219, 220b.
[7] Feet of F. Div. Co. Mich. 15 & 16 Hen. III, no. 89.
[8] Feet of F. Surr. Trin. 21 Edw. I.
[9] Ibid. Mich. 30 Edw. I.
[10] *Vide* Witley, Artington, and Cattishull.
[11] *Cal. Pat.* 1292–1301, pp. 66, 67, 69.

[12] Ibid. 1313–18, p. 470.
[13] Chan. Inq. p.m. 16 Edw. II, no. 66 ; *Cal. Close,* 1323–7, p. 16.
[14] *Vide infra.*
[15] Egerton MS. 2033, fol. 5b.
[16] *Cal. Close,* 1341–3, p. 541.
[17] Chan. Inq. p.m. 21 Edw. III (1st nos.), no. 58 ; *Cal. Close,* 1346–9, pp. 315, 316. She must have acquired the reversion.

Arundel, son of his sister Alice and Edmund, late Earl of Arundel. Richard accordingly inherited the manor,[18] a settlement being made in 1349 on his younger son, Sir John de Arundel, in tail male.[19] Sir John perished at sea in 1379, and was succeeded by his son John,[20] who received during his minority an annual grant of 40 marks for his maintenance from Richard Earl of Arundel, 'being the amount of his farm for the manor of Bokeland, Surrey, in the king's hands by reason of the said minority.'[21] Eleanor widow of the first Sir John married Reginald Lord Cobham as her second husband,[22] and he at his death in 1402–3 was seised of a third of the manor of Buckland in the right of his wife.[23] The major part of the manor continued to be held by the second Sir John de Arundel, and at his death passed to his son John, who became twelfth Earl of Arundel.[24] The latter died in 1421.[25] His widow Eleanor married Sir Richard Poynings, who was assessed for the manor in 1428 ;[26] after his death she married Sir Walter Hungerford, and died in 1455, when William, her second son by the twelfth earl, inherited the manor.[27] He had become fifteenth Earl of Arundel in 1438,[28] and the manor appears to have remained in the hands of succeeding earls until 1564. Henry Earl of Arundel settled the manor on his daughter Jane, who had married John Lord Lumley.[29] In 1567 Lord Lumley and Jane conveyed the property to Herbert Pelham and Roger Dallender.[30]

FITZ ALAN, Earl of Arundel. *Gules a lion or.*

Pelham quitclaimed his right to Dallender in 1569,[31] and the latter held until his death in 1599,[32] when his son William inherited his lands, a settlement having been made in 1589 on the marriage of William with Margaret Leigh.[33] William died in 1618, and his son Ralph succeeded him.[34] Ralph Dallender in 1654 joined with several other members of the family in a sale to George Browne,[35] who married a daughter of Sir Ambrose Browne of Betchworth. Ambrose and John Browne, son of George, held the manor successively.[36] On the death without issue of John Browne in 1736 his estates passed to the family of his sister Philippa, who had married William Jordan of Gatwick ; their son Thomas Jordan died unmarried in 1750, when his sisters Elizabeth wife of William Beaumont and Philippa wife of John Sharp became his heirs.[37] The manor of Buckland became the property of the former, Philippa and John Sharpe having released their claim to her in 1753.[38] From that time until the

present the manor has been held by descendants of William and Elizabeth Beaumont, remaining usually in the younger branch of the family.[39] Mr. F. H. Beaumont is at present lord of the manor.

BROWNE. *Sable three lions passant bendwise between two double cotises argent.*

BEAUMONT. *Azure powdered with fleurs de lis argent and a lion argent.*

A mill in Buckland is recorded in the Domesday Survey, when its value was stated to be 6s.[40] It was probably identical with the mill in Hartswood, parcel of the manor of Buckland, of which later record is found (*vide infra*). In 1268 John de Wauton and his heirs received a grant of free warren in his demesne lands in Buckland and elsewhere.[41] Guy Ferre received a grant of free warren in his demesne lands of Buckland in 1291,[42] nearly two years before the formal grant of the manor was made him by John de Wanton. In 1350 a complaint was made by the Earl of Arundel that his free chases and warrens at Buckland had been entered by trespassers who hunted and took away the deer, hares, rabbits, pheasants, and partridges.[43] In 1390 it was found that the manor was charged with a payment of 2d. yearly, then due to Richard Chamberlayn, who was custodian of the warren there.[44]

HARTSWOOD, lying in the ecclesiastical parish of Sidlow Bridge, originally formed part of the manor of Buckland. The name occurs early in the 13th century, when John de Wauton, lord of the manor of Buckland, granted to Robert de Hartswood, for his homage and service, a field called Rudene lying between the mill of 'Herteswode' and a field called Pegesull.[45] There is no further mention of this mill, which apparently fell into disuse. In 1379 John de Arundel, lord of Buckland, received licence to inclose his wood of 'Herteswode,' and to impark 360 acres of land adjacent thereto.[46] An extent of the manor of Buckland made in 1380 includes 100 acres of land there among the appurtenances.[47] Hartswood remained part of the manor until 1569, when it seems to have been conveyed by Roger Dallender, as lands in the parish of Buckland, including 300 acres of wood, to John Skinner[48] ; the latter died in 1583–4 seised of the manor, park, and demesnes of

[18] Chan. Inq. p.m. 21 Edw. III (1st nos.), no. 58 ; *Cal. Pat.* 1348–50, p. 517.
[19] Chan. Inq. p.m. 50 Edw. III (1st nos.), no. 52b.
[20] Ibid. 3 Ric. II, no. 1.
[21] *Cal. Pat.* 1377–81, p. 564.
[22] Dugdale, *Baronage,* ii, 316–25.
[23] Chan. Inq. p.m. 4 Hen. IV, no. 34.
[24] Ibid. 14 Ric. II, no. 1.
[25] Ibid. 9 Hen. V, no. 51.
[26] Ibid. ; *Feud. Aids,* v, 121.
[27] Chan. Inq. p.m. 33 Hen. VI, no. 35 ; Feet of F. Div. Co. East. 26 Hen. VI.
[28] G.E.C. *Complete Peerage.*
[29] Ibid. ; Feet of F. Surr. Hil. 6 Eliz.

[30] Feet of F. Surr. East. 9 Eliz. ; Pat. 9 Eliz. pt. ix, m. 34.
[31] Pat. 11 Eliz. pt. vii, m. 30.
[32] Chan. Inq. p.m. (Ser. 2), cclvii, 48.
[33] Ibid. ; Pat. 31 Eliz. pt. xiv. ; Feet of F. Surr. Mich. 31 & 32 Eliz.
[34] Chan. Inq. p.m. (Ser. 2), ccclxxii, 142 ; Recov. R. Trin. 19 Jas. I.
[35] Feet of F. Surr. East. 1652 ; Hil. 1654 ; Mich. 1654.
[36] Berry, *Surr. Gen.* 29, 82 ; Feet of F. Surr. Mich. 1 Jas. II ; Recov. R. Mich. 1 Jas. II, rot. 7.
[37] Berry, *Surr. Gen.* 29, 82.
[38] Feet of F. Surr. Mich. 27 Geo. II.

[39] Recov. R. East. 12 Geo. III, rot. 260 ; Manning and Bray, *Hist. of Surr.* ii, 218 ; Burke, *Peerage and Baronetage* and *Landed Gentry.*
[40] *V.C.H. Surr.* i, 316.
[41] *Cal. Chart.* 1257–1300, p. 88.
[42] Chart. R. 19 Edw. I, 43, m. 10 ; *Cal. Chart.* 1257–1300, p. 389.
[43] *Cal. Pat.* 1348–50, p. 517.
[44] Inq. p.m. 14 Ric. II, no. 1.
[45] Add. Chart. 24586.
[46] *Cal. Pat.* 1377–81, p. 380.
[47] Chan. Inq. p.m. 14 Ric. II, file 62, no. 1.
[48] Feet of F. Surr. Hil. 11 Eliz.

Hartswood in Buckland.[49] In 1589 William Poyntz, brother-in-law and heir of Skinner, was lord of the manor;[50] it afterwards passed to Richard Elyot of Albury, nephew, and in default of male heirs to Poyntz's son John, heir of the same John Skinner,[51] being the son of his sister Elizabeth. Richard died in 1608.[52] The manor was afterwards held by his brother or uncle Thomas Elyot,[53] and in 1620 was, with the park, conveyed by him and other members of this family to Sir William Garway.[54] In 1632 it was held by Lionel Wright, who sold it in that year to John Hatt and Elizabeth his wife, receiving in the following year a ninety-nine-years' lease of the capital messuage and mansion house belonging to the manor.[55] By 1653 it was in the possession of the family of Moore.[56] Susan daughter and heir of Thomas Moore, who died about 1676, married Robert Bristow.[57] After her husband's death, she and trustees conveyed the manor in 1718 to Sir William Scawen,[58] in whose family it remained until 1781, when James Scawen sold it to Sir Merrick Burrell.[59] Sir Peter Burrell, great-nephew of Sir Merrick, inherited the latter's estates in 1787,[60] and sold the manor shortly afterwards to William Clutton.[61] The property is still in this family. Mr. Ralph William Clutton is present owner.

SCAWEN. *Argent a chevron gules between three griffons' heads razed sable, those in chief facing each other.*

CHURCH The church of OUR LADY consists of a chancel 22 ft. 2 in. by 19 ft. 6 in., small north transept or vestry 11 ft. by 9 ft., nave 44 ft. 6 in. by 21 ft. 8 in., and a south porch.

The church was rebuilt in 1860, and has no architectural details earlier than this date, and all the fittings are modern. The walls are built of ironstone rubble, and the window tracery is of 14th-century style. The bells are hung in a shingled wood turret with a spire, rising above the roof at the west end of the nave, and supported on wooden posts from the floor.

In two of the windows is some old stained glass. The south-west window of the nave has a figure of St. Peter holding the two keys; the head and keys, although old, have the appearance of being later than the rest of the figure; the canopy work (with the name below) is generally modern, but has some old foliage in red and blue set in it; the head of the canopy is apparently old. The other window at the north-east of the nave has the figure of St. Paul; on this again the head and sword are less worn than the rest of the figure. There are six bells, all by Warner; the three largest were recast in 1900 from three by William Eldridge dated 1681; the third is dated 1900, the second 1860, and the treble 1892.

The plate was stolen in 1850, but a set was given to replace it by the then rector, Dr. Hulse, consisting of a cup and cover, a paten, a flagon, and two plates. There are also two silver candlesticks of 1691, a paten of 1894, two cruets of 1893, and a flagon of 1907. There is a note in the register mentioning the complete restoration of the church and rebuilding of the chancel in 1859–60, at a cost of £2,253.

The registers date from 1560, but are an 18th-century transcript. The first volume contains two books of unequal size in parchment bound together; the first part has baptisms, marriages, and burials to 1667 with one baptism of 1675, and the second baptisms and burials to 1776 and marriages to 1753. The second book contains marriages from 1754 to 1812, and the third baptisms and burials from 1777 to 1812.

ADVOWSON The Domesday Survey records the existence of a church at Buckland.[62] From its foundation it belonged to the manor of Buckland, and was held with it as 'the church of the manor,' until 1567,[63] the patronage being in the hands of the lord of the manor.[64] When Lord Lumley conveyed the manor to Pelham and Dallender in 1567, however, he retained the advowson of the church, and was possessed of it at his death in 1609.[65] His heir was Henry Lloyd, son of his sister Barbara.[66] In 1628 Henry Lloyd *alias* Fludd held the advowson.[67] Lloyd sold it to All Souls College, Oxford, for £335, on 18 February 1639.[68] But in 1658 the Parliamentary Commissioners found that George Browne, lord of the manor, held the advowson.[69] Probably the royalist college had been deprived during the Civil War. In 1661 Lloyd had resumed possession, presumably as a step in the restoration of the advowson to the college, which held it in 1674,[70] and still holds.

ALL SOULS COLLEGE, OXFORD. *Argent a chevron between three cinquefoils gules.*

CHARITIES In 1704 Laurence Denton left 30s. a year rent from a meadow since called Poor's Land, for relief of poor not receiving parish relief. It is now worth £6 6s. a year. In 1733 Mr. John Brown, lord of the manor, left three acres for a similar purpose. This is now represented by a sum in consols. A Mr. William Cooke left £65 4s. 4d. consols.

The above are all consolidated with Smith's charity, and applied for general purposes of medical relief, nursing, provident clubs, or temporary loans.

Smith's charity is distributed as in other Surrey parishes.

[49] Chan. Inq. p.m. (Ser. 2), cciv, 123.
[50] Ibid.; Feet of F. Surr. Trin. 31 Eliz.
[51] Chan. Inq. p.m. (Ser. 2), cciv, 123; cccxi, 116. [53] Ibid.
[54] Recov. R. East. 11 Jas. I; Harl. MS. 1561, fol. 23*b*, 50.
[55] Feet of F. Surr. Mich. 15 Jas. I; East. 18 Jas. I; Recov. R. East. 18 Jas. I, rot. 48. [55] Com. Pleas D. Enr. East. 11 Chas. I, m. 1.
[56] Feet of F. Surr. Hil. 1653.
[57] Surr. Arch. Coll. xi, 180; Manning and Bray, Hist. of Surr. ii, 221.

[58] Feet of F. Surr. Mich. 5 Geo. I; Recov. R. Hil. 5 Geo. I, rot. 87.
[59] Close, 21 Geo. III, pt. iii, m. 9.
[60] Ibid. 30 Geo. III, pt. i, m. 14.
[61] Manning and Bray, Hist. of Surr. ii, 221.
[62] Pope Nich. Tax. (Rec. Com.), 238; Abbrev. Plac. (Rec. Com.), 219; Feet of F. Surr. Trin. 21 Edw. I; Chan. Inq. p.m. 14 Ric. II, no. 1; Feud. Aids, v, 114; Cal. Close, 1323–7, p. 16; Chan. Inq. p.m. 50 Edw. III (1st nos.), no. 52b.
[64] See above refs.; Wykeham's Reg.

(Hants Rec. Soc.), i, 183, 202, 209, 211, 227; Egerton MSS. 2031, fol. 53; 2032, fol. 132b; 2033, fol. 5b, 76; 2034, fol. 34, 72b, 123b, 137b, 161; Cal. Pat. 1391–6, p. 52.
[65] Feet of F. Div. Co. East. 5 Jas. I; Chan. Inq. p.m.(Ser. 2), cccxi,109. [66] Ibid.
[67] Feet of F. Surr. East. 4 Chas. I; Recov. R. East. 4 Chas. I.
[68] All Souls College Books per Rev. A. H. Johnson, Fellow of All Souls.
[69] Church Survey, Lambeth, vol. 21, fol. 5. [70] Inst. Bks. P.R.O.

BURSTOW

Burstowe and Burghstowe (xiv cent.) ; Byrstowe (xv cent.) ; Bristowe (xvii cent.).

Burstow is a country parish on the Sussex border. The church is 7 miles south-east of Reigate, and about 2 miles south-south-east of Horley Junction. It is bounded on the north and east by Blechingley, on the east by Horne, on the south by the county of Sussex, on the west by Horley, a detached part of Horne, and Nutfield. It measures about 6 miles from north to south, and is about 1 mile broad at the north and 2 miles at the southern part. It contains 4,750 acres. The soil is the Wealden Clay over most of the parish, but in the south-east where the ground rises to Copthorne Common it is Hastings Sand. Across the northern part of the parish a ridge of higher land runs from east to west, formed by a bed of Paludina Limestone. It yields stone, usually called Sussex marble, which is susceptible of polish ; but, as is generally the case in the Surrey examples of this stone, it is too friable for architectural work. The parish as a whole is a typical Wealden parish, formerly thickly wooded with oak, which furnished the massive framework and rafters of the farms ; in the absence of building stone the houses were probably all oak-framed. The upper waters of the Mole drain Burstow, but on the eastern side the streams and ditches communicate with the upper Medway. No main road or railway is actually in the parish, for the main Brighton line and road pass to the west of it, the South Eastern line to the north of it. It is purely agricultural, with a few brickfields. Copthorne Common is now inclosed in Burstow, though part of the common across the Sussex border in Worth parish is still open. Part of it is called Effingham Park, from an Effingham on the county border, but this has no connexion with the village of Effingham in Surrey. There is some open ground at Outwood Common. The village is not at all compact ; there are a few houses near the church, others are about Copthorne or Smallfield, or are scattered farms. The parish was formerly one of the seats of the iron industry in the Weald, which flourished about Copthorne,[1] though no forge or furnace of importance in the 16th-century lists can be located exactly in Burstow parish. The name Blacksmith's Farm probably refers to a forge, and ornamental iron fire-dogs, fire-backs, &c., were till recently common in the farms and cottages.

There seem to be no records of prehistoric antiquities, though it is unlikely that such should not be found about the higher and drier soil of Copthorne ; but this part of Surrey has been much less thoroughly explored, archaeologically, than the west and north.

The antiquarian feature of the parish is the comparatively large number of moated houses. Many of the older houses possessed this characteristic feature, the abundance of water, and the retentive nature of the clay soil, made moats the natural defence ; the

moats remain in whole or in part around several of them. Burstow Lodge is moated. On the west of Smallfield Place there appear to be the remains of a moat. Rede Hall is situated in the middle of a very large moated inclosure ; the old house has been lately rebuilt. Court Lodge Farm, just north of Burstow Church, shows traces of an extensive moat, and south of the church is a moated inclosure in which there is now no house, but which is probably the site of the old manor-house of Burstow Court, taken down in 1786.[2] Burstow Hall is the seat of Mr. D. M. Jackson ; Smallfield Place of Mr. W. Leslie Moore ; Burstow Lodge of Mr. Lord John Sanger, the well-known owner of wild beasts ; The Gables, where there is a preparatory school, of Mr. E. C. Marsh. About Copthorne and Effingham a considerable number of modern houses have been built.

There was an Inclosure Award, 15 August 1855,[3] inclosing waste at Copthorne and Burstow Common Fields. It is interesting as one of the rare appearances of any common fields in the Weald, and it may be noted that they were on a manor which was from its earliest mention attached to a manor (Wimbledon) in the old settled part of the county.

There are Baptist chapels at Burstow and at Fernhill, and a mission room near Smallfield.

The school at Smallfield was built as a Church school in 1859, and added to in 1861. A School Board was formed, which took it over in 1874.

Outwood is an ecclesiastical district formed from the parishes of Blechingley, Burstow, Horley, Horne, and Nutfield (19 August 1870). The church is in Burstow parish, and the northern part of Burstow parish is included in the district.

The church (St. John the Baptist) was built in 1869. It is of stone in 13th-century style, with a tower. There is also a Baptist chapel built in 1879. The school, built in 1876, was under the Burstow School Board. Brightleigh is the seat of Miss Collingwood ; Ashcroft of Mr. W. H. Maw ; Axeland Park of Mr. D. Wardlaw Wardlaw. Abbot's Hospital, Guildford, has land in Outwood.

MANORS No mention of Burstow occurs in the Domesday Survey,[4] but the manor appears to have been held as early as the reign of Richard I by a family who took their name from the land. Sir Edward Bysshe, a descendant of this family,[5] writing from the evidence of documents and seals in his possession, states that Stephen de Burstow, whose name appears in the seals as Stephen Fitz Hamo, held the manor in the latter part of the 12th century, and that he was succeeded by his son Roger and his grandson John, the latter holding during and prior to the reign of Henry III.[6] Of John de Burstow there are other records. He made a grant of lands in Burstow about the year 1205.[7] In 1210-12 John de Burstow held half a

---

[1] *V.C.H. Surr.* ii, 272.

[2] Manning and Bray, *Hist. of Surr.* ii, 279.

[3] *Blue Bk. Incl. Awards.*

[4] This is probably accounted for by the fact that it was a part of Wimbledon which was then included in the manor of Mortlake. The large number of pigs, 55, due from the pannage in Mortlake points to a large forest holding, perhaps in the Burstow Weald. The manor of Sutton in like manner had *cubilia porcorum* in Thunderfield in Horley parish in the Weald (Birch, *Cart. Sax.* iii, 470), and

Banstead had its mill in the Weald at Leigh.

[5] Sir Edward Bysshe, Clarenceux King-of-Arms.

[6] Bysshe, *Notae in N. Uptonem. De Studio Militari,* 67 (1654).

[7] Add. Chart. 7620.

knight's fee 'in Wimbledune' of the Archbishop of Canterbury.[8] This entry seems to refer to the service rendered for the manor of Burstow, which was held of the archbishop as of his manor of Wimbledon.[9] In 1247 a John de Burstow was lord of the manor,[10] though whether this is the John mentioned above or the son of the same name who, according to Bysshe, succeeded his father, is not evident. In 1255 a settlement was made between John de Burstow and Peter de Burstow, possibly a younger brother, by which John was to hold the manor, paying an annual rent of 4 marks to Peter, John and his heirs to be quit of payment on Peter's death.[11] From the account of this family given by Bysshe it appears that the second John married Joan Burnevalle and had a son Roger,[12] who married Matilda Chastillon and was succeeded by his son John, who served in the French wars under the Black Prince and won great distinction.[13] The next records of the manor, in 1350 and 1358, show it to have been held at that time by Richard de Burstow,[14] whose name, however, does not appear in Bysshe's pedigree, and whose relationship to John de Burstow is not apparent.

BURSTOW. *Gules three falcons close argent.*

In 1366 the reversion of the manor was conveyed by Richard de Burstow to Sir Nicholas de Loveyne.[15] Margaret daughter of Nicholas Loveyne married Sir Philip St. Clere, and they held the manor in the right of Margaret, who was her father's heir.[16] When Sir Philip St. Clere died in 1408, very shortly after his wife, he was holding the manor of Burstow 'of the Archbishop of Canterbury by paying £6 yearly at his manor of Wimbledon.'[17] John St. Clere, son and heir of Philip, died in 1418, and was succeeded by his brother Thomas.[18] In 1424–5 Thomas St. Clere, whose children were then all minors, granted the manor to William Cheyne, kt., John Aston, and Geoffrey Motte, in trust for himself and his heirs, 'in order to defraud the king and other lords of those fees (i.e. the manor of Burstow and others) of the custody thereof and the marriages of the heirs.'[19] Aston's share was afterwards conveyed to John Hall,[20] while Geoffrey Motte remitted his to the other trustees.[21] Thomas St. Clere died in 1435, leaving three daughters and no sons.[22] The second daughter,

Eleanor, inherited the manor of Burstow; she married John Gage, who was seised of it at his death in 1475, when, his wife having predeceased him, their son

ST. CLERE. *Azure the sun in splendour or.*

GAGE. *Party saltire-wise azure and argent a saltire gules.*

William became lord of the manor.[23] John Gage, who was the son and heir of William and who was afterwards knighted, succeeded to the manor at the death of his mother Agnes, on whom it had been settled by her husband.[24] The manor descended from Sir John to his son Sir Edward Gage, who as Sheriff of Surrey and Sussex, 1557–8, was concerned in the Marian persecutions. He died in 1568.[25] His son John married Margaret daughter of Sir Thomas Copley, of the noted recusant family, and died without issue, his heir being his nephew John Gage, who in 1614 conveyed the manor to Sir Edward Culpepper[26] of Wakehurst.[27] He died in 1630, when his eldest surviving son, Sir William Culpepper, created a baronet in 1628,[28] inherited the manor.[29] Another son Edward seems to have held some share in the manor, settled on him doubtless on his marriage with Mary Bellingham ;[30] in 1638 he was apparently lord of the manor,[31] but it certainly reverted afterwards to the elder branch, and in 1696 Sir William Culpepper, fourth baronet, sold it to Sir Richard Raines,[32] LL.D., Judge of the Prerogative Court of Canterbury.

CULPEPPER. *Argent a bend engrailed gules.*

Henry Raines, son of Richard, inherited the manor at his father's death,[33] and in 1733 conveyed it to Joseph Kirke,[34] to whom Raines's widow Susan quitclaimed her right in 1745.[35] Kirke, by will

[8] *Red Bk. of Exch.* (Rolls Ser.), 473.
[9] *Vide infra*; *Feud. Aids*, v, 121.
[10] *Cal. of Chart.* 1226–57, p. 326.
[11] Feet of F. Surr. 39 Hen. III, no. 12.
[12] Bysshe, *Notae in N. Uptonem. De Studio Militari*, 67.
[13] Ibid. But see account of Smallfield below.
[14] Chan. Inq. p.m. 24 Edw. III, no. 91 ; ibid. 32 Edw. III, no. 40.
[15] Feet of F. Div. Co. 40 Edw. III, no. 25. Richard died after 1379 ; see under Redhall Manor below.
[16] Wrottesley, *Ped. from the Plea Rolls*, 376, 434 ; Feet of F. Div. Co. 2 Hen. IV, no. 20.
[17] Chan. Inq. p.m. 9 Hen. IV, no. 44.
[18] Ibid. ; Chan. Inq. p.m. 1 Hen. VI, no. 30.
[19] Close, 3 Hen. VI, no. 22 ; Chan. Inq. p.m. 17 Hen. VI, no. 56.

[20] Feet of F. Div. Co. 6 Hen. VI, no. 72 ; Close, 8 Hen. VI, m. 15.
[21] Close, 7 Hen. VI, m. 8.
[22] Chan. Inq. p.m. 17 Hen. VI, no. 56.
[23] Ibid. 15 Edw. IV, no. 26.
[24] Ibid. (Ser. 2), xiii, 103, 106 ; Feet of F. Surr. Hil. 19 Hen. VIII.
[25] Chan. Inq. p.m. (Ser. 2), clii, 144.
[26] Feet of F. Surr. East. 12 Jas. I.
[27] Berry, *Sussex Gen.* 136.
[28] G.E.C. *Baronetage*, ii, 60.
[29] Chan. Inq. p.m. (Ser. 2), ccclv, 80.
[30] Berry, *Sussex Gen.* 136 ; Feet of F. Div. Co. East. 6 Chas. I ; Trin. 22 Chas. I ; *Cal. of Com. for Compounding*, 2458 ; Feet of F. Div. Co. Hil. 18 & 19 Chas. II.
[31] Recov. R. Mich. 14 Chas. I. rot. 16.
[32] Ibid. East. 1 Will. and Mary, rot. 95 ; Feet of F. Div. Co. East. 2 Will. and Mary ; Close, 8 Will. III, pt. i, no. 33 ; *Sussex Arch. Coll.* x, 154. The

pedigree of the Culpeppers of Wakehurst given in G.E.C. *Baronetage* states that Sir William, first baronet, died in 1651, confusing him with Sir William Culpepper of Aylesford ; an article in the *Sussex Arch. Coll.* x, 154, however, gives the date of his death as 1678, and this statement is borne out by the fact that the document referred to in note 30 of 18 & 19 Chas. II refers to a Sir William Culpepper, baronet, then living. G.E.C. (op. cit. ii, 60) also says that the next Sir William, the fourth baronet, did not succeed his grandfather Sir Edward, younger son of the first Sir William, until 1700 (?). It appears, however, that he must have succeeded to the title as early as 1694, when he sold Wakehurst.
[33] Manning and Bray, *Hist. of Surr.* ii, 280.
[34] Com. Pleas D. Enr. Trin. 3 & 4 Geo. II, m. 5 d. ; Recov. R. Trin. 7 Geo. II, rot. 229.
[35] Feet of F. Surr. Mich. 19 Geo. II.

proved in September 1765, devised Burstow to his cousin James Harris, with remainder to the latter's sons, and in default of such to Mrs. Bridget Hand, sister of James Harris, and her sons in turn.[36] By 1779 the manor was in possession of Christopher, the elder son.[37] After his death the second son James became lord, and held as late as 1808.[38] Thomas Bainbridge, who died in 1830, is described as of Burstow,[39] and his son John Hugh Bainbridge was lord of the manor in 1841.[40] He sold it before his death in 1877, for in 1870, and as late as 1887, Henry Kelsey of Burstow Park was lord of the manor. It was sold in 1888 by Mr. Kelsey's executors to Mr. Alfred Howard Lloyd, who holds at present.

In 1247 a grant of free warren was made to the lord of the manor and his heirs; at the same time he also received a grant of a weekly market on Tuesdays and an annual fair to be held on the vigil, feast, and morrow of St. Michael.[41]

In 1329 Roger son of Roger atte Logge of Burstow granted to Roger son of Ralph Salaman lands and tenements in Burstow, Nutfield, and Horley, consisting of a messuage, 360 acres of land, 12 acres of meadow, 10 acres of wood, and 20s. rent, part of which formed the dower of Agnes wife of Roger atte Logge.[42] These are evidently the lands and tenements called 'La Logge' of which Roger Salaman died seised in 1343,[43] and which were afterwards known as the manor of LODGE or BURSTOW LODGE. Roger Salaman held of John de Burstow, lord of the manor of Burstow, by service of 26s. and suit of court.[44] His son Roger left a daughter and heir, who married Thomas Codyngton of Codyngton[45] and brought the manor to this family, though it evidently passed to a different branch afterwards, as Thomas Codyngton left an only child Rose, married to John Jordan of Gatwick, who does not appear to have held the manor. According to Manning a settlement was made by which, in default probably of male heirs to Codyngton, the manor passed to another Thomas Codyngton, a goldsmith in London.[46] In 1470 Margaret widow of Thomas Codyngton quitclaimed to her son John Codyngton 'the manor called le Logge' in Surrey.[47] He held a court as late as 1491–2.[48] In 1538 the manor was held by Richard St. Myghell alias Codyngton.[49] It is probable that the manor had passed to an heiress, perhaps Elizabeth Cornwayles, who is said to have held a court in 1511,[50] and whose son by a second husband, or perhaps her grandson, Richard St. Myghell, on inheriting his mother's lands, took her maiden name in addition to his own.

In 1538 Richard St. Myghell alias Codyngton and

Elizabeth his wife enfeoffed Thomas Fromond of the manor;[51] he held it of Sir John Gage of Burstow for rent of 39s. 8d., and died in 1542, leaving a son Bartholomew,[52] who was in turn succeeded by his son William and grandson Bartholomew.[53] The latter died before 1652, by which date his widow had married again, her second husband being William Howard, who held the manor for some years.[54] After the death of William and Elizabeth the manor passed to Mary daughter and co-heir of Bartholomew Fromond and Elizabeth, who had married Richard Walmesley.[55] Catherine, granddaughter of Richard and Mary and sole heir to her father Bartholomew Walmesley, who died in 1701 and whose son died in infancy, married Robert, Lord Petre,[56] and held the manor in her own right.[57] She lived until 1788,[58] but before that time she had vested the manor in her grandson and heir Robert Edward, ninth Lord Petre, as in 1785 he joined with his son Robert Edward in conveying it to Melancthon Saunders,[59] who was a representative of the younger branch of the Sanders of Charlwood.[60] He held it in 1808.[61] It now no longer exists as a manor.

Land in Burstow called BURSTOW PARK belonged at an early date to the Archbishops of Canterbury, to whose manor of Wimbledon it was attached.[62] In the early 13th century reference is made to land in Burstow 'lying to the south of the park of H. Archbishop of Canterbury,' the reference evidently being to Hubert, who was archbishop until 1205.[63]

During the vacancy of this see in the time of Edward I or Edward II an account of 51s. 7d. was rendered for the sale of three oaks and ashes in the archbishop's park of Burstow.[64] In 1328 a commission was issued against evil-doers who had entered the parks of the archbishop's 'manors' of Croydon, Wimbledon, Burstow, Wyke, &c.[65] In 1531 Burstow Park was leased to Sir John Gage of Burstow for a term of eighty years at an annual rent of £11, 'the deer therein being reserved to the Archbishop of Canterbury until the following Christmas.'[66] In 1536 the archbishop made an exchange of lands with the king, the latter receiving, among other lands, the manor of Wimbledon and all parcels and members of the said manor.[67] The king

SEE OF CANTERBURY. *Azure the cross of the archbishop having in head or and in chief a staff argent surmounted by the pall of a metropolitan argent having edges and fringes or and four crosses formy fitchy sable upon it.*

[36] P.C.C. 336 Rushworth.
[37] Recov. R. East. 19 Geo. III, rot. 295; Manning and Bray, *Hist. and Antiq. of Surr.* ii, 280. [38] Ibid.
[39] Burke, *Landed Gent.*
[40] Brayley, *Hist. of Surr.* iv, 293.
[41] *Cal. of Chart.* 1226–57, p. 326.
[42] Feet of F. Surr. 3 Edw. III, no. 42.
[43] Chan. Inq. p.m. 17 Edw. III (1st nos.), no. 45. [44] Ibid.
[45] Ibid.; Harl. MS. 1561, fol. 120; Berry, *Surr. Gen.* 28.
[46] Manning and Bray, *Hist. of Surr.* ii, 283.
[47] Anct. D. (P.R.O.), B. 1159.
[48] Manning and Bray, *Hist. of Surr.* ii, 283, from Court Rolls in hands of Mr. Glover.

[49] Feet of F. Surr. East. 30 Hen. VIII.
[50] Manning and Bray, *Hist. and Antiq. of Surr.* ii, 283 from Court Rolls, but see manor of Lodge in Horley.
[51] Ibid.
[52] Chan. Inq. p.m. (Ser. 2), lxvii, 122.
[53] Feet of F. Div. Co. Trin. 4 Jas. I; Recov. R. Trin. 21 Jas. I, rot. 49; Hil. 14 Chas. I, rot. 76; *Visit. of Surr.* (Harl. Soc. xliii), 30.
[54] *Cal. of Com. for Compounding,* 2678; Recov. R. East. 1657, rot. 140; Mich. 1658, rot. 131.
[55] Recov. R. Mich. 1658, rot. 131; Berry, *Essex Gen.* 38, 39.
[56] Ibid. The Fromonds were a recusant family under Elizabeth, and seemingly remained Roman Catholic.

[57] Feet of F. Div. Co. Trin. 5 Geo. I.
[58] Burke, *Peerage.*
[59] Com. Pleas D. Enr. East. 25 Geo. III, m. 136; Recov. R. East. 25 Geo. III, rot. 237; Com. Pleas D. Enr. Trin. 25 Geo. III, m. 200.
[60] Berry, *Surr. Gen.* 40, 41.
[61] Manning and Bray, *Hist. and Antiq. of Surr.* ii, 284.
[62] Chan. Inq. p.m. 21 Ric. II, 137, m. 114.
[63] Add. Chart. 7620.
[64] Mins. Accts. (Gen. Ser.), bdle. 1128, no. 2.
[65] Cal. Pat. 1327–30, p. 295.
[66] L. and P. Hen. VIII, v, 128.
[67] *Stat. of the Realm,* iii, 712.

in the same year granted these lands to Thomas Cromwell, when the previous act was stated to have referred ' not only to the manor of Wimbledon, but also to the manor of Burstow.'[68] A few years later Cromwell was attainted, and his lands became forfeit to the Crown. By this time probably part of the estate had been disparked and tenants had settled there, for in 1542 a court with view of frankpledge, evidently an offshoot of the court at Wimbledon Manor, was held at Burstow, which then included the tithings of Southborough, Middleborough, and Northborough.[69] A curious entry in a Court Roll occurs for the year 1547, when after the usual entries under Wimbledon it is stated that at Burstow no one was amerced that year *causa infirmitatis.*[70] In 1590 Elizabeth granted to Sir Thomas Cecil and his heirs the manor of Wimbledon and ' all those our lands in Bristowe *alias* Burstowe called le Parke.'[71] Later in the same year Cecil received licence to alienate the manor of Burstow to Sir Thomas Shirley and his heirs.[72] Shirley, who had been appointed Treasurer-at-War to the English army in the Low Countries in 1587, had in that capacity become inextricably involved in debt to the Crown, and his pecuniary embarrassments grew greater as the years passed on ; in 1596 it was stated that ' he owed the queen more than he was worth.'[73] In satisfaction of £800 11s. 8d. remaining due to her, the queen accepted, among other lands, this manor, which was therefore conveyed to her in March 1602 by Shirley and John Quarles,[74] whom Shirley had previously enfeoffed.[75] In the following month the queen granted the manor to William Bowes and others in consideration of the payment by them to the Crown of the above sum.[76]

These grantees were evidently trustees for Quarles, to whom they conveyed the manor in 1603.[77] It remained in his possession until 1606, in which year he conveyed it to William Turner,[78] from whom it passed, four years later, to Richard Infield or Innyngfield.[79] The latter in 1625 made a settlement on himself in tail, with contingent remainder to his brother and to his nephew Innyngfield Falconer, son of his sister Agnes.[80] He died in 1625 and was succeeded by his brother.[81] Henry and Agnes Falconer were seised of the manor in 1633.[82] It was conveyed by Falconer to Edward Payne in 1649, when the Park is mentioned as still existing.[83] Richard Payne, perhaps his son, was owner in 1669.[84] In 1697 Richard's son John Payne was holding it,[85] and in 1701 settled it on his intended wife, Anne Gage.[86]

Owing to a family dispute the manor was sold, and bought by John Smith, husband of Elizabeth Smith and grandson of John Payne by his first wife Blanche.[87] In 1743, apparently after the death of Ann and Eliza-

beth, John Smith, with his son and various trustees, conveyed the manor to Walter Harris,[88] from whom in 1765 it passed to Daniel Hailes.[89] The latter conveyed in 1779 to Thomas Dickson, who held it as late as 1807.[90] It was soon afterwards sold by him to Henry Kelsey, who died in 1827, and whose son, of Burstow Court Manor (q.v.), owned the estate in 1841[91] and held it as a farm until 1887, when he died. It was bought from his family by Mr. Alfred Howard Lloyd in 1888.[92]

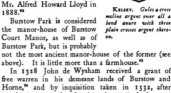

KELSEY. *Gules a cross moline argent over all a bend azure with three plain crosses argent thereon.*

Burstow Park is considered the manor-house of Burstow Court Manor, as well as of Burstow Park, but is probably not the most ancient manor-house of the former (see above). It is little more than a farmhouse.[93]

In 1328 John de Wysham received a grant of free warren in his demesne lands of Burstow and Horne,[94] and by inquisition taken in 1332, after his death, he was found to have been seised of 1 messuage, 160 acres of land, 6 acres of meadow, and 22s. rent in Burstow known as the manor of *REDHALL* near Burstow, which he held, jointly with Hawisia his wife, of John de Burstow.[95] His son John de Wysham, afterwards knighted, inherited the manor, and in 1370 granted it to John Pecche, citizen and alderman of London.[96] In 1379 John Pecche died· seised of the manor, which he held of Richard Burstow by fealty, and by service of rendering thence yearly to the said Richard 42s., and by suit at his court of Burstow every three weeks. His son Sir William Pecche was his heir.[97]

The history of the manor during the next century is not apparent. It passed, however, out of the hands of the Pecches and became the property of the family of Welles. Mention is made in 1447 of a Henry Welles of Burstow.[98] Edward Welles was lord of the manor in 1595-6,[99] and it afterwards passed to John Welles, who held it in 1613.[100] In 1650 it was in the possession of Edward Payne the elder and Hannah his wife,[101] and it continued to be held by this family until the late 18th century.[102] Thomas Holles Payne, by his will, proved in May 1800, devised the manor of Redhall, including a capital messuage or mansion-house called Redhall, and a messuage called Cophall, to Sophia Elizabeth Beard and her heirs for ever.[103] The said messuages, &c., were in 1799, when the will was made, in the occupatiou of himself and Richard King, and mention is

68 *Stat. of the Realm,* iii, 713.
69 Ct. R. (P.R.O.), bdle. 205, no. 39, 40.
70 Ibid. bdle. 205, no. 41.
71 Pat. 32 Eliz. pt. xvii, m. 37.
72 Ibid. pt. xiv, m. 43 ; Feet of F. Surr. Hil. 33 Eliz.
73 *Dict. Nat. Biog.*
74 Close, 44 Eliz. pt. xxviii ; Pat. 44 Eliz. pt. xiii, m. 1.
75 Ibid. ; Feet of F. Div. Co. Trin. 40 Eliz. ; Hil. 43 Eliz. ; S.P. Dom. Eliz. cclxviii, 126 ; Pat. 43 Eliz. pt. xiii, m. 1.
76 Pat. 44 Eliz. pt. xxiii, m. 1.
77 Close, 45 Eliz. pt. ix.
78 Feet of F. Surr. Hil. 3 Jas. I.
79 Ibid. 7 Jas. I.

80 Recov. R. Hil. 22 Jas. I, rot. 67 ; Chan. Inq. p.m. (Ser. 2), dxxv, 80.
81 Ibid.
82 Feet of F. Surr. Mich. 9 Chas. I.
83 MS. abstract of title.
84 Manning and Bray, *Hist. of Surr.* ii, 282. 85 Recov. R. Hil. 9 Will. III.
86 MS. abstract of title.
87 Feet of F. Surr. East 13 Geo. I ; and MS. abstract of title.
88 Feet of F. Surr. Trin. 16 & 17 Geo. II ; and MS. abstract of title.
89 Feet of F. Surr. Trin. 5 Geo. III.
90 Ibid. East. 47 Geo. III ; Manning and Bray, *Hist. of Surr.* ii, 282 ; information from Mr. A. H. Lloyd.

91 Brayley, *Hist. of Surr.* iv, 293.
92 Information from Mr. A. H. Lloyd.
93 Ibid.
94 Chart. R. 2 Edw. III, m. 17, no. 59.
95 Inq. p.m. 6 Edw. III (1st nos.), no. 53 ; *Cal. Close,* 1330–3, p. 516 ; 1333–7, p. 454.
96 Close, 44 Edw. III, m. 15.
97 Inq. p.m. 3 Ric. II, file 10, no. 54.
98 *Cal. of Inq. Hen. VII,* 177.
99 Inq. p.m. (Ser. 2), ccxlvii, 52.
100 Feet of F. Surr. East. 11 Jas. I.
101 Ibid. East. 1650.
102 Ibid. East. 3 Jas. II ; ibid. Mich. 3 Will. and Mary ; Div. Co. East. 11 Geo. I.
103 P.P.C. Adderley, 393.

also made of two freehold tenements in Burstow which were included among the appurtenances of the manor.[104] Sophia Elizabeth Beard and her husband Richard Beard held the manor in 1801,[105] and Mrs. Beard was still lady of the manor in 1808.[106] It was occupied as a farm throughout the 19th century.[107] It is at present held by Mr. William Tebb. The house is surrounded by a broad moat inclosing a considerable area of ground.

The estate of *SMALLFIELD* in this parish belonged in the 16th and 17th centuries to the family of Bysshe, who were said to be descended from the de Burstows, lords of the manor of Burstow in the 13th and 14th centuries, through the marriage of an heiress of the latter family with John Bysshe. They said that the land had been given to their ancestor John de Burstow, who served under the Black Prince in the French wars, and who was promised a gift of some small field or piece of land in return for services rendered by him to Bartholomew Lord Burghersh. Land in Burstow called Crullinges was accordingly granted him, the name being changed to 'Smallfield' to meet the terms of the promise.[108]

The house, Smallfield Place, was erected there apparently in the 17th century [109] by Edward Bysshe, a successful Chancery lawyer, the father of Sir Edward Bysshe. The latter, who was born there in 1615, was M.P. for Blechingley and also held the offices of Garter King-of-Arms and of Clarenceux King-of-Arms; he was knighted in 1661,[110] in which year he made additions to the house, which bore

Bysshe. *Or a cheveron between three roses gules.*

that date. Manning states that part of the house was pulled down, the remainder being occupied in his time as a farm, and owned by Isaac Martin Rebow, M.P., of Colchester, who died in 1781.[111] His daughter Mary Hester married General Francis Slater, who took the name of Rebow and owned Smallfield Place when Brayley wrote, in 1841. He died in 1845. By a second wife he left a daughter Mary, who married John Gurdon, who also took the name of Rebow. He died in 1870. His son was Hector John Gurdon Rebow, from whom Mr. William Leslie Moore, the present owner, bought Smallfield Place in 1898.[112]

The house, which had been only a farm, was converted again into a gentleman's house by Mr. W. Leslie Moore. It is an interesting house of local sandstone with a roof of Horsham slabs. With its three embattled and mullioned bay windows, its gabled porch, and the fireplaces, staircase, and panelling in the interior, it ranks, although but a fragment, among the more important remains of domestic architecture in Surrey. It has a good staircase and much old panelling in good preservation.[113] On it are the initials E.M.B. and the arms assumed by Bysshe, a cheveron between three roses. The old Bysshe coat was Ermine a chief battled gules with three leopards' heads or therein.[114] During the ownership of the Rebow family the house was occupied as a farm by a family named Hooker, one of whom used to manage the Burstow Harriers before they became the Burstow Foxhounds.

The church of *ST. BARTHOLOMEW CHURCH* consists of a chancel 30 ft. by 14 ft. with a small vestry on the north side, a nave 38 ft. by 18 ft. with a south aisle 8 ft. 10 in. wide, a timber west tower, and a south porch.

The plan of the nave, and probably that of the chancel, dates from c. 1120, and the north and part of the west walls of the nave, with the west half of the north wall of the chancel, are for the most part of this time. Two original windows remain, one in the chancel and one in the nave; but nearly all the rest of the building, including the south aisle, belongs to the 15th century, and has been connected, though apparently on no direct evidence, with Archbishop Chicheley. The church was restored in 1884, the east wall of the aisle and the eastern quoins of the chancel being rebuilt.

The vestry and the south porch are modern additions. The east window of the chancel is of 15th-century date, and has three cinquefoiled lights under a flat drop arch with moulded label. The easternmost north window is a single trefoiled light, and the only other window in this wall is a narrow round-headed 12th-century light which now looks into the vestry.

Beneath the sill of the north-east window is a recess with two trefoiled openings separated by a mullion, and with moulded jambs and square head; it has served as a cupboard, and possibly also for the Easter sepulchre. West of it is a modern doorway to the vestry, and near the west end of the north wall, in an unusual position, is another aumbry set low in the wall, with rebated jambs and a square head.

[104] P.P.C. Adderley, 393.
[105] Feet of F. Surr. East. 41 Geo. III.
[106] Manning and Bray, *Hist. of Surr.* ii, 284.   [107] *Directories of Surrey.*
[108] Bysshe, *Notae in N. Uptonem. De Studio Militari,* 67, 1654; *Surr. Arch. Coll.* iii, 381. Aubrey (op. cit. iii, 7) disbelieves his pedigree altogether, and says the family sprang from farmers of the neighbourhood. That there was an ancient family of De Bysshe in Burstow, and that Bysshe Court was a house there, perhaps bears out his suspicions, for it is not the same as Smallfield Place. Wood (*Athenae Oxonienses,* ii, 483) is also severe upon Bysshe for inventing pedigrees. Aubrey says that the arms borne by him, and placed on his house, were not the ancient arms of De Bysshe. Wood adds

that he fell into disgrace for falsifying heraldry and genealogies, and died very poor. There are many Bysshes, later on, living as farmers about or in Burstow. One of the family, however, kept a status as a gentleman, and was an ancestor of the poet Shelley.

Roger Bysshe

Helen = John Shelley
(co-heiress)
|
Timothy Shelley
(b. 1700)
|
Sir Bysshe Shelley
(b. 1731)

Sir Timothy Shelley
(b. 1752)
|
Percy Bysshe Shelley

[109] *V.C.H. Surr,* ii, 480.
[110] *Dict. Nat. Biog.*
[111] Manning and Bray, *Hist. of Surr.* ii, 285.
[112] Private information. Mr. Isaac Martin Rebow, M.P., was son of Isaac Rebow, M.P., who died in 1734, and Mary Martin. It is possible that the Martins bought from the son of Sir Edward Bysshe, Clarenceux, who died poor.
[113] *V.C.H. Surr.* ii, 480.
[114] Cott. MS. Tib. D. 10.

The south-east window of the chancel is like the east window, but of two lights, and the other south window is of four lights of the same character. Near the east end of the south wall is a piscina with a small quatrefoiled basin and a chamfered shelf. The lower portion has plain chamfered jambs, but above the shelf they are trefoiled and the head is trefoiled, under a square lintel. It is of 15th-century date. Beneath the sill of the first window is a canopied seat which has moulded jambs and a very flat arched head.

Between the two south windows is a small 15th-century priest's doorway with a four-centred arch under a square head, and now blocked on the inside.

The vestry has a small single trefoiled east window, the jambs being of old stones re-used, but the head and sill are modern.

The 15th-century chancel arch has shafted and moulded jambs with octagonal moulded bases and capitals to the shafts. On either side of it are shallow trefoiled recesses to contain images over the nave altar, that on the south having a second recess below it, while in the south-east arcade of the nave is a piscina. At the north-east end of the north wall of the nave is an arched recess, common in this district, designed to give more room for the altar here.

The north-east window of the nave has two cinquefoiled lights under a flat head with a moulded label, and near the west end of the north wall is a window of four cinquefoiled lights under a square head with a moulded label, all but the foiled heads and the label being modern. Immediately to the east of it is a small blocked 12th-century window with a semicircular head, the western jamb of which must have been destroyed when the four-light window was inserted. Nothing of it can be seen on the inside. There is no trace of a doorway in this wall.

The south arcade is of three bays with columns formed of four attached shafts set square with the wall over, and not diagonally after the usual fashion; their moulded bases and capitals are single octagons, not following the plan of the shafts, the arrangement being unusual, but quite satisfactory in effect. The arches are four-centred and are moulded with a hollow casement between two hollow chamfers, and above the capitals at the springing level there are plain shields, and in a similar position on the south side of the east respond is a large carved head.

The east and west windows of the aisle are modern and have each two cinquefoiled lights, and the south-east window is like that in the north wall, of four cinquefoiled lights, of which only the heads are old; to the east of it is a piscina with chamfered jambs and four-centred head and a small quatrefoiled drain.

The south doorway is of 15th-century date and has moulded jambs and a two-centred arch under a square head, the spandrels being filled with quatrefoils.

At the west end of the nave is a modern Gothic tower arch, set within the lines of a four-centred arch evidently coeval with the south arcade. It was made

to contain a deal screen of poor Gothic character, now set up in the west side of the tower. The tower is a very interesting piece of timber construction, probably of 15th-century date, the supporting beams and posts being very massive. As usual, the lower stage is wider than the upper, the main posts coming down within its lines, and being connected by heavy ground sills with a most picturesque effect. The ground stage must have been almost entirely dark before the narrow cinquefoiled windows were pierced in the north and south walls within recent years. The stairs to the belfry are in the north-west corner, and do not rise above the first floor; in the west wall is a wooden doorway with moulded jambs and a three-centred head with trefoiled spandrels. The upper part of the tower is covered with oak shingles lately renewed (1902), and has small angle pinnacles, and an octagonal shingled spire, on the east side of which a large flagstaff is set up. The fittings of the church, except the font, are of modern date, but under the tower is kept an old chest with an arched lid heavily strapped with iron, and doubtless of considerable age.

The font is of 15th-century date, octagonal with

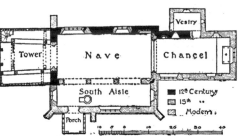

PLAN OF ST. BARTHOLOMEW'S CHURCH, BURSTOW

quatrefoil panels on each side, and leaf *paterae* at the base of the bowl.

There are six bells in the tower, the treble by Gillett and Johnson, 1906, and the second by the same founders, 1899, who at this date recast the other four bells, preserving their original inscriptions. The third was by John Daniell of London, c. 1450, inscribed, ' Sancte Thome ora pro nobis,' with Daniell's cross and stop, and the royal arms of England; the fourth had the three names ' Thos. Gelman, John Bhyss, and Wyllum Rofe '; the fifth was by William Mears, and the tenor by William Eldridge, 1681.

The plate is as follows :—A silver cup of 1667 ; a paten probably belonging to it, but the hall-mark, if any, is almost obliterated. There is also a stand paten of 1899 and a flagon of 1898. There is a pocket Communion set of plated white metal.

The registers are contained in six books, the first having entries of baptisms, marriages, and burials from 1549 to 1600. This is a paper book in very good condition. The second book is of parchment, and contains all three entries from 1547 to 1685, and is a copy of the first with additions both at the beginning and end of the book. The third book has marriages and burials from 1685 to 1756 and baptisms from 1685 to 1797. The fourth has marriages on printed forms from 1757 to 1798, the fifth continues marriages from 1798 to 1812, and the sixth has entries of baptisms and burials from 1798 to 1812.

The churchyard is small, surrounded by tall trees, and on the east side is a modern wooden lych-gate.

Close to the church on the south, and at a lower level, stands the rectory, an old building of several periods, the middle being probably 16th-century work, and of timber construction. Additions were made by Flamsteed the astronomer, formerly rector here, and by several later rectors. To the west of the house is a rectangular site surrounded by a moat still full of water, on which ancient foundations are said to exist ; it is at present a rose garden, and adds greatly to the beauty of the grounds of the vicarage.

ADVOWSON The church of Burstow was probably built by the Archbishop of Canterbury on his land at Burstow, as it was always a peculiar of the see of Canterbury.[116] In 1121, when the earliest mention of the church occurs, Ralph, Archbishop of Canterbury, granted it to the Cluniac priory of St. Pancras at Lewes.[116] In the confirmation of its charters made to this house from 1129 to 1171 it appears as holding Burstow Church.[117] It is not apparent how long the monks continued to do so, but it is possible that the archbishop reclaimed it towards the end of the 13th century, as from

1286 onwards the alien priory of Lewes was liable to have its possessions seized when there was war with France.[118] Presentation was made to Burstow by the king in the 14th century during voidance of the see of Canterbury.[119] The church came finally into possession of the Crown in 1536, being given up by the archbishop with his manor of Burstow Park.[190] Except during the time of the Commonwealth, when the right of presentation was vested in the Lord Protector,[191] the patronage has since that time remained in the Crown, presentation being now made by the Lord Chancellor.[192] The living ceased to be a peculiar to the see of Canterbury in 1851, when it was united to Winchester. By the rearrangement of dioceses in 1878 it was joined to Rochester. One eminent man, John Flamsteed, the famous astronomer, was rector of Burstow from 1684 to 31 December 1719, when he died.

CHARITIES Smith's Charity is distributed as in other Surrey parishes.

In 1684 Ralph Cooke, rector of Burstow, left money to buy large upper coats for a widower and a widow yearly.

In 1718 John Flamsteed, rector and Astronomer Royal, left money to buy new coats for two poor Christian people.

In 1728 Mrs. Margaret Flamsteed, widow of the rector, left money for clothing for two poor women.

CHARLWOOD

Cherlewude (xiii cent.) ; Cherlwude (xiii & xiv cent.) ; Chorlwode (xiv cent.) ; Charlewood (xviii cent.).

Charlwood is a parish on the Sussex border. The village is 7 miles south-west-by-south from Reigate, and rather more south-west from Dorking. The parish is bounded on the north and east by Horley, on the south by Rusper in Sussex, on the west by Newdigate. An outlying portion is surrounded by Newdigate and Rusper, and another by Leigh and Horley. The main part of the parish is about 4 miles from east to west, and 3 miles from north to south. The whole contains 6,875 acres. The Mole forms part of the eastern boundary, and tributaries of the same river run through the parish. The soil is entirely the Wealden Clay, but in the middle of it a ridge of Paludina Limestone makes a very considerable elevation, rising to 385 ft., called Stan Hill, Norwood Hill, and Horse Hill. The same ridge continues to the south-west of the village, as Rug or Russ Hill, and reaches about the same height there. Between the two parts of the hill is a depression through which a tributary of the Mole runs past Charlwood village.

The village is compact, and of a considerable size for the district, but farms and cottages are widely scattered also over the parish ; on the ridge mentioned there are

several considerable gentlemen's houses built in recent years. The parish is agricultural, with some brick works, and there is a large nursery garden, of Messrs. Cheal & Son, near Lowfield, in Charlwood.

Charlwood Common was a large village green by Charlwood village, but is now all inclosed except a small recreation ground. Hookwood Common still open ground, 2 miles north-east of Charlwood village ; Johnson's Common and White's Common were roadside wastes, now inclosed.

The Brighton Road, through Reigate and Crawley, passes through the parish. The part between these two towns was the first road in Surrey made under a Turnpike Act.[1] The object was to make a way for riding out of the Hastings Sand of Sussex over the clay on to the hard ground in Surrey. But to save the causeway from being cut up by wheels posts were to be fixed along it, so that it might be passable only for horses.[2] It was not made a driving road till the reign of George II. The main Brighton line just comes into a corner of Charlwood parish.

The bones of an elephant have been found in Charlwood,[3] and similar finds not exactly recorded are said to have been made. Remains of human antiquity are not on record, but about 1890 a vessel of Paludina Limestone (Sussex marble) was found on the

115 V.C.H. Surr. ii, 3.
116 Anct. Chart. (Pipe R. Soc.), 14.
117 V.C.H. Surr. ii, 11 ; Cal. of Doc. France, 509.   118 V.C.H. Surr. ii, 68.
119 Cal. Pat. 1348–50, pp. 353, 355, 400, 424, 434.
190 Stat. of the Realm, iii, 712, 713.
191 Surr. Arch. Coll. xvii, 97.

192 Inst. Bks. (P.R.O.) ; Clergy Lists.
1 Stat. 8 Will. III, cap. 15.
2 Reigate is on the sand, and Crawley on the clay is close to the edge of the sand. The Wealden roads used to be quite impassable in bad weather. There is a letter at Loseley (undated) from Sir Robert More to his father, Sir George, at

Loseley, from some place near Horsham, saying that he could not drive home in a coach with his wife the nearest way because it had rained ; but that he would go to East Grinstead, whence he could find a road to Reigate by Godstone, and would come home that way.
3 Topley, Geology of the Weald, 195.

estate of Mr. Young at Stanhill, which the finders regarded as an ancient font, but which was perhaps a stone mortar.

Manning and Bray [4] mention the tradition that the Timberham Bridge was formerly known as Killman-bridge because of a slaughter of the Danes there. It does not appear, however, that there is any documentary evidence for the improbable name 'Killman-bridge,' and it is unlikely that Charlwood was inhabited at the time of Danish invasions. It is not mentioned in Domesday, and was probably a forest district of the manor of Merstham, which to the present day reaches into the parish.

The Sanders or Sander family of Charlwood were, if not Catholic recusants, closely allied by marriage and sympathies with recusants. Nicholas Sander the famous controversialist was of a younger branch of the family, and his sister, who married John Pitts of Oxfordshire, was mother of John Pitsaeus, Dean of Liverdun in Lorraine and Bishop of Verdun. The squire's family evidently preserved the pre-Reformation inscription on the church (see church).

Another curious trace of ancient manners is that Charlwood, with lands in Leigh and Newdigate, was conveyed in the first year of Edward VI 'with the bondsmen and their families.' [5]

Charlwood Place, formerly the seat of the Sanders family, is a moated house. At Charlwood House there was apparently a moat, part of which only remains.

In the outlying part of Charlwood between Leigh and Horley parishes, east of Barnland Farm and west of the Mole, between the Mole and the Brighton road, there are the remains of a moated inclosure.

Charlwood was in the Wealden iron district, though none of the principal forges and furnaces named seem to be in it. [6] But it was one of the iron-working parishes exempted from the Act of 1 Elizabeth against cutting timber of a certain size.

Of late years a completely new feature has been brought into the parish by the making of the Gatwick Race Course, which was opened in 1891, after the closing of the old Croydon Race Course at Woodside.

Some common land was inclosed, according to Brayley,[7] in 1844, but the chief inclosure award was dated 5 February 1846, under the General Inclosure Act of 1843.[8] Other waste was inclosed 12 January 1854,[9] when Shellwood Manor in Leigh was inclosed, including waste in Betchworth, Charlwood, Horley, Leigh, and Newdigate. There was a common meadow, but common arable fields are not mentioned.

There are both Baptist and Congregational chapels at Charlwood.

Farmfield is a Home for female inebriates acquired by the London County Council.

The Cottage Hospital opened in 1873 is at present closed.

Charlwood Boys' School was built in 1840. Charlwood Girls' and Infants' School was built in 1852 and enlarged in 1893.

Lowfield Heath School was built in 1868.

Charlwood House is the seat of Mr. G. H. Beckhuson; Russ Hill of Mr. H. N. Corsellis, part of whose house is of the middle of the 17th century; Stanhill Court belongs to Mr. A. F. Hepburn; Gatwick Manor House is the seat of Mr. E. G. MacAndrew; Norwood Hill House of Major Mac-Micking; Ricketswood of Sir A. M. Rendel, K.C.I.E.; Norwood Hill of Mr. C. F. Wakefield; Charlwood

CHARLWOOD CHURCH FROM THE NORTH-EAST

Park of Mr. Herbert Musker. The Misses Sanders of Hookwood House belong to the old Sanders family of Charlwood. Charlwood Place itself is now a farmhouse.

Lowfield Heath was a large common about 2 miles south-east of Charlwood village, on the Sussex border, inclosed in 1846. As several houses lay about it at some distance from the church a chapel of ease, St. Michael and All Angels, was built in 1868. It is of brick with stone dressings, a tower and spire, in the French 13th-century style.

[4] Hist. of Surr. ii, 187.
[5] Deed formerly in possession of Duke of Norfolk, copied by the Rev. T. R. O'Fflahertie of Capel.
[6] V.C.H. Surr. ii, 219, etc.
[7] Hist. of Surr. iv, 267.
[8] Blue Bk. Incl. Awards.
[9] Ibid.

MANORS

CHARLWOOD seems to have been held from an early period by the Prior and convent of Christchurch, Canterbury, as member of the manor of Merstham (q.v.).[10] In 1231 the Prior of Christchurch or Holy Trinity, received licence to send letters to his freemen of 'Cherlewud,' desiring them to render him aid to get quit of the debts with which he was burdened.[11] A ten-years' lease of the manor of Merstham and its member of Charlwood, made in 1396 by the prior, records many particulars concerning the 'live and dead stock' existing at both places (*vide* Merstham), and mentions, among other things, that the 'digging of iron at Cherlwood' was to remain the right of the prior and convent.[12] The prior surrendered his possessions in July 1539,[13] and in the following month Henry VIII granted Merstham and Charlwood to Sir Robert Southwell and his heirs.[14] In 1542 the manor of Charlwood was quitclaimed to Southwell by Henry de la Hay,[15] who was possibly the lessee of the prior. This deed marks the separation of Charlwood, henceforth held as a separate manor, from the manor of Merstham, their subsequent descent being entirely distinct. In 1547 Sir Robert Southwell and Margaret his wife alienated the manor of Charlwood to Henry Lechford,[16] whose family had held land in Charlwood as early as the reign of Edward III.[17] He died seised of the manor in 1567 and was succeeded by his son Richard,[18] who was afterwards knighted. It descended in 1611 to the latter's grandson Richard, his son Henry being already dead.[19] The second Sir Richard Lechford conveyed the manor in 1625 to Edmund Jordan,[20] who was already seised of the manors of Gatwick and Shiremark in Charlwood, and was also possessed either then or soon afterwards of the manor of Hook (q.v.). These manors remained in the Jordan family, passing from father to son, until the death without issue of Thomas Jordan in 1750.[21] His sisters and

CONVENT OF CHRIST-CHURCH, CANTERBURY. *Azure a cross argent with the monogram* ✠ *sable thereon.*

LECHFORD. *Sable a chevron between three leopards' heads argent.*

co-heirs, Elizabeth Beaumont and Philippa Sharp, divided his inheritance, the manors in Charlwood becoming the property of the latter, who held them with her husband John Sharp until her death without issue in 1759.[22] Her husband continued to hold the manors, and by will of 1770, having disinherited his eldest son by a former marriage, entailed them on John and James, sons of William Jennyngs Sharp, his second son.[23] On his death in 1771[24] his eldest grandson, John Sharp, succeeded and held the property intact until 1806,[25] when he sold the manors of Charlwood, Hook, and Shiremark to Thomas Kerr.[26] They afterwards passed to James Woodbridge, from whom they were purchased by Michael Clayton before 1841.[27] He died without issue in 1847, when the estate apparently passed to the family of his younger brother Richard,[28] whose grandson, Major Edward Clayton, afterwards held the manor. The present lord is Mr. G. S. Clayton, brother of the last owner.[29]

Grants of free warren in their demesne lands of Charlwood were made to the Prior and convent of Christchurch during the reigns of Edward II and Edward III.[30] In 1592 mention is made of a fair which was held annually on the feast of St. James, the profits of which belonged to the lord of the manor.[31] It seems, however, to have long been discontinued.

In 1241 Richard de Warwick and Juliana his wife and Joan her sister quitclaimed a messuage, 4 acres of meadow, and 18 acres of land in Charlwood to John de Gatwick and his heirs.[32] This land was probably part of that which was afterwards known as the manor of *GATWICK* and which was held by the de Gatwicks until the 14th century. It is probable that a John de Gatwick who held during the reign of Edward II married Joan de Ifeld, and that their daughter and heir Elizabeth married Thomas de Cobham.[33] In 1363 the manor of Gatwick was granted to William son of Elizabeth, daughter of John de Gatwick, by the vicars of Charlwood and Horley and by William Jordan; it was stated that the latter parties held the manor of the gift and feoffment of Thomas de Cobham.[34] In 1396 Reginald de Cobham, son of William, held the manor,[35] of which he suffered a temporary forfeiture for debt.[36] In the reign of Henry VII Gatwick was held by Joan widow of Reginald Cobham, son and heir of John,[37] and presumably grandson of the first Reginald.[38] Joan Cobham after her husband's death brought a suit against John Jordan, John Lechford, Richard Sanders, and others on the grounds that they,

[10] *Cal. Pat.* 1225–32, p. 429; Chart. R. 10 Edw. II, no. 24; 38 Edw. III, no. 15; Ct. R. bdle. 204, no. 66, 67, 68; Pat. 31 Hen. VIII, pt. iii, m. 28; Pat. 31 Hen. VIII, pt. i, m. 6.

[11] *Cal. Pat.* 1225–32, p. 429.

[12] Manning and Bray, *Hist. of Surr.* ii, 255 (quoting from a 'long roll marked 85 in Lambeth Palace').

[13] Pat. 31 Hen. VIII, pt. iii, no. 28.

[14] Ibid. pt. i, m. 6.

[15] Feet of F. Div. Co. Mich. 34 Hen. VIII.

[16] Pat. 1 Edw. VI, pt. viii, m. 15.

[17] Feet of F. Surr. 31, 37 Edw. III; Ct. R. bdle. 204, no. 67, 68; Early Chan. Proc. bdle. 100, no. 79; Star Chamb. Proc. Hen. VII, no. 31; bdle. 17, no. 85.

[18] Chan. Inq. p.m. (Ser. 2), cxlv, 13.

[19] Ibid. cccxxv, 195.

[20] Close, 1 Chas. I, pt. xviii, no. 18.

[21] Feet of F. Surr. Trin. 1 Will. and Mary; Com. Pleas D. Enr. Mich. 5 Geo. II, m. 9; Recov. R. Mich. 5 Geo. II, rot. 124; Berry, *Surr. Gen.* 28, 29.

[22] Feet of F. Surr. Mich. 27 Geo. II; *Surr. Arch. Coll.* xi, 22; Berry, *Surr. Gen.* 29, and monument in Charlwood Church.

[23] P.C.C. 357, Trevor.

[24] Ibid.

[25] Recov. R. East. 25 Geo. III, rot. 259; Com. Pleas D. Enr. Hil. 26 Geo. III, m. 113–14; Recov. R. Hil. 45 Geo. III, rot. 197.

[26] Manning and Bray, *Hist. of Surr.* ii, 189.

[27] Brayley, *Hist. of Surr.* iv, 264.

[28] Burke, *Landed Gentry.*

[29] Ibid.

[30] Chart. R. 10 Edw. II, m. 24; 38 Edw. III, no. 15.

[31] Pat. 34 Eliz. pt. iv, m. 21.

[32] Feet of F. Surr. East. 25 Hen. III.

[33] Wrottesley, *Ped. from the Plea R.* 244; Feet of F. Surr. 4 Edw. III, no. 41; Close, 7 Ric. II, m. 20 d.

[34] Close, 7 Ric. II, m. 20 d.

[35] Chan. Inq. p.m. 20 Ric. II, no. 63; Wrottesley, *Ped. from the Plea R.* 244.

[36] Chan. Inq. p.m. 20 Ric. II, no. 63; *Cal. Pat.* 1401–5, p. 162.

[37] Star Chamb. Proc. Hen. VII, no. 31.

[38] *Surr. Arch. Coll.*; Feet of F. Surr. 9 Hen. V, no. 50.

'by crafty meanes,' occupied the manor and took the profits to their own use ; the defendants maintained that Reginald Cobham had disposed of the manor to them by various sales and mortgages.[39] The result of the suit is not apparent. It is probable that John Jordan, whose actual claim is not stated, eventually acquired the whole manor, as it was in his family by the latter half of the 16th century.[40] Edmund Jordan, his descendant in direct line,[41] held the manor in 1625, when he acquired also the manor of Charlwood (q.v.) and that of Shiremark (q.v.). The manors followed the same descent until 1806,[42] when John Sharp, whose grandmother Philippa was the sister and co-heir of the last of the Jordans,[43] sold all his manors in Charlwood except that of Gatwick to Thomas Kerr.[44] Reference is made in 1785 to a capital messuage called Gatwicks with houses, &c., belonging, then in possession, as was the manor itself, of the second John Sharp.[45] According to Manning a new manor-house, called Timberham House from its vicinity to Timberham Bridge, was erected by this owner, the site of the old manor-house being in the east of the parish. Brayley, writing in 1841, mentions 'Gatwick house' as having been recently sold by John Sharp to Alexander Fraser,[46] who occupied it as late as 1859. The Gatwick Race Course Company bought the Gatwick estate and the manor-house in 1890 from Mr. John King Farlow of Egham. They do not appear to have bought the manorial rights, and it seems as if these had fallen into abeyance.[47]

JORDAN. Sable an eagle bendwise between two coties argent and a chief or with three oakleaves vert therein.

The family of Sander, from whom the manor of SANDERS PLACE took its name, was established at Charlwood as early as the 14th century. A court roll of 1388 records that Stephen Sander was called upon to answer for a plea of trespass,[48] and a reference is found in 1434 to Thomas Sander of Charlwood,[49] apparently his son.[50] In 1446 land called Sloghterwyk in Charlwood was granted to Thomas Sander and William his son by Richard son of Thomas Cokeman,[51] and about the same time they received

a grant of 4 acres from Thomas White.[52] In 1565 Sir Thomas Sander, kt. died seised of 'the manor of Charlwood called Sander's manor,' held as of the manor of Charlwood by fealty and rent of 15s. 1¼d.[53] Edmund his son and heir succeeded to the property, which passed successively to Edmund's son Thomas and grandson Edmund.[54] The latter died without issue in 1662, having devised all his 'lands and tenements in Charlwood' to his sister Elizabeth Bradshaw,[55] from whom they evidently passed to Sir William Throckmorton, son of her aunt Dorothy,[56] as in a conveyance of this property in 1673 from Sir Andrew King to Francis Lord Aungier, it was stated that Sir Andrew had obtained it from Throckmorton.[57] The deed of 1673 describes the property as 'the site and the remaining part of the late capital messuage . . . called Charlwood Place, with all fields, &c. called the Great Parke, the Little Parke, the Knowe, the Great Godfreyes, the Lesser Godfreyes, the Greater Biggle Hawe, the Lesser Biggle Hawe, Bush Field, the Granthams, the Skewles mead and Lyons Riddles Mead,' containing altogether about 300 acres. According to Manning the estate afterwards passed, with the church, to the family of Wise. This family held these lands in 1828, by which time, apparently, a new house had been built, as reference is made to 'all that capital messuage, and site and late remaining part of the late capital messuage called Charlwood Place.[58]

Land called HOKE or LA HOKE existed in Charlwood at an early date, as the name Walter atte Hoke, or Walter de la Hok, occurs as that of a witness to deeds in the early 14th century,[59] and in 1333 Walter atte Hoke contributed to the lay subsidy for Surrey.[60] In 1335 the custody of a messuage and 45 acres at la Hoke, possibly in Charlwood, was granted to Thomas de Flaynsford.[61] In the late 15th century the family of Lechford held at least a portion of the lands afterwards called the 'manor of Hook.'[62] In 1546 the 'manor of Howke,' then in the possession of Henry Lechford, was sold by him to Henry Amcotts ;[63] he retained, however, a parcel of ground in Hook called Backworth and Littleworth. In 1614 William Hewett died seised of the manor, which was held of the manor of Charlwood by suit at court and yearly rent of 11s. 10d.[64] According to Manning, William Hewett son of the above William conveyed it in 1627 to Symonds, from whom it afterwards passed to the family of Jordan.[65] It descended with the

[39] Star Chamb. Proc. Hen. VII, no. 31.

[40] Recov. R. Hil. 30 Eliz.

[41] Visit. of Surr. (Harl. Soc. xliii), 123. These arms quartered with Codington, Berwick, Hussey, Nesfield and Hussey, stand at the head of the pedigree of Jordan (Harl. MS. 1561, fol. 120 and 120b) ; but the chief was 'taken away' by St. George Clarenceux (Harl. MS. 1433, fol. 67b), and in 1628 a new coat Azure a lion between nine crosslets or was granted by Segar Garter to Edmund Jordan of Gatwick.

[42] Vide Charlwood, Feet of F. Surr. Trin. 1 Will. and Mary; Recov. R. Mich. 5 Geo. II, rot. 124; Com. Pleas D. Enr. Mich. 5 Geo. II, m. 9 ; Feet of F. Surr. Mich. 27 Geo. II ; P.C.C. 357 Trevor ; Recov. R. East. 25 Geo. III, rot. 259 ; Com. Pleas D. Enr. Hil. 26 Geo. III, m. 113, 114; Recov. R. Hil. 45 Geo. III, rot. 197.

[43] Berry, Surr. Gen. 28, 29.

[44] Manning and Bray, Hist. of Surr. iii, 188.

[45] Com. Pleas D. Enr. Hil. 26 Geo. III, m. 113, 114.

[46] Brayley, Topog. Hist. of Surr. iv, 264.

[47] Information from Mr. G. H. Verrall, secretary to the company.

[48] Ct. R. bdle. 204, no. 67.

[49] Cal. Pat. 1429–36, p. 381.

[50] Berry, Surr. Gen. 40.

[51] Sloane Chart. xxxii, fol. 30. The name 'Sloghterwyk' occurs as that of a witness to deeds in the early 14th century, see Add. Chart. 18588–91. A MS. in private hands contains a list of inscriptions taken down 15 December 1622 : Thomas Sander and his wife Johanna (in the church porch, no date) ; Johanna Sander, 1470 ; Margaret wife of John Sander, d. 1477 ; Richard Sander, d. 1480 ; William Sander, d. 1481 (husband of Johanna above) ; Agnes (wife of Richard above), d. 1485 ; James Sander, third son of Richard Sander, d. 1510 ; Nicholas

Saunder (d. 1553) and Alice his wife, father and mother of Sir Thomas Saunders, King's Remembrancer of the Exchequer.

[52] Feet of F. Surr. 24 Hen. VI. no. 17.

[53] Chan. Inq. p.m. (Ser. 2), cxli, 29.

[54] Feet of F. Surr.Trin. 43 Eliz. ; Chan. Inq. p.m. (Ser. 2), cccxcii, 129.

[55] P.C.C. 28 Land.

[56] Berry, Surr. Gen. 40, 41 ; Le Neve, Knights (Harl. Soc. viii).

[57] Close, 25 Chas. II, pt. iv, no. 6.

[58] Com. Pleas D. Enr. Trin. 9 Geo. IV, m. 4.

[59] Add. Chart. 18588, 18590–1, 18600.

[60] Subs. R. Surr. bdle. 184, no. 4, xv⁰ & x⁰.

[61] Add. Chart. 24596.

[62] Early Chan. Proc. bdle. 100 ; no. 79 ; Close, 38 Hen. VIII, pt. i, no. 63.

[63] Close, 38 Hen. VIII, pt. i, no. 63 ; Feet of F. Div. Co. Mich. 1 Edw. VI.

[64] Chan. Inq. p.m. (Ser. 2), cccxliv, 66.

[65] Manning and Bray, Hist. of Surr. ii, 188.

other manors in Charlwood which were held by this family,[64] and probably became united with the main manor. It is named on the tomb of Philippa Sharp in 1759, and in the sale of 1806.

No mention of *SHIREMARK* as a separate manor is found until the 16th century, and it was probably included in the manor of Charlwood, being evidently situated in that part of the parish which borders Sussex. In 1542 Shiremark was quitclaimed, with the manor of Charlwood, to Sir Robert Southwell and Margaret by Henry de la Hay.[67] The manor of Shiremark passed to Henry Lechford before the latter obtained that of Charlwood from Sir Robert Southwell, as in 1546 Lechford sold it to Henry Amcotts.[68] In 1616 Sir Thomas Hewett, then holding the manor, conveyed it to William Mulcaster,[69] whose son Thomas was rector of the church of Charlwood.[70] In 1625 it passed from William Mulcaster to Edmund Jordan of Gatwick,[71] with whose manor of Charlwood it has since descended.[72]

ROWLEY is another reputed manor in this parish which was held of the manor of Charlwood. In 1429–30 Reginald Cobham of Charlwood made an agreement with the Abbot of Chertsey concerning the right to repair the banks of a certain brook which flowed past a meadow of Reginald Cobham and into the main stream, called Emel stream (the Mole), flowing from a mill called Rowle Mill to one belonging to the abbot in Horley.[73] It is possible from this account that the mill marks the position of lands afterwards known as ' the manor of Rowley,' the manor of Gatwick, close by, being held at that time by Cobham. In 1497 the 'manor' of Rowley was held by the family of Culpepper.[74] John Culpepper died seised of it in 1565 and was succeeded by his son Thomas.[75] The manor descended in this family until 1648,[76] when Sir William Culpepper, bart., with his brother and other trustees conveyed it to Thomas Luxford.[77] George Luxford held the manor in 1683, when he conveyed it to Thomas Jordan,[78] and it appears to have been in this family as late as 1770.[79] In 1820 it was held by George Maximilian Bethune of Worth in Sussex in the right of his wife, Anna Maria.[80] It is now a farm.

In 1295 Master Clement de Wyk held 21s. rent in Charlwood.[81] In 1357 an inquisition taken on John son and heir of John de Brewes states that he held a tenement called *WYKES* in Charlwood consisting of a toft, a garden worth 4d., 100 acres of arable land, 5 acres of meadow worth 5s., and 20s. rent ; mention is also made of one Richard de Sloghterwyk who held land in Charlwood of John de Brewes, paying an annual rent of 2s. at the tenement called Wykes.[82]

At the end of the 15th century land called Wyke-land is referred to as being parcel of the manor of Gatwick ;[83] it is probable that it was identical with the Wykes before named. In 1539–40 Henry VIII granted the 'manor of Wykland '[84] in Surrey to Sir Robert Southwell in fee.[85]

Sir Robert Southwell was so notorious a recipient of monastic lands that the grant raises a suspicion that ' Wykland' answered to the 60 acres once held in Newdigate by Merton Priory (see under Newdigate). But a messuage in Charlwood, 'Wykelandes in Charlwood,' and Lowfield Common had been granted for life that same year to Agnes widow of Walter Whyght, lately in occupation of the same, by Thomas Nudygate, John Skynner, and others, and by a deed of 10 October 1541 the reversion of the life interest of Agnes, now wife of William Wever, was confirmed to Sir Robert Southwell and his heirs for the sum of £100 paid to William Wever and Agnes.[86]

Sir Robert Southwell, in 1547, received licence to alienate the manor to Henry Lechford[87] together with that of Charlwood (q.v.), with which Wyklond, or Weekland, has since been held.[88]

EDOLPHS, a well-known farm in Charlwood, derives its name from the family of Edolf, who were settled in Charlwood in the early 14th century.[89] John Edolf made a grant of land in Charlwood in 1318,[90] and in 1371 Stephen Edolf, or Edolfi, quitclaimed land there to William Walsshe.[91] At the end of the 15th century a messuage and lands called Edolfi's was held by Henry Lechford, whose family afterwards held the manor of Charlwood.[92]

Occasional reference is found to a *RECTORY MANOR* in Charlwood. The earliest mention of land belonging to the rectory occurs in 1316–17, when a grant of land in Charlwood, bounded on one side by that of the rectory, is recorded.[93] Manning states that in 1406–7 Richard, vicar of the parish, held lands of the manor of the rectory.[94] In 1535 Philip Mesurer, rector, gave the annual value of the rectory as £20 13s. 4d., of which the house with garden and cemetery of the church was worth 20s.[95] A conveyance of the rectory, made in 1629, includes ' all manors, views of frankpledge, courts leet and baron &c. belonging,'[96] and a deed of 1828 also mentions the ' manor of the rectory.'[97] According to Manning courts were held by most of the rectors from quite early times.[98]

The church of *ST. NICHOLAS* CONsists of a chancel (now used as a vestry and organ chamber) 28 ft. 4 in. long by 16 ft. 7 in., south chapel (now serving as the chancel) 26 ft. 5 in. by 19 ft. 2 in., central tower 16 ft. 8 in.

[64] Recov. R. East. 25 Geo. III. rot. 259 ; Com. Pleas D. Enr. Hil. 26 Geo. III, m. 113–14.

[67] Feet of F. Div.Co. Mich.34 Hen. VIII.

[68] Close, 38 Hen. VIII. pt. i, no. 63 ; Feet of F. Div. Co. Mich. 1 Edw. VI.

[69] Feet of F. Div. Co. Hil. 13 Jas. I.

[70] Surr. Arch. Coll. xi ; Dict. Nat. Biog. (Hy. Hesketh).

[71] Close, 1 Chas. I, pt. xviii, no. 17.

[72] Vide Charlwood Manor.

[73] Exch. K.R. Misc. Bks. vol. 25, fol. 367.

[74] Feet of F. Surr. Mich. 13 Hen. VII.

[75] Chan. Inq. p.m. (Ser. 2), cxlii, 91.

[76] Ibid, clix, 50 ; Recov. R. Trin. 33 Eliz. rot. 17 ; Chan. Inq. p.m. (Ser. 2),

cccclv, 80 ; Feet of F. Div. Co. East. 6 Chas. I ; Trin. 22 Chas. I.

[77] Feet of F. Surr. Mich. 24 Chas. I.

[78] Ibid. Mich. 35 Chas. II ; Recov. R. Mich. 35 Chas. II, rot. 45.

[79] Feet of F. Div. Co. (K.S.B.) Mich. 10 Geo. III.

[80] Feet of F. Surr. East. 1 Geo. IV.

[81] Ibid. East. 23 Edw. I, no. 38.

[82] Chan. Inq. p.m. 31 Edw. III (1st nos.), no. 49.

[83] Star Chamb. Proc. Hen. VII, no. 31.

[84] It seems that the manor of Wyklanda, and some at least of the land called Wykelandes, must be distinguished. The former may have been partly in Newdigate, the latter in Charlwood.

[84] L. and P. Hen. VIII, xiv (1), 590.

[85] Close, 33 Hen. VIII. pt. i, no. 66.

[87] Pat. 1 Edw. VI, pt. viii, m. 15.

[88] See Newdigate parish.

[89] Add. Chart. 17303, 17307, 18588, 18590, 18600.

[90] Add. Chart. 8816.

[91] Feet of F. Surr. 45 Edw. III, no. 87.

[92] Early Chan. Proc. bdle. 100, no. 79.

[93] Add. Chart. 18590.

[94] Manning and Bray, Hist. of Surr. ii, 192.

[95] Valor Eccl. (Rec. Com.), ii, 43.

[96] Close, 5 Chas. I, pt. xxvi, no. 13.

[97] Recov. R. East. 9 Geo. IV, rot. 314.

[98] See note 94.

north to south by 15 ft. east to west, nave (the present north aisle) 37 ft. 4 in. by 22 ft. 8 in., south aisle 16 ft. wide below the nave, and a south porch ; all these measurements are taken within the building.

The plan is of much interest, preserving the aisleless nave and the tower of a church of c. 1100, the tower having been set between the chancel and nave, with the same internal width as the former, but being externally wider owing to the greater thickness of its walls. The nave is 6 ft. wider than the tower, and the tower itself is not accurately square, being about 2 ft. less from east to west than from north to south. Its greatest inclusive measurement is 24 ft., a size which occurs so often in 12th-century towers that it has claims to be considered normal. In the beginning of the 14th century a south aisle 16 ft. wide was added to the nave, and the chancel seems to have been lengthened and probably rebuilt some thirty years later. The south porch is a 15th-century addition, and about 1480 a large south chapel of the full width of the south aisle was added, and arches opened to it from the old chancel and tower. It is inclosed on the line of the east wall of the tower by a screen, and was doubtless the Lady chapel. In modern times, owing to its greater convenience, it has become the chancel, the old chancel being used as an organ chamber and vestry. Cracklow notes that the church was repaired and a gallery erected in 1716.

A certain amount of modern repair has been done, much of the external firestone ashlar being in a bad state of decay, whilst there are several cracks over the tower arches.

The old chancel has a 15th-century east window of three trefoiled lights under an elliptical head with moulded labels inside and out ; the jambs outside have a wide casement mould ; and the external label and outer order of the arch are modern restorations. On either side of the window are 15th-century image-niches about 4 ft. high with trefoiled and square heads ; they are only 7 in. deep, but the projecting brackets which formerly existed beneath them have been cut away. A fireplace is now placed across the south-east angle. The first of the two north windows, much restored, dates from c. 1330, and has two ogee trefoiled lights with a half-quatrefoil between them under a square head, the jambs and head being of one hollow-chamfered order, with a scroll moulded label and head stops, now much perished. The second north window is a 16th-century insertion of two plain lights with four-centred arches in a square head ; below it the wall has been pierced by a modern doorway of very poor character. An arcade of two bays divides the old chancel from the south chapel (present chancel) ; its middle pillar is octagonal, each face being concave, and has a moulded base and capital of late section ; each respond consists of rather more than half of a similar pillar, and the capitals, especially that of the west one, are set back as far as possible, in a peculiar manner, to obtain a wider arch thereby ; the arches are four-

centred and of two chamfered orders ; and on the north side (towards the original chancel) they have a moulded label, while there is none on the south.

The east window of the chapel has three trefoiled four-centred lights under a depressed four-centred arch ; it has been partly repaired outside. In the south wall is a small square recess with moulded edges, which has no drain and seems to be a credence rather than a piscina recess.

The first and second windows in the south wall have details like those of the east window, and are of three lights under square heads, their masonry being to a large extent old.

The ground stage of the tower has a two-light 15th-century window in its north wall, and arches in the other three, that to the old chancel being much altered and made up with roman cement ; it is round-headed, and springs from square imposts, being evidently the original opening ; while the west arch of the tower is also original, but much more perfect, with small attached shafts with cushion capitals to the inner order ; the shafts have chamfered bases dying on the splayed plinth of the jamb ; and the

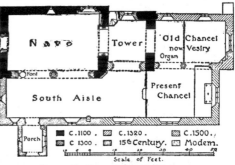

PLAN OF ST. NICHOLAS' CHURCH, CHARLWOOD

semicircular arch is of two square orders. The south arch dates from the addition of the chapel, and has semi-octagonal responds with chamfered bases and plainly moulded capitals which bear signs of 17th-century or later recutting ; the arch is a pointed one of two hollow-chamfered orders.

The tower stair is a modern one of wood inclosed in the north-west corner, accessible only by an external square-headed doorway. The ringing chamber has two rectangular lights on the north, a small round-headed light looking into the nave in the west, and the upper half of a blocked round-headed window on the south ; the bell-chamber or third story is lighted in each wall by pairs of round-headed lights ; those in the east wall have brick jambs, but the others are of stone in a more or less decayed condition ; the parapet has a moulded string and embattled coping of 15th-century date or later.

The early nave walls are very well preserved, except on the south, the original sandstone quoins showing at the western and north-eastern angles. The only original window, however, is that in the north wall, a small round-headed light set about midway in its length.

At the north-east is a very beautiful two-light window of c. 1300 with a quatrefoil in the head, set in a tall arched recess which seems to be of earlier date, possibly of the first half of the 13th century ; adjoining it in the west wall of the tower is a smaller arched recess, both being connected with the altar which formerly stood at the north-east of the nave. The recess in the north wall is much taller than is commonly the case, but there seems no reason to suppose that it was ever intended to open to a chapel on the north-east, as has been suggested. It may have been heightened when the window was inserted.

The south arcade, c. 1300, is of two bays with an octagonal pillar and semi-octagonal responds ; the bases and capitals are moulded, and the arches are two-centred and of two chamfered orders. The west doorway of the nave is an early 15th-century insertion, and has double-chamfered jambs and a pointed arch of two double-ogee orders with a label ; and over it is a 15th-century window of three cinquefoiled lights with cusped tracery in a two-centred arch.

The south aisle has a piscina near where its former east wall stood ; it has moulded jambs and a two-centred arch with trefoiled soffit cusps, and a filleted roll hood mould forming a straight-sided gablet over the arch ; the sill containing the octofoiled basin projects and is moulded below ; halfway up is a shelf, above which the recess deepens. The window west of this piscina is contemporary with the aisle, and is of two trefoiled lights with a cinquefoiled circle in the pointed head ; the splayed jambs have hollow-chamfeted edges, and the internal label is a scroll mould with mask stops ; outside is a similar label with one volute and one mask stop. The south doorway is a pointed one with moulded jambs and arch, and has a scroll mould label with corbel stops, and the west and south-west windows are trefoiled lancets with soffit cusps, all being contemporary with the aisle.

The porch is a 15th-century addition ; it has an east window of two plain pointed lights in a square head, and a broken holy-water stoup which was moulded like a capital on three sides. In the west wall is a tiny quatrefoil piercing the outer archway, having moulded jambs and pointed head ; it has been much repaired with cement. The porch is built of sandstone ashlar, and contrasts with the rest of the walling, which is of thin shaly rubble with stone dressings. There was formerly an inscription on the porch,[99] ' Orate pro anima(bus) Thome Sander et Johannae uxoris eius et pro animabus omnium fidelium defunctorum.' This inscription survived the Reformation, for it is noticed in a MS. description of the church written on 12 December 1622 (now in private hands), but was probably destroyed in the Civil Wars.

The east wall of the old chancel is coated with new cement. All the roof timbers are old, those of the present chancel and south aisle being of the date of the building of the chancel, c. 1500, while those of the nave and old chancel are probably somewhat earlier ; all seem to have been underdrawn with plaster ceilings. Under the tower is a modern flat panelled ceiling.

Across the entrance to the present chancel is a fine contemporary screen of eighteen panels (four of which

are over the central opening) with ogee cinquefoiled heads and trefoiled tracery. The cornice is painted and gilded ; the lower part carved with a running vine pattern, and the upper has the initials R.S. (for Richard Sander, who died in 1480) several times repeated between pairs of winged dragons. Over the central opening, which retains its double doors, are the letters IHS and a crowned M supported by angels, and there are also two shields on the cornice, with the arms of Sander—Sable a cheveron ermine between three bulls or, tongued gules, impaling Carew—Or three lions passant sable. The lower panels of the screen are plain and solid, and the middle rail is carved with a band of quatrefoiled lozenges.

The altar table is of dark oak, and is apparently of late 18th-century date. The pulpit is an octagonal one made up with ornamental carved cartouche panels containing painted texts of about 1620, and seven earlier linen panels probably of the 16th century.

In the chapel is an ancient chest 4 ft. by 1 ft. 8 in. by 1 ft. 8 in. with a three-sided lid, bound by plain iron straps and having three locks.

The seats are modern.

On the south wall of the south aisle are a set of very interesting wall paintings, for the most part contemporary with the aisle. To the east of the window by the pulpit are scenes from the story of St. Margaret, arranged in bands one above another. The highest shows the governor Olybrius hunting, and sending his huntsman to bring Margaret to his palace. Below, Margaret is being beaten and imprisoned, and swallowed by the dragon, whose body bursts and the saint comes forth unharmed. The lowest range, which is very indistinct, shows the beheading of the saint.

To the west of the window are some much-damaged scenes, perhaps from the story of St. Nicholas, with later paintings on a larger scale of the Three Living and the Three Dead, and apparently part of a St. Christopher or St. Edmund. The paintings were in very fair condition when uncovered, but have unfortunately been treated to a so-called preservative process, and have suffered in consequence.

The font is a small one with a plain octangular bowl on a square shaft ; it appears to be modern. In the west window of the former nave are some fragments of ancient glass, a portion of the figure of a saint, and several other odd pieces, including two words of an inscription. Also in the first window of the north wall are two small eyelets containing roses and leaves.

On the south wall of the chapel, or present chancel, is the brass of Nicholas Sander, 1553, and his wife Alys Hungate, with four sons and six daughters ; there are shields with Sanders quartering Carew, and another with Hungate, a cheveron engrailed between three sitting hounds, a molet for difference. On a separate plate is the Sander crest, a demi-bull holding a flower. In the old chancel is a brass plate to William Jordan, 1625, and Katherine his wife, 1626, and in the south aisle one to Nicholas Jeale, 1615. Lost inscriptions to the Sander family are given by Aubrey.[100]

There are six bells ; of these the treble and second are by Thomas Janaway, 1764 ; the third, fourth, and fifth by William Eldridge, 1697, 1668, and 1662

[99] Recorded by J. L. André in Surr. Arch. Coll. xi.

[100] Hist. of Surr. iv, 258.

CHIPSTEAD CHURCH : THE FONT

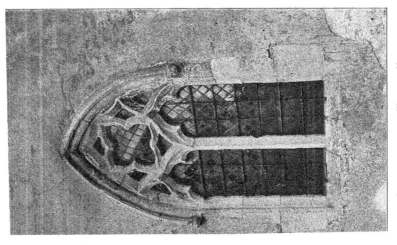

HARLWOOD CHURCH : 14TH-CENTURY WINDOW IN NAVE

respectively; and the tenor by Thomas Mears, 1835.

The communion plate consists of a cup, two patens, and a flagon of 1703–4.

The registers date from 1595.

ADVOWSON   The advowson of the church belonged with Charlwood Manor to Christchurch, Canterbury.[101] A vicarage was ordained by the monks before 1308–9, as reference is made in that year to the land of the vicar of Charlwood.[102] After the dissolution of Christchurch the advowson was apparently granted to Sir Robert Southwell with the manor, as in 1547 he alienated both to Henry Lechford,[103] whose son Sir Richard conveyed the advowson to Richard Dallender in 1609.[104] In 1615 Dallender quitclaimed to Robert Hatton,[105] from whom in 1622 it returned to the Lechfords.[106] Sir Richard, when he sold the manor of Charlwood in 1625, retained the advowson, selling it, however, in 1629 to Edmund Sander of Charlwood Place.[107]

In 1644 the rectory of Charlwood was sequestered, the rector, Thomas Mulcaster, having been proceeded against by 'five or six of the very scum of the parish,' according to his own account.[108]

His son-in-law, Henry Hesketh, who was chaplain in ordinary to Charles II, was afterwards rector of the parish.[109] In 1661 Edmund Sander devised all his lands and tenements in Charlwood, including the property of the rectory, to his sister Elizabeth Bradshaw,[110] from whom they passed to her cousin Sir William Throckmorton, who sold in 1672 to Sir Andrew King.[111] In 1716 the rectory and advowson were conveyed to Henry Wise from various parties,[112] who were according to Manning trustees of Francis Lord Aungier, to whom Sir Andrew King had conveyed them.[113] The property remained with the Wises until 1884, during which time the church was often served by members of that family.[114] It passed in 1884 to the Rev. E. M. Gibson,[115] and the living, which is still in his gift, has been held by him since that time.

The living was a peculiar of Canterbury till 1846, when it was transferred to Winchester. By the rearrangement of dioceses in 1878 it was again transferred to Rochester.

CHARITIES   Smith's Charity is distributed as in other Surrey parishes.

Four houses for the use of the poor were returned as existing in 1786, but are now lost.

The Rev. John Bristowe, rector from 1624 to 1637, left a schoolhouse and 5 acres of land to educate poor children, and Michael Earle, rector 1598 to 1624, left £2 annually charged on land for the poor.

CHIPSTEAD

Tepestede (xi cent.) ; Chepstede, *Testa de Nevill;* Chypstede (xiii cent.) ; Chipstede (xv cent.) ; Chepstid (xvi cent.).

Chipstead is a small parish, 4 miles north from Redhill, and 6 miles south-west of Croydon. It is bounded by Banstead and Woodmansterne on the north, by Coulsdon and Merstham on the east, by Gatton on the south, and by Kingswood in Ewell on the west. It measures 3 miles north-east and southwest by 2 miles north-west to south-east, and contains 2,419 acres. It lies upon a high ridge of down between 500 and 600 ft. above the sea, on the chalk which is crowned by clay with flints and a large patch of sand, between the curiously dry depression in the chalk on the east through which the Brighton and South Eastern line and the road from Croydon to Merstham run, and the valley called Chipstead Bottom on the west and north-west. The former depression, called Smitham Bottom lower down, is purely in the chalk, but in the bottom of the latter is a continuous strip of gravel and sand, showing that though now dry a stream has run down it at no very remote time. Even in the historical period, and during recent years, the water level in the chalk has sunk appreciably.

The parish is agricultural. There can hardly be said to be a village. There is a farm near the church, which occupies a commanding position on the hill, and there are scattered houses. Mugswell, which formerly was called Muggs Hole, and before that Monks Hole, is a hamlet 2 miles south-west of the church. There is a considerable amount of wood upon the sand and clay that caps the chalk. Upper Gatton Park extends into the parish, and a road runs by it from Reigate along the high ground of Chipstead towards Woodmansterne. Gatewick Heath, now inclosed, upon it, and Gatton, and Gatwick due south on the same line in Charlwood and Horley, may indicate an old track-way.

A few flakes and a celt of micaceous grit have been found about Chipstead.[1] The Chipstead Valley and Tattenham Corner branch of the South Eastern and Chatham Railway runs through the parish, and there is a station, opened in 1899, called Banstead and Chipstead, but situated in Woodmansterne parish; Kingswood Station is in Chipstead.

The land is now nearly all inclosed, except Starrock and Parsonage Green, although no Inclosure Act or Award is extant. Above Chipstead Bottom are artificial balks along the face of the chalk slope, which may be traces of ancient cultivation.

There are several gentlemen's houses. Shabden, standing in a large park, is the seat of Mr. William Milburn, J.P.; Pirbright of Mr. W. A. McArthur, M.P.; Court Lodge Farm of Mr. Frank Brown. Manning and Bray[2] consider this to be the site of the old manor house of Beauchamps. The Old Rectory, at Mugswell, 2 miles from the church, is the seat of Mr. E. Campbell Cooper. It is an old house, part of it dating

101 *V.C.H. Surr.* ii, 9; Add. Chart. 18600; Manning and Bray, *Hist. of Surr.* ii.
102 Add. Chart. 18600.
103 Pat. 1 Edw. VI, pt. viii, m. 15.
104 Feet of F. Div. Co. East. 7 Jas. I.
105 Feet of F. Surr. Mich. 13 Jas. I.
106 Close, 20 Jas. I, pt. xxxvii, no. 40.

107 Close, 1 Chas. I, pt. xviii, no. 18; 5 Chas. I, pt. xxvi, no. 13.
108 *Surr. Arch. Coll.* ix, 256.
109 Ibid. ; *Dict. Nat. Biog.*
110 P.C.C. 28 Land.
111 Close, 24 Chas. II, pt. xxv, no. 6.
112 Feet of F. Surr. Trin. 2 Geo. II.

113 Manning and Bray, *Hist. of Surr.* ii.
114 Ibid. ; Inst. Bks. (P.R.O.) ; Com. Pleas D. Enr. Trin. 9 Geo. IV, m. 4 ; Recov. R. East. 9 Geo. IV, rot. 314.
115 Close, 47 Vict. pt. xxxiii, m. 35.
1 *Proc. Soc. Antiq.* (Ser. 2), v, 374–5.
2 *Hist. of Surr.* ii, 244.

from the early 17th century. The Rev. Peter Aubertin, rector in 1808, was the first resident rector for some time, and found the old rectory converted into two labourers' cottages. He recovered it for the proper use and spent money on repairs.[3] But in 1902, owing to its distance of 2 miles from the church, leave was obtained to sell it, and the present rectory was built.

The Aubertin Memorial Church Hall was built in 1906, chiefly at the expense of Miss Aubertin, in memory of her father, the late rector.

Among the monuments in the church is one to the memory of Sir Edward Banks, who raised himself from the position of a labourer to become the builder of Waterloo, Southwark, and London Bridges. He is said to have first observed the pleasant situation of Chipstead when working as a labourer on the Merstham railway about 1803. He died in Sussex in 1835, and was buried at Chipstead by his own express direction.

Alice Hooker, eldest daughter of the author of the *Ecclesiastical Polity*, was buried here in 1649.

In 1746 Mrs. Mary Stephens left a farm for teaching six poor children to read, providing them each with a Bible, and putting out such apprentices from among them as the trustees should think fit. This is the origin of the endowed school of Chipstead, now carried on according to a scheme under the Endowed Schools Acts, of 7 July 1874, in which year the present school was built.

MANOR — The manor of *CHIPSTEAD*, according to Domesday, was held of King Edward by one Ulnode. At the time of the Survey it was in the possession of Richard de Tonbridge,[4] and as part of the honour of Clare was held in chief by his descendants until the beginning of the 16th century. In 1290 Gilbert de Clare, having married as his second wife Joan of Acre, daughter of Edward I, surrendered all his estates in England and Ireland to the king, who in several grants restored them to him or his wife and heirs.[5] Amongst the places so surrendered mention is made of 'Chepestede in Kent,' but it seems certain that this is an error for the Surrey Chipstead, the mistake being made in the first grant and never corrected. This would appear to be the case from the fact that there is no further evidence at any other date of the Clares having had possession of the Kent Chipstead, which was held of the Archbishops of Canterbury. It is not mentioned in 1217 amongst the Kentish possessions for which Richard de Clare did homage at Otford,[6] neither is it alluded to in any other documents than those referring to the lands of Gilbert de Clare, who at the time of his death was seised of the manor of Chipstead in Surrey,[7] and whose son, killed at Bannockburn, died seised of the same.[8] This Gilbert, the last Clare Earl of Gloucester and Hertford, left three sisters and co-heirs, and his peerage dignities passed to

CHIPSTEAD CHURCH FROM THE SOUTH-WEST

[3] Before the Rev. Peter Aubertin became resident rector in 1808, Chipstead was served from Croydon. It is related that the dead used to be brought to the church and left there till the parson next came round. He used to give out the next meet of the hounds from the pulpit, and cricket matches were played on the church green just outside the church, while the church itself was used as a pavilion where beer and bread and cheese could be had by the players. It is said the matches were 'notched' on the edge of the altar ! (Information by Mrs. Watson, granddaughter of Mr. Aubertin.)

[4] *V.C.H. Surr.* i, 316.

[5] *Cal. Chart. R.* ii, 350; *Cal. Pat.* 1281–92, pp. 351, 360.

[6] Chartul. of Christchurch, Canterbury, Stowe MS. 924, p. 233.

[7] Doc. relating to Surr. MS. 6167, fol. 89.

[8] Inq. p.m. 8 Edw. II, no. 68.

the Crown. In 1337, however, Hugh de Audley, the second husband of Margaret de Clare, was created Earl of Gloucester.[9] Chipstead appears to have fallen to the share of Margaret, for her grandson Hugh, Earl of Stafford, the son of her only daughter Margaret, died seised of the manor in 1386, when his son Thomas succeeded to his title and estates.[10] This Thomas married Anne the daughter of Thomas of Wood- stock, Duke of Gloucester, and she, after his death, became the wife of his brother and heir, Edmund Stafford. Their son Humphrey, who was created Duke of Buckingham,[11] in 1458 conveyed the manor to William Catesby for the purpose of settling it upon his youngest son John, Earl of Wiltshire.[12] After his father's death John held the manor jointly with his wife Con- stance, who survived him for two years.[13] Edward Stafford, the second Earl of Wiltshire, who at his mother's death in 1474–5 was only five years old, died without children in 1499, and Henry the younger son of his cousin the second Duke of Buckingham then became Earl of Wiltshire.[14] Chipstead, how- ever, passed into the possession of Henry's eldest brother Edward,[15] who had at that time succeeded to the dukedom. In 1521, when the duke was attainted and beheaded, Chipstead with the rest of his lands was forfeited to the king,[16] who in 1528 granted it to Sir John Bourchier, Lord Berners.[17] Lord Berners, the translator of Froissart's Chronicles, has left several records of a varied experience ; in 1518, while envoy in Spain, he wrote home accounts of the court sports and entertainments there, and in the following year he sent a description to the Privy Council of the Field of the Cloth of Gold. In 1520 he became deputy of Calais, where he did much in superintending the fortifications. At the time of the grant of Chipstead he was, and had been for many years, heavily indebted to the Crown, and it seems possible that the king took the manor back into his own hands when Lord Ber- ners became seriously ill in 1532–3.[18] It is perhaps more likely that Lord Berners never actually entered into possession, as besides the original grant, which may not have been immediately acted on, there is a bill to the same purport dated 1532, but unsigned.[19] In any case, there is no mention of Chipstead in his will, drawn up a few days before his death, although the reversion of two or three other manors was bequeathed

STAFFORD. Or a cheve- ron gules.

to the king in payment of the debt.[20] From 1542 to 1547 John Ledes and Ann his wife held courts at Chipstead.[21] In 1558 Thomas Matson and Ann his wife conveyed the manor of Chipstead to Thomas Copley in mortgage ;[22] another document of the same year a few weeks earlier conveying it to Thomas Percy and Reginald Heygate is probably part of the same transaction.[23] In the following year Matson conveyed it to William Frank,[24] and he, while re- taining the ownership of Chipstead Court,[25] sold the manor in 1562–3 to John Turner of the Inner Temple in trust for Sir Richard Sackville,[26] whose wife Winifred surviving him held it until her death in 1586.[27] In 1571 her son Thomas Sackville, Lord Buckhurst, sold the reversion to John Skinner of Reigate,[28] who, however, never owned the manor in fee, as he died in 1584, two years before the death of Winifred, then Marchioness of Winchester.[29] The manor was settled after his death upon his wife Alice and her sons, should she have any, with remainder to her brother William Pointz, and after him to his son John.[30] In 1613 John Pointz sold Chipstead to John Huntley,[31] who with his wife Margaret con- veyed it two years later to Sir Henry Burton.[32] According to Manning and Bray it then became part of the estates of the Owfields of Upper Gatton, Samuel Owfield holding his court there in 1635.[33] He died in 1645. His son William, who died in 1664, con- veyed it in turn to his father-in-law, Maurice Thomp- son, whose son Sir John held his first court there in 1681.[34] By him it was sold to Paul Docminique,[35] and henceforth it apparently followed the same de- scent as Merstham, becoming the property of Rachel Tattersall and her husband John,[36] and later that of William Jolliffe, with whose descendants it has re- mained up to the present day, Lord Hylton being now lord of the manor (vide Merstham).

For a short period the manor of Chipstead seems to have been held in subfee from the Clares by the Dammartins. In 1230 it was quitclaimed to Mar- gery widow of Odo de Dammartin as part of her dower by Roger de Clare and his wife Alice, daughter of Odo, formerly wife of John de Wauton.[37] In 1248 Alice Dammartin conveyed the manor of Chip- stead to Thomas de Warblington,[38] who probably afterwards surrendered it, for in an undated document Richard de Clare, Earl of Gloucester and Hertford, granted the manor of Chipstead to Nicholas de Leuk- enore to hold as two knights' fees.[39] This grant must have been made by Richard, who became Earl of Gloucester in 1230 and who died in 1262, as he was the only Richard de Clare who bore the title.[40]

[9] G.E.C. Peerage, Gloucester.
[10] Ibid. Stafford ; Cal. Pat. 1385–9, p. 365.
[11] G.E.C. Peerage, Buckingham.
[12] Feet of F. Div. Co. Trin. 36 Hen. VI ; Chan. Inq. p.m. 38 & 39 Hen. VI, no. 59 ; 13 Edw. IV, no. 13.
[13] Chan. Inq. p.m. 15 Edw. IV, no. 44.
[14] G.E.C. Peerage, Wiltshire.
[15] Mins. Accts. Harl. MS. 1667.
[16] G.E.C. Peerage, Buckingham.
[17] Pat. 19 Hen. VIII, pt. i, m. 18 ; L. and P. Hen. VIII, iv, 3991 (15).
[18] Dict. Nat. Biog. Sir John Bourchier ; and see in West Horsley.
[19] L. and P. Hen. VIII, v, 858.
[20] P.C.C. 10 Hogan.
[21] Court Rolls penes Lord Hylton. They were patrons of the living in 1552.

[32] Manning and Bray, Hist. of Surr. ii ; Feet of F. Surr. East. 4 & 5 Phil. and Mary.
[23] Feet of F. Surr. Hil. 4 & 5 Phil. and Mary.
[24] Feet of F. Surr. Hil. 1 Eliz.
[25] Chan. Inq. p.m. (Ser. 2), ccxlii, 33.
[26] Close, 8 Eliz. pt. i.
[27] Feet of F. Surr. Trin. 13 Eliz.; G.E.C. Peerage, Winchester.
[28] Ibid.
[29] Chan. Inq. p.m. (Ser. 2), cciv, 123 ; G.E.C. Peerage, Winchester.
[30] Pat. 32 Eliz. pt. xvi, m. 36.
[31] Feet of F. Surr. Mich. 11 Jas. I.
[32] Ibid. Trin. 13 Jas. I.
[33] 21 Oct. 11 Chas. I ; Court Roll penes Lord Hylton. The two Owfields were both M.P. for Gatton. For deaths see Com.

Journ. 3 Sept. 1645, and return of election of Sir Nicholas Carew vice W. Owfield, deceased 1664.
[34] 19 May 1681 ; ibid. The courts from 1663 to 1681 were all held by Ed- ward Thurland, 'Seneschal.' He con- tinued as 'Seneschal' after 1681, but the lord's name appears again.
[35] Close, 3 Anne, pt. i, no. 14.
[36] P.C.C. 96 Ducie.
[37] Feet of F. Div. Co. Mich. 15 & 16 Hen. III, no. 89. The Testa de Nevill (Rec. Com.), 219, 220b gives Alice Dam- martin holding a knight's fee in Chipstead of the honour of Clare.
[38] Feet of F. Surr. East. 32 Hen. III, 50.
[39] Add. Chart. 20039. See Effingham.
[40] G.E.C. Peerage.

CHIPSTEAD COURT, also called a manor, was retained by William Frank when he sold the manor in 1563 (*vide supra*), and held by him at his death in 1595, when his son Robert succeeded him.[41] In 1639 Ferdinand Heybourn died seised of this estate, leaving as heirs his elder brother John's three daughters—Elizabeth wife of George Morton, Hester wife of Henry Burley, and Mary wife of Francis Mascall.[42] It must have been reunited to the manor, for as Court Lodge Farm it was bought from the Tattersall trustees by William Jolliffe in 1788.

BEAUCHAMPS.—In the 14th century the family of Beauchamp of Hatch in Somerset held property in Chipstead, which also afterwards came to be called the manor of Chipstead. A mention of this estate occurs in 1301, when John de Beauchamp complained that, during his absence in Scotland, Thomas de Wotton and several others had cut his corn at Chipstead and driven away 200 sheep.[43] The property was apparently at this time in the tenure of his mother

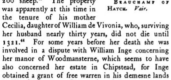

BEAUCHAMP OF HATCH. *Vair.*

Cecilia, daughter of William de Vivonia, who, surviving her husband nearly thirty years, did not die until 1321.[44] For some years before her death she was involved in a dispute with William Inge concerning her manor of Woodmansterne, which seems to have also concerned her estate in Chipstead, for Inge obtained a grant of free warren in his demesne lands in Woodmansterne, Chipstead, and Ewell in 1314. Cecilia, however, must have won her cause here as at Woodmansterne, for the ownership eventually remained with the Beauchamps.[45]

Her son and grandson, both named John, succeeded her in turn, the latter dying childless in 1361. The property was then divided between his sister Cecilia wife of Sir Richard Turberville, and his nephew John Meriet, the only son of Eleanor Beauchamp.[46] Cecilia granted her half of the estate at farm to Peter atte Wode, his wife Laurencia and their son Peter, in survivorship, and Peter atte Wode accounted for the manor of Chipstead in 1364.[47] Some years later, in 1381–2, Peter and his son both being dead, Cecilia Turberville quitclaimed the manor to Hugh Queche of London, mercer, Laurencia's son by her second husband.[48] In 1387–8 there is a conveyance of Chipstead from Hugh Queche to John Gardyner,[49] probably for the purpose of settlement upon Hugh's daughter Joan Norton, who at his death in 1402

inherited his estates.[50] Joan's daughter carried the property to the Colcok (or Caldecote) family by marriage,[51] and Richard Colcok settled Chipstead upon his eldest daughter Joan and her husband John Skinner, of Reigate, who died about 1472.[52] The property then descended to their son Richard Skinner, who settled it upon his son William with remainder first to William's brother Michael, and after him to their eldest sister Anne, sometimes called Agnes. William and Michael both died childless, and about eighteen months later Anne with her husband Bartholomew Chaloner brought a suit against her sister Elizabeth the wife of John Scott, who, they complained, had taken possession of the premises, disregarding the elder sister's right.[53] The dispute was settled by dividing the estate, and in 1505–6 the moiety of Chipstead Manor was settled upon Anne and her second husband Roger Leigh and their children, with remainder to her two sons by her first husband, Henry and William Chaloner,[54] while in 1513–14 John Scott the elder settled half of the manor of Chipstead upon his son and heir, also John Scott.[55] The latter John Scott died in 1558,[56] and was succeeded in turn by Richard Scott and his son Thomas, both of whom died within a couple of years, and Edward Scott, Richard's brother, inherited the property,[57] which he held apparently in 1571, when he presented to the living. It is not possible to trace it further. A house called Noke, near the church, may have been the same.

A fair was held in Chipstead in the reign of Edward I, and is again referred to in 1584.[58] A court leet and view of frankpledge are said to have belonged to the manor in the 16th century,[59] but according to Brayley no such court was held there, and consequently the constable for Chipstead, who is now appointed at the quarter sessions, used to be chosen at the sheriff's tourn for the hundred of Tandridge.[60]

In 675 Frithwald, *subregulus* of Surrey, gave 5 hides of land in Chipstead to the abbey of Chertsey,[61] and this seems to have been the property which was afterwards known as the manor of *PURBRIGHT* (Purybrith, Pirifrith, xiii cent.). In 933 a similar grant from Athelstan to the abbey speaks of the vill of Chipstead.[62] In 967 Edgar confirmed a gift of 10 hides,[63] while under Edward the extent is again estimated at 5 hides.[64] These variations appear to be different estimates of the value of the same land, as in Domesday the Abbot of Chertsey is said to hold Chipstead, which, though assessed at 5 hides under King Edward, was rated at 1 hide only at the time of the Survey.[65] It was then held at farm of the abbot. The abbey remained overlord of the manor[66] and received from the rector of Chipstead all the tithes

[41] Chan. Inq. p.m. (Ser. 2), ccxlii, 33.
[42] Ibid. dxxx, 198.
[43] Cal. Pat. 1301–7, p. 79.
[44] G.E.C. *Peerage,* Beauchamp of Somerset ; Chan. Inq. p.m. 14 Edw. II, no. 38.
[45] Rot. Parl. (Rec. Com.), i, 304a, 322a ; Chart. R. 8 Edw. II, m. 22. no. 53.
[46] G.E.C. *Peerage,* Beauchamp of Somerset ; Add. Chart. 23729. No mention of the second half of the estate is extant, but it is possible that it was quitclaimed to Cecilia, and became the property of Hugh Queche with the rest.
[47] Mins. Accts. bdle. 1092, no. 3.
[48] Close, 5 Ric. II, m. 24 d.
[49] Ibid. 11 Ric. II, pt. i, m. 45 d.

[50] Chan. Inq. p.m. 4 Hen. IV, no. 25 ; Feet of F. Div. Co. 4 Hen. IV, no. 65.
[51] Manning and Bray, op. cit. quoting Rawlinson's MSS. in the Bodleian, no. 425, fol. 104.
[52] Harl. MS. 897, fol. 140.
[53] Star Chamb. Proc. bdle. 19, no. 86. This is dated reign of Henry VIII, but internal evidence proves that it must have occurred before 1505. In the Visitation (Harl. 1561, fol. 50) Bartholomew is called Thomas Chaloner.
[54] Feet of F. Surr. Hil. 21 Hen. VII.
[55] Ibid. Hil. 5 Hen. VIII.
[56] Chan. Inq. p.m. (Ser. 2), cxxi, 148.
[57] Ibid. cxxxi, 191.

[58] Plac. de Quo War. (Rec. Com.), 740 ; Chan. Inq. p.m. (Ser. 2), cciv, 123.
[59] Ibid. cxlv, 11 ; Feet of F. Surr. Trin. 13 Eliz. ; Close, 8 Eliz. pt. i.
[60] Brayley, *Hist. of Surr.* iv, 299.
[61] Birch, *Cart. Sax.* i, 64 ; Kemble, *Cod. Dipl.* v, 19. But see notes on Chertsey for the doubtful character of the alleged earliest Chertsey charters.
[62] Ibid. ii, 193.
[63] Ibid. iii, 6 ; Birch, *Cart. Sax.* iii, 469.
[64] Kemble, *Cod. Dipl.* iv, 151.
[65] V.C.H. Surr. i, 310.
[66] Testa de Nevill (Rec. Com.), 220b, 221b ; Chan. Inq. p.m. 20 Edw. I, no. 25.

of the lands of Purbright and Lovelane,[67] until its dissolution in 1538, when the abbot and twelve monks were transferred by the king to his new foundation at Bisham, which was endowed with the abbey lands. In the following year the new monastery also surrendered to the king.[68]

The immediate tenants of the manor before 1066 were Turgis and Ulf, the former belonging to the abbey, while Ulf could 'seek what lord he pleased.' The two estates seem to have been united later, and were held from the abbot by William de Wateville, who, however, relinquished the land before 1086. It was then farmed out at 40s.[69] In the 13th century Peter de Pirifrith, from whom it must have taken the name of Purbright, held one quarter of a knight's fee in Chipstead of the abbot.[70] Peter granted one carucate of land in Chipstead to Thomas de Leukenore in 1247, and in 1252-3 he gave 10 librates of land there to Joan the daughter of Henry Lovel for the yearly rent of a pair of white gloves.[71] In 1291 the manor of Purbright was amongst the possessions of Hamo de Gatton, his son and heir, also Hamo, being at that time twenty-six years of age.[72]

The next reference to Purbright is given by Manning and Bray, who quote the Court Rolls of Coulsdon. According to these one Gilbert Malevyle was distrained in 1360 for fealty for lands in Chipstead called Puribrit, and again in 1389 Sir Thomas Brewes was distrained for the same cause.[73] These lands were probably the manor, for Coulsdon was held at that time by Chertsey Abbey, and a tithing-man for Chipstead was chosen at the Coulsdon court leet.[74] Nothing further appears touching the descent of this manor until 1505, when one-half of it was in the possession of Anne and Roger Leigh, Purbright, presumably, having been divided at the same time as Chipstead between them and the Scotts[75] (q.v.). In 1590 it was in the hands of Thomas Best, who, in his will dated 11 March of that year, left it to his wife Ann for eighteen years, while she brought up his son and heir William.[76] In 1618 William Best died seised of the manor of Purbright, which was said to be held of the lords of the manors of Gatton, Coulsdon, and Merstham.[77] His son and heir William, who at his father's death was aged a little over four years,[78] conveyed the manor to the use of Sir Samuel Owfield and his wife Katherine, with remainder to their sons, and in Katherine's will dated 1662, and proved 1664, she confirmed the settlement of the property on her second son Samuel.[79] About three years later the Owfields conveyed Purbright to Thomas Manning and Samuel Salter,[80] possibly trustees for Sir John Thompson, afterwards Lord Haversham,

CHERTSEY ABBEY. *Party or and argent St. Paul's sword argent, its hilt or, crossed with St. Peter's keys gules and azure.*

who sold it in 1704 to Mr. Docminique.[81] With Chipstead it became the property of William Jolliffe, but was sold in lots by the present Lord Hylton.

The church of *ST. MARGARET* is a fine cruciform building, with a chancel 30 ft. by 16 ft. 10 in., crossing 16 ft. 10 in. square; north transept 17 ft. 10 in. by 14 ft. 4 in.; south transept 15 ft. 3 in. by 14 ft. 4 in.; nave 53 ft. 9 in. by 17 ft.; north aisle 52 ft. by 9 ft. 5 in.; south aisle 53 ft. 2 in. by 7 ft. 10 in., and a south porch, all the measurements being internal.

The west wall of the nave, from the evidence of a doorway formerly existing here, and shown by Manning and Bray (drawing dated 1794), appears to be in part of 12th-century date, and the north doorway of the nave, now reset in the north aisle, is work of c. 1180. The north aisle itself is a modern addition, as is the south porch, and the south transept has been for the most part rebuilt, but all the rest of the church belongs apparently to one design consisting of chancel, central tower with transepts, and nave with south aisle, begun early in the 13th century, and carried through without any obvious pause in the work. The north transept is not square with the tower, for some reason which is not now clear, but otherwise the setting out is very regular and there is no deviation from the axis of the old work. The outer walls of the south aisle have perhaps been rebuilt in the 15th century, and there has been a good deal of modern repair, the tower bearing the dates 1631, 1827, and 1903.

The stone chiefly used is the firestone of the district, which while very good for internal work stands the weather badly, and has had to be very largely renewed.

The east window of the chancel is of partly restored 15th-century work, of three cinquefoiled lights with tracery in a two-centred head; at the angles of the inner sill are the moulded bases of a 13th-century shaft belonging to the original east window, probably a group of three lancets.

In the side walls of the chancel are tall and very narrow lancets, five on each side according to the original design, but one on the south-west has been destroyed for the insertion of a modern priest's door with a round window over it, the rear arch of which is that of the old lancet. The external jambs and heads are chamfered and rebated and have all been renewed, but the firestone weathers badly and is already crumbling to pieces. The inside splays are original and have triangular heads instead of two-centred or segmental rear arcades, a very unusual feature. Beneath the sills is a plain roll string-course, and the external hood-moulds run as horizontal strings between the windows.

Near the east end of the south wall is an aumbry with jambs, sill, and square head rebated for a shutter. To the west of this is a 13th-century piscina with a circular basin and a chamfered trefoil head. On either side of the western half of the chancel is a stone seat contemporary with the rest of the work,

[67] Index, Winton Epis. Reg.; Egerton MSS. 2031-34, i, fol. 61; ii, fol. 46, &c.; *Valor Eccl.* (Rec. Com.), ii, 56; Exch. K.R. Misc. Bks. xxv, fol. 30, &c. In a confirmation of these tithes by William Giffard, Bishop of Winchester, 1107-29, they are said to have been given to the abbey by Robert Oil of Larreu.

[68] *L. and P. Hen. VIII*, xii (2), g. 1311 (22); Dugdale, *Mon.* vi, 526.
[69] *V.C.H. Surr.* i, 310.
[70] *Testa de Nevill* (Rec. Com.), 220b, 221b.
[71] Feet of F. Surr. East. 32 Hen. III; *Abbrev. Plac.* (Rec. Com.), 133.
[72] Chan. Inq. p.m. 20 Edw. I, no. 25.

[73] Manning and Bray, *Hist. of Surr.* ii, 245.
[74] Ibid.
[75] Feet of F. Surr. Hil. 21 Hen. VII.
[76] P.C.C. 28 Kidd.
[77] Chan. Inq. p.m. (Ser. 2), dix, 168a.
[78] Ibid.
[79] P.C.C. 117, Bruce.
[80] Close, 19 Chas. II, pt. ii, no. 31.
[81] Ibid. 3 Anne, pt. i, no. 14.

the ends carved with a single long 'palm leaf' of unusual character, fitted to the hollow curve of the back end. The southern seat now runs no farther west than the new south door.

The four crossing arches have jambs of two stop chamfered orders continuous with the two-centred arches, and an abacus splayed on both edges at the spring. There is a label of similar section on the east side of the chancel arch.

The crossing is covered with a stone vault having wide and shallow diagonal ribs with splayed edges and a beautiful carved boss at the crown.

The north transept has two lancet windows in its east wall which are similar to those of the chancel, and in the north wall are three lancets with modern external stonework dating from 1854, but the inner east and west jambs are original and have shafts with moulded bases and capitals. The two intermediate shafts are modern. The rear arches are rebated and have a large roll moulding in the angle, and the moulded label continues as a horizontal string. Above these windows is a modern circular quatrefoil,

All this work is modern, the transept having been destroyed, as it is said, by fire in the 17th century, and rebuilt in 1855. A half arch, now blocked, formerly opened from the transept to the south aisle, and the wall south of the arch is thickened, having in it a stair entered from a door high up on its west face, and looking into the aisle and leading to the space above the crossing. Part of the west wall of the transept projecting beyond the south wall of the aisle, and containing the rear arch of the blocked lancet, seems to be old, but Manning and Bray's view shows no projection at the angle of the aisle.

The south arcade of the nave is of four bays, with circular columns having moulded bases and capitals, and two-centred arches of two chamfered orders with a chamfered label on the nave side only. Above the arches, but now below the aisle roof, are three circular clearstory windows, contemporary with the arcade, inclosing quatrefoils and having an external rebate and semicircular rear arches.

The north arcade is a modern copy of that on the south, but has no clearstory windows above it. The

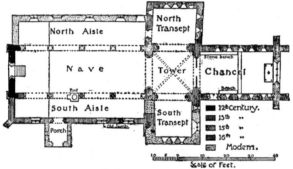

PLAN OF ST. MARGARET'S CHURCH, CHIPSTEAD

and in the apex of the gable a small loop, and there is a west lancet like those in the east wall, but it has had its rebate cut out to widen it. In the east wall of the transept near the south angle is a small square-headed piscina with a circular basin, and at the east end of the north wall are two lockers one above the other, square-headed like that in the chancel. In the west wall is a doorway formerly external, but now opening to the north aisle, with jambs of two chamfered orders, the outer continuous with a two-centred arch on the west face, while the inner is carried up to form a trefoiled head on a tympanum with a segmental soffit. The priest's door on the south side of the chancel is copied from this doorway. Above the arch is a circular window inclosing a quatrefoil rebated for a frame like the rest, the rear arch being triangular.

The south transept has two blocked lancets like those of the chancel, one in the east wall and the other in the west. The east wall has also a modern two-light tracery window of 14th-century design, and in the south wall is a triplet of lancets more or less copied from the corresponding ones in the north transept, with a quatrefoil circle in the gable above.

west doorway of the nave is modern, of 16th-century style, replacing that shown by Manning and Bray, which had a round arch with a roll moulding, shafts in the jambs, and some ornament not specified on the arch. It seems to have been of fairly early 12th-century date, and over it was a window of three trefoiled lights, now replaced by one of three cinque-foiled lights with tracery in a two-centred head.

The north wall of the north aisle contains three modern two-light windows of 15th-century design, and at the east end of the same wall is a doorway, also modern. Between the second and third of these windows is set the late 12th-century doorway already referred to, with a round arch of two roll-moulded orders springing from slender jambshafts with carved capitals, two having the form of heads, and two ornamented with foliage; the bases are lost. The arch has a label enriched with dog-tooth ornament and is a great deal repaired. In the old north wall of the nave there was a round-headed window towards the west, and three narrow lancets farther east.

The windows of the south aisle have modern tracery, two being of 15th-century and one of 14th-century

CHIPSTEAD CHURCH : THE CHANCEL

CHARLWOOD CHURCH : NAVE LOOKING EAST

design. The inside Jambs, however, appear to be old in each case. Below the sill of the eastern of these windows is a small splayed recess in the wall with a square head and remains of colour on the Jambs, and on the outer face of the wall below the second window are a few stones of what seems to be the east jamb of a destroyed doorway. The existing south doorway is of late 15th-century character, with moulded jambs and four-centred arch under a square head with a heavy moulded label. The modern porch has quatrefoiled side lights and a south entrance with moulded jambs and two-centred arch.

The tower rises one stage above the ridge of the nave roof, this stage being now mostly of brick, only a few of the old stone quoins remaining. One of the 13th-century lancets, however, still remains in the west face above the roof line, and the Jambs of another in the same face and of one window in each of the other three sides of the tower may still be seen on the inside, though they are now blocked up. The top stage has a modern window in each face consisting of two trefoiled lights under a square head, and is furnished with a modern stone parapet. The date 1653 is shown on the west parapet of the tower in Manning and Bray's illustration.

The walls of the north aisle and west front are of flint with stone dressings, and the main body of the other walls is also faced with flint, but in the older work the mortar Joints are larger. All the roofs are modern and are covered with tiles.

Across the east arch of the tower is set a good 15th-century screen, with three cinquefoiled lights on each side of the central opening, and a moulded cornice on which is fixed an 18th-century carved wooden achievement of the royal arms of England.

The pulpit and reading desk are of late 16th-century date and have moulded panels, and ornamental pilasters and rails and a dentil cornice.

The font is of 14th-century date and has a large octagonal bowl, each having a shallow sunk panel filled with tracery patterns, all different. It stands on a circular stem with moulded base.

In the south windows of the south transept are some small pieces of late 13th-century glass with figures of St. Peter and St. Paul, and in the east window of the chancel some fragments of 15th-century glass, among modern imitations.

There are also some old quarries in the windows of the south aisle.

On the north wall of the chancel is a small tablet to 'Christopher Shawe Citizen of London embroderer,' who died in 1618.

In the churchyard, near the porch, is a coffin slab with a double hollow-chamfered edge, and on the top are traces of a raised cross, now almost defaced. Outside the east end of the south aisle are two fragments of another large coffin slab on which was a raised flowered cross with a stepped base.

The tower contains a ring of five bells : the treble and second by John Hodson, 1658 ; the third by

William Mears, 1785 ; and the fourth and tenor by Robert Eldridge, 1607 and 1595.

The plate comprises a cup of 1664, with a stand paten of 1714, and a silver mounted flagon.

There are six books of registers, the first containing baptisms from 1656 to 1804, the second marriages from 1663 to 1754, the third burials from 1656 to 1804, the fourth baptisms from 1804 to 1812, the fifth marriages from 1805 to 1811, and the sixth burials from 1805 to 1812.

The churchyard is large and contains several elm trees, and a large yew on the north side. There is an entrance on the west side with a lych-gate.

ADVOWSON The advowson of the church of Chipstead has generally followed the descent of the manor. Towards the end of the 13th century Ralph de Monthermer, who had married Joan widow of Gilbert the Red, and in her right was called Earl of Gloucester, presented to

MONTHERMER. *Or an eagle vert.*   AUDLEY. *Gules fretty or.*

Chipstead Church.[82] At the beginning of the following century it was in the gift of Hugh de Audley, Earl of Gloucester,[83] through his marriage with Margaret de Clare, and from their daughter Margaret descended with the manor to the Earls of Stafford.[84] In 1402 it seems to have been leased to John Norton and his wife Joan, and in the following year to John Fremingham.[85] In 1422 it was mentioned amongst the right and possessions of Sir Hugh Stafford.[86] Sir John Bourchier presented in 1519,[87] John Ledes and Agnes his wife in 1552.[88] In 1558 Thomas Matson conveyed the advowson in mortgage to Thomas Copley,[89] in the next year selling it to William Frank.[90] It was then held in turn by the Sackvilles[91] and by William and John Poyntz.[92] Edward Scott presented in 1571, Lord St. John and Winifred his wife in 1573, and Lord Dacre in 1586. The advowson was conveyed in 1613 to John Huntley. After the resale of the property in 1615 the right of presentation no longer belonged to the lord of the manor. In 1658 it was owned by George Moore,[93] and in 1664 was still held by his wife Margaret, then a widow.[94] The Crown presented in 1678, and Thomas Middleton in 1740. Anthony Nott had the advowson in 1747 and 1753. William Jolliffe bought it about 1790 and his descendant Lord Hylton now holds it. Anne Aubertin presented in 1808 by agreement with Col. Hylton Jolliffe.[95]

[83] Index Winton Epis. Reg. Egerton MSS. 2031-4, i, fol. 61, 62 ; G.E.C. *Peerage,* Gloucester.

[88] Ibid. ; Index Winton Epis. Reg. Egerton MSS. 2031-4, ii, fol. 46, 47.

[84] Ibid. ; *Wykeham's Reg.* i, 232 ; *Cal. Pat.* 1467-77, p. 543.

[85] Feet of F. Div. Co. Trin. 4 Hen. IV, 65 ; *Wykeham's Reg.* i, 241.

[86] Chan. Inq. p.m. 1 Hen. VI, no. 33.

[87] Winton Epis. Reg. Fox, iv, fol. 3*b.*

[88] See Chipstead Manor, and Winton Epis. Reg. Poynet, fol. 4*a.*

[89] Feet of F. Surr. East. 4 & 5 Phil. and Mary.

[90] Ibid. Hil. 1 Eliz.

[91] Ibid. Trin. 13 Eliz.

[92] Pat. 32 Eliz. pt. xvi, m. 36 ; Feet of F. Surr. Mich. 11 Jas. I.

[93] Parl. Surv. of Surr. Living, Lambeth MSS. Cert. vol. 21, fol. 5.

[94] Feet of F. Div. Co. Hil. 1652; Recov. R. Trin. 16 Chas. II, rot. 135.

[95] Inst. Bks. (P.R.O.), and information supplied by Lord Hylton.

195

In the Taxation of Pope Nicholas and in Wykeham's Register the spiritualities of Chipstead were rated at £18 13s. 4d., the tithes being £1 17s. 4d.[96] In 1428 the church was taxed at £21 6s. 8d. and paid a subsidy of £1 17s. 4d.[97] Under Henry VIII the value was nearly the same, being £18 3s. 6d.; 2s., however, was due yearly to the Bishop of Winchester and 7s. 7½d. for the procurations of the archdeacon, reducing the net value to £17 13s. 10¾d. Of this, the house and grounds

were worth 30s.; the tithes of grain amounted to £9. and private baptisms brought in about 6s. 8d. yearly.[98]

The commissioners of 1658 recommended the union of Chipstead and Kingswood in Ewell.

CHARITIES Smith's Charity is distributed as in other Surrey parishes. Christopher Shaw, embroiderer, who died 31 July 1618, and was buried at Chipstead, left an annual rent-charge of 16s. for the poor.

GATTON

Gatetune (x cent.); Gatone (xi cent.); Gatton (xii cent.).

Gatton is a small parish 2 miles north-east from Reigate. It is bounded on the north by Chipstead, on the east by Merstham, on the south by Reigate, and on the west by Kingswood in Ewell. It is on the crest and southern slope of the chalk downs, and extends southwards on to the Upper Green Sand and Gault. The church and such village as there is stand on the Green Sand. The parish measures about a mile from east to west, and a trifle more from north to south, and contains 1,200 acres of land and 32 of water. A tongue of the parish ran southwards, south of Merstham to the boundary of Nutfield, but was added to Merstham (q.v.) in 1899.

The situation of Gatton is highly picturesque. The upper part of the parish, on the chalk hills, is upwards of 700 ft. above the sea. A great part of the centre of the parish is taken up by Gatton Park, which covers 550 acres, nearly a half of the whole acreage. In it is the lake formed by damming up water from small springs which ultimately flow down to the Mole. There are two other ponds. The parish is very well wooded with various kinds of trees.

The village is represented by a small group of houses at the north-eastern gate of the park; but there is no shop, no public-house, and now no school. There are five gentlemen's houses, one vacant, besides Gatton Park and the rectory, and one farm. There were undoubtedly other houses in the ground now covered by the park, but though Gatton was a borough there is no evidence that it was ever a place of any importance or of any large population.

The so-called town hall is an open portico supported on pillars in the pseudo-classical style, and may date from the 18th century, when the proprietor was usually the only voter. In it now is an urn 'in memory of the deceased borough.'

The same stone which is dug at Merstham is also found and worked in Gatton parish.

The road which skirts the north-eastern side of Gatton Park is apparently part of the old line of communication along the chalk downs, and the Ordnance map marks it as called in Gatton, 'The Pilgrims' Way.' This does not appear to be justified. The old way left the present road at a point near the north-east corner of the park and crosses the park to the present lodge, whence it continues still eastward to Merstham. The old line of road is clearly visible in the park. In the northern part of the parish

British coins have been found, some way north of the old road. Close to the former school, much nearer the road and lodge entrance to the park just mentioned, both British and Roman coins have been found. In the park, near Nutwood House, is an ancient well which has what is supposed to be Roman masonry round the upper part. Roman tiles have been picked up, and the late rector, Mr. Larken, had a bronze ring which he found in the park, which was said by the late Sir A. W. Franks of the British Museum to be part of Roman ornamental horse trappings, intended to hold two straps together. There is therefore reason to believe that Gatton was occupied during the Roman dominion in Britain.

Practically the whole of Gatton is the property of the lord of the manor. Upper Gatton, standing in a park, was formerly the capital mansion of a separate manor (see below). It is now the seat of Mr. Alfred Benson. Nutwood Lodge is the seat of Capt. Charles Francis Cracroft Jarvis. The house called Gatton Tower is used as the rectory. The old rectory near the church was pulled down by Sir James Colebrooke, owner 1751–61, who also turned most of the glebe into the lake which he made, and altered the interior of the church, destroying all the old monuments. The Tower was originally what its name indicates, and probably built as a summer-house for the view on an eminence in the park, but has had a house attached to it.

There is now no school. The late Lord Oxenbridge supported a national school of about twenty children. It was started as an infant school about fifty years ago and made a mixed school about ten years later. It was his private property and sold with the estate. After the Act of 1902 it was discontinued. The few children attend Merstham or Chipstead School.

BOROUGH So far as can be judged from somewhat scanty records there appear to be no traces of burgage tenure in Gatton before the middle of the 15th century, when it first sent two burgesses to Parliament, and subsequently there are no signs of a corporate community except in respect of the distinct Parliamentary representation of the 'borough.'

In 1086 the only tenants of the manor were 6 villeins and 3 bordars[1] and later extents do not show any peculiarity of tenure. The town inhabitants, numbering seventeen, were assessed in 1332 for a tenth as a town, instead of the fifteenth then levied from rural districts,[2] but the term 'borough' was

[96] *Pope Nich. Tax.* (Rec. Com.), 207; *Wykeham's Reg.* i, 379.
[97] *Feud. Aids,* ii, 114.
[98] *Valor Eccl.* (Rec. Com.), ii, 46.

[1] *V.C.H. Surr.* i, 303.
[2] *Lay Subs. R. bdle.* 184, no. 4, m. 3, 11. But the assessment is very low, £3 0s. 2d., less than rural parishes like

Merstham, which was not of much greater size than Gatton and was assessed at £4 8s.

not apparently applied to Gatton till 1450, when it returned two burgesses.[3] The returning officer was the constable,[4] who was at first appointed in the sheriff's tourn at Tandridge and afterwards in the quarter sessions.[5]

From 1450 until the Reform Act of 1832 Gatton returned two burgesses to Parliament. The first extant return, that of 1452-3,[6] was made by the constable 'with the assent of the whole borough.'[7] From the first it must have been a 'pocket' borough. In 1536 the Duke of Norfolk, then lord of the neighbouring borough of Reigate, noted Gatton, 'where Sir Roger Copley dwelleth,' among the towns for 'which in times past he could have made burgesses.'[8] In 1539 Sir Roger Copley found the privilege burdensome, for there was only one house to be any help in paying the members' wages.[9] In 1547 Sir Roger, as 'burgess and only inhabitant of the borough and town,' elected Richard Shelley and John Tyngelden,[10] and after his death his widow nominated the burgesses, one of them in 1558, her own son, then under age.[11] After the death of Sir Thomas Copley in 1584 his widow was not allowed to elect burgesses, since she was a recusant, but members were nominated in 1584 by Lord Burghley as chief officer of the Court of Wards.[12] In 1586 the lords of the Council recommended two members to the deputy-lieutenants of the county, but two others of similar loyal opinions were in fact returned.[13] The Copleys, who were always notorious recusants, never regained their right of nomination, though their influence must have been considerable, for in a dispute concerning the election of 1620 it was stated that six out of the seven houses in the 'town' were occupied by tenants of William Copley, although the right of election was decided in favour of the freeholders,[14] and in 1696 it was agreed that the franchise was in the freeholders of the borough not receiving alms and occupying their own freeholds.[15] In 1832 the borough was disfranchised as having, with its twenty-three houses, the unenviable position of fourth from the bottom of the list of 'rotten boroughs.'

There is no evidence of a charter of incorporation.

MANOR One hide at Gatton was bequeathed by Alfred the Ealdorman to Ethelwald his son between the years 871 and 889.[16] In the time of Edward the Confessor Gatton was assessed at 10 hides. It was held by Earl Leofwine, brother of Earl Harold, who held the earldom of the county.[17] He fell at Hastings, and Gatton became the land of Bishop Odo of Bayeux, of whom it was held by a certain Herfrey.[18]

The bishop forfeited the overlordship of Gatton with his other English possessions through his complicity in the Norman rebellion of 1088. Probably it was then held of his manor of Ospringe, co. Kent, to which the lord of Gatton was said to owe suit of court from the 13th century onwards.[19] Both Ospringe and Gatton were members of the honour of Peverel in Dover.[20]

The actual tenant in 1086 was Herfrey. His son or grandson Hamon gave a moiety of the manor to Ralph de Dene in marriage with his elder daughter Joan, reserving to himself the other moiety for life, with remainder to Ralph. The agreement was confirmed by Henry II,[21] but Hamon's heir 'male, Robert de Gatton,[22] evidently took possession of his moiety, but was ousted c. 1190 by Geoffrey de Beauvale in right of his wife Idonea. She was mother of Robert de Dene,[23] and probably connected with Ralph de Dene, for in 1220 the heirs of Ralph de Dene, Geoffrey Sackville, Richard de Cumberland, his wife Sibyl, and Parnel de Beauvale, granddaughter of Geoffrey de Beauvale, impleaded Hamon son of Robert de Gatton for his failure to keep an agreement concerning a moiety of the manor with Robert de Dene.[24] The plea was postponed on account of the minority of Parnel, whose mother Margery had recovered seisin of one carucate at Gatton against Hamon before 1223.[25] In that year he recovered this carucate from Parnel, since her father Ralph son of Geoffrey de Beauvále, a spendthrift who hated his heirs, had restored it to Robert de Gatton for £28 in the time of King John.[26] In 1227 she joined with the other heirs of Ralph de Dene in a release of the whole manor to Hamon de Gatton.[27] He was appointed escheator of the Crown for Surrey in 1232,[28] but died in or before 1235, when his lands, saving the dower of his widow Beatrice, were given into the custody of William of York during the minority of his heir.[29] This heir was probably Robert de Gatton,[30] who died seised of the manor in or before 1264.[31] His son and heir Hamon, Sheriff of Kent in 1285,[32] was holding the manor at his death shortly before 1 February 1291-2.[33] He was succeeded by a son of the same name, whose infant son Edmund inherited Gatton upon his death, c. 1299.[34] The custody of all Hamon's lands with the exception of Gatton Park was granted in 1301 to the executors of Edmund Earl of Cornwall in part payment of the king's debt to him.[35] They conveyed it to Sir William Milksop, kt., who sold it to John Northwood.[36] Edmund de Gatton did not live to enjoy his inheritance, which was divided between his two sisters and co-heirs, Elizabeth wife of William de Dene, and Margaret wife of Simon Northwood, brother or son of

[3] Original Parl. Returns, 29 Hen. IV.
[4] Ibid. 31 Hen. VI; 31 Chas. II; Carew, Hist. Acct. of Rights of Election, 244.
[5] Manning and Bray, Hist. of Surr. ii, 227.
[6] No separate return exists for 1450, although the names of the two members, Thomas Bentham and Hugh Huls, are recorded with those of the other Surrey burgesses on a membrane attached to the writ to the sheriff.
[7] Parl. Returns, 31 Hen. VI.
[8] L. and P. Hen. VIII, x, 816.
[9] Ibid. xiv (1), 645.
[10] Ret. of Memb. of Parl. i, 376.
[11] Ibid. 394; in 1552 she had presided over a jury to inquire respecting the state

of Gatton Church (Hist. MSS. Com. Rep. vii, App. 608a).
[12] Add. MS. (B.M.), 5702, fol. 86-7.
[13] Hist. MSS. Com. Rep. vii, 642b.
[14] Carew, Hist. Acct. of Rights of Elections, 244.
[15] Wm. Bohun, Debates touching Rights of Electing, 7.
[16] Kemble, Cod. Dipl. 317.
[17] Freeman, Norm. Conq. ii, 568.
[18] V.C.H. Surr. i, 303a.
[19] Chan. Inq. p.m. 29 Edw. I, no. 58; ibid. (Ser. 2), cccv, 159.
[20] Red Bk. of Exch. ii, 617, 709; Testa de Nevill (Rec. Com.), 220, 226.
[21] Curia Regis R. 78 (Mich. 4 & 5 Hen. III), m. 10.
[22] Ibid. 83 (Mich. 7 & 8 Hen. III), m. 7 d.

[23] Pipe R. 2 Ric. I, m. 13 d. Her name occurs in Curia Regis R. 83, m. 7 d.
[24] Curia Regis R. 78, m. 10.
[25] Feet of F. Surr. 8 Hen. III, 28.
[26] Curia Regis R. 83, m. 7 d. and Feet of F. Surr. 8 Hen. III, 28. Hamon, however, paid her 30 marks for the quitclaim.
[27] Feet of F. Surr. 11 Hen. III, 38.
[28] Cal. Close, 1231-4, p. 130.
[29] Cal. Pat. 1232-47, p. 130; Excerpta e Rot. Fin. i, 292.
[30] Cf. Feet of F. Surr. 32 Hen. III, 4.
[31] Chan. Inq. p.m. 48 Hen. III, no. 20.
[32] List of Sheriffs (P.R.O.), 67.
[33] Chan. Inq. p.m. 20 Edw. I, no. 25.
[34] Ibid. 29 Edw. I, no. 58.
[35] Cal. Pat. 1292-1301, p. 603.
[36] Ibid. 1301-7, p. 338.

John Northwood.[37] Gatton was evidently assigned to the latter, for her husband was holding the manor in 1327,[38] and her son Sir Robert Northwood, kt., was holding in 1344,[39] and was summoned to do homage for it in 1345.[40] He died in 1360, leaving a son and heir Thomas.[41] The latter's sisters and co-heirs, Agnes Northwood and Joan wife of John de Levedale, conveyed the manor to Richard, Earl of Arundel and Surrey, in 1364,[42] and Gatton was among the lands seized by the Crown on the attainder and execution of his son Richard in 1397.[43] His son Thomas, Earl of Arundel, was restored to his father's lands in 1399,[43a] and so probably to Gatton, although no record mentions his tenure of it. At his death in 1415 his lands were divided among his three daughters and co-heirs, the eldest of whom, Elizabeth, married Thomas Mowbray, Duke of Norfolk. Her great-grandson, John, Duke of Norfolk, probably granted Gatton about 1446[44] to his retainer John Timperley,[45] who in 1449 had licence to inclose the manor.[46]

John Timperley conveyed the manor[47] to feoffees to the use of Roger Copley and his wife Anne and their heirs.[48] Roger Copley, son of the former Roger and Anne, in May 1537 en-tailed it on his son Thomas ; after his death, which took place in 1548,[49] his widow Elizabeth nominated the bur-gesses, and Thomas Copley re-presented Gatton in 1554, 1557-8, and 1562-3.[50] Un-der Queen Mary he was com-mitted to the custody of the Serjeant at Arms for indiscreet words in favour of the Lady Elizabeth in Parliament.[51] He had scruples about the oath of supremacy, left England without licence in 1569 and became a leader among the English fugitives, was created Baron Copley of Gatton by the King of Spain, and died in Flanders in 1584.[52] His son and heir William Copley settled the manor on his younger son William in 1615, but the latter died in 1623 in his lifetime, leaving two infant daughters, Mary and Anne.[53] His estate had been sequestered for his recusancy c. 1611, and an annuity of £160 from it granted to Sir William Lane, who had evidently procured the sequestration.[54]

COPLEY. *Argent a mill-rind cross sable.*

Captain Henry Lane, son of Sir William, petitioned for a lease of Gatton Manor in 1630.[55] Apparently he was unsuccessful, for in 1632 William Copley the elder was pardoned his recusancy and permitted to hold Gatton for twenty-one years for an annual rent to the Crown.[56] Meanwhile his granddaughters Mary and Anne had been left under the guardianship of Sir Richard Weston, who married them to his two sons John and George, in spite of the protests of their grandfather.[57] Their estates were again sequestered for their recusancy, c. 1650.[58] John Weston's moiety was purchased from the Treason Trustees by John Carrill in 1653.[59] Finally, a partition of the lands of William Copley the younger assigned Gatton to John and Mary Weston,[60] who joined with John Carrill and others in a sale to Thomas Turgis in 1654.[61] He died in 1661[62] leaving a son Thomas, who in 1669 obtained a release of the manor from Richard Weston.[63] By his will[64] dated 1703 he bequeathed it to his kinsman William, eldest son of George Newland of Smithfield. He left it to his brother Dr. George Newland for life, with remainder to the sons of his own daughters in tail male. The estate was sold after his death to James Colebrooke,[65] who was created baronet in 1759. His two daughters, Mary wife of John Aubrey and Emma wife of Charles, Earl of Tankerville, sold Gatton to their uncle Sir George Colebrooke, bart., from whom it was purchased in 1774 by Sir William Mayne, afterwards Baron New-haven of Ireland.[66] It was then successively purchased by a Mr. Percy and a Mr. Graham.[67] Mary and George Graham sold to Robert Ladbrooke of Portland Place in 1789.[68] He sold the manor to John Petrie in February 1796,[69] and it was purchased in 1808 by Mark Wood, later Sir Mark Wood, bart.[70] After his death it was purchased by trustees for John, fifth Baron Monson.[71] It was sold in 1888 by the seventh Lord Monson, created Viscount Oxenbridge in 1886, to Mr. J. Colman, since created Sir J. Colman, bart., the present owner.

A house of considerable importance was attached to Gatton Manor in 1220,[72] and a deer-park existed in 1278.[73] The custody of the park was entrusted to John Berwick, a clerk of the king, from 1301 on-wards during the minority of the heirs of Hamon de Gatton.[74] The hall was divided between the sisters of Thomas de Northwood in 1362.[75] Possibly John Timperley wished to enlarge the park in 1449 when

[37] *Plac. Abbrev.* (Rec. Com.), 318.
[38] Chan. Inq. p.m. 1 Edw. III (1st nos.), no. 35.
[39] Chan. Misc. Inq. file 151 (18 Edw. III, 2nd nos.), no. 95.
[40] *Cal. Close*, 1343-6, p. 528.
[41] Chan. Inq. p.m. 34 Edw. III (1st nos.), no. 72.
[42] Close, 37 Edw. III, m. 38-40 ; Feet of F. Surr. 38 Edw. III, 39.
[43] Chan. Inq. p.m. 21 Ric. II, 137, m. 11c.
[43a] *Cal. Pat.* 1399-1401, p. 134.
[44] It was at this date that he granted Flanchford in Reigate.
[45] He was M.P. for Reigate in 1453 and 1460.
[46] Chart. R. 27-39 Hen. VI, no. 41.'
[47] It is strange that as late as 1468-9 Gatton is included in lands granted by the Duke of Norfolk to Thomas Hoo and others, apparently to a certain John Charlys in exchange for a manor in Suf-

folk (Feet of F. Div. Co. 8 Edw. IV, 64; Early Chan. Proc. bdle. 137, no. 4). Whether this inclusion is an error or not it is difficult to say, but in 1518 Roger Copley received a quitclaim from Michael Denys and his wife Margery (Feet of F. Surr. Mich. 10 Hen. VIII) which may represent Charlys' interest.
[48] Feet of F. Surr. Mich. 10 Hen. VIII ; Berry, *Surr. Gen.* 85.
[49] Chan. Inq. p.m. (Ser. 2), lxxxix, 139.
[50] *Ret. of Memb. of Parl.* i, 391, 394, 398, 406.
[51] *Cal. S.P. Dom.* 1580-1625, p. 66.
[52] *Dict. Nat. Biog.* xii, 189 ; *Cal. S.P. Dom.* 1580-1625, p. 66.
[53] Chan. Inq. p.m. (Ser. 2), ccccv, 159.
[54] Ibid. 1629-31, p. 427.
[55] Pat. 8 Chas. I, pt. iv, no. 2.
[56] *Cal. S.P. Dom.* 1638-9, p. 41 ; *Cal. of Com. for Compounding* i, 252.
[57] Ibid.
[58] Ibid. iii, 2171.

[59] Title deeds quoted by Manning and Bray, *Hist. of Surr.* ii, 231.
[60] *Close*, 1654, pt. xl, no. 10.
[61] Title deeds quoted by Manning and Bray, *Hist. of Surr.* ii, 231.
[62] Feet of F. Surr. Trin. 21 Chas. II.
[63] Quoted by Manning and Bray, loc. cit.
[64] Private Act, 24 Geo. III, cap. 39.
[65] Title deeds quoted by Manning and Bray, loc. cit.
[66] Brayley, *Hist. of Surr.* iv, 310.
[67] Com. Pleas D. Enr. Trin. 29 Geo. III, m. 264.
[68] Ibid. Hil. 36 Geo. III, m. 298, 308. Petrie immediately mortgaged it to Lad-brooke.
[69] Manning and Bray, *Hist. of Surr.* ii, 232.
[70] Brayley, loc. cit.
[71] Curia Regis R. 78, m. 10.
[72] *Cal. Pat.* 1272-81, p. 294.
[73] Ibid. 1292-1301, p. 597.
[74] Close, 37 Edw. III, m. 38 d.

GATTON CHURCH : THE PULPIT

GATTON CHURCH : WEST SCREEN

he obtained licence to inclose the manor, 360 acres of land, 40 acres of meadow, and land at Merstham, together with a grant of free warren there.[76] It has already been stated that the Copleys lived for some time at Gatton. Aubrey, writing late in the 17th century, mentions a fine manor-house there, and states that it was built on the site of a former castle ; but of this there is no proof.[77] The house, then known as Gatton Place, was the residence of Dr. George Newland.[78] The present Gatton Park is a very fine example of the Italian style of house. It seems to have been begun by Sir Mark Wood, owner in 1808, whose predecessor, Mr. Petrie, had pulled down part of the older house.[79] The house of Sir Mark Wood was a good deal reconstructed, if not quite rebuilt on a grander scale, by Lord Monson, for what are known as Sir Mark Wood's cellars are outside the wall of the present house. Lord Monson, who died in 1841, left it unfinished, and it was completed by his successor. The Marble Hall, entirely lined by Italian marbles, is very fine, and there was a good collection of pictures and statuary.

UPPER GATTON was the property of Samuel Owfield, afterwards Sir Samuel, who represented Gatton in every Parliament from 1623 till his death in 1644.[80] He acquired the neighbouring manor of Chipstead (q.v.), and Upper Gatton was the seat of the lords of that manor and descended with it till after the death of the Rev. James Tattersall in 1784, when Chipstead was sold to William Jolliffe, and Upper Gatton to Lord Newhaven, owner of Lower Gatton, with which it has remained united. The estate of Upper Gatton is surrounded now by a park of 100 acres in the parishes of Gatton and Chipstead.[81]

The church of ST. ANDREW has a CHURCH chancel 12 ft. 4 in. deep by 12 ft. wide, nave 48 ft. 6 in. by 40 ft., small north and south transepts, the latter containing the vestry, a north-west porch, and a west tower 8 ft. square. The general appearance is that of an early 19th-century Gothic building, almost every trace of antiquity being absent. There is, however, a piscina in the chancel which seems to be of late 13th-century date, and the east window of the north transept may be of 15th-century date, and a good part of the walling of the nave and chancel is probably ancient. The font at the west end under the tower has a band of good 13th-century foliage below the bowl, though it is otherwise much altered. The most noteworthy part of the building is the woodwork, which was brought together and presented to the church by the late Lord Monson in 1834.

The altar table and pulpit came from Nuremberg. The latter is carved with the Descent from the Cross, in three panels ; it projects from a gallery over the vestry in the south transept, from which it is entered, and is finished with a pendant below. On the altar table is another part of the same scene, showing the women at the foot of the cross. The chancel is lined with oak panelling, the framing, cornice, &c. of which are modern, but the panels, for the most part old, of late French Gothic work : there are three ranges of

twelve panels on each side, the lowest being plain linen panels, the middle ones also linen panels but of a much more elaborate character, while the top panels have very rich tracery of various designs, containing lilies, crowned Ω's, diaper pattern, passion emblems, &c.; two have AΩ and another IHS.

The nave is seated quirewise : there are three rows of seats on each side, the highest being a set of sixteen stalls backed by panelling and a canopy, and divided by arms carved with cherubs' heads; they are fitted with misericordes carved somewhat plainly in foliage and faces ; the second row is divided into three blocks, the two western of which have stalls like those of the back row ; and the front row has plain open benches. The panelling behind the stalls, brought from Belgium, has traceried heads of elaborate and delicate character ; and the cornice has a moulded top member in which is an inscription in Gothic lettering bearing the date 1515. At the west end of the nave is a screen below the organ gallery ; it is divided into five bays, the middle one with a pair of doors ; each bay is subdivided into four openings with cinquefoiled heads and tracery.

The front of the organ gallery over is modern, but a high screen rising above it contains some old tracery of the same character as the rest. The north transept is used as a private pew to the hall adjoining, and contains some panelling with 17th-century strapwork carving ; and the door of the vestry in the south transept space is made up with some elaborate linen panelling. Beside the altar table there are two chairs in the sanctuary, with carving like that of the surrounding panelling, and the altar rails are carved and traceried ; they are said to have been brought from Tongres. The church also possesses some good early 16th-century glass, brought from a religious house at Aerschot near Louvain. There are two bells ; the smaller only is rung, and was made by William Eldridge in 1665. The other is used as a clock bell and is hung high up in the wooden spire.

The plate is all of modern date and includes a cup of 1825, a standing paten of 1835, an almsdish of the same date, and a small flagon of 1870.

The registers date from 1599.

There is a clump of fir-trees in the churchyard screening the church from the hall adjoining. Part of the churchyard was destroyed by Sir George Colebrooke, brother and successor to Sir James Colebrooke, to improve the access to the house, close by which the church stands.

A church at Gatton is mentioned ADVOWSON in the Domesday Survey.[82] The advowson evidently belonged to Herfrey as lord of the manor, for he granted it to the priory of St. Pancras founded at Lewes by William de Warenne.[83] The gift was confirmed by the successive lords of Gatton in the 13th century.[84] In 1291 the church was valued at £10,[85] and a yearly pension of 30s. was due from it to the priory.[86] The advowson apparently remained vested in the prior until the surrender of his house in November 1537,[87] and in February 1537–8 it was among the

---

[76] Chart. R. 27–39 Hen. VI, no. 41.
[77] Hist. and Antiq. of Surr. iv, 217.
[78] Private Act, 24 Geo. III, cap. 39.
[79] Manning and Bray, op. cit. ii, 233, say that one Moffatt, who did not buy the estate, began to pull down the house.
[80] It was possibly divided from the original manor when the Copley estates were sequestrated for recusancy in the early 17th century.
[81] From deeds of Lord Hylton communicated by him.
[82] V.C.H. Surr. i, 303a.
[83] Anct. Chart. (Pipe R. Soc.), 13 ; cf. V.C.H. Suss. ii, 64.
[84] Cott. MS. Vesp. F. xv, 173–4.
[85] Pope Nich. Tax. (Rec. Com.), 208.
[86] Cott. MS. Vesp. F. xv, 174, 198 ; Valor Eccl. (Rec. Com.), ii, 46.
[87] Egerton MSS. 2033, fol. 99 ; 2034, fol. 16, 53, and 87 ; V.C.H. Suss. ii, 69.

A HISTORY OF SURREY

late possessions of Lewes granted with the site of the priory to Cromwell.[88] Nevertheless Michael Denys, who released the manor to Roger Copley in 1518, presented a rector in 1512.[89] It is clear that he had had a grant of the advowson for one turn only, for the priory presented in 1530.[90] Cromwell was attainted and executed in July 1540. Lord William Howard possibly had a grant or lease of the advowson, for he presented a rector in February 1550.[91] In 1551 a new royal grant of the advowson was made to Thomas Bill and his wife Agnes,[92] who immediately conveyed it to Elizabeth widow of Sir Roger Copley,[93] and she presented in 1552,[94] but it was not returned among her possessions at her death.[95] Thomas Copley presented in 1562,[96] but in 1571 the queen presented by reason of his recusancy.[97] In 1581 Michael Harris and his wife Margaret conveyed the advowson to Richard

More,[98] and again in 1596 Michael and Margaret Harris conveyed to Richard More,[99] but in 1615 the Crown presented by lapse.[100] The Rev. Nehemiah Rogers, who was himself turned out by the Parliament from St. Botolph's Without Bishopsgate, petitioned for confirmation of his title in the advowson in 1635, stating that he had acquired it by conveyances and assurances in law, possibly from Michael and Margaret Harris.[101] He presented it to St. John's College, Oxford, at the instance of Archbishop Laud, who reserved to himself the nomination of the incumbent during his lifetime.[102] Presentation was made under the Great Seal in 1648,[103] but the college presented a rector in 1666. Thomas Turgis had acquired the advowson before 1668,[104] and since his time it has remained vested in the successive lords of the manor.

CHARITY Smith's Charity is distributed as in other Surrey parishes.

HORLEY

Horley, Horlie, and Horle (xiii cent.) ; Horlee (xiv cent.) ; Horle (xv cent.).

Horley is a village 5 miles south of Redhill. The parish, which is one of the largest in Surrey, is bounded on the north by Reigate, on the east by Nutfield, Burstow, and a detached portion of Horne, on the south by Worth in Sussex, and on the west by Charlwood and Leigh. It is of irregular form, with western extensions running into Charlwood and Leigh, but the greatest length from north to south is 6 miles, and the greatest breadth from east to west 4 miles. It contains 7,957 acres of land and 25 of water. It is a Wealden parish, on the clay, with strips of sand and alluvium which stretch along the course of the Mole and its tributaries. The various branches of the Mole, those which flow from the Surrey chalk range at first southward and then westward, that coming eastward from Charlwood, and those flowing northward from Crawley and Worth in Sussex, all come into Horley and unite in the parish, which is consequently much intersected by streams. There are numerous bridges. The character of the parish has been changed by the opening, in 1841, of the Brighton Line, which runs through it, having a station at Horley, and another, also in Horley, for the use of the Gatwick race-meetings, though Gatwick is in Charlwood. Horley Village, or Horley Street, was a small place clustered round the church, east of the Brighton road and west of the Cuckfield road. East of it was an extensive common. This is now inclosed, and the station is on its site. Here a new village has grown up. Farther north, and stretching nearly all the way to Earlswood Common and Reigate parish, are frequent groups or rows of small houses and cottages. There is a Horley District Gas Company, established in 1886.

The road through part of Horley parish from Crawley to Reigate was the first turnpike road in Surrey, made by the Act 8 & 9 Will. III, cap. 15, but available then only for horses, posts being fixed in it to prevent its being subjected to the wear and tear of wheels. The road from Horley Common to Cuckfield was made a turnpike road by stat. 49 Geo. III, cap. 94, but there was an old road on this line. Probably a very old track had led from the Sussex coast in this direction, and some habitations had been made near the line of it. Thundersfield, for instance, though deep in the forest and the clay, had been accessible in Athelstan's time, if it is the Thundersfield where he held a Witan ;[1] and there is stronger reason for supposing that it is the Dunresfelda of Alfred's will. It is half a mile from the road, just outside Horley parish. The Ordnance map records Roman pottery found west of the road in Horley parish. South of Horley Station, north of Holyland Farm, a British sepulchral urn, flint arrowheads, and bronze Roman coins were found when the line was being made in 1839-40 ; and a British gold coin has been found in Horley [2] and another in Horne not far away.[3] The implements and pottery indicate dwellers in the Weald, the coins possibly show that traffic passed through it. Of the old village, not many houses remain. On the outskirts of the parish, a mile to the north of the church, are one or two old cottages close to the blacksmith's forge, and close by is a picturesque old inn, with the sign of 'The Chequers,' parts of which are of the 16th century. Adjoining the churchyard is the picturesque Six Bells Inn, dating back to the 15th century or earlier, with its steep roof of Horsham slabs, half-timbered walls and fine brick chimney. Inside is to be seen a large beam, perhaps part of a screen, bearing a battlemented moulding. The quaintness of the building is en-

[88] L. and P. Hen. VIII, xiii (1), g. 384 (74).
[89] Winton Epis. Reg. Fox, iii, fol. 7b.
[90] Ibid. Wolsey, fol. 55a.
[91] Egerton MS. 2034, fol. 164b.
[92] Pat. 5 Edw. VI, pt. vi, m. 34.
[93] Chan. Inq. p.m. (Ser. 2), ccx, 85.
[94] Winton Epis. Reg. Poynet, fol. 5b.
[95] Chan. Inq. p.m. 2 Eliz. pt. i, no. 145.

[96] Winton Epis. Reg. Horn, 7b.
[97] Ibid. quoted by Manning and Bray, Hist. of Surr. ii, 239.
[98] Feet of F. Div. Co. Mich. 23 & 24 Eliz.
[99] Ibid. East. 38 Eliz.
[100] Inst. Bks. P.R.O.
[101] Pat. 11 Chas. I, pt. xxiv, no. 28.
[102] Laud, Works (ed. Oxford, 1860), vii, 242.

[103] Lords' Journ. x, 11b.
[104] Inst. Bks. (P.R.O.). The Parliamentary Survey of 1658 says that Thomas Turgis was then patron (Surr. Arch. Coll. xviii).
[1] Thorpe, Dipl. Angl. Sax. i, 217.
[2] Evans, Coins of the Ancient Britons, 69.
[3] Ibid. 61.

hanced by tile-hanging of diamond pattern covering the upper stories; and the same kind of tiling occurs upon the walls of a large old house on the opposite side of the road.

Heaverswood Common was inclosed by an Award of 21 September 1858, parts of Earlswood Common which extended into Horley by an Award of 15 July 1886.[4] Horley Common and Thundersfield Common have been inclosed since the first issue of the Ordnance Maps.

Christ Church, Salford, was built as a chapel of ease for the northern part of the parish in 1881, and enlarged in 1892.

There is a Baptist chapel built in 1881, a Primitive Methodist chapel, and a meeting-place of the Plymouth Brethren.

There is a Cottage Hospital for the district.

In the parish are the Reigate Borough Isolation Hospital, at White Bushes, built in 1900, and the Reigate District Isolation Hospital, built in 1885.

Duxhurst has been acquired by Lady Henry Somerset as a Home for Female Inebriates, and additional houses built for the same purpose.

Horley National Schools were established in 1834. In 1872 a School Board was formed, and the schools passed under it. In 1905 they were rebuilt by the county authority.

In 1876 a school was built at Salford, and enlarged in 1886.

In 1884 a girls' school was built in Albert Road, and in 1890 an infants' school was added.

In 1896 a National School was built at Sidlow Bridge.

HORLEY is not mentioned in Domes-
MANORS day, unless it be the nameless land then in Tandridge Hundred held by Chertsey Abbey.[5] Thundersfield on the borders of Horley and Horne was granted to Chertsey by Athelstan in 933,[6] and was confirmed to the abbey by Edgar in 967,[7] when the amount of land named—30 *mansae*—must have extended into Horley,[6] the earliest references to which show that it was in the possession of the abbey.

In 1263 the Abbot of Chertsey acquired lands in Horley which he annexed to his manor of Horley;[9] John de Rutherwyk also, who was abbot from 1307 to 1346, obtained several tenements which he attached to his lordship.[10] He also reclaimed divers lands and tenements there formerly held in villeinage but occupied for a long time since by freeholders, being alienated from tenant to tenant by charter. The abbot, on behalf of the monastery, ordered these tenants to come into court and surrender their holdings; then, a fine having been paid, he gave them back to the tenants, to be held in future of the abbot himself for a fixed annual rent.[11]

The Abbot and convent of Chertsey continued to hold the manor until in 1537 the abbot surrendered his lands, including Horley, to the king.[12] Later in the same year Henry VIII granted this manor to Sir Nicholas Carew in tail male.[13] On the disgrace and death of Carew in 1538-9, his lands reverted to the Crown, and though the attainder was afterwards reversed his son Sir Francis Carew[14] did not inherit Horley. In July 1539 the king granted the manor to Sir Robert Southwell,[15] who alienated it in 1544 to Robert Bristowe.[16] The latter died in 1545, and his son and grandson succeeded to the property in turn.[17] Robert the grandson died a minor in 1563, his heirs being his aunts on his father's side, Joan Jordan, Margaret Woodman and Anne Taylor, and his cousin Thomas Twyner, son of Agnes, another aunt who had died before this date.[18] Each of these heirs received a fourth part of Horley. George Taylor and Anne conveyed their share to the Woodmans in 1564,[19] and when John Woodman, who survived his wife Margaret, died in 1587, he was therefore seised of a fourth of the manor in the right of his wife, and of another fourth in his own demesne as of fee.[20] Their son Richard alienated both parts to Matthew Carew in 1590,[21] and in the same year Henry Jordan, presumably the son of Joan and Thomas Jordan, conveyed the reversion of this fourth of the manor to Carew also.[22] In 1598 Carew obtained the remaining fourth from Thomas Yonge and Agnes, and the heirs of Agnes,[23] the latter being the daughter and heir of Thomas Twyner, who had died in 1582.[24] Carew, Doctor of Law and Master in Chancery, conveyed to James Cromer in 1600,[25] and two years later it passed from the latter to the Mayor and Commonalt of London as Governorsy of Christ's Hospital,[26] and they have remained lords of the manor to the present day.

CHRIST'S HOSPITAL. *Argent a cross gules with a sword gules upright in the quarter (which are the arms of the city of London) with chief azure having a Tudor rose between two fleurs de lis or therein.*

An early 13th-century deed records that Robert son of Walter de Horley granted the mill at Horley to Alfred son of Robert for the rent of a silver mark, together with a meadow and plough-land close by, to be held for the rent of 16*d.*[27] Alice, daughter of 'Alfred of Horley Mill,' afterwards received a grant of the mill and lands.[28]

In 1309 William de Newdigate, by deed dated at Horley Mill, granted to Thomas atte Mulle, evidently the miller, a messuage, with garden, croft, &c., which Thomas and his heirs were to hold of Newdigate and his heirs for 200 years at the rent of 12*d.*[29] In 1317 William de Newdigate alienated to Chertsey Monastery the water-mill called Newdigate's Mill or Horley Mill, together with the 12*d.* rent due from Thomas atte Mulle.[30] It passed with the manor to Sir Robert Southwell after the Dissolution,[31] and was alienated

4 *Blue Bk. Incl. Awards.*
5 *V.C.H. Surr.* i, 307 and note.
6 Kemble, *Cod. Dipl.* no. 363.
7 Ibid. no. 532.
8 Part of what was lately Thundersfield Common is in Horley parish.
9 Exch. K.R. Misc. Bks. xxv, fol. 73.
10 Ibid. fol. 353*b*, 361*b*, 363, 364.
11 Ibid. fol. 354; Lansd. MS. 435, fol. 29–38.
12 Feet of F. Div. Co. Trin. 29 Hen. VIII.
13 *L. and P. Hen. VIII,* xii (2), g. 1150 (3).

14 Harl. MS. 1561, fol. 17.
15 *L. and P. Hen. VIII,* xiv (1), g. 1354 (46).
16 Ibid. xix (1), g. 80 (64); Feet of F. Surr. Hil. 35 Hen. VIII.
17 Chan. Inq. p.m. (Ser. 2), lxxii, 85; cxxiv, 189.
18 Ibid. cxl, 176; clxxxiii, 54.
19 Feet of F. Surr. Mich. 6 & 7 Eliz.; Pat. 6 Eliz. pt. vii, m. 32.
20 Chan. Inq. p.m. (Ser. 2), ccxvi, 70.
21 Pat. 32 Eliz. pt. xiv, m. 42; Feet of F. Surr. Trin. 32 Eliz.

22 Pat. 32 Eliz. pt. xxi, m. 12.
23 Chan. Inq. p.m. (Ser. 2), cxcvii, 69.
24 Feet of F. Surr. Hil. 42 Eliz.
25 Ibid. East. 44 Eliz.
27 Add. Chart. 24587.
28 Ibid. 24589.
29 Lansd. MS. 435, fol. 48*b*.
30 Ibid. fol. 48; *Cal. Pat.* 1317–21, p. 319.
31 *L. and P. Hen. VIII,* xiv (1), g. 1354 (46).

by him to Robert Bristowe in 1541.[32] On the death of Bristowe's grandson Robert, John, half-brother to the latter, received the mill as his share of the inheritance which was divided up among co-heirs.[33] John Bristowe, in 1586, alienated to John Kerrell and Nicholas his son the mill and its appurtenances, which included land called Mill Eye, the mill-house, and all watercourses, ponds, ways and passages belonging to the mill and all its profits and commodities.[34]

In 1259 Roger de Stomnîhole and Isabel his wife granted a messuage and a virgate of land in Horley to John de Bures.[35] The land was in that part of Horley adjacent to Hartswood, as a deed relating to the latter place refers to a wood of John de Bures close by,[36] and Stumblehole in Leigh, held of Banstead, is also near. Another 13th-century deed records a grant of land in Horley, made to William, son of Roger del Mahone by John de Bures.[37] It is probable that the family of de Bures held, for at least another century, land in Horley, afterwards known as the manor of *BURES*, or *BEERES*. In 1314 land called Burilond in Horley is mentioned.[38] In 1358 an extent for debt, taken on the lands of John son of John de Bures, states that he held in Horley a messuage with 3d. per annum beyond reprises, 80 acres of land worth 20s., 25 acres of wood worth 4s. 2d., and 1s. 7d. from rent of free tenants there.[39]

In 1487 John Holgrave, baron of the King's Exchequer, died seised of the manor of Bures in Horley which he devised to his son Thomas.[40] The latter died in 1505, and was succeeded in the lordship of the manor by Robert his son.[41] In 1544 the manor was held by Richard Broke and Elizabeth his wife in the right of Elizabeth,[42] daughter and heiress of Thomas or Robert Holgrave ;[43] they conveyed it in that year to Richard Bray and his wife Joan.[44] In 1581 Sir John Bray, their son, granted the reversion of the manor, after the death of Joan his mother, to John Skinner of Reigate, who died in 1584, his nephew Richard Elyott of Albury being one of his heirs.[45] The latter was seised of the manor at his death in 1608 ;[46] his grandson Richard died unmarried in 1612.[47] Thomas Elyott, brother of the elder Richard,[48] held in 1613.[49] By deeds of 1617 and 1620 Thomas Elyott, Rachel Elyott widow of Richard, and her remaining children conveyed the manor to Sir William Garway.[50] In 1622 Garway sold to Nicholas Charrington 'the manor of Beres alias Buryes and

that capital messuage and farm called Beres . . . all of which premises are, or lately were, in the tenure of Nicholas Charrington and his assigns or farmers.'[51] The manor has since remained in the Charrington family ; Mr. E. S. Charrington holds it at present.[52]

Occasional reference is found to a manor or farm called *DUXHURST* in Horley and Charlwood.[53] Peter de Duxhurst was one of those whose lands were reclaimed by the Abbot of Chertsey[54] on the grounds that they were held of the tenement which Gilbert atte Mathe had held of the abbot's predecessors in villeinage ; the abbot granted them back to Duxhurst, to be held of the abbey.[55] In 1604 Sir John Holmden settled the manor to the use of himself and his heirs.[56] Giles Fraunces died seised of the manor or farm of Duxhurst and certain lands belonging to Horley and Charlwood in 1616.[57]

A survey of the manor, taken much later, mentions the site of the manor-house with courtyard, barn, stable, and garden and lands.[58] It was afterwards acquired with the manor of Horley, by the governors of Christ's Hospital.[59] It is now used as Lady Henry Somerset's Home for Female Inebriates.

The priory of Merton, which had certain lands and tenements in Horley from which rent and services were due, included a wood called *LANGSHOTT* among its possessions at an early date.[60] By a deed without date the prior granted Robert son of Walter of Horley 4 acres of land at Langshott to be held for the annual rent of 2s.,[61] and Roger Salaman died in 1343 seised of land in Horley held of Merton.[61a]

At the Dissolution the possessions of the priory included a farm called 'Langshott' in Horley and Horne.[62] John Cooper farmed it of the priory, by an indenture of 1525, by which it was leased to him for thirty years.[63] In 1538-9 the lands were granted by the king to Richard Gylmyn for thirty years.[64] In 1550 William Sakevyle conveyed to Thomas Yngles and Katherine and their heirs ' all those lands, meadows, pastures, woods, &c., called Langshott *alias* Landshott, and Pryers landes *alias* Pryern in Horley.'[65]

In 1669 the land was held as a 'manor' by Richard Evelyn and Elizabeth in the right of Elizabeth,[66] the daughter of George Minne.[67] It seems to have passed soon after to the family of Barnes ; William Barnes of Horley married Sarah Bridges and she, after her husband's death, devised Langshott to her nephew Alexander Bridges,[68] who held in 1733,[69] and

---

[32] L. and P. Hen. VIII, xvi, g. 1056 (4).
[33] Vide Horley ; Chan. Inq. p.m. (Ser. 2), cxl, 176 ; clxxxiii, 54.
[34] Pat. 29 Eliz. pt. ½, m. 5.
[35] Feet of F. Surr. 44 Hen. III, no. 2.
[36] Add. Chart. 24586.   [37] Ibid. 24588.
[38] Lansd. MS. 435, fol. 27.
[39] Chan. Inq. p.m. 31 Edw. III (1st nos.), no. 55. Earlier inquisitions on this family contain references which must mean this manor (Chan. Inq. p.m. 6 Edw. III [1st nos.], no. 174 ; 19 Edw. III [1st nos.], no. 54). After mentioning land in Banstead, and a tenement called Stumblehole in Leigh, the inquisitions continue, 'and there are there : assize rent per annum 47s. 2d. due from two free tenants at Banstead, 9 at La Legh, 5 at Sandon and 1 customary at La Legh.' Bures is adjacent to Stumblehole. Probably the manor-house now in Horley parish, which is not mentioned in the earlier inquisitions, had been built before 1358, causing the manor in the two much

intermixed parishes to be spoken of as in Horley. The family of Bures continued in Banstead (q.v.), but perhaps through debt sold the Leigh and Horley lands.
[40] P.C.C. 4 Milles.
[41] Exch. Inq. p.m. file 1065, no. 6.
[42] Feet of F. Surr. Mich. 35 Hen. VIII.
[43] Burke, Family Rec., 108.   [44] Ibid.
[45] Feet of F. Surr. Mich. 23 & 24 Eliz.; Chan. Inq. p.m. (Ser. 2), cciv, 123.
[46] Ibid. cccxi, 116.   [47] Berry, Surr. Gen. 25.
[48] Harl. MS. 1561, fol. 216, &c. ; Berry, Surr. Gen. 25.
[49] Recov. R. East. 11 Jas. I, rot. 23.
[50] Berry, Surr. Gen. 5 ; Visit. of Surr. (Harl. Soc. xliii), 25 ; Surr. Arch. Coll. vi, 316 ; Feet of F. Surr. Hil. 11 Jas. I ; Mich. 15 Jas. I ; East. 18 Jas. I ; Recov. R. East. 18 Jas. I, rot. 48.
[51] Close, 20 Jas. I, pt. xxiv, no. 4.
[52] Feet of F. Surr. East. 13 Geo. I ; Hil. 7 Geo. III ; Manning and Bray, Hist. of Surr. ii, 195 ; Brayley, Hist. of Surr. (ed. E. Walford, 1878), iv, 64.

[53] The present house is in Horley.
[54] Vide Horley Manor.
[55] Lansd. MS. 435, fol. 35b.
[56] Com. Pleas D. Enr. East. 2 Jas. I, m. 14.
[57] Chan. Inq. p.m. (Ser. 2), ccclxi, 98.
[58] Harl. MS. 2192, fol. 23.
[59] Brayley, Hist. of Surr. loc. cit.
[60] Cott. MS. Cleop. C. vii, fol. 88b, 103.
[61] Ibid. fol. 93.
[61a] Chan. Inq. p.m. 17 Edw. III, no. 45.
[62] Dugdale, Mon. Angl. vi, 248.
[63] Mins. Accts. 33-4 Hen. VIII, no. 169.
[64] Ibid. 36-7 Hen. VIII, no. 187. Com. Pleas D. Enr. Hil. 3 Edw. VI, m. 15. Prior's land was quite separate from Langshott.
[65] Feet of F. Surr. Trin. 21 Chas. II.
[66] Misc. Gen. and Her. (Ser. 2), iv, 125 ; v, 209 ; Betham, Baronetage, iii, 161, &c. Monument at Epsom.
[67] Burke, Landed Gentry.
[68] Recov. R. Hil. 7 Geo. II, rot. 216.

whose descendant in the fourth generation, John Henry Bridges, now holds the lands which are known as Langshott Manor.

At the end of the 13th century 40 acres of land in Horley, and a messuage there worth 13*d.* were held of Fulk de Archek, lord of Woodmansterne, by suit at the court of Woodmansterne.[70] It is possible that this land was part of what was afterwards known as the manor of *KINNERSLEY* in Horley. Fulk held his lands in the right of his wife, and they were afterwards inherited by her family, passing at length to John Skinner.[71] During this time no trace of the lands in Horley can be found, but in 1506 Agnes, a daughter and co-heir of John Skinner, then wife of Roger Leigh and formerly wife of Thomas Chaloner, held Woodmansterne together with the 'moiety of Kynworsley in Horley.'[72] In 1556 Henry Lechford and Clemency his wife held 80 acres of land in Horley called 'Kenersley' and Ladyland, in the right of Clemency daughter of Huchar,[73] who was Lechford's second wife.[74] They demised the land in 1556 to Richard Hever on a ten-year lease for a rent of £12 per annum.[75] In 1563 they conveyed the reversion of 'the manor of Kinnersley' from themselves and the heirs of Clemency to John Cowper;[76] in the following year Hever brought a suit against the latter for wrongfully entering on the premises.[77]

Cowper sold Kinnersley in 1566 to John More.[78] Edward More and Mary his wife conveyed to George and Jasper Holmden in 1584,[79] and they, with others, to Matthew Carew, Master in the Court of Chancery, in 1587.[80] The manor changed hands many times at the beginning of the 17th century. It passed successively from Carew to James Cromer,[81] William Southland,[82] George Huxley,[83] and finally, in 1606, to Sir William Mounson,[84] a distinguished admiral, who had served under Essex in the Cadiz expedition, and was at this time in command of the fleet in the narrow seas, a post which he held until 1615. In this year he fell under suspicion of being implicated in the murder of Overbury and was committed to the Tower in 1616. He was, however, released in the following year and made vice-admiral of the narrow seas, remaining in the navy until 1635, when he retired to Kinnersley and spent the last seven years of his life compiling naval tracts.[85] He died in 1642 seised of the manor of Kinnersley, which he held jointly with his son John, who died three years later.[86]

Anne, daughter and heir of John Mounson, married Sir Francis Throckmorton; they, with Ann Mounson, widow, conveyed the manor in 1667 to Arthur Kettleby and George Petty,[87] from whom it passed, in 1675, to Benjamin Bonwick,[88] whose son Benjamin, according to Manning, left two daughters and co-heirs.[89] In 1740 Charles Mason and Sarah his wife conveyed a moiety of the manor to Richard Ireland;[90] he obtained the other moiety from Samuel Duplock and Mary his wife in 1765.[91] At his death in 1780 the manor passed by will to his niece Ann Jones,[92] whose son Arthur held in 1797,[93] when he sold to Robert Piper,[94] and the latter's family held it as late as 1829.[95] During the next ten years it passed through the hands of Gibson, Fosket and Clark.[96] John Clark held until after 1845. It became the property, before 1855, of J. C. Sherrard, who held until after 1874. It passed soon after to the Brocklehurst family, and is at present held by Mr. Edward Brocklehurst.[97]

From the 16th century onwards the right of free fishery at Horley is mentioned as appurtenant to Kinnersley.[98]

In 1263 Mary daughter of William de Dammartin received a grant of a water-mill and a carucate of land in Horley to be held of Roger de Loges and his heirs for the annual rent of a pair of gold spurs, or 6*d.* and foreign service.[99] It was probably part of the lands afterwards known as the manor of *LODGE* in Horley; a water-mill was included among the appurtenances of this manor in the 16th century.[100] A tenement called Labbokland, which Roger son of Roger atte Logge had quitclaimed to the Abbot of Chertsey in 1324,[101] was also held with the manor about 1590.[102] Evidently this family, who held the manor of Lodge in Burstow (q.v.) in the 14th century, gave their name to their lands in Horley also. These latter lands they may have held of the Abbot of Chertsey, while their under-tenants held of them as mesne lords. In the 15th century Lodge in Horley was held of the lord of the manor of Lodge in Burstow,[103] while in the next century it was held of Sir Robert Southwell,[104] to whom the manor of Horley had been granted at

70 Chan. Inq. p.m. 21 Edw. I, no. 37; 32 Edw. I, no. 28.
72 *Vide* Woodmansterne; Manning and Bray, *Hist. of Surr.* ii, 460, 461.
73 Feet of F. Surr. Hil. 21 Hen. V; Manning and Bray, *Hist of Surr.* ii, 244.
70 Ct. of Req. bdle. 41, no. 26; *Visit. of Surr.* (Harl. Soc. xliii), 43.
74 Chan. Inq. p.m. (Ser. 2), cxlv, 13; *Visit. of Surr.* (Harl. Soc. xliii), 43. The fact that his first wife had been Mary, daughter of a Thomas Chaloner (*Visit. of Surr.* [Harl. Soc. xliii] 43) suggests that the moiety of 'Kynworsley' held by Agnes, co-heir of John Skinner and at one time wife of Thomas Chaloner, passed by marriage of a daughter Mary to Lechford, and that he obtained different moieties of the manor with each of his wives, Clemency having acquired hers from Elizabeth Scott, the second co-heir of John Skinner. There is also a manor of Kinnersley in Carshalton, of which John Scott died seised in 1532, but in spite of this coincidence the descents do not seem to have been otherwise the same, for John Scott acquired this Kinnersley

from Edward Burton and his wife Isabel, who were holding in the right of Isabel.
74 Ct. of Req. bdle. 41, no. 26.
76 Feet of F. Surr. Trin. 5 Eliz. Cowper's mother was also named Clemency. She was the daughter of — Engler, so was not the same as Clemency Lechford. In 1549 she bought land in Horley of Robert Hawkes as Clemency Cowper (Feet of F. Surr. Mich. 3 Edw. VI). In 1566 Cowper sold the land which his mother, Clemency Cowper, had bought of Hawkes (Feet of F. Surr. Hil. 8 Eliz.). Richard Cowper, her husband, who held Roys in Horley of the manor of Banstead, died in 1549. His youngest son and heir, 'according to the custom of the manor,' was Robert (Banstead Ct. R. 2 May 1549). He also held Langshott in Horley (q.v.). John and Richard were other sons.
77 See note 75.
78 Feet of F. Surr. Hil. 8 Eliz.
79 Ibid. Trin. 26 Eliz.
80 Ibid. Trin. 29 Eliz.
81 Ibid. Hil. 42 Eliz.

82 Ibid. Trin. 43 Eliz.
83 Ibid. Trin. 1 Jas. I.
84 Ibid. Mich. 4 Jas. I.
85 *Dict. Nat. Biog.*
86 Ibid.; Feet of F. Surr. Hil. 7 Chas. I; Chan. Inq. p.m. (Ser. 2), xxxii, 26.
87 Feet of F. Surr. Trin. 19 Chas. II; Brydges, *Collins Peerage*, vii.
88 Feet of F. Surr. East. 27 Chas. II.
89 Manning and Bray, *Hist. of Surr.* ii, 90.
90 Feet of F. Surr. Hil. 14 Geo. II.
91 Ibid. Trin. 5 Geo. III.
92 P.C.C. 323 Collins.
93 Recov. R. East. 29 Geo. III, rot. 312; Feet of F. Surr. Trin. 37 Geo. III.
94 See note 89.
95 Feet of F. Surr. Mich. 8 & 9 Geo. IV.
96 Brayley, *Hist. of Surr.* iv, 283.
97 Kelly, *Directories of Surr.*
98 See above references.
99 Feet of F. Surr. Hil. 47 Hen. III.
100 Chan. Inq. p.m. (Ser. 2), cxxiv, 189.
101 Exch. K. R. Misc. Bks. xxv, fol. 361b.
102 Pat. 32 Eliz. pt. xxi, m. 12.
103 Chan. Inq. p.m. 11 Edw. IV, no. 42.
104 Ibid. (Ser. 2), lxxii, 85; cxl, 176.

A HISTORY OF SURREY

the dissolution of Chertsey Monastery. Probably the mesne lordship lapsed before the Dissolution, as the de Burstows of Horley, who are known to have held the manor of Lodge in that place in the 15th century and afterwards, held at an earlier date a considerable amount of land there direct of the abbot, who was lord of Horley Manor. In 1336, for instance, William de Burstow held land called Spiresland of the abbot, and died leaving a son John.[105] In 1339 John de Burstow made an exchange of lands with the abbot by which the former received lands called Mutheslond, Blakemores and Joyneres, to be held of the abbot for a rent of 7s. 5d.[106] In 1417 Robert de Burstow is referred to as holding a messuage called Muthesland.[107]

In 1471 John Bury died seised of the manor of ' Loge ' in Horley, held, as has been said, of John Codyngton, then lord of the manor of Lodge in Burstow, and of 50 acres of land called Blakemores and Joyneres and a toft and 20 acres called Speryslond held of the Abbot of Chertsey.[108] He had been enfeoffed of the manor to the use of himself and his heirs, in 1458, by Robert de Burstow of Horley, Viscount Beaumont and Sir Ralph Boteley, the two latter being probably trustees.[109] He left two daughters and co-heirs, Elizabeth and Alice.[110] Possibly Elizabeth married Robert Cornwaleys, as, according to Manning, courts were held in 1501 by Robert Cornwaleys and Elizabeth his wife, and in 1510 by Elizabeth, when a widow, for the manor of Burstow Lodge.[111] This may be Lodge in Horley, which was sometimes called Burstow Lodge, from the chief holding being in Burstow. Robert and Elizabeth certainly held other land in Horley in the right of Elizabeth,[112] while there is no trace of them in Burstow. In 1526 the manor, again called Burstow Lodge but evidently in Horley, was held by John Mounteney and Agnes in the right of Agnes,[113] possibly the heiress of Elizabeth Cornwaleys. It seems to have passed back to the family of Burstow or Bristowe soon after, as, in 1546, Robert Bristowe died seised of it.[114] On the death of his grandson, in 1563, this manor was divided, as was that of Horley (q.v.) among four co-heirs.[115] The part belonging to the Jordans descended with the main manor of Horley (q.v.), and doubtless became united with it. John Woodman and Margaret conveyed their quarter to John Cowper in 1564,[116] from whom it passed, three years later, to Peter Bonwick.[117] Henry Bonwick, his son, held a fourth in 1607.[118] In 1574 Thomas Francke and Anna widow of George Taylor conveyed a fourth part of Lodge to John Woodman,[119] but the latter, on his death in 1587, was seised of no part of this manor.[120] This part must have passed previously to John Kerrell, who presumably had also obtained the quarter belonging to Agnes daughter and heir of Thomas Twyner,[121] as in 1618 John Kerrell and Henry Bonwick held the ' manor of Lodge.'[122]

According to Manning Bonwick afterwards obtained the whole manor, and died in 1663, leaving it to his cousin John Shove, who died in 1700 having devised to his son Henry Shove.[123] The latter died in 1752 seised of ' the manor or reputed manor of Lodge in Horley,' which he bequeathed to his wife for life with remainder to his godson John Shove, eldest son of John Shove, and his heirs.[124] The latter conveyed in 1769 to John Yeoman, whose grandson in 1791 sold to William Bryant ; the property then passed successively to Henry Byne,—Spiller and—Adams who held in 1804.[125] After that date it frequently changed hands ; it was at one time owned by the Rev. H. des Voeux, who sold to George Birch before 1845, and his family held until 1878.[126]

The family of atte Holyland, who were seised of lands in Nutfield (q.v.), also held land in Horley in the 14th century.[127] In the early 17th century and until 1760 land called Holylands in Horley was the property of the Needler family,[128] the last of whom, Henry Needler, was a musician of some renown.[129] The name Holyland is still preserved in Horley.

In 1334 Alleyn de Warewyk and Emma his wife granted to the priory of Reigate the reversion of an estate consisting of a messuage, a mill, 155 acres of land, 9 acres of meadow and 9 acres of wood in Horley and Burstow.[130] At the time of the Dissolution the estate appears still to have been called by the name Allen of Warwick, the tenant being Thomas Michell.[131]

The church of ST. BARTHOLO- CHURCH MEW stands at the end of a narrow lane leading off the main road to Brighton, and close to the River Mole. The churchyard, which is narrow on the north side, where its boundary is partly composed of the actual wall of the old Six Bells Inn (the windows of which look into the churchyard in a very unconventional fashion), has been considerably extended towards the south and east of late years. It is bordered by tall elms to the south, and there are public paths, stone flagged, through it, the whole bearing a well-tended appearance. In the more ancient parts are numerous quaint wooden ' bedheads,' one with a most elaborate scrolled top, some large old railed tombs and many ancient headstones, one of which, with stone posts and a slab between, is a curious example of local taste, being evidently derived from the wooden ' bed-head.' Most of these are of 17th and 18th-century dates. At the western end of the churchyard are two fine yew trees.

Although there is no mention of a church in Domesday there is practical certainty of the existence of one on this site by the middle of the 12th century, but it was probably of timber, like the existing tower at the end of the north aisle ; at any rate no stones bearing the tooling of that period are observable, but, owing to the walls being plastered externally in the older parts, this must not be taken

[105] Lansd. MS. 434, fol. 84.
[106] Exch. K.R. Misc. Bks. xxv, fol. 365.
[107] Ibid. fol. 357b.
[108] Chan. Inq. p.m. 11 Edw. IV, no. 42.
[109] Ibid.   [110] Ibid.
[111] Manning and Bray, Hist. of Surr. ii, 283.
[112] Feet of F. Surr. 11 Hen. VII, no. 8.
[113] Ibid. Mich. 18 Hen. VIII.
[114] Chan. Inq. p.m. (Ser. 2), lxxvii, 85.

[115] Ibid. cxxiv, 189 ; cxl, 176.
[116] Feet of F. Surr. Mich. 6 & 7 Eliz.
[117] Ibid. Mich. 9 & 10 Eliz.
[118] Ibid. Mich. 5 Jas. I.
[119] Ibid. Hil. 16 Eliz.
[120] Chan. Inq. p.m. (Ser. 2), ccxvi, 70.
[121] Ibid. cxcvii, 69.
[122] Feet of F. Surr. Mich. 16 Jas. I.
[123] Manning and Bray, Hist. of Surr. ii, 198.

[124] P.C.C. 140 Butterworth.
[125] See note 123.
[126] Brayley, Hist. of Surr. (ed. Walford), iv, 64 ; Dir. of Surr. 1845.
[127] Feet of F. Surr. 8 Edw. II, 128.
[128] Chan. Inq. p.m. (Ser. 2), cccci, 92.
[129] Dict. Nat. Biog.
[130] Pat. 8 Edw. III, pt. ii, m. 24.
[131] MS. list of Priory lands inspected by editor.

as conclusive evidence. The construction of the walls being masked, it can only be assumed that they are built of local sandstone rubble in the old parts, as in the new, the original dressings being of Reigate stone, and those in the new parts of Bath stone. The timber tower, where it rises from the aisle roof, is covered with oak shingles and crowned by a slender shingled spire set well within the walls. The modern west porch is of stone with a half timber gable, and it, together with the rest of the church, is roofed with tiles, but Horsham slabs remained upon the roofs down to the restoration of 1881–2, when they were most unfortunately removed. The church was enlarged in 1901 (Sir A. Blomfield), and this extension, which took the form of a wide south aisle, organ chamber and vestry, more than equal in area to the old nave, has necessarily entirely altered its appearance. Until 1901 the plan consisted of a nave about 61 ft. long by 19 ft. at its eastern end, and 20 ft. 7 in. throughout the greater part of its length ; chancel about 31 ft. long by 18 ft. wide, a transept on the south of the nave at its eastern end about 17 ft. by 14 ft., and a large north aisle and chapel under a parallel gabled roof, 70 ft. long by 18 ft. 8 in. wide, having a small but lofty north porch, 7 ft. 8 in. by 7 ft. 3 in. In the west end of the aisle was, and is, the timber tower, inclosing a space about 15 ft. square. Of this structure, the spacious north aisle contained the earliest work, and it has therefore been somewhat hastily assumed that it formed the nave and chancel of the original church, and that the coeval arcade on its southern side opened into a narrow south aisle, which subsequently gave place to a wide nave and chancel, tacked on to what thus became an ordinary aisle.[132] There is no evidence worth considering to support this far-fetched theory of plan development, and it may be taken for certain that the north aisle always has been an aisle, its chapel or chancel forming the chantry of the Salaman family, by whom it was probably built ; and it was added in the ordinary way to a church of 12th or 13th-century date, possibly then of timber construction, which afterwards was either rebuilt in stone, or entirely altered in the 15th century. Practically all the old features of the nave and chancel were of one or more dates between 1400 and 1500, while the transept had lost its old windows with the exception of one that has been preserved as the east window of the modern organ chamber—a two-light 15th-century opening. It should be recorded that two of the large three-light windows now in the south wall of the modern south aisle originally stood in the same relative positions in the south wall of the nave. They differ slightly in design, and the character of the tracery in the heads is somewhat unusual. The west window of the nave has modern tracery, the opening in Cracklow's view showing a wooden frame, while the doorway below, now within the porch, is ancient and has a plain four-centred arch. The buttresses and the west window of the south aisle are of course modern. The east window of the chancel is of three lights, and appears to have been entirely renewed in Bath stone

in 1881–2, and the original plain design (c. 1500) was not strictly reproduced. The window in the north wall, of two lights with tracery, has been more or less renewed, but upon the old lines, and its design is somewhat unusual and earlier than the other (c. 1390). On the opposite side the evidence has been obliterated by restoration and subsequent enlargements, but prior to these works there were two two-light windows and a small priest's door between then ; the windows, if one may judge by the solitary restored specimen now remaining, being of plainer and later character than that in the north wall. The existing piscina is modern.

The transeptal chapel with gabled roof, on the south of the nave, known as the Bastwick Chapel (possibly the original Lady Chapel), removed in 1901, seems to have had features of late date, but perhaps incorporated 13th-century stonework in its walls. It opened to the nave, not by an arch, but by a timber framing of a beam and posts. The nave wall at its Junction with this transept was thickened out, so as to form a projection of about 2 ft. on the inside, perhaps to contain a newel-stair in connexion with the rood-loft ; no trace of this now remains. The modern south aisle has been built with an arcade of four arches on octagonal piers, in general conformity with the 15th-century period.

The chief interest of the church centres in its beautiful north aisle, which presents a very valuable and regularly designed example of early 14th-century work. Most unfortunately, its elaborate and graceful window tracery, which was in Reigate stone and in excellent preservation, was almost entirely renewed in 1881–2 in Bath stone, when the ancient corbels, carved as human heads, that formed the termination to the hood-mouldings on the outside, were destroyed, and their places taken by square blocks, not even carved to imitate the destroyed heads. From drawings of the old work that have been preserved,[133] it is some consolation to observe that the ancient design of the tracery was closely copied, while the internal arches and Jambs were suffered to remain in the original stone. It has been supposed that the aisle and its chapel were the work of John de Rutherwyk, 'the very prudent and very useful lord and venerated Abbot,' as he is styled in the deed of 1313, when the Abbot and convent of Chertsey, the patrons of the church, obtained licence to appropriate this church and that of Epsom. But this seems somewhat unlikely on various grounds, partly from the great dissimilarity in style between the work here and that in the chancel of Great Bookham Church, which is actually proved to have been reconstructed by this great church-builder in the year 1341.[134] More probably the aisle was erected by the Salaman family as their burying-place, and the chancel or chapel at its eastern end as the chapel of St. Katherine. It is quite possible, of course, that Chertsey Abbey co-operated in the work. The exact date is about the year 1315, but possibly it occupied some years in building. The east window, for example, bears a somewhat later stamp than the arcade to the nave.

[132] Paper by the late Major Heales, F.S.A., in *Surr. Arch. Coll.* vii, 169.

[133] Reproduced with an account of the church in its pre-restoration state, by the late Major Heales, F.S.A., in *Surr. Arch. Coll.* vii, 172–3.

[134] As is recorded on the well-known dedication stone built into the chancel wall at Great Bookham. A similar dedication stone, with the date 1327, at Egham, preserves the record of the rebuilding of the chancel of that church (destroyed in 1817) by John de Rutherwyk, traces of whose work were visible also in Sutton and Epsom Churches, prior to their 19th-century re-construction.

It is of three somewhat lofty lights, having ogee trefoiled heads, and is a thin edition of the west window of the tower at Cranleigh. In the apex of the head of both windows are three cusped vesica-shaped figures, and beneath these at Horley are six irregular flamboyant piercings, the whole tracery plane being recessed, within a moulded arch and jambs, and a hood-moulding with returned ends inclosing the head.[185] In the north wall are four windows, much shorter and of quite different tracery, two on either side of the porch, which is about in the centre of the wall ; and in the west wall, within the space inclosed by the wooden tower, is another window of the same design, but loftier. These windows are of two ogee trefoiled lights, over which is a spherical triangle inclosing a trefoil with 'split' or 'curled' cusps, and straight bars radiating to the angles of the triangle. The hood-moulding of these windows prior to 1881 used to terminate in the carved heads above mentioned. The tracery belongs to a type usually called 'flowing,' but its peculiar interest lies in its partaking also of a local form, called 'Kentish.'[186] The internal treatment of the splays is also unusual, as instead of running out to a plain angle, they are finished by a plain semi-octagonal member, which receives the rear-arch of the head, a very effective treatment.

The north porch, also of c. 1315, has a plain outer door with simply chamfered head and jambs, and in its side walls are small lancets with pointed heads, which in another situation might have been assigned to an earlier date. These have very flat splays on the inside, and below them are stone seats, apparently coeval. The inner doorway is peculiar in many of its details, particularly has not been touched in the restoration. Its arch has a springing line about 8 in. below the level of the top of the capitals, and as the outer order of mouldings is continuous, this leads to slight distortion. The shafts to the inner order are reduced to mere bead-mouldings, 1 in. in diameter, but they have complete and delicately moulded capitals and tiny bases very minutely worked. The arch mouldings are very good, and the wide hood-moulding terminated in carved heads now defaced, while there is a characteristic stop to the wave-moulding on the outer order of the jamb. The inner arch and jambs are chamfered.

The arcade of this aisle is of four slender arches, on peculiarly graceful hexagonal columns with responds of semi-octagon plan. The arches, like that of the doorway, are struck from a line well below the level of the capitals, and are of two chamfeted orders with well-moulded capitals and bases, the latter, like the capitals, taking a hexagonal form, but brought out to the square in a plinth course by means of bold wave-like stops, similar to those in the doorway. At the east end of this arcade is a tomb-arch with pointed segmental head, between the respond and the east wall of the aisle. It is chamfered in the same manner as the aisle windows, and adjoining it in the aisle wall are the remains of an image niche.

At the west end of the north aisle, within the walls and the last bay of the arcade, is the remarkably massive wooden tower, standing upon great balks of oak, which rest upon huge squared blocks, braced together by arches of timber, above which is some elaborate oak framework. A date in the 15th century has been assigned to this tower, but there seems no reason for doubting that it is coeval with the aisle, i.e. about 1315. This supposition is strengthened by the general resemblance of the work to the timber tower of Rogate Church, Sussex, which is unquestionably of early 14th-century date.

The roofs of the north aisle, nave, and chancel, are in the main composed of the ancient timbers, of great size and strength, the aisle roof being probably coeval with the walls, and the others perhaps of 15th-century date. A beautiful and very perfect roof of c. 1315 remains over the porch, formed of rafters and collars with curved braces, which make a complete pointed arch.

Before 1881-2 there existed the lower part of a par-close screen, which inclosed the eastern end of the north aisle, in which is the fine Salaman tomb. This screen, which was of 15th-century date, had a return end to the respond of the arcade, and showed 'traces of its original colouring of red and green.'[187] Also there were a good number of the old seats, 'disguised by the addition of a top-gallant bulwark to keep out draughts and curiosity, and facilitate a quiet snooze. One lofty pew with carved upper panels' bore the date 1654, and the initials 1 f, which may indicate one of the Fenner family, who were people of some importance in the parish.[188] No relic remains of these old pews to which so much old parish history clung : pitch pine seats have taken their place. Galleries, which were comparatively modern, have been swept away, and are hardly to be regretted, especially one, 'handsomely painted to resemble mahogany.' 'The communion table, rails, and a wainscot against the east wall,' described as 'neat,' which were 'given in 1710 by the Governors of Christ's Hospital, the patrons of the living and lay rectors,' have also been removed from the church, together with a late 17th-century screen on the east side of the timber tower.

Remains of a simple pattern in red-brown, painted on the east respond of the arcades, still exist, but other traces of mural paintings uncovered in the chancel were not preserved. The north doorway shows signs of having been painted in black and other colours. Some rare fragments of painted glass in the trefoil figure of the tracery of the north aisle windows, after a temporary disappearance, consequent upon the restoration of 1881-2, have been recovered, and are now to be seen in their old places. They have a design of three fleurs de lis in rich flash-ruby glass, radiating from a circle in which is framed a golden leopard's head, the arms of the Salaman family. The pattern in the spandrels was in black and white, with a ribbon of light yellow beads inclosing a geometrical tracery pattern.[189] These seem to have disappeared, but there are other fragments such as roses, flaming suns, &c., in the west window of the aisle.

---

[185] Cf. the east window of Old Dorking Church, illustrated in Surr. Arch. Coll. xvi, 1.

[186] Found at Chartham : but also at Winchelsea, Sussex, and as far afield as Sandiacre, Derbyshire. The presumption is that a Kentish architect or masons, imported from that county, had to do with these windows. They are unlike anything else of the period in Surrey.

[187] Surr. Arch. Coll. viii, 241.

[188] Ibid. vii, 180. Major Heales gives the date as 1656 in a drawing of the lettering, and suggests that the initials are those of Thomas Saunders's son or descendant, but they seem to be т ғ, not т s.

[189] Surr. Arch. Coll. vii, 172 ; paper by the late Major Heales, F.S.A.

The font, of Sussex marble, small and square in form, on a circular stem and plinth, may be of 13th-century date, but it has lost its angle shafts, and has been otherwise mutilated.

The monuments are of exceptional interest, the earliest being a very finely carved and well-preserved stone effigy of a knight of the Salaman family, which lies beneath the arch at the east end of the north aisle. It used to lie upon the pavement, but has been very properly set upon a stone base. 'It is upon a table slightly ridged *en dos d'âne*, forming doubtless the lid of the coffin or tomb, and is recumbent in the usual manner, the head resting on a cushion, with a lion at the feet.'[140] The figure, which is life-size, is in Reigate stone, in a free and unconventional attitude.

'The shield, of an intermediate size between the small heater-shape and the long one almost covering the body, is incurved and emblazoned with a double-headed eagle displayed, charged on the breast with a leopard's head.' The arms are those of the Salaman family, who held land in the parish, but which member of that family is represented is uncertain—probably the father of Roger Salaman, who died 1343–4, seised of the manor of Imworth next Kingston, and of land in Horley held of the Prior of Merton.[140a] His Christian name is unknown. The date of the effigy is about that of the aisle—c. 1315.[141]

The fine brass of a lady beneath an elegant canopy, which formerly lay in the north aisle, afterwards in the floor of the chancel, and which has lately been embedded, with its slab, in a vertical position in the north wall of the chancel, is also in all probability a memorial of another member of the Salaman family, its date being about a century later than the stone effigy, viz. c. 1415. The inscription at the foot does not belong to it. Her hands are conjoined in prayer, and she wears the horned head-dress looped up in an unusual manner at the back, with pads or inclosures for the hair projecting considerably on either side. On her neck is a collar of SS.[142] The canopy is of a single cusped arch, from which rises a crocketed pediment, surmounted by a finial, and the whole supported by long shafts ending in pinnacles.

On the south wall of the chancel is now fixed a small brass figure of a man, the inscription being lost. He is in the civilian costume of the end of the 15th century, and has a long furred dress, girdled at the waist. The inscription wrongly attached to the other brass has been also mistakenly associated with this. It runs :—'Of yo' charite pray for the soule of Johā fienner late wyf of Joñn ffenner gent' which Johan deceased the ij day of juley in the yere of our Lord m'v'xvj on whose soule Jh̄u have mercy. amen.'

On a small stone let into one of the buttresses of the modern south aisle is the following in capital letters :—

'Here lyeth Alyce theldest daughter of . . . . Gilmyn gent : late wife of Thomas Taylor of Horly the yovnger. Bvried the 18 day of Janvary : 1615 :

and Thomas the sonne of her and of Thomas Taylor above writen her husband buried the 1 day of Febrya : 1615.'

On a stone of the north wall of the chancel inside is the curious inscription on a sunken panel with a moulded border to William Brown, 1613, 'pastor' of Horley 50 years, and his two wives, Magdalen, 1604, and Margaret, 1611. Below is a table of his descendants.

There is a small cross upon the east Jamb of the north door, and several others more rudely scratched. Also on the same jamb is a very curious little unfinished carving, 5¾ in. high, of the design of a traceried window, coeval with the doorway on which it has been cut.

In the inventory of the commissioners of Edward VI there were : 'In the steple iiij belles and iiij hand belles.' Now there are eight, dated 1812 and 1839, by Thomas Mears of London, with the exception of the fifth, which is inscribed, 'Henry and John Shove gave the original 3ᵈ Bell 1673 James P Brazier John Newnham Church Wardens.'

The church plate is not of much interest. It comprises a silver cup, paten and flagon, of 1714, each bearing the letters IHS and the inscription 'Sam Billingsley, vicar. Jnᵒ Humphrey, James Wood, Church Wardens. Jnᵒ Charington, Tho. Beadle, overseers. Anno Domini 1714.'

The registers date from 1578. More interesting are the churchwardens' accounts, from 1507 to 1702, now at the British Museum.[143] There are, however, disappointingly few references to the church fabric, and these chiefly consist of repairs to the glazing and leadwork, a 'lok,' and 'yerns' (irons). One entry has : 'The su' of the Ryngg̃s a pon the crose, is liij,' and another, 'Of the sylt̃' that is a pon the crose, ij̃s jᵈ—iiij pessis of a whope' [? hoop]. These probably refer to a processional cross.

Later entries (1604 and 1934) contain interesting memoranda as to the appropriation of the seats, showing that they went with the estates and farms in the parish, and 'the repaire of the church and steeple' (1669), which cost £40 13s. 4d., a further repair (1686) costing £6 14s. 1d. In 1632 'John Ansty is chosen by consent of yᵉ minister & Parishoners, to see yᵗ yᵉ younge men & boyes behaue themselves decently in yᵉ church in time of Diuine service & Sermon, and he is to have for his paines ij'.' There are several records as to apprentices ; and some of the earlier entries refer to the parish cow and to the 'stock,' or common funds of parochial gilds, which was to be placed in the treasure chest.

ADVOWSON   In 1190 Pope Clement III granted permission to the Abbot and convent of Chertsey to retain in their own hands the parish churches of Horley, Epsom, Bookham, &c., reserving the benefices thereof to their own use 'provided that they elect vicars thereto.'[144] This permission was recited in a licence for the appropria-

---

[140] Fully described in a paper by the late J. G. Waller, F.S.A., *Surr. Arch. Coll.* vii, 184.

[140a] Chan. Inq. p.m. 17 Edw. III, no. 45.

[141] This remarkable effigy, undoubtedly the most interesting and the finest as a work of art remaining in Surrey, should be compared with the mutilated effigy of a knight in St. Peter's, Sandwich, with

the brass of Sir John Northwode at Minster-in-Sheppey, and with that of Sir John d'Abernon the younger, in Stoke d'Abernon Church, Surrey, 1327. See Stothard, *Monumental Effigies* ; and *Arch. Journ.* viii, 231.

[142] Fully described by the late J. G. Waller in *Surr. Arch. Coll.* vii, 189. Mr. Waller compares with this brass as an example of female costume of the

period the brasses of Lady Peryent, at Digswell, Herts., 1415, and Millicent Meryng, East Markham, Notts. ; also the brass to Robert Skerne's wife in Kingston Church, Surrey, 1420, and Sir Nicholas Carew's lady, at Beddington, 1432.

[143] Add. MS. 6173. Published by Mr. A. R. Bax, in *Surr. Arch. Coll.* vii, 243.

[144] Pat. 20 Edw. I, m. 11 ; Exch. K.R. Misc. Bks. xxv, fol. 16 d.

tion of the churches of Horley and Epsom made to Chertsey Abbey by the Bishop of Winchester and confirmed by the Crown in 1313,[145] the concession being due to the decrease in the revenues of the monastery incidental to floods, to pestilence among the cattle, and to other misfortunes from which the Chertsey lands had lately suffered.[146] Confirmation was also made by the Archbishop of Canterbury, and the abbot was inducted into the churches on St. Dunstan's Day, 1313, by the Archdeacon of Surrey.[147] The church of Horley, surrendered with the manor in 1537,[148] was granted with it (q.v.) to Sir Nicholas Carew, and has since followed the same descent, the present patrons and lay rectors being the governors of Christ's Hospital.

In 1316 the abbot purchased of Michael le Waps a certain messuage with garden, curtilage, and a croft of arable land which he assigned as a manse for the vicar of Horley.[149] Thomas Cowper of Horley, in his will, proved in March 1499, desired to be buried ' in the church of the Blessed Mary at Horley in the chapel of St. Katherine' ; he bequeathed to the high altar 20d., to each of the four lights in the same church 4d., and for two torches 13s. 4d.[150] The early churchwardens' accounts of Horley contained frequent memoranda of sums received for St. Katherine's and St. Nicholas' lights in the church ; in 1518, for instance, 47s. was received for St. Katherine's light, kept by two of the married women of the parish, and 34s. 8½d. for St. Nicholas' light, kept by two men.[151] A will of 1534 records bequests to the lights of the Holy Cross and of the Blessed Mary in the church.[152]

CHARITIES Smith's Charity is distributed as in other Surrey parishes.

LEIGH

Leghe (xii cent.) ; Legh and Leygh (xiv. cent.) ; The Lea, 1499 ;[1] Lye and Lee (xvi cent.).

Leigh is a small village, 3 miles south-east of Reigate. The parish, which is of irregular form, is bounded on the north by Reigate, on the east by outlying portions of Buckland and Charlwood and by Horley, on the south by Horley and Newdigate, on the west by Capel, and on the north-west by Betchworth. It measures about 3 miles west and east, by 2 miles north and south, but a tongue runs down south into Newdigate for nearly a mile further. It contains 3,412 acres.

The soil is Wealden Clay, with the exception of some sand and alluvium on the banks of the Mole and its tributaries, which traverse the parish. The Mole, running generally from east to west, bounds the parish on the north-east. Brooks flow into it from Charlwood on the south and the Holmwood Common on the west.

The village consists only of a small cluster of houses about the green near the church ; there are cottages at Dawes Green to the west, and scattered farms and houses. Shellwood Mill stands on high ground, which was once Shellwood Common, but is now inclosed, and is that somewhat rare survival in these times, a working windmill.

The extensive commons formerly in Leigh have been inclosed, except Westwood Common and some roadside waste.

The roads of the parish are now as good and hard as any others, though liable to interruption in places by actual flood in a wet season. Formerly they were almost a byword, even in the Weald, for the impassable character of this deep clay after the rain of any autumn or winter.

Leigh is not named in Domesday, but was no doubt partly inhabited there for that date. Shellwood Manor, which includes the greater part of it, was part of Ewell. Banstead Manor included Dunshot tithing in Leigh,

Stumblehole, part of the Leigh Place estate, and other farms. The manors of East Betchworth and Reigate also extend into Leigh, both mentioned in the Domesday Survey ; and Brockham and Charlwood, which were not manors in 1086, are partly in the parish.

Elizabethan coins have been found on the site of Shellwood Manor House, and the adjacent farm called Shellwood Manor is a good old gabled house of perhaps 17th-century origin.

At Shellwood Common in Leigh the last stand of the abortive Royalist insurrection of 1 August 1659 was made, but was overcome without fighting. The original rendezvous of the Royalists at Redhill had been occupied by troops beforehand, but a few men had apparently ridden on here, only to scatter when the soldiers appeared.[2]

Leigh was one of the parishes where the iron industry existed. It was among those excepted from the operation of the Act 1 Eliz. cap. 15 against conversion of timber of a certain size into charcoal for the purposes of iron smelting. During the 16th century ironworks existed at Leigh on lands 8 acres in extent, called Burgett and Grove Lands, a lease of which had been obtained in 1551 by George and Christopher Darell, who were engaged in developing the iron industry in this part of Surrey.[3] Hammer Bridge in Leigh, on a branch of the Mole, above the village, commemorates perhaps a hammer of Mr. Darrell's works at Ewood in Newdigate, a little higher up the same stream.[4] In 1635 it was presented at the court baron that there had formerly been great woods, now cut down, of oak, alder, and other trees, in Shellwood, Westwood, Leigh Green, Dawes Green, and other places, where the tenants used to feed swine and had since pastured their cattle.[5] This felling of the woods must no doubt be associated with the ironworks, so that Darrell's preservation of his woods, referred to in the statute of 23 Elizabeth, cap. 5, had not been successfully imitated.

[145] Cal. Pat. 1307-13, p. 556 ; Exch. K.R. Misc. Bks. xxv, fol. 16 d.
[146] Ibid. fol. 16 d., 17.
[147] Ibid. fol. 18.
[148] Feet of F. Div. Co. Trin. 29 Hen. VIII.
[149] Lansd. MS. 455, fol. 51 ; Cal

Pat. 1317-21, p. 319 ; Coll. Topog. and Gen. iv, chap. xviii, 164.
[150] P.C.C. 39 Horne.
[151] Surr. Arch. Coll. viii, 244.
[152] Ibid. 246.
[1] Will of Richard Arderne, P.C.C. 5 Moone.

[2] V.C.H. Surr. i, 423.
[3] Surr. Arch. Coll. xvii, 30-1 ; V.C.H. Surr. ii, 263-4.
[4] Ibid. 269.
[5] Manning and Bray, Hist. of Surr. ii, 180.

The extensive wastes of Shellwood Manor were inclosed under an award of 12 january 1854.[6] There is no evidence of common fields.

There are some good houses in the parish. Mynthurst is the property of Mr. Henry Bell, J.P. ; Denshott (properly Dunshott), of Mr. Cecil Brodrick ; Burys Court of Mrs. Charrington ; Nalderswood of Mr. A. G. Fraser.

The present school (National) was founded in 1845. On 20 October 1849 the Duke of Norfolk conveyed a site on the waste of Shellwood Manor to the National Society for the schoolhouse. It has been enlarged in 1872 and 1885.

        The earliest records of *SHELLWOOD MANORS* show it to have been a member of the manor of Ewell ; it is not mentioned in the Domesday Survey, but was probably included in Ewell, which was ancient demesne of the Crown. In 1156 Henry II granted the manor of Ewell with its members of Kingswood and Shellwood to the Prior and convent of Merton, Surrey.[7] In 1324 john le Dene, one of the prior's tenants at Shellwood,[8] received licence to build a chapel in the 'manor of Leigh.'[9] Shellwood was held by the prior until the surrender of the monastery in 1538.[10] In 1539 the king made a grant to Sir Thomas Nevile, for £400, of the manor of Shellwood with land called Deneland, Manwood, and Fynchland, and tenements called Ryvesland and Hokesferm in Leigh, to hold for an annual rent of £3 7s. 7¾d., with reversion to Sir Robert Southwell and Margaret his wife, daughter and heir of Sir Thomas Nevile, and Margaret's issue : the grantee was charged with a life annuity of 40s. granted by the late priory to James Skinner.[11] In 1547 Sir Robert Southwell and Margaret received licence to alienate to Henry Lechford,[12] in whose family the manor remained until 1634,[13] when Sir Richard Lechford, great-grandson of Henry, conveyed to Sir Garret Kempe and John Garnett.[14] They in the same year conveyed to Penning Alston and Spencer Vincent, trustees of Dr. Edward Alston, the estate being then charged with an annuity of £70 to Mary, Lady Blount.[15] It was sequestered for her delinquency in 1644 ; in 1651 the trustees complained that they had paid £40 per annum to the State ever since, and that though Lady Blount's term had expired, yet the sequestration of two-thirds was continued on a false pretext of the recusancy of Edward Cotton, the tenant.[16] The latter seems, however, to have been a recusant, and petitioned to contract for his estate in January 1654.[17] Later in the same year he, with the trustees of Shellwood, conveyed Shellwood to George

MERTON PRIORY. Or fretty azure with eagles argent at the crossings of the fret.

Browne of Spelmonden, Kent,[18] whose sons, Ambrose and john, both held after him.[19]

Both died childless ; the survivor, John, who died in 1736, devised the property to Thomas Jordan, son of his sister Philippa.[19] Jordan also died without issue in 1750, his sisters Elizabeth Beaumont and Philippa Sharp were his co-heirs.[21] Shellwood became the property of the Beaumonts, to whom John Sharp and Philippa quitclaimed their right in 1753.[22] The manor descended to the son and grandson of Elizabeth Beaumont,[23] and was sold in 1806 to the Duke of Norfolk.[24] The present duke is now lord of the manor.

During the 13th and early 14th centuries the customs and services due from the men of Shellwood to the Prior of Merton seem to have been a constant subject of dispute. In 1223 Gilbert de Covelinden and others were summoned to answer to the prior for their refusal to do the services which he exacted of them for the tenements which they held of him, as he said, in villeinage. The men, however, denied all villeinage (*defendunt omne villenagium*), and said they held freely. The prior maintained that the manor of Ewell, of which the lands of Fifhide and Shellwood were members, was held in villeinage, and demanded judgement as to whether the members of a manor could be freer than the chief holding. The men asked that an inquisition might be taken to discover what services and customs their ancestors had performed when first the lands came to the prior.[25] An account of the inquiry, enrolled on a Curia Regis Roll for 1226, gives an interesting description of these services.[26] The prior claimed that besides paying the ordinary rent of 5s. per virgate for their lands, every tenant should come in harvest time, with his entire household, exclusive of his wife and his shepherd, to the 'bedripe' (the wheat harvest) of the lord, and should then be allowed two meals, the first with ale, the second without, that each man should assist in making a house called the 'Sumerhus,' or pay 6d. towards the same, at the choice of the prior, that they should cut down brushwood in the wood of Shellwood and bring it to Tadworth, and should inclose a rood of land around the court of Ewell, and that they should send a man of their household to till the fields of Ewell both in winter and in Lent, the prior finding them food. They also owed him pannage at the rate of one hog in every ten, or, if they had less than ten, 1d. for every hog. No son or daughter of a tenant might marry without the prior's licence ; each man also owed Peter's pence— 1d. so long as his wife was alive, ½d. after her death. Moreover the prior claimed that every man should come to the court of Ewell to make the court when summoned by the prior's bailiff. They were not allowed to sell ox or horse without the prior's leave, and the best ox in each man's possession, or horse if he had any, could be taken as a heriot by the prior

---

[6] *Blue Bk. Inc. Awards.*
[7] *V.C.H. Surr.* ii, 95 ; Cart. Antiq. U, 6 ; *Plac. de Quo War.* (Rec. Com.), 739.
[8] *Vide infra.*
[9] Winton Dioc. R. Stratford, 8*b.*
[10] Maitland, *Bracton's Note Bk.* no. 1661 ; *Abbrev. Plac.* (Rec. Com.), 325 ; *Valor Eccl.* (Rec. Com.), ii, 48. See note 7.
[11] *L. and P. Hen. VIII,* xiv (2), g. 651 (50).

[12] Pat. 1 Edw. VI, pt. viii, m. 15 ; Feet of F. Surr. Trin. 1 Edw. VI.
[13] Chan. Inq. p.m. (Ser. 2), cxlv, 13 ; Feet of F. Surr. Hil. 45 Eliz. ; Chan. Inq. p.m. (Ser. 2), cccxxv, 195 ; Feet of F. Surr. Hil. 20 Jas. I.
[14] Feet of F. Surr. Mich. 10 Chas. I.
[15] *Cal. of Com. for Compounding,* 2735.
[16] Ibid.   [17] Ibid. 3179.
[18] Feet of F. Surr. Trin. 1654 ; Berry, *Surr. Gen.* 81.
[19] Ibid. ; Feet of F. Surr. Mich. 1

Jas. II ; Recov. R. Mich. 1 Jas. II, rot. 171.
[20] Berry, *Surr. Gen.* 81 ; P.C.C. 124 Derby.
[21] Berry, loc. cit.
[22] Feet of F. Surr. Mich. 27 Geo. II.
[23] P.C.C. 400 Harris ; Recov. R. East. 12 Geo. III, rot. 260.
[24] Manning and Bray, *Hist. of Surr.* ii.
[25] Maitland, *Bracton's Note Bk.* no.1661.
[26] Ibid. note ; Cur. Reg. R. 94, Hil. 10 Hen. III, m. 8.

at death of a tenant. Lastly, they were not to cut down oaks in Shellwood without his permission.

The men of Shellwood allowed that they owed for the farm of the land 5*s.* per virgate, or 100*s.* for 5 hides. They said that when the prior had need of their aid for the requirements of the church they gave it freely, not by reason of their villeinage, but rather from courtesy. They allowed the claims for pannage and Peter's pence, but said that they came to the court of Ewell as free men, at the election of the prior's bailiff, to act as Jurors.

The jurors for the inquest denied the prior's claim for work from his tenants in harvest time, and they stated that the brushwood cut down by the men should be taken by them over the hill called Bridelcumbe. The other services were allowed to the prior. The men of Shellwood were said to owe tallage whenever the men of Ewell did so, and it was not voluntary, but compulsory; they were also required to plough the lands of Ewell if the prior wished it, bringing their own horses and ploughs.

In 1311 john de Dene, a tenant of the prior in Shellwood, was remitted certain of these services in consideration of an increase on his annual assize rent of 8*d.*, payable at four terms of the year.[17]

In 1316 the men of Shellwood accused the prior of exacting from them other services than those which they were required to perform. The prior, however, said that he exacted no more than those allowed to his predecessor in the suit of 1223, and Judgement was given in his favour.[18]

It may be that the memory of an ancient dispute caused the careful insertion in the conveyance from Southwell to Lechford in 1547 of the words 'with the bondmen and their families.' The liberation of the tenants from the essential villein service of attendance at the *bedrip* probably means that in 1223 it was recognized that they were not technically *villani*, had no share in the common fields, but were yet servile tenants.

Free warren in all their lands of Merton, Ewell, Kingswood and Shellwood was granted to the prior and convent in 1252.[19] In a plea of 'quo warranto' in 1279 the prior claimed assize of bread and ale and gallows on the ground that Henry II had granted them Shellwood with soc, sac, &c., and quittance of shires and hundreds, and that these liberties had been confirmed by Richard I.[20]

The capital messuage of Shellwood was separated from the manor itself during the 18th century. According to Manning, Ambrose Browne obtained an Act of Parliament in 1712 enabling him to sell a manor in Kent and the capital messuage of Shellwood, which was therefore vested in Jemmett Raymond,

second husband of Elizabeth, widow of George Browne.[21] From Raymond it passed, in 1755, to John Winter,[22] who conveyed it in 1781 to Richard Simpson.[23] It passed in 1796 to his nephew Cornelius Cayley, and was sold three years later to the Duke of Norfolk,[24] and thus became reunited to the manor. It is not now standing (see above), but the farm next to it is of about 17th-century date, and perhaps had superseded the original manor-house before the separation from the manor.

The messuage and farm of *LEIGH PLACE* was the residence of the Ardernes in the 15th century.[25] John Arderne, who was high sheriff of Surrey in 1432, was of Leigh Place. By his will, which was proved in 1449, he directed that if he died at or near Leigh he should be buried in the church there. His son John inherited the estate, and was in turn succeeded by his son Richard,[26] who died in 1499 seised of 3 messuages, 255 acres of land, &c., in Leigh. Richard Arderne by his will bequeathed all his lands to his wife joan, requiring her 'to fynd an honest pryst to pray for me &

ARDERNE. *Argent a fesse checky or and azure.*

all my friends & all cristyn sowlys deuryng her lyf'; after her death his stepbrother John Holgrave was to fynd the priest, who was to receive an annual sum of £6 13*s.* 4*d.*[27] There is apparently no record of any such chantry in Leigh Church. Leigh Place soon after became the property of the Dudleys.[28] By an Act of 1512, reversing the attainder of Edward Dudley, john Dudley his son, subsequently Duke of Northumberland, was restored to his father's lands.[29] He sold the estate of Leigh Place to Edward Shelley of Findon in Sussex in 1530.[30] The deed recites that in 1527 Sir john Dudley had conveyed the manor of Findon, which had belonged to his father, to Edward Shelley, that Shelley had agreed to re-sell it to Dudley, in consideration of which sale Dudley agreed to sell to Shelley 'a messuage called Lye Place[31] with appurtenances in the parish of Lye, Surrey.' In an account made in 1534, of defaults of bridges in Surrey, a reference occurs to 'the bridge before Mr. Shellie's place, Lye.'[32] Elizabeth, daughter of Sir William Shelley and niece of Edward Shelley, married Sir Roger Copley of Gatton,[33] and in 1540 Edward Shelley and Anne Cobbe (possibly his daughter-in-law) made a settlement of Leigh Place on them.[34] The property is described as a messuage, 200 acres of land, 40 acres of meadow,

17 Cott. MS. Cleop. C vii, fol. 158.
18 *Abbrev. Plac.* (Rec. Com.), 325.
19 *Cal. of Chart.* 1226–57, p. 391.
20 *Plac. de Quo War.* (Rec. Com.), 739, 748.
21 Manning and Bray, *Hist. of Surr.* ii, 180; Berry, *Surr. Gen.*; *Stat. of the Realm*, x, 1005.
22 Manning and Bray, *Hist. of Surr.* ii, 180.
23 Feet of F. Surr. East. 21 Geo. III.
24 See n. 32.
25 *Surr. Arch. Coll.* xi, 141 et seq.; *Cal. Pat.* 1429–36, p. 380. It has been stated that the family of de Braose, or Brewes, held Leigh Place in the 13th and 14th centuries (Brayley, *Hist. of Surr.*

iv, 282). There does not seem to be much documentary evidence in proof of this assertion. However, John son of John de Braose died in 1358 seised of a tenement in Leigh called Erneshewed, consisting of — and a garden worth 12*d.* and 40 acres worth 20*s.* (Chan. Inq. p.m. 31 Edw. III [1st nos.], no. 49), and as the Braoses were succeeded by the Ardernes in other places, this holding may be the Leigh Place estate. Moreover, the arms of the Cookseys, who were descended from the Braoses, used to be in the parish church, and the Cookseys and the Ardernes were both Warwickshire families.
26 Chan. Inq. p.m. 15 Hen. VII,

no. 101; P.C.C. 5 Moone; *Surr. Arch. Coll.* xi, 141.
27 P.C.C. 5 Moone.
28 For a possible connexion between Ardernes and Dudleys, see *Surr. Arch. Coll.* xi, 149.
29 *Stat. of the Realm*, iii, 42.
30 *Surr. Arch. Coll.* xi, 150 (quoting from deed in possession of owners of estate).
31 Also Flanchford in Reigate, and Hartswood in Buckland.
32 L. and P. Hen. VIII, vii, 42.
33 *Visit. Surr.* (Harl. Soc. xliii), 121; Berry, *Surr. Gen.* 85; *Surr. Arch. Coll.* xi.
34 Chan. Inq. p.m. (Ser. 2), ccx, 85.

100 of pasture, 20 of wood in Leigh, and 40 acres of pasture in Betchworth, the said messuage and lands being known as that mansion, messuage or farm with dovecot called ' Le Ley,' held of the manor of Banstead by service of 11*l*. Elizabeth Copley survived her husband, and died in 1559, Sir Thomas Copley being her son and heir.[45] He was M.P. for Gatton in 1554, 1557-8, and 1562-3. Under Mary he was a supporter of the rights of succession of Elizabeth,[46] who was his third cousin twice removed through the marriage of Sir Geoffrey Boleyn with his great-great-aunt Anne, daughter of Lord Hastings. But he had scruples about subscribing to the Acts of Supremacy and Uniformity,[47] and left England in 1569 and spent the rest of his life abroad, dying in Flanders in 1584.[48] William Copley, eldest surviving son of Thomas, inherited the estate.[49] It was settled on his son William on the marriage of the latter with Anne Denton in 1615.[50] In 1620, however, William Copley the father, having married as his second wife Margaret Fromond, appears to have made a second settlement of the estate, this time on himself and his wife Margaret and the survivor of either of them for life, with reversion to his son by his first wife.[51] The son, who had predeceased him, had left two daughters and co-heirs—Mary, who married John Weston, and Anne, wife of Sir Nathaniel Minshull.[52] William Copley the father died in 1643, and his widow Margaret apparently entered on Leigh Place. In 1649, Mary Weston, to whom on the partition of estates Leigh Place had been allotted, conveyed the reversion, expectant on the demise of Margaret Copley, widow, to John Woodman.[53] The latter in 1651 conveyed to Thomas Jordan in trust for Robert Bristowe, and at the end of the same year Margaret Copley agreed to sell to the latter her life interest in the estate.[54] From Susanna Moore, daughter and heiress of Robert Bristowe, Leigh Place passed in 1706 to Edward Budgen, who by will of 1716 devised to his grandnephews in turn. Thomas, the youngest, married Penelope Smith, and in 1806 his grandson, Thomas Smith-Budgen, conveyed the estate to Richard Caffyn Dendy,[55] in whose family it remains, Sir John Watney, the present owner, having married Elizabeth, a daughter and co-heir of Stephen Dendy.[56]

Leigh Place is the remains of a 15th-century house surrounded by a moat. Part of the house was pulled down about 1810, and the interior as restored and modernized is not of any great interest ; there is, however, some fine woodwork. In a room on the ground floor is a large fireplace of 18th-century design, and on the first floor a large room now divided into three bedrooms has a four-centred arched ceiling, and over it a bell turret. It used to be approached by a drawbridge, which is now superseded by a permanent way. Old maps show the house to have been foursquare with a central courtyard, and the view in Manning

and Bray shows the entrance front as it existed about 1806, with the drawbridge over the moat.[56a] The Copleys being Catholic recusants accounts for a cupboard near the chimney in the hall which was called the Priest's Hole. Robert Southwell the Jesuit and poet was son of Bridget, sister of Sir Thomas Copley of Leigh and Gatton, and may have been here.

STUMBLEHOLE.—In 1325 R. de Stumblehole held a tenement at Stumblehole of Banstead Manor.[57] A messuage and lands at Stumblehole were held by the de Bures family as parcel of lands at Burgh in Banstead in the 14th century.[58] The property seems to have afterwards belonged to the Leigh Place estate, as Bray, writing in the early 19th century, states that it had then been sold as a farm to William Brown by John Smith-Budgen of Leigh Place.[59]

The church of *ST. BARTHOLOMEW CHURCH* has a chancel 25 ft. 6 in. by 18 ft. 2 in., a south vestry, a nave 54 ft. 3 in. (of which 10 ft. at the west end is covered by the tower and divided from the nave by an arch) by 21 ft., and south and west porches.

The building is of 15th-century origin, but has been much modernized. The nave was formerly about three-quarters of the present length, and had a west tower with a stone base and upper part of wood. The tower had a west doorway, and over it a three-light traceried window, and its west wall was flush with that of the nave. At a later date the wooden part was replaced by one of stone. When the church was lengthened in 1890 the tower was demolished and replaced by the present wooden erection above the nave roof : the arch opening to the nave appears to have been re-used, but no other part of the work is old.

The east window of the chancel is a modern one in 15th-century style, of three lights under a traceried head. The two north windows are both partly restored 15th-century work : the first is of two cinquefoiled lights under a traceried pointed head with a label, the external jambs and arch having a wide casement moulding, while the second window is of two trefoiled lights under a square head. The south-east window is quite modern and similar in design to that opposite. In this wall, near the chancel arch, is the doorway to the modern vestry. The chancel arch has chamfered jambs with moulded bases and capitals, and the arch is two-centred of two chamfered orders. The bases and some other stones are modern, the rest may be original.

The two easternmost of the north windows of the nave are both old, of three cinquefoiled lights under pointed segmental heads, the third window is a new one of similar character but of two lights. The south-east window is an old one of three lights like that opposite, and below it is a small cinquefoiled and square-headed piscina. The south doorway is original, and has two moulded orders continuing round the

[45] Chan. Inq. p.m. (Ser. 2), cxxvi, 145 ; P.C.C. 5 Mellershe.
[46] Com. *Journ.* i, 50.
[47] Loseley MSS. ix, 19, 20. Letters dated 17 and 23 Nov. 1569.
[48] *Dict. Nat. Biog.*
[49] Chan. Inq. p.m. (Ser. 2), ccccv, 159.
[50] Ibid.
[51] Ibid. The *Surr. Arch. Coll.* states that the deed of 1620 settled the estate not only on William Copley, senior, and Margaret for life, but on their issue,

remainder being to William Copley, junior, the issue by the father's first marriage. This account also states that, after the death of the latter, the first settlement was disputed, and that of 1620 was finally allowed. The inquisition on the son and the subsequent history do not, however, show that the children by the father's second marriage ever had any right to the estate.
[52] Ibid. ; Chan. Inq. p.m. (Ser. 2), ccccv, 159. Minshull was apparently Anne's second husband. *See* Gatton Manor.

[53] *Surr. Arch. Coll.* xi, 177-8 (deed in possession of owners of estate).
[54] Ibid. 179.
[55] Ibid. 183.
[56] Burke, *Landed Gentry.*
[56a] See *Surr. Arch. Coll.* xi, 141-84.
[57] Add. Chart. 16532.
[58] Chan. Inq. p.m. 6 Edw. III (1st nos.), no. 54 ; 19 Edw. III (1st nos.), no. 54.
[59] Manning and Bray, *Hist. of Surr.* ii, 184.

two-centred arch and jambs. The porch is comparatively modern. just west of it is the junction of the old walling with the new, although the old nave was some 10 ft. or 12 ft. longer than this. The south-west window is a new two-light one, similar to that opposite.

The arch dividing off the western portion of the nave has old stones re-used, and is of like detail to the chancel arch, except that the bases have a plain hollow chamfer. The space to the west of it has a three-light square-headed south window and a west doorway; on the north side is a stair to the gallery, which contains the organ; this gallery has a modern panelled traceried front. Over it the bell-turret rises; it has battering sides covered with oak shingles, and the bell-chamber is lighted on each side by two-light windows. Over it is an octagonal spire also covered with shingles, the whole being of modern construction.

Both the roofs are modern, and are covered with Horsham stone slabs. All the furniture is modern. The font has an octagonal bowl of grey marble with shallow trefoiled panels in 13th-century style, carried on a central stone stem and a cluster of shafts.

There are three monumental brasses in the chancel; the slab on the north side of the altar has the figures of john Arderne and Elizabeth his wife; he wears a long cloak with a high collar and loose sleeves gathered in close at the wrists, and his tunic underneath is held by a waistbelt enriched with rosettes. She wears a mantle fastened across the breast by a cord which descends below her waist and finishes with tasselled ends, and a close-fitting gown with a high belt. A shield above the man is charged with a fesse checky between three crescents, for Arderne, that above the woman is missing, as is also the main inscription. Below are the mutilated figures of three sons and the inscription: 'Thomas johñes et Henricus, filii jobis Arderne Armig'i et Elizabeth ux'is sue,' and the figures of three daughters inscribed 'Anna, Birgitta, et Susanna filiae jobis Arderne et Elizabeth ux'is sue.'

Between the figures is a shield with the Arderne arms impaling a quarterly coat, of which the first and fourth are blank and the second and third paly of six. The slab south of the altar has lost the brass figures of a man and woman, but the inscription below remains intact and reads: 'Orate pro Animabus Ricardi Ardern Gentilman et johanne uxoris ejus qui quidem Ricardus obiit xxii die Mensis Novembris Anno Dñi Millaño ccccº l xxxxixº Quorū Animabus Propiciet' deus Amen.' From the woman's mouth issues a scroll inscribed 'Fili redemptor mūdi deus miserere nobis,' and from the man's, 'Ut videntes Ihūm semper Colletemur.' Above is a small reptescutation of the Trinity between two shields, the first Arderne as before, and the second with the same impaling a cheveron between three harts tripping. These two shields also occur in reverse order at the bottom.

The third brass is a small one west of the communion rail, and is to Susanna the daughter of John Arderne, and shows her whole-length figure. It is undated, but she is doubtless the same lady as the

third daughter on the john Arderne slab; a scroll above her head is inscribed 'Mercy Jhū et graunt m'cy.'

The stained glass in the windows is modern, but in the vestry are preserved a few fragments of old glass, chiefly borders of three cinquefoiled heads, with red roses and jessant de lys repeated continuously.

There are five bells, all cast by Mears & Stainbank in 1889; the second was formerly by Lester & Pack, 1756; the third by William Eldridge, 1687; and the fourth by Bryan Eldridge, 1638.

The communion plate includes a cup of 1606 with an egg-and-tassel ornament around the foot; below the top edge is pricked the inscription 'TEH PARICH OF LEIGH + GC + WN.' There are also a standing paten of 1773, a flagon of 1899, both of silver, a small modern plate of base metal, a large plated flagon (now used to serve the font), a pewter plate, and a pewter bowl.

The first book of the registers has paper leaves and begins in 1579. The entries are much mixed up, but the baptisms appear to run from 1579 to 1703, the marriages from 1584 to 1643, and 1648 to 1653, and burials from 1584 to 1670 and 1674 to 1675. There are also some churchwardens' accounts dating from 1586 in the same volume. The second book contains baptisms from 1702 to 1800, marriages 1704 to 1754, and burials 1704 to 1800. The third book has the marriages from 1754 to 1812, and the fourth baptisms and burials from 1801 to 1812.

ADVOWSON The advowson of the church was granted to the priory of St. Mary Overy, Southwark, by charter of Hamelin de Warenne in 1202;[60] it is not evident when it ceased to belong to this priory, but the church was in the hands of the Prior and convent of Newark next Guildford by 1262,[61] and so remained until the Dissolution.[62] The cure of the parish was habitually served by one of the canons, the successive priors thus 'saving to themselves the stipend of a curate.'[63] Richard Arderne of Leigh Place, who died in 1499, expressed a desire in his will to be buried before the image of St. Katherine in the parish church of Leigh.[64] john Grave, elected prior in 1534, demised the rectory for ninety-nine years to Edward Shelley of Leigh Place, who afterwards granted his term of years to Edmund Saunders.[65] By the terms of the lease, according to Manning, the tenant of the rectory was to find a priest, provide wine and wax, to repair the parsonage and the chancel, and to find food for men and horses when the prior's servants came to collect rent.[66]

At the Dissolution, when the property came to the Crown, there seems to have been some uncertainty regarding the benefice of Leigh, as the advowson of the 'vicarage' was granted apart from the rectory to Sir Thomas Nevile, with remainder to the daughter Margaret, wife of Sir Robert Southwell;[67] the latter conveyed it to Henry Lechford,[68] from whom it passed to Richard his son.[69] Henry son of Richard in 1599–1600, during his father's lifetime, joined with Robert Casey in purchasing the rectory of Leigh 'with the mansion there,' &c., from the Crown for themselves

60 V.C.H. Surr. ii, 10; Pat. 3 Edw. IV, pt. iii, m. 21   61 V.C.H. Surr. ii, 103.
62 Valor Eccl. (Rec. Com.), ii, 33; Dugdale, Mon. vi, 383–4.
63 Chan. Proc.(Ser. 2), bdle. 154, no. 34.
64 P.C.C. 5 Moone. His tomb is on the south side of the chancel.
65 See n. 63.
66 Manning and Bray, Hist. of Surr. ii, 184.
67 Pat. 30 Hen. VIII, pt. vii, m. 7; Pat. 42 Eliz. pt. xv, m. 34.
68 Chan. Proc. (Ser. 2), bdle. 154, 34; Feet of F. Surr. Trin. 1 Edw. VI.
69 Chan. Inq. p.m. (Ser. 2), cxlv, 13.

and their heirs.[70] Casley seems to have quitclaimed his right to Lechford. The latter predeceased his father Sir Richard, who, already possessed of the advowson,[71] held the rectory also after his son's death,[72] probably during the minority of his grandson Richard. Henceforth the rectory and advowson were presumably held together, the benefice reverting to its original curacy, for which the lay rectors were responsible.[73] Sir Richard Lechford conveyed in 1610 to Richard Dallender,[74] who in 1627 sold to Sir Ralph Freeman ' the rectory and parsonage impropriate of Leigh with the capital messuage called the parsonage house.'[75] After this time the property frequently changed hands, passing from Freeman to George Smith in 1630,[76] and from the latter to Edward Bathurst in 1638.[77]

The Parliamentary Surveys of Church Lands made during the Commonwealth record in 1658 that ' the parish of Leigh . . . is an impropriation. That Mr. Anthony Bathurst of Dogmershfield in the county of Southampton is Impropriator thereof. That Tithes and Gleabe Land thereof are worth threescore pounds by the yeare. That john Bonwicke Clerke is Curat there to whome the said Mr. Anthony Bathurst giveth of his free will ffive pounds everie quarter of the year.'[78]

In 1691 members of the Bathurst family conveyed to Mary Tainturier, widow, and Daniel Tainturier,[79] and from the latter the rectory passed to Thomas Scawen in 1711–12.[80] James Scawen held it in 1779,[81] and conveyed it in that year to Cartwright,[82]

from whom it passed in 1790 to the Duke of Norfolk.[83] It passed from trustees of the duke in 1819 to the Rev. joseph Fell.[84] Fell conveyed to joseph Hodgson in 1823, and the latter, in the same year, to R. C. Dendy, of Leigh Place,[85] in whose family the patronage remained for many years. After the death of Stephen Dendy it passed to his third daughter and co-heir, Elizabeth wife of John Watney.[86] She died in 1896 ; her husband, who was knighted in 1900, still holds the advowson.[87] The living was created a vicarage in 1869. The benefice, as has been said, had previously been a perpetual curacy, the impropriator of the rectory holding both great and small tithes.[88]

Smith's Charity is distributed as in other Surrey parishes. In 1786 three *CHARITIES* houses, with orchards, from one benefaction, and one house, with no orchard, from another, were held for the poor ; but the donors were unknown. Two houses on the road from Leigh to Charlwood were called the Poor's Houses in living recollection, but they have been long in private hands, and were probably sold after 1834.[89]

Earl's Charity, date unknown, was £1 12s. charged on land for the poor. This is not known to exist at present.

In 1637 the Rev. Thomas Bristowe, by will, left a schoolhouse with 5 acres of land for the education of four poor children. This is lost apparently.

S. Dendy, by will, proved 1861, left stock producing £11 0s. 3d. yearly for the school.

MERSTHAM

Merstan (xi cent.) ; Mestham and Merstham (xii cent.) ; Meyrstham and Merystham (xiv cent.)

Merstham is a village 3½ miles north-east of Reigate, 8 miles south-by-west from Croydon, on the road between the two. The parish is bounded on the north by Coulsdon, on the east by Chaldon and Blechingley, on the south by Nutfield, on the south-west by Gatton, on the north-west by Chipstead. It measures 3 miles from north to south, and 2 miles from east to west, and contains 2,015 acres.

In 1899[1] a small readjustment of boundaries was made between Merstham and Gatton, part of each parish being transferred to the other. Merstham is in situation one of the typical parishes of the southern side of the chalk range. The parish runs from the chalk across the Upper Green Sand and Gault, into the Lower Green Sand, the outcrop of the Gault being unusually wide. The church and old village stand on the Upper Green Sand, at the foot of the chalk. The chalk is generally here crowned with an unusual thickness of clay with flints, but in the southern escarpment the chalk is on the surface.

Alderstead Heath is still an open common, and Worstead Green, or Wood Street Green, as it was anciently called, is a long strip of roadside waste. The Wellhead,

at the foot of Church Hill, was a valuable spring feeding one of the branches of the Mole, but has been much diminished by the workings of water companies and by the railway tunnel. An intermittent burn used to issue from the foot of Merstham Hill in wet weather, as at Croydon, on the other side of the chalk. But though both still flow occasionally, the water companies have permanently lowered the level of water in the chalk and interfered with all such natural overflows.

The Merstham quarries are in the Upper Green Sand formation, and though the parish was and is agricultural for the most part, the stone quarries are the most striking industrial part of Merstham, particularly on account of the general scarcity of good building stone in the county.

The Upper Green Sand yields stone of varying qualities throughout the whole of the outcrop of the bed. Lingfield had its quarries at the time of the Domesday Survey, but Godstone and Merstham have been more famous since as sources of supply. It is often called firestone, for it used to be in request for the beds of furnaces, especially in glass-houses. In West Surrey the same stone is called Malm stone. It is a calcareous sandstone, containing green silicate of

[70] Pat. 42 Eliz. pt. xv, m. 34 ; Cal. S.P. Dom. 1598–1601, p. 237.
[71] Vide supra.
[72] Feet of F. Surr. Mich. 4 Jas. I ; ibid. Hil. 7. Jas. I.   [78] Vide infra.
[74] Feet of F. Surr. Hil. 7 Jas. I.
[75] Close, 3 Chas. I, pt. ix, no. 22.
[76] Feet of F. Surr. Trin. 6 Chas. I.
[77] Ibid. 14 Chas. I.

[78] Surr. Arch Coll. xvii, 97.
[79] Feet of F. Surr. Trin. 3 Will. and Mary.
[80] Feet of F. Surr. Hil. 10 Anne.
[81] Ibid. East. 19 Geo. III.   [82] Ibid.
[83] Manning and Bray, Hist. of Surr. ii, 185.
[84] Brayley, Hist. of Surr. iv, 283 ; Inst. Bks. (P.R.O.).

[85] See preceding note.
[86] Clergy Lists ; Burke, Peerage, &c., Landed Gentry.
[87] Ibid.
[88] See note 82 ; Clergy Lists. .
[89] Information from Sir John Watney.
[1] Loc. Govt. Bd. Order 39880 ; Mark Hedge Shaw is an existing name on the boundary between Merstham and Gatton.

iron and plates of mica. It is very differently judged by different authorities as a building stone. It in fact differs in quality. It is quite soft when first dug, and requires seasoning, and must be laid as it lay in the quarry, if it is to last. Stone from the Merstham quarries was used in 1259 for the king's palace at Westminster, and in 1359 for Windsor Castle ;[2] also for Old St. Paul's and London Bridge. The Reigate stone frequently mentioned as employed at Windsor and Westminster, and by Henry VIII at Nonsuch, was of the same kind, and no doubt some of it of the same Wealden origin, for John and Philip Prophete, who supplied the stone in the 14th century, were masters of the quarries at Merstham.[3] Stone is still worked here.

Ironstone was found on Merstham Manor as early as the 14th century, and in 1362 the Earl of Arundel asked permission of the abbot to work it.[4] In a lease at Lambeth[5] of 1396 it appears that the iron was at Charlwood, land at Charlwood being in Merstham Manor. It could not occur in Merstham parish itself, for geological reasons.

The chalk at Merstham has also been long famous for its lime. The lime produced is not quite equal to the Dorking and Betchworth, but superior to the Guildford product. The lime used to be extensively used as manure, and is still so employed. Cement is also now made from it.

The mineral works at Merstham helped to bring about improved means of conveyance. The mediaeval line of carriage was by cart to Battersea for conveyance by water to Windsor. In both cases the line lay over a fairly dry and hard country.[5a] In 1807 the high road to Croydon was improved by Act of Parliament.[6] This road, new for a great part of its course, avoided the steep hill into Reigate, which was descended by the Reigate and Sutton road, and also the steeper portion of the Merstham hill, passing by the depression near the west end of the church, cutting off a little of Gatton Park, and entering Reigate over Wray Common.

Before this road was made, a railroad, worked by horse traction, and following the same depression in the chalk, had been laid down, connecting Merstham with Croydon, and, by a branch, with Wandsworth. This was opened in 1805, and was perhaps the earliest public railroad in England. Similar lines in the north were used only for particular collieries or mines. Though the Merstham stone and lime works were intended primarily to benefit by the line, it took goods of any ownership or description. Fullers' earth from Nutfield (q.v.) was conveyed upon it ; but through the cost of carriage and transhipment into the trucks, and further removal from the trucks and carriage at the other end, it was said to offer no great saving of expense. The mistake lay in not continuing the line, as was once suggested, to reach the Wey and Arun Canal in West Surrey, and so communicate with the southern coast. Also allowance was not made for the fact that there was no great quantity of goods to furnish a return traffic from the Thames to Merstham.

The line was taken over at last by the London and Brighton and South Eastern Companies, whose joint line runs upon part of it, but near Merstham the old railway is still visible in an inclined cutting. The rails, of course, have been removed.

The Locomotive Engine Railway was opened in 1842. Merstham Tunnel, now doubled, is a well-known feature of the line. There is a station at Merstham.

Close to the station is a place called Battle Bridge, originally in Gatton, about which traditions, incapable of verification, have gathered, concerning a defeat of the Danes. It is perhaps worth mentioning that there is an Ockley Wood in the east part of Merstham parish. But the great defeat of the Danes in 852, 'hard by Ockley Wood,' was no doubt at Ockley in West Surrey.

Neolithic flints are not uncommon about Merstham. They are very common about Redhill and Reigate, and precise attention to parish boundaries is not paid when flints are picked up.

The trace of greatest antiquity, perhaps, in the parish is connected with communications. An ancient trackway is to be observed along the chalk downs, which, crossing Gatton Park, enters Merstham and is used for some distance as a footpath, but appears in traces only south of the church. The line seems to continue, generally in use, into Chaldon parish, where it was called Pilgrim Lane. This is no doubt part of the old cross-country communication west and east along the Downs, but it is not until it reaches Chaldon that it used to be called the Pilgrims' Way. On the Ordnance map, however, and elsewhere, it is so called from West Surrey onwards.[7]

The village is picturesque, and stands on a hill or plateau at some elevation above the railway and the surrounding valleys. A few old-fashioned cottages remain, notably the half-timbered blacksmith's forge (now converted into a modern house), probably of the latter part of the 15th century, with a projecting upper story, and massive curved braces and story posts.[8] Much rebuilding, including the Feathers Inn, and the development of a picturesque building estate, in which are many well-designed houses, has taken place within recent years.

Close to the church is Merstham House, the seat of Lord Hylton. At Alderstead, ¾ mile to the north-east, is a picturesque farm-house, which preserves a few old features. There were ancient manor-houses here and at Albury in this parish.

At Albury Farm, south of the village, are well-marked remains of a moat which surrounded the destroyed manor-house of Albury.

South-west of the church is Court Lodge Mead, where traces of the terraces of the old manor-house garden are still visible.

There are numerous gentlemen's houses about Merstham. Merstham House, the property of Lord Hylton, is at present occupied by Mr. Andrew Walker; Battle Bridge House is the seat of Mr. Richard Trower ; the Gables, of Mr. Frederick Adams ; Ockley House, of Mrs. Pelley.

The property called Netherne—'Lez Nedder' in 1522—has been acquired by the Surrey County

[2] Pat. 33 Edw. III, pt. iii, m. 7.
[3] V.C.H. Surr. ii, 277–8.
[4] Lit. Cant. (Rolls Ser.), vii, 420.
[5] Quoted by Manning and Bray, Hist. of Surr. ii, 255.

[5a] V.C.H. Surr. ii, loc. cit.
[6] 47 Geo. III, cap. 25.
[7] Manning and Bray (op. cit. ii, 253) say that the name Pilgrims' Lane is used in this parish.

[8] See an excellent wood-cut of this, before it was modernized, in Palgrave's Handbook to Reigate, p. 124.

Council for an asylum; the quit-rent of 11s. 1d. recorded in 1522 was enfranchised from the present lord by the council.

A school (national) was established in 1849. A School Board was elected in 1889, which took over and enlarged the National School. The present building was erected in 1898.

South Merstham is an ecclesiastical parish made in 1898 out of Merstham parish and a portion of Gatton. The church (All Saints) was built that year. It is of brick in 13th-century style, and when completed will include chancel, nave, transepts, and spire. The chancel and transepts and one bay of the nave are completed at present. The basin of the font is a Tridacna Gigas shell brought from the Philippine Islands by Mr. William Willox. Battle Bridge is in the part of Gatton transferred to Merstham and included in this district.

A rental of Merstham of 1522,[9] and a map in Lord Hylton's possession, of 1760, show that the parish was much subdivided into small holdings in open fields about Ashted Hill and also elsewhere. About Worstead Green were many cottages which have disappeared. Townend Meads are marked in the Ordnance map west of the village. Towney Meads seems to be their usual name, but the rental of 1522 calls them Townman Meads ; obviously the meadows of the villani. Both 'Common Fields' and 'Cotman Mead,' with several 'shots' in each, appear in the 1522 rental.

There is no Inclosure Act, but William Jolliffe, who bought the manor in 1788 and died in 1802, consolidated the holdings in large farms as leases fell in ; a process completed after his premature death caused by an accident.[10]

The earliest mention of *MERSTHAM MANORS* (Mearsdethan, x cent. ; Mersthan, Domesday Survey ; Mesham, xiii cent. and later) occurs in 675, when Frithwald, *subregulus* of Surrey, and Erkenwald, Bishop of London, granted 20 hides there to the abbey of Chertsey.[11] In 947 20 hides were bestowed by Eadred upon Oswig his minister,[12] while the grant to Chertsey was confirmed in 967 by Edgar, and again in 1062 by Edward.[13] Some of this property came ultimately into the possession of the abbey of Christchurch, Canterbury. According to Dugdale, who prints a charter to that effect, the manor was granted to the monastery by Athelstan, more usually known as Lifing, Archbishop of Canterbury, in 1018.[14] At the time of Domesday Survey it was held by the archbishop for the clothing of the monks,[15] and after the separation of the lands of the archbishop from those of Christchurch,[16] it remained part of the abbey estate until the beginning of the 16th century.[17] In 1539 Thomas, Prior of Christchurch, surrendered Merstham Manor to Henry VIII, who granted it to Sir Robert

Southwell, Master of the Rolls, and Margaret his wife, in exchange for the rectory of Warnham in Sussex, which the king then bestowed upon the abbey in fee.[18] Sir Robert died before his wife, who married William Plumbe and held the manor jointly with her second husband for the term of her life.[19] In 1569 her two sons Francis and Robert Southwell alienated the reversion to Thomas Copley,[20] who apparently entered into immediate occupation of the house, for a complaint was raised by William Rychebell to the effect that Copley had turned him out, seized his household goods, and spoiled his crops. Rychebell, who had married Alice, the eldest daughter of Christopher Best,[21] pleaded that the estate, excepting the courts leet and rents of assize, had been let to his father-in-law for a term of fifty years, and that he himself now held the lease 'by good law.'[22] The result of his petition does not appear. In 1584 Thomas Copley died in Flanders seised of the reversion, bequeathing it to his wife Katherine for her life.[23] In 1604 William Copley, son of Thomas, conveyed the property to Nicholas Jordan and John Middleton.[24]

Two years later the manor was sold by these to John Hedge,[25] who settled it upon his son Anthony 16 December 1619. John Hedge died in the following January, and a few months later the manor was re-settled by trustees upon Anthony on his marriage with Margaret Fountayne.[26] In 1650, Merstham was held by another John Hedge, presumably his son.[27] By 1673-4 the manor was divided between two coheiresses, Jane the wife of Henry Hoare and Mirabella the wife of John Gainsford, junior,[28] and as Jane was daughter and co-heiress of John Hedge[29] it seems probable that Mirabella was her sister. John and Nicholas Gainsford sold Merstham 30 May 1678 to Sir John Southcote,[30] who died seised of property in Merstham in 1685. He left everything to his wife Elizabeth,[31] who died in the following year and was succeeded by her eldest son Edward.[32] A partition was made between Sir Edward Southcote and Henry Hoare in 1705, by which the manor and some of the lands were ceded to the former, and the remainder of the property was retained by Hoare.[33] The manor was first mortgaged in two moieties, and then sold in successive portions to Paul Docminique and to his son Charles,[34] who died without children in 1745, his cousin Paul Humphrey inheriting the property. Paul Humphrey also died without issue, and the manor passed into the possession of his sister Rachel and her husband John Tattersall.[35] They too left no children, and the estate devolved upon John's brother the Rev. James Tattersall, who, dying in 1784, left the estates for sale.[36] They were purchased in 1788 from trustees by William Jolliffe, who was succeeded in 1802 by his son Hylton. Hylton Jolliffe died without issue in 1843. His nephew Sir W. G. H. Jolliffe, bart.,[37]

[9] Communicated by Lord Hylton to the *Surr. Arch. Soc. Trans.* xx.
[10] *Surr. Arch. Coll.* loc. cit. ; Manning and Bray, op. cit. ii, 252.
[11] Birch, *Cart. Sax.* i, 64 ; Kemble, *Cod. Dipl.* v, 19.
[12] Ibid. ii, 27 ; Birch, *Cart. Sax.* ii, 584.
[13] Kemble, *Cod. Dipl.* iii, 6 ; iv, 151.
[14] Dugdale, *Mon.* i, 97.
[15] *V.C.H. Surr.* i, 300.
[16] Somner, *Antiq. of Cant.* 122.
[17] Bibl. Cott. Galba E. iv, fol. 33, &c.
[18] L. *and P. Hen. VIII*, xiv (1), 1286 ; (2), g. 113 (21) ; xv, g. 282 (84).

[10] Pat. 10 Eliz. pt. vi, m. 40.
[20] Ibid.; Chan. Inq. p.m.(Ser. 2), ccx, 85.
[21] P.C.C. 6 Street.
[22] Chan. Proc. (Ser. 2), bdle. 28, no. 13.
[23] Chan. Inq. p.m. (Ser. 2), ccx, 85 ; Pat. 31 Eliz. pt. xiv, m. 20.
[24] Feet of F. Surr. Hil. 1 Jas I. The Copleys were recusants, paying heavy compositions, and gradually forced to sell lands.
[26] Close, 4 Jas. I, pt. i ; Pat. 4 Jas I, pt. xii.
[26] Chan. Inq. p.m. (Ser. 2), cccclxxxvi, 117.

[27] Feet of F. Surr. Trin. 1650.
[28] Ibid. East. 25 Chas. II ; Mich. 29 Chas. II ; Hil. 29 & 30 Chas. II ; Hil. 2 Will. and Mary.
[29] Ct. R. in Lord Hylton's hands.
[30] Deeds in Lord Hylton's hands.
[31] P.C.C. 77 Cann.
[32] Ibid. 7 Lloyd.
[33] Manning and Bray, *Hist. of Surr.* ii, 257.
[34] Ibid. ; information, Lord Hylton.
[35] P.C.C. Ducie.
[36] Manning and Bray, *Hist. of Surr.* ii, 257.
[37] Ibid.

was created Baton Hylton and held the manor until 1876. His heir the second baron died in 1899, and his son the present Lord Hylton is lord of the manor.[38]

William jolliffe, after his purchase in 1788, built what was called the Great House, west of Merstham Street. This was pulled down in 1834 and the remains sold to Lord Monson for building Gatton Park. The present Merstham House is what was called the Cottage, built by the Rev. W. J. jolliffe, father of the first Baron Hylton, and subsequently enlarged.[39]

JOLLIFFE, Lord Hylton. *Argent a pile vert with three right hands or thereon.*

There are three grants of free warren to the Abbots of Christchurch in their demesne lands at Merstham, the earliest from Henry II, and the two others bearing the dates 1316 and 1364.[40] The prior had a prison[41] at Merstham, and kept a strict watch over his rights there. In 1335 in a case depending on a writ of tight, granted at the petition of John Passelew, the suitors had assumed to themselves the right of giving an award before the process had been begun by the prior's bailiffs, to whom the writ was addressed, and the prior wrote indignantly that this was done 'in prejudice of us and infringement of our position which is not to be patiently borne.'[42] On another occasion a special representative was sent to the court as the abbot understood that 'certain matters of high import' were impending.[43]

A mill worth 30d. at Merstham is mentioned in Domesday,[44] and in the conveyance to Thomas Copley two water-mills and two horse-mills are spoken of.[45] One water-mill also went with the moiety of the manor which was owned by Henry and Jane Hoare in 1705.[46]

In 1348 Alexander Hanekyn was granted licence to alienate some 28 acres of meadow, woodland, &c., to the Prior of Christchurch for the sustenance of seven chaplains to celebrate divine service daily in the chapel of St. Thomas the Martyr, to pray for the souls of Edward II and his ancestors.[47]

At the beginning of the 14th century the reputed manor of *ALBURY* (Aldebury, Aldbury, xiv–xvi cents.) was held of the Prior of Christchurch by Sir Edmund de Passelew or Passelee, together with his son John, for service of 16s. a year and suit of court every three weeks at Merstham. Sir Edmund also held 40 acres of land in Merstham parish jointly with his second wife Margaret. john de Passelew inherited the manor at his father's death about 1327,[48] and in 1339 he conveyed all his right in it to Richard de Burton,[49] transferring to him an annual rent of 20 marks from

John le French, who held the tenement of Albury on a seven years' lease from the preceding year, 1338.[50] It seems that either this lease was renewed or else John le French acquired the manor in fee, for we find later that Nicholas le French granted the manor for eight years at a rent of 50s. to Fulk Harwode, who in 1365-8 conveyed his right to Nicholas de Lovayne.[51] It does not appear who next succeeded as lord of the manor, but Manning and Bray, quoting the Court Rolls of Merstham, say that Albury was held by John Timperley,[52] who in the reign of Henry VI was granted licence to impark 40 acres of wood, 100 of land, 80 of pasture, and 30 of meadow in Merstham, with 'pales and ditches.' At the same time Timperley received a grant of 'waif and stray,' of free warren in all his lands in Merstham,[53] with the further privilege that he should not be 'put on assizes, juries, &c.'[54]

Quoting the same Court Rolls, Manning and Bray say that Timperley conveyed the manor of Albury to John Elingbridge, who settled it upon his second wife Anne, the daughter of john Prophet and widow of Ralph St. Leger.[55] This john died in 1473, and was succeeded by his grandson Thomas, who died in 1507 leaving one daughter, Anne. A son john was born to him posthumously, but died in the same year.[56] Anne, who then became heiress of the estates, afterwards married her guardian, john Dannett,[57] knighted in 1529, who marshalled a muster of thirty-eight men from Merstham, reviewed in 1539.[58] Albury remained in the possession of the Dannetts until 1579, when it was sold by Leonard Dannett and Christiana his wife to john Southcote, one of the judges of the Queen's Bench.[59] Southcote died in April 1585, and Albury was settled upon his son John and his wife Magdalen, one of the daughters of Sir Edward Waldegrave.[60] Apparently the estate was sequestered by the Crown under Charles I, for two-thirds of it, with several other estates, were regranted in 1633-4 to John Southcote and Edward his son, recusants, at a yearly rent of £100.[61] john Southcote lived until january 1637-8, the manor having been settled on the preceding December on his grandson john,[62] and it remained the property of this family[63] until 1727, when it was sold to Paul Docminique.[64] It eventually became the property of William jolliffe and was united to the manor of Merstham (q.v.), Lord Hylton being the present owner.

The site of the old manor-house is marked by a moated inclosure.

According to Manning and Bray, who quote deeds in the register of the Dean and Chapter of Canterbury, the reputed manor of *ALDERSTEAD* was held by the Passelew family about 1287.[65] In the 13th century it was in the possession of Sir Robert

[38] G.E.C. *Peerage.*
[39] Information, Lord Hylton.
[40] Stowe MS. 924, p. 212 ; Chart. R. 10 Edw. II, m. 24, no. 60 ; 38 Edw. II, m. 8, no. 15.
[41] *Cal. Pat.* 1301-7, p. 172.
[42] *Lit. Cant.* (Rolls Ser.), ii, 102.
[43] Ibid. ii, 272. [44] *V.C.H. Surr.* i, 300.
[45] Pat. 10 Eliz. pt. vi, m. 40.
[46] Recov. R. Trin. 4 Anne, rot. 103.
[47] *Cal. Pat.* 1345-8, p. 447.
[48] Chan. Inq. p.m. 1 Edw. III (1st nos.), no. 35 ; Add. MS. 6167 fol. 20.
[49] Add. MS. 6167, fol. 245 ; *Cal. Close,* 1339-41, p. 338.

[50] Ibid.
[51] Close, 39 Edw. III, m. 26 and 25.
[52] Manning and Bray, *Hist. of Surr.* ii, 258.
[53] Fishery and free warren in Albury was owned by the family of Medley in the 16th century. See Feet of F. Sutt. 5 Edw. VI.
[54] Chart. R. 27-39 Hen. VI, no. 41. The rental of 1522 gives Albury as Dannet's, late Illingbridge, formerly Corve.
[55] Chan. Inq. p.m. (Ser. 2), xxi, 118.
[56] Aubrey, *Antiq. of Surr.* iv, 233-4.
[57] Manning and Bray, *Hist. of Surr.* ii,

259. He held in 1522 (Rental, *Surr. Arch. Coll.* xx, 92).
[58] *L. and P. Hen. VIII,* xiv (1), 294.
[59] Recov. R. Hil. 22 Eliz. rot. 534 ; Feet of F. Surr. Mich. 22 & 23 Eliz. ; Hil. 22 Eliz.
[60] Chan. Inq. p.m. (Ser. 2), ccvi, 25.
[61] Pat. 9 Chas. I, pt. xvi, no. 2.
[62] Chan. Inq. p.m. (Ser. 2), ccccIxxxvii, 181.
[63] Recov. R. Hil. 1652, rot. 98 ; Feet of F. Surr. Hil. 1652 ; East. 1687.
[64] Close, 1 Geo. II, pt. i, no. 18 ; Feet of F. Surr. Mich. 1 Geo. III.
[65] Manning and Bray, *Hist. of Surr.* ii, 257.

Passelew, whose wife Christiana or Custance held it in dower after his death, and at the beginning of the following century their son Sir Edmund granted the reversion to Robert, his son by his second wife.[66] In 1335 this Robert complained that his step-brother John, then lord of Albury, had broken his close, mowed his grass and carried it away with other of his goods.[67] Nothing further is known about this estate until the 15th century, when according to Manning and Bray, who quote Court Rolls of Merstham, William Best died seised of it in 1487. Richard Best was holding in 1522,[68] and in 1572 and 1587 it appears as the property of Nicholas Best. Another Nicholas Best died and was succeeded in 1670 by his son Nicholas. In 1678 it was sold to Joseph Reeve, who bequeathed all his estates to his only son John, making provision for his daughter Sarah,[69] who eventually succeeded her brother. She married secondly George Ballard, and in 1749 her eldest son by him sold the estate to Samuel Nicholson. By 1773 it was in the possession of Sir James Colbroke, who died in 1761. His brother Sir George conveyed it to Lord Newhaven. The manor then became the property of John Lefevre, who bequeathed it to his son-in-law Shaw, who took the name of Lefevre and was holding the estate in 1808.[70] The Rev. W. J. Jolliffe, second son of Mr. Jolliffe who bought Merstham, bought Alderstead between 1820 and 1830. He died in 1835. His son was the first Lord Hylton, and Alderstead, which was always held of Merstham Manor, was united to it by him in 1843.[71]

In 1522 Sir John Leigh held CHILBERTON (Chylbertons) as a manor of the Prior of Christchurch.[72] According to Manning and Bray, Henry Drake conveyed it to William Franke in 1625. In 1658 he by will devised it to his youngest son William. In 1677 he and his son conveyed it to William Bowman, who in 1710 left it to his youngest son William. In 1735 Benjamin Bowman conveyed to Charles Docminique, from whom it passed to the Tattersalls and so to the Jolliffes with the main manor.[73] It is called 'the reputed manor of Chilvertons,' but a court has been held for it in recent years. The manor-house, on the west side of Merstham street, is little more than a cottage, with the date 1598 upon it. In 1905 it was bought by Mr. Paxton Watson, who has carefully restored the house.

In the rental of 1522 and the Court Rolls, NORTH and SOUTH WORTH appear as holdings in Merstham Manor. It is possible that an error has been made in treating Orde, in Reigate Hundred, in the Domesday Survey, as Worth in Sussex, counted in Surrey by error or by an indeterminate boundary. It is at least equally probable that this Worth, now commonly called The Wor, is meant.

The church of ST. KATHERINE CHURCH stands in a strangely isolated position on the Brighton road, at some distance from the village, upon a green knoll surrounded by tall old elms. A modern lych-gate gives access to the churchyard from the east, and broad gravelled paths lead to the south porch, with long flights of steps from the

south, rendered necessary by the steep pitch. The churchyard, which has been extended towards the south within the last half-century, and must now be one of the largest in the county, is very nicely planted and carefully tended. It contains a few old and many modern tombstones. The ground rises above the church to the north, and falls rapidly to the southward, and the whole hill is formed of the Merstham stone, lying beneath the chalk, from which the church, with many other local buildings, has been built.

This stone is, externally and internally, the most conspicuous of the materials used in the building. In the original dressings and walling it appears throughout, mixed in the latter with flints from the chalk, and only partly replaced in the former by Bath stone in modern restorations. All things considered, the old stone has not weathered badly. The south chapel and parts of the chancel are faced with ashlar in this stone. The roofs of the nave and south chapel are covered with stone slabs, probably dug from the neighbouring hills, and like those known as Horsham slabs, the chancel, north chapel, and porch being roofed with tiles, and the aisles with lead. The well-proportioned timber spire is shingled.

The church consists of nave, 42 ft. 8 in. by 19 ft. 9 in., with aisles about 1 ft. longer by 7 ft. 9 in. wide, having a good sized porch 10 ft. by 8 ft. 3 in., and a western tower 15 ft. by 14 ft. 9 in., with walls no less than 4 ft. 6 in. thick, chancel 30 ft. 6 in. by 19 ft., north (or Albury Manor) chapel 21 ft. 10 in. by 15 ft. 8 in. and south or St. Katherine's (or Alderstead Manor) chapel, 19 ft. 9 in. by 11 ft. At the west corner of the north aisle vestries have been built within recent years. The whole building is of exceptional height and dignity for a Surrey church.

Probably the predecessor of the present church, that mentioned in Domesday, or one built, perhaps, towards the end of the 11th century, consisted of a nave of the same size, but with a shorter and narrower chancel. These, with the exception of the angles of the nave walls, were swept away in the closing years of the 12th century, when a complete new church, substantially that which exists, took the place of the primitive building, the fine massive tower of three stories, the nave arcades of three bays, the lofty chancel arch, and parts of the chancel being the most prominent of the features of this period. The date may be set down at about 1200, but there are points in the work—such as some voussoirs with enriched cheveron ornament now lying loose—which suggest a slightly earlier date. In the case of the particular detail referred to, however, it may be that the stones belonged to a doorway inserted in the early nave wall (about 1180) before the aisles were thrown out.[74] The south porch and north and south chapels were added, and the aisles and chancel greatly altered at various dates between c. 1390 and c. 1500. It is a debatable point whether the aisles were not widened, as well as heightened, in this later period. From the presence of a piscina of the earlier period in the south chapel it is possible that there may have been a smaller chapel on this site, rebuilt in its present form c. 1500; or perhaps the piscina was removed from the end of the south aisle

---

[66] Chan. Inq. 1 Edw. III (1st. nos.), no. 35.
[67] Cal. Pat. 1334-8, p. 205.
[68] Rental, Surr. Arch. Coll. xx, 97.
[69] P.C.C. 9 End.

[70] Manning and Bray, Hist. of Surr. ii, 260, 261. [71] Lord Hylton, information.
[72] Rental, Surr. Arch. Coll. xx, 98.
[73] Manning and Bray, Hist. of Surr. ii, 261, from the Ct. R.

[74] These enriched cheveron voussoirs should be compared with those in the arch of south doorway at Shiere Church (q.v.), illus. in V.C.H. Surr. i, 433.

when the new chapel was built. The church has passed through several 'restorations' of more or less destructive character between 1840 and the present time, and the tower was repaired in 1908. The tower is of great architectural interest, and the shingled spire with which it is crowned, probably a century later in date, forms a beautiful finish. Square at the eaves, it is splayed off to an octagonal plan above. Beneath the eaves is a corbeltable, which originally perhaps supported a low parapet, as at Witley, the corbels being all of the same general design—a sort of billet set within a broad hollow, crowned by a quirked bead. Below this there are in each face of the top stage three lancets under conjoined hood-mouldings, the centre lancet a mere recess that has never been pierced.[75] The stringcourse upon which these lancets rested is at present of moulded form, but the mouldings appear to be in ' Roman ' cement, and the original section was probably a semi-octagon. The lancets themselves have

a very beautiful and interesting doorway, 4 ft. 6 in. wide in the clear, somewhat injured, together with most of the other stonework, by retooling in about 1840. In design it is unusual, consisting of a pointed arch of two orders under a label, the outer order chamfered and the inner having a dog's-tooth moulding on the angle, resting on a nook-shaft, within these being a third order consisting of a trefoiled arch, with a bold roll-moulding continued down the jambs. The shape of the trefoil is peculiar, the head being a broad horse-shoe in shape, and the sides flat curves of much smaller radius. The label terminates in the heads of a man and a woman, and is of a section which suggests a 14th-century restoration—possibly when the window over it was inserted, but the heads appear to be original. The mouldings of the capitals and bases to the shafts also appear to have been re-cut, and the sill was probably lower originally.[76] The oak door is coeval and still retains its beautiful wrought-iron scrollwork, hinges, straps, and key-plate, the C-shaped curves of the hinges and the ends of the scroll-pieces in the upper part of the door terminating in dragons' heads. The latch-handle and the bottom hinges are plain work of the 14th or 15th century. The tower arch is of pointed form, chamfered, and has semicircular responds. There is now no staircase visible, and it is doubtful if one ever existed, but in Cracklow's view (c. 1824) there are indications of what may have been a staircase in the south-west angle.

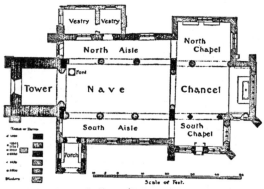

PLAN OF ST. KATHERINE'S CHURCH, MERSTHAM

The nave arcades are of about the same date (c. 1200) and the same general design, and of two chamfered orders and a label of semi-octagonal

been a good deal repaired in stone and cement except on the north side. In the middle stage is a single lancet of similar design, which originally had a label, also standing upon a string-course of semicircular section ; and another lancet appears in the upper part of the bottom stage. In the two upper stories there are plain quoins, but in the lower are wide buttresses of shallow projection, two on the west face and one on the south, but none on the north ; in addition to which a small buttress-like projection occurs at the eastern end of both north and south sides. In the bottom stage on the west side is a three-light tracery window of 15th-century date standing upon a stringcourse that has been cased in cement. Below this is

section, but the piers on the north side are of octagonal plan, while those on the south are circular, the moulded capitals also being of different design ; and on the north there is a square western respond, while on the south it takes a semicircular form, there being at the east end no responds, but corbels of heavy design, on the north octagonal, and on the south semicircular.[77] Above the arcades is a clearstory in which are quatrefoil and trefoil windows—some of the quatrefoils 'lying on their sides '—set in tall, splayed, round-headed internal openings, four on each side, over the columns and responds.[78] The chancel arch is very wide and exceptionally lofty, the half-columns of its jambs being somewhat out of the perpendicular, giving the acutely

[75] The corbel-table and lancets in this top stage resemble those in the tower of Southwick, Sussex, of slightly earlier date.
[76] The whole design of the doorway resembles that to the frater in the monastic buildings at Rochester, the work of Prior Helias in the first few years of the 13th century.
[77] Cf. the arcades in the neighbouring

churches of Chipstead and Betchworth, coeval in date. The sections of arches, capitals and bases of the south arcade at Merstham are almost identical with those at Chipstead, and the capitals of the north arcade greatly resemble those in the nave of Betchworth.
[78] Cf. the similar clearstory lights on the south side at the sister church of Chip-

stead, where the internal openings are plain square-edged and round-headed, and the external quatrefoils set in a circle with a surrounding moulding, all now inside the church, as were the clearstory lights at Merstham till a recent restoration, when the aisle roofs were lowered, so as to make the clearstory windows fulfil their original purpose.

MERSTHAM CHURCH : WEST DOOR OF TOWER

MERSTHAM CHURCH FROM THE SOUTH-EAST

pointed arch a slightly horse-shoed form. This arch is of two orders with unequal chamfers, and retains a good deal of its original colour decoration in patterns. The capitals are very curious, being of an irregular outline, not semicircular on plan, but waved in form and having a tall bell, upon which are three separate sprays of peculiar foliage resembling the classical acanthus. These so closely resemble the carving on the stone seat-elbows in the chancel of Chipstead Church and a scallop-shell ornament on the chancel arch piers at Letherhead—both works of the same date—as to render it almost certain that all were carved by the same hand.[79] Taken with the palm-branch foliage at Reigate hard by, they point to the influence of Eastern art through the Crusades. In the chancel itself the only traces of the work of this 1200 period are the partly destroyed blind arcades in the eastern part of the south wall and the beautiful double piscina. The wall arcades are lofty, with plainly chamfered arches, and resemble those in the chancel of Merton Church, and a group of other examples in Surrey and Kent. One capital of the shafts between the blank arches remains on the south side, circular in form and of good moulded section.[80] The piscina, which is certainly one of the best remaining of an early series in Surrey,[81] has a 'shouldered' head, boldly moulded, a credence shelf, and two drains in the form of projecting bowls beautifully carved in undercut foliage of a somewhat uncommon type. The small plain piscina in the south chapel, with projecting chamfered sill, is of the same period. It is almost triangular, with arched sides, measuring 12 in. wide by 7 in. and 4 in. deep. Part of a lancet window of this date remains in the west wall of the north aisle, beneath a modern two-light opening. The corresponding two-light opening in the south aisle is an insertion of c. 1340.

The two-light window, inserted perhaps in the place of an earlier lancet, in the wall-arch on the south side of the chancel, with cusped heads and a pointed quatrefoil under an inclosing arch, dates from about 1340, and is the only other feature of that period. To c. 1390 the porch in the end bay of the south aisle may be ascribed. It has a lofty outer archway of pointed form under a square label, with plain heater-shaped shields within quatrefoils in the spandrels, the jambs having a shaft with capital and base and good mouldings, repeated on the inner side. The doorway within is a plain example of the same date, and in the side walls, set very low down, are quatrefoil windows. The porch would appear to have been higher originally, and perhaps had a parvise over it. An image niche over the entrance is blocked by a sundial. This porch should be compared with the south porch of Oxted Church.

Slightly later, about 1450, the north and south aisles were remodelled if not rebuilt on a wider plan,

and to this date may be ascribed the windows and other features. The south aisle has square-headed two-light windows in its south wall, while those in the north aisle are of three lights under pointed segmental heads. The north chapel, perhaps dedicated to St. Mary Magdalen, was probably also built at this time, and has similar windows to those in the north aisle. In its north wall is the arched tomb recess of John Elinebrygge (Elingbridge), 1473.[82] To the same period belongs the very large and handsome east window of the chancel. It is of five lights, doubled in the head, in which two quatrefoils of the width of the lower lights are placed. The arches dividing the north chapel from the chancel are of very unequal spans and coarse design. The south chapel, which appertained to the manor of Alderstead, and is dedicated to St. Katherine, dates from c. 1500. It is faced externally with ashlar, has a small priest's door in the south wall, with four-centred arch, the jambs and head of which stand out from the wall in an unusual manner; and right and left tall two-light windows with moulded jambs and square heads, having four-centred arches to the lights. Its east window of three lights under a pointed head is of more ordinary type. On the east wall to the left inside are the remains of an image niche with a good deal of ancient red colour, and there are other indications that this wall was richly decorated with a reredos of carved stonework, and coloured and gilt. The arches between the south chapel and chancel are of the same period, and are more elaborate than those on the opposite side; the pier and respond have attached shafts, quatrefoil fashion, alternating with hollows, the capitals, bases and arches being characteristically moulded. The same inequality of span is observable in these as in those opposite, the smaller arch to the west being doubtless reduced in span in order to minimize the thrust upon the east wall of the nave. The arches at the east end of the aisles opening into these chapels are of four-centred form, set very high up on moulded corbels, and belong to the dates of the chapels respectively; that to the north having two hollow-chamfeted orders and the southern plain chamfers.

The aisle roofs are modern, but those of the nave, chapels, and chancel are mainly composed of the old timbers, the chancel roof being ceiled with plaster over the timbers, but showing one tie-beam and moulded wall-plates as evidence of antiquity. The north chapel has a roof with tie-beams, and octagonal king-posts having curved braces to the principal and ridge. The porch roof has trussed rafters of good design. Except in the aisles, which are covered with lead, the pitches of the roof are somewhat steep. Oak parclose screens of 15th or early 16th-century date have been destroyed within the last fifty years, but fragments of one have been made into a lobby to the priest's door.[83] All the seating in the body of the

[79] For illustrations of all three see V.C.H. Surr. i, 451.

[80] Ibid. 453. These lofty blind wall-arches, as part of the wall construction, are not to be confounded with ordinary wall arcades of a more or less decorative character, and usually about 5 ft. or 6 ft. high. They occur at the following Surrey churches : Blechingley, Chaldon, Charlwood, Merstham, Merton, and Couldon—the last being later (c. 1260), and all the others quite early in the 13th century. The late Mr. G. E. Street first drew attention to the connexion of some of

these Surrey churches with a group in Kent, where the same blind arches occur, as at Cliffe-at-Hoo and Brasted, and the writer has discovered other examples at Hartlip, St. Mary Cray, Horton Kirby, Dartford, Rainham, Upchurch, Newington and Sittingbourne, also in work of the early part of the 13th century.

[81] Good double piscinas of the period, c. 1190–1220, occur at Carshalton, Cobham, Ockham, and Okewood Chapel ; and single-drain examples at Fetcham, Chipstead, Chiddingfold, and Godalming.

[82] His grandson, Thomas Elinerugge or

Elyngbrigge (he is called by both names on his brass, post), directed by his will that he should be buried in the 'North Chauncell wᵗ in the church of Merysthm afore the pictur of Mary Magdalen.' He bequeaths to the 'high aultar of or lady of Merysthm, 3s. 4d. and to the repacōn of the church, 10s.' This is dated 1507, and may assist in fixing the time when St. Katherine's Chapel was built.

[83] The screen between the north aisle and the north chapel is said to have been even later than these—perhaps of 17th-century date, like that at Wotton.

church, the quire fittings, pulpit, &c., are modern. Besides the painted patterns on the chancel arch and the colouring still visible on the east wall of the south chapel, there are traces of extensive figure paintings in the nave. On the north-west column is a cross patée, no doubt a consecration cross, about 6 in. in diameter ; and on the same column is a female figure wearing a hat and wimple. These date from about 1200. On the corresponding pillar on the south side was a figure of a bishop, in the attitude of benediction ; on the east face of the chancel arch pier on the south side was a painting of the Blessed Virgin and Child ; and along the whole of the south aisle traces of painting were visible, among which is said to have been a representation of the Martyrdom of St. Thomas of Canterbury and other scenes, of which a man drawing a sword was the most distinct figure. It seems likely that the story of St. Katherine, the patroness of the church, was here represented. Mr. Reginald Palgrave, writing in 1860, says :—' If this be so the easternmost compartment represents the first act of her martyrdom, when an angel descending from heaven broke in pieces the instruments of torture. The figures to the right . . . with hands uplifted, and faces upturned, would form the astonished spectators of the miraculous interposition ; more in the centre appears the persecuting tyrant Maximin, distinguished by a crown and shield. The centre compartment is sadly destroyed ; but the forms of a colossal Virgin and Child are just traceable. The third division . . . would represent the saint's death by beheading, if the soldier drawing his sword may be thus interpreted.'[84] All except the first-named fragments have disappeared during the last forty years. Cracklow, writing in 1824, states that there were formerly ' some exquisite devices in stained glass, of which only a few fragments' were then remaining. There are still in the east window of the south chapel figures of the Blessed Virgin and Child, St. Peter, and another saint. In the chancel and other windows the modern stained glass is of poor quality, but in the nave some glass recently put in is of better design and colouring.

The font, of Purbeck marble, in good preservation, dates from the end of the 12th century. It has a square body, with a circular basin, and elegant trefoil leaves filling the spandrels on the top. The sides, which overhang, have a shallow round-arched arcade, and rest upon a central drum and four angle-shafts, the whole standing on a moulded base and square moulded plinth. Altogether it is an exceptionally good example of a common type ; cf. Beddington, Great Bookham, Frensham, and Mickleham.

The oldest monument is a sadly mutilated stone effigy of a civilian, said to be that of Nicholas Jamys, mayor and alderman of London, and father to the first wife of John Elingbridge. Its date has been placed between 1420 and 1430. When this was discovered, in about 1800, it was lying face downwards, the back of the slab forming part of the chancel pavement. It is described at that time as having the hands raised in prayer, and bright scarlet colouring on the robes, both of which details have disappeared. There was also a bird with outspread wings at the

feet, and the head was supported by two angels, but these have been almost destroyed by the ill-usage that the effigy has received. It would seem that the figure was habited in a scarlet alderman's gown bordered with fur, which can still be seen at the foot, and a very interesting detail remains in the gypcière, attached by straps to the waist girdle and hanging from the right side. This effigy now rests upon a very richly carved frieze or cornice, which itself lies loose upon the pavement of the north chapel. This, although its history is uncertain, may well have formed the cornice to the wall-tomb belonging to this effigy. It is about 18 in. high and 9 ft. in length originally, the upper part moulded, and the lower most beautifully carved with an undercut vine trail, a fine vigorous piece of work. In the middle is a demi-figure of an angel with curly locks, in alb and apparelled amice holding a plain ridged heater-shaped shield ; while at the left end is sculptured an heraldic casque bearing the crest of an eagle or falcon, perched upon a cap of maintenance, perhaps with reference to the deceased having filled the high office of mayor of London. Other fragments which may have formed part of this tomb are lying on the floor of the north aisle to the westward, and among them the richly-carved voussoirs of the 12th-century doorway above noticed. The tomb probably stood either in the western part of the north chapel, against its north wall, or else in the sanctuary of the main chancel.

In the chancel is a small brass to John Ballard and his wife. He is in civilian dress, and the wife in the ordinary costume of the period. The black letter inscription reads :—

' Hic jacent Iohēs Ballard qui obiit xxı° die marcii Anno dñi Millm̄o cccclxiij°, Et Margareta uxᵍ eiᵍ qᵒr aiᵍ abȝ ppicieꝛ deᵍ ameᵍ.'

On the high tomb in the recess in the eastern part of the north chapel, under a segmental moulded arch, is the following brass inscription in black letter :—

' Hic jacet Iohēs Elinebrygge armiger qui obiit viijᵒ die Februarii Aᵒ dñi Mᵒccccᵒ lxxıiij. Et Isabella uxor eius que fuit filia Nichi Jamys quondaᵍ Maioris et Aldermanᵍ Londonᵍ que Obiit viiᵒ die Septembris Aᵒ dñi Mᵒccccᵒ lxxiiᵒ et Anna uxōr eiᵍ que fuit filia Johēī Prophete Gentilman que obiit [blank] Aᵒ dni Mᵒccccᵒ [blank] quornᵍ animabus ppicietur Deus.'

There were three figures above, but that of the husband, who was in civil costume, although described as esquire, has long been lost. The two wives are precisely similar as to figure and costume, and have scrolls proceeding from their mouths, bearing the invocation, ' Sancta Trinitas—Unus Deus—Miserere Nobis.' Beneath is a group of seven daughters, rather quaintly drawn, with ' butterfly ' head-dresses, but the corresponding group of sons has disappeared. The front of the tomb beneath the slab is ornamented with four large quatrefoils, containing heater-shaped shields, standing on a moulded plinth.[85]

A grandson of John, Thomas Elingbridge, is commemorated by a brass effigy, together with that of his wife (originally in the north chapel, but now in the chancel), and the following inscription :—

' Hic jacent Thoffis Elinerugge Armiger alias dict.ᵍ Thoffis Elyngbrigge filius et heres Thome

[84] *Handbk. to Reigate*, 128–9.
[85] The Elingbridge family, who were settled at a place of the same name, a chapelry of Dodderhill, Worcs., as far

back as the 13th century, spelt their name in at least fifteen different ways during three hundred years. Their arms are Checky argent and sable, and they were

settled in Surrey during the 15th and 16th centuries, having lands in Merstham, Carshalton and Beddington ; in all of the three churches they have left memorials.

220

Elinerugge, et Johanna uxōr ei} qui quidem Thomas obit xxvii die marcii Aᵒ dñl мᵒ vᶜ vii quoruⁿ} aiⁿ} abus ppicietur deⁿ}. Amen.'⁸⁶

He is shown as in armour, but with head and hands uncovered, and without spurs, and his wife wears the ordinary dress of the period. Of the four shields of arms which originally lay at the corners of the slab, the lower one on the right only remains: it bears Checky argent and sable, impaling Lozengy and a chief with a saltire with the ends cut off charged with five roundels, which seem to be the arms of Overton.

In the chancel is the brass effigy to Sir John Newdegate, 1498. It is unusually small and the figure, which is badly proportioned, is in armour, the head resting on a helmet. The Newdegate arms are Gules three lions' paws razed or. The inscription, in black letter, runs :—' Hic Iacet Johēs Newdegate Armiger nup dñs de Herfeld in Cõm Midd qⁱ obiit xxiᵒ die mens} Februarii Aᵒ dñi мᶜccccᵉ ʟxxxxviii FAᵒ regni reḡ Henⁱ VII, xiiij, cuiⁿ} aīe ppiciet⁹ de.' The manor of Harefield, Middlesex, was acquired by the Newdegates in the 14th century. They took their name from the village of Newdigate in this part of Surrey, where also they held lands from an early date.

There is also a brass to Peter and Richard Best, two children of Nicholas Best of Alderstead, 1585–7. The figure of Peter, who is represented as a little child in a quaint long gown with a handkerchief tied to his girdle, still remains, but that of his brother was stolen about 1839. It represented a 'chrysom' child.⁸⁷ The inscription, in Roman capitals, runs :— ' Here lyeth the bodyes of Peter Best and Rychard Best his brother sonnes of Nycolas Best & Elizabeth his wyfe of Alderstead in yᵉ Parryshe of Merstham in the countie of Surrey wᶜʰ Peter deceased the xiiᵗʰ day of August Aᵒ Dñi 1585. And the said Rychard his brother deceased the xxiiᵗʰ of June Aᵒ Dñi 1587.'

There is a stone let into the east wall of the south chapel which is engraved with the arms and crests of Southcote and Waldegrave, and bears the initials s. м. s., denoting the purchase of the manor of Albury from Leonard Dannett in 1579 by John Southcote. The stone appears to have been shifted from the Albury Manor chapel to that of the manor of Alderstead. A piece of carving from old London Bridge is preserved in the church.

The bells, five in number, are inscribed : 1. Bryanvs Eldridge me fecit 1657; 2. ✠ Sancta

Katerina Ora Pro Nobis ; 3. Robertus + mot + me + fecit + 1597 O; 4. Pack & Chapman of London Fecit — Nichᵗ Feldwick & Jnᵒ Eastland Church Wardens 1774; 5. Bryan Eldridge made mee 1640. Nicholas Best Richard Sharp Chvrch Wardens.

No. 2 is a 14th-century bell, resembling others at Chelsham and Limpsfield.

Among the church plate is a silver cup of 1623 bearing the inscriptions :—' Deo sacrauit & gregi suo dedit 1623 ;' and ' Tho : Goad Srᵃᵉ Theolᵐ Dʳ Rector eccliæ pochialis de Mestham Comitat Surrey.' There is a paten of 1714 given by the Rev. Henry Mills, M.A., rector, in 1728. He was rector from 1724 to 1742, and was buried in the chancel. There is also a silver flagon of 1762, the gift of Jer. Milles, D.D., rector, 1763. Besides these there are many modern pieces.

The registers date from 1539, though not continuous at the beginning, and irregularly kept, especially under the Commonwealth. They are printed by the British Record Society.

The right of presentation to the *ADVOWSON* church of Merstham has always belonged and still belongs to the Archbishop of Canterbury.⁸⁸

The earliest mention of a church there occurs in Domesday. In 1255 dispensation to hold the living of Merstham at the same time as that of 'Gerolweston' was granted at the request of the archbishop to his physician, Master William de Twytham.⁸⁹ In 1294 the parson there was Robert de Segre,⁹⁰ who, having purchased land in Merstham from the prior and several other persons, took possession of it without the king's licence, after the passing of the Statute of Mortmain ; the same thing was done by his successor, Edward Dacre, who petitioned for pardon and obtained it at the price of 6s. 8d.⁹¹

Under Henry VIII the rectory-house with orchard, garden, and 9 acres of glebe-land was worth £2 14s. 4d. The tithes of grain amounted to £12 3s. 4d. Tithes of pigs and geese came to 6s. 8d. A yearly payment of 16d. was required by the Prior of Christchurch, and 6s. 8d. was due to the Archdeacon of Surrey for procurations, &c. With the rest of the tithes, oblations, &c., the living was worth in all £22 1s. 8d.⁹²

CHARITIES Smith's Charity is distributed as in other Surrey parishes.

---

⁸⁶ His will, dated the same day and year as those of his death given on the brass, contains the direction that he should be buried in the 'North Chauncell,' and there the brass remained probably till as late as 1840.

⁸⁷ Woodcuts of both children appear in Haines's *Manual of Monumental Brasses*, 219. An earlier chrysom child remains at Stoke D'Abernon, illustrated in *Surr. Arch. Coll.* xx, 46.

⁸⁸ *Cal. Pat.* 1330–4, pp. 477, 481 ; *Wykeham's Reg.* (Hants Rec. Soc.), i, 146 ; Inst Bks. P.R.O. 1723, &c.

⁸⁹ *Cal. of Papal Letters*, i, 325.
⁹⁰ *Cal. Pat.* 1292–1301, p. 122.
⁹¹ Ibid. 1345–8, p. 271 ; *Abbrev. Rot. Orig.* (Rec. Com.), ii, 190.
⁹² *Valor Eccl.* (Rec. Com.), ii, 43.

NUTFIELD

Notfelle (xi cent.) ; Notfeud, Nutfield and Notfeld (xiii cent.) ; Nutefeld and Nuttefeld (xiv cent.).

Nutfield is a village 3¼ miles east of Reigate. The parish is bounded on the north by Gatton and Merstham, on the east by Blechingley and Burstow, on the south by a detached portion of (formerly) Horne, on the west by Horley and Reigate. It measures 5 miles from north to south, 2 miles from east to west in the northern part, and less than 1 mile in the southern part. It contains 3,576 acres.

The parish of Nutfield extends from the Upper Green Sand at the foot of the chalk range, over the Gault, the outcrop of which is wider here than is usually the case in Surrey, the Lower Green Sand, and the Wealden Clay, which forms the soil of the lower half of the parish. On the ridge of the Lower Green Sand there is a considerable width of the sandy clay known as the Sandgate Beds. This is the soil in which fullers' earth is found. It is in Nutfield that this has been most extensively worked, but it occurs, more or less, wherever the Sandgate Beds can be traced, and can be followed from West Surrey to Maidstone ; its existence no doubt had a great deal to do with the formerly flourishing clothing trade of Surrey. The quality of the earth dug from the Nutfield pits, as well as the quantity, made them famous.[1] The industry was formerly of great importance, though not now so considerable ; fullers' earth is still in demand however, owing to its peculiar properties in absorbing oil and grease. Pits are still worked in Nutfield parish, and close to the parish in Reigate. The Fullers' Earth Union, and the Surrey Fullers' Earth Company, are the principal proprietors.[2]

The village and church of Nutfield lie upon the Green Sand hill on the road between Blechingley and Reigate, which follows the top of the ridge, and is probably an ancient way. There is scarcely any open ground in the parish. The South Eastern Railway, Redhill and Tunbridge branch, runs through the parish from east to west ; it was opened in 1842, but the station, at South Nutfield, some distance from Nutfield village, was only opened twenty years ago.

The hamlet called Ham, 2 miles south-west of Nutfield village, was an outlying part of Blechingley, added to Nutfield in 1894.[3]

The history of Nutfield, so far as it exists, is the history of the fullers' earth industry. But in 1755 nearly 900 Roman brass coins of the later empire were found in an earthen vessel crushed by a wheel in the road between Nutfield and Ham.[4] As roads were usually mended with stone from the nearest quarter, the vessel was

probably brought with the stone from the Upper Sand ridge.

No Inclosure Act or Award is known. When Manning and Bray wrote,[5] there was waste at Nutfield Marsh where certain tenants only had rights of common.

The ridge of the hill at Nutfield offers a pleasant situation for houses, of which there are several of a good character. Nutfield Court is the seat of Mr. J. T. Charlesworth ; Nutfield Priory, which stands in a park, of Mrs. Fielden ; Woolpits, where was an old house, of Mr. Frederick Scrutton ; Holmsdale House of Miss Sharwood. The Rev. E. Sandford, instituted in 1792, rebuilt the rectory ; it stands in a small park. At South Nutfield, nearer the railway, a large number of gentlemen's houses have been built of late years. There is a cemetery under Parish Council management.

The school (national) was built in 1863.

South Nutfield, or Lower Nutfield, is an ecclesiastical district in the middle part of the parish, near to and south of the railway. It was made an ecclesiastical district in 1888. The church (Christ Church) consecrated in 1888, is in 13th-century style, in red brick, consisting of nave, chancel, and north porch, with a shingled belfry and spire. The church stands near the old hamlet of Ridge Green.

An infant school (Church of England) was opened in 1889.

The southern part of the parish is in the ecclesiastical district of Outwood, formed in 1870 (see Burstow).

MANORS
NUTFIELD was held of the king by Ida of Lorraine, wife of Count Eustace II of Boulogne.[6] Nutfield was afterwards held of the Crown as of the honour of Boulogne,[7] when that honour came to the king by forfeiture.[8] In the time of King Edward Ulwi had held Nutfield for 13½ hides ; it was afterwards assessed for 3, but its value had increased from £13 to £15.[9] There were 10 serfs attached to the land, a somewhat large proportion.[10]

During the reign of Henry I the manor was granted by the king, at the petition of the Countess Ida, to the priory of St. Wulmar at Boulogne.[11] In 1195 Hubert de Anestie rendered account to the Exchequer of £16 for the farm of Nutfield, held of the abbot, and of £4 of that farm for the past year when the land was seized into the hands of the King of England because the abbot was of the land of the King of France.[12] Hubert de Anestie, still living in 1211–12, when he held the lordship of Nutfield,[13] left as heiress Denise, who married Warin de Monchensey.[14] In 1246–7 the Abbot of St. Wulmar

[1] Topley, Geol. of the Weald, 130–3.
[2] V.C.H. Surr. ii, 279–80.
[3] By Loc. Govt. Bd. Order 31855.
[4] Manning and Bray, Hist. of Surr. ii, 266, and local information.
[5] Hist. of Surr. ii, 266.
[6] V.C.H. Surr. i, 312b, and note 5.
[7] Vide infra ; Chan. Inq. p.m. Edw. II, file 34, no. 7.
[8] After the death of William son of King Stephen in 1159 the honour was in diminio Regis ; Pipe Roll 8 Hen. II, m. 1 d.

[9] See note 6.
[10] V.C.H. Surr. i, 314, n. 2.
[11] Cart. Antiq. A. 30.
[12] Pipe R. 7 Ric. I, m. 18 d.
[13] Red Bk. of Exch. (Rolls Ser.), 582.
[14] Ibid. 500 ; Cal. of Chart. 1226–57, p. 288 ; Abbrev. Plac. (Rec. Com.) 252. This Warin de Monchensey is stated, in the pedigrees, to have married Joan, sister of the Earl of Pembroke, by whom he had a daughter Joan. It is, however, quite evident from the documents above cited that he must have married, as his second

wife, Denise who was the mother of his son William. A pedigree of the Monchenseys in Lansd. MS. 860, fol. 166, confuses this Denise de Anestie, who married into the family, with the Denise who married Hugh de Vere and who was really granddaughter of the first Denise. Hubert de Anestie's wife was also called Denise (Add. Chart. 24606), but it was certainly his daughter, not his widow, who married Warin de Monchensey. See also note on Holilond, infra.

quitclaimed to Monchensey and his heirs the £16 rent in Nutfield and all right which the abbot or his successors might have in the manor.[15]

Denise survived her husband Warin de Monchensey and her son William and, in 1288, after the death of the latter, was granted the custody of her son's lands during the minority of Denise, daughter and heir of William.[16] In 1290 Joan, half-sister of William de Monchensey,[17] and William de Valence, Earl of Pembroke, her husband, protested against the right of the younger Denise to inherit her father's lands on the plea of illegitimacy, which was, however, disallowed.[18] In 1290 Denise was married to Hugh de Vere,[19] and in 1304 after the death of her grandmother, Denise de Monchensey, inherited the manor of Nutfield.[20] Denise the granddaughter died in 1314 and, her husband being already dead, the manor passed to her cousin Aymer de Valence, Earl of Pembroke, son of Joan Countess of Pembroke.[21] He died ten years later, but in the inquisition made on his lands at the time of his death there is no mention of Nutfield, though it is not evident when he parted with it. He held in 1316.[22] In 1325–6 it was held by John de Cobham,[23] to whom it had been demised by Sir Ralph de Cobham,[24] presumably his brother.

The latter seems to have been a younger brother of Stephen de Cobham of Rundale, but this is not certain.[25] He died before 1329, in which year, in a suit concerning the manor, John de Cobham, senior, stated that he held the manor for life, calling to warrant John, son and heir of Sir Ralph, then a minor.[26] At the same time Mary, widow of Sir Ralph and wife of Thomas Earl of Norfolk, Marshal of England, claimed to hold a third as dower.[27] In 1359, probably after the death of John de Cobham, senior, the manor was held by Sir John de Cobham, son and heir of Ralph and Mary, usually referred to as the son of the Countess Marshal.[28] He alienated the manor to Fulcon Horwode in that year.[29] This was apparently a grant for life only,[29] as Sir John de Cobham, who served in the French wars under the Black Prince, conveyed the reversion of his lands to the Crown

COBHAM. *Gules a cheveron or with three stars sable thereon.*

in 1359,[30] 'by reason,' as was stated in 1377, when the matter came before Parliament, 'of the great love and good affection he bore towards the prince, eldest son of the said King' (Edward III).[31] Sir John surrendered his lands by giving the king a gold ring for livery of seisin, a procedure which Parliament, in 1377, stated to be legal and valid without any document, especially when such a surrender was made to the king himself.[32] The manor of Nutfield was among those so conveyed,[33] but though the king had re-granted the manor to Cobham for life,[34] it was seized into the king's hands in 1363, as it was found that the alienation to Fulcon de Horwode in 1359 had been made without royal licence,[35] and early in 1364 the manor was granted by the Crown to Sir Nicholas Lovayne,[36] to whom Horwode quitclaimed all right in 1365.[37] In 1367 William Strete presented to the church as lord of Nutfield.[38] It is probable that Strete obtained the manor in consequence of a debt incurred by Lovayne. In 1372 and for several years afterwards the manor was in the hands of trustees, who had been enfeoffed by consent both of Lovayne and of Strete, apparently for the purpose of raising the sum of £550 due to Strete from Lovayne.[39] In 1375 Strete acknowledged the payment of £275,[40] but soon after, possibly in payment of the remainder of the debt, Strete seems to have obtained full possession of the manor, as he held it in 1377, though it was still in the hands of trustees.[41] An inquisition taken in that year on the death of Sir John de Cobham, recording the grant of his lands to the Crown, states that William Strete held the manor of Nutfield.[42] In 1380 trustees quitclaimed the manor of Nutfield to Sir Nicholas Carew and his son Nicholas ;[43] possibly this was also a mortgage. William Strete by his will, 1383, desired that his manor of Nutfield should be sold for £900, but that if the purchaser were Nicholas Carew the price should be £800.[44] Edmund Strete, kinsman and heir of William, quitclaimed all his right to the Carews in 1384.[45] Sir Nicholas the father died in 1390.[46] His son in 1432 settled the manor on himself and Mercy his wife and their issue ;[47] it seems, about this period, to have been frequently in the hands of trustees.[48] The manor passed to his son and grandson ; the latter died in 1466 and left a son, also called Nicholas,[49] who died soon after. The major part of his lands, including Beddington, then passed to his uncle, James Carew.[50]

The manor of Nutfield was, however, divided

[15] Feet of F. Surr. 31 Hen. III, no. 309.
[16] *Cal. Pat.* 1281–92, p. 292.
[17] See note 14 ; G.E.C. *Peerage*, &c.
[18] *Rolls of Parl.* i, 38*b.*
[19] *Cal. Pat.* 1280–92, p. 376.
[20] *Abbrev. Plac.* (Rec. Com.), 252 ; *Abbrev. Rot. Orig.* (Rec. Com.), i, 133.
[21] Chan. Inq. p.m. Edw. II, file 34, no. 7.
[22] Harl. MS. 6281.
[23] Close, 19 Edw. II, m. 4.
[24] De Banco R. 275, m. 39 d.
[25] Banks, *Dormant & Ext. Bar.* i, 270 ; Dugdale, *Bar.* ; G.E.C. *Peerage*, &c.
[26] De Banco R. 275, m. 39 d.
[27] Ibid. Most pedigrees (G.E.C., Dugdale, &c.), state that Ralph de Cobham probably lived till after 1338, when Thomas Earl of Norfolk died ; and that Cobham then married the latter's widow. It is clear, however, from the above that Cob-

ham died before 1329, and that Mary was his widow when she became the wife of Thomas, Earl of Norfolk.
[28] Add. Chart. 23615, 23619–20 ; G.E.C. *Peerage*, &c.
[29] Add. Chart. 23619–20.
[30] Chan. Inq. p.m. 1 Ric. II, no. 146*b.*
[31] *Rolls of Parl.* iii, 8*a.*
[32] Ibid.
[33] Add. Chart. 23621 ; Esch. Enr. Accts. Surr. & Suss. bdle. 5, no. 14 ; Chan. Inq. p.m. 1 Ric. II, no. 146*b.*
[34] See notes 30 and 32.
[35] *Abbrev. Rot. Orig.* (Rec. Com.), ii, 275 ; Esch. Enr. Accts. Surr. and Suss. bdle. 5, no. 14.
[36] *Cal. Rot. Pat.* (Rec. Com.), 176*b* ; Esch. Enr. Accts. Surr. and Suss. bdle. 5, no. 15.
[37] Close, 39 Edw. III, m. 26 and 25.
[38] Egerton MS. 2030, fol. 97 ; Winton Epis. Reg. Wykeham, i, fol. 6*b.*

[39] Add. Chart. 23622 ; Close, 45 Edw III, m. 11.
[40] Add. Chart. 23623.
[41] Chan. Inq. p.m. 1 Ric. II, no. 146*b* ; Add. Chart. 23624–8.
[42] Chan. Inq. p.m. 1 Ric. II, no. 146*b.*
[43] Add. Chart. 23267–8.
[44] *Coll. Topog. et Gen.* iii, 100.
[45] Add. Chart. 23629.
[46] Chan. Inq. p.m. 14 Ric. II, file 63, no. 10.
[47] Close, 10 Hen. VI, m. 4 ; Feet of F. Surr. 10 Hen. VI, no. 14.
[48] Ibid. ; Close, 6 Hen. V, m. 6, 13. Add. Chart. 23632, 23633, 23635. Nicholas Carew died in the year of settlement, 1432. (Monumental inscription at Beddington.)
[49] Chan. Inq. p.m. 6 Edw. IV, file 21, no. 40.
[50] *Cal. of Inq. Hen. VII,* i 362.

among his sisters and co-heirs,[61] Sancha wife of John Iwardby or Ewerby, Anne wife of Christopher Tropenell, and Elizabeth wife of Walter Twynyho.[62] In 1508-9 Nutfield was held by John Ewerby, Anne Tropenell and Walter Twynyho.[63] The Ewerbys seem to have conveyed their share of the manor in equal portions to the other co-heirs, as complete moieties were soon after held by the Tropenell and Twynyho families.[64]

The manor was not again united until 1619. The Tropenell moiety descended to Thomas, also called Giles, son of Christopher and Anne, and to his daughters and co-heirs, Ann wife of John Eyre, Elizabeth wife of William Charde, Mary wife of John Young, and Eleanor wife of Andrew Blackman, all of whom were holding a moiety jointly in 1557.[65] The Chardes seem to have relinquished their share soon afterwards. In 1570 John Young and Mary conveyed a third of a moiety to Thomas Bristow.[66] In 1576 Richard Mompesson and Susan daughter and heir of Andrew Blackman[67] conveyed a third of the moiety to William Gawton,[68] who in 1583 obtained the third which belonged to the Eyres.[69] Gawton died ten years later seised of two-thirds of a moiety ;[70] his son William[61] obtained Thomas Bristow's third in 1597,[62] and died seised of a complete moiety of the manor in 1610.[63] Richard Gawton, his son and heir,[64] conveyed this moiety in 1619 to Daniel Bassano and Thomas Turner.[65]

In the meantime the Twynyho moiety had passed from Walter Twynyho and Elizabeth to their son Edward, and to his son Anthony.[66] Anthony Twynyho died in 1529, and his sisters and co-heirs, Ann wife of Henry Heydon, and Katherine wife of John Dauntesay, each became seised of a moiety of a moiety.[67] That of the Heydons descended to Francis Heydon, their son and heir, while Bridget, daughter and heir of John and Katherine Dauntesay, married Hugh Hyde and inherited her mother's fourth share.[68] These parties held the moiety in 1564,[69] but Heydon probably quitclaimed his share soon after, as in 1566 Hugh Hyde and Bridget conveyed the entire moiety to Nicholas Best.[70] Apparently Nicholas at his death left the property to three sons in equal parts ; Christopher Best, who died in 1598, held a third of a moiety of Nutfield, which he left to Nicholas his son

and heir.[71] William Best was probably another son, and seems to have obtained both the share of his other brother and that of his nephew Nicholas, as he died in 1602 seised of a moiety of Nutfield,[72] and Henry, his son,[73] is referred to in 1603 and 1609 as holding an entire moiety.[74] In 1619 Henry Best and Etheldreda his wife conveyed this moiety to Daniel Bassano and Thomas Turner, who,[75] at the same time, obtained the Tropenell moiety as already shown. Bassano, barrister of the Inner Temple, was evidently a trustee as, in 1641, presumably after the death of Thomas Turner, he conveyed Nutfield to John Turner, eldest son of John Turner of Ham in Blechingley, to the second son, also called John, and to the third son Thomas.[76]

The eldest son died before 1651,[77] and John and Thomas Turner held Nutfield jointly in 1658.[78] Thomas the survivor, by will proved December 1671, devised the manor to John, George, and Thomas Turner, sons of his brother John, late of Ham.[79] The survivor John conveyed in 1707 to his son John in fee ; the latter died in 1713, his sister Charity, wife of Joseph Cooke, being his heir.[80] On the death of the latter in 1740 without issue the manor was divided between Cooke's sisters and co-heirs, Elizabeth Eboral and Mary Gotty.[81]

Elizabeth's son William died in 1775 and he by will devised to his niece Mary Eliza who held this moiety in 1808.[82] William Gotty and Mary conveyed their moiety to Sir George Colebrook, bart.,[83] in 1763.[83] Colebrook in 1774 conveyed half to Anthony Aynscomb and half to John Clement ; Aynscomb left his share to his wife, who died in 1800, with remainder to her sister Bett Tyler, afterwards wife of William Burtt, and she held this fourth part in 1808.[84] John Clement's fourth descended to his son and grandson, the last selling in 1805 to John Perkins.[85] The parts held by Mary Eliza and the Burtts afterwards passed either to John Perkins or John Newton, as these two held the manor in 1841.[86] Newton afterwards obtained Perkins' share, and Mr. John Newton was lord of Nutfield until after 1895, after which date it passed to Jervis Kenrick, who held in 1899. Mr. Henry Partridge of Castle Hill, Blechingley, was recently lord of the manor, but it is now held with that house by Mr. A. P. Brandt.

[61] By the *Visit.* of *Surr.* (Harl. Soc. Publ. xliii) 17, it would appear that Nicholas, James's brother, had no male issue and left three daughters only. An inquisition on James, however (*Cal. of Inq. Hen. VII*, i, 362), states that the latter obtained Beddington, &c., after the death of his *nephew* Nicholas, which makes it probable that those pedigrees giving Nicholas, James's brother, a son as well as three daughters are correct. See also Chan. Inq. p.m. (Ser. 2), xxxv, 52.

[62] Berry, *Surr. Gen.* 3 ; *Visit. of Gloucester* (Harl. Soc. xxi), 263 ; Lysons, *Environs of Lond.* i, 53 ; *The Tropenell Cart.* (Wilts. Arch. Soc.), Introd. and vol. ii.

[63] Chan. Inq. p.m. (Ser. 2), xci, 118.

[64] Chan. Proc. (Ser. 2), xc, 10 ; Feet of F. Div. Co. East. 3 & 4 Phil. and Mary, vide infra. John St. John, however, descendant of the Ewerbys, afterwards held a rent of 4 marks from the manor of Nutfield (Feet of F. Surr. Trin. 32 Eliz.) vide the church.

[65] *Tropenell Cart.* ii (Wilts. Arch. Soc.) ; Feet of F. Div. Co. East. 3 & 4 Phil. and Mary.

[66] Feet of F. Surr. Hil. 12 Eliz.

[67] *Visit.* of *Surr.* 1623 (ed. Geo. Marshall), 97.

[68] Feet of F. Surr. Trin. 18 Eliz.

[69] Ibid. Mich. 25 & 26 Eliz.

[60] Chan. Inq. p.m. (Ser. 2), ccxlvii, 21.

[61] Ibid.

[62] Feet of F. Surr. Mich. 39 & 40 Eliz.

[63] Chan. Inq. p.m. (Ser. 2), cccxiv, 144.

[64] Ibid.

[65] Feet of F. Surr. Trin. 17 Jas. I.

[66] *Visit. Gloucester* (Harl. Soc. xxi), 263 ; Chan. Proc. (Ser. 2), bdle. 40, no. 10 ; Close, 17 Chas. I, pt. xv, no. 16. Chan. Inq. p.m. (Ser. 2), i, 84.

[67] Ibid.

[68] Chan. Proc. (Ser. 2), bdle. 40, no. 10.

[69] Ibid.

[70] Feet of F. Surr. East. 8 Eliz. As late as 1639 a fine occurs (Feet of F. Surr. Mich. 14 Chas. I) in which Richard and Anthony Hyde, heirs of Hugh and Bridget (Berry, *Hants Gen.* 108) quitclaim their right in a moiety of Nutfield to William Best, who, according to Manning and Bray, was son to Henry Best. The latter's conveyance of 1619 must have

been in trust, and the original title had to be confirmed to make it absolute.

[71] Chan. Inq. p.m. (Ser. 2), cclv, 35.

[72] Ibid. ccvii, 7.

[73] Ibid.

[74] Ibid. cccxiv, 126 ; ccxc, 124. In a recovery in 1617 of a moiety of the manor between Henry Best and another, Nicholas Best was called to warranty, the deed being probably a surrender of all his claim in the manor preparatory to its sale by Henry (Recov. R. East 15 Jas. I, rot. 125).

[75] Feet of F. Surr. Trin. 17 Jas. I.

[76] Close, 17 Chas. I, pt. xv, no. 16.

[77] Cal. of Com. for Compounding, 2870.

[78] Surr. Arch. Coll. xvii, 188.

[79] P.C.C. 150 Duke.

[80] Manning and Bray, *Hist. of Surr.* ii, 271 ; Feet of F. Surr. Mich. 12 Anne.

[81] Manning and Bray, *Hist. of Surr.* ii, 271.

[82] Ibid.

[83] Feet of F. Surr. Trin. 3 Geo. III.

[84] See notes 81, 82.

[85] Ibid.

[86] Brayley, *Hist. of Surr.* iv, 331.

William Charde and Elizabeth his wife, descendants of Ann Tropenell, held a moiety of the site and capital messuage of Nutfield in 1557.[87] According to Manning and Bray, using Mr. Glover's deeds,[88] it passed to a daughter of William Best above named, Mary wife of Richard Jewell. He left a son John, whose son, also John, married Mary Tyler and died without issue. She married Anthony Ayascomb, see above. It is now the property of Mr. J. T. Charlesworth.

The family of Hadresham or Hedresham was settled in Nutfield at the end of the 12th century, their lands there being afterwards known as the manor or reputed manor of *HATHERSHAM*. In the reign of Richard I Hubert de Anestie granted a wood in Nutfield called Widihorn to John de Hadresham and his heirs,[89] and about the same time John also received a grant of a mill there, the names of Robert and Peter de Hadresham appearing among the witnesses to this deed.[90] In 1271–2 Peter de Caterham and Alice his wife quitclaimed 6 acres of land in Nutfield to Bartholomew de Hadresham,[91] and in 1316 John, son of James de Hadresham, received a grant of a meadow there called Merchauntesmead.[92] In 1358 John de Hadresham died seised of a tenement in Nutfield, held of the chief manor, consisting of a capital messuage, 60 acres of land of which 20 could be cultivated, 4 acres of meadow, 20 of pasture, and 10 of wood. The tenement was said to be worth 23s. per annum.[93] The same amount was paid in the 17th century as the annual rent of the manor of Hathersham.[94] John left a son and heir, William de Hadresham.[95] The lands afterwards passed to the Asshurst family. William Asshurst held land in Nutfield in the early 15th century,[96] and in 1507 John Asshurst, son of William, died seised, among other lands, of the 'manor of Hadresham'; he left no issue.[97] Agnes, widow of John Asshurst, afterwards married John Skinner,[98] and seems to have brought this land to his family. Sir Thomas Wyatt the poet held the manor in 1538,[99] but he was possibly a trustee, his father, Sir Henry Wyatt, having acted as such for John Skinner and Agnes in the conveyance of property which they held in East Betchworth.[100] In 1556 the manor of Hathersham was held by James Skinner and Margaret his wife,[101] and on James's death without issue in 1558 passed to the family of his brother.[102] John Skinner, nephew of James according to the inquisition taken at his death, died seised of the manor in 1584.[103] Richard Elyot of Albury was a nephew and heir.[104]

In 1603 Richard and Thomas Elyot conveyed the manor of Hathersham to Henry Drake and Charles Evans,[105] Sir Thomas Palmer and Alice his wife, widow of John Skinner, surrendering their claim.[106] Drake and Evans seem to have divided the manor, as in 1609 Drake died seised of a moiety,[107] which his son Edward conveyed to Richard Killick in 1614,[108] and in 1616 it passed from Killick to Henry Shove.[109] Shove apparently acquired the other moiety also, as his family afterwards held the entire manor, of which they retained possession until the latter part of the 18th century.[110] It was held in 1768 by Henry Shove and Ann his wife.[111] According to Manning, Shove died in 1771, when, by the terms of his will, Hathersham was sold, becoming the property of Robert Smith.[112] In 1790–1 Robert Smith the son and Elizabeth his wife sold to Sir Sampson Wright,[113] whose widow, Lady Wright, held the property in 1808.[114] It passed after her death to Mr. S. Simms.[115] It is now held as a farm.

In 1350 Thomas de Wolbergh died seised of a tenement in Nutfield which he held of the lord of Nutfield for the service of 33s. 9d.[116] His son, John de Wolbergh, was witness to a deed in 1359.[117] In 1364 Cecily de Beauchamp held five acres of meadow in Nutfield of John de Wolbergh.[118] In 1463 William Sydney died seised of the manor of *WOLBERGH* leaving two daughters and co-heirs, Elizabeth afterwards wife of John Hampden, and Anne, afterwards wife of William Uvedale.[119] The Uvedale moiety remained in this family until after 1528.[120]

In 1572 the whole manor was held by William Jeale.[121] In 1602 William and Ovington Jeale, probably sons of the first William, conveyed to George Evelyn,[122] who settled Wolbergh shortly after on his daughter Katherine on her marriage with Thomas Stoughton.[123] Stoughton, who survived his wife, died in 1611 seised of the 'manor or manor of Woolboro,' George Stoughton, his brother, being his heir.[124] The latter conveyed the manor in 1623 to John Turner,[125] from whom it passed to Thomas Turner of Nutfield. The latter by will of 1671 left 'the messuage, &c., containing 160 acres in Nutfield in occupation of Anne Barnes called Woolborough,' to his nephew Thomas Turner.[126] The latter, according to Manning, conveyed in 1685 to William Barnes, whose son conveyed to William Lukyn in 1722.[127]

From Thomas and Robert Lukyn the property passed, in 1740, to Helen Shelley,[128] daughter of Robert Bysshe, wife of John Shelley, and grandmother of Sir Bysshe Shelley, who died in 1815.[129] He was

[87] Feet of F. Surr. East. 3 & 4 Phil. and Mary.
[88] Manning and Bray, *Hist. of Surr.* ii, 272.
[89] Add. Chart. 24606.
[90] Ibid. 24606.
[91] Feet of F. Surr. Mich. 56 Hen. III.
[92] Add. Chart. 24608.
[93] Chan. Inq. p.m. 32 Edw. III (1st nos.), no. 40.
[94] Ibid. (Ser. 2), cccxiv, 126.
[95] Ibid. 32 Edw. III (1st nos.), no. 40.
[96] Feet of F. Surr. 7 Hen. V, no. 34.
[97] Chan. Inq. p.m. (Ser. 2), xx, 24.
[98] Feet of F. Surr. Trin. 3 Hen. VIII; East. 4 Hen. VIII.
[99] Ibid. Trin. 30 Hen. VIII.
[100] See note 98.
[101] Chan. Inq. p.m. (Ser. 2), cciv, 123.
[102] Ibid.
[103] Ibid. He was really a great-nephew

(Berry, *Surr. Gen.* 25; *Visit. of Surr.* [Harl. Soc. xciii] 59).
[104] Ibid.
[105] Feet of F. Surr. Trin. 1 Jas. I.
[106] Chan. Inq. p.m. (Ser. 2), cccxiv, 126; Manning and Bray, *Hist. of Surr.* ii, 273.
[107] Chan. Inq. p.m. (Ser. 2), cccxiv, 126.
[108] Ibid.; Feet of F. Surr. Trin. 12 Jas. I.
[109] Ibid. Hil. 13 Jas. I.
[110] Manning and Bray, *Hist. of Surr.* ii, 273; P.C.C. Henchman 64; Feet of F. Surr. East. 2 Geo. III.
[111] Ibid. Mich. 8 Geo. III.
[112] Manning and Bray, *Hist. of Surr.* ii, 273.
[113] Feet of F. Surr. Mich. 31 Geo. III.
[114] See note 112.
[115] Brayley, *Hist. of Surr.* iv, 332.
[116] Chan. Inq. p.m. 24 Edw. III (1st

nos.), no. 91; *Cal. of Close,* 1249–54, p. 182.
[117] Add. Chart. 231619–20.
[118] Chan. Inq. p.m. 38 Edw. III (1st nos.), no. 8.
[119] Esch. Inq. (Ser. 1), file 1805, 3 Edw. IV; Chan. Inq. p.m. 17 Edw. IV, no. 38.
[120] Ibid. (Ser. 2), l, 120.
[121] Feet of F. Surr. Trin. 14 Eliz.
[122] Ibid. Hil. 44 Eliz.
[123] Chan. Inq. p.m. (Ser. 2), ccxc, 124; Feet of F. Surr. East. 3 Jas. I.
[124] Chan. Inq. p.m. (Ser. 2), cccxxiv, 159; cccxcvii, 17.
[125] Feet of F. Surr. Mich. 21 Jas. I.
[126] P.C.C. 150 Duke.
[127] Manning and Bray, *Hist. of Surr.* ii, 273.
[128] Feet of F. Surr. Mich. 15 Geo. II.
[129] See note 127 (private deed); *The Shelley Pedigree* (privately printed 1816).

succeeded by Sir Timothy Shelley, whose eldest son, Percy Bysshe Shelley, the poet, was drowned in 1822. Sir Timothy, at his death in 1844, was therefore succeeded by his grandson, Sir Percy Florence Shelley.[130]

HOLILOND.—The family of atte Holilond was settled in Nutfield in the early 13th century. In an inquiry concerning their lands, made in the reign of Edward III, it was stated that during the reign of King John Denise de Monchensey[131] had alienated to Reginald de Holilond a messuage, 42 acres of land, 8 acres of meadow, 10 of pasture and 1 of wood in Nutfield, parcel of the manor of Nutfield, to hold to him and his heirs at the rent of the true value.[132] This alienation was made in 1202–3, the charter being enrolled 'in a certain missal' of Battle Abbey, the abbot of which, Richard atte Holilond, was brother to Reginald.[133] The property was afterwards held by Robert son of Reginald, and John son of Robert.[134] John atte Holilond in 1349 obtained a pardon from the Crown for having entered into the said premises without licence from the king; both his father and grandfather had been similarly in fault.[135] The name of Thomas atte Holilond appears as witness to a deed in 1359,[136] and in 1400 John atte Holilond held land in Nutfield.[137]

The subsequent ownership of these lands is not apparent, but they clearly had given their name to the family which held them so long, and the present Holland House, or Hall Land House, in Nutfield is the survival of the name.

The church of ST. PETER and ST. PAUL stands on a site with a steep northerly slope, close to the road, in a very pretty and well-planted churchyard, and some way below the crest of the ridge on which the village is built. It consists of a chancel 36 ft. 4 in. long by 17 ft 4 in. wide, north vestry and organ chamber, nave 40 ft. 2 in. by 22 ft. 3 in., north aisle 12 ft. 9 in. wide, south transept 10 ft. 3 in. deep by 14 ft. 11 in wide, south aisle 15 ft. 5 in. wide, south porch and a west tower 14 ft. 1 in. by 13 ft. wide. All these dimensions are taken within the walls.

The plan of the nave doubtless dates from the 12th century, but the oldest architectural details are to be found in the chancel, which inclines southward from the axis of the nave, and seems to have replaced the 12th-century chancel early in the 13th century. It was about 26 ft. long originally, but was lengthened 10 ft. early in the 14th century.

A north aisle was added to the nave about 1230; the arcade still remains, but the aisle walls have been removed at a widening of the aisle in the 15th century. The chancel arch was widened to its utmost limits early in the 14th century. A south transept was added in the 15th century, about 1450, and the west tower is the work of the latter half of the same century. The south aisle was built in 1882, and the north vestry and organ chamber are also modern. The tower has been repaired at different times, the upper part being much rebuilt late in the 18th century; in recent years a great deal of restoration work

has been undertaken, with the result that nearly all the window tracery has been renewed.

The east window of the chancel has three cinquefoiled lights with tracery under a pointed head of 15th-century style, but all of modern stonework. The north-east window is of two trefoiled lights with a quatrefoil in the head under a two-centred arch, but only the inner jambs and hollow-chamfered rear arch are old. just west of the window is a straight joint in the wall, which has been stripped of its plaster, marking the line of the east wall of the 13th-century chancel. In the 13th-century walling is one complete lancet, tall and narrow, with a plain chamfer on the outer face, now looking into the vestry, and close to it on the west the head of a second lancet of different detail, with an external rebate, and perhaps of earlier date. It is evident that the complete lancet was the eastern one of a pair, the springing of the rear arch of the second window being yet visible, but the window head just noticed is too near it to allow for a splay of equal angle, which would be natural in a pair of contemporary windows, and has either been moved eastward at the insertion of the modern arch to the organ chamber, or belongs to an older arrangement. As at present set, it is accurately half-way between the chancel arch and the east wall of the 13th-century chancel, a fact which suggests that it is in position, and that the complete lancet is a slightly later addition. This is also possible from the way in which the sill of the complete lancet breaks into the head of a recess in the sill below, which though now much altered was originally a locker with two arched openings, the eastern of which is now represented by its sill only, while the western has lost its inner order and is masked by a modern memorial brass hinged to serve as a door to it. Two cinquefoiled arches, one large and one small, open into the modern vestry and organ chamber.

Only the lower part of the 13th-century south wall of the chancel remains, the upper part having been rebuilt when the chancel was lengthened, with three windows, two of a single trefoiled light and one at the south-east of two cinquefoiled lights. Only the east jamb of the western of the two trefoiled lights is left, the window having given place to a two-light 15th-century window, but both the other windows preserve their old jambs and rear arches, the external masonry being modern. Below the south-east window is a 15th-century piscina with a shallow half-round basin in the sill and a shelf. Below the middle window is a 14th-century tomb recess with jambs of two chamfered orders, broach stopped, with a two-centred arch, dying on the chamfer of the jambs; in the recess is a contemporary slab with a floriated cross in low relief, and on its hollowed edge a partly destroyed inscription:—

'SIZE THOM[AS DE R]OLEHAM GIST ICI DEU DE SA ALME EYT MERCI.'[138]

The chancel arch is a 14th-century insertion, having half-octagonal jambs with broach stops at the base, and moulded bell capitals with scroll-moulded abaci;

[130] Brayley, Hist. of Surr. iv, 332.

[131] It seems quite impossible that this can be the Denise, Anestie's daughter who died in 1304. It can scarcely have been her mother, Denise, wife of Hubert de Anestie. It is very difficult to account for, as it seems to connect the Monchen-

seys with Nutfield before the marriage of Denise with Warin de Monchensey. Perhaps the inquisition is wrong in its dates, but Richard was abbot 1215–35.

[132] Cal. Pat. 1348–50, p. 288; Inq. a.q.d. file 288, no. 3.

[133] Chan. Inq. p.m. 2 Edw. III (2nd nos.), no. 4.

[134] Ibid.; Feet of F. Surr. Trin. 24 Edw. I.

[135] Cal. Pat. 1348–50, p. 288; Abbrev. Rot. Orig. (Rec. Com). ii, 204.

[136] Add. Chart. 23615.

[137] Feet of F. Surr. 2 Hen. IV, no. 11.

[138] The complete inscription is given in Manning and Bray, op. cit.

NUTFIELD CHURCH FROM THE SOUTH-EAST

the arch is double-chamfered on both sides and has no label.

The 13th-century north arcade of the nave is of three bays with circular pillars, water-moulded bases, and bell capitals ; there is no east respond, the arch dying on the east wall face, but on the north face of the return in the aisle is a short length of chamfered abacus which looks to be of earlier date than the arcade, and may have belonged to an arch opening to a former north transept. The west respond is half-round with a capital like those of the pillars, but the base is buried beneath the floor. The arches are two-centred and of two chamfered orders.

The south arcade is of three bays, and is all modern except the east arch and respond, which has chamfered edges and a moulded capital of 15th-century detail. The pillars are circular with moulded capitals and bases ; the eastern pillar having an attached shaft on its south side to receive the modern arch between the transept and aisle.

All the windows of the north aisle have been modernized outside ; the first and third on the north are of two lights, and the middle one of three lights, all with traceried pointed heads of 15th-century style ; the inner jambs are old, as are also the rear arches, which are hollow-chamfered, and the west window has two lights of 14th-century character with old inner jambs and arch. A modern arch-way opens from the aisle into the organ chamber.

The south transept has a 15th-century east window of two cinque-foiled ogee-headed lights with old tracery in a pointed head ; the jambs are of two hollow cham-fers, and the window has a moulded label outside. The south window of the transept has two lights under a geometrical traceried head ; the inner jambs are old, but the outer stonework is all modern. Under the window are two recesses each 6 ft. 3 in. long with four-centred arches, doubtless sepulchral, but now empty; the chamfered jambs have broach stops at the base. On the outer face of the gable of the transept is a sundial dated 1758.

The south doorway is of the 15th century, moved out with the wall, and has moulded jambs and a two-centred arch. The two south windows of the aisle are square-headed, the first of three lights and the second of two ; the west window is of three lights under a traceried pointed head ; all three windows are modern.

The west tower is of three stories, but rises without a break. It is strengthened by diagonal buttresses at the western angles and has a stair-turret at its north-east corner. The arch opening into it from the nave has chamfered jambs and a two-centred arch of two hollow chamfers with a wide hollow between, and

the west doorway is of two hollow-chamfered orders and has a four-centred head with a modern window of three lights over it. The second story is lighted on the north, south, and west by single trefoiled lights, and the third story by two-light windows with cinquefoiled four-centred heads. The diagonal but-tresses are faced with stone slabs bearing inscriptions, now partly hidden by the cement coating, referring to some late 16th or 17th-century repairs,[139] and the tower is tied by iron rods, on the straps of which is the date 1740. Later repairs are shown by a small stone panel on the south side below the bell-chamber window bearing the date 1786, and this date also occurs on several rain-water heads. Over the tower is a shingled wood spire changing from square to octagon above the parapet, and crowned by a weather vane with the date 1767. The tower is coated with cement, which has fallen away here and there, showing that the parapet and upper parts of the buttresses have been repaired with brickwork. The north wall of the aisle, in addition to its east diagonal buttress and the two at the western angle, has been strengthened

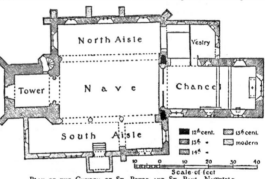

PLAN OF THE CHURCH OF ST. PETER AND ST. PAUL, NUTFIELD

by raking buttresses of brick between the windows. The south porch is a modern one of wood. Owing to the slope of the ground there are several steps down from the south doorway to the floor level of the aisle.

The roof of the chancel is covered with Horsham stone slabs and has a modern wood-panelled ceiling ; a moulded tie-beam across the middle appears to be old. The nave roof, also covered with Horsham slabs, is open timbered, a plaster ceiling having been removed ; two of its tie-beams are old. The north aisle has a gabled roof with collar-beam trusses, formerly plastered ; the timbers are old and plain, and the south aisle roof is modern. Both aisle roofs are tiled.

There is a good deal of interesting woodwork in the church.

In the chancel is a seat made up with two old bench-ends with carved poppy-heads, probably of early 16th-century date, and the 15th-century rood-screen still stands across the chancel arch. Its door-way has a two-centred pointed head with traceried

139 Cracklow gives the date as 1594, on the north-west buttresses.

spandrels, and the arch springs from carved bunches of foliage on the doorposts, on the inner faces of which are three sunk quatrefoils, an unusual detail. The side bays are each divided into two trefoiled openings, with a quatrefoil over in the traceried pointed head of the bay; the middle rail is moulded, and the plain boarding below it is modern in the south half of the screen. The muntins are all moulded : on the face of the northernmost is a short length of half-octagonal shaft with a moulded capital, from which sprang a vaulted cove below the loft; on the moulded cornice stands a line of brattishing, but the rest of the loft has, as usual, been removed. The space above the screen was evidently once boarded, as in the soffit of the chancel arch is a row of square holes (now filled in) in which the uprights were fixed.

The font is dated 1665, but the octagonal panelled bowl is clearly some two centuries earlier, and the date doubtless records its return to the church after having been thrown out by Puritan fanatics in the time of the Commonwealth.

The hexagonal pulpit contains a number of early 16th-century linen-pattern panels in two tiers, one pair of panels being modern; the framing of the pulpit appears to be modern also.

The middle window of the north aisle contains a few fragments of 15th-century glass in the two piercings over its middle light.

On the south wall of the chancel is a brass plate inscribed : ' Orate p' aiabz Willi¯ Graffton qndȝ Clici hui' ecclesiae et Johē ux eius et Johis filii eordm qor aiabz ppiciet deus amȝ.' Above it is the figure of a man in a long cloak girt at the waist and with fur trimming; his hands are clasped in prayer; also a woman in long high-waisted gown and a loose head-dress hanging down behind her. Over the man is a shield charged with a cheveron, and over the woman one charged with a cheveron impaling a saltire. On the south wall of the south aisle is a small 17th-century brass with a Latin inscription to Edmund Molyneux.

On the north wall of the chancel is a chalk panelled tablet to Charles Gillman, son of Anthony Gillman of Reigate. The date of his death was left blank, and has been roughly scratched in at a later date— ' 13th April 1631.' The inscription finishes : ' as by yᵉ monumᵗ of yᵉ said Anthony in Reigat apears ' ; the shield over is charged with a leg cut off at the thigh, booted and spurred.

There are six bells; the treble by Mears and Stainbank, 1897; the second by William Eldridge, 1663; the third, Thomas Mears, 1793; the fourth, C. and G. Mears, 1848; the fifth and the tenor, Wm. Eldridge, 1662.

The oldest piece of the communion plate is a cup with a trumpet stem with the hall-mark of 1665; it has a cover dated 1666; there is also a chalice and paten of 1849. In the vestry are kept two wooden collecting boxes with handles, of the usual 17th-century type; both have painted inscriptions,

' Pray remember the poore,' with the name of the parish.

The registers date from 1558.

ADVOWSON The Domesday Survey mentions the existence of a church at Nutfield,[140] but no other early record of it is found. It was valued at £8 12s. in the Taxatio of 1291.[141] It is not mentioned in the gift of the manor to the priory of St. Wulmar of Boulogne, nor in the surrender of the manor by the abbot to Warin de Monchensey, but there is nevertheless some reason for supposing that the advowson became the property of the priory and was retained after the surrender of the manor. John de Warenne, Earl of Surrey, presented to the church in 1328,[142] and it is possible that he had received a grant of the advowson when the possessions of alien priories had been seized by the Crown some years before; another advowson which he held in 1328 had come into his possession in that manner.[143] In 1337, at the beginning of the Hundred Years' War, the Sheriff of Surrey was ordered to restore church, goods and chattels to Giles de Fossato, parson of Nutfield Church, whose possessions had been seized because he was 'a native of the power of the king of France.'[144] As a reason for this concession it was stated that the king had considered the poverty of Giles and wished to have compassion on him.[145]

It is not evident how the advowson passed to the lord of the manor, but it had become his property by 1363,[146] and was held by successive lords until the death, in 1466, of Nicholas Carew.[147] His son, who died shortly after, left, as has been shown, sisters and co-heirs who married into the families of Ewerby, Tropenell, and Twynyho, and each sister retained a third of the advowson.[148] The portions belonging to the two latter families descended with their respective shares of the manor (q.v.).[149] Of the latter property each of the two families afterwards held a complete moiety, which probably accounts for the fact that their shares of the advowson were constantly referred to as moieties also, though in reality they were thirds only. In 1580 William Best presented on a grant from William Charde and Elizabeth, one of the Tropenell heiresses.[150] These two thirds were finally conveyed to the Turner family in 1619.[151] The third held by the Ewerbys passed to the family of St. John by the marriage of Joanna the daughter and heir of Sir John Ewerby with John St. John.[152] The son of John and Joanna, also called John,[153] presented to the church in 1550,[154] and in 1590 conveyed one moiety of his third to Henry Burton and the other to Walter Cole.[155] In 1620 Walter Cole and William his son and heir sold their share to Sir Thomas Penruddock, Sir George Stoughton, and George Duncombe, trustees of Ann, Dowager Countess of Arundel.[156] In 1626 presentation was made by Sir Julius Caesar by virtue of a grant made him by Burton and Cole,[157] presumably before the latter gave up his right in the advowson. The king presented by

140 *V.C.H. Surr.* i, 312b.
141 *Pope Nich. Tax* (Rec. Com.), 208b.
142 Egerton MS. 2032, fol. 67 (Winton Epis. Reg. Index); Manning and Bray, *Hist. of Surr.* ii, 274.
143 *Cal. Pat.* 1327–30, p. 315.
144 *Cal. Close,* 1337–9, p. 160.
145 Ibid.
146 Add. Chart. 23621.

147 *Vide* manor of Nutfield; Egerton MSS. 2033, 2034.
148 *Vide infra.*
149 Feet of Div. Co. 35 Hen. VIII; Chan. Proc. (Ser. 2), xc, 10; East 3 & 4 Phil. and Mary; Mich. 6 & 7 Eliz.
150 Add. MS. 6167, fol. 317.
151 Feet of F. Surr. Trin. 17 Jas. I, 2.
152 Berry, *Hants Gen.* 230.

153 Ibid.
154 Egerton MS. 2034, fol. 169; Manning and Bray, *Hist. of Surr.* ii, 274.
155 Feet of F. Surr. Trin. 32 Eliz.
156 Close, 18 Jas. I, pt. iii, no. 37; Feet of F. Surr. Trin. 18 Jas. I; G.E.C. *Peerage*; Manning and Bray, *Hist. of Surr.* ii, 509.
157 Add. MS. 6167, fol. 317.

NUTFIELD CHURCH: NAVE LOOKING EAST

lapse in 1634 because Christopher Best had not sued out livery of the advowson.[158] Henry Lord Mowbray, grandson of Ann, Dowager Countess of Arundel,[159] presented in 1640,[160] and this family seems to have acquired Burton's share also, as in 1658 the Earl of Arundel held a full third turn of presentation, the other two-thirds of the advowson being held, as has been said, by John and Thomas Turner.[161] In 1660 the Crown presented.[162] According to Manning, Henry Lord Maltravers, Earl of Norwich, and Henry Howard his son granted the next turn to West and Keck in trust for Burbury in 1676,[163] and in 1677 John and Thomas Turner granted their turn to Henry Hesketh, who afterwards purchased Burbury's interest and sold to William Hollingsworth.[164] The latter presented in 1711 and again in 1731.[165] Lord Mowbray[166] finally conveyed his share to William Beckford in

trust for Sir Lionel Jenkins who, by will, devised it to Jesus College, Oxford. The Turners' share descended with the manor (q.v.), and after the death of William Hollingsworth presentation was made both by Joseph Cooke, as lord of the manor, and by Jesus College. The case was brought before a commission of six clergy and six laymen, but as these decided equally in favour of the college and lord of the manor, nothing was settled.[167] Finally, however, a decision in Cooke's favour seems to have been made, as his incumbent continued to hold the living.[168] The college afterwards treated with him for purchase, but the transaction was not completed until after his death, his sisters conveying to the college shortly after 1740.[169] Jesus College has since held the advowson.[170]

CHARITIES Smith's Charity is distributed as in other Surrey parishes.

REIGATE

Cherchefelle or Crechesfeld (xi–xii cent.) ; Reygate (xiii cent.) ; Reigate or Riegate (xvii–xviii cent.).

Reigate is a municipal borough, formerly a parliamentary borough, 6 miles east from Dorking, and 23 miles south by road from London. The parish is bounded by Kingswood in Ewell and Gatton on the north, by Nutfield on the east, by Horley, Buckland (detached), and Leigh on the south, by Betchworth and Buckland on the west. It measures 4 miles east and west, by 3 miles north and south, and contains 5,871 acres of land and 34 of water. The parish extends from the crest of the chalk, over the Upper Green Sand, the Gault, Lower Green Sand and Atherfield Clay, on to the Wealden Clay. The top of the down where the suspension bridge crosses the old London road is 700 ft. above the sea, and the highest point of Reigate Hill is 762 ft. ; the level in the town of Reigate, which lies on the Lower Green Sand, is 270 ft. South of the town is a ridge of sand, the western end of which, Park Hill, is 411 ft., the eastern, Redhill Common, 478 ft. above the sea. The land then falls to under 200 ft. in the southern part of the parish. The depression in the chalk and sand to the east of the parish is taken advantage of by the railway and the new London road. Four hundred and eighty acres of common exist still on Reigate Heath to the west, Wray Common to the north-east, Redhill Common to the east, Earlswood and Petridge Wood Common, the latter on the borders of Horley, to the south-east. The last two were woodland in the Weald, but the trees were cut down in the 17th century by Lord Monson.

Redhill and Earlswood Commons were in part inclosed by an Award of 15 July 1886, as part of the scheme for making them a public park. Numerous ancient encroachments on the waste are represented by houses, cottages, and gardens about Earlswood Common, Wray Common, and Reigate Heath.

The industry of Reigate was formerly that of a country market town ; oatmeal is said to have been made in large quantities, and the fine sand of the soil was and is in demand for building, gardening, and glass-making. But in general industries have now rather gravitated towards Redhill, the new town in the eastern part of the parish (q.v.), where are breweries, tanneries, timber yards, printing works, fullers' earth works, and the necessary adjuncts of a large railway station.

The old town of Reigate consisted of one main street, the High Street, running east and west, south of the eminence on which the castle stood, and north of the opposite ridge on the lower part of which was the priory. Bell Lane ran from the south to the eastern corner of High Street, the newer Town Hall stands at the intersection of the two. Nutley Lane ran north from the western end of High Street, up the hill, to join the old main road east and west on the chalk downs, which only in modern times has been called the Pilgrims' Way. The name Reigate is not in Domesday ; it is there evidently represented by the place called Cherchefelle. The town is manifestly the creation of the lords of the castle, consisting of a row of houses clustering for protection under the walls of the fortress and faced by a religious house, and may be compared with Lewes, which lies between a castle and a religious foundation of the same lords, the Earls of Warenne and Surrey. The church of the original Cherchefelle stood south-eastward of the castle, on a sandy knoll not unlike that on which the castle stands, but lower. The habitations clustered under the castle, not near the church. The High Street retains its name and position ; eastward it is continued as Church Street, westward as West Street. These were east and west lines of communication. Bell Lane, High Street, and Nutley Lane, now the London road, were north and south lines, equally dominated by

---

[158] Winton Epis. Reg. Neile, fol. 9a. As Christopher Bert died in 1598 this was rather a flagrant case of raking up of old claims by the Crown, characteristic of the period of personal government, when the rule 'nullum tempus regi obstat' was pushed to an extreme.
[159] G.E.C. Peerage.

[160] See note 157.
[161] Surr. Arch. Coll. xvii, 98.
[162] Inst. Bks. (P.R.O.).
[163] Manning and Bray, Hist. of Surr. ii, 275.   [164] Ibid.
[165] Inst. Bks. (P.R.O.). The Visitation of 1725 says the Hollingsworths had the advowson for two lives only.

[166] Henry Howard was created Lord Mowbray in 1679.
[167] Manning and Bray, Hist. of Surr. ii, 274 (quoting from Mr. Cooke's papers in private hands).
[168] Ibid.
[169] Ibid.
[170] Inst. Bks. (P.R O.).

the castle. Manning and Bray, apparently quoting MSS. in the hands of Mr. Glover, the antiquarian solicitor of Reigate, and Aubrey say that there were three chapels in Reigate town.[1] The chapel of St. Thomas of Canterbury stood where the Town Hall stands in the middle of High Street, at the east end.[2]

At the western end of the High Street stands the Red Cross Inn, an ancient building much modernized, which was probably the hospice of the Canterbury pilgrims. In Slipshoe Street, West Street, and Bell Street are other old houses, half timber, tile-hung or brick fronted, the tile-hanging taking the form of diamond scales. There are several picturesque old inns with Georgian fronts, such as 'The Crown,' 'The Swan,' and 'The Grapes.'

A deed of 1588 referred to the old Market Place at the west end of High Street. The new one was therefore in existence then, but the present ugly brick building was put up in 1708.[3] At the place where the old Market House stood, between West Street and Slipshoe Lane, are parts of a very old clunch wall, and within their line is a pit, once a saw-pit, now a motor pit, in the side of which appears early stone vaulting, the remains of an old crypt or cellar. The chapel of the Holy Cross was said to be represented by two old houses at the end of High Street, looking down it eastward, which were recently demolished to improve the entrance into West Street. St. Lawrenee's Chapel is said to have been in Bell Lane. Here, next the 'White Hart,' in a chemist's shop occupied by Mr. Fisher, are the remains of the stone corbels and tie-beams of a wide spanned roof, and the party walls of the house are very thick and ancient.[4] Opposite the present entrance to the castle is Cage Yard, where till recently a two-storied house of detention for accused persons was standing. Access to the town from the north, and now from the railway station, was materially improved in 1823 by driving a tunnel under the eastern part of the castle hill, whereby traffic came directly into High Street opposite Bell Lane, or Bell Street as it is now called, instead of circling round the castle. The northern approach to the tunnel, however, destroyed part of the eastern outworks of the castle. As in the case of other Surrey towns a large number of gentlemen's houses have sprung up of late in the outskirts of Reigate, and the streets have been in several places widened by the pulling down of old-fashioned houses. Slipshoe Lane, however, still retains some ancient cottages.

The town is spreading along the valley and northwards, and there are many good modern houses, as well as several new churches and chapels.

Among the larger houses, Minster Lea is the seat of Lady Jennings; The Wilderness of Mr. J. W. Freshfield; Northcote of Mr. F. C. Pawle, J.P.; Shermanbury of Sir John Watney; Normanton of Mr. F. E. Barnes, J.P.; Woodhatch House of Mr. R. P. Evans, J.P.; Colley of Mr. W. H. Nash, J.P. Near Redhill, High Trees is the residence of Mr. M. Marcus; Redstone Manor of Miss Webb; Shenley of Major Foster, J.P.; The Mount of Mr. E. C. P. Hall, J.P.; Lorne House of Captain Brodie.

Reigate might have been served by the Brighton line, when it was first projected, but opposed its too near approach to the town. It remained 2 miles from the railway at Redhill, till in 1849 the South Eastern Railway Company made the branch line from Redhill to Reading, with a station at Reigate. The road from Crawley to Reigate was the first turnpike road in Surrey, made in 1696,[5] but was then only passable for horses in the southern part. It is the road which enters Reigate by Bell Street. The communication to London went on up Nutley Lane, and so up Reigate Hill. But the present road up the hill was made in 1755.[6] The road from Reigate to Merstham, into the new road to Croydon, by way of Wray's Common, was made in 1807.[7] The communication of the London road with the town was improved by the tunnel made in 1823.

The borough was constituted a municipal borough in 1863, four years before it was destroyed finally as a parliamentary borough by the second Reform Act. The municipal buildings were erected in 1902 at a cost of over £25,000. In 1861 the Public Hall had been built at a cost of £5,000. It contains a library, and accommodates a literary institution and friendly societies. The cemetery adjoining the churchyard was opened in 1855.

The Isolation Hospital is in Horley parish; it was opened in 1900; Mrs. Kitto's Free Convalescent Home was moved to South Park in Reigate in 1880.

The Brabazon Home for invalid members of the Girls' Friendly Society was founded in 1885. It is in Lesbourne Road, and was founded by The Countess of Meath. The Victoria Almshouses were built by public subscription to celebrate the Diamond Jubilee of her late Majesty. They stand in Deerings Road.

Reigate and Redhill neighbourhoods have yielded a great number of prehistoric remains, and there was clearly a large settlement of primitive people on the dry soil. Between 1848 and 1860 Mr. John Shelley made large discoveries of Neolithic flakes near Redhill Junction, on ground now covered by houses, and two sites of barrows were opened, revealing at 18 in. below the soil calcined bones, burnt flints, and a corn crusher. Sir John Evans described them to the Society of Antiquaries.[8] But various implements, including leaf-shaped arrow-heads, a hammer, and traces of hut floors were also found.[9] Two bronze armlets and British coins have also been found on Reigate Heath,[10] and on the heath are seven barrows, four easily visible, and three less clearly marked but discernible. There are pine trees on them, and guide books say that when the trees were planted glass beads and ashes were found. Flint flakes occur on the spot, which is a sand-hill to which the flints have been brought.

The subsequent history of Reigate is to be found in the possession of the manor and castle by the Earls of Warenne and Surrey.

From the utter destruction of the *CASTLE* stonework it is impossible to date the castle, which has always belonged to the lords of the manor. It occupies a natural sand-hill,

[1] Manning and Bray, op. cit. i, 288–9; cf. Symmes, Add. MS. (B.M.), 6167.
[2] In 1873 old foundations were found under and in front of the Town Hall.
[3] Local information.
[4] Personal observation. Mr. Fisher's shop is undoubtedly an ancient building formerly comprising only one large chamber running east and west. It probably was the chapel. Some niches and other features suggest an early 14th-century date.
[5] Stat. 8 Will. III, cap. 15.
[6] Stat. 28 Geo. II, cap. 28.
[7] Stat. 47 Geo. III, cap. 25.
[8] Proc. (Ser. 2), i, 69–72.
[9] Ibid.; Evans, Stone Imp. 244, 277, 378.
[10] Ibid.

which has been artificially scarped, forming a plateau of about 300 ft. from east to west, by 200 ft. wide at the western end and 150 ft. at the eastern end. At the foot of the scarp is a ditch, of varying widths, from 60 to 30 ft. The crest of the scarp had a stone wall round it at one period. This formed the inner ward of the castle. The entrance was to the east, by the causeway, perhaps once broken by a drawbridge, across the ditch. There was an entrance tower standing here 120 years ago. The dwelling-house was latterly, and probably always, at the wider western end. Outside the north-western part of the ditch, up the hill, was an extensive outwork. This part of the site is partly covered by private grounds, and has been cut into by building and a road, and is hard to define exactly. From this outwork or barbican a wet ditch ran eastwards, and then southwards in a curve. The south ditch of the inner ward is continued eastward for about 320 ft., and has a short limb reaching north and divided from the south-eastern extremity of the wet ditch by a bank. The wet ditch and extended dry ditch inclose an outer ward of nearly twice the area of the inner ward, and lying north-east and east of it.

From the northern outwork or barbican a wall was carried round the west and south sides of the castle on the outside of the dry fosse round the inner ward, making a narrow outer ward here also. Some small parts of this outer wall seem to remain in the garden walls of the houses on the south side of the castle, being the only stonework left *in situ* with any claims to antiquity.

The castle was an important place in the line of fortresses between London and the south coast. It immediately commanded a way north and south, by Bell Lane and Nutley Lane up the downs ; a natural line of communication on the dry ground ran east and west immediately below it, through Reigate High Street, and it was not far from the great cross-county route along the chalk to the north. It surrendered to the French and the barons 8 June 1216.[11] It passed back into the regent's hands in 1217. In the campaigns of 1264 it is not mentioned, but was probably held for the king till after Lewes, while its near neighbour, Blechingley, de Clare's castle, was certainly held for the barons. In 1263, after the violent affray in Westminster Hall, when Alan de la Zouche was attacked by the Earl of Surrey and his men, and received wounds from which he ultimately died, the earl shut himself up in Reigate Castle and defied justice till Edward, the king's son, appeared before his walls, and Henry of Cornwall and the Earl of Gloucester persuaded him to surrender.[12] As in so many other cases, the decay of the castle was so gradual that no definite period can be assigned to it. Roland Lenthal stated in 1441 that the houses within the castle were ruinous.[13] Camden described it as 'now neglected and decayed with age.' A survey of 1622[14] calls it 'a decayed castle with a very small house.' This is the interior dwelling-house, rebuilt at some earlier period. In 1648 the Earl of Holland's Royalist insurrectionaries came to Reigate and skirmished with Major Audley's soldiers on Redhill. The Royalists occupied the decayed castle, which was no doubt in some sense defensible, but

abandoned it next day, when the pursuing Parliamentary commander Livesay thought it worth while to leave a garrison in it.[15] While this was in progress, 4 July 1648, Parliament referred to the Derby Home Committee an order to make Reigate Castle, among other places, incapable of being used as a fortress.[16] This order no doubt completed the ruin. In 1782 Watson[17] gives a contemporary view from the south, which shows the small house, a one-storied building with two wings, the Gate Tower, apparently of about 14th-century date, in good preservation, a round tower to the south-west and a bit of ruinous wall between these two towers. It is badly drawn, and the Gate Tower is in the wrong place, according to his own plan, and judging from the existing causeway over the ditch.

Some French *jetons* and a large mediaeval spur have been found in the castle.

The caverns are under the western part of the inner inclosure. There is an entrance from the middle of the castle, and another, perhaps more recent, from the western ditch. The sandstone of the hill yields readily to excavation, and is hard enough to stand unsupported. The caverns were in all probability dry cellars and storehouses to begin with, enlarged later from busy idleness, which is also responsible for the sham antique gateway of the castle, or merely from commercial desire to dig and sell the fine sand which is in great request. The survey of 1622 mentions 'special white sand within the lord's castle.' The tradition that William de Warenne's castle was made a rendezvous for a secret meeting of the barons who were about to demand the Great Charter from the king, is equivalent to saying that the Reform Bill of 1832 was elaborated in the Carlton Club. Moreover the combined barons went nowhere near Reigate except in legend.

Some of the same uncertainty which prevails about the date of the castle exists about the date of the foundation of the priory. This can be more approximately dated, however, for it was founded by William de Warenne, who died in 1240, and by Isabel his wife.[18] It was grievously decayed before the Suppression, when its revenues were only £68 a year, and there were only the prior and three Austin Canons residing in it. The Priory House, on its site, the property of Lady Henry Somerset, is not the old Priory.

When Lord William Howard, first Lord Howard of Effingham, obtained the priory estate by grant from Henry VIII he must have demolished a great part of the buildings, including probably the church, and transformed what remained into a mansion for his own use, and this house was in turn almost entirely rebuilt or refronted in 1779. The main or south front of this last period is of pleasing elevation in Reigate stone, consisting of a long central portion with a pediment in the middle, above which rises a cupola, and projecting wings, the whole under a steep-pitched tiled roof. The simple and dignified style suggests a date of a century earlier. Parts of the walls in the rear are those of the priory buildings—perhaps of the refectory—in particular a range of plain stone corbels, and what appears to be the lower part of a corbelled-out chimney belonging to an upper story.

[11] *Ann. Mon.* (Rolls Ser.), ii, 285.
[12] *Flores Hist.* (Rolls Ser.), iii, 18.
[13] Mins. Accts. Gen. Ser. bdle. 1120, no. 2.
[14] Copied in the Ct. R.
[15] *V.C.H. Surr.* ii, 418-19.
[16] Whitelocke, *Memorials*, date cited.
[17] In his *Hist. of the Earls of Warren*.
[18] *V.C.H. Surr.* ii, 105-6.

The house contains a fine 16th-century mantel-piece with the royal arms on it, which tradition says came from Blechingley Place.[19] The royal arms are France and England quarterly, which shows the date to be previous to James I, and on the lower part, to which the overmantel was added, are the Howard arms.

The survey of Reigate Manor in 1622 mentions the old park, south of the town, well stored with timber and deer, with 'a faire pond' stocked with fish. It covered 201 acres, including a portion of the waste laid to it. It was leased by the Earl of Nottingham, who lived at the Priory, of the Earl of Dorset. It is obviously the park about the Priory, which properly belonged to Reigate Manor, not to the Priory. Sir Roger James was then tenant of the castle, and of the 'connie warren.'

The present buildings of the Reigate Free School were erected in 1871, when a new scheme was sanctioned for the management of the school.[20] The earlier history of the school (given in another volume) can be supplemented from the vestry books and a MS. which has come under the writer's notice. The litigation in Chancery which followed the refusal of the heirs of Sir Edward Thurland, the original trustee of the school funds in 1675, to recognize the trust, resulted in a decision of 18 April 1687 establishing the vicar, churchwardens, and six of the principal inhabitants as trustees. The school was started shortly afterwards, previous to 1744, the date given in the earlier volume of this history. Andrew Cranston, vicar from 1697 to 1708, who established the library in the church, was master of the school, which was kept in a house devised for the purpose by Robert Bishop in 1698, when four boys had to be taught freely. Mr. John Parker in 1718 added two more free scholars supported by an endowment, and there were then thirty paying boys. It was ordered that year by the vestry that the master should teach the Catechism twice a week and see that the boys went to church on Sundays, holidays, and weekly prayer days. The election of the master was in the hands of 'the whole parish,' but as there were three masters between the death of the Rev. John Bird, vicar and master in 1728, and the appointment of the Rev. John Martin in 1732, the relations between the master and the vestry were probably not easy. The masters were expected to do repairs of the schoolhouse, and did not do them. In 1778 the vestry voted that the repairs were to fall upon the master, and that the last executed had been in 1733, when £60 was laid out 'from an unknown source.' Mr. Thomas Sisson signed as master on those terms. The desire of the masters was clearly to neglect the free scholars, and to take paying pupils. It would seem that at this date (1778) the Rev. Mr. Pooles was nominally master, drawing the small endowment and probably taking private pupils, and had put in Mr. Sisson to teach the free boys. The vestry put in Mr. Sisson as master, but ultimately[21] had to undertake the repairs.

Reigate (British) School, High Street, was built in 1852, enlarged in 1888.

Reigate (national) School, London Road, was built in 1859.

St. Mark's (national) School, Holmesdale Road, was built in 1869.

Holmesdale (British) School, was built in 1870, and rebuilt in 1900.

St. Luke's (national) School, Allingham Road, was built in 1873, enlarged 1883.

Heathfield (Church) School, Reigate Heath, was built in 1873.

Lesbourne Lands (national) School for Infants was built in 1880.

The Wesleyan chapel in High Street was built in 1884, in place of an older chapel in Nutley Lane.

The Primitive Methodist chapel was built in 1870; there is also a Congregational church in Allingham Road.

Two societies of Nonconformists in Reigate have a more ancient history. George Fox came to Reigate in 1655, and his friends were numerous in the neighbourhood. Reigate, Dorking, Capel, Ockley, Newdigate, Charlwood, all had early adherents of the Society of Friends in them. There is a record of a meeting in Reigate in 1669. Mr. Thomas Moore, a Justice of the peace, mentioned in Fox's *Journal*, let some land at a nominal rent for a permanent meeting-house as soon as the Toleration Act of 1689 made it lawful. A burial-ground was attached to it. The original building lasted till 1798, when it was rebuilt or considerably altered. In 1856 the building was pulled down and replaced by the present meeting-house, on the same site, on the road to Redhill.[22]

A congregation of Independents claims to have existed in Reigate since 1662. From the records of the present church it appears that the Rev. James Waters was the first minister. The list of meetings which Sheldon procured in 1669, and the licences under the Indulgence of 1672, show no meetings in Reigate.[23] But Mr. Waters is not said to have entered upon regular ministrations till 1687, after James's Declaration of Indulgence. Meanwhile, however, he had been tutor in the family of Denzil Lord Holles, who was a Presbyterian, and chaplain to Mr. Evelyn of Nutfield. In 1715 there were Presbyterian and Friends' meetings in Reigate, but no Independents.[24] In 1725 the returns to Willis' Visitation[25] show the same. It is pretty obvious that this is another of the Presbyterian meetings which for want of a real Presbyterian organization passed into Congregationalism. The chapel was repaired in 1819 by Mr. Thomas Wilson, and reopened after having been closed about twenty years. It was rebuilt altogether by Mr. Wilson in 1831, and has since been enlarged.[26]

Redhill was, as the name conveys, a hill of the sand formation, and Redhill Common was a large open space in Reigate parish, of some fame historically as the scene of a skirmish, or of the meeting at least, of hostile picquets of Royalists and Parliamentarians in 1648, or of a projected Royalist meeting in 1659.[27] The coming of the railways turned the neighbourhood of a country common into one of the most important towns in Surrey. In 1841 the

---

[19] Evelyn says (*Diary*, 21 Aug. 1655) that the work came from Blechingley, and as Blechingley Place and the Priory belonged to the same owner (Lady Peterborough), this is probably true.

[20] *V.C.H. Surr.* ii, 217–18.
[21] Ibid. 217.
[22] MSS. formerly in hands of Mr. Marsh of Dorking.
[23] *V.C.H. Surr.* ii, 38–40.

[24] *Surr. Arch. Coll.* xiv (2).
[25] MS. Farnham Castle.
[26] Waddington, *Surr. Cong. Hist.* 281.
[27] *V.C.H. Surr.* i, 418, 423.

Brighton line was opened with stations at Battle Bridge and Hooley, the former now disused, the latter a goods siding, north of Earlswood station. In 1842 the South Eastern line to Dover, which had obtained running powers over the Brighton line as far as a point north of Hooley Station, was carried from what then became Redhill Junction to Dover. Earlswood station was opened at a later date. The districts of Reigate parish called Woodhatch, and Linkfield, the latter including the hamlets of Linkfield Street and Wiggey, and Mead Vale and Earlswood, were those which were immediately affected by the line, and population soon increased in them. In 1844 there being about 1,200 people in Linkfield and Woodhatch, the ecclesiastical parish of St. John the Evangelist was formed. In 1867 St. Matthew's ecclesiastical parish was formed out of the northern part of St. John's, and the ecclesiastical parish of Holy Trinity was formed in 1907 out of St. Matthew's. The population served by these three churches is nearly 20,000.

The Roman Catholic church, St. Joseph's, was consecrated in 1898, in place of one built in 1860.

St. Paul's Presbyterian Church of England was built in 1902.

The Congregational chapel in Chapel Road was built in 1862 ; the Baptist chapel in London Road in 1864. There are other Baptist chapels in Station Road, Hatchlands Road, and Mead Vale ; two Wesleyan, and three Primitive Methodist chapels ; and meeting-places for the Plymouth Brethren and Salvation Army.

The Reformatory of the Philanthropic Society for Reformation of Juvenile Offenders, founded in St. George's Fields, Southwark, in 1788, and incorporated in 1806, was removed to a site at Earlswood in 1849. It consists of five separate houses, each holding sixty boys.

The Royal Asylum of St. Anne, established in Aldersgate in 1702, for the support and education of children of both sexes, was removed in 1884 to buildings close to Redhill Station, which were opened by King Edward VII, then Prince of Wales.

The Earlswood Asylum, the national home for the feeble-minded, was founded on Earlswood Common in 1847. The buildings were opened by the Prince Consort. It was considerably enlarged in 1870 and 1877, and altered from 1903 to 1906. It accommodates 600 patients.

Reigate Union Workhouse is also on Earlswood Common.

On Earlswood Common there is a station on the Brighton line, which serves the southern part of Redhill and the numerous houses springing up towards Horley parish.

Redhill has a Market Hall, built in 1860 and enlarged in 1891 and 1903. It gives accommodation to the post office, the county court, and several societies. There is a market every alternate Wednesday. The Market Field, with a house exclusively for the purpose of a market, is at the back of the Hall.

The Colman Institute was presented to Redhill by Sir Jeremiah Colman, bart., of Gatton Park, in 1904. In it the Literary Institution, founded in 1884, now meets. It is in the London Road, and is of red brick and terra cotta.

The County Council Technical Institute is on Redstone Hill.

The top of Redhill Common was taken by the War Office in 1862 for the erection of a fort. This design was never carried out, and in 1884 the Reigate Corporation acquired it for a public park. The Board of Conservators, appointed under the provisions of a private Act, have planted some of the ground, and acquired and improved the sheet of water on Earlswood Common as a bathing and skating pond.

St. John's (national) school was built in 1846, enlarged 1861 and 1884.

St. Matthew's (national) Boys' School, built in 1872, was enlarged in 1884 ; Girls' and Infants', started in 1866, was rebuilt in 1884.

St. Joseph's (Roman Catholic) School, built in 1868, was rebuilt in 1902.

The Wesleyan School, Cromwell Road, was opened in 1867.

Frenches Road (Church) School was built in 1903. St. John's (Infants) School is at Mead Vale. There is also at Battle Bridge a (Church) mixed school.

BOROUGH   Reigate was for many centuries a mesne borough entirely under the power of the successive lords of the manor. Apparently the burgesses had no charter until 1863.[38]

The borough was evidently of little importance before that date. Its extent was inconsiderable as compared with that of the whole parish, and although it contained the more thickly-inhabited district round the castle, it is noteworthy that it excluded the old parish church.[39] The Domesday name of the manor, Cherchefelle, suggests that the church was the centre of the original settlement, and that the borough grew up under the walls of the castle, where it is closely clustered. There were only ninety separate tenements in it in 1622. Beyond its limits the rest of the parish, known as the 'foreign,' was divided into the 'boroughs' or tithings of Santon, Linkfield, Woodhatch, Hooley, and Colley.[40] In 1832 the parish boundary was adopted for parliamentary purposes.[41]

Previous to 1863 the privileges of the burgesses of Reigate beyond that of the parliamentary franchise were very limited. They had no court of their own but attended the court leet of the lord,[42] in which their officers were elected.[43] The court leet at Michaelmas elected a bailiff, constables, two for the borough, one for the 'foreign,' six headboroughs, a fish-taster, a flesh-taster, a searcher of leather, a sealer of leather, and two ale-conners.[44] They had no common lands until their purchase of Redhill Common from the Crown in 1867,[45] but in 1678–9 they were granted the tolls of a monthly market and yearly fair.[46] The burgesses were chiefly distinguished from the other tenants of the manor, the majority of whom were copyhold tenants,[47] by the rents which

---

[38] The charter has been printed.

[39] A plan of the old borough and parish appears in the *Boundary Rep.* of the Commission on Parliamentary Representation, *Parl. Papers,* 1831-2, xl, 35. The area of the borough was only 65 acres, while that of the parish was 5,415 acres.

[40] Ct. R. (Land. Rev.), bdle. 70, no. 2 et seq.

[41] *Parl. Papers,* 1831-2, xl, 35.

[42] *Rep. of Com. on Publ. Rec.* 1837, App. p. 477.

[43] Ct. R. (Land. Rev.), bdle. 70, nos. 2-12.

[44] Reigate Ct. R.

[45] *Ret. of Boroughs possessing Com. Lands, Parl. Papers,* 1870, lv, 24.

[46] See below.

[47] *Rep. of Com. on Publ. Rec.* 1837, p. 477. It is of note also that the garden of each burgage tenement paid a certain fixed tithe (Exch. Dep. Hil. 11 & 12 Will. III, 7).

they paid. The liberties of the lord within the borough in 1279 included infangtheof, gallows, the custody of prisoners, view of frankpledge, and free warren, which last. extended in the case of Reigate over the lands of the freemen as well as the demesne lands of the manor.[39] Return of writs was granted to John Duke of Norfolk, when lord of the manor in 1468.[39]

The first known mention of Reigate as a borough is in 1291, when the men of the borough complained of exactions by the sheriff.[40] In 1295 they first returned two burgesses to Parliament.[41] The returning officers in 1452 were the two constables.[42] The bailiff of the borough appears to have supplanted them shortly afterwards, for Richard Knight, bailiff, was returning officer in 1472.[43] It has been said that it was customary for the presiding constable to be elected bailiff each year,[44] but the rolls show that the bailiff was not the same man as either constable in certain years at least. The two constables and the bailiff chosen in the lord's court leet[45] were the principal municipal officers until the incorporation charter of 1863 established a council of mayor, aldermen, and councillors.

From 1295 till 1832 two burgesses were returned for Reigate, the franchise being vested in the burgage holders.[45] Under the Reform Act of 1832 the borough boundary was extended to include the whole parish,[47] and the number of representatives reduced to one, and in 1867 Reigate was disfranchised.[48]

The growth of the borough was evidently due to the protection afforded by the castle. It may also have acquired importance through the neighbouring stone quarries worked in the 13th and 14th centuries and its position on cross roads.[49] It was a market town before 1276,[49] and shortly afterwards Earl Warenne proved his claim to a prescriptive weekly market on Saturdays and fairs on Tuesday in Pentecost week, the eve and day of St. Lawrence (10 August), and the eve and day of the Exaltation of the Cross (14 September).[51] The first and last continue still. In 1313 John Earl of Surrey had a new grant of a market on Tuesdays,[52] which is still extant. Another market was established at Redhill by a private company in 1859,[53] and is now held on alternate Wednesdays.

A monthly market and a cattle fair on Wednesdays in Easter week were granted to the burgesses in February 1678–9.[54] A fair is still held on 9 December. The weekly market granted to the burgesses seems to have been merged in the Tuesday market.

MANORS The manor of *REIGATE* appears in the Domesday Survey under the name of Cherchefelle. It was then held in demesne by the king, and had formerly belonged to Queen Edith.[55] Probably William II granted it to William de Warenne when creating him Earl of Surrey, c. 1088.[56] The statement in *Testa de Nevill*, that Reigate had pertained to the barony of Earl Warenne from the time of the Conquest,[57] points to its having formed part of the earl's original endowment, but the earliest known reference to Reigate Manor as a possession of the Earls of Surrey[58] is that of the inquest of 1212, where it is returned among the lands of William .Earl of Surrey, son of Isabel, great-granddaughter of the above-mentioned earl.[59] An account of the family and its close connexion with the county will be found in the article on the Political History of Surrey.[60]

In 1316 John Earl of Surrey surrendered Reigate with other lands to the king and had a regrant for life, with remainder to John de Warenne, his illegitimate son by Maud de Nerford.[61] This settlement was altered in 1326 in favour of his lawful wife Joan, Countess of Bar, granddaughter of Edward I,[62] who after his death held Reigate in dower.[63] In accordance with the settlement of 1326 and a charter of Edward III,[64] it passed at her death in 1351 to the earl's nephew Richard, Earl of Arundel,[65] afterwards styled

WARENNE. *Checky or and azure.*

Earl of Surrey. His son and heir, Richard, the distinguished naval commander of the later French wars, having incurred the enmity of Richard II fled to Reigate, but having been treacherously persuaded to leave the castle[66] was arrested, attainted, and beheaded September 1397.[67] His lands thus forfeit to the Crown[68] were granted to John Holand, Duke of Exeter.[69]

The latter was himself beheaded at Pleshey for conspiracy against Henry IV in January 1399–1400, and in the following October Thomas, son of the last-named Richard, Earl of Arundel, was restored to his father's honours, and probably to his lands.[70] After his death, which occurred in 1415,[71] Reigate formed part of the dower of his widow Beatrice.[72]

Soon after her death, which occurred in 1439, par-

---

[38] *Plac. de Quo War.* (Rec. Com.), 737, 745.

[39] Chart. R. 8–10 Edw. IV, no. 14.

[40] Assize R. 893.

[41] *Ret. of Memb. of Parl.* i, 6.

[42] Orig. Parl. Ret. 31 Hen. VI.

[43] *Ret. of Memb. of Parl.* i, 362.

[44] Carew, *Hist. Acct. of Rights of Elec.* 86.

[45] In Jan. 1485–6 William Clifton was appointed constable of the castle and bailiff of the 'town' by Hen. VII, to whom was forfeited one-fourth of the manor (see below), *Mat. for Hist. of Hen. VII* (Rolls Ser.), i, 251; but his office may only have been the stewardship of the manor or honour; *Cal. Close,* 1313–18, p. 101.

[46] Orig. Ret. of M.P. 12 Edw. IV; 31 Chas. II; Partic. of Present and Proposed Parl. Boroughs, *Parl. Papers,* 1831–2, xxxvi, 301. It is noteworthy, however, that the electors in 1541–2 were the

burgesses 'and others of the commonalty gentlemen being burgesses' and in 1620–1 the burgesses and inhabitants. (Orig. Ret. 33 Hen. VIII; 18 Jas. I.)

[47] See Parl. Papers, 1831–2, xl, 35.

[48] 30 & 31 Vict. cap. 102.

[49] *V.C.H. Surr.* ii, 277.

[50] In that year inquiry was made into the value of tolls paid by the men of the Archbishop of Canterbury at certain fairs or markets; they paid 1 mark at Reigate (Misc. Inq. xxxiv, 22).

[51] *Plac. de Quo War.* (Rec. Com.) 737.

[52] Chart. R. 6 Edw. II, no. 66.

[53] *Report on Markets and Tolls,* 1891 xiii (2), 512.

[54] Pat. 31 Chas. II, pt. iii, no. 16.

[55] *V.C.H. Surr.* i, 297.

[56] Cf. G.E.C. *Baronage,* vii, 322. The endowment of the earldom seems to have consisted of all Edith's manors in Surrey.

[57] *Testa de Nevill* (Rec. Com.), 226.

[58] That it was held by Isabel and her husband Hamelin, Earl Warenne, between 1164 and 1199 may be deduced from their gift of the church to St. Mary, Southwark, see below.

[59] *Red Bk. of Exch.* (Rolls Ser.), 561.

[60] *V.C.H. Surr.* i, 329.

[61] Harl. Chart. 57, E. 33; *Cal. Close,* 1313–18, p. 347; *Cal. Pat.* 1313–17, p. 528.

[62] Ibid. 1324–7, p. 271; *Cal. Close,* 1323–7, p. 573.

[63] Ibid. 1346–9, pp. 314, 316.

[64] *Cal. Pat.* 1345–8, p. 221.

[65] Cf. Feet of F. Div. Co. 40 Edw. III, 17.

[66] *Chron. S. Albani* (Rolls Ser.), ii, (Trokelowe), 202.

[67] G.E.C. *Peerage,* vii, 329.

[68] Chan. Inq. p.m. 21 Ric. II, no. 137.

[69] Pat. 22 Ric. II, pt. ii, m. 23.

[70] G.E.C. *Peerage.*

[71] Chan. Inq. p.m. 4 Hen. V, no. 54.

[72] Ibid. 18 Hen. VI, no. 28.

tition was made of the estates which she had held in dower between her husband's co-heirs, the descendants of his three sisters, viz. john, Duke of Norfolk, grandson of one sister Elizabeth, who had married Thomas, Duke of Norfolk; Lady Elizabeth Nevill, granddaughter of Joan, Lady Abergavenny, a second sister ; and Edmund Lenthal, son of Margaret with Sir Roland Lenthal, a third sister.[73] Since Edmund Lenthal was then a minor Sir Roland Lenthal, perhaps his father,[74] had the custody of his lands till he came of age, 16 June 1441.[75] Among these was one-third of certain houses within the castle of Reigate,[76] and Edward Lord Abergavenny held at his death by right of his wife Lady Elizabeth Nevill another third of the castle and liberties.[77] No further trace of tenure either by the Lenthal or Nevill families has been found, but in a later plea it is stated that by an agreement between the three sisters, Elizabeth, joan, and Margaret, the whole of Reigate was assigned as the purparty of Elizabeth and her husband, Thomas Duke of Norfolk.[78] The whole manor seems to have been in the possession of the latter's great-grandson, John Duke of Norfolk,[79] who, in September 1474, settled it on his wife Elizabeth.[80] In 1477 she conveyed her life interest to Elizabeth (Wydeville), Queen of Edward IV,[81] but in the same year Katharine, widow of the late duke's grandfather and sister-in-law of the queen, was holding the manor in dower.[82] The remainder was then settled on Anne, the duke's only daughter and heir, at her betrothal to Richard the unfortunate Duke of York, murdered in 1483.[83] The co-heirs of Anne were the representatives of her great-aunts, viz., William Marquess of Berkeley, John Howard, created Duke of Norfolk in 1483, Thomas Earl of Derby, and Sir John Wingfield. The manor was apparently divided between them, for William Marquess of Berkeley was in possession of one-fourth in 1489.[84] His brother and heir Maurice, from whom he endeavoured to alienate this inheritance,[85] recovered one-fourth of Reigate from the Crown in 1503.[86] In the following year he conveyed this purparty to Sir Edward Poynings, kt.,[87] and others, probably to sell, for he is said to have

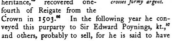

BERKELEY. *Gules a cheveron between ten crosses formy argent.*

parted with his quarter to Thomas Howard, Earl of Surrey, son of John Duke of Norfolk.[88]

John, Duke of Norfolk, fell at Bosworth, August 1485, and was attainted in the following November.[89] His interest in Reigate thus fell to the Crown,[90] but was not regranted to Thomas with his father's other lands in 1489.[91] Henry VIII granted the manor of Reigate to Agnes, widow of Thomas, in dower.[92] His son, Thomas Duke of Norfolk, was attainted in January 1546-7,[93] and the farm of his moiety of the manor was granted in March 1550-1 to his half-brother William Howard, afterwards Baron Howard

HOWARD. *Gules . bend between six crosslets fitchy argent.*

of Effingham.[94] His widow Margaret held a court in 1574.[95] Their son and heir Charles, Lord High Admiral, created Earl of Nottingham in 1596, held one moiety of the manor in his own right and leased the other moiety from the Earl of Derby.[96] He settled his moiety on his wife Margaret,[97] who, after his death in December 1624, married William, afterwards Viscount Monson[98] of Castlemaine. After her death in 1639[99] this half of the manor appears to have reverted to her husband's heir male, Charles, second Earl of Nottingham, whose half-brother, the third earl of that name, sold it to John Goodwyn[100] in 1648.[100a] The latter held a court jointly with James, Duke of York, in 1672, and in 1683 his interest was vested in Dean Goodwyn,[101] who with Charles Goodwyn released his moiety to James shortly after his accession to the throne.[102]

Thomas Earl of Derby, the third co-heir to the lands of Anne Mowbray (see above), appears to have acquired the Wingfield quarter of the manor in addition to his own.[103] He was succeeded by his grandson Thomas, who died seised of this moiety in 1521.[104] His widow held it in dower.[105]

STANLEY. *Argent a bend azure with three harts' heads caboshed or thereon.*

During the lifetime of his son and ultimate heir, Henry fourth Earl of Derby, the Earl of Nottingham had a lease of it.[106] After the death of his son

[73] Cal. Pat. 1436–41, p. 483.

[74] Sir Roland, the father, is said to have married a second time (Devon Visit. [Harl. Soc. vii], 169). His second wife seems to have been named Lucy (Cal. Pat. 1429–36, p. 446).

[75] Cal. Pat. 1436–41, p. 562.

[76] Mins. Accts. (Gen. Ser.) bdle. 1120, no. 1.

[77] Chan. Inq. p.m. 16 Edw. IV, file 66, m. 22.

[78] Plac. in Cancellaria (Rolls Chapel Ser.), bdle 1, no. 29.

[79] Feet of F. Div. Co. 8 Edw. IV, 64; cf. Chart. R. 8–10 Edw. IV, no. 14.

[80] Add. Chart. (B.M.), 7619, 7629. In the settlement on the Duke of York it is called 'the halvendale' or moiety of Reigate; cf. also Chan. Proc. Eliz. H. h. xvii, 3.

[81] Feet of F. Div. Co. 16 Edw. IV, 116.

[82] Parl. R. (Rec. Com.), vi, 168b.

[83] Ibid.

[84] Feet of F. Surr. Mich. 5 Hen. VII.

[85] Fosbroke, Lives of the Berkeleys, passim.

[86] Parl. R. (Rec. Com.), vi, 529 ; Placita in Cancellaria, bdle. 1, no. 29.

[87] Feet of F. Div. Co. Trin. 19 Hen. VII.

[88] Manning and Bray, Hist. of Surr. i, 276.

[89] G.E.C. Peerage, vi, 47.

[90] Parl. R. (Rec. Com.), vi, 336 ; Mat. for Hist. of Hen. VII (Rolls Ser.), ii, 138.

[91] Parl. R. vi, 426b.

[92] L. and P. Hen. VIII, xv, 498 (p. 220).

[93] Agnes the dowager duchess died in the preceding May, and it appears from the terms of the grant to William Howard that the duke held the farm of Reigate until his attainder.

[94] Partic. for Grants (Aug. Off.), 1710 ; Chan. Inq. p.m. (Ser. 2), clxv, 172. It had been leased to John Skynner in 1547.

[95] Ct. R.

[96] Chan. Proc. Eliz. H. h, xvii, 3.

[97] Chan. Inq. p.m. (Ser. 2), cccclxii, 69.

[98] Hist. MSS. Com. Rep. iv, 386.

[99] G.E.C. Peerage, v, 334.

[100] M.P. for Godalming 1640, for Reigate 1656. He was a buyer of church lands and sequestrated estates. See Farnham.

[100a] Feet of F. Surr. Hil. 23 Chas. I.

[101] Ct. R. 1683. He was M.P. for Reigate 1678–81.

[102] Feet of F. Surr. Mich. 2 Jas. II.

[103] He was first lord with Thomas Earl of Surrey in 1496 (Manning and Bray, op. cit. i, 278); and from Chan. Proc. Eliz. H. h., xvii, 3, it appears that, by that time, there were only two moieties, owned respectively by the Earl of Derby and Charles, Earl of Nottingham.

[104] Chan. Inq. p.m. (Ser. 2), xxxix, 110.

[105] L. and P. Hen. VIII, iii, 2820.

[106] See above.

Ferdinand, the fifth earl, without issue male it was purchased in 1600 by John Gawber, an agent or trustee for Thomas, created Earl of Dorset in March 1603-4.[107] Gawber died before the conveyance was completed, but his daughter and heir Margaret, wife of John Harris, conveyed it to Richard Earl of Dorset, grandson of the above Thomas, in 1613.[108] In 1611 he had already obtained a royal grant of it.[109] A survey of the manor was made for him in 1622. Earl Richard died in March 1623-4,[110] and in 1628 his estate in Reigate was sold, probably for the payment of his debts, to Sir John Monson and Robert Goodwyn.[111] They conveyed it in 1646 to William Viscount Monson,[112] whose wife, as widow of Charles Earl of Nottingham, had held the other moiety until her death in 1639. Viscount Monson was one of the regicide Judges and was accordingly degraded and imprisoned for life after the Restoration,[113] and his moiety of Reigate was immediately acquired by James Duke of York, who was endowed with the estates of the regicides.[114] He appointed a steward of the manor in March 1661,[115] and in 1686, after his accession as James II, acquired the other moiety.[116]

The whole manor thus united was granted 24 April 1697 by William III to Joseph Jekyll[117] (knighted in the same year), possibly in trust for his brother-in-law John Lord Somers, in whose name courts were held.[118] At his death in 1716 it was inherited by his two sisters, Mary wife of Charles Cocks and Elizabeth wife of the above-mentioned Sir Joseph Jekyll, kt.[119] Courts were held in their names until the death of Mrs. Cocks, 1717, after which Sir Joseph Jekyll, until his death, and subsequently his widow, held courts. She died in 1745,[120] and was succeeded by her nephew James Cocks,[121] M.P. for Reigate. He died 1750. His son James died unmarried 1758, when Charles, son of John the brother of James above-mentioned, succeeded. He was M.P. for Reigate from 1747 to 1784. He was created a baronet in 1772, and Baron Somers in 1784. His son and successor, John, was created Earl Somers July 1821 and died 1841. The manor descended to his son and grandson; on the death of Charles, third Earl Somers, in 1883, without male issue, it devolved upon one of his daughters, Lady Henry Somerset, the present owner.

Cocks. *Sable a chevron between three pairs of harts' horns argent.*

The ' honour ' of Reigate evidently comprised those lands of the honour of Warenne which were directly held of Reigate Manor. These included the manors of Dorking, Fetcham, Cranleigh, Vachery, Bradley in Dorking, Ashtead, and the Priory, Hooley, Redstone, Frenches, and Colley in Reigate.[107]

Most of the lands of the *PRIORY* in Reigate were probably granted to it by William de Warenne, Earl of Surrey, and his wife Isabel, at the foundation of the house before 1240.[113] At the suppression of the Priory in July 1536 it had lands both in the parish and in the borough, and courts were held for the tenants of these.[114] Lord Edmund Howard was then steward, but a lease of the Priory was made to John Marten in January 1537-8.[115] In 1541 it was granted to Lord William Howard, afterwards Lord Howard of Effingham, younger son of Thomas second Duke of Norfolk, and his wife Margaret in tail,[116] with lands in Reigate, Dorking, Capel, Betchworth, Horley, Burstow, Headley, Nutfield, Mickleham, Ashtead and Letherhead. In the following year he was attainted for complicity with his niece Katherine Howard,[117] but in 1543 the Priory was regranted to his wife, and in 1544 the original grant to them both was renewed.[118] Lady Howard died at Reigate in 1581,[119] and their son Charles, first Earl of Nottingham, Lord Admiral, held the Priory at his death in 1624, and habitually resided there, though he died at Haling. It was inherited by his granddaughter Elizabeth, Countess of Peterborough, ' a lady of extraordinary beauty.'[120] She tried to cut off the entail on the Priory in favour of her younger son, John Viscount Mordaunt,[121] a Royalist who made unsuccessful attempts to raise the country on behalf of Charles in 1658 and 1659.[122] His mother's estates were seized for his recusancy in 1659, but after the Restoration he was granted the remainder of the Priory at her death.[123] From his trustees it was purchased by Sir John Parsons, Lord Mayor of London in 1703.[124] It was inherited by his son Sir Humphrey, a brewer of note, who was twice Lord Mayor, and represented Reigate in many Parliaments.[125] He died in 1741, having bequeathed the Priory to his wife Sarah,[126] after whose death in 1759 her two daughters, the wives of Sir John Hinde Cotton and James Dunn, inherited it.[127] They are said to have sold it in 1766 to a Mr. Richard Ireland, who bequeathed it to his niece, Mrs. Jones.[128] Her son Arthur conveyed it in 1801 to Thomas Eden, Francis Webber, and Henry Ley,[129] in trust for sale to Mr. Mowbray, from whom it was purchased c. 1808 by Lord Somers,[140] since when it has descended with the manor. (q.v.).

[107] Recov. R. East. 42 Eliz. m. 94; Feet of F. Surr. Trin. 42 Eliz.; Chan. Inq. p.m. (Ser. 2), cclxxxix, 79.

[108] Feet of F. Surr. Trin. 11 Jas. I. There is no evidence that it was ever held by Robert the second earl, son of Thomas and father of Richard. He was earl less than one year, April 1608 to Feb. 1609.

[109] Pat. 9 Jas. I, pt. xxxvi, no. 5.

[110] Chan. Inq. p.m. (Ser. 2), cccv, 153.

[111] Feet of F. Surr. Mich. 4 Chas. I.

[112] Close, 22 Chas. I, pt. i, no. 28.

[113] G.E.C. *Peerage*, v, 334.

[114] *Hist. MSS. Com. Rep.* v, App. 205; but the estates of Viscount Monson are not specially mentioned in the Act of 1660 vesting certain forfeited estates in the duke, nor in the patent for the same purpose; Pat. 13 Chas. II, pt. v, no. 15.

[115] *Hist. MSS. Com. Rep.* viii, App. i, 280.

[116] See above.

[117] Pat. 9 Will. III, pt. ii, no. 11.

[118] Manning and Bray, op. cit. i, 283.

[119] G.E.C. *Peerage*, vii, 167; Feet of F. Surr. Mich. 4 Geo. I.

[120] Ct. R. The courts were held in the name of a single person, but it does not follow that the estate was not jointly held.

[121] Ct. R.; Recov. R. Trin. 32-3 Geo. II, m. 201; Trin. 15 Geo. III, m. 160.

[122] Ct. R.; Surv. of 1622.

[123] *V.C.H. Surr.* ii, 105.

[124] Mins. Accts. Surr. 28-9 Hen. VIII, bdle. 108, m. 5.

[125] L. and P. Hen. VIII, xiii (1), 588.

[126] Ibid. xvi, g. 947 (12).

[127] G.E.C. *Peerage*, viii, 235; cf. L. and P. Hen. VIII, xvi, 1444.

[128] Ibid. xvii, g. 443 (5); xix (1), g. 278 (5).

[129] G.E.C. *Peerage* iii, 235; Chan. Inq. p.m. (Ser. 2), cxcvii, 75.

[130] Ibid. ccclxiii, 69.

[131] *Cal. S.P. Dom.* 1645-7 pp. 571-2; 1660-1, p. 138; 1663-4, p. 487; 1666-7, p. 422.   [132] *Dict. Nat. Biog.*

[133] *Cal. S.P. Dom.* 1660-1, p. 138.

[134] Aubrey, *Hist. and Antiq. of Surr.* iv, 192.

[135] *Dict. Nat. Biog.*

[136] P.C.C. Wills, 74 Spurway.

[137] Bill of Sale, 1766.

[138] Add. MS. 34237 (Hist. of Reigate), fol. 5.

[139] Feet of F. Surr. Trin. 41 Geo. III.

[140] Add. MS. B.M. 34237, fol. 5; Com. Pleas D. Enr. East. 51 Geo. III, m. 2.

The manor of COLLEY[141] (Colle, xiii cent.) was a member of the honour of Reigate. It seems to be identical with 2 hides of land held by Walter of Colley in 1217–18.[142] In that year he gave three-fourths of a virgate there to Roger son of Alfred.[143] Roger of London evidently acquired the manor, for he was holding half a knight's fee in Reigate late in the 13th century,[144] and obtained a release of land there from Thomas son of Walter of Colley in 1326.[145] Roger's widow Eleanor, in consideration of a yearly rent to herself and her son Roger of London, conveyed the manor to Ralph son of Roger of London in 1332, with contingent remainder to Ralph's brother Roger and others, and finally to Eleanor's son Roger.[146] A Roger of London with his wife Alice[147] sold the manor to Richard, Earl of Arundel, in 1348,[148] and it was settled on his younger son Sir John Arundel, kt., in tail male, together with the manor of Buckland.[149] The grandsons of Sir John Arundel became successively Earls of Arundel, and it was held by the earls till 1566, when Henry, the thirteenth earl, after the death of his only son, sold it to Thomas Copley of Gatton.[150] With his heirs male[151] it remained for more than a century. At the partition of the estates of William Copley the elder between his two granddaughters, Mary wife of John Weston, and Anne wife of George Weston and afterwards of Sir Nathaniel Minshull, Colley was assigned to Mary Weston.[152] Her husband died in 1690,[153] and her grandson John Weston was in possession of Colley in 1702.[154] He died in 1730, leaving an only daughter, Melior Mary Weston, who died unmarried in June 1782.[155] Under her will Colley passed to John Wehbe, who took the name of Weston. His son John Joseph Webbe Weston sold it in 1842 to Henry Lainson.[156] He died in 1850, and was succeeded by his son Mr. Henry Lainson, whose nephew Mr. William H. Nash succeeded him in 1890, and almost immediately broke up the property. The manor is now lost. Mr. Frederick Horne at present lives in Colley Manor House.

The reputed manor of COMBES was held for several centuries by the lords of Flanchford[157] (vide infra). Possibly it was identical with the messuage and land conveyed to Henry Flanchford by William Combe and his wife Alice in 1408–9,[158] but the Priory of St. Mary Overy had a grange at Combe.[159]

The house called Minster Lea is reputed to be on their land.

The reputed manor of FLANCHFORD (Flaunch-ford or Flaunchworth, xvii cent.), a member of Reigate, was held by Hugh Flanchford,[160] and afterwards granted by John Earl Warenne to Brice his cook and his wife Alice.[161] In 1446 it was given by John Duke of Norfolk, lord of the manor of Reigate, to John Timperley, who represented Reigate in Parliament in 1453 and 1460. In February 1453–4 the manor was conveyed by feoffees to John and Alice Arderne of Leigh (q.v.).[162] Richard Arderne, son of John, died in 1499, and left his estates to his half-brother John Holgrave,[163] from whom this must have passed to the Dudleys (of Leigh Place). John Dudley sold to Edward Shelley of Findon in Sussex in 1530. Anne widow of Reginald Cobham (Cobbe?) of Blechingley, and possibly daughter-in-law of Edward Shelley, conveyed it to Sir Thomas Sander of Charlwood in 1539;[164] his eldest son Edmund sold it in 1601 to Martin and Christopher Freeman,[165] who alienated in the following year to Thomas, afterwards Sir Thomas Bludder, kt., a commissioner of the Victualling Office.[166] He died at Reigate 2 November 1618, and was succeeded by his son Sir Thomas Bludder, kt.[167] After his death in 1655 it was sold to Sir Thomas Hooke, bart.,[168] who in 1666 conveyed it to Sir Cyril Wyche, one of the six clerks in Chancery.[169] He is said to have sold it in 1676 to Thomas Lord Windsor, afterwards created Earl of Plymouth.[170] From his younger son, Thomas Viscount Windsor (in Ireland), it was purchased by Sir William Scawen in 1720.[171] His heir male, James Scawen, sold in 1781 to Sir Metrik Burrell, bart., of West Grinstead Park, co. Sussex, who bequeathed it to his great-nephew Sir Peter Burrell, bart., from whom it was bought in 1790 by William Browne.[172] It was afterwards owned by a Mr. William John Clutton, deceased, whose executors held it till recently.

FRENCHES was a reputed manor held of Reigate by fealty, suit of court, and 24s. rent. It belonged in 1596 to Nicholas Pope and his wife Mary, who conveyed it in that year to Charles Tingilden.[173] From the latter it was shortly afterwards acquired by Henry Drake, who died seised in 1609, and was succeeded by his son Edward.[173a] There was an in-

[141] Derived doubtless from Collis. The manor lies on the hill north-west of Reigate town.

[142] Chan. Inq. p.m. 14 Ric. II, no. 1.

[143] Feet of F. Surr. 2 Hen. III, 4.

[144] Testa de Nevill (Rec. Com.), 221b. It is worthy of note that some of the manorial lands were still known as London Lands in 1565 (Close, 8 Eliz. pt v, m. 12 d.).

[145] Feet of F. Surr. 20 Edw. II, file 41, no. 23.

[146] Ibid. 6 Edw. III, no. 77.

[147] Very probably Roger son of Eleanor, for Ralph's brother Roger died before him, and neither Ralph nor his brother left issue (De Banco R. East. 6 Hen. V, m. 117).

[148] Feet of F. Surr. 22 Edw. III, 22. In 1476 Edward Lord Abergavenny was said to have the service of half of half a knight's fee formerly held by William de Loundres. The Christian name here is evidently incorrect (Chan. Inq. p.m. 16 Edw. IV, 66, m. 22).

[149] Chan. Inq. p.m. 50 Edw. III (1st nos.), no. 52b.

[150] Feet of F. Surr. East. 8 Eliz. At the time of the sale it was mortgaged to Sir John White, kt., of London (Close 8 Eliz. pt v, m. 12 d.).

[151] See Gatton.

[152] Title deeds quoted by Manning and Bray, Hist. of Surr. i, 313.

[153] Berry, Surr. Gen. 55.

[154] Feet of F. Div. Co. Trin. 1 Anne. His father Richard died in 1701. Monument at Guildford.

[155] Berry, Surr. Gen. 55; Com. Pleas D. Enr. Hil. 15 Geo. III, m. 251, 255.

[156] Manning and Bray, op. cit. i, 313: Recov. R. Mich. 46 Geo. III, m. 36. See Sutton, in Woking. Brayley, Hist. of Surr. iv, 228.

[157] See Manning and Bray, Hist. of Surr. i, 308.

[158] Feet of F. Surr. 10 Hen. III, 35.

[159] Cott. MS. Faust. A. viii, fol. 154b.

[160] Henry Flaunchford was a party to conveyances of land in Reigate in 1394–5 and 1408–9 (Feet of F. Surr. 18 Ric. II, 64; 10 Hen. IV, 35). Possibly he was a member of the same family.

[161] Deeds penes R. Barnes of Reigate,

quoted by Manning and Bray, Hist. of Surr. i, 305. The name is here given as Cobham, but see Inq. p.m. Ct. of Wards xxi, 249. This Anne may be the widow of Edward's son Henry.

[162] Ibid.

[163] P.C.C. Moone, fol. 5.

[164] Manning and Bray, op. cit. i, 305.

[165] Feet of F. Surr. Trin. 43 Eliz. By his father's will it had been left to younger brothers, but had probably reverted to him (Chan. Inq. p.m. [Ser. 2], cxli, 25.)

[166] Feet of F. Surr. Hil. 44 Eliz.

[167] Chan. Inq. p.m. (Ser. 2), ccclxxx, 114.

[168] Feet of F. Surr. Hil. 22 Chas. I; Mich. 14 Chas. II.

[169] Aubrey, Hist. and Antiq. of Surr. iv, 209; Feet of F. Surr. East. 18 Chas. II.

[170] Manning and Bray, Hist. of Surr. i, 307.

[171] Feet of F. Surr. East. 6 Geo. I.

[172] Manning and Bray, op. cit. i, 307.

[173] Feet of F. Surr. East. 1596.

[173a] Ibid. Mich. 1596; Chan. Inq. p.m. (Ser. 2), cccxiv, 126.

scription in the church, now covered by seats, to Henry Drake of Frenches, father of Edward Drake. In 1630 Edward Drake sold the manor to Timothy Cartwright,[173b] who conveyed it in 1646 to john Parker.[174] john Parker died seised in 1679, his son James in 1689, his son John in 1718.[174a] The last is said to have left it by will to john Shaw of Eltham. Richard Ladbroke 'of Frenches' died in 1730. His 'kinsman' Richard Ladbroke died in 1765, and the latter's son Richard Ladbroke in 1793.[175] Richard Ladbroke, junior, left Frenches by will[176] to the children of his sisters Elizabeth Denton and Mary Weller in succession.

The so-called 'manor' of HOOLEY (Houlegh, xiv cent. ; Houghley, xv cent.) was held by john son of John de Brewes c. 1357,[177] but had been acquired by Richard, Earl of Arundel, before his death in 1397,[178] and thenceforward descended with the main manor of Reigate (q.v.). There is no record of separate courts, although in the deeds relating to Reigate and Hooley they are always distinguished as two separate manors. The manor-house of Hooley was conveyed to Richard Savage, yeoman, as a tenant of the manor in 1702. In 1729 his widow was admitted. In 1733 Charles Boone was admitted, and in 1752 his sons sold their interest to John Burt Tanner.[179] When Manning and Bray wrote[180] Henry Byne held it. In 1838 it was bought by the London, Brighton and South Coast Railway.

The reputed manor of LINKFIELD, held of the Priory Manor and of Gatton Manor, is probably identical with the tenement held by Nicholas de Linkfield, whose rent Earl Warenne granted to the prior in 1315.[181] In February 1506–7 Thomas Fulbourne, his wife Katherine, and his daughter Anne sold the manor of Linkfield to John Couper,[182] and in 1560 Thomas Engles and his wife, Katherine daughter of john Couper, were in possession.[183] He died 26 September 1575.[184] She was still living at Reigate in 1575,[185] and had a son James. But in accordance with a settlement on his first wife Linkfield descended to their daughter Anne wife of Philip Moys of Banstead. It remained in their family till 1648, when Henry Moys conveyed it to Roger James and Edward Thurland,[187] as trustees for Thomas Turges. In the following year he alienated it to John Parker.[188] His son Ambrose Parker, who succeeded in 1684,[189] mortgaged it in 1717 to Turges Newland of Gatton, who shortly afterwards became the owner.[190] It descended with Lower Gatton to Robert Ladbroke.[191] Brayley[192] says that Mr. Robert Ladbroke left it to Miss Ladbroke, who married Mr. Weller, and he took the name

of Ladbroke, and owned it in 1841. But Mary Ladbroke, cousin to Robert, married the Rev. james Weller in 1767, and he, under the name of Weller, from 1774 to 1824, when he resigned. Possibly his son changed his name. The capital mansion of Linkfield no longer exists.

The reputed manor of REDSTONE was evidently held in 1292 by john de Montfort, for in that year he had grant of free warren in Ashtead, Newdigate, and Redstone.[193] It is probably identical with the messuage and carucate of land granted in 1273–4 by Peter de Montfort, father to the said john, and his wife Maud to Martin Odo of Westminster for life, with remainder to his brother Thomas and contingent reversion, failing the heirs of Thomas, to Peter and Maud and the heirs of Maud.[194] John de Montfort did not hold it at his death, unless it was then included in Ashtead.[195] John Birt sold it in 1528 to Thomas Michell and others,[196] and in 1584 John Michell of Cuckfield conveyed it to John Hussey of Cuckfield.[197] George, brother and heir of john Hussey, son of George son of the above-mentioned john, alienated to Richard Heath c. 1632.[198] It remained in his family until 1713, when George Heath conveyed to Robert Bicknell.[199]

The house with the site of the manor passed to Sir Evelyn Alston in 1720, when the lands of the manor were broken up.[200] Mr. Thomas Peyto became owner of part of them.[201] Thomas Okes died in 1759 owner of Redstone,[201a] and his widow was in possession till 1768. The house was eventually acquired by the Colebrookes of Gatton, with which it descended to Mary Graham and George Graham, who in 1794 sold it to Ebenezer Whiting.[202]. In 1883 it was the property of Mr. Henry Webbe, and since 1891 has been owned by his daughter Miss Webbe.

The RECTORY MANOR had its origin in the enfeoffment of the priory of St. Mary Overy by Hamelin, Earl Warenne and his wife Isabel, of the church of 'Crechesfesd,' with the tithes and land appurtenant[203] (1164–99). In 1535 the rectory was valued at £20.[204] After the surrender of the monastery, October 1539, the rectory apparently remained in the Crown until 17 December 1552, when it was granted to James Skinner.[205] He settled

SKINNER of Reigate. *Sable a chevron wavy argent between three griffons' heads razed or with three fleurs de lis azure on the chevron.*

173b Feet of F. Surr. Mich 6 Chas. I.
174 Ibid. Mich. 22 Chas. I.
174a Inscriptions describing them as of Frenches.
175 Inscriptions in church.
176 Proved 1793, P.C.C.
177 Chan Inq. p.m. 31 Edw. III (1st nos.), no. 49a
178 Ibid. 21 Ric. II, no. 137.
179 Ct. R.
180 Op. cit. i, 309.
181 Dugdale, *Mon.* vi, 518.
182 Feet of F. Surr. 22 Hen. VII, 11.
183 Ibid. Mich. 2 & 3 Eliz.
184 Ct. R.
185 Chan. Inq. p.m. (Ser. 2), cxci, 75.
186 Ibid. ccxxix, 127.

187 Feet of F. Surr. Mich. 24 Chas. I.
188 Ibid. Mich. 1649.
189 Ct. R.
190 Reigate MS., summary of title ; Recov. R. Hil. 4 Geo. I, m. 122 ; Manning and Bray, op. cit. i, 310.
191 See the accounts of Gatton ; Com. Pleas D. Enr. Mich. 35 Geo. III, m. 39.
192 Op. cit. iv, 228.
193 Cal. Chart. R. 1257–1300, p. 428.
194 Feet of F. Surr. 2 Edw. I, 13.
195 Chan. Inq. p.m. 24 Edw. I, no. 59. He died seised of the manor of Ashtead, which descended in his family.
196 Feet of F. Surr. Hil. 19 Hen. VIII.
197 Ibid. Div. Co. East. 26 Eliz.

198 Ibid. Surr. East. 8 Chas. I ; for the pedigree cf. Feet of F. Div. Co. Trin. 34 Eliz. ; Chan. Inq. p.m. (Ser. 2), cccl, 64.
199 Feet of F. Surr. Hil. 12 Anne ; Recov. R. Hil. 12 Anne, m. 103.
200 Add. MS. 34237, fol. 7b.
201 MS. in Reigate papers in hands of Messrs. Walford, New Oxford Street.
201a Monumental inscription at Reigate. See under Church.
202 Com. Pleas D. Enr. Hil. 35 Geo. III, m. 23.
203 Dugdale, *Mon.* vi, 172.
204 Valor Eccl. (Rec. Com.), ii, 61.
205 Orig. R. 6 Edw. VI, pt. ii, m. 99.

238

it on his nephew john in 1556 subject to his own life interest. John died in 1584,[206] and was succeeded by one of his nephews and co-heirs, Richard Elyot of Albury.[207] The latter's son Richard Elyot the younger died in February 1612–13,[208] and his heirs sold the rectory in the following year to Sir Roger James, kt.,[209] who was succeeded in 1636 by his son Roger.[210]

In 1679 it was settled on his son Haestreet james on his marriage. Haestreet died in 1721. In 1730 his son of the same name conveyed the land, but not the tithes[211] nor advowson, to Sir Thomas Scawen.[212] The tithes are said to have been sold in 1720 to Sir William Scawen, uncle of Sir Thomas Scawen,[213] who left them by will to the latter. He gave them to his brother Robert, in whose hands the whole of the rectory was therefore reunited. Under his will, however, the land was sold in 1780 to Gawen Harris Nash,[214] who bequeathed it to his cousin Charles

of the soft calcareous sandstone quarried in the locality, with modern dressings and refacing (as in the tower) of Bath stone, its roof being still for the most part covered with the stone slabs usually called ' Horsham,' but somewhat similar to stones which were also dug in the Middle Ages from the Surrey Hills.[217] The church was repaved and repewed in 1770, owing to a legacy left by Mrs. Mary Okes of Redstone, and at this time the building was full of galleries to which, between 1804–18, others were added, disfiguring alterations being made in the structure, and the tie-beams of the roofs removed, nearly causing the nave to collapse. From Cracklow's view of about 1824, it would appear that the walls were at that date plastered externally for the most part. The church underwent a very destructive ' restoration ' in 1845, under the late Mr. H. Woodyer, and between 1877 and 1881 was again completely restored, chiefly under the direction

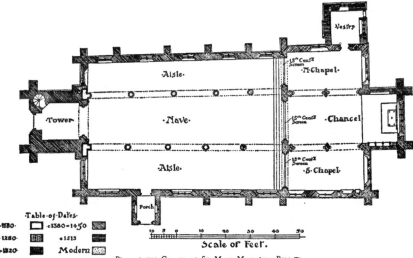

PLAN OF THE CHURCH OF ST. MARY MAGDALEN, REIGATE

Goring, from whom it was purchased by Charles Birkhead of Walton-on-Thames.[215]

The tithes were sold separately in 1787,[216] and are now said to be divided among twelve different owners.

The church of *ST. MARY MAGDALEN*, which ranks with Farnham, Godalming, St. Mary's Guildford, Dorking, Kingston and Lambeth, as one of the largest ancient parish churches in Surrey, is chiefly constructed

CHURCHES

of the late Sir Gilbert Scott, the latter's work being in the main of a conservative character, some of the mischief of the earlier ' restoration ' being undone. At the time of writing further works are in contemplation, involving the extension of the north aisle and the building of an organ chamber.

The plan presents many curious and puzzling features. It consists of a nave, 77 ft. 6 in. on the north and 77 ft. on the south side, 18 ft. wide at the west end,

[206] Chan. Inq. p.m. (Ser. 2), cciv, 123.
[207] Ibid. cccxi, 116.
[208] Chan. Inq. p.m. (Ser. 2), ccciii, 34.
[209] Feet. of F. Surr. Hil. 11 Jas. I; East. 12 Jas. I; Hil. 14 Jas. I.
[210] Chan. Inq. p.m. (Ser. 2), ccccxxx, 106.
[211] Exch. Dep. Mich. 2 Geo. I, 8; Recov. R. Mich. 5 Geo. I, m. 80; Feet of F.

Surr. Trin. 8 Geo. I; Trin. 10 Geo. I; MS. abstract of Reigate deeds seen by editor.
[212] William James appears to have retained some interest in the rectory in 1756 (Recov. R. East. 29 Geo. II, m. 292), although Robert and William Scawen suffered recovery in 1740 (Recov. R. Trin. 13 & 14 Geo. II, m. 292).

[213] Manning and Bray, *Hist. of Surr.* i, 322.
[214] Com. Pleas D. Enr. East. 20 Geo. III, m. 209.
[215] Manning and Bray, loc. cit.
[216] Ibid.; cf. Exch. Dep. Mich. 2 Geo. I, m. 8.
[217] From Chaldon for example, whence they were brought to Westminster Abbey.

and spreading in width to 20 ft. at the east, the walls being 2 ft. 6 in. thick ; north aisle of the same length, 11 ft. 8 in. wide at the west, and 12 ft. at the east end ; a south aisle of the same length by 15 ft. 6 in. wide ; western tower 15 ft. from west to east by 14 ft. 6 in., the walls being 4 ft. 9 in. thick ; south porch 10 ft. by 7 ft. 6 in. ; chancel 44 ft. 6 in. by 19 ft. ; north chapel 30 ft. by 15 ft. 3 in. at west and 15 ft. 6 in. at east ; south chapel 30 ft. 6 in. by 15 ft. 6 in. at west, and 16 ft. 3 in. at east. On the north of the north chapel is that comparatively rare feature— a vestry, or sacristy, built in 1513, double-storied, 13 ft. 3 in. from north to south and 11 ft. 8 in. from east to west. From these figures it will be seen that the walls of the body of the church are not parallel, but diverge towards the east, and that this peculiarity is repeated in the outer walls of the north and south chapels. In Compton Church the divergence of the walls of the pre-Conquest nave is in the reverse direction, and in both cases it is so marked as to be evidently intentional, and not due to a mistake in setting out. The axis of the chancel inclines slightly to the north. Another peculiarity is the irregular spacing of the nave arcades, none of the columns of which are opposite to each other, the width between each pair on the north side being about 15 ft., and on the south from 13 ft. 2 in. to 14 ft. 2 in.—and this in spite of the fact that the two arcades must either have been built at once or within a few years of each other, the date of commencement being about 1180, and the execution of the work probably occupying about ten years. Three arches and three columns on the north, with the western respond, belong to this period, and four arches with four columns and both responds on the south ; the two eastern arches on the north side and the easternmost arch and half the easternmost column on the south representing an extension eastwards of the nave about two hundred years later. It would appear probable that the church before 1180 consisted of an aisleless nave, the same width as the present, and about 70 ft. long, with a long chancel, possibly a low central tower and almost certainly shallow transepts. There is no proof of the early church, which was probably here in the 11th and 12th centuries, having been of stone, excepting a fragment of interlaced carving preserved in the room over the vestry,[318] but it seems likely that the arcades were pierced through existing walls.[319] There is practical certainty that they represent the church re-edified on an extended plan by Hamelin Plantagenet, half-brother to Henry II, who in 1164 acquired the title of Earl de Warenne and Surrey by marriage with Isabel, the first earl's great-granddaughter. The character of the work and its resemblance to the dated work (1175–8) in the quire of Canterbury Cathedral sufficiently fix the date at about 1180, and the south arcade as the later of the two. The western respond of this is a square pier, with very peculiar foliage to its square capital, exactly like a similar square respond-capital in the quire of Canterbury Cathedral. The column next to this, which is octagonal, has a singularly beautiful capital, with moulded abacus of octag-

onal form, the bell of the capital being carved with foliage in a mixture of the English trefoil and the French 'Corinthianesque' variety so well represented at Canterbury. The second column—circular, with a round capital—has ruder foliage of a more experimental type curiously like one of the capitals at Carshalton Church, where the work generally resembles this and is evidently by the same masons.[320] The third column is of a kind of quatrefoil plan, the four 'foils' being flat segments of a circle joined by sharp hollows, which at first sight look as though intended to receive slender marble shafts, but the evidence of the capital, the necking of which is on the same plan, negatives this idea. Here the carving is an experimental sort of stiff-leaf consisting of a row of knops on separate stalks, and in this case alone the upper member of the abacus is square-edged in section, with pear-shaped members below, all the other abaci excepting that of the west respond of the north arcade having rounded or pear-shaped members, the work recalling in these and other respects the coeval quire arcades of New Shoreham Church, Sussex. The respond of this south arcade, of octagonal section, was turned into a whole pillar when the nave was extended eastwards in the 14th century, and the eastern half of the capital has been fashioned in accordance with the prevailing style, but a crosslet carved upon the south face of the cap is modern, having been cut by a workman in 1845 out of a projecting knob of stone originally hidden in the west wall of the demolished transept. Both arcades were practically rebuilt stone for stone at the later restoration by Sir Gilbert Scott, and a piece of interesting evidence was then obliterated in the shape of a vertical joint from top to bottom of this hybrid pillar, by which the two dates were clearly displayed. The eastern arch, which has no respond, but dies into the chancel arch pier, is of two hollow-moulded orders, with a deep hollow between. What gives the original arches of this south arcade additional interest is that the outer of their two orders is carved with conventional palm-branches which form an ornamental band all round, exactly as in the arches of the north quire arcade at New Shoreham, the only instance of the employment of this ornament now remaining in Surrey, although formerly it was to be found as the hood-moulding to the prior's doorway at St. Mary Overy, Southwark.[321] All the bases have been restored, from evidence found by Sir Gilbert Scott. The arches themselves are pointed, and have a pear-shaped member on the angles of the inner order, and a quirked hollow to the outer order on the aisle side.

On the north side the arcade is somewhat differently treated, and probably was not begun till the south arcade was finished. Its arches, also pointed, are of two orders, but with narrow chamfers in place of mouldings, stopped just above the springing ; the western respond also is semicircular on plan instead of square as on the south side, the three succeeding columns being alternately octagonal and circular, and the fourth or easternmost, which, with the two eastern arches, belongs to the period 1380–1420, is again

[318] This fragment may be only a piece of a coffin lid of 9th or 10th-century date, re-used as old material, and may well have been laid down originally within or outside a timber church.

[319] The advowson was given by the second Earl of Warenne to the monastery of St. Mary Overy early in the 12th century, and the partially destroyed prior's door and the work in the western bays of the nave of the priory church, now Southwark Cathedral, bears a close resemblance to that of these arcades.

[320] The capital referred to is one thrown out of the church at the recent enlargement.

[321] Crusading influence no doubt accounts for all three cases, as it does also for several instances which occur in Kent along the Dover road, as at Bapchild, Milstead, Frinstead, Rodmersham and Hartlip.

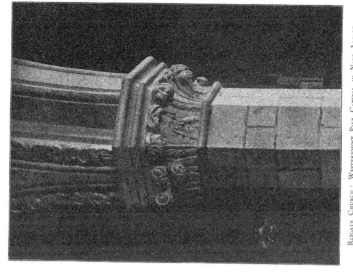

REIGATE CHURCH : WESTERNMOST PIER CAPITAL IN NAVE ARCADE,
SOUTH SIDE

REIGATE CHURCH : SOUTH ARCADE OF NAVE

octagonal. In the capitals the sections of the abaci and the character of the foliage are of the same early type, but not so experimental in design as on the south side. No other work of this interesting early period remains in the church, except a voussoir of one of the entrance doors with quirked hollow and bold bowtell mouldings, now preserved in the chamber over the vestry. The original aisles were comparatively narrow, and the outer walls of the north aisle, with a lean-to form of roof, probably stand on the old foundations; but the south has been rebuilt on a much higher and wider plan, with a span roof of low pitch. The west window of the north aisle is an insertion of about 1280, as is evidenced by its internal hood-moulding and corbel heads.

Work of the succeeding period (c. 1320) is found in the north and south chapels, which are earlier than the main chancel and the arcades which divide them from it, and must therefore have been coexistent with the early transepts, central tower, and chancel. In the north chapel is the only window in the church retaining its original net tracery, of about 1330, in the soft Reigate stone. It is of two lights, wide and lofty, the central ogee-shaped figure of the head being octo-foiled and the ogee heads of the lights having similar foliations. The tracery of the two two-light windows in the opposite south chapel wall, with ogee heads and an ogee quatrefoil over, is modern, but apparently a restoration, although the mouldings and their stops inside are old, and the character of the work suggests a slightly earlier date, c. 1320, which is borne out by that of the niche, or sedile, and piscina in its south wall. Both side chapels probably had sculptured stone reredoses, and remains of that in the north chapel, together with niches right and left of the window and beautiful fragments now in the room over the vestry, date from this period. The buttress at the end of the south wall of the south chapel is an old one restored, but that on the east face is modern; and the east window of this chapel, which in Cracklow's view is shown as with wooden bars in place of tracery, is now fitted with tracery of early 14th-century character.

· Late in the 14th century and at subsequent dates in the 15th century, extensive alterations and extensions took place. The central tower was removed, the present fine and lofty western one taking its place, the south aisle re-built on an enlarged scale, with a new porch, and the north transformed by the insertion of five two-light windows; the chancel was extended eastwards or perhaps only rebuilt, and the arches from it opening into the side chapels were made to take the place of earlier arches. At about the same date the extension of the nave and aisles eastward, which as above mentioned involved the destruction of the early central tower and transepts, was carried out, and this probably caused the chancel to be pushed out a bay further to the east. It also necessitated the building of the present lofty chancel arch and of new arches opening from the nave aisles to the north and south chancels. A striking feature is the series of three steps stretching across the church from wall to wall at the entrance to the chancel and chapels. The south wall of the south aisle contains four handsome three-light windows with arched heads and super-tracery, renewed in Bath stone, and there is another in the west wall. The buttresses are also of this period, with one

exception, which is modern. This south wall was heightened early in the 19th century. The second bay from the west is occupied by a small but well-proportioned porch which has an outer doorway, with pointed arch, except a square label, with traceried spandrels, above which is an image niche.

The north wall of the north aisle is lower, and the windows, of two lights with segmental heads, are plainer than those in the opposite wall. All these works, which externally at least entirely changed the appearance of the church, were probably spread over the period c. 1380 to c. 1480, but the bulk appears to have been done before the end of the 14th century, the extension of the chancel showing many points of resemblance to the contemporary work in Arundel parish church and the Fitzalan chancel, especially in the handsome range of sedilia and piscina, with their ogee-crocketed canopies, pinnacles, and miniature vaulting. These are elaborately coloured and gilt, in attempted reproduction of the original decoration. Adjoining, on the east wall, is a beautiful stone reredos, brought to light in 1845, previously to which it had been concealed by a later altar-piece and a coating of plaster. It is about 8 ft. in height and is in two stages, the lower plain stone panelling consisting of a series of shallow-arched compartments, with a blank space in the centre for the altar; and the upper of ogee-crocketed niches, with finials and slender pinnacles, six narrow ones on either side of a wide central niche, with pedestals in their sills, no doubt originally containing images of the twelve apostles, now represented by modern figures painted on the backs of the niches, and our Lord, or the Blessed Virgin and Child, in the centre. Above is an enriched cornice, with carved paterae and a cresting of the Tudor flower ornament. This reredos is flanked by large and lofty canopied niches, originally containing figures of the patron and another saint; and over them, right and left of the east window, are others which also had images. The whole of this stone tabernacle work, which was most elaborately decorated in gold, silver, and colours, was somewhat harshly restored in 1846, and the original colouring scraped off, while at the same time the great east window, of six handsome lights under a pointed head of 15th-century date, was replaced by one of five lights in an incongruous late-13th-century design, the east windows of the north and south chancels being similarly treated.[123] The result is most unhappy and historically misleading. The north and south windows of the sacrarium, of three transomed lights and dating from about 1400, were fortunately spared and give some idea of the character of the destroyed work. The piers of the quire arches and of those between the nave and aisles and the chancels are of the quatrefoil plan, with hollow mouldings between the shafts, commonly met with in the work of this period, the arches being moulded with the double ogee bands and deep hollows and having grotesque heads of monkeys and other animals as terminations to the hood-mouldings. Besides the three steps at the entrance to the chancel there is another in the middle of the quire, and a fifth at the sacrarium, while the altar is elevated on a pace, and these appear to be the ancient levels.

The tall, handsome western tower, perhaps the best of its period in Surrey, was built before the end of the 14th century. It has lost interest through having

---

[123] The internal jambs and arch of the great east window, however, appear to be those of the former opening.

been refaced with Bath stone by Sir Gilbert Scott, who found the original Reigate stone much weathered and coated with brown cement; but the original mouldings and other features were reproduced with painstaking exactitude, even to a singular group of grotesques upon the wall-surface on the north side. The tower is in four stages, the two lower open to the ceiling, and including a good tracery window of four lights and a large west doorway. In the topmost stage are tall two-light openings under pointed arches, with tracery in the heads, and transoms. The stage below has a small square-headed window. There is a pair of buttresses at each angle, save on the east side, which stop at the string-course below the top stage, and from the north-west angle rises an octagonal stair turret, formerly capped by a lead cupola, which was removed at the restoration, its place being taken by a spirelet and vane. In the cornice beneath the battlements carved paterae are introduced, and the hood-mouldings of the windows have square stops, not very common in Surrey. They occur in a window of this period in the south wall of the nave at Chelsham, Surrey.

The vestry is entered by a doorway in the north wall of the north chancel, over which is a brass plate with a Latin inscription, which may be translated as follows :—

'Be it remembered that in the year 1513 John Skinner, gent., as well as with £10 given for the soul of Richard Knight, 40s. for the soul of William Laker, Esq., with 18s. 6d. for the soul of Allice Holmenden, also with 13s. 4d. for the soul of George Longeville, left to be disposed of by the aforesaid John Skinner, as well as with 10s. and 4d. of his own money for the souls of his own parents, hath for the honour of God caused this porch to be built. On all whose souls God have mercy.—Amen.'[223] This ' porch ' or vestry is of two stories, the upper being fitted up to contain the valuable parish library, established in 1701 by Mr. Andrew Cranston, then vicar both of Reigate and Newdigate, the vicar himself being librarian. It was founded for the use of the clergy of the old rural deanery of Ewell and of the parishioners, and the books now number about 2,300 volumes, a large proportion of which were contributed by all the neighbouring gentry during the first year of the library's existence. The names of Sir John Parsons, Mr. Speaker Onslow, the Evelyns, Mr. Jordan of Gatwick, Scawens and Thurlands are found among the donors. The lesser folk of the town contributed after their fashion to the upkeep of the library and its contents, for, according to the register, Russell the blacksmith gave the bar and fastenings to the window; and Ward, the Reigate carrier, 'cheerfully carried all parcels gratis from London to the library.' There are a few MSS., and some early printed books, but perhaps the most interesting item is the first Lord Howard of Effingham's Prayer Book, the Psalms at the end of the prayers bearing date 1566. The book appears to have been retained till about the middle of the 17th century in the use of a member of the Howard family, for an old metrical version of the Psalms, printed in 1637, is inserted at the end. The coat of arms impressed on the original covers is that of the Howard family, quartering Brotherton, Warren, and Bigod; the initials W.H., the encircling garter, and the old Howard motto, *Sola Virtus invicta*, indicate the

first possessor of the book. The volumes are chiefly standard theology of the 17th and 18th centuries including such controversial works as Bugg's *Quakerism Drooping*; but also including history, classical authors, travels and literature in general. There are a few curious MSS., such as Stephen Birchington's Historical Collections, c. 1382, with the satirical homily on Scottish affairs. This was presented by Mr. Jordan of Gatwick, and presumably came out of Reigate Priory originally, whence also a MS. Vulgate may have come. The library is open for reference or consultation of books on the spot on application to the vicar. In this upper room, as already mentioned, are deposited many architectural fragments found in 1845 and 1877, ancient keys and other curiosities. The door to this vestry from the north chancel has a good pierced tracery lock, with chiselled straps having square rosette bolt-heads coeval with the vestry. Most of the external stonework, which is in the soft local stone, seems to have been renewed, but the three-light window, with square heads and shields as label terminations, and iron stanchions and cross-bars, and the adjoining ogee-headed doorway in the east wall of the lower story, appear to be original features.

The roofs have been greatly interfered with in the successive 19th-century alterations, but the chancel roof, now concealed by an arched and panelled ceiling of wood and plaster, dating from 1845, is ancient (c. 1380) and of massive construction, there being between each pair of rafters a plank of oak with the remains on the whole of decoration in vermilion. Its original tie-beams have been removed and iron tie-rods substituted. The south chapel roof is of early 14th-century date, but is concealed by modern boarding, leaving the heavy cambered tie-beam and king-post visible, the latter having a capital and base, moulded in a peculiar fashion. The roof of the north chapel is modern, as are also those of the aisles and the greater part of the nave roof; but the original timbers of late 14th-century date in the latter have been grouped together at the western end. All the tie-beams are modern, the old ones having been sawn off early in the 19th century, much to the injury of the fabric. The three screens extending across the openings to the chancel and chapels are good examples of 15th-century woodwork although much restored. They are of oak, heavily moulded with traceried and boarded lower parts, and tracery in the heads of the square upper panels. The moulded and nail-studded oak doors in the west doorway are original.

The church must have been rich in painted decoration, on walls, roofs, and fittings, but nothing of this is now visible. A record has fortunately been preserved of the original decoration upon the stone reredos and the adjoining niches,[224] giving the chief colours as blue, vermilion, and green, with powderings of stars, rosettes, and fleurs de lis in gold and silver. 'The centre niche is coloured vermilion, powdered with silver stars. The thirteen pedestals are green ornamented with rosettes of gold. The niches on each side' of the centre '. . . are coloured vermilion, but without stars.' The groined canopies were coloured blue, the bosses being gilt. 'The background above the niches is filled with a flowing pattern of great elegance upon a slate-coloured ground, grey stalks, and grey and red flowers; a sash of red

[223] Rev. J. W. Pickance, 'Reigate Church and Monuments,' *Surr. Arch. Coll.* xi, 194. Corrected from the inscription. [224] *Brit. Arch. Assoc. Con.* vol, 1845, p. 256.

and gold running above, being coloured cobalt, is divided by gold paterae, each space being charged with two silver palm branches with the stems together. The foliated crest is gilt. The buttresses and pedestals of the four large niches,' i.e. those right and left of the window, ' are painted murrey colour, and have silver panels on them, ending in ogee heads, with singularly ugly tracery and silver flowers springing from the apex of each ogee. The triangular cinquefoil heads above terminate with a buttress and crocketed finial in the centre, and terminate below in a gilt rose. The backs of these four niches are painted blue, . . . with a diaper composed of thin gold embossed, four leaves making a pattern, which was again powdered with silver stars of an inch and a half diameter, having six rays, each ray embossed and laid on separately ; ' under these four niches were apparently the names of the saints whose images they were made to contain, the letters RIE—probably part of the name MARIE being visible under one of them. ' On one of the twelve small niches, that to the right of the centre, the letters IHC are very plainly to be seen in gold upon the pedestal.' ' A very fine encaustic tile was found in the rubble work with which the niches were stopped up, and an octagonal column and capital of about six inches in diameter painted all over each surface of the octagon, having flowers and crosses alternately of red and silver, and upon the angles between them lozenges of blue.' The canopied niches of the north chancel, remains of which were brought to light in 1845, and also a fine stoup to the east of the south door in the aisle, in 1873, were found to have been richly coloured and gilt. The shields with painted coats of arms on the chapel ceiling are modern.

There is no ancient glass remaining in the church, and the modern stained glass is not of a very high class ; the east window in particular, which dates from 1845, is interesting as an early essay in the revived art of glass painting, but in itself is very ugly, and the same may be said of the east window of the south chapel.

The font, at the west end of the south aisle, is modern, and copied from an unfortunate model, the octagonal bowl and stem being carved with flamboyant tracery and the bowl with twenty-four grotesque heads leering and putting out their tongues. In old work this sort of thing might be deemed quaint, but in a modern font it is surely rather childish. The pulpit, lectern, altar, and quire-stalls are modern, but some carvings imported from Belgium are worked up into the latter. The large organ almost fills the western part of the north chapel, hiding the large monument on its northern wall. All the seating in the church is modern. The oldest monument in the church is a stone coffin lid, of 13th or 14th-century date, now lying in the tower.

The John Skinner who helped to build the vestry had an inscription in his memory, no longer to be found : ' Orate pro animâ Johñ Skynner generosi qui obiit 8 die mensis Martii, 1516, anno regis Henrici octavi octavo, cuJus aniē propicietur Deus.—Amen.' Another formerly existing inscription ran :

' Here lieth buried Mary, the wife of George Holmeden, of Longfield, in the Countie of Surrey, gent., and one of the daughters of John Skynner, late of Rigate Esq., deceased, while he lived, who departed this mortal life at Riegate, 1578.' There was also formerly a monument containing various escutcheons, viz., Skinner, impaling Colcoke, the same impaling Barley, Newdigate, Poyntz, &c., and bearing the inscription on brass :

' This monument was erected by Alice, one of the daughters of John Poyntz, of Alderley, in the County of Gloucester, Esq. in memorie of hir loveing husband Joh Skynner, Esq., the onely sonne of John Skynner Esq., one of the Clerk-controvlers of the household to the high and mightie Prince Queene Elizabeth, which John deceised the 19 day of May, A.D. 1584.'

This john Skinner represented Reigate in the Parliament of 14 Elizabeth, and his monument is referred to again by Manning and Bray [225] as follows : ' At the east end of the north chancel is a large altar tomb of Sussex marble, on each side are 3 coats of arms, and one at the end, but entirely defaced. The inscription also round the edge (if in reality there ever was one) is totally illegible.' [226] On a brass plate in a gravestone in the chancel, prior to 1804, was inscribed :—' Orate pro Anima Katherine Skynner Vidve, nuper uxoris johannis Skynner Armigeri que obiit viii. die Septembris Ao. 1545. Cujus a'ie propicietur Deus. Amen.' Another bore the following :—' Pray for the soule of Elizabeth Skynner, second wife of james Skynner, of Rigate, Esq., which Elizabeth deceased the 29 of Avgvst in the yeare of ovr Lord God 1549. On whose soule Christ have mercy. Amen.' And on another were the words : ' Here lieth buried James Skynner of Rigate in the Countie of Surrey, Esquire, which died the xxx. day of July in the year of ovr Lord God 1558. Upon whose sovle ovr Lord have mercy. Amen.' None of these inscriptions are now known to be in existence. The Skinners became possessed of the impropriation of the rectory of Reigate at the dissolution of the Priory of St. Mary Overy, Southwark.

The Elyots of Reigate and Albury, who were connected by marriage with the Skinners, left a tomb which till 1845 stood against the north wall of the sacrarium, but was then taken down, its beautiful canopy destroyed, and the remains, including the recumbent figures of the two Richard Elyots, father and son, who lived at the mansion called the Lodge and died respectively in 1608 and 1612, placed in the north chancel.[227] The statue of the father, with hands joined, in

ELYOT. Azure a fesse or.

prayer, is a good piece of work. Upon the front of this tomb were the kneeling figures of Rachel, widow of Richard Elyot, senior, daughter of Matthew Poyntz, of Alderley, Gloucestershire, and their six surviving daughters.

[225] Hist. of Surr. i, 319.
[226] Rev. J. W. Pickance (' Reigate Church and Monuments,' Surr. Arch. Coll. xi, 195) quotes from an annotated copy of Manning and Bray, Surr., a pencil note by Ambrose Glover to the effect that this monument was 'taken down by Mr. (Bryant), the antiquary mentioned in the preface to Manning and Bray, and literally broken to pieces. The inscript.on was then gone.'
[227] Richard Elyot the younger was in the service of Henry, Prince of Wales, elder brother of King Charles I.

Close by this in the sacrarium was the tomb, with a canopy of alabaster or coloured freestone, of Katherine the elder, erected by her sister Rachel, wife of Roger Trappes, late of Chatham.[228] The kneeling figure, a good example of the dress of the period, and finely carved—the features showing a family likeness to those of the other Elyot effigies—is now very incongruously placed in the niche, or sedile, in the south chapel. She 'put off this mortal life at her age of 28 years,' A.D. 1623. Above these Elyot tombs in the sacrarium was a tablet to Sir Edward Thurland, kt., solicitor to James, Duke of York, afterwards James II, and a baron of the Exchequer.[229] His only son Edward was married to Elizabeth, another daughter and co-heiress of Richard Elyot, who died in 1641. Edward died 1682, his son Edward Thurland, gent., in 1687, leaving three sons, the eldest of whom, Edward, 'married Frances daughter of Sir Edward Alford of Offington, Sussex.' Frances died in 1694, and their son Edward, the last of the race in the male line, 19 December 1731, aged 62. Their tombstones lie before the altar.

On the left of the Elyot tomb, at the east end of the north chapel, is that of Sir Thomas Bludder and his wife Mary, the daughter of Christopher Herries, esq., of Shenfield, Margaretting, Essex. Sir Thomas, who was First Commissioner of the Victualling Office in the reign of James I, purchased the manor of Flanchford (q.v.) His wife died Saturday, 25 October 1618, and he just a week later. In a window sill in the north chancel is the diminutive figure of a female child, removed from its position at its parents' feet on this monument. Over the vestry door was the tablet to the memory of Sir Thomas Bludder, the younger (died 29 September 1655), erected by his third wife, Elizabeth daughter of Robert Bret.

There is a small brass inscription on the north wall of the north aisle : 'To the memory of Anthony Gilmyn. 23 August 1575.' It is said that there was formerly a second tablet bearing this inscription on the north side of the chancel.

The monument to Richard Ladbroke, esq., of Frenches (d. 1730), unfortunately almost entirely hidden from view by the organ, is a fine piece of 18th-century allegorical sculpture, costing £1,500. It stands against the western part of the north wall of the north chapel. That 'zealous member of the Church of England' is habited in Roman costume and attended by justice and Truth, with angels, and trumpets, suns and palm-branches.

There is a monument, formerly in the south chapel, but now in the bell-ringers' chamber, to Lieut. Edward Bird, d. 1718, whose claim to fame rests on the fact that he 'had the misfortune to kill a waiter near Golden Square,' in a disreputable tavern, and was hanged for this deed in February 1718, thereby achieving what a writer unkindly calls 'a County History immortality.' Bird, who was a lieutenant

in 'the Marquis of Winchester's regiment of horse,' appears against a background of warlike instruments, a half-length figure, truncheon in hand, in armour, full-bottomed wig, with a cravat round his neck, which popular belief has converted into a halter.[230]

In a large vault beneath the chancel [231] lie buried Lord Howard of Effingham and the first and second Earls of Nottingham. It is strange that although Lord Howard left directions that a monument should be raised to him, neither he nor his family had been commemorated in this fashion, until in 1888, the tercentenary of the defeat of the Spanish Armada, a brass tablet was set up on the south wall of the sacrarium in memory of Elizabeth's famous Lord High Admiral. There are three lead coffins in the vault, standing one upon another, and 'the lowermost of the three is supposed to contain the body of the first Lord Howard of Effingham, who died in 1573, as the other two are known by their inscriptions.' [232] One of the other coffins bears the following inscription : 'Heare lyeth the body of Charles Howarde, Earle of Nottinghame, Lord High Admyrall of Englande, Generall of Queene Elizabethe's Navy Royall att Sea agaynst the Spanyard's invinsable Navy, in the year of our Lord 1588 ; who departed this life att Haling Howse, the 14 daye of December, in ye yeare of oure Lorde 1624. Œtatis sve 87.'

There are many other tablets and other memorials in the church and bell-chamber, but of no special interest.

A few masons' marks and other scratchings are visible internally, as in the porch, where interlaced triangles are found, and the soft Reigate stone has in general preserved the axe and broad chisel tooling in the early work of the nave arcades.

The eight bells were recast in 1784, but the first bears date 1789. Their inscriptions record consecutively the names of the donors, contributors, vicar, churchwardens and founder, Robert Patrick of London. In the Edwardian inventory it is recorded that there were ' In the steple iiij belles and ij hand belles.'

The plate is modern, with the exception of a silver spoon-strainer, of c. 1770, resembling one at St. John's, Richmond, being originally intended for removing obstructions from the spout of a teapot.

The registers, which commence in 1546, contain many entries of exceptional interest relating to the Howard interments.[233]

The churchyard is of great size and is still used for interments. It contains many 18th-century and later monuments, among them an obelisk to Baron Maseres (d. 1824), the editor of some valuable tracts relating to the periods of Elizabeth and Charles I.

The chapel of St. Cross on Reigate Heath was formerly known as Mill Chapel, the original building used having been a mill. There is also an iron church on the heath. These are both served from the church.

The church of St. Mark, built in 1860, is in stone in 14th-century style, with chancel, nave, aisles, transepts, and tower with a slender spire.

[228] Manning and Bray say 'alabaster,' but Ambrose Glover says 'freestone.' The inscription is given at length by Manning and Bray.

[229] Mr. R. F. D. Palgrave (Handbook to Reigate) writes : ' Even the stone in honour of Sir Edward Thurland, a faithful servant of Charles I, and an esteemed friend of Jeremy Taylor, has been swept away, though

his were those " silent excellencies," which so specially need commemoration.'

[230] The story is not without its true pathos. Bird seems to have sunk into dissipated courses owing to being left a widower at twenty-two years of age. His mother on every anniversary of his execution came and shut herself up alone in the church for hours.

[231] This vault, belonging to the manor of the Priory, was 'made by the Lord Howard of Effingham, the first grantee of that estate.' Manning and Bray, Hist. of Surr.

[232] Ambrose Glover, MS. Hist. of the Priory.

[233] See Surr. Arch. Coll. xi, 189-201.

A mission church in Nutley Lane was built and endowed as a chapel of ease to St. Mark's, chiefly at the cost of the late Mr. W. Phillips.

The church of St. Luke, South Park, was built in 1871 in a style similar to that of St. Mark's.

St. John the Evangelist, Redhill, built in 1843, is of white brick and Caen stone. It was restored, the chancel rebuilt, and the roof raised, and a new front built in 1889 by the late Mr. J. L. Pearson. The tower and spire were completed in 1895. The seven stained windows in the chancel were finished in 1907. The church was originally designed in 15th-century style.

St. Matthew's Church, Redhill, is in Reigate and Bath stone, in 14th-century style, with a tower and spire.

Holy Trinity Church, Redhill, in memory of the Rev. Henry Brass, vicar of St. Matthew's, is of red brick and Bath stone in 15th-century style. It is still incomplete.

ADVOWSONS No church is mentioned in the Domesday Survey of Reigate, but in the latter end of the 12th century, Hamelin Earl Warenne with his wife Isabel, great-granddaughter of the first Earl Warenne, granted the church of 'Cherchesfeld' to Southwark Priory.[234] The right of presentation remained with the successive priors until the dissolution of the house in October, 1539.[235]

A vicarage had been ordained before 1291.[236] The vicar was to provide a second priest.[237] In 1347 Bishop William of Wykeham issued a monition to the parishioners against forsaking their parish church to attend mass at the chapel of Reigate Priory.[238]

After the surrender of the priory the advowson was still held by the successive owners of the rectory (q.v.), but, perhaps in 1724, it was separately sold to the Rev. John Bird, then vicar.[239] His executors, widow, and his widow's second husband, presented successively till 1782, unless it was the son of the last who then presented. The Rev. Geoffrey Snelson, instituted in

1782, married a daughter of the patron, and inherited the advowson. His wife Mary joined with Anne wife of John Marshal in a conveyance of it to William Bryant in 1788,[240] but it reverted to the Snelson family, who owned the benefaction by Brayley wrote, c. 1842. It is now in the hands of the Church Patronage Society.

The other churches of which particulars have been given are all in the gift of the Bishop of Rochester.

CHARITIES Smith's Charity was formerly distributed in Reigate as in other Surrey parishes, but it has been diverted to the school.

1663 : Mrs. Philippa Booker left £6 14s. yearly for twelve poor women over sixty. James Relf about doubled the benefaction at an unknown date.

1673 : Mrs. Magdalen Cade left £100 for bread, since applied for apprenticing boys and girls.

1698 : Robert Bishop left two houses for bread, and one house for teaching poor boys ; both since applied to the school.

1717 : Mrs. Susanna Parsons left £2 yearly to poor girls in the charity school, or in default to poor widows.

1718 : John Parker left £500 invested in land for the school.

1730 : Richard Ladbroke left £5 yearly for keeping up family monuments, the residue for bread. This has been since employed for apprenticing. He also left £1 yearly for repairing the church bell ropes.

William Cooke, at an unknown date, left money for bread in Reigate and Buckland charged on a long leasehold which expired in 1862, when the annuity ceased.

1820 : Francis Maseres, Cursitor baron of the Exchequer, gave £1,010 to provide for sermons after evensong in Reigate Church, and for bread to the poor.

1835 : Sir James Alexander left £200 for the poor. — Charrington, esq., left a charity, extinct by the cessation of long annuities in 1860.

[234] See the account of the Rectory Manor.
[235] Index to Winton. Epis. Reg. ; Egerton MSS. 2031–4, *passim*.
[236] *Pope Nich. Tax.* (Rec. Com.), 208. The church was valued at £13 6s. 8d. ; the vicarage at £5.

[237] Egerton MS. 2033, fol. 29 ; *Wykeham's Reg.* (Hants Rec. Soc.), ii, 438.
[238] Ibid. ii, 220–1.
[239] Monument to Mr. Bird. Manning and Bray (op. cit. i, 323) state that he had purchased it in 1715, possibly a misprint for 1725, for the owners of the

rectory had it in 1724 (Recov. R. Trin. 10 Geo. I, rot. 44). John Bird returned himself as patron in March, 1725 (Visit. Answers, MS. at Farnham). If the purchase was in 1725 it was therefore before March of that year.
[240] Feet. of F. Surr. Hil. 28 Geo. III.

THE HUNDRED OF COPTHORNE[1]

CONTAINING THE PARISHES OF

ASHTEAD	EPSOM	LETHERHEAD
BANSTEAD	EWELL	MICKLEHAM
CHESSINGTON	FETCHAM	NEWDIGATE (part of)
CUDDINGTON	HEADLEY	WALTON ON THE HILL

This hundred has undergone some change in its area since 1086,[2] when it included part of Weybridge, the rest being entered under its later hundred of Elmbridge, and also West Betchworth, which is now in Wotton Hundred. 'Mideham,' the identification of which is uncertain, was in Copthorne.[3] Newdigate is not named in Domesday, and Chessington was included in the hundred of Kingston.

Copthorne was a royal hundred, and remained in the hands of the Crown, though leased for 21 years to Thomas Jenkins in 1617.[4] In a subsidy roll of

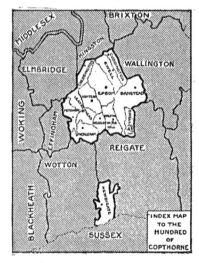

the 14th century it was said to be worth £47 15s. 6¼d., and with Effingham Hundred it was assessed for ship - money at £136 16s. 4d. in 1636.[5]

The honour of Wallingford extended into the hundred at Chessington,[6] and in 1300 the Earl of Cornwall was said to have 4s. from a view taken here at Easter, and pertaining to the honour.[7] The Abbot and convent of Chertsey[8] had view of frankpledge in Horton in Epsom, and Robert Darcy received a similar grant from Edward III for his lands in Letherhead.[9] John D'Abernon had view of frankpledge at Fetcham in 1279,[10] and in the same year presentment was made that his father William D'Abernon had withdrawn his suit at the hundred court for land in Headley.[11] The grant in 1547 to John Rychbill of the land of the Abbot of Boxley in Chessington included view of frankpledge.[12]

---

[1] This list is taken from the *Pop. Ret.* of 1831.
[2] Ibid. 325.
[3] *Plac. de Quo Warr.* (Rec. Com.), 741.
[4] Chart. 1–20 Hen. VI, no. 26.
[10] *Plac. de Quo Warr.* (Rec. Com.), 747.
[12] Pat. 38 Hen. VIII, pt. iii, m. 8.

[4a] Pat. 15 Jas. I, pt. xxxi.

[5] *V.C.H. Surr.* i, 308, 319, 320–1.
[6] Ibid. 442.
[7] Inq. p.m. 28 Edw. I, no. 44.
[8] Ibid. 2 Edw. III, no. 20.
[11] Assize R. 876, m. 47.

246

ASHTEAD

Stede (xi cent.), Akestede (xiii cent.), Ashstede (xiv cent.), Asshested (xv cent.).

Ashtead is a village 2 miles south-west from Epsom, a mile and a half north-east of Letherhead. The parish measures 3 miles from north-west to south-east, and rather under 2 miles from south-west to north-east, and contains 2,645 acres.

The parish lies in the normal way for parishes on the north side of the chalk downs, with one end upon the chalk, the village and church upon the narrow belt of the Woolwich and Thanet beds, and the other extremity reaching on to the London Clay, which rises in Ashtead Common to a height of 270 ft. On the common is a spring of the nature of the Epsom well. Here there is a large extent of open common and wood, but the open fields and open chalk land pastures at the south-eastern part of the parish have been inclosed.

The parish is mainly agricultural, but there are brickfields and special brick and tile manufactories at the Ashtead Brick Works in Barnett Lane. Messrs. Peto & Radford have electrical accumulator works, and Messrs. Cadett & Neall photographic dry-plate and paper works.

The road from Epsom to Letherhead passes through Ashtead, and the joint London and South Western Railway and London, Brighton, and South Coast Railway Companies' line has a station at Ashtead opened by the London and South Western Railway Company in 1859.

On the top of Ashtead Common is a camp, or inclosure. Coarse hand-made pottery, calcined flints, and flint flakes occur in and near it. Round the church is a well-defined rectangular inclosure. In 1830, when the church was restored, a considerable number of Roman tiles and part of a hypocaust were found in the inclosure, with fragments of tile ornamented with a raised pattern, and in one case figures of animals. The last is figured by Brayley.[1] The trackway or road across the downs, described under Mickleham, is about half a mile to the north-east. The rectangular inclosure, with these Roman remains, is worth comparison with the rectangular inclosure at Pachevesham described under Letherhead. The fields immediately outside it are called the Upper and the Lower Bury Fields.

Samuel Pepys records in his diary a visit to Ashtead, his 'old place of delight,' where he was obliged to stay owing to Epsom being too full to accommodate any more visitors. He found a lodging with a Farmer Page in a little room in which he could not stand upright. The house of a cousin of his, who had formerly lived in Ashtead, was then occupied by Mr. Rouse, called the Queen's Tailor.

In a map of the late 18th century,[2] Ashtead Common Field is marked south of the church and south-east of the village. It was inclosed before the Tithe Commutation of 1836, but no Act or Award is known.

Ashtead Park, the seat of Mr. Pantia Ralli, is a house built late in the 18th century in place of the old house which stood rather nearer the church.

Ashtead Grange is the seat of Mr. W. T. Birts; Forest Lodge of Mr. Augustus Meyers; Caen Wood of Captain Warner. Many new houses are springing up about Ashtead.

Near the station is an extensive recreation ground, which is a favourite resort of schools and other parties from London during six months of the year. There is an institute and a working-men's club in the village.

The parish is supplied with gas by the Epsom Company, and with water by the Letherhead Company.

The chapel of ease of St. George, near the station, was built in 1905. It is a red brick building in the 13th-century style. There is also a Baptist chapel, which was built in 1895.

The old Rectory House at Lower Ashtead was replaced by the present house, the gift of Colonel Howard, in 1823. The rectory was enlarged in 1845.

In 1725 Mr. David White, who had been a bricklayer of Ewell, left South Sea Annuities for the education of 8 poor children. A school was then started, the first in the parish.[3] The present school was built in 1853, at the cost of the Hon. Mrs. Howard, and enlarged in 1861, 1895, and 1900. Another school was built in 1906. They are both under the County Council.

MANORS A manor of *ASHTEAD* is mentioned in Domesday: it had been held by Turgis of Earl Harold, and after the Conquest it became the property of the Bishop of Bayeux, who granted it to his canons of Bayeux.[4-6]

If this was the manor of Great Ashtead, the canons must have lost it before the end of the 13th century,[7] for it is then found as part of the honour of Reigate, being held of the Earls of Surrey in socage by the service of 1 mark.[8] It so continued for a century, until in 1397 Richard Earl of Surrey and Arundel, grandson of Edmund Earl of Arundel (who married Alice heiress of the Warennes Earls of Surrey), was attainted and beheaded,[10] and his estates passed to the Crown.[11] Thomas son of the Earl of Arundel was restored to the title, but dying in 1415 without issue, his Warenne estates passed to his sisters and co-heirs. One of these, Elizabeth, had married Thomas Mowbray, created first Duke of Norfolk. Ashtead ultimately remained with the Mowbray family, until John fourth Earl of Norfolk dying (1475) without male issue, his estates passed to his only daughter Anne: she died childless in 1481, and her co-heirs were the representatives of her two great-aunts, the daughters of Thomas Mowbray, first Duke of Norfolk, and Elizabeth Arundel.[12] The estates were divided, and the chief rent payable by the manor of Ashtead came to the Howards, Dukes of

<hr>

[1] *Surr.* iv, 396.
[2] In the possession of Mr. H. E. Malden.
[3] Bishop Willis's Visitation, of that year.
[4-6] *V.C.H. Surr.* i, 304a.
[7] The tenure of the canons probably did not survive the forfeiture of Odo in 1088.
[8] Chan. Inq. p.m. 24 Edw. I, no. 59.
[9] Ibid. 43 Edw. III, no. 19.
[10] G.E.C. *Peerage,* i, 147.
[11] Chan. Inq. p.m. 2 Hen. IV no. 46
[12] G.E.C. *Peerage,* v, 413.

A HISTORY OF SURREY

Norfolk.[13] Thomas the eighth Duke of Norfolk was attainted in 1546, and although he was restored on the accession of Queen Mary, his moiety of the honour was retained by the Crown, and after this the manor was held of the Crown in chief.

At the beginning of the 13th century the manor was held in sub-fee by Henry de Mara, who, dying before 1260, left a daughter or granddaughter Matilda.[14] In 1260 Peter son of Peter de Montfort forcibly took possession, ejecting Walter de la Hyde and his wife Joan from a moiety of the same, which Walter and Joan held by virtue of the wardship of Matilda. Possibly Peter the younger was already at this date the husband of Matilda.[15] In 1286 Peter settled the manor on his son John and the heirs of John by his wife Alice de la Flaunche[16]: this John obtained a grant of free warren in 1292.[17] He leased the manor to his brother William, and died in 1296, before the lease had expired, so that at his death the manor was in the hands of Robert Winchelsey, Archbishop of Canterbury, and the co-executors of William's will.[18] His son John was five years old when he succeeded to the property: he joined in the murder of Piers de Gaveston, but was pardoned and summoned to Parliament, 1313.[19] The following year he was killed at Bannockburn, and, leaving no issue, was succeeded by his brother Peter, who was in holy orders, but who obtained a dispensation, and was knighted.[20] Peter's only son Guy married Margaret daughter of Thomas Beauchamp, Earl of Warwick,[21] a marriage arranged to put an end to many suits which were constantly taking place between the two families, who were related, and whose estates in many places adjoined.[22] Peter settled the manor of Ashtead on Guy and Margaret in tail, with reversion to the Earl of Warwick. Guy died before his father, and his widow took the veil at Shouldham, co. Norfolk,[23] upon which the earl entered into possession, and obtained in 1352 a grant of free warren.[24] He died in 1369, and his son Thomas Beauchamp conveyed the estates to Sir Baldwin Freville and Sir Thomas Boteler, heirs of Peter de Montfort.[25] Freville was son of Peter's sister Elizabeth, who had married Sir Baldwin Freville, and Sir Thomas Boteler was husband of Joan granddaughter of Maud, the other sister, who had married Bartholomew de Sudeley.[26] These two made a partition of the Montfort estates, and the manor of Ashtead fell to the share of Sir Baldwin Freville. He was twice married, and left a son, who died in 1400, leaving a son[28] (two years old) and three daughters. The son died a minor and with-

out issue, and the Freville estates were divided among the daughters,[29] Ashtead remaining ultimately with Joyce wife of Sir Roger Aston.[30] Their son Robert

FREVILLE. Or a cross paty gules.

ASTON. Party chevronwise sable and argent.

held a court as lord of the manor in 1442,[31] and died seised of the manor 1464–5[32]; he was succeeded by his son John, who died in 1483,[33] and whose son, John Aston,[34] was made a Knight of the Bath on the marriage of Arthur, Prince of Wales, 1501.[35] He died in 1522, leaving a son and heir Edward,[36] who granted the site of the manor to Thomas Frank and his wife Agnes for their lives, for a yearly payment of 23 marks: in this grant mention is made of the commons and warrens as belonging to the site.[37] In 1543 Aston granted to the king in exchange for other lands the manor of Ashtead: he discharged the king of all rents except 13s. 4d. yearly payable to the Duke of Norfolk as chief lord.[38]

The following year the king granted the reversion of the manor for 21 years after the death of Thomas Frank and his wife to William Tanner of Nonsuch, rendering yearly £15 9s. 4d.[39] In the same year the manor was augmented by the purchase of lands in Ashtead from Nicholas Leigh, 'the king's servant.'[40]

Philip and Mary (1556) granted to Anne widow of Edward, Duke of Somerset, in full satisfaction of her dower, the reversion of the site of the manor, and also the manor itself, which by an error is described as 'parcel of the lands and possessions lately purchased of the Abbot of Bermondsey.'[41] In 1563 Elizabeth granted to Henry, Earl of Arundel, for the sum of £725 8s., the reversion of the site and manor to hold by the service of one-fortieth of a knight's fee.[42] His son died before him, without issue, and he divided his estates between his two daughters—Joan wife of John, Lord Lumley, and Mary wife of Thomas Howard, Duke of Norfolk. He settled Ashtead on himself, with remainder to the Duke of Norfolk,[43] but the duke being attainted and beheaded in 1572[44]

[13] See grant 1562, also Chan. Inq. p.m. 15 Hen. VIII (Ser. 2), xl, 96.

[14] Coram Rege R. 11, m. 14d; Abbrev. Plac. (Rec. Com.), 152. Matilda is here given as the daughter and heir of Henry de Mara, but according to the pedigree given in De Banco R. 926, m. 427, she was the daughter of Matthew son of Henry.

[15] That they were subsequently married is shown by the above-mentioned pedigree. De Banco R. 926, m. 427.

[16] County Placita, Surr. portf. no. 42, 43; Feet of F. Div. Co. 14 Edw. I, no. 32.

[17] Cal. Chart. R. 1257–1300, p. 428.

[18] Chan. Inq. p.m. 24 Edw. I, no. 59.

[19] Ibid.

[20] Ibid.

[21] Ibid.

[22] Manning and Bray, Surr. ii, 626.

[23] Burke's Dormant and Extinct Peerages (1883), 31.

[24] Chart. R. 26 Edw. III, m. 10.

[25] Manning and Bray, Surr. ii, 626. Peter died in 1367, not 1358 as Manning and Bray say.

[26] G.E.C. Peerage, v, 349. De Mara Chantry, Surr. Arch. Coll. xix.

[27] Dugdale, Baronage, i, 103. William de Beauchamp, brother of Thomas, evidently had a life interest in the manor (ibid.) which probably took effect after the lease of three years made to Thomas by his trustees in 1372. Close, 46 Edw. III, m. 15 (bis).

[28] Chan. Inq. p.m. 2 Hen. IV, no. 46.

[29] See Feet of F. Div. Co. Trin. 13 Hen. VI, no 63.

[30] See Mins. Accts. bdle. 1010, no. 4.

[31] See Ct. R. portf. 204, no. 30, for a court held by him.

[32] Chan. Inq. p.m. 4 Edw. IV, no. 24.

[33] The date of his death is given as 1485 in an inquisition taken in 1512. Exch. Inq. p.m. (Ser. 2), bdle. 1069, no. 4.

[34] Ct. R. portf. 204, no. 31.

[35] Shaw, Knights, i, 145.

[36] Chan. Inq. p.m. (Ser. 2), xl, 96.

[37] See Pat. 2 & 3 Philip and Mary, pt. viii, m. 22.

[38] Pat. 34 Hen. VIII, pt. xii, m. 15; Deeds of Purchase and Exch. (Aug. Off.), c. 49; Feet of F. Surr. Mich. 35 Hen. VIII; Mins. Accts. 34, 35 Hen. VIII.

[39] L. and P. Hen. VIII, xix (i), 648; see also Pat. 2 & 3 Philip and Mary, pt. viii, m. 22.

[40] Pat. 38 Hen. VIII, pt. xxviii, m. 29.

[41] Pat. 5 Eliz. pt. i, m. 46.

[42] Manning and Bray, Surr. ii, 628.

[43] G.E.C. Peerage, vi, 53.

the remainder escheated to the Crown. Philip, Earl of Arundel, son of the duke, prayed the queen to grant him the remainder that he might sell the manor to pay his debts ; [45] she granted the site and demesne lands to William Dixe in trust for him, [46] and in 1582 Philip conveyed these to Lord Henry Seymour, second son of Edward, Duke of Somerset, for £1,390.[47] He sold them to John Ballett,[48] who, according to the plea of Edward Darcy in a suit which took place in 1601, conveyed them in 1593 to Edward Darcy and his wife Elizabeth.[49]

In 1601 Henry Newdigate laid claim to the site and demesnes of the manor on the ground that Philip, late Earl of Arundel, and William Dixe had sold them to Francis Newdigate, second husband of the late Duchess of Somerset. Francis dying without issue was succeeded by his nephew John ; this John conveyed the premises to his son Henry, the plaintiff, and his heirs after him. He affirmed that the deed of conveyance had come into the hands of Edward Darcy, who took possession of the premises ; [50] Edward Darcy evidently proved his title, for he still had the site of the manor in 1605.[51] In 1639 it was in the possession of Christopher Fitzgerald and his wife Mary, who in that year conveyed it to Henry, Lord Maltravers.[52]

Meanwhile the queen in 1595 granted the manor to Elizabeth Darcy and her sons Robert and Christopher for their lives,[53] but James I soon after his accession restored Thomas son of the attainted Philip, Earl of Arundel, to his blood and the title of Earl of Arundel and Surrey,[54] and granted the manor to him,[55] and he probably acquired the site and demesne lands. His mother and he exhibited their bill in Chancery against Richard Turner, Augustine Otway, and others, tenants of the manor, to ascertain the customs depending upon view of the Court Rolls of the manor of Ashtead ; [56] the matter was referred to the Attorney-General Coventry, who settled it as follows :—

1. That the copyholders' estates should be reduced to be estates of inheritance in fee simple, and that in regard thereof the lord of the manor should have two years' value of the copyhold tenements according to a moderate valuation.

2. That all the fines ought to be arbitrable.

3. That heriots ought to be paid for copyholds that have no messuages upon them in the same way as for messuages and lands.

4. That copyholders might take timber upon their customary tenements (except the coppices of which the lords used to have the woods) for reparation of their houses, and for ploughbote, firebote, and other botes incident to the tenements by law and custom, without assignment by the lord's officers, as long as they committed no waste or needless consumption of the timber and woods growing upon their lands.

This opinion was, by the consent of all parties, ratified and confirmed on 20 November 1622 by

John, Lord Bishop of Lincoln, Lord Keeper of the Great Seal, and by a decree in Chancery the defendants and their heirs and assigns were bound to carry out the decision.[57]

Thomas, who in 1644 was created Earl of Norfolk, was succeeded by his son Henry whose son Thomas (1652) settled the manor on Henry, Earl of Kingston, and others in trust for a wife.[58] Charles II restored this Thomas to the title of Duke of Norfolk ; he died unmarried (1677), and was succeeded by his brother Henry.[59] In 1679 a bill was brought before the House of Lords for vesting this manor among other of his estates in trustees for the payment of certain mortgages and debts, with power to sell for that purpose. The bill appears to have dropped ; [60] but in 1680 the duke sold Ashtead Manor to Sir Robert Howard, kt.,[61] son of the first Earl of Berkshire, who the following year received licence to inclose a common-way leading from Epsom to Ashtead, and to hold the same so inclosed to himself and heirs on condition that he provided a similar road elsewhere or on his own land.[62] Sir Robert immediately built a new house, which Evelyn visited in 1684.[63] His only son and heir died in 1701, leaving the manor to his widow Diana, daughter of the Earl of Bradford ; she married William Fielding, and after the death of the son of her first marriage, Thomas Howard, restored the manor, with the site, free fishery, and free warren, to the Howard family, settling it on Henry Bowes, Earl of Berkshire,[64] with remainder to his fifth son, Thomas Howard, in tail male. This Thomas, who eventually succeeded to the earldom of Berkshire, left no son, and the manor of Ashtead passed to the daughter of an elder brother ; she married (1783) Richard Bagot, who assumed the name of Howard and held Ashtead in right of his wife. He rebuilt the manor-house almost completely in 1790. Their only daughter and heir married the Hon. Colonel Fulk Greville Upton, who also took the name of Howard.[65] She survived till 1877. The manor then passed to her cousin, Lieut.-Colonel Ponsonby Bagot. He sold it in 1880 to Mr., afterwards Sir Thomas, Lucas, who sold it in 1889 to Mr. Pantia Ralli, the present lord of the manor.

A park was inclosed before 1650, when it was included in a conveyance of the manor.[66] It is mentioned also in a settlement of 1693.[67] In a survey of Great Ashtead [68] of the reign of Edward VI it is mentioned that the farmers of the site of the manor rendered the equivalent of 12 couple of rabbits and 12 pairs of pigeons, probably in respect of the warren of Ashtead.

By the custom of the manor the copyholds descend to the youngest son,[69] and daughters of copyholders are co-heirs.[70]

LITTLE ASHTEAD, or *PRIOR'S FARM*, a reputed manor, was in the possession of the Prior and

[45] Manning and Bray, *Surr.* ii, 628.
[46] Pat. 23 Eliz. pt. vii, m. 10.
[47] Close, 24 Eliz. pt. xix.
[48] Pat. 36 Eliz. pt. vii, m. 26.
[49] Chan. Proc. Eliz. Nn. 3, no. 31.
[50] Ibid.
[51] Pat. 3 Jas. I, pt. viii ; Feet of F. Div. Co. Trin. 3 Jas. I.
[52] Feet of F. Surr. Mich. 15 Chas. I.
[53] Pat. 37 Eliz. pt. iv, m. 11 ; *Cal. S.P. Dom.* 1595–7, p. 8.
[54] G.E.C. *Peerage*, vi, 54. He was created Earl of Norfolk by Charles I in 1644.
[55] Pat. 2 Jas. I, pt. xvii, m. 37.
[56] Chan. Decrees A 1621, p. 524 d.
[57] Add. MS. 6167, fol. 49.
[58] Feet of F. Div. Co. Trin. 1652.
[59] G.E.C. *Peerage*, vi, 55.
[60] *Hist. MSS. Com. Rep.* xi, App. ii, 139 ; Recov. R. Mich. 32 Chas. II, rot. 256.
[61] Feet of F. Surr. Mich. 32 Chas. II.
[62] Pat. 33 Chas. II, pt. vi, no. 11.
[63] Evelyn, *Diary*, 11 Dec. 1684.
[64] Recov. R. Hil. 1 Geo. II, rot. 124.
[65] Brayley, *Surr.* iv, 394.
[66] Feet of F. Surr. Mich. 32 Chas II ; see Com. Pleas D. Enr. Mich. 32 Chas. II, m. 11–14.
[67] Feet of F. Surr. East. 5 Will. and Mary.
[68] Surv. of Edw. VI. Land Revenue Office, Surr. vol. 2.
[69] Ct. of Req. bdle. 94, no. 8.
[70] Add. MS. 6167, fol. 43.

canons of Merton before 1291, as in the Taxation of Pope Nicholas they were rated 13*s.* 4*d.* in respect of it.[71] In the 14th century reference is found to the Prior of Merton's lands and tenements in Ashtead.[72] The Commissioners of Henry VIII valued the farm at £6 per annum.[73] At the dissolution of the monastery in 1538 it passed to the Crown,[74] and Queen Mary gave it to Anne Duchess of Somerset for life.[75]

In 1578 Elizabeth granted it to Robert Newdigate and Arthur Fountain,'s who afterwards conveyed it to Francis Newdigate, husband of the late Duchess of Somerset. He died without issue, having devised it to Henry grandson of his eldest brother. Henry granted the manor to George Cole (1604),[77] who is mentioned as holding it of the king as of l is manor of East Greenwich, and leaving it by will to his second son Thomas.[78] In 1650 Thomas conveyed it to John Wall in trust for Peter Evans,[79] who died 1661, leaving a son and heir Peter. This Peter conveyed the estate to Leonard Wessell,[80] and it was sold by him to Robert Knightley (afterwards knighted), whose grandson John (1713) suffered a recovery of the manor, and probably sold it to Aquila Wyke,[81] who settled it on his daughter on her marriage with Charles Brown ; she died childless, and it descended to Aquila Dackambe as heir-at-law of Aquila Wyke. His grandson of the same name held it. It is now part of the Ashtead Park estate.

There was a customary messuage in Ashtead called ' le Howse ' *alias* Talworth, and also a tenement called ' Dicks,' which were the subject of a lawsuit in the reign of Queen Elizabeth.[82]

The church of *ST. GILES* has a CHURCH chancel 29 ft. 3 in. by 13 ft. 4 in. inside, north vestry, north chapel (now organ-chamber) ; nave, 53 ft. 2 in. by 18 ft. 9 in. ; north transept, 34 ft. 2 in. deep by 15 ft. 10 in. wide, and a short aisle, 17 ft. 9 in. wide, connecting it with the organ-chamber ; south porch, and west tower 11 ft. 5 in. by 10 ft. 3 in.

A number of Roman bricks mixed with the flint and stone of the south wall of the nave, and a window on the north side with Roman bricks in the head (as at Fetcham), removed in 1862, suggest an early origin for the building, and there is a slight change in the walling west of the south doorway and porch, pointing to the lengthening of the nave before the tower was added. The chancel is not square with the nave, but bends southward, and was probably rebuilt in the 13th century, a lancet window formerly in its walls having been removed, it is said, to the modern vestry.

The arch in the north wall of the chancel appears to be old, and probably opened into a 15th-century

chapel ; but Cracklow's plan (1829) shows the church as consisting only of chancel, nave, north porch, and west tower, the last having been built in the early part of the 16th century. The north transept dates from 1862, and in 1891 a general restoration took place, when the vestry was added, and all the windows which had not previously been modernized were replaced by new work.

The chancel has an east window of three trefoiled lights under a pointed segmental arch, a south-east window of two trefoiled lights, and a square-headed south-west window of three cinquefoiled lights, all the tracery being modern. The chancel arch is also modern, with square jambs and a pointed two-chamfered arch, and the axial line of the chancel is to the south of that of the nave and also deflects to the south.

The nave retains no ancient features beyond the south wall already mentioned, and the south doorway, which is of the 15th century, with moulded jambs and two-centred arch. The jambs inside retain the old draw-bar holes.

The tower is of three stages, and is coated with cement ; its two western angle-buttresses and the south-east stair-turret are of brick ; the west doorway is of two hollow-chamfered orders, and has a three-centred arch in a square head with a modern label ; the door is also old, and has vertical ribs studded with square-headed nails. The window over it is a modern one of three plain lights under a square head, and in the second stage are two modern lancets piercing the west wall. The third stage is lighted on each side by similar lancets, and the parapet is of flint and stone, and is embattled.

The cedarwood of the roofs came from Woodcote Park, and the design is intended to reproduce 15th-century work ; the chancel has arched and foiled trusses and a panelled ceiling with moulded ribs and carved bosses. The nave has traceried trusses with angels at the wall-plates, and is likewise panelled, and the transept has a similar roof ; the faint aromatic smell of the wood is exceedingly pleasant.

The 18th-century altar-table was brought from Woodcote Hall, and has shaped, curved legs, and the octagonal font is of the 15th century, with quatrefoiled panels on the bowl inclosing roses and shields ; on the chamfer beneath are carved faces and shields alternately ; the stem is also panelled and the base moulded, and over it is a tall, modern oak canopy.

The glass in the east window of the chancel comes from Herck near Maestricht, and appears to date from c. 1550 ; the main subject is the Crucifixion, with the figures of St. Mary and St. John ; on each side are panels with (1) St. George and the Dragon, (2) St Anne, the Virgin and Child, (3) an abbess kneeling, behind her a Cistercian abbot with a small dog by his side ; and a shield charged quarterly (1) sable (?) a lion gules ; (2) quarterly 1 and 4 argent a lion sable, 2 sable a lion or, 3 barry of six, over all a lion sable ; (3) gules five fusils in fesse argent ; (4) gules ten

MERTON PRIORY. *Or fretty azure with eagles argent at the crossings of the fret.*

[71] *Pope Nich. Tax.* (Rec. Com.), 206.
[72] *Exch. of Pleas,* Plea R. 25 Edw. III, m. 17 ; 27 Edw. III, m. 8 d.
[73] *Valor Eccl.* (Rec. Com.), ii, 48 ; Dugdale, *Mon.* vi, 248.
[74] See *Mins. Accts.* Surr. rot. 115, m. 33 d. (29–30 Hen. VIII).
[75] Pat. 2 & 3 Philip and Mary, pt. viii, m. 22 ; *Mins. Accts.* Mich. 2 & 3 to Mich. 3 & 4 Philip and Mary.
[76] Pat. 20 Elis. pt. ii, m. 19.
[77] Feet of F. Surr. Hil. 1 Jas. I.
[78] *Chan.* Inq. p.m. (Ser. 2), ccccvi, 56.
[79] Feet of F. Surr. Mich. 1650 ; *Hist. MSS. Com. Rep.* xi, App. ii, 164.
[80] Feet of F. Surr. Hil. 23 & 24 Chas. II.
[81] Brayley, *Surr.* iv, 401.
[82] *Chan.* Proc. Eliz. G g. 4, no. 47 ; G g. 10, no. 49 ; Ct. of Req. bdle. 96, no. 3.

bezants, in dexter chief a canton argent with two embattled bars sable.

In the chancel floor are two small brass inscriptions, the first reading :

> BODLÆI CONJUX, FROMOUNDI FILIA, CHRISTI SERVA SUB HIS SAXIS ELIZABETHA JACET.
>
> UNDER THIS STONE LIES ELIZABETH BEREFTE OF MORTALL LIFE,
>
> CHRIST'S FAITHFULL SERVAUNT FROMOUND'S CHILD AND BODLEY'S LOVING WYFE.
>
> DIED THE 2ND MARCH ANNO DNI 1591.

The other brass is inscribed : HERE LYETH BURYED THE BODYE OF JOHN BROWNE ESQUIER LATE SARGEANT OF HER MAJESTIES WOOD YEARD AND EDITH HIS LATE WIFE W^CH EDITH DECEASED THE . . . OF JULY 1590.

There are several 18th-century and later gravestones. On the north wall of the chancel is a brass plate to Dorothy wife of Robert Quennell, 'Pastor of this church,' 1640 ; and there are other monuments to Henry Newdigate, second son of John Newdigate of Harefield, Middlesex, 1629 ; William Duncomb, rector, 1698–9, and Philadelphia his wife, 1724–5 ; Lady Diana Fielding, daughter of the Earl of Bradford, 1733, and others.

There are eight bells by Mears and Stainbank, 1874.

None of the pieces of the Communion plate are of great age, the earliest being a standing paten of 1710 ;

there are also a cup of 1847, a flagon of 1889, an almsdish of 1847, and a Victorian stand-paten with an illegible hallmark.

The first book of the registers contains baptisms from 1662 to 1698, and marriages and burials, 1662 to 1699 ; the second book has baptisms 1699 to 1784, marriages 1691 to 1754, and burials 1699 to 1783 ; the third contains the printed forms of marriages from 1754 to 1812 ; and the fourth continues the baptisms and burials from 1782 to 1812.

ADVOWSON   The church of Ashtead is mentioned in the Taxation of Pope Nicholas, where it is valued at £13 6s. 8d.[82] The advowson of the church belonged to the lord of the manor. From 1302, and probably before then, a vicar was presented by the rector, whose benefice in 1331 was endowed by the bishop with the small tithes. The last institution of a vicar appears to have taken place in 1482.[83] In 1291 the tithes were held by the executors of the will of William de Montfort,[85] to whom John de Montfort, his nephew and lord of the manor, had leased the manor of Ashtead.[86]

In 1543 Sir Edward Aston conveyed to the king the advowson of the church with the manor,[87] and in the various grants of the manor in this and the three following reigns the Crown always reserved the advowson ;[88] but when James I granted to Thomas Earl of Arundel the manor of Ashtead he must have included the advowson, for the earl held it in 1624.[89]

ASHTEAD CHURCH FROM THE SOUTH-EAST

[82] *Pope Nich. Tax.* (Rec. Com.), 208.
[84] Manning and Bray, *Surr.* ii, 634.
[83] *Pope Nich. Tax.* (Rec. Com.), 209.
[86] See Chan. Inq. p.m. 24 Edw. I, no. 59.
[87] Feet of F. Surr. Mich. 35 Hen. VIII.
[88] See Pat. 2 & 3 Philip and Mary, pt.
viii, m. 22 ; 5 Eliz. pt. i, m. 46 ; 37 Eliz. pt. iv, m. 11.
[89] Feet of F. Surr. East. 22 Jas. I.

In 1619 Peter Quennell presented and again in 1647,[90] the lord of the manor having the alternate presentation in 1639.[91] The MSS. of the House of Lords contain an application for an order for William King to be instituted and inducted to the rectory of Ashtead in 1647.[92] He was a Puritan minister ejected for nonconformity in 1662,[93] when Elkanah Downes was presented to the living by — Downes, merchant.[94] He died in 1683, and the next presentation was by Sir Robert Howard, kt., who had bought the advowson from Henry Duke of Norfolk.[95]

For nearly a century more it remained with the Howard family, as lords of the manor. In 1782 and 1826 the bishop presented, and in 1822 the Hon. F. Grenville.[96] The living is now in the gift of the Rev. F. G. L. Lucas, the present incumbent.

King Edward VI granted to Sir Anthony Archer one acre of land called 'Cotton Acre' in the common field, formerly applied to maintaining a lamp in Ashtead Church.[97]

There was in the parish church a perpetual chantry of the value of 5 marks.[98] This was evidently the chantry established in 1261, when the Prior of Newark undertook to maintain three chaplains in the 'chapel of Estede,' to pray for the soul of Henry de Mara, his ancestors and heirs.[99] The keeping up of the chantry was the occasion for continual litigation, which went on from 1364 till 1493, between the heirs of De Mara and successive Priors of Newark. The dispute began on account of the original endowment of a sum of 250 marks, which presumably the Prior of Newark spent, so that the endowment for chaplains was not forthcoming.[100] It would seem that before 1364 there had been continual irregularity in providing chantry priests, for Bishop Edington had to ordain two in 1346 and two in 1347, which looks as if his predecessor had neglected to fill up vacancies.[101] In 1493 the complainants, John Aston and others, obtained a writ compelling the prior to provide an endowment.[102] No chantry, however, seems to have existed in Ashtead Church at the time of the suppression of the chantries.[103]

Smith's Charity is distributed as in other Surrey parishes.

In 1712 Mrs. Sarah Bond left £500 for the relief of the poor.

In 1733 Lady Diana Fielding left money for the support of six poor widows, for whom a house was built on the Epsom road. It has since been rebuilt for the accommodation of eight poor widows.

CHARITIES

BANSTEAD

Benestede (xi cent.), Banested (xii cent.), Benested and Bansted (xiii cent.), Bendestede (xiv cent.), Bansted (xviii cent.).

Banstead is a village 3½ miles south of Sutton on the east of the road to Reigate. The parish measures 6 miles from north to south, and varies in breadth from 3 miles to a few yards at the southern apex, where it forms an acute angle between Kingswood and Walton. The acreage is 5,552. The whole of Banstead is situated upon the chalk downs, and with Walton and Headley adjoins that row of parishes whose sides lie at the northern front of the downs. The ground rises in places to nearly 600 ft. above the sea level, while much of it is over 400 ft. The soil is chalk, with surface deposits of clay, gravel, and brick-earth.

In 1086 the parish was counted in Wallington Hundred, and it is so entered in the returns of 1316 and 1428.[1] In 1636 it was entered in Copthorne, but Aubrey in 1718 placed it in Croydon Hundred.

Banstead Downs are still a wide extent of open land, though much reduced since the time when they made one unbroken expanse with Epsom Downs, and the old 4-mile race-course, marked on Norden's map, ran from a point between Banstead village and the railway station into the present 'straight' of Epsom race-course.

The downs, now appropriated chiefly for golf, formerly fed sheep in abundance. The old inn in Banstead village, a building which may well date from the 17th century, is called the 'Wool Pack,' a survival of a past trade. In 1324 the Abbot of Chertsey impleaded John de la Lane, bailiff to Isabella the Queen at Banstead, and others, for taking 1,500 of his sheep at Evesham (Epsom), driving them to Banstead and imparking, or, as we say, impounding, them, till from want of food some of them died. The bailiff answered that he took them on Banstead Down by way of distress as the abbot had been impleaded for trespass in the queen's manorial court 'at Banstead, but had not answered. In the king's court, to which the case was transferred, the abbot obtained damages.[2] In 1338 it was ordered that the officers taking wool for purveyance should exact none from the queen's (Philippa's) manors of Witley and Banstead.[3] The high quality of the wool is shown by a petition of the Commons in 1454, in which they prayed that a sack of wool of the growth of Banstead Down might not be sold under 100s., as the price of such wool was greatly decayed.[4] The reputation of Banstead Downs for sheep is referred to by Pope in the Imitations of Horace, and by others.

Historically Banstead Downs were the scene of sport. When Holland's ill-contrived royalist rising of 1648 took place at Kingston, the original plan had included a muster of adherents, as for a horse race, on Banstead Downs. Rumour was rife as to the time of such an assembly being formed, and that Holland had marched thither from Kingston. But in fact he had marched to Dorking, and Major Audeley, who was on his track, went over Banstead

90 See Inst. Bks. P.R.O.
91 See Recov. R. East. 15 Chas. I, rot. 38.
92 Hist. MSS. Com. Rep. vi, App. 177a.
93 Manning and Bray, Surr. ii,635, note L.
94 See Inst. Bks. P.R.O.
95 Feet of F. Surr. Mich. 32 Chas. II.
96 See Inst. Bks.
97 Pat. 3 Edw. VI, pt. iii, m. 29.

98 Manning and Bray, Surr. ii, 634.
99 Feet of F. Surr. 45 Hen. III, no. 158.
100 It was Peter de Montfort, who had thrown up holy orders and married, who first in 1364 betrayed anxiety about the due provision of masses, after he had arrived at seventy years of age.
101 Winton Epis. Reg. Edington, ii, Ord. A, F, and G.

102 De Banco R. 926, m. 427, Mich. 9 Hen. VII.
103 Surr. Arch. Coll. xix, article on De Mara Chantry.
1 Feudal Aids (1284–1431), v, 110, 125.
2 Abbrev. Plac. (Rec. Com.), 346.
3 Cal. of Close, 1337–9, p. 496.
4 Parl. R. (Rec. Com.) v, 275, 1454.

Downs without finding him or the assembly. The rising had in fact exploded prematurely.[5]

There is evidence of races at Banstead as early as 1625,[6] but the subject more properly belongs to Epsom. When the great question of the exclusion of the Duke of York from the succession was before the House of Lords, in 1678, the Duke of Ormonde wrote to Colonel Cooke that he tried to delay the first reading by pointing out the thinness of the House owing to a Dog Match at Hampton Court, and a Horse Match on Banstead Downs. He himself did not attend the Horse Match, where 12 horses ran for 3 plates, 'owners up,'[7] apparently, but he sent a description of it. Two horses fell, one nearly killing his jockey, and 'the Duke of Monmouth escaped narrowly,' so apparently he also was riding.

Hares and partridges were also preserved on the downs. Henry Saunders was made keeper of a portion of the downs at £30 a year under the Protectorate, as a reward for trying to seize a highwayman,[8] and in 1668 a gamekeeper was appointed by the Duchy of Lancaster, at the same salary, to preserve hares and partridges.[9] In 1669 the king was hawking there, it not being then the custom to shoot partridges.[10]

The downs were also used as a muster-place for the Surrey Militia in 1670, when an inspection of the troops was made by the King and Prince Rupert. The formation of a camp of the regular army under the Duke of York or the Duke of Monmouth was discussed in 1678, but it is uncertain whether the plan was carried out.[11]

The parish is now agricultural, with a considerable number of new small houses in it. The road from Sutton to Reigate, the old Brighton road, passes through the parish, traversing Burgh Heath. The Sutton and Epsom branch of the London, Brighton, and South Coast Railway has a station at Banstead, on the downs; and the Tattenham Corner branch of the South Eastern and Chatham Railway cuts through the middle of the parish. Tattenham Corner station, opened in 1901, is on the borders of Banstead.

From its position on the hills Banstead can never have been well watered. There are no streams in the higher and larger part of the parish. The primitive water supply must have depended entirely upon rain and dew-ponds, and the later supply was dependent on wells. The village well is said to be 350 ft. deep. The Domesday Mill was no doubt at Beddington, where there was a mill called Vielmille held of the manor of Banstead in 1318.[12] Similarly the Woodmansterne Mill was at Carshalton. But the absence of a good water supply did not hinder settlement, possibly even very ancient, on the high ground near Banstead. At Great Burgh many neolithic flint implements have been found; and on Banstead Heath, knives, two saws, a borer, an axe-head, seven arrow-heads, and other implements and flakes, implying a considerable settlement.[13] Banstead Downs have been

much disturbed by digging for gravel in the brick-earth, by the making of the Epsom Downs railway, and by the laying out of golf links. But to the west of the road to Sutton, north of the railway bridge, were three barrows, one of which has recently been nearly destroyed. Others are said to have existed, and the remains of one seem to exist close to the railway bridge. An old map, reproduced by Manning and Bray, shows a great many barrows and a long bank about Preston Downs (which are now inclosed), the bank continuing on to the now inclosed Ewell Downs. 'Tumble Beacon,' a large mound crowned with Scotch firs near Nork Park, is an unmistakable barrow, and one of the largest in the county. It used to be the site of a fire beacon, and at the manor court a man was appointed to keep the beacon ready for use. Traces of hut-circles are reported to have been observed on Banstead Downs, but have never been explored and verified. One trace of a more remote antiquity still is undoubted, a fossil oyster shell which the writer himself picked up where the ground had been disturbed. John Evelyn reported that he heard from the Shepherds that near Sir Christopher Buckle's house, that is near West Burgh, 'divers medals have been found both copper and silver, with foundations of houses, wells, &c. Here indeed anciently stood a city of the Romans.'[14]

In 1903 mediaeval remains were discovered south of Banstead Church, consisting of tiles, broken glass, and carved chalk. They are in the St. John's Gate, Clerkenwell, Collection, owing to a supposed connexion with a house of the Hospitallers, who had lands near the church,[15] but possibly they belonged to the manor-house.

At Burgh in this parish there was a church to which rectors were instituted in the 14th and 15th centuries,[16] but there is no evidence of its having been a separate parish from Banstead after 1414. An entry in Wykeham's Register[17] in 1379 speaks of the poverty of the benefice and the ruinous character of the buildings. Aubrey says that the church at Burgh existed in his time,[18-20] and that there had been a chapel of St. Leonard at Preston, mentioned in deeds, which had quite disappeared. Salmon, in 1736, said that the Burgh chapel existed, turned into a barn. The return to Bishop Willis's visitation, 1725, described it as in ruins, no service having been held there within living memory. The ruins of St. Leonard's chapel do, however, still exist, in spite of Aubrey's assertion, in Chapel Copse near Preston, with which manor it was conveyed in 1440. Bergh or Burgh Church was between Little Burgh House and Church Lane, where the foundations remained supporting a barn till about 1880.

Tadworth is a hamlet on the Reigate road, included now in the ecclesiastical district of Kingswood. Tadworth Court was built by Mr. Leonard Wessells in 1700 (see manor).

The land to the north of the village on the edge of the downs was common field as late as 1841.[21]

[5] V.C.H. Surr. i, 418.
[6] The parish registers contain the burial in this year of a man, who in running the race fell from his horse and broke his neck.
[7] Hist. MSS. Com. Rep. vi, App. 740b.
[8] Cal. S.P. Dom. 1657–8, p. 88.
[9] Ibid. 1667–8, p. 353.

[10] Hist. MSS. Com. Rep. xii, App. vii, 46.
[11] Ibid. xi, App. vi, 39; xii, App. v, 44.
[12] Cal. of Close, 1313–18, p. 534.
[13] Neolithic Man in North-East Surr. 132, 167.
[14] Evelyn's Diary, 27 Sept. 1658.
[15] See Survey of 1421, penes Col. F.A.H. Lambert. In 1535 the Prior of St. John's

had 2s. rent in Banstead. Valor Eccl. (Rec. Com.), ii, 404.
[16] Winton Epis. Reg. Pontoise, 230; G. Beaufort Inst. fol. 105–6.
[17] Wykeham's Reg. (Hants Rec. Soc.), ii, 175a.
[18-20] Aubrey, Nat. Hist. and Antiq. of Surr. ii, 97.
[21] Tithe map of 1841.

No Inclosure Act is known, but a great deal of open heath and down has been inclosed.

From 1850 to 1890 the common rights of most of the tenants of Banstead Manor in Leigh and Horley, called *Walda*, i.e. the Weald, in the Survey of 1325, were bought out by private arrangement.

There are a considerable number of gentlemen's houses. Court House is the residence of Mr. B. A. Goad ; Banstead Hall of Mr. D. V. James ; The Larches of Mr. H. Lambert, C.B. ; Tadworth Court of Mr. C. D. Morton ; Banstead Place of Mr. Justice Neville.

There were two private schools in 1725 in which reading and writing were taught. In 1837 Lady Arden of Nork endowed a Church school at Burgh Heath with £205 ; it was rebuilt in 1885, and enlarged in 1901. In 1857 a school, now County Council, was built in the village, and enlarged in 1906. In 1874 a School Board was formed for Banstead, Tadworth, and Kingswood, and in 1875 Tadworth and Kingswood School was opened by the Board. A Wesleyan school was built at Burgh Heath in 1880 The Kensington and Chelsea Pauper Children's School, built in 1880, is in Banstead. It is in a fine position, arranged in 23 separate Homes, with chapel, swimming bath, workshop, laundry, gymnasium, &c. The Boys' Surgical Home was opened in 1895. There is a Church Institute, which was opened in 1906.

A great feature of Banstead is the London County Lunatic Asylum on Banstead Downs, originally opened in 1877. It now consists of nineteen blocks of buildings, with a chapel, and houses for the attendants, and will hold 2,240 patients. It is built of white brick.

There is a Baptist mission room in the village, and a Baptist chapel at Tadworth.

The earliest records of *BANSTEAD MANORS* refer to gifts of land there, the first being a grant, in 680, from Caedwalla, King of Wessex, to Bishop Wilfrid ;[25] a grant made by Frithwald, *subregulus* of Surrey, and Bishop Erkenwald to Chertsey Monastery, in augmentation of the lands given at the foundation of the abbey, the lands mentioned in this second gift being ' xx mansas apud Benesteda cum Suthmaresfelda,'[26] of which confirmation was afterwards made by King Edgar.[27] It does not appear, however, that the monastery held land at Banstead in later times.

Banstead Manor was held, prior to the Conquest, by Alnod, very possibly identical with ' Alnod Cild,' who was one of the largest landowners in Surrey in the time of King Edward.[28] In 1086 Banstead, in Wallington Hundred, was held by Richard of Odo, Bishop of Bayeux.[29] Among the appurtenances of the manor was a house in Southwark worth 40d.[30] Alnod,

when he had held the manor, had had a demesne house in London, which Adam son of Hubert held of Odo.[30] In the time of Henry I Tirel del Maniers gave the church to the monastery of St. Mary Overy,[31] but there is no other proof that he was lord of the manor. It was held in 1169–70 by Nigel de Mowbray, whose wife Mabel had received it from her father as her marriage portion.[30] She seems to have been the daughter of Roger, Earl of Clare ; it is therefore possible that the Richard of 1086 was the great Richard of Tonbridge himself.[30a]

William de Mowbray son of Nigel was one of the barons who opposed King John in 1215 ; he was among the twenty-five who were appointed executors of the great charter, and as such was excommunicated by the pope. He was afterwards taken prisoner at the battle of Lincoln, but, by promising to give Banstead to Hubert de Burgh, lord chief justice, he redeemed his other lands before the general restoration later in the year.[31]

In 1226–7, after William's death, Nigel de Mowbray his son quitclaimed all right in the manor to Hubert.[32] The master and brethren of the Knights Templars were given seisin of the manor in 1233, to hold as security for the debts which Hubert de Burgh owed them.[33] He seems, however, to have recovered the manor, as he died at Banstead in 1243,[34] and, after the death of his widow Margaret, his son John de Burgh held the manor,[35] receiving a grant of free warren there in 1260.[36]

DE BURGH. *Gules seven lozenges vair.*

In 1272 John de Burgh alienated Banstead without royal licence to William de Appeltrefeld,[37] who was ordered to hold until the king's return to England.[38] The next year John de Burgh granted the manor to the king and his heirs, with the exception of lands to the value of 100s. given to Anselm de Gyse.[39] Pending the completion of the conveyances Appeltrefeld was allowed to hold,[40] but John de Burgh finally quitclaimed his right in 1274.[41] Appeltrefeld later surrendered all claim in it, for which remission the king pardoned him 1,000 marks, in which he was bound in the King's Jewry.[42] The king seems to have visited the manor soon after he acquired it. In 1276 the reeve of Banstead rendered account of his expenses there, which included 67s. 11d. for repairs in the hall, kitchen, and other rooms 'against the coming of the king' ; money spent on tiling and carpentering and on the carriage of materials was also accounted for, and 33s. 4d. was spent in making glass windows for the hall.[43] The manor-house was probably close to Banstead Church.

[25] Birch, *Cart. Sax.* i, 81.
[26] Ibid. i, 64. But see under Chertsey for the doubtful character of the early charters. [26] Ibid. iii, 469.
[27] *V.C.H. Surr.* i, 282, note 1.
[26] Ibid. 302a, note 9, and p. 287.
[27] Ibid. 285–6. [30] Ibid. 302b.
[30] Manning and Bray, *Hist. of Surr.* ii, 582. *Rolls in the King's Court* (Pipe R. Soc.), xiv, 42. This roll is, in places, very illegible, but in view of Manning's deeds and those concerning Southmerfield and the Prior of Southwark (see rectory), there seems no doubt that the places

referred to in the roll (. . . feld and . . . stud) are Southmerfield and Banstead, particularly as they are stated to have belonged to Tirel del Maniers and after to Nigel de Mowbray.
[30] Manning and Bray, *ut supra* ; *Pipe R.* 16 *Hen. II* (Pipe R. Soc.), xv, fol. 129.
[30a] Cott. MS. Cleo. Col. iii, fol. 302.
[31] Ibid. Matt. Paris, *Chron. Maj.* iii, 22; *Dict. Nat. Biog.*; *Cal. of Close,* 1231–4, p. 166. It may be noted that he did not derive his name from Burgh in this parish, nor did Burgh derive its name from him.

[32] Feet of F. Surr. East. 11 Hen. III.
[33] Close, 17 Hen. III, m. 13.
[34] Matt. Paris, *Hist. Angl.* (Rolls Ser.), ii, 477 ; *Dict. Nat. Biog.*
[35] Chan. Inq. p.m. 44 Hen. III, no. 14.
[36] *Cal. of Chart.* 1257–1300, p. 27.
[37] *Abbrev. Rot. Orig.* (Rec. Com), i, 20.
[38] Ibid. 21.
[40] *Cal. of Pat.* 1272–81, p. 41.
[40] *Cal. of Close,* 1272–9, p. 64.
[41] Feet of F. Div. Co. East. 2 Edw. I.
[42] *Cal. of Close,* 1272–9, p. 170.
[43] Mins. Accts. (Gen. Ser.), bdle. 1010, no. 8.

On the east of the churchyard there used to be a pit called traditionally the cellars of Hubert de Burgh; but the remains referred to above, which must have belonged to a considerable house, were found south of the church. In October 1275 the manor was assigned as dower to the king's consort, Eleanor of Castile.[44] In 1299 it formed a portion of the dowry granted to Margaret of France on her marriage with the king,[45] and she held until her death.[46] Edward II and Edward III subsequently granted Banstead to their queens as dower.[47] In 1378 Richard II confirmed to Nicholas Carew a grant of Banstead made to him in 1376 for life, 'saving to the Prior of Merton the term granted to him.'[48] This latter grant, made evidently after the death of Queen Philippa, was not, probably, of long duration, as in 1378–9 Carew was tenant of the manor and was ordered to pay 100s. yearly out of the issues of the manor to Stephen de Haddele, yeoman of the chamber to the late queen.[49] In 1390, after the death of Carew, the manor and park of Banstead were granted for life to Sir Reginald Braybrooke; if, however, the issues exceeded 40 marks annually, the surplus was to be paid to the Exchequer.[50]

In 1399 confirmation was made of a grant of 1397 to Sir William de Arundel and Agnes his wife of the same manor,[51] and on their death shortly after without issue, the grant was extended to Sir Richard de Arundel, brother of William, for life,[52] and on his death to his widow Alice, who died in 1436.[54] The king in the following year demised the manor to Sir Ralph Rochefort.[55] The reversion was granted in November 1437 to John Merston and Rose his wife in survivorship,[56] and Rochefort quitclaimed his life interest to them in 1438.[57] In 1448 Henry VI granted the reversion, after the death of John Merston, Rose being already dead, to his new foundation of Eton College.[58] This grant was, however, cancelled by Edward IV, and the manor was resumed in 1464.[59] His queen received the manor as dower in 1466;[60] in 1471 it was given to George, Duke of Clarence,[61] after whose death it remained in the Crown until Henry VIII, in the first year of his reign, assigned it to Queen Katharine.[62] She continued to hold after her divorce, and in 1532 leased the manor to Sir Nicholas Carew for ninety-nine years, should she live so long.[63] This deed seems to have been made at the king's desire, as two months later he granted the re-

Carew. Or three lions passant sable.

version of the manor, after Katharine's death, to Sir Nicholas Carew in fee.[64] When it came to the Crown on the attainder of Carew the manor was annexed to the honour of Hampton Court.[65] It was given back to Sir Francis Carew on the reversal of the attainder in 1549, and continued to be held by this family with their manor of Beddington until 1762, when Sir Nicholas Hacket Carew died.[66] By the terms of his will the manor of Banstead was sold, according to a previous agreement, to Rowland Frye of Beddington,[67] who died in 1777, when his brother and heir William inherited the manor.[68] It passed in 1795 to their nephew Rowland Frye, and on his death in 1801 to the latter's nephew, William Morris Newton, who took the name of Frye,[69] and was lord of the manor in 1808.[70] At his death in 1820 it passed to his daughter, wife of Captain Spencer, and she held in 1841.[71] The property was subsequently sold before 1874 to Sir William Craddock-Hartopp, who held until after 1882. It passed soon after to mortgagees, the trustees of Lady Lavinia Bickersteth, the present lady of the manor. The manor of Banstead included extensive holdings in Horley and Leigh. Sir William Craddock-Hartopp between 1874 and 1878 paid over £13,000 to buy up rights over Banstead Wastes from the following lands: Part of Leigh Place, Dunshott, Flatguns, Sawyers and Skeats, in Leigh, and Horshill, part of Christmas Farm, West Green, Tylers, Fetheridge, Watts, Gawlers, Axes, Crutchfield, Flanchford, Rydens and Banfield, in Horley,[72] a total of 720 acres. Woolvers Farm, Stumblehole, Collendean Farm, and Duxhurst were also in Banstead Manor.[73]

The first mention of the *PARK* of Banstead occurs in 1299,[74] when it was included with the manor in the grant made to Margaret of France by the Crown. It was probably imparked after Banstead had been granted to the king by John de Burgh in 1274. An action for trespass in the queen's park was brought in 1305.[75] In 1348 and 1349, when Queen Philippa held the manor, a writ of aid for one year was granted to the clerk of the great wardrobe to enable him to have timber brought to her wardrobe in La Rioll, London, from her park at Banstead.[76] In 1439 John Merston and Rose, then holding Banstead, received licence to inclose the park, stated to be in great need of repair, with paling and hedge, and to cause trees and oaks required for the purpose to be felled both within and without the park, under the survey of the Prior of Merton.[77] The park was included in the grant in fee made to Carew in 1532.[78] In 1623 John Lambert received a lease of the part of the park called Banstead Old Park.[79] The manor-house, which succeeded the older manor-house near the

[44] *Cal. of Chart.* 1257–1300, p. 192.
[45] *Cal. of Pat.* 1292–1300, p. 452.
[46] Ibid. 1301–7, p. 355; 1307–13, p. 216; 1313–17, p. 135.
[47] Ibid. 1317–21, p. 115; *Cal. of Close,* 1318–23, p. 149; 1318–23, p. 57; *Cal. of Pat.* 1327–30, p. 476; 1330–4, p. 55; 1334–8, p. 206.
[48] *Cal. of Pat.* 1377–81, p. 143; Chan. Inq. p.m. 7 Ric. II, no. 14.
[49] Close, 2 Ric. II, m. 35.
[50] *Cal. of Pat.* 1388–92, p. 299.
[51] Ibid. 1399–1401, p. 266.
[52] Ibid. 1399–1401, p. 547.
[53] Ibid. 1422–9, p. 159.
[54] Chan. Inq. p.m. 15 Hen. VI, no. 27.
[55] *Cal. of Pat.* 1436–41, p. 122.

[56] Ibid.
[58] Pat. 27 Hen. VI, pt. i, m. 16; *Parl. R.* (Rec. Com.), v, 160a.
[59] *Cal. of Pat.* 1461–7, pp. 430, 48t.
[61] Ibid. 1467–77, p. 241.
[62] Pat. 24 Hen. VIII, pt. ii, m. 12.
[63] Ibid.
[65] L. *and P. Hen. VIII,* xv, g. 498 (36).
[66] Feet of F. Surr. Hil. 17 Chas. I; Hil. 18 Chas. II; Recov. R. Hil. 6 Anne, rot. 106; Add. Chart. 22918, etc., etc.
[67] P.C.C. 370 St. Eloy. By a fine of 1763 (Surr. Trin. 2 Geo. III) James Earl of Lauderdale and Mary Turner his wife appear as holding the manor in Mary's right. She was a daughter and co-heir of

[57] Ibid. p. 138.
Sir Thomas Lombe, who seems to have held a mortgage on Carew's estate of Banstead (P.C.C. 370 St. Eloy), which presumably devolved upon his daughter Mary after his death.
[66] P.C.C. 507 Collier.
[68] Ibid. 165 Newcastle.
[70] Ibid. 174 Abercrombie.
[71] Brayley, *Hist. of Surr.* iv, 340.
[72] Private information.
[73] B.M. Add. MS. 16532.
[74] *Cal. of Pat.* 1292–1301, p. 452.
[75] Ibid. 1301–7, p. 355.
[76] Ibid. 1348–50, pp. 5, 183, 393.
[77] Ibid. 1436–41, p. 347.
[78] Pat. 24 Hen. VIII, pt. ii, m. 12.
[79] Add. Chart. 22910.

church stood in the park ; it is now the bailiff's house. The new house called Banstead Wood was built by the Hon. Francis Baring in 1884–90, and is now owned together with the park by Mr. Charles Garton.[79a]

At the time of the Domesday Survey the manor of *BURGH* or *GREAT BURGH* (Berge, xi cent. ; Bergh, Burgh, Barewe, Berewe, xiii cent. ; West Bergh, Great Bergh, xiv. cent. ; Borowe, Westborowe, Westburgh, xvii cent. ; Burrowe, Westburgh, xviii cent.) was held of Odo of Bayeux by his vassal Hugh de Port for 2½ hides.[80] Before the Conquest three freemen had held it and could seek what lord they pleased, the assessment then being for 5 hides.[81] The three manors were held as one in 1086.[82] The holders of Burgh during the 12th century do not appear. Possibly the Mowbrays had it with Banstead, and enfeoffed one of the family of de Bures, as, between the years 1216 and 1243, John de Bures held a knight's fee in Burgh or Barewe of Hubert de Burgh as of the honour of Mowbray.[83] In 1276 John de Bures died seised of the whole land of Burgh which he held for the service of one knight's fee and for which he paid 12s. castle ward to Rochester.[84] His son John succeeded him. In 1325 an extent of the manor of Banstead included a messuage and a carucate of land at Burgh held by de Bures for the service and rent above mentioned and, in addition, for an annual rent of 2s. and suit at the court of Banstead.[85] His son inherited in 1332,[86] dying in 1345, when the extent of the tenement at Burgh included a capital messuage and a garden newly planted.[87] The next John de Bures seems to have become involved in debt to Robert Boteler. In 1346–7 the king pardoned the latter for acquiring for life without licence land of John de Bures at Burgh consisting of a messuage, 240 acres of land, 32 acres of wood, and 12s. rent,[88] and, by an extent for debt taken on de Bures' lands in 1357, Boteler was found to hold a part of those in Burgh.[89] The reversion, after the death of Boteler, was granted by de Bures, called John de Bures of Surrey, kt., to John de Bures of London, citizen and fishmonger.[90] The grant was made before 1362, in which year, Boteler being dead, de Bures of London entered the premises without licence, but was permitted to retain them,[91] the licence being extended to his heirs in 1368–9.[92] In 1384 his son[93] conveyed the manor by means of trustees to Thomas Hayton,[94] who in 1428 was said to hold the 'half-fee in Berewe which Robert Boteler formerly held of the king in the said vill,'[95] and in 1432 he died seised of 'the manor of Westbergh.' Agnes, then wife of John Exham or

Hexham, was his daughter and heir.[96] She seems to have afterwards married Thomas Sayer, as in 1450 they conveyed lands in Westbergh, held in the right of Agnes, and identical in extent with those mentioned in 1346, to Richard Ford and Mercy his wife, William Sander and Joan his wife, and John Collard.[97] Mercy and Joan were daughters of Agnes by her first husband, Thomas Carew.[98] These parties released the property in 1466 to Henry Merland and others.[99]

Richard son and heir of Henry Merland died in 1506, having left the lands to his wife Elizabeth for life with remainder to his brother Nicholas.[100] Nicholas survived and died seised of the manor in 1524, Edward being his son and heir.[101] Edward married Frances Leigh, and in 1543 settled the manor on her with remainder to their sons.[102] After his death his widow married Robert Moys ; her son William Merland inherited at her death in 1596, her elder sons Arthur and Matthew having predeceased her.[103] In 1614 Merland, with other members of his family, conveyed to Christopher Buckle,[104] whose family continued to hold this manor with others in Burgh until the middle of the 19th century.[105] Christopher Buckle, 1684–1759, built Nork House, where his son, Admiral Matthew Buckle, died. The property descended in the direct line until the death without issue, in 1816, of Christopher Buckle, the fifth of that name to hold Burgh,[106] when it passed to his sister, wife of Captain Crowe.[107] A year later it went to the Rev. William Buckle, a cousin, representing the younger branch of the family, and he held until his death in 1832.[108] His son, the Rev. William Lewis Buckle, held this manor, with others in Banstead and with the church, until 1847,

EUCKLE. *Sable a chevron between three chaplets argent.*

PERCEVAL, Earl of Egmont. *Argent a chief indented gules with three crosses formy or therein.*

when it became the property of the Earl of Egmont.[109] From his successor, the fourth earl, it passed (about 1900) to Mr. F. E. Colman, and Mrs. Colman now holds it. Dr. Burton, author of the *Iter Surriense*, in

79a Information from Col. F. A. H. Lambert.
80 *V.C.H. Surr.* i, 304b and note 7.
81 Ibid.   82 Ibid.
83 *Testa de Nevill* (Rec. Com.), 220, 221b.
84 Chan. Inq. p.m. 4 Edw. I, no. 19.
85 Add. Chart. 16532.
86 Chan. Inq. p.m. 6 Edw. III (1st nos.), no. 54; *Cal. of Close,* 1330–3, p. 475.
87 Chan. Inq. p.m. 19 Edw. III (1st nos.), no. 54; *Abbrev. Rot. Orig.* (Rec. Com.), ii, 173.
88 *Abbrev. Rot. Orig.* (Rec. Com.), ii, 191; *Cal. of Pat.* 1345–8, p. 354.
89 Chan. Inq. p.m. 31 Edw. III (1st nos.), no. 55.

90 Inq. a.q.d. cccxlii, 3; ccclxv, 4.
91 Ibid.
92 Inq. a.q.d. ccclxv, 4; *Abbrev. Rot. Orig.* (Rec. Com.) ii, 305.
93 Chan. Inq. p.m. 7 Ric. II, no. 14.
94 Chan. Inq. p.m. 13 Ric. II, no. 14; Inq. a.q.d. ccccviii, 12; *Cal. of Pat.* 1388–92, p. 99.
95 *Feud. Aids,* v, 125.
96 Chan. Inq. p.m. 10 Hen. VI, no. 19.
97 Feet of F. Surr. 28 Hen. VI, no. 33.
98 Berry, *Surr. Gen.* 4.
99 *Cal. of Pat.* 1461–7, p. 518; Feet of F. Surr. 6 Edw. IV, no. 13.
100 Exch. Inq. p.m. mlxv, 7.
101 Chan. Inq. p.m. (Ser. 2), xliii, 85.
102 Recov. R. Hil. 34 Hen. VIII, rot.

100; Chan. Inq. p.m. (Ser. 2), ccxlvii, 95.
103 Chan. Inq. p.m. (Ser. 2), ccxlvii, 95.
104 Feet of F. Surr. Hil. 12 Jas. I.
105 Feet of F. Div. Co. Hil. 1653; 32–33 Chas. II; Recov. R. Trin. 12 Anne, rot. 149; Hil. 4 Geo. III, rot. 144; Hil. 58 Geo. III, rot. 160.
106 There were six of the name of Christopher, but the third died,v.p. in 1706.
107 Brayley, *Hist. of Surr.* iv.
108 Com. Pleas D. Enr. Hil. 58 Geo. III, m. 60; Recov. R. Hil. 58 Geo. III, rot. 160; *Visit. of Surr.* (Harl. Soc. xliii); Berry, *Surr. Gen.* 18, 19, 20.
109 *Parish Reg. of Banstead* (Par. Reg. Soc.), i, vi.

Greek, in 1752 stayed at Nork House, and describes at length the ingenious waterworks by which water was raised from a very deep well and distributed over the slopes of a dry down.

Record is found of a capital messuage at Burgh in 1345.[110] In 1432 Beatrice widow of Thomas Hayton held part of the site of the manor as dower, her portion including two high rooms and two low ones in the south part of the hall (aula), a third part of the kitchen, of the 'Baggehous' and of the oven, two gerners, a barn, a stable covered with tiles, parts of buildings called the 'Sidyrhous,' the 'Wrengehows,' and the 'Wellehous,' with a third of the garden opposite the hall and various other inclosures.[111]

The later house was probably built by William Merland, who held the manor from 1598 to 1614. It is said to have been a Jacobean house. In the windows were the arms of the Buckles. It was pulled down by the late Lord Egmont about twenty-five years ago.

A manor called LITTLE BARROW[112] was held in demesne as of fee by Thomas Barowe in the 15th century.[113] By his will Katherine, a daughter of William Broke, was to receive the issues and profits of the manor for 28 years after his death, or, if she married, they were to be delivered to her husband. Barowe enfeoffed Thomas Wode to carry out these provisions. Katherine married James Warner, who received all issues from 1473 until 1486, when, by agreement, he sold them to John son and heir of Thomas Barowe.[116] John then brought a suit against Thomas Wode, who refused to be party to the transaction,[118] but the result is not apparent. Manning states that a rental of 1531 gives Richard Covert as lord of this manor, his son George afterwards holding. According to the same authority, Christopher Buckle of Burgh held in 1661.[116] The manor of Little Barrow afterwards descended with Burgh (q.v.), with which it is at present held.

The manor of PERROTTS in this parish belonged in the 16th century to the family of Charlwood. The earliest court of which record exists was held in 1447.[117] In 1515 Nicholas Charlwood sold it to John Lambert of Woodmansterne, who possibly was connected with the family of Lampet, Lomputte, or Lampert, who were settled in Banstead in the 14th century.[118] It descended from John Lambert, the purchaser, to Roger his second son, who married Katherine Causton. Roger, the eldest son of Roger, sold the manor to the second son John, the quit-claim being made in 1573.[119] John the eldest son of this John

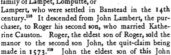

LAMBERT. Gules three sexfoils argent.

married Katherine Moys of Canons (q.v.). He was Marshal of the Hall to King James I, and fought for King Charles. To escape sequestration of his estates he conveyed Perrotts to a younger brother Edward.[190] It afterwards passed to the latter's fifth son Daniel, who purchased it from his elder brother Nicholas.[191] Thomas eldest son of Daniel sold the manor to his brother Daniel, the third son, who was Lord Mayor of London in 1741, and was knighted in 1743.[192] He died without issue in 1750, leaving Perrotts to his nephew, also named Daniel, who died in 1765.[193] The manor is still in possession of this family. Mr. Daniel Henry Lambert, son of the late Benjamin Lambert, of Well House, at present holds. The last court was held about 1866, the last copyhold tenant, Mr. Bonsor, M.P., enfranchised not long since; only a bare seignory therefore remains to the lord.[194] The manor-house mentioned in a deed of 1680 as having been recently rebuilt stood on the slope facing Rydon Hill. It was pulled down about 1760, when the family moved to the Well House in Banstead.

The first mention of the manor of PRESTON occurs in 1316–17, when John de Chetwode, sen., settled it on himself for life with remainder to his son John and Lucy his wife and their heirs.[195] Almost a century previously a Ralph de Chetwode had held 10s. rent in Burgh, so it is probable that the family had long been holding land in Banstead.[196] In 1346 Sir John de Chetwode, kt., and Lucy his wife, settled the manor on Nicholas, apparently their son, and Elizabeth his wife.[197] In 1384 John de Bures was said to hold a cottage at Burgh of Thomas Hayton as of the manor of Preston.[198] Hayton, however, who afterwards held Burgh (q.v.), did not die seised of Preston ;[199] probably, therefore, he was a trustee for the Chetwode family, or held the manor for a term of years only, as, according to Manning, Sir Thomas Chetwode, grandson of Nicholas, afterwards held the manor, and in 1473 his sister and heir Elizabeth, then wife of William Woodhall, released it to Richard Illyngworth and others, trustees for Henry Merland.[190] Richard son of Henry Merland died seised of the manor in 1506, holding also that of Burgh,[191] and the two manors have since been held together.[192]

William de Braose, lord of Bramber, held Tadorne (NORTH TADWORTH) in 1086 as half a hide, Halsart being his tenant ; Godtovi had held it of King Harold and could seek what lord he pleased.[193] In the early 13th century William Haunsard held a fee in Bookham and Tadworth of the honour of Brembre

CHETWODE. Quarterly argent and gules with four crosses formy countercoloured.

[110] Chan. Inq. p.m. 19 Edw. III (1st nos.), no. 54.

[111] Ibid. 11 Hen. VI (add.), no. 59.

[112] In 1086 Adam son of Hubert held a house in Banstead, and he also held of the bishop one hide in Wallington Hundred, which had never paid geld. This hide may probably be added to the 29 of Banstead to make up the usual round number, and is very probably Little Barrow or Burgh. V.C.H. Surr. i, 303–14.

[113] Early Chan. Proc. lxxiv, 39.

[114] Ibid.

[115] Ibid.

[116] Manning and Bray, Hist. of Surr. ii, 588.

[117] Ibid. 589. Information from Mr. D. H. Lambert and Col. F. A. H. Lambert.

[118] Information from Mr. H. Lambert.

[119] Feet of F. Surr. East. 15 Eliz.

[190] Ibid. Trin. 10 Chas. I.

[191] Information from Col. F. A. H. Lambert.

[192] Burke, Landed Gentry.

[193] Ibid. ; Recov. R. Trin. 6 Geo. III, rot. 338 ; East. 9 Geo. III, rot. 223.

[194] Information from Mr. D. H. Lambert.

[195] Feet of F. Surr. 10 Edw. II, 187.

[196] Ibid. East. 13 Hen. III, 89.

[197] Ibid. Hil. 20 Edw. III.

[198] Chan. Inq. p.m. 7 Ric. II, 14.

[199] Ibid. 10 Hen. VI, 19.

[190] Manning and Bray, Hist. of Surr. ii, 586 ; Misc. Gen. and Her. v, 69 et seq.

[191] Exch. Inq. p.m. mlxv, 7.

[192] See Burgh.

[193] V.C.H. Surr. i, 321a, 282.

3   257   33

(Bramber).[134] Later in the century, but before 1243, he was stated to hold two fees in Tadworth of Hubert de Burgh, of the honour of Mowbray.[135] In 1273 John and James, sons of William Haunsard, gave a carucate of land, 2 acres of pasture, 12 acres of wood, and 20s. rent in North Tadworth and Little Bookham to the Prior of St. Mary Overy.[136] The priory continued to hold North Tadworth as a manor until the Dissolution. In 1524 it was demised with the rectory of Banstead to William Coltson and Richard Moys and Elizabeth his wife for a term of forty years.[137] After the Dissolution the manor was granted by the Crown to Thomas Walsingham and Robert son and heir of Richard Moys in fee ;[138] Walsingham soon after released to Moys,[139] who died in 1596 leaving a son Philip.[140] John son of Philip died without issue,[141] and Henry, another son, held in 1648.[142] At Henry's death the manor passed to his five sisters and co-heirs.[143] In 1659 Sir Henry Hatton and Elizabeth his wife, daughter and heir of Robert Hazard and Ann, a sister of Henry Moys,[144] John Ireland son of another sister, John Kyme son of Mary, a third sister, and Paul Tracey son of Margaret, a fourth,[145] conveyed four-fifths of the manor of North Tadworth to Christopher Buckle of Burgh.[146] In 1663 Christopher Buckle acquired the remaining fifth from John Bushell and Joyce his wife,[147] daughter and heir of Edward Lambert, who was the son of John Lambert and Catherine, the fifth sister of Henry Moys.[148] Since that time North Tadworth has been held with the manor of Burgh (q.v.).

In 1086 Ralph held Tadeorde, probably SOUTH TADWORTH, of Odo of Bayeux for 1½ hides ; before the Conquest two brothers had held it of King Edward for 5 hides.[149] Its value had decreased from 40s. to 30s.,[150] and it was still taxed for the latter sum in 1291 when the Prior of Merton held the land.[151] It is not evident how the prior acquired it, but possibly it had been granted him by the lord of Banstead, as the prior held the land of that manor.[152] South Tadworth was certainly held by Merton before 1274, as in that year the Prior of Southwark brought a plea of novel disseisin against the Prior of Merton for common pasture in Banstead, North Tadworth, and South Tadworth.[153] In 1428 the Prior of Merton held a quarter of a knight's fee here.[154] The manor remained in possession of the priory until the Dissolution,[155] after which, on coming to the Crown,

it was annexed to the honour of Hampton Court.[156] In 1553 Edward VI made a grant in fee to Edward Harendon or Herrenden.[157] The manor was settled in 1569 on his son Henry, who married Mary Digby.[158] In 1587, after the death of Millicent Herendon, widow, Edmund was stated to be her son and heir.[159] He, with Henry Herendon, senior and junior, levied a fine of the manor in the same year.[160] The deed was possibly a surrender of Henry's claim, as Edmund still held in 1618.[161] In 1620 John Herendon conveyed to Thomas Hawes.[162] From the latter the manor passed in 1631-2 to Thomas Grymes or Crymes,[163] who died seised in 1644.[164] His son, Sir George Grymes, kt., inherited,[165] but before 1650 the manor had come into the possession of Robert Wilson and Katherine his wife.[166] The Wilsons conveyed in 1694 to Leonard Wessel,[167] who still held in 1704. Leonard Wessel, about 1700, built the house there known as Tadworth Court.[168]

By 1724 the manor was the property of John Fleetwood, who died in 1725 having devised to his sons John and Gerard Dutton Fleetwood in tail male with reversion to his daughter Anne Maria wife of William Bury, or his sons' daughters.[169] The second John Fleetwood died in 1752 leaving an only child Emilia, wife of Giuseppe Calenda. The Calendas and the Burys in 1755-6 conveyed their interest to Gerard Dutton Fleetwood, who was unmarried,[170] and he in 1756 procured an Act of Parliament enabling him to sell the manor to William Mabbot.[171] Mabbot died at Tadworth Court in 1764,[172] having devised his property to his wife, Lady Rhoda Delves, with reversion to her daughter Rhoda wife of Philip Carteret Webb.[173] The daughter afterwards married Edward Beaver,[174] and in 1773, after the mother's death, they, with William Wright and Charles Scrase, executors, conveyed the manor to Sir Henry Harpur.[175] It passed soon after to Robert Hudson, who held in 1808,[176] his son and his son's widow holding after his death ; Mrs. Hudson was lady of the manor in 1841,[177] and seems to have held until after 1860. Before the end of the 19th century Sir Charles Russell, afterwards Lord Russell of Killowen, bought the manor, which is now in the possession of his widow, Lady Russell of Killowen. The house which Leonard Wessel built is now owned by Mr. C. D. Morton.

[134] Red Book of Exch. (Rolls Ser.), 561.
[135] Testa de Nevill (Rec. Com), 220, 221b.
[136] Feet of F. Div. Co. 1 Edw. II, 11.
[137] Mins. Accts. Surr. 31-32 Hen. VIII, bdle. 146, m. 59.
[138] Pat. 3 Edw. VI, pt. xi, m. 17.
[139] Manning and Bray, op. cit. ii, 538.
[140] Berry, Surr. Gen. 102.
[141] Ibid. ; Close, 20 Chas. II, pt. xiv, m. 35 ; Visit. of Surr. (Harl. Soc. xliii), 186.
[142] Ibid. ; Feet of F. Surr. Mich. 24 Chas. I.
[143] See note 141.
[144] Close, 20 Chas. II, pt. xiv, m. 35 ; Le Neve, Ped. of Knights (Harl. Soc. viii), 125.
[145] Harl. MS. 1561, fol. 210b and 211. G.E.C. Baronage. According to Aubrey and G.E.C. Baronage Paul Tracey son of Paul Tracey, who married Margaret Moys, died in 1618. The Paul Tracey

mentioned in 1659 may have been the husband of Margaret. It is possible that another son, born after the death of the first, was also called Paul, as the Close Roll of 1668 distinctly says that the Paul Tracey of 1659 was Margaret's son.
[146] Close, 20 Chas. II, pt. xiv, m. 35.
[147] Feet of F. Surr. Hil. 14 & 15 Chas. II.
[148] Close, 20 Chas. II, pt. xiv, m. 35.
[149] V.C.H. Surr. i, 304a, 289.
[150] Ibid.
[151] Pope Nich. Tax. (Rec. Com.), 206.
[152] Feud. Aids, v, 126.
[153] Pat. 2 Edw. I, m. 23.
[154] Feud. Aids, v, 126.
[155] Dugdale, Mon. vi, 245 ; Valor Eccl. (Rec. Com.), ii, 48.
[156] Pat. 7 Edw. VI, pt. iii, m. 12.
[157] Ibid.
[158] Chan. Inq. p.m. (Ser. 2), ccxii, 53 ; Feet of F. Surr. Trin. 14 Eliz.
[159] Chan. Inq. p.m. (Ser. 2), ccxii, 53.

[160] Feet of F. Surr. Trin. 29 Eliz.
[161] Ibid. Hil. 15 Jas. I.
[162] Ibid. Mich. 18 Jas. I ; Recov. R. Mich. 18 Jas. I, rot. 75.
[163] Feet of F. Surr. Hil. 7 Chas. I.
[164] Feet of F. Div. Co. Mich. 13 Chas. I ; Chan. Inq. p.m. (Ser. 2), xxxii, 22.
[165] Ibid.
[166] Feet of F. Surr. Hil. 1650.
[167] Ibid. Mich. 6 Will. and Mary.
[168] Manning and Bray, Hist. of Surr. ii, 588.
[169] Private Act, 29 Geo. II, cap. 30.
[170] Ibid. ; Feet of F. Surr. Hil. 29 Geo. II.
[171] See note 169.
[172] Musgrave's Obit. (Harl. Soc.).
[173] P.C.C. 474 Simpson.
[174] Ibid. 47 Taverner.
[175] Ibid. ; Feet of F. Surr. Mich. 13 Geo. III.
[176] Manning and Bray, Hist. of Surr. ii, 589.
[177] Brayley, Hist. of Surr. iv, 342.

RECTORY MANOR, alias *SOUTHMERFIELD,* alias *CANONS.* The Prior and canons of St. Mary Overy were possessed, as early as the 12th century, of a considerable amount of land in Southmerfield in Banstead. In 1194 Mabel de Mowbray, after the death of Nigel, claimed against the prior two carucates of land in Southmerfield, as well as the advowson of the church, as having been given her by her father as her marriage portion.[178] The prior said that no lord had previously intermeddled with the church there, but she was finally allowed to hold three parts of the land for life; the rest she quitclaimed to the prior.[179] In the first year of King John's reign Sewel son of Robert of Southmerfield quitclaimed to the prior and his successors two virgates in Southmerfield, with the house belonging, which he had previously demised to the prior for a term of four years.[180]

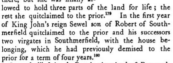

PRIORY OF ST. MARY OVERY. *Argent a cross indented gules with a lozenge gules in the quarter.*

In 1269[181] John de Burgh, then lord of Banstead, released the prior and his successors from the customary rent, services, and suit at court by which the priory lands in Banstead Manor were held. A rental of the priory in the reign of Edward I shows that its lands in Banstead amounted to nearly two hundred acres.[182] Of these, 17 acres were held of the gift of John de Burgh, 16 of the fee of John de Bures for the rent of 2*s.* and a rose, and 7 acres of the fee of Robert Walton for the rent of 12*d.*[183] The land belonging to the Waltons lay in Southmerfield.[184] In 1317–18 Juliana widow of Robert de Walton received licence to have divine service celebrated at a portable altar in her houses of Holeghe (in Coulsdon) and Southmerfield.[185]

In 1524 the rectory, with the house in Southmerfield, was demised to William Coltson and Richard Moys and Elizabeth, together with the priory's manor of North Tadworth.[186] In 1549, after the surrender of the priory, these lands were granted to Robert son and heir of Richard Moys and Thomas Walsingham, the latter releasing his share soon after.[187] The deed of 1549 refers to the lands of the manors of North Tadworth and Southmerfield and the rectory and church of Banstead. They passed successively to

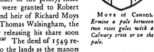

MOYS of Canons. *Ermine a pale between two roses gules with a Calvary cross or on the pale.*

Philip, John, and Henry Moys, and finally to the five sisters and co-heirs of Henry.[188] In 1661 the descendants of four of these sisters conveyed four-fifths of the rectory to Francis Beard.[189] According to Manning this portion passed from Beard in 1663 to Frances Moys widow of John Moys, and she, out of her share of the impropriation, endowed the vicarage with an annuity of £20.[190] By 1702 Henry Read held four-fifths of the rectory,[191] and he still held in 1724.[192] In 1726 he and Lydia his wife, with Christopher Buckle, levied a fine of four-fifths of the manor of Southmerfield and of the rectory and advowson.[193] This was probably part of a conveyance of the rectory from the Reads to Buckle, as he afterwards held both this and the advowson (q.v.). The remaining fifths of the rectory and advowson, the portion of Henry Moys's sister Katherine Lambert, passed to her daughter and heir Joyce,[194] who, with her husband, John Bushell, conveyed in 1663 to trustees of Richard Parr and Elizabeth his wife, widow of Henry Moys.[195] Parr and his trustees sold in 1668 to Robert Wayth.[196] In 1732 Edward Fulham, son and heir of Anne daughter and eventually heir of Robert Wayth, sold his fifth to Christopher Buckle.[197] After this time the entire rectory descended with the advowson, and the Earl of Egmont is the present impropriator of the great tithes with the exception of those in South Tadworth, which apparently passed out of the hands of the owner of the rectory in 1551.[198]

The house in Southmerfield, acquired in 1199–1200 by the prior and convent,[199] evidently became the site of the rectory manor, as in 1203 record is found of the prior's house in Southmerfield, where his bailiff collected or paid rent.[200] After the Dissolution, this house, called the capital messuage of the rectory, was known by the name of Canons or Southmerfield.[201] It descended with the rectory. Land called Canon's Hatch belonging to the priory is mentioned in the late 13th century.[202] A farm, Canhatch, was afterwards held by the Moys family with the church lands.[203]

GARRATTS HALL [203a] (Gerardes, Garades) represents a tenement held of the manor of Banstead, apparently according to the custom of borough English. It preserves the name of a family settled in Banstead in the 15th century. Their estate passed to the Calcokes of Chipstead, and descended from Richard Calcoke to his youngest son Alan, who joined with his mother in conveying it to Jeffery Lambert of Woodmansterne in 1534. From this latter it passed to the youngest son of his nineteen children, Samuel, and after Samuel's death it descended to his son John, born in 1638, who left one daughter, Elizabeth, the wife of Sir Robert Wilmot, Lord Mayor of London. John Lambert rebuilt the mansion-house and conveyed the property to his nephew Thomas, a

[178] *Rolls in the King's Court* (Pipe R. Soc.), xiv, 42. See account of the manor.
[179] Feet of F. Surr. Mich. 7 Ric. I, file 1; Trin. 9 Ric. I, file 1.
[180] Cott. MS. Nero C. iii, fol. 197.
[181] Harl. Chart. 47 E, 35.
[182] Cott. MS. Faust. A. viii, fol. 156.
[183] Ibid.; Cott. Chart. xvi, 45.
[184] Feet of F. Surr. 9 Ric. I, file 1.
[185] *Reg. of Sandale and Asserius* (Hants Rec. Soc.), 83.
[186] Mins. Accts. Surr. bdle. 146, no. 59.
[187] Pat. 3 Edw. VI, pt. xi, m. 17; Com. Pleas D. Enr. Trin. 5 Edw. VI, m. 2.

[188] See North Tadworth.
[189] Feet of F. Surr. East. 13 Chas. II.
[190] Manning and Bray, *Hist. of Surr.* ii, 590.
[191] Feet of F. Surr. East. 1 Anne; Recov. R. East. 1 Anne, rot. 17.
[192] Feet of F. Surr. Mich. 11 Geo. I.
[193] Ibid. Hil. 12 Geo. I.
[194] Close, 20 Chas. II, pt. xiv, m. 35.
[195] Ibid.; Feet of F. Surr. Hil. 1663.
[196] Close, 20 Chas. II, pt. xiv, m. 35; Feet of F. Surr. Trin. 20 Chas. II.
[197] Close, 6 Geo. II, pt. xii, no. 12; Recov. R. Trin. 6 Geo. II, rot. 155.

[198] Com. Pleas D. Enr. Trin. 5 Edw. VI, m. 2.
[199] Cott. MS. Nero C. iii, fol. 197.
[200] Campb. Chart. xvi, 2.
[201] Close, 20 Chas. II, pt. xiv, m. 35.
[202] Cott. MS. Faust. A. viii, fol. 156.
[203] See note 201. Canhatch is the name of a gate from which the farm was familiarly known. It is properly Canon Farm.
[203a] The account of this estate and those following in this parish have been kindly supplied by Col. F. A. H. Lambert.

merchant of London, son of his elder brother Samuel. Thomas Lambert died in 1704, and his son, John Lambert, sold Garratts to his cousin, John Ludlow, whose son Lambert Ludlow died without issue, leaving three sisters and co-heirs. These ladies conveyed to Isaac Hughes of London, merchant, who married a Buckle of Burgh, and left a son John. The estate passed shortly afterwards to the Ladbrokes, and then to the Clowes, from whom it was bought back by Thomas Lambert of Banstead (see Perrotts) about 1850. He gave the property to his brother, John Lambert, an active magistrate and great benefactor to the parish, who left one son, Wilmot Lambert, after whose death his trustees sold it to the late Mr. F. Lambert. His son, Colonel F. A. H. Lambert, is the present owner. The house has a handsome Queen Anne staircase and some Jacobean panelling. In the chapel is a 15th-century triptych, an ancient crucifix, and some pictures. The house is occupied by Mrs. Davies, and used for a girls' school.

BANSTEAD PLACE (formerly Carpenters) was an estate of the Wilmots early in the 17th century. It passed through an heiress to Elizabeth wife of Gabriel Bestman, and afterwards to her niece, Hannah Wilmot, who married Sir Samuel Prime, a well-known lawyer in the reign of George III. The property passed later to the Westons, and then to John Motteux, of Beachamwell and Sandringham, co. Norfolk, whose trustees sold it to W. S. H. Fitz Roy, from whom it was acquired by John Lambert of Garratts Hall. Is now the property of the Hon. Mr. Justice Neville.

The *WELL HOUSE* was a farm which came into the possession of the Lambert family through the marriage of Mary, daughter and co-heir of John Wilmot, with Sir Daniel Lambert. The latter built the present dining and drawing-room, leaving the old house, an early 16th-century building, practically intact. It is now the residence of the Hon. Mrs. Arthur.

NEWLANDS belonged in the 17th century to the family of Harris, who were connected with Winchester. Richard Harris, M.D., of Newlands, married a sister of Sir Edward Bysshe, of Smallfield Place, in Burstow, and left a son, Thomas Harris, a secondary of the Court of Exchequer, who married Anne, sister of Sir Timothy Thornhill, bart., and widow of John Wilmot. He died in 1727, and his son John twenty years later. The property subsequently came into the possession of the Aubertins, a Huguenot family, one of whom, the Rev. Peter Aubertin, rector of Chipstead, married a daughter of Mr. Lambert of Banstead. His son, Peter Aubertin, also rector of Chipstead, sold Newlands to Mr. Nisbet Robertson, whose widow is the present owner.

ALL SAINTS' church is a fine building consisting of a chancel 33 ft. 7 in. by 13 ft. 4 in. with a north chapel 21 ft. 6 in. by 13 ft. and a south chapel 21 ft. by 13 ft. 2 in., a nave 37 ft. 10 in. by 16 ft. 8 in. with a north aisle 10 ft. 9 in. wide and a south aisle 11 ft. 2 in. wide, a west tower 14 ft. 4 in. by 14 ft., and to the north of it a vestry. The north and south entrances have porches.

CHURCHES

The church has been over-restored, but is still of very great interest, the nave and chancel arcades being of a very uncommon type. The nave, as usual, probably retains the plan of a building considerably earlier than any detail now existing, the great height and comparative thinness of its walls suggesting a possible pre-Conquest origin. The arches of the nave arcades and the west arch of the north chapel show distinctive late 12th-century tooling, and are the oldest features to which a date can now be given, and the church must have been brought to its present plan, except as regards the aisles and north-west vestry, somewhere between the years 1190 and 1220. The north aisle seems to have been widened in the 15th century, the south aisle has been rebuilt in modern times, and the vestry is also modern. The south chapel was rebuilt in 1837, and brought to its present form in 1868, and both porches are modern. Cracklow mentions that the chancel was repaired in 1631, and the church beautified by subscription in 1716, and again repaired at a later date.

An old cork model of the church in the vestry shows a 13th-century lancet and a 15th-century three-light window in the north wall of the north chapel, and the east and south chancel windows as of 15th-century date with three cinquefoiled lights.

At present there are three modern lancets in the east wall of the chancel, two in the north wall, partly old, and shown in Cracklow's drawing, and two entirely modern in the south wall.

The arcade between the chancel and north chapel is of two bays with a very interesting and unusual octagonal central column, the faces of which are sunk and hollowed alternately, leaving fillets about an inch wide on either side of

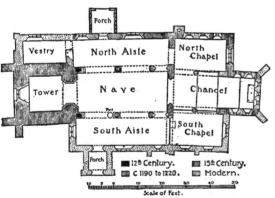

PLAN OF BANSTEAD CHURCH

Porch
Vestry
North Aisle
North Chapel
Tower
Nave
Chancel
Font
South Aisle
South Chapel
Porch

■ 12ᵗʰ Century.   ■ 15ᵗʰ Century.
▦ C 1190 to 1220.   ▨ Modern.

Scale of Feet.

each angle. The base is roll-moulded and is now below the floor line, and the bell capital is also moulded and has scrolls of 13th-century foliage at the four cardinal angles curving outwards from the bell of the capital. The responds are quite plain and have simple moulded capitals, and the arches are two-centred of one order with slightly chamfered edges, and with plain labels on both sides.

The opposite arcade is similar, but the faces of the central column are not recessed; it has a water-moulded base and an octagonal moulded capital without foliage, and the arches have no labels. Just above the capital on the chancel side can be traced one of the consecration crosses.

The chancel arch has jambs of two chamfered orders which continue round the arch with a moulded abacus at the springing. It is of early 13th-century date, and the wall in which it is set is square with the chancel and not with the nave. The east window of the north chapel is of 15th-century date, and has three cinquefoiled lights under a four-centred head with a moulded label. On either side of it are stones bearing the outlines of image-brackets which have been cut back to the wall face.

In the north wall are three lancet windows, the eastern of which may be in part old, while the other two replace a 15th-century three-light window. The rear arches are chamfered, and that of the middle window springs from small moulded corbels.

The arch from this chapel into the north aisle has plain square jambs and a pointed arch; the stone is darker than that used in the rest of the building, and the 12th-century diagonal tooling on it is very distinct.

The south chapel dates only from the rebuilding of 1837, and its windows from 1868; its opening from it to the south aisle has a modern pointed arch on old jambs, attached to each of which is a small modern shaft and moulded base with good foliate capitals of 13th-century date.

The nave arcades are of two bays with narrow arched openings in the east responds. It is to be noted that the setting out of the arcade follows the line of the east wall of the nave, which is not square with the side walls, so that the arches are not opposite to one another. The arches and inner order of the jambs of the narrow eastern openings are modern, but the openings themselves seem to be old, and may have been made to give more room for nave altars, like the recesses which are often found in the walls of aisleless naves in this position.

The arcades are finely proportioned with tall octagonal columns and water-moulded bases or square sub-bases with angle spurs. The capitals are square with moulded abaci, beneath the projecting angles of which are volutes springing from the necking, of very plain detail, only one being carved into leaves.

The responds are plain and have moulded abaci at the springing, while the arches are of a single square order and are two-centred, the diagonal tooling of the masonry being well preserved. The two north windows of the north aisle are modern, the first having three lights and the second two, all with trefoiled heads, while the west window, now looking into the vestry, is 15th-century work of two lights. The north doorway is also of 15th-century date, and has a large hollow chamfer in the jambs which changes to a double ogee moulding in the four-centred arch.

The porch is modern, built of timber on low flint and stone walls.

From the west end of the aisle a plain modern doorway leads to the vestry, which is lighted by a three-light window of the same design as those in the

Banstead Church   Capital of Nave Arcade.

north wall of the adjacent aisle. The south aisle and porch are entirely modern.

The tower arch is two-centred, of three chamfered orders continued from the jambs with splayed bases and moulded abaci, all of early 13th-century date; and above it is a blocked doorway which opened from the first floor of the tower. All the walls of the tower are extraordinarily thick, being doubtless intended to be carried up to a greater height than they now are. The west wall measures 6 ft. 5 in., and in it is a modern two-light window.

The tower is of two stages, and has a low-pitched roof from which rises a small octagonal spire, covered with oak shingles. In the upper stage are lancets on the north, west, and south aisles, old within, but with their outer stonework renewed, and on the east side is a modern window of two trefoiled lights under a square head.

The roofs are tiled, the timbers of the chancel, north chapel, and nave being old, and the former having a deep moulded cornice, while the south chapel has a modern panelled ceiling, and the aisles modern lean-to roofs.

All the internal fittings are modern except the font, which has a 14th-century octagonal bowl on modern round stem and base. The top and bottom of the bowl are moulded, and each of the sides has a panel filled with tracery of a different pattern. The effect is not very successful, but a fair number of similar fonts exist up and down the country—Chipstead is a neighbouring example.

In the lower part of the east window of the north

chapel are some remains of 17th-century glass, one piece bearing the date 1619. It came from Great Burgh, and has some modern heraldic glass set with it.

There are many monuments in the church, of which the following are the oldest or most noteworthy. In the vestry a quaint little marble wall-tablet to Paul Tracy, 1618, son of Paul and Margaret Tracy and grandson of Sir Paul Tracy of Stanway, Gloucestershire. At the foot is his figure in low relief in a chrism robe. Another, a black marble tablet in an alabaster frame, is to Robert Smyth, fourth son of Richard Smyth of Backton, Suffolk, 1603; and in the north aisle is a wooden panel to Ruth (Lambert) wife of George Brett, citizen and goldsmith of London, 1647, with a set of twelve couplets of somewhat extravagant eulogy, and a shield with the arms—Argent a cheveron azure with three bezants thereon, impaling Gules three sexfoils (narcissi) argent.

In the south chapel are several monuments of the Lambert family, including one to Mrs. Judith Lambert, daughter of Daniel and Elizabeth Lambert, 1725; and one on the south wall of the aisle to Sir Daniel Lambert, Lord Mayor of London 1741, died 1750.

There are eight bells hung on a modern iron frame : the treble and second by Warner 1892, the third by Bryan Eldridge 1638, the fourth by William Carter 1613, the fifth by Thomas Mears 1791, the sixth by Lester & Pack 1756, the seventh by Robert Mot 1585, and the tenor by William Eldridge 1651.

The communion plate is a silver-gilt set of 1788 given by Richard Ladbroke in 1789, and comprising a cup, paten, almsdish, and a large helmet-shaped flagon.

The first book of the registers contains baptisms, marriages, and burials from 1547 to 1618, the second baptisms from 1616 to 1783, and burials from 1663 to 1783; third baptisms and burials 1663 to 1712, and marriages 1663 to 1711, fourth marriages 1754 to 1772, fifth marriages 1773 to 1811, sixth baptisms 1784 to 1812, seventh burials 1789 to 1812, and eighth marriages 1811 to 1837.

The church of *ST. MARY* at *BURGH HEATH*, successor of the ancient church, was begun in April 1908 and opened in 1909. It is built of flint and stone, and has a chancel, nave, two aisles, vestry, &c.

There was a church in existence
ADVOWSONS at Banstead in 1086.[204] Tirel del Maniers granted the advowson to the Prior and convent of St. Mary Overy during the reign of Henry I,[205] and this grant was afterwards confirmed by Nigel de Mowbray, lord of Banstead.[206] After his death his widow Mabel seems to have claimed the advowson against the prior,[207] but without success (see under Banstead Manor), and the prior continued to hold it.[208] A vicarage was ordained before the end of the 13th century.[209] In 1549, after the Dissolution, the advowson was granted, with the rectory (q.v.), to Robert Moys,[210] whose descendants held until 1661, when four co-heirs[211] conveyed fourfifths of the advowson to Francis Beard.[212] Frances

Moys presented to the church in 1663,[213] and, according to Manning, she had acquired the four-fifths held by Beard and conveyed them soon after to her brother Christopher Buckle.[214] His grandson presented to the church in 1714,[215] and held four-fifths of the advowson in 1726,[216] obtaining the remaining fifth both of rectory and advowson in 1732.[217] The rectory and advowson remained in possession of the Buckles[218] until 1855–6, when they passed to the Earl of Egmont, the present earl being patron of the vicarage.

Nigel de Mowbray, at the close of the 12th century, granted the advowson of the church of Burgh to the priory of St. Mary Overy,[219] presentation being made to the church by the prior and convent during the 14th and 15th centuries.[220] After the Dissolution it became the property of the lords of the manor of Burgh, being held by the Merlands and afterwards by the Buckles,[221] but no incumbents were instituted after the 15th century.

A chapel dedicated to St. Leonard was attached to the manor of Preston in the 15th century.[222] The advowson was held with the manor, the last record of it being, apparently, in the conveyance from the Merlands to Christopher Buckle.[223]

CHARITIES   These are recorded in the church as follows :—

1693.   Mr. Samuel Wilmot left £50 for 5 poor men and 5 poor widows.
1699.   Mr. Robert Wilmot gave £35.
1725.   Mrs. Judith Lambert left £10 for 10 poor housekeepers, at the town end of the parish.
1741.   Simon Wilmot, merchant, left £100 for the poor.
1750.   Sir Daniel Lambert left £100 for 16 poor people not receiving parish relief.
1770.   Dame Mary Lambert, his widow, left £50 for the same purpose.
1785.   Mr. Edward Lambert left £100 for the same purpose.
1793.   Mr. J. Motteux left £100 for bread on the first Sunday in February.
1805.   Mrs. Lucy Burr gave £5 a year for the poor on the first Monday in Advent.
1814.   Mr. John Hewitt, £100.
1815.   Mr. Wilmot Lambert, £50.
1818.   Mr. Richard Pairy, £100.
1822.   Rev. J. E. Francis (vicar), £100.
1823.   Mrs. Katherine Motteux, £150 for bread on the first Sunday in December.
1824.   Mrs. Lucy Motteux, £150 for bread on the second Sunday in the year.
1829.   Mrs. Martha Jones, late wife of Mr. W. Lambert, £100.
1833.   Mr. Thomas Lambert, £100.

In 1725 £30 a year from a Mr. Lambert was returned to Bishop Willis, but is not in this table.

Smith's Charity is distributed as in other Surrey parishes.

[204] V.C.H. Surr. i, 302b.
[205] Dugdale, Mon. vi, 169, 172 ; Rolls in the King's Court (Pipe R. Soc.), xiv, 42.
[206] Dugdale, Mon. vi, 169.
[207] Rolls in the King's Court (Pipe R. Soc.), xiv, 42.
[208] Egerton MS. 2031-34 (Index Winton Epis. Reg.).
[209] Cott. MS. Faust. A. viii, fol. 156.
[210] Pat. 3 Edw. IV, pt. xi, m. 17.
[211] See North Tadworth.
[212] Feet of F. Surr. East. 13 Chas. II.
[213] Inst. Bks. (P.R.O.).
[214] Manning and Bray, Hist. of Surr. ii, 590 ; Visit. of Surr. (Harl. Soc. xliii), 186.
[215] Inst. Bks. (P.R.O.).
[216] Feet of F. Surr. Hil. 12 Geo. I.
[217] Close, 6 Geo. II, pt. xii, no. 12, vide rectory.
[218] See Burgh.
[219] See note 206.
[220] Egerton MSS. 2031, fol. 3 d. 52 ; 2033, fol. 4b, 75b (Index Winton Epis. Reg.) ; Manning and Bray, Hist. of Surr. ii, 591.
[221] Feet of F. Surr. Mich. 8 Jas. I. ; see description of the parish.
[222] Exch. Inq. p.m. mlxv, 7.
[223] Feet of F. Surr. Hil. 12 Jas. I. ; see description of the parish.

BANSTEAD CHURCH : NAVE LOOKING EAST

EPSOM PARISH CHURCH FROM THE NORTH-EAST IN 1824

(From Cracklow's View)

CHESSINGTON

Cisendene and Cisedune (xi cent.), Chissendon (xii cent.), Chesinden (xiii cent.), Chesingdon (xiv cent.), Chyssyndon (xv cent.).

Chessington is a very small village about 3 miles south from Surbiton Station, and 2 miles west of Ewell. The parish, which is a chapelry to Malden, measures 3 miles from north-east to south-west, and barely a mile in any part from north-west to south-east, and contains 1,645 acres. This includes a detached part of Malden, round the farm called Rushett, which lies south of Chessington, and was added to the parish in 1884.[1]

The soil is entirely London Clay, undulating considerably. A brook which flows into the Hoggsmill stream runs through the parish, which is traversed throughout by the road from Kingston to Letherhead. Rushett Common now only exists as roadside waste on each side of this road.

On a little hill covered with wood south-east of the church, and on the other side of the stream, is a small inclosure or camp, about 100 yds. by 30 yds. in extent. Brayley[2] says that a Roman brass coin was found near it, and that it was known as Castle Hill. If so, the name has been disused, and it is now called Four Acres Wood. The stream has hollowed out a valley in the clay close by, and across the valley there was thrown a very substantial dam, perhaps the site of the mill of which Robert de Watevile held half in 1086. But the dam, now cut through at each end, is more than enough for a mill-dam, and may have been made a pool for the better protection of this side of the fortification above.

In the 18th century Mr. Samuel Crisp, the friend of Dr. Burney, lived at Chessington Hall, and Miss Burney is said to have written part of Cecilia in a summer-house in the garden which is still standing. Her father composed the epitaph upon Mr. Crisp which is in the church, and her Diary contains many references to him and to her visits to the house.

The inclosure was made by an award dated 1 August 1825.[3] A map in possession of Mr. Chancellor of Chessington Hall shows the parish largely cut up into very small holdings of villagers whose names correspond to those in the earlier registers.

Chessington Hall is now the seat of Mr. Horatio Chancellor; Chessington Lodge of Mr. D. R. Cameron; Strawberry Hill of Mr. A. E. Clerk.

A Church of England school was founded by subscription in 1822, and for a time was divided into two parts for primary and more advanced teaching. The latter was discontinued about fifty years ago. The present building was erected in 1863.

There is an iron parish room in the village.

The manor of CHESSINGTON was held in the reign of Edward the Confessor by one Erding, and in 1086 by

MANORS

Richard de Tonbridge, ancestor of the Clares, Earls of Gloucester.[4] In 1439 it was included among the knights' fees held by Isabel Countess of Warwick, through descent from Eleanor wife of Hugh le Despenser and co-heiress of Gilbert de Clare[5]; after the death and attainder of Richard Nevill, husband of Anne daughter and heiress of Isabel, the overlordship apparently escheated to the Crown.

In 1086 Robert de Watevile was holding this manor under Richard de Tonbridge,[6] and his descendants continued to hold both this manor and Malden until 1240, when a grant of Malden, evidently including Chessington, of which a whole or a part was a member of that manor, was made by William de Watevile and Peter de Malden, his subtenant, to Walter de Merton,[7] who received a grant of free warren there in 1249.[7a] In 1262 licence was granted by Richard de Clare for the presentation of Malden with its member of Chessington to the 'House of Scholars' which Walter de Merton was founding at Malden,[8] and in 1264 Walter de Merton assigned them by charter to this house, for the support of 20 scholars at Oxford.[9] The manors thus became part of the endowment of Merton College, Oxford, the estate at Chessington being subsequently known as CHESSINGTON PARK.

In 1287 Richard de Merplesdon, Warden of the House of the Scholars of Merton, in Oxford, was holding 3 fees in Farley, Malden, and Chessington, of William de Watevile, as mesne lord between the said Richard and Gilbert de Clare.[10] In 1279 the master and scholars of Merton claimed Chessington as a park pertaining to their manor of Malden, with warren in all their demesne lands there by charter of Henry III.[11]

Edward I confirmed these estates to the scholars of Merton in 1290,[12] and they are mentioned among the fees held by Merton College of the descendants of Richard de Clare in 1314,[13] 1375,[14] 1428,[15] and 1439.[16] In 1578 the college ceded their manors of Malden and Chessington Park for a term of 5,000 years to the Earl of Arundel, from whom they passed to Lord Lumley, and shortly after to the family of Goode. As a result of legal proceedings commenced against Sebastian Goode in 1621, with a view to evading the terms of this lease, the college finally recovered this estate in 1707, and retain it to the present day.[17]

In 1086 Robert de Watevile was holding of Gilbert de Clare in Chessington half a mill worth 10s.,

Merton College, Oxford. Or three chevrons party and counter-coloured azure and gules.

1 Local Govt. Bd. Order 16490.
2 Hist. of Surr. iv, 402.
3 Blue Bk. Incl. Awards.
4 V.C.H. Surr. i, 317b.
5 Exch. Inq. p.m. 18 Hen. VI, no. 3.
6 V.C.H. Surr. i, 317b.
7 Feet of F. Surr. 31 Hen. III, no. 306; Kilner, Acct. of Pythagoras School, 157, 160.

7a Cal. Chart. R. 1226–57, p. 345.
8 Kilner, Acct. of Pythagoras School, 157; Heywood, Foundation Charters of Merton College, Oxford, 3; Parl. R. (Rec. Com.), i, 11a.
9 Harl. Chart. 53, H. 12. Chessington is not mentioned by name in this charter, being evidently included in Malden.
10 De Banco R. East. 15 Edw. I.

11 Plac. de Quo Warr. (Rec. Com.), 741; Cal. Chart. R. 1226–57, p. 345.
12 Cal. Chart. R. 1257–1300, p. 354.
13 Exch. Inq. p.m. 8 Edw. II, no. 68.
14 Chan. Inq. p.m. 49 Edw. III, pt. ii, no. 46.
15 Feud. Aids, v, 122.
16 Exch. Inq. p.m. 18 Hen. VI, pt. iii.
17 Kilner, Acct. of Pythagoras School, 64–5.

263

but it is not mentioned in connexion with the manor after this date.

Another estate in Chessington, probably part of the original manor, was acquired by Merton Priory,[18] whose lands in the 16th century are entered in the monastic accounts under the name of the manor of CHESSINGTON-AT-HOKE.

In 1521 the manor was leased by the Prior of Merton to Thomas Rogers for a term of 21 years at a rental of £5 0s. 6d., chargeable with 20s. 6d. in fee-farm rent due to the king,[19] and this lease was renewed to Richard Rogers on the same terms in 1525[20] and in 1536.[21] The manor was surrendered to the Crown with the rest of the possessions of the priory in 1538, and in 1552 was held at farm by Richard Hewer for the sum quoted above.[22]

George Rigley made a request to purchase this manor in 1553–4,[23] but nothing appears to have resulted, and in 1557 it was granted to William Rigges and Peter Gearing.[24]

Rigges and Gearing may have been trustees for Nicholas Saunders of Ewell, who was holding the manor in 1590, at which date he mortgaged it to Thomas Fletcher of London.[25] In 1601 Nicholas Saunders conveyed the manor to Benedict Haynes, gentleman,[26] son of William Haynes and Alice his wife,[27] and in 1610–11 it was held by William Haynes, brother of Benedict, who settled it upon himself and Anne his wife in that year.[28] William died in 1611, his son and heir William being then aged 13 years. The latter died two years later, leaving Matthew his brother and heir, aged 12 years.[29] Matthew died in 1617, and the estate was divided among his four sisters, Alice, Jane, Ann, and Thomasine.[30] Thomasine married John Evelyn, and in 1622 conveyed her fourth part of the manor to Robert Hatton,[31] serjeant-at-law, co. Thames Ditton,[32] who had married Alice, and who in 1628 acquired the remaining fourth parts from Ann (wife of Thomas Samwell) and Jane Haynes.[33] Robert and Alice had a son Sir Richard Hatton, who married Anne daughter of Sir Kenelme Jennour of Great Dunmow, Essex, bart.[34] Their son Sir Robert Hatton, afterwards Sheriff of Surrey, was holding the manor in 1679,[35] and, dying without issue, was succeeded by his nephew, Robert Hatton, a serjeant-at-law.[36] The latter died in 1701,[37] and was succeeded by his son Thomas Hatton,[38] who in 1742 conveyed this manor to Edward Northey of Epsom.[39] William Northey, son of Edward, sold in 1797 to Joseph Smith Gose, a distiller of Battersea,[40] who died in 1812,[41] and was succeeded by his son Henry Gosse, who held the manor in 1813.[42] His granddaughter

married Mr. John Maude, and they are now lords of the manor.

Appurtenant to the prior's manor were certain woods called Lynell Coppice (18 acres), Fusgrove Coppice (7 acres), Beatrice Hill Coppice (2 acres 7 roods), and 'Le Hedgerowe' in Alderfield (1 acre), which in 1552 were held on a lease granted by the prior to John Garroway;[43] also a wood called Gosborough Hill Wood, leased in 1537 to William Saunders, with liberty to fell the timber, on condition of leaving thirty 'standers' (trees left for increase) on every acre.[44] In the accounts of the manor for 1544 there is reckoned £4 13s. 4d. from eighty old oaks called 'Storbedd Okes,' suitable for firewood, situated on that parcel of the manor called Epsom Common.[45]

In a dispute which arose in the 16th century with regard to certain lands called 'Maulthayes' in Chessington, it was declared to be the custom of this manor that the youngest son should inherit.[46]

FREAM, formerly *FREREN*.—Land in Chessington was held of Edward the Confessor by Magno Suert, and in 1086 (when it was assessed for 1 hide, though in the time of King Edward it had been assessed for 5) was included among the estates of Miles Crispin, who appears to have claimed it without warrant in right of his father-in-law Wigod of Wallingford, as the jurors declared that Wigod was not holding it when William I came into England.[47]

This land descended with the honour of Wallingford, and in 1279 was in the possession of Edmund Earl of Cornwall.

In 1300 the tenant of the earl in Chessington was Rowland Huscarl,[48] and later it was held of the honour of Wallingford by Roger Apperle.[49] Before 1428 it seems to have been granted to the Abbot of Boxley, co. Kent, who in that year was assessed for half a knight's fee formerly held by Roger Apperle.[50] As early as 1189 the abbot had held land in Chessington granted by Robert of Chessington and confirmed in that year by Richard I[51] and subsequently by other kings.[52] In 1291 the possessions of the monastery in Boxley were taxed at £1 4s., and in 1329 the abbot was pardoned for acquiring a rent of 13s. 2d. there from Clement le Taillour and Nicholas son of Osbert atte Wodehall.[53]

The possessions of Boxley in Chessington are not described as a manor until 1535, when they are

BOXLEY ABBEY. *Argent a bend indented gules and a quarter gules with a crozier or therein.*

---

[18] Eudo de Malden, who granted the advowson to Merton, and who was evidently an early sub-tenant of the manor, may have granted lands also to the priory.
[19] Mins. Accts. 29–30 Hen. VIII, no. 115.
[20] A. C. Heales, *Records of Merton Priory*, 338.
[21] Harl. MSS. 606, fol. 125.
[22] Misc. Bks. (Exch. K.R.), vol. 168, p. 210.
[23] Partic. for Gts. 2225.
[24] Pat. 4 & 5 Philip and Mary, pt. vii, m. 34.
[25] Close, 32 Eliz. pt. xvi.
[26] Feet of F. Surr. East. 43 Eliz.
[27] Close, 40 Eliz. pt. v.

[28] Chan. Inq. p.m. (Ser. 2), cccxxiv, 168.
[29] Ibid. cccxxxiv, 55.
[30] Ibid. ccclxi, 101.
[31] Feet of F. Div. Co. Mich. 20 Chas. I.
[32] Le Neve, *Knights*, 317.
[33] Feet of F. Div. Co. Hil. 3 Chas. I.
[34] Le Neve, *Knights*, 317.
[35] Feet of F. Surr. Hil. 30–31 Chas. I; List of *Sheriffs*, P.R.O. 138.
[36] Manning and Bray, *Hist. of Surr.* ii, 685; Feet of F. Surr. Mich. 36 Chas. II.
[37] Chan. Enr. Decrees, 1901, no. 4, pt. ii.
[38] Ibid.
[39] Manning and Bray, *Hist. of Surr.* ii, 685.
[40] Ibid.
[41] *Gent. Mag.* lxxxii (i), 604.

[42] Recov. R. Hil. 53 Geo. III, no. 7.
[43] Harl. MSS. 606, fol. 125.
[44] Harl. Chart. 112, C 28.
[45] Mins. Accts. 36–7 Hen. VIII, no. 44, m. 65 d.
[46] Ct. of Req. bdles. 39, no. 2, 124, no. 54.
[47] *V.C.H. Surr.* i, 325b.
[48] Chan. Inq. p.m. 28 Edw. I, no. 44. The family of Huscarl also held under the honour of Wallingford in Beddington.
[49] *Feud. Aids*, v, 122.
[50] Ibid.
[51] Cart. Antiq. Q. 8.
[52] Cal. of Chart. R. 1257–1300, p. 354.
[53] Pat. 3 Edw. III, pt. i, m. 32; Inq. p.m. 3 Edw. III (2nd nos.), no. 134.

included among the monastic lands under the name of the 'Manor of Friern,' and valued at £6.[54]

In 1538 the manor was surrendered to the king by John Dobbys the abbot,[55] and in 1547 was granted to John Rychbell,[56] to hold in chief for a fortieth part of a knight's fee.[47] John Rychbell died seised of it in 1554, leaving a son and heir William Rychbell, aged six years.[58] In 1575 William Rychbell alienated to Henry Harvey,[59] who died seised of the manor in 1589, leaving a son and heir William.[60] The latter was succeeded in 1590 by his son William Harvey,[61] who in 1594 conveyed it to William Haynes.[62] From this date the descent of the manor follows that of Chessington down to the time of Thomas Hatton, who sold Chessington (*vide supra*) in 1742, but not Fream. He died in 1746. Fream was bought shortly afterwards by Mr. Christopher Hamilton, with whom lived Samuel Crisp, Miss Burney's friend. Mr. Hamilton was succeeded by his sister, who died in 1797. The house was called Chessington Hall by Mr. Hamilton, and the property has since been known by that name. It was used as a farm, and the old house, said to date from 1520, became ruinous and was pulled down in 1833-4. The present house was then built on the old foundations; the old brickwork is visible in the cellars. Mr. Horatio Chancellor bought Fream or Chessington Hall in 1851 and still owns it.[63]

In 1279 Edmund Earl of Cornwall claimed in Chessington his free monthly court of the honour of Wallingford, return of the king's writs, view of frankpledge, and the right to imprison in his Castle of Wallingford all taken and convicted of felony in Chessington, and was confirmed in all these liberties, save only the free monthly court.[64] In 1300 the same earl is stated to have 4*s.* from a certain view taken at Easter in Beddington and Chessington, and pertaining to the honour of Wallingford.[64]

In 1359 the Abbot of Boxley had a charter for free warren in Chessington,[66] and the grant to John Rychbell in 1547 included court leet, view of frankpledge, and warren in Fream and Chessington.[67]

The deed of alienation from William Rychbell to Henry Harvey in 1575 included among the appurtenances to the manor one water-mill, two dovehouses, and twenty fisheries.[68]

The church of *ST. MARY THE CHURCH VIRGIN* consists of a chancel 24 ft. 11 in. by 11 ft. 11 in. with a small north vestry, and a nave 42 ft. 3 in. by 15 ft. 2 in. with a south aisle 12 ft. wide, and a south porch. Over the west end of the nave is a wooden bell-turret.

The south aisle was added in 1870, and the north vestry is also modern, but the rest of the building dates from the beginning of the 13th century, with later 13th-century alterations, and a few inserted windows, &c., of more recent date. The nave has been lengthened, but the completeness of the renewal of the external stonework throughout the church has

destroyed all evidence. The walls are of flint rubble and the roofs are tiled.

A sketch in the church, c. 1740, shows it with no aisle, but with a west doorway to the nave and a large south porch of wood. Cracklow says that there was a pointed arch like the chancel arch between the nave and the wooden belfry, and the date 1636 on the ceiling, and Manning and Bray note that this date was on the north side of the ceiling.

The east window of the chancel is a 16th or 17th-century insertion, of two plain lights with three-centred heads, and to the north of it is a large semi-octagonal moulded image bracket of 15th-century date. There is a narrow lancet with a semicircular rear arch about midway in the north and south walls, of early 13th-century date, these being probably the only side-windows in the chancel as first built. To the east a wider lancet has been inserted in both cases, having a wooden lintel on the inside, and this alteration seems to have taken place about the middle of the 13th century. At the same time two recesses were made in the south wall near the west end, each about 3 ft. 6 in. wide by 1 ft. deep, and each lighted

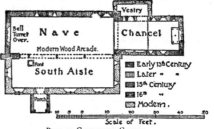

PLAN OF CHESSINGTON CHURCH

by a small lancet at the back. Their object is clearly to give more room for seats, the chancel being less than 12 ft. wide.

In the north wall part of a similar recess remains, but it has been cut through to make a doorway into the vestry; to the west of it is an original doorway, with plain chamfered jambs and semicircular head, adjoining which is a small square opening, rebated externally, and of the same date as the doorway. Its internal jambs are splayed, and it doubtless belongs to the category of low side-windows, though of unusual character. At the north-east of the chancel is a locker with rebated jambs in which is one of the hanging hooks for the wooden door, and a groove for a wooden shelf. The vestry has small modern single lights in its east and west walls and a two-light window with a wood frame to the north. The chancel arch has old masonry in its jambs, probably re-used from the earlier and narrower opening, and the arch, which is two-centred and of one chamfered

54 *Valor Eccl.* (Rec. Com.), i, 79.
55 Feet of F. Div. Co. Hil. 29 Hen. VIII.
56 Orig. R. (L.T.R.), 38 Hen. VIII, pt. iii, no. 5.
57 Pat. 38 Hen. VIII, pt. iii, m. 8.

58 Inq. p.m. 2 & 3 Philip and Mary, pt. ii, no. 61.
59 Feet of F. Surr. Hil. 17 Eliz.; Pat. 18 Eliz. pt. xi, m. 20.
60 Inq. p.m. 34 Eliz. pt. i, no. 50.
61 Chan. Inq. p.m. (Ser. 2), ccxxvii, 201.

62 Feet of F. Surr. Mich. 36 & 37 Eliz.
63 Information from Mr. Chancellor.
64 *Plac. de Quo Warr.* (Rec. Com.), 741.
65 Inq. p.m. 28 Edw. I, no. 44.
66 *Cal. Rot. Chart.* (Rec. Com.), 183.
67 Pat. 38 Hen. VIII, pt. iii, m. 8.
68 Feet of F. Surr. Hil. 17 Eliz.

3

34

order, also has some old stones, but the abaci are entirely modern.

There are four windows in the north wall of the nave, but no traces of a doorway. The western of the four windows is a single light with a semicircular rear arch, probably contemporary with the early windows in the chancel, but that next it to the east has a wooden lintel inside, and is perhaps of the later 13th-century date. The north-east window, of two pointed lights, may be a 15th-century insertion, and the fourth window, a little to the west, is also of two lights, and perhaps late 13th-century work. The complete renewal of all the outer stonework makes any dating doubtful. The west window is a modern triplet of lancets, and there is no trace of a west doorway.

The modern wooden arcade between the nave and the south aisle is of three bays with pairs of posts carrying the plates of the nave and aisle roofs, and the only old feature in the aisle is the south doorway, which has chamfered jambs and a two-centred head, probably of 13th-century date.

The porch is constructed of wood with plaster panels resting on low flint and stone walls.

The bell-turret on the west end of the nave is finished with a small octagonal shingled spire.

Two panels of English alabaster carving are preserved in the church, both of the 15th century, and probably from the Nottingham workshops. One, in the vestry, is part of a representation of the Nativity, and the other, on the south wall of the chancel, very much repaired, shows the Annunciation.

The font has a 13th-century moulded base from which rise a modern circular stem and four small detached shafts supporting a modern square bowl. All the other internal fittings are modern, the lectern being in the form of an angel with the book-rest on its wings. It was presented in 1898 and was carved in London.

There are eight bells in the turret which were cast by Warner in 1894.

The oldest piece of plate is an Elizabethan cup of 1568 which is kept at Malden. It is not quite 3½ in. high, and probably one of the smallest Elizabethan cups in existence. There are also two plated patens, a plated cup, flagon, and salver, two brass almsdishes, and a pewter flagon dated 1635.

Of the four books of registers the first contains baptisms from 1656 to 1754, marriages 1656 to 1756, with a gap between 1749 and 1756, and burials from 1656 to 1751. The second book contains baptisms 1754 to 1791, and burials 1752 to 1812, the third has marriages, not on printed forms, from 1756 to 1811, and the fourth contains baptisms from 1791 to 1812.

ADVOWSON The church of Chessington has always been a chapel to Malden, and was confirmed with that church to Merton Priory by Eudo de Malden[69] (of whom Peter de Malden [see manor] was the cousin and heir).

In 1265 the priory made over the advowson of the church of Malden to Walter de Merton,[70] who assigned it as part of the endowment of Merton College, which has held the advowson both of Malden and of the annexed chaplery of Chessington ever since. In 1279 a vicarage for Malden and Chessington was ordained by Nicholas of Ely, Bishop of Winchester.[71] In a survey of church lands taken 1649–58 the chapelry of Chessington is stated to be worth £60 per annum, and the commissioners appointed to make inquiries recommended that the chapelry should be divided from Malden and made a parish by itself.[72] This suggestion was, however, never complied with.

In 1595 the tithes of sheaves, grain, and hay in Chessington were conveyed by Thomas Vincent to Edward Carleton, together with the manor of Berewell in Kingston,[73] and a lease was still held by the owners of that manor in 1774.[74]

CHARITIES Smith's Charity is distributed as in other Surrey parishes.

CUDDINGTON

Codintone (xi cent.) ; Cudintone, Codington (xiii cent.) ; Codynton or Codyngton (xiv cent.).

Cuddington measures nearly 4 miles from north-west to south-east, and is scarcely a mile in breadth. It contains 1,859 acres, and extends over the usual variety of soils, the southern part being upon the chalk downs, the centre on the Woolwich and Thanet beds, the rest upon the London clay. There is no village of Cuddington ; Henry VIII pulled down the church, the old manor-house, and the village, to make Nonsuch Palace.[1] It appears possible from its position that the destroyed church and village were in this neighbourhood, and if this was the case they were placed in the usual situation, close to the foot of the chalk, either on the chalk itself or on the Thanet beds. There is no instance, on the northern side of the chalk-hills, where the parishes extend from the chalk on to the clay, of the old church and village

being on the clay. It is unlikely that Cuddington was differently placed from the others, but no map older than the time of Henry VIII exists. The Manor Farm is on the chalk and the Thanet sand, and may show the neighbourhood of the old manor-house.

The South Western Railway line from Wimbledon to Letherhead crosses the parish, with a station at Worcester Park, opened in 1859 ; and the London, Brighton, and South Coast Railway line to Epsom passes through it. This was first opened as the Croydon and Epsom Railway in 1848.

The early history, and the history of the inclosure, are summed up together in the story of Nonsuch Palace.

After the destruction of Nonsuch in 1671–2 the land in the parks was thrown into farms, of which more than one had evidently existed before outside

69 A. C. Heales, *Rec. of Merton Priory*, 27.
70 Ibid. App. p. lxxix.
71 Percival, *Stat. of Merton College*, 130.
72 *Surr. Arch. Coll.* xvii, 101, 105.
73 Feet of F. Surr. East. 37 Eliz.
74 Ibid. Mich. 14 Geo. III.
1 Most of the parks were on the clay ; the site of the palace was on the Thanet sand.

the park pales. The place, however, existed in name only. There was no ecclesiastical parish; the land was taxed with Ewell, but separately rated, with its own overseers.

The present house, known as Nonsuch Park, is the property of Captain W. R. G. Farmer. It is not on the site of the palace, but is on the confines of the old Little Park, in which the palace stood. It was built for Mr. Samuel Farmer by Sir Jeffrey Wyattville, in supposed 16th-century style, early in the 19th century (1802–6).

In the last fifty years, as railways extended, houses have grown up near the site of Worcester Park and have received the name of Cuddington. Worcester Court is the residence of Mrs. Hanney, and Homesteads that of Mr. C. A. Harris, C.B., C.M.G. In 1894 a church was built at Worcester Park, which is now the parish church, though certainly upon a very different site from the original one: There is also a Primitive Methodist chapel.

In Cuddington is the Joint Isolation Hospital for the Sutton, Carshalton, Letherhead, and Epsom District Councils.

Cuddington and Nonsuch Park were, according to Leland, the site of pits for obtaining fire-clay. Subsequently Nonsuch pottery and tiles were known, but they were in reality made in Ewell.[1a] There used to be gunpowder works on the Hoggsmill Stream, called generally the Malden Mills or the Long Ditton Mills, but they were actually in Cuddington parish.[2]

There are no schools peculiar to Cuddington. Cheam and Cuddington (National) School for Boys was built in 1826, and that for girls and infants in 1869. But they are the original Cheam schools.

The earliest mention of CUDDINGTON MANOR is in connexion with Chertsey Monastery, the alleged first endowment of which by Frithwald, *subregulus* of Surrey, and Bishop Erkenwald included thirty dwellings at Ewell cum 'Cotinton.'[3] The confirmation of this charter by Athelstan in 933[4] mentions the village of 'Cudintone'; and Edward the Confessor in 1062 confirmed to the monastery six dwellings at 'Cudintone.'[5] No further mention of Chertsey in connexion with Cuddington occurs after this date, however,[6] and in the Domesday Survey it is declared to have been held in the time of Edward the Confessor by Earl Leofwine, the younger brother of Harold.[7] At the date of the Survey (1086) it was held by Ilbert de Laci, lord of Pontefract, of Odo of Bayeux,[8] and on the forfeiture of his estates for high treason by Robert son of Ilbert, was bestowed by Henry I on Hugh de Laval.[9]

In 1203 Guy de Laval forfeited his English estates for joining with the French king against John,[10] who in the same year granted Cuddington to William de St. Michael, who was to render to Roger de Lacy, Constable of Chester (who had claimed the estates of Guy as his right by inheritance), the same farm which he, William, had been wont to render to Guy.[11] Laurence de St. Michael was holding land in Surrey in 1233,[12] and in 1236–7 he appears as party to a fine concerning lands in Cuddington.[13] He or his son died in 1283, leaving a widow Margaret, four sons—Laurence, William, Thomas, and John—and four daughters.[14] It was probably the eldest son Laurence who in 1289 sought to replevy his land in Cuddington which had been taken into the king's hands for default.[15] In 1331, 1332, and 1333 courts were held in the name of Thomas de St. Michael,[16] who in 1333 settled the manor upon himself for life, and after his death upon Laurence son of John de St. Michael and Joan his wife and their heirs.[17] In 1337 the manor was held by Laurence,[18] who appears indifferently in records of this period under the name of Codington (Cuddington) or St. Michael, the latter, however, occurring but rarely after this date.

CODINGTON. *Gules a cross or fretty gules.*

In 1355 courts were held in the name of Sir Simon de Codington (Sheriff of Surrey in 1353 and 1362) and Katherine his wife.[19] Sir Simon married, secondly, Idonea, and died before 1378, in which year the manor was settled by trustees on Ralph son of Simon (Sheriff of Surrey in 1400) and Anne his wife.[20]

In 1470 the manor was surrendered to John Codington by his mother Margaret widow of Thomas Codington.[21] The manor was finally sold in 1538 by Richard Codington and Elizabeth his wife to Henry VIII,[22] who annexed it to the honour of Hampton Court, and commenced there the erection of the magnificent palace of Nonsuch.

In 1547 a messuage and lands in the manor of Nonsuch *alias* Cuddington were granted by Edward VI to Sir Thomas Cawarden (who was Sheriff of Surrey in 1547) to hold for 21 years for a rent of £5 5s. 8d. In 1550 Cawarden was appointed Keeper of the King's House of Nonsuch, 'called the Banketyng House within the Park there.'[23] The Banqueting House was a separate building from the Palace, which was not completed until later. In 1556 the reversion of Cawarden's lease, with the additions of the capital mansion of Nonsuch or Nonsuch Place, with appurtenances in Nonsuch, Ewell, Cuddington, and Cheam, and all that park called the Little Park of Nonsuch, was bestowed on Henry, twelfth Earl of Arundel,[24] Lord Chamberlain to

[1a] *V.C.H. Surr.* ii, 282, 293–4.
[2] Ibid. 327.
[3] Birch, *Cart. Sax.* i, 64. But see in Chertsey for the authenticity of these early charters.
[4] Kemble, *Cod. Dipl.* ccclxiii; Birch, *Cart. Sax.* ii, 397.
[5] Kemble, *Cod. Dipl.* dcccxii.
[6] A possible supposition is that Ulwin who in 1086 held 1 hide of 'Codintone' may have been the same Ulwin who held Byfleet of Chertsey, and this may have been the Chertsey holding in Cuddington.

[7] *V.C.H. Surr.* i, 304a.
[8] Ibid.; *Engl. Hist. Rev.* xiv, 430.
[9] *Engl. Hist. Rev.* xiv, 429.
[10] *Rot. de Liberate* (Rec. Com.), 44.
[11] Ibid.; Dugdale, *Baronage*, i, 100.
[12] *Cal. Close*, 1231–4, p. 250.
[13] Feet of F. Surr. 21 Hen. III, file 10.
[14] R. R. Sharpe, *Cal. of London Wills*, i, 67; Chan. Inq. p.m. Edw. I, file 33, no. 11.
[15] *Cal. Close*, 1288–96, p. 52.
[16] Ct. R. portf. 204, no. 44.
[17] Feet of F. 6 Edw. III, no. 105.
[18] Inq. p.m. 11 Edw. III, no. 39.

[19] Ct. R. portf. 204, no. 44.
[20] Close, 51 Edw. III, m. 6 d.
[21] Anct. Deeds, P.R.O. B. 1159.
[22] Pat. 30 Hen. VIII, pt. iii, m. 31; Treas. Roll of Accts. pt. i, m. 11 d; Feet of F. Surr. Mich. 30 Hen. VIII; L. *and* P. *Hen. VIII*, xiii (1), g. 1519 (10); xv, 498 (36).
[23] Original patent at Loseley.
[24] Pat. 3 & 4 Philip and Mary, pt. iii, m. 36; Orig. R. 3 & 4 Philip and Mary, pt. iv, no. 71. Cawarden died in 1559. His lease expired in 1568.

Henry VIII and Lord High Steward of the Household to Mary and Elizabeth. The Earl of Arundel died in 1580,[25] having bequeathed all his manors and lands to his son-in-law Lord Lumley, upon whom he had already settled Nonsuch. Lord Lumley died in 1609, and was succeeded by his nephew, Splandian Lloyd.[26] The latter dying without issue was succeeded by his brother Henry Lloyd,[27] whose grandson of the same name died in 1704. Robert Lumley Lloyd, son of Henry, was rector of St. Paul's, Covent Garden, and chaplain to the Duke of Bedford, whose patronage he acknowledged by bequeathing to him all his possessions in Surrey, including this estate.[28] In 1755 the manor, rectory, and advowson of the vicarage were sold by the duke to Edward Northey of Epsom,[29] who died in 1772, leaving this estate to his son William Northey.[30] The latter died in 1808,[31] and was succeeded by his cousin William Northey, on whose death the estate passed to his brother, Rev. Edward Northey, Canon of Windsor.[32] Edward Richard Northey, son of the latter, was holding the manor in 1821,[33] and his son, Rev. E. W. Northey, M.A., of Epsom, is lord of the manor at the present day.

LLOYD. *Quarterly or and azure four harts countercoloured.*

NONSUCH.—The whole of the former village of Cuddington, with its mansion and church, were swept away by Henry VIII to make room for the palace afterwards known as Nonsuch, and its two parks—the Great Park or Worcester Park (containing 911 acres), and the Little Park (containing 671 acres). The palace was never completed by Henry VIII, but had already attained sufficient splendour to evoke from Leland the lines—

'Hanc quia non habeat similem, laudare Britanni Saepe solent, *nullique parem* cognomine dicunt.'

During the next reign Sir Thomas Cawarden, Keeper of the Banqueting House, in accordance with a royal mandate entertained there 'at the Quenes Majestie's House,' the French ambassador, M. de Noailles, and his wife.[34]

In 1556 the reversion of Cawarden's lease was granted to the Earl of Arundel, with the additional grant of the Little Park and the palace (*vide supra*) which he is said to have completed.[35] He in 1559 entertained there Queen Elizabeth, when, we are told, 'her grace had as gret chere every nyght and bankets; but ye sonday at nyght my lord of Arundell made her a grete bankett at ys coste as ever was sene, for soper, bankete, and maske, w' drums and flutes, and all ye mysyke yt cold be, tyll mydnyght; and as for chere,

has not bene sene nor heard. On Monday was a great supper made for her, but before night she stood at her standing in the further park, and there she saw a course. At nyght was a play of the Chylderyn of Powlles and theyr mysyke master Sebastian Phelyps and Mr. Haywode; and after, a grete banket, w' drumes and flutes and the goodly bankets and dishes as costely as ever was sene, and gyldyd. . . . My Lord of Arundell gayfe to ye Quene grace a cubard of plate.'[36] Queen Elizabeth paid frequent subsequent visits to Nonsuch, and in 1590–2 purchased the palace and park of John, Lord Lumley, heir of the Earl of Arundel, in exchange for lands to the value of £534.[37]

In 1599 Mr. Roland White wrote to Robert Sydney: 'Her Majestie is returned again to Nonesuch, which of all other places she likes best'; and it was on the occasion of this visit that the Earl of Essex, having returned from Ireland without the queen's permission, burst into her bedchamber at ten o'clock in the morning, and though received kindly at the time, was committed four days later to the custody of the Lord Keeper.[38]

Lord Lumley was appointed Keeper of the Palace and Little Park by James I, who was frequently resident there for hunting and racing, which probably took place on Banstead Downs (*vide* Banstead).

On 1 December 1606 the Earl of Worcester was appointed Keeper of the Great Park at Nonsuch, whence no doubt it acquired the name Worcester Park, and the lodge in it the name of Worcester House.[39]

The estate formed part of the jointure of Queen Henrietta Maria, and was visited by Charles I in 1625, 1629, 1630, and 1632. During the Commonwealth the palace was at first leased to Algernon Sidney for £150 per annum. The Government soon afterwards assigned the whole place to Lilburne's regiment, then in Scotland, as security for the men's pay. A letter is extant from Colonel Robert Lilburne to General Lambert, in which he offers on behalf of the regiment to sell Nonsuch to him. The men, it was thought, would be willing to accept 12s. in the £ for their debentures.[40] Certainly the Little Park and Palace were purchased by Major-General Lambert,[41] and in 1654–6 the Great Park and Worcester House were purchased by Colonel Thomas Pride,[42] who died in 1658 at Worcester House, the house in the Great Park.

At the Restoration Nonsuch House and Parks were restored to Queen Henrietta Maria. In 1663 the reversion of part of the estate (under the name of Nonsuch Great Park or Worcester Park, land called the Great Park Meadow, and the mansion-house called Worcester House) was leased by Charles II for a term of 99 years to Sir Robert Long, his late companion in exile, and at this date Chancellor of the Exchequer;

25 Feet of F. Div. Co. East. 8 Eliz.; Hil. 13 Eliz.; Will P.C.C. 1 Arundell.
26 Chan. Inq. p.m. (Ser. 2), cccxi, 109; G.E.C. *Complete Peerage*, v, 178.
27 Feet of F. Surr. East. 4 Chas. I; Recov. R. East. 4 Chas. I, no. 33.
28 Close, 29 Geo. II, pt. iii, no. 11; 34 Geo. II, pt. iv, no. 9.
29 Ibid.; Recov. R. Mich. 1 Geo. III, rot. 147.
30 Will P.C.C. 403 Bargrave.
31 Manning and Bray, *Surr.* i, 471.
32 Burke, *Landed Gentry*, 1906.

33 Recov. R. Mich. 2 Geo. IV, rot. 160; ibid. Hil. 3 & 4 Geo. IV, rot. 219.
34 A. J. Kempe, *The Loseley MSS.* 157.
35 Camden, *Brit.* (ed. Gibson), 158.
36 *Gent. Mag.* (New Ser.), viii, 139 (from the MS. life of the Earl of Arundel).
37 A. J. Kempe, *The Loseley MSS.* 147; Feet of F. Surr. Hil. 34 Eliz.
38 Strickland, *Lives of the Queens of Engl.* iv, 717.
39 Pat. 4 Jas. I, pt. xxiv. Lord Lumley

had had a lease of the Great Park Lodge; *Shrewsbury Letters*, iii, 207. Lumley died in 1609, and Worcester's keepership must have co-existed with his lease and lasted beyond it, to allow the name Worcester Park to remain. The lodge is called the Earl of Worcester's house in 1642. B.M. Thomason Tracts, E. 127 (39).
40 Firth, *Cromwell's Army*, 206; *Letters from Officers in Scotland* (Bannatyne Club), 59.
41 *Gent. Mag.* (New Ser.), viii, 143.
42 *Commons' Journ.* viii, 73.

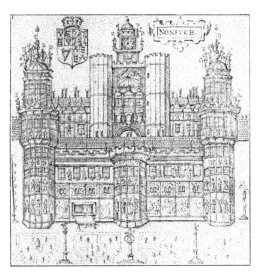

CUDDINGTON : NONSUCH PALACE IN 1611

(From Speed's 'Theatre of the Empire of Great Britain')

one of the conditions of the lease being that Sir Robert should from time to time convert part of the premises into pasture without destroying the trees and bushes, so that the same might become fit for deer in case the king were minded to restore and make the same park a park as formerly, Sir Robert to be keeper of the park and have herbage and pannage.[42] During the plague year of 1665 Nonsuch Palace was fitted up temporarily for the offices of the Exchequer. In 1670 Sir Robert Long pleaded for another life in his lease, at the same time representing that during the late disturbed times the site had been converted into tillage, the wood all down, and that he, Sir Robert, had compounded with the queen for her interest, bought out the keepers, and paid £2,500 for repairs of the house.[43]

Sir Robert Long died in 1673, and his will[44] mentions that he settled his lease on his nephew. But in 1670 the palace and fee simple of both parks were bestowed by Charles II on Viscount Grandison and Henry Brounker, in trust for Barbara Villiers, Duchess of Cleveland,[45] in that year created Baroness of Nonsuch, by whom as a means of settling her pecuniary difficulties the house was entirely dismantled, its contents sold, and the park divided up into farms.[47]

In 1710 the parks were held by Charles, Duke of Grafton, grandson of the duchess,[5] whose son in 1731 sold Worcester Park to John Walter his former steward. John Walter died in 1745, and was succeeded by his son George, afterwards knighted. The latter left two daughters, one of whom died single in 1749, while the other married Rev. — Clarke, who sold to Mr. Taylor, from whom it passed to William Taylor, who died in 1764. Mr. Taylor set up here a large gunpowder factory.[48] His heir, William Taylor, built a new house, called Worcester Park, in 1797. The property has long been divided. Worcester Park House is now the residence of Miss Wheeler.

The Little Park was sold by the Duke of Grafton in 1731 to Joseph Thomson, who built a house here and left it to his nephew, the Rev. Joseph Whateley, on condition that he should take priest's order. On the death of Mr. Whateley the estate was sold to Mr. Farmer, who built a new house,[50] and is now the property of his descendant, Captain William R. G. Farmer.

FARMER of Nonsuch. *Argent a fesse sable between three lions' heads razed gules.*

Some idea of the splendour of Nonsuch Palace may be gathered from the eulogies of contemporary writers, such as Leland and Camden, while it is described at length by Braun in *Civitates Orbis Terrarum*.[51] The Survey of 1650 gives a detailed account of the house and grounds. The commissioners' admiration of the splendid building and anxiety for its preservation can be clearly seen through the dry official language of their report. The 'capitall messuage or royal mansion house, commonly called Nonsuch [they say], consists of one fayer stronge and large structure of build-

ing of freestone of two large stories high, well wrought and battled with stone and covered with blue slate, standing round a court of 150 foote long and 132 foote broad, paved with stone, commonly called the Outward Courte,' and also of 'one other faire and very curious structure or building of two stories high, the lower storie whereof is of good and well wrought freestone, and the higher of wood, richly adorned and set forth and garnished with variety of statues, pictures, and other antick formes of excellent art and workmanship, and of no small cost ; all which building lying almost upon a square, is covered with blue slate, and incloseth one faire and large court of one hundred thirty seaven foot broad, and one hundred and sixteen foot long, all paved with freestone, commonly called the Inner Court.'

The uses of the various rooms are noted ; in the outer court on the ground floor were the buttery, the wine cellar, and fifteen other rooms occupied by Lady Holland's servants, the housekeeper, the gentlemen ushers, the quarter waiter, the groom porter, and Mr. Henry Jermyn. On the first floor twenty-one rooms are mentioned, three for Lady Denbigh, three for Lady Holland, a dining-room, drawing-room, and bedchamber for Lady Carlisle, two rooms for her servants, four rooms for the lord chamberlain, Lord Dorset, two for the queen's almoner, two for the maids of honour, and two for the housekeeper.

The outer court was entered through a three-story gatehouse, 'very strong and graceful,' with embattled turrets at the angles, and a large room on the top floor 'very pleasant and delectable for prospect.'

The rooms of the inner court, being the royal apartments, were 'very faire and large,' many of them panelled and having 'spacious lights both inwards and outwards,' i.e. towards the court and towards the park. Another gatehouse stood between the two courts, an ascent of eight steps leading up from the outer to the inner court. This gatehouse was of freestone with corner turrets and a clock turret in the middle, and was 'of most excellent workmanship and a very speciall ornament to Nonsuch house.'

The rooms of the inner court were on the ground floor a guard chamber, two rooms for Lady Cary, two for 'Madam Nurse' the queen's back stairs, two for Madam Vautlet the queen's dresser, two for Dr. 'Myerne,' two for Madam Conget, two for the queen's priests, two for the master of the horse, two for the queen's robes, two for Madam Cyvet, two for the queen's 'querrier,' the queen's kitchen, a room for 'Mr. Cooke,' and one for the queen's waiters. On the first floor were the presence chamber, the privy closet, the privy chamber, the privy gallery, the queen's bedchamber, the queen's back stairs, the king's bedchamber and back stairs, the queen's chapel, and two rooms for the Marchioness Hambleton. The inner court had wooden battlements covered with lead, adding 'a very great grace and special ornament to the whole building,' and had large angle turrets at east and west, five stories high, of timber covered with lead, 'the chiefe ornament of the whole house.' In the west turret was a large lead cistern, serving the whole house, including a white marble fountain in

[42] Orig. R. L.T.R. 15 Chas. II, pt. iv, no. 4 ; Pat. 15 Chas. II, pt. v, no. 1.
[43] Cal. S.P. Dom. 1670, p. 298.
[44] Proved 20 Dec. 1673, P.C.Canterbury.
[44] See Feet of F. Surr. Trin. 3 Jas. II.
[5] Dict. Nat. Biog.
[48] Recov. R. East. 9 Anne, rot. 117.
[49] Manning and Bray, Hist. of Surr. ii, 607.
[50] Ibid.
[51] Braun and Hogenburg, Civitates Orbis Terrarum, V, 1.

the inner court, supported by two brass dragons, and having a lead-lined marble basin on three steps. A 'belcone' in the middle of the privy gallery seems to have been specially designed to give a view of this fountain.

In addition to these two courts was a third and smaller kitchen court, adjoining the outer court on the east. The lay-out of the grounds is described. In front of the outer court was a stone balustrade with a bowling-green, 'railed with good postes, rails, and lattices of wood,' from which an avenue of trees led directly to the park gate. The privy garden, inclosed by a 14-foot brick wall, lay round and adjoining unto the three outsides of the inward court,' and was divided into 'allyes, quarters, and rounds set about with thorne edges,' rather neglected at the time, as was to be expected, but easily capable of repair. To the north lay the kitchen garden, also walled, and to the west a wilderness, its trees lately felled by 'one Mr. Bond, one of the contractors for sale of the late king's goods.'[53] North of the wilderness was an orchard.

In the privy garden, on the west side of the great turret at the west angle of the inner court, was a marble basin with a pelican through which the water was supplied, and near it a 'piramide' or spired pinnacle of marble. There were also two other marble 'piramides' called the 'Fawlcon perches,' having between them a white marble fountain set round with 'six trees called black trees, which trees beare no fruite but only a very pleasant flower.'

In the highest part of the park was a foursquare banqueting house, timber-built in three stories, with three cellars on the ground floor, a hall and three other rooms above, and on the top floor five rooms, with a lantern on the roof. Nearly all the rooms were panelled and amply lighted, and at each of the four corners of the house was a 'belcone placed for prospect.' The banqueting house was surrounded by a brick wall with projecting angle bastions. This wall is the only part now remaining. There were also a well-house, 'with a wheel for winding up of water,' and a wash-house close by.

Other buildings in the park were the under-house-keeper's house, with the saucery house for the yeomen of the saucer, and a well-house with a deep well, the stables, 'a little remote upon the north-east,' with barns and outhouses, and the keeper's lodge.

All the buildings were in a very good state, and 'not fit to be demolished or taken down,' and the value of their materials was estimated at £7,020.

By 1665 Evelyn speaks of the gardens as 'ruined,' and though he remarks upon the wonderful preservation of the bas-reliefs in plaster, considering their age, he implies that they were perishing. The house must have needed a great outlay to keep it in repair. The description and the picture alike convey the idea of a somewhat barbaric magnificence overloaded with ornament.

The house was destroyed by orders of the Duchess of Cleveland, but not immediately after she received it.[53] That some of it, or of the separate banqueting house, was standing about the time of James II is proved by a MS. note in Aubrey's *Wiltshire*, by P. le Neve, Norrey, who writes : 'I saw it in james II's time or thereabouts. It was done with plaister work made of rye dough, in imagery, very costly.'[54] As late as 1757 the foundations of it could be traced round the courtyards.[54a]

CHURCH Of the original church the exact site cannot be determined at the present day.

It was, with the old manor-house, at the foot of the downs between the villages of Cheam and Ewell.[55] It was swept away with the rest of the village in the reign of Henry VIII to make room for the palace and park of Nonsuch.

The present church of *ST. MARY THE VIRGIN* is an unfinished building dating from 1895, and situated at Worcester Park. It is in the style of the 13th century, and has flint-faced walls with bands of red brick and dressings of stone. It consists of an apsidal chancel, with organ chamber, south chancel-aisle, nave and aisles of three bays out of the five requisite to complete the building, the west end being closed by a temporary brick wall and west porch. The chancel has a wood-vaulted ceiling ; its east walls are lined with marble ; the reredos is of white marble and alabaster. Carved oak screens span the chancel arch. The nave has a clearstory of lancets and a panelled oak ceiling. The roofs are tiled. Over the nave roof is an oak fleche with a spirelet covered with lead. The pulpit is of carved stone ; the font of stone with marble shafts. The churchyard is a triangular grass plot in which stands a tall elm and a few young trees. The communion plate is electro-plated, and consists of a cup, two patens, and a flagon.

ADVOWSON The church of Cuddington was granted in the early 12th century by Hugh de Laval to Bernard the Scribe in trust for the Prior and convent of Merton, by whom it was retained from that date until the Dissolution.[56] By a charter dating between 1186 and 1198 the prior and convent granted to one, Master Hamo, a lease of the church for four years in consideration of 6 silver marks per annum.[57] In 1284 Pope Martin IV, upon a petition from the prior and convent, pleading poverty, consented to their appropriating the church to their own uses, reserving, however, a suitable sustentation for a vicar, and sufficient for the payment of ecclesiastical dues and other burdens, this appropriation being confirmed by letters patent in 1309.[58] The church was valued at £14 13s. 4d. in the Taxation of 1291.[59] In 1311 an episcopal ordinance was issued for the endowment of a vicarage, and Low Thomas of Kingston, priest, was presented to the same.[60] In 1346 a suit took place between the king and the Prior of Merton, the king claiming the presentation to the vicarage by reason of the last vicar having resigned at a time when the temporalities of the monastery were in the king's hands during a vacancy of the priorship.[61] The court adjudged the presentation to the king.

[52] Evelyn on his visit in 1665 remarked on the destruction of trees.
[53] The Duchess of Cleveland, supplanted in Charles's favour by the Duchess of Portsmouth, resided abroad 1677 to 1684. It may have been after her return to England that she completed the destruction to raise money. She survived till 1709.
[54] *Gent. Mag.* 1837, ii, 146 ; Aubrey, *Wilts.* ii, 218.
[54a] Pocock's *Travels in England* (Camd. Soc.), ii, 262.
[55] Survey communicated by Mr. Whateley to Mr. Manning.
[56] H. C. Heales, *Rec. of Merton Priory*, 9.
[57] Ibid. 43.
[58] Ibid. 166 ; *Cal. Pat.* 1307–13, p. 162.
[59] *Pope Nich. Tax.* (Rec. Com.), 270b.
[60] H. C. Heales, *Rec. of Merton Priory*, lxviii.
[61] *Cal. Pat.* 1345–8, pp. 168, 232 ; De Banco R. 348, m. 44a.

PALATIVM REGIVM IN ANGLIÆ REGNO APPELLATVM NONCIVTZ,
Hec effi indicium facit.

CUDDINGTON : NONSUCH PALACE

(From an old Print)

In 1428 the church was exempted from taxation on the ground that there were not at that time ten inhabitants in the parish having dwellings.

At the Dissolution the rectory and advowson were valued at a total of £10, from which the vicar received £8 in a money payment of 2s. and a cottage for his dwelling.[62] At this time, or very shortly after, the rectory appears to have been held at farm by one William Cowper of Westminster and Cecilia his wife, who in 1539 resigned the remainder

of their term in the same in consideration of other estates.[63]

In 1586 the rectory and the church, which had been pulled down, and the advowson, with tithes of grain, hay, &c., which in 1571 had been leased to Roger Marshall for twenty-one years, were granted by Queen Elizabeth to Sir Christopher Hatton,[64] who the next day conveyed the same to John, Lord Lumley,[65] and from this date the descent of the rectory followed that of the manor.

EPSOM

Evesham (xi cent.) ; Ebbesham (xiii cent.) ; Ebsham, Ebesham, and Ebbesham (xiv cent.) ; Ebbisham, Eppesham, and Ebsame (xvi cent.) ; Ebsham (xvii cent. and xviii cent.) ; Epsom (late xvii cent.).

Epsom is a town 16 miles north-east of Guildford, 7 miles south-by-east of Kingston, 15 miles from London. The parish measures 4 miles from north to south, and 2 miles from east to west, and contains 4,413 acres. It lies upon the chalk downs, the Woolwich and Thanet Beds, and the London Clay. The church is on the chalk, but the greater part of the old village is on a patch of gravel and sand of the Thanet Beds. The building of later days has had a tendency to spread up the chalk. A branch of the Hoggsmill River flows from Epsom. Besides agriculture, brick-making and brewing are carried on ; but the chief importance of Epsom since it ceased to be a small country village has been, first, that of a watering-place ; and, secondly, that of a horse-racing town. Epsom Common is still to a great extent open ground, lying on the clay, and adjoining Ashtead Common to the west of the town. Epsom Downs are a noble expanse of chalk country, comprising 944 acres of open land.

The road from London to Dorking passes through Epsom. This road was evidently passable for carriages when Epsom was a fashionable watering-place, in the latter part of the 17th century ; but it was not passable, except with difficulty, beyond Epsom till 1755, when an Act[1] was passed for carrying on the turnpike road from the watch-house in Epsom. In the same year[2] the road from Epsom to Ewell, and thence into the Kingston road, was re-made.

The London, Brighton, and South Coast Railway came to Epsom by the Croydon and Epsom line in 1847. The Epsom Downs branch was opened in 1865. The London and South-Western Railway came to Epsom in 1859. The stations of the two companies are some distance apart, but the lines converge just before reaching the London and South-Western Railway Station, and continue together till Letherhead, the Dorking extension to Horsham having obtained running powers over the South-Western Railway line.

Epsom is now a flourishing country town. It was constituted an urban district under the Public Health Act of 1848 on 19 March 1850. By the Local Government Act of 1894 it was put under a Local District Council of nine members, increased to twelve

in 1903. It is essentially a town, supplied with gas by the Epsom and Ewell Gas Company, formed 1839; with electric light by a company in Church Street ; with water from the chalk by works belonging to the Council. There is a cemetery in Ashley Road, first opened in 1871. The County Court was built in 1848 ; the Town Hall, in red brick and terra cotta, in 1883. The Technical Institute and Art School was opened in 1897. The sewage of the town is disposed of by an irrigation system on part of the Epsom Court farm lands, the purified effluent is discharged into the Hoggsmill River. The District Council's Isolation Hospital is in the Hook Road. The Union Workhouse is near the Dorking Road. Horton Manor, lying west of the town, has been acquired by the London County Council for an asylum, and the Manor Asylum has been built for 2,100 patients. The Colony for Epileptics, in the same neighbourhood, lying partly in Ewell Parish, was opened in 1902, and can accommodate 366 patients in separate houses. A large suburb of cottages is growing up in the neighbourhood of the asylums. There is another outlying hamlet about Epsom Common.

The wide High Street is still a picturesque feature of the town. Up till 1848 a watch-house, with a sort of wooden steeple, stood in the middle of it, where the present clock tower stands. There was also a large pond, drained in 1854. In this street, as well as in South Street and Church Street, are many interesting old houses and inns. A fair is still held in the town on 25 July and two following days.

Historically, Epsom was unimportant till the 17th century. Neolithic flakes and implements have been found, but few only, near Woodcote. Toland, in his letter descriptive of Epsom in 1711, speaks of Roman remains at Epsom Court Farm. The old trackway (see under Mickleham) which came over the Downs headed for the western side of Epsom Race-course, but is not to be clearly traced beyond it. It is called the Portway in a rental of 1495-6.[3] When the church was being enlarged in 1907 a dene hole was discovered in the churchyard. The depth was some 16 ft. to the bottom of the shaft, and chambers ran each way from the bottom of the shaft for 12 ft. or 13 ft. The shaft and most of the chambers had been filled in with loose soil, and a mediaeval grave had been dug to a great depth and reached the top of one of the chambers, whence the bones found there had been let

[62] Valor Eccl. (Rec. Com.), ii, 41, 48 ; H. C. Heales, Rec. of Merton Priory, App. ciii.

[63] L. and P. Hen. VIII, xiv(1), g. 651(36).
[64] Pat. 28 Eliz. pt. ii, no. 2.
[65] Close, 28 Eliz. pt. xi.

[1] 28 Geo. II, cap. 45.
[2] Ibid. cap. 57.
[3] Chertsey Chart. fol. 392b.

through to the bottom. Nothing else was found but a little loose charcoal, and two or three small pieces of hand-made pottery.

Epsom Well, to the discovery of which the place owed its later fame, is on Epsom Common, some distance from the village. It is in the London Clay. Water charged with sulphate of magnesia is not uncommonly found in this soil, as at Jessop's Well, on Stoke D'Abernon Common, which is probably as powerful as the Epsom spring. The situation of Epsom, however, on the edge of the downs, made it a pleasant resort, and so gave greater fame to its waters. The current story is that the well was discovered in 1618 by one Henry Wicker, who observed that cattle would not drink of it. Dudley North, third Lord North, asserts in his *Forest of Varieties*, published in 1645, that he first made the Tunbridge Wells and Epsom waters known to the world at large. Aubrey drank the water in 1654. After the Restoration the Epsom Wells became a fashionable resort, Epsom being nearer to London than Tunbridge Wells. Nonsuch, so long as it remained standing, was a royal house in the near neighbourhood, and it was an easy ride from Hampton Court. Charles II, James II, as Duke of York, and Prince George of Denmark, all visited Epsom. Pepys, of course, went there; he paid his first visit in 1663, when the town was so full that he had to seek a lodging in Ashtead. In 1667, he writes, on 14 July, 'to Epsom by eight o'clock to the Well, where much Company. And to the town, to the King's Head; and hear that my lord Buckhurst and Nelly' (Nell Gwynne) 'are lodged at the next house, and Sir Charles Sedley with them; and keep a merry house.' In 1663 he had remarked on the large number of citizens 'that I could not have thought to have seen there; that they ever had it in their heads or purses to go down thither.' The New Inn in High Street dates from about this period. It is now called Waterloo House, and is occupied by shops. It is now mainly an 18th-century two-story building of red brick with plastered quoins, and a low gable in the middle of the front; in the roof are attics lighted by good dormer windows. There is a good gable end over the original entrance, which led into a narrow courtyard in the centre, whence there is an exit at the opposite end. On the first floor, approached by a fine staircase with carved balusters, was the Assembly or Ball Room, now cut up by partitions. In 1690 Mr. Parkhurst, lord of the manor, built an Assembly Room at the Wells, erected other buildings, and planted avenues of elms and limes, which were mostly cut down for timber in the early 19th century. The popularity and fashion of Epsom at this time is sufficiently attested, not merely by the names of visitors, but by the announcement in the *Gazette*, 19 June 1684, that a daily post would go to and from Epsom and Tunbridge Wells respectively and London during the season for drinking the waters, that is, during May, June, and July. This was the earliest daily post outside London.

In 1711, Toland, the famous deistical writer, gives a very flowery description of the beauties of Epsom in a letter to 'Eudena.' But by this date Epsom had come to rely upon its general attractions for pleasure seekers, rather than upon its medicinal waters. A quack doctor named Levingston sank a rival well, of no particular quality, near the town in

1706, built an Assembly Room and shops near it, and in 1715 got a lease of the old well and closed it till his death in 1727. Queen Anne visited Epsom during this period, but the place decayed as a fashionable resort. The neighbouring gentry, however, used to visit the old well when it was reopened, after 1727. Clearly it continued to be a very different kind of place from any other country town in Surrey. In 1725 Bishop Willis, in his Visitation questions, asked for the names of resident gentry in every parish, and for Epsom, Lord Yarmouth, Lord Guilford, Lord Baltimore, Sir John Ward, eight gentlemen, and eight well-to-do widows are returned, whilst nothing like the same number are returned for any other parish; eight for Kew is the nearest to it. The invention of sea-bathing, about 1753, was finally fatal to Epsom as a watering-place. The Old Well House, however, was not pulled down till 1804, when a private house was built on the spot, a successor to which still occupies the ground. A part of the old brickwork seems to survive in one of the greenhouses in the garden.

Among the recreations of Epsom in its glory were gambling, cudgel-playing, foot-races, cock-fighting, and catching a pig by the tail, besides horse-racing. Robert Norden's map, of the 17th century, marks 'the Race,' extending in a straight line from Banstead Downs on to Epsom Downs. In 1648 a horse-race on Banstead Downs, evidently a usual occurrence, was made the prelude to Lord Holland's rising against the Parliament.[4] The races were one of the regular diversions of the company at the Wells, and they used to witness two or three heats in the morning, return to dinner in the middle of the day, and come up to the Downs for more heats in the afternoon. These were run in 1730 either on the old straight course, or on what Toland in 1711 calls the 'new orbicular course.' In those days the runners started above Langley Bottom behind the Warren, and, going outside the Bushes, ran by way of Tattenham Corner to the winning-chair. The original Derby course was the last mile and a half of this track, the starting-post being out of sight of the grand stand. The Derby and the Oaks races were founded in 1780 and 1779 respectively, and were called after the Earl of Derby and his seat at Banstead.

In 1846 Mr. Henry Dorling, the clerk of the course, made, on the advice of Lord George Bentinck, a course for the Derby, the whole of which lies on the eastern side of the Warren and in full view of the stands. This, which is now known as the old course, was used until 1871. For the present Derby course, first used in 1872, the horses start on slightly higher ground at the high-level starting-post, and run into the old course at the mile-post. The first half-mile and the last five furlongs of this track are in the manor of Epsom; that part of it above the Bushes, from the City and Suburban starting-post to the old five-furlong start, lying on Walton Downs within the manor of Walton, is owned by the Epsom Grand Stand Association.

The antiquities and history of the race-meetings have been sufficiently treated already.[5] The popularity of the races survived the popularity of the watering-place. Dr. Burton[6] speaks enthusiastically of the crowds of spectators, even from London, and, as he is writing in Greek, is irresistibly reminded of the Olym-

⁴ *V.C.H. Surr.* i, 417, &c.   ⁵ See *V.C.H. Surr.* ii, under 'Sport.'   ⁶ In *Iter Surriense*, 1752.

272

p:c Games. Greater crowds than ever used to attend now flock to Epsom races, for the population within reach is larger, and the means of access by railway much facilitated. But probably the almost national importance of the Derby reached its height in the last generation. It was while Lord Palmerston and Lord Derby were political leaders that the House of Commons regularly adjourned for the Derby day. The fashion outlived Lord Palmerston, but it ceased under Mr. Gladstone's rule, and not even in joke can London now be said to be empty on the Derby day.

As a result of the races, rather than that of the old watering-place life, Epsom is an extension of London into Surrey. The county is now permeated by Londoners, but up to about thirty years ago the speech of the country was different north and south of a line drawn about Epsom. An exact demarcation, of course, could not be made.

Epsom Common Fields, which were on the slopes of the chalk in front of the present Medical College, between it and the town, were among the last to survive in Surrey. They were inclosed by an Award of 4 September 1869, under an Act of 1865.[7] A certain amount of inclosure on the lower part of the downs and on Epsom Common has been made, probably from the watering-place era onwards, by private purchase and arrangements.

Woodcote House is the residence of the Rev. E. W. Northey, J.P.; Woodcote Grove, of Mr. A. W. Aston, J.P.; Hookfield, of Mr. B. Braithwaite, J.P.; The Wells, of Mrs. Jamieson. This last is a new house on the site of the old well-house. Pit Place is the seat of Mr. W. E. Bagshaw. The lions at the entrance and some interior work are said to be from Nonsuch. It was the scene of the well-known story of Lord Lyttelton's apparition.

The Roman Catholic Church (St. Joseph's), Heathcote Road, was built in 1857.

The Congregational church, in Church Street, has taken the place of a Presbyterian chapel, where a congregation met, it is said, from James's Indulgence in 1688, and certainly in 1725.[8] No trace is found of it after 1772. In 1815 the old chapel, which had been closed, was bought and fitted up for a Congregational use. In 1825 it was rebuilt.[9] It was again rebuilt in 1904, in red brick with stone dressings, in a quasi-Decorated style. It has chancel, nave, aisles, and tower with a small spire. The first stone was laid by Mr. Evan Spicer. There are also chapels of the Wesleyans and Baptists, and a Baptist congregation meets in the Gymnasium Hall.

Epsom College, incorporated by Act of Parliament in 1855, and by a new Act in 1895, is a first-class public school, with fifty foundation scholarships open to the orphans of medical men, and taking the sons of medical men at a slight reduction. There are five leaving scholarships to the universities, and ten to the hospitals. The buildings are of red brick and Caen stone in 16th-century style, fitted with chapel, laboratories, gymnasium, swimming-bath, and all the

accessories of a school. They occupy a fine site on the downs east of the town.

A National School was built in 1828, but a school had been carried on certainly since before 1725.

The present elementary schools are Hook Road (boys), built in 1840 as a mixed school in place of the one above, enlarged in 1886 and 1896; Ladbrooke Road (girls), built in 1871, recently enlarged; West Hill (infants), built in 1844, enlarged in 1872; Hawthorne Place (infants), built in 1893; Hawthorne Place (junior), built in 1904, a temporary iron building. The schools are under a committee of trustees of charities and elected managers. They are endowed, by the original bequest of Mr. John Brayne in 1693, with land in Fetcham, for teaching poor children to read and write, and binding them as apprentices; by bequest of Mr. David White (see also Ewell) in 1725, with a freehold estate; by bequest of Mrs. Elizabeth Northey, in 1764, with £100 for books; by Mr. Thyar Pitt, with £225; by Mrs. J. Elmslie, with £105 by gift, 1851, and one-fourteenth part of £1,236 15s. 1d. by will in 1858, both sums to the infants' school.

MANORS — In 727 Frithwald, subregulus of Surrey, and Bishop Erkenwald, are said to have granted to their newly founded abbey of Chertsey twenty mansas of land in Epsom;[10] this was confirmed by King Edgar in 967,[11] and in the Domesday Survey EPSOM is mentioned among the possessions of Chertsey Abbey.[12] Henry I granted the abbot leave to keep dogs on all his land inside the forest and outside, to catch foxes, hares, pheasants, and cats, and to inclose his park there and have all the deer he could catch, also to have all the wood he needed from the king's forests.[13] In the reign of Edward I the abbot's right to free warren in Epsom was called in question, and it was found that only in his park he had the right;[14] this was confirmed later (1285).[15] In 1291 the abbot resumed the possession of 9 acres of land (part of the demesne land of the abbey) which he, or a predecessor, had granted to Hugh de la Lane.[16] In 1323–4 the abbot brought a suit against John de la Lane, bailiff of the queen, for distraining him by 1,500 sheep, for his default in not appearing when impleaded in the queen's court of Banstead, and driving them as far as Banstead, where for lack of nourishment some of them died; the abbot was adjudged £1 in compensation.[17]

Grants of land in Epsom were made to the abbot in 1338 by Peter atte Mulle and Richard de Horton.[18] In 1535 the rents of the manor were valued at £20 12s. 5½d.[19] and the perquisites of the court amounted to £2 10s. 4d.; two years later the manor was surrendered to the king.[20]

CHERTSEY ABBEY. Party or and argent St. Paul's sword argent its hilt or crossed with St. Peter's keys gules and azure.

[7] Blue Bk. Incl. Awards.
[8] Bishop Willis's Visitation, Farnham Castle MS.
[9] Waddington, Hist. of Congregationalism in Surr. 203.
[10] Birch, Cart. Sax. i, 64. But see under Chertsey for the authenticity of the earliest charters.
[11] Ibid. iii, 469.
[12] V.C.H. Surr. i, 308a.
[13] Cart. Antiq. D, 142.
[14] Plac. de Quo Warr. (Rec. Com.), 744b.
[15] Cal. Chart. R. 1257–1300, p. 305.
[16] Inq. a.q.d. 19 Edw. I, xv, 20; Cal. Pat. 1281–92, p. 482.
[17] Abbrev. Plac. (Rec. Com.), 346. See Banstead.
[18] Cal. Pat. 1338–40, pp. 45, 47½
Abbrev. Rot. Orig. (Rec. Com.), ii, 129.
[19] Valor Eccl. (Rec. Com.), ii, 56.
[20] Feet of F. Div. Co. Trin. 29 Hen. VIII.

' Henry VIII granted it in 1537 to Sir Nicholas Carew, K.G., in tail male ; [21] but in 1539, in consequence of his attainder, the manor returned to the Crown, and the next year was annexed to the honour of Hampton Court.[22] Queen Mary, however, granted it in 1576 to Francis Carew (afterwards knighted),[23] eldest son of Nicholas,[24] and his heirs male, with reversion to the queen and her successors.[25] In 1589 the reversion (Francis Carew being unmarried) [26] was granted to Edward Darcy, groom of the Privy Chamber [27] and son of Carew's sister Mary,[28] who held the manor after the death of Sir Francis in 1611 and died seised in 1612,[29] having settled it on his wife Mary with remainder to his second son Christopher and contingent remainder to his eldest son Robert.[30]

Robert died in 1618 [31] seised of the reversion of the manor after the death of Mary widow of Edward, from which it appears that Christopher, who was alive in 1623,[32] must have quitclaimed to Robert. Robert's widow and son Edward levied a fine of the manor in 1632.[33] The rent of the manor (£40) was settled on Queen Anne by James I,[34] and on Queen Catherine by Charles II.[35] Edward Darcy sold the manor to Mrs. Anne Mynne, widow of George Mynne of Horton Manor,[36] and daughter of Sir Robert Parkhurst, who left it by will to her daughter Elizabeth wife of Richard Evelyn, brother to John Evelyn the diarist. He resided at Woodcote. Courts of the manor were held in his name in 1667 and 1668.[37] Elizabeth survived him and held courts as lady of the manor until 1691 ; [38] she, at her death in 1692, devised the estate to Christopher Buckle of Banstead and his son Christopher as trustees for her sister Ann for her life, with remainder first to her nephew John Lewknor and then to John Parkhurst of Catesby, co. Northants.[39] The trustees held the courts of the manor until 1706,[40] when John Parkhurst succeeded to the estate ; his grandson John was holding it in 1725.[41] This John devised the manor to Sir Charles Kemys Tynte, bart., and another trustee for his wife Ricarda during her lifetime, after her death to be sold and the proceeds divided between his two younger sons.[42] He died in 1765, and in 1770 the manor was sold to Sir Joseph Mawbey, bart.,[43] who was succeeded by his son John in 1798. John had no male heir, and was followed first by his daughter Emily and then by Ann, in right of whom her husband, John Ivett Briscoe,[44] held the manor till past the middle of the 19th century. It was afterwards held by his trustees, and then went to Charles Vernon Strange, who held it in 1874. From him it passed to James Stuart Strange, who died in 1908 leaving three daughters.

Two mills were in existence at the time of Domesday,[44] but only one is afterwards mentioned in the records of the manor.[45] Charles II granted Elizabeth Evelyn, then lady of the manor, the right to hold a weekly market and two fairs at Epsom ; the grant was renewed by James II, together with a grant to hold a court of pie-powder at each of the fairs.[47]

Epsom Court, the old manor-house, was not sold with the property in 1770, but by a family arrangement descended to the Rev. John Parkhurst, eldest son of John and Ricarda Parkhurst (see above), and the great tithes and the advowson went with it. It is now a farm-house.

The manor of HORTON in this parish belonged to the Abbot and convent of Chertsey, but there seem to be no early records relating to it,[48] unless the lands granted by Richard de Horton in 1338 (*vide supra*) formed part of it.

According to a charter of the early 15th century, the Abbot and convent of Chertsey owned the hamlet or township of Horton, co. Surrey, with 168 acres of land, 60 acres of pasture lying in common fields of Horton and in two fields called West Crofts and Sampsones, 3 acres of wood called Burnet Grove, 13s. 8d. rent of free tenants there, and 12s. 3d. rent proceeding from the manor of Brettgrave and the lands of Adam Whitlokke in Ewell and 100 acres furze and heath in ' Ebbesham Common ' opposite the township of Horton ; also another small parcel of land containing 1 rood in ' Ebbesham ' near the parish church, parcel of a tenement called Rankyns, with court and view of frankpledge there, ' wayf and strayf ' fines, &c. These lands together made the manor of Horton.[49]

In 1440 the abbot granted it to John Merston, the king's esquire, and his wife Rose, and their heirs, to hold of the king by payment of 3d. yearly for all service. Free warren in all the demesne lands of Horton was also granted by the king to John and Rose, and licence to inclose 100 acres of land for a park.[50]

After the death of Rose, who survived her husband, the manor passed to William Merston and his wife Anne ; [51] he died in 1495, leaving a son William,[52] who inherited on his mother's death. He died in January 1511–12, leaving Horton to his wife Beatrice for her life, with remainder to his daughter Joan and her heirs.[53] Joan married first Nicholas Mynne,[54] secondly William Sander of Ewell,[55] and died in 1540 leaving a son John

MYNNE. Sable a fesse dancetty paly argent and gules of six pieces.

21 L. and P. Hen. VIII, xii (2), 1150 (3).
22 Ibid. xv, 498.
Shaw, Knights of Engl. ii, 77.
Pat. 1 Mary, pt. viii, m. 35.
23 See Pat. 31 Eliz. pt. v, m. 16.
24 Berry, County Gen. Surr. 5.
25 Pat. 31 Eliz. pt. v, m. 16 ; Hist. MSS. Com. Rep. v, App. 266.
26 Berry, County Gen. Surr. 5 ; The Genealogist (New Ser.), xvi, 243.
27 Chan. Inq. p.m. (Ser. 2), ccccxxviii, 157, and W. and L. do. xviii, 85.
28 Chan. Inq. p.m. (Ser. 2), ccclxxii, 151, and W. and L. do. xxvi, 202.
31 See. Chan. Inq. p.m. (Ser. 2), ccclxxii, 151.

32 Christopher was knighted 29 Sept. 1623 ; Shaw, Knights, ii, 182.
33 Feet of F. Surr. Mich. 8 Chas. I.
34 Pat. 11 Jas. I, pt. xiii, no. 4.
35 Pat. 17 Chas. II, pt. ix, no. 1.
36 Feet of F. Surr. East. 1659.
37 Ct. R., quoted by Manning and Bray, op. cit. ii, 611.
38 Ibid.
39 Manning and Bray, Surr. ii, 611.
40 Ct. R. quoted by Manning, op. cit. ii, 611.
41 Recov. R. East. 11 Geo. I, rot. 193.
42 Manning and Bray, Surr. ii, 612.
43 Feet of F. Surr. Hil. 11 Geo. III.
44 Recov. R. East. 3 Geo. IV, rot. 147.

44 V.C.H. Surr. i, 308a.
46 Recov. R. Trin. 4 Jas. II, rot. 178.
47 Pat. 1 Jas. II, pt. vii, no. 19.
48 Conveyances of land in Horton occur in Feet of F. Surr. Hil. 13 Hen. III, no. 30, 31 ; Trin. 23 Hen. III ; 10 Edw. I ; 25 Edw. I ; B.M. Sloane Chart. xxxii, 29.
49 Chart. R. 1–20 Hen. VI, no. 26.
50 Ibid.
51 Chan. Inq. p.m. 11 Hen. VII, no. 37.
52 Cal. Inq. p.m. Hen. VII, i, 521.
53 Chan. Inq. p.m. (Ser. 2), xxvi, 27, and Exch. Inq. p.m. (Ser. 2), mlxxvii, 3.
54 Manning and Bray, Surr. ii, 612.
55 Visit. of Surr. (Harl. Soc. xliii), 18.

by her first marriage, during whose minority William Sander was granted an annuity of £4 issuing from the manor of Horton, with wardship and marriage of the said John.[56] This John Mynne was holding the manor in 1564 ;[57] he died in 1595,[58] leaving a son and heir William,[59] whose son John succeeded his father in 1618.[60] John married Alice daughter of William Hale and settled various lands and tenements on her, among them the manor-house of Horton ;[61] but in order to pay his debts he with the consent of William Hale sold these estates[62] to George Mynne[63] of Woodcote (1626). George Mynne left two daughters, co-heiresses ;[64] Elizabeth married Richard Evelyn[65] and Anne married Sir John Lewknor. On the division of the estate the manor of Horton fell to the share of Elizabeth,[66] who, having survived her husband and children, left the manor to Charles Calvert,[67] fourth Lord Baltimore, a great-grandson of Anne, daughter of George Mynne of Hertingfordbury, a connexion of her family.[68]

His grandson Charles, the sixth Lord Baltimore, died in 1751, and his son and heir Frederick, Lord Baltimore, who left the country after a celebrated trial in 1768, sold the estates.[69] During the next twenty years Horton Manor changed hands several times, and was finally bought by Mr. Trotter, an upholsterer in Soho ;[70] his son James, high sheriff in 1798, succeeded him in 1790.[71] He was succeeded by his son John, M.P. for West Surrey 1841–7, from whom it passed to William S. Trotter. The estate has been recently bought by the London County Council for asylums.

TROTTER of Horton. *Argent a crescent gules and a chief indented azure with three pierced molets argent therein.*

The old manor-house of Horton was a large building surrounded by a moat. It was in the low ground north of Epsom. The Mynnes seem to have lived at Woodcote, for Richard Evelyn married their heiress there in 1648,[72] and he is said to have rebuilt the house at Woodcote.[73]

Later, when Woodcote Park had been separated from Horton, Mr. John Trotter, owner of Horton, built a new mansion, called it Horton Place, and inclosed land around it for a park.[74]

The manor of BRETTGRAVE (Bruttegrave, Bertesgrave, Brottesgrave, Bryddesgreve, xiv and xv cent.) belonged to the abbey of Chertsey as parcel of their manor of Epsom.[75] It was held of the Abbot of Chertsey in the reign of Henry III by John de Tichemarsh.[76] Later in the century it was in the tenure of Reginald de Imworth, who died before 1287, leaving a son John, then a minor.[77] In a suit brought in 1346 by the Abbot of Chertsey against Nicholas de Tonstall, Joan his wife, and Thomas de Saye, this John was said to have granted the manor in fee to Henry Gerard, chaplain, and John his illegitimate son, who were holding in the reign of Edward II by services due.[78] After the death of John son of Henry, John the then abbot entered upon the manor as an escheat,[79] and continued his seisin until forcibly and unlawfully disseised by Joan and her first husband, Henry de Saye, who carried off his crops, impounded the beasts from his ploughs, and otherwise persecuted him, until by a writing he released his right in the manor. As the release was obtained by force, and without the consent of the convent, it was not held valid by the jurors, and the abbot recovered seisin of the manor with damages. In the same year the abbot and convent received licence to grant the manor to Guy de Bryan the younger to be held of the king in chief by the rent of 8s. 3d. ;[80] they probably reserved to themselves a rent of 12s. 3d. from the manor, as this is afterwards stated to belong to their manor of Horton,[81] and this may have led to Brettgrave being considered a parcel of the manor of Horton, which was denied by the jurors in an inquisitiou taken in 1517.[82] Guy de Bryan had licence to have Mass celebrated in his chapel in Brettgrave in Epsom in 1348,[83] but in the same year enfeoffed John Gogh and other clerks of the manor,[84] probably in trust for Henry, Earl of Lancaster, who in 1350 received a grant of free warren in his demesne lands of Brettgrave.[85] Henry was created Duke of Lancaster in 1352, and died seised of the manor in 1361.[86] He left no son, and his eldest daughter Maud, wife of the Duke of Bavaria, dying the following year,[87] the estates passed to her only sister Blanche, wife of John of Gaunt, Earl of Richmond,[88] created Duke of Lancaster in 1362, father of Henry IV.[89] The manor thus became part of the Duchy of Lancaster, leases of it being granted by successive kings.[90] Ultimately the fee-simple seems to have been acquired by William Merston, whose father John Merston (vide Horton) had held the lease of it.[91] William died in January 1511–12.[92] It descended through his daughter Joan, wife of Nicholas Mynne, to John Mynne, the

DUCHY OF LANCASTER. *England with a label azure.*

[56] *L. and P. Hen. VIII*, xvi, 1056 (68).
[57] Recov. R. East. Eliz. rot. 614.
[58] Chan. Inq. p.m. ccli, 158.
[59] Chan. Inq. p.m. ccclxxi, 105 ; W. and L. Inq. xxviii, 163.
[60] Ibid. ; Feet of F. Surr. Mich. 21 Jas. I ; Recov. R. Mich. 21 Jas. I, rot. 65.
[61] B.M. Add. Chart. 36438.
[62] Ibid. 36439.
[63] Feet of F. Surr. Hil. 2 Chas. I.
[64] Feet of F. Div. Co. Trin. 1652 ; ibid. Trin. 15 Chas. II.
[65] Berry, *County Gen. Surr.* 79.
[66] Manning and Bray, *Surr.* ii, 612.
[67] Recov. R. Hil. 1 Geo. II, rot. 40.
[68] G.E.C. *Peerage*, i, 296 (George Mynne of Woodcote's daughter Anne married Sir John Lewknor, *not* Lord Baltimore).
[69] D. Enr. Hil. 9 Geo. III (1769).
[70] Manning and Bray, *Surr.* ii, 614.
[71] Brayley, *Surr.* iv, 351.
[72] Evelyn's *Diary*, 16 Aug. 1648.
[73] Burke, *Visit. of Seats*, i, 231.
[74] Brayley, *Surr.* iv, 351.
[75] *Cal. Pat.* 1345–8, p. 155.
[76] Ibid.
[77] *Cal. Close*, 1279–88, p. 490.
[78] *Cal. Pat.* 1345–8, p. 155.
[79] *Cal. Close*, 1279–88, p. 490.
[80] Inq. a.q.d. ccclxxxi, 11 ; Feet of F. Surr. Trin. 21 Edw. III ; *Cal. Pat.* 1345–8, p. 217 ; Add. MS. 6167, fol. 141.
[81] See Chart. R. 1–20 Hen. VI, no. 26.
[82] Exch. Inq. p.m. mlxxii, 3. Locally its boundaries make it a long way off Horton, but near Woodcote.
[83] Winton Epis. Reg. Edington, pt. ii, 168.
[84] *Cal. Pat.* 1348–50, p. 206.
[85] Chart. R. 24 Edw. III, pt. i, no. 3.
[86] *Cal. Inq. p.m.* (Rec. Com.), ii, 236 ; Add. MS. 6167, fol. 151 d.
[87] *Cal. Inq. p.m.* (Rec. Com.), ii, 247.
[88] Add. MS. 6167, fol. 151 d.
[89] G.E.C. *Peerage*, v, 8.
[90] Duchy of Lanc. Misc. Bks. xvi, 102 (pt. iii) ; xviii, 135 d, 136 d ; *Cal. Pat.* 1422–29, p. 455.
[91] Duchy of Lanc. Misc. Bks. xxi, 184 d.
[92] Exch. Inq. p.m. mlxxii, 3.

great-grandson of Joan.[93] He sold it with the manor of Horton to George Mynne,[94] whose daughter and co-heir Elizabeth, wife of Richard Evelyn, owned it in 1652.[95] From that time it may have been merged with the manor of Horton,[96] for now no trace of the manor or place of that name can be found. In a survey of Epsom[97] a boundary point is Brettegraves-herne—that is, Brettegrave's Corner, otherwise called Wolfrenesherne. The next mark on the boundary is Abbot's Pit, which on an old map is the name for the disused chalk-pit called Pleasure Pit on the Ordnance map.[97a]

The estate called *DURDANS* in this parish, held of the manor of Horton, is probably the property consisting of a messuage, a dovecote, two gardens, two orchards, 12 acres of land with meadow, pasture, and wood, which Sir William Mynne, lord of Horton, conveyed to Elizabeth, Lady Berkeley, in 1617.[98] She in 1634-5 settled Durdans on her daughter Theophila, wife of Sir Robert Coke, and her heirs and assigns.[99] Theophila died without issue, Sir Robert Coke surviving. He, by his will of 1652, left Durdans to his nephew George Berkeley, afterwards Earl of Berkeley ; he also devised a messuage called the Dog House, in Epsom, which he had lately acquired (probably by fine from John and Thomas Hewett),[99a] to be fitted up as a library and kept for any of the ministers of the county of Surrey, to use on week-days between sun-rising and sun-setting.[100] The books left for this purpose however, which probably formed part of the library of his father, the famous lawyer, Sir Edward Coke), seem to have remained at Durdans until 1682, when George, Earl of Berkeley, gave all or part of them to Sion College.[100a] George, Earl of Berkeley, entertained Charles II here in 1662, when John Evelyn records in his diary being invited to meet the King and Queen, Duke and Duchess, Prince Rupert, Prince Edward, and abundance of noblemen.[101] Charles II also dined with the Earl of Berkeley at Durdans in 1664.[101a] This was probably at the old house, for the Earl of Berkeley is said to have built a new residence with materials from the palace of Nonsuch,[102] which was pulled down by the Duchess of Cleveland after 1669. During the Earl's tenure of Durdans, it was the scene of the notorious intrigue between his daughter, Lady Henrietta Berkeley, and her brother-in-law, Lord Grey of Wark.[103] By will of 1698 the earl left the property to his son Charles, afterwards earl, who in 1702 sold Durdans with ' the little park paled in ' to Charles Turner of Kirkleatham, co. York. He in 1708 conveyed it to John, Duke of Argyll and Earl of Greenwich, reserving the Dogghouse or Dagghouse Farm.[103a] Before 1712 it seems to have

been acquired by Lord Guilford,[103b] and Bishop Willis's Visitation calls him a resident of Epsom in 1725. His son, Lord North and Guilford, succeeded him in 1729. He was lord of the bedchamber to Frederick, Prince of Wales, from 1730 to 1751, during which time the prince seems to have had a loan or lease of the house,[103c] but the tradition that he owned it is incorrect.

Alderman Belchier pulled down Lord Berkeley's house after 1747. The new house was bought by Mr. Dalbiac in 1764, and later, in 1799, was acquired by Mr. George Blackman, who sold it in 1819 to Sir Gilbert Heathcote, bart., M.P. From the cousins and heirs of his son Arthur Heathcote it was bought by Lord Rosebery in 1874,[104] and he is the present owner.

PRIMROSE, Earl of Rosebery. *Vert three primroses or within the royal tressure of Scotland for* PRIMROSE, *quartered with* Argent *a lion* sable *with a forked tail for* CREWY.

The capital messuage of *WOODCOTE* in Epsom was held of the manor of Horton.[105] In the first half of the 16th century it belonged to one John Ewell of Horton, and continued in his family until 1591, when it was the cause of litigation between Agnes Tyther, a descendant of John Ewell, and Roger Lamborde.[106] It was in the possession of John Mynne, lord of the manor of Horton, in 1597, and he settled it on his son William on his marriage.[107] It passed with Horton Manor to Elizabeth wife of Richard Evelyn (1648), who built there a new mansion. Mrs. Evelyn bequeathed Woodcote to Lord Baltimore, a remote connexion of her family.[108] After the seventh Lord Baltimore left England in 1771 it was sold to Mr. Monk, then to Mr. Nelson, in 1777 to Mr. Arthur Cuthbert, and in 1787 to Mr. Lewis Teissier, a merchant of London, having been separated from the manor of Horton. Mr. Teissier's son, created by Louis XVIII the Baron de Teissier, was owner at the beginning of last century.[109] It was sold by the Baron de Teissier in 1855 to Mr. Robert Brookes, and is now the property of his son, Mr. Herbert Brookes, J.P.

The church of *ST. MARTIN* has a nave with aisles and a north-west tower ; the church has lately been considerably enlarged eastward, the new work consisting of an addition to the nave, a chancel and north chapel, a south organ chamber, and aisles. The only old part of the present building is the tower, which dates from the 15th century, but has been recased

CHURCHES

[93] Terrier of lands in Surrey ; Donat MS. B.M. 4705, fol. 145, 146.
[94] Feet of F. Surr. Hil. 2 Chas. I.
[95] See Feet of F. Div. Co. Trin. 1652.
[96] See Feet of F. Div. Co. Trin. 15 Chas. II.
[97] K. R. Misc. Bk. vol. 25, fol. cccxcv d.
[97a] The line continues by Seburghes *super montem*, the Kingston and Reigate road, Dene or Deuelonds, the Portway, Motschameles hedge, corner called Merlesherne *iuxta* Ashtead, Werehull on the heath by the Kingston and Walton road, Cheseldene parkhatch, Kocshete, and so back to Brettegravesherne.

[98] Feet of F. Surr. Trin. 18 Jas. I.
[99] Chan. Inq. p.m. (Ser. 2), dxxviij, 38.
[99a] See Feet of F. Surr. Trin. 23 Chas. II.
[100] P.C.C. Brent, 294.
[100a] See Inner Temple MSS. 538, 17, fol. 347, and the account of Sion College by the Rev. W. H. Milman in *Lond. and Midd. Arch. Soc.* 1880.
[101] Evelyn's *Diary*, 1 Sept. 1662.
[101a] *Hist. MSS. Com. Rep.* xv, App. vii, 173.
[102] Brayley, *Surr.* iv, 352, quoting Aubrey, who was contemporary.
[103] *State Trials*, ix, 127-86. But it was perhaps at another house of Lord

Berkeley's in Epsom. See Manning and Bray, *Surr.* ii, 614.
[103a] Close, 7 Anne, pt. ii, no. 13.
[103b] See *Hist. MSS. Com. Rep.* xi, App. v, 309.
[103c] See Pococke's *Travels through Engl.* (ed. Wright, Camd. So:.), ii. 171. See Lord Rosebery's Introd. to Gordon Home's *Epsom*.
[104] Local information.
[105] Ct. of Req. 1, bdle. 95, no. 61.
[106] Ibid.
[107] Chan. Inq. p.m. (Ser. 2), ccli, 158.
[108] G.E.C. *Peerage*, i, 226.
[109] Brayley, *Surr.* iv, 351.

and much modernized. The present nave and aisles were built in 1824, when the old church was pulled down; a print of about this date shows it to have had a nave with a north aisle, and a north-west tower. The chancel was evidently of the 13th century, and had a lancet window midway in its north wall, but all the other windows shown in the chancel and aisle are wide ugly single lights fitted with iron casements. The aisle had been raised to contain a gallery and a second tier of windows added. The nave of 1824 has arcades of four bays with plastered piers and arches; the aisles are lighted by two-light pointed windows, and are filled with wooden galleries, shortly to be removed. The walling of the nave and aisles is of flint and stone, and that of the new portion is of rubble with stone and brick dressings, the chancel and nave having alternate bays of cross and barrel vaulting; the new work is soon to be extended to the present nave and aisles. The jambs of the openings into the tower from the nave and north aisle are moulded and the arches are blocked. The tower is of flint and stone, and has cemented angle buttresses and a north-west octagonal stair turret; an old oak door opens into the turret, the steps of which are inscribed with various names and 18th-century dates, and a stone records the recutting of the steps in 1737. The bell-chamber is lighted by plain pointed windows of two lights, and surmounted by a plain parapet, from which rises a very slender wooden spire covered with oak shingles.

Under the tower is a 15th-century font; it is octagonal with quatrefoiled sides to the bowl and a hollowed under-edge on which are carved heads, a shield, a fish, &c. There is also a fine chest of carved mahogany; on the lid are carved—in the middle—Adam and Eve in the garden, and in the two side panels David and Goliath; on the front are other figures in late 16th-century dress.

On the floor on the north side is a small brass with an inscription to William Marston, or Merston, 1511, and there are wall monuments to Richard Evelyn of Wootton, 1669; Robert Coke of Nonsuch, grandson of Lord Chief Justice Coke, 1681; Robert Coke, 1653; Richard Evelyn, 1691; and others.

There are eight bells: the treble is by Samuel Knight, 1737; the second by R. Phelps, 1714; the third by Thomas Janaway, 1781; the fourth has no date, and is inscribed: 'Although I am but small I will be heard above them all'; the fifth is dated 1737; the sixth by R. Phelps, 1714; the seventh by Thomas Swain, 1760; and the tenor by Richard Phelps, 1733.

The plate is all modern, consisting of a chalice and paten of 1904 given by the parishioners, and a chalice and paten given by Lord Rosebery in 1907, besides six Sheffield plate almsdishes and two cups and an almsdish about a hundred years old.

The first book of the registers contains baptisms and marriages from 1695 to 1749 and burials to 1750; the second repeats the baptisms from 1695 to 1749 and the marriages from 1695 to 1719; the third has baptisms and burials from 1750 to 1773 and

marriages 1750 to 1754; the fourth, baptisms 1773 to 1812; fifth, burials 1773 to 1812; the sixth, marriages 1754 to 1783; and the seventh continues them to 1812.

The greater part of the churchyard, which surrounds the building, lies to the north of it. The west entrance is towards the road, and is approached by a flight of stone steps and a flagged landing. There are several large trees about it.

CHRIST CHURCH, originally built as a chapel of ease to the parish church in 1843, is now the church of a separate parish. It was rebuilt in 1876. It is a small building of flint and stone situated on the edge of Epsom Common, and consists of a small chancel with a north transept and south organ chamber, nave of four bays with north and south aisles and a clearstory, and a south-west tower and porch. At the west end is a passage-way containing the font. There are eight bells by Mears & Stainbank, 1890.

ST. JOHN'S, chapel of ease to St. Martin's, is a small building of red brick and stone, off East Street, erected in 1884.

ST. BARNABAS, Hook Road, is a chapel of ease to Christ Church.

ADVOWSON Two churches on the abbey estate are mentioned in Domesday,[110] but all trace of one has disappeared; there was a Stamford Chapel in Epsom, near or on the lord's waste, close to where Christ Church, Epsom, now stands, belonging to Chertsey Abbey, which may have been the second church.[111] Licence to appropriate was granted to the convent by a bull of Clement III,[112] 1187–91, and a vicarage was ordained before 1291.[113] A further endowment was carried into effect in 1313[114] when John Rutherwyk the then abbot was inducted.[115] In 1537, when Henry VIII acquired Epsom Manor from the convent of Chertsey, the rectory and the advowson of the church were included,[116] and he granted them with the manor to Sir Nicholas Carew,[117] from which time they have always been included in the grants and sales of the manor till 1770, when the manor went to Sir Joseph Mawbey, and the great tithes and advowson to John Parkhurst. They descended to the Rev. Fleetwood Parkhurst, vicar of Epsom, 1804–39. The advowson has since belonged to the Rev. Wilfred Speer and Captain Speer, and now belongs to Mr. H. Speer.

In 1453 John Merston received a grant for founding a chantry in Epsom Church, to be called 'Merston's Chantry,' and for purchasing lands to the value of 10 marks for the use of it.[118] There is no record of the chantry at the time of the suppression under Edward VI.

CHARITIES Smith's Charity is distributed as in other Surrey parishes.

In 1691 Mrs. Elizabeth Evelyn left a rent-charge of £10 a year for clothing six poor women.

Since 1692 the rent of a piece of land called Church Haw has been received by the churchwardens, now by the local authority, for the use of the poor.

---

[110] V.C.H. Surr. i, 308a. [111] Ibid. note 2. [112] Pat. 20 Edw. I, m. 11 (1292). Inspeximus and confirmation of letters patent of the Bishop of Winchester reciting the bull.
[113] Pope Nich. Tax. (Rec. Com.), 209. [114] Cal. Pap. 1307–13, p. 556. [115] Winton Epis. Reg. Woodlock, fol. 179b.
[116] Feet of F. Div. Co. Trin. 29 Hen. VIII. [117] L. and P. Hen. VIII, xii (2), 1150 (3). [118] Manning and Bray, Surr. ii, 612.

In 1703 Mr. John Levingston, the quack doctor mentioned above, built almshouses for twelve poor widows in East Street on a piece of land granted by the parish. The almshouses were rebuilt about 1863. They are further supported by the Church Haw rent, by that of 'Workhouse Field,' the site of the old parish workhouse, and by the bequests of Samuel Caul (£500) in 1782, Mr. Langley Brackenbury (£300) in 1814, Mr. Story (£100), 1834, Mrs. Margaret Knipe (£300), 1834, the last to be devoted to this purpose after providing for the upkeep of vaults and monuments in the church.

In 1728 Mrs. Mary Dundas left copyhold premises in Epsom for providing coals.

In 1790 Mrs. Elizabeth Culling left £150, part of which was to be set aside to accumulate, for the church, vicar, sexton, churchwardens, and the surplus for apprenticing children and for bread.

In 1803 Mrs. Mary Rowe left £188 18s. 11d. for bread and meat and firing.

In 1835 Sir James Alexander left £200 for clothing for five men and five women, who had to appear in church.

In 1884 Baron De Teissier left £90 for six poor communicants.

Mittendorf House was presented to the National Incorporated Society for Waifs and Strays (Dr. Barnardo's Homes) by Miss Mittendorf.

Epsom and Ewell Cottage Hospital was built in 1889 by public subscription.

EWELL

Etwelle (xi cent.) ; Awell (xii cent.) ; Ewell (*Testa de Nevill*).

Ewell is a village a mile north-east of Epsom and 5 miles south-east of Kingston. The parish is nearly 4 miles from north to south, and almost a mile wide, and contains 2,427 acres. This is the compact parish of Ewell, excluding the detached liberty of Kingswood, which is treated separately. The parish lies in the ordinary position of the neighbourhood as regards soils. The southern part is on the chalk downs ; the old village was on the extremity of the chalk, on a tongue of that soil extending into the Thanet Sand, and the parish crosses the Thanet and Woolwich Beds, reaching on to the London Clay. There is a strong spring, one of the principal sources of the Hoggsmill River, which rises in the village and has good trout ; other springs feed the same stream. There are extensive brick, tile, and pottery works, called the Nonsuch Works, and two flour mills worked by water and steam. There were formerly also gunpowder mills, which have now ceased to exist.[1]

The roads from Kingston to Epsom and from London to Epsom meet in Ewell. The Wimbledon and Letherhead, branch of the London and South-Western Railway, and the Portsmouth line of the London, Brighton, and South Coast Railway, opened respectively in 1859 and 1847, both pass through the parish, the stations being about a mile apart.

Ewell was a market town when Speed's map was made (early 17th century) and when Aubrey wrote. In 1618 Henry Lloyd, lord of the manor, was granted licence to hold a market in Ewell.[2] A curious entry exists in the parish registers for 1654 of banns published in Ewell Market, preparatory to a marriage before a justice of the peace, Mr. Marsh of Dorking. The market was held on Thursdays. It seems to have died a natural death early in the 19th century, the small market-house which stood at the intersection of Church Street and High Street having been removed at a slightly earlier date. The old watch-house, however, is still to be seen, facing the place where the market-house stood. Fairs are said to have been held on 12 May and 29 October in a field near the Green Man Inn.[3] The village of Ewell still retains some of the picturesque appearance of an old market town.

Pits have been found in Ewell containing Roman pottery, bones, and a few other remains, which have been taken to the British Museum. Ewell lay possibly on the Roman road from Sussex to the Thames, diverted at Epsom from the British trackway, though it is matter of inference rather than proof.

It was probably once a place of some importance, as it gave its name to one of the old Surrey deaneries, but in Domesday there is no church named. Letherhead Church, however, we are told was annexed to the king's manor of Ewell. Shelwood Manor in Leigh was also part of Ewell Manor.[4]

Richard Corbet, Bishop of Oxford from 1628 to 1632, and of Norwich from 1632 to 1635, was born at Ewell in 1582. He was the son of a gardener, but became a Queen's scholar at Westminster, and then a student of Christ Church. As a bishop he is said to have had 'an admirable grave and reverend aspect,' but it is told of him that after he was a Doctor of Divinity he disguised himself as a ballad singer in Abingdon market. He was certainly a wit, and to some extent a poet ; his *Iter Boreale* and *Journey into France* show the former, the *Fairies' Farewell* the latter character.

Amongst the modern houses is Ewell Castle, built by Mr. Thomas Calverley in 1814 in an imitation castellated style. It is now vacant. The grounds, which extend into Cuddington parish, cover part of the former Nonsuch Park, and include the site of the Banqueting House, which stood apart from the palace of Nonsuch, and the remains of the pool called Diana's Bath. Ewell Court is the seat of Mr. J. H. Bridges, J.P. ; Tayle's Hill of Major E. F. Coates, M.P. ; Rectory House of Sir Gervas Powell Glyn, bart. ; Purberry Shot of Mr. W. M. Walters.

The inclosure of common fields (707 acres) and of waste (495 acres) was carried out in 1801.[5] The common fields lay east of the village.

There is a Congregational chapel in the village, with a school and lecture hall adjoining, built in 1864. Archbishop Sheldon's Returns in 1669[6] show that there was a Nonconformist congregation of fifty, ministered to by Mr. Batho, the ex-rector of Ewell.

[1] In connexion with the industries of the parish may be noted an inquisition taken in 1390 on the death of Thomas Stapelton, which records that he held in Ewell one messuage, 12 acres of land and
[2] *Cal. S.P. Dom.* 1637, p. 40.
[3] Local Information.
'unum instrumentum pro textoribus vocatum Handwork' ; Chan. Inq. p.m. 14 Ric. II, no. 69.
[4] *Testa de Nevill* (Rec. Com.), 225 ; Coram Rege R. 10 Hen. III, rot. 8.
[5] Act 41 Geo. III, cap. 41.
[6] *V.C.H. Surr.* ii, 39.

Bishop Willis's Visitation of 1725 mentions 'about 50 Presbyterians,' an unusual instance in rural Surrey of the continuance of a large body of Nonconformity between those dates.

The village is supplied with gas by the Epsom and Ewell Gas Company, and with water by the Sutton Water Company.

The Chelsea and Kensington Workhouse Schools are in the parish.

In 1811 a National School was established on the strength of Mr. White's and Mr. Brumfield's benefactions. Mr. Calverley gave a further benefaction, which became available in 1860. The schools at present existing were built in 1861, one for boys and girls, and the other for infants. The former was enlarged in 1893. They still continue Church of England Schools.

Kingswood Liberty is a completely detached part of Ewell parish, bounded on the west and north by Banstead, on the east by Chipstead and Gatton, on the south by Reigate. It measures less than 3 miles from north to south, and is under a mile broad, of a fairly regular form. It contains 1,821 acres. It lies upon the chalk hills, but the chalk is here in general crowned with a deposit of brick-earth and of clay with flints.

Kingswood is traversed by the old Brighton road which came up Reigate Hill and went to Sutton. It has now a railway station on the Tattenham Corner branch of the South Eastern and Chatham Railway, opened as far as Kingswood in 1899. The neighbourhood which used to be singularly sequestered and rural is fast becoming residential, especially since the opening of the railway. But the majority of the new houses are in the part of Banstead included in the ecclesiastical parish of Kingswood, not in the old portion of Ewell.

In 1838 an ecclesiastical district was formed from Kingswood with a portion of Banstead, and a new church, St. Andrew's, was built in 1848 by the late Mr. Thomas Alcock. The old church is used as a parish room. The church is endowed with a glebe of 31 acres. There is also a Methodist chapel, built by the late Mr. H. Fowker.

Kingswood Warren, built about 1850 by Mr. H. Alcock, M.P., is the fine seat of Mr. Henry C. O. Bonsor, J.P.

Lower Kingswood School was built in 1893 and enlarged in 1903. Tadworth and Kingswood School (in Banstead parish) was built in 1875. Both are County Council Schools.

MANORS The manor of *EWELL* is named in Domesday as part of the royal demesne,[7] and as such William I secured it as the alleged heir of Edward the Confessor.[8] Henry II granted it to the Prior and canons of Merton in frankalmoign and as free from aids and customs as it had been when Crown property.[9] This grant was augmented by one from Richard I of 101 acres of land, without impeachment of assart and quit of all

aids and escheats, &c.[10] Henry III granted to the prior the right of free warren in his manor of Ewell,[11] this grant being confirmed by Edward I.[12]

Richard tenth Earl of Arundel, who was executed as a traitor in 1398, held the manor of the Prior and convent of Merton at the time of his death.[13]

With the manor of Ewell Henry II had granted to the convent of Merton, as parcels of the same manor, two pieces of land called Fifhide[14] and Selswood (Shelwood).[15] In the reign of Henry III the prior claimed that the men on these lands were his villeins and owed him villeins' service; this the men denied, affirming that they owed him only the service of free men, and that what the men of Ewell, who were their equals, gave they would give, and no more.[16] An inquisition held later on the services due to the Prior of Merton determined that the men of Selswood and Fifhide were subject to the tax of Peterpence, and that they might not marry son or daughter out of the township without the prior's licence, but that their taxation should be the same as that of the men of Ewell.[17]

At the dissolution of Merton in 1538, the prior surrendered all the lands of the convent to the king, and this manor was annexed to the honour of Hampton Court,[18] Henry purchasing from William Cooper his lease of the manor.[19] In 1540 Ralph Sadler was appointed bailiff of the manor,[20] and he was granted a lease for twenty-one years of the site of the manor where not inclosed in Nonsuch Park.[21]

Edward VI granted a lease of the site of Ewell Manor to Henry Collier and Agnes his wife for the rent of 69s. 9d. yearly, which lease was renewed by Philip and Mary.[22] In 1563 Elizabeth granted the manor to Henry, Earl of Arundel, and his heirs, for the sum of £885 12s. 10d.[23] He had only one child, Jane, who married John, Lord Lumley;[24] these died without issue surviving, and the estates passed, 1609, to Splandian Lloyd, Lord Lumley's nearest kinsman, son of his sister Barbara;[25] Splandian died childless, and his brother Henry succeeded,[26] the manor then continuing in his family in direct male line to Robert Lumley Lloyd, D.D. He presented a claim to the peerage, being a direct descendant of Barbara sister and heir of Lord Lumley; it was disallowed on the ground that the barony was limited to John, Lord Lumley, in tail male.[27] Dr. Lloyd died in 1730, and left his estates to his three sisters for their life, with reversion to Lord John Russell, afterwards Duke of Bedford. By him they were sold in 1755 to Edward Northey,[28] in whose family they have remained, the present lord of the manor being the Rev. E. W. Northey of Epsom.

NORTHEY. *Or a fesse azure between three panthers standing and powdered with stars argent with a pansy or between two lilies argent on the fesse.*

7 *V.C.H. Surr.* i, 297*b*.
8 Ibid. 279.
9 Cart. Antiq. U, 6. This was not the whole of the royal property, see below.
10 Cart. Antiq. GG, 18; RR, 10.
11 Chart. R. 36 Hen. III, m. 11.
12 *Plac. de Quo Warr.* (Rec. Com.), 739.
13 Chan. Inq. p.m. 21 Ric. II, bdle. of forfeitures, no. 11 e.
14 *Abbrev. Plac.* (Rec. Com.), 35a.

15 Maitland, *Bracton's Note Book*, no. 1651. See under Leigh parish.
16 Ibid.
17 Cur. Reg. R. 94, Hil. 10 Hen. III.
18 Manning and Bray, *Surr.* i, 455.
19 *L. and P. Hen. VIII*, xiv (1), g. 651 (36).
20 Ibid. xvi, p. 714. 21 Ibid. xvii, p. 695.
22 Pat. 4 & 5 Phil. and Mary, pt. xii, m. 58.

23 Pat. 5 Eliz. pt. ii, m. 45.
24 Feet of F. Div. Co. East. 8 Eliz. See also Chan. Proc. Eliz. Cc. ii, 18.
25 G.E.C. *Peerage*, v, 178 (e); Chan. Inq. p.m. Surr. 7 Jas. I.
26 Recov. R. East. 4 Chas. I, rot. 33; Feet of F. Surr. East. 4 Chas. I.
27 G.E.C. *Peerage*, v, 178 (c).
28 Manning and Bray, *Surr.* i, 457.

It appears that Henry II made another grant of land which later was called a manor, but which does not appear as a separate property after the 13th century. He gave to Maurice de Creon [29] 43s. 1½d. rent [30] to hold of the king in chief [31] as an instalment of 4 librates which he had promised him. Maurice gave the rent to his son-in-law, Guy de la Val, [32] who sub-enfeoffed William St. Michael ; [33] this grant was confirmed by the king's writ in 1205, [34] and also on the death of Guy without issue, when the king granted the manor to Peter de Creon son of Maurice to hold of the Crown as his father had done. [35] William St. Michael continued to hold possession until he was disseised in 1222. [36]

Peter was succeeded by his brother Almaric, [37] whose heir, Maurice, lord of Creon, gave all his hereditary right in the manor to Sir Robert Burnell, clerk, and his heirs, to be held of the king by the services due therefrom, and by rendering to Maurice and his heirs 1d. yearly at Easter. [38]

Robert Burnell the same year, 1272, restored the lands to the king, who bestowed them on John de la Linde to be held by him and his heirs by the service of one-fourth part of a knight's fee. [39] From this time the manor seems to have been attached as a member to Wallington [40] (q.v.).

Two mills at Ewell are mentioned in Domesday, and later there appear to have been more ; Adam Tychesey gave one to the Prior and convent of Merton. [41]

There is a reputed manor in Ewell called BOT-TALS [42] (Battailes, Buttalls, Butolphs, xvii cent.), of which there is no certain history until 1659, when it was held by Henry Sanders ; [43] he sold it to Thomas Turgis, [44] who dying childless left it to his kinsman William Newland. He had no son, and his two surviving daughters were his heirs ; they married respectively Philip Cantillon [45] and Robert Dillon, and their children sold the manor to Anthony Chamier of Epsom. [46] He died in 1780 without issue, having left his estates in trust for his wife, and after her decease to his nephew John des Champs or Chamier. [47] They sold it with the manors of Fitznells and Rookesley to Thomas Calverley, whose son Thomas built Ewell Castle on the site of the old family mansion. [48] He was succeeded by his nephew William Bower Monro, who sold the estate to James Gadesden. [49] Mr. James Philip Gadesden of Burley, Newbury, Berks., is the present owner.

As early as 675 we have mention of 30 mansas of land in Ewell, afterwards known as the manor of FITZNELLS (Venelles, [50] Fenelles, [51] xv cent. ; Fenys, [52] xvi cent.), being granted by Frithwald subregulus of Surrey and Bishop Erkenwald to the newly-founded

abbey of Chertsey. [53] In 1331 Robert de FitzNeel died seised of one messuage, 250 acres of land, 6 acres of meadow, and one water-mill, which he held after his wife's death of the inheritance of his daughter Grace ; of these he held the capital messuage, 100 acres of land, and 4 acres of meadow of the Prior of Merton by the service of 15s., and 50 acres of land and one mill of the Abbot of Chertsey by the service of 6s. 8d. [54] It was from this family that the manor took the name of Fitznells. Robert's daughter Grace had at the time of her father's death a son and heir, Robert, [55] who was probably the father of Robert Leversegge, who died seised of a tenement called Fenelles, lying in the parishes of Ewell, Cuddington, and East Cheam. [56] His son Richard was imbecile from his birth, but held the estate in demesne as of fee until 10 June 1438, on which day John Iwardby (alias Everby) took possession and was succeeded by his son John, who affirmed that his father held the manor of the gift of Robert Leversegge. [57] In 1542 it was held by Dame Joan St. John, [58] who was daughter and heir of Sir John Iwardby, [59] and her son John sold it (1562) to Edmund Horde, [60] in whose family it remained for more than a century, [61] Thomas Horde settling it on his son William in tail male in 1639. [62] The Hordes were holding the manor as late as 1662, when Thomas Horde conveyed it to Jane Hope, widow. [63]

In 1693 John Harvey and his wife Mary quit-claimed an annual rent in the manor to Thomas Turgis, warranting it against themselves and all other claimants for Edmund and Thomas Horde, deceased. The manor was in the possession of Thomas Turgis at the time of his death, 1704, he having devised it to his kinsman, Mr. William Newland, [64] from which time the history of this manor is the same as that of Bottals and Rookesley.

FITZNEEL. Paly argent and gules a fesse azure.

IWARDBY. Argent a saltire engrailed sable and a chief sable with two molets argent therein.

HORDE. Argent a chief or with a raven therein.

[29] Pipe R. 20 Hen. II (Pipe R. Soc.), 3.
[30] Testa de Nevill (Rec. Com.), 225b.
[31] Rot. Lit. Pat. (Rec. Com.), 142.
[32] Testa de Nevill (Rec. Com.), 225b.
[33] Ibid.
[34] Rot. Lit. Claus. (Rec. Com.), i, 45b.
[35] Rot. Lit. Pat. (Rec. Com.), 142.
[36] Excerptae Rot. Fin. (Rec. Com.), i, 88.
[37] Rot. Lit. Claus. (Rec. Com.), i, 484b.
[38] Chart. R. 56 Hen. III, m. 4.
[39] Ibid. m. 3.
[40] See Chan. Inq. p.m. (Ser. 2), xiv, 44.
[41] Chan. Inq. p.m. 16 Ric. II, pt. ii, no. 133.
[42] The name 'Butele' occurs in 1205–6. See Cal. Rot. Chart. (Rec. Com.), i, 166.

[43] Recov. R. Surr. East. 1659, rot. 15.
[44] Feet of F. Surr. Trin. 1659.
[45] Feet of F. Div. Co. Hil. 27 Geo. II.
[46] Feet of F. Surr. Trin. 5 Geo. III ; Hil. 6 Geo. III.
[47] Will of Anthony Chamier, dated 9 Oct. 1780, P.C.C. 465 Collins ; see also Recov. R. Surr. Mich. 22 Geo. III, rot. 37.
[48] Burke, Visit. of Seats and Arms (1855, Ser. 2), ii, 203.   [49] Ibid.
[50] Chan. Inq. p.m. 28 Hen. VI, no. 3 ; Plac. in Canc. file 30, no. 11.
[51] Early Chan. Proc. bdle. 41, no. 110.
[52] Feet of F. Surr. Mich. 6 Hen. VIII.
[53] Birch, Cart. Sax. i, 64.   But see

note on Chertsey for the authenticity of the charter.
[54] Chan. Inq. p.m. 5 Edw. III, 75.
[55] Ibid.
[56] Chan. Inq. p.m. 28 Hen. VI, no. 3.
[57] Early Chan. Proc. bdle. 41, no. 110.
[58] Chan. Proc. Eliz. Bb. xxviii, 60.
[59] Manning and Bray, Surr. i, 460.
[60] Feet of F. Surr. East. 4 Eliz.
[61] See Bodl. Chart. 10, 11, 12 ; Feet of F. Surr. East. 12 Jas. I ; Hil. 10 Chas. I.
[62] Chan. Inq. p.m. (Ser. 2), ccclxxxviii, 12.
[63] Feet of F. Surr. Mich 1662 ; Recov. R. Mich. 14 Chas. II, rot. 217.
[64] Manning and Bray, Surr. i, 460.

There is no mention of the so-called manor of SHAWFORD (Standeford, Shaldeford, Rokesley, xv cent. ; Rixley, xvi cent.) until the middle of the 15th century ; but as early as 1229 John de Scaldeford is mentioned as owning half a hide of land in Ewell,[65] and twenty years later William de Standeford claimed common of pasture in Ewell, of which his uncle Joceus de Standeford (whose heir he was) was seised as of fee as pertaining to his free tenement in 'Scaldeford,' the day on which he died.[66]

Manning and Bray,[67] quoting an undated deed in the Rawlinson MSS., give a grant by Henry Picot of Chessington of a tenement in 'Schaldeford,' in the parish of Ewell, and of a mill in 'Schaldeford,' in Long Ditton, to John de Rokesle. The witnesses, John d'Abernon and William Ambesas, date the deed about 1297, when those two were knights of the shire.

In 1458-9 Simon Melbourne and others released to John Merston and Rose his wife for the term of their lives, with remainder to William, nephew of the said John, and Anne his wife, all right in the 'manor of Shaldeford alias Rokesley,' formerly called 'Standeford,' in the parish of Ewell, without impeachment of waste.[68] This manor was then worth 5 marks and included a barn worth 4s. and two tenements, 100 acres of land, 26s. 8d. rent in the parishes of Ewell and Cuddington worth 5 marks, and was said to be held of the Prior of Merton, service unknown. John and Rose died so seised and William and Anne entered and were seised in fee tail. William died 26 October 1495, and was succeeded by his son William.[69] About fifty years later it was owned by Edward Jenens, who, dying without issue, left it to his aunt Jane wife of Robert Kempe. Her only daughter and heir married John Wight, and they had one son Rhys.[70] Then it seems to have come into the possession of John, Lord Lumley, at that time lord of Ewell Manor, for in 1593 he quitclaimed it to Margaret Sanders, widow,[71] for the sum of £100. In 1714 William Newland[72] was holding the manor, and thenceforward its history follows that of the manors of Bottals and Fitznells.

At the Domesday Survey 'the men of the Hundred' deposed that the reeves of the king's manors had abstracted two and a quarter hides of the manor of Ewell with appurtenances.[73] This is believed to be the manor of KINGSWOOD, which Henry II granted with Selswood as parcel of the manor of Ewell[74] to the Prior and canons of Merton.[75] It was augmented by 5 acres of wood granted by Richard de Bures, 1208.[76]

In 1291 the Prior and convent of Merton were granted licence to inclose their wood of Kingswood, which was of their own soil and without the bounds of the forest, and which they held by grant of the king's progenitors.[77]

In 1535 Kingswood Manor was worth £14 6s. 8d.,[78] including the perquisites of court valued at 14s. 8d. The manor continued in the priory till its dissolution, when it was annexed by Henry to the honour of Hampton Court. Queen Elizabeth granted it to William Lord Howard of Effingham and Lady Margaret his wife for the service of one-fortieth part of a knight's fee[79] ; it descended to their son, who was created Earl of Nottingham. His son Charles died seised of it in 1642,[80] having settled it on his second wife Mary daughter of Sir William Cockayne.[81] She held a court there as lady of the manor.[82] On her death, 1651, the manor should have passed to Sir John Heydon, the reversion of the manor having been granted to him in consideration of the military services of his brother Sir William Heydon,[83] but as Sir John Heydon had been a Royalist partisan, and died in 1653,[84] it is doubtful if he was ever in possession. His name, according to Manning, does not appear in the court rolls. In 1656 the manor was conveyed by Charles Cockayne and his wife Mary to Sir Thomas Bludworth,[85] another Royalist partisan, who held a court as lord in October 1660. He lived at Flanchford, Reigate (q.v.). He was succeeded by his son Charles, who held his first court 1698, and in 1703 conveyed the manor to Richard Lynch and Thomas Brandon, possibly trustees for Thomas Harris, who held a court in 1708 ; it then descended to his son Thomas, whose nephew John Hughes[86] in 1791 sold the manor to William Jolliffe, whose son Hylton Jolliffe was owning it in 1804.[87] It was sold about 1830 to Mr. Thomas Alcock,[88] from whose executors it was bought by Sir John Hartopp, and from his trustees by Mr. H. Cosmo Bonsor. The manorial rights are in abeyance.

The old parish church of ST. MARY CHURCHES THE VIRGIN, has been pulled down, all except the tower, which is of 15th-century date, and is built of flint with stone dressings in three stages. The west doorway is original, and has moulded jambs and a two-centred arch, but is restored with plaster. The window over it, also old, has three cinquefoiled lights with tracery under a two-centred arch. On the east side there are remains of the nave walls, which are now used as buttresses and to form the sides of a porch. There is also part of the west wall of the south aisle.

The middle stage has single cinquefoiled lights on the north-west and south sides, but a good deal of the stone has been plastered over. The top stage has two-light windows of similar character in each face. The stair turret is on the south-west, and the top of the tower has a much-repaired parapet and angle pinnacles.

The two-centred tower arch is of typical 15th-century character, the moulded jambs having attached shafts with octagonal moulded bases and capitals.

[65] Feet of F. Surr. 13 Hen. III, no. 35.
[66] Cur. Reg. R. 135, m. 22.
[67] Surr. i, 460.
[68] Close, 37 Hen. VI, m. 21.
[69] Cal. Inq. p.m. Hen. VII, i, 521.
[70] Chan. Proc. (Ser. 2), cxciii, 41.
[71] Feet of F. Surr. Hil. 35 Eliz.
[72] Recov. R. Mich. 1 Geo. I, rot. 125.
[73] V.C.H. Surr. i, 290.
[74] The three portions of the manor of Ewell, Ewell itself on the northern side of

the chalk, Kingswood detached from it on the summit and southern side, and Shelwood further detached, down in the Weald, indicate the isolated condition of human habitation in the 11th and even 12th centuries.
[75] Plac. de Quo Warr. (Rec. Com.), 739.
[76] Feet of F. Surr. Trin. 10 John.
[77] Pat. 19 Edw. I, m. 10.
[78] Valor Eccl. (Rec. Com.), ii, 48.
[79] Pat. 6 Eliz. pt. iv, m. 3.

[80] Chan. Inq. p.m. (Ser. 2), dxx, 2 ; see also Recov. R. Trin. 9 Chas. I, rot. 60
[81] B.M. Add. Chart. 5638.
[82] Court Rolls quoted by Manning and Bray, Surr. i, 461.
[83] Pat. 6 Chas. I, pt. viii, m. 5.
[84] Dict. Nat. Biog.
[85] Feet of F. Surr. Mich. 1656, pt. ii.
[86] See Feet of F. Surr. Hil. 30 Geo. III.
[87] Recov. R. Trin. 44 Geo. III, rot. 283.
[88] Brayley, Surr. iv, 272.

3

36

Inside the tower. is an early 17th-century pulpit, with ornamental arched and square panels, but spoilt by being grained and varnished. Amongst other slabs on the floor is one to Margaret Craydon, 1690.

There is an old print in the vestry of the new church which shows the original building to have been a small, plain structure. There was a 15th-century south window with a flat head to the chancel, and there was a south porch.

The new church of *ST. MARY* is built not far to the north of the old one, and dates from 1848. It is in 14th-century style, and consists of a chancel with a south vestry, nave of five bays, north aisle which is extended eastwards, and has a north organ-chamber and quire-vestry, and at the west end of the aisle is a tower ; there is also a south aisle with a south porch, and a new porch lately built at the west end of the nave.

The material throughout is grey stone with ashlar dressings and the roofs are tiled.

There are several fittings inside which came from the old church. The altar is a Jacobean wood table, dated 1612, and has large carved legs, and the chancel-screen is of late 15th-century date with cinquefoiled, ogee-headed lights, and a moulded cornice with leaf cresting. The solid panelling at the base has been pulled out, and modern pierced work substituted.

The font is also 15th-century work from the old church. It is octagonal, each side of the bowl having quatrefoiled panels inclosing square leaf ornaments, and there are similar ornaments on the moulded base of the bowl, while the stem has narrow, trefoiled panels on each side.

In the chancel are several mural monuments from the old church, the most important being a large one to Sir William Lewen, who died in 1721. On the same tablet his nephew Charles and his wife Susannah are commemorated. Below is a recumbent figure of Sir William.

At the west end of the south aisle are several old brasses on stone slabs, placed on the walls. The first on the south wall has the following inscription in black letter : ' Pray for me lady Jane Iwarby sũtyme wife of Sʳ Johñ Iwarby of Ewell Knyght dought⁹ of Johñ Agmondeshm̃ sũtyme of ledered in Surrey sqer which Jane dyed the viii day of May in yᵉ yere of oure lord mᵛᶜxix of home Jhū have mᵉci.' Above is her figure kneeling in prayer, with a kennel head-dress and a heraldic mantle with the arms of Agmondesham. On one side of her is a scroll bearing the words ' lady helpe me and you ' ; the scroll on the opposite side is missing. Above are two shields, the first bearing the arms : Quarterly (1) Argent a cheveron azure between three boars' heads sable with five cinquefoils or upon the cheveron (Agmondesham) ; (2) Party with a lion countercoloured ; (3) A cheveron with three millrind crosses thereon ; (4) A cheveron between three martlets with five cinquefoils on the cheveron.

The other shield has Agmondesham impaling the second coat.

The next brass has the black letter inscription : ' Hic jacet Margeria Treglistan nup⁹ consors Johannis | Treghistan que quidem Margeria obiit xxiii die | Octobris Anno Domini mᵒvᶜxxiᵒ cujus anime propicietur deus Amen.' Above is a figure of a lady wearing a long, loose head-dress and gown with fur cuffs.

On the west wall is the following brass black-letter inscription : ' Of your charite pray for the soule of Edmond dows gentilmᶻ oon of the clerkᶜ of the signett with Kyng harry the vii whiche decessed the xiiii day of May the yere of our lord god m̃cccc and x on whose soule Jhu have mercy Amen.'

On the return wall of the north side of the aisle is a large stone slab on which are several brasses. Near the centre is an inscription in black letter as follows : ' Here lyeth the lady dorothe Taylare widow and Edmonde | Horde her seconde sonne the which Edmond deceassed the 29 day of October Aᵒ 1575, and she beinge ye dawghter of Thomas Roberdẹ of Wylesdon in Mydellsexe Esquyre late the wyffe of Syr Lawrence Taylare of doddington in ye countye of Huntington Knyght and before wyffe unto Allen Horde of ye myddle Temple esquire and bencher ther, ye yeres of her age was lxx and deceased ye xiᵗ of Maye Aᵒ 1577.' Above is her figure with her five sons and five daughters, with their names above them : Thomas, Edmond, Alyn, William, and John, and Ketheren, Elizabeth, Mary, Dorothe, and Ursula. All the children are named Horde. Near the top of the slab are two shields, both bearing the same arms : three pheons, and in chief a greyhound collared (Roberts). Near the bottom of the slab are the figures of a man and his wife. Beside the man are three boys, with their names, Arthur, Alyn, and Edmond, and the initial ' ḣ ' after each ; and by the woman is an indent of three girls, with part of the name-plate over. When complete the three names were Dorothe, Elizabeth, and Anne. Between the man and the woman is a shield : Quarterly (1 and 4) Argent on a chief or a raven sable ; (2) Gules a cheveron between three leopards' heads or with three molets sable on the cheveron (Perrell) ; (3) Azure a lion with a forked tail or (Stapylton) ; over all a fleur de lis for difference.

A brass, now lost, of which a rubbing is preserved in the collection of the Society of Antiquaries, was inscribed : ' Hic jacet Johẽs Tabard et Johanna ux⁹ ei⁹ q⁰ aĩab; ꝓpicieͭ dc⁰ amẽ⁹.'

There is a ring of eight bells in the tower, the treble and second being by Mears & Stainbank, 1890. The third and fifth are dated 1767, and, together with the fourth, which is probably of the same date, are by Lester and Pack. The sixth is by T. Mears, 1767, and the seventh and eighth are re-casts from old ones, by Mears and Stainbank, 1890. All the old bells came from the tower of the old church.

The oldest piece of plate is a standing paten of 1764. All the rest, consisting of two chalices, two patens, three standing patens, a fiagon, and a spoon, date from 1844.

There are four books of registers, the first containing baptisms, marriages, and burials, from 1604 to 1641. There is one baptism of 1597 and one of 1600, and between 1604 and 1608 there is a gap. There are also a few Kingswood marriages and baptisms for 1638. The second book contains baptisms and burials from 1669 to 1723, and marriages from 1697 to 1723. The third book has all three entries from 1723, the marriages to 1754, and the other entries to 1812. The marriages are continued on printed forms in the fourth book from 1754 to 1812.

The parish church of *ST. ANDREW, KINGS-WOOD,* is a building of flint and stone, built in 1848–52, in the 14th-century style, by Mr. Thomas

Alcock. It is cruciform in plan, having a chancel, transepts, nave, and central tower. The nave is of less length than the chancel. The central tower has a tall octagonal spire of stone. The building stands to the east of the Banstead and Reigate road. It is endowed with a glebe of 31 acres.

At Lower Kingswood is a small mission church, dedicated in honour of *ST. SOPHIA OR THE WISDOM OF GOD*, built in 1891 by Mr. H. C. Bonsor of the Warren and Dr. Edwin Freshfield. Its material outside is red brick with stone dressings. It has a small chancel, with a round apsidal east end and small vestries on either side, and a nave with narrow aisles divided from the nave on each side by an arcade of two large and two small round-headed bays of Ham Hill stone ; the middle shaft is of dark-green marble, the others of stone ; all three are circular.

The lower part of the apse, to about a height of 10 ft., is lined with marble of various tints, mostly dove-coloured ; the upper part is treated with mosaic, having a rose-tree pattern on dark-blue ground ; the semi-dome is lined with gold mosaic, in which is a cross in red outline between the letters I C X C N I K A. The east wall on either side of the apse is also treated in a similar manner. The floor is paved with various-coloured marbles, and which are continued down the centre passage of the nave. At the west end, beside the three entrances and lobbies, is a small baptistery also lined with marble, in which is a font of yellow marble of a cylindrical shape, with slightly wavy sides of five lobes.

The furniture of the chancel is of a dark-brown wood, inlaid with lozenges of mother-of-pearl. In the church are nine Byzantine capitals, &c., brought to England by Dr. Freshfield, of which a short description has been written by Mrs. Freshfield. The two largest are capitals closely resembling those of the Corinthian order ; they were brought from Ayasolook, the north quarter of ancient Ephesus, in which stood the Temple of Diana of the Ephesians ; they formed part of a church screen, and were erected by the Emperor Constantine. The third capital, a smaller one, belonged to a second church, of the 6th century. Two other small capitals came from the monastery of St. John of the Stadium, near the Seven Towers at Constantinople, erected about the time of the Emperor Theodosius ; the capitals date from between the 5th and 8th centuries. The sixth capital is from the platform on which the imperial palace of Blachernae stood, in the west quarter of Constantinople. The seventh capital is a small one from Bogdan Serai, Constantinople, and dates from the period of the Comneni. The eighth is a beautiful little capital from near the site of the church of the Blachernae, and was probably part of an internal ornament. The ninth stone is a piece of ornament from the great triple church of the Pantocrator at Constantinople, the mausoleum of the family of the Comneni, dating probably from the 11th century. A small cross over it was from another church built by the Comnenus family ; it was in the church now called the Eski Imaret Djami.

The bell belonging to the church hangs in a detached wooden turret in the churchyard.

The chapel of ease of *ALL SAINTS* is situated about three-quarters of a mile west of the parish church. It is a small, unfinished building of red brick and stone, erected at the expense of Mr. J. H. Bridges of Ewell Court and the Rev. John Thornton, vicar of Ewell, in 1894, and of the style of the end of the 13th century. It consists of a nave of four bays, north aisle, north porch, and a temporary sanctuary and south organ-chamber ; provision is made for a future south aisle. The roofs are tiled, and at the west end is an oak-shingled bell-turret with an octagonal spirelet. The font is of various marbles ; the other furniture is more or less temporary. The churchyard is small, and has a wooden fence on the north side towards the road.

The church was apparently not situated on the royal domain at Ewell, but on the property of the Abbot of Chertsey there. A bull of Pope Clement III, which was confirmed by letters patent of John, Bishop of Winchester dated 1 April 1292, licensed the abbot and convent to retain in their own hands the parish church of Ewell, to reserve the benefice to their own use, and to appoint vicars to the church.[89] In the reign of Richard I we have mention of a suit concerning the building of a wall on some land which the Prior of Merton, lord of Ewell Manor, claimed against William the vicar of Ewell.[90]

ADVOWSON

In 1380 the abbot and convent received confirmation for the appropriation in mortmain of the church which was of their own advowson.[91] In 1415 they gave the advowson to the king,[92] reserving to themselves an annual pension of 20s., to be paid by future rectors. The following year Henry V granted the church to the Prior and convent of Newark, who continued to pay the pension to the Abbey of Chertsey until its dissolution.[93] In 1458 the endowment of a vicarage took place under the direction of Bishop Wayneflete,[94] and was ratified by the Prior and convent of Newark as rectors of Ewell.

After the Dissolution the advowson remained with the Crown[95] until 1702, when Queen Anne granted it to the Earl of Northampton in exchange for the advowson of the rectory of Shorncutt, co. Wilts,[96] the Crown reserving one turn.[97] In 1703 it was purchased by Barton Holliday,[98] and passed with his other estates to the Glyn family.[99]

Lady Dorothy Brownlow, of Belton, co. Lincs., gave a sum of money to be disposed of by Henry Compton, Bishop of London, for the benefit of this vicarage ; with part he bought the tithes of the liberty of Kingswood,[100] with the remainder a small farm in Malden, the rents of which were appropriated to the same use. In 1843 the Malden Farm was exchanged for a house and land adjoining Ewell Church for the use of the vicar.

After the suppression of Newark Henry VIII granted to his new monastery of Bisham the ' tithes of the church of Ewell, one of the possessions of the late Abbey of Chertsey.'[101] But on the almost immediate suppression of that house also they reverted to

88 Pat. 20 Edw. I, m. 11.
89 Rolls of the King's Ct. (Pipe R. Soc. xiv), 1.
91 Pat. 4 Ric. II, pt. i, m. 27.
92 Close, 3 Hen. V, m. 21.

93 Valor Eccl. (Rec. Com.), ii, 34.
94 Winton Epis. Reg. Wayneflete, (2), fol. 52.
95 See Inst. Bks. (P.R.O.) 1614, 1633, 1663, 1676, 1696.

96 Pat. 1 Anne, pt. ix, no. 52.
97 Inst. Bks. (P.R.O.), 1722.
98 Close, 2 Anne, pt. i, no. 15.
99 See rectory.   100 Ibid.
101 L. and P. Hen. VIII, xii (2), 1311 (22).

the Crown. In 1558 Queen Mary granted the rectory to John Bishop of Winchester,[102] but he was deprived in 1559 and died in January 1560, and it reverted to the Crown. In 1560 Elizabeth granted the rectory and church to Thomas Reve and George Evelyn and their heirs, to be held in chief by the service of a fortieth part of a knight's fee.[103] These were probably trustees, for soon after Nicholas Saunders was seised of the rectory, from whom Sir William Gardiner purchased it,[104] and left it by will, proved 1622, to his son,[105] who was holding it in 1628.[106] A descendant of his of the same name sold it to Barton Holliday in 1691,[107] who conveyed it to Sir Richard Bulkeley, bart.[108] A few years after Sir W. Lewen bought it, and in 1722 devised it to his nephew George, whose daughter and sole heir married, in 1736, Sir Richard Glyn of London,[109] and with her it passed to the Glyn family, with whom it still remains.

When the rectory was granted to Thomas Reve and George Evelyn in 1560, the sum of £11 was reserved out of the profits, to be annually paid to the vicar.[110] The vicarage fell very low after that time, for we have the humble petition of the inhabitants and parishioners of Ewell for the 'relief of the most miserable state of their poor vicarage'—the vicar was Richard Williamson,[111] who held the living from April 1584 to April 1589.

There was a chapel in the far-removed hamlet of Kingswood, which had existed long before the middle of the 15th century; for when the vicarage of Ewell was endowed in 1458, it is mentioned as of long standing. It was then stipulated that the vicar should not be obliged to minister to the hamlet of Kingswood or to celebrate Mass in the chapel there; that when any of the Sacraments of the Church were to be administered to the people of that place, the rectors (Prior and convent of Newark) should provide a priest for the purpose; and in case of the death of any inhabitant of Kingswood and his removal to Ewell for burial, the vicar should meet the body at Provost's Cross, on the south side of Ewell, which had been the custom

from ancient time.[112] The subsequent history of this chapel remains obscure.

CHARITIES

Smith's Charity is distributed as in other Surrey parishes. Mr. Thomas Dickenson's rent-charge of £2 2s. for the poor, presented as existing in 1725, was left in 1631.

Mr. Mason, in 1733, gave £3 a year from South Sea Stock for the poor.

Two fields, Chamber Mead and Parish Close, were rented for the benefit of the poor from an unknown date.

In 1725 Mr. David White left money for educating poor children. There was no school at Ewell, and the bequest led to protracted Chancery suits, with no benefit to the parish till 1816, when Mr. Bromfield's bequest had also became available for a school.

Mr. Bromfield, by will of 1773, left £350 for the vicar of Ewell, or, if he did not preach on Sundays at evensong, for the poor not receiving parish relief, and five shares in the Sun Fire Office for six poor widows and the education of ten poor children.

Mrs. Hellena Tindall, in 1798, left £1,758 19s. 6d. Three per Cent. Stock for widows and poor not receiving parish relief.

Bromfield's charity is, according to a scheme sanctioned by the Charity Commissioners, 3 January 1905, divided between a payment made to the vicar, educational purposes, and poor relief. Under the second head prizes and exhibitions for the higher education of scholars are given, and a balance is held over to provide against possible demands under the Act of 1902. White's bequest is now held in reserve for the same contingency. Chamber Mead was sold in 1883, and the price invested in consols, the income being applied in relief of the poor rate. Parish Close, awarded to the parish under the Inclosure Act of 1801, was exchanged in 1885 for a field at Beggar's Hill, which is let in allotments, the rent, £8, being also used for the relief of the poor rate. The total of the charities amounts to over £300 a year, given in bread, clothing, and school scholarships and prizes.

FETCHAM

Feecham (xi cent.); Fecham (xiii cent.); Feecham (xiv cent.); Fetcham, 1499.

Fetcham is a small parish and village, the latter a mile from Letherhead. It measures nearly 4 miles from north to south, and under 2 miles from east to west, tapering to the south, and includes 1,817 acres of land and 22 of water. Roreing House Farm, a small detached portion of Great Bookham, was transferred to Fetcham under the Act of 1882. The Mole forms part of the eastern and northern boundary. The village lies on the Woolwich Beds at the foot of the chalk, but the greater part of the parish to the south is upon the chalk hills, and the northern part and eastern fringe are upon the London Clay and alluvium of the Mole. It is a purely agricultural

parish. The mill, close to Letherhead, is worked by the overflow of a pond formed by several strong springs rising in it, which runs into the Mole in the course of a few yards. The springs do not seem to be connected with the swallows in the bed of the Mole, as they are unaffected by the rising or falling of the river. Fetcham Downs were a large tract of open chalk down, of which much has been inclosed, cultivated, or planted. The road from Letherhead to Guildford passes through the parish, and also the South-Western Railway from Effingham Junction to Letherhead. The London, Brighton, and South Coast Railway line to Dorking also just touches the parish.

Fetcham is rich in prehistoric antiquities. Anglo-

102 Pat. 5 & 6 Phil. and Mary, pt. iv.
103 Pat. 2 Eliz. pt. iv.
104 Chan. Proc. Eliz. Ll. i, 38.
105 Brayley, *Surr.* iv, 380.
106 Feet of F. Surr. East. 4 Chas. I; East. 7 Chas. I.
107 Feet of F. Mich. 3 Will. and Mary.
108 Recov. R. Hil. 4 Anne, rot. 231.
109 G.E.C. *Baronetage*, v, 114.
110 Brayley, *Surr.* iv, 380.
111 *Hist. MSS. Com. Rep.* vii, App. 666a; Loseley MSS. ii, 14.
112 Winton Epis. Reg. Wayneflete, i (2), fol. 52.

Saxon burial has already been noticed[1] at Hawkshill in Fetcham. Since the publication of the earlier volume, however, additional remains have come to light. The earliest record is the finding of some twenty skeletons in 1758 when the road from Letherhead to Guildford was being first made as a really passable driving road. A small pike-head and some blades of knives were found with them. The remains were probably Anglo-Saxon. Other skeletons were found on the inclosing of the Common Fields in 1803.[2] Subsequent discoveries have been made which confirm these, but also show more ancient remains at and about Hawkshill. In the year 1900 two hut circles were excavated on the lawn of Hawkshill House, under the supervision of Mr. Reginald Smith of the British Museum. The discoveries included bones of animals, fragments of hand-made pottery, burnt grains of wheat, oats, and barley, and loom weights of burnt clay. The pottery corresponded to fragments found elsewhere of the late Celtic period. Other pits seem to exist, and a larger ring was excavated in the meadow, but the ground had been ploughed formerly, and though traces of fire and a bone were found, the remains here had been scattered. When the house was built twenty years earlier some remains were found, but not properly observed or recorded.[3] On the downs in the neighbourhood are some deep holes which seem to be collapsed dene-holes, as on Ranmore Common, but though in the neighbourhood they are outside Fetcham parish. There used to be a barrow on Standard Hill near the Guildford road.[4] These late Celtic remains, of a period rather before the Roman Conquest, are distinct from the Anglo-Saxon burials, which indicate a considerable settlement in the neighbourhood. In these a bronze wheel-shaped ornament, an inlaid glass bead, a coin of Constantine, several small iron knives, and a small hand-made black vase were found. Many skeletons were unearthed when the house was built, others have since been discovered, and in laying down pipes for the road six more were found in 1906. The bodies lay with heads to west-by-south and south-west, and Mr. Smith attributes the burials to the 5th or 6th century.[5]

The neighbourhood was probably continuously occupied, for subsequent in date to the Celtic huts there are Roman bricks in considerable quantities in Fetcham Church, remains of Anglo-Saxon architecture in the church, and a road coming from the north and crossing the Mole by a ford, which passes close by the small rectangular camp or inclosure near Pachevesham Farm in Letherhead, close by which Roman coins and bricks have been found. It may be noticed, however, that Deadwoman's Lane, near Hawkshill, was named from a recent suicide, and that the skeleton found in a coffin farther along the road towards Bookham is recent, probably that of a criminal or suicide. Gallows Bush Shot was the name of a field abutting on the Guildford road.[6]

There were large common fields at Fetcham inclosed in 1801.[7] There were then found to be 316

acres of common arable, 26 of common meadow, and 330 waste. All was inclosed except part of the waste. (The award seems to be wrongly dated in Sir John Brunner's *Return* as in 1813. It was carried out in 1803.)

Fetcham Park, adjoining the church, is the seat of Mr. J. B. Hankey, J.P., lord of the manor ; Ballands Hall of Lieut.-Col. Sir F. S. Graham Moon, bart., son of the late rector, the Rev. Sir Edward Graham Moon ; and Hawkshill of Sir E. E. Blake, K.C.M.G.

Fetcham School was founded as a Church school in 1854, and passed under a School Board in 1883. The building was enlarged in 1886. There is also a reading-room in the village.

FETCHAM is mentioned in the MANORS Domesday Survey, when it was held as three manors by the king, Odo of Bayeux, and Oswold the Thegn.[8] The manor which the king held in 1086 had been the property of Edith widow of Edward the Confessor,[9] and in 1088–9 was bestowed upon William de Warenne with the rest of her late possessions.[10] In the 13th century a knight's fee in Fetcham is found to be held of the honour of Warenne.[11] The holding was in the hands of John d'Abernon, a minor in ward of John de Gatesden, and the bishop's fee in Fetcham was in the same manor (see below). The two were considered as one manor, and parts were said to be held of different lords. In the 15th century a fourth part of the manor was held of the Earls of Warenne and Surrey, and through Elizabeth, sister and co-heir of Thomas Earl of Surrey,[12] the lordship passed to the Dukes of Norfolk. In 1476 John Duke of Norfolk died seised of this fee,[13] and in 1553 this part of the manor is said to be held of Thomas Duke of Norfolk, Edward Earl of Derby, and Henry Nevill first Lord Abergavenny[14] (to whom the Norfolk estates had come by partition) as of their manor of Reigate.

The second manor had been held by Biga of Edward the Confessor, and in 1086 was in the hands of Odo of Bayeux, the Conqueror's half-brother, of whom it was held by Richard de Tonbridge, lord of Clare, and ancestor of the Earls of Gloucester.[15] In the 13th century a fee in Fetcham is said to be held of the honour of Clare by John d'Abernon,[16] and in 1314 the manor is included among the fees held of the same honour.[17] In the 15th century three parts of the manor are said to be held of the honour of Clare,[18] as a part of which it apparently became merged in the Crown on the accession of Edward IV.

At an early period the two manors appear to have been included in the estates of the d'Abernon family, and the bishop's manor was one of the

D'ABERNON. *Azure a chevron or.*

four knights' fees in Surrey held by the Earl of Gloucester of which Ingelram d'Abernon died seised in

---

[1] *V.C.H. Surr.* i, 267.
[2] Manning and Bray, *Surr.* i, 482.
[3] *Surr. Arch. Coll.* xx, 119.
[4] Manning and Bray, *Surr.* i, 482.
[5] *Surr. Arch. Coll.* loc. cit.
[6] Tablet of charities in the church.
[7] By Act of 41 Geo. III, cap. 126.

[8] *V.C.H. Surr.* i, 297, 304, 327.
[9] Ibid. 279, 297.
[10] Ibid. 340.
[11] *Testa de Nevill* (Rec. Com.), 220a.
[12] Chan. Inq. p.m. 3 Hen. V, no. 37 ;
6 Hen. V, no. 30 ; *Feud. Aids,* v, 125.
[13] *Cal. Inq. p.m.* (Rec. Com.), iv, 313.

[14] Memo. R. Mich. 19 Eliz. rot. 87.
[15] *V.C.H. Surr.* i, 304b.
[16] *Testa de Nevill* (Rec. Com.), 219b.
[17] *Cal. Inq. p.m.* (Rec. Com.), i, 266.
[18] Chan. Inq. p.m. 3 Hen. V, no. 37 ;
6 Hen. V, no. 30 ; *Feud. Aids,* v, 125.

1234,[18] and which passed to Gilbert d'Abernon, uncle of Ingelram, by reason of Jordan d'Abernon, the rightful heir, having surrendered his claim.[19] Gilbert paid a relief of 40 marks to the sheriff in 1235 on taking up this inheritance, and on his death, in the next year, the custody of his land and of his heir was granted to John de Gatesden, then sheriff of Surrey and Sussex.[21] The heir of Gilbert was probably the John d'Abernon who in 1252 granted to William d'Abernon a tenement in Fetcham,[22] and who claimed liberties in the manor in 1252–3.[23] He was sheriff of Surrey and Sussex in 1266,[24] and was apparently dead in 1279, when his son John was made a knight.[25] The elder John had also been a knight.[26] The son John claimed the same rights as his father in 1279.[27] In 1314 John d'Abernon the son was holding the manor,[28] and in 1326–7 died seised of it as a holding consisting of half a messuage, 100 acres of land worth 25s. per annum, 8 acres of meadow, and 19s. from rent of free tenants, leaving a son and heir of the same name.[29] The latter was sheriff of Surrey and Sussex in 1330 and 1334,[30] and in 1339 settled Fetcham on his grandson William son of John and Margery wife of William.[31]

William died in 1358,[32] leaving a daughter Elizabeth then wife of William Croyser, and afterwards of John de Grey of Ruthyn.[33] In 1395 William son of Elizabeth and William Croyser was holding the manor,[34] of which he died seised jointly with his wife Edith in 1415, leaving a daughter and heir Anne,[35] then aged nine years, and before her thirteenth year the wife of Ingram Bruyn, son of Sir Maurice Bruyn.[36] Anne subsequently married Sir Henry Norbury, and died in 1464, leaving a son and heir Sir John Norbury,[37] afterwards Vice-Marshal to Richard III,[38] who inherited these estates and married Jane daughter of Sir Otes Gilbert. Their daughter Anne married Richard Hallywell of Devon, and had a daughter Joan,[39] who in 1514–15 was holding the manor jointly with her husband Edmund Lord Bray. In a bailiff's account of Lord Bray's manors of Fetcham and Letherhead for this date the rents of assize for the two manors amounted to £11 11s. 1¼d.; the farm of the manor and the demesne lands was £8 a year.[40]

In 1548 Joan settled the manor upon herself and her husband for their lives, with remainder to John Bray their son and heir.[41] The latter married Anne daughter of Francis fifth Earl of Shrewsbury, and was summoned to Parliament as a baron from 1545 to 1555, but on his death without issue in 1557 his estates were divided among his six sisters and co-heirs,

Fetcham falling to the share of Frances, the youngest, who married Thomas Lyfield.[42] In 1575 a settlement was made on Thomas Vincent and Jane his wife, daughter of Thomas and Frances, with remainder to Francis Vincent and Bray Vincent, sons of Thomas and Jane. Francis married Sara daughter of Sir Amias Paulet in 1589,[43] and in 1617 settled this manor on his son Anthony on the occasion of his marriage with Elizabeth daughter of Sir Arthur Ackland.[44] Anthony was sheriff of Surrey and Sussex in 1636–7.[45] He was named as a sequestrator of delinquent estates by the Long Parliament, but died in 1642, and was succeeded by his son Sir Francis. He married Catherine daughter of George Pitt and died in 1670,[46] having settled this manor on his fourth son Thomas Vincent,[47] who in 1693, jointly with his wife Mary, conveyed it to Thomas Folkes,[48] the latter probably acting in the interest of Francis, fifth Baron Howard of Effingham, for whose widow he was executor in 1727.[49]

Thomas, Lord Howard, son of the said Francis, suffered a recovery of the manor in 1721,[50] and died without issue four years later. His nephew, Thomas Howard, Earl of Effingham, was seised of it in 1742.[51] In 1801 Richard, nephew of Thomas and last Earl of Effingham,[52] conveyed the manor to James Laurell,[53] who made his seat at Eastwick Park in Great Bookham, and subsequently sold this property to the family of Hankey of Fetcham Park,[54] whose descendant, Mr. John Barnard Hankey, is lord of the manor at the present day.

HANKEY. *Party gules and azure a leaping wolf erminois wounded in the shoulder.*

In 1252–3 John d'Abernon received a grant of free warren in his demesne lands of Fetcham,[55] and the privilege is mentioned as appurtenant to the manor in a conveyance of 1607.[56] In 1279 John d'Abernon claimed in addition to have view of frankpledge and all things pertaining thereto from time immemorial.[57]

In 1303 Henry de Gildford had a grant of free warren in his demesne lands in Fetcham,[58] but there is no other trace of his connexion with Fetcham, except that in 1284–5 he was appointed custodian of Robert d'Abernon, rector of Fetcham, who was under age at the time of his admission to the rectory.[59]

At the time of the Domesday Survey the king's manor included 4 mills worth 4s., and Richard de Tonbridge received 6s. 6d. from another mill,[60] which

[18] *Excerpta e Rot. Fin.* (Rec. Com.), i, 270. There is an exhaustive article on the d'Abernons by C. S. Percival, Dir.S.A. and formerly Fellow of Trinity Hall, in *Surrey Arch. Coll.* v, 53.
[19] *Excerpta e Rot. Fin.* (Rec. Com.), 272.
[21] Ibid. 305.
[22] Feet of F. Surr. 30 Hen. III, no. 31.
[23] Chart. R. 37 Hen. III, m. 3 (1).
[24] *Madox, Hist. of Exch.* 24, § 4.
[25] *Parl. Writs* (Rec. Com.), i, 216, 218; Pat. 7 Edw. I, m. 21 d.
[26] Add. Chart. 5547.
[27] *Plac. de Quo Warr.* (Rec. Com.), 747.
[28] *Cal. Inq. p.m.* (Rec. Com.), i, 266.
[29] Chan. Inq. p.m. Edw. III, file 3, no. 1.
[30] *Lists of Sheriffs*, 135, 136.

[31] Feet of F. Div. Co. 13 Edw. III, no. 267.
[32] Chan. Inq. p.m. file 139 (1st nos.), no. 23.
[33] Ibid.
[34] De Banco R. 538, m. 338a.
[35] Chan. Inq. p.m. 3 Hen. V, no. 37.
[36] Ibid. 6 Hen. V, no. 30.
[37] *Surr. Arch. Coll.* x, 282.
[38] *Cal. Pat.* 1476–85, p. 392.
[39] *Visit. of Surr.* (Harl. Soc. xliii), 221.
[40] Manning and Bray, *Hist. of Surr.* i, 480.
[41] Feet of F. Div. Co. Mich. 35 Hen. VIII.
[42] *G.E.C. Complete Peerage*, ii, 111; Feet of F. Surr. East. 3 & 4 Phil. and Mary.
[43] Chan. Inq. p.m. (Ser. 2), ccxlvii, 99.
[44] Ibid. ccccxcii, 106.

[45] *List of Sheriffs*, 138.
[46] G.E.C. *Complete Baronetage*, i, 158.
[47] Will P.C.C. Penn, 68.
[48] Feet of F. Surr. Hil. 5 Will. and Mary.
[49] *Surr. Arch. Coll.* ix, 432.
[50] Recov. R. Mich. 7 Geo. I, rot. 267.
[51] Ibid. East. 15 Geo. II, rot. 191.
[52] G.E.C. *Complete Peerage*, iii, 237–8.
[53] Feet of F. Surr. Trin. 41 Geo. III.
[54] Brayley, *Hist. of Surr.* iv, 415.
[55] Chart. R. 37 Hen. III, m. 3 (1).
[56] Feet of F. Surr. Hil. 5 Jas. I.
[57] *Plac. de Quo Warr.* (Rec. Com.), 747.
[58] *Cal. Rot. Chart.* (Rec. Com.), 74.
[59] Manning and Bray, *Hist. of Surr.* ii, 486 (quoting from the episcopal register).
[60] *V.C.H. Surr.* i, 279, 297.

passed with Richard's share of the manor to the d'Abernons, and is probably referred to in the grant by Adam le Jeune to Sir John d'Abernon in 1293 of ' my half of the mill which is called cutte, with half of the pond and of the ditches pertaining thereto.'[61] In the bailiff's account of Sir Edmund Bray's manor of Fetcham and Letherhead for 1514-15, the water-mill called cutt-mill is said to be let out for £5, and is probably the same as that conveyed by Arthur Moore to Jabez Cellier[62] in 1717. The flour-mill which exists at the present day near Letherhead Bridge, and which is worked by the overflow from a spring-pond, probably stands upon the ancient site.

On the bishop's manor in Domesday were also the sixth part of a mill and the third part of another mill. These were probably fractions of the dues from the Pachevesham mills[63] in the Mole between the manors.

The manor of CANNON COURT probably represents that portion of Fetcham which had been held of Edward the Confessor by Oswold, brother of Wulfwold, Abbot of Chertsey, and was retained by him in chief after the Conquest.[64] By the 12th century, however, it appears to have been acquired by Merton Priory, which had possessions in Fetcham as early as 1167, when William, Prior of Merton, made a grant of certain tenements in Fetcham to one Guarnerius,[65] and in 1178 Robert, Prior of Merton, conceded to Alexander, a clerk of Fetcham, certain lands in the manor, amounting to a quarter of a virgate, which Gilbert le Blond had given him in fee and inheritance at a quit-rent of 12d. a year.[66] In 1291 the possessions of the prior at Fetcham and Letherhead were taxed at £3,[67] and in 1301 the tenants of Fetcham contributed 6s. 8d. towards the loan of £50 from the prior to Edward I.[68] In the reign of Henry VIII the manor was let out at farm for the sum of £13 6s. 8d. by the prior, who had in addition 6s. 5d. for perquisites from the court.[69] The priory was dissolved in 1538,[70] and in 1541 the manor was granted in tail male to Uriah Brereton (who already held the manor of Fetcham in right of his wife Joan late wife of Sir Edmund Bray), to be held of the king for a tenth part of a knight's fee and a yearly rent of £6 1s. 10d.[71] It appears to have formed part of the marriage portion of Jane, granddaughter of Joan, who married Thomas Vincent,[72] and from this date it continued with the lords of Fetcham. In 1700 ' Cannon Farme' is included in the estates of Thomas Vincent.[73] This property appears to have been leased out at various times. In 1560 John Edsawe complained that his father of the same name had occupied the site and demesne lands of the manor of Fetcham called Cannon Court by lease from the Prior and convent of Merton for a term of twenty-one years to commence in the year 1543, but that he, the plaintiff, had been forcibly dis-

possessed by his stepmother and her sons. Whereupon an award was made that John should for the remainder of his term occupy certain parcels of land, including two closes, of which one called ' Cokkes Close,' containing 6 acres, probably represents the wood now known as Cocklane Shaw, while the other, called ' Bykney,' also containing 6 acres, is frequently mentioned in connexion with this manor.[74] (See below.) It was probably this manor which Francis Crosse, of Stoke D'Abernon, who must have been a lessee, granted in 1582 under the name of ' the manner place, fermehouse and lands of Fetcham' to John Dewe of Fetcham, who assigned his interest by lease to Robert Gavell of Cobham.[75]

The prior had a grant of free warren in his demesne lands of Fetcham in 1252,[76] and the privilege is mentioned as appurtenant to the manor in 1590 and in 1607.[77]

At the time of the Domesday Survey, Oswold received 6s. 6d. from a mill,[78] which passed with his manor to Merton Priory, and in 1167 William, Prior of Merton, granted his part in the mill at Fetcham, with a certain acre of land, to one Guarnerius, the latter rendering 5s. yearly and grinding all the corn required for the use of the priory free of charge.[79]

In the accounts of the prior's manor for 1537-8 certain lands called Bykney Magna are stated to be farmed for £1 6s. 8d.,[80] and in the grant of the manor in 1541, following the dissolution of the priory, a reservation was made of the lands and meadows called ' Moche Bykney,' parcel of the manor, and then or lately in the tenure of Christopher Parker.[81] In 1544 Sir Anthony Browne, son of Sir Wistan Browne of Abbess Roding and Langenhoe in Essex, received a grant of the tenement of Great Bickney in Fetcham to be held of the Crown in chief by socage at an annual rent of 2s. 8d., being valued at £1 6s. 8d. per annum.[82] Later documents refer to it as a manor. In 1714 Dr. Hugh Shortrudge suffered a recovery of the ' manors of Slyfield and Bigney,'[83] and by a deed of trust dated 1715 between Dr. Shortrudge and Sir Francis Vincent the manor of Great Bickney was included among certain estates vested for charitable purposes.[84] The tenement of Great Bickney was afterwards held by the Howards, together with the manor of Fetcham, with which it was sold to James Laurell in 1801,[85] and passed with Fetcham to the Hankey family.

The mansion known as FETCHAM PARK is said to have been built by one of the Vincent family, by whom it was sold to Arthur Moore the famous economist and politician, who in 1718 enlarged the property and planted the park ; but his profuse expenditure more than exceeded his means, and he died in 1730 ' broken in all respects but in his parts and spirit.'[86] The property was put up for sale by his son

[61] Add. Chart. 5573.
[62] Manning and Bray, Hist. of Surr. i, 480 ; Feet of F. Surr. Trin. 3 Geo. I.
[63] V.C.H. Surr. i, 304.
[64] Ibid. 327b.
[65] H. C. Heales, Rec. of Merton Priory, 24-5.
[66] Cott. MS. Cleop. C. vii, 20.
[67] Pope Nich. Tax. (Rec. Com.), 206.
[68] A. C. Heales, Rec. of Merton Priory, 187.

[69] Ibid. App. clii, p. cxxxv ; Valor Eccl. (Rec. Com.), ii, 43.
[70] V.C.H. Surr. ii, 101.
[71] L. and P. Hen. VIII, xvi, g. 678 (20) ; Pat. 32 Hen. VIII, pt. viii, m. 23.
[72] Feet of F. Surr. Hil. 32 Eliz.
[73] Will P.C.C. Nod, 147.
[74] Ct. of Req. bdle. 77, no. 66.
[75] Anct. D. (P.R.O.), A. 12297.
[76] Chart. R. 36 Hen. III, m. 11.
[77] Feet of F. Surr. Hil. 32 Eliz. ; Hil. 5 Jas. I.

[78] V.C.H. Surr. i, 327b.
[79] Add. MSS. 6167, fol. 122.
[80] H. C. Heales, Rec. of Merton Priory, App. clii, p. cxxvii.
[81] L. and P. Hen. VIII, xvi, g. 98 (40).
[82] Manning and Bray, Hist. of Surr. i, 482 ; L. and P. Hen. VIII, xix (1), g. 1035 (11).
[83] Recov. R. Mich. 1 Geo. I, rot. 66.
[84] Manning and Bray, Hist. of Surr. i, 479 ; ii, 700. [85] Ibid. i, 482.
[86] Dict. Nat. Biog.

William Moore, under the description of 'The mansion house and offices of the late Arthur Moore, Esq., dec^d., being a beautifull building from the design of the late Mr. Tollmen, consisting of many rooms on a floor, a large hall and staircase, painted by the late famous · Laguerre, with a saloon and gallery, and several other rooms finely painted by the same hand, particularly one wainscoted with japan, with Tartarian tapestry silk. Together with the gardens and park, containing by estimation about 100 acres, the whole being finely adorned with canalls, basins, statues, vases, iron gates, pallisades, etc., and laid out in the most elegant manner ; with three ponds, containing the space of six acres, in which are several clear and deep springs, which by large engines serve the canalls, basins, reservoirs, etc., and furnish the house with water convey'd in strong leaden pipes.'[87]   It was purchased by Thomas Revell, agent victualler at Gibraltar and member for Dover in 1734, 1741, and 1747,[88] and on his death in 1752 his immense wealth was inherited by his only daughter Jane, who married George Warren, of

with quoins and dressings of thin red bricks, no doubt Roman, set in wide mortar joints.

About 1150–60 a south aisle was added to the nave; and towards the end of the same century the tower was built. The present chancel dates from the early years of the 13th century ; and the transept seems contemporary with it. The north arcade of the nave is work of c. 1300, of unusual character, but it seems probable that a north aisle was built before that date, perhaps when the transept was added. The tower has been much altered and rebuilt in the 17th and 18th centuries, and the south aisle became ruinous and was pulled down, not being rebuilt till 1872. The vestry and porch are modern, and a good deal of renewal of stonework has been carried out in modern times.

The east window of the chancel is of 15th-century date, with three pointed cinquefoiled lights under a two-centred arch, probably replacing an original triplet of lancets, but the two north windows of the 13th-century work remain, tall narrow lancets with an external rebate. Under the north-east window is a modern doorway to the vestry, and to the east of it an original locker with rebated jambs and flat head, arranged for two doors, modern successors of which are now fitted to it.

There is only one window on the south of the chancel, and this is modern with three wide cinquefoiled ogee lights under a square head ; below it are three sedilia in modern stonework of 13th-century design, with detached shafts having moulded capitals and bases and carrying two-centred arches.

Near the east end of the south wall is a piscina probably of 15th-century date with a shallow rectangular basin. The flat head and part of the jambs are quite plain, but below a wooden shelf which has been inserted the jambs have been chamfered.

The north transept opens to the chancel by a two-centred arch of two continuous chamfered orders with a chamfered abacus at the springing, and is lighted on the north by a pretty window of two trefoiled lights with a quatrefoil over, c. 1320. In the east wall are two lancet windows like those in the north wall of the chancel, and between them a wide arched recess with chamfered jambs and dogtooth ornament on the angles, marking the position of the altar formerly here.

In the north wall, east of the window, is an aumbry with rebated jambs and a wooden lintel, which was originally taller than at present, and at the south-east of the transept is a piscina which has stop-chamfered jambs and a triangular head with an old wooden shelf at the springing. The basin is very shallow, square at one end and semicircular at the other.

The arch opening to the aisle from the transept is quite plain and has been modernized.

PLAN OF FETCHAM CHURCH

Poynton, co. Chester, afterwards created K.B.[89] Their daughter and heir, Elizabeth Harriet, in 1777 married Viscount Bulkeley,[90] but in 1788 joined with her father in the sale of this estate to John Richardson.[91] Shortly after it was sold to Thomas Hankey, a London banker, whose great-grandson, Mr. John Barnard Hankey, holds it at the present day.

The church of ST. MARY consists CHURCH of a chancel 26 ft. by 13 ft. 6 in. at the east, and 13 ft. 10 in. at the west, at which point it is flanked on the north by a transept 17 ft. 4 in. by 16 ft. 10 in., and on the south by a tower 12 ft. 10 in. by 10 ft. 2 in. ; a nave 33 ft. 7 in. by 20 ft., and north and south aisles 10 ft. 2 in. wide. There is also a north-east vestry and a north porch. All the measurements are internal.

The west wall and the upper part of the south and probably of the east wall of an early nave still remain, and belong perhaps to the beginning of the 11th century, the walls being of plastered flint-work,

[87] Notes and Queries (Ser. 4), ix, 307.
[88] Brayley, Hist. of Surr. iv, 414.
[89] Gent. Mag. 1752, p. 44.
[90] G.E.C. Complete Peerage, ii, 74.
[91] Brayley, Surr. iv, 414.

FETCHAM CHURCH : NAVE LOOKING NORTH-EAST

The tower is of three stages, the two upper being largely of 18th-century date, with red brick quoins and battlements, but the ground stage is of late 12th-century date, and opens to the aisle by a plain round-headed arch, the western face of which, formerly exposed to the weather, has been restored, and to the chancel by a pointed arch of three chamfered orders, the outer order only being ancient.

At the south-west angle of the tower, and opening from the chancel, is the lower entrance to the rood-stair, the steps of which still exist, though the upper doorway facing the nave is blocked up.

The ground stage of the tower has one window in the east wall and two in the south, tall narrow round-headed lights of plain character, belonging to the original work; the space they light is now blocked up by an organ.

The chancel arch has plain jambs in modern stone and a two-centred arch, which looks like 14th-century work, of two splayed orders without corbels or abaci at the springing. It is evidently the successor of a narrower and doubtless earlier arch, for on the nave side its north jamb has destroyed the larger part of a small 13th-century arched recess springing at the north-east from a cone-shaped corbel set across the angle. There was evidently a second recess in the north wall of the nave, destroyed when the present north arcade was built; the object of both recesses was to give more room for the north nave altar.

The north arcade of the nave is of two wide bays with a slender octagonal shaft and responds to match, worked with a single broad chamfer which continues round the two-centred arches, there being no capitals or strings at the springing. A moulded label of good early 14th-century section is the only ornamental detail of the arcade, which is of very uncommon character.

The south arcade of the nave is of three bays with circular columns and large flat scalloped capitals with chamfered abaci; the arches are of one plain semicircular order with chamfered edges, the chamfers being a later addition. Above the eastern column of the arcade is a window belonging to the early aisleless nave, widely splayed towards the nave with plastered jambs and a round arch of Roman bricks set with a wide mortar joint. Towards the aisle it shows as a narrow round-headed light with jambs and arch of Roman bricks, originally intended to be plastered over.

The windows lighting the nave and aisles are entirely modern, except the west window in the north aisle, which has old inside splays, perhaps of 13th-century date. The west window of the nave is of three trefoiled lights with tracery of 14th-century style.

The north doorway is of 13th-century date, having jambs and arch of two splayed orders with a small chamfered label; the moulded abaci at the springing are modern, and all the stones have been retooled.

The nave and chancel roofs have Horsham slabs near the eaves, but are covered with tiles above, and the other roofs have tiles only.

Internally the roofs are modern open timber, except that to the north transept, where the timbers are hidden by plaster. The western portion of the chancel roof is not quite continuous with the rest, the break occurring just above the east jamb of the arch to the north transept.

All the internal fittings are modern.

On the south wall of the chancel is a monument with Corinthian pillars flanking an oval which contains the half-figure of Henry Vincent, 1631. Above the niche is a defaced shield of arms.

On the north wall of the chancel is a black

FETCHAM CHURCH : SOUTH ARCADE OF THE NAVE, SHOWING EARLY WINDOW

marble tablet with a round-headed recess flanked by pilasters and containing an inscription to Anthony Rous, who died in 1631.

There are three bells in the tower, the treble bearing the inscription 'William Eldridge made mee 1665,' and the second 'Robertus Mott me fecit 1588.' The third is by William Land, 1613.

The plate is all modern, and comprises a chalice, paten, and flagon.

The registers are contained in three books. The first, which is of parchment and is a copy up to about 1600, has entries of baptisms, marriages, and burials from 1559 to 1712. The second has baptisms and burials from 1712 to 1812, and marriages from 1712 to 1753. The third book contains marriages from 1754 to 1812 on the usual printed forms.

A HISTORY OF SURREY

ADVOWSON In 1338 the advowson was held by John d'Abernon, lord of the manor of Fetcham,[92] and from that date descended with the manor at least until 1654, when Thomas Vincent presented to the living.[93]

Shortly after it was held by William Heckford in right of his wife Elizabeth, with whom, in 1711, he joined in conveying it to Thomas Cooke, clerk, and Joshua Draper, gentleman.[94] The latter in the same year sold it for the sum of £580[95] to Arthur Moore of Fetcham Park, who presented to the living in 1720, 1724, and 1726.[96]

The advowson was acquired with the rest of Arthur Moore's Fetcham property by Thomas Revell, who presented to the living in 1737 and 1748,[97] and descended to his son-in-law Sir George Warren, who presented in 1772,[98] and is said to have sold it in 1788 to Mrs. Ann Kirkpatrick, under whose will it passed to Rev. Abraham Kirkpatrick Sherson, rector of Fetcham, in 1794. Before 1818 it was acquired by John Bolland, whose son Rev. J. G. Bolland presented to the living in 1829. On the death of the latter in 1833 it was sold by his executors to Rev. Robert Downes, incumbent at that date.[99] The patronage was acquired in 1864 by Alderman Sydney,[100] trustee for Lady Moon, wife of the late rector. Lady Moon presented in 1904. It is now in the hands of her son, Lieut.-Colonel Sir F. S. G. Moon, bart.

In 1535 the farm of the rectory with the accompanying glebe land was valued at £21 19s. 11½d. There was also a pension of 6s. 8d. due to Chertsey Monastery,[101] which after the Dissolution was granted to the new foundation at Bisham.[102]

Dr. Thomas Turner, a devoted royalist, was instituted rector of Fetcham in 1634, and after having been deprived of this with his other benefices during the Commonwealth, was reinstated after the restoration of the Monarchy and became Dean of Canterbury.[103]

Samuel Lisle, afterwards Bishop of Norwich, was rector from 1726 till 1737,[104] and Dr. J. Conybeare, the famous metaphysician and defender of revelation, was curate for a short time under the rectorship of Dr. Shortrudge.[105]

In 1358 Robert de Leddrede, the king's sergeant-at-arms, had licence for making a chapel at his house at Fetcham,[106] the site of which is probably that now occupied by the Sun ale-house. Salmon, writing in 1736, says, 'In this parish is an old chapell, now turned to an ale-house which may however supply in excise more than ever it paid in tenths.'[107]

CHARITIES The almshouses, for six poor persons, were founded in 1886 by the Rev. Sir Edward Graham Moon, bart., Mr. J. B. Hankey, and Mr. Gervas Parnell.

Smith's Charity is distributed as in other Surrey parishes, but in the case of Fetcham it was endowed with parcels of lands in the common fields and inclosed fields in the parish. It is commemorated on a tablet in the church.

In 1690 a decree in Chancery confirmed the will of Sir George Shiers, bart.,[108] who left rents of land amounting to £24 2s. for apprenticing boys, marrying maids who had lived in the same family for seven years, and relieving the poor not in receipt of parish relief.[109]

HEADLEY

Hallega (xi cent.) ; Hadlee and Hadlig (xiii cent.) ; Hedleghe (xiv cent.) ; Hedley (xvii cent.).

Headley is a small parish on the top of the chalk downs. The village is 2 miles north of Betchworth station, and about three miles south-east of Letherhead. The parish measures about two miles from north to south, under a mile and a half from east to west, and contains 2,066 acres. The subsoil is that of the chalk downs, which is on the surface in the valleys and on the slopes of the hills, but in the higher parts is crowned with brick earth and hill-sand deposits. The church, and the few houses which form the centre of a scattered village, stand on the brow of a steep slope some 600 ft. above the sea, at the head of the valley up which the road from Juniper Hall in the Mickleham valley runs to Walton-on-the-hill. The church is a conspicuous landmark for many miles round. Headley Heath is a large extent of still open ground to the south of the parish, lying back from the southern edge of the chalk range.

The parish is agricultural, and formerly fed large numbers of sheep.

On Headley Heath, and scattered at other points in the parish, are numerous neolithic implements and flakes, and fragments of a coarse earthenware vessel have been found near Toot Hill.[1] Less than a mile south-west of the church, west or north-west of Headley Heath, on the slopes of the valley up which the road from Juniper Hall comes, excavations have revealed the inclosing trench of a large inclosure. In the loose soil overlying the undisturbed chalk Mr. Gordon Home, of Epsom, found in 1907 fragments of hand-made pottery, with bones of many different animals, and one worked flint. At a higher level he found the broken point of a bronze weapon. Near the trench, but not in it, he found some good glazed pottery, and in another place several signs of fires, burnt stones, and charcoal. A young plantation unfortunately is on the spot. The names Toot Hill, and Elderbury, and Nore Wood (a name often found in close juxtaposition to old fortifications, for which we may compare Nore under the banked hill at Hascombe) suggest an ancient settlement or settlements.

No Inclosure Act or Award is on record.

92 Feet of F. Div. Co. 13 Edw. III, file 40, no. 268.
93 Inst. Bks. P.R.O.
94 Feet of F. Surr. Trin. 10 Anne.
95 Close, 10 Anne, pt. i, no. 6.
96 Inst. Bks. P.R.O.
97 Ibid. 98 Ibid.
99 Brayley, Hist. of Surr. iv, 415.
100 Clergy Lists.

101 Valor Eccl. (Rec. Com.), ii, 32.
102 L. and P. Hen. VIII, xii (2), g. 1311 (22).
103 Dict. Nat. Biog.
104 Ibid.
105 Ibid. ; Gentleman's Magazine Library, pt. 12, p. 30.
106 Manning and Bray, Hist. of Surr. i, 482 (quoting from Episcopal Register).

107 Salmon, Antiq. of Surr. 90.
108 Died 1685, monument in Great Bookham Church.
109 It is commemorated on a tablet in the church.
1 Neolithic Man in North-east Surr. 154–62 ; and personal observation. There seem to be traces of terracing on the sides of the slopes.

Headley Court is the seat of Mr. Walter Cunliffe, Headley Park that of Mr. J. N. Mappin, and Headley Grove that of Miss Bridge.

There is an iron Congregational chapel ; and there is an institute and club in the village.

A school (Church of England) was built in 1868. In 1725 there was a school of 20 gentlemen's sons kept by Mr. Stubbs.

MANOR Before the Conquest the Countess Goda held *HEADLEY* in chief of King Edward, and at the time of the Domesday Survey it was in the hands of Ralph de Felgeres.[2] By the end of the 12th century it was held by Gilbert de Tilers, who paid 40s. for it into the king's treasury in 1199.[3] His daughter Agnes, who married Philip de Crois,[4] was one of his heirs.[5] Another daughter Joan married Thomas Malesmains, who held land in Headley in 1210, which had been given to him with the daughter of Gilbert de Tilers by the king's grant.[6] Hilary, one of Agnes's daughters, succeeded to part of the manor, including the capital messuage, and her husband James de Banelingham did homage for it in 1233.[7] James was an alien, and in 1246 the estate had escheated to the king.[8]

In 1253 John d'Abernon was granted free warren in his demesne lands at Headley,[9] and twenty-five years later his son John was summoned to prove his right to this privilege.[10] This, however, may not refer to the manor, but to a half-carucate of land there which Giles d'Abernon acquired in 1217–18 from Martin and Eva de Covenham, possibly one of the heiresses of Agnes de Tilers.[11] The next mention of Headley occurs amongst the possessions of John de Plesey, who held it for the service of a quarter of a knight's fee. John died in 1313–14,[12] leaving three sons : Edmund his heir, Robert from whom were descended the owners of Headley at a later date, and John.[13]

De Plesey. *Argent six rings gules.*

At the death of Edmund, who was said to have held in free socage owing no service to the king,[14] two parts of the estate were assigned in dower to his widow Maud.[15] He was succeeded by his son Nicholas, at whose death in 1357 the property was taken into the king's custody on account of the minority of the heir,[16] John de Plesey, who died shortly after. Nicholas his brother also died without attaining his majority, and Headley then passed to their sister Joan,[17] the wife of John Hameley. Hameley continued to hold the manor after her death for service of a quarter of a knight's fee, until he himself died in 1398–9.[18] As Joan's only son had died unmarried before his father, the property should then have reverted to Peter de Plesey, Joan's uncle, and Sir Nicholas's only brother. Peter, however, apparently never held the manor, for having no son to succeed, he granted it to Joan's distant cousin, John de Plesey, who being descended in a direct line from Robert, Edmund's younger brother, was the next heir after Peter.[19] From about this date the estate is referred to as 'three parts of the manor,' and it is possible that one quarter was settled upon Elizabeth, Joan Hameley's daughter and only surviving child.[20]

John de Plesey died in 1406, and his son John succeeded him.[21] This John left no children, and the manor reverted in 1417 to his father's first cousin, John Camel.[22] In 1438 Camel conveyed one-third of the manor to William Wikes and John Aleyn,[23] and a William Wikes died seised of the property in 1518, his uncle, Richard Wikes, being his heir.[24] In 1526 Richard received licence to alienate the manor and lands to Sir David Owen and others,[25] probably in trust for Andrew Windsor, afterwards Lord Windsor, who died seised of the manor of Headley, also called Wikes Manor, in 1543–4.[26] The year before his death he likewise became possessed of property in Headley which had formerly belonged to the Abbot of Westminster, who had claimed liberties there as early as 1278–9,[27] Henry VIII granting him these lands with all the other possessions of the dissolved abbey in a forced exchange for the manor of Stanwell.[28] In this document this monastic land is said to be one quarter of Headley Manor ;[29] it may have been so called from the fact that since John de Plesey had inherited the estate in 1398–9 it had only consisted of three-quarters of the manor ; the remaining fourth seems to have been lost sight of, and when Lord Windsor acquired the Westminster land it was accounted for in this way.[30]

Lord Windsor was succeeded by his son William, who in 1554 acquired Headley Farm from the trustees of Nicholas Leigh, the heir of one Michael Leigh,[31] who had held it ten years before. This farm had

[2] *V.C.H. Surr.* i, 326.
[3] Pipe R. 6 Ric. I, m. 1.
[4] Add. Chart. 5527.
[5] Ibid. 5526.
[6] *Testa de Nevill* (Rec. Com.), 225 ; *Red Bk. of Exch.* (Rolls Ser.), 562.
[7] *Excerpta e Rot. Fin.* (Rec. Com.), i, 246.
[8] Chan. Inq. p.m. 31 Hen. III, no. 8.
[9] *Cal. of Chart.* 1226–57, p. 434.
[10] *Plac. de Quo Warr.* (Rec. Com.), 738 ; Symmes' Coll. for *Hist. of Surr.*; Add. MS. 6167, fol. 215.
[11] Feet of F. Surr. East. 2 Hen. III. There may have been another manor in Headley, as in 1204–5 the sheriff of Surrey was ordered to deliver seisin to Richard de Clare 'quod de feodo suo est' (Close, 6 John, m. 12, no. 110). This de Clare holding, which does not, however, appear in the inquisitions on later Earls of Clare and Gloucester, possibly explains the appearance at Headley of the d'Abernons, their sub-tenants in other places. The holding of the d'Abernons, who were lords of Albury, may have included the land in Headley called Eldebury, which afterwards appears amongst the possessions of the Pleseys, in which case it would seem that the two holdings became united.
[12] Chan. Inq. p.m. 7 Edw. II, no. 5.
[13] Berry, *Surr. Gen.* 56 ; *Visit. of Surr.* (Harl. Soc. xliii), 7.
[14] Chan. Inq. p.m. 1 Edw. III (1st nos.), no. 42.
[15] Ibid.
[16] *Abbrev. Rot. Orig.* (Rec. Com.), ii, 244.
[17] Chan. Inq. p.m. 36 Edw. III, pt. ii (1st nos.), no. 15.
[18] Ibid. 22 Ric. II, no. 25. In this inquisition Headley is said to be held of the honour of Boulogne, a reminiscence of its having been held before the Conquest by the Countess of Boulogne, Goda (Godgifu), Edward's sister, though it had not apparently gone to her son Earl Eustace.
[19] Ibid. ; Berry, *Surr. Gen.* 56.
[20] Ibid.
[21] Chan. Inq. p.m. 8 Hen. IV, no. 63.
[22] Ibid. 4 Hen. V, no. 31 ; Feet of F. Div. Co. Hil. 10 Hen. VI.
[23] Chan. Inq. p.m. 29 Hen. VI, no. 32.
[24] Ibid. (Ser. 2,) xxxiii, 87.
[25] *L. and P. Hen. VIII,* iv, 2673 (2).
[26] Chan. Inq. p.m. (Ser. 2), lxviii, 28.
[27] *Plac. de Quo Warr.* (Rec. Com.), 745.
[28] *L. and P. Hen. VIII,* xvii, 285 (18) ; Harl. MS. 1880 [copy of indenture].
[29] The property was possibly granted to the abbey with the advowson by one of the heirs of Agnes de Tilers.
[30] Or this quarter may have been acquired by Westminster at some time after 1398–9.
[31] Pat. 36 Hen. VIII, pt. xxviii, m. 29.

previously been in the possession of John Wikes,[32] having apparently been excepted from the sale of the manor by Richard Wikes in 1526.

In 1560 Edward, Lord Windsor, leased the manor to the family of Puttenham,[33] and seven years later he sold it to John Vaughan and Anne his wife.[34] Anne was the daughter of Sir Christopher Pickering, and had been three times married : first to Francis Weston,[35] who had been involved in the accusation against Anne Boleyn ; secondly to Sir Henry Knyvett ; and thirdly to John Vaughan.[36] By a curious chance Francis Weston was descended from John Camel's daughter Katherine, sometimes called Anne, who married Edmund Weston.[37]

Anne Vaughan outlived her third husband, and dying in 1582 she was succeeded by her son Henry Weston.[38] His son Richard became lord of the manor in 1592,[39] and he probably conveyed it to William Stydolf, amongst whose lands it is mentioned on his death in 1600–1.[40] In 1677 William's grandson Sigismond settled the manor on himself and his wife Margaret, daughter of Sir Francis Rolle,[41] and having no issue he left it to her in fee.[42] She married secondly Michael Hyde,[43] and thirdly Thomas Edwin, who owned Headley after his wife's death in 1734.[44] He died shortly afterwards, childless, and his nephew Charles Edwin inherited the estate. Charles Edwin died in 1756, leaving the remainder at the death of his wife Lady Charlotte, daughter of the Duke of Hamilton, to his nephew Charles Windham, who took the name of Edwin,[45] and who in 1784 sold the estate to Henry Boulton.[46] The mansion house was sold by Boulton to Colonel Alexander Hume, who, having married the daughter of William Evelyn of St. Clare, Kent, took the name of Evelyn.[47] Colonel Evelyn afterwards sold it to Robert Ladbroke, who, having purchased the rest of the estate in 1804 from Mr. Boulton, was lord of the manor in 1809.[48] Not long after the manor, but not the manor-house, was again sold, and passed into the hands of Richard Howard of Ashtead.[49] He was the brother of Sir William Bagot the first Lord Bagot of Bagot's Bromley, Staffordshire, who on his marriage with the heiress of Ashtead had assumed the name of Howard.[50] His only child and heir, Mary, married in 1807 the Hon. Fulk Greville Upton, who also took the name of Howard on his marriage.[51] Mary Howard survived her husband a great many years, dying at the age of ninety-two in 1877.[52] Headley then became the property of Colonel Charles Bagot, one of the sons of her first cousin, also Charles Bagot.[53] After his death in 1881 the manor was purchased by the Hon. Henry Dudley Ryder, who succeeded his brother as fourth Earl of Harrowby on 26 March 1900. He died on

11 November following, and his widow the Dowager Countess of Harrowby is the present lady of the manor.

A fair held at Headley on 24 August is mentioned by Symmes.[54]

The manor-house, where Mr. Ladbroke resided after the manor was sold, is now the property of Mr. Walter Cunliffe. It has been turned into a farmhouse. When Mr. Cunliffe bought it the strong-room with arrangements for securing the prisoners' hands was still existing.

The church of *ST. MARY THE CHURCH VIRGIN* consists of a chancel 31 ft. by 15 ft. 9 in. with a small north vestry, a nave 59 ft. 6 in. by 25 ft. 6 in. with a south porch, and a west tower 13 ft. square inside.

The present building was erected in 1855, excepting the tower, which was added a few years later. The nave is in 13th-century style. The tower, the ground story of which serves as a porch, is capped by a shingled wooden spire changing from square to octagonal above the eaves. The former church had a low square tower at its west end, and is said to have been much dilapidated before it was pulled down. All that is left of it is set up in the churchyard over the grave of the late rector, the Rev. Ferdinand Faithful, who died in 1871, in the form of a small rectangular ivy-covered building with a 15th-century arch at the west, and in it are preserved a few details, such as the tracery of a two-light window with trefoiled heads, and the bowl of an 18th-century font. The present font is modern.

In the vestry are preserved two painted wooden mural tablets, one to Elizabeth Leate, daughter of Mr. Nicholas Leate, Turkey merchant, 'a worthy and eminent citizen of London,' and aunt of a former rector, Richard Wyld ; she died in 1680. The other is to Margaret daughter of William and Mary Warren of London, who died in 1675. There are several 18th-century monuments retained and reset in the tower.

In the tower is a mediaeval bell used for striking the hour only. It is inscribed 'Sancta Katrina ora pro nobis,' and bears the 'cross and ring' shield of Richard Hille of London, c. 1430. There is also a set of eight cup-shaped gongs, put up in 1876.

The communion plate consists of a cup of 1752, a standing paten of 1706, a flagon of 1854, and a small cover paten without hall marks.

The registers date from 1663.

The right of presentation to the *ADVOWSON* church of Headley belonged from the beginning of the 14th century to the abbey of Westminster,[55] until its dissolution in 1539–40.[56] In 1350, during a vacancy in the abbacy,

[32] Pat. 1 Mary, pt. xiv, m. 21.
[33] Feet of F. Div. Co. Mich. 2 Eliz.
[34] Ibid. Surr. East. 9 Eliz. ; Recov. R. Trin. 9 Eliz. rot. 141.
[35] *Visit. Surr.* (Harl. Soc. xliii), 7.
[36] Manning and Bray, *Hist. of Surr.* ii, 640 ; Chan. Inq. p.m. (Ser. 2), cc, 60 ; Pat. 29 Eliz. pt. xiii, m. 11.
[37] *Visit. Surr.* (Harl. Soc. xliii), 7.
[38] Chan. Inq. p.m. (Ser. 2), cc, 60 ; Pat. 29 Eliz. pt. xiii, m. 11.
[39] Two documents, Pat. 31 Eliz. pt. vi, m. 17, and Feet of F. Surr. Trin. 31 Eliz. record a conveyance of Headley to Thomas Foster and Thomas Cowper, but from the wording of the inquisition on Henry,
and from the fact that Thomas Cowper acted as trustee formerly for Lady Vaughan, it seems most probable that this transaction was for the purpose of settlement upon Richard.
[40] Chan. Inq. p.m. (Ser. 2), cclxiv, 175.
[41] Feet of F. Surr. Mich. 29 Chas. II.
[42] P.C.C. 193 Smith.
[43] Aubrey, *Antiq. of Surr.* ii, 303.
[44] Manning and Bray, *Hist. of Surr.* ii, 640 ; Brayley, *Hist. of Surr.* iv, 421.
[45] Ibid. ; Recov. R. Trin. 24 Geo. II, rot. 262 ; P.C.C. 164, Glazier.
[46] Feet of F. Surr. East. 25 Geo. III.
[47] Manning and Bray, *Hist. of Surr.* ii, 640 ; Brayley, *Hist. of Surr.* iv, 421.
[48] Ibid.
[49] Ibid. 422.
[50] *Records of the Ashtead Estate and its Howard Possessors,* 173 ; Burke, *Peerage.*
[51] *Records of the Ashtead Estate and its Howard Possessors,* 176 ; Burke, *Peerage.*
[52] Ibid.
[53] Ibid. *Surr. Dir.* 1878, 1882.
[54] Symmes MS., Add. MSS. 6167, fol. 215.
[55] Index Winton Epis. Reg. ; Egerton MSS. 2031–2034, ii, 8, 58, 138 ; iii, 17, 88, 138 ; iv, 15, 45, 78.
[56] Dugdale, *Monasticon,* i, 280.

Nicholas de Plesey tried to establish a claim to the advowson, declaring that his great-grandfather Robert had given the benefice to a certain Bartholomew de Plesey, and that the advowson had passed with the manor to Robert's son John, and from John to Edmund, Nicholas's father. It was proved, however, that the last incumbent was there by the gift of the abbot, and the temporalities being for the moment in the king's hands, that the king ought to present.[57] Nicholas, however, seems to have tried to assert his right in spite of this judgement, for the next entry in the index to the episcopal registers of Winchester shows that Nicholas actually did present to Headley,[58] while certain officers were in this same year to arrest anyone who attempted to uphold the claims of de Plesey against the court's decision.[59] Immediately after the Dissolution the advowson was granted to Thomas Thirlby, Bishop of Westminster,[60] who seems to have ceded his right, as Henry VIII granted it in the same

year, with the rest of the estates of the abbey of Westminster, to Andrew, Lord Windsor;[61] and from this date, excepting a lease of the right to the Bishop of London in 1550 and 1553,[62] the living has always been in the gift of the lords of the manor,[63] until the death of Colonel Bagot in 1881, after which the advowson passed into the possession of Mr. H. Thompson.[64] The present patron is Mr. H. St. John O. Thompson.

Headley Church was rated at £5 in the 13th century,[65] and in 1428 it was taxed for the same amount, paying a subsidy to the king of 6s. 8d.[66] Under Henry VIII the total value was said to be £8 7s. 6d.[67]

CHARITIES Smith's Charity is distributed as in other Surrey parishes.

There is also a small rent-charge of £4 12s. 2d. on the manorial estates, it is supposed in compensation for a right of cutting brushwood on certain waste, given in bread and coals.

LETHERHEAD

Leodride (x cent.); Leret (xi cent.); Lereda, Lerred (xii cent.); Ledred and Leddered (xiii cent.); Ledered alias Letherhed (xv cent.); Lethered and Letherhed (xvii and xviii cents.); Leatherhead (xix cent.).

Letherhead is a small town or large village 4 miles south-west of Epsom and 5 miles north of Dorking. The parish measures 4 miles from north-west to south-east, from 2 to 1¼ miles across, and contains 3,481 acres. It lies across the Mole valley, and is traversed by the river in its southern part. The south-eastern part is on the chalk downs; the village is at the foot of the Chalk and partly on the Thanet and Woolwich Beds, and the parish extends northwards on to the London Clay. The immediate valley of the river is alluvium. The clay rises at the northern extremity of the parish into an open common, with some wood on it, called Letherhead Common. The open grass-land on the downs has been partly inclosed, but there is still some on Letherhead Downs. The yew grows thickly on the chalk downs about Cherkley Court.

The village consisted originally of one long street, with a cross-street running down to the bridge over the Mole, but building has recently been extended in several directions, especially to the north and east. It is governed by an Urban District Council, under the Act of 1894, and is supplied with gas by a company started in 1850 and incorporated by Act of Parliament in 1901, and with water by a company formed in 1883, the wells of which are in Fetcham. There are a brewery and brick and tile works; the parish is otherwise agricultural. The main road from London to Horsham, through Epsom and Dorking, traverses the main street. The London and South Western Railway line from Wimbledon and Worcester Park had a terminus in Letherhead, opened in 1859.

It had been intended to take this line on to Dorking, but it was never done by the original company. In 1867 the through-route by Epsom, Dorking, and Horsham to Portsmouth was completed by the London, Brighton, and South Coast Railway Company using part of the South Western line, but with a separate station at Letherhead. This route had been originally surveyed for the first line to Brighton, which was to have gone through Shoreham Gap in the South Downs, but this plan was defeated chiefly through the exertions of Letherhead people and a Parliamentary counsel whose father lived at Thorncroft.[1] The South Western Railway line was continued to Guildford in 1887.

Neolithic flints have been found on Letherhead Downs, and British coins have also been found.[2] The Anglo-Saxon remains found at Fetcham (q.v.) lay close to Letherhead parish. Near Pachevesham, not far from the Mole, in a wood by the side of a small stream is a rectangular inclosure of a single bank and ditch measuring about 80 yds. by 75 yds. At the nearest point of the Mole to this work there is a ford, by the side of Randall's Park. Stone 'pot-boilers' are said to have been picked up in the square inclosure,[3] and the ordnance map records that Roman coins were found in the field south-west of it in 1859. Fragments of Roman tile are not at all uncommon in that and the adjoining field, and Pachevesham, now only a farm-house, gave its name to the Domesday manor, indicating that the chief settlement of the neighbourhood had been here by the road leading to the ford.

Part of the south-east of the parish is traversed by the Roman or British track across the downs, described under Mickleham, and near it on Letherhead Downs are two barrows, of which one to the west of the

57 De Banco R. 360, m. 79 d.(23-24 Edw. III); Index Winton Epis. Reg.; Egerton MSS. 2031-34, iii, 17.
58 Ibid.
59 Cal. Pat. 1348-50, 597.
60 Pat. 32 Hen. VIII, pt. vii; L and P. Hen. VIII, xvi, 503 (33).
61 L. and P. Hen. VIII, xvii, 285 (18); Harl. MS. 1880.
62 Pat. 4 Edw. VI, pt. iv, m. 16; 1 Mary, pt. iv, m. 16.
63 Feet of F. Surr. East. 9 Eliz.; Chan. Inq. p.m. (Ser. 2), cclxiv, 175; cc, 60; Recov. R. Trin. Eliz. rot. 141; Inst. Bks. P.R.O. 1663, etc., etc.
64 Clergy List, 1885.
65 Pope Nich. Tax. (Rec. Com.), 280.
66 Feud. Aids, v, 114.
67 Valor Eccl. (Rec. Com.), ii, 39.
1 Family information.
2 Evans, Coins, 83, 169.
3 Neolithic Man in North-east Surrey, 82, where the description of the site and of the parish in which it is are both erroneous.

road is in good condition. The other has been opened. . The ordnance map marks three tumuli east of the road, but this is the only one visible now.

. Historically, Letherhead has claimed consideration as the old county town, but it is doubtful whether the County Court was ever held there continuously. In 1259 a complaint was made that the County Court was held at Guildford instead of at Letherhead, ' Comitatus qui semper solebat teneri apud Leddrede.' [4] But it may be remarked that the mediaeval *semper* is a loose term, and it is quite certain that in 1195 the king's justices had sat at Guildford, not Letherhead, and in 1202 Guildford Castle was the county gaol.

. Letherhead was quite possibly the meeting-place of the Hundred Court of Copthorne.[5] It is also geographically near the centre of the county, and a

'THE RUNNING HORSE,' LETHERHEAD.

convenient place for the meetings of influential people in Surrey, as in 1642 on the eve of the Civil Wars,[6] and in 1685 for a county election, though Evelyn seems rather to complain of the election being held at an obscure place.[7]

A character famous at least in literary history lived at Letherhead, Eleanor Rummyng, celebrated by Skelton, poet-laureate to Henry VIII, in the poem called *The Tunnyng of Elynour Rummynge*. Her traditionary inn is now called 'The Running Horse,' and is near the bridge. Part of the fabric is as old as the 16th century, and there is no reason to doubt that the brewster was a real woman. The name Rumming occurs in the Lay Subsidy assessments in

the neighbourhood, and is in the parish registers as late as 1669. A John Skelton was assessed in Kingston in 1524–5, but the poet was in orders, so this is probably not the same man.

Letherhead Bridge is carried on fourteen arches, with stone piers and brick parapets, over a wide part of the Mole, where formerly there was a ford. According to a common practice, the bridge used to be closed by a bar except in flood time, when the ford was dangerous. In 1362 a licence was granted to collect money for the repair of a bridge here.[8] An unknown benefactor left land in Fetcham for its repair, but in 1782 an Act was passed[9] making it a county bridge, providing for its widening, and for the sale of the land given for its maintenance. As it is said to have been let at the time for 18s. a year,[10] the parishes of Letherhead and Fetcham, in which the bridge lies, must have really kept it up.

Letherhead had a large common on the downs, common fields on the slope of the chalk, a common meadow by the river, a common called Letherhead Common, which still exists, and is mentioned above, and a common on the manor of Thorncroft. Under an Act of 1859 the common fields were inclosed : the date of the award was 20 November 1862 ; and the commons were inclosed by an award of 4 May 1865.[11] The common fields were among the last extensive common fields in the county.

There are a large number of gentlemen's houses in the parish besides those belonging to the old manors. Gravel Hill is the seat of Admiral Booth ; Cherkley Court was that of the late Mr. A. Dixon ; The Priory is that of Mr. A. H. Tritton, J.P. ; Pachesham Park, of Mr. F. C. Ramsey ; Wrydelands, of Mr. S. Le Blanc Smith ; Givons, formerly Gibbon's Grove, of Mr. H. P. Sturgis. Letherhead Court, at the western extremity of the parish, is a large ladies'-school, kept by Miss Tullis.

St. John's School, Letherhead, was established first in St. John's Wood in 1852, and after being held at Clapton from 1858 to 1872, was moved to Letherhead. It provides a gratuitous education to a certain number of sons of clergy of the Church of England, receives clergymen's sons beyond the number of foundationers on low terms, and admits other boys also. The foundation depends upon voluntary support. It is carried on as a first-class public school. The head master is the Rev. E. A. Downes, University College, Oxford. The buildings, begun in 1872, and added to in 1890 and 1894, are in 16th-century style in brick with stone dressing. There is a handsome chapel.

The School for the Blind, Highlands Road, was founded in St. George's Fields, 1799, incorporated by royal charter in 1826, and removed to Letherhead in 1902. The first stone of the new buildings was laid by H.R.H. the Princess Christian.

The Literary and Scientific Institute was given by the late Mr. Abraham Dixon, of Cherkley Court, in 1892.

All Saints' chapel of ease, on the Kingston Road, was built in 1889 by the late Sir Arthur Blomfield.

---

[4] Assize R. 873, 43 Hen. III.
[5] Possibly in the manor of Thorncroft, i.e. Tornecroft ; in Domesday Tornecrosta, named from the sheriff's tourn.
[6] Loseley MS. vi, 81, 133.
[7] Diary, 8 April, 1685.
[8] Pat. 35 Edw. III, pt. ii, m. 24.
[9] 22 Geo. III, cap. 17.
[10] Manning and Bray, Surr. ii, 666.
[11] Blue Bk. Encl. Awards.

LETHERHEAD : SWAN INN, FRONT VIEW

LETHERHEAD : SWAN INN, BACK VIEW

There is a Wesleyan chapel and hall, a Baptist chapel, and a Congregational chapel, which was built in 1844, but represents an older congregation.

The Victoria Memorial Cottage Hospital was built in 1903.

Mr. John Lucas, by will, endowed a school with £500 in 1797. The Highlands Road School (National) was built by subscription in 1837–8. It is now used as the boys' school. The girls' school in Poplar Road was built in 1883. Fairfield Road (infants) is on a site given to the vicar and churchwardens by Mr. John Henderson of Randalls Park; and All Saints', Kingston Road (infants), was built when the chapel of ease was built. The schools were regulated under a scheme of the Charity Commissioners in 1873.

MANORS   The earliest mention of Letherhead occurs in the will of King Alfred, who bequeathed land at 'Leodrian' to his son Edward,[12] but it is uncertain with which part of the Letherhead land mentioned in Domesday this is connected.

The Bishop of Bayeux was overlord of the manor of PACHESHAM, later called MAGNA PACHE-VESHAM, in Letherhead, at the time of the Domesday Survey.[13] Hugh held Pachevesham under the bishop. His holding was that which had belonged to Ælmer under the Confessor.[14] A certain Baingiard also held part of Pachevesham, that which Ælmer had held of King Harold. Both owned moieties of mills.[15] Subsequently (probably when Odo's lands were forfeited to William II) Pachevesham came into the king's hands. In 1203 King John granted 60 solidates and 2 denariates of land in Letherhead to Brian de Therfield for rent of a sparrowhawk.[16] In the reign of Henry III the royal estate seems to have been held for three serjeanties. William Frankelen then held certain land by finding a hall for the county court, then held in Letherhead. Walter le Hore held land by finding a prison for prisoners taken at the sheriff's tourn, and William de Oxencroft [17] held his land by finding a pound for cattle taken for the king's debt.[18] The whole of the land held by the serjeanties and the sparrowhawk passed to Walter de Thorp.[19] He subinfeudated to Eustace de Hacche, who held the manor in 1292–3,[20] when he was accused before the justices itinerant of seizing upon horses and carts that did not belong to him in Kingston market-place, for carrying timber to his 'manor of Pachevesham.'[21] He made a warren in Pachevesham.[22] He also appears to have acquired a rent [23] of 10s. which King Richard granted to William d'Eyo,[24] afterwards held by Eustace d'Eyo [25] and Matthew Besill.[26]

The next lord of Pachevesham of whom there seems to be any record was the favourite of Edward II—Piers Gaveston. To him free warren in his lands in Pachevesham was granted by Edward in the year he came to the throne. On Gaveston's marriage with Margaret sister of the Earl of Gloucester,[27] two years later, the king confirmed Gaveston's grant of Pachevesham to Robert Darcy and Joan his wife.'s Charters of Edward III gave to Darcy free warren,[29] view of frankpledge,[30] a weekly market on Fridays, and a yearly fair upon the festival of St. Peter ad Vincula at Letherhead.[31] Dying in 1343, Robert Darcy left a daughter Margaret,[32] who married Sir John Argentine or Argentham,[33] who held the manor in 1347.[34] He died in 1382–3,[35] leaving three co-heirs, two grandchildren, and his daughter Maud, the wife of Sir Ivo Fitz Warin, kt., who held the manor in his wife's right until his death in 1414.[36] They left a daughter Eleanor, who had married John Chideok.[37] She presumably alienated the manor, since William Massey [38] seems to have been lord of Pachevesham in 1420, and Eleanor Chideok did not die till 1433.[39]

Possibly William Massey left co-heirs, for it seems that John Bacon and Reginald Rakett owned, in right of their wives, Dorothy and Joan, three parts of the manor of Magna Pachevesham in 1538, which they conveyed by fine to Thomas Stydolf, who left it in 1545 to his son John.[40] There exists an account of the boundaries of part of the manor at this time.[41] The lane called 'Bygnallane,' the regia via from Great Bockham to Kingston, appears to have formed a boundary. This is the road that runs from Bookham, over Hawks Hill, through Letherhead, and on to Kingston. Probably the Letherhead part of the road was 'Bygnallane.' Following the same boundaries that divided the parishes of Letherhead and Stoke d'Abernon, the manor stretched to places named 'Page Grene,' 'Charlewood Corner,' 'Horns-hyll,' and 'Ravennest,' and so to where the ditch divided Pachevesham Common from the common of Chessington. It crossed the old highway from Dorking to Kingston, reaching Ashtead Common and 'Asshested Crosse,' and so on to the ditch which severed Pachevesham Common from that of Thorncroft, another Letherhead manor. Thence it stretched to a bridge named 'Woodbrydge,' and so by copses to 'Bygnallane' again. By this it seems that the manor comprised all the northern part of Letherhead parish, but did not extend south of the village.

Stydolf having three parts of the manor, there remained a fourth part, which was acquired by John

---

[12] Kemble, Codex Dipl.
[13] V.C.H. Surr. i, 303.
[14] Ibid.   [15] Ibid.
[16] Chart. R. 5 John, m. 24.   The same king also made a gift of 60s. rent in Letherhead to Richard Lewer for rent of a sparrowhawk; Testa de Nevill, 225.
[17] The name of Oxencroft survived for many years in a plot of land so called, which with land named Poteszland escheated to the Crown, and was leased by Henry VII and Henry VIII to John Iwarby and Richard Hest and to Christopher Smyth for terms of years. It was granted by Edward VI to Sir William Sackville (see Fine R. 1 Hen. VII, m. 11; 37 Hen. VIII, m. 16; and Pat. 7 Edw. VI, pt. xiii, m. 16). After this date there is no further trace of the serjeanties.

Various overlords are afterwards mentioned of Pachevesham : Hamo de Gatton before 1310, the Prior of Merton and Robert de Northwode, lord of Gatton in 1343. In 1509 the manor was said to be partly held of Merton and later of the Crown ; Subs. R. Surr. bdle. 184, no. 4 ; Chan. Inq. p.m. 17 Edw. III (1st nos.), no. 54 ; (Ser. 2) xxiv, 46 ; 16 Hen. VIII, no. 40.
[18] Blount, 'Tenures of Land and Customs of Manors,' fol. 191.
[19] Assize R. 892.
[20] Ibid.   [21] Ibid.   [22] Ibid.
[23] Feet of F. Surr. Hil. 20 Edw. I.
[24] Testa de Nevill (Rec. Com.), 225.
[25] Ibid. 227.   [26] Assize R. 865.
[27] Chart. R. 1 Edw. II, no. 7.
[28] Pat. 3 Edw. II, m. 20.

[29] Chart. R. 1 Edw. III, no. 42.
[30] Ibid. 2 Edw. III, no. 20.
[31] Ibid. 5 Edw. III, no. 47.
[32] Chan. Inq. p.m. 17 Edw. III (1st nos.), no. 54.
[33] Brayley and Britton, Hist. of Surr. iv, 427.
[34] Chan. Inq. p.m. 21 Edw. III (2nd nos.), no. 48.
[35] Ibid. 6 Ric. II, no. 5.
[36] Ibid. 2 Hen. V, no. 38. The extent of the manor then comprised a house and dovecote, 200 acres of arable land, 12 acres of meadow, 4 acres of pasture, 20 acres of wood, and a water-mill.
[37] Ibid.   [38] Add. Chart. 27759.
[39] Chan. Inq. p.m. 12 Hen. VI, no. 38.
[40] Ibid. 37 Hen. VIII, no. 89.
[41] Ibid.

Agmondesham from the heirs of Joan wife of Sir Robert Pynes, probably one of the co-heirs of Massey.[42] His son John Agmondesham, who died in 1519, was described as holding the fourth of the manor which had descended to him from his father.[43]

The heir of the younger John Agmondesham was his son Edward, a child of seven years,[44] who, later, died childless, so that his sisters became his co-heirs, one of whom, Jane, who had married Thomas Sandes, died in 1557[45] possessed of a third of the fourth part of the manor, which descended to her son Robert.[46] Another of the co-heirs was probably Mary wife of William Husee, who alienated in 1570 another third of the fourth part of the manor to Sir John Godwyn;[47] he, in 1572, alienated it to Robert Sandes, who thus became possessed of two thirds of the fourth.[48]

The remaining third of that part had become the property of the Herberts, for in 1561 William and Matthew Herbert alienated it to John Stydolf,[49] who thus held the three parts (which had descended to him from his father), and a third of the remaining fourth part of the manor. His son Thomas Stydolf acquiring from Robert Sandes in 1586 the remaining two thirds of the fourth part,[50] the whole manor became the property of the Stydolfs. The descent of Pachevesham Magna then is identical with that of Mickleham and Norbury, the neighbouring manors of the Stydolf family.[51] In the reign of Anne it was the property of Sir Richard Stydolf's grandson, James Tryon, who devised the manor to his nephew Charles Tryon.

According to Manning and Bray, Mr. Tryon sold the estate to Anthony Chapman in 1766, who sold it in 1773 to Benjamin Bond Hopkins. Of him Henry Boulton of Thorncroft bought it in 1781.[52] Mr. Robert Ladbroke bought it from Mr. Henry Crab Boulton's trustees after 1828, according to Brayley;[53] but Mr. Richard Boulton, his son, was lord in 1833.[54] Mr. Felix Ladbroke, son of Robert, sold the manor in 1857 to Mr. Robert Henderson; his son, Mr. John Henderson, is the present lord of the manor, which is now amalgamated with Parva Pachevesham.

PARVA PACHEVESHAM or RANDALLS.—

AGMONDESHAM. *Argent a cheveron azure between three boars' heads sable with three cinqfolls or upon the cheveron.*

The origin of the estate called Randalls seems to be found in the hide and virgate which Randulf held of Bishop Odo in 1086.[55] The name of Randulf still remained in connexion with Letherhead in the reign of Edward III. John Randulf seems to have possessed a several fishery and land in Letherhead.[56] William Randulf later in the same reign owned two mills and lands in Letherhead and Fetcham,[57] and in the reign of Henry V Nicholas Randolf, who in Fuller's *Worthies* is described as J.P., was holding land there.[58] The holding of the Randulfs is never described as a manor, although they must have been persons of some importance, as John Randulf 'of Packlesham' had licence for an oratory in his mansion at Letherhead.[59] Their lands became amalgamated with another estate called Parva Pachevesham, being represented by the messuage and property within the manor known as Randalls. Parva Pachevesham was evidently formed from a manor of Letherhead which was held with Fetcham (q.v.) by the d'Abernons. John d'Abernon, in 1331, claimed that he and his ancestors had enjoyed from time immemorial the right to a pillory in Letherhead, which pillory Robert Darcy (lord of Magna Pachevesham) had broken down.[60] Robert Darcy declared that the pillory had been set up in his ground.[61] Sir Edmund Bray, heir of the d'Abernons, held this manor in 1538,[62] and it descended to Frances Lyfield, sister of John, Lord Bray.[62a] After this it became amalgamated with Fetcham.[63] Of this manor John Agmondesham held lands at his death in 1509[63a] which in the inquisition on Jane Sandes, one of the co-heirs of John Agmondesham, are called Patesham, or Pachevesham Parva.[64] Jane Sandes's third part descended to her son Robert.[65] Another third was owned by William or Matthew Herbert, who sold it in 1561 to John Stydolf[66] of Magna Pachevesham. By William Husee, who was evidently the husband of another of the co-heirs, the remaining third was granted to Sir John Godwyn, who alienated it in 1571 to Robert Sandes.[67] John Stydolf's third descended to his son Thomas.[68] According to Manning and Bray he alienated it to Robert Sandes, but according to the inquisition taken at his death he died in possession of it.[69] However, alienated it evidently was at some time, for John son of Robert Sandes held the whole manor, which included the capital messuage called Randalls in Letherhead.[70] The manor descended to his son and grandson, Thomas and John Sandes,[71] the latter of whom, with his wife Elizabeth, conveyed the manor of Parva Pachevesham or Randalls by fine in 1700 to Arthur Moore,[72] whose

[42] Feet of F. Surr. Hil. 21 Hen. VII; East. 23 Hen. VII; Trin. 14 Hen. VII. Sir Robert Fynes held the fourth, or part of it, for life, the reversion being made over to Agmondesham.
[43] Chan. Inq. p.m. 16 Hen. VIII, no. 40.
[44] Ibid.
[45] Ibid. (Ser. 2), clxxxvii, 64.
[46] Ibid.
[47] Pat. 13 Eliz. pt. ii, m. 20.
[48] Feet of F. Surr. East. 14 Eliz.
[49] Ibid. Mich. 3 & 4 Eliz.; Pat. 2 Eliz. pt. i.
[50] Feet of F. Div. Co. East. 28 Eliz.
[51] *Vide* Mickleham.
[52] Manning and Bray, *Hist. of Surr.* ii, 669.
[53] *Hist. of Surr.* iv, 428.
[54] Private information.

[55] *V.C.H. Surr.* i, 303.
[56] De Banco R. 356, m. 275 d.
[57] Feet of F. Surr. East. 51 Edw. III.
[58] Ibid. Mich. 2 Hen. V.
[59] Egerton MS. 2033.
[60] De Banco R. 284, m. 110 d.
[61] Ibid. 286, m. 139.
[62] Feet of F. Div. Co. Mich. 30 Hen. VIII.
[62a] She and her husband by deed of 10 Sept. 1572 granted a house and acre of land to William Skyte of Letherhead (Manning and Bray, *Surr.* ii, 669), to be held of their manor of Letherhead.
[63] See the later extents of Fetcham, which mention free warren in Pachevesham, &c.
[63a] Chan. Inq. p.m. (Ser. 2), xxiv, 46 (1 Hen. VIII).

[64] Chan. Inq. p.m. (Ser. 2), clxxxvii, 64.
[65] Ibid.
[66] Feet of F. Surr. Mich. 3 & 4 Eliz.
[67] Pat. 13 Eliz. pt. ii, m. 20; Feet of F. Div. Co. Mich. 13 & 14 Eliz. Husee and Godwyn made sale of Magna and Parva Pachevesham at the same time; the words used in the deeds of sale are 'the third part of the fourth part of the manors of Letherhead and Pachevesham,' but it was the third of the fourth part of the one manor and the third of the other.
[68] Inq. p.m. W. & L. 1 Jas. I, bdle. 7, no. 174.
[69] Ibid.
[70] Chan. Inq. p.m. (Ser. 2), cccclxix, 127.
[71] Manning and Bray, *Hist. of Surr.*; Recov. R. Mich. 24 Chas. II, rot. 168.
[72] Feet of F. Surr. East. 12 Will. III.

widow Theophila and son William sold to the Hon. Thomas Pagett in 1736.[72] By Caroline daughter of Thomas Pagett and her husband Sir Nicholas Bayly in 1753 Parva Pachevesham was sold to George Lord Carpenter, Earl of Tyrconnel,[74] whose son conveyed to Lewis Montolieu in 1788.[75] He sold it in 1792 to Henry Casmajor, who conveyed the mansion house in 1795 to Thomas Kingscote, from whom it passed by sale in 1802 to Sir John Coghill.[76] In 1812 Sir John sold to Nathaniel Bland, who in 1829 pulled down the old house, which was a timbered one close to the river, and built the present house called Randalls Park on a new site. Rather before this the road leading to the ford across the Mole and to Fetcham had been diverted to the westward, but still crosses the river at the old ford.[77] The manor was bought in 1856 from Bland's trustees by Mr. Robert Henderson, whose son, Mr. John Henderson, is now lord of the manor.

HENDERSON of Randalls. *Gules three piles issuing from the sinister or and a chief engrailed ermine.*

THORNCROFT, a manor in Letherhead, formed part of the lands of Richard de Tonbridge, lord of Clare.[78] Of the honour of Clare the manor was continuously held.[79] Jordan son of Amfred held half a virgate in Letherhead in the reign of Henry III.[80] This half-virgate William le Moine in 1226 claimed against Henry son of Jordan,[81] and in 1228 William Monk or le Moine quitclaimed his right in a virgate of land in Letherhead to John de Chereburg or Cheleburg,[82] who according to the *Testa de Nevill* held half a knight's fee there of the honour of Clare. He alienated all his Letherhead property to Sir Philip Basset and the Lady Ela his wife, Countess of Warwick.[83] The countess and Sir Philip in 1267 granted two carucates of land in Letherhead to Walter de Merton for the support of the house of his scholars at Oxford.[84] Merton College, Oxford, still holds the manor.[85] Sir Thomas Bludder (*vide* Reigate) lived there, also Mr. Henry Crab Boulton (*vide* Headley), who rebuilt the house in 1772. It was occupied in the 19th century by Colonel Drinkwater Bethune, author of *The Siege of Gibraltar*.

MYNCHIN.—In 1195 Ailric of Leddrede claimed and obtained half a hide of land in Letherhead against his brother Baldwin.[86] Baldwin's son, however, seems to have owned it later, if this was the same half-hide that William the son of Baldwin granted to Ralph de Bradele in 1248.[87] Whether or not this was the land which was shortly afterwards in the possession of the Apperdele family cannot be ascertained. The Apperdeles held in Letherhead at the end of the

reign of Henry III when Henry de Apperdele claimed against William de Apperdele and Maud his wife various parcels of land in Letherhead which he declared he had given to them when he was 'non compos mentis, et extra se et extra mentem suam.' He also thought that the Prior of Holy Cross, Reigate, ought not to retain the 26 acres in Letherhead which Alexander, Henry's son, had given him, because he (Henry) had given them to Alexander when he was mentally unbalanced, and that gifts made at such a time were quite invalid. The other parties, however, said that Henry had not been out of his mind at the time, and had himself afterwards ratified his son's grant to the prior, and five years after his grant to William had further assured the same to him. The jury not inclining to the excuse of mental aberration sent Henry to prison.[88]

Roger de Apperdele in the 14th century founded a chantry in Letherhead Church,[89] and in 1365 granted a messuage, 30 acres of land, 8 acres of meadow, and 13*s*. 4*d*. rent in Letherhead to the Prior and convent of Kilburn.[90] Roger de Apperdele held some of his land of Sir John Argentine as of his manor of Pachevesham and some of Merton Priory.[91] Part of the land given to the prioress seems to have been rather poor ground: some of the pasture was too stony to be sown, and some lay in so dry a place that it could only be mown in a wet season.[92] This lay in the north of the parish bordering on Letherhead Common, which is poor land; other Apperdele land was between the river and the Dorking road, now called Aprils.[93] The property remained with Kilburn until its dissolution, when it was granted under the name of the manor[94] of Minchen to Thomas Stydolf, and then followed the descent of Pachevesham[95] and the other Stydolf property.

The priory of Merton had an estate in Letherhead which in the 16th century is called the manor of *PAKENHAM*. In 1535 the possessions of the monastery in Pachevesham were valued at 20*s*.[96] In 1579 'the lordship and manor of Pakenham in Letherhead, late part of the possessions of the monastery of Merton,' was granted to Edmund Downing and John Walker and their heirs.[97] There seems to be no further trace of this manor.

CHURCHES
The church of *ST. NICHOLAS* consists of a chancel 48 ft. by 16 ft., north transept 30 ft. 5 in. by 16 ft. 4 in., south transept 17 ft. 8 in. by 13 ft. 2 in., nave 54 ft. 2 in. long on its north side by 23 ft. 9 in., north aisle 9 ft. 5 in. wide, north porch, south aisle 10 ft. 7 in. wide, and a west tower 17 ft. 9 in. wide by 12 ft. 10 in. deep; all these measurements are internal.

The plan of the nave, apart from the interruption caused by the irregular setting of the tower, is doubtless of the 12th century, as the early 13th-century arches

[72] Manning and Bray, *Surr.* ii, 671.
[74] Ibid.
[75] Feet of F. Surr. Trin. 28 Geo. III.
[76] Manning and Bray, *Surr.* ii, 671.
[77] Private information.
[78] *V.C.H. Surr.* i, 319.
[79] *Testa de Nevill* (Rec. Com.), 219; Chan. Inq. p.m. 8 Edw. II, no. 68.
[80] Feet of F. Surr. 3 Hen. III.
[81] *Rot. Lit. Claus.* (Rec. Com.), ii, 210.
[82] *Testa de Nevill* (Rec. Com.), 219.
[83] Anct. D. (P.R.O.), A, 4586.
[84] Feet of F. Div. Co. Hil. 51 Hen. III;

Coram Rege R. Trin. 52 Hen. III, rot. 24.
[85] See Pat. 9 Chas. I, pt. v, no. 23.
[86] Pipe R. 7 Ric. I, m. 18 d.
[87] Feet of F. Surr. Trin. 32 Hen. III.
[88] Assize R. 874, rot. 10 d.
[89] Egerton MS. 2833.
[90] Chan. Inq. p.m. 39 Edw. III (and nos.), no. 34.
[91] Ibid. Certain land in Letherhead was owned by Roger de Apperdele at the time of his death, viz. a field of 30 acres named Long Aperdele said to be held of

the Prior of St. John of Jerusalem, and an acre and a half of meadow in Buschemede and a house in Letherhead held of the Abbot of Netley. Chan. Inq. p.m. 45 Edw. III (2nd nos.), no. 37.
[92] Ibid.
[93] Local knowledge.
[94] Pat. 33 Hen. VIII, pt. i.
[95] *Vide* Pachevesham Magna.
[96] *Valor Eccl.* (Rec. Com.), ii, 48.
[97] Pat. 21 Eliz. pt. vi, no. 1. Perhaps this grant was in trust for Robert Darcy, for see Pat. 30 Eliz. pt. xvi, m. 17.

of the arcades are clearly pierced in an older wall, which was leaning outwards, especially on the south side, at the time. To counteract this lean the inner order of the south arcade is built as nearly vertically as the conditions allow, while the outer order has of necessity to follow the line of the wall above, giving a curious twisted effect to the arches. That this is not a late alteration is shown by the fact that it occurs in the western arch of the arcade, which is partly buried in the west tower, an addition of c. 1500; it is of course possible that it may have been done between the 13th and the 16th century, but it is perhaps more likely to be an original expedient. The north arcade is of somewhat earlier character than the south, dating from the opening years of the 13th century, and was originally of three bays only. It does not, however, seem likely that the nave was any shorter at the time of its building than when the south arcade was set up. In the first half of the 14th century the church was

have been added to this tower before the 14th-century alterations, and preserved its plan, though apparently rebuilt with the rest of the eastern parts of the church. Manning and Bray record that when Leeds Priory obtained the advowson of the church in 1346 they rebuilt the tower, transepts, and chancel; the chancel looks some twenty years earlier than this date, but 'restorations' may account for this. The existing tower is of much later date.

The aisles of the nave seem to have been widened in the 15th century, being made equal in width to the transepts, and the west tower belongs to the end of this century or the early years of the next. Its oblong plan and the violent angle at which it is set to the nave are evidently due to the necessity of preserving space for a procession path round the churchyard, the boundary of which comes close to the west end of the church, and the builders did not hesitate to cut into the west bay of the south arcade in order

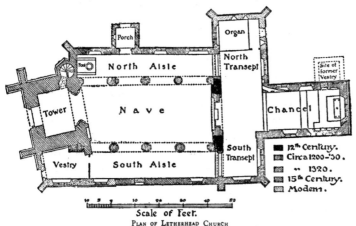

PLAN OF LETHERHEAD CHURCH

Scale of Feet.

■ 12ᵗʰ Century.
■ Circa 1200-'50.
■ „ 1320.
■ 15ᵗʰ Century.
■ Modern.

considerably enlarged on the east, the old chancel giving place to a larger one flanked by transepts on the north-west and south-west, and with a north-east vestry, its axis being deflected northward from that of the nave. It is to be noted that the east wall of the nave is not at right angles to the north and south arcades, but this may be due to an irregularity in the original setting out. The transepts also are not of equal width with each other, and while the north transept is set at right angles with the chancel, the south transept follows rather the lines of the nave. There is also a break in the chancel wall near its junction with this transept, and while it is clear that the chancel and north transept are of one build, it is quite possible that the plan of the south transept is of earlier date. There may, indeed, have been a church here in the 12th century of the same kind of plan as Charlwood, with a tower between nave and chancel, and the thickness of the existing east wall of the nave points in this direction. The south transept may

to effect their purpose; the west respond of the arcade is to be seen on the west side of the south-east buttress of the tower, in which it is partly buried.

A general repair was carried out in 1701-2, and in later times a great deal of restoration work to the windows and external stonework, so that the only windows retaining their original external stone are one of the 15th century in the north aisle, and a later one in the porch. The tower was plastered over in 1766, but has been stripped and the flintwork pointed; the north transept has been lengthened to take an organ, and other work has been done to the roofs, &c.

The east window of the chancel is a modern one of three cinquefoiled lights under a pointed head with net tracery. In the north wall are two windows with modern tracery of two cinquefoiled lights, and 14th-century jambs and rear arches; in the south wall are two similar windows, the western of which is entirely modern, while the other has old jambs. At the north-east of the chancel there has been a contemporary vestry, 8 ft. square, the blocked door-way of which remains. It seems to have been of two stories, and a shallow cupboard recess remains in the outer face of the chancel wall at some height from the ground. A wide arched recess on the inner face of the wall, now much modernized, has served as a cupboard and probably as an Easter sepulchre. Two pieces of dog-tooth ornament are built into the wall above the site of the destroyed vestry. In the south wall of the chancel are a modern trefoiled piscina and three sedilia with marble shafts.

A scroll-moulded string-course runs round the chancel below the windows, much repaired, but some of the original work remains. In the north-west corner is cut a double squint from the transept at a very acute angle; it has two openings separated by a mullion towards the chancel, and the eastern opening commands the site of the high altar, while the other gives a view of the sedilia. There are no arches across the openings to the transepts, but they were doubtless inclosed by screens in former times. The north transept has an inserted 15th-century east window of three lights under a traceried head, the tracery and outer stonework being modern, while the inner jambs and hollow-chamfered rear arch are old; between it and the squint is a small square recess with chamfered edges, and north and south of the window, but below the level of its sill, are plain chamfered image-brackets. The modern extension of the tran-sept is used as a vestry.

The south transept has a modern east window of three lights resembling that of the chancel, and a south window of four lights with a four-centred head and moulded label, also modern; and there are 14th-century arches opening to the aisles from both transepts, each of two wave-moulded orders. The chancel arch is of 13th-century date, with two moulded orders and a string at the springing, the chamfers of the western jambs being stopped below the string with a pretty shell ornament; the wall is very thick and probably older than the arch, but the ashlar courses on its west face run through from the arch to the respond of the south arcade of the nave at the level of its capital; the broken courses below are probably due to the former existence here of a recess behind the south nave altar. To the north of the chancel arch the facing ranges neither with the jambs of the arch nor with those of the north arcade, but appears to be of later date than the latter, against which it ends with a straight joint. Above the springing level of the chancel are shallow arched recesses to the north and south, now apparently quite modern, but perhaps representing entrances to the rood-loft. They now contain painted figures of our Lady and the Angel of the Annunciation.

The north arcade of the nave has four bays, the western bay being modern, cut through a wall which was previously blank. The other three bays are early 13th-century work, the east and west responds being semi-octagonal with moulded bases and capitals, while the first pillar is round with a moulded base, and a capital enriched with a line of beautiful trefoil foliage; the second pillar is octagonal and has a moulded capital without carving. All the bases are modern, but the rest of the arcade is old, the arches being two-centred, with a chamfered inner order, and an outer order with an undercut keeled roll towards the nave, and a chamfer towards the aisle, hollow in the

eastern bay. The levels of the bases rise from west to east in this and the south arcade, following the rise of the ground, as commonly happens in old churches, the necessity of a level floor being a tenet of the modern 'restorer' only.

The south arcade is of four bays; the responds are semi-octagonal, the middle pillar octagonal, and the other two circular; all have moulded bases and capitals, the former renewed in modern times; the arches are, pointed and of a slightly more elaborate section than those of the other side, the edge roll of the outer order having a side fillet and an additional small roll or bead. The west respond and part of the arch are partly buried in the stonework of the tower which cuts into it, and are somewhat distorted, per-haps by a settlement of the newer work. The curious treatment of the inner order of the arches has been already remarked upon. Of the three north windows in the north aisle only the middle one is old, of 15th-century date, with two cinquefoiled lights, and the north doorway is modern or modernized, with mouldings of 15th-century style.

The north porch appears to be of the late 15th or 16th century, and has a pointed archway and a plain square-headed west window; the lower part of the porch is of brick, the rest of flint and stone. In the south aisle only the doorway is old, of simple 15th-century style, and there is a modern vestry at the west end of the aisle.

The tower is of three stages, the western angles are strengthened by pairs of deep buttresses, and the stair rises on the north-east corner; at the south-east a buttress cuts into the south arcade, and the tower arch has a low four-centred head with jambs of two orders, and moulded with a series of rolls and hollows of very dry detail. In the wall south of the arch is a large recess 14 in. deep with a four-centred arch, and a seat or ledge about 3 ft. above the floor. The stair is entered through a four-centred doorway within the tower, opening to a rib-vaulted passage leading to the stair foot.

The west doorway is a modern one with a four-centred arch in a square head, and over it outside is an inscription in memory of Edward Rickards, 1893. The window above is of four lights divided by a transom, the lights below the transom and also in the head are cinquefoiled; the arch is four-centred and filled with perpendicular tracery; it is all now of modern stone except the rear arch and jambs. In the north wall inside, higher up, is a wide recess with a rough four-centred arch, entered from the stair, and showing marks of use as a ringing-gallery. In the second stage is a modern west window of two trefoiled lights under a square head; the bell cham-ber is lighted by windows of three plain lights with four-centred heads; the parapet is embattled and the roof pyramidal; the stair turret stands up above the parapet and has a pointed roof.

The chancel has a modern open-timbered cradle roof covered with tiles; at the crossing the roof is of collar-beam type. The transepts have panelled ceilings; the north transept is covered with Horsham stone slabs and tiles, the southern with tiles only. The nave has a modern collar-beam roof with trusses, the king-posts of which have capitals and bases; in it, on the north side, are two gabled dormer windows, each of three lights, and one on the south side. The aisles have lean-to roofs, that on the north covered with stone slabs, and in the south aisle is a four-light dormer window with a transom.

The altar-table is modern, and behind it is a modern reredos of stone. An old altar-slab is preserved in the church. The pulpit is a modern one of stone and marble, and the font appears to be of 15th-century date; it is octagonal with a panelled bowl moulded on its upper and lower edges; the stem is plain and the base moulded. Under the tower is an old chest covered with leather, and bearing in nail-heads the date 1663. Preserved in cases are a Book of Homilies of 1683 and a Book of Common Prayer of 1669 ; both had been removed from the church, and were restored in 1885.

At the west end of the north aisle, against the wall, is a stone slab, on which is the brass figure of a man in civil dress, c. 1470, and the indent of the figure of his wife ; below are the small figures of their three sons and three daughters, and near the top of the slab is a small circular indent. A modern inscription in brass is attached to the stone : 'Hic jacet Matild Hamildun . . . ux Thomae at Hull que obiit . . . die mens Octob Anno Dni мccccx cujus anime propicictur (sic) Deus Amen.' Incised at the foot of the slab is a record of its removal from the middle aisle in 1873.

Two pieces of the inscription of a brass, c. 1340, were found lately in excavations on the site of the vestry; they read : '[Mar]garete . . . nre seig[neur].'

On the east respond of the south arcade is a curious inscription on brass to Robert Gardner, chief serjeant of the cellar to Queen Elizabeth, 1571 :

'Here fryndly Robartt Gardnar lyes, well borne of
ryghtt good race
Who sarvd in cowrtt wyth credytt styll, in worthi
rowlm and place
Cheeff Sargantt of the Seller longe, whear he dyd
duetty shoe
Wyth good regard to all degrees, as ffar as powre
myghtt goe
He past hys youth in sutch good ffraem, he cam to
aeged years
And thearby porchaest honest naem, as by reportt
a peers
A ffrynd whear any cawse he ffownd, and corttes
unto all
Of myrry moode and pleasantt spetch, howe ever happ
dyd ffall
Ffowr chyldern for to ffornysh fforth, the table rownd
he had
Wyth sober wyeff most matrenlyk, to mak a man
ffull glad
Prepaerd to dye longe ear his day, whych argues
greatt good mynd
And told us in the other world, whatt hoep he had
to ffynd
We leave hyme whear he loektt to be, our lord
receyve hys spreett
Wyth peace and rest in habram's brest, whear we att
leynth may meett.

'Qd Churchyard

He departed owte of thys transetory worlde the xth daye of November anno dm̃i 1571 being then of the age of LXXIII yeres.'

Over the inscription is a shield with the arms—Sable a cheveron between three hunting-horns argent on a pile argent a covered cup gules all within a border or charged with eight roundels sable. His helm, with the crest of a goat's head, is on a bracket above.

In the tower are ten bells, five of which are by T. Mears, 1816, and the other five by Warner & Sons, 1877.

The communion plate comprises a large cup of 1661, large flagon of 1704, three chalices of 1871, 1872, and 1891 respectively, three patens of 1832, 1890, and 1891, and a small paten without a mark or date ; besides these are four pewter plates, two of which are dated 1711.

In the first book of the registers the baptisms begin regularly in 1656, but there are individual entries in the years 1626, 1647, and 1649 ; they continue to 1793 ; the marriages date from 1626 to 1753, and the burials 1626 to 1794 ; the book is of paper. The second book contains marriages from 1754 to 1792, the third continues them to 1812, and the fourth has baptisms and burials from 1794 to 1812.

ALL SAINTS' church is a medium-sized, modern building of flint and stone in the style of the 13th century, consisting of a chancel, nave, south chapel and aisle, vestry, and north porch. Over the chancel arch is a wooden bell-turret with one bell ; the inside of the building is lined with red brick.

ADVOWSON The church of Letherhead, at the time of the Domesday Survey, was appurtenant to the manor of Ewell, and, together with 40 acres of land, was held by Osbern de Ow.[98] It later became the property of the abbey of Colchester, to whom it was granted by Eustace de Broc.[99]

Brother Robert, Abbot of Colchester, granted the advowson in 1287 to the king (Edward I),[100] who presented before 1304.[101] The advowson remained with the Crown[102] until Edward III in 1341, at the request of his mother, Queen Isabel, and to recompense the priory of Leeds, Kent, for losses sustained when Edward II besieged the castle of Leeds in order to avenge an insult offered to the queen, granted the advowson to the Prior and convent of Leeds[103] with licence to appropriate the church, and the monastery continuously presented to the church until its dissolution.[104] Henry VIII then gave the rectory and church and advowson of the vicarage of Letherhead to the Dean and Chapter of Rochester,[105] who are the present patrons.[106]

Besides their advowson, the Prior and convent of Leeds owned land in Letherhead. Edward III granted them free warren,[107] which shows they had a considerable estate. The prior held, as glebe land, fields and crofts named Morescroft, Bunteynesland, and Necrofts in Letherhead.[108]

CHARITIES Smith's Charity is distributed as in other Surrey parishes.

In 1608 John Skeet left £140 to buy land to provide bread for the poor.

In 1642 Charles, Earl of Nottingham, left £50 to the poor. It was not paid till 1679, when the parish added £20 and bought a house for an almshouse. In

98 V.C.H. Surr. i, 297.
99 Manning and Bray, Surr. ii, 673.
100 Feet of F. Surr. 15 Edw. I, no. 10.
101 Egerton MS. 2031.
102 Ibid. 2032.
103 Cal. Pat. 1340–3, pp. 333, 346, 356.
104 Egerton MSS. ; Winton Epis. Reg. Wykeham, ii, fol. 571.
105 Pat. 33 Hen. VIII, pt. ix.
106 See Inst. Bks. P.R.O.
107 Chart. R. 41 Edw. III, no. 158.
108 Chan. Inq. p.m. 4 Edw. IV, no. 57.

LETHERHEAD CHURCH : NAVE LOOKING EAST

1725 it was let for 15s. a year for the use of the poor. In 1807 it was sold, and a new house of industry built, which existed until the passing of the Poor Law of 1834.

In 1692 Edward Hudson left £3 a year to the trustees of Skeet's Charity to provide beef for the poor at Christmas, Easter, and Whitsuntide, and £1 to the vicar and parish clerk for saying evening prayer on the eve of those festivals.

In 1777 Elizabeth Rolfe gave the interest of £400 to maintain a monument in the church and for distribution among ten poor families.

In 1786 William Denne left £250 for coals to the poor.

In 1797 John Lucas, the founder of the school, endowed a midwife with £100, and left £100 for bread, the latter sum being diverted to the school in 1815.

In 1812 Richard Toye left £1,200 for monthly grants to six poor and aged persons.

In 1842 Richard Emberton left £300, the interest to be laid out in beautifying the church.

In 1843 James Roberts left £89 10s. for the benefit of four poor widows with dependent families.[109]

Mr. John Sandes, after 1725, left a rent-charge of 50s. for bread.

In 1715 Dr. Shortrudge gave a benefaction to the vicars of Letherhead, Great Bookham, Effingham, and Shalford.

The total of the charities amounts to £300 a year.

MICKLEHAM

Michelham and Micelham (xi cent.) ; Mikeleham (xii cent.) ; Mikelham and Micheham (xiii cent.) ; Mykeleham (xiv cent.).

Mickleham is a small parish and village midway between Dorking and Letherhead, and 21 miles from London. It measures about 3 miles east and west and 2 miles from north to south, and contains 2,825 acres.

The village lies in the Mole valley, and the parish comprises the valley and the downs rising on either side of it, where the Mole makes its way in a deep depression through the chalk downs. The soil in the valley is river alluvium, calcareous rubble, sand, and Wealden Clay washed down by the Mole, and on either side is chalk, with some small patches of brick-earth on the higher parts. The valley is peculiarly picturesque (see Frontispiece of Vol. II). On the west side the well-wooded slopes of Norbury Park rise in places steeply from the stream, and at its southern extremity on the east the side of Box Hill is almost precipitous in places, particularly 'The Whites,' overlooking Burford, which consists of loose chalk thickly overgrown with box and yew. Elsewhere it sweeps upwards in smooth, grassy slopes, studded with box, yew, and other dark-foliaged trees and shrubs. Amid thick woods of box, yew, and beech on the summit, overlooking Dorking, is a fort and magazine recently constructed, and still more recently abandoned. The well-known view from the top extends southward over the Weald, which, from that height, seems to drop away into a plain bounded by the South Downs, while to the south-west Redlands, and other hills near Dorking, covered with wood, rise to the greater height of Leith Hill. Ranmore Common and Norbury face the spectator from the east across the valley. The top of Box Hill is not more than 700 ft. above the sea, but the steep descents to the east and south, and the absence of any high ridge of sand immediately in front of it, give an impression of greater elevation. Dr. Burton, who in 1752 wrote in Greek of his travels through Surrey and Sussex, calls it, with pardonable exaggeration, the brow of a mountain.

On a spur of Box Hill, overlooking Juniper Hall, is a round tower, said to have been built by Mr. Thomas Broadwood.

It is in Mickleham chiefly that the River Mole burrows in the way which has suggested the popular etymology of its name.[1] From the foot of Box Hill at Burford to Norbury Park there are holes, called swallows, through which the water sinks, making its way by subterranean clefts in the chalk. Some of these swallows are in the bed of the stream, others in bays in the banks of the river, which only come into operation in times of flood. One of the largest of these latter is in Fredley Meadows, some 200 yards up-stream from the railway bridge, close to which, before the pathway from Dorking to Mickleham was diverted, stood the wooden 'Praybridge.' Near Thorncroft, in Letherhead, the water rises again in the bed of the stream. In normal summers the bed of the river for 3 or 4 miles is dry ground and stagnant water. In the grounds of Burford House and Fredley are hollows some way from the stream, in which the water rises when the river is full. The peculiarity of the river, that its whole volume normally ran underground for some miles, has been exaggerated. The Mole is well known by the notice of poets, Spenser and Drayton writing at length upon it, and Milton and Pope mentioning it. Miss Drinkwater-Bethune of Thorncroft privately printed a poem, 'The Mole or Emlyn Stream,' in 1839, with sensible topographical and antiquarian notes, which deserves to be better known.

In Norbury Park is a famous grove of giant yews of great age, known as the Druid's Walk, which no doubt mark part of the track which, leaving the main east and west road, called in modern times 'The Pilgrim's Way,' near Bagden Farm, crossed the river near the Priory, and thence led over Letherhead Downs to Epsom and London. Norbury is also noted for some giant beeches.

On Box Hill, and north of it upon Mickleham Downs, is a great deal of still open grass-land, though plantations and inclosures upon the downs have curtailed it greatly in recent years.

The main road from Dorking to London traverses the Mickleham valley. This was made a passable

[109] The above are recorded in the church.
[1] Perhaps the oldest form of the name known is Emlyn Stream (Emele aqua) ; Lansd. MS. 435, fol. 130a, in a grant of 1331. The name 'Mole' may come from 'Molinae Aqua'; compare the Welsh 'Melin.'

road in 1755.[2] Up to that time it was not available for wheeled traffic in bad weather,[3] and to judge from the traces of the old road it needed courage to drive along it at all. Till the bridge at Burford Bridge, together with the approach to it, was raised some twenty years ago, it was frequently overflowed by the Mole in time of flood.

The old west and east line of communication across the country by the chalk downs passed south of the village, past Bagden Farm and Chapel Farm, to a ford on the river south of Burford Lodge, at the foot of Box Hill.

The London, Brighton, and South Coast Railway line from London to Portsmouth also passes through the Mickleham valley. The line was completed in 1867. There is a station at West Humble in Mickleham, now called Box Hill and Burford Bridge, to distinguish it from Box Hill on the South Eastern line, more than a mile distant.

Mickleham is fairly rich in antiquities. In 1788 William Bray, the historian of Surrey, became possessed of some brass Roman coins of the later Empire, which had recently been ploughed up on Bagden Farm,[4] and neolithic flakes are not uncommon both about this place, near Norbury, and on Box Hill. The ancient road which, as the Roman Stone Street, runs from Sussex past Ockley to Dorking (q.v.) headed for the Mole valley through a gap in the chalk, though it does not appear that it has been actually traced between Dorking and Burford Bridge. A ford over the Mole is still visible at the place where Burford Bridge stands, and a little further north, at Juniper Hall, a lane leaves the present road on the right and ascends the downs. It is called Pebble Lane. At the point where it emerges upon the high ground it becomes a well-marked track carried on a causeway over declivities. Flints with cement clinging to them occur upon it, as farther south on the same road in Capel (q.v.). It is still a bridle road, and leads in nearly a straight line to Epsom race-course. After this point it is supposed to have led to the right, in a curve following the top of the downs, past Banstead to Woodcote. It probably represents a British trackway utilized by the Romans as the line of a small road, though the Roman way probably continued straight on at Epsom towards Ewell, and so to London. In 1780, when Juniper Hall was being built, two skeletons

[2] Act 28 Geo. II, cap. 45.
[3] Manning and Bray, Surr. iii, App. p. lii.
[4] Ibid. p. xlvii.

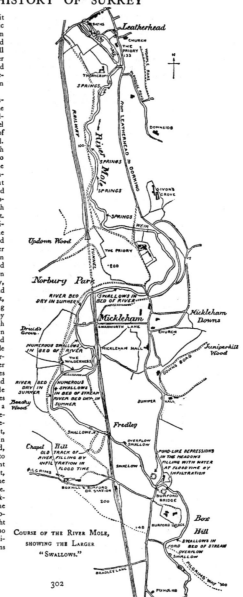

COURSE OF THE RIVER MOLE, SHOWING THE LARGER "SWALLOWS."

MICKLEHAM : BURFORD BRIDGE HOTEL FROM GARDEN

and a spear-head were found, called by Brayley 'exuviae of warfare,'[5] but were probably Anglo-Saxon interments, as at Fetcham (q.v.). At Chapel Farm, near West Humble, in Mickleham, are the very ruinous remains of part of the east, south, and west walls of a chapel. The history of its origin and decay is obscure. The priory of Reigate possessed a messuage and rents which were called the manor of West Humble, and the chapel has been supposed to have been built by the priory. But it more probably belonged to Merton, which held the manor of Polesden Lacy. In 1566 lands called Capel were held with this manor,[6] and these would appear to be Chapel Farm, close by which the remains stand. The building is about 48 ft. by 16 ft. ; the greater part of the gabled west wall, a portion of the south wall, and part of the east wall still stand ; the material is flint and sandstone. There are no architectural details left, excepting a small light in the head of the west gable, too much worn to be dated ; it has one jamb, and part of what appears to have been a trefoiled head. Below it is a round hole, and in the east wall a gap formed by a single light, of which no dressings remain ; also another gap in the south wall. The flints of the walling are not split, and are set in fairly even courses. The building probably dates from the 13th century.

The Running Horse Inn, in the days before the advent of railways, was a favourite stabling for horses racing at Epsom. On Mickleham Downs were, until recently, some training gallops.

At the beginning of the French Revolution Mickleham became the refuge of several distinguished French émigrés. M. de Narbonne, ex-minister of war, was the most celebrated among them, and Talleyrand also was here for a short time, and Madame de Staël. Juniper Hall had been taken by some of them, but several settled in other houses. Among them was M. d'Arblay, who married Fanny Burney, famous then as the authoress of 'Evelina.' M. and Madame d'Arblay, after a stay at Great Bookham, settled at a newly-built house in West Humble, which they named Camilla Lacey, because it was provided by the profits of 'Camilla,' her third novel. It is now occupied by Mr. Leverton Harris.

Fredley Cottage was the home of Mr. Richard Sharp, F.R.S., M.P., known from his talents as 'Conversation Sharp.' During his lifetime many celebrated men visited Mickleham. He died in 1853. On a tree in the garden are the initials W. W. carved in the bark by Wordsworth.

James Mill and his son John Stuart Mill lived for a time in a house behind the Running Horse Inn. Hazlitt stayed at the Burford Bridge Hotel ; there also Keats wrote the latter part of 'Endymion,' and Nelson spent some of his last days in England. It was then called 'The Fox and Hounds' and has since been very much enlarged. The literary traditions of Mickleham were continued by Charles Mackay, who lived in a cottage at the foot of Box Hill, since destroyed, and by the residence of the late Mr. George Meredith at Flint Cottage, where he died in 1909. The Grove, the seat of Mr. Edward Arnold, on the border of Dorking and Mickleham, was once the

residence of the Marquis Wellesley. But the old house has been pulled down.

Mickleham Hall is now the residence of Mr. H. H. Gordon Clark, J.P. ; Norbury, of Mr. Leopold Salomons, J.P. ; High Ashurst, of the Dowager Countess of Harrowby ; Burford Lodge, with its famous collection of orchids, of Sir Trevor Lawrence, bart. ; Juniper Hall, famous for its cedars of Lebanon, of Mr. George McAndrew ; Juniper Hill, of Mr. L. Cunliffe ; The Priory, of Mrs. Grissell ; Fredley, of Mrs. Kay and Miss Drummond.

'The Old House,' now the residence of Mr. Gordon Pollock, is situated on the east side of the main road south of the church ; it bears the date 1636. It is of two stories and an attic, and is built entirely of red brick. Its west front towards the road has a slightly projecting wing at each end with moulded strings and cornices and shaped gables, and there are two similar gables in the main block. The present entrance is in the south wing and is modern ; the windows are square with modern wood frames and have moulded brick labels, those on the gables to the third story having pediments over them. The garden or east front is practically on one plane, with a gable head at either end and a small middle gable ; each of the side gables has three shallow brick pilasters with moulded capitals formed by breaking the string-course or cornice at the foot of the gables round the pilasters. To the south of the building is a modern extension. The arrangement of the rooms has been somewhat altered since the house was built, and there is nothing of note inside excepting one original brick fire-place with moulded jambs and three-centred arch ; this was discovered a short time ago. The original gateway of the grounds towards the road has some good posts with carved brick Ionic capitals.

In a deed of 1585–6 reference is made to Mickleham Common Fields. No Inclosure Act or Award seems to be in existence. Inclosure of waste on Mickleham Downs has taken place bit by bit.

Mickleham Village Hall was built by Mrs. and Miss Evans of Dalewood, in memory of the late Mr. David Evans.

The school, national, was built by subscription in 1844 and enlarged in 1872. There is a small infants' school at West Humble.

MICKLEHAM alias HIGH ASH-MANORS URST alias LITTLEBURGH.—At the time of the Domesday Survey one of the two manors then called Mickleham was held of Odo, Bishop of Bayeux.[7] After his forfeiture under William II the manor was held of the king in chief, the tenant paying 12s. yearly on St. Andrew's Day for ward of Rochester Castle.[8]

Ansfrig had held Mickleham under the Confessor, and Nigel held it under the bishop,[9] but there is no trace of subsequent tenants until the Testa de Nevill, which under the heading of escheats gives Robert and Matthew de Micheham holding a hide in Mickleham by the grant of 'King Henry the Elder.'[10] This was the nucleus of the considerable property of the family in Mickleham in later reigns. Documents of the time of Edward I show that Robert de Mickleham held a messuage, 20 virgates

5 Op. cit. iv, 457.
6 See manor of Polesden Lacy.
7 V.C.H. Surr. i, 304.
8 Exch. Enr. of Inq. rot. 4, m. 7,

21 Edw. I ; Testa de Nevill (Rec. Com.), 228 ; Chan. Inq. p.m. 21 Edw. I, no. 38.
9 V.C.H. Surr. i, 304.
10 Testa de Nevill (Rec. Com.), 228.

Henry I is probably meant. Henry II is called in Testa de Nevill 'Henricus rex pater Domini Regis.'

of land, 10 acres of pasture, and 2 acres of wood in Mickleham.[11] Robert's property descended to his son Gilbert,[12] who augmented it by his marriage with Alice daughter of Peter de Rival, with whom he received 30 acres of land and rent and services of John Adrian and. others.[13] He and his wife were also conjointly enfeoffed by William de Bures of 4s. rent of assize.[14] He died in 1292 or 1293,[15] and was succeeded by his son John. In 1332 John conveyed the manor of Mickleham (certain premises afterwards known as the manor of Fredley excepted) to Roger de Apperdele. Roger son of Roger de Apperdele settled it on his son Richard to hold during his father's lifetime.[16] Richard evidently died without issue, as it came to his brother John,[17] who forfeited Mickleham when he was outlawed as a felon in 1366.[18] The king, having the manor as an escheat, granted it, first to Simon de Bradestede,[19] then to William Croyser.[20] Afterwards Roger de Apperdele appears to have tried to regain the manor by denying that he had made any grant to his sons.[21] Evidently he was not successful, as Edward III about that time granted it to William, Bishop of Winchester.[22] Before this date Fredley and West Humble (see below) had both been separated from the manor of Mickleham, which is now referred to as half, and sometimes as two thirds or two parts. In 1402 the bishop received pardon for alienating what is termed half the manor to Nicholas Wykeham[23] and five other clerks.[24] From these clerks the manor or portion of the manor passed to another clerk, John Brommesgrove, described as holding two parts of the manor.[25] Brommesgrove, in 1431, alienated it to Lawrence Doune, who is said to have held two-thirds of the manor.[26] Half of this was bought from him by Ralph Wymeldon and Isabel his wife in 1464.[27] In 1481 Richard Wymeldon died seised of a third of the manor known subsequently as Littleburgh alias Mickleham.[28] He left a son Thomas, whose daughter Isabel married Thomas Stydolf.[29] The other part of the manor, which belonged to Laurence Doune, seems to have been acquired by William Ashurst, who held it in 1485.[30] Together with land which William Ashurst already held in Mickleham[30a] it descended under the name of Mickleham alias High Ashurst to his son John.[31] In 1511 William brother of John Ashurst quitclaimed his right to Robert Gaynesford, whose son Henry in 1535 conveyed it to Thomas Stydolf.[32] From this

time Littleburgh and Ashurst are sometimes treated separately and sometimes as different names for the same manor.

In 1538 Thomas Stydolf appears as owner of two parts of one part of the manor of Mickleham, formerly

WYMELDON. *Argent a cheveron azure between three eagles sable.*

STYDOLF. *Argent a chief sable with two wolves' heads rased or therein.*

the land of John de Mickleham, Henry Burton and John Walk being trustees, to his use.[33] At his death in 1545 he is described as holding a third of the manor of Mickleham alias High Ashurst.[34] John Stydolf succeeded his father Thomas, being followed by his son, another , who was succeeded by his son, Sir Francis.[35] Thomas

John Evelyn gives an account of a visit to Sir Francis Stydolf at Mickleham in August 1655. He says : 'I went to Boxhill to see those rare natural bowers, cabinets, and shady walks in the box copses : hence we walked to Mickleham, and saw Sir F. Stidolph's seate environ'd with elme-trees and walnuts innumerable, and of which last he told us they receiv'd a considerable revenue. Here are such goodly walkes and hills shaded with yew and box as render the place extremely agreeable, it seeming from these ever-greens to be summer all the winter.'[36] This description is one that might have been written yesterday, for Surrey's lovely hill is still as fair in winter as in summer.

In the following century Sir Richard Stydolf left two daughters, Frances wife of James, Lord Astley,[37] and Margaret wife of James Tryon, and to the two sons of the latter, Charles and James Tryon, the Stydolf lands descended.[38] In 1705 the two sons made a partition of the property, the manor of Mickleham alias High Ashurst alias Littleburgh falling to James.[39] From James

[11] Kirby's Quest, fol. 97. Besides his service to the king, he owed rent and suit at the court of Betchworth to ' Lord John de Berewyk,' and also rent to William Agulham for a certain tenement in the manor.
[12] Exch. Enr. of Inq. rot. iv, m. 7.
[13] Exch. Enr. of Inq. rot. iv, m. 11 ; Inq. p.m. 21 Edw. I, no. 129. His wife Alice apparently afterwards married William de Clyvedene (Inq. a.q.d. 1 Edw. II, no. 86). .
[14] Exch. Enr. of Inq. rot. iv, m. 11.
[15] Chan. Inq. p.m. 21 Edw. I, no. 38.
[16] Cal. Pat. 1348–50, p. 421 ; Chan. Inq. p.m. 21 Edw. III (2nd nos.), no. 48.
[17] Ibid.
[18] Chan. Inq. p.m. 40 Edw. III (1st nos.), no. 60.
[19] Ibid.
[20] Abbrev. Rot. Orig. (Rec. Com.), ii, 288.
[21] Plac. in Canc. file v, Hil. 41 Edw. III, no. 5. .
[22] Chan. Inq. p.m. 43 Edw. III, pt. i, no. 21.

[23] Cal. Pat. 1401–5, p. 227. Before this date conveyances were made to two of these clerks, Nicholas de Wykeham and Master John Campeden, by Roger de Friddele and John Apperdele son of John Apperdele of Letherhead, of 133 acres of land, 150 acres of pasture, 6 acres of wood, and 14s. rent in Mickleham (Feet of F. Surr. Trin. 14 Ric. II ; Mich. 15 Ric. III). This is the same as the extent of the two thirds afterwards given, so that the fines were probably for assurance of title.
[24] Ibid.
[25] Chan. Inq. p.m. 10 Hen. VI, no. 43.
[26] Chan. Inq. p.m. 9 Hen. VI, no. 12. The extent here given, viz. 133 acres of land, 150 acres of pasture, 6 acres of wood and 14s. rent is the same as that in the fines mentioned above ; but in the inquisition taken after Brommesgrove's death the two parts were said to consist of 120 acres of arable land, 200 acres of pasture, and 15 acres of wood.
[27] Cal. Pat. 1436–41, p. 545.
[28] Chan. Inq. p.m. 20 Edw. IV, no. 71.

He had acquired it from Isabel Wymeldon in 1464 (Fine R. 4 Edw. IV, m. 1 ; Cal. Pat. 1461–7, p. 321). Why it is called Littleburgh is unknown. There is no reason to connect it with Berge in Domesday.
[29] Manning and Bray, Surr. ii, 651.
[30] Chan. Inq. p.m. (Ser. 2), xx, 24.
[30a] The Ashursts had land in Mickleham, called High Ashurst, of which there is record in 1439 and 1477 (Deeds quoted by Manning and Bray, Surr. ii, 656).
[31] Ibid.
[32] Manning and Pray, Surr. ii, 656.
[33] Mem. R. (L.T.R.) East. 30 Hen. VIII, rot. 1.
[34] Chan. Inq. p.m. 36 Hen. VIII, no. 89.
[35] Chan. Inq. p.m. (Ser. 2), cclxxv, 69 (1 Jas. I) ; clxxv, 66 (18 Eliz.).
[36] Evelyn's Diary, (Ser. 2), xx, 24.
[37] He died 1674 (monument at Mickleham).
[38] Close, 4 Anne, pt. iii, no. 16. .
[39] Ibid. .

MICKLEHAM 'OLD HOUSE': WEST FRONT

MICKLEHAM 'OLD HOUSE': EAST FRONT

Tryon, according to Manning and Bray, the manor descended to his nephew, Charles Tryon, whose son Charles, in 1766, sold it to Anthony Chapman of London for £35,000. Chapman sold Mickleham Manor to Benjamin Bond Hopkins of Paine's Hill in 1775, and he in 1779[40] sold it to Charles Talbot, afterwards a baronet. He died in 1798. His family held the manor till 1871, when the baronetcy being extinct the Misses Talbot sold it to Mr. R. H. Mackworth Praed, the present lord. Mickleham Hall, built by Sir C. H. Talbot, was bought at the same time by the late Mr. Gordon W. Clark, and is now the seat of his son, Mr. H. H. Gordon Clark.[41]

TALBOT, baronet. *Gules a lion in a border engrailed or with the difference of a crescent.*

Meanwhile Ashurst had been separated, as a reputed manor, but bearing the name of Mickleham, and had been sold by Chapman in 1776 to Mr. Robert Botall.[42] From him it passed to George Morgan,[43] and in 1804 was conveyed by John Morgan to F. R. V. Villebois.[44] In 1817 it was bought by Mr. Andrew Strahan, the king's printer. In 1855 it was purchased from his nephew by Sir Henry Muggeridge ; it passed in 1862 to Sir Richard Glass, and in 1872 to J. C. Wilson. It is now the seat of the Dowager Countess of Harrowby.[45]

NORBURY was evidently the estate in Mickleham which in 1086 belonged to Richard son of Earl Gilbert ; it was then assessed for two hides.[46] From Richard de Tonbridge the overlordship descended to the De Clares, Earls of Gloucester,[47] from them to the Despensers,[48] and in the reign of Henry VI belonged to their descendant Isabel, Countess of Warwick.[49] As her ultimate heir was Anne Beauchamp who married Warwick the King-maker, the overlordship must have fallen to the Crown after his death and attainder in 1471 ; but in the 16th century it was said to belong to the warden and scholars of Merton College, Oxford, and Norbury to be held as of their manor of Thorncroft ;[50] this is evidently an error.

At the time of the Domesday Survey Norbury was held under Richard de Tonbridge by Oswold, who had formerly been the tenant under Edward the Confessor. The next holder of whom anything is known was Odo de Dammartin, who during the 12th century granted to the monks of St. Pancras a third of his tithe in Mickleham.[51] His daughter, Alice de Dammartin, held half a fee there,[52] and Margery widow of Odo de Dammartin had as her dower, among other lands, the manor of Mickleham.[53]

From the Dammartins the manor passed to William Husee, who in 1314 held ' the manor called Le North Bury ' in Mickleham as half a knight's fee of Earl Gilbert de Clare.[54] He was granted free warren there by Edward II,[55] and had licence for an oratory in his manor between 1323 and 1333.[56]

In 1349 the manor was held by Isabel Husee,[57] and in 1376 by another William Husee.[58] The next holder of Norbury appears in Thomas Stydolf, who died seised of it in 1545.[59] He has been connected by Manning and Bray with William Husee, in direct descent. According to these historians Isabel daughter of William Husee married William Wymeldon, the grandchild of whose son Ralph, Isabel Wymeldon, married Thomas Stydolf who died in 1545.[60] The Stydolfs held Norbury with their other Mickleham manors until the latter half of the 17th century.[61] In 1705 the manor became the property of James Tryon, grandson of Sir Richard Stydolf.[62] According to Manning and Bray James Tryon devised Norbury to his nephew Charles Tryon, who settled it upon his wife. She lived at Norbury till 1764, and then granted her life interest to her son Charles,[63] who with his wife Rebecca, in 1765, levied a fine to Sewallis Shirley.[64] In 1766 the estate was sold (according to Manning and Bray) to Anthony Chapman, who sold it to William Locke in 1774. Mr. Locke built the present house.[65] In 1819 his son sold Norbury to Mr. E. R. Robinson, who, however, sold it again in 1822 to Mr. E. Fuller Maitland, who exchanged it with Mr. H. P. Sperling for Pace Place, near Henley-on-Thames. Mr. Sperling made great improvements in the beautiful grounds. In 1848 he sold it to Mr. Thomas Grissell, whose family sold it in 1890 to Mr. Leopold Salomons.[66]

FREDLEY.—In 1336 John de Mickleham, after having granted the manor of Mickleham with the exception of a messuage, 120 acres of land, and 4 acres of wood, to Roger de Apperdele, granted the excepted premises, also under the name of the ' manor of Mickleham,'[67] to his son-in-law John Dewey, husband of Margery de Mickleham.[68]

In 1365 John Frychele or Fridlee *alias* Dewey settled a house, 80 acres of land, and 4 acres of wood in Mickleham on himself and his wife Joan, by Hugh

40 In 1779, not 1780, as Manning and Bray say, for in 1779 Talbot, as owner, made an agreement with the parish about a right of way (Parish Books).
41 Private and local knowledge.
42 Com. Pleas D. Enr. Hil. 16 Geo. III, m. 133. Botall himself seems to have told Manning that he bought it from Hopkins.
43 Feet of F. Surr. East. 21 Geo. III.
44 Recov. R. Mich. 44 Geo. III.
45 Private and local information.
46 V.C.H. Surr. i, 317.
47 Testa de Nevill (Rec. Com.), 219, 220 ; Chan. Inq. p.m. 8 Edw. II, no. 68.
48 Ibid. 23 Edw. III (pt. 2, 1st nos.), no. 169.
49 Ibid. 18 Hen. VI, no. 3.
50 Chan. Inq. p.m. (Ser. 2), clxxv, 66. Thorncroft includes lands in Mickleham now, but not Norbury.
51 Cal. of Anct. Deeds, iii, A. 3978.

52 Testa de Nevill (Rec. Com.), 219. Robert de Mickleham also seems to have held half a fee (according to Testa de Nevill) of the honour of Clare.
53 Feet of F. Div. Co. 15 & 16 Hen. III, 89.
54 Chan. Inq. p.m. 8 Edw. II, no. 68.
55 Chart. R. 11 Edw. II, m. 9, no. 42.
56 Egerton MS. 2032.
57 Chan. Inq. p.m. 23 Edw. III (pt. 2, 1st nos.), no. 169.
58 Chan. Inq. p.m. 49 Edw. III (pt. 1, 2nd nos.), no. 46.
59 Chan. Inq. p.m. (Ser. 2), clxxv, 89.
60 Manning and Bray, Hist. of Surr. ii, 651. From deeds, apparently. The Visitation in Harl. MS. 1561, fol. 38b, also connects Thomas Stydolf with Husee in descent through the Wymeldons, but makes Isabel Wymeldon marry George Stydolf, their son being Thomas Stydolf.

61 Chan. Inq. p.m. (Ser. 2), clxxv, 66 ; cclxxx, 69 ; Feet of F. Div. Co. Trin. 14 Chas. I.
62 Close, 4 Anne, pt. iii, no. 16.
63 Manning and Bray, Hist. of Surr. ii, 652.
64 Feet of F. Surr. Hil. 5 Geo. III.
65 On the hill. The old house was near the river. Part of it was preserved and is now a farm-house.
66 Local and private knowledge.
67 Compare the common use of the name, the manor of Mickleham for Mickleham and Ashurst later.
68 Feet of F. Surr. Trin. 10 Edw. III ; Abbrev. Rot. Orig. (Rec. Com.), ii, 108 ; Cal. Pat. 1334–8, p. 232. This 'manor' was subsequently held of the king by half of the original service owed by the manor of Mickleham. See Chan. Inq. p.m. 39 Edw. III (2nd nos.), no. 38.

atte Sonde, his feoffee.[69] The manor was held by his son and grandson John Dewey and Roger Dewey *alias* Fridlee.[70] Roger Fridlee granted the manor to James Janyn and Nicholas Glover, who enfeoffed John Wydoweson and Isabel his wife.[71]

In 1449 John Wydoweson was in possession of the manor then first called the manor of Fredley (Frydelees) in Mickleham,[72] and the following year he and his wife Isabel granted the manor (then simply styled Mickleham) to William Wydoweson.[73] A William Wydewson presented to the living in 1492,[74] so was perhaps still holding Fredley. He is buried in Mickleham Church, where his wife also was buried in 1513.

Nothing more is known of the manor till 1528, when Sir John Mordaunt granted a lease of land in it,[75] and in 1571 Lewis, Lord Mordaunt, his grandson, alienated the manor to William Lever or Leaver.[76] From William Leaver the manor of Fredley descended to his son and grandson, John and Thomas Leaver, the latter inheriting it in 1640.[77] Documentary evidence of the descent is wanting, but according to Manning and Bray Thomas Leaver left sisters, Mary and Joan Leaver, as his heirs. The former married Edward Arnold,[78] the latter Edward Turner. The Arnolds in 1682 sold their moiety to Mr. John Spencer of Dorking, who in 1691 purchased Turner's moiety. On the same authority Spencer devised to Margaret wife of Gilbert Parker.[79] They sold Fredley to Samuel Hawkes in 1721.[80] Hawkes, according to Manning and Bray, was succeeded by his nephew Samuel Lamb, by whom Fredley was again sold in 1762 to Cecil Bisshop, afterwards Sir Cecil Bisshop, and Susannah his wife.[81] Cecil Bisshop is distinguished for building the famous Juniper Hall on the site of the old Royal Oak Inn. This fine old house afforded a kindly shelter to French *émigrés* in troubled times.[82] Sir Cecil Bisshop died in 1779. Mr. David Jenkinson, a lottery agent, bought the property, and built Juniper Hill. In 1803, on the death of his son, the property was broken up. Mr. Worrall bought Juniper Hall and sold it in 1814 to Mr. Thomas Broadwood, from whom it was bought by Miss Beardmore. Her heir conveyed it in 1868 to Mr. F. Richardson, who in 1882 sold it to Mr. George McAndrew. Juniper Hill was bought by Sir Lucas Pepys, bart., M.P., who married the Countess of Rothes and took the name of Leslie. It passed through them and Colonel Lambton to Mr. J. H. Bryant in 1884, and in 1899 to Mr. Leonard Cunliffe.

A third portion was ultimately bought by Mr.

Sharp, F.R.S., 'Conversation Sharp.' He left it to his adopted daughter, Mrs. Drummond, who built the house now called Fredley. It is the property of her daughter, Mrs. Kay.

As early as 1253 the priory of Reigate held a tenement in Mickleham of Robert de Watevile.[82] Their property, afterwards known as the manor of *WEST HUMBLE*, was augmented by the grant of John de Mickleham, who gave to the Prior and convent of Reigate a house and 1s. 8d. rent with the advowson of the church in Mickleham.[84] Licence for the alienation was granted by the king in 1345 at the request of Queen Philippa.[85] The priory held their land until the Dissolution. Before that event, earlier in the reign of Henry VIII, it had been leased by the priory, under the name of the manor of 'West Humble in Mikelham,' to Thomas Stydolf for 99 years. Stydolf's right in certain lands in Mickleham was contested by John Arnold, who declared that he had been unjustly ousted by Stydolf from the peaceful occupation of his land in Mickleham, leased to him, so he said, for 99 years, by the Prior of Reigate in the March of 1521.[86] He accused Stydolf of having set his servants to kill him, one of whom assaulted him with a sword and 'strake' him 'upon the raynes of his bak' and 'there cut his coot,' his enemies' intention being to cut his head off, and 'playe at the foteball therewith,' according to the admission of Stydolf's own daughters. Stydolf's reply was that the lease of the lands in question had been made to him in August 1516.[87] An audit of rents of the late priory of Reigate in 1537 shows three years' rent from Thomas Stydolf and John Stydolf his son for the manor of West Humble £15 15s.[88]

After the dissolution of Reigate Priory the Stydolfs remained as tenants of the manor, which they held of Lord William Howard and his successors,[89] to whom the lands of the dissolved priory were granted in 1551.[90] The lease seems to have been renewed at the end of the ninety-nine years, as in 1681 a rent of £6 3s. 8d. was still paid to the successors of the Howards.[91]

The Stydolfs now held the three manors in Mickleham—Norbury, High Ashurst, and West Humble—all Mickleham, in fact, except Fridley. As Norbury and Ashurst, so West Humble passed, in Anne's reign, to the grandson of Sir Richard Stydolf,[92] James Tryon, whose nephew, Charles Tryon, in the reign of George III, 1765, levied a fine of the same manor to Sewallis Shirley for purpose of sale.[93] According to Manning and Bray the manor was sold to Chapman in 1776, in 1780 to Hopkins, and in 1781 to

[69] Chan. Inq. p.m. 39 Edw. III (2nd nos.), no. 38.
[70] De Banco R. Mich. 5 Edw. IV and 44 Hen. VI, m. 619.
[71] Ibid.
[72] Close, 27 Hen. VI, m. 109. He appears to have been enfeoffed by Richard Horton, who was probably a trustee, as were, doubtless, Janyn and Glover.
[73] Feet of F. Surr. East. 28 Hen. VI.
[74] Winton Epis. Reg. Courtney, 43d.
[75] Deed in private hands. See also Exch. (L.T.R.) Memor. R. East. 29 Hen. VIII, rot. 6.
[76] Pat. 13 Eliz. pt. xi.
[77] Inq. p.m. (Ser. 2), cxxxvi, 150; eccxcii, 54.
[78] Edward Arnold, 'of Fridley,' was churchwarden in 1670. The Arnolds had

farmed Fridley in the previous century. From 1549 to 1635 there are 68 baptisms of Arnold children.
[79] Manning and Bray, *Surr.* ii, 655.
[80] Feet of F. Surr. Hil. 7 Geo. I.
[81] Ibid. 12 Geo. III. A fine between John Matthews and Cecil Bisshop occurs in 1772.
[82] Hill, *Juniper Hall*.
[83] Feet of F. Surr. East. 37 Hen. III.
[84] Inq. p.m. 17 Edw. III (2nd nos.), no. 86.
[85] *Cal. Pat.* 1343–5, p. 526.
[86] Ct. of Req. bdle. 11, no. 46.
[87] Ibid.
[88] *L. and P. Hen. VIII,* xiii (2), 1264.
[89] Chan. Inq. p.m. (Ser. 2), clxxv, 66 (18 Eliz.) ; cclxxx, 69.
[90] Pat. 33 Hen. VIII, pt. vii, m. 1; Mar-

garet wife of Lord William Howard was succeeded by her son Charles, Lord Howard of Effingham, from whom the priory's lands descended to his granddaughter, Elizabeth wife of the Earl of Peterborough (Pat. 12 Chas. II, pt. xviii, no. 16). Charles II in 1660 made a grant of these lands to Viscount Mordaunt de Avalon, son of the Countess of Peterborough (Pat. 12 Chas. II, pt. xviii, no. 16), by whom they seem to have been conveyed, by fine, in 1681, to John Parsons (Feet of F. Surr. Mich. 33 Chas. II), who also, in the same year, levied a fine to Grace Pierpoint (Feet of F. Surr. Hil. 33 & 34 Chas. II).
[91] Feet of F. Surr. Mich. 33 Chas. II.
[92] Close, 4 Anne, pt. iii, nq. 16.
[93] Feet of F. Surr. Hil. 5 Geo. III.

Sir Francis Geary of High Polesden, who died in 1796, being succeeded by his son Sir William, who sold to Richard Brinsley Sheridan in 1809. In 1816, after Sheridan's death, it was sold to Mr. Thomas Hudson, along with Chapel Farm, which was in Polesden Lacy Manor. The manorial rights and part of the property were sold by Mrs. Hudson's trustees in 1874 to Mr. J. Leverton Wylie, by whom courts were held occasionally. He died recently, and his relative, Mr. F. Leverton Harris, is now lord of the manor.

In the reign of John the priory of Merton held land in Polesden,[94] later described as the manor of *POLESDEN LACY*.[95] At the dissolution of the monastery in 1538 the manor was granted by Henry VIII to William Sackvyle, who purchased the manor of Polesden Lacy and farms called Capelland and Bowetts.[96] William Sackvyle died in 1556.[97] His son in the same year had licence to alienate the manor and messuages and land called Capelland and Bowetts to Gilbert and Richard Sackvyle,[98] by whom it was sold to Henry Stydolf in 1564.[99] He died without male issue,[100] having settled the manor on a certain John Stydolf, with remainder to his brothers William and Thomas successively.[101] William died in seisin of it at the end of Elizabeth's reign;[102] Thomas himself, at his death in 1603, only possessed land in Polesden, which descended to his son Sir Francis Stydolf.[103] William Stydolf, son of William, had Polesden Lacy in 1657.[104] His son Sigismund Stydolf in 1689 settled the manor on himself and his wife Margaret, daughter of Sir Francis Rolle, and at his death left it to his wife.[105] She married three times, her third husband being Thomas Edwin, upon whom she settled the manor after her death, in default of issue from the marriage. She died in 1734, and as she left no children Mr. Edwin became seised of the manor, which descended to his nephew Charles Edwin.[106] Charles Edwin bequeathed his estates to his wife Lady Charlotte, with remainder to his issue, in default to his sister Catherine Edwin and her male issue, and in default to his nephew Charles Wyndham. Lady Charlotte died in 1777, and Catherine Edwin being dead without issue,

Charles Windham succeeded to the estates and took the name of Edwin. In 1784 he sold the manor to Admiral Sir Francis Geary, who held the manor of High Polesden in Great Bookham, after which the descent of the two manors is identical (q.v.).

The church of *ST. MICHAEL* consists of a chancel 28 ft. 9 in. by 16 ft. 9 in., with vestries on the north side and a circular organ-chamber on the south; a nave 42 ft. by 17 ft. 10 in., with a north aisle 30 ft. 6 in. by 15 ft. 6 in., at the east end of which is a chantry 16 ft. by 10 ft.; a south aisle 7 ft. 6 in. wide, and a west tower 16 ft. 7 in. by 14 ft. 2 in., having over its west doorway a porch 10 ft. 9 in. by 8 ft. 7 in.

The oldest part of the building is the west tower, dating from c. 1140, while the chancel is some forty years later. All the rest of the church except the west porch, a 15th-century addition, and the north chapel, which is of early 16th-century date, has been rebuilt in modern times—1872 and 1891—the north aisle having been widened at the latter date. A

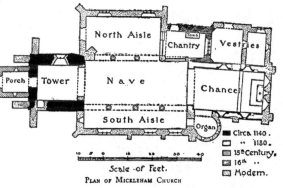

PLAN OF MICKLEHAM CHURCH

Scale of Feet.

Circa 1140.
" 1180.
15th Century.
16th "
Modern.

former north doorway was taken away in 1891, and has been set up in the grounds of Fredley, in the parish.

Parts of a large circular column with a scalloped capital, now in the tower, were found in excavating for the new arcade, and show that an aisle existed in the 12th century, evidently on the south side, as the north aisle was a very late addition, none existing when Manning and Bray wrote.

The chancel has a marked deviation to the south from the line of the nave and tower, and doubtless

[94] Feet of F. Surr. 3 John; *Abbrev. Plac.* (Rec. Com.), 93.

[95] *Valor Eccl.* (Rec. Com.), ii, 48; Mins. Accts. Surr. 29 & 30 Hen. VIII, no. 115, m. 7. It is probably what is meant at an earlier date by East Polesden; *vide* Feet of F. Surr. 13 Edw. II, no. 10 (*Surr. Arch Coll. Vol. of Fines,* 89).

[96] Aug. Off. Partics. of Grants, 38 Hen. VIII, no. 972; Pat. 4 Edw. VI, pt. viii, m. 38.

[97] Chan. Inq. p.m. 2 & 3 Phil. and Mary, cx, 148. He held the manor and woodlands called the Hooke Grove, the Lower Prunes, the Upper Frunes, Capell Grove, and Malbrydynge Coppice in Mickleham and Polesden, and messuages and tenements called Capellande and Bowetts.

[98] Pat. 3 & 4 Phil. and Mary, pt. iv, m. 17; Com. Pleas D. Enr. East. 6 Eliz. m. 28 d.

[99] Pat. 6 Eliz. pt. ix, m. 9; Com. Pleas D. Enr. East. 6 Eliz. m. 28 d.

[100] Chan. Inq. p.m. (Ser. 2), clxxv, 66.

[101] Mem. R. (L.T.R.) 10 Eliz. rot. 157.

[102] Chan. Inq. p.m. (Ser. 2), cclxiv, 175.

[103] Ibid. cclxxx, 69.

[104] Recov. R. Trin. 1657, rot. 59.

[105] Manning and Bray, *Surr.* ii, 657; Feet of F. Div. Co. Mich. 29 Chas. II.

[106] Manning and Bray, *Surr.* ii, 658. The history of the tenure from the Stydolfs to the Edwins is identical with that of Headley (q.v.).

replaced a narrower building coeval with or older than the west tower. Its east wall is almost entirely modern, and contains three round-headed lights with a circular wheel-window over, in 12th-century style. The north and south walls of the chancel are for the most part old, and in each are two round-headed windows, modern on the outside, but with old internal jambs having shafts at the angles with moulded bases and carved foliate capitals of several types, c. 1180.

The rear arches are semicircular, and have moulded outer orders with billet-moulded labels, which continue between the windows as a string-course. Below

the sills of the windows is another string, being in section a keeled roll.

Near the east ends of both walls are rectangular lockers with plain rebated jambs and square heads, fitted with modern doors ; and between the two north windows is a modern doorway leading to the vestries, with moulded jambs and pointed arch.

At the west end of the south wall of the chancel is a modern opening to the organ-chamber in 12th-century style, and above it an open arcade of interlacing round arches.

The organ-chamber is circular on plan, lighted by four narrow round-headed windows, and by a series of small circular windows high in the wall. On the west side of the chamber is a tall narrow opening to the south aisle with a semicircular arch and scalloped capitals.

The chancel arch is semicircular, and is of three orders, the two inner ones being modern and having moulded edge rolls, but the outer order on the west face is a pretty piece of late 12th-century work, with a lozenge pattern with leaf-carving in the spandrels between it and the label, which has a line of dogtooth ornament on the chamfer. The jambs are of old stonework and quite plain, with modern scalloped capitals and corbels.

The north and south arcades of the nave are entirely modern, and are of four bays with semicircular arches and round columns having moulded bases and scalloped or carved capitals, with corbels to correspond at each end. The eastern bay on the north side opens to the north chapel, and instead of a column has a square pier to take the western arch of the chapel.

The chantry has an early 16th-century east window of four cinquefoiled lights with a traceried four-centred head and a moulded label, the inner jambs being worked with a large casement moulding, and on the north side of the window is a canopied niche, now without a base ; the canopy has trefoiled ogee arches with crockets and finials and small crocketed pinnacles between. Manning and Bray note that in their time there was a corresponding niche on the south side. Two plaster figures of St. Peter and St. Paul, now in the vestry, are said to have stood in these niches.

Against the north wall of the chapel is a canopied tomb, which is described below ; and to the west of it a plain contemporary doorway with a three-centred arch ; while above it is a window of two cinquefoiled lights in a square head. The arch opening to the aisle is modern, and corresponds to the adjacent arches of the nave arcade.

The north aisle has two modern windows in its north wall, each having three cinquefoiled ogee lights under a square head ; and at the west end of the aisle is a modern doorway.

The three windows of the south aisle are likewise modern, except the small west window, which is old work reset, its inner splayed jambs and rear arch being perhaps of 13th-century date.

The tower opens to the nave by a modern round-headed arch, and has in its north wall a modern two-light window of 12th-century design.

In the south wall of the tower near the west end is an old doorway, now leading into a cupboard in the wall, but originally intended to open to the stairs to the belfry.

The 12th-century west doorway in the tower has jambs of two square orders with engaged shafts having scalloped capitals and chamfered abaci ; the arch is semicircular, and has a heavy roll between two plain orders. It opens to a porch with small loop-lights in each side wall, and a western arch with chamfered jambs and a modern moulded label.

The tower is low in proportion to its width, and

MICKLEHAM : BURFORD BRIDGE AND BOX HILL
(EARLY 19TH CENTURY)

MICKLEHAM CHURCH : CHANCEL ARCH

has on the north, south, and west two small lights, one above the other, which have what seem to be 16th-century heads externally, but retain their 12th-century rear arches.

On the east face is one window of the same character just above the nave roof. The western angles of the tower are strengthened by pairs of deep buttresses, which have been largely rebuilt, but their internal angles have old stones ; they are probably 15th-century additions, and the tower is finished with a low pyramidal roof from which rises a slender octagonal shingled spire. The roof of the nave and the west porch are covered with Horsham stone slabs, while the chancel and organ-chamber are tiled, and the aisles have lead roofs and stone parapets.

The fittings of the church are for the most part modern. In the pulpit are five panels carved in high-relief, representing scenes from the New Testament. At the angles are figures in canopied niches, and the moulded cornice has a form of acanthus-leaf ornament in low-relief.

In the north chapel is some panelling from St. Paul's School in London, c. 1680.

The font is of 13th-century date, and has a shallow square bowl with tapering sides ornamented with arcades in low-relief, and standing on a central and four angle shafts with moulded bases. Near the font is an old wooden eagle lectern fixed to a modern iron stem and base ; and on the south wall of the chancel is the banner and helmet of Sir Francis Stydolf, who died in 1655.

The tomb in the north chapel is a panelled Purbeck marble altar-tomb in a canopied recess, the panels being square with feathered quatrefoils inclosing shields, once painted, but now almost plain. The recess above has a four-centred head with tracery spandrels, and a cornice with a vine-trail and a Tudor flower cresting. On a brass plate in the recess is the following inscription : 'Here lyth the body of Wyllyam Wyddowsoun cytezein and mercer of londn & of ye parych of Mekyllham late patorne & also here lythe ye body of Jone hys wyfe the wyche dyssesyd the xxvii day of septebyr the vᵗʰ yere of kyng hary the VIII on whoys soullys goᵈ have mercy ame.'

Above is the figure of a man in a long fur-trimmed cloak praying at a desk. A scroll issues from his mouth on which is the prayer : ' Dne deus miserere suῥ animabs.' To his right is a woman with a long head-dress and a tight-fitting dress with a loose waist-belt ; on the scroll from her mouth is, ' Ihs xps miserere sup animabs.' Between the two figures is a brass shield on which are the arms of the Mercers' Company, and above are indents for other shields now lost.

There are two floor-slabs near the east end of the nave, one to Thomas Tooth, who died in 1685, and the other to Peter de Lahay, 1684. Near the west end of the nave is a mediaeval coffin-lid on which is the indent of a long cross with foliated ends. In the west porch are two marble coffin-slabs of the 14th century, with raised crosses, and edges which are twice hollow-chamfered. On one of them are

remains of an inscription in Gothic capitals. . . . . ICΥ DEU DALME EIT MERCI AMEN.

The tower contains three bells, the treble being by C. and G. Mears, 1850. The second has the inscription, ' Bryanus Eldridge me fecit 1624,' and the third has ' Wilhelmus Carter me fecit 1610 ' in Gothic capitals.

The plate is as follows : Two cups, one of 1666 and the other of 1870 ; two patens, one of 1701 and the other a year later ; and two flagons, the first being of 1614 and the other of 1702. There is also an almsdish of 1700.

There are four books of registers, the first a long paper volume containing very irregular entries ; first is a group of burials from 1612 to 1629, then there are baptisms from 1549 to 1629, and next come more burials from 1549 to 1605, and finally baptisms, marriages, and burials from 1634 to 1660. At the other end of the book are some briefs, churchwardens' accounts, &c. The second book, which is mostly a copy on parchment of the first, contains baptisms from 1549 to 1698, with a gap between 1658 and 1660 ; marriages from 1549 to 1713, with a gap between 1647 and 1663 ; and burials from 1549 to 1712, with a gap as in the baptisms. At the other end are accounts and tithe rents from 1637. The third book contains baptisms and burials from 1713 to 1812 and marriages from 1713 to 1753, and the fourth book contains the marriages from 1754 to 1812.

Mr. Samuel Woods, one of the founders of the London Institution, who lived in Mickleham, made an index to the registers.

The churchyard surrounds the church, and it is entered from the road at the north-west corner and by a lych-gate at the south-west corner.

ADVOWSON   A church at Mickleham is mentioned in the Domesday Survey.[107]

At the time of the taxation of Pope Nicholas it was assessed at £18 13s. 4d.[108] The early owners and patrons of the church were the De Micklehams, John de Mickleham presenting in the 14th century.[109] He alienated the advowson in 1344[110] to Reigate Priory that prayers might be daily sung in the priory church for the souls of his family, and the priors presented continuously until the Dissolution, with two exceptions, when Laurence Doune and William Wydoweson presented in the 15th century.[111] Wydoweson claimed the advowson, which he said John de Mickleham had alienated to John Dewey, from whose descendants it had passed to himself.[112] The owners of Fridley Manor had claimed some right in it in 1449,[113] and William Wydoweson presented in 1492.[114] Henry VIII after the dissolution of Reigate Priory granted the advowson of the rectory and parish church of Mickleham, with West Humble Manor, to Lord William Howard and Margaret his wife.[115] It passed by descent to Elizabeth, Countess of Peterborough.[116] Charles, Viscount Mordaunt of Avalon, her grandson, sold the advowson to John Parsons in 1681,[117] and in 1698 Sir John Parsons presented to the living.[118] The next presentation, in 1744, was made by Thomas Walton,

107 *V.C.H. Surr.* i, 304.
108 *Pope Nich. Tax* (Rec. Com.), 208.
109 Egerton MS. 2032.
110 Inq. p.m. 17 Edw. III (2nd nos.), no. 86.
111 Egerton MS. 2034.

112 De Banco, Mich. 5 Edw. IV ; 44 Hen. VI, m. 619.
113 Feet of F. Surr. 28 Hen. VI, no. 30.
114 *Vide supra* under Fridley.
115 Pat. 33 Hen. VIII, pt. vii, m. 1 ; Chan. Inq. p.m. (Ser. 2), cxcvii, 75.

116 Pat. 12 Chas. II, pt. xviii, no. 16 ; Inst. Bks. (P.R.O.). She presented in 1669.
117 Feet of F. Surr. Mich. 33 Chas. II.
118 Inst. Bks. (P.R.O.). He levied a fine in 1681 to Grace Pierpoint.

merchant of London, *hac vice*. According to Manning and Bray, Parsons devised the rectory to his daughters, Sarah wife of James Dunn, and Anne, who married John Hynde Cotton, afterwards knighted.[119] Sir John Hynde Cotton presented in 1771,[190] and sold the advowson to Sir Charles Talbot in 1786,[191] and Lady Talbot, the widow of Sir Charles, presented in 1800 and 1802. In 1813 Mr. Henry Burmester presented his son, having bought the next presentation from Sir George Talbot.[192] It passed with the manor till 1899, when Mr. H. H. Gordon Clark of Mickleham Hall bought the advowson from Mr. Praed.

CHARITIES Smith's Charity is distributed as in other Surrey parishes. In 1586

Richard Woodstock left 5*s.* annually charged on land in Mickleham common fields for the repair of the church. It appears that the fields were by the river. After the parish was brought into the Dorking Union by the Poor Law of 1834 the old poorhouse at Bytom Hill became useless, and proposals were made for converting it into an almshouse. The matter was delayed till the old building fell down, and it was not till 1851 that the almshouses were actually opened, built chiefly by the generosity of Sir George Talbot, and endowed by Miss Talbot. They were burnt down in 1864, and were rebuilt by Mr. H. P. Grissell of Norbury, whose family further endowed them. They accommodate eight persons.

NEWDIGATE

Newdegate (xiii cent.), Newedegate and Neudegate (xv cent.), Nudgate (xvi cent.).

Newdigate is a village nearly 6 miles south-east of Dorking, 2½ miles from Holmwood Station, on the London, Brighton, and South Coast Railway. The parish is on the borders of Sussex, and is bounded on the north by Leigh, on the east by Charlwood, on the south by Rusper in Sussex, on the west by Capel. An outlying part of Charlwood is in the southern part of it, surrounded by Newdigate and Rusper. It measures about 4 miles from north to south and 2 miles from east to west, and contains 4,732 acres. The soil is the Wealden Clay. The parish is still thickly wooded, and is purely agricultural, except for brick and tile works. A branch of the Mole in the parish is called the Rithe. The only commons are some strips of roadside waste. No main road leads through the parish, but there was an old way from Ockley, through Capel, and past Eutons into Newdigate, and by Parkgate towards Reigate. The name Rodgate Field appears upon its course ; and though Parkgate may be named from the park at Ewood, this road marked in old maps as the only one across this line of country, although now in places no more than a bridle-road, suggests an exception to the alleged non-use of the word 'gate' for a road in southern England. Gatwick in Charlwood is on another old way to Reigate and Gatton.

Newdigate is for the most part in the hundred of Copthorne, forming an outlying portion of it. But the hamlet of Parkgate and the part of the parish near it are in Reigate Hundred. The place does not appear at all in Domesday, and the connexion with Copthorne is a probable result of the holding by the Montfort family of Newdigate together with Ashtead Manor, while Parkgate was held with Reigate and Dorking by the Earls of Warenne and Surrey.

In the 16th century Ewood, or Iwood, was the seat of an important iron forge and furnace.[1] Newdigate was among the parishes excepted by name from the Act 1 Elizabeth against cutting of timber, and the works at Ewood were excepted by name from a later

Act on the same matter owing to the good management of the woods.

Ewood Pond, an extensive sheet of water, artificially dammed for the use of these works, long survived the industry. It was drained *circa* 1850–60, but was marked on ordnance maps long after that date.

In the older farms and cottages there is much massive timber-work. The tower of the church (q.v.) is one of the finest examples of oak building in the county. Cudworth Manor House is a moated house apparently of the 16th century, though considerably altered at different times. Newdigate Place, the house of the family of that name, was a large house standing round a courtyard, but was almost entirely demolished near the end of the 18th century. In 1807 the Duke of Norfolk began to build a house at Ewood, but it was never completed, and the part built was pulled down after the duke's death in 1815. Traces of it, however, still remain.

Of modern houses Newdigate Place, close to the site of the old house, is the property of Mrs. Janson ; the Red House of Mr. Leopold Goldberg ; Cudworth Manor of Mr. H. Lee-Steere. Lyne House (see Capel) is on the border of that parish and Newdigate. At Parkgate, a hamlet north-east of the village, there is a Congregational mission room.

The old poor-house was between the village and Parkgate. The whole labouring population were in receipt of out-door relief in the earlier 19th century, and the rates reached 19*s.* in the pound.[2]

MANORS There is no mention in the Domesday Survey of the manor of *NEWDIGATE* ; it probably then formed part of Dorking. In the 12th century the overlordship belonged to the Earls Warenne and Surrey,[3a] whose descendants continued to hold it until the end of the 16th century.[3] In 1347 the male line of the Warennes died out, and Richard, Earl of Arundel, the son of Alice de Warenne, succeeded to the title and estates.[4] In 1415, on the death of his grandson Thomas, the Warenne and Surrey estates were divided between his three sisters,[5] Newdi-

119 Manning and Bray, *Surr.* ii, 659.
190 Inst. Bks. (P.R.O.).
191 Manning and Bray, *Surr.* ii, 659. (The date by a misprint is here given as 1766.) In 1788 a fine occurs between Daniel Vandewall and Sarah his wife and La-

zarus Venables of the rectory of Mickleham.
192 Inst. Bks. (P.R.O.), and private information.
1 *V.C.H. Surr.* ii, 269–70 ; *Surr. Arch. Coll.* xvii, 28.

2 Churchwardens' accounts.
3a Cott. MS. *Nero,* C. iii, fol. 188.
3 Chan. Inq. p.m. 43 Edw. III, no. 19 ; (Ser. 2) clxxix, 76 ; ccxxxiii, 74.
4 Berry, *Gen. Peerage,* 88 ; G.E.C. *Peerage,* Arundel. 5 Ibid.

gate apparently falling to the share of Joan the widow of William Beauchamp, Lord Abergavenny, as in 1576 the manor was held of her descendant, Henry Nevill, then Lord Abergavenny.[6] The early history of the tenants of Newdigate in subfee is difficult to trace. In 1292 John de Montfort was granted free warren in his demesne lands in Newdigate.[7] He was succeeded by his son John, who was slain in battle at Bannockburn in 1314[8]; he left no children, and was succeeded by his brother Peter, who is said to have become a knight on inheriting. He married Margaret the daughter of Lord Furnival. By her he had one son Guy, who died in his father's lifetime.[9] Guy had married Margaret Beauchamp,[10] and on his death Peter settled the reversion of his estates on her father, Thomas Beauchamp, Earl of Warwick.[11] Peter died in 1367[12] and the earl succeeded, holding of the Earl of Arundel. In 1369 he enfeoffed John de Bokyngham, Bishop of Lincoln, and several others, of the manor of Newdigate,[13] probably in order to settle it upon his son Thomas, who inherited at his death in 1369.[14] At this point Dugdale states that Baldwin de Freville, son of Elizabeth one of the sisters and heirs of Peter de Montfort, claimed and recovered the manor of Newdigate with that of Ashtead, and that from him it passed to the family of Aston[15] (vide Ashtead). Aubrey also says in his book on Surrey that the manor of Newdigate was left by the Baldwin de Freville, who died in 1400, to his son Baldwin, who died a minor, leaving three sisters co-heirs, of whom Joyce the wife of Roger Aston inherited this manor.[16] There is, however, no mention of property in Newdigate in any of the subsequent inquisitions on the Frevilles and Astons, but this might arise from the fact that the manor was small and appurtenant to Ashtead. That they actually did hold Newdigate is proved by the settlement of one third of the manors of Ashtead and Newdigate made in 1419 by Hugh de Willoughby and his wife Margaret, one of the sisters of Baldwin de Freville, upon themselves and their heirs male. Ultimately the whole of Ashtead went to the Aston family, who inherited through Joyce another sister of Baldwin de Freville.[17] In 1543, when Sir Edward Aston conveyed Ashtead to the king, he also conveyed rents and appurtenances in Newdigate.[18] Tradition exists that these same lands were granted by Henry VIII to Trinity College, Cambridge, and were identical with the manor of Marshlands, which the college subsequently held.[19] Unfortunately no grant to the college exists,

TRINITY COLLEGE, CAMBRIDGE. *Argent a cheveron between three roses gules and a chief gules with a leopard between two bibles or therein.*

but the fact that part of that estate held by the family of Newdigate, which came to be called the manor of Newdigate, was held of the manor of Marsh-lands,[20] appears to corroborate the presumption that Marshlands was the original manor of Newdigate. The manor remained in the possession of Trinity College until the middle of the 19th century, when it was sold to Mr. Henry Fowler Broadwood, whose father and grandfather had held it on lease,[21] and whose grandson is the present owner.

At Trinity College there are several surveys of the manor of Marshlands, and these show its gradual decay and deterioration. In 1564 their estate at Newdigate was divided amongst various tenants who paid quit-rents, heriots, and owed suit of court. In 1702 the manor-house, then in good repair, was let to Dr. Akehurst, and sublet to Joseph Peter, and the estate included three other farms—Naylors, Horseland, and Bearland. By 1756, however, the manor and farms, of which there were then only two besides the manor farm, were falling into ruin. Naylors seems to be now incorporated with Horseland or Horseyland. The soil had apparently never been fertile, but incompetence and neglect, and the increasing poverty of the tenant, had hastened the general deterioration. Reference is made to quit-rents worth about 30s., which had been collected by Mr. Capon, a recent tenant, but it was no longer precisely known who had paid them. A court had been called within the last twenty years, but no one had attended it. Cattle had been brought to the pound, but the tenant had refused to admit them; the pound was now ruinous and part of it had been carried away. It was then suggested to unite the manor farm and one of the others, which appears to have been done. The estate was much improved during the tenancy of the Broadwoods, who gave great care and attention to the timber.

The second reputed manor of NEWDIGATE was not called a manor until the 16th century. It appears to have originated in lands which were held there at a very early date by the family of Newdigate, whose name is derived from the place. Mr. Budgen showed various documents to Manning,[22] which prove that they were holding property in Newdigate from the 13th century, and besides these there is a conveyance in 1234–5 of half a carucate of land by Roger de London to Richard de Newdigate,[23] while further lands there were granted to William de Newdigate and his brother Richard in 1335–6.[24] The Newdigates evidently continued to acquire various tenements which they held of different overlords, and in time their estate came to be called a manor. The inquisition taken in 1592

NEWDIGATE of New-digate. *Gules three lions' legs razed argent.*

[6] Chan. Inq. p.m. (Ser. 2), clxxix, 76; clxxxiii, 74.
[7] Cal. of Chart. R. 1257–1300, p. 428; Chart. R. 21 Edw. I, 86, m. 3.
[8] Surr. Arch. Coll. xix, 29; Banks, Dormant and Extinct Peerage, i, 376.
[9] Ibid.   [10] Ibid.
[11] Add. Chart. 20422.
[12] Not in 1357 as in Banks, op. cit. He went to law in 1364. See under Ashtead.
[13] Close, 43 Edw. III, m. 8 d.

[14] Chan. Inq. p.m. 43 Edw. III, no. 19; Close, 46 Edw. III, m. 15 (bis).
[15] Dugdale, Baronage, ii, 105.
[16] Aubrey, Hist. and Antiq. of Surr. iv, 262.
[17] Feet of F. Div. Co. Trin. 13 Hen. VI, no. 63.
[18] Aug. Off. Deeds of Purch. and Exch. c. 49; Feet of F. Surr. Mich. 35 Hen. VIII, no. 19.
[19] Gent. Mag. Aug. 1811, p. 100. Letter to Trin. Coll. Cambridge from Mr.

Broadwood, 1876 (Docs. re Marshlands at Cambridge). See deed of Mr. Budgen's quoted by Manning and Bray, op. cit. 171.
[20] Chan. Inq. p.m. (Ser. 2), clxxix, 76, ccxxxiii, 74; Docs. re Marshlands in New-digate at Trin. Coll. Cambridge.
[21] Docs. at Trin. Coll. Cambridge.
[22] Manning and Bray, op. cit. ii, 173.
[23] Feet of F. Surr. Mich. 19 Hen. III.
[24] Add. Chart. 17303. See also article on the Newdigate family, Surr. Arch. Coll. vi, 227.

on Walter de Newdigate helps to prove this supposition by giving an account of his lands in Newdigate and of whom they were held, the principal overlord being Lord Abergavenny.[25]

The first authentic mention of the property as a manor is in a deed dated 1569, which appears to be a settlement of the manor by Thomas de Newdigate on his son Walter.[26] At Thomas's death in 1576 he was said to be seised of the site of the manor, and of all those lands that constituted the manor of Newdigate, which he was holding of Henry Nevill, Lord Abergavenny. A water-mill which he left to his wife Agnes, and certain fisheries, were appurtenant to the manor, which passed to his son Walter. He also bequeathed a house called Newdigate Place to his wife.[27] In 1588 Walter subscribed £25 towards the fleet raised against the Armada.[28] His son Thomas, who succeeded him in 1590, had only two daughters, Mary and Ann,[29] who married respectively William Steper and William Smithiman. Thomas bequeathed the manor to his brother Richard's son West, who succeeded him.[30]

In 1636 West Newdigate united with Henry Darrell, who had married Thomas Newdigate's widow Mary,[31] and William and Mary Steper, in a conveyance of the manor to John Budgen.[32] From this date Newdigate was held by the Budgen family[33] until 1810, when John's descendant, Thomas Budgen, sold the manor to Charles, Duke of Norfolk,[34] who in 1815 was succeeded by his cousin, Bernard Howard.[35] The present lord of the manor is the great-grandson of the latter, Henry FitzAlan Howard,[36] Duke of Norfolk. The old manor-house was pulled down by Mr. John Budgen, owner between 1772 and 1805. It stood close to Newdigate Place.

BUDGEN. *Party vert and argent a cheveron ermine and in the chief three crescents counter-coloured.*

The manor and park of *IWOOD* or *EWOOD* in Newdigate belonged to the Earls Warenne and Surrey, and was used by them as a centre for hunting, hawking, and fishing.[37] It constantly appears in the Dorking Court Rolls as 'Dorking Iwode,' contrasted, apparently, with 'Dorking Homewode.'

In 1312 and 1314 commission of oyer and terminer was granted for the prosecution of poachers who had entered the free warren of John de Warenne at Newdigate.[38] This property descended like the manor of Newdigate (q.v.) through the Arundels to William Beauchamp through his wife Joan Arundel and to the Nevills, Lords Abergavenny. In 1476 Edward Nevill,

Lord Abergavenny, died seised of the park of Iwood.[39] His great-grandson Henry conveyed the estate to George and Christopher Darrell,[40] who in June 1554 leased it to John Stapley of Framfield for ninety-nine years at a rent of £66 13s. 4d.[41] A month later Christopher Darrell sold his half of the property to Thomas Collet,[42] and George Darrell sold the remainder to Anthony Pelham.[43] Anthony was succeeded by his son Herbert Pelham,[44] but Collet conveyed his share in 1567 to John Heathe,[45] who in May 1574 conveyed it back to Christopher Darrell and Sir Thomas Browne.[46] In the following December Christopher bought what had been his brother George's share from Herbert Pelham.[47] A few months later a survey was taken of the messuages and buildings, including the ironworks, furnace, forge, and hammer, which were then worked by Robert Reynolds, who was occupying the mansion-house and park, and who also held the brew-house and water-mill for grinding corn. The ironworks were then said to be worth £40 yearly. The owners claimed view of frankpledge there.[48] In 1575 Christopher Darrell, who was indebted to the Crown for £2,000, conveyed three parts of the estate and view of frankpledge, estimated at £800, to the queen.[49] This portion of the manor she granted in 1582, after Christopher's death, to Henry Darrell of Scotney for the sum of £700, at the same time transferring the debt of £2,000 to Edmund Pelham, with power to exact the money from Darrell, though without distraining his lands at Iwood.[50] Apparently Darrell did not pay the £700 to the queen, for in 1594 she granted the same land to Edmund Pelham and James Thetcher on condition of the payment of £200 by certain dates.[51] According to Manning and Bray this latter sum was never paid, and the estate remained in the royal possession[52] until it was granted to Mary Goche and her son Barnaby in 1605.[53] The farm and lands of Iwood were later on divided between John Gratwicke with his wife Mildred and Elizabeth Richards, widow, with John Hetherington.[54] One moiety afterwards descended to Dr. Morton, who was succeeded by his son Richard.[55] At Richard's death the estate was sold to Thomas Grinstead, whose son Joseph Valentine Grinstead sold it to the Duke of Norfolk in 1786.[56] The other moiety became the property of Richard Hurst, and was sold by his son to General Smith. This portion of the estate was also bought by the Duke of Norfolk in 1786,[57] and

DARRELL. *Azure a lion or having a crown gules.*

[25] Chan. Inq. p.m. (Ser. 2), ccxxxiii, 74.
[26] Recov. R. East. 1569, rot. 706.
[27] Chan. Inq. p.m. (Ser. 2), clxxix, 76.
[28] Surr. Arch. Coll. xvi, 249.
[29] Chan. Inq. p.m. (Ser. 2), ccclxxi, 93.
[30] P.C.C. 26 Capel; Chan. Inq. p.m. (Ser. 2), ccclxxxviii, 9. Manning and Bray are of opinion West Newdigate did not hold the manor, but this inquisition states that he did inherit. Also the note of Livery, sued out by Mary Steper, quoted by them, is of money still unpaid.
[31] Manning and Bray, Hist. of Surr. ii, 172.

[32] Feet of F. Div. Co. Trin. 12 Chas. I; Recov. R. Hil. 14 Chas. I, rot. 77.
[33] Com. Pleas D. Enr. East. 3 Geo. I, m. 14.
[34] Feet of F. Surr. Hil. 50 Geo. III.
[35] G.E.C. Peerage, Norfolk.
[36] Ibid.
[37] Symmes, Coll. for Hist. of Newdigate, Add. MS. 6167, fol. 256.
[38] Cal. Pat. 1307–13, p. 531; 1313–17, p. 236.
[39] Chan. Inq. p.m. 16 Edw. IV, 66.
[40] Surr. Arch. Coll. xvii, 28.
[41] Close, 1 & 2 Philip and Mary, pt. iv, no. 21.
[42] Ibid.
[43] Ibid. no. 22.

[44] Close, 17 Eliz. pt. xii.
[45] Ibid. 10 Eliz. pt. xxi, m. 1.
[46] Ibid. 16 Eliz. pt. ix.
[47] Ibid. 17 Eliz. pt. xii.
[48] Exch. Spec. Com. no. 2242.
[49] Feet of F. Surr. Trin. 17 Eliz.
[50] Pat. 24 Eliz. pt. xiii, m. 10.
[51] Ibid. 37 Eliz. pt. vii, m. 14.
[52] Manning and Bray, Hist. of Surr. ii, 174.
[53] Pat. 2 Jas I, pt. x, m. 30.
[54] Exch. Spec. Com. 29 Chas. II, no. 6500.
[55] Manning and Bray, Hist. of Surr. ii, 174.
[56] Ibid.
[57] Ibid.

since then has been united to Newdigate under one lord of the manor.

In 1298–9 Walter de la Poyle died seised of the site of the manor of CUDWORTH or CUDFORD, in Newdigate and Rusper, Sussex, which he held of the Abbot of Chertsey in socage, the house, court, and garden then being worth 7s. The lands were held of various overlords, 50 acres from the abbot, 30 from the Earl Warenne of Surrey, 20 from John de Montfort, &c.[58] His son and heir was John,[59] who presumably inherited the manor, though there is no mention of it amongst the possessions he held in demesne at his death in 1317–18.[60] Some years later licence was granted to Henry de la Poyle to have mass celebrated in the oratory of his manor of Cudworth,[61] and in 1360, at his death, he was holding the manor of the king, the Abbot of Chertsey, the Earls of Arundel and Warwick, &c., for various rents.[62] After this there is no further mention of the estate until 1574, when Thomas Bowett died seised of the manor, which his father Richard had bought, and which was said to be held of Sir Francis Carew.[63] Bowett's brother Nicholas succeeded him, and in 1579 sold the property to John Thorpe.[64] In 1622 the lord of the manor was still a John Thorpe,[65] whether the same or his successor does not appear, and in 1636 the estate was purchased by Mr. Ede.[66] The extant court rolls begin with courts of John Ede in 1763 and 1773. In 1775[67] it was sold to Mr. Lee Steere Steere, who died in 1785. It was left to his wife for her life, and at her death passed into the possession of his grandson Lee Steere Witts, who took the name of Steere ; he died in 1842. His son Mr. Lee Steere Steere succeeded. The grandson of the latter, Henry Lee Steere of Jayes Park, is now lord of the manor. The manor-house is of some age, and is surrounded by a moat. It was long occupied as a farm, but was converted again lately into a gentleman's house.

STEERE of Jayes Park. *Ermine two bars sable with three besants or thereon and a quarter argent with a chief sable and thereon a cross formy between two martlets or.*

There was also a farm or tenement in Newdigate called GREENES, sometimes referred to as a manor, with lands in Newdigate and Capel. In 1449–50 John Grene held land in Newdigate,[68] and the family again appears in 1457 and 1497. Towards the end of the 16th century one half of Greenes was held by Thomas Boorde, who died in January 1601–2.[69] His son Ninian held it till his death in 1606, and left a son and heir Herbert, then about four years old.[70] By 1642 the property was in the possession of

Christopher Wheeler, yeoman, and he bequeathed it in his will of that year, in tail male,[71] to his grandson Robert, who was holding it in 1663.[72] In 1694 the manor of Greenes was conveyed by John Hill of Hurstpoint, gentleman, and Mary his wife, the daughter of Robert Wheeler, to Thomas Patching.[73] Thomas Patching became a bankrupt in 1706, and his property was conveyed to trustees for the benefit of his creditors.[74] In 1714 it was conveyed by them to John Woods, and by him to Ezra Gill, as the manor of Greenes. In 1729 Greenes was settled on the children of a marriage between Ezra Gill and Mary Woods,[75] daughter of John Woods. It descended in the Gill and Frankland family (see Eashing and Temple Elfold in Capel) till 1832, when J. H. Frankland sold it to Mr. James Tschudi Broadwood of Lyne, whose great-grandson is now owner.[76]

In 1291 it was found that the Prior of Merton held a messuage and 60 acres of land in Newdigate, which was of the ancient demesne of the Crown, and Richard de la Sterte held it of him.[77] KINGSLAND, by its name, may answer to this ancient demesne, but subsequent possession by Merton does not appear.[77a] On 14 January 1573–4 Matthew Wrighte of Newdigate, yeoman, conveyed to Nicholas Bryne of Reigate, tanner, his tenement in Newdigate, called Kingsland, in the occupation of William Wood. On 5 October 1584 William Dible of Newdigate, husbandman, gave a lease to William Wood, tanner, of his messuage, barns, &c., and one half of his lands called Kings Lands in Newdigate, ' as it lyeth divided by the king's highway leading between Nudigate and Capell on the south, and one pond and lymepitte on the north,' in the occupation of William Wood.[78] Kingsland so lies on the present road. In 1619 Thomas Constable and Agnes his wife sold it to Sir Thomas Bludder, whose widow and her second husband sold it in 1655 to the former's mother, Mrs. Hester Shaw. By will of 1659 Mrs. Hester Shaw of London left Kingsland in Newdigate, consisting of two messuages, barns, &c., and 50 acres of land, in trust for her daughter Elizabeth, Lady Bludder, then the wife of George Farrington, who by deed of 12 April 1687 made an appointment of the property, charging it with an annuity to her son, and naming trustees, who on 10 June 1696 conveyed it, subject to the said payment, to Thomas Patching, from whom it descended as Greenes above. Thomas Patching became bankrupt in 1706. On 25 August 1714 Kingsland and other property of Thomas Patching was conveyed by trustees for his creditors to Ezra Gill, Preston Patching, and George Arnold. On 26 September 1716 Kingsland was released to the use of Ezra Gill, and descended in his family with his manor of Temple Elfold, adjoining, in Capel (q.v.).[79]

[58] Chan. Inq. 27 Edw. I, no. 44.
[59] Ibid.
[60] Ibid. 11 Edw. II, no. 17. The inquisition says that he had no other land than Guildford and Stoke in his own hands, implying that there were others.
[61] Index Winton Epis. Reg. Egerton MS. 2031–4, iv, 58.
[62] Chan. Inq. p.m. 34 Edw. III (1st nos.), no. 71.
[63] Chan. Inq. p.m. (Ser. 2), cxci, 95.
[64] Feet of F. Surr. Trin. 21 Eliz.
[65] Chan. Inq. p.m. (Ser. 2), cccxcii, 123.

[66] Manning and Bray, Hist. of Surr. ii, 175.
[67] Feet of F. Surr. Trin. 1 Will. and Mary ; Manning and Bray, Hist. of Surr. ii, 175.
[68] Feet of F. Surr. 21 Hen. VI.
[69] Chan. Inq. p.m. (Ser. 2), cclxv, 145 ; Fine R. 44 Eliz. pt. i, no. 33.
[70] Chan. Inq. p.m. (Ser. 2), ccxcii, 159.
[71] Chan. Inq. p.m. 19 Chas. I, pt. xvi, no. 145 ; (Ser. 2) dxxi, 145 ; P.C.C. 88 Rivers.

[72] Recov. R. East. 15 Chas. II, rot. 28.
[73] Feet of F. Surr. Trin. 6 Will. and Mary.
[74] Com. under Great Seal, 3 July 1706.
[75] See Feet of F. Surr. Mich. 1 Geo. I.
[76] Deeds in private hands.
[77] Chan. Inq. p.m. 19 Edw. I, no. 75.
[77a] Unless this is the manor of Wykelond : see under Charlwood.
[78] Deeds in private hands.
[79] Ibid.

CHURCH The church of *ST. PETER* consists of a chancel 23 ft. 3 in. by 13 ft. 7 in., with a vestry (and organ-chamber) to the north of it, nave 33 ft. by 17 ft. 6 in., north aisle 8 ft. 6 in. wide and south aisle 7 ft. 2 in., south porch, and a west tower of wood. All the measurements are internal.

The nave and chancel are of 13th-century origin. The south aisle, despite the massiveness of its arcade, made to carry the early thick wall above, appears to be an addition of the latter half of the 14th century. When the west tower was added is not evident; but its inner timbers are old, although the outer boarding and the windows, &c., are modern. The church was repaired in 1877, when the north aisle and vestry were built.

The east window of the chancel is a modern one of three lancets, but has an old round-headed rear arch and quoin stones; the north-east and south-east windows are single lancets, apparently original, but restored; below the latter is a plain pointed piscina with a modern basin.

The second south window has modern tracery of two lancets with a circular piercing over, but its head and jambs are old. The priest's doorway west of this is old, and has a pointed head of a single chamfered order; its western jamb inside is partly cut away for a squint from the south aisle. A modern arch opens to the organ-chamber on the north; and the chancel arch is also modern. The roof of the chancel is a modern one with plain panelling below.

The south arcade of the nave has two bays with a large circular column and chamfered responds, the moulded base of the column is modern, and its capital (an octagonal one) is of late 14th-century character like those of the responds; the arches are two-centred and of two orders, the outer small and hollow-chamfered, the inner large and plain. The wall east of the east respond is carried by a low arch, in order to allow for the squint to the chancel. The north arcade is a modern copy of the other, but has a small pointed arch east of the east respond. The north aisle is lighted by two three-light north windows and a two-light window at the west, all with modern tracery.

The south aisle (the walls of which are comparatively thin) has an east window of two trefoiled ogee-headed lights; the sill and mullion are modern, but the rest appears to be of the 14th century, as does also the piscina in the south wall of the aisle, which has a trefoiled ogee head and a quatrefoil basin.

The two south windows are modern, that east of the doorway has three lights, and the other two are both under square heads. The south doorway of two orders has simple continuous mouldings and a two-centred arch; it is of the date of the south wall. The west window of the aisle is also old, of two cinquefoiled lights under a two-centred segmental head.

The original west wall of the nave has been almost all removed for the tower, and what is left at the angles slopes back above to the side walls. The four legs of the tower inclose a space about 11 ft. square, and are tied together by cross braces in a most picturesque way. About 5 ft. outside them on the north, west, and south are the smaller timbers of the ground story with upright studs boarded horizontally. On the second stage these are roofed over and covered with oak shingles; on the north and south are plain rectangular windows, and on the west a doorway. The main posts run up to form an upper stage for the bells, which is boarded, and lighted by plain square windows, and capped by an octagonal wood spire. The south porch is a modern one of wood. In the north-east window of the north aisle is a little 15th-century glass, including the arms of Newdigate. The walling of the older portions of the church is of Bargate stone with sandstone quoins, and the timbers of the nave roof are old, covered with stone slates. The aisles have modern lean-to roofs. All the furniture is modern, including the octagonal stone font. Under the tower is an old wooden chest, cut from a single log; it is quite plain and has three locks.

The only old monuments are a small brass inscription in the chancel to Joan wife of George Steere, a former rector, died 1634; a small lead plate on the west respond of the south arcade to Margaret wife of Henry Darrell of Scotney, died 1616, probably a coffin plate; and one or two 18th-century mural monuments.

There are six bells, all by Thomas Mears, 1803.

The communion plate comprises two cups, two patens, and a flagon of 1891 now in use, and—disused—a cup and paten of 1699, a metal paten of 1886, and a metal flagon.

The registers date from 1559, baptisms; 1560, burials; 1565, marriages. They contain some notes, and the churchwardens' books have interesting matter in them.

The rectory was rebuilt north of the old site in 1880.

ADVOWSON In the 12th century Hameline, the natural son of Geoffrey of Anjou, and Earl of Surrey in right of his wife Isabel de Warenne, granted the church of Newdigate to the Prior and monks of St. Mary Overy, Southwark,[90] and the right of presentation remained with them throughout the Middle Ages.[91] Licence to appropriate was granted to the prior by Edward II, but a vicarage does not seem to have been ordained there.[92] Newdigate rectory was included amongst the temporalities of the monastery in the estimate made under Henry VIII, and was then said to be worth £8 18s. 4d.[93] At the dissolution of Southwark in 1539,[94] the advowson passed into the king's possession, and the benefice has remained in the royal gift up to the present day.[95]

There was also a chapel of St. Margaret in Newdigate, referred to in Newdigate wills of 1482, 1516, and 1521. It is described in 1516 as in the churchyard of Newdigate. Salmon says that one of the Newdigates pulled it down.

CHARITIES Smith's Charity is distributed as in other Surrey parishes.

The village club and reading-room was built by the widow of the late Mr. W. Farnell Watson of Henfold, Capel, in 1901, in memory of her husband, whose estate extended into Newdigate.

The Rev. George Steere, rector, gave in his lifetime a school-house to Newdigate, and by his will,

90 Cott. MS. *Nero* C. iii, fol. 188; G.E.C. *Peerage*, Surr.; Symmes, Coll. for Hist. of Surrey, B.M. Add. MS. 6167, fol. 257.

91 *Index Winton Epis. Reg.* Egerton MSS. 2031-4, iv, 51, 101, 117, 168.
92 *Abbrev. Rot. Orig.* (Rec. Com.), 200.

93 *Valor Eccl.* (Rec. Com.), ii, 62.
94 Dugdale, *Mon.* vi, 169.
95 Inst. Bks. P.R.O.

November 1661, he confirmed the possession of the school to trustees for the parish, and left £6 13s. 4d. a year charged on land called Clarke's and Squire's Piece, for teaching four children. Mr. George Booth, who had acquired the land, left £100 by will, 31 December 1681, to teach three more children. His executors obtained a decree in Chancery, February 1683, enabling them on the payment of £200 to free the land in Newdigate from the charge, and to acquire an estate called Scallow, in Worth, Sussex, which was to be held in trust for the purposes of the school. The master was elected by the parishioners.[66] In 1838 the school had become ruinous, and Mr. J. T. Broadwood of Lyne rebuilt it and endowed it with £200 more. In 1872 the present school building was erected.

The Rev. George Steere, founder of the school, was entered at Trinity College, Cambridge, in 1599, and appointed rector by King James in 1610. He copied out the earlier registers into the present book. In 1614 he repaired and ceiled the chancel at his own cost, and in 1627 contributed to two new windows. He held the living through the Civil War, and was nominated a member of the Dorking Presbyterian Classis in 1648.[67] He was buried 13 January 1662.[68]

He further, by his will, left an exhibition of £10 a year for a student at Trinity College, Cambridge, to be chosen by the incumbents of Newdigate, Ockley, Dorking, and Rusper from Newdigate, or, in default of a fit candidate, from a circle of 15 miles round Newdigate Church. The payment was charged upon an estate called Blackbrooks in Dorking, and Manning and Bray state that 'it continues to be paid when there is a claimant to it.' The late Rev. L. S. Kennedy, rector of Newdigate, made special inquiries after it, but in vain ; neither the Charity Commissioners nor Trinity College have any record or knowledge of it.

Modern charitable effort is exemplified by the establishment in Newdigate of a farm colony in connexion with the Church Army.

WALTON-ON-THE-HILL

Waltone (xi cent.) ; Wanton (xiii cent.), Waleton and Walleton (xiii and subsequent cents.).

Walton, called Walton-on-the-Hill to distinguish it from Walton-on-Thames, is a village 5 miles north-west of Reigate, 4½ miles south of Epsom, and a parish lying entirely upon the high ground on the top of the chalk hills. It measures over 3 miles from north to south, and 1 mile from east to west, being, roughly, a parallelogram. It contains 2,606 acres. The subsoil is chalk, but in the greater part of the parish the chalk is covered by brick earth, clay, and gravel.

The parish is agricultural, and like the neighbouring hill parishes, formerly fed large numbers of sheep. Walton Heath is a large expanse of open land, 613 ft. above the sea at one point, much overgrown by gorse, and is continuous with Banstead Heath ; over it extend some training gallops. The situation is a very fine one, with bracing air and extensive views, and has been utilized for a golf club and links, which have more than a local celebrity. In the northern part of the parish Walton Downs are open land in continuation of Epsom Downs, and a small part of Epsom Racecourse is in Walton parish.

The road from Dorking to Croydon crosses the parish.

The village lies compactly round the church, at a height of 580 ft. above the sea.

In accordance with the practice in some other hill parishes, as Banstead (q.v.), land in the weald was attached to the manors in Walton. It is still so connected, and lies in Horley and Charlwood. No mill is mentioned in Domesday, but if there was one it was in the weald. There is no stream capable of turning the smallest mill in Walton parish ; the water is wholly derived from wells and ponds. The name Mere Pond, on the boundary of Walton and Banstead, may be noticed.

This poor water supply, except at great expense and trouble of sinking deep wells, interfered no more with early settlement in the neighbourhood than it did in Banstead and Headley. A few neolithic flakes and one knife have been found in the parish ;[1] and there are considerable Roman remains. In 1772 Mr. Barnes contributed to the Society of Antiquaries[2] a notice of discoveries of Roman remains on Walton Heath, about a mile west of the road from Reigate to London, and half a mile east of the pool called Pintmere Pond. They included a small brass figure of Aesculapius, the memory of which is preserved in Walton as 'a golden image,' and tiles, a coin of Vespasian, and fragments of glass and metal. Further digging on the spot took place in 1808,[3] resulting in the discovery of part of the flue of a hypocaust and more tiles ; and again, it is said, in 1864. The remains were surrounded by a rectangular inclosure, of which two sides are fairly perfect. At a point further south on the heath Roman coins have been found.

There are three more rectangular inclosures, which may fairly be mentioned here, as being connected in all probability with the settlement of which this villa was part, though they are actually over the border of Banstead parish. Two of these are south of the two windmills south of Tadworth. They are well-marked, nearly square inclosures, with a mound and ditch and gateways to the east or south-east. They are east of the road from Betchworth to Banstead. The third is west of the road, and very close to Walton village ; but though on land known commonly as Walton Heath, is actually on the Banstead side of the boundary. It is larger than the others, less well-preserved, and with a gateway to the north-west. Roman tiles may be found in or near all three. These inclosures have been commonly referred to as the 'Roman

---

[66] Local records and Bishop Willis's Visitation Answers, 1725.

[67] Shaw, Church under the Commonwealth, ii, 433.

[68] Registers.

[1] Neolithic Man in North-East Surrey, 132.

[2] Arch. ix, 108.

[3] Manning and Bray, Surr. ii, 645.

Camps[1] on Walton Heath, but it is not obvious that they were camps. Fortified inclosures against banditti or wild beasts, or both, might be nearer the truth. They are worth comparison with the inclosures round Ashtead Church and near Pachevesham, Letherhead. Within the boundary of Walton parish there is a well, now dry and mostly filled up, with no modern house near it, which may belong to the same period of settlement.

No Inclosure Act or Award seems to be known, but undoubtedly some inclosure of common fields and waste has taken place. The names in the register and churchwardens' accounts seem to point to holdings of *shots* in common fields in the 17th and 18th centuries, and the tithe map of 1839 shows common fields, called North and West Common Fields, with small holdings in them. The road to the common fields was mended by the parish in 1835.

Frith Farm, a 17th-century house with a park, is the seat of Mr. W. Stebbing. Street Farm is another 17th-century house. Of other large properties may be mentioned Walton Lodge (Mr. H. J. Broadbent), Hurst (Mr. H. C. Lyall), Feeble Combe (Mr. E. J. Coles), and Lovelands (Hon. H. S. Littleton).

There was a village shepherd still in 1792.[5]

There is a Congregational mission room in the village.

The schools (National) were built in 1878, and enlarged in 1898.

The manor of *WALTON-ON-THE-MANOR HILL* (Waleton, Wauton, xi–xvi cent.) was held in 1086 by Richard de Tonbridge,[6] and descended from him to the Earls of Gloucester and Hertford. At the death of the last Gilbert de Clare, his estates were divided among his sisters and co-heiresses. Walton-on-the-Hill passed to Hugh le Despenser, who had married Eleanor the

CLARE. *Or three cheverons gules.*

DESPENSER. *Quarterly argent and gules, the gules fretty or, with a bend sable over all.*

earl's sister. Hugh, their son, died seised of Walton in 1349.[7] His descendant, Thomas le Despenser, created Earl of Gloucester by Richard II, was murdered and attainted in 1400, when, his land being confiscated to the Crown, this manor seems to have passed to the Earls of Stafford, the descendants of Margaret,

sister of Gilbert de Clare,[8] who were still the overlords in 1403.[9] By 1437, however, the manor was said to be held of the Crown.

The manor was held under Richard in 1086 by a certain John,[10] who seems to have been the ancestor or predecessor of the Dammartin family. (See Buckland in Reigate Hundred.)u John de Walton, who married Alice daughter of Odo de Dammartin,[11] is said to have founded the church of Walton,[12] and in 1268 free warren in Betchworth, Buckland, and Walton was granted to John de Walton, probably his son, and his heirs.[14] Ten years later he was called upon to show by what right he claimed this privilege.[15] In 1293–4 John de Walton senior conveyed the manor to John de Lovetot senior, who died seised of it shortly after, and was succeeded by his son and heir, also John.[16]

The next tenant under the De Clares was John Drokensford, Bishop of Bath and Wells. He had a grant of free warren here in 1307.[17] He was tenant of the Gilbert de Clare who fell at Bannockburn in 1314,[18] and the inquisition taken on his lands shows him dying in possession in 1330.[19]

What next occurred in the descent is extremely difficult to trace. John de Braose, a minor, and the ward of John de Warenne, Earl of Surrey,[20] was heir to the manor of Walton at the death of the latter in 1347.[21] This John was half-witted,[22] and after the Earl's death Mary, Countess Marshal, the widow of John's great-grandfather Sir William de Braose, who had since married Thomas of Brotherton, Duke of Norfolk,[23] occupied the manor for four years, and later it was held by Sir Thomas de Braose, apparently, however, as guardian, and only for the life of his witless cousin John.[24] After this the Braoses disappear, and the next lord of the manor was Richard, Earl of Arundel, nephew and heir to John de Warenne, Earl of Surrey, whose only sister Alice married Edmund, Earl of Arundel.[25] Richard's son John succeeded him, and settled one-third of the manors of Buckland, West Betchworth, and Walton, upon his wife Eleanor. She married, secondly, Sir Reginald Cobham, who died in 1403 seised of these estates in his wife's right. Eleanor survived him two years.[26] Her second son William appears to have had the remaining two-thirds of Walton Manor, with the reversion of his mother's dower ; for in 1401, he having lately died, all his share in Walton was granted to his next brother Richard and his wife Alice for life, which grant was confirmed and renewed at several subsequent dates.[27] Alice outlived her husband over twelve years, and held the manor until her death in 1437, when it reverted to the king.[28]

In the spring of that year Walton was granted in lease by Henry VI to Ralph Rocheford to hold for seven years, but in the following November the grant was changed to one for life, with remainder, on the

[4] Overseers' Accts.

[5] *V.C.H. Surr.* i, 316.

[7] *Vide* Chipstead. Chan. Inq. p.m. 21 Edw. III (1st nos.), no. 58 ; 23 Edw. III (1st nos.), no. 169.

[8] *Vide* Chipstead.

[9] Chan. Inq. p.m. 4 Hen. IV, no. 34.

[10] *V.C.H. Surr.* i, 316.

[11] He held also Woldingham in Tandridge Hundred.

[12] See Buckland.

[13] Inscription in Walton Church.

[14] *Cal. of Chart. R.* 1257–1300, p. 88.

[15] *Plac. de Quo Warr.* (Rec. Com.), 737, 747.

[16] Feet of F. Surr. Hil. 22 Edw. I ; Chan. Inq. p.m. 23 Edw. I, no. 33.

[17] Chart. R. 35 Edw. I, no. 66.

[18] Chan. Inq. p.m. 8 Edw. II, no. 68.

[19] Ibid. 3 Edw. III, no. 41.

[20] Chan. Inq. p.m. 21 Edw. III (1st nos.), no. 58 ; 23 Edw. III (1st nos.), no. 169.

[21] Ibid. 21 Edw. III (1st nos.), no. 58.

[22] Manning and Bray, *Hist. of Surr.* ii,

[23] Index Winton Epis. Reg. Egerton MS. 2031–4, iii, fol. 37.

[24] G.E.C. *Peerage,* Norfolk ; Manning and Bray, *Hist. of Surr.* ii, 77.

[25] Chan. Inq. p.m. 31 Edw. III (1st nos.), no. 49.

[26] Ibid. 21 Edw. III (1st nos.), no. 58 ; Berry, *Gen. Peerage,* 88.

[27] Nichols, *Topog. at Gen.* ii, 318 ; Chan. Inq. p.m. 4 Hen. IV, no. 34.

[28] Berry, *Gen. Peerage,* 88 ; *Cal. Pat.* 1399–1401, p. 347 ; 1422–9, p. 205.

[29] Chan. Inq. p.m. 15 Hen. VI, no. 27.

same terms, to John and Rose de Merston, who had consented 'to marry according to the king's intent.'[29] In the following year Rocheford transferred all his right to Rose and John.[30] By 1464 the manor was again disposed of to Richard Harleston and Thomas Bradbrigge, yeomen, to hold for life.[31] In the next year, however, it was granted to Elizabeth Woodville 'in part support of her expenses of her chamber'; and in 1470, during the brief return to the throne of Henry VI, the sum of £45 yearly was granted to the Keeper of the Great Wardrobe from the custody of the manors of Banstead, Walton, &c.[32] In 1471 the king gave the manor to George, Duke of Clarence,[33] and it reverted to the Crown on his attainder in 1478.

In the reign of Henry VIII it became part of the possessions of Catherine of Aragon, given to her apparently in 1509.[34] In 1513 the queen granted a lease of the manor to Richard Carew of Beddington at a rent of £48 yearly.[35] About twenty years later she granted it at the same rent to his son Nicholas, Master of the Horse to Henry VIII, for a lease of ninety-nine years, which was afterwards changed to a grant of the reversion to hold after Catherine's death at a rent of £40.[36] This rent seems to have formed part of the jointure of Henry's queen, Jane Seymour, for Walton is included in a valuation of the lands that had contributed to her dowry.[37] In 1539 Sir Nicholas Carew was attainted and beheaded, and the king annexed the manor to the honour of Hampton Court, which he had lately created,[38] and it was consigned to the charge, first of Sir Ralph Sadler one of the king's secretaries,[39] and in 1544 of Thomas Cawarden of the Privy Council.[40]

CAREW. Or three lions passant sable.

Queen Mary in 1553 restored his father's estates to Sir Francis Carew,[41] and he was holding the property under Elizabeth.[42] He never married, and his sisters Mary, Elizabeth, and Anne were his heirs. Elizabeth had no children, but the sons of Mary the wife of Sir Arthur Darcy and Anne the wife of Sir Nicholas Throgmorton inherited.[43] In 1615 Sir Francis Carew alias Darcy conveyed all his right in Walton to Sir Nicholas Carew alias Throgmorton of Beddington,[44] and from this date until the end of the 18th century the manor was held by the direct descendants of the latter.[45] In 1762 Sir Nicholas Hacket Carew died, leaving one only daughter Katherine. By his will he

THROGMORTON. Gules a chevron argent with three gimel bars thereon.

left the estate to William Pellat in trust for her, with remainder to the sons of his cousin John Fountain, Dean of York, and after them to Richard the son of his cousin Richard Gee of Orpington.[46] In 1769 Katherine Carew died unmarried, and in 1780 the only son of the Dean of York also died without issue. Richard Gee then inherited the manor and took the name of Carew.[47] Mr. Richard Gee Carew dying unmarried in 1816 left all his estates to the widow of his brother. She died in 1828 and left them to her cousin Admiral Sir Benjamin Hallowell. He died in 1834, and was succeeded by his son Captain Charles Hallowell, who assumed the name of Carew by royal licence. In 1865-6 the Carew estates were broken up. Mr. Henry Padwick was lord of the manor in 1891, but sold it shortly afterwards to Mr. H. Cosmo Bonsor, the present owner.

BONSOR. Six pieces azure and argent with three lions' heads rased in the azure and a chief indented erminois with three roses gules therein.

The manor-house was occupied in the 17th century by other members of the Carew family who were not the lords. A somewhat distant relative, George Carew, Baron Carew of Clopton and Earl of Totnes, was living here. His arms are on the house. In 1643 Mr. Nicholas Carew of the manor-house died in Walton. Mr. James Ede of the manor-house died in 1825.[49] In 1865 Mr. Cumberland bought the house, and in 1890 it was acquired by Mr. W. Rolle-Malcolm, J.P., the present owner.

The manor-house is a most interesting building, containing amid much modern work a stone-built hall of c. 1340, 38 ft. by 21 ft., with a contemporary chapel at its south-east corner. At the west or lower end of the hall are the three original doorways once leading to the buttery, pantry, and kitchen passage, and at the south-east is an original doorway to the chapel, while at the east end of the north wall is a fifth doorway which opened to a newel stair. This stair led to another doorway exactly over that last named, opening either to a gallery across the east end of the hall, over the dais, or perhaps merely to a landing in the north-east angle. A fine 14th-century doorway in the east wall of the hall opened on to this gallery or landing, and doubtless formed the main approach to the great chamber, which must have been at the north-east of the hall, on the first floor. A passage must also have run outside the east wall of the hall at the first floor level to a door in the north-west corner of the chapel, leading to the west gallery in which the household would sit. The chapel retains considerable parts of an east window, a north window, and two on the south, all original work, and has had an external door at the south-west. In the

[29] Cal. Pat. 1436-41, pp. 121, 138, 160, 347.
[30] Ibid. p. 238.
[31] Ibid. 1461-7, p. 328.
[32] Pat. 5 Edw. IV, pt. i, m. 18; Cal. Pat. 1467-77, p. 237.
[33] Cal. Pat. 1467-77, p. 241.
[34] Pat. 24 Hen. VIII, pt. ii, m. 12.
[35] Add. Chart. 22629.
[36] Pat. 24 Hen. VIII, pt. ii, m. 12; L. and P. Hen. VIII, v, 1207 (13).
[37] L. and P. Hen. VIII, xii (2), 975.
[38] Coll. Topog. et Gen. iv, 361; L. and P. Hen. VIII, xv, 498 (36).
[39] L. and P. Hen. VIII, xvi, 714; xvii, 695.
[40] Ibid. xix, 643.
[41] Pat. 1 Mary, pt. viii.
[42] Add. Chart. 23703, 22903, 23232, 23234.
[43] Berry, Surr. Gen. 56; Feet of F. Surr. Trin. 7 Jas. I.
[44] Add. Chart. 23720; Feet of F. Surr. Trin. 13 Jas. I.
[45] Add. Chart. 23721, 22906, 22907, 23718, 23719, 23725; Recov. R. Trin. 35 Chas. II, rot. 183; Hil. 6 Anne, rot. 106; Feet of F. Surr. Hil. 15 Geo. II.
[46] P.C.C. 370 St. Eloy.
[47] Manning and Bray, Hist. of Surr. ii, 527; Brayley, Hist. of Surr. iv, 288.
[48] Parish Reg.

latter part of the 16th century the hall was cut in two by a large chimney stack with two fireplaces in it, and at the same time or a little later a three-light window was inserted at the south-east; over it are the arms of George Carew, Earl of Totnes, dated 1636. A projection to the west of this, apparently of late 16th-century date, may represent an earlier (though not original) chimney breast. At the south-west of the hall is a large modern bay.

Close to the house on the north-east is a circular mound with a ditch. The possibility of its being a garden mount must not be overlooked, but it is not unlikely that it is of much earlier date, and marks the site of the dwelling-place of the Domesday lord of the manor.[49]

The first reference to a *PARK* at Walton-on-the Hill occurs in 1436, when it is mentioned with the manor amongst the possessions held at her death by Alice widow of Richard, Earl of Arundel.[49a] Free warren however was granted to the lords of the manor as early as 1268,[60] and in 1358 a rabbit warren, worth 6s. 8d., was part of the estate. The park and warren were granted to Rose and John de Merston in 1437,[61]

PLAN OF MANOR HOUSE, WALTON-ON-THE-HILL

and again are mentioned in the conveyances from Queen Catherine to Richard and Nicholas Carew.[62]

In 1294–5 the pleas and perquisites of the court of Walton-on-the-Hill were worth 6s. 8d.[58] and in 1358, 8s., while in an account rendered to Sir Francis Carew by his bailiff in 1587 the profit of 'one court holden for the same manor the 19th daye of Oct. in the 27th yeare of the queene's majestic that nowe is,' amount to £4 4s. 8d.[54] In 1770 a general court baron was held there by William Pellat, executor to Sir Nicholas Hacket Carew, in which certain waste land was leased with the consent of the tenant to Sir Richard Barnes, 'for the purpose of searching for the remains of some works of antiquity, of which discovery hath lately been made.'[55]

A windmill is mentioned in the 13th century,[56] and again in the 17th century,[57] and in 1358 a dovecot is amongst the appurtenances of the manor.[58]

The church of *ST. PETER* consists **CHURCH** of a chancel 33 ft. 6 in. by 18 ft. 2 in., nave 31 ft. 6 in. by 22 ft. 6 in., small north vestry, north aisle of two bays, 13 ft. 8 in. wide, and a west tower 12 ft. square, all measurements being internal. The chancel dates probably from the 15th century, but has been much modernized; the nave was rebuilt and the greater part of the tower added in 1817; the tower fell into decay rapidly and was partly pulled down and rebuilt in 1895. The north aisle is an addition of 1870. The east window of the chancel is modern of four traceried lights with a transom. Of the three south windows the first two are of two cinquefoiled lights with tracery under a pointed head, while the west window in this wall is square-headed with modern tracery of two lights, below it is a blocked low side window. The three north windows match with those opposite; west of them is a small blocked low side window, and below the third window is a door to the north vestry. In the south wall is a range of three plain arched sedilia of 15th-century date, with an ogee-headed piscina to the east, which has a single drain and a stone shelf. The chancel arch has a round shaft in each jamb with octagonal moulded capitals and bases of 15th-century character; the arch is two-centred with a wide hollow between its two hollow-chamfered orders. The buttresses of the chancel have been refaced in red brick, but one on the south side has been destroyed; the walling is of flint with blocks of Reigate stone. Below the north-east window of the chancel is an external recess containing an old coffin lid; a modern stone bears an inscription (now almost obliterated) to Johannes de Walton . . . 1268. The nave has three south windows, one of two tall cinquefoiled lights between two plain single lights. The modern arcade between the nave and aisle is of two bays, in 15th-century style, and the aisle is lighted by two two-light north windows and a western one of three lights.

The lowest stage of the tower is vaulted in brick with stone ribs, and is apparently work of 1817. There is a west doorway which forms the principal entrance to the church. The tower is in three stages and has a low pyramidal roof. The roofs of the nave chancel and aisle are modern, and all the window tracery has been renewed at various dates.

The most interesting thing in the church is the 12th-century lead font, cylindrical in shape, with its sides divided into eight and three-quarter panels, each

49 See *Surr. Arch. Coll.* xxiii.
49a Chan. Inq. p.m. 15 Hen. VI, no. 27.
50 *Cal. of Chart. R.* 1257–1300, p. 88; *Plac. de Quo Warr.* (Rec. Com.), 737, 747; Chan. Inq. p.m. 31 Edw. III (1st nos.), no. 1.
51 *Cal. Pat.* 1436–41, pp. 138, 347.
52 Add. Chart. 22629; Pat. 24 Hen. VIII, pt. ii, m. 12; L. *and* P. *Hen. VIII,* v, 1207 (13).
53 Chan. Inq. p.m. 23 Edw. I, no. 33; Chan. Inq. p.m. 31 Edw. III (1st nos.), no. 49.
54 Add. Chart. 22903.
55 Ibid. 24648.
56 Chan. Inq. p.m. 23 Edw. I, 33.
57 Add. Chart. 23716.
58 Chan. Inq. p.m. 31 Edw. III (1st nos.), no. 49.

WALTON-ON-THE-HILL CHURCH: THE LEADEN FONT

under a round arch on twisted shafts with volute capitals ; the spandrels are filled with foliage, and there are bands of foliage around the top and bottom edges. In each bay is the seated figure of a saint, each fourth figure repeating. Three out of each four have books, but there is no distinctive feature to show whom they are intended to represent. In two places on the top are the attachments for the staples of the cover. The font stands on a modern stone base at the south-west of the nave. Opposite to it is a desk made up of 17th and 18th-century carved woodwork, on which is a large chained Bible ; the chain is an old one brought from Salisbury Cathedral, but the Bible dates only from 1795, having been given to the church in 1803.

All other fittings of the church are modern, except that in the south-east window of the nave are some fragments of old glass, including a seated figure of St. Augustine in late 15th-century white and gold glass. The rest is chiefly 17th- and 18th-century work, and is said to have been dug up when the excavations were made for the new north aisle. There is a shield: Argent a saltire sable, on which is an escutcheon Argent a cheveron between three voided lozenges sable ; a crescent for difference. A second has Party cheveronwise azure and gules three covered salts argent, the arms of the Salters' Company ; and a third, Azure a cheveron ermine between three scallops argent impaling a doubtful shield. There are small panels with the Creation, the Last Judgement, the Works of Mercy, and part of the story of the Prodigal Son. In the south-west window of the nave is a shield bearing the arms of Dacres: Argent a cheveron sable between three roundels gules, each charged with a scallop argent.

There are three bells, the treble by William Eldridge 1681, the second blank, and the tenor by Robert Mott 1591.

The communion plate includes a cup of 1568, a standing paten of 1905, two plated salvers, and a copper-plated flagon.

The first book of the registers contains baptisms from 1581 (a parchment copy of 1618), but the first four pages and some of the entries for 1585 have been cut out ; they end in 1702. The marriages and burials begin in 1631 and run to 1701.

The second book contains mixed entries from 1700 to 1754, and thence baptisms and burials to 1802 ; there is a hiatus from 1743–46, when no entries were recorded ; the third book has marriages from 1754 to 1812, and the fourth baptisms and burials from 1804 to 1812.

ADVOWSON Walton Church is said to have been founded by John de Walton in the first half of the 13th century,[58] and the right of presentation has always belonged to the lord of the manor until the latter part of the 19th century.[59] In 1880 the advowson came into the possession of the Rev. H. J. Greenhill, who is the patron at the present day.

In the Taxation of Pope Nicholas Walton Church was rated at £13 6s. 8d.[61] In 1428, when the church paid a subsidy of £1 6s. 8d. to the king, the yearly value was the same.[62] Under Henry VIII the living was estimated to be worth £12 6s. 3½d., including a house with 30 acres of land.[63]

CHARITIES Smith's Charity is distributed as in other Surrey parishes.

[59] Inscription in Walton-on-the-Hill Church, but the inscription is of no authority.
[60] Chan. Inq. p.m. 23 Edw. I, no. 23 ;

15 Hen. VI, no. 27 ; Index Winton Epis. Reg. Egerton MS. 2031-4, &c.; Inst. Bks. P.R.O. ; Clergy Lists, &c.

[61] Pope Nich. Tax. (Rec. Com.), 208.
[62] Feud. Aids, v, 114.
[63] Valor Eccl. (Rec. Com.), ii, 37.

common
Tithingm
ance of t
Court th
their tow
find that
they beli

THE HUNDRED OF EFFINGHAM

CONTAINING THE PARISHES OF

EFFINGHAM   GREAT BOOKHAM   LITTLE BOOKHAM

The Hundred of Effingham is usually classed with Copthorne and described as a half-hundred: i.e. perhaps 50 hides, for in the time of Edward the Confessor the total assessment worked out at 47 hides. In 1086, in addition to the three parishes of Effingham, Great Bookham, and Little Bookham, which compose it at the present day, it included the two unidenti_fied places of 'Driteham' and 'Pechingeorde.'[1] It was a royal hundred, and in a document of the reign of Edward I is stated to have been farmed formerly for half a mark per annum, but then for 10s. per annum.[2] The same document states that all the free tenants of the Abbot of Chertsey used to come twice a year to the sheriff's tourn at 'Lethe Croyce,' but had for five years past withdrawn their suit, and that the abbot had royal liberties in Great Bookham, including gallows, assize of bread and ale, and other things pertaining to the view of frank-pledge. A Subsidy Roll dated 1428 includes Fetcham in this hundred, probably by a scribal error, as no other instance of it occurs.[3] In 1628 the borough of Kingston received a grant of jurisdiction within the hundred of Copthorne and Effingham in compensation for

INDEX MAP
TO THE
HUNDRED
OF
EFFINGHAM.

their loss of the privilege of court leet in Richmond and Petersham,[4] and this grant was confirmed by Charles I to Kingston in 1638, and held good until within recent years. In a survey taken in 1651 Effingham Hundred is described as late parcel of the possessions of Charles I, and was found to include Little Bookham, Effingham, and 'the township or tithing of Churchlond,' the last undoubtedly representing Great Bookham, which in the early Subsidy Rolls is more usually entered as 'the vill of the Abbot of Chertsey.' The survey also states that the court leet for the two hundreds of Effingham and Copthorne was kept at Leithepitt at the usual times, 'and the lord thereof may call and keep a court leet within any of ye towneshipps or tithings which payeth any

[1] V.C.H. Surr. i, 309a, 309b, 318b, 320a, 321a, 327b. The neighbourhood of the latter can be surmised from Pickett's Hole, the hollow in the chalk in the place where the old road comes up from Wotton.
[2] Assize R. 897.
[3] Subsidy R. bdle. 184, no. 75.
[4] Cal. S.P. Dom. 1628-9, p. 399.

common fines. At which said Court at Michaelmas all Constables and Tithingmen for ye yeare past are discharged and others sworn for ye performance of their severall offices for ye ensuing year.' At the said Michaelmas Court the constables or tithingmen were to deliver to the lord all dues from their townships or tithings. The jurors further declared that they could not find that there was ever held any three weeks' court for these hundreds, though they believed that the lord might hold one if he pleased [1]

EFFINGHAM

Fingeham, Epingeham (xi cent.).

Effingham is 3½ miles south-south-west from Letherhead, 8 miles north-east from Guildford, upon the road between the two places, the village being fairly compactly placed about the road and a cross road which runs from over the downs northward. The parish is bounded on the north by East Horsley and Cobham, on the east by Little Bookham, on the south by Wotton and Abinger, on the west by East Horsley. It measures quite 4 miles from north to south and one from east to west. It contains 3,183 acres.

The southern limit of the parish is on the summit of the chalk range, which is here extensively covered with beds of clay and gravel. It reaches over the northern face of the chalk down, across the Thanet and Woolwich Beds, down on to the London Clay. The church and village were on the beds between the chalk and the clay, but the houses have spread upwards on to the former. The Guildford and Epsom road, and the Guildford and Letherhead Railway traverse the parish.

Neolithic implements have been found. On the chalk were several dene holes, and a round barrow is recorded near the road from Guildford,[1] but these seem to have disappeared except for depressions which may mark filled-in dene holes. Manning and Bray record the discovery of a small camp on the downs near Mare House, to the left of the road from Guildford to Dorking, that is on White Downs. The ground has since been cultivated. Lord William Howard, who had property here from the spoils of Chertsey Abbey, resided near at hand in Bookham, and was created Lord Howard of Effingham. The most interesting side of the place, however, historically, is in connexion with the social history of England. Little more than one hundred years ago Effingham was still an open parish almost entirely, such as used to be called 'champion.' Its geographical position is fairly typical of the whole group along the northern side of the chalk range : an elongated parish, with its open fields and waste on the chalk, its settlement, church, and closes on the comparatively dry soil just below the chalk, its waste again on the clay beyond.

There was an Inclosure Act in 1800,[2] and another in 1802,[3] inclosing the wastes and common fields of Byfleet Manor in Effingham parish, and wastes of Effingham East Court respectively. There was a further inclosure in 1814,[4] and another in 1815.[5]

In Lee Wood, towards the northern end of the parish, on the clay, are the remains of a wet moat, inclosing a square of 60 or 70 yds.

Effingham Hill, built by General de Lancey on the estate of Tib Farm, is the residence of Mr. Caesar Czarnikow. It took the place of the manor-house of Effingham East Court. Effingham Lodge is the residence of Mr. G. Pauling ; Dunley Hill of Mr. C. J. Allen. Opposite the Plough Inn is an old house called Widdington ; it has a large projecting brick porch of about 1600 to 1620. The pilasters of brick on each side of the doorway resemble those on Slyfield House. There is a Wesleyan chapel, built in 1854. A national school was built in 1857.

The manor of *EFFINGHAM EAST MANORS COURT* was held at the time of the Domesday Survey, of Richard de Tonbridge, Lord of Clare,[6] by Oswold, who also held the manor of La Leigh,[7] but it appears to have been acquired very shortly after by the Dammartin family. In 1166 William de Dammartin was holding 11½ knights' fees in Surrey of the honour of Clare,[8] and in 1230–1 the manor of Effingham was confirmed to Margery widow of Odo de Dammartin, the founder and benefactor of Sandridge Priory and son of William de Dammartin,[9] as dower, by Alice her daughter and Roger de Clare husband of Alice.[10] In 1231 Margery was summoned to answer a charge of waste and alienation in this estate, preferred by Alice and Roger, when Margery declared that the heronry had been destroyed by her first husband Odo, and that the alienation had been made by her second husband Geoffrey de Say, from whom she was divorced, but that no proof was forthcoming that waste had been made by her during her widowhood, and consequently no case could be proved against her.[11] Alice appears to have been holding this manor for a knight's fee shortly after, and in 1248 conveyed it to Thomas de Warblington.[12] Shortly afterwards Richard de Clare, the overlord, took the manor into his own hands,[13] and between 1250 and 1260 regranted it to Sir Nicholas de Leukenore,[14] keeper of the wardrobe to Henry III,[15] to hold with the manor of Chipstead by the service of two knights' fees. In 1279 William

[1] Aug. Off. Parl. Surv. Surr. (2).
[1] Manning and Bray, *Hist. and Antiq. of Surr.* ii, 708.
[2] 39–40 Geo. III, cap. 87.
[3] 42 Geo. III, cap. 76.
[4] *Tithe Commutation Rct.* (Bd. of Agric.).
[5] Sir John Brunner's Return, 1903.

[6] *V.C.H. Surr.* i, 320b.
[7] Ibid.
[8] *Red Bk. of Exch.* (Rolls Ser.), 405.
[9] Dugdale, *Mon.* vi, 604.
[10] Feet of F. Div. Co. 15 & 16 Hen. III, no. 30. Alice was formerly married to John de Wauton.

[11] Maitland, *Bracton's Note Bk.* 574.
[12] Feet of F. Surr. 32 Hen. III, no. 50.
[13] *Plac. de Quo Warr.* (Rec. Com.), 743.
[14] Add. Chart. 20039.
[15] *Cal. Close, 1272–9,* p. 90.

de Hevre, apparently the successor of Leukenore, was holding Effingham,[16a] but not long after the De Clares seem to have resumed their possession, for in 1295 a capital messuage and tenements in Effingham were held by Gilbert de Clare, Earl of Gloucester, as member of Blechingley,[16] and in 1306, during the minority of his son and heir Gilbert, the manor was held by John Pichard[17] (who in 1278 had been acting as attorney for the late earl[18]) by service of one fee, of the honour of Blechingley, then in the king's hands. The said Gilbert in 1314 died seised of lands at Effingham held as member of Blechingley, including a messuage, 112 acres of arable land, of which 50 were worth 25s. per annum or 6d. per acre, and 62 were worth 20s. 8d., or 4d. per acre ; 4 acres of meadow worth 10s. or 2s. 6d. per acre ; 30 acres of boscage worth 5s., or 2d. per acre ; 74s. 4d. rent of assize ; customary work worth 32s. 9d. per annum ; pleas and perquisites of the court worth 3s.[19]

In 1317 Thomas de Geddyng was holding at Effingham a third of a curtilage called 'Bellosehagh' containing ⅓ rood of land held of the inheritance of the Earl of Gloucester by service of 4d., and owing suit every three weeks at the East Court, 'which is in the king's hands by the death of the said Earl.' He also held of the said court 7 acres of land called 'Golereslond' by service of 5s. 5½d., owing suit as above.[20] In 1347 Hugh de Audley, Earl of Gloucester,

CLARE. Or three chevrons gules.   AUDLEY. Gules fretty or.

died seised of tenements in Effingham held respectively for a quarter and a tenth of a knight's fee, which he had by his wife Margaret daughter and co-heir of Gilbert de Clare. In 1372 Ralph de Stafford died seised of this tenement, having married Margaret daughter of the said Hugh.[21]

Their son Hugh died in 1386,[22] and on the death of his son Edmund, Earl of Stafford, the manor was taken into the king's hands by reason of the minority of Humphrey son of Edmund, afterwards Duke of Buckingham.[23] The latter settled this manor after the death of his eldest son Humphrey, Earl of Stafford, at St. Albans, 1455, on his third son John, Earl of Wiltshire, and Constance his wife.[24] Their son Edward

dying without issue in 1498–9,[25] the manor reverted to Edward, Duke of Buckingham,[26] who was attainted for high treason and beheaded in 1521.[27] In 1528 the manor was granted to John Bourchier, Lord Berners,[28] on whose death in 1533 it was conveyed by his executor Francis Hastings, and Joan his wife, to Henry, Marquis of Exeter.[29] The latter in 1535 settled it on himself and Gertrude his wife and their heirs,[30] but on his attainder in 1538 it was forfeited to the Crown, and in 1547 was granted by Edward VI to Sir Anthony Browne,[31] one of the knights of the Bath at the Coronation, created in 1554 Viscount Montagu.[32]

STAFFORD. Or a chevron gules.

Anthony, Viscount Montagu, his grandson, conveyed the manor in 1618 to Henry Weston and Thomas Grey.[33] In 1625 Thomas Grey and William Grey conveyed the manor to William Wall and John Fielder,[34] apparently trustees, for William Grey died seised of the manor and capital messuage of Effingham East Court in 1645, leaving a son and heir Thomas, aged eighteen.[35]

In 1660 Thomas Grey sold to Matthew Tayler, grocer of London, for the sum of £3,000, the manor of Effingham East Court, a tenement and farm called Nice Court in Effingham, and the rectory and parsonage of Effingham.[36] Matthew died in 1678, having bequeathed this manor, with the farm of Nice Court and the rectory, to his grandson Thomas White, younger son of Thomas White and of Margaret daughter of Matthew.[37] Thomas White suffered a recovery in 1692,[38] and manorial courts were held in his name in 1696, 1697, and 1698.[39] In 1732 William White son of Thomas[40] suffered a recovery of the manor,[41] and by his will dated 1758 devised it to trustees to sell for the payment of debts and legacies.[42] In 1790 William White son of William sold to William Bryant,[43] who resold in 1793 to Gerard Dutton Fleetwood of Letherhead. The latter died in 1796, and was succeeded by John Fuller,[44] who with Dinah his wife made a conveyance of the manor in 1799 to William Lyson.[45] The manor was subsequently purchased by General Oliver de Lancey, Barrack-Master General, whose estates were, however, seized for debts to the Crown in 1806, and vested in trustees for sale.[46] This manor was purchased by Miles Stringer, who died in 1839, but it was acquired by the Maxse family before 1874, when Lady Caroline Maxse, daughter of the fifth Earl of Berkeley and widow of James Maxse, was lady of the manor.[47] Her son Admiral Maxse held the manor in 1891,[48] and died in 1900. Shortly

16a Cal. Close, 1272–9, pp. 90, 739.
16 Inq. p.m. 24 Edw. I, no. 107. He was also receiving 10 marks rent paid by Roger de Horne from a manor in Effingham.
17 Subs. R. 34 Edw. I, bdle. 242, no. 44.
18 Cal. Close, 1272–9, p. 489.
19 Exch. Inq. 8 Edw. II, no. 68.
20 Chan. Inq. p.m. Edw. II, file 54, no. 6.
21 Ibid. 21 Edw. III, no. 57.
22 G.E.C. Complete Peerage, vii, 210.
23 Mins. Accts. bdle. 1123, no. 11.
24 Chan. Inq. p.m. 38 & 39 Hen. VI, no. 50.
25 G.E.C. Complete Peerage, viii, 165.

26 Chan. Inq. p.m. 13 Edw. IV, no. 13.
27 Exch. Inq. p.m. 12 & 13 Hen. VIII, file 1074, no. 5.
28 L. and P. Hen. VIII, iv (2), 3991 (15) ; Pat. 19 Hen. VIII, pt. i, m. 11.
29 Feet of F. Surr. Trin. 35 Hen. VIII.
30 Pat. 27 Hen. VIII, pt. i, m. 27.
31 Pat. 1 Edw. VI, pt. vii, m. 13.
32 G.E.C. Complete Peerage, v, 359.
33 Feet of F. Surr. East. 15 Jas. I.
34 Feet of F. Div. Co. Hil. 1 Chas. I.
35 Chan. Inq. p.m. (Ser. 2), Misc. dxxxvii, 13.
36 Close, 12 Chas. II, pt. x, no. 34 ; Feet of F. Surr. Hil. 12 & 13 Chas. II.

37 P.C.C. Will Reeve 58.
38 Recov. R. 4 Will. and Mary, rot. 190.
39 Add. MSS. 23751.
40 Manning and Bray, Hist. of Surr. ii, 712.
41 Recov. R. 5 Geo. II, rot. 213.
42 Manning and Bray, Hist. of Surr. ii, 712.
43 Close, 30 Geo. IV, pt. i, no. 10.
44 Burke, Landed Gentry, 1886, p. 693.
45 Feet of F. Mich. 39 Geo. III.
46 Pub. Gen. Acts, 47 Geo. III, sess. 2, cap. 69.
47 Surr. Dir. 1874.
48 Ibid. 1891.

afterwards it was acquired by Mr. Caesar Czarnikow, the present lord of the manor.[49]

In the 13th century there appears to have existed some doubt as to the legality of the franchises of the de Clares in Effingham, and when William de Hevre in 1279 claimed view of frankpledge, assize of bread and ale, and other liberties in this manor, it was declared on evidence that when the Dammartins and Thomas de Warblington held the manor they were geldable and came twice a year to the sheriff's tourn, to which they paid 8s. yearly, but that Richard de Clare, father of Gilbert the present earl, after he had taken the manor unto his own hands, had unlawfully appropriated the said rent. Moreover, it is stated that William I had given this manor to Odo Dammartin, his knight and member of his household, who with his descendants had always had seisin of these liberties.[50] In view of the Domesday entry the alleged grant to Odo by the Conqueror can hardly be correct.

EFFINGHAM PLACE COURT alias *EFFINGHAM.* About 1316 Thomas de Geddyng died seised of lands in Effingham, including 29 acres of land at La Place, held of the manor of La Leigh by the service of 2s., 4 acres of land held of the Lord de Berners (Lord of West Horsley Manor in Woking Hundred) by the service of 12d., also a hall, chamber, granary, fishery, and dovehouse at La Place. His heir was Walter de Geddyng, son of his brother Walter.[51] In 1320 Walter de Geddyng conveyed his lands in Effingham under the name of a messuage, 80 acres of land, 60 acres of wood, and 6s. rent to Master John Walewayn to hold for life, with remainder to William son of Humphrey de Bohun and his issue.[52] William de Bohun had a grant of free warren in his demesne lands of Effingham in 1328.

In 1347 Humphrey son of Humphrey de Bohun granted the reversion of certain lands to Sir John de Pulteney,[53] a distinguished citizen of London and five times lord mayor, and apparently a similar transaction took place in regard to some of William's lands also, for in 1362 Sir William de Pulteney conveyed the manor of Effingham (said to be formerly of John his father) to trustees.[54] In 1363 these trustees settled it on Nicholas de Lovayne and Margaret his wife, widow of Sir John de Pulteney,[55] for their lives, with remainder to William de Pulteney, and failing issue to him, to Guy de Lovayne and his heirs.[56] William died without issue in 1367. Whether Lovayne succeeded is not clear, for in 1478 Lawrence Downe died seised of the manor, said to be held of John de Berners as of his manor of West Horsley, leaving his grandson John son of Thomas Downe his heir.[57] In 1491 John Downe and Joan his wife sold the manor to John Leigh,[58] who in 1544 conveyed it to the Crown.[59]

In 1550 Edward VI granted the manor to Lord

William Howard,[60] who died seised of it in 1573,[61] having in 1554 received the title of Baron Howard of Effingham as a reward for his services in suppressing Wyatt's rebellion.[62] His son and heir, Charles Howard, distinguished as commander-in-chief against the Spanish Armada and created in 1588 Earl of Nottingham,[63] suffered a recovery of this manor in 1622,[64] and on his death in 1624 it passed to his eldest surviving son Charles, second Earl of Nottingham.[65] The latter was succeeded by his half-brother Charles, third Earl of Nottingham, who in 1647 conveyed the manor to Thomas Turgis.[66] The latter, by will dated 1703 and proved in 1705, gave the manor to William, third son of Thomas Urry of Gatcombe in the Isle of Wight,[67] subject to such interest as his wife Mary had in some part of it.[68] William suffered a recovery in 1704,[69] but leaving no children the manor passed to Thomas Urry, who died unmarried

HOWARD, Earl of Nottingham, bore the arms of HOWARD with the difference of a molet.

in 1776, having bequeathed his estates to his niece Elizabeth, wife of Windsor Heneage, with instructions that the court for his manor of Effingham should be kept every three years.[70] Elizabeth had by her husband, Windsor Heneage of Haynton, two daughters, Elizabeth and Mary, who became co-heirs. Elizabeth married Basil Fitzherbert Squire, of Swynnerton, Staffordshire, and Mary married William Fitzherbert Brockholes of Claughton Hall, Lancashire.[71] Thomas Fitzherbert Brockholes, son of Mary and William, suffered a recovery of this manor in 1832,[72] but in the same year the estate, comprising upwards of 800 acres, was disposed of in lots, the manor and manor-house (included in the homestead of the Upper Farm), with the woods and other lands to the extent of 358 acres, being purchased by Sir Thomas Hussey Apreece, bart.,[73] who died in 1833, leaving an only son, Sir Thomas G. Apreece, who died unmarried in 1842.[74] The manor is now held by Colonel E. Latimer Parratt.

The manor of *EFFINGHAM-LA-LEIGH* was alleged to be Chertsey property as early as 675, when Frithwald, Subregulus of Surrey, and Bishop Erkenwald were said to have granted to the abbey twenty dwellings at Bookham-cum-Effingham.[75] But

APREECE, baronet. Sable three bloody spearheads argent.

[49] *Surr. Dir.* 1907.
[50] *Plac. de Quo Warr.* (Rec. Com.), 739, 743.
[51] Exch. Inq. 10 Edw. II, no. 42.
[52] Feet of F. Surr. 14 Edw. II, no. 21.
[53] *Cal. Pat.* 1317–21, p. 255.
[54] Close, 36 Edw. III, m. 20; Feet of F. Div. Co. 36 Edw. III, no. 100.
[55] *Cal. Close,* 1349–54, p. 249.
[56] Feet of F. Div. Co. 37 Edw. III, no. 628.
[57] Chan. Inq. p.m. 18 Edw. IV, no. 14.
[58] Feet of F. Surr. Trin. 6 Hen. VII.

[59] Feet of F. Div. Co. East. 36 Hen. VIII; Pat. 35 Hen. VIII, pt. x, m. 33.
[60] Pat. 4 Edw. VI, pt. ix, m. 48; Lansd. MSS. no. 49.
[61] Chan. Inq. p.m. (Ser. 2), cxlv, 172.
[62] *Dict. Nat. Biog.*
[63] Ibid.
[64] Recov. R. Trin. 20 Jas. I, rot. 15.
[65] Chan. Inq. p.m. (Ser. 2), cccclxii, 69.
[66] Feet of F. Surr. East. 23 Chas. I.
[67] H. B. Wilson, *Hist. of Merchant Taylors' School,* 1172; Berry, *Hants Gen.* 357.

[68] Manning and Bray, *Hist. of Surr.* ii, 709. Mary quitclaimed all right in the manor to William Urry after the death of Thomas. Close, 3 Anne, pt. ii, no. 20.
[69] Recov. R. Mich. 3 Anne, rot. 49.
[70] P.C.C. Will Collier, 289.
[71] Manning and Bray, *Hist. of Surr.* i, 709; H. B. Wilson, loc. cit.
[72] Recov. R. Mich. 3 Will. IV, rot. 368.
[73] Brayley, *Hist. of Surr.* iv, 486.
[74] G.E.C. *Baronetage,* v, 233.
[75] Birch, *Cart. Sax.* i, 64.

the grant is very suspicious (see Chertsey). In 1086 it was held of the Abbot of Chertsey by Oswold, who had it in the time of Edward the Confessor;[76] but Chertsey does not appear to have exerted any overlordship after this date, and it is possible that Oswold had merely placed himself under the protection of Abbot Wulfwold, who was his brother.[77] Oswold or one of his successors apparently sub-infeudated, for La Leigh appears subsequently as held of the manor of Wotton, which was among Oswold's possessions in 1086.[78] Early in the 12th century Oswold de la Leigh, the immediate tenant, granted to Hugh, Abbot of Chertsey, a tithe of his demesne lands in Effingham.[79] In the reign of John, Maud de Camoys had custody of the heir of Gilbert de la Leigh and of his tenement in Effingham-La-Leigh and Polesden.[80]

In 1285 Nicholas le Gras had a grant of free warren in the manor of 'La Leye,'[81] which he held at fee-farm of William de la Leigh, who in that year recovered it from him, Nicholas having for two years failed to pay his farm.[82] John de la Leigh, son of William, was acting in the service of Humphrey de Bohun in 1314,[83] and in 1320 released all his right in the manor of La Leigh to Master John Walewayn,[84] apparently with remainder as in Effingham Place Court, to William de Bohun, who in 1328 had a grant of free warren in all the demesne lands of Effingham and La Leigh.[85] La Leigh then descended with Effingham Place Court to Lawrence Downe, who died seised of it in 1478.[86] From this date there is no trace of La Leigh as a separate manor, and it apparently became amalgamated with Effingham Place Court.

The moated inclosure in Lee Wood (already mentioned) is probably the site of the old manor-house of La Leigh.

Aubrey, writing in 1718, mentions a small fair at Effingham on the feast of St. Lawrence (10 August),[87] the patron saint of the church, which was transferred before the end of the 15th century to 15 July,[88] and has since been abandoned.

The church of ST. LAWRENCE has a chancel 26 ft. 7 in. by 16 ft. 1 in., CHURCH south organ chamber and vestry, nave 43 ft. by 21 ft. 6 in., south transept 27 ft. 6 in. deep by 18 ft. 10 in. wide, south aisle 8 ft. 6 in., south porch and a west tower 8 ft. 9 in. by 8 ft. 1 in.; these dimensions are within the walls.

Owing to the great amount of modern reconstruction which the building has undergone the history of the fabric is for the greater part lost, but enough remains to prove that it dates at least from the 13th century, the large south transept having the remains of windows of that date; no old features are left in the nave, but the proportion of two squares is suggestive of a 12th-century date. The chancel was repaired about 1388, but has an early 14th-century window at the north-west, and the masonry of the walls may be considerably earlier. No other details are left to give a clue to the history of the building,

but the tower appears to have been built (or rebuilt) in 1757, on the evidence of a stone recording that date; it was again reconstructed in 1888; a brass inscription on the wall states that it was erected at that time. The nave was wholly modernized in 1888, the south aisle added, and the chancel partly rebuilt; the vestry, east of the transept, was added in 1899.

The east window of the chancel is a modern one of three lights under a traceried pointed head; but the north-east and south-east windows clearly belong to the work of 1388, which was done by order of William of Wykeham, and in their simple and rather heavy detail have much of the spirit of his work at Winchester Cathedral. Each is of two cinquefoiled pointed lights with a quatrefoiled spandrel under a two-centred segmental arch; the inner jambs and mullions are moulded, and the outer are double-chamfered with a moulded label. The north-west window is an earlier one of two trefoiled pointed lights with a plain pierced spandrel on a two-centred arch; the jambs are of two chamfers, and the label is a filleted round. A modern archway with moulded and shafted jambs and a four-centred arch opens into the organ-chamber at the south-west, and the chancel arch is also modern with similar jambs and a two-centred arch.

The nave has three modern north windows each of two lights with foiled spandrels in pointed heads. The south arcade, also modern, is of four bays with round pillars of grey stone having white stone moulded bases and capitals; the arches are pointed and of two chamfered orders.

The organ-chamber has a doorway in its west wall to the transept, and another in its south wall to the vestry; this has an outer doorway on the east and a three-light south window.

The transept has a 15th-century window at the south-east, now looking into the vestry, of two cinquefoiled lights under a square head with a label. In the south wall is a small square piscina with a projecting corbel basin, 11 in. by 10 in., probably contemporary with the transept. Of the two lancets which pierce this wall the eastern has modern jambs inside and old jamb stones outside, and the western old inner jambs and modern outer; only one light existed here formerly, and the two seem to have been made from it. In the west wall are two lancets, of which the north one has old inner jambs and modern outer, and the other is wholly modern. The walls of the transept are unusually thick, the south wall being 3 ft. 6 in.; the others have been thinned above a line about 6 ft. above the floor, but they were originally over 3 ft. thick. The south-west angle seems to have fallen into disrepair in the 17th or 18th century, as it has been repaired with red brick, and the square buttresses supporting the angles are modern. The aisle has two lancets in the south wall and a west window of two lights and tracery, all modern. The south-west doorway is also modern. East of it is an

[76] V.C.H. Surr. i, 309b.
[77] Ibid. 283.
[78] See Cal. Inq. Edw. II, 192; Chan. Inq. p.m. 18 Edw. IV, no. 14.
[79] Misc. Bks. (Exch. K.R.), xxv, 35.
[80] Abbrev. Plac. (Rec. Com.), 72.
[81] Cal. Rot. Chart. (Rec. Com.), 114.
[82] De Banco R. 60, m. 127.
[83] Cal. Pat. 1313-17, p. 113.

[84] Cal. Close, 1318-23, p. 342. William's widow Maud married Walter de Geddyng (See Assize R. no. 888). He had a grant of free warren in the demesne lands of Effingham in 1305 (Chart. R. 33 Edw. I, m. 90) and died in 1311 (Chan. Inq. p.m. file 26, no. 29). Maud, who was remarried to Roger de Stretton, was still holding the manor in dower in 1320.

Walter de Geddyng, her grandson, and at that date her heir, quitclaimed all right in the reversion to John de Walewayn. Feet of F. Surr. 14 Edw. II, no. 18.
[85] Chart. R. 2 Edw. III, no. 60.
[86] Chan. Inq. p.m. 18 Edw. IV, no. 14.
[87] Aubrey, Collections for Surr. ii, 282.
[88] Manning and Bray, Hist. of Surr. ii, 709.

old square recess with chamfered edges in which is set a modern sill with a basin and drain.

A modern arch opens into the tower from the nave. The west doorway is a modern one with a pointed arch in a square head; the window over is of three lights with cusped tracery of 15th-century style in a two-centred head, all modern except for some old stones in the jambs; over this window is a clock. The bell-chamber is lighted by three lancets in each wall except the east, which is unpierced, and the parapet is embattled. The chancel and nave roofs are both gabled and have modern panelled ceilings, the transept has a low gabled ceiling of plaster and appears to be old, but the single tie-beam has been cased; the aisle has a panelled lean-to roof. The south porch is modern, and has pairs of lancet windows on each side and a pointed entrance arch.

The altar table is modern, and a former table (of no great age) serves as a side altar in the transept. There remains an old bench end with a fleur de lis head and part of another, of 15th-century work or perhaps earlier; these have been copied in the modern chancel seats. The font is modern with a bowl of a fine piece of alabaster and a marble stem.

In the nave floor is an early coffin-lid; the inscription around is almost illegible, but is said to read:

+ VATER : DE : GEDDINGCES : GIT : ICI
OXV : A : SA : ALME : FACE : MERCI.

In the tower are placed most of the old monuments; the most interesting perhaps are seven small square tablets to the children of William Walker, formerly vicar; the inscriptions read thus: 'Hic jacent Su^ma W. ob. 1670 aet 8 an—Robt. W. ob. 1686 aet 3 an—Rob. W. ob. 1688 aet 2 hebs.—Gu. Walker huius eccle iam : iam vicario 1693.' They are roughly cut, and are possibly the work of the vicar himself. There are two other small stones, one with initials, apparently, H M or H W dated 1651, and another stone is inscribed: 'Thos. Bonney, vicar—Thos. Killick Geo. Monk Churchwardens 1757' and refers to the rebuilding of the tower. A large broken stone slab with chamfered edges, lying in the churchyard south of the transept, appears to be ancient, but has no inscription.

There are also three small brass inscriptions, the oldest reading: 'Pray for the soull of John Aley which decessid the xxvi day of Apriell the yere of oure Lord MCCCCCVII on whose soull Ihu have mercy Ame.' Another has the inscription: 'Here lyeth buried the body of John Agmondesham late of Rowghbarnes in the County of Surr Esquire, somtymes reader of New Inne and after an aprentice in the lawe who dyed the first day of August Anno dni 1598.' The third is in Roman type as follows: 'John Cooke and Frances his wife was buried ye xxv day of April 1629.'

There are five bells, all by Gillett of Croydon, 1890.

Among the communion plate is a silver cup of 1569, with a cover paten dated 1570; there are also a cup, standing paten, and flagon of 1828.

The registers begin in 1565, the first book containing baptisms, marriages, and burials from that date

to 1725. The first portion is a copy of 1624; the book is of paper. The second book contains baptisms and burials from 1660 to 1812, and marriages from 1660 to 1772; the third has the marriages from 1754 to 1812.

The churchyard is not large, and surrounds the building; to the south are some large chestnut and other trees; an iron railing bounds the ground towards the road on the west side, and has two gates.

The church of Effingham was *ADVOWSON* bestowed on Merton Priory by William de Dammartin,[89] and in 1269 the advowson was granted to the prior by Gilbert de Clare,[90] probably in confirmation of the original grant. In 1291 the church was held by the priory and valued at £14 13s. 4d. with a pension of 26s. 8d.[91] The same valuations were given on an inquiry taken six years later as to whether it would be to the king's loss if the prior and convent were to appropriate the church to their own uses.[92] On a further inquiry, however, in 1299, the church was found to be worth only 20 marks (£13 6s. 8d.), and the prior and convent had licence to appropriate accordingly.[93]

MERTON PRIORY. *Or fretty azure with eagles argent at the crossings of the fret.*

In 1297 the bishop issued an ordinance for the endowment of the vicarage, under which the vicar was to receive for his maintenance all the altarage of the church, and all small tithes and profits pertaining to the altarage, with the tithe of the produce of crofts and gardens dug in the parish by foot and spade; also the tithe of all hay and produce of the lands of William Wrenne in the parish, and 18½ acres of arable land with common pasture pertaining to the church, free and quit of tithe, as the rector of the place used to hold them, with herbage of the cemetery, and also a competent site near the church, to be assigned by the monks of Merton, whereon to build a suitable vicarage within the space of a year.[94]

In 1308 John de Rutherwyk, Abbot of Chertsey, conceded to the Prior of Merton the tithes both great and small from those demesne lands within the limits of the parish church of Effingham, formerly of Philip de la Leigh and Oswold de la Leigh, the prior rendering in return to Chertsey Monastery 50s. per annum,[95] and on the dissolution of Chertsey this payment was included among the possessions of the monastery granted to the new foundation at Bisham.[96] In 1317 the prior mortgaged to Philip de Barthon, Archdeacon of Surrey, the tithes of corn or fruit of the great tithes in Effingham, with the court or manse there, for a term of six years, in consideration of a sum of £26, the prior to be responsible for all extraordinary expenses and for the pension of 50s. to the Abbot of Chertsey; the archdeacon to be responsible for all ordinary payments and for the sustenance of all houses and other buildings.[97]

In 1388 the prior was severely censured for neglect-

89 Cartul. of Merton, Cott. MS. Cleop. C. 7.
90 Feet of F. Surr. Mich. 53 Hen. III, no. 27.
91 *Pope Nich. Tax.* (Rec. Com.), 208b.
92 Inq. a.q.d. 23 Edw. I, xxiii, 12.
93 Inq. p.m. 27 Edw. I, no. 61; Pat. 27 Edw. I, m. 30.
94 Cott. MS. Cleop. C. vii, fol. 210.
95 Misc. Bks. (Exch. K.R.), bk. 25, p.35.
96 L. and P. Hen. VIII, xii (2), 1311 (2).
97 Surr. Arch. Soc. ix, 371.

ing to repair the chancel, which had fallen into such a state of ruin that the parishioners complained that divine service could not be celebrated there.[96]

In 1535 the Prior of Merton granted to John Holgate a lease of the rectory, with all tithes and profits, excepting the presentation of the vicar and mortuaries, to hold from Midsummer 1544 for a term of twenty-one years, at a rental of £12 6s. 8d., but chargeable with a pension of 26s. 8d. to the vicar.[99] In the same year the vicarage was found to be worth with its appurtenances £7 18s. 9d.,[100] while the farm of the rectory was worth £10.[101] After the dissolution of Merton Priory the king retained the patronage of the living.[102] In 1551 the rectory and church were granted by Edward VI to John Poynet, Bishop of Winchester, and his successors,[103] and this grant was confirmed in 1558 by Philip and Mary.[104]

But this grant was apparently afterwards revoked, for a grant of the rectory appears to have been acquired by William Hammond, who in 1574 bequeathed the remainder of it to Rose Cave his step-daughter.[105] Rose married Laurence Stoughton, in conjunction with whom she is said to have conveyed the rectory to Thomas Cornwallis of East Horsley,[106] who in 1588, as farmer of the king's rectory of Effingham, recovered three cartloads of peas, three cartloads of barley, one cartload of oats, &c., to the value of 30s., of the tithes of the rectory,[107] and again in 1592 recovered forty sheaves of peas to the value of 20s. of the tithes of the rectory.[108] In 1626 Lady Catherine Cornwallis died seised of the rectory, from the inheritance of her late husband, the said Thomas, having settled the same in 1625 on her nephew Thomas, Earl of Southampton.[109] The latter, however, in 1629, conveyed the rectory with tithes to Carewe Raleigh,[110] by whom it is said to have been conveyed to William

Grey,[111] who in 1645 died seised of the rectory and tithes together with the manor of Effingham East Court,[112] with which it descended from that date. The patronage of the living was, however, reserved to the Crown,[113] until in 1866 it was acquired by A. Cuthell.[114] Since 1891 it has been in the gift of the Rev. E. F. Bayly, the present incumbent.

In 1607 a fee-farm rent reserved from the rectory, of the annual value of £11, was granted by the king to William Blake and George Tyte, gentlemen.[115] Under the Commonwealth Act for the sale of fee-farm rents, it was sold in 1651 to Walter Kempson and his heirs,[116] but Charles II granted it to Queen Catherine for life.[117] Subsequently, it appears to have been acquired by James, Duke of Chandos, who in 1732, jointly with Cassandra his wife, conveyed to Sir Matthew Deckes, bart., his annual rents from the rectory of Effingham.[118] In 1790 the fee-farm rent of £11 payable from the rectory was in the hands of Lord FitzWilliam and his heirs.[119]

In 1658 it was proposed to unite the parishes and churches of Effingham and East Horsley, when the commissioners appointed to make inquiries reported that the two parishes were distant about a mile, and neither alone sufficient to maintain 'an able and godly preaching minister,' the real yearly values of both being not above £85 a year.[120] The project was however abandoned.

CHARITIES Smith's Charity is distributed as in other Surrey parishes. There were some small tenements near the church used as a poor-house. They were rebuilt in 1774, the proceedings being the cause of a lawsuit which ended in the expense being disallowed.[121] Later, a workhouse for Effingham stood on the southern verge of the parish, on the brow of the downs.

GREAT BOOKHAM

Bocheham (xi cent.) ; Bocham (xiii cent.) ; Bokeham (xvi cent.).

Great Bookham is a village 2 miles south-west of Letherhead. The parish is bounded on the north by Stoke D'Abernon and the River Mole, on the east by Fetcham and Mickleham, on the south by Dorking, on the west by Little Bookham. It measures 5 miles from north to south ; in the southern part it is a mile wide, diminishing to half a mile near the north. It contains 3,281 acres. It extends from the brow of the Chalk, here capped by clay and gravel, across the Thanet and Woolwich beds, on which the church and village lie, over the London Clay, to the alluvium of the Mole. Bookham Common is still an extensive open space in the middle of the parish, and Ranmore Common, on the Chalk Down, is chiefly in Bookham. In this part of the parish are extensive plantations on

the property of the Hon. Henry Cubitt, Lord Lieutenant of Surrey.

The road from Letherhead to Guildford, and the London and South-Western Railway between the same places pass through the parish. Bookham Station was opened in 1885. Roreing House was transferred from Great Bookham to Fetcham in 1882.

Neolithic flints are not very uncommon in the southern part of the parish, and there are cavities in the chalk which may be caused by collapsed dene holes. Roman brass coins, of Gallienus chiefly, but also of some later emperors, are said to have been found in an earthen pot about 1750, at Bagden Farm.[1] Anglo-Saxon interments were found in making the high road from Letherhead to Guildford in 1758. These probably belong to the discoveries recently made in Fetcham (q.v.).

[96] V.C.H. Surr. ii, 101 ; Winton Epis. Reg. Wykeham, ii, fol. 23b.
[99] A. C. Heales, Records of Merton Priory, 339.
[100] Valor Eccl. (Rec. Com.), ii, 29.
[101] Ibid. ii, 48.
[102] Surr. Arch. Coll. ix, 378.
[103] Pat. 5 Edw. VI, pt. vi.
[104] Pat. 5 & 6 Phil. and Mary, pt. ii, m. 6.
[105] P.C.C. Will 19 Pyckering.
[106] Manning and Bray, Hist. of Surr. ii, 713.
[107] Exch. of Pleas 30 & 31 Eliz. Mich. m. 19. [108] Ibid. 34 Eliz. East. m. 25.
[109] Chan. Inq. p.m. (ser. 2), ccccxxii, no. 19.
[110] Feet of F. Surr. Trin. 5 Chas. I.
[111] Manning and Bray, Hist. of Surr. ii, 713.
[112] Chan. Inq. p.m. (Ser. 2) Misc. dxxxvii, 13.
[113] Inst. Bks. P.R.O.
[114] Clergy Lists.
[115] Pat. 5 Jas. I, pt. xix, m. 39.
[116] Close, 1653, pt. x, no. 27.
[117] Pat. 15 Chas. I, pt. xiv, no. 1.
[118] Feet of F. Div. Co. Trin. 6 Geo. II.
[119] Close, 30 Geo. III, pt. i, no. 10.
[120] Surr. Arch. Coll. xvii, 103.
[121] Manning and Bray, op. cit. ii, 718.
[1] Manning and Bray, Hist. of Surr. ii, 688.

The road (called Paternoster Lane in Mickleham) which passes Bagden Farm[2] and leads to a ford in the Mole in Sir Trevor Lawrence's grounds, is the probable line of the great west and east road along the Downs, sometimes now called the Pilgrims' Way.

Bookham Grove, south-west of the church, is the seat of Mr. Sydney C. Bristowe ; Old Dene of Mr. C. E. Cuthell ; Millfield House of Mrs. Hansard ; Merrycourt of Sir Stephen Mackenzie, M.D. Sole Farm, on the west side of the village street, is a picturesque old-fashioned gabled house. Miss Fanny Burney, after her marriage with M. D'Arblay, lived for a short time in a cottage at Bookham.

The kennels of the Surrey Union Foxhounds, of which Mr. F. G. Colman is master, are in Great Bookham.

Extensive open fields existed, and were inclosed by an Act of 1821. The award is dated 19 March 1822.[3]

An infants' school was built in 1830, and was enlarged in 1882. A National school with residence for the master was built in 1856 by Viscountess Downe, the Hon. Lydia Dawnay, and the Hon. P. Dawnay, in memory of William Henry, Viscount Downe.

Ranmore is an ecclesiastical parish, formed in 1860 from the parishes of Great and Little Bookham, Effingham, Dorking, and Mickleham. It lies upon the high ground of the chalk range, but extends into the lower ground towards Dorking and Mickleham. The church, St. Barnabas, is in Great Bookham.

Near the church is a village dispensary and training school for domestic servants. Ranmore Common is a large open space on the brow of the hill.

The schools (National) are private property of the owner of Denbies and were built in 1858, an infants' department being added in 1874.

The earliest alleged mention of MANORS GREAT BOOKHAM is in a charter dated 675, by which Frithwald, Sub-regulus of Surrey, and Bishop Erkenwald granted to Chertsey Abbey twenty dwellings at 'Bocham cum Effingham.'[4] The grant was confirmed by Offa in 787, by Athelstan in 933,[5] by Edgar in 967,[6] and by Edward the Confessor in 1062,[7] and in the Domesday Survey the manor of 'Bocheham'[8] is included in the possessions of the monastery.[9] In 1537 it was surrendered to the Crown by John, Abbot of Chertsey,[9] with the rest of the monastic lands, and in 1550 was regranted to Lord William Howard,[10] son of the Duke of Norfolk, who settled it on his second son, Sir William Howard,[11] in whose line it remained until 1801, when it was sold by Richard Howard, last Earl of Effingham, to James Laurell.[12] In 1811–12 James Laurell and his wife jointly conveyed the manor to John Harrison Loveridge,[13] probably in trust for Holme Sumner, who in the Court Rolls appears as lord of the manor until 1828. Within the next year it was acquired by Louis Bazalgette, who died in 1830. It was evidently bought from his executors[14] by David Barclay, who was lord of the

GREAT BOOKHAM CHURCH FROM THE SOUTH-WEST

2 Terrier of Bookham Glebe, 1638 in registers.

3 Sir John Brunner's Ret., 1903.

4 Kemble, Cod. Dipl. dccccxxxviii ; Birch, Cart. Sax. i, 64,349. But this charter is doubtful. See in Chertsey.

5 Kemble, Cod. Dipl. ccclxiii.

6 Ibid. dxxxii.

7 Ibid. dcccxii.

8 V.C.H. Surr. i, 309a.

9 Feet of F. Div. Co. Trin. 29 Hen. VIII.

10 Pat. 4 Edw. VI, pt. ix.

11 Chan. Inq. p.m. (Ser. 2), cclxxi, no. 154 ; G.E.C. Complete Peerage, iii, 326 n.

12 Feet of F. Surr. Trin. 41 Geo. III.

13 Ibid. Hil. 52 Geo. III.

14 See Eastwick.

manor in 1834. His grandson, Mr. H. Barclay, sold the manor in 1882 to Mr. William Keswick, M.P.,[16] to whom it now belongs.

The monks of Chertsey obtained a grant of a weekly market on Tuesday, and a two-days' fair on the eve and day of Michaelmas.[16] The latter was maintained until 1792, but abandoned very shortly after.[17]

In the survey of Surrey taken in 1549, it is stated that John Gardyner, sen., holds in Great Bookham a curtilage formerly of John Gardyner, on which was built a horse-mill, and a cottage with a curtilage formerly belonging to the schoolhouse.[18]

The reputed manor of *EASTWICK* in Great Bookham appears to have been held by the Dabernon family, certainly as early as the reign of Edward I, and John Dabernon, kt., was holding land in Bookham in 1273.[19]

In 1327 Sir John Dabernon, his son (see Stoke D'Abernon), died seised of 80 acres of land in Eastwick in Bookham, held of the Abbot of Chertsey, leaving his son and heir of the same name of full age,[20] who in 1335 conceded to Robert de Aylynchagh and Walter atte Welle a curtilage called 'Clerke-shagh' and a field called 'La Vynye' at Aylynchagh in Great Bookham,[21] the latter probably representing the messuage and lands called 'Vines' mentioned as forming part of the manor of Eastwick in 1571,[22] and the name of which is preserved to the present day in Phenice Farm.

William Dabernon, son of John, died in 1359, leaving a daughter Elizabeth, wife of William Croy-ser,[23] and afterwards of John de Grey de Ruthyn, in conjunction with whom in 1391 she conveyed the manor of Eastwick to trustees.[24] William Croyser, son of Elizabeth and William,[25] had a daughter Anne,[26] who married first Sir Ingelram Bruyn,[27] and afterwards Sir Henry Norbury, in conjunction with whom in 1436 she conveyed the manor to trustees,[28] who in 1439 re-conveyed the manor to Henry and Anne and their heirs.[29] Sir John Norbury, son of Henry and Anne, had a daughter Anne, married to Sir Richard Haleighwell,[30] by whom she had a daughter and heir, Joan, or Jane, who settled the manor upon herself and her first[31] husband, Sir Edmund Bray, kt., Lord Bray, for their lives, with remainder to their son and heir, John, Lord Bray.[32] The latter in 1547 sold all his lands in Effingham and Bookham to Thomas Lyfield,[33] who married Frances, sister and co-heir of Lord Bray,[34] with whom in 1571 he joined in conveying the manor to Ralph Stevyn.[35] In 1584 John Stevyn and Elizabeth his wife were in possession of the manor,[36] and in 1608 Edward Stevyn,

husbandman, son and heir of John Stevyn, yeoman, deceased, in conjunction with his brothers John, 'shereman,' William, husbandman, Ralph, husband-man, and Richard, weaver, sold the manor and farm of Eastwick to John Browne of Esher for the sum of £320.[37] At a court of survey held for the manor of Great Bookham in 1614, John Browne was found to hold the whole and entire manor and demesnes of Eastwick, with the rents and services of the free and customary tenants, as it lay intermixed in the parish and fields of Great Bookham.[38]

In 1626 John Morrice and Grace his wife and William Cooke conveyed the manor to Sir Francis Howard, lord of Great Bookham, who made Eastwick his residence, and from this date the history of the manor follows that of Great Bookham until 1809, when Mr. Laurell (*vide* Great Bookham) sold East-wick to Louis Bazalgette, who died in 1830.[39] In 1833 it was purchased of his executors by Mr. David Barclay.[40] His son, Mr. H. D. Barclay, died as owner of Eastwick in 1873. Mr. H. Barclay, his son, sold the property, and it now belongs to Mr. William Keswick, M.P., being merged in the manor of Great Bookham.

Eastwick Park is the site of the old manor-house, occupied formerly by the Lords Howard of Effingham. The old house was re-faced and altered by Mr. James Laurell after 1801, and further rebuilt by the late Mr. David Barclay after 1833. There is no vestige of the older building, but the house is now a good example of the Italian style.

The manor of *SLYFIELD* was probably held by the family of that name of the lords of Great Book-ham from very early times, but few records remain to throw light upon its early history. In 1201 Ralph son of Walter de Cunton conveyed to William le Fancier a virgate of land in 'Slifeld,'[41] and in 1217 William son of Roger Testard proved his claim to half a hide in 'Slifeld.'[42]

In 1368 Nicholas atte Houke and Hawisa his wife, and Walter Rykhous and Alice his wife, made con-veyance to Nicholas de Slyfield and his heirs of a messuage and 50 acres of land in 'Bokeham,' which Joan widow of Thomas le Frye was holding for life,[43] and a later document shows that Nicholas held this tenement jointly with the manor of Slyfield and its appurtenances, extending to a watercourse called Emlyn Streame (the Mole), which marked the boundary between this manor and Stoke D'Abernon, and that Nicholas and his ancestors had held the same from time immemorial.[44] From this date the manor continued with the Slyfield family, and Edmund son of John Slyfield, who was sheriff of the county in

[14] Information kindly supplied by the Rev. G. S. Bird, M.A., rector of Gt. Bookham.
[16] *Cal. Pat.* 1232–47, p. 380.
[17] *Rep. of Com. on Market Rights and Fairs,* i, 206.
[18] *Misc. Bks.* (Exch. T. R.), vol. 168, p. 106.
[19] Add. Chart. 5569.
[20] Inq. p.m. 1 Edw. III, no. 53. (This inquisition has become almost entirely illegible, and the name Estwyk is only to be found in the Calendar.)
[21] Add. Chart. 5596.
[22] Manning and Bray, *Hist. of Surr.* ii, 688. [In 13 Eliz. — Lyfield granted to — Marter a messuage and lands called

Vines, being the demesne lands of the manor of Eastwick; Mr. Glover, from the deed].
[23] Chan. Inq. p.m. 32 Edw. III (1st nos.), no. 23.
[24] Feet of F. Div. Co. 14 Ric. II, no. 40.
[25] De Banco R. 538, m. 338 d.
[26] Chan. Inq. p.m. 3 Hen. V, no. 37.
[27] *Surr. Arch. Soc.* x (2), 283.
[28] Feet of F. Div. Co. 14 Hen. VI, no. 184.
[29] Add. Chart. 5618.
[30] *Surr. Arch. Coll.* x, pt. ii, 283.
[31] She afterwards married Sir Uriah Brereton; Feet of F. Surr. East. 3 & 4 Phil. and Mary.
[32] Feet of F. Div. Co. Mich. 35 Hen. VIII.

[36] Exch. Dep. 3 Eliz. East. 5.
[37] Chan. Inq. p.m. (Ser. 2), ccxlvii, no. 99.
[38] Feet of F. Surr. Mich. 13 & 14 Eliz.
[39] Ibid. Mich. 26 & 27 Eliz.
[40] Close, 6 Jas. I, pt. xii, no. 42; Feet of F. Surr. Mich. 6 Jas. I.
[41] Manning and Bray, *Hist. of Surr.* ii, 688.
[42] Monument in church.
[43] Brayley, op. cit. iv, 469.
[44] Feet of F. Surr. 2 John, no. 20.
[45] Maitland, *Bracton's Note Bk.* 1348, no. 3.
[46] Chan. Proc. (Ser. 2), bdle. 158, no. 27.

1582, by his will proved in 1590 directed his executors not to pull down or deface any manner of wainscot or glass in or about his house of Slyfield.[45] In 1598 Henry Slyfield his son died seised of the capital messuage, manor or farm called Slyfields, held of Sir William Howard as of his manor of Great Bookham, leaving a son and heir Edmund,[46] who in March 1614 sold the manor to Henry Breton and his heirs for the sum of £2,000.[47] In November of the same year Henry Breton conveyed these premises, for the sum of £380, to George Shiers,[48] who died in 1642 leaving his second son Robert his heir.[49] George Shiers, son of Robert, was created a baronet 1684, and, dying unmarried in 1685, aged twenty-five, left his estates to his mother, Elizabeth Shiers, who died in 1700, having devised this estate to Hugh Shortrudge, clerk in holy orders,[50] rector of Fetcham. The latter suffered a recovery in 1714, and in 1715 conveyed the estate to trustees for charitable uses, but chiefly for the benefit of Exeter College, Oxford, thereby carrying out an intention of Mrs. Elizabeth Shiers, who is commemorated at Exeter College, Oxford, as a benefactor.[51] The present occupants of Slyfield Manor House are Mr. Edward J. M. Gore and the Hon. Mrs. Gore.

Slyfield House is situated on the main road between

SLYFIELD. *Gules a fesse engrailed argent between three saltires or.*

Letherhead and Cobham on the banks of the Mole, and is near Stoke D'Abernon Church. It now consists of quite a small portion of the original house, which was quadrangular or ⊏-shaped in plan, the present dwelling-house representing about one-half of the south side, while the block which is now used as farm-buildings formed the north-east angle.

The arms of Shiers occur in two rooms of the house, while there is no instance of the Slyfield coat; and there is nothing to suggest that any parts of the existing buildings are earlier than the advent of the Shiers in 1614. The house is built of red brick, the south front being of two stories divided into bays by Ionic pilasters standing on high plinths, and running up to a moulded cornice under deep-projecting eaves with modillions, with a very picturesque effect. The pilasters have a considerable entasis, and at

SHIERS of Slyfield, baronet. *Or a bend azure between a lion sable and three oak leaves vert with three scallops or on the bend.*

half height shields in slightly raised brickwork with lions' heads and fleurs de lis, a treatment recalling Inigo Jones's work on the west side of Lincoln's Inn Fields. The western part of this front has a curved brick gable, and the pilasters are differently treated, having simple moulded Tuscan capitals ; this was evidently the central feature of the front, the western half being now represented only by the lower part of its façade

SLYFIELD HOUSE, GREAT BOOKHAM

[45] Surr. Arch. Coll. v, 45 ; vii, 61.
[46] Chan. Inq. p.m. (Ser. 2), cclx, no. 131.
[47] Close, 12 Jas. I, pt. xxiv, no. 55 ;

Recov. R. East. 12 Jas. I, rot. 51 ; Feet of F. Surr. Mich. 12 Jas. I.
[48] Feet of F. Surr. Hil. 12 Jas. I ; Close, 12 Jas. I, pt. xxxviii, m. 31.

[49] Chan. Inq. p.m. (Ser. 2), d, 23 ; inscription in church.
[50] Surr. Arch. Coll. vii, 61.
[51] Manning and Bray, Hist. of Surr. ii, 692.

with remains of the pilasters dividing the bays. The windows have for the most part 18th-century sashes, but some of the cut-brick heads and sills remain, and the first-floor window in the gable, though possibly not original, has an arched head and square-faced wooden mullions and transom, with leaded casements. The remainder of the exterior is of no great interest, a new wing has been added on to the east end, and the whole of the west wall, in which is the entrance, is modern.

The hall is now quite small, being only a fragment of the original. At the top of the north wall is a wooden balustrade, which is now blocked up on one side. All the doors opening into the rooms from the hall are panelled and hung in solid carved frames. The landing above is supported by a massive beam which rests on carved and moulded pilasters, and at the end of the hall is a massive staircase with large square-carved newels and moulded tops, and in the place of balusters there are carved pierced panels of

winged amorino in a wreath, and others occur in the ceiling, among swags of fruit, gryphons, &c. The tympanum at the east end has similar strapwork and a shield bearing the arms of Shiers with helm, crest, and mantle.

The bedroom over the dining-room has a flat ceiling with a moulded dentil cornice and wide moulded ribs enriched with running patterns of fruit and festoons, and in the centre is a large oval wreath containing a female figure holding a palm branch in her right hand and some uncertain object in her left. The room over the kitchen, used as a nursery, has also an ornamental ceiling with flowered ribs.

The out-buildings to the north-west of the house are L-shaped, built of brick with the exception of the lower portion of the north side, which is of flint. They appear to be of somewhat earlier date than the rest, perhaps c. 1600, and retain a good deal of Gothic character.

The front is divided into two stories by a moulded

OUTBUILDINGS, SLYFIELD HOUSE, GREAT BOOKHAM

strapwork. At the foot of the stairs are original dog-gates.

The drawing and dining rooms on the south side of the ground-floor are panelled, and the former has also a fine plaster ceiling with fleurs de lis, swags, &c., in guilloche borders, and in the centre is a figure of 'Plenty.' Over the fireplace of this room are the arms of Shiers carved in oak, impaling those of Rutland of Mitcham, which are Gules a border engrailed or with an inescutcheon of the like coat. The dining-room fireplace has plain black marble jambs and white marble moulded shelf, and is apparently original.

On the first floor all the rooms are panelled, and several of them have very fine ceilings, the best one being in the south-west room over the drawing-room and entrance. It is coved and has an intricate strapwork design with a central cartouche containing a

brick frieze with architrave and cornice, the lower story having at the east end a pair of rusticated brick pilasters with Ionic capitals and moulded bases, presumably marking one jamb of an opening now otherwise destroyed, the building having been cut short at this point and made up with later brickwork. The windows in both stories are nearly square with moulded brick labels and wood frames with leaded casements, the labels in the upper story being continuous, breaking up over the windows and over shallow round-headed recesses which alternate with the windows in the eastern part of the range. There is a deep modillion cornice under the eaves as on the principal building. The west front is like the north, but is of brick throughout, and has a plainer cornice and a doorway with a three-centred head.

The Domesday Survey mentions a mill at Great

GREAT BOOKHAM: SLYFIELD HOUSE, CEILING OF BEDROOM OVER DINING-ROOM

Bookham worth 10*s.*, which afterwards became appurtenant to Slyfield Manor, and with regard to which a lengthy dispute arose between the Slyfields and the lords of the manor of Stoke D'Abernon. The mill, on the Mole, was on the boundary of Stoke D'Abernon and of the Slyfield property which lies on the river bank. In the early 16th century John Slyfield alleged that Sir Edmund Bray had wilfully turned away from his water corn-mill the stream called Emlyn Streame, which worked the mill and which formed the boundary between the manors of Slyfield and Stoke D'Abernon, and it was represented that when in 1375 Nicholas Slyfield had granted the reversion of certain lands in Great Bookham to William Croyser and Elizabeth his wife, it had been on the expressed condition that Nicholas and his heirs should not be disturbed in their possession of a wharf extending from the north part of the water running to their mill to the south-east angle of the wood of the said William and Elizabeth called ' the parke.'[52] In 1614 there were appurtenant to the manor of Slyfield two water corn-mills and one fulling-mill, called 'Slyfield Mills.'[53]

The manor of *POLESDEN* (High Polesden, Bookham Polesden) was in 1470 conveyed by Thomas Slyfield and Anne his wife to John Norbury,[54] who in 1491–2 enfeoffed trustees to hold it to the use of Robert Castleton and Elizabeth his wife[55] (daughter of Sir Henry Norbury[56]). John Castleton, son and heir of Robert and Elizabeth, died in 1545 seised of the manor of 'Pollesdon,' held of the king as of. his manor of Great Bookham, his son and heir William Castleton being then aged seven years.[57] William Castleton and Elizabeth his wife joined in conveyances of the manor in 1572 and 1584,[58] and in 1630 William Castleton (presumably a son of the above)

with Phoebe his wife conveyed the manor to Anthony Rous and Anne his wife.[59] Samuel Rous, the son of Anthony, jointly with Elizabeth his wife, made a conveyance of the manor in 1680.[60] In 1713 Edward Symes and Elizabeth his wife, daughter of Samuel Rous,[61] suffered a recovery of the manor, and in 1723 Elizabeth Symes, then a widow, jointly with Thomas Harris, her son by her first husband, Thomas Harris, of Gray's Inn, sold the estate to Arthur Moore, in 1729. The latter, who died in 1735, was succeeded by his nephew, William Moore, M.P. for Banbury, whose executors in 1747 were empowered by Act of Parliament to sell the estate for the payment of his debts.[62] It was purchased in the same year by Francis Geary,[63] Captain R.N., afterwards Admiral Sir Francis Geary. He died in 1796, aged eighty-six. In 1804 it was conveyed by his son Sir William Geary, bart., to the trustees of the Right Hon. R. B. Sheridan. In the particulars of the sale in 1804 it is stated that the mansion-house and principal part of the land contained about 341 acres, the terrace walk in the pleasure ground being 900 ft. in length. Mr. Sheridan died in 1816, and in 1818 the estate was purchased by Mr.

BONSOR. *Six pieces azure and argent with three lions' heads razed or in the azure and a chief indented ermined with three roses gules therein.*

Joseph Bonsor, who rebuilt the mansion-house, and was succeeded in 1835 by his son of the same name.[64] It was subsequently bought by Sir Walter Farquhar, bart., and after his death in 1896 was

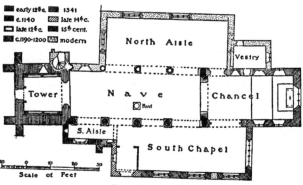

early 12th c.   1341
c.1140   late 14th c.
late 12th c.   15th cent.
c.1190-1200   modern

North Aisle

Vestry

Tower

Nave

Font

Chancel

S. Aisle

South Chapel

Scale of Feet

PLAN OF ST. NICHOLAS'S CHURCH, GREAT BOOKHAM

[52] Chan. Proc. (S:r. 2), bdle. 158, no. 27.

[53] Recov. R. East. 12 Jas. I, rot. 51 ; Close, 12 Jas. I, pt. xxiv, no. 55.

[54] Feet of F. Surr. Hil. 9 Edw. IV, no. 18.

[55] Chan. Inq. p.m. (Ser. 2), lxxii, 79.

[56] *Visit. of Surr.* (Harl. Soc. xliii), fol. 50*b*.

[57] Chan. Inq. p.m. (Ser. 2), lxxii, 79 ; 1 Edw. VI, pt. iii, no. 56.

[58] Feet of F. Surr. Mich. 14 & 15 Eliz. ; Trin. 26 Eliz.

[59] Feet of F. Surr. Mich. 6 Chas. I.

[60] Ibid. Trin. 32 Chas. I.

[61] Manning and Bray, *Hist. of Surr.* ii, 689.

[62] Feet of F. Surr. Trin. 9 Geo. I ; Close, 10 Geo. I, pt. iii, no. 26.

[63] Statute 20 Geo. II .cap. 15.

[64] Manning and Bray, *Hist. of Surr.* ii, 689.

[65] Brayley, *Hist. of Surr.* iv, 471.

acquired by Sir Clinton E. Dawkins, K.C.B. Captain the Hon. Ronald H. Fulke-Greville bought it in 1906. The manor of High Polesden was in 1784 united with the reputed manor of Polesden Lacy in Mickleham, and is now commonly called Polesden Lacy.

The church of *ST. NICHOLAS CHURCHES* has a chancel 34 ft. 8 in. by 17 ft. 6 in., north vestry, south chapel 19 ft. by 18 ft. 8 in., nave 52 ft. 8 in. by 18 ft. 9 in., north aisle 48 ft. 10 in. long and 19 ft. wide. The south aisle forms a continuation of the south chapel, and is of the same width for 35 ft. 6 in. in length, the remainder of the aisle at the west end being of the original 5 ft. 9 in. in width. There is a west tower 16 ft. 6 in. wide by 15 ft. 6 in. deep. All these dimensions are internal.

The church is mentioned in Domesday, and it is not improbable that the present nave is of the same size as that of the 11th-century building, and may have some of the original stones incorporated in its walling. The first addition to the plan was a south aisle and the existing arcade between the years 1140 and 1150, and about one-third of this narrow aisle still remains at the west. Some thirty or forty years later a north aisle followed. Two of the pillars of the north arcade are octagonal, but the middle pillar is square on its east side and semi-octagonal to the west; it is evident that the two western bays were completed first, with the semi-octagonal east respond, and that the intention was to make this respond into an octagonal pillar when the two other bays were added. The octagonal pillars have two whole and two half scallops on each face of their capitals; it will be seen that the scallops on the middle pillar were similarly treated with a view to the ultimate splaying off of the eastern angles to complete the octagon. This was, however, not done, and the scallops were continued round a square-edged block forming the east half of the column. The reason was perhaps the difficulty experienced in bringing the arches, cut in the older and thicker wall, on to the octagonal abaci of the capitals. It is probable that the west tower was also an addition of the end of the 12th century. The next increase was in the chancel, which is a most valuable instance of dated 14th-century work, an inscription on its east wall recording that it was built in 1341 by Abbot John de Rutherwyk, of Chertsey. Late in the 14th century a south porch with a parvise over was added. When, late in the 15th century, a large south chapel was set out, the eastern half of the aisle was pulled down and the new south wall brought out to the width of the porch, which was included in the chapel by the removal of its east wall and the abolition of its upper chamber. It is not certain whether the tower was ever carried higher in masonry than at present; but if so it was pulled down to its present level and the existing timber structure and spire built in the 15th or following century. A small archway at the west end of the north wall of the chancel is also of late 14th-century workmanship; it is very narrow, and presumably opened into a small chapel, perhaps made by lengthening the north aisle eastward.

The westernmost bay of the north arcade is now blocked; this is said to have been done to form a vestry there (now removed), and dates probably from the beginning of the last century. The narrow aisle was pulled down and the present wider one built

about 1845, when the former late 15th-century windows appear to have been re-used. The vestry is also a modern addition; and time and weather have necessitated the repair partly or wholly of many of the windows and other external stonework.

The east bays of both arcades of the nave have been altered, probably to accommodate a rood-loft passage, and are both higher and wider than the rest.

The east window of the chancel is an original one (c. 1341) of three ogee trefoiled lights under a two-centred head filled with net tracery; the jambs and arch are double-chamfered outside, and the latter has a moulded label with large bearded head-stops, nick-named locally 'the Parson and the Clerk,' of very coarse rough work, and later in date than the window. The easternmost of the three north windows (which are all coeval with the chancel), is of two cinque-foiled sharply-pointed lights with a quatrefoiled span-drel in a two-centred head. The second window is like it, but has been closed up with stone, doubtless when the vestry was added; the third window is a cinquefoiled single light like the others, but somewhat differently drawn, and perhaps due to a later altera-tion. Below it is a low-side window. To the west of it is a late 14th-century arch with semi-octagonal jambs, moulded bases and capitals, and a moulded two-centred arch of two orders—a wave mould and a double ogee—with a wide hollow between. A modern doorway between the second and third windows opens into the vestry, which has a two-light east window and a north doorway.

In the south wall is a piscina with old chamfered jambs stopped out above the sill, and a modern tre-foiled head. The two south windows are like those opposite, and at the south-west is a wide late 15th-century arch to the south chapel.

The chancel arch is entirely modernized, and has plain chamfered jambs, the chamfers on the east side having splayed stops, and on the west side broach stops; the arch is pointed and of two chamfered orders, the inner springing from moulded corbels.

The north arcade of the nave has four bays; the east respond is square, and of modern stonework with a chamfered abacus; the first arch is of square section, and is pointed. The first pillar is octagonal with a base-mould of two rounds, and a chamfered sub-base, and the scalloped capital is octagonal with a cham-fered abacus; the second pier is square on its east side, and half-octagonal to the west, the base is as that of the other pillar, but is not continued round the east side; the capital is scalloped, with the irregu-larity in the spacing of the scallops already referred to on its north and south faces; the third pillar is partly buried in the filling of the western bay, and it is octagonal, like the first; and the west respond is wholly buried. The arches are pointed and of a single chamfered order, and the filling of the western bay is pierced by a modern window of two plain pointed lights.

The south arcade also consists of four bays, and has a modern square east respond, and an east arch wider and higher than the rest; the pillars are circular, and the west respond corresponds with them; the bases are square with a moulding following the form of the pillars, and leaf spurs at the angles; the scalloped capitals are square above, and have chamfered abaci; and the arches are semicircular of a single square order.

The north aisle is lighted by two north windows,

GREAT BOOKHAM CHURCH, LOOKING SOUTH-WEST

and one in each end wall ; they are all of three cinque-foiled lights under two-centred heads, and appear to be of late 15th-century date with some modern stones, though they are said to be entirely modern ; they have a wide casement moulding inside and out.

The east window of the south chapel is apparently modern, and contains stained glass in memory of Lord Raglan (Commander-in-Chief in the Crimean War), dating from 1859 ; it consists of five cinque-foiled lights with cusped vertical tracery above, in a two-centred head ; the jambs are moulded with a wide hollow.

In the south wall is a 15th-century piscina with an eight-foiled basin and stone shelf in a trefoiled ogee-headed recess with pierced spandrels, and the three windows on the south side of the chapel or widened aisle are each of three cinquefoiled lights under seg-mented heads ; they have moulded jambs, arches, and labels, and have been partly repaired with cement. The doorway at the south-west corner was that to the former porch ; it has two double ogee orders separated by a hollow in the jambs and pointed arch. In the western wall are two windows, one above the other, each of two cinquefoiled lights, and of modern stone-work. The blocked doorways to the former parvise still remain in place ; the lower opens from the narrow part of the aisle, and the upper is in the west wall of the wider portion ; the stair has been re-moved. The south-west window (in the narrow portion of the aisle) is modern, and has two trefoiled lights with a quatrefoil over in a pointed head. The west window is a tiny round-headed light dating from the 12th century, and probably contemporary with the aisle.

The tower opens to the nave with a depressed pointed arch, perhaps of late 12th-century date, with two chamfered orders, at the springing of which has been a string, now cut away. The base mould is, however, preserved. In the north wall is a small modern round-headed light, and the west doorway, with chamfered jambs and four-centred arch, is per-haps early 16th-century work. Over it is a modern window of two elliptical-headed lights ; and the angles of the tower are strengthened by heavy but-tresses, that at the north end of the west wall being a raking one of brick, while the others are old, of stone repaired with brick in places ; a modern stair turret rises in the north-east angle. The masonry walls stop at the first floor, and the upper part of the tower is of timber carried up within the lines of the masonry tower on heavy oak posts from the floor, and covered with modern boarding ; the parts gathered in over the walls are covered with stone slabs, while the tower is crowned by an octagonal shingled spire.

Most of the walling of the church is of flint and stone, but the lower parts of the chancel are faced with blocks of Heath stone—a crystalline sandstone—and the north-east angle has some very large quoins in this stone, and in a pebbly conglomerate deeply coloured with iron.

The chancel has a modern plastered collar-beam roof with moulded wood ribs. The nave also has a plastered collar-beam roof with moulded trusses, ap-parently modern.

The south chapel roof is gabled and ceiled below, and dates in part from the building of the aisle and chapel ; it has an old moulded tie-beam over the first arch of the arcade ; the space above the tie is filled with modern wood tracery ; the narrow south aisle has a flat ceiling, and the north aisle has a modern gabled roof like the others.

The altar table, chancel screen, pulpit and seats are all of modern workmanship ; across the south chapel are the remains of the lower part of a 15th-century oak screen having eight bays of closed panels with feathered trefoiled heads ; the main cusp points had roses attached, but most of these have been destroyed ; the posts and rails are moulded ; some of the former have panelled buttresses on their faces ; one of the panels has the remains of the original painting, and the rest contain modern decoration. The font has a late 12th-century grey marble bowl ; it is square, chamfered and rounded to a circle in its lower edge, with the plain capitals of four shafts cut out of the solid ; the stem and base are modern.

The oldest of the inscribed stones and monuments is that in the east wall of the chancel recording the building of the chancel ; it reads :—'Hec : domus : Abbate fuerat : constructa : Johanne : de Ruther-wyka : decus ob : Sancti : Nicholai : Anno : Mil-leno : triceno bisqz : viceno : primo : ꝝc : ei paret hinc sedem requiei.'

On the rail of the old screen in the south chapel is fixed a small brass inscription reading in black letter :—'Pray for the soule of John Barmsdale and Marion his wyf the which John desseced in August in the yere of oure Lord m cccc lxxxi ᵭ whos soules Jhu have m . . ' In the nave floor, near the chancel screen, is a brass inscribed 'Hic jacet Elizabeth nup ux Thome Slyfield ac quonda ux Georgii Brewes armig'i filia Edwardi Seynt John milit' que obiit xxvii die mēs' Augusti Aᵒ dñi Mᵒ iiiiᶜ xxxiii' ; above the inscription is the figure of a lady in a cushion head-dress, high-waisted loose dress, and loose hanging sleeves. Under the south arch to the chancel is a brass inscrip-tion :—'Here lieth buried Henry Slyfield Esq. and Elizabeth his wife who was the daughter of Richard Buckfold citizen of Lond : the said H. was of ye age of 56 yeres and deceased AnᵒDni 1598 and had issue by his wife 6 sonnes and 4 daughters.' Over it is his figure in a gown and ruff, and his hands in prayer ; and her figure in a tight bodice, full farthingale and ruff ; below are the children in one plate. There are three shields of arms, the first being Slyfield quartering Weston of West Clandon, Sable a cheveron or between three lions' heads razed argent ; the second has the quartered coat of Slyfield impaling Buckfold, Party cheveronwise argent and sable three bucks' heads countercoloured with their horns or ; the third has Slyfield impaling Cobb, Party cheveronwise gules and sable with two swans argent in the chief and a her-ring or in the foot.

Further east is a brass inscription to Elizabeth Slyfield wife of Edmund Slyfield and daughter of Walter Lambert, of Carshalton ; it bears no date, but from other sources the date 1597 is known.

On the south side of the east respond of the south ar-cade is a brass inscription to Edmund Slyfield, who died 1590 ; it has a quaint epitaph in 50 lines beginning:—

'Of Slyfield Place in Surrey soile
Here Edmond Slyfeld lyes
A stout Esquier who allweys sett
Godes feare before his eyes
A Justice of the Peace he was
From the syxt Kinge Edwards dayes
And worthely for vertues use
Dyd wyn deserved prayse.' . . .

In the south aisle is a brass inscription to Robert Shiers, a Bencher of the Inner Temple, who died in 1668; over the inscription he is represented in a large brass wearing a lawyer's gown and holding a book; on a shield are the arms of Shiers impaling a fesse wavy ermine between three crescents ermine.

There is also a floor slab to Edward Shiers, second son of Robert Shiers, died 1670, and a large white marble monument in the north aisle. Robert Shiers, of Slyfield, died 1668, Elizabeth his wife 1700, and Sir George Shiers, bart., his son, died 1685. There is another to Sir Francis Howard, kt., son of Lord Howard of Effingham, died 1651. Among the later monuments may be mentioned Colonel Thomas Moore, of Polesden, 1735; William Moore, 1746; and Cornet Francis Geary, eldest son of Admiral Geary, who fell in the American War in 1776, and the monument has a bas-relief showing the incident which caused his death.

Outside in the churchyard is an ancient coffin-lid on which is a floriated cross in relief, but without an inscription; it is probably of the 14th century.

In the tower are two bells, and space where there was formerly a third; one of them bears no mark or inscription, the other was cast by William Eldridge in 1675.

The communion plate includes a cup, evidently of the 17th century, but without a hallmark; the maker's mark is R A over a star; it has a cable band on the lower edge of the cup, and a trumpet-shaped stem; there is also a paten with mark of 1675 dated 1677, a flagon of 1762, and cup of 1859, all of silver; besides these there exist two pewter plates, one dated 1730.

The first book of the registers is a parchment copy containing baptisms and marriages from 1632 to 1711 and burials to 1680; the second has baptisms from 1695 to 1812, marriages 1695 to 1753, and burials 1680 to 1812; in it is a note that the yew tree and five walnut trees (south of the churchyard) were planted in February 1733-4; the third book has marriages from 1754 to 1812. There is also a vestry book, in which are recorded the names of all the churchwardens from 1631.

In 1632 Samuel Cherrie was vicar. In 1633 six of his parishioners were excommunicated, but the cause is not given. One of them was absolved in 1635.

The church stands in the midst of a roughly triangular churchyard, the south and west boundaries are on the road sides, and at their angle is a lych gate of 1897.

The church of ST. BARNABAS, RANMORE, was built in 1859 by Lord Ashcombe, then Mr. George Cubitt, from the designs of Sir Gilbert Scott. It is a handsome stone church, with chancel, nave, and aisles in 13th-century style, with a tower and spire which form a conspicuous landmark. The tower is vaulted and treated as a lantern over the crossing.

ADVOWSON The church of Great Bookham was appurtenant to the manor in 1086,[46] and in 1292 was confirmed with its issues to the Abbot and convent of Chertsey, under letters patent from John de Pontoise, Bishop of Winchester, reciting a bull of Clement II given the fourth year of his pontificate.[47]

An endowment of the vicarage in the same year by Philip de Barthou and John de Pontoise secured to the vicar all offerings made upon the altar of the church, with all the small tithes, except hay and wool, which belonged to the abbot and convent, and a house near the court once belonging to the rector of the church.[48] The rectory and advowson having been surrendered to the king in 1537 by John, Abbot of Chertsey,[49] were regranted in the same year to Bisham, the new foundation,[50] and on the dissolution of the latter a draught was made for a grant to Sir Christopher More for life, to be held in chief for the twentieth part of a knight's fee.[51] This was apparently not completed, for in 1544 a grant of the rectory and advowson to Richard and John Sackvile is recorded.[52] They seem to have conveyed it to Sir Christopher More, who died in 1549 seised of the rectory.[53] His son, William More, in 1560, in conjunction with Margaret his wife, obtained licence to alienate to Thomas Lyfield and Frances his wife and their heirs.[54] Thomas died in 1596, having settled the rectory and advowson on his grandson Sir Francis Vincent,[55] whose grandson Sir Francis Vincent[56] in 1657 conveyed it to Francis and Samuel Rous.[57] Francis Rous, who was provost of Eton College, died in 1659, having bequeathed £40 per annum out of the parsonage or tithe to maintain two scholars at Pembroke College, Oxford. The remainder of the tithe he bequeathed to the minister of the parish, the patronage of the living to his kinsman Samuel Rous, and his lands and interest in the parsonage to Colonel Anthony Rous.[58] Samuel Rous presented to the living in 1663,[59] and in 1713 Edward Symes and Elizabeth his wife, of Polesden, suffered a recovery of a moiety of the rectory, with all the tithes pertaining thereto and the advowson of the vicarage, together with the manor of Polesden,[60] with which it descended until sold by Sir William Geary in 1803 to James Laurell, who in 1812 conveyed it in trust to John Harrison Loveridge, together with the manor of Great Bookham.[61]

Before 1821 the advowson was bought by William Heberden, M.D., F.R.S., who in that year gave the living to his son, the Rev. W. Heberden, who succeeded to the advowson also in 1845, and died in 1879. It was bought by the late Viscount Downe, who died in 1900, and in 1903 by Mr. Arthur Bird, of the Grange, Great Bookham.[62]

The living of St. Barnabas is a rectory in the gift of Lord Ashcombe.

CHARITIES Smith's charity is distributed as in other Surrey parishes.

In 1625 Mr. John Brown, of

46 V.C.H. Surr. i, 309a.
47 Misc. Bks. (Exch. Q.R.), vol. 25, p. 48; Cal. Pat. 1281-92, p. 493.
48 Misc. Bks. (Exch. Q.R.), vol. 25, p. 48.
49 Feet of F. Div. Co. Trin. 29 Hen. VIII.
50 L. and P. Hen. VIII, xii (2), g. 1311 (22).
51 Ibid. xviii (1), 54; Hist. MSS. Com.

Rep. vii, App. 604a. The draught is in Loseley MSS.
52 Pat. 36 Hen. VIII, pt. iii; L. and P. Hen. VIII, xix (1), g. 1035 (31); Aug. Off. Partics. for Grants, 970.
53 Chan. Inq. p.m. (Ser. 2), lxxxix, 134. Copy among Loseley MSS. ix, 50.
54 Pat. 2 Eliz. pt. ii, m. 28/9; Feet of F. Surr. Hil. 3 Eliz.

55 Chan. Inq. p.m. (Ser. 2), ccxlvii, no. 99.
56 Ibid. dxcv, no. 106.
57 Feet of F. Surr. Commonw. Mich. 1657.
58 P.C.C. Will 51 Pell.
59 Inst. Bks.
60 Recov. R. Trin. 12 Anne, rot. 121.
61 Feet of F. Surr. Hil. 52 Geo. III.
62 Clergy Lists.

Great Bookham, left 30s. yearly, charged upon land in Eastwick Manor.

Sir George Shiers, bart., of Slyfield, left in 1685 an annual rent-charge of £36 3s. (less land tax) upon land in Hertfordshire for Great Bookham, to apprentice children, to portion poor maids, and to relieve the aged poor or those with large families who had not come upon the rates. It is commemorated by a tablet in the church, dated 1717.

In 1715, by deed enrolled in chancery, a settlement was made by Dr. Shortrudge, Sir Francis Vincent and others, of land in Hertfordshire and in Bookham for the use of various charities, the residue to go to the vicars of Great Bookham, Effingham, Letherhead, and Shalford for ever, on condition that they read the Common Prayer in their churches on Wednesdays and Fridays ; that they preach sermons proper for the several days on Good Friday and 30 January ; that the vicar of 'Lethered' administers the Holy Sacrament, according to the form of the Church of England, in the parish church there on the first Sunday of every month. This charity is commemorated by a tablet in the church, by order of the trustees. There is a similar tablet in Shalford Church. The second condition, as to 30 January, is not now observed.

LITTLE BOOKHAM

Bocheham (xi cent.) ; Bokham (xiii and xiv cent.).

Little Bookham is a small parish 2¼ miles south-west of Letherhead. It is bounded on the north-west by Cobham, on the north by Stoke D'Abernon, on the east by Great Bookham, on the south by Dorking and Wotton, on the west by Effingham. The area of the parish is 926 acres. It runs from the brow of the Chalk, across the Thanet and Woolwich Beds and over the London Clay, and touches the alluvium of the Mole valley, which river bounds the parish on the north. The Guildford and Letherhead road, and the Guildford and Letherhead line pass through it.

The village is on the Thanet and Woolwich Beds immediately below the Chalk, on to which it has extended in recent times. Part of Bookham Common to the north is still open land, and there is some open land to the south on the top of the Chalk near Ranmore Common. Though separately held from Great Bookham in Domesday Little Bookham is evidently a slice cut off the latter ; its shape and soil illustrate the usual arrangements of the settlements which subsequently became parishes. There were extensive common fields on the Chalk which are mentioned as existing by James and Malcolm in 1794, but not mentioned in Stevenson's *View of the Agriculture of Surrey* in 1809. They would seem to have been inclosed with Great Bookham in 1822.[1]

The manor-house is the seat of Mr. Meredith Townsend ; the Lane Cottage of Lady Yule ; Inglewood of Mr. W. F. A. Archibald ; Rickleden of the Hon. D'Arcy Lambton. The old rectory house, probably of the 18th century, is too large to have been built for a rectory. Preston House was a preparatory school for boys kept by Mr. De Brath Stanley. The school (under the County Council), for infants only, was founded by the late Mr. T. Mashiter, and opened in 1884. The elder children attend the school at Great Bookham.

The manor of *LITTLE BOOKHAM MANOR* is stated in the Domesday Survey to have been held by Godtovi of Earl Harold, and in 1086 was held by Halsard of William de Braose, lord of Bramber.[2] In 1275 Sir John Haunsard held

part of the manor of the lord of Bramber for one knight's fee, part of the Earl of Gloucester for a quarter of a fee, and part of the Abbot of Chertsey.[3] The Braose overlordship was sold in 1324 as part of the barony of Bramber to Hugh le Despenser, one of the heirs by marriage of the Gloucester property, by Oliva daughter of William de Braose and wife of John de Mowbray.[4] After the forfeiture of his estates following the attainder of Hugh in 1326,[5] the overlordship was confirmed to John de Mowbray, Duke of Norfolk, son of Oliva, and remained with the Dukes of Norfolk until it was acquired by Richard Duke of York, second son of

MOWBRAY. *Gules a lion argent.*

Edward IV, who was affianced to Anne, only daughter and heir of John de Mowbray, Duke of Norfolk, at the age of six years.[6] The manor is said to have been held of Richard in 1480,[7] and after his death in the Tower in 1483 appears to have become vested in the Crown.

The part of the manor which was held of the Earl of Gloucester was a carucate of land which extended into the parish of Effingham[8] and formed part of his fee there.[9] It is sometimes mentioned separately from the manor of Bookham. In 1306 this carucate was said to be held by John Pykard,[10] probably as representing the Earl of Gloucester,[11] and in 1326 was in the king's hands by the forfeiture of Hugh de Audley, who had acquired part of the Gloucester estates by marriage.[12] The Braose and Gloucester portions thence fell to the Crown by contemporaneous forfeitures, and were treated as one manor. Three virgates of land in the manor were held of the Abbot of Chertsey for 12d.[13] annual rent and suit of court at Cobham and Great Bookham.

The subtenancy of the manor appears to have continued with the descendants of Halsard, the Domesday tenant. In 1189 William de Braose accounted to the sheriff of Surrey for £8 7s. 4d. of the amercement of William Hansard, whose heir was in

[1] *Sir John Brunner's Ret.* 1903.
[2] *V.C.H. Surr.* i, 321a.
[3] Chan. Inq. p.m. 3 Edw. I, no. 65.
[4] Pat. 17 Edw. II, pt. ii, m. 9, 6.
[5] G.E.C. *Complete Peerage,* iii, 91.
[6] *Suss. Arch. Coll.* xxvi, 261.

[7] Chan. Inq. p.m. 20 Edw. IV, no. 72.
[8] See Ibid. 19 Edw. II, no. 90.
[9] *Cal. Close,* 1272–9, p. 501.
[10] Chan. Inq. p.m. 33 Edw. I, no. 264.

[11] John Pykard was acting as attorney for the Earl of Gloucester in 1278 ; *Cal. Close,* 1272–9, p. 489.
[13] Close, 19 Edw. II, m. 2.
[14] Chan. Inq. p.m. 3 Edw. I, no. 65 ; ibid. 7 Ric. II, no. 15.

his custody,[14] and this heir was probably the William Hansard who is found holding a fee in 'Bocheam' (Bookham) and Cateworthe of the honour of Bramber in 1210–12,[15] and again between 1234 and 1241. In 1273 John and James, sons of William Hansard, made a joint conveyance of lands in Little Bookham to the Prior of St. Mary Southwark,[16] and in 1275 John (here Sir John) died seised of the manor of Bookham,[17] leaving as his heir his nephew James son of James Hansard.

It seems however that James Hansard, the elder, had already made a grant to William de Braose (the overlord),[18] and in 1291 Mary widow of William de Braose had livery of the manor, which she is said to have held jointly with her husband before his death in 1290,[19] and of which she enfeoffed Ralph de Camoys and Margaret her daughter, wife of Ralph, in 1303.[20] In 1306 Ralph and Margaret obtained licence to regrant the manor to Mary for life, with reversion to themselves and heirs of Margaret.[21]

In the next year, consequent upon an assize of novel disseisin having been brought against them by James Hansard with regard to this manor, Ralph and Margaret summoned Mary to secure them against loss, and Mary thereupon agreed that if they or their heirs should be deprived of the manor, she and her heirs would make good such loss out of her manor of Wynesthorp in Yorkshire.[22]

This is the last mention of the Hansards in connexion with the manor, which, however, in 1399 appears under the name of Bookham Hansard.[23] Mary de Braose died in 1326, her next heir being her grandson Thomas son of Peter de Braose, then aged 26.[24] Ralph and Margaret however had seisin of this manor in accordance with the above settlement,[25] but before 1334 it was acquired from them by the said Thomas de Braose, who in that year had licence to convey it to Robert de Harpurdesford,[26] for the purpose of settlement on himself and Beatrice his wife and their heirs.

Thomas died seised of the manor in 1361, leaving a son John, who died in 1367, and in 1372–3 the manor was conveyed by Sir Peter de Braose and others to Beatrice, widow of Thomas, for her life, with remainder to her children, Thomas, Peter, Elizabeth, and Joan, and their heirs respectively, and in default of such to the right heirs of Thomas.[27] Beatrice died in 1383,[28] and in 1395, on the death of her son Thomas, and of his infant children Thomas and Joan a few weeks later,[29] the manor passed to Elizabeth, the daughter of Beatrice mentioned above and now wife of Sir William Heron. Elizabeth died without issue on 8 July 1399,[30] and in the inquisition taken

the next year on the Duke of Norfolk, one of the heirs of the Braoses, this manor was said to be held by Sir William Heron,[31] on whose death in 1404[32] it reverted to the Braose line represented by George son of John son of Peter de Braose.[33]

George died in 1418 seised of this manor, which he held jointly with his wife Elizabeth,[34] when his next heir was found to be Hugh Cokesey, aged 15, son and heir of Walter Cokesey, son of Isabella wife of Walter Cokesey, kt., and daughter of Agnes wife of Uriah Seyntpere and sister of the said George. Hugh died in 1445,[35] and his widow Alice, who had married Sir Andrew Ogard, in 1460,[36] when the manors passed to Joyce Beauchamp, sister and heir of Hugh, and afterwards wife of Leonard Stapelton, but at this date a widow. Joyce died in 1473, leaving a son and heir, Sir John Grevyle, kt.,[37] aged 40, who died in 1480 seised of the manor,[38] leaving a son and heir Thomas, who appears to have taken the name of Cokesey, and who was one of the Knights of the Bath at the coronation of Henry VII, and was created a knight banneret for his services at the battle of Stoke.[39] On the death of Thomas without issue in 1498, Thomas, Earl of Surrey (afterwards Duke of Norfolk) and Sir Maurice Berkeley, as cousins and heirs of George Braose, had special livery of his estates.[40] Little Bookham, to the overlordship of which they had a claim as representatives of the Mowbrays, fell to the former, who settled it for life on his second son William Howard,[41] afterwards Lord Howard of Effingham and Lord Chamberlain. On the attainder of the Duke of Norfolk the grant was renewed by the king, and was confirmed by Edward VI in 1553[42] to William and his heirs. Lord Howard subsequently became involved in pecuniary difficulties, and in 1566, after rendering an account of his Surrey possessions to his great-nephew Thomas, Duke of Norfolk, begged that an estate might be found for his wife out of his manor of Little Bookham and his moiety of Reigate, the former being then 'lette into for certaine rent-corne for provisions of my house' and worth £21 per annum.[43] Lord Howard of Effingham died seised of the manor in 1573,[44] leaving a son and heir Charles, afterwards Earl of Nottingham, who in 1622[45] settled the manor on himself and his second wife Margaret for their lives, with remainder to his eldest surviving son Charles, Lord Howard. The said earl died in 1624,[46] and his widow married William, Viscount Castlemaine, courts for the manor being held in their names in 1633 and 1635.[47] The reversion, however, appears to have been purchased by Benjamin Maddox, whose son Howard Maddox died seised of this manor in 1637, leaving

[14] Pipe R. 1189–90 (Rec. Com.), 218.
[15] Red Bk. of Exch. (Rolls Ser.), 561.
[16] Feet of F. Div. Co. 1 & 2 Edw. I, no. 11.
[17] Chan. Inq. p.m. Edw. I, file 11, no. 1.
[18] Cal. Close, 1272–9, p. 501.
[19] Ibid. 1288–96, pp. 160, 162.
[20] Cal. Pat. 1301–7, p. 147; Chan. Inq. p.m. 31 Edw. I, no. 68.
[21] Chan. Inq. p.m. 33 Edw. I, no. 264; Cal. Pat. 1301–7, p. 442; Feet of F. Surr. Trin. 34 Edw. I, 134, 13.
[22] Add. Chart. 20036.
[23] Chan. Inq. p.m. Hen. IV, file 17.
[24] Ibid. 19 Edw. II, no. 90.
[25] Cal. Close, 1323–7, p. 437. Peter

father of Thomas had claimed the manor against Ralph and Margaret in 1306 (Feet of F. Surr. 39 Edw. I, no. 13).
[26] Cal. Pat. 1334–8, p. 62; Feet of F. Div. Co. 11 Edw. III, no. 22.
[27] Add. MSS. 5705.
[28] Chan. Inq. p.m. 7 Ric. II, no. 15.
[29] Ibid. 19 Ric. II, no. 7.
[30] Suss. Arch. Coll. viii, 100.
[31] Chan. Inq. p.m. 1 Hen. IV, no. 71b.
[32] Ibid. 6 Hen. IV, no. 21.
[33] Pat. 24 Hen. VI, pt. i, m. 28; Suss. Arch. Coll. viii, 101.
[34] Chan. Inq. p.m. 6 Hen. V, no. 48.
[35] Ibid. 24 Hen. VI, no. 36.
[36] Ibid. 38–9 Hen. VI, no. 49.

[37] Ibid. 13 Edw. IV, no. 32.
[38] Ibid. 20 Edw. IV, no. 72.
[39] Dugdale, Warw. (2nd ed.), 707.
[40] Coll. Topog. and Gen. vi, 74; Pat. 14 Hen. VII, pt. ii, m. 4; Suss. Arch. Coll. viii, 100.
[41] L. and P. Hen. VIII, ix (1), 278 (51).
[42] Pat. 7 Edw. VI, pt. ix, m. 12.
[43] Lansd. MSS. ix, 49.
[44] Chan. Inq. p.m. (Ser. 2), clxv, no. 172.
[45] Recov. R. 20 Jas. I, rot. 15; Feet of F. Surr. 19 Jas. I.
[46] Chan. Inq. p.m. (Ser. 2), ccclxxi, no. 69.
[47] Manning and Bray, Hist. of Surr. ii, 704.

Benjamin Maddox his brother and heir, then aged 5 months.[48] Benjamin was created a baronet in 1675,[49] and in 1684, in a court-book for the manor of Effingham East Court, is stated to hold the manor of ' Brewers Court '[50] (evidently a corruption of Braose Court). Benjamin died in 1717,[51] leaving two daughters, the younger of whom, Mary wife of Edward Pollen, inherited this manor. In 1727 Benjamin Pollen son of Mary suffered a recovery[52] of the manor, and died in 1751, leaving a daughter Anne, who died unmarried in 1764. She bequeathed this estate to her step-mother Mrs. Sarah Pollen, with re- mainder to Rev. Thomas Pol- len, son of her grandfather Edward Pollen, by his second wife, with remainder to George Pollen, son of Edward Pollen of New Inn, another son of Edward the grandfather.

Mrs. Sarah Pollen died in 1777, and the estate came to the said Thomas, and a few years later, on his dying with- out male issue, to the said George.[53] George died in 1812, and was succeeded by his grandson, Rev. George Augustus Pollen, who died in 1847, and was suc- ceeded by his son John Douglas Boileau Pollen.[54] Mr. Henry C. W. Pollen is now lord of the manor.

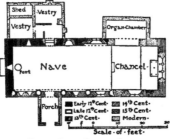

Pollen of Little Book- ham. *Azure a bend co- tised or between six lo- zenges argent each charged with a scallop sable and with six scallops vert on the bend.*

The church of *LITTLE BOOKHAM*, CHURCH of unknown dedication, is a small build- ing consisting of a chancel and a nave all under one roof, measuring 59 ft. 3 in. by 17 ft. 9 in., with a wooden bell-turret at the west end. On the north side of the chancel is an organ-chamber, and further west are the vestries. To the south of the nave is a porch.

The north and west walls of an early 12th-century aisleless nave, to which a south aisle was added about the year 1160, are still standing, but the chancel which was contemporary with it was pulled down in the 13th century, and replaced by another of the same width as the nave, the east wall of the nave

being entirely removed. By the latter half of the 15th century the south aisle was perhaps in bad repair and was pulled down, the spaces between the columns of the arcade being walled up. A 13th- century window, no doubt from the old aisle, has been set in one bay of the blocking.

The vestries, porch, and organ-chamber are modern, the latter having been added in 1901.

The east window of the chancel is a modern inser- tion of 13th-century design, and has three high tre- foiled lancets within a two-centred outer arch. The internal jambs and mullions have shafts with moulded capitals, bases, and rear arches.

In the north wall of the chancel is the modern arch to the organ-chamber, copied from the 12th- century north arcade. The organ-chamber has modern single east and west lights, but the square-headed north window of two trefoiled lights is of 15th- century date, and has been moved from the north wall of the chancel. There are three other windows of this type, one in the south wall of the chancel, the head and sill only being old, and the other two at the north-east and south-east of the nave, the north-east window having a modern head. At the south-east of the chancel is a piscina with two drains, probably of 13th-century date, over which is a four-centred, cinquefoiled head with sunk tracery in the spandrels, of the 15th century.

At the south-west is a blocked window which shows outside as a single light, with a trefoiled ogee head of 14th-century date. The groove for the glass and the holes for the window-bars remain in the reveals and soffit.

The north-east window of the nave is set in an arched recess reaching from the apex of the window to the floor, 9 ft. 6 in. wide, doubtless designed to give more room for the north nave altar ; similar recesses occur in several churches in the neighbour- hood. To the west of it is a single-light 14th- century window like the blocked one in the chancel. Near the west end is a third north window of early 12th-century date, a narrow deeply-splayed round- headed light, which now looks into the vestry. In the west wall of the nave is another original window, and beneath it a block of masonry of comparatively modern date, added as a buttress.

The arcade in the south wall of the nave is of four bays with large circular columns, the bases of which are hidden, but the scalloped capitals with hollow chamfered abaci show both within and without the building. The columns project from the wall on the inside only, being completely covered on the outside. The arches are semicircular of one order, chamfered towards the nave, but externally square, and flush with the wall face. The 15th-century window in the blocking of the first bay has been described ; that in the second bay is a 13th-century lancet with a keeled moulding to the inner jambs and arch, and a chamfered label, the moulding ending in simply- moulded bases. In the western bay are two modern round-headed lights, with detached shafts to the inside jambs, of 12th-century design. The south doorway is 15th-century work, with plain chamfered jambs and two-centred arch.

PLAN OF LITTLE BOOKHAM CHURCH

(plan labels: Shed, Vestry, Vestry, Organ-Chamber, Nave, Font, Chancel, Porch; legend: Early 12th Cent., Late 12th Cent., 13th Cent., 14th Cent., 15th Cent., Modern; Scale of feet)

[48] Chan. Inq. p.m. (Ser. 2), ccclxxxvi, 24.
[49] G.E.C. Baronetage, iv, 74.
[50] Add. MSS. 23751, fol. 5.
[51] G.E.C. Baronetage, iv, 74.
[52] Recov. R. Mich. 1 Jas. II, rot. 279.
[53] Manning and Bray, Hist. of Surr. ii, 705.
[54] Burke, Peerage.

The entrance to the vestries, opposite the south doorway, has plain square jambs and semicircular arch, the stones being old on the nave side, and is the original north doorway of the nave much altered.

The walls of the main building are of flint plastered over, except in the case of the west wall, and the gable over it is of weather-boarded timber running up to a square bell-turret which has a pointed, shingled roof. All the other roofs are tiled, and the nave and chancel roofs inside are panelled with modern boarding ; but two of the tie-beams are old, and a third one has been cut away.

The modern stone pulpit is lined with 17th-century carved panels, and other carved woodwork of the same date has been used in the vestry door.

The font is circular, with a peculiar clumsy outline, the bowl being held together by cleverly-designed modern straps of iron and copper. All the other fittings are modern.

There is one bell in the turret, but it bears no mark by which its age can be told.

The plate is modern.

The registers date from 1636, but are imperfect in the earlier part.

The churchyard is small, with entrances on the east and west sides. At the west end of the church is a very fine yew tree of great age, and to the north there are two large cedars, besides other trees.

ADVOWSON   In 1306 the advowson of the church of Little Bookham was in-cluded in the fine confirming the grant of the manor to Ralph de Camoys and Margaret his wife by Mary de Braose,[66] and the presentation of the living has continued with the owner of the manor from that date down to the present day. In 1535 the rectory was valued at £10 16s. 6d.,[66] from which was deducted 9s. 8d. for procurations and synodals paid to the Archdeacon of Surrey. In 1657, a project having been formed for uniting this parish with that of Great Bookham, the jurors commissioned to make necessary inquiries reported the living to be worth £50 a year.[67] This scheme was, however, abandoned.

CHARITIES   Smith's Charity is distributed as in other Surrey parishes. Sir Benjamin Maddox, lord of the manor, who died in 1717, left the rent of certain tenements in All Hallows Lane, London, one-half to the rector and his successors, four-eighths in equal parts for the repair of the church and churchyard fence, the use of the poor, the repair of roads and bridges, and to the parish clerk ' for the better setting and singing of psalms in the church,' and for reading the testator's will on some Sunday between All Saints and Christmas.[68]

The tenement is now a stable in All Hallows Lane, let for twenty-one years at £120, which is duly paid in the proportions stated.[69]

Three almshouses were erected by Edward Pollen in 1730. They do not seem to exist at the present day.

66 Feet of F. Surr. 34 Edw. I, no. 134.
66 *Valor Eccl.* (Rec. Com.), ii, 32.

67 *Surr. Arch. Coll.* xvii, 102.
68 *Char. Com. Rep.* xiii, 475.

69 Information from Mr. C. A. Cook, Charity Commissioner.

LITTLE BOOKHAM CHURCH FROM THE SOUTH-EAST

THE HUNDRED OF WOKING

The places given in Woking Hundred at the time of the great Survey differ somewhat from the above list. In Domesday Book, Ockley and Lodesorde (which has been identified with Lodsworth in Sussex), find a place in the list, while Worplesdon, with its members of Wyke and Burgham, is classed in Wotton;[2] but the difference is probably only due to an error in transcription. In the time of the Confessor the hundred was worth £88 10s., and by 1086 its assessment had risen to £125 10s.; the actual payment, however, in some cases exceeded the assessment.[3] The sum contributed by the hundred to a 14th-century aid amounted to £45 16s. 6½d.[4] This did not include Guildford borough, which paid £15 2s. 9½d. In 1636 the taxable value of the hundred was £297 2s. 8d.[5]

The descent of the hundred followed that of Blackheath Hundred, q.v.

The Hundred Court was held at Harmeshatch,[6] later called Harmesheath, near the borders of Ockham and Cobham parishes, on the verge of the hundred, as in the case of the court of Blackheath, q.v.

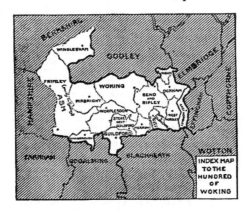

INDEX MAP TO THE HUNDRED OF WOKING

---

[1] *Population Returns*, 1831, ii, 636.
[2] e.g. Guildford was assessed at £30, but rendered £32.
[3] *V.C.H. Surr.* i, 442.
[4] 'Ad Hundredum domini regis de Hameshatch vocatum Wokynge Hundredum.' Chan. Inq. p.m. 50 Edw. III, no. 10.
[5] *V.C.H. Surr.* i, 313.
[6] Ibid.

A HISTORY OF SURREY

ASH

Esche, Assche (xiii cent.) ; Asshe (xiv cent.).

Ash is a parish on the western border of the
county, 36 miles south-west from London, 8 miles
from Guildford, bounded on the north by Frimley,
formerly part of the same parish, on the east by
Pirbright and Worplesdon, on the south by Wanborough and Seale, on the west by Aldershot in
Hampshire. The shape is irregular, but the furthest
extension west to east is over 4 miles, from north
to south over 3 miles. The southern part of the
parish, including St. Peter's Church and Ash village,
is on the London Clay ; but the greater portion,
once including Frimley, covers the western side of the
ridge of Bagshot Sands, which is divided from Chobham Ridges by the dip through which the Basingstoke
Canal and Railway run, and is known as Ash Common,
Fox Hills, Claygate Common. The high land,
largely covered by heather with plantations of conifers,
slopes westward to the alluvium of the Blackwater
River between Surrey and Hampshire. The parish
is traversed by the road from Guildford to Aldershot ;
by the Basingstoke Canal ; by the London and South
Western Railway, with Ash Green station opened
1852 ; by the London, Brighton, and South Coast
Railway, with Ash station opened 1849, and Aldershot North Camp station ; and by the Pirbright,
Aldershot, and Farnham branch, 1879 ; and the
Ascot, Frimley, and Aldershot North Camp branch,
1878.

The area of the parish is 6,292 acres, including
the district of Wyke, formerly in Worplesdon, but
added to Ash in 1880.[1]

The making of Aldershot Camp has revolutionized
the whole of this neighbourhood. The camp itself
is in Hampshire, but ranges have been established in
Ash parish, and houses in connexion with the camp
have turned what were desolate heaths into a succession of straggling villages or even towns. Henley
Park (q.v.) lies on the other side of the parish. It is
one of the numerous parks formed in the Surrey
bailiwick of Windsor Forest. Cobbett, the famous
political and social reformer, farmed land at Normandy in this parish.

Of prehistoric antiquities only a few neolithic
implements, in the Surrey Archaeological Society's
Museum at Guildford, have been recorded.

There was an Inclosure Act (Ash and Frimley),
1801, making large inclosures of waste, but reserving
certain rights of fuel (turf) to the inhabitants.

There are Wesleyan and Congregational chapels in
the village. There are also Wesleyan chapels in Ash
Street and Normandy. Wyke is an ecclesiastical parish
formed out of Ash, Worplesdon, and Wanborough in
1847 (vide infra).

Henley Park is the seat of Sir Owen Roberts ;
Normandy Park of Mr. P. G. Henriques, J.P.;
Westwood House of Lieut.-Colonel Coussmaker.

Ash School (National) was built in 1835 ; Ash
Vale School (also National) was built in 1860, and
enlarged 1897 ; Wyke School (National) was built
in 1874, and enlarged 1896.

The Victoria Hall was built in 1897 as a Jubilee
Memorial. It is used for meetings and entertainments.

Frimley, though formerly part of Ash, was in
Godley Hundred, not in Woking, which justifies a
presumption that it may have become the property of
Chertsey Abbey at an earlier date than Ash.

The parish, separated from Ash in 1866, is bounded
on the north-west by Berkshire, on the north-east by
Windlesham, on the east by Chobham and Pirbright,
on the south by Ash, on the west by Hampshire. It
is 30 miles from London. It contains 7,800 acres,
and measures 4 miles from north to south, and
3 miles from east to west. The parish covers the
western side of Chobham Ridges, and extends down
into the valley of the Blackwater, which bounds the
county. The soil is, therefore, Bagshot sand and
alluvium, with patches of gravel and large beds of
peat. In the latter conifers and rhododendrons
flourish exceedingly. The Heatherside Nurseries,
where are some of the finest Wellingtonias in England,
may be taken as the typical industry of the neighbourhood, which is otherwise a residential district, or
occupied by those connected with Aldershot, the
Staff College, which is in the parish, and Sandhurst
which lies just outside it. A very great part of
the parish was open land, heather-covered, before
the Inclosure Act of 1801. Much of it is still
uncultivated. The main road from London to
Southampton crosses the northern part of the parish.
It is substantially on the line of the Roman road.
On the top of the hill, near the Golden Farmer Inn,
named after a notorious highwayman, the road to
Farnham branches south from it, and passes through
Old Frimley village. The main line of the London
and South Western Railway cuts the middle of the
parish. The Ascot, Aldershot, and Farnham branch
traverses it from north to south. The Basingstoke
Canal also passes through Frimley.

Palaeolithic flints have been found in the drift
gravels on the hills, and a few neolithic implements
at places unspecified in the parish. On the hill, near
the southern end of Chobham Ridges, is a very large
round barrow called Round Butt ; south of it Main-
stone Hill probably preserves the name of the Standing
Stone, which formed a boundary mark of Chobham
in the early Chertsey charter. Dr. Stukeley, in his
Itinerarium Curiosum, records a Roman urn and coins
as found here.

Frimley Manor House is the seat of Mrs. Burrell,
Frimley Park of Mr. N. Spens, Watchetts of Mr.
H. J. B. Hollings, Prior Place of Mr. F. H.
Goldney.

The Royal Albert Orphan Asylum was built by
subscription in 1864. It has about two hundred
inmates, boys and girls. A farm is attached to it.
Schools (National) were built in 1842, and enlarged
in 1897.

The common fields were inclosed under an Act
passed in 1826.

York Town with Camberley is a small town
which has grown up on the road in the north-
western part of Frimley parish, and increased owing
to the proximity of the Military College, Sandhurst,
over the Berkshire border, the Staff College at Camberley, and the Albert Asylum.

The Royal Military College, founded by Frederick, Duke of York, was removed under his direction to Sandhurst, close to this neighbourhood (but in Berkshire), in 1812. The houses which grew up near it in Surrey were called after him, York Town. When under a later royal commander-in-chief, the Duke of Cambridge, the Staff College was built in 1862, the extension of York Town was called Cambridge Town, but was soon changed to Camberley for postal convenience, and under that name has become the most important place of the district.

Schools (Provided) were built at York Town in 1883 ; at Camberley in 1897 ; at Camberley, Infants, in 1902. There is a Roman Catholic school, built in 1877. There was a Church school at York Town from 1818 to 1883.

Frimley, York Town, and Camberley form an urban district under an Urban District Council, by the Act of 1894.

It seems probable that the manor of *MANORS* ASH (Esche, xii cent.; Asshe, Assche, xiv cent.) was included under Henley in the land which the Domesday Commissioners say that Azor granted for his soul to Chertsey in the time of King William.[2] The fact that the parish was known as Ash by Henley[3] in the 14th century lends colour to the suggestion that Henley in early times was regarded as the more important place.

Ash was definitely asserted to be the property of the abbey in 1279, when the abbot with his men was declared to be quit of all forest dues in his vill of Ash.[4] The chartulary of Chertsey Abbey[5] records that shortly after the statute, 'vulgarly called Mortmain,' 11 acres in Ash with sufficient common pasture for his flocks and herds were held by Robert de Zathe, while Geoffrey de Bacsete (Bagshot) and his brother William had 28. The Atwaters of West Clandon also held land in Ash.[6]

In 1537 the abbey granted Ash with its other lands to Henry VIII,[7] and for a few years it seems to have remaiucd as Crown property. Edward VI, however, shortly

CHERTSEY ABBEY.
Party or and argent St. Paul's sword having in hilt or crossed with St. Peter's keys gules and azure.

WINCHESTER COLLEGE.
Argent two cheverons sable between three roses gules.

after his accession granted it to Winchester College,[8] which still holds it.

There is no mention of a mill under Henley in Domesday Book, but it is certain that a mill existed at Ash from comparatively early times, for in 1322 the Abbot of Chertsey ordered a new windmill to be built at Ash.[9] Windmills were comparatively new in England then, and it may have been in place of a small water-mill of earlier date. There seems no later record of it.

HENLEY (xi cent. onwards; Henle, xiv cent. ; Suth henle and Henle on the Heth) was granted in William's reign to Chertsey by Azor, a wealthy Englishman who had retained land after the Conquest.[10]

It would appear that before the 14th century the abbey had sublet the manor and certain lands at Fremelesworth (Frimley) to a family who were known as 'of Henley.'[1] Deeds in the possession of Mr. Woodroffe of Poyle (q.v.), quoted by Manning,[11] refer to a John of Henley, and in 1306 to a William de Henley, and in 1324 William enfeoffed Edward II of it.[12] The document further states that since the transfer the rent of 22s. 8d. and 12 measures (*lagenae*) of honey[13] due to the abbey had been in arrears, which furnishes a significant comment on the lawlessness of the end of the reign of Edward II. In 1338 Edward III granted the manor to John de Molyns, together with view of frankpledge and fines for breach of the assize of bread and ale.[14] In the next year other privileges followed, including the right of erecting gallows on the soil of the manor, and of passing judgement on malefactors apprehended there.[15]

In 1343 the manor was reported to be in the king's hands owing to 'the rebellion' of John de Molyns, who was one of the ministers disgraced in 1340 for alleged misappropriation of money, and the abbot took advantage of his tenant's disgrace to renew his demands for rent; he pointed out that Henley had been held of his church since the time of its foundation for the service of paying a sum of money with twelve gallons of honey yearly, and suit at the abbey's court at Ash.[16] The rent is said to have been wrongfully withdrawn by John de Molyns.

John de Molyns' disgrace appears to have been of only short duration. In 1343 the manor was again granted to him to hold in the same way as before,[17] and the next year he obtained a confirmation of that grant.[18] Possibly the manor or part of it may have been granted to Henry de Stoughton[19] during de Molyns' disgrace ; at any rate, in 1349 Henry released to him all his right in the manor.[20] Some two years later John granted Henley to the king in return

[2] *V.C.H. Surr.* i, 311a.
[3] *Cal. Pat.* 1381–5, p. 385.
[4] *Plac. de Quo Warr.* (Rec. Com.), 744.
[5] Exch. K.R. Misc. Bks. vol. 25, fol. 30. See also Feet of F. Surr. 32 Hen. III, 30.
[6] Feet of F. Surr. 8 Edw. II, 29.
[7] Feet of F. Div. Co. Trin. 29 Hen. VIII. [8] Pat. 5 Edw. VI, pt. v.
[9] Exch. K.R. Misc. Bks. vol. 25, fol. 170.
[10] *V.C.H. Surr.* i, 311. It is true that 'Heniei' is included with other lands of the original grant to Chertsey by Frithwald, *subregulus* of Surrey, c. 675, in a charter which is dated 727 (Birch, *Cart. Sax.*

i, 64). But this charter, attested by two kings who were reigning and one of whom died fifty-two years earlier, and by a Bishop Humfrith who was not a bishop till seventeen years later, includes land which was certainly granted to Chertsey at later dates. It is a composition of some time after the Conquest. The early Chertsey charters are more than suspicious. The abbey was sacked by the Danes once or twice. The earliest in reputed date (Birch, op. cit. i, 55–8) grants land in Chertsey, Thorpe, Egham, and Chobham only, giving the boundaries in English, which is not English of the 7th century, and mentioning Giffreus de

la Croix, who was alive when Testa de Nevill was compiled, and the hedge of Windsor Park. But these may contain a re-edited form of the traditional earliest grants. See under Chertsey.
[11] *Hist. of Surr.* iii, 69.
[12] Chan. Inq. p.m. 1 Edw. III (2nd nos.), no. 143.
[13] *Coll. Topog. et Gen.* iv, 164.
[14] Chart. R. 12 Edw. III, m. 4, no. 3.
[15] Ibid. 13 Edw. III, m. 5, no 10.
[16] *Cal. Pat.* 1343–5, p. 89.
[17] Ibid. 543.
[18] Chart. R. 20 Edw. III, no. 141.
[19] Lord of Stoughton in Stoke (q.v.).
[20] Close, 23 Edw. III, pt. ii, m. 9.

for special privileges in his Buckinghamshire property,[31] and in 1359 the king levied a fine against William son of John,[32] by which he made his possession more secure.

From that time Henley Manor remained Crown property for upwards of three centuries, and the evidence for its history consists chiefly of appointments of stewards and parkers. In 1633 Charles I granted to Robert Tyrwhitt and Arthur Squib,[33] who sold it soon after to Sir John Glynn.[34] In 1724 the Duke of Roxburgh, Lord Justice in the absence of George I from England in 1723 and 1725, seems to have been residing at Henley Park.[35] Bowen's map of about 1736 also names him as occupier. Sir John Glynn's son left three daughters, two of whom died unmarried, and the manor passed to Dorothy, the third daughter, who married Sir Richard Child, created Earl of Tylney in 1731. In 1739 the earl sold the manor to Mr. Solomon Dayrolles,[36] who in 1784 conveyed to Henry Halsey.[37] The Halsey family are still owners, but the late Lord Pirbright lived in the house, and Sir Owen Roberts is the present tenant.

In 1338 John de Molyns received licence to impark his woods of West Grove and Goddard's Grove in the manor of Henley.[38] In 1356, after the manor had returned into the king's hands, he bought out twenty tenants, and seems to have laid all the land into the park, granting the rector of Ash compensation for the loss of tithes.[39] The office of park-keeper, with a residence in the manor-house, was a valuable piece of preferment bestowed among others upon Sir Thomas St. Leger by his brother-in-law, Edward IV, on Sir Reginald Bray by Henry VII, and on Viscount Montagu by Queen Mary. Montagu frequently resided at Henley, and it was notoriously the refuge of recusants and suspected priests[30] during his tenure. Henley Park is among those surveyed by John Norden in 1607.[31] The house may contain some ancient walls, but it was mostly rebuilt by Mr. Dayrolles in 1751, the year of his marriage, and bears the date upon it. Lord Pirbright made further additions during his tenancy.

The manor of CLAYGATE (Cleygate) was apparently of late formation. In 1399 a grant was made to Richard Rayle and Nicholas Churchill of lands called Claygate lying at Henley.[32] These lands probably came into the hands of Jasper Tudor, Earl of Pembroke, later Duke of Bedford, and on his attainder in 1461 lapsed to the Crown. In 1475 Sir Thomas St. Leger received a grant of the manor of Claygate[33] for his expense in keeping the game in Guildford Park.[34] Claygate returned into the possession of Jasper, Duke of Bedford,[35] on the reversal of his attainder in 1485. He died in 1495.[36] It is said, however, that Claygate was granted for life to Sir

Reginald Bray in 1488 with the custody of Guildford and Henley Parks.[37] Bedford died without issue, and his lands passed to his nephew, King Henry VII. Elizabeth granted the manor to Edward Lord Clynton and Saye, afterwards Earl of Lincoln.[38] A deed of 1564[39] records that Lord Clynton owed money to a certain Christopher Draper, citizen and alderman of London. The manor was in Draper's hands in the same year,[40] so that probably Claygate was ceded to him in payment for debt. Draper apparently lost little time in selling, for a year later William Harding of Wanborough was in possession.[41] He died seised in 1593,[42] leaving by his wife Catherine daughter of Sir John White of London a son and heir William, who died unmarried in 1610, when the manor passed to his sister Mary.[43] Mary married Sir Robert Gorges, who in 1620 joined with her in conveying the manor to Sir Thomas White.[44] According to Manning and Bray,[44] who had access to Mr. Woodroffe's papers, Sir Thomas settled it on his cousin, Robert Woodroffe, son of Catherine wife of William Harding, by her second marriage with Sir David Woodroffe. From him it descended in the family through Poyle[44] (q.v.).

The manor of FRIMLEY, although part of the parish of Ash, is in Godley Hundred, and is reckoned in it in a court roll.[47] It may have been the land in Ash purchased for Chertsey Abbey by Bartholomew de Winton, the abbot, in 1277, from a Sir Walter Raleigh.[48] William de Henley ' held land in Fremelesworth ' of the abbey, together with Henley (q.v.), in 1324. It came into the possession of Henry VIII in 1537[49] with other monastic lands, and was apparently held by the Crown in demesne for some years. It was granted to Sir John White of Aldershot,[50] who died seised of it in 1573,[51] leaving a son and heir Robert, then aged twenty-eight. Robert died in 1599,[52] when the manor passed to his daughters Helen and Mary, who had respectively married Richard and Walter Tichborne.

The manor remained in the Tichborne family until 1790, when Sir Henry Tichborne and Elizabeth his wife joined in conveying it to James Laurell.[53] He died in 1799 leaving a son and heir James.[54] He sold the Manor House to Mr. Tekell. This and the manor were subsequently bought about 1858 by Mr. J. F. Burrell. The manor has since been sold to Messrs. Pain & Brettell, solicitors at Chertsey.

TICHBORNE. *Vair a chief or.*

The reputed manor of FORMANS in Ash does not appear before the 16th century. Henry Vyne died seised of it in 1571, leaving a son and heir

31 Close, 25 Edw. III, pt. i, m. 4.
32 Feet of F. Surr. 33 Edw. III, 41.
33 Pat. 8 Car. I, pt. ix.
34 Private Deed quoted by Manning and Bray.
35 Willis, Visit. 1724.
36 Deed quoted by Manning and Bray.
37 Feet of F. Surr. Trin. 25 Geo. III.
38 Pat. 11 Edw. III, pt. iii, m. 19.
39 Close, 29 Edw. III, pt. i, m. 14, 15 d. ; pt. ii, m. 25.
30 Loseley MSS. *passim.*
31 Harl. MS. 3749.
32 Cal. Pat. 1399-1401, p. 109.
33 Ibid. 1467-77, p. 548.
34 Accts. &c. Exch. K.R. 516, no. 11.
35 Chan. Inq. p.m. (Ser. 2), ccxxxvi, 79.
36 Ibid. xxiii, 280.
37 Manning and Bray, *Hist. of Surr.* quoting Antis MS.
38 Pat. 2 Eliz. pt. i.
39 Close, 6 Eliz. pt. x.
40 Pat. 6 Eliz. pt. vi.
41 Ibid. 7 Eliz. pt. vi.
42 Chan. Inq. p.m. (Ser. 2), ccxxxvi, 79.
43 Ibid. cccxxiv, 131.
44 Feet of F. Surr. Trin. 18 Jas. I.
44 Hist. Surr. iii, 69.
44 V.C.H. Surr. ii, 618.
47 Ct. R. (P.R.O.), portf. 204, no. 53.
48 Excheq. K.R. Misc. Bks. xxv, 67b.
49 Feet of F. Div. Co. Trin. 1537.
50 He was Lord Mayor 1563. His brother, also John, was Bishop of Lincoln and Winchester; deprived 1559. The grant is probably of Mary's reign.
51 Chan. Inq. p.m. (Ser. 2), clxv, 174.
52 Ibid. cclvii, 112.
53 Feet of F. Surr. Trin. 29 Geo. III.
54 Manning and Bray, *Hist. Surr.* iii, 77.

Stephen.[54] In 1598 Jane Vyne, presumably the widow of Stephen, joined with her son Ralph in conveying the manor to Robert White of Aldershot.[55] At his death it came with Frimley into the hands of the Tichborne family, who alienated to Sir Thomas White in 1609.[57] From that date it seems to have followed the descent of Poyle in Tongham. It is now a farm.

The church of *ST. PETER ASH*

CHURCHES consists of two parts, an old and a new. The former has a chancel 18 ft. by 15 ft. 7 in., nave 42 ft. 10 in. by 20 ft. 6 in., west tower 14 ft. 9 in. by 13 ft. 7 in., and the latter, consisting of a large modern chancel, nave, and vestry, has been added to it on the north side. The new chancel is 30 ft. long by 14 ft. 3 in. wide, and the nave 58 ft. long by 24 ft. wide. The older part of the church has been a good deal repaired, but has been an aisleless building of nave and chancel of 12th-century date, the tower, built of Heath stone, being a 15th-century addition. The earliest details are in the south door and a lancet in the old chancel, both of early 13th-century date, and in the new north wall of the nave is reset a small 12th-century round-headed light, much repaired.

The east window of the old chancel is modern, of three lights in late 13th-century style. On the north are two double bays vaulted between, with foliate or moulded capitals, opening into the new chancel. West of this is a modern squint directed towards the new chancel. In the south wall is a 13th-century lancet with external rebate, in which are a few old stones. The south door is modern and has a continuous chamfer; and west of it is a square-headed window of two trefoiled lights, 15th-century work repaired. Under the lancet is a small piscina with pointed head and half-projecting bowl. The chancel arch is of two chamfered orders with modern moulded capitals and bases and half-octagonal responds; the jambs perhaps date from the 14th century. The north arcade is modern, of four bays, each of two chamfered orders and with moulded circular capitals, ornamented with heads carved in high relief.

In the south wall are three modern two-light windows. The south door dates from c. 1200, and is round-headed, of two orders, the inner with an edge-roll on jambs, the outer with a filleted roll between two hollows in the arch, and filleted shafts with foliate capitals in the jambs. The porch has wood framing, probably of 16th-century date, filled in below with brick, and is covered with ivy. The tower arch is of two chamfered orders with half-octagonal responds and moulded capitals and bases. The tower is a fine massive building of Heath stone, modernized as regards its windows, with a tall shingled broach spire. The modern chancel has a five-light traceried window in the east wall. On the north and south walls is a wall arcade, and there is also a single traceried light on each side. The north vestry has a single and a two-light window. The chancel arch, in 15th-century style, rests on moulded

corbel capitals. In the north wall is inserted a small 12th-century light, and there are also three modern three-light windows, with a similar one of two lights in the west wall. The roofs are all of steep pitch and modern. The font is of wood, as at Chobham in this neighbourhood, probably of 17th-century date, the bowl octagonal, cut from one piece and lined with lead ; there is a central stem with eight octagonal detached shafts.

On the south wall of the old chancel is a brass tablet to Thomas Manory, 1516 ; below is another to Anne Vyne, his daughter and heir. A shield above these bears an engrailed cross.

There are five bells, all of which were cast by Thomas Mears, 1798.

The plate consists of a silver cup and silver cover of 1575, a silver paten of about 1674, a silver flagon of 1734, and a brass almsdish.

The registers date from 1580. There is an iron church at Ash Vale, built in 1885.

The church of *ST. PETER FRIMLEY.*—The present church was built in 1825 in place of the old chapel and is of stone with a low west tower of debased design. It was restored and added to in 1882, 1884, and 1888. The old chapel was a picturesque timbered building with a thatched roof ; a good engraving of it is preserved in Cracklow's *Surrey Churches.*

A new church, *ST. PAUL'S*, was built in 1903 near the north boundary of Frimley.

There is an iron church at Frimley Green, built in 1889.

The church of *ST. MARK WYKE* is of stone, with a belfry, erected in 1847.

The church of *ST. MICHAEL YORK TOWN* dates from 1851. It is of stone, in 13th-century style.

The church of *ST. GEORGE CAMBERLEY* was built in 1893.

The advowson of Ash, like the *ADVOWSONS* manor, belonged first to Chertsey Abbey[58] and later to Winchester College.[59] In 1311 the presentation was in the king's gift ' by reason of the late voidance of the abbacy of Chertsey.'[60]

Under Edward III some supplementary provision was made for the parson of Ash, after the inclosure of Henley Park (q.v.), on condition of his celebrating divine service daily within the king's manor of Henley.[61] This grant was confirmed under Richard II[62] and subsequently.[63]

There was a chapel at Frimley, built at an unknown date. After the foundation, but again at an unknown date, a chantry called John Stephen Chantry was founded in the chapel, worth £5 14s. 11½d. in the time of Edward VI.[64] It was served by an ex-canon of Newark. It was not demolished when the chantry was suppressed, for by the registers baptisms took place there in 1590. In 1607 Bishop Bilson licensed the chapel and churchyard for marriages and burials, the inhabitants undertaking to raise £6 and the rector of Ash to contribute £4 a year for a curate, Winchester College, the patron of Ash, consenting.[65] In 1636 the warden and fellows

54 Chan. Inq. p.m. (Ser. 2), clix, 48.
55 Deed supplied by Mr. Woodroffe to Manning and Bray.
57 Feet of F. Surr. Trin. 7 Jas. I.
58 *Wykeham's Reg.* (Hants Rec. Soc.), i, 22.
59 Inst. Bks. (P.R.O.).
60 *Cal. Pat.* 1307–13, p. 330.
61 In 1357. See Henley Park.
62 *Cal. Pat.* 1381–5, p. 385.
63 Ibid. 1399–1401, p. 549; also 1422–9, p. 98.
64 Chant. Cert. Aug. Off. xlviii, 5.
65 Winton Epis. Reg. Bilson, fol. 21b. A note on the cover says that the chapel was consecrated 8 March 1606–7. But the building had existed before.

of the college protested to Archbishop Laud against the inhabitants of Frimley, who had petitioned him ' for the allowance of a yearly stipend pretended to be due from the parson of Ashe, for the maintenance of a chaplaine at their chappell of ease in Frimley.' It was pointed out that the people of Frimley, like the other inhabitants of Ash, ought to repair to the parish church. The archbishop's decision is not recorded. Services were intermittent ; but in 1735 an agreement was made by which the rector of Ash was to pay £10 a year for a curate, the inhabitants £8, and the bishop £2.[66] The inhabitants appointed the curate ;[67] but the patronage is now in the hands of Winchester College. It was made a separate parish in 1866.

The ecclesiastical parish of Wyke was formed out of Ash, Worplesdon, and Wanborough in 1847. The greater part of it was in Worplesdon, but was surrounded by Ash and is part of the civil parish. The living is in the gift of Eton College.

York Town was made an ecclesiastical parish in 1851. The living is in the gift of the Bishop of Winchester, and includes Camberley.

CHARITIES   Smith's Charity exists as in other Surrey parishes.

Dr. Michael Woodward, rector in 1643, who died or retired before 1662, left £2 10s. annually to the poor, charged on land.

Mr. Edward Dawe left £20 in 1721, laid out in land, for persons not receiving regular relief.

Mr. Thomas Stevens in 1747 left a charge of £3 annually on land for distribution of bread to the poor.

A parcel of land in Ash, called Parish Close, was let for the benefit of the poor of Ash and Frimley.[68]

EAST CLANDON

Clanedun (xi cent.) ; Clendon, and Clandon Abbatis (xii cent.).

East Clandon is a small parish 5 miles east-by-north of Guildford. It is bounded on the north by Send and Ripley, on the east by West Horsley, on the south by Shere and Albury, on the west by West Clandon. It measures about 2 miles from north to south and about a mile from west to east. It contains 1,444 acres.

The parish extends from the summit of the chalk downs over the northern slope of the chalk and the Thanet and Woolwich Beds on to the London Clay. Clandon Downs on the chalk are still partly open ground, and East Clandon Common to the north is fairly well covered with oaks. The Guildford and Epsom road (see West Clandon) runs through the parish. The Guildford and Cobham line cuts the northern part of it.

The village, which includes several picturesque timbered and thatched cottages, lies as usual just on or below the limit of the chalk.

Hatchlands, in East Clandon, is often spoken of as the site of the old manor-house. When Sir Thomas Heath conveyed the manor to Lord King, in 1720, he retained this house. His son Richard sold it, and in 1749 it was bought by Admiral Boscawen. He pulled down the old house and built the present. After his death it was sold to Mr. W. B. Sumner in 1770, and it continued in the Sumner family for some generations. It is now the property of Lord Rendel. It is extremely improbable that it was the site of the manor-house ; the name indicates a different property, and on the original

RENDEL, Lord Rendel of Hatchlands. *Six pieces parted nebuly fessewise sable and argent with a ragged staff between two demi-lions in the chief and a demi-lion between two ragged staves in the foot all countercoloured.*

manor of the abbey, farmed by the *villani* (*vide infra*), there was probably no manor-house at all.

High Clandon is the residence of Mr. F. B. Eastwood, who did much for the restoration of the church. The schools (National) were opened in 1863, and enlarged in 1902.

The manor of EAST CLANDON MANOR (Clandon Abbatis, xi–xiv cent.) is included among the estates which purport to have been granted to Chertsey at the foundation in 675, but appears for the first time in the copy of the charter ascribed to 727,[1] which is undoubtedly a later edition and includes all the Chertsey lands of 1086, some of which were certainly acquired long after 675. At the time of the Survey the abbey was still holding, and it was recorded that under Edward the Confessor the abbot had bought two hides in East Clandon and 'laid them in the manor.'[2] In 1201 Martin, Abbot of Chertsey, granted the manor to John Chaper for life, with reversion to the abbey.[3] Otherwise the history of East Clandon during the Middle Ages consists for the most part of a recital of grants and licences for alienating lands in mortmain. In 1537, after a reputed tenure of over eight hundred years, the abbey ceded East Clandon Manor to the king.[4] In July 1544 Henry granted it to Sir Anthony Browne,[5] who a few weeks later alienated it to George Bigley and Elizabeth his wife.[6] George Bigley's tenure was marked by a dispute in connexion with the copyhold of certain lands in the manor,[7] but seems to have been otherwise uneventful. He died in 1558, leaving two daughters and co-heirs, Dorothy and Mary ; the manor, in default of issue, was to remain to Edmund son of Richard Sutton, with contingent remainders to his brothers John, James, and Jasper.[8] At the death of Elizabeth Bigley,[9] some five years later, Dorothy Bigley had become the wife of Robert Gavell, while Mary had married Edward Carleton. There is record of a fine in the year 1565

66 Correspondence quoted by Manning and Bray, *Surr.* iii, 78.   67 Ibid.
68 Manning and Bray, *Hist. of Surr.* iii, 76.
1 Birch, *Cart. Sax.* i, 94.

2 *V.C.H. Surr.* i, 310b.
3 Feet of F. Surr. 2 John, no. 21.
4 Feet of F. Div. Co. Trin. 29 Hen. VIII.
5 *L. and P. Hen. VIII*, xix (1), p. 616.

6 Ibid. p. 641.
7 Chan. Proc. (Ser. ii), bdle. 183, no. 27.
8 Chan. Inq. p.m. (Ser. 2), cxv, 63.
9 Ibid. (Ser. 2), cxxxv, 18.

in which George Carleton and Edmund Sutton appear as the plaintiffs, while Robert and Dorothy Gavell with Edward and Mary Carleton defended.[10] Probably this suit represented a division of property, since the manor was afterwards in the possession of the Carletons. Edward Carleton died in 1582,[11] and in the inquisition taken at his death[12] his wife Mary is mentioned as having been seised of the manor jointly with him.[13] Their son Edward, who had just come of age at the time of his father's death,[14] evidently sold the property, and it came into the hands of Francis Lord Aungier, who died seised of it in 1632.[15] The Aungiers were Royalists and suffered accordingly. From Gerard son of Francis Lord Aungier it came into the possession of Thomas Earl of Pembroke, whose son sold it in 1692 to Sir Richard Heath of Hatchlands in East Clandon.[16] The Heath family did not keep the manor long; it was conveyed in 1718 under a private Act[17] by Sir Richard's sons to Sir Peter King,[18] whose descendant, the Earl of Lovelace, is the present owner.

Clandon gives an interesting case in Domesday of a manor entirely in the hands of the tenants in villeinage. There is no demesne land mentioned, but the *villani* paid rent. There was a small separate holding in Clandon claimed by Chertsey Abbey, the overlord of the main part, but taken by Odo of Bayeux. John de Rutherwyk, the stirring and reforming Abbot of Chertsey, temp. Edward II and Edward III, bought out the rights of the *villani* in the common field called Siggeworth, 1315. But common fields continued to exist at East Clandon, and are marked on old maps. Between James and Malcolm's *General View of the Agriculture of Surrey*, 1794, and Stevenson's *General View* in 1809, 150 acres were inclosed at Clandon, perhaps the common fields of the two Clandons.[19] But there is no reference in Sir John Brunner's *Return*, 1903. In this, however, the final award of the inclosure of the waste is noted on 21 May 1867.

The church of *ST. THOMAS OF CANTERBURY* has a chancel 31 ft. 3 in. long by 18 ft. 8 in. wide, nave 36 ft. 4 in. by 20 ft. 5 in., a short north aisle 10 ft. wide, with a vestry to the west of it, and a south porch; all internal measurements.

The nave, which is short for its breadth, is evidently of early origin, probably dating from the end of the 11th century; but no architectural details of the original building are left to give a clue to its exact age. The building originally consisted of this nave and a small chancel, but the latter was rebuilt and considerably enlarged about the year 1220, and a few years later a north aisle with an arcade of two bays was added. The western bay is now closed up, and there is nothing to show when this was done; but it may have occurred as far back as the 15th century, when the present wooden bell-turret seems to have been constructed.

The aisle is now modern, having been rebuilt in 1900, when the vestry also was added and the church restored and re-seated.

In the east wall of the chancel are two 13th-century lancet windows with splayed inner jambs and arches. One of the external jamb stones of the south lancet is made of the small pointed head of a rebated and splayed lancet of very early 13th-century or late 12th-century date. On either side of the chancel are two lancets contemporary with the east window, all four more or less renewed. The pair on the north side have plain square jambs and are very much patched. To the south-west is a rectangular low side window with chamfered jambs and lintel, inserted probably in the 14th century. Opposite to this is a blocked doorway with a shouldered lintel, probably of the date of the chancel.

The chancel arch, also of the same period, has chamfered jambs and a two-centred arch with a plain chamfered label; the angles of the jambs have been partly repaired with oak, and the abaci are now entirely replaced by modern oak copies.

The arch to the north aisle has a half-round east

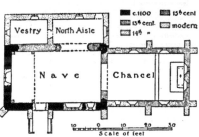

PLAN OF EAST CLANDON CHURCH

respond and a circular pillar partly buried for its west respond; the filling in of the other bay is plastered on both faces and shows no indication of a blocked arch; the responds have moulded bases and capitals, and the arch is a pointed one of two chamfered orders with a grooved and hollow-chamfered label; in the east respond is a vertical groove (now filled in) showing where the arch was boarded up in later times. A plain opening in the wall above, to the east of the arch, is the passage-way to the former rood-loft from the aisle, and contains several steps in the thickness of the wall.

There are two windows in the south wall of the nave; the first is a single trefoiled light near the east, and was inserted presumably to light the pulpit; it is modern externally, but has an old pointed hollow-chamfered rear arch of clunch; the second is an insertion close to it dating from the 15th century and consisting of three trefoiled lights much renewed under a square head with a square-cut moulded label;

[10] Feet of F. Surr. Hil. 7 Eliz.
[11] Parish Register.
[12] Chan. Inq. p.m. (Ser. 2), ccxxxviii, 20.
[13] Ibid. (She remarried, as lady of the manor, in 1583. Parish Register.)
[14] Ibid.
[15] Ibid. ccclxvii, 39.
[16] Feet of F. Surr. Mich. 4 Will. and Mary.
[17] 3 Geo. I, cap. 12.
[18] Feet of F. Surr. Mich. 4 Will. and Mary.
[19] The two Clandons are not distinguishable by name in Domesday. The disputed land had been acquired by the abbey apart from their original holding, and seems to have been in what is now West Clandon.

the jambs outside have been partly restored with cement.

The south doorway appears to have been renewed in chalk, and has a pointed head and jambs of a single chamfered order. The west window is of two trefoiled lights with a quatrefoil over in the pointed head, and is entirely modern. Below it is a blocked late 16th-century doorway of two chamfered orders in red brick with a four-centred arch.

In the north aisle is a small 13th-century piscina next to the respond with a mutilated round basin. The east window of the aisle is all modern except its inner jambs, which are of chalk; it has two trefoiled lights under a pointed head inclosing a quatrefoil. On the north side are a doorway and a square window of two lights, and at the west a doorway into the vestry, which is lighted by a north window of two lights and a single west light.

The walling of the nave is of flint and stone, some of the flints in the south wall being set more or less in herringbone fashion, and the masonry has a very early look about it; this wall has been strengthened by modern buttresses of brick and flint. The chancel walls are also of unbroken flints, and have similar modern buttresses.

The roofs of the chancel and nave are gabled and have open collar trussed rafters, which were formerly plastered on the under side. The aisle has a modern lean-to roof. Above the west end of the nave is a square wood bell-turret supported on posts from the floor of the nave; the posts against the west wall are old, but the eastern pair are modern; the turret is covered with oak shingles and is crowned by a four-sided spire, also shingled.

The altar table is a modern one of oak. The altar rails, date from the last half of the 17th century and have turned balusters of good section flanked by scrolled brackets. A modern desk in the chancel also contains some pieces of 17th-century carving of a honeysuckle pattern. The pulpit is modern. The font dates from the 18th century and is of stone, with a small cup-shaped bowl on a turned baluster stem.

There are three bells : the treble is a pre-Reformation bell from the Reading foundry, c. 1500, inscribed 'Sancte Toma or'; the second is by Eldridge, 1679, and the tenor by R. Phelps, 1737.

The communion plate includes an Elizabethan cup and cover paten of 1569, also a cup of 1661 ; a paten of 1776, a standing paten of 1675, of which it is possible that the foot is older than the top, and an electro-plated paten of 1883.

The earliest book of the registers contains baptisms from 1558 to 1707, marriages to 1690, and burials to 1711 ; the second continues the baptisms to 1754 and marriages and burials to 1787 ; the third has all three from 1788 to 1812. There is also a vestry book from 1591.

ADVOWSON The church of East Clandon, which is mentioned at the time of Domesday, was, like the manor, held by Chertsey Abbey until the Dissolution.[20] Henry VIII granted it to Sir Anthony Browne with the manor, with which it has descended ever since.

CHARITIES Smith's Charity is distributed as in other Surrey parishes. Greethurst's Charity, consisting of £20, was supposed to have been left by a person of the name resident in East Clandon, the name occurring in the registers. The interest was given to the poor.

A convalescent home for children suffering from hip disease, called 'Welcome,' was founded in 1902. It is in connexion with the Alexandra Hospital, London.

WEST CLANDON

Clandun (xi cent.) ; Clandon Regis (xiv cent.).

West Clandon is a small parish 4 miles east-by-north of Guildford. It is bounded on the north by Send and Ripley, on the east by East Clandon, on the south by Albury, on the west by Merrow. It measures 2 miles from north to south and rather over half a mile from east to west. It contains 1,003 acres.

The parish meets Albury on the top of the chalk down, and extends over the northern slope of the chalk, across the Thanet and Woolwich Beds, on to the London Clay. The church and village, according to the usual rule, lie just below the chalk, or on its extreme boundary. The village is scattered along a road from north to south with many picturesque old cottages. Clandon Downs, on the chalk, are still partly open common. The Guildford and Epsom road runs through Clandon. It was made a turnpike road in 1758,[1] and diverted in places out of the narrow ravine into which, as usual, the old unmade road was worn down. The old line can be seen in places in this and the neighbouring parishes by the side of the modern road.

Clandon station, on the Guildford and Cobham line, opened in 1885, is at the north end of the village street, and the line passes through the parish.

The old maps mark 'Common Fields' on the chalk downs. The only inclosures, however, recorded are of the Park (see below).

The Woking Water Works are in West Clandon parish. They draw water from the chalk, and supply not only Woking but the two Clandons, the two Horsleys, part of Merrow, Send, and part of Worplesdon. The works have seriously diminished the flow of springs on both sides of the chalk range.

MANORS At the time of the Domesday Survey *WEST CLANDON* was held of Edward of Salisbury by a certain Hugh ; Fulcui had held it in the time of the Confessor.[2]

The later mentions of the overlordship represent it as belonging to the family of Giffard of Brimsfield.[2]

Giffard of Brimsfield. *Gules three lions passant argent.*

²⁰ *Wykeham's Reg.* (Hants Rec. Soc.), i, 238.

¹ Stat. 31 Geo. II, cap. 77.
² *V.C.H. Surr.* i, 325a.

³ Chan Inq. p.m. 36 Edw. III, pt. ii (1st nos.), no. 75 ; ibid. (Ser. 2), ii, 10.

EAST CLANDON CHURCH : THE CHANCEL

WEST CLANDON CHURCH FROM THE EAST IN 1824
(From Cracklow's View)

This manor was also called CLANDON REGIS,[4] and it was stated in 1279 that part had been in the king's hands,[5] and part in those of William de Braose in his manor of Bramley. It is a fact that some houses are in the manor of Tangley, which represents William's Bramley manor.[5a] In 1255 Christina de Alsefeld released to Matthew de Bovill one messuage and lands in West Clandon,[6] which seem to have been part of the original manor. Matthew de Bovill left a daughter Alice, who in 1294 was the wife of William de Weston.[7] She had, however, made two previous marriages.[8] Her first husband was John de Aqua,[9] who was probably a member of the Atwater family, who in later years tried to assert their claims to this manor. She married secondly Robert de Boclynton,[10] and in 1290 a settlement was made, probably on their marriage, by which the manor was secured to them for life with remainder to the heirs of Alice. Robert was found dead at Send in the autumn of 1290, having been slain by William Atwater 'qui percusit dictum Robertum in capite et praeterea in sinistra parte collis cum hachia quae vocatur polhax.'[11] The sheriff of Surrey was afterwards ordered to release Atwater, on the grounds that his attack had been provoked.[12]

The Atwater family seem to have had certain rights in the manor; in 1279 John Atwater claimed to have liberty to buy and sell in Guildford without payment of tolls 'for himself and his men of Clandon,' and won his case.[13] It therefore seems as though the quarrel which proved fatal to Robert de Boclynton may have originated in some dispute touching the manor. At any rate, after Robert's death, William and Alice de Weston enjoyed peaceable possession of the manor.[14] Their son William, who succeeded them, married first Isabel, daughter of Walter Burgess, by whom he was the father of another William, who inherited West Clandon, and secondly Margery de Romaine,[15] who was custodian of the manor during the minority of her stepson. In 1336 the elder William made a settlement of the manor on himself and his wife with remainder to his son William, and contingent remainders to Edmund and Richard his sons by Margery.[16]

After William's death the old Atwater dispute reappeared. Robert son of William Atwater brought a suit against Margery de Weston, with intent to recover the manor of West Clandon, into which, so it was declared, 'she would not have had ingress but for the disseisin wrongfully wrought by Robert de Boclynton and his wife Alice on Robert Atwater, grandfather of the plaintiff.'[17] Some six years later Robert released to Margery and to William son of William de Weston all his right in the manor.[18] Margery died seised in 1361.[19]

The manor seems to have descended in the Weston family from father to son until the death of John de Weston, great-grandson of William son of William and Margery, in 1441.[20] John left no male issue, and his lands were apparently divided among his three daughters, Agnes wife of John Athall of Horsham, Joan wife of John Skynner, and Agnes, who carried West Clandon to her husband Thomas Slyfield of Great Bookham.[21] His son Henry was given possession by his father's trustees in 1487.[22]

In 1531 John Slyfield, presumably his son, died seised of the manor, leaving Edmund his son and heir.[23] He had entered into an agreement with one Walter Lambert, citizen and goldsmith of London, by which the one of John's three sons, Edmund, John, or Richard, who first reached the age of fifteen was to take to wife either of Lambert's two daughters, Elizabeth or Margaret.[24] Edmund the eldest was only ten years old at the time of his father's death, and there seems no record to show whether the agreement was ever carried out. In 1598 Henry Slyfield, who was the eldest son of Edmund,[24a] died seised, leaving Edmund as his son and heir, then aged eighteen.[25] By Henry's will, dated 1598, the manor was secured to his wife Elizabeth for life with remainder to his son Edmund and contingent remainders to his other sons Thomas and John.[26] Elizabeth soon afterwards became the wife of Henry Vincent,[27] brother of Sir Thomas Vincent of Stoke D'Abernon, and appears as Elizabeth Vincent in the list given by Symmes of persons who held their court at West Clandon as late as 1631.[28] Of Henry's younger sons, Thomas died in 1608,[29] and John, who had become a member of Gray's Inn, was convicted of felony and murder and attainted; he contrived to escape the extreme penalty of the law, but his lands and remainders were forfeited to the Crown.[30] West Clandon was not affected, not being his, and in 1615 Edmund and William Slyfield united in conveying the reversion after their mother's death to George Duncumbe,[31] who held courts from 1638 to 1645.

The Duncumbes, however, did not retain possession long. Sir Richard Onslow had bought the Lodge in the park in 1642,[32] and a series of transactions with the Onslow family, begun in 1650,[33] was finally concluded in 1711 by the transference of the manor to Sir Richard Onslow.[34] The Earl of Onslow, a descendant of Sir Richard, still holds it.

ONSLOW, Earl of Onslow. *Argent a fesse gules between six Cornish choughs.*

---

[4] Inq. p.m. 36 Edw. III, pt. ii (1st nos.), no. 75.

[5] Plac. Cor. 7 Edw. I, rot. 31.

[5a] Historically the name Clandon Regis is puzzling, for if it is true that it had been in the king's hands, one would have expected a grant of it to have been on record. The part belonging to William de Braose must have been at first a separate holding attached to the manor of Tangley which have been included in the original manor of Bramley.

[6] Feet of F. Surr. 39 Hen. III, no. 9.

[7] Ibid. 22 Edw. I, no. 29, also Harl. Soc. Publ. xliii, 215.

[8] Brayley, Hist. of Surr. ii, 81–8 (pedigree supplied by Weston family).

[9] Ibid.

[10] Ibid.

[11] Assize R. 906.

[12] Cal. Close, 1288–96, p. 373.

[13] Plac. de Quo Warr. (Rec. Com.), 747.

[14] Feet of F. Surr. 22 Edw. I, no. 29.

[15] Visit. of Surr. (Harl. Soc. xliii), 215.

[16] Feet of F. Surr. Trin. 10 Edw. III.

[17] De Banco R. 351, m. 333.

[18] Close, 27 Edw. III, m. 18.

[19] Chan. Inq. p.m. 36 Edw. III, pt. ii, (1st nos.), no. 75.

[20] Ibid. 19 Hen. VI, no. 5.

[21] Ibid.

[22] Deed quoted by Manning and Bray, op. cit. iii, 74.

[23] Chan. Inq. p.m. (Ser. 2), ii, 10.

[24] Ibid.

[24a] Monument in Great Bookham Church.

[25] Chan. Inq. p.m. (Ser. 2), cclx, 131.

[26] Exch. Spec. Com. 4974. [27] Ibid.

[28] Add. MSS. 6167, fol. 443.

[29] Exch. Spec. Com. 4974. [30] Ibid.

[31] Feet of F. Surr. Trin. 13 Jas. I.

[32] See below.

[33] Ibid. Mich. 1650; Recov. R. Mich. 29 Chas. II, m. 240, &c.

[34] Ibid. Trin. 10 Anne.

The second Lord Onslow built the house in 1731 from designs by Giacomo Leoni. The house is of red brick with stone dressings, and has the merits of its style, with large and lofty rooms and good ornament.

The second manor in West Clandon, represented originally by the manor of William de Braose, noticed above, is described under Bramley, of which it was part.

On 25 May 1530 Sir Richard Weston of Sutton had licence by charter to impark his land at Merrow and Clandon. The Clandon Park so formed, chiefly in Merrow, was disparked later. In 1642 a later Sir Richard Weston, the agriculturist and canal projector, sold this land to Sir Richard Onslow, the recusant naturally giving place to the Parliamentarian, who inclosed the park again.

CHURCH The church of *ST. PETER AND ST. PAUL* has a chancel 24 ft. 1 in. by 18 ft. 5 in., nave 50 ft. 8 in. by 23 ft. 4 in., north-east vestry, north tower 13 ft. 9 in. by 13 ft. 6 in. and south porch; all these measurements are internal.

PLAN OF WEST CLANDON CHURCH

The church is mentioned in the Domesday Survey of 1086, but of this building nothing is now left.

The earliest portion of the present structure is the nave, which dates from about 1180; it is of its original size, but now only retains (of the date) the north and south doorways; the chancel is a rebuilding of about the year 1200, and may have superseded a small apsidal chancel to the first building, or more probably the wooden chancel of the earlier Saxon building which may have been left standing after the nave was rebuilt in stone; of this date a lancet window in the north wall remains; the tower was probably added at the same period, but it has since been re-cased and much altered. Windows were inserted in the south wall of the nave and in the two side walls of the nave about 1250, and the sedile in the chancel was put in at the same time. The east window of the chancel is the work of about 1330, three original lancets being destroyed to make room for it, and it is probable that the angle buttresses against this wall were work of the same period. The porch, although it has since been reconstructed, may contain timbers of 13th-century date. Much restoration of the windows has taken place, and the chancel arch has

been considerably widened; the vestry is a modern addition.

The east window is a mid-14th-century one of three trefoiled ogee lights under a two-centred arch containing cusped net tracery; it is of two chamfered orders and has a moulded label outside. The tracery has been almost wholly restored with clunch and the jambs partly, in Bath stone. To the north and south of it in the same wall are the remains of the original lancet windows. In the north wall is a complete original lancet modernized outside; under it is a plain square recess with rebated edges, all of chalk; it has the holes for the hinge staples and bolts, and another deep hole in its head. To the west of these are the modern doorway and archway to the vestry and organ chamber.

In the south wall are two ancient piscinae; the eastern has a plain round head chamfered like the jambs and a half-round basin; it is also set higher in the wall than the other, which is shallower and of a square shape with chamfered edges and a three-quarter round basin. Both basins have three grooves in the bottom radiating from the drain; the sedile west of these is of mid-13th-century date and has an engaged shaft in each jamb (between two hollow chamfers) with moulded base of three rounds and moulded bell capital with a scroll mould abacus; the arch is of two hollow-chamfered orders and has a head and scroll mould label with mask stops. The first of the two south windows is a lancet, inserted or enlarged about the same time, whilst the other lancet in the same wall was also replaced by the present trefoil headed light. The chancel arch is modern and is pointed.

The vestry has a two-light window in its north wall and a doorway to the east; a modern arch opens into it from the tower through the east wall of the latter. The tower has its north angles strengthened by modern square buttresses and a vice rises in its south-west angle. The arch opening into it from the nave is of chalk in two chamfered orders without imposts in capitals; the chamfers are finished with pyramidal stops a short distance above the floor. In the north wall of the tower is a modern window of three lights and tracery; there was formerly a lancet in the east window, now removed for the vestry arch; the stone portion of the tower has been heightened and recased in modern times and has a modern cornice over which is a timber bell-chamber with an octagonal spire. The north doorway of the nave has a round head of two chamfered orders continuous with the jambs; they are now modernized outside in chalk with stone bases. The only window north of the nave is a 13th-century lancet either re-cut or modernized outside.

The first window in the south wall of the nave is of three ogee trefoiled lights with intersecting tracery and a two-centred arch with a moulded label; the tracery is of modern stone and the label in chalk. On a keystone in the external arch is a curious shield carved with the arms of the Westons: a cheveron between three lions' heads, the whole very rudely carved.

In the east jamb is a piscina of late 12th-century date ; it is the square head of a former pillar piscina beautifully carved with leaf ornament ; a rudely pointed arch is cut out of the jamb over.   The south doorway is similar to the north doorway and has an old arch with a moulded label, but modern jambs outside.   East of it is a portion of a 14th-century holy-water stoup under a pointed head ; the front half of the basin has been cut away.   On one of the stones inside are three cuttings which appear to be wide sundials.   The westernmost south window has two pointed lights re-tooled or modernized outside. The west window was inserted late in the 15th century, and has three cinquefoil lights under a flat segmental arch.   It is largely glazed with heraldic glass of the 18th century, placed there by an Earl of Onslow.

The walling is of flint with stone dressings ; diagonal buttresses strengthen the angles at both ends ; the one to the north-west of the nave is modern ; in the modern square buttress against the south-east of the nave is a stone on which is cut an early circular sun-dial probably of the 12th century ; it has three circles and is divided in twenty-four spaces by radiating lines ; four dots mark the hour of noon and a small cross that of six p.m.

The south porch has ancient timbers ; it is open at the sides, in which were formerly balusters or posts.

The roof of the chancel is of low pitch and with heavy timbers, and may date from the 14th century. The nave roof is of late 15th-century date, although it appears to have been reconstructed in 1716 ; the wall plate has a handsome embattled cornice fixed to it, probably original.

The font has a bowl of Sussex marble, square, with shelving sides, in which are arcades of shallow circular-headed arches which have been partly chiselled off ; it is of the earliest date of the building ; the stem and base are modern.

In the chancel are preserved, in a glass case, some ancient panels of oak ; it is doubtful whether they belonged to a 'table' behind an altar or to a rood screen ; but they appear to be of late 13th or early 14th-century date ; the figures upon them are un-doubtedly those of St. Peter and St. Paul on either side of St. Thomas of Canterbury ; the two apostles bear their respective emblems, the keys and the sword ; the martyred archbishop between them has his right hand raised in benediction, while the left holds the cross staff ; there are traces of gold on the nimbus of each saint, and the figures are coarsely outlined in black.   Much of the pewing in the western part of the nave is nicely carved in dark wood imported from abroad by a former Earl of Onslow.

The six bells were all by Thomas Lester, 1741, but the third, fourth, and fifth were re-cast by Mears and Stainbank in 1875.   One is inscribed in capitals ' At propper times my voice Il raies, unto my bennifactor praise.'

The communion plate includes an Elizabethan cup and cover paten of the date 1569 ; also another Paten of 1712 given by Sir Richard Onslow.

The registers begin in the unusually early year of 1536.   In the first book, which is of parchment, the baptisms, marriages, and burials are mixed thence to 1583, then written separately from 1584 to 1699, followed by a short gap, the baptisms continuing from 1700 to 1755, marriages 1701 to 1735, and burials 1700 to 1746.   In a second parchment book are baptisms and burials from 1653 to 1663 and mar-riages 1654 to 1657 ; there are also two baptisms of 1675.   The third book has baptisms and burials from 1756 to 1807 ; the fourth has marriages from 1778 to 1812 ; the marriages between 1735 and 1778 appear to be missing.   The fifth continues the bap-tisms and burials from 1807 to 1812.

ADVOWSON   The advowson of the church of West Clandon always descended with the manor.

CHARITIES   Smith's Charity is distributed as in other Surrey parishes.

Land was purchased for the benefit of the poor at an uncertain date, and vested in the churchwardens (now not known).

— Balcuin left about £25 to the churchwardens for the poor at an unknown date.

William Stovall left money for bread, for the poor, also at an unknown date, and Lord Onslow gave a small piece of land for the same object.[26]

The various charities produce about £30 a year.

EAST HORSLEY

East Horsley is bounded on the north by Cobham and Ockham, on the east by Effingham, on the south by Shere and Abinger, on the west by West Horsley. It measures 4 miles from north to south, and three-quarters of a mile from east to west.   It contains 1,826 acres.   The elongated form is common to it with the other parishes along the northern slope of the Chalk, and like the others it reaches from the crest of the hill across the Chalk, the Thanet and Woolwich Beds, and on to the London Clay.   The village is be-low the Chalk or just upon its lower edge.   On the sum-mit of the Chalk however hereabouts occurs a bed of clay with frequent flints.   The village is compact and well built on the whole.   The Guildford and Epsom road and the Guildford and Cobham line run through the parish.   East Horsley Station, opened in 1885, is nearly a mile north of the village.   The station called Effingham Junction is also in East Horsley, and was opened the same year.

Green Dean is the name of a farm in the parish. The name occurs at an early date.   John de Grendon held land in East Horsley in 1305,[1] and Peter de Grendene appears in an inquiry by Christchurch, Canterbury, under Edward III.[3]

Horsley Towers is a large house standing in a park of 300 acres, the seat of the Earl of Lovelace.   The old house was rebuilt about 1745.   The present house was built by Sir Charles Barry for Mr. Currie on a new site, between 1820 and 1829, in Eliza-bethan style.   Mr. Currie, who owned the combined manors, 1784–1829, rebuilt most of the houses in the village and restored the church.

26 Parl. Ret. 1786.   1 Feet of F. Surr. 33 Edw. I, 112.   3 Manning and Bray, Hist. of Surr. iii, 29.

In 1792 an Inclosure Act [3] enabled Mr. Currie to inclose most of Horsley Common at the northern end of the parish and the common fields and waste at the southern part, on the Chalk. The parsonage and glebe were at the same time removed, by exchange, to other sites.

The school (National) was established by Mr. Currie.

MANORS The entry in Domesday Book touching the manor of *EAST HORSLEY* (Horslei, xiii cent. ; Horslegh, xiv cent. &c.) reports it to have been held at that date by the Archbishop of Canterbury for the sustenance of his monks of Christchurch.[4] It is said to have been granted for the purpose by Thored in 1036.[5] But it was later in the hands of the monks of Christchurch, not of the archbishop himself.

In 1129 Edith of Horsley gave a virgate of land in Horsley to Geoffrey, Prior of Canterbury, to hold for a rent of 40s. during her life, of which he was to be quit after her death.[6] Edward II granted to the Prior of Christchurch the right of having free warren in his demesne lands,[7] a privilege which was afterwards confirmed by Edward III.[8]

CHRISTCHURCH, Canterbury. *Azure a cross argent with the monogram ℔ sable thereon.*

East Horsley was taken into the king's hands at the time of the Dissolution, and formed part of Queen Mary's grant to the priory of Sheen when it was refounded.[9] Under Elizabeth the Crown resumed possession, and the manor was granted to John Agmondesham,[10] whose family had held the manor of Rowbarnes in East Horsley (q.v.) for some years. His tenure was marked by an attempt to inclose part of the common land of East Horsley ; a project passed by the Earl of Lincoln and Lord Montagu, who as actual and contingent holders of West Horsley were interested in the question.[11] He died without issue in 1600, when the manor passed to his sister Mary wife of William Muschamp.[12] At Mary's death in 1620 she left a son and heir Agmondesham,[13] who was then forty years of age. He had a son William who in 1646 made a settlement of the manor on his son Agmondesham and Hester his wife.[14] According to Manning and Bray [15] Agmondesham died in 1648 before his father, who died in 1660, and was succeeded by his grandson Ambrose. In 1701 Ambrose conveyed the manor to Frances, Viscountess Lanesborough, widow of his brother Denny Muschamp.[16] Lady Lanesborough bequeathed her Surrey estates in remainder to Sackville Fox the youngest son of her daughter Frances by Henry Fox.[17] Sackville died in 1760,[18] his son James, who was then a minor, being heir to his lands. James, shortly after his coming of age,

sold the manor to Robert Mackereth,[19] who in his turn conveyed it to Thomas Page of Cobham. Page died in 1781, and East Horsley was sold to Charles Dumbleton,[20] from whom it passed in 1784 to William Currie.[21] Brayley,[22] writing about 1840, states that shortly after Mr. Currie's death in 1829 [23] the manor was purchased by Lord Lovelace, with whose family it remains.

The *BISHOP'S MANOR* in East Horsley seems to have belonged to the see of Exeter throughout the Middle Ages. It has been conjectured that the Domesday entry to the effect that 'Bishop Osbern of Exeter holds Woking' should more properly be referred to this manor, since there is no trace of any land held by the Bishop of Exeter in Woking.[24] In 1243 the bishop was summoned to show by what

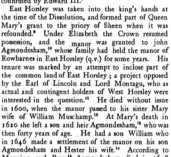

SEE OF EXETER. *Gules St. Paul's sword erect surmounted by St. Peter's keys.*

warrant he held the moiety of East Horsley Manor, and it was then said to pertain to his chapelry of Bosham in Sussex.[25] About the same time the manor was assessed at a quarter of one knight's fee.[26] Domesday Book mentions two homagers who each held four hides of the bishop,[27] but since this is the only mention of tenants it seems reasonable to suppose that the manor was farmed for the bishop.

Manning [28] states that in the time of Henry VIII the bishop sold the manor to Henry, Marquis of Exeter ; and in that case it was forfeited to the Crown with the marquis's other lands in 1538. Edward VI granted it to a certain Thomas Fisher,[29] who in 1555 alienated to William Walter.[30] Walter did not long retain possession, but in 1555 joined with Sir Nicholas Throckmorton, to whom it had possibly been leased, in conveying the manor to Joan Hamond, widow.[31] Her son William Hamond left it by will (5 May 1575) to Sir Laurence Stoughton, husband to his step-daughter Rose Ive, and they were in possession in 1580.[32] Sir Laurence Stoughton sold the manor in 1584 to Thomas Cornwallis,[33] who died in 1596.[34] His widow died seised of it in 1626, when her great-nephew Thomas Earl of Southampton came into possession.[35] He sold the manor three years later to Carew Raleigh,[36] who afterwards purchased the manor of West Horsley (q.v.). He kept possession of the bishop's manor for about fifteen years, and then conveyed it through trustees to Henry son of Sir Christopher Hildyard of Winestead in Holderness.[37] At Henry's death in 1674 it was inherited by his second son Philip.[38] His estates were sold under a private Act of Parliament,[39] and East Horsley was bought by Sir William Brownlow, bart. He in 1698 conveyed to Denny Muschamp and the Viscountess Lanesborough

[3] 39 & 40 Geo. III, cap. 11.
[4] *V.C.H. Surr.* i, 300a.
[5] Canterbury, Treasury Reg. ii, 351.
[6] Feet of F. Surr. 1 John, no. 3.
[7] Chart. R. 10 Edw. II, m. 24, no. 60.
[8] Ibid. 38 Edw. III, m. 156.
[9] Pat. 5 & 6 Phil. and Mary, pt. iv, m. 9.
[10] Pat. 2 Eliz. pt. v.
[11] Loseley MSS. Letters, viii, 67 ; x, 34.
[12] Chan. Inq. p.m. (Ser. 2), cclvii, 86.
[13] Ibid. ccclxxxviii, 120.
[14] Feet of F. Div. Co. Mich. 22 Chas. I.
[14] *Hist. of Surr.* iii, 31.

[16] Chan. Proc. Reynardson, clxiii, 52.
[17] P.C.C. 10 Marlbro'.
[18] Gent. Mag. xxx, 594.
[19] Manning and Bray, *Hist. of Surr.* iii, 31.
[20] Ibid.
[21] Feet of F. Surr. Trin. 24 Geo. III.
[22] *Hist. of Surr.* ii, 66.
[23] *V.C.H. Surr.* i, 300.
[24] *Plac. Abbrev.* (Rec. Com.), 118b.
[25] *Testa de Nevill* (Rec. Com.), 220a.
[26] *V.C.H. Surr.* i, 300.
[27] *Hist. of Surr.* iii, 30.

[29] Pat. 3 Edw. VI, pt. vi, m. 16.
[30] Feet of F. Surr. 5 Edw. VI.
[31] Ibid. East. 1 & 2 Phil. and Mary ; Add. Chart. 25505.
[32] Feet of F. Surr. East. 2 Eliz.
[33] Ibid. Trin. 26 Eliz.
[34] Tomb at East Horsley.
[35] Chan. Inq. p.m. (Ser. 2), cccxxii, 19.
[36] Feet of F. Surr. Trin. 5 Chas. I.
[37] Ibid. 18 Chas. I ; Div. Co. Mich. 22 Chas. I. See also Foster, *York. Ped.* under Hildyard.
[38] Foster, *York. Ped.*
[39] 3 & 4 Will. and Mary, cap. 35.

West Clandon : Clandon Park

East Horsley : Horsley Towers

his wife,[40] by which the manor was united to the other manor of East Horsley.

The origin of the so-called manor of ROW-BARNES (Ruebern, Rughberne) in East Horsley is somewhat obscure. In 1215 Ralph de Kameis (Camois) and Matilda his wife claimed land in Rowbarnes of Peter de Rowbarnes.[41] Ralph de Camois held Wotton,[42] and Rowbarnes still pays quit-rent to the manor of Wotton.

In 1229 Walter de Rowbarnes granted to Matilda de Kalcham half a virgate of land in Horsley.[43] According to the pedigree of the Agmondesham family, given in the *Visitations of Surrey*,[44] Ralph, great-grandson of Walter Agmondesham, who lived in the time of Henry III, gained possession of Rowbarnes Manor by his marriage with one Isabel, whose parentage is unfortunately not stated. This family was still at East Horsley in 1411 when the jurors at the archbishop's court declared that the highway was liable to be flooded owing to the default of Philip Agmondesham.[44] Philip, according to the pedigree, was the son of Ralph and Isabel.

Another Ralph, grandson of Philip, died seised of Rowbarnes in 1498, leaving a son and heir John, then twenty-three years of age.[46] John died without issue,[47] and the manor passed to his brother Thomas, who survived him only for a few years. The inquisition taken at Thomas's death states that he left an infant daughter Barbara,[48] but it seems probable that she died soon after her father, since the Agmondesham pedigree represents him as dying without issue. In any case Rowbarnes came into the possession of John son of Thomas's brother Henry,[49] who also obtained the archbishop's manor by a grant from Queen Elizabeth.[50] From that date the two manors have the same descent.

Gervase of Canterbury mentions a convent of Black Nuns at Horsley. By a process of elimination, because Canterbury and Exeter held the rest, this has been supposed to have been at Rowbarnes, but there is no other record of it.

CHURCH

The church of *ST. MARTIN* consists of a chancel 29 ft. 3 in. by 15 ft. 9 in., a nave 49 ft. 8 in. by 16 ft., with a north aisle 10 ft. 4 in. wide, a west tower 16 ft. 2 in. by 10 ft. 4 in., and a south porch.

Much repair and rebuilding has obscured the history of the building, but before 1869 the chancel was of 13th-century date, and the nave, which was not entirely rebuilt, is probably older. The west tower is so covered with plaster that little can be said of its history; it opens to the nave by a modern arch, above which is a blocked pointed arch, presumably of 13th-century date. A third arch, now quite covered up, is said to exist above the pointed arch, and on the strength of this a pre-Conquest date has been claimed for the tower. It would be interesting if any proof could be obtained. The windows of the tower are small lancets, in great measure modern, but in the west wall is what looks like a round-headed window opening,

the lower part of which has been destroyed by the insertion of a west doorway late in the 13th or 14th century. The plan of the tower is unusual, being much wider from north to south than from east to west.

The north aisle seems to have been originally of two bays, and the chapel east of it, which now is thrown into the aisle, must have existed in some form from the 13th century, though it seems to have been rebuilt in the 15th. The aisle was probably widened in the 15th century, and the chapel was entirely rebuilt in 1869. The chancel and nave are practically of equal width, a fact which suggests a rebuilding of the former in the 13th century round an older chancel, while the nave has preserved its original plan. The difference of axis between nave and chancel points in the same direction.

In the east wall of the chancel is a triplet of lancets with diapered inner splays, while the north wall contains two and the south wall three lancets, all being repaired and reset in new walls in 1869. There was formerly a third lancet on the north and a north doorway.

To the west of the north windows is a shallow modern recess for the organ, the arch opening to it having attached shafts with moulded bases and capitals. The three east windows are recorded to have been of equal height before 1869.

The chancel arch has re-tooled 13th-century jambs with attached semi-columns having original moulded capitals but modern bases. The arch has been rebuilt and is two-centred and of two chamfered orders.

The north arcade of the nave is of four bays with octagonal columns which have splayed bases, of which only one is original, and heavy hollow-chamfered square-edged abaci. The arches are two-centred and are of two orders, the inner hollow-chamfered and the outer with a plain chamfer. Only the two western bays of the arcade are old, the other two dating from 1869; so that no evidence of the former history of this part of the church remains. The old work is in chalk, of very broad and plain detail, and in spite of its square-edged abaci is probably not earlier than the middle of the 13th century, the section of the arches being by no means of early character.

The south wall of the nave has three pairs of lancet windows under inclosing arches dating from 1869, and replacing two-light windows of 15th-century style; between the second and third of these windows is the south doorway, which is also modern and has plain chamfered jambs and a pointed arch in Bath stone. The porch of 1869 is of timber construction and replaces one which was apparently ancient, and had a roof of Horsham stone slabs.

The east window of the north chapel, now forming the east end of the north aisle, is modern, of 14th-century design, and the north window is a modern copy of a 15th-century original, of three lights with a transom under a square head : west of it is a modern copy of a 15th-century doorway. Further west in the same wall, in the aisle proper, are two late 15th-century windows, each of two cinquefoiled lights under a square head, and in the west wall is a similar window with a moulded label.

Some of the features of the tower have been already noted. A modern lancet has been cut in its south

AGMONDESHAM. *Argent a cheveron azure between three boars' heads sable with three cinqfoils or on the cheveron.*

[40] Manning and Bray, *Hist. of Surr.* iii, 31.

[41] Feet of F. Surr. 15 John, no. 97.

[42] *Testa de Nevill* (Rec. Com.), 219.

[43] Feet of F. Surr. East. 13 Hen. III, no. 69.

[44] *Harl. Soc. Publ.* xliii, 53.

[45] Eccl. Com. Ct. R. bdle. 18, no. 6.

[46] Chan. Inq. p.m. (Ser. 2), xiii, 67.

[47] *Harl. Soc. Publ.* xliii, 54.

[48] Chan. Inq. p.m. (Ser. 2), xxii, 32.

[49] *Harl. Soc. Publ.* xliii, 54.

[50] Pat. 2 Eliz. pt. v.

wall to light the ground stage, and the west doorway has jambs and a pointed arch of two very small chamfered orders, perhaps cut from a single order, and a modern label in Roman cement. In the angles of the tower are large posts framed and braced together and carrying the wooden bell-cage above, independently of the tower walls ; they are obviously of considerable age, but their date can only be conjectured.

The tower is of three stages, but has no dividing string-courses ; in the middle stage is a narrow loop light on the north, west, and south sides. These are of brick, but they are set in old, probably 13th-century, jambs. The top stage is of brick with a window in each face, and is crowned with an embattled parapet ; it dates from early in the last century.

The roofs are tiled, all the timbers being modern.

All the internal fittings are modern except two jacobean chairs in the chancel, which have carved backs and baluster legs and arm rests. There is also a small table in the vestry, which is possibly older still. The chancel screen was set up in 1897 in memory of the Rev. Freeman Wilson, rector, who died in the church on Sunday 11 October 1896.[31]

There are several interesting brasses, the most important being a small one on the north wall of the chancel, on which is represented a kneeling bishop in mass vestments and with a mitre and his pastoral staff. On a shield opposite him are the arms of Booth—Three boars' heads razed with a label.

Below is an inscription : ' Quisquis eris qui transieris sta plege plora. | Sum q^d eris fuerī. q͠ q^d es : pro me precor ora. | Hic jacet Johēs Bowthe quōdā Eps̄ Exoniēn qui | Obiit v° die mes̄ Aprelis A° dn̄i M° cccc° LXXVIII.'

On the north abutment of the chancel arch is a brass demi-figure of a civilian of the time of Richard II in a loose gown buttoned down the front with sleeves and a hood. He has a forked beard and a moustache, with short hair, and wears buttoned mittens. The inscription which is unfortunately lost, was as follows : ' Hic jacet Robertus de Brentyngham, Frater Reverendi Patris Thome Exon Episcopi. Cujus anime propicietur Deus.' Thomas was Bishop of Exeter from 1370 to 1394.

There are also two brasses of the Snelling family, one in the north aisle having the inscription : ' Pray for the sowllis of john Snellyng and Alys hys wyfe the whych desecyd the VIII day of ffeveryll in the yer of owr lorde M° cccc° LXXXVIII on whose sowllis god have mercy.'

SNELLING. Gules three griffons' heads rased or and a chief indented erminois.

Above are the figures of John and Alice, and below are those of their six sons and five daughters.

The other brass is on the south wall of the nave and has the following inscription : ' Of your charity pray for the soulis of Thomas Snellinge late of the Fatishe of Est Horsley smith and Jone his wife which Thomas diseased the XXVIII day of May in ye yere of our lorde MCCCCCIIII. And for the soules of the faders and moders of the foresaid Thomas and jone with all

theyr childerne on whoes sowlys Almyghty Jhū have mercy Amen.'

Below are the figures of eight sons and five daughters, but those of the parents are now missing, with the upper part of the stone.

In the north aisle are the alabaster effigies and other fragments of a fine alabaster tomb of Thomas Cornwallis, esq., and Lady Katherine his wife, daughter of Thomas Wriothesley, Earl of Southampton and Lord Chancellor of England, and their two sons Robert and Henry. She died in 1626 ' and was 30 years a widdow.' Above are the arms of Cornwallis impaling those of Wriothesley, with the crests of a stag and a bull, which are also set at the feet of the effigies. On the north wall of the aisle is a monument to Henry Hildyard, eldest surviving son and heir of Sir Christopher Hildyard, of Winestead, co. York. He died in 1674.

In the window near the Cornwallis tomb is a fragment of glass dated 1573, and three quarries with the crest of Acton of Worcestershire : An arm in armour holding a sword on which is a boar's head, with the motto ' Vaillance avance.' There are also several small pieces of old heraldic glass, too broken for identification.

There are four bells in the tower, the treble being inscribed ' Bryan Eldridge made mee 1648 ' ; the second and tenor are by William Eldridge 1703 ; and the third is by Richard Hille of London, c. 1450, and has a black letter inscription : ' Sit nomen Domini benedictum ' with the ' cross and ring ' shield.

The plate comprises a cup and paten of 1640, and a cup, paten, and two large flagons of 1649.

The registers are contained in three books ; the first having baptisms from 1666 to 1752, marriages 1668 to 1752, and burials from 1666 to 1753. The second has baptisms and burials from 1753 to 1787, and one or two marriages ; and the third book contains baptisms, marriages, and burials from 1788 to 1812.

In 1666 the registers record the death of eight persons from the plague.

A small yard surrounds the church, which is entered from the road on the west side, and there are large trees on the adjoining property on the south and east sides.

ADVOWSON The advowson of East Horsley was in the hands of the archbishop, except in 1349, when the king presented twice, ' because of the vacancy in the archbishopric.'[32] It was the year of the Black Death. Henry VIII probably took over the advowson with the manor in 1538. In 1551 it was granted to Thomas Fisher,[33] grantee of the Bishop's Manor (to which it had not been attached before), and it descended for some years with this manor. After the Restoration the advowson was successfully reclaimed by the archbishop, who presented in 1662,[34] and continued to do so till 1876, when it was transferred to the Dean and chapter of Canterbury.[35]

CHARITIES Smith's Charity is distributed as in other Surrey parishes. There is a rent-charge on land called Bishop's Mead, supposed to be the gift of Bishop Booth of Exeter, who is buried in the church, for the relief of the poor ; and another small charge on other land for the same purpose.

31 The Rev. F. Wilson, rector of East Horsley, died suddenly in church on the same day on which Archbishop Benson died in church at Hawarden.
32 Pat. 23 Edw. III, pt. ii, m. 20.
33 Pat. 5 Edw. VI, pt. vi.
34 Inst. Bks. (P.R.O.).
35 Lond. Gaz. 4 Aug. 1876, p. 4370.

WEST HORSLEY

Horsaleges (ix cent.) ; Orselei (xi cent.) ; Horslegh (xiii cent.).

West Horsley lies 6 miles north-east of Guildford and the same distance south-west of Letherhead. It is bounded on the north by Ockham, on the east by East Horsley, on the south by Shere, on the west by East Clandon and Send and Ripley. Blackmoor Heath, in the north of it, was transferred to Ockham 15 March 1883,[1] and an outlying fragment of Wisley which bordered on West Horsley was also made part of Ockham at the same time. The parish is over 3 miles from north to south, and over one mile from east to west, and contains 2,672 acres. Like its neighbours east and west it reaches from the top of the Chalk Downs, across the chalk, the Thanet and Woolwich Beds, and part of the London Clay. The church is just upon the edge of the chalk, the scattered village on the next soil. Netley Heath, however, which is in the parish, is a bed of sand and gravel lying upon the chalk. There is still some open ground upon the Downs, but the greater part of the commons has been inclosed. The village is scattered about the lanes, but a few houses are clustered together at Horsley Green. The church has very few houses near it, except West Horsley Place, and is close to the border of East Horsley parish.

The road from Guildford to Epsom passes through West Horsley, and the Guildford and Cobham line is in the northern part of the parish.

West Horsley Place (see below) has literary interests connected with it. It was the seat of john Lord Berners, who made the first English translation of Froissart's Chronicle in the reign of Henry VIII. It was shortly afterwards the house of the Earl of Lincoln, whose wife, in whose right he held it, was the widow of Sir Anthony Browne, and was by birth Lady Elizabeth Fitzgerald, daughter of the Earl of Kildare, celebrated by Surrey the poet as the ' Fair Geraldine.' She resided at West Horsley after her husband's death, and corresponded in very unpoetic style with Sir William More at Loseley, where several of her letters are preserved, including an invitation to Sir William to come to her house during the crisis of the Spanish invasion of 1588, dated 30 july, and expressing the consternation in the court at the news that the Spaniards were over against Dover in Calais Roads. Carew Raleigh, son of Sir Walter, was a later owner, and he sold it to Sir Edward Nicholas, Secretary of State to Charles I, who died in 1669. Sir Edward's son, Sir john, was Clerk to the Privy Council and died in 1704. His son Edward, who died in 1726, was Treasurer to Queen Mary. Their correspondence was preserved at West Horsley, and a schedule of the papers was drawn up by Edward Nicholas in 1720.[2] A considerable part of the collection was purchased for the British Museum in 1879, and now forms part of the Egerton MSS. 2533–2562. But it is unfortunately only a part of what once existed. The

whole collection seems to have passed into the possession of Sir John Evelyn of Wotton, after the death of William Nicholas in 1749. Dr. Thomas Birch made transcripts and a catalogue of the papers in 1750–1, describing them as in the possession of Sir john Evelyn. Some of them are still at Wotton, and were printed by Bray at the end of his edition of John Evelyn's Diary and Correspondence, 1818. The rest are supposed to have been returned to West Horsley, whence they passed to the Museum in 1879, but a great many papers referred to by Birch, whose transcripts are in the British Museum,[3] are now lost. The missing part included a History of the Long Parliament, covering 285 pages in Sir Edward Nicholas's own hand. Only fragments of this and of three letter-books, from 1648 to 1658, survive.

Extracts from the papers have been edited for the Camden Society and the Royal Historical Society in 1886, 1892, 1897, and a fourth volume is in the press. Inferior to the Loseley MSS. in local interest, they are by far the most valuable general historical collection preserved in any Surrey house.

There is a valuable collection of historical portraits at West Horsley of the Nicholas family and 17th-century persons of note, Raleigh, Weston Earl of Portland, Clarendon, Hobbes, Compton Bishop of London, Ben jonson, Anne of Denmark, Nell Gwynn, and others.

Woodcote Lodge in this parish is the residence of the Rt. Hon. Sir Henry Roscoe. The Rectory house was built by the Rev. C. H. S. Weston in 1819, a mile away from the church, near Horsley Green.

In West Horsley were 362 acres of common fields and 16 acres of common meadow. The Inclosure Act was in 1802.[4] By it 79 acres of common arable and 88 acres of waste on Netley Heath were appropriated as a glebe. Five acres and a half are assigned for the repairs of the church.

There is a Wesleyan chapel in this parish.

Broomhouse on the Epsom road is the property of Lord Rendel, and is used as a convalescent home for Poor Law children.

In 1786[5] a house and orchard were recorded as left for a school by an unknown donor. In 1813 Mr. Weston Fullerton built and endowed a school. The Rev. C. H. S. Weston further endowed a school with £760 in 1845. The present school (National) was built in 1861. Mr. Weston's endowment is paid to this, and it seems that Mr. Fullerton's school had been previously amalgamated with Mr. Weston's.

The earliest mention of WEST HORS-MANOR LEY occurs in the 9th century, when a certain Dux Alfred granted it to Werburg his wife.[6] Bricsi held it in the time of Edward the Confessor,[7] and at the time of the Survey it was in the possession of Walter son of Other,[8] from whom the family of Windsor descended.[9] Hugh de Windsor, grandson of Walter,[10] held a knight's fee in West

[1] Loc. Govt. Bd. Order 14283.
[2] Not by William his younger brother as usually stated ; see Introduction by Dr. Warner to vol. i of Nicholas Papers (Camden Series), 1886.
[3] Add. MSS. 4180.
[4] 42 Geo. III, cap. 48.
[5] Return to Parl.
[6] Kemble, Cod. Dipl. no. 317.
[7] V.C.H. Surr. i, 323.
[8] Ibid.
[9] Collins, Hist. Coll. of Fam. of Windsor, i.
[10] Ibid. 7.

Horsley in 1166. Hamo de Wudecote in 1232 brought a suit against Hugh de Windsor, who seems to have been a younger son of the Hugh last mentioned, concerning services which Hugh claimed from him.[11] Some ten years later Hugh de Windsor bought the right of common pasture in eighty acres of land in West Horsley.[12] In 1271 Hugh son of Hugh de Windsor granted the manor to Ralph de Berners and Christina his wife in return for an annual rent of £10 during the life of Hugh.[13] This Christina was probably the daughter of Hugh de Windsor ; most of the old historians agree in asserting that the manor passed to the Berners family by reason of the succession of heirs female.[14] The manor still continued to be held of the main line of the Windsor family.[15] In 1297 Ralph de Berners died, leaving a son and heir Edmund,[16] who was reported to be in Normandy at the time of his father's death, although it was uncertain whether he were alive or dead.[17] Christina wife of Ralph survived both her husband and her son, and in 1317 was party in a fine with Richard de Berners touching lands held by him in West Horsley and elsewhere.[18] In 1325 another fine was levied : Christina had died in the meanwhile, and the manor had passed to her grandson john son of Edmund.[19] A final conveyance of these lands was not made until some ten years later, when Thomas son of Richard released all his right to John.[20] In 1332 John settled the manor on himself and his wife Elizabeth, probably on the occasion of their marriage.[21] He died in 1361, and the manor passed to his grandson james, who was then a minor.[22] james de Berners grew up to be a person of some influence in the government, but was accused of taking advantage of the youth of Richard II for his own purposes, and was beheaded in 1388.[23] His lands were forfeited to the Crown, but his widow Anne secured West Horsley by a special grant from the king.[24] Henry IV confirmed this grant, while deprecating the fact that his predecessor had alienated the manor without the consent of Parliament.[25] Anne de Berners married a second husband, john Bryan, who seems to have held the manor jointly[26] with her until her death[27] in 1403, when her son Richard de Berners came into possession. Bryan released his right in the manor to Richard in 1406.[28] Three years later Richard enfeoffed trustees of his estate to the use of himself and his wife Philippa, with remainder to their heirs.[29] He died in 1417.[30] Philippa married a second husband,[31] Thomas Leukenore,[32] but did not live long afterwards, and at her death Margery daughter of Richard de Berners was found to be her heir. Margery while still a child

was married to John Fereby,[33] who held his first court at West Horsley in 1420.[34] He died in 1441,[35] and she then became the wife of Sir John Bourchier. In 1442 certain trustees released the manor to Sir john

BERNERS. *Quarterly or and vert.*

BOURCHIER. *Argent a cross engrailed gules between four water-bougets sable.*

Bourchier, called Berners, summoned to Parliament in 1455 as Baron Berners, and to Margery his wife, which was probably a form of marriage settlement.[36] By her second husband Margery had issue Humphrey, who, however, died before his mother, being killed at Barnet in 1471, so that at her death in 1475 the manor passed to her grandson john Bourchier, Baron Berners, then a child of eight.[37] john, known as the translator of Froissart, was also a distinguished soldier and courtier in the expensive court of Henry VIII, and in 1518 he mortgaged the manor to Thomas Unton[38] and others. He died in 1522.

Thomas Unton was probably father of Alexander Untou who married Mary, Lord Berners' daughter, who died childless. joan, his other daughter, married Edmund Knivett and had livery as heiress to the estate in 1534.[39] The Lady Knivett's steward is referred to in a document at about this date.[40] The manor afterwards passed into the possession of Henry, Marquis of Exeter, who was seised of it at his attainder in 1539.[41] His estates were forfeited to the king, who in 1547 granted West Horsley to Sir Anthony Browne.[42] His widow, daughter of the Earl of Kildare, Surrey's 'Fair Geraldine,' married Lord Clinton, afterwards Earl of Lincoln, and held West Horsley for life. She and her husband resided here till her death, which took place after 8 December 1589.[43] Her stepson Viscount Montagu succeeded and died here in 1592. His grandson and heir succeeded. His son, who made great sacrifices for the king in the Civil War, apparently mortgaged some of his estates to Sir John Evelyn and sold West Horsley in 1656[44] to Carew Raleigh[45] son of the great Sir Walter, who conveyed it to Sir Edward Nicholas[46] in 1664.[47] Sir Edward died in

11 Feet of F. Surr. Trin. 16 Hen. III, 9.
12 Ibid. Mich. 27 Hen. III, 9.
13 Ibid. Mich. 56 Hen. III, 15.
14 e.g. Collins, *Hist. Coll. for family of Windsor.*
15 Chan. Inq. p.m. 22 Ric. II, no 52.
16 Ibid. 25 Edw. I, no. 39.
17 Ibid.
18 Feet of F. Surr. Hil. 10 Edw. II, no. 14.
19 *Parl. R.* (Rec. Com.), i, 425a.
20 Close, 10 Edw. III, pt. ii, m. 39 d.; Feet of F. Surr. Mich. 11 Edw. III.
21 Ibid. Hil. 6 Edw. III, 114.
22 Chan. Inq. p.m. 50 Edw. III (1st nos.), no. 10.
23 *Parl. R.* (Rec. Com.), iii, 241–3.
24 Ibid. 245. This James was father of Lady Juliana Berners, Prioress of Sopwell,

the celebrated authoress ; Pat. 13 Ric. II, pt. iii, m. 28 ; 16 Ric. II, pt. iii, m. 11.
26 *Cal. Pat.* 1399–1401, p. 81.
26 Ibid.
27 Chan. Inq. p.m. 4 Hen. IV, no. 18.
28 Feet of F. Surr. Hil. 7 Hen. IV, 11.
29 Close, 10 Hen. IV, m. 9, 10 d.
30 Chan. Inq. p.m. 5 Hen. V, no. 8.
31 Ibid.
32 Chan. Inq. p.m. 9 Hen. V, no. 24.
33 Ibid.
34 Ct. R. (P.R.O.), gen. ser. portf. 204, no. 59.
35 Esch. Inq. p.m. (Ser. i,) file 1222, no. 7.
36 Feet of F. Div. Co. 20 Hen. VI, 70.
37 Chan. Inq. p.m. 15 Edw. IV, no. 35.
38 Anct. D.(P.R.O.), A. 3993, 3981, &c.
39 Pat. 25 Hen. VIII, pt. ii, m. 17.

40 Harl. MS. 1561, fol. 262.
41 Esch. Inq. p.m. file 1088, no. 3. The marquis shortly before his attainder had received large grants in Surrey, including the adjacent manors of Effingham and Ockham. Blomefield (*Hist. of Norf.*) says that Berners died in debt to the Crown, which may explain the addition of West Horsley to those grants.
42 Pat. 1 Edw. VI, pt. ix.
43 Loseley MSS. numerous letters.
44 Cf. Aubrey, op. cit. iii, 253, who misdates the sale apparently. Carew Raleigh was of the dominant party.
45 Feet of F. Surr. East. 1656.
46 Secretary of State to Charles I and Charles II, collector of the Nicholas Papers.
47 Feet of F. Surr. Hil. 1664.

1669 and was succeeded by his son john. john, clerk to the council, married Penelope daughter of the Earl of Northampton, and died in 1704. He left three sons : Edward, who died unmarried in 1726, john, who left daughters and died in 1742, and William, who succeeded his brother and died in 1749.[48] He left West Horsley by will to Henry Weston, son of john Weston of Ockham.[49] Weston died in 1759, and was succeeded by his son Henry Perkins. After Henry's death in 1826 the manor passed in turn to his sons Ferdinand Fullerton and Charles Henry Samuel.[50] The latter died in April 1849,[51] leaving his nephew Henry Weston, father of the present owner, as his heir. The manor is now in the possession of Mr. Henry Macgregor Weston, of the ancient Surrey family of Weston of Weston in Albury and Ockham, not to be confounded with Weston of Sutton who held land in West Clandon (q.v.).

West Horsley Place, lately the residence of Mrs. Fielder, is also the property of Mr. H. M. Weston, who himself resides at Cranmere. West Horsley Place used to be commonly known as the Sheep Leze, from the flat meadow in front of it next the road ; but West Horsley Place is the name in the 16th century. It is a large red-brick building which has been much altered from time to time. Some parts of the back are of timber, and possibly of 16th-century date, but the front was rebuilt in 1749. It faces south-east, and it has projecting wings at each end, which, however, have been shortened. The west wing originally had a long gallery, which has since been divided up into rooms. The front is of two stories, separated and crowned with large moulded brick cornices. The upper story is divided into bays by projecting pilasters with moulded bases and Ionic capitals. Over the centre is a large gable, and the wings have smaller and plainer gables. All the windows have square heads and wood frames.

It appears to have been largely rebuilt in the early 17th century by the second Lord Montagu, who resided there. The two wings formerly projected farther than they do now : foundations exist outside them. Probably Montagu built the gallery in the west wing. Henry Weston who succeeded in 1749 is said to have made alterations.[52] He probably cut down the wings, destroying the gallery, and built the present 18th-century brick façade. It was again altered in the 19th century.

The church of *ST. MARY THE VIRGIN* has a chancel 31 ft. 10 in. by 16 ft. 2 in., south vestry, south chapel 16 ft. by 13 ft. 10 in., nave 47 ft. 3 in. by 19 ft. 8 in., north aisle 16 ft. 6 in. wide, north porch, south aisle 13 ft. 10 in. wide, west tower 12 ft. 10 in. square, and a west porch ; all these measurements are internal.

The plan is very irregular and difficult to analyse, the centre line of the tower being about 1 ft. to the north of that of the nave, which is itself 15 in. north of that of the chancel. The tower, which is of the 12th century, is built against the west wall of the nave, which is therefore of earlier date than the tower. The length of the nave, and the line of its north wall, probably represent those of an early aisleless nave, and the north wall of the chancel may also stand on the foundations of an equally early chancel.

A north aisle was added to the nave about 1210,

WEST HORSLEY CHURCH FROM THE SOUTH-WEST

48 *Gent. Mag.* 1750, p. 43.
49 Manning and Bray, *Hist. of Surr.* iii, 41.
50 Brayley, *Hist. of Surr.* ii, 79.
51 *Gent. Mag.* (New Ser.), xxxi, 662.
52 Manning and Bray, *Hist. of Surr.* iii, 41.

at which time the chancel was rebuilt in a very irregular way, its north wall preserving the line of the older chancel, while the south wall fell partly beyond that of the nave. The south aisle and south chapel were both built in the 16th century, but probably the aisle preceded the chapel by a few years ; the north aisle has been widened in modern times, the 13th-century north doorway moved out with the wall, while the stonework of the north arcade has been for the greater part either recut or renewed.

The external wrought stonework of the angles and window dressings has been renewed, for the most part in chalk, which is already in very bad condition ; the window tracery has been renewed in Bath stone, and the whole church except the tower is covered with modern plaster.

The east wall of the chancel is pierced by three 13th-century lancet windows, their inner jambs having detached shafts with moulded bases and capitals, and

WEST HORSLEY CHURCH : WEST PORCH

pointed chamfered rear arches ; and there are two contemporary lancets, set close together, at the north-east and south-east, but these have no internal shafts ; a plain roll string-course runs along the eastern half of the chancel below the windows on both sides. The third window in the north wall is of three cinquefoiled lights under a pointed head filled with flowing tracery of mid-14th-century style, the tracery being renewed, but the inner jambs are old and have moulded angles brought out square above the window-ledge by semicircular stops. Below the window is a contemporary tomb recess with a feathered cinquefoiled arch and a crocketed label containing a raised tomb on which lies the effigy of a priest in mass vestments ; his hands are broken off, and now lie loose on the figure. In the opposite wall is an arch opening into the south chapel and contemporary with it, of very poor late Gothic detail, four-centred, and of two chamfered orders. Across the chancel runs a step of Purbeck marble. The chancel arch dates

from the 13th century ; it has double chamfered jambs and a pointed arch with chamfered bases and abaci. The south chapel has an original south window of three cinquefoiled lights in a four-centred arch ; the jambs are of equal depth inside and out, and are moulded with a wide casement moulding on both sides : there are traces of a vertical joint outside, marking its junction with the south aisle. The nave has a north arcade of four bays, the pillars circular, and the responds half round with water-moulded bases and moulded capitals. The westernmost of the three pillars is the only one that shows signs of age and preserves traces of red colour ; all the rest, together with the pointed arches, have a clean, sharp appearance and have been retooled or renewed. The south arcade has three bays with octagonal pillars, hollow-chamfered bases, and capitals of a coarse section like those of the arch to the south chapel from the chancel ; the arches are four-centred and of two chamfered orders.

All the windows of the north aisle are modern, the eastern being set high up in the wall and having wheel tracery in a two-centred arch ; the two north windows are each of two trefoiled lights with tracery. The north doorway is of 13th-century date with jambs of three orders, the middle one with an edge roll and the other two chamfered ; in the arch the middle order has a keeled edge roll ; the label is grooved and hollow-chamfered. The porch is modern.

The three windows in the south aisle are coeval with the south arcade, and each of three cinquefoiled lights under a square head. All have been partly restored. The west window is a modern one of badly weathered chalk, of three cinquefoiled ogee lights under a two-centred traceried head.

In the west wall of the nave is a 13th-century doorway entered from the tower ; its jambs and arch are of two chamfered orders with a moulded abacus, and grooved and hollow-chamfered label. Over it is a modern doorway presumably to a former gallery. The tower is of three stages, setting back on the outside at each stage ; it is not bonded in with the west wall of the nave, its north and south walls being built against its plastered face.

The west doorway has jambs of two chamfers, changing in the pointed arch to a double ogee and wave mould. The tower is exceedingly plain, having single pointed openings in each face of the upper stage, and a curious shingled spire which is four-sided in the lower half and octagonal in the upper. The west porch is of wood set on a low wall of flint and stone repaired with brick ; and has a cusped barge-board ; the sides have lost the vertical studs which formerly closed them in.

The chancel roof is open-timbered and appears to be modern ; the nave and aisle have semicircular plaster ceilings with old tie-beams ; the north aisle roof is modern.

The rood screen is early 16th-century work with twelve traceried bays, four of which are over the central opening, which retains its double doors and a moulded cornice. On either side of the chancel are stalls, returned against the screen, and the south chapel is closed in by screens on the north and west. The font has a retooled 13th-century circular bowl with tapering sides on a modern stem flanked by four shafts with scalloped capitals.

WEST HORSLEY PLACE

In the nave hangs a very good brass chandelier said to have been presented by William III ; it bears the following inscription : ' Martin Kaisinx et Anne Chacon son epouse, 1652 : Pour parvenir au roiaume sans fin j'esper en Dieu. Fai a Namur par Pierre Rock maistre fondeur de cuivre et potin.' In the south chapel is an ancient chest with plain iron bands around it.

In the east window of the chancel are two small panels of 13th-century glass, one of the martyrdom of St. Katherine, and the other of the Last Supper, and in the 14th-century north window is the kneeling figure of a man wearing a mail hauberk, plate arm and leg defences, and a surcoat of his arms ; below is the inscription : ' Jacobus Berners patronus istius eccl'ie.' Above is his crest, a lion standing. The date must fall between 1361 and 1388, when James Berners was beheaded.

On the east wall of the nave is a small panel of English alabaster of 15th-century date ; it represents the Nativity. On the floor are two small brass inscriptions ; one is inscribed : ' Pray for ye soules of Martyn Whyth and Annes his wyf ye which Martyn decessid ye xi day of May ye 3ere of oure Lord mccccc & vi on whos sowles ihū have mercy Amen,' while the other reads : ' Hic jacet Henricus Darckam qui obiit ix° die Augusti a° dni m v° iiii° cui' aie ppicietur deus.' There are two large monuments in the south chapel, one on the east wall to Edward Nicholas, 1669, and the other on the south side to John and Penelope Nicholas, who died in 1704 and 1703 respectively.

There are three bells, hung in an old cage ; the first is by Bryan Eldridge, 1645, the second by William Eldridge, 1687, and the third by Bryan Eldridge, 1621 ; the last is cracked and disused.

The communion plate comprises a silver cup and stand paten of 1634 and a large flagon and stand paten of 1666.

The first book of the registers contains baptisms from 1605 to 1754, marriages from 1600 to 1754, and burials from 1600 to 1686 ; the second repeats the baptisms and burials from 1653 to 1660, and the marriages for 1654. The third has burials from 1682 to 1783, of which ten years were omitted. The fourth has marriages from 1754 to 1783, the fifth baptisms from 1755 to 1783, the sixth continues them to 1812 ; and the seventh has marriages from 1784 to 1812 ; the eighth has burials to 1812.

The churchyard surrounds the building and runs a long way to the south, evidently a modern extension. The roadway passes to the north of the church and along it are some tall elm trees.

ADVOWSON There was a church at West Horsley at the time of Domesday. Edward II claimed the presentation in 1309, and actually presented twice,[62] but the archbishop ordered the Bishop of Winchester to institute the nominee of Christina Berners.[64] This rector, Roger de Berners, a relative clearly, was removed for dilapidating the church and rectory and for marriage in 1317.[65] The lord of the manor has presented since.

CHARITIES Smith's Charity is distributed as in other Surrey parishes.

The Rev. Weston Fullerton in 1817 gave £3,200 in the 3 per cents. for the relief of three men and three women, housekeepers of sixty years of age and upwards.

MERROW

Merwe and Merewe (xiii cent.) ; Merroe (xviii cent.).

Merrow is a village 2 miles east of Guildford. The parish is bounded on the north-west by Worplesdon, on the north-east by Send and Ripley, on the east by West Clandon, on the south by Albury and St. Martha's, on the west by Stoke. It measures about 1½ miles from east to west, and 2 miles from north to south. It contains 1,792 acres. The southern boundary of the parish is on the ridge of the chalk down. It extends northward over the Woolwich and Thanet Beds to the London Clay. The village is just on the lower border of the chalk.

Merrow Common is open roadside land, with many trees upon it, in the northern part of the parish. The Guildford and Cobham line of the London and South-Western Railway intersects it. Merrow Downs, to the south, are a fine expanse of chalk down, partly covered with trees and brushwood. Newlands Corner, where the road from Albury passes up the down, is famous for the view. St. Martha's, crowned by the church, is to the right ; the valley in the foot of the chalk escarpment runs eastward with the spire of Shere Church appearing among the trees. The Leith Hill range is across the south-eastern horizon. In front the rising ground of the sand, at a lower level than the chalk, is backed by the woodlands of the Weald, with the Sussex Downs beyond. Hindhead and Blackdown are to the south-west, Crooksbury Hill and the high ground near Farnham to the west.

Further north upon the downs the old Guildford race-course can still be traced. The races used to take place on the Tuesday, Wednesday, and Thursday after Whitsunday. William III gave a King's Plate of 100 guineas, which, having apparently lapsed under Queen Anne, was renewed by King George I. The races used to fill Guildford with a crowd of visitors, but the growth of Epsom and establishment of Ascot, near the same time, diminished this popularity. The Plate, however, was given as a Queen's Plate in Queen Victoria's reign. The grand stand was taken down more than sixty years ago, and the last meeting was held in 1870.

At a very early period Merrow was clearly an inhabited place. Neolithic flints are not uncommon. There is one large round barrow, or possibly two barrows, rifled, at Newlands Corner. In the valley in the downs, called Walnut Tree Bottom, are earthbanks and a barrow opened by General Pitt-Rivers, in which a sepulchral urn was found. Near here the remains of an extensive cemetery with Roman-British urns was found in 1895. Unfortunately much of the find was lost or destroyed

---

[62] Pat. 2 Edw. II, pt. i, m. 7, 3.   [64] Winton Epis. Reg. Woodlock, fol. 12b.   [65] Ibid. Sendale, fol. 17a, 20b, 23b.

before being notified.[1] The main road in the county, east to west, ran along the downs, and the road from Guildford to Epsom runs through Merrow village.

Of existing houses the inn near the church, 'The Horse and Groom,' is much the most curious. The newel staircase and the interior suggest a date as old as the 15th century. There is some old panelling, and the exterior bears the date 1615. A great part of Clandon Park is in Merrow parish. Among modern houses Levylsdene is the residence of Sir C. H. Stuart Rich, bart. ; Woodlands, of Mr. James Cholmeley-Russel ; Merrow House was the seat of the late Miss Thrupp.

There is a Congregational chapel, built in 1876. The National School was built in 1853 and enlarged in 1886 ; the Infants' School in New Down Road was built in 1884 and enlarged in 1896.

There is no mention of *MERROW MANOR* (Merwe, xiii cent.) in Domesday Book ; probably it formed part of Stoke at that date, since both were royal demesne. Henry II granted part of his demesne land at Merrow to William de St. John,[2] who granted it to Walter son of Ingard for one knight's fee. Walter had two daughters, of whom the elder married Roger Craft and had half the land which at the time of the *Testa de Nevill* was held by Roger the son of Roger Craft.[3] The other daughter and co-heiress died young, and her land was granted to William de Feogières, who afterwards forfeited it to Richard I.[4] John granted it to William de Leycester,[5] whose holding in Merrow was assessed early in the 13th century at £4.[6]

Merrow was thus divided into three portions, in the hands of the king, William de Leycester, and Roger Craft respectively ; the over-lordship of the second had apparently passed to the priory of Boxgrove by successive grants of the St. Johns. Roger Craft granted his portion to the Templars in 1241.[7] By charter (c. 1250–60) Henry III confirmed Boxgrove and the Templars in possession, and granted the royal third to the Benedictine Priory of nuns of Ivinghoe in Buckinghamshire, with the advowson.[8] The grant was confirmed by Edward I.[9]

The first grant of land in Merrow to the priory of Boxgrove in Sussex was made apparently in the time of Henry II, when William de St. John gave half a virgate of land for the sustenance of fifteen monks.[10] It should be noted that the family of St. John was connected by ties of marriage with the de Haia family who founded Boxgrove Priory.[11] In the time of Richard I Simon de Seynluz granted property in Merrow, which he had acquired of the

THE TEMPLARS. *Argent a cross gules and a chief sable.*

gift of William de St. John, to Boxgrove ;[12] it comprised four messuages, six tofts, one carucate of land, 30 acres of pasture, 10 acres of wood, and 12s. rent.

Cravenhurst in Merrow was held by Elgar de Utterworth (in Cranleigh) in 1285,[13] and Lucia de Say gave 17s. a year out of Cravenhurst in Merrow to the Templars.[14] The fortunes of Cravenhurst are otherwise unknown.

After the dissolution of the Templars, their lands passed to the Hospitallers. All three manors in Merrow were thus ecclesiastical property, and after the Dissolution they all seem to have been acquired by the Westons of Sutton. Henry VIII granted a lease of the Hospitallers' Manor (*TEMPLE COURT*) for sixty years to Sir Richard Weston.[15]

THE HOSPITALLERS. *Gules a cross argent.*

Queen Mary restored the Hospitallers, and resumed this manor, which she granted to Sir Thomas Tresham, the prior, and the order in 1557.[16] The order was again dissolved on the accession of Elizabeth, and the manor was re-granted to Sir Henry Weston of Sutton in 1559.[17] In 1564 he was granted the Boxgrove manor,[18] and in 1582 he presented to the living. The rectory manor, which had been in the hands of the nuns of Ivinghoe, had therefore come to him probably by purchase from Sir John Daunce[19] (or Dauncey), for the latter presented to the rectory in 1561 and 1562.[20] It does not seem quite certain however whether the land[21] in Merrow belonging to the priory had not already been amalgamated with the rest of the property. At any rate Sir Henry Weston died in 1593 seised of Merrow, Temple Court, and Boxgrove.[22] Sir Richard Weston, his grandson, the famous agriculturist and canalizer of the Wey, recusant and delinquent in the Civil War, sold Temple House, but not the manor, to Sir Richard Onslow in 1642. His son John sold the Boxgrove part to George Duncombe of Weston in Albury (q.v.). It passed through his family to the Steeres and to the Chatfields, finally rejoining the rest in the hands of Lord Onslow.[23]

The church of *ST. JOHN THE EVANGELIST* consists of a chancel 18 ft. 5 in. by 16 ft., with north and south chapels each 19 ft. 5 in. by 14 ft., a nave 40 ft. 3 in. by 19 ft. 10 in., with north and south aisles 13 ft. 2 in. wide, and a west tower 11 ft. 5 in. square. There is also a north porch.

The church is almost entirely modern, having been rebuilt in 1842 with the exception of the south arcade and the south chapel. There are, however, a few remains of a 12th-century building, which have been re-used. Probably the church of this date consisted merely of a chancel and nave, to which were added at the beginning of the 13th century a south aisle and

[1] *Surr. Arch. Coll.* xiii, 26.
[2] *Testa de Nevill* (Rec. Com.), 225.
[3] Ibid.   [4] Ibid.   [5] Ibid.
[6] *Red Bk. of Exch.* (Rolls Ser.), ii, 562.
[7] Feet of F. Surr. 25 Hen. III, no. 37.
[8] Cott. MS. Claud. A. vi, fol. 102.
[9] Pat. 8 Edw. I, m. 2.
[10] Dugdale, *Mon.* iv, 646.
[11] *Suss. Arch. Coll.* xv, 20.

[12] *Cal. Pat.* 1343–5, p. 534.
[13] Pipe R. 31 Hen. II.
[14] Dugdale, *Mon.* vi, 833.
[15] Chan. Proc. (Ser. 2), bdle. 79, no. 27.
[16] Pat. 4 & 5 Phil. and Mary, pt. xiv.
[17] Ibid. 2 Eliz. pt. viii.
[18] Ibid. 6 Eliz. pt. x.
[19] Manning and Bray, op. cit. iii, 60.

[20] Winton Epis. Reg. Horne, fol. 2b, 6b.
[21] There was land besides the advowson. See above and *Pope Nich. Tax.* (Rec. Com.), 207.
[22] Chan. Inq. p.m. (Ser. 2), ccxxxv, 90.
[23] Manning and Bray, op. cit. iii, 60, 61 ; Frederic Harrison, *Annals of an old Manor House*, 121.

chapel; the arcade of this aisle still stands, and apparently part of the walls of the chapel. Owing to the rebuilding nothing of the later history of the church can be traced. In Cracklow's time it consisted of chancel with south chapel, nave with south aisle, and west tower and spire. He notes a repair in 1665. In 1881 the north aisle was added and further restoration was done.

The modern parts of the building are chiefly in 14th-century style with traceried windows, but those in the south and east walls of the south aisle are of 13th-century design.

Beneath the east window of the north chapel are built in two short 12th-century shafts with ornamental scalloped capitals, one having a scalloped base and the other a moulded one. At present they form the sides of a recess, which contains a wooden cupboard.

The only other 12th-century work is the semi-circular arch of the north doorway, which has an edge roll and zigzag ornament on both sides of the order. The chamfered label is also old. The modern jambs have shafts with moulded bases and scalloped capitals.

The south arcade of the nave is of three bays with circular columns having moulded bases and capitals, and the arches are semicircular with two chamfered orders and grooved and chamfered labels on each side.

The arch at the east end of the south aisle is apparently contemporary with the south arcade, and is two-centred and of two splayed orders with a chamfered label on the west face. The jambs are of the same section as the arch, but are either recut or modern ; on the east side of the arch are traces of painting.

The inner jambs of the lancet windows in the south chapel are apparently old, and below the sill of the south-east lancet is a piscina or aumbry, but only the upper part shows above the pews.

The walls throughout are of flint with stone dressings, and the roofs, which are of modern open timber construction, are covered with tiles.

The tower has an octagonal shingled spire.

The north porch is roofed with Horsham slabs and has a fine 15th-century barge-board enriched with a series of trefoils. There are six bells ; the first

was cast by Bryan Eldridge in 1650, the second by Richard Eldridge, and the third, which is badly cracked, is inscribed ' Johannes est nomen eius.' The three others were added in 1897 as a jubilee memorial.

The oldest piece of plate is a paten dated 1683 and having the initials of the maker, R.P., but there is no hall-mark. Besides this there are a cup, paten, and flagon of 1842 and an elaborate altar cross set with amethysts, given in 1886 in memory of Viscount Cranley and Katherine his wife, by their children.

There are three books of registers, the first being dated 1536, but there are no entries earlier than 1544, at which date the baptisms and burials begin, the former continuing fairly regularly until 1643 and the latter to 1645, and following this are marriages from 1541 to 1636. The latter half of the book contains very irregular entries of baptisms, marriages, and burials from 1643 to 1731. The second book contains marriages from 1754 to 1812, and the third has baptisms from 1754 and burials from 1753, both to 1812.

ADVOWSON The first mention of Merrow Church seems to be in 1208, when it was said to be in the gift of the king.[34] In 1233 Henry III granted it to the Prioress and nuns of St. Margaret Ivinghoe,[35] who retained it[36] until the Dissolution. It was granted with the other Ivinghoe lands to Sir John Daunce (see above), Sir Henry Knevitt presented in 1574 and 1577, but by 1582 it was in the possession of Sir Henry Weston.[37] In 1642 Sir Richard Weston conveyed it to Richard Onslow,[38] in whose family it has since remained.

CHARITIES Smith's Charity is distributed as in other Surrey parishes. A donor, unknown, gave £30, the interest to go to the poor.

In 1776 Lord Onslow made an agreement with the parish by which he inclosed 19 acres of Merrow Common in Clandon Park, and gave the parish a house for a poor-house. In 1786 two families lived here rent free, and a third paid a small rent which was given to the poor-rate.[39]

OCKHAM

Bocheam (xi cent.) ; Occam (xiii cent.).

Ockham is a parish on the east side of the Wey Valley, 7 miles north-east from Guildford, 20 miles from London. It is bounded on the north by Pyrford, Wisley, and Cobham, on the south-east by the two Horsleys, on the south-west by Send and Ripley. It is of very irregular shape, but the greatest breadth from east to west is a little over, and the greatest distance from north to south just about, 3 miles. It contains 2,871 acres. A detached portion of Wisley was added to Ockham in 1883 ;[1] and Blackmoor Heath, a projecting tongue of West Horsley, was transferred to Ockham.[2] A piece of Ockham, far away on Holmbury Hill, was also added to Abinger[3] (q.v.). The soil of Ockham Common in the north of the parish is Bagshot Sand. The southern part of the parish is on the London Clay. Part of the Wey Valley in the west of the

parish and the banks of a stream which joins it from the east are alluvial. The road from London to Guildford runs through Ockham. The village, lying some little distance east of the church, which is in Ockham Park, is very small, and the population scanty. It is purely agricultural.

Ockham Common was inclosed by an Act of 1815-16. The Award is dated 3 March 1817.[4] The common was in the southern part of the parish next to Horsley Common, and is to be distinguished from Ockham Heath adjoining Wisley Common to the north, which is still uninclosed. There are wells on the clay which yield Epsom Salts. Historically Ockham may claim some celebrity as the probable birth-place of William of Ockham, perhaps of John Occam and Nicholas Occam. All three were Franciscans and nearly contemporary. Nicholas Occam (flourished

³⁴ *Rot. Lit. Pat.* (Rec. Com.), i, 78b.
³⁵ *Cal. Chart. R.* 1226–57, p. 186.
³⁶ *Wykeham's Reg.* (Hants Rec. Soc.), i, 23, 208, 210.
³⁷ Winton Epis. Reg. Home, fol. 101a, 106b ; Watson, fol. 8b.
³⁸ Feet of F. Surr. Trin. 17 Chas. I.
³⁹ *Return to Parl.* 1786.
¹ By Loc. Govt. Bd. Order 14282.
² By Order 14283.
³ By Order 14281.
⁴ *Sir John Brunner's Return,* 1903.

circa 1280) is also called Nicholas de Hotham, which renders the tradition of his birthplace here more uncertain. John Occam (flourished *circa* 1340) was a doctor of civil and canon law. William of Ockham was the most famous, and has the best claim to be a native of Surrey, if he was a fellow of Merton College, Oxford (which is very doubtful), for natives of the diocese of Chichester were not eligible for fellowships at Merton, so that Okeham in Sussex could not have been his birthplace, and Oakham in Rutland has never been mentioned as claiming him. His was the last great name among the schoolmen. He was a Nominalist, but is better known for his controversy with the Popes John XXII and Benedict XII. The former he charged with seventy errors and seven heresies. He subsequently submitted, but the next pope admitted the incaution of his predecessor's language. Ockham warmly supported the Emperor, Lewis of Bavaria, the ally of Edward III, in his quarrel with the papacy on the imperial election. He died at Munich about 1349.

Evenwood House is the residence of Mr. B. Noel ; Southend, of Mr. W. H. Morgan.

In 1836 elaborate schools were planned by Ada, Lady King, daughter of Lord Byron. Besides the ordinary village school, they included workshops where the children were taught carpentry, the use of the lathe, and gardening. The subjects of school lessons were also more advanced than was then common in village schools, and there was a gymnasium. As children were attracted from neighbouring parishes, accommodation for boarders was provided. There were masters' houses, in one of which infants were taught up to seven years old. After Lord Lovelace had removed from Ockham to Horsley Towers the schools were superintended by the Misses Lushington, daughters of Dr. Lushington, who lived at Ockham Park. After his death they were unfortunately given up, in 1874, and an ordinary National School carried on in the same buildings, where it still continues.

MANOR OCKHAM At the time of the Domesday Survey Ockham Manor was held by Richard de Tonbridge,[5] and it remained in the possession of the Clares for several centuries. It was part of the property surrendered by Gilbert de Clare on his marriage with Joan of Acre, daughter of Edward I, 1290, and resettled on her and her heirs. Gilbert died seised in right of his wife in 1295,[6] and it passed with his other possessions to his wife Joan during the minority of his son Gilbert. About this time the manor was leased by Joan widow of Gilbert to a certain Jordan le Bacheler, who died in 1297.[7]

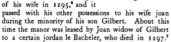

CLARE. *Or three cheverons gules.*

Joan herself died in 1307,[8] leaving a son and heir Gilbert, then seventeen years of age. He died at Bannockburn without issue in 1314.[9]

The heirs of Gilbert de Clare were his three sisters : Eleanor wife of Hugh le Despenser, Margaret widow of Piers Gaveston, and Elizabeth formerly wife of John de Burgh.[10] In 1320 the sisters were confirmed in their possession, Margaret by that time having become the wife of Hugh de Audeley.[11] A division of the Clare lands took place in which Ockham must have fallen to Margaret's share, for in 1326 Ockham appears in the king's hands owing to the minority of Hugh de Andeley's heir.[12] Margaret, the only child of Hugh de Audeley, became the wife of Ralph de Stafford, who paid a relief for her lands

AUDLEY. *Gules a fret or.*   STAFFORD. *Or a cheveron gules.*

in 1347.[13] The date of Margaret's death is doubtful : the inquisition taken in 1364 gives it as September 1347,[14] but since the king received homage for her lands in December of that year[15] this is evidently a mistake. It is, however, certain that she was succeeded by her son Hugh,[16] who died seised of the manor in 1387, leaving a son and heir Thomas, then aged eighteen.[17] Thomas died without issue, and the manor passed in turn to his brothers William and Edmund.[18] Edmund was slain at Shrewsbury in 1403,[19] fighting in the king's army. His son Humphrey, who was not quite two years old at the time of his father's death, was created Duke of Buckingham by Henry VI in 1444, and met his death at the battle of Northampton in 1460.[20] His son Humphrey had been killed at the first battle of St. Albans five years before,[21] so that the manor passed to his grandson Henry, then a child of four.[22] Henry led the rebellion of 1483 against Richard III and was beheaded,[23] when his lands were forfeited to the Crown.[24] Ockham was granted to a certain William Cowper in return for his services to the Crown,[25] but he did not hold it for long.

After the accession of Henry VII, Edward son of Henry Stafford was restored as Duke of Buckingham,[26] and had his father's estates on coming of age in 1499 ;[27] he was, however, beheaded for treason in 1521, and his lands were forfeited.[28] Henry VIII granted Ockham in 1528 to John Bourchier, Lord Berners,[29] who held the manor of West Horsley, and from him it passed

[5] *V.C.H. Surr.* i, 320*b*.
[6] Chan. Inq. p.m. 24 Edw. I, no. 107*a*.
[7] Ibid. 25 Edw. I, no. 19.
[8] Ibid. 35 Edw. I, no. 47, pt. ii, m. 36.
[9] Ibid. 8 Edw. II, no. 68.
[10] Ibid.
[11] *Cal. Pat.* 1317–24, p. 532.
[12] Ibid. 1324–7, p 273.
[13] Originalia R. 21 Edw. III, m. 25.

[14] Chan. Inq. p.m. 37 Edw. III, pt. i (1st nos.), no. 67.
[15] Fine R. 21 Edw. III, m. 8.
[16] *Vide* Inq. above.
[17] Chan. Inq. p.m. 10 Ric. II, no. 38.
[18] Ibid. 22 Ric. II, no. 46 ; *vide* also G.E.C. *Complete Peerage.*
[19] Chan. Inq. p.m. 4 Hen. IV, no. 41 ; also G.E.C. op. cit.
[20] Chan. Inq. p.m. 38 & 39 Hen. VI, no. 59 ; G.E.C. *Complete Peerage.*

[21] G.E.C. *Complete Peerage.*
[22] Chan. Inq. p.m. 38 & 39 Hen. VI, no. 59.
[23] Ibid. Ric. III, V. O. no.17 ; G.E.C. *Complete Peerage.*
[24] Ibid.
[25] *Cal. Pat.* 1476–85, p. 488.
[26] G.E.C. *Complete Peerage.*   [27] Ibid.
[28] Exch. Inq. p.m. file 1074, no. 5. Act of Attainder, 14–15 Hen. VIII, cap. 20.
[29] Pat. 19 Hen. VIII, pt. i, m. 18.

into the possession of Henry Marquis of Exeter.[30] In 1538 the Crown was once more in possession, owing to the attainder of the marquis :[31] and Ockham was in 1545 leased to Gregory Reavill.[32] Edward Courtenay, son of the marquis, was restored by Queen Mary as Earl of Devon in 1553, but died abroad, without heirs, in 1556. In 1560 the manor, then said to have been lately a possession of Edward Courtenay, Earl of Devon, was granted to Anthony Crane and Elizabeth his wife.[33] In 1566 Crane obtained a licence to alienate Ockham to Thomas Knevett and Francis Vaughan to the use of John Vaughan and Lady Anne his wife, with remainder to the heirs of Lady Anne.[34] The actual conveyance took place in 1567.[35] Anne Vaughan died seised in 1582,[36] when Henry Weston, her son by a previous marriage with Francis son of Sir Richard Weston of Sutton[37] (q. v.), was found to be her heir.[38] Henry died in 1592, leaving Ockham to his son Richard, then twenty-five years old.[39] From Richard the manor passed to his son of the same name[40] who in 1621 conveyed it to Henry[41] son of john Weston,[42] of quite a different family—the Westons of Albury, Send in Surrey, and of Sussex. Henry died in 1638, and his brother Edward was found to be his heir.[43] Edward died in 1640 ; he is buried at Speld-hurst, Kent. His son Henry was Sheriff of Surrey in 1661. From Henry the manor passed to his son John,[44] who under an Act of Parliament (9 Anne, cap. 31) sold the manor to Sir Peter King in 1710.[45] His descendant, Lord Lovelace, is the present owner.

WESTON of Ockham. *Sable a cheveron between three lions' heads rased argent.*

By the inquisition on the death of Henry Weston in 1638 (*vide supra*) it appears that he held 54 acres of land and two messuages in Ockham, besides the manor, with tithes in Pirford Mead, all late the property of Newark Priory, and granted by Parliament to Cardinal Reginald Pole.

Ockham Park, the seat of the Countess of Lovelace, was largely rebuilt by Lord Chancellor King, who died in 1734, and more completely altered by the late Lord King, ancestor to the Earl of Lovelace, who died in 1833. It is a fine specimen of Italian architecture, and the gates from the Guildford road are well-known examples of ironwork.

KING, Earl of Lovelace. *Sable three spear-heads argent with drops of blood and a chief or with three battleaxes azure therein.*

Two water-mills at Ockham are mentioned in the inquisition taken at the death of Gilbert de Clare in 1296 ; they appear to have always descended with the manor. In 1296 they were worth 40s.[46]

Two fisheries worth 10d. are mentioned in Domesday ; but in 1296 there was only one, which was then worth 2s.

CHURCH

The church of *ALL SAINTS* consists of a chancel 27 ft. 11 in. by 17 ft. with a north chapel 16 ft. 2 in. by 12 ft. 5 in., a nave 31 ft. 11 in. by 18 ft. 2 in. with a north aisle 12 ft. 3 in. wide, and a west tower 10 ft. 6 in. by 10 ft. 3 in. ; to the north of the aisle is a transept 12 ft. 9 in. square and a small porch.

The plan of the nave probably represents that of a 12th-century church, the chancel of which gave place at the beginning of the 13th century to that now standing. A north aisle was added to the nave about 1220, and in the middle of the century the original triplet in the east wall of the chancel was replaced by the beautiful group of seven lancets which forms the most striking feature of the church. About 1350 the south wall of the nave seems to have been rebuilt, and in the 15th century the north aisle was enlarged and the west tower added.

To the north of the aisle is an 18th-century tomb-chamber built by Peter, Lord King, whose monument it contains, and in 1875 the aisle was lengthened eastwards, overlapping the chancel, and a north porch added.

The walls are built of flint rubble, plastered on both faces, the old external ashlar dressings of freestone having been to a great extent replaced by new stone or brick. The stonework of the tower is, however, in great measure old and weatherworm. The roofs are of high pitch and covered with red tiles, and the tower has a flat leaded roof.

The lower parts of the original east windows of the chancel may be seen on the outer face of the wall below the sill of the beautiful seven-light window which succeeded them. The lights are graduated, the middle one being the tallest, having its springing line a few inches higher in the wall than the heads of the lancets on either side, and the same proportion is observed between the other lights. Outside they are simply chamfered, and have no inclosing arch over the group, but inside there are Purbeck marble shafts on the faces of the mullions with moulded bases and foliate capitals of different designs, from which rise beautifully moulded arches with dog-tooth ornament and labels, the whole composition being inclosed by a wide chamfered rear arch of three-centred form.

In the north wall of the chancel is the semicircular rear arch of an original early 13th-century window, in which is inserted tracery of c. 1320 of two trefoiled lights with a quatrefoil over. To the west is a modern arch to the north chapel, and at the west end of the chancel is a squint from the chapel.

The south wall contains two windows, the easternmost being square-headed and of 15th-century style with three cinquefoiled lights and vertical tracery over, only the head and jambs being old. The other window, c. 1320, has tracery like that in the north wall,

[30] Feet of F. Surf. Trin. 25 Hen. VIII.
[31] L. and P. Hen. VIII, xix (1), 372.
[32] Ibid.   [33] Pat. 2 Eliz. pt. xv.
[34] Ibid. 8 Eliz. pt. vi, m. 34.
[35] Feet of F. Surr. Hil. 9 Eliz. ; Memoranda R. L.T.R. 10 Eliz. m. 92.
[36] Chan. Inq. p.m. (Ser. 2), cc, 60.

[37] The first of this family of Weston, of Essex and Lincolnshire, to come into Surrey.
[38] Chan. Inq. p.m. (Ser. 2), cc, 60.
[39] Ibid. ccxxxv, 90.
[40] Ibid. cccxxxiii, 20.
[41] Feet of F. Surr. Mich. 19 Jas. I.

[42] Pedigree supplied by Mr. Weston to Brayley (*Hist. of Surr.* ii, 86).
[43] Chan. Inq. p.m. (Ser. 2), ccclxxxvi, 142.
[44] Mr. Weston's pedigree.
[45] Feet of F. Surr. Hil. 9 Anne.
[46] Chan. Inq. p.m. 24 Edw. I, no. 107d.

3   46

but is entirely of 14th-century date, with a straight-sided rear-arch. Its sill is carried down lower than that of the south-east window.

Between these two windows is a blocked doorway apparently of 13th-century date, having plain chamfered jambs and a two-centred arch, and below the south-east window is a double piscina of 13th-century date with stop-chamfered jambs and two trefoiled arches ; one drain is a quatrefoil and the other circular, but the projecting portions of both have been broken off. To the west is a single seat, the sides of which run up to the window-sill above.

The chancel arch is of 13th-century date and has semicircular responds with moulded bases and capitals, and the two-centred arch is of two chamfered orders. To the north of it is the upper entrance to the rood loft, and below are the remains of a 15th-century canopied niche hacked off almost flush with the wall face, but still showing the mark of the dowel which kept the image in position.

The three-light east window of the north chapel is modern, and to the south of it has been set a fine

chamfered jambs with a moulded label which stops on grotesque faces.

Below the sill of the south-east window is a 15th-century piscina with moulded jambs and cinquefoiled ogee head, the projecting portion of its drain having been cut away, and at the west end of the south wall is a small blocked four-centred doorway coeval with the tower.

The west and only window of the north aisle is modern, and has three trefoiled lights with tracery over under a square head. The north doorway is also modern, opening to a shallow porch, but to the west of it the jamb of an older opening shows in the wall. The 18th-century tomb-chamber already referred to is immediately to the east of the doorway, and opens to the aisle by a round-headed arch. It has a vaulted plaster ceiling springing from pilasters at the angles, and is lighted from the west, with blank recesses on the north and east. Against the north wall is set the white marble monument of Peter first Lord King, 1734, with life-size figures of himself and his wife seated with an urn between them.

A 15th-century doorway with moulded jambs and a two-centred arch under a square head opens from the tower to the nave, with a very tall round-headed rear arch towards the nave. The whole seems to be of the date of the tower, but the lower parts of the wall on either side are possibly older.

The tower is of three stages, with an embattled parapet, and a rectangular stair-turret at the south-east. In each face of the top stage is a square-headed window of two cinquefoiled lights, and in the middle stage a west window of two cinquefoiled lights ; the west doorway below is of plain 15th-century character.

The chancel has a modern boarded ceiling ; but the east bay of the nave roof and the whole of that of the north aisle are of 15th-century date, with canted panels framed by moulded ribs ornamented at their intersections with carved bosses. These take the form of single roses in the aisle, but in the nave they are more elaborate, and include fleurs de lis, Stafford knots, &c. The panels are all painted with a running zigzag pattern on a dark ground, now much faded. The rest of the nave roof is old, but has no panelling or ornament. The east wall of the nave round the chancel arch from the floor of the rood loft to the tie-beam retains a great deal of 15th-century colouring, with a pattern of flowers on a red ground, and traces of colour also remain on the back of the mutilated canopy at the north-east of the nave. On the west wall of the nave, to the south of the doorway to the tower, is painted a line of trefoiled arches, which seems of 14th-century character, though the small corbelled shafts from which they spring suggest a later date.

The font now in use is modern, but placed in the chancel are the remains of one of early 13th-century date, consisting of a circular Purbeck-marble stem on a square base-stone, on which are the moulded bases of four detached shafts. In the tracery of the south-

Scale of feet

PLAN OF OCKHAM CHURCH

15th-century niche from the old east wall of the aisle. It has a projecting base elaborately carved with foliage, shafted jambs with moulded capitals and bases, and a large canopy with crocketed gables and pinnacles. The north window of the chapel is also modern, and has two trefoiled lights with tracery in a square head. To the west of it is a small modern doorway.

The north arcade of the nave is of two wide bays, the arches and the capitals of the responds being in chalk, while the pillar, the responds, and the capital of the pillar are of sandstone. The pillar is circular with a simply moulded base and capital and semicircular responds to match, the base of the west respond being at a higher level than the rest. The arches are two-centred, with a springing line a little below the capitals, of two chamfered orders, the labels having the hawk's-bill moulding characteristic of early 13th-century work. There are marks of screens in both bays, showing that the aisle was partitioned off from the nave, and the label of the eastern arch has been cut away for the rood loft. In the south wall of the nave are two mid-14th-century windows of three cinquefoiled lights, with flowing double-cusped tracery, and double-

OCKHAM CHURCH : EAST WINDOW

OCKHAM CHURCH : NAVE LOOKING EAST

east window there are six small figures of angels in 15th-century glass, a good deal repaired. One angel holds a harp, another cymbals, another a viol, and the fourth pipes. Of another figure only head and wings remain, and the sixth is a seraph with four wings and a feathered body, holding a crown in each hand. The heads of the main lights also contain some old glass consisting of red borders and diamond quarries. The 14th-century south-west window of the chancel preserves a little original glass, a lion's head, and a border of Stafford knots and vine pattern in yellow stain on a dark background. The north window of the chancel also contains part of a border of vine pattern and a lion's head of the same period. Both the south windows of the nave contain a good deal of Dutch glass of 17th- and 18th-century date, but the middle light in the head of the south-east window preserves its original glazing in blue and yellow, c. 1350, and there are other fragments of mediaeval quarries.

The wood fittings of the church are modern, except for a pair of early 14th-century stall arms belonging to a set of stalls of unknown origin, worked into seats one on each side of the chancel. On the chancel floor at the north side of the altar is a brass half-figure of a priest in richly ornamented mass vestments, with the following inscription : 'Hic jacet dn̄s Walterus Frilende quondā rector istius ecclīē et factor huī capelle cuius aīē ppicietur deus.' On the opposite side of the chancel are the brass figures of a man in armour and his wife, with an inscription 'Hic jacent Johēs Weston fili' et heres Willi Weston qui obi . . . primo die Junii a° dn̄i m cccclxxxiiii° et Margareta uxor ei . . . qe obiit penultimo die Januarii a° dn̄i mcccclxxv° q' aīabz ppiciet . . .' The end of the brass is broken off so that the last letters of each line are missing. There are three shields, the first and third bearing the cheveron and lions' heads of Weston, while the second has the same impaling the quarterly coat of Metford of Ockham.

On the north wall of the chancel is a small brass bearing the inscription 'Orate pro aīa dn̄i Roberti Kellett quondm̄ rectoris isti' ecclīē qui obiit xviī° die Septembris an° dn̄i mv°xxv° cui' aīe propiciet' deus.'

On the south wall of the north chapel is another small brass inscribed 'aīa Johīs Wexcombe hic qui tumulat' vite ppetue xpi m'ito dirigatur.'

On the north wall of the chapel is a black marble tablet to Henry Weston, 1638, and others of his family.

The tower contains four bells by R. Phelps 1719, and a tenor by T. Mears 1811. The plate consists of a cup of 1854, with a paten and flagon of 1861. The registers date from 1567.

There was a church on the manor *ADVOWSON* of Ockham at the time of Domesday. The advowson has always followed the descent of the manor.

CHARITY Smith's Charity is distributed as in other Surrey parishes.

PIRBRIGHT

Pirifrith and Pirifright (xiii cent.) ; Purifright (xiv cent.).

Pirbright is a parish, formerly a chapelry of Woking, 5¼ miles north-west of Guildford. It contains 4,674 acres, and measures about 3 miles each way. It is bounded on the north by Chobham and Bisley, on the east by Woking, on the south by Worplesdon and Ash, on the west by Ash and Frimley. It is almost entirely upon the Upper and Middle Bagshot sands, and is therefore generally unproductive. It lies upon the western side of the ridge of Bagshot sand-hills, of which Chobham Ridges is the general name, and a great deal of it is open heath-land. No less than 3,070 acres, nearly three-quarters of the parish, have been acquired by H.M. War Office for military purposes, training and musketry especially. An encampment of the Brigade of Guards is permanently maintained here, and extensive rifle ranges are laid out.

Pirbright Common and Cow Moor (the latter name appears in the boundaries of the earliest Chertsey charter) are the names of the principal wastes.

The main line of the London and South Western Railway and the Farnham line pass through it ; and it is also crossed by the Basingstoke Canal.

The village lies in the only fertile part of the parish, between higher ground both east and west, in the valley of a small stream. A by-road leads west from the village for a short distance to the church, which stands in a large graveyard, recently extended and thickly planted with a variety of shrubs. It is long and wedge-shaped, being widest at the west, where a small stream runs along its southern boundary. At the east end is the grave of Sir H. M. Stanley, the African explorer, a great block of unworked stone bearing his name cut deeply on it.

The Court House, now called the Manor House, is the seat of Major Armstrong. It is a stone house of 16th-century date, but on the site of an earlier house surrounded formerly by a moat. The manorial courts were formerly opened here.

Heatherside is the residence of Mr. F. C. Selous, the famous African big-game hunter, and contains a remarkable collection of hunting spoils and native African curiosities. The Lodge is the residence of Mrs. Mangles, widow of the late Mr. Ross Mangles, V.C., of the Indian Civil Service. In the 18th century this house was the property of Admiral Byron, the explorer, grandfather of Lord Byron. He planted an avenue of Scotch firs, still called the Admiral's Walk, which extends for a mile over the Government land attached to the ranges.

There is a Congregational chapel in the parish.

A drinking-fountain on the village green was presented by Lord and Lady Pirbright as a memorial of the Diamond Jubilee, 1897. The same benefactors, then resident at Henley Park in Ash, presented a village hall and recreation ground in 1899, completed in 1901 as a memorial of the accession of H.M. King Edward VII. The Church of England Institute, at the Guards' Camp, was built in 1892, enlarged in 1894, and rebuilt in 1902.

Schools (Provided) were built in 1870, and enlarged in 1889. An infants' school was built in 1902.

The manor of *PIRBRIGHT* (Piri- MANOR fright, xiii cent.) does not seem to occur earlier than the 13th century, when it was reported to be held of the honour of Clare by Peter de Pirbright.[1] John Trenchard died seised of it under the Earl of Gloucester in 1301–2.[2] His heir was Henry, aged 18 ; but in 1314 John Bishop of Bath and Wells held it.[3] The overlordship passed to Hugh le Despenser, who was holding in 1324.[4] After Hugh le Despenser's forfeiture in 1326 the manor was granted to Edmund, Earl of Kent,[5] who not long afterwards was executed for treason and lost his estates.[6] Sir John Mautravers in 1330 received Pirbright from Edward III,[7] but this grant was probably only temporary, since Sir John's name does not occur in a descent given less than a century later.[8] Edmund son of Edmund was restored in blood and to all his lands in the same year in which his father had been executed. He died a minor. His brother John succeeded, and died in 1352 holding Pirbright.[9] His wife Elizabeth had Pirbright in dower,[10] but subject to her right of dower it passed to Joan, Princess of Wales, John's sister, whose son by her first husband, Thomas Holand, Earl of Kent, died seised of it in 1397.[11] He was succeeded by his sons Thomas and Edmund in turn, but they both died without issue,[12] and from

HOLAND. *Gules three leopards or in a border argent.*

MORTIMER. *Barry or and azure a chief or with two pales between two gyrons azure therein and a scutcheon argent over all.*

them the manor passed into the family of Mortimer by the marriage of their sister Eleanor with Roger Mortimer, Earl of March.[13] Edmund, Earl of March, son of Eleanor, died seised of the manor in 1425,[14] leaving three co-heirs : Richard, Duke of York, son of his sister Anne, and his two surviving sisters, Joan wife of Sir John Grey, and Joyce wife of Sir John Tiptoft.[16] Probably some deed of partition was exe- cuted by virtue of which this manor was assigned to the Duke of York, for some years later it was held by his widow Cecily as part of her dower ;[16] and passing later to her son Edward IV, became merged in the possessions of the Crown. Edward inclosed a great part of the lands pertaining to the manor for a park, and appointed Sir Thomas Bourchier first keeper.[17] There had been a park before, disparked under Richard II.[18]

During the reign of Henry VIII the manor changed hands several times. It formed part of the marriage portion of Queen Katharine of Aragon,[18] and was later successively in the possession of Sir Thomas Boleyn[20] and Sir William Fitz William.[21] Finally it was granted to Sir Anthony Browne, afterwards Viscount Montagu,[22] with whose family it remained until the middle of the next century. In 1677 Francis, Lord Montagu, great- grandson of Sir Anthony, con- veyed it to John Glynne of Henley Park.[23] At Mr. Glynne's death the manor de- scended to his daughter Doro- thy,[24] who became the wife of Sir Richard Child, afterwards Earl Tylney of Castlemaine.[25] The earl sold Pirbright in 1739 to Solomon Dayrolles (see Henley),[26] who in 1784 disposed of it to Henry Halsey.[27] The Halsey family are still in possession.

BROWNE, Viscount Montagu. *Sable three lions passant bendways be- tween two double cotises argent.*

The church of *ST. MICHAEL AND* CHURCH ALL ANGELS consists of chancel with north vestry, organ bay and south chapel, nave, north aisle with gallery extending also round the west end, west tower, and south porch. The building is of little architectural interest, being mostly of 18th-century date or later, the chancel and tower being of Heath stone and the nave of red brick with a stone plinth. The chancel is in 15th-century style with an east window of three traceried lights, a moulded arch and door on the north to the vestry and organ bay, and a similar but wider arch to the chapel on the south. The chancel arch is of 15th- century style, and consists of two moulded orders, which continue nearly to the ground.

The north arcade is formed by three wooden Tuscan columns carrying a panelled architrave. The north aisle has three large round-headed windows, and in the south wall of the nave are two like them, and between them a round-headed brick doorway opening to a simple but pleasing wooden porch. All internal fittings, including the octagonal font by the south door, are modern.

The tower has a tall round-headed west doorway, the upper part glazed, plain round-headed belfry lights, and two circular lights in the second stage. It is finished with a small shingled spire and battlements. On the exterior of the south walls of the nave and tower, which have been recently in part repaired, are various initials and the date 1785. In the south aisle of the chancel is a plain and ancient three-lock chest of oak.

The six bells are modern, by Mears & Stainbank.

The plate comprises a chalice made in 1654, with L LR pricked on the bowl, a small flat paten made in 1739, a modern paten and modern flagon. There are also two London pewter plates and a pewter flagon.

[1] *Testa de Nevill* (Rec. Com.), 219, 220b.
[2] Chan. Inq. p.m. 30 Edw. I, 32.
[3] Ibid. 8 Edw. II, 68.
[4] Feet of F. Surr. Trin. 17 Edw. II.
[5] Chart. R. 1 Edw. III, 82.
[6] G.E.C. *Complete Peerage.*
[7] *Cal. Pat.* 1327–30, p. 517.
[8] Chan. Inq. p.m. 4 Hen. VI, no. 36.
[9] Ibid. 26 Edw. III, 54.
[10] Close, 27 Edw. III, m. 25.
[11] Chan. Inq. p.m. 20 Ric. III, no. 30. For connexion between Thomas and Ed- mund see manor of Sutton in Woking.
[13] G.E.C. *Complete Peerage.*
[13] Ibid.
[14] Chan. Inq. p.m. 3 Hen. VI, no. 32.
[15] Ibid.
[16] *Cal. Pat.* 1476–85, p. 278.
[17] Ibid. 333.
[18] Harl. MS. 433, fol. 200.
[19] L. *and* P. *Hen. VIII,* i, 22.
[20] Ibid. 373.
[21] Ibid. iii, 414.
[23] Pat. 1 & 2 Phil. and Mary, pt. xv.
[23] Manning and Bray, *Hist. Surr.* i, 148.
[24] Aubrey, *Hist. Surr.* iii, 215.
[25] G.E.C. *Complete Peerage.*
[26] Manning and Bray, *Hist. Surr.* i, 149.
[27] Feet of F. Surr. Hil. 25 Geo. III.

The first book of registers contains mixed entries 1574 to 1600, the second is a transcribed copy of this book, but contains baptisms to 1655, burials to 1642, and marriages to 1641. There are also further burial entries 1650 to 1664 ; the third book contains mixed entries 1653 to 1733, the fourth baptisms and burials 1733 to 1812, the fifth marriages 1733 to 1754, and the sixth marriages 1754 to 1812.

ADVOWSON The chapel of Pirbright was in early times attached to the church of Woking, and was granted by Peter of Pirbright to the Prior of Newark in 1240.[58] It was still part of the priory possessions in 1535, and was then worth £6 8s. 4d.[59] It was served separately from Woking, and after the Dissolution was in all respects a parish served by a perpetual curate.

In 1640 the family of Stoughton were holding the advowson ;[60] in 1694 they released it to George Martin,[61] in whose descendants it remained till 1779, when George Tate, second husband of the widow of Martin's grandson, presented. It was probably bought by the Halseys with the manor, they being now patrons.

In Pirbright were two plots of land called Torch Plot and Lamp Plot, let at 12d. and 8d. a year respectively for lights in the church. They do not appear among lands devoted to such uses in Surrey in the certificates of Edward VI. They were granted by Elizabeth to John Dudley and john Ascough, 17 May 1575.

CHARITIES Smith's Charity is distributed as in other Surrey parishes. There is a charity of about £6, left by Mr. George Poulton of Pirbright, which is distributed in clothing to old persons.

SEND WITH RIPLEY

Sande (xi cent.) ; Sandes and Saundes (xiii cent.) ; Sende (xiv cent.).

Send is a parish with two villages, Send lying about 3 miles and Ripley about 5 miles north-east of Guildford. It is bounded by Woking on the north-west, Pyrford to the north, Ockham to the north-east, West Horsley on the east, the two Clandons and Merrow on the south, and Worplesdon on the south-west. It measures 3½ miles from east to west, and about 4 miles north to south in the widest part. It contains 5,139 acres. Ripley and the north of the parish are on the sand and gravel of the Wey Valley, Send on a patch of Bagshot Sand ; the southern part of the parish is on the London Clay. The River Wey skirts the western side of the parish, and in part bounds it. The road from London to Guildford runs through it, and the London and South-Western Railway line by Cobham to Guildford cuts the extreme south of the parish. There are brickfields on the London Clay. Ripley Green is a well-known open space in the parish.

The neighbourhood of Send has yielded several neolithic flints, some of which are in the Archaeological Society's Museum at Guildford. Salmon says that Roman coins were found there.[1] The site of Newark Priory is just within the border of the parish. It had evidently occupied another site, also possibly in the parish, but was rebuilt on a new site and called De Novo Loco, Newark, Newstead, or New Place. The foundation was anterior to the benefaction by Ruald de Calva and his wife Beatrice de Sandes, under Richard I, and the Winchester Registers[2] say that it was founded by a Bishop of Winchester. Bishop Godfrey de Lucy, who died in 1204, gave a grant of land to the house under the name of Aldbury. Andrew Bukerel, son of Andrew, citizen of London, mayor 1231–7, or the son of the mayor, gave a grant to the house De Novo Loco.[3] The site and remains of the Priory buildings have lately been placed under the protection of the Ancient Monuments Acts.

The parish was the scene of a nearly forgotten skirmish. On 14 June 1497 the Cornish rebels marching upon Kent from the west had reached Guildford, and had a skirmish with the outposts of the royal troops on the road from Guildford to London. The latter evidently fell back, for they had lost touch of the rebels on the 16th and were looking for them on the Guildford road again near Kingston when they were actually on the border of Kent.[4] Old maps mark the place where the road crosses the stream which joins the Wey near Send as St. Thomas's Waterings, a name which occurs in the London suburbs. It is now not used, but its occurrence here shows that it had no connexion with pilgrimages to St. Thomas's shrine.

By the Inclosure Act for Send and Ripley, passed in 1803, 600 acres of common and common fields were inclosed.[5]

There is a Congregational chapel at Cartbridge, built in 1875.

Send Grove is the property of and occupied by the Misses Onslow. General Evelyn, a son of Sir John Evelyn of Wotton, resided at this house, and he laid out the grounds. On his death, in 1783, it was bought by Admiral Sir Francis Drake, second in command to Rodney in his victory of 1782 over De Grasse. Woodhill is the seat of the Dowager Countess of Wharncliffe.

Ripley was formerly a chapelry of Send. There are Baptist and Wesleyan chapels there. Earl Ligonier, the famous Huguenot refugee and military commander, was Baron Ripley.

Dunsborough House is the seat of Mr. G. H. Maitland-King ; Ripley Court of Mr. R. M. Pease ; Ripley House of Captain Herbert D. Terry, Inspector of Constabulary for England and Wales.

Ripley (National) School was built in 1847 and enlarged in 1898. Send (National) School was built in 1834 and enlarged in 1892.

MANORS The early history of SEND begins with the 10th century, when Athelstan sold lands which he held at Send to the Archbishop of Canterbury.[6] But at the time of Domesday the tenant in chief was Alured de Merle-

[58] Feet of F. Surr. Trin. 24 Hen. III.
[59] Valor Eccl. (Rec. Com.), ii, 33.
[60] Feet of F. Surr. Mich. 15 Chas. I.
[61] Ibid. Mich. 6 Will. and Mary.

[1] Salmon, Antiq. of Surr. 142.
[2] Winton Epis. Reg. Woodlock, fol. 141b, 1720.
[3] Inspeximus of 14 Edw. II, Chart. 26.

[4] V.C.H. Surr. i, 366.
[5] In the Com. Ret. (Bd. of Agric.).
[6] Birch, Cart. Sax. 1063.

bergh, of whom Rainald held it.[7] There were two other sub-tenants, Walter and Hubert, whose holdings may be the origins of Papworth and Dedswell.

Alured's property in Send followed the descent of his Herefordshire estate at Ewyas Harold.[8] Robert de Tregoz married Sibyl daughter of Robert de Ewyas,[9] and about 1207 confirmed the endowment of Newark Priory in Send.[10] Robert de Tregoz his grandson was killed at Evesham in 1265. In 1290 his son John de Tregoz granted a knight's fee in Send to Newark,[11] and some ten years later he died seised of two knights' fees in Send, leaving two co-heirs, his daughter Sibyl wife of Otho de Grandison, and John son of another daughter, Clarissa wife of Roger De La Warr.[12]

TREGOZ. *Azure two gimel bars or with a lion passant or in the chief.*

In 1359 the Prior of Newark and Roger son of John De La Warr[13] are mentioned as being lords of Send,[14] so that probably Sibyl de Grandison had by that date released her rights. In 1398 John De La Warr son of Roger[15] died holding rents only in Send,[16] and since the Priors of Newark are the only lords mentioned between that date and the Dissolution it seems reasonable to suppose that the De La Warr family endowed the priory with any other property that they possessed.

Henry VIII granted the manor, called Send and Jury, to Sir Anthony Browne in 1544.[17] It remained in his family until 1674, when the impoverishment of the family necessitated its being vested in trustees with a view to sale.[18] Accordingly in 1711[19] Francis Browne, fourth Viscount Montagu, conveyed it to Sir Richard Onslow, together with the manor of Ripley and the farms called 'Chapel Farm, Send Barnes, Jury Farm, Ride Farm, and Newark Priory.'[20] The manor has remained in the Onslow family, but Newark was sold to Lord King, ancestor of the Earl of Lovelace, in 1785.

There are traces of various tenants of land in Send during the 13th century. Ruald de Calva and Beatrice his wife, the benefactors of Newark, evidently held land in Send as well as the advowson of the church.[21] Their charter to the priory mentions a certain William Maubaunc as their heir.[22] Geoffry Maubaunc, John Dedeswell, and Simon Pypard are mentioned in the inquisition of John Tregoz as having formerly each held two-thirds of his two knights' fees.[23] In 1290 Ruald Maubaunc is mentioned, who left three daughters and co-heirs ; Alice wife of Thomas de Send is known to have been his daughter,[24] while the others may possibly have been the wife of John de Dedswell,[25] and Dionisia wife of John le Blund, for in 1290 Robert de Lodenham held of John Tregoz, and John le Blund and John de Dendeswell are named as holders under him with Thomas de Sende.[26]

The earliest mention of the manor of *RIPLEY* (Rippelege, xiii cent.) seems to be in 1279, when the Prior of Newark claimed to have suit at his court of Ripley.[27] Henry III in 1220 granted to the Prior of Newark the right of holding an annual fair at the feast of St. Mary Magdalen.[28] In 1279 the prior also claimed the right of having a market in Ripley, which he had received by charter from Henry III, but it was of no value, as no one came to it.[29] This manor subsequently descended with Send (q.v.).

There was apparently a manor of *NEWARK* in Send, since in 1279 the prior claimed to have free warren in his 'manor of Newark.'[30] This manor probably consisted of the land immediately adjacent to the priory. It is not described as a manor at the Dissolution, and in the 18th century appears as the farm called Newark Priory,[31] which was purchased by Sir Richard Onslow and subsequently sold to Lord King (*vide supra*).

The remains of the church of Newark Priory stand in the midst of level fields almost wholly surrounded by streams, and belong entirely to the early years of the 13th century, though the plan shows evidence of an older building, set at a slightly different axis, represented by the quire and nave of the existing church. The plan is noteworthy in several respects. The quire, which seems to represent the presbytery and possibly also the quire of a simple 12th-century church, is flanked, as regards its two eastern bays, by the 13th-century transepts, but is separated from them by walls solid for some 10 ft. from the ground to take the stalls, above which pairs of arches open to the upper parts of the transepts, while its third or western bay forms the first bay of the nave, and has a cross arch at the west, under which the *pulpitum* stood. The 13th-century enlargements were a three-bay presbytery east of the quire, flanked by pairs of square-ended chapels *en échelon*, on the east of the transepts. A very unusual feature of these chapels, which were covered with barrel-vaults, is that they have separate side walls, a space being left between each pair of chapels. The aisles of the nave were probably 13th-century additions, but have quite disappeared except for a length of the wall of the south aisle, which having no foundations has unfortunately fallen over bodily quite recently.

The walls are of well-built flint rubble, but nearly all the ashlar dressings have been picked out, reducing windows and doors to ragged holes in the wall.

The presbytery, which has lost its east wall, was of three bays, forming a continuation of the quire, which was also of three bays, both having been vaulted with quadripartite rib vaults springing from wall-shafts with Purbeck marble capitals. In each of the bays is a gap on either side left by the removal of the stonework of the lancet windows, which apparently were of three orders with splayed rear-arches, and had steeply sloping sills inside. Under the second or middle north window is a gap opening to the north chapel. In the third or western bay on both sides are

7 *V.C.H. Surr.* i, 326b.   8 Ibid. 281.
9 Glouc. Chart. ; *Testa de Nevill* (Rec. Com.), 69.
10 Dugdale, *Mon. Angl.* vi, 383.
11 Chan. Inq. a.q.d. file 14, no. 30.
12 Chan. Inq. p.m. 28 Edw. I, no. 43.
13 G.E.C. *Complete Peerage.*
14 Chan. Inq. p.m. 32 Edw. III (2nd nos.), no. 83.

15 G.E.C. *Complete Peerage.*
16 Chan. Inq. p.m. 22 Ric. II, no. 53.
17 Pat. 36 Hen. VIII, pt. xxvi, m. 20.
18 Lords' *Journ.* xix, 271b.
19 Under an Act 9 Anne, cap. 30.
20 Close, 11 Anne pt. iii, no. 18.
21 Dugdale, *Mon. Angl.* vi, 383.   22 Ibid.
23 Chan. Inq. p.m. 28 Edw. I, no. 43 (as above).

24 Chan. Inq. a.q.d. file 14, no. 30.
25 See below.
26 Inq. a.q.d. 19 Edw. I, no. 52.
27 *Plac. de Quo Warr.* (Rec. Com.), 737.
28 *Rot. Lit. Claus.* (Rec. Com.), i, 413.
29 *Plac. de Quo Warr.* (Rec. Com.), 747.
30 Ibid.
31 Close, 11 Anne, pt. iii, no. 18.

the openings which were the upper quire entrances. In the middle bay of the south side a ragged hole represents the sedilia. At the west of the presbytery a cross arch marked the eastern limit of the quire; the first two bays had lofty pointed archways opening into the transepts, but only those on the south side are standing; between the bays are the toothings of buttresses which must have projected into the transepts. The third or westernmost bay, left standing on the south side, has a lower archway of equal width with the others, opening into the east end of the aisle. The dwarf wall closing its lower half is pierced below the west jamb of the arch by a

range of three lancet windows on either side, and another lancet high up in the south gable end. This portion had a high-pitched wooden roof, now of course all gone.

Of the two chapels to the east of the transept very little remains. The northern one extended behind two bays of the presbytery, being divided into two by a cross arch supporting the buttress between the bays. Of this arch and the east wall only the toothings on the presbytery wall are left; the chapel had a semi-circular barrel-vault running from east to west, of which a few springing stones remain. Over it was a lean-to roof against the presbytery wall. On

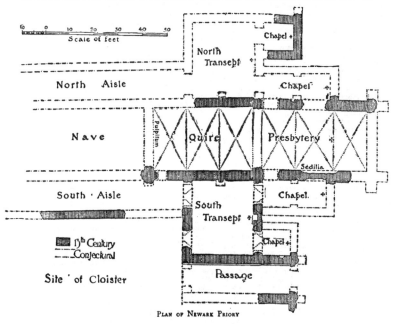

PLAN OF NEWARK PRIORY

pointed doorway. Over the archway are the remains of a lancet window which gave light to a clearstory above the aisle roof.

The south transept is more complete than any other part, its three outer walls being almost intact excepting where they have been robbed of all the dressed stones. In the east wall were two pointed archways —now mere gaps—opening into the chapels; between them are the remains against the wall of a small stone altar 5 ft. long, and over this altar is a square recess 2 ft. 6 in. wide. Another archway at the north end of the west wall opened from the nave aisle.

In the south wall of the transept, near the south-west angle, is the doorway connected with the night-stair from the dorter. The transept is lighted by a

the transept wall are the marks of two such roofs, one steeper than the other, and evidently of different dates.

The southern chapel was only of one bay in depth; its south wall still stands with a few angle stones indicating the return of the east wall; in it are the remains of a piscina. There are also the springing stones of a pointed barrel vault springing from a grooved and hollow-chamfered string-course. Over this vault, but not central with it, was a gabled wood roof, the outline of which is to be seen on the transept wall, and the gap between the two chapels is very clearly shown, the east face of the transept wall retaining its external plinth, which must have returned round the outsides of the chapels.

On the south face of the transept and chapel wall is the mark of the barrel-vault of the passage to the cemetery, 12 ft. wide, part of the east wall of which remains : the gable line of the dorter range also shows on the transept wall, but except for this all traces of the priory buildings have disappeared.

The north transept has entirely gone, and the only part left on that side is the north chapel to the east of the transept ; of this much of the three outer walls still stands, but they possess no details of note.

The only part of the nave still left is a length of the south aisle wall, and this has now fallen ; the toothings where it came against the transept wall remain in place, but for a space of 24 ft. the wall is missing, the remaining portion running thence westward for 34 ft. On the transept wall are the marks of the lean-to roof of the aisle ; it cuts across the north-west lancet window into the transept.

The dimensions of the church were : Presbytery, 43 ft. by 24 ft. 4 in. ; quire, 40 ft. by 26 ft. ; north and south transepts, 30 ft. deep by 25 ft. 4 in. wide ; north-east chapel off the south transept and south-east chapel off the north transept, 26 ft. by 10 ft. 6 in., the other two chapels 12 ft. by 10 ft. 6 in. ; nave length uncertain, width probably that of the quire, and south aisle 12 ft. wide.

In the south transept lies a heavy 14th-century cross slab of very rough work, being made of the intractable crystalline stone which occurs in isolated blocks in various parts of the county and elsewhere.

The so-called manor of *PAPWORTH* (Pappeworth, xiv cent.) may have been the holding of Walter or of Hubert in 1086. In 1271 Ruald de Calva granted the 'hamene of Papworth' to Newark Priory.[33] The priory granted it to the Westons of West Clandon, for in 1331 William de Weston had land in Send,[33] and in 1363 Margery widow of William de Weston died seised of a 'tenement called Papworth,' which she held of Newark.[34]

Papworth followed the descent of West Clandon Manor (q.v.) until the beginning of the 17th century, when Edmund Slyfield, lord of West Clandon, conveyed it to Henry Weston of Ockham.[35] The Westons held it until 1711, when John Weston sold it with Ockham to Sir Peter King.[36] Early in the 19th century Lord King, a descendant of Sir Peter, exchanged it with Lord Onslow for the manor of Wisley.[37]

The reputed manor of *DEDSWELL* (Dodswell, Dadswell, xvi cent.), possibly the other small holding of Domesday, received its name as land held of John de Tregoz by John de Dedeswell for the service of one-third of two knights' fees.[38] This service was in 1290 granted by John de Tregoz to the Prior of Newark.[39]

In 1351 Thomas de Weston of Albury married Joan daughter and heiress of John Dedswell of Send.[40] This Thomas was of a younger branch of the Westons of Send. At the death of William de Weston without issue in 1485 [41] Dedswell passed to his sister Margaret,

who married first William Welles of Buxted in Sussex and second John Appesley. She died in 1512 leaving a son and heir John Welles.[42] In 1539 Thomas Welles son of John conveyed the manor to Sir Richard Weston of Sutton in Woking.[43] It remained with the Westons of Sutton until 1661, when John Weston conveyed it to Arthur Onslow.[44] The Onslow family has retained possession until the present day.

The reputed manor of *JURY* in Send is mentioned among the lands lately belonging to Newark Priory which were granted to Sir Anthony Browne at the Dissolution.[45] Probably it represents the grant of a messuage with 100 acres of land made to the Prior and convent of Newark in 1333 by William Diry,[46] whose name was apparently attached to the holding, and became corrupted into Jury in process of time. This tenement descended with the manor of Send.

The Domesday Survey of Send (q.v.) mentions a mill, which in the 13th century appeared as a water-mill in the possession of Thomas and Alice de Send.[47] This mill, which they granted to the priory, was Newark Mill. The grant to Sir Anthony Browne (q.v.) mentions a mill in Ripley which may refer to the same. There was another mill on one of the smaller holdings.

The church of *ST. MARY THE VIRGIN, SEND,* is a small building consisting of a chancel 17 ft. 6 in. by 24 ft. 9 in. and an aisleless nave 38 ft. 3 in. by 31 ft. 2 in. with a west tower 10 ft. by 9 ft. 3 in., and a south porch.

The chancel seems to have been built about the year 1240, and is the oldest part of the church. The whole nave was rebuilt late in the 14th century, being unusually wide for its length, and the tower was added somewhat later. The south porch, which is of timber, was probably added late in the 15th century, and the church was restored in 1847.

The east window of the chancel was inserted apparently in old jambs in 1819. It has three cinque-foiled lights and tracery of a curious semi-gothic character in a two-centred head. The north wall of the chancel has two original lancets, the eastern-most one having chamfered and rebated jambs and the other plain rebated jambs.

In the south wall are two lancets of 13th-century date like those in the opposite wall, the easternmost one in this case having unchamfered jambs, while all have external shafts. At the west end of this wall is a small coeval low side window.

Near the east end of the north wall of the chancel is a plain projecting corbel, which was probably intended to support a figure. Opposite this in the south wall is a piscina with stop-chamfered jambs and pointed head. The basin was circular, but the projecting portion has been lopped off. Between the first and second windows of the south wall is a small 13th-century priest's doorway which has chamfered jambs of sandstone, and a four-centred head. The ashlar elsewhere, except in some of the lower quoins,

33 Dugdale, *Mon. Angl.* vi, 383.
33 Winton Epis. Reg. Stratford, fol. 55*b.*
34 Chan. Inq. p.m. 36 Edw. I, pt ii (1st nos.), 75.
35 Close, Jas. I, pt. xxxix, m. 2.
36 Feet of F. Surr. Hil. 9 Anne.
37 Manning and Bray, *Hist. of Surr.* iii, 109.
38 Chan. Inq. p.m. 28 Edw. I, no. 43.
39 Chan. Inq. a.q.d. file 14, no. 30.
40 *Harl. Soc. Publ.* xliii, 28, 216, and Weston Genealogy ; Brayley, op. cit. ii, 82.
41 Chan. Inq. p.m. (Ser. 2), xxvii, 61.
42 Ibid.
43 Feet of F. Surr. Mich. 31 Hen. VIII.
44 Ibid. Trin. 13 Chas. II.
45 Pat. 36 Hen. VIII, pt. xxvi, m. 20.
46 Chan. Inq. a.q.d. file 213, no. 24 ; Pat. 5 Edw. III, pt. ii, m. 24.
47 Chan. Inq. a.q.d. file 14, no. 30.

SEND: NEWARK PRIORY, SOUTH TRANSEPT AND PRESBYTERY FROM SOUTH-EAST

SEND: NEWARK PRIORY, SOUTH TRANSEPT FROM SOUTH-WEST

is of chalk. There is no chancel arch ; but that one originally existed is proved by the remains of squints on either side at the western angles of the chancel.

The north wall of the nave contains three windows, the easternmost being one of two plain lights with a square head set low in the wall. The head, sill, and mullion are chamfered, but the jambs are rebated as well as if to receive a shutter. The other two windows have each three trefoiled lights under a square head with a moulded label. They have both been restored in places. The windows of the south wall of the nave are similar to those of the north just described, except that the small south-east window is of one light only. The south doorway has plain chamfered jambs and a pointed four-centred head, and the porch retains its original moulded wall plates and uprights, but the lower parts have been replaced by plastered brickwork. The cusped barge-board at the south gable end is original. The tower arch is of two continuous chamfered orders, and in the north wall of the tower is a small doorway with a four-centred head which leads to the stair turret.

In the west wall of the tower is a plain doorway, much repaired, with two continuous hollow-chamfered orders and a moulded label. Above it is a 15th-century window partly restored, having three cinquefoiled lights under a four-centred head with a moulded label. The tower is of three stages with angle buttresses and a modern embattled parapet. In each face of the top stage is a window with a modern outer order and four-centred head of two wide trefoiled lights, the tracery of which is masked by modern louvres. The second stage has a single cinquefoiled light on the north and south, the former having a two-centred head and the latter one of ogee shape.

The walls throughout are of flint rubble, a few pieces of 13th-century detail being built into those of the nave ; some of the heavy Horsham slabs remain on the lower parts of the nave roof, but elsewhere red tiles are used. The nave roof has old tie-beams and embattled wall plates, and is plastered between the rafters ; and the tie-beam at the west end of the chancel is supported on curved brackets.

The chancel screen has been rebuilt, most of the upper portion being modern, but the traceried heads to all the lights and part of the moulded cornice are of 13th-century date. There are no mullions now, but modern carved pendants take their place, the holes where the original mullions tenoned into the middle rail being filled up ; below the rail is plain solid panelling. The moulded posts at each end of the screen show the marks of former parclose screens returning westwards.

The font is apparently of 13th-century workmanship, but the octagonal bowl has been entirely recut ; the lead lining, however, is old. One side of the moulded base has been cut away.

Over the west end of the nave is an early 17th-century wood gallery with a turned baluster front, now reached by modern stairs.

In the tower is an ancient chest constructed out of roughly finished log timber and bound with iron straps.

It has two lids made out of half tree-trunks, the curved surface being uppermost.

A stone on the north wall of the chancel has a brass attached to it which bears the following black-letter inscription : ' Here lyeth Laurence Slyffeld gent' & Alys he wyfe which Laurenc̄ decessid ye xiii day of Novēbr' aº dn̄i mº vᶜ xxi ō whōs soule Jh̄u have m'ci.' Above are the figures of the man and his wife, and below are three boys.

Above this brass is another with inscription : ' Pray for the Soule of Sʳ Thomas Marteyn late Vycar of Sende the which decessed the xxix day of September the yere of our lord mˡ vᶜ xxxiii on whos soule Jh̄u have m'ci.'

To the south of the tower in the churchyard is an indent of a half-figure and an inscription plate.

The westernmost window of the north wall of the nave has in the top of its centre light a few fragments of old painted glass.

The tower originally contained a ring of five bells, all cast by Phelps in 1711 ; but three of these are now missing, and one is known to have been sold. The tenor was cast by T. Mears in 1803.

The oldest piece of plate is a paten of the Britannia standard, but the date-letter is worn away. It is

PLAN OF SEND CHURCH

inscribed 1845. There is also a cup of 1844, a flagon of the same date, and a plate or almsdish which is not silver.

There are six books of registers, the first, which is of parchment, containing in the beginning entries of births from 1633 to 1659 copied from an old book. Following this are baptisms from 1666 to 1683, marriages from 1654 to 1700 with a gap between 1659 and 1666, and burials from 1653 to 1700 with a gap as in the marriages. The second book contains baptisms, marriages, and burials all from 1700 to 1762, 1754, and 1764 respectively. The third book contains marriages from 1754 to 1769 ; the fourth baptisms and burials from 1792 to 1812 ; the fifth has marriages from 1762 to 1791 ; and the sixth continues them from 1792 to 1812.

The church of *ST. MARY THE VIRGIN, RIPLEY,* consists of a chancel, nave, south aisle, and north porch; and was rebuilt in 1845-6, except the chancel, which dates from about 1160 and was intended to have a stone vault of two bays, the vaulting shafts of which yet remain, although it is not certain whether the vault was ever completed. The east window is an insertion of c. 1230 and is too high to have co-existed with any stone vault; the vault must therefore have been removed by this time if it was ever completed at all. The window consists of three lancets separated by wide rebated and chamfered mullions, all under one two-centred rear arch; the two jambs inside have a deeply undercut roll with a somewhat formless base, and stopped out below the springing. The two north windows are original, and have round heads with shallow rebated outer jambs, and wide inner splays with engaged shafts at the angles, which have scalloped capitals with grooved and chamfered abaci. The two south windows are contemporary with the east window; the first is restored outside, but has an inner edge roll like that of the east window; the other has plain angles. West of the latter is a 15th or 16th-century priest's doorway, now opening from the modern vestry. The vaulting shafts divide the chan-

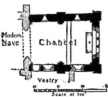

PLAN OF THE CHANCEL OF RIPLEY CHURCH

cel into two bays; the middle pilaster is a foot wide and projects about seven inches, and has an engaged half-round shaft on its face, flanked by detached round shafts 5 in. in diameter, and similar detached shafts stand in the angles at the east and west ends of the chancel; they all have good moulded bases with projecting spurs at the corners of the square sub-bases; the capitals are richly scalloped and have hollow chamfered square abaci. The richest detail of the whole chancel is the elaborately carved string-course running round the chancel below the windows; it is large and half-round in section, ornamented with interlacing spiral bands filled in with diamond-shaped leaves; the string is carried round the vaulting shafts and finishes against the chancel arch. The eastern angles of the chancel have shallow clasping buttresses, and there are shallow buttresses behind the intermediate shafts; the two side walls are about 2 ft. 8 in. thick and the east wall about 3 ft., the walling is flint mixed with conglomerate with chalk dressings, and all the dressings inside are of chalk.

The chancel arch and the nave generally are modern, excepting perhaps the rear arch of the north doorway which appears to be of the 13th century; it is of chalk and has a pointed edge roll with deep hollows on either side of it and another small roll on the outermost edge. Three lancet windows pierce

the north wall, the doorway with a pointed head coming between the second and third. An arcade of four bays divides the nave into the aisle; it has round pillars and pointed arches of 13th-century character. The east wall of the aisle is pierced by a traceried circular window, and the south wall has four windows each of three lights under traceried heads. At the west end of the nave is a pointed doorway below an organ gallery, and on the west wall is a bellcot in which hangs a small modern bell.

The roofs are all modern, as are the altar, pulpit, font, &c.

There are no ancient monuments, the earliest being two gravestones in the chancel, one to Nicholas and Elizabeth Fenn, 1705, and the other to Burleigh Fenn, who died in 1708.

The communion plate comprises a silver cup and stand flagon of 1846 and a plated flagon and paten.

The older registers are incorporated with and kept at the mother parish of Send.

ADVOWSON The advowson of the church of Send was granted to the Prior of Newark by Ruald de Calva.[48] It remained with the priory until the Dissolution,[49] when it was granted with the manor (q.v.) to Sir Anthony Browne. It has followed the descent of the manor from that time.

The chapel at Ripley was granted to Newark Priory by Ruald de Calva.[50] Its advowson descended with the manor of Send after the Dissolution, when the Newark possessions were granted to Sir Anthony Browne.

The chapel was included as a chantry chapel at the time of the Commissions of Edward VI, and a revenue of £6 was confiscated as a chantry foundation. The building survived and was made the church of an ecclesiastical parish in 1878.

CHARITIES A table in the church records Smith's Charity, distributed as in other Surrey parishes; and the following benefactions:

A house near the church which was exchanged with General Evelyn for a house at Three Ford, 1772, for the use of the poor. It was probably the old parish workhouse.

William Boughton gave 40s. a year from the rent of a house called Keep House.

Sarah Hale gave £20, the interest to be for poor widows. A return of 1786 says that this was lost by a defaulting churchwarden.

Dame Anne Haynes gave £300 to bind poor children as apprentices. This property is now worth £50 a year.

Mrs. Legat gave £200, the interest to be devoted to poor widows not receiving regular relief.

General Evelyn gave 20s. a year for the repair of his monument, the surplus for the poor on Christmas Day.

48 Dugdale, *Mon.* vi, 383.
49 *Wykeham's Reg.* (Hants Rec. Soc.), i, 36, 66, &c.; Egerton MSS. 2031, fol. 268,
101 d.; 2032, fol. 74 d.; 2033, fol. 29 d., 63, 69; 2034, fol. 58 d., 87 d., 171.
50 Dugdale, *Mon. Angl.* vi, 383.

OCKHAM CHURCH FROM THE SOUTH-EAST

SEND CHURCH FROM THE SOUTH-EAST

STOKE JUXTA GUILDFORD

Stochae (xi cent.) ; Stok (xiii cent.).

Stoke is a parish lying across the River Wey just below Guildford. It is bounded on the west and north by Worplesdon, on the east by Merrow, on the south by St. Martha's, Shalford, and the Guildford parishes. It measures 3 miles from north-west to south-east, and 1¼ miles from south-west to north-east. The total area of the whole parish is 2,301 acres. It extends from the ridge of the chalk down east of Guildford across the Thanet and Woolwich beds, the London Clay, and the sand and alluvium of the Wey Valley. It is intersected by the river, and by the railways and roads which enter Guildford from the north and east. The Cobham and Guildford line, with a station in the London Road, Guildford, in Stoke parish, was opened in 1885. Stoke is now largely a town or suburban parish, or parishes, for by the Local Government Act of 1894 it was divided into two parishes. Stoke Within is part of the borough of Guildford, and contains 252 acres. It comprises the southern part of the old parish. Stoke next Guildford is the more outlying suburban and country part of the parishes, and contains 2,049 acres. No Inclosure Act is known, but Stoke Fields, now built over, suggest common fields by their name. Neolithic implements have been found in the parish.

Wood Bridge is a brick bridge on an old line of road where a bridge has long existed. It was repaired by the neighbourhood and not by the lord of the manor.[1] It is now a county bridge and was rebuilt in brick in 1847–8.[2] When the property of Stoke Park and Stoke Mills was purchased by Mr. Aldersey in 1780 the road ran between his house and the east end of Stoke Church, and passed the river by a ford with a long narrow wooden bridge by the side of it for use in flood time. He diverted the road to the west end of the church, where it now is, and built Stoke Bridge of brick.

On the site of Stoughton Manor House are the remains of the old moat. Stoke Park is now the seat of Mrs. Budgett. It is not the site of the old manor-house ; this was at Warren Farm on the chalk down east of Guildford, where the courts used to be held. The name Stoke Park was not used in 1762,[3] when the place was called the Paddocks. Mr. Dyson, the owner, laid out the park about that time. Stoke Hill was the seat of the late Rev. F. Paynter ; Woodbridge Park is the seat of Mrs. Blount. Mrs. Charlotte Smith, who died at Elstead in 1806, and was well known formerly as a poetess and writer, was a native of Stoke, and has a monument in the church.

Stoke Church Institute in the Foxenden Road was opened in 1895. There is a Roman Catholic chapel (St. Joseph's) in Chertsey Street, where also is a

Primitive Methodist chapel. There is a Baptist chapel in Martyr Road, and one in Commercial Road.

Stoughton is an ecclesiastical parish formed from Stoke in 1893. There is a Wesleyan chapel founded in 1895. The cemetery in Stoughton was purchased and laid out in 1880–2. It comprises 8 acres.

Stoughton Barracks are the dépôt of Regimental District No. 2, the 1st, 2nd, and 3rd Battalions of the Royal West Surrey. Guildford Union Workhouse is in Stoke Within.

Stoke (Church) School was built in 1856 and enlarged in 1895. Sandfield School (Provided) was opened in 1901. Stoke Hill School (Church) was built in 1870, Stoughton School (Provided) in 1885, and St. Joseph's (Roman Catholic) in 1885.

At the time of Domesday STOKE MANORS formed part of the royal demesne.[4] It continued to be a Crown possession until the time of King John, who granted it to the Bishop of London and his church of St. Paul.[5] By 1222, however, the rights of St. Paul's in Stoke had apparently ceased to exist, since there is no mention of the manor in the Domesday of St. Paul's drawn up about that date.[6] The Bishops of London continued to be the lords of the manor of Stoke[7] until the 16th century, when Bishop John Aylmer released it to Queen Elizabeth.[8] It seems

SEE OF LONDON. *Gules two swords of St. Paul crossed having hilts and pomels or.*

to have been granted shortly afterwards to Thomas Vyncent of Stoke D'Abernon, who in 1587 conveyed it to Laurence Stoughton,[9] lord of the manor of Stoughton in Stoke, q.v.

The manor of STOUGHTON in Stoke seems to have originated in land called 'Stocton' which was part of the manor of Stoke, and was afforested under Richard I.[10] King John granted it with Stoke to the Bishop of London,[11] and it was continuously held as of that manor.[12]

The first record of immediate lords occurs in 1345, when Henry de Stoughton settled the manor on himself and his wife Joan and their heirs.[13] In 1415 Walter Stoughton, probably son of Henry, died seised of the manor, leaving a son Thomas, then twenty years of age, to succeed him.[14]

The manor apparently passed through Gilbert son of Thomas[15] to Laurence Stoughton,[16] who held it in the 16th century.[17] He died in 1571, leaving a son Thomas,[18] who survived him only five years.[19] The manor had in 1575 been settled in tail male on Laurence son of Thomas on his marriage with Rose

[1] Pleas of the Manor, East. 5 Ric. II, R. 14.
[2] Diary of Mr. J. More-Molyneux, J.P.
[3] Rocque's Map. [4] V.C.H. Surr. i, 296a.
[5] Cal. Rot. Chart. (Rec. Com.), 147 ; Cart. Antiq. MM, 18 ; A, 11 ; A, 6 ; AA, 47 ; SS, 13.
[6] W. H. Hale, Dom. of St. Paul, 1 et seq.

[7] Cal. Close, 1232, p. 40 ; 1348, p. 353 ; Chan. Inq. p.m. 32 Edw. I, no. 90.
[8] Feet of F. Div. Co. East. 33 Eliz.
[9] Ibid. Surr. Trin. 29 Eliz.
[10] Rot. Lit. Claus. (Rec. Com.) ii, 59.
[11] Ibid.
[13] Chan. Inq. p.m. 3 Hen. V, no. 1 ; Chan. Inq. p.m. (Ser. 2), clv, 49.

[14] Feet of F. Surr. 19 Edw. III, no. 20.
[14] Chan. Inq. p.m. 3 Hen. V, no. 11.
[16] Publ. Harl. Soc. xliii, 85.
[16] Ibid. ; son of Gilbert.
[17] Chan. Inq. p.m. (Ser. 2), clxxxvii, 84.
[18] Harl. Soc. Publ. xliii, 86.
[19] Chan. Inq. p.m. (Ser. 2), clxxix, 81.

Ive,[20] and it accordingly passed to him.[21] At his death in 1615[22] he was succeeded by his third son George,[23] who died in 1624 without issue.[24] His brother Nicholas barred the entail in order to secure the manor to his daughter Rose, wife of Arthur Onslow, but on the failure of her issue it passed to Nicholas son of Anthony eighth son of Laurence Stoughton.[25] He was created a baronet in 1661, and died in 1685, leaving one son Laurence and four daughters.[26] Laurence died childless in 1692,[27] and by a Parliamentary decree his estates were vested in trustees to be sold for the double purpose of paying his debts and providing portions for his sisters.[28]

STOUGHTON, baronet.
Azure a cross engrailed ermine.

The now combined manors of Stoke and Stoughton were bought by Edward Hubbald in 1698.[29] He died in 1707. His son William died in 1709, and shortly after his death in 1711 an Act was passed for the sale of his estates.[30] Nicholas Turner purchased the manors in 1718, and his son sold them about 1760 to Jeremiah Dyson.[31] Mr. Dyson died in 1776. His son sold in 1780 to Mr. George Vansittart, who sold immediately to Mr. William Aldersey (*vide supra*). The latter also purchased parts of Stoughton which had been alienated since 1700 and had passed to Lord Onslow, including the site of Stoughton Place, which had been pulled down after the sale in 1692. Mr. Aldersey died in 1800. His widow sold next year to Mr. Nathaniel Hillier. Colonel the Hon. C. T. Onslow married in 1812 Susannah second daughter and co-heiress of Mr. Hillier. Colonel the Hon. G. A. C. Onslow, who died in 1855, succeeded, and his son, the present Earl of Onslow is now lord of the manor. No separate courts have been held for Stoughton since 1615.

In 1324 there is mention of a messuage and 5 acres of land in Stoke called *WOODBRIDGE*. This tenement was held of the family of La Poyle,[32] who had lands in Guildford and Tongham. The earliest tenant seems to have been Thomas de Woodbridge, who was holding about 1264; Juliana his daughter and heir married Roger de Rypon.[33]

About the end of the 16th century Henry Stoughton was in possession of this property,[34] which passed from him to his son Thomas, who died seised of it in 1612. Woodbridge, with certain lands appurtenant, was settled on his wife Alice, with remainders to various members of the Stoughton family.[35]

Manning[36] speaks of Woodbridge House as having been the property of Jeremiah Dyson in the 18th century. It was afterwards in the possession of Mr. Allen and Mrs. Smith, and in Manning's time belonged to John Creuse.[37] It was subsequently the

residence of Colonel the Hon. E. M. Onslow, of Colonel Annand, and now of Mr. H. Porter.

The church of *ST. JOHN THE EVANGELIST, STOKE JUXTA GUILDFORD*, consists of a chancel 15 ft. 5 in. by 33 ft. 2 in., with a north chapel 24 ft. 10 in. by 13 ft. 10 in.; south vestry and chapel formed by a prolongation of the aisle; a nave 40 ft. 6 in. by 19 ft. 6 in.; a north aisle 18 ft. 7 in. wide; a south aisle 17 ft. 6 in. wide; a west tower 12 ft. 8 in. by 10 ft. 3 in., and a south porch. Like so many churches in the neighbourhood it has suffered severely at the hands of the restorer, and externally is almost completely modern. The earliest details now to be seen are in the arcades of the nave and south chapel, which are of early 14th-century date. Late in the 15th century the tower was added, and the north chapel is probably work of a century later. In comparatively recent years the north aisle has been completely rebuilt and widened, and the whole church greatly modernized. The south porch and south-east vestry are completely modern, but the latter is evidently on the site of an earlier and similar structure.

The east window of the chancel is of five lights, of 15th-century style, with sub-mullions and smaller lights in the two-centred head. The north wall is in three bays, the first being blank and the other two filled with an arcade with a circular column and half-round responds, plainly moulded capitals, and arches of two chamfered orders. The bases are now buried under the floor. On the south is a similar arrangement, but the arcade is of earlier date, and has arches of two wave and ogee moulded orders. The capitals are of good profile, and the bases have a roll-moulding, all being circular on plan. There is no corner arch, a cambered beam of late 16th-century date supporting the eastern gable of the nave.

The nave is of three bays, with arcading of similar date but plainer detail than the south chancel arcade. The arches are of two plain chamfered orders, and the columns circular with moulded capitals and bases. The tower arch is of late 15th-century date, and of two continuously moulded orders, separated by a three-quarter hollow.

The north chapel has a two-light window to the east and a four-light to the north, both transomed, and with square heads of late 16th-century date. Between the chapel and the aisle is a plastered arch, either of brick or lath-and-plaster. At the north east is an external door with a segmental head.

The north aisle has, to the north, two modern windows of two lights with tracery of 14th-century detail. The west window is of four lights, also of 14th-century design.

The south aisle and chapel, in one range, have an east window of which the opening is apparently original and at such a height above the floor as to clear the vestry. The tracery and external jambs are

[20] Feet of F. Surr. East. 17 Eliz.
[21] Chan. Inq. p.m. (Ser. 2), clxxix, 81.
[22] Ibid. ccclv, 49.
[23] His eldest son Laurence died s.p. in 1597, and his second son Thomas in 1610. Thomas has a monument in the church.
[24] Entry in Stoke Ch. Reg. copied in Symmes, MSS. (Add. MSS. 6167, fol. 405 d.); Harl. MSS. 1561, f. 76.
[25] G.E.C. Complete Baronetage. The inscription to Nicholas at Stoke Church

records how he was disinherited in favour of Rose, but succeeded at last *Deo volente, hominibus invitis.*
[26] Ibid. (1) Elizabeth, wife of Timothy Whitfield; (2) Frances, wife of Charles Ventris; (3) Henrietta; (4) Sara. See also Feet of F. Surr. Mich. 11 Will. and Mary.
[27] G.E.C. Complete Baronetage.
[28] Journ. of House of Lords, xv, 614a, 668b.

[29] D. Jan. 1697–8; Manning and Bray, Surr. i, 168. The deaths of Edward and William Hubbald are in Stoke Reg.
[30] Journ. of House of Lords, xix, 216, 301b.
[31] Hist. of Guildford (publ. 1801), 276.
[32] Cal. Close, 1324, p. 241.
[33] Ibid.
[34] Chan. Inq. p.m. (Ser. 2), dxvii, 36.
[35] Ibid.
[36] Hist. Surr. i, 173.   [37] Ibid.

quite modern, and of 14th-century detail. In the south wall are four two-light windows, all of the same 14th-century design. There are perhaps some old stones in the internal splays, but otherwise they are completely modern. The west window is of the same design and date as that of the north aisle. The south door, between the western pair of windows, and the porch are modern, and of 15th-century design. At the north-east of the aisle is a small door, possibly of late 14th-century date, restored with a pointed chamfered head, leading into the vestry. The latter is quite modern, and has a three-light modern window to the east, and a small external door to the south.

The tower is of three stages, with an embattled parapet, and buttresses, and a south-east turret stair-case. The walling is worked in a checker of flints and blocks of Heath stone. The belfry windows, which are very much restored, are of two four-centred uncusped lights, in a square-headed chamfered reveal. In the second stage is a small single light of similar detail, and below it is the west window, which is quite modern, and of four lights with tracery. The west door, also modern, is of 15th-century design, with a two-centred head within a square outer order, and spandrel sinkings, &c.

The font is a late 18th-century one, and has a small black marble octagonal bowl on a baluster stem of white marble. The base is also of black marble. The other fittings and the seating are all modern, except the communion rails, which are of early 18th-century date. A table of the same period also remains. The roofs of the nave and chancel are both of late date, probably early 17th or late 16th century, while those of the aisles, &c., are modern.

In the north chapel are a number of incised wall slabs to members of the Stoughton family. One is to Sir Nicholas Stoughton of Stoughton, 1647, married, first, to Brigid Compton; secondly, to Anna Evans. Six shields, arranged round the frame of the inscription, give the arms of Stoughton, Compton of Godalming, and other families. Another slab is to Brigid (Compton), wife of the above, 1631, who had four children, John, George, Rose, and Brigid. There are two shields, the first, Stoughton impaling Compton, and Compton. Also three slabs close together, one to Sir Laurence Stoughton, 1615, and Rose Ive his wife, 1632, with Stoughton impaling Party cheveronwise sable and argent three elephants' heads razed and countercoloured with crowns or; a second to Thomas Stoughton, second son of Sir Laurence Stoughton and his wife Catherine Evelyn, who had five children and both died in 1610, with the arms of Stoughton and Evelyn on separate shields; and the third to Sir George, third son and heir of Sir Laurence Stoughton, 1623-4. There is also, in the chancel, a monument to George Barnes, 1683, eldest son of George Barnes of Wassage, and grandson of Sir George Barnes of London. The arms are Azure three leopards' heads argent impaling Ermine a cheveron azure. In the south aisle is an achievement of the royal arms, with the initials A.R., and the date 1702.

The tower contains four bells, the treble, second, and third cast by Bryan Eldridge in 1620, and the tenor dated 1790.

The plate consists of a chalice of 17th-century type with illegible date-letter, a modern copy, a paten made in 1701, a very large flagon made apparently in 1631 and presented in 1702, and a plated paten.

The first book of registers contains mixed entries, 1662 to 1726; second, 1727 to 1812, marriages stopping 1748; the third, marriages 1754 to 1776; the fourth, banns and marriages 1776 to 1800; the fifth, marriages 1801 to 1812. There are also two small books, the first, 1727 to 1748, containing baptisms; the second, similar, but with burials also, 1764 to 1803.

The church of *ST. SAVIOUR, WOODBRIDGE ROAD,* is of stone, in 14th-century style, with a tower and spire. It was consecrated in 1899. A church room was built in 1892.

The church of *EMMANUEL, STOUGHTON,* is built in stone by Mr. W. Gilbert Scott in 14th-century style. It was consecrated in 1904. A brick church on the other side of the road was formerly used.

CHRIST CHURCH is a chapel of ease to Stoke, built in the Waterden Road, Guildford, in 1868. It is in 13th-century style, of stone, with a tower.

ADVOWSONS The church of Stoke is mentioned in the Domesday Survey.[38]

It was afterwards in the gift of the priory of St. Pancras at Lewes,[39] who at the Dissolution released it to the king.[40] It was afterwards granted to Robert Lord.[41] The mayor of Guildford presented in 1633,[42] Sir Nicholas Stoughton in 1662, William Hubbald, son of William who died in 1709, in 1712.[43] In 1719 Henry Sherrat conveyed it to Nicholas Turner.[44] John Russell presented in 1749, and George West in 1795.[45] In 1826 George West conveyed it to Francis Paynter.[46] Samuel Paynter presented in 1831.[47] The advowson is now in the hands of Simeon's trustees.

St. Saviour's was formed into an ecclesiastical parish in 1893 from Stoke and the formerly extra-parochial liberty of the Friary. The living is in the gift of Simeon's trustees.

Stoughton parish was formed from Stoke in 1893. The patron was then the late Rev. Francis Paynter of Stoke Hill.

CHARITIES Parsons' Almshouse for poor widows was established by William and Henry Parsons in 1796. They were brothers engaged in business in Guildford. Henry died in 1791, leaving money by will for the purpose, which was carried out by William. The building, in Stoke Road, is of brick, with a turret and clock in the centre, and is not unpleasing.

Smith's Charity is distributed as in other Surrey parishes.

In 1767 Mr. James Price left £400 3 per cent. stock for the benefit of poor housekeepers not receiving parish relief.

Dr. James Price, his nephew, in 1783 added £800 to this charity. Dr. Price was really named Higginbotham, but took his maternal uncle's name. He pretended to discoveries in the transmutation of metals. He was a F.R.S., and when a committee of the society was appointed to test his experiments, committed suicide.

[38] *V.C.H. Surr.* i, 296a.
[39] *Wykeham's Reg.* (Hants Rec. Soc.), i, 189.
[40] Feet of F. Div. Co. Mich. 26 Hen. VIII.
[41] Pat. 36 Hen. VIII, pt. iv.
[42] Inst. Bks. (P.R.O.).   [43] Ibid.
[44] Feet of F. Surr. Hil. 6 Geo. I.
[44] Inst. Bks. (P.R.O.).
[46] Feet of F. Surr. Trin. 6 Geo. IV.
[47] Inst. Bks. (P.R.O.).

WANBOROUGH

Weneberge (xi cent.) ; Waneberg (xii–xiii cent.) ; Wamberge (xiii cent.); Wanbergh (xiv cent.) ; Wanborowe (xvii cent.).

Wanborough is a small parish, 4 miles west of Guildford, containing 1,823 acres and measuring about 3 miles from east to west and one from north to south. It is bounded on the north by Ash and Worplesdon, on the east by Compton, on the south by Compton and Puttenham, on the south-west and west by Seale. It throws out a tongue, however, between Compton and Puttenham which just touches Godalming. The South Eastern Railway, Redhill and Reading line, runs through it, with a station opened in 1849. It is traversed by the high road from Guildford to Farnham along the Hog's Back, the *via regia* of early deeds and Hundred Rolls. The greater part of the parish is on the chalk of the Hog's Back, but it reaches the sand south of the ridge, where Puttenham Heath is partly in Wanborough, and a further distance north on to the London Clay. The small hamlet of Wanborough lies on the north side of the Hog's Back. It is an exception to the almost universal rule of the church and village lying south of the chalk hills with a parish reaching over the chalk or on to it northwards. The village and church are to the north, as is most of the parish. It is doubtful whether it is an ancient parish. It was perhaps a chapelry of Puttenham, though in a different hundred (but for this compare Ash and Frimley).

Neolithic flint implements were found in 1870 near the church, and others at various times and places. A palaeolithic ovate implement is in the Charterhouse Museum and a small bronze palstave in the Archaeological Society's Museum, Guildford.

MANOR *WANBOROUGH* was in the early stages of its history held as two manors by two brothers, Swegen and Leofwine, possibly Harold's brothers ; after the Conquest, however, these two manors were united in the possession of Geoffrey de Mandeville.[1] Probably the overlordship of the manor remained with the Mandevilles, and passed with the earldom of Essex from their family to the de Bohuns,[2] for Humphrey, Earl of Hereford and Essex, held four knights' fees in Wanborough, Clapham, and Carshalton in 1372,[3] and the connexion still existed under Henry IV.[3] Geoffrey son of Eustace, Count of Boulogne, married

Bohun. *Azure a bend argent between cotises and six lioncels or.*

a daughter of Geoffrey de Mandeville. He received with her the Mandeville land at Carshalton,[4] and his grandson Faramus of Boulogne[5] appears as sub-tenant of the Mandeville land at Wanborough also, for in or about 1130, just after the foundation of Waverley Abbey, he sold it, with the permission of his overlord, to the abbey, for the sum of one hundred marks.[5] This sale was some years later ratified by Pope Eugenius III.[7] In 1279 the abbey's possessions in Wanborough were increased by the gift of a capital messuage with appurtenances from William de Abbecroft.[6]

In 1346 the Abbot of Waverley claimed to have view of frankpledge in his manor of Wanborough by right of immemorial custom without charter ; and this claim obtained recognition from the king's treasurer and chamberlain.[9]

At the dispersion of the abbey lands in 1536, the major portion of them, including Wanborough Manor, was assigned to Sir William Fitz William, afterwards Earl of Southampton.[10] At his death in 1542 the manor passed to his half-brother, Sir Anthony Browne,[11] in whose family it remained for some sixty years. His grandson, the second Viscount Montagu, demised the manor to a certain Richard Amye[12] for a term of twenty-one years from Michaelmas 1603 ; but before the expiration of the lease the ownership of the manor had been transferred to John Murray, keeper of the privy purse to King James I,[13] who created him Earl of Annandale. In 1625 he mortgaged the manor to Thomas Bennett for the sum of £4,200,[14] and after his death his son James sold it to his cousin James Maxwell,[15] who a few years later became Earl of Dirletoun.[16] His widow Elizabeth survived him for some years, keeping the manor in her possession.[17] At her death it passed under the terms of her husband's will to their daughter Elizabeth, wife of the second Duke of Hamilton.[18] The Duchess took as her second husband Thomas Dalmahoy,[19] to whom she bequeathed Wanborough in trust to sell.[20] He conveyed it to Mrs. Elizabeth Colwall,[21] from whom it passed in due course to her grandson Daniel Colwall.[22] Daniel in his will devised it to his half-brothers, Arthur and Richard Onslow, sons of Foot Onslow.[23] The manor was shortly afterwards sold to Thomas Onslow,[24] ancestor of the present Earl of Onslow, who is lord of the manor.

Shortly before the Dissolution the monks of Waverley obtained the privilege of holding an annual fair with court of pie powder on the feast of St. Bartholomew, in whose honour the church is dedicated.[26] The manor house, a fine old gabled house near the church, is now the seat of Sir Algernon West, G.C.B.

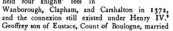

[1] *V.C.H. Surr.* i, 324b.
[2] G.E.C. *Complete Peerage.*
[3] Esch. Inq. p.m. file 146 (51), m. 20. Note also Chan. Inq. p.m. 46 Edw. III (1st nos.), no. 10.
[4] *V.C.H. Surr.* i, 324.
[5] See *Genealogist* (New Ser.), xii, 145–51, article by Mr. J. H. Round.
[6] Dugdale, *Monasticon,* v, 342.
[7] Lansd. Chart. 27.
[8] *Annales Mon.* (Rolls Ser.), ii, 392.
[9] *Cal. of Pat.* 1345–6, p. 220.
[10] L. and P. Hen. *VIII,* xi, 88.

[11] Chan. Inq. p.m. (Ser. 2), lxx, 29.
[12] Chan. Proc. Jas. I, m. xxii, 24. Richard Amye was a parishioner in 1600. A daughter of a Henry Amye was buried at Wanborough in 1630, and a John Amye in 1634.
[13] Ibid. ; see also Add. MSS. 6167.
[14] Com. Pleas Recov. R. Hil. 22 Jas. I m. 11.
[15] Close, 18 Chas. I, pt. xviii, no. 20.
[16] G.E.C. *Complete Peerage.*
[17] Add. MS. 6167.
[18] Ibid.

[19] Ibid.; see also G.E.C. *Complete Peerage*
[20] Add. MS. 6167.
[21] Ibid. [22] Ibid. [23] Ibid.
[24] Ibid. This part of the history of Wanborough was added to Symmes's Collections (Add. MSS. 6167) after his death, but since the MS. was in the possession of the Onslow family until the beginning of the 19th century, it seems reasonable to suppose that had these facts been incorrect the Onslows would have taken steps to rectify them.
[26] Chart. R. 207, m. 8, no. 16.

WANBOROUGH CHURCH : EAST WINDOW

The church of *ST. BARTHOLOMEW CHURCH* is a small rectangular building measuring inside 43 ft. 5 in. by 18 ft. 4 in. with a screen placed 17 ft. 8 in. from the east wall to separate the chancel from the nave.

All the walls are of 13th-century date, except that at the west, this having been rebuilt in modern times. There is no evidence of the existence of a chancel arch. The building was disused for two centuries, from 1674 to 1861.

The east window is a late 15th-century insertion with three peculiar cinquefoil lights and a square head without a label. The inside jambs are splayed and have a flat segmental chamfered rear arch.

In the north wall are three 13th-century lancets, one in the chancel and two in the nave, the first and easternmost having plain chamfered jambs and head and inside splays with a semicircular rear arch. The second is rather wider and has chamfered and rebated jambs and head and a chamfered rear arch, which with the internal splays is either modern or retooled. The third window is similar to the first except that the jambs are rebated only and the inside stonework is either modern or has been retooled. Between the first and second of these windows is a 13th-century doorway, originally external, but now used as an entrance from the vestry, which is built of wood and corrugated iron. The jambs and pointed arch of the doorway are moulded with an edge roll.

The south wall has four windows, two in the chancel and two in the nave. The easternmost dates from about 1330 and has two trefoiled lights with a quatrefoil over and a scroll-moulded label. The second window is apparently of 15th-century date and has a single cinquefoiled light. The sill is low down and the inside is rebated for a shutter, one of the hooks for hanging it still remaining in position. The third and fourth windows are similar to the opposite ones in the nave except that in the third the jambs are chamfered only and the rear arch is semicircular.

Between these last two windows is a doorway similar to that in the north wall of the chancel, but wider, and having a grooved and hollow-chamfered label. The jambs are modern.

Below the sill of the south-east window is a small recess with plain chamfered jambs and square head. The sill is plastered, but it no doubt once held the circular piscina basin which is now lying loose on the window-sill above.

To the west of this is a similar but wider recess with a stone sill which was probably used as a single seat.

The west window of the nave is modern and has two cinquefoiled lights and a two-centred head with tracery of late 14th-century design.

The walls are of flint in mortar with stone dressings, except the west wall, which is of brick with a tile-hung gable, from which projects a small bell-cot with one bell. The buttresses to the south wall are modern. The roof is of modern open timber-work and is covered outside with tiles.

The chancel screen has a panelled lower portion, above which are six lights on either side of the central opening. Each light has flowing tracery in the head, and the mullions and cornice are moulded. The central doorway has a flat four-centred head with carved leaves in the spandrels, and is of 15th-century date, but the rest of the screen is for the most part modern, including all the tracery to the lights.

All the other interior fittings are modern. There are no monuments of any importance, but in the churchyard outside the west wall is a long tapering stone which was probably once used as a coffin lid.

PLAN OF WANBOROUGH CHURCH

The Communion plate is modern and is not silver.

The first book of registers is dated 1598; the entries, however, are from 1561 and consist of baptisms, burials, and marriages, which continue until 1646. During the Commonwealth the only entries are the births of the children of a certain Joseph Freakes, but after the Restoration other entries continue up to 1674.

ADVOWSON The church was early appropriated to Waverley,[27] but it does not appear in Pope Nicholas's Taxation of 1291. The abbey appointed a vicar in 1327,[28] but vicars do not appear to have been instituted afterwards, and it was probably treated as a donative, with perpetual curates presented by Waverley without episcopal institution. The 'advowson' which was granted with Waverley to Fitz William at the Dissolution probably means the advowson of Wanborough, for there was no parish of Waverley. Richard Harding, who lived as a tenant in the abbey buildings, was married and had his children baptized at Wanborough, and in 1600 William Hampton and Joan Smith, both of Waverley, were married after having had their banns published in Wanborough Church. Some of the other names in the fragmentary register are suspected as being of Waverley, which was extra-parochial, but of which this seems to have been still commonly considered the church. The lay impropriators paid no regular stipend to curates. The names of two survive for 1598–1600 and 1612–13, but services were often performed by clergy of other parishes. By the exertions of the Rev. G. C. R. Chilton, vicar 1861 to 1895, a small endowment fund was raised. The church was disused altogether for about 200 years, but the parish always remained separate, and the advowson of the now restored church is in the hands of Mr. G. McKibben.

[27] A chaplain of Wanborough, Richard, witnessed a 12th-century *deed* now in the Loseley MSS.
[28] Winton Epis. Reg. Stratford, fol. 101 *b*.

WINDLESHAM

Wyndesham (xiii cent.) ; Wyndelesham (xiv cent.); Wynsham (xvii cent.).

Windlesham is a parish on the north-west border of the county, 25 miles from London. It contains 3,672 acres, and measures 5 miles from north-east to south-west, and 3 miles from north-west to south-east. It is bounded on the north-west by Berkshire, on the east and south by Chobham, on the west by Frimley. It is in Woking Hundred,[1] but is isolated in Godley Hundred, to which Chobham and Frimley belong. This corner of the county appears, from absence of notice in Domesday, to have been very sparsely inhabited. Godley Hundred was the land of the abbey of Chertsey, and when Chertsey early acquired property the hundred was extended. Windlesham and Bagshot, never belonging to Chertsey, were never incorporated into the hundred. But the boundary between Surrey and Berkshire was known, and was delineated as the boundary of Windsor Forest by the perambulations of 1226 and 1327.[2]

The neighbourhood has yielded bronze implements, now in the Archaeological Society's Museum, Guildford, and a certain number of neolithic flints.

The village of Windlesham is a scattered one, and though almost entirely modern, is picturesquely situated in rolling and well-wooded country. The church is some distance from the village, on high ground. The plan of the village defies analysis, and is of very recent growth. A few examples of late 18th-century work remain, but these are rapidly giving place to modern cottages and villas. The roads and lanes by which the parish is traversed, though erratic in their course, are picturesque in the extreme, with magnificent hedges and well shaded by fine timber.

The soil of Windlesham and Bagshot is the barren Bagshot sand, with extensive peat beds. Digging in the peat reveals the former existence of a forest of small oaks. The peat produces the only important industry of to-day, the raising of rhododendrons, azaleas, and so on, in nursery gardens—those of Messrs. Fromow and Messrs. Waterer employing a great deal of labour. Bagshot Heath, part of which was called Windlesham Heath, covered a great deal of the parish ; there is still some uncultivated land, and the heaths extend beyond the parish. The great south-western road from London passes through the parish. The London and South Western Wokingham and Reading line cuts its extreme end, and the Ascot, Aldershot, and Farnham branch runs through it for some distance, with a station at Bagshot, opened in 1878. Sunningdale station, on the Wokingham branch, is just inside the parish. It was opened in 1856.

The old road had been the source of great prosperity in Bagshot till it was superseded by the railway. Thirty coaches a day passed through, and there were many inns, since closed. The most interesting

history of the place is in connexion with Windsor Forest, and its bailiwick in Surrey. The tenure of Bagshot in the Red Book of the Exchequer is *per serjentiam veltrariae*, i.e. providing a leash of hounds. The later history is full of the exploits of highwaymen, who found the wild country hereabouts specially favourable for their purposes.

The Inclosure Act of 1812 inclosed much of Bagshot Heath, and also inclosed the common fields of Windlesham.[3] Inclosure had begun before, for in 1768 the lords of the manors and the freeholders gave land inclosed from the waste for charitable purposes.[4]

There are a considerable number of gentlemen's houses about Windlesham. The Camp is the residence of Sir Joseph Hooker, F.R.S., &c., &c. ; Ribsden, of Mrs. Christie ; The Towers, of Lady Elvey. Woodcote House is a boys' school.

There are an Institute and Reading-room built in 1880, and enlarged in 1901 ; the Institute and Reading-room at Bagshot were founded in 1862. The schools (built as National Schools in 1825, now Provided) were taken over by a board in 1871. They were enlarged in 1889.

Bagshot was a tithing of Windlesham. There is a church there dedicated to St. Anne, and also a Wesleyan Methodist chapel.

Bagshot Park, long the property of the Crown, was formerly the residence of the Duke of Gloucester, son-in-law to George III, and now of H.R.H. the Duke of Connaught.

Pinewood is the residence of Lady Elphinstone ; Penny Hill of Mr. L. Floersheim ; Hall Grove of Mr. Stephen Soames.

A school was built at Bagshot in 1870, and taken over by the newly-formed Windlesham School Board in 1871. It was enlarged in 1893.

The manor of *WINDLESHAM MANORS* (Winlesham, xiii cent. ; Winsham, xvii cent.) belonged in the Middle Ages to the small convent of Broomhall in Berkshire. Land in Bagshot was granted to the Prioress of Broomhall by Henry III in 1228.[5] But Windlesham appears among the manors granted to Westminster by Edward the Confessor in his foundation charter. It was apparently transferred to Broomhall at an unknown date.

The priory of Newark had a grant of land in Windlesham in 1256,[6] and had the advowson of the church.[7]

Joan Rawlyns, Prioress of Broomhall, made a voluntary surrender of the property of her house in 1522.[8] In the next year Windlesham was granted to St. John's College, Cambridge,[9] who still hold it.

The manor of *BAGSHOT* in early times was royal demesne, and may have formed part of the forest of Windsor.

There are traces of two distinct holdings in Bagshot. About 1211 one Hoppeschort held 30s. worth of land in Bagshot,[10] which, according to *Testa de*

---

[1] Subs. R. of 14th century.

[2] *V.C.H. Surr.* i, 357–9. Bromhall, on this boundary (now Broomhill), is the proper name of the manor of Windlesham, held by St. John's College, Cambridge.

[3] Tithe Commutation Ret., Bd. of Agric.

[4] Parl. Ret. of Char. 1786.

[5] *Cal. Chart. R.* 1226–57, p. 70.

[6] Harl. Chart. 55, B. 41.

[7] *V.C.H. Surr.* ii, 103.

[8] Chan. Inq. p.m. (Ser. 2), xxxvii, 132.

[9] Pat. 14 Hen. VIII, pt. ii, m. 5.

[10] *Red Bk. of Exch.* (Rolls Ser.), ii, 456.

Nevill,[11] had been granted by Henry II out of his demesne lands to a certain Ralph. This land was bought from Hoppeschort by Robert de Basing.[12] In 1218 Geoffrey Aurifaber sued Robert de Basing for the possession of 3½ hides of land in Bagshot, but judgement was entered for Basing.[13] Some three years later, however, Robert de Bagshot, evidently the same person as Basing, granted the 3½ hides to Geoffrey with the consent of Hoppeschort.[14] But this grant was only of a temporary nature, for at the time of the *Testa de Nevill*[15] Robert son of Robert de Basing was holding, and in 1365 Geoffrey de Bagshot died holding the manor.[16]

The other part of Bagshot was granted to John Belet by Henry III, and descended to his son Michael.[17] Both these holdings seem to have reverted to the Crown early in the 14th century, and from that date Bagshot followed the descent of Sutton in Woking (q.v.).

The return for the aid taken for marrying of Blanche daughter of Henry IV states that 'terras et tenementa que quondam fuerunt Hoppesort.'[18] Unfortunately the name is torn off, but it seems probable that the reference is to Bagshot.

The reputed manor of FOSTERS in Windlesham appears first in 1557, when Alan Fryday and Margaret his wife released one-seventh of it to John Taylor.[19] In 1603 George Evelyn at his death was reported to have been in possession of three-fifths of it.[20] This portion passed under the terms of a settlement made before his death to George second son of his second son John.[21] The whole manor was in the possession of the Evelyns in 1637,[22] but apparently was sold in the year that George died to James Lynch,[22a] who died seised of it in 1648,[23] and in 1650 his nephew James Lynch conveyed it to John Lovibond.[23] Heneage Finch, Lord Guernsey, held a court here in 1714.[25] In 1717 Mr. John Walter bought it,[26a] and his son Abel Walter sold it in 1752 to Sir More Molyneux.[26] He was a trustee of the Onslow property,[26a] and probably purchased in that capacity, for it belonged to Lord Onslow later.[27]

There is mention in 1650 of a ' manor ' in Windlesham which was held by the Dean and Canons of Windsor.[28] They were said to have received it of the gift of Queen Elizabeth, and to have afterwards leased it to Edward Harward. 'Those entrusted with the abolishing of the Deans and Chapters' granted it to Walter Harward, possibly the son of Edward.[29]

St. George's, Windsor. *Argent a cross gules.*

The so-called manor of FREEMANTLES in Windlesham had its origin in land held by Richard Freemantle in the time of Edward II.[30] His grandson Richard, son of John, released to William Skrene and Robert Hewlett all his right in the manor of Windlesham.[31] In 1467 Edmund Skrene, probably son of William, quitclaimed his right to Robert Hewlett,[32] and from that time until the Dissolution the manor apparently formed part of the endowment of Hewlett's gild in this parish.[33]

After the dissolution of gilds and chantries the manor seems to have been granted out in two parts. In 1549 George Molyneux was in possession of one moiety,[34] and in 1561 William Molyneux released it to John Attefield.[35] During the next hundred and fifty years it passed successively through the Whitfield,[36] Quinby, and other families,[37] none of whom, however, retained possession for any length of time. Finally it came into the hands of Francis Bartholomew,[38] who conveyed it to Leonard Child, an attorney in Guildford, in 1719.[39]

The other moiety was granted by Queen Elizabeth to George Evelyn in 1560,[40] and seems to have followed the history of the manor of Fosters (q.v.).[41]

The church of ST. JOHN THE CHURCHES BAPTIST, Windlesham, consists of a modern chancel with a north vestry and south chapel, a nave with north and south aisles, a south porch, and a south-western tower. The south chapel and aisle are the chancel and nave of a small church, the date of which is given on a board in the tower, which bears the inscription : ' Burnt by lightning in 1676. Rebuilt 1680 John Atfield Richard Cotherell.' The tower dates from 1838, and, like the rest of the church, is of brick. The 17th-century walls are faced with a chequer of black and red bricks ; the aisles have projecting stone quoins. In the south wall of the old nave are four windows of Gothic style, two of three lights in 15th-century style with square heads, and two of late 13th-century style with a quatrefoiled circle over the trefoiled lights. They are in part modern, in part old work reset. The porch has small balustered openings on either side.

The roofs, seating, and fittings throughout are modern, and of no particular interest. The sanctuary has been somewhat elaborately decorated in recent years, and has a high dado of marble and mosaic. Preserved in a glass case in the nave is a chained copy of Jewel's *Apology*, found in the floor of the tower at the time of the enlargement of the church. There are no monuments of any interest.

The tower contains a sanctus bell by William Eldridge, 1686, and one large bell by Warner, 1875.

11 Op. cit. 225. Hoppeschort held by the service of providing the king with a leash of hounds. 12 Ibid.
13 *Bracton's Note Bk.* (ed. Maitland), 10; *Rot. Lit. Claus.* (Rec. Com.), i, 378a.
14 Feet of F. Surr. 5 Hen. III, no. 9.
15 Op. cit. 227b.
16 Chan. Inq. p.m. 39 Hen. III, no. 26.
17 *Testa de Nevill* (Rec. Com.), 225.
18 Rentals and Surv. Surr. portf. 15, no. 31.
19 Feet of F. Surr. East. 3 & 4 Phil. and Mary.
20 Chan. Inq. p.m. (Ser. 2), ccxc, 124.
21 Ibid.

22 Feet of F. Surr. Hil. 12 Chas. I.
22a Manning and Bray, op. cit. iii, 82.
23 Chan. Inq. p.m. (Ser. 2), ccccxcii, 41.
24 Feet of F. Div. Co. Hil. 1650.
25 Manning and Bray, op. cit. iii, 82.
26a Ibid. ; See Chobham and Woking for the Walters.
26 Feet of F. Surr. Trin. 25 & 26 Geo. II.
26a Private information.
27 Inclosure Act, 52 Geo. III, cap. 166.
28 Close, 1650, pt. xlvi, no. 16.
29 Ibid.
30 *Parl. Writs*, vol. ii, div. iii, p. 337.
31 Close, 21 Hen. VI, m. 21.

32 Ibid. 6 Edw. IV, m. 17.
33 *Cal. Pat.* 1476–85, p. 204.
34 Feet of F. Surr. East. 1549.
35 Ibid. East. 1561.
36 Ibid. Trin. 38 Eliz.
37 Ibid. East. 34 Eliz.; Trin. 38 Eliz. ; East. 12 Chas. II ; Mich. 11 Jas. II.
38 Ibid. Mich. 4 Geo. I.
39 Ibid. Mich. 5 Geo. I.
40 Pat. 2 Eliz. pt. iv, m. 27.
41 Chan. Inq. p.m. (Ser. 2), ccxc, 124 ; Feet of F. Surr. Mich. 20 Jas. I ; Hil. 21 Jas. I ; Mich. 2 Chas. I ; Hil. 12 Chas. I ; Div. Co. 1650 ; Surr. East. 29 Chas. II.

The church plate is a silver-gilt set given by H.R.H. the Duchess of Gloucester in 1841, and consists of two cups with paten covers of 1841, a paten of 1840, a flagon of the same date, an almsdish undated, but part of the set, and a cup of 1896.

The first book of the registers contains baptisms from 1677 to 1689 ; a second, all entries from 1695 to 1747 ; a third, baptisms and burials from 1749 to 1783, and marriages from 1749 to 1753 ; a fourth, baptisms from 1783 to 1810 ; a fifth, burials from 1793, and baptisms from 1810 to 1812. There are also two printed marriages and banns books from 1754 to 1802, and from 1802 to 1812.

When the old church of Windlesham was struck by lightning and burnt in 1676, the registers were burnt, and now date only from that time.

There is a chapel of ease, St.Alban's, on the Bagshot Road.

ST. ANNE'S, BAGSHOT, is red brick with Bath stone dressings, a tower, and spire. The east window, in memory of H.R.H. the Duke of Albany (ob. 1884), was given by King Edward VII and the other brothers and sisters of the late duke.

ADVOWSONS The earliest mention of the church of Windlesham is in 1230, when it was reported that Hoppeschort, who held land in Bagshot, granted the advowson to Sherborne Priory in the time of Henry II.[43] The priory's right of presentation, however, was successfully disputed by Newark Priory in 1230,[43] and in 1262 the living was, it is said, appropriated to Newark.[44] The advowson was, however, in private hands after that date. In 1443 the church reappears attached to the manor of Freemantles in Windlesham.[45] It was still so attached in 1539.[46] In 1536 John Quinby, who held Freemantles, presented.[47] But on the death of the rector in 1598 the queen presented,[48] and the patronage has since continued in the Crown.

Presentations were always to Windlesham, *cum capella de Bagshot.* The chapel at Bagshot was dedicated to Our Lady. Hewlett's or Hulot's chantry was founded in the chapel of Our Lady at Bagshot, and endowed with half the manor of Freemantles.[49] In 1467 Edmund Skrene released all his rights in the manor of Freemantles to Robert Hewlett.[50] He, or one of his family, founded the chantry. The chapel at Bagshot probably fell with the chantry in it, though a tradition of its site lingered here in the middle of the 18th century.[51] In 1820 a new chapel was built. Bagshot became a separate ecclesiastical parish in 1874. In 1884 a new church, that of St. Anne, was built (see above).

CHARITIES Smith's Charity is distributed as in other Surrey parishes. Half an acre of land was vested in the parish for the use of the poor at an unknown date.

Mr. George Newton, by will 1754, left £5 a year charged on land for the distribution of bread quarterly on Sundays in the churchyard. A tablet in the church commemorates the bequest.

In 1757 Lady Amelia Butler, residing in Bagshot Park, gave £100 for building a pest-house. One room was set apart for wayfaring men suffering from smallpox.

In 1761 James Butler gave a house for an almshouse. These benefactions seem to have been amalgamated into six almshouses.

In 1804 the Rev. Edward Cooper by will gave five guineas annually for educating poor boys.

In 1809 Mrs. Strange gave by will £100 bank annuities for providing clothing for six poor widows.

WISLEY

Wiselei (xi cent.) ; Wyseleye (xiii cent).

Wisley is a small parish 4 miles south-west from Weybridge station. It contains 1,076 acres. In shape it is roughly triangular, the apex southwards, and each side about two miles in length. It is bounded on the north by Walton-on-Thames and Byfleet, on the east by Cobham and Ockham, on the south and west by Ockham and Pyrford. The soil is mainly the alluvium, sand, and gravel of the Wey valley ; the old natural course of the river runs through it, and Wisley Common on the south-east side is on the patch of Bagshot Sand which makes St. George's Hill and Cobham Common. There is no village of Wisley ; merely some scattered farms and cottages. The road from London to Guildford, through Cobham and Ripley, passes through the parish.

Neolithic flints have been found in Wisley. One fine polished celt is in the Archaeological Society's Museum, Guildford. In 1906 an ancient dug-out canoe was found in the old river bed of the Wey. It is still, 1911, in the possession of the farmer on whose land it was found.

The parish is ecclesiastically attached to Pyrford. Slade Farm and a cottage were transferred from Wisley to Ockham 25 March 1883.[1] The children of Wisley Common attend Byfleet School.

Fox Warren is the seat of Mrs. Charles Buxton.

MANOR The manor of *WISLEY* was held at the time of Domesday by Oswold, lord of Wotton ;[2] and the overlordship follows the descent of Wotton (q.v.). Early in the 13th century Roger de Somerey was holding in sub-fee and demised the manor to Robert de Briwes,[3] who in 1243 leased it to Walter le Basle and Denise his wife.[4] Apparently this grant was for Walter's life, since Denise after her husband's death gave up her rights in the manor.[5]

43 *Bracton's Note Bk.* 769.
43 Ibid. 416. There is record of an earlier suit in 1226 ; *Rot. Lit. Claus.* (Rec. Com.), ii, 145*b.*
44 *V.C.H. Surr.* ii, 103.
45 Close, 21 Hen. VI, m. 21d.

46 Feet of F. Surr. Mich. 1 Hen. VIII.
47 Winton Epis. Reg. Gardiner, fol. 26a.
48 Ibid. Bilson, fol. 6b.
49 Particulars for Sale of Chantries, Index, vol. ii, P.R.O.
50 Close, 6 Edw. IV, no. 17.

51 Manning and Bray, *Hist. of Surr.* iii, 85.
1 Loc. Govt. Bd. Order 14282.
2 *V.C.H. Surr.* i, 328a.
3 *Cal. of Inq. p.m. Hen. III,* 20.
4 Feet of F. Surr. Mich. 23 Hen. III.
5 Ibid. East. 42 Hen. III.

Robert de Briwes died in 1275 holding it of Ralph Camoys of Wotton, and left a son and heir John, then forty years of age.[6] In 1282 John effected a settlement of the manor on his daughter Beatrice,[7] who soon after became the wife of Robert son of William Burnel.[8]

The exact date at which Wisley passed from the Briwes family is uncertain.[9] Lands in Somerset held by John de Briwes in 1285 were less than twenty years later in the possession of Robert Fitz Payne,[10] to whom Wisley ultimately passed.[11] In 1328 Robert Burnel, who had acquired the manor in right of his wife Beatrice, brought an action against Robert Fitz Payne, who had apparently ousted him from it.[12] The end of the suit has not been discovered, but since the Fitz Paynes remained in possession, they evidently established their right to the estate.

Robert Fitz Payne married Ela daughter of Sir Guy de Bryan,[13] but had no male heirs, and at Ela's death in 1355 the manor passed to her cousin[14] Robert second son of Lord Grey of Codnor, under the

CAMOYS. *Argent a chief gules with three bezants therein.*

terms of a settlement made in 1324.[15] Robert de Codnor assumed the name of Fitz Payne[16] and died seised of the manor in 1392,[17] when the manor passed to his daughter Isabel, wife of Richard de Poynings. She did not long survive her father, but died seised of the manor in 1393,[18] holding of Thomas de Camoys, lord of Wotton. She left a son and heir Robert then fourteen years old. In 1434 Robert de Poynings settled the manor on his daughter Eleanor on her marriage with Henry Percy, son and heir of the Earl of Northumberland.[19] She died in 1483, and was succeeded in the possession of the manor by her son Henry Earl of Northumberland.[20] The earl was murdered in a riot in 1489, and shortly afterwards a dispute arose among the descendants of Sir Guy de Bryan touching the lands inherited from him.[21] Two of the parties in this suit were the Earls of Northumberland and Ormond, and in the ensuing division of property Wisley was evidently assigned to Ormond, for John Covert died in 1503 seised of the manor by Ormond's grant.[22] At Covert's death the manor passed to his

COVERT. *Gules a fesse ermine between three martlets or.*

WISLEY CHURCH FROM THE SOUTH-EAST

6 Chan. Inq. p.m. 4 Edw. I, no. 46.
7 Feet of F. Surr. East. 11 Edw. I.
8 Esch. Inq. p.m. Roll i, no. 193.
9 Probably about 1324; see note 11.
10 e.g. Manor of Staple Fitz Paine; see Feud. Aids, iv, 272, 313.
11 In 1324 Richard de Fitz Payne and Ela his wife paid half a mark for a writ

of entry to their Surrey lands (Fine R. 17 Edw. II).
12 Parl. R.
13 G.E.C. Complete Peerage.
14 Son of Elizabeth sister of Sir Guy de Bryan (G.E.C. Complete Peerage).
15 Chan. Inq. p.m. 30 Edw. III, no. 14.

16 G.E.C. Complete Peerage.
17 Chan. Inq. p.m. 16 Ric. II, no. 12. pt. i.
18 Ibid. 17 Ric. II, no. 46.
19 Close, 13 Hen VI, m. 4.
20 Chan. Inq. p.m. 1 Ric. III, no. 26.
21 Close, 4 Hen. VII, pt. i, no. 8.
22 Cal. of Inq. Hen. VII, i, 431.

son John, who died in 1503,[33] leaving only daughters. Wisley passed to his cousin Richard Covert, who died in 1547.[34] The manor then became the property of Giles Covert, a distant cousin of Richard, who retained possession until his death in 1556,[35] when he was succeeded by his brother Richard.[36] Richard Covert in 1594 joined with his son Anthony in conveying the manor to Sir John Wolley and Elizabeth his wife, daughter of Sir William More.[37] On the death of Sir John in 1596 his son and heir Francis, then thirteen years old, succeeded him.[38] Francis died without lawful issue in 1609, leaving descendants of his father's three sisters-in-law as his heirs.[39] Wisley passed to Sir Arthur Mainwaring, son of his mother's sister Anne, who was in possession in 1610.[30]

Sir Arthur conveyed the manor in 1641 to Sir Robert Parkhurst,[31] who died in 1651. His son died in 1674, and in 1677 it was sold to Denzil Onslow.[32] It passed under his will, after his widow's death in 1729, to Thomas Lord Onslow, and early in the 19th century it was exchanged for the manor of Papworth in Send with Lord King,[33] whose descendant the Earl of Lovelace is the present owner.

PLAN OF WISLEY CHURCH

A mill and a fishery were attached to the manor at the time of Domesday ; they do not, however, appear again.[34]

In 1252 Robert de Briwes received a grant of free warren in his demesne lands of Wisley, provided that the lands were not in the king's forest.[35] Wisley, partly on the west bank of the Wey (old river), was to that extent in the forest of Windsor.

In 1199 King John granted the Earl of Leicester the right of free chase in Wisley ;[36] and various members of the royal family seem to have enjoyed rights there at different times.[37]

The dedication of the church of WIS-CHURCH LEY has been lost. It is a very small building consisting of a chancel 15 ft. 7 in. by 11 ft. 4 in., and a nave 31 ft. 5 in. by 14 ft. 1 in., both of late 12th-century date, to which has been added a wooden north porch, probably in the 17th century,

and a small modern south vestry. The church was restored in 1872.

The east wall of the chancel has a two-light window, c. 1600, with a transom, set in the splayed jambs of the original round-headed 12th-century opening, the head of which has remains of 'masonry pattern' decoration, every third course being ornamented with four-leaved flowers as a diaper. The north and south walls of the chancel have each two 12th-century round-headed windows, repaired in the heads and sills, with splayed jambs and semicircular rear arches, also having remains of colour. At the south-east of the chancel is a square patch of the diaper pattern left free from whitewash, giving it the effect of a cross. At the south-west there is a blocked square-headed window low down in the wall, which seems to be a 13th-century insertion.

The chancel arch has jambs and semicircular arch of one plain order with a chamfered abacus at the springing, and on the west face of the jambs are incomplete two-centred arched recesses, adjoined by others in the north and south walls of the nave ; they seem to be of 13th-century date, and were designed to give more room for the nave altars. In the north recess is a small star, the remains of painted decoration.

The side walls of the nave have each one window which is similar to the east window of the chancel, and the north doorway has been almost entirely restored in Bath stone, the only old parts being the 12th-century label, and the inner jambs and splayed head. The outer jambs are of two recessed orders with detached shafts having moulded bases and scalloped capitals, and the semicircular arch has zigzag ornament. The north porch is of plain timber construction, the lower portion being filled with modern brickwork.

The round-headed doorway to the vestry in the south wall is quite plain, and seems to be modern. Near its east jamb is a low round-headed recess of uncertain date, and west of the doorway is a consecration cross painted on the wall, which seems to be one of the original set. In the west wall of the nave are two round-headed windows with original inner jambs and rear arches, but modern outside, with small shafts in the jambs. Over the west end of the nave is a small wooden bell-turret containing one bell, and capped by an octagonal shingle spire, with the sides of the turret, is covered with shingles. All the walls are built with a dark brown ironstone conglomerate roughly plastered, and have no dressed stone angles, and the roofs, which retain much of their old timbers, are tiled. The internal fittings are all modern except a late 16th-century wrought-iron hour-glass bracket fixed on the wall near the pulpit.

The plate comprises a cup of 1713, a paten of 1714, and a plated flagon.

There are two books of registers, the first containing entries of baptisms, marriages, and burials from 1666 all mixed together ; after which follow separately

[33] Chan. Inq. p.m. (Ser. 2), xxiii, 263.
[34] Berry, Suss. Gen. 321.
[35] Chan. Inq. p.m. (Ser. 2), cxiv, 42.
[36] Ibid.
[37] Feet of F. Surr. East. 36 Eliz.

[38] Chan. Inq. p.m. (Ser. 2), ccxlix, 74.
[39] Ibid. ccccxxxiv, 60.
[30] Feet of F. Surr. Mich. 8 Jas. I.
[31] Ibid. Trin. 17 Chas. I.
[32] Ibid. 29 Chas. II.

[33] Manning and Bray, Hist. of Surr. iii, 110. [34] V.C.H. Surr. i, 328a.
[34] Cal. Chart. R. 1226–57, p. 391.
[36] Cal. Pat. 1327–30, p. 459.
[37] Cal. of Close, 1346–49, p. 566.

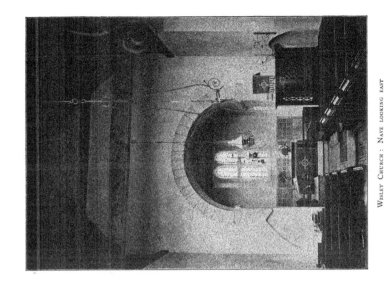

WISLEY CHURCH : NAVE LOOKING EAST

WISLEY CHURCH : THE PORCH

marriages from 1669 to 1752, baptisms from 1670 to 1798, and burials from 1699 to 1798. The second book contains marriages from 1754 to 1812. The baptisms and burials from 1798 to 1812 are missing. There is also a book of churchwardens' accounts from 1669, and in another book are the affidavits for persons buried in woollen from 1680 to 1697.

ADVOWSON   There was a church at Wisley at the time of Domesday.[38] The advowson followed the descent of the manor (though the Black Prince presented in 1345 and in 1370) until the beginning of the 19th century, when the manor was transferred to Lord King. The Onslow family then retained the advowson and still hold it. The living is now held with Pyrford.

Smith's Charity is distributed as in *CHARITIES* other Surrey parishes.

The parish books record the request, 2 May 1837, to the Poor Law Commissioners for leave to sell a double tenement which had belonged to the parish from time immemorial, and a single tenement erected on land inclosed from the waste about thirty years before, for the advantage of the parish. The present advantage resulting is unknown.

WOKING

Wocingas (viii cent.) ; Wochinges (xi cent.) ; Wokynge, Wockynge, Wochynghe, &c. (xiii and xiv cent.).

Woking is a large parish giving its name to the hundred, 6 miles north from Guildford. It contains 8,802 acres, and is in extreme dimensions 6 miles from east to west and 4 miles from north to south. It is bounded on the north by Bisley and Horsell, on the east by Pyrford and Send and Ripley, on the south by Worplesdon, on the west by Pirbright. There is still a little open land about Woking Heath, but it is being covered rapidly with houses. Farther west there is more open land towards Pirbright Common and Brookwood. The soil is mainly Bagshot Sand, with alluvium in the Wey Valley. The river and the artificial navigation run through the parish. The Basingstoke Canal also runs through it. It is traversed by the main line of the South Western Railway, made in 1838, and carried by a branch to Guildford from a station at Woking Junction in 1845. Worplesdon Station on this line to Guildford, and Brookwood Station on the main line, are also in Woking Parish. The road also from Guildford to Chertsey passes through it.

Woking is ruled by an Urban District Council under the Local Government Act of 1894. In 1901 part of Horsell was added to the Woking district.[1] There are eighteen members chosen from five wards.

The parish is agricultural, where not occupied by new houses on the former waste. A certain number of small businesses have grown up in the new town. In Old Woking Village is an extensive printing establishment of Messrs. Unwin, the Gresham Press. Old Woking Mill is a paper mill. Woking Broad Mead is the old common pasture of 150 acres along the river, also called Send Mead. It is on the border of the parishes, and Woking and Send have rights in it. The old practice was, after the hay was cut, to close it till 18 September, then to throw it open to pasture for the occupiers till March, when it was closed again for the grass to grow. The waste in Sutton in Woking was inclosed in 1803.[2] The Inclosure Awards of 29 September 1815, Pyrford and Woodham, and that of Sutton in Woking, 1803, affected waste in the parish of Woking.

The parish was divided into nine tithings : Town Street, the old village ; Heathside, the rising ground north of it towards the railway ; Goldsworth or Goldings, to the west of Woking Junction ; Kingfield, north-west of Woking ; Sackleford, at the west end of Woking Street ; Mayfield, south-west ; Hale End, near Goldings ; Crastock, in the part of the parish near Brookwood ; and Sutton, on the Wey.

The character of the parish has been entirely transformed in about sixty years by the railway. Woking village lies on the river (on the old river, not on the navigation), and is out of the way, on no frequented road. It was a market town, but obscure even when Aubrey wrote, and is probably quite unknown to many people who pass through or stay in the modern Woking near the railway. In addition to the market house of 1665, which still stands in Woking village street, there are other picturesque old houses, notably a considerable brick gabled house of the 17th century, near the west end. On the hill above Hoe Bridge Place stood a brick beacon tower, said to have been built by Sir Edward Zouch to burn a light for directing messengers for James I, when staying with him, across the trackless wastes from Oatlands. It was more probably a beacon tower for the public service. It was ruinous and inaccessible for many years in the 19th century, and was finally taken down in 1858.

Whitmoor House is the property of Mr. Philip Witham, owner of a considerable estate in Woking. Sutton Park Cottage is the seat of Sir Joseph Leese, K.C., M.P. ; Little Frankley, Hook Heath, of the Rt. Hon. Alfred Lyttelton, K.C., M.P. ; Uplands, Maybury, of Sir A. T. Arundel, K.C.S.I. ; Hook Hill, Hook Heath, belongs to His Grace the Duke of Sutherland ; and Fishers Hill is a modern house built by the Right Hon. G.W. Balfour for his own occupation.

St. Edward's Roman Catholic Church in Sutton Park was built by Captain Salvin in 1876. There is an iron Roman Catholic chapel, St. Dunstan's, in Woking Town. There is a Baptist chapel built in 1879. Mount Hermon Congregational Church was built in 1903. There are also two chapels of the Wesleyans at Woking and Knapp Hill, three of the Primitive Methodists at Brookwood, Maybury, and Woking, and a meeting-place of the Plymouth Brethren. The Mosque at Maybury was built in 1889. The extensive buildings here were opened as the Dramatic College for the training of actors in 1865 ; but failing to answer its purpose the place was transformed by the exertions of Dr. G. W. Leitner, in 1886, into the Oriental Institute, for the accommodation of Indian subjects of the Crown visiting England, with two separate departments for high-caste Hindus and for Mohammedans respectively. The Public Hall, Woking, was built by a company in Commercial Road in 1896.

---

[38] *V.C.H. Surr.* i, 328a.   [1] By Local Govt. Bd. Order 41688.   [2] Tithe Commutation Returns, Bd. of Agric.

The Mayford Industrial School, for destitute boys not convicted of crime, was established at Wandsworth in 1867, removed to Byfleet in 1871, and to its present site near the line to Guildford south of Woking Town in 1886. It accommodates over one hundred boys, and has a farm and workshops. A cottage hospital was opened in 1893 in the Bath Road, and was transferred to quarters in the Chobham Road in 1897 as the Victoria Cottage Hospital, in commemoration of the Diamond Jubilee. St. Peter's Memorial Home, for sick poor, in connexion with the Kilburn Sisterhood, was opened in 1885 and enlarged in 1894, with additional rooms for ladies in bad health and narrow circumstances. At Brookwood is the Surrey County Asylum for Pauper Lunatics, opened in 1867 and much enlarged in 1903. It has a water tower 90 ft. high, which forms a conspicuous landmark. The convict prisons, male and female, at Knapp Hill, first opened in 1859, are now transformed into barracks. An Orphanage for the children of servants of the London and South-Western Railway was opened close to Woking Junction in 1909.

Woking Waterworks Company was established in 1882. It draws its chief supply from the chalk near Clandon.

Brookwood Necropolis adjoins the Brookwood Station. In 1854 a company purchased 2,000 acres in Woking and Pirbright, of which 400 acres have been laid out as a cemetery, and well planted with rhododendrons and conifers. In 1889 the Woking Crematorium was built. A public recreation ground was laid out in 1906–7 between Woking Town and Old Woking Village.

The oldest provided school in the village of Woking was opened in 1848 as a Church school. It was enlarged in 1901. St. John's was built as a Church school in 1870 and enlarged in 1876. Maybury was built in 1874, by the first elected School Board, and enlarged in 1881, 1886, and 1893. Knapp Hill was built in 1877, enlarged in 1884. Westfield was built in 1884, and enlarged in 1891 and 1895; the infants' school was built in 1896. Goldsworth Road was built in 1898.

MANORS The manor of *WOKING* seems to have been Crown property from very early times. When the Domesday Survey was taken Woking was in the king's hands, and the Confessor was also reported to have held it. It remained in the hands of the Crown for several centuries. King John shortly after his accession made a grant of the manor of Woking to Alan Basset, who held it for half a knight's fee. His eldest son Gilbert was holding it in 1236–7. He died in 1242. It was held by his brother Fulk, who was Bishop of

London and died in 1259. His younger brother Philip succeeded. On the death of Philip, who left no heirs male, the manor descended to Aliva his daughter, who was married twice. Her first husband was Hugh le Despenser the Justicier, killed at Evesham, to whom she bore the son who was afterwards popularly known as the elder Despenser. She married, secondly, Roger Bigod, Earl of Norfolk, against whom Elaine, wife of Philip Basset, brought a suit for the dower which she ought to have enjoyed in Woking Manor. Aliva's death, which occurred in 1281, was the signal for a dispute over her estates. The earl brought a suit against Hugh le Despenser, Aliva's son and heir, on the grounds that he himself had had issue by his wife, but withdrew his claim.

Hugh le Despenser was executed in 1326 in the troubled time when Edward II was deposed, and Woking reverted to the Crown. Edward III in the first year of his reign granted the manor of Woking, then said to have been forfeited by Hugh le Despenser, to his uncle, Edmund of Woodstock, Earl of Kent. Under Mortimer's régime, however, Edmund was soon afterwards attainted and executed. His son Edmund was restored in 1330, but died in 1333 while yet a minor, and was succeeded by his brother John. After John's death without issue in 1352 the manor became the right of his sister Joan, then married to Sir Thomas Holand, who was summoned to Parliament as Earl of Kent in her right. But his widow Elizabeth kept part of it as dower till her death in 1410–11. The son of Joan and Thomas was Thomas, second Earl of Kent in the Holand line.

Joan died in 1386, and although the king is named as her heir in the inquisition taken after her death, many of her lands apparently passed to her other son; Thomas de Holand was certainly holding Woking at the time of his death some ten years later. In the next year the Despensers released to Thomas his son and heir all rights which they possessed in Woking Manor.

After the accession of Henry IV Thomas, whom Richard had created Duke of Surrey and whom Henry had deprived of the dignity, joined in the conspiracy of 1400 against the king and was beheaded as a traitor, and Woking was forfeited among his other lands. Henry IV, however, restored it to Alice widow of Earl Thomas, and she continued to hold until her death in 1416. She left her husband four sisters as co-heirs, and it seems as though some deed of partition must have been made, since Woking Manor remained intact in the possession of the Beaufort Dukes of Somerset, who descended from Margaret, one of the co-heirs aforesaid.

3 *V.C.H. Surr.* i, 296a.
4 *Rot. Chart.* (Rec. Com.), 37 ; *Testa de Nevill* (Rec. Com.), 225.
5 *Pipe R.* 21 Hen. III.
6 *Testa de Nevill* (Rec. Com.), ii, 55.
7 Chan. Inq. p.m. 9 Edw. I, no. 9 ; *Plac. de Quo Warr.* (Rec. Com.), 740.
8 *Abbrev. Plac.* (Rec. Com.), 200.
9 Ibid. 10 Ibid.
11 Feet of F. Div. Co. 56 Hen. III, no. 69.
12 *Abbrev. Plac.* (Rec. Com.), 200.
13 Ibid.
14 Chart. R. 1 Edw. III, m. 43, no. 82.
15 *Dict. Nat. Biog.* xvi, 413.
16 Close, 6 Edw. III, m. 31.
17 Chan. Inq. p.m. 26 Edw. III (1st nos.), no. 54.
18 Ibid.
19 *Dict. Nat. Biog.* xxvii, 156.
20 Inq. p.m. 12 Hen. IV, no. 35.
21 Ibid.
22 Chan. Inq. p.m. 9 Ric. II, no. 54.
23 Ibid. 20 Ric. II, no. 30.
24 Close, 21 Ric. II, pt. ii, m. 18 d.
25 Exch. Inq. file 160, no. 16.
26 *Cal. Pat.* 1399–1401, p. 392.
27 Chan. Inq. p.m. 4 Hen. V, 51.
28 *Vide infra.*
29 G.E.C. *Complete Peerage.* See pedigree below.

Margaret Holand = John (1st Earl of Somerset)

Henry (Earl of Somerset)   John (1st Duke of Somerset)   Edmund (2nd Duke)

Margaret = Edmund Tudor (Earl of Richmond)   Henry, ob. 1464   Edmund, ob. 1471   John, ob. 1471

WOKING : SUTTON PLACE, THE SOUTH OR GARDEN FRONT

WOKING : SUTTON PLACE, QUADRANGLE LOOKING SOUTH

Edmund, Duke of Somerset, son of Margaret, was slain at the first battle of St. Albans,[30] and it was recorded at the time of his death that he held Woking Manor of the king by the service of paying him one clove gillyflower a year. He was succeeded by his son Henry,[31] who also embraced the Lancastrian cause, and was attainted in 1461, restored in 1463, but beheaded after the battle of Hexham in 1464, and attainted after his death by an Act annulling his former restoration.

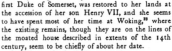

BEAUFORT. France quartered with England in a border gobony argent and azure.

Woking passed to the Crown. The rightful heir, Margaret Beaufort, daughter of John first Duke of Somerset, was restored to her lands at the accession of her son Henry VII, and she seems to have spent most of her time at Woking,[32] where the existing remains, though they are on the lines of the moated house described in extents of the 14th century, seem to be chiefly of about her date.

At Margaret's death in 1509 the manor once more became Crown property.[33] Henry VIII appears to have made it a favourite residence, to judge from the number of his letters which are dated thence,[34] and it was when Wolsey was on a visit to his royal master at Woking that he received the news of his nomination to the Sacred College.[35]

The Tudors continued to hold Woking in demesne, for it was Elizabeth's own house in 1583.[36] James I, however, made a grant of it in 1620 to Sir Edward Zouch, who died in 1634.[37] From him the manor passed to his son James, who married Beatrice daughter of Lord Mountnorris.[38] He died in 1643, leaving two sons, of whom Edward, the elder, died in 1658,[39] and James, the second son, succeeded to the inheritance at his brother's death.[40] This James became a person of mark in the county of Surrey; he filled the office of High Sheriff, and Symmes, the local historian of the time, speaks of him with considerable respect.[41] He died in 1708. In 1671 James had granted the reversion of his property to the king, and Charles II leased it for 1,000 years to Lord Grandison, among others, to hold in trust for his cousin, the notorious Duchess of Cleveland, and her children.[42] She held a court in 1709, but died the same year. The trustees held courts down to the year 1715, when they conveyed Woking to John Walter, who held his first court in May 1716. He was followed by his son Abel Walter, who in 1748 obtained an Act of Parliament[43] granting him the fee simple in place of the 1,000 years' lease which his father purchased. He sold to Lord Onslow in 1752.[44] It has remained in the Onslow family down to the present day.

Domesday Book mentions the existence of a mill at

Woking. At the end of the 14th century the manor possessed a water-mill and a fulling-mill[45]; it seems possible, however, that one of these was really in Sutton, and should be identified with the mill which was there at the time of the Survey. Henry VIII leased Woking mills to Thomas Spencer,[46] and the water-mill was again granted out by Elizabeth[47] and James I.[48] The fact that the two mills were separated after the grant of Sutton Manor to Sir Richard Weston again seems to suggest that one of these mills was in Sutton. This one would then be the mill near Trigg's Lock, the other the mill on the old river just south of Woking village.

Henry VI in 1451 granted to Edmund Duke of Somerset and his heirs the privilege of having a fair every Whit Tuesday.[49]

James Zouch in 1662 received the grant of a fair on 12 September and a weekly market on Friday,[50] and in 1665 he built the market-house which still stands in Woking village street.

The old royal residence at Woking Park lay down the river a mile from old Woking village. An early 14th-century survey was seen by Symmes[51] in very bad condition, and copied. It has now perished. It appears from it that there were extensive buildings, with two chapels, within a double moat. The double moat is shown in the survey of Woking Park by Norden of 1607,[52] and the remains of it are still visible at Woking Park Farm. There were a corn-mill and a fulling-mill on the manor, and a deer park. The park extended from the manor-house along the river to Woking village and up over the high ground nearly to the present railway line. In addition to the royal visits mentioned above,[53] Edward VI was there in 1550,[54] and Elizabeth in 1569[55] and 1583.[56] In what is now a farm building is a marble gateway of the earlier 15th century, much dilapidated, leading into a building with a barrel vault of small bricks of a rather later date, and communicating with what is now a barn of old chalk, brick, and timber work. But the whole is in very bad repair. Sir Edward Zouch, probably finding the manor-house in a ruinous state, built a new house with two courtyards nearly a mile away on higher ground at Hoe Bridge Place. James Zouch his grandson built a third house contiguous to this, on a smaller scale, the date of which is fairly determined by mythological paintings on the staircase attributed to Antonio Verrio, who decorated Hampton Court for James II and William III, and by a painting on the ceiling of a drawing-room, attributed to Sir Godfrey Kneller, and certainly celebrating the peace of Ryswick under allegorical forms. Some part of the second house perhaps remains in the stable buildings and its foundations. James Zouch died in 1708, and Hoe Bridge Place passed to his niece Sophia, who in 1718 conveyed it to James Field, who sold it in 1730 to John Walter; he cleared away the remains of the second house and altered the existing building. It is now the residence of Mr. F. H. Booth, who has

[30] G.E.C. Complete Peerage.
[31] Chan. Inq. p.m. 33 Hen. VI, no. 38.
[32] Dict. Nat. Biog. iv, 48.
[33] Chan. Inq. p.m. (Ser. 2), xxv, 46.
[34] e.g. L. and P. Hen. VIII, iii (1), 357.
[35] Add. MSS. 6167, fol. 457.
[36] Loseley MSS. viii, 59.
[37] Pat. 18 Jas. I, pt. ii.
[38] Chan. Inq. p.m. (Ser. 2), dxxxviii, 136.
[39] Registers, Woking.
[40] Add. MSS. 6167, fol. 457.
[41] Ibid.
[42] Pat. 23 Chas. II, pt. ix.
[43] 21 Geo. II, cap. 9.
[44] Ct. R. and deeds in possession of Lord Onslow.
[45] Esch. Inq. p.m. file 160, no. 16.
[46] L. and P. Hen. VIII, iv (2), g. 2927 (12).
[47] Pat. 35 Eliz. pt. ix.
[48] Ibid. 7 Jas. I, pt. xxxiii.
[49] Chart. R. 27–39 Hen. VI, no. 30.
[50] Pat. 13 Chas. II, pt. xvi, no. 5.
[51] Add. MSS. 6167.
[52] Harl. MS. 3749.
[53] See descent of the manor.
[54] Cott. MS. Nero, C. 10.
[55] Rawlinson MS. A. 195, C. 4, fol. 287.
[56] Loseley MSS. (4 Aug. 1583), viii, 52.

made further alterations. The park was destroyed at the time of the Civil Wars, when the Zouch family was royalist.[57]

The manor of *SUTTON* was held at the time of Domesday by Robert Malet; Wenesi had held it of King Edward.[58] Robert's lands were confiscated for his adherence to the side of Duke Robert in 1102. Sutton, which was held as of the honour of Eye, was granted to Stephen, afterwards king. It passed to his only surviving son William, who married the heiress of de Warenne. On his death, 1159, it reverted to the Crown,[59] and although it was still of the honour of Eye was granted separately by Henry II to a certain Master Urric.[60] His son died without heirs, and King John granted Sutton to Gilbert Basset, son of the holder of Woking.[61] It descended to his brother Fulk, Bishop of London, and to his younger brother Philip,[62] and to Aliva, Philip's daughter, who married first Hugh le Despenser, and secondly Roger Bigod, Earl of Norfolk, who claimed it after her death in 1281,[63] but whose claim was disallowed in favour of Hugh, Aliva's son by her first husband. It was forfeited with Woking, and with it was granted by Edward III to the Earl of Kent. They continued to be held together for nearly 200 years. In 1521 however Henry VIII granted Sutton to Sir Richard Weston,[64] at whose house he was afterwards forced to take refuge when an outbreak of the sweating sickness drove him from Guildford.[65] The manor remained in the Weston family until the end of the 18th century, when Melior Mary Weston, the last of her line, bequeathed it to John Webbe on condition that he assumed the name and arms of Weston.[66] The male line of Webbe-Weston became extinct in 1857. The manor passed to F. H. Salvin of Croxdale, Durham, a grandson of the first John Webbe-Weston. He died in 1904, and was succeeded by his niece's son, Mr. Philip Witham.

WESTON of Sutton. *Ermine a chief azure with five besants therein.*

Owing no doubt to the manors of Woking and Sutton having being held together before the reign of Henry VIII, the old manor-house of Sutton had been allowed to fall into decay. In 1329, after the death of Edmund, Earl of Kent, the house was ruinous and worth nothing. It stood near St. Edward's Chapel, a quarter of a mile from Sutton Place. The field is called Manor Field, and traces of foundations, old encaustic tiles, and an old well exist.

Sutton Place was built by Sir Richard Weston, most probably about 1523–5, at one of the most interesting periods of English architectural history, and is from every point of view a notable house. Alike in detail and in plan it shows the meeting of the old and new schools; the ornament is Italian, but the construction is Gothic. There is a hall which had screens, kitchen, and offices after the mediaeval type, but its plan is affected by the desire for exact symmetry and balance which its external elevation to the courtyard shows, and in place of stone all windows, parapets, etc., are of terra cotta.

The plan was quadrangular, four ranges of buildings, with the gatehouse and entrance on the north, inclosing a court 81 ft. square. The hall and kitchen were in the south wing, the great chamber and principal rooms in the east wing, and on the north and west were sets of living rooms called lodgings. A fire damaged the north and east wings in 1560, and they were never thoroughly repaired, and the north wing with its gatehouse, after standing in a ruinous state for many years, was pulled down in 1782, throwing the courtyard open to the north, as it remains to-day.

Though the general arrangement of the original house is certain, many points in it are far from being so, and some of these are of particular importance in the history of house-planning. An inventory of 1542, taken at the death of the builder, Sir Richard Weston, is unfortunately not so explicit as could be wished, making no mention of a great hall or dining chamber of any sort, and, as in the contemporary inventory of the Vyne in Hampshire, the word 'chamber' seems to be used for ground- and first-floor rooms alike. The great hall as it appears to-day is a fine room two stories in height (31 ft.), 51 ft. long by 25 ft. wide, lighted on the north by three-light windows and a four-light bay window in each story, and on the south by two three-light windows and a four-light bay also in each story. The exact repetition of these windows may perhaps be set down to the exigencies of symmetry, for, especially in the bays, the internal effect is far from satisfactory, but the fact that all the details of panelling, etc., are of the early part of the 17th-century raises a question as to whether there was not a first floor over the hall in its original state. The fact that the hall chimney-stack on the south side has not one but three chimneys points in the same direction. The hall fireplace accounts for one of these, and though it is true that there is a cellar under the hall, it is most unlikely that it should have had two fireplaces, and the former existence of a first-floor fireplace seems therefore very probable.

The upper floor of the east wing is now arranged as a 'long gallery,' 152 ft. by 21 ft., but although Wolsey had built galleries at Hampton Court before this time, it seems clear that such a room formed no part of the 16th-century house here. Its present form dates only from 1878, and part of it was used as a chapel during the 19th-century.

In spite of the evidences of Italian influence, the general aspect of the house is Gothic, showing everywhere the simple directness and absence of ostentation which mark the mediaeval English country house. The gatehouse was a stately building, as existing drawings show, being nearly twice as high as the rest of the house, but its treatment was absolutely straightforward, and no attempt was made to impress anyone approaching the house with a sense of magnificence, all the elaborate ornament being characteristically reserved for the inner walls of the courtyard. Even here there is a certain artlessness in the way it is used

[57] Aubrey, op. cit.
[58] V.C.H. Surr. i, 325a.
[59] Testa de Nevill (Rec. Com.), 296.
[60] Ibid. 225.
[61] Ibid. 227; Close, 6 Hen. III, m. 3.

[62] See Woking, above.
[63] L. and P. Hen. VIII, iii (1), g. 1324 (17).
[64] Ibid. vi, 948.
[65] Manning and Bray, Hist. of Surr. i,

[66] Ibid.

131. Mr. Wehbe was descended in the female line from the Westons of Prested Hall, Essex, who were related to the Westons of Sutton (Frederic Harrison, Annals of an Old Manor House, 143).

WOKING : SUTTON PLACE, DETAILS OF A BAY WINDOW

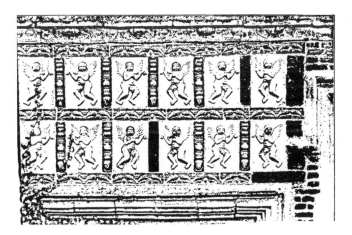

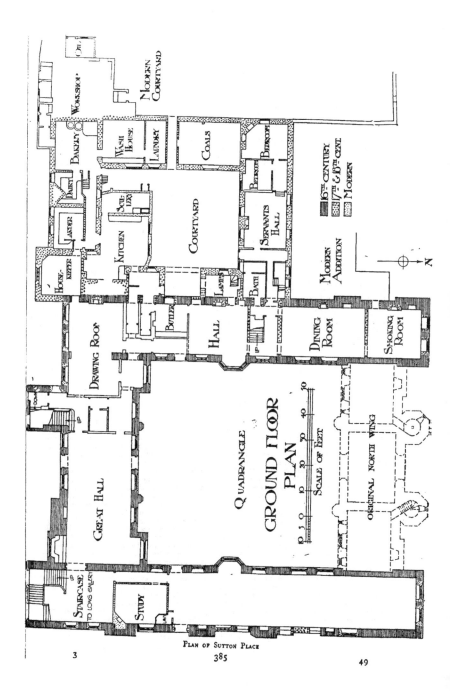

STAIRCASE
TO LONG GALLERY

GREAT HALL

STUDY

DRAWING ROOM

HOUSE-KEEPER

LARDER

BUTLER

KITCHEN

SCULL-ERY

DAIRY

BAKERY

WORKSHOP

OIL.

HALL

LARDER

COURTYARD

WASH HOUSE

LAUNDRY

COALS

MODERN COURTYARD

BATH

SERVANTS HALL

BEDROOM

BEDROOM

DINING ROOM

SMOKING ROOM

MODERN ADDITION

16TH CENTURY
17TH & 18TH CENT
MODERN

N

QUADRANGLE

GROUND FLOOR PLAN

SCALE OF FEET

0 5 10   20   30   40   50

ORIGINAL NORTH WING

which is entirely native to the soil. The hall doorway, flanked by three-light windows and distinguished by a double row of terra-cotta amorini above its head, is framed by a pair of half-octagonal terra-cotta buttresses running up beyond the general lines of the elevations, and capped by domed pinnacles, having between them a high embattled parapet, forming as it were the centrepiece to the whole design. Yet the very centre of the composition, the façade of the first floor over the hall doorway, where a Palladian architect would have put forth his full strength, is a blank expanse of brickwork.

The original windows are all of three lights, except in the projecting bays, and are worked in terra-cotta. All have transoms with trefoiled heads beneath them, but the upper lights on the first floor are trefoiled, while those on the ground floor are cinquefoiled. Heads, sills, and mullions are enriched with a line of Italian ornament in low relief, adding a peculiar distinction to the work. The line of the first floor is marked by a string-course of Gothic section decorated with tuns (a Weston rebus) set in Italian floral scrollwork, and there is a similar string-course at the base of the parapet, but without ornament, except on the façade of the hall. On the east and west sides of the courtyard this string runs just over the first-floor window-heads and below it and between the windows is a line of lozenge-shaped panels with leaf ornament. On the hall façade, as formerly on the south front of the gatehouse range, the string is at a higher level, and the line of lozenge-shaped panels runs unbroken over the windows. The parapet itself is solid, ornamented with similar lozenge panels or with quatrefoiled panels; its outline was originally broken by pinnacles, of which only the stumps now remain, while the higher parapet above the hall door has a further band of trefoiled panels containing amorini, and lozenge panels on the battlements. The masonry of the half-octagonal buttresses which flank it is moulded with cusped panels containing the initials of the builder, R.W., or bunches of grapes, and the same detail occurs on the bays at either end of the façade of the hall, and on the north ends of the east and west wings; otherwise the external elevations of the house have no ornament, except the south elevation, where the existing parapet of the hall block is, however, of mid-17th-century date. The modelling of the floral ornament leaves little to be desired; but that on the quoins is markedly inferior, and the amorini are very stiff and clumsy and evidently some way from their Italian originals. That a good deal of this renaissance work was carried out by English workmen is known, as at Hampton Court, where, however, Richard Ridge and his fellow workmen wrought the pendants of the great hall roof of Henry VIII in masterly style; but here at Sutton it must be confessed that the lesson has not been so thoroughly learned.

The terra-cotta work has, with little exception, stood nearly four centuries of English weather in a wonderful way. A good deal of the window tracery, especially on the external elevations, was at one time or another taken out and replaced by sash-windows, but these in their turn have nearly all given way to modern copies of the original work.

It seems probable that the principal alterations to the house, other than those of quite recent date, took place in the 17th century, after the sale of Clandon in 1641, and of Gatton in 1654, when John Weston had command of money. The parapet on the south side of the hall, with its large mill-rind crosses, is clearly of this time, the crosses being the arms of Copley, whose heiress married John Weston in 1637. A great deal of panelling in the house is also of this time, and the impaled arms of Weston and Copley are painted over the fireplace in the small hall in the west wing. The second or kitchen court was doubtless added at this time; being set against the west side of the house, it is quite unpretentious, and makes no attempt to harmonize with the 16th-century work.

The partition walls dividing the original house were as usual of timber, the only internal masonry walls being those which separated the north and south wings from the east and west. Apart, therefore, from the fire of 1560, the chances of alteration of the original arrangements must have been many, particularly as regards the staircases, none which now exist being older than the 17th century. The disposition of the house at present is that the principal entrance is from the court at the south end of the west wing, the doorway opening to a narrow lobby which leads directly to the small hall on the north, and going northward from the hall are successively a staircase, the dining-room, and the smoking-room. The dining-room is furnished with very good oak panelling, a recent importation, but the stair, which is good 18th-century work, has its south wall covered with early 17th-century panelling which seems to be *in situ*. The drawing-room is on the ground floor at the south-west angle of the old building, a fine modern room, and between it and the great hall is a lobby opening to a staircase in a projecting bay, the woodwork showing its date to be c. 1700. This with the other staircases is doubtless part of the work of John Weston, 1701–30.

The great hall is approximately two squares on plan, and its arrangement, as already noted, is abnormal, as its entrance doorways on the north and south are two bays east of the line of the screens, and could never have opened into anything of the nature of a passage. The present panelling is in part of Jacobean date, and the rest of later 17th-century work with 18th-century alterations. From the inventory of 1542 it is clear that the hall was hung with tapestry, and there was probably no panelling in the first instance. But the principal attraction of the hall is its glass; a great deal of this was evidently put in after the marriage of Richard Weston and Mary Copley in 1637, but some pieces are of earlier date, and may be in their original position, in which case they must have been made about 1530. Some also, which may have come from the royal manor-house at Woking, are apparently older than this, and there are Onslow arms and others which are doubtless added from various sources.

The set of Tudor arms and badges is extremely good, and the arms of Richard III as Duke of Gloucester also occur. The glass was repaired in 1724 by John Weston, and again in 1844.[66a] The fireplace is part of the original work, and has in its spandrels the Weston rebus and the pomegranate.

The east wing, as already noted, was practically abandoned for a long time, and only partly refitted early in the 18th century by John Weston, to whom

---

[66a] For a complete and thorough description of it see Mr. Frederic Harrison's *Annals of an Old Manor House.*

Woking : Sutton Place, Interior of Great Hall

WOKING : SUTTON PLACE, THE LONG GALLERY

WOKING : SUTTON PLACE, STAIRHEAD LEADING TO LONG GALLERY

the fine staircase at its south end is due. The stair-head and the long gallery take up the whole of the upper floor, and the tapestries and panelling are of great interest; about half of the lower floor is now made into a library. The house is full of fine furniture, pictures, etc., which cannot here be adequately described. The quadrangle of offices on the west side of the house is said to be the work of John Weston, 1652–90, and though quite unpretending, is very picturesque. The principal gardens lie to the west of it, and part of their inclosing walls is of 16th-century date and of the same character as the house, but the lay-out of the Tudor garden is unfortunately not now recoverable. The house is now the residence of Lord Northcliffe, to whom the recent restoration is due.

There was a mill at Sutton in the time of Domesday, which does not however appear to be mentioned afterwards. It may perhaps be included with the Woking mills (q.v.).

The manor of *CRANSTOCK, CRASTOCK* or *BRIDLEY* was apparently the land recorded in the extent of Woking Manor[67] as bought by Fulk Basset of the fee of Pirbright, which was part of the honour of Clare; for Cranstock owed suit and service to the Lord of Pirbright.[68] Both Pirbright and Woking were granted to Edmund, Earl of Kent,[69] and Pirbright descended to Joan his daughter, who married Edward, Prince of Wales, of whom Cranstock was held in 1366. There was apparently always a sub-tenancy, for in 1219 Gilbert de Chayham and Alice his wife granted half a hide in Cranstock to William de Cranstock,[70] and some years later Ralph son of William de Tinchingfeld leased the manor of Cranstock to Roger son of William de Cranstock for life.[71] Apparently the manor did not remain long with either of these families, for in 1321 a certain Lambert de Thrikyngham sold it to John de Latimer and Joan his wife, with remainder to their son Edmund.[72] The manor remained as a possession of the Latimers for some little time; and in 1366 Robert Latimer died seised of it, leaving Robert his son and heir, then only a child.[73]

Little can be traced of the history of Cranstock for some time after the death of Robert Latimer. In 1469 it appears in the hands of John White, who died in that year, leaving his son Robert as his heir.[74] In 1531 Henry White conveyed to Walter Champyon, William Roche, Thomas Pierpoint and Anthony Eliot, possibly as trustees,[75] and until the beginning of the next century the manor seems to have remained with them and their successors. In 1611 William Engler and William Skynner released to James Hobson,[76] and Christopher Hobson, presumably the heir of James, sold in 1641 to Francis Williamson.[77] He in 1652 joined with his wife Martha in conveying the manor to Paul Carell[78] (or Caryll), who held his

first court in August 1652, and Paul Carell is said to have bequeathed the manor to his cousin John of Great Tangley Manor, Wonersh.[79] John was also seised of Bramley Manor and other Surrey lands, most of which were divided at his death among his three daughters and co-heirs, Lettice wife of John Ramsden, Elizabeth wife of Peter Farmer, and Margaret wife of Henry Ludlow. Cranstock was among the lands divided.[80]

Between 1678 and 1680 John Child of Guildford purchased three parts of the manor, which passed to his son Leonard, who died in 1730. Leonard left it to his nephew Charles, who held a court in 1742. He sold it to John Tickner about 1758, and from him it was purchased by Richard (? Philip) Hollingworth, who sold it to Sir Fletcher Norton, first Lord Grantley.[81] Lord Grantley's Surrey estates were sold about 1884. Major Ewings' trustees sold Bridley or Crastock to Mr. Garton in 1894, who conveyed it in 1900 to Mr. Richards. Most of the land has been bought by Mr. Anderson, who resides at Bridley Manor.[82]

In the 13th century Geoffrey de Pourton held *MAYFORD* in chief of the king,[83] by grand serjeanty. In 1231 and 1238 the sheriff accounted for 10s. 3d. from the land of the late Henry Kinton in Mayford.[84] Henry Kinton and Walter de Langeford were Geoffrey's heirs.[85] Walter de Langeford sold his moiety to John de Gatesden.[86] The serjeanty was acquired by Fulk Basset,[87] and in the survey of Woking in 1280–1,[88] Mayford is called part of Woking Manor. It remained hereafter attached to Woking.

The tithing of Mayford appears in 1666.[89] Tenements in Mayford occur frequently in Feet of Fines.

The reputed manor of *RUDEHALL* or *HOLLANDS*, really a part of Woking, possibly originated in land held by William de la Rude in Woking in the 13th century.[90] It is at Hale End, which is perhaps a corruption of Holland or Hollands. In the reign of Henry VIII the Heyward family released their rights in the manor of Rudehall to John Grover.[91] In 1601 William Grover conveyed it to William Collyer,[92] and in 1622 it passed to Sir Edward Zouch.[93] It afterwards came into the hands of the Covert family, who were holding it in 1690,[94] when they sold it to Robert Royden.[95] Royden in 1724 alienated it to John Coussmaker.[96] In 1745 Nathanael Newnham conveyed it to William Collyer,[97] who in 1748 sold to Philip Hollingworth[98] (see Cranstock, above). It probably subsequently descended in the same way as Cranstock.

The parish church of *ST. PETER* CHURCHES has a chancel 28 ft. by 20 ft. 1 in., modern north vestry, nave 49 ft. 8 in.

[67] Inq. p.m. 9 Edw. I, no. 9.
[68] Chan. Inq. p.m. 40 Edw. III (1st nos.), no. 38.
[69] See Woking, above.
[70] Feet of F. Surr. Hil. 3 Hen. III, 11.
[71] Ibid. East. 29 Edw. I, 7.
[72] Ibid. East. 14 Edw. II, 30.
[73] Chan. Inq. p.m. 40 Edw. III (1st nos.), no. 25.
[74] Ibid. 9 & 10 Edw. IV, no. 25. It was then still held of the manor of Pirbright.
[75] Feet of F. Surr. Mich. 23 Hen. VIII.
[76] Ibid. Div. Co. Mich. 9 Jas. I.

[77] Ibid. Surr. Mich. 17 Chas. I.
[78] Feet of F. Surr. Trin. 1652.
[79] Manning and Bray, Hist. of Surr. i, 127, who quote court rolls as their authority.
[80] Exch. Spec. Com. 30 Chas. II, 6484. See Recov. R. Hil. 1654, m. 57.
[81] Manning and Bray, op. cit. i, 128; probably a mistake for Philip Hollingworth, banker of Lombard Street.
[82] Private information.
[83] Testa de Nevill (Rec. Com.), 225.
[84] Pipe R. 21 Hen. III.
[85] Fine R. 12 Hen. III, m. 4.

[86] Testa de Nevill (Rec. Com.), 227 and 229, where it is called Maioford.
[87] Inq. p.m. 9 Edw. I, no. 9.
[88] See Woking.
[89] Exch. Dep. 18 Chas. II, Mich. 18.
[90] Cat. Anct. Deeds, A. 9738.
[91] Feet of F. Surr. Hil. 12 Hen. VIII; 15 Hen. VIII.
[92] Ibid. Surr. Mich. 43 & 44 Eliz.
[93] Ibid. Surr. Hil. 19 Jas. I.
[94] Ibid. Surr. Hil. 2 Will. and Mary. [95] Ibid.
[96] Feet of F. Surr. East. 10 Geo. I.
[97] Ibid. Mich. 19 Geo. II.
[98] Ibid. Mich. 22 Geo. II.

by 29 ft. 11 in., south aisle 12 ft. 8 in. wide, south porch, and west tower 12 ft. 9 in. square—all inside measurements.

The earliest part of the building dates from the beginning of the 12th century, at which time it consisted of an aisleless nave, the present one, and a chancel; the latter was probably smaller than the present chancel, which is a rebuilding of about a hundred and twenty years later. The lower part of the existing tower was also added in the 13th century, about 1240, and may have had a timber upper stage until the present stone addition over it was built about 1340.

.The east window of the chancel is an insertion of the second quarter of the 14th century, and is a fine example of the style; it is set rather to the south of the axial line of the chancel, and this may have been a piece of subtlety on the part of the builders to make it appear central with the nave, as it will be noticed that the centre line of the nave passes through that of the window, which it would not have done had it

The 14th-century east window is one of three trefoiled lights under a two-centred arch filled with flowing tracery, now modern; it has two chamfered orders outside and a scroll-mould label; the inside jambs are old and the pointed rear arch is chamfered. In the north wall is a plain square locker, partly restored; the 13th-century lancet in this wall has its glass two inches from the outside, but a groove in the jambs shows that it had formerly been set farther in. On the south side are two original lancet windows like that opposite. Below the first is a modern arched recess with an old sill having a piscina drain in the west half, and a plain surface on the east, while between the windows is a blocked doorway not visible outside owing to the modern coating of cement; it has a segmental arched head inside of square section like the jambs, and is probably contemporary with the windows. At the west end of this wall is a low window of a single trefoiled light with much deeper chamfered jambs outside; it has been a good deal

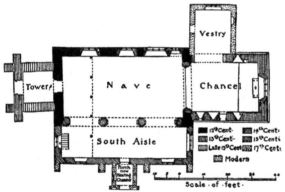

PLAN OF WOKING CHURCH

been in the middle of the wall. The large window in the north wall of the nave is of the same period, but has modern tracery. At the beginning of the 15th century the south aisle was added, with the present arcade, and at the same time the chancel arch was widened to its utmost limits. Soon after this the rood loft was set up and a passage way pierced through the wall above the east respond, the bases of the chancel arch being cut to accommodate the screen. Two other windows were inserted in the north wall in the same century, the easternmost evidently to light the north nave altar.

The west gallery was put up in 1622, and the south porch was probably added at the same time; when the modern vestry was built the 13th-century lancet, displaced by the organ arch, was reset in its east wall. A certain amount of necessary restoration to several of the windows has been carried out and other work done to put the building in good repair. The only entrance to the church (a fairly large one) besides the small door in the vestry is that in the west wall of the nave, approached through the tower.

knocked about, but is probably a 14th-century insertion.

The vestry has a three-light window in its north wall, the reset 13th-century lancet already mentioned in its east, and a doorway to the west. In the vestry are preserved two bases of small shafts contemporary with the early nave, and one 13th-century base.

The chancel arch has semi-octagonal jambs with moulded bases and capitals of a heavy section, the latter with ogee abaci; the wall above is evidently of the date of the arch and not older work pierced, and the arch is of three chamfered orders, the inner order considerably wider than the others.

The first of the four north windows of the nave is a 15th-century insertion of two trefoiled lights under a square head with sunk spandrels; the window is set low in the wall and the wall below the sill thinned to form a recess for the nave altar. The second window is a large 14th-century insertion of three lights; the outer order of the double chamfered jambs is old, but the tracery is modern; the inner

388

WOKING CHURCH FROM THE SOUTH-EAST

quoins of the jambs and the pointed chamfered rear arch are also old. The third window is another 15th-century insertion of two cinquefoiled lights with a quatrefoil over in a four-centred arch, and the last or north-west window is of the 13th century, with two plain pointed lights and a pierced spandrel over in a two-centred arch; like the third window the jambs are of a single chamfered order outside.

The south arcade is of three bays with octagonal pillars, fine massive work in chalk, with simple details and semi-octagonal responds, the bases, capitals, and arches being of similar detail to those of the chancel arch. The bases have been mutilated in the responds; on the south side of the east respond the base mould is splayed back to the wall instead of ending square, but there seems no obvious reason for the treatment. The haunch above this respond is pierced by a square passage-way through the wall to the former rood loft. The west doorway of the nave is part of the original work; its jambs have been cut to enable the door to open outwards, and were originally of two orders; in the angles of the remaining order are round shafts with chamfered bases and cushion capitals, the chamfered abaci of which have been much mutilated for the fitting of the door; the arch is round and of one order with a large edge roll and no label.

The wood door itself is evidently very old, and probably with its iron work contemporary with the doorway. It is made of oak planks, half an inch thick, bound together by iron straps of ornamental design on both faces, the hinge straps being the least important part of the work. There are five large horizontal bands, three of which are attached to large C-straps like those shown in early MSS.; all the bands and straps have forked and curled ends, and small curled sprigs of iron spring from them at irregular intervals. In the upper part of the door are a cross, a saltire, and a spider's web with an insect in it. The rounded head of the door is fixed, but probably opened with the rest orginally, when it was hung in the east side of the doorway.

The east window of the south aisle is one of three lights under a traceried pointed head; all modern outside except the outer order of the head and the upper half of the jambs; the inner jambs, quoins, and the pointed chamfered rear arch are old. In the south wall is a piscina with a cinquefoiled pointed arch in a square head with sunk spandrels; half of the sill with its round basin has been cut away. The three windows are alike, each of two cinquefoiled lights with a quatrefoil over; all modern outside, but have old inner jambs and pointed rear arches, the latter being almost straight-sided. The middle window has been reduced a half for the insertion below it of a doorway with a two-centred segmental arch; it was probably inserted shortly before the 17th-century porch was built, and is now blocked up. The porch is of narrow red bricks with a stepped gable and has an outer archway with moulded jambs and elliptical arch, flanked by low small arched recesses. The side walls were pierced by windows with wood frames, but that in the east wall is now filled in and the porch used as a boiler room for heating purposes. The west window of the aisle resembles the others and is entirely modern outside; in its flat inner sill is set the plain round drain of a piscina, which must have been brought to the church from elsewhere.

The tower has no break or string-course in its height, the lower part being strengthened by pairs of angle buttresses. The west doorway has jambs of two orders, the outer hollow chamfered, the inner square, the two-centred arch has a much decayed scroll mould label; the door is a modern one, but has a handle and plate inscribed R D F V 1731. The window over is a square one of brick, probably of the 17th century. The first-floor chamber is lighted by a small rectangular light in each wall, that to the south having been repaired with brick; and over these on the north and west sides are clock faces. The windows of the bell-chamber are each of two trefoiled lights with a quatrefoil above in a two-centred head; the north window is old, but the others are partly or wholly modernized; the parapet is embattled and has a moulded string-course. The lower part (less than a half) of the tower is of flint and iron conglomerate with stone quoins and dressings; the buttresses, which are of two stages, have been repaired in places with brick and are covered with tiles; the bottom of the north wall has also been patched in brick, while the upper part of the tower is of square-coursed rubble or rough ashlar.

The north wall of the nave is a good specimen of early masonry, built of whole flints and pieces of iron-stone conglomerate, but the chancel walls have been newly cemented outside, and their character thus hidden.

The roof of the chancel is gabled, and has a modern plaster panelled ceiling with moulded wood ribs and moulded tie-beam; the nave has a plastered collar-beam ceiling and modern trusses dividing it into three bays. The gabled aisle roof also had a modern ceiling, but the plaster has been stripped off, revealing the old timbers. The gallery at the west end has an inscription upon it recording its erection by Sir Edward Zouch in 1622; it runs right across the west end of the nave and aisle, the front being carried on five oak posts; but only that part which is in the nave is old.

The altar-table has thin turned legs, and is probably of the 18th century, but the pulpit is six-sided and evidently of the same date as the gallery. The font is modern, of carved and panelled stone on marble shafts.

In the tower is an ancient oak chest of plain design with a plain strap to the lock.

In the quatrefoil in the head of the middle window of the south aisle is a fragment of old glass, probably original with the aisle—a six-petalled double rose, yellow and white, a piece of border with a lozengy or fret pattern, and other flowers.

In the blocked doorway of the south aisle is set a small brass inscription which reads :—' Pray for the soules of john Shadhet et Isabell hys wyfe the which john decessed the xi day of Marche yn the yere of our lord MVᶜxxvii on whos soullᶜ jhu have mercy.' Above it are two standing figures praying; the man has long hair, and wears a long fur-trimmed cloak with sleeves; the lady has a long linen head dress, fur cuffs, and a loose belt about her dress at the waist with ends reaching to the ground; below is part of an indent, probably that of the children. By the side of this brass is another inscription :—' Pray for the soules of Henry Purdon and johan hys wyfe which Henry deceessed the vii day of Noveber the yer of ō lord MVᶜxxiii on whose soules Jhu have mercy, Amen.' Over it were two figures, but that of the man is missing; the lady is dressed like the other. Between these two brasses are the figures of four girls.

In the chancel is a brass inscription to Sir Edward Zouch who died in 1634 ; it has a long eulogistic epitaph in Latin ; also a mural monument to Sir John Lloyd, bart., who died in 1663. There are several later monuments.

There are six bells : the treble, second, third and fifth were cast by William Eldridge 1684, the fourth is dated 1766 and has the initials I F cut in ; this is said to have been cast near the church ; the tenor was by Eldridge 1684, but was recast by Warren in 1887.

The church possesses no old plate, the set in use comprising two silver cups and a standing paten of 1837, a plate of 1805, and a plated flagon.

The first book of the registers contains baptisms, marriages, and burials from 1653 to 1672 ; the second has baptisms from 1673 to 1770, marriages 1673 to 1754, and burials 1673 to 1786 ; the third has marriages 1754 to 1763 ; fifth, marriages 1763 to 1787 ; sixth, the same to 1812 ; seventh, baptisms from 1770 and burials from 1787, both to 1808 ; eighth, baptisms 1809 to 1812 ; and ninth, burials for the same period.

ST. JOHN THE BAPTIST'S CHURCH, of stone in 13th-century style, was built by Sir Gilbert, then Mr., Scott, in 1842 at Goldsworth, and enlarged in 1879 and 1883.

The present church of *CHRIST CHURCH* parish was built in red brick in 1889.

ST. PAUL'S, MAYBURY HILL, built of red brick with Bath stone windows and quoins, was erected in 1895 as a chapel of ease to Christ Church.

An iron church, Holy Trinity, was built at Knapp Hill in 1855.

ADVOWSONS The church of Woking from early times seems to have had the Prior and convent of Newark in Send as its patrons.[99] After the dissolution of that monastery in the 16th century, it generally followed the history of the manor. A few exceptions must, however, be noted. Thus it was granted by Philip and Mary to John White, Bishop of Winchester.[100] Elizabeth seems to have resumed the patronage, and towards the end of her reign granted it to Francis Aungier,[101] afterwards Baron Longford. Under James I two persons, named respectively Francis Maurice and Francis Phelips,[102] received it from the Crown, but this grant was possibly in trust for the lord of the manor, for James Zouch presented in 1637,[103] and from that date it has been united with the manor.

The parish of St. John the Baptist was formed from the old parish in 1884. The living is in the gift of the vicar of Woking.

Christ Church parish was formed out of the same district in 1893. In 1877 it was served by a temporary church. The living is in the gift of trustees.

CHARITY Of old charities only Smith's, distributed as in other Surrey parishes, appear to exist.

WORPLESDON

Werpesdune (xi cent.) ; Werplesdone and Werplesden (xii cent.).

Worplesdon is a parish lying 3 miles north-west from Guildford. It contains 5,253 acres, and is about 5 miles east to west, and 3 miles north to south in extreme measurement. The village and church stand upon an abrupt hill of Bagshot sand (the Bracklesham Beds), but round it the soil is lower Bagshot sand. To the south the parish is on the London Clay, and to the east there is alluvium of the Wey valley. The river runs through the parish for a short distance, and is joined by a brook, sometimes called Worplesdon Brook. There are brick and tile works, and cement works in the parish, and nursery gardens. It is otherwise agricultural, and a great part of it is waste land. Whitmoor and Broad Street Commons are extensive wastes. The Guildford and Aldershot road passes through it, and the main London and South-Western Railway line from London to Portsmouth. There is a Worplesdon station, which lies however, in Woking parish.

The parish was divided into four tithings : Perry Hill, about the hill on which the church stands ; Burpham, on the east side ; West End ; and Wyke. The last, which was separated from the rest of the parish, was added to Ash (q.v.) in 1890.

The heaths are rich in archaeological remains. Aubrey[1] mentions a trench and bank, the bank on the west side running through this parish from south-east to north-west. It is still visible on Whitmoor Common, though it is now curtailed at both ends by

extended cultivation, and at the south end has been apparently incorporated into the bank of a lane. It is roughly parallel to the railway line, on the west side of it, some 400 yds. from it. The existing portion is about 600 yds. long, too long for one side of an inclosure, more probably a boundary ditch. There are also Bronze Age tumuli which have been opened, and pottery found there is now in the Pitt-Rivers collection, Oxford. Arrow-heads and implements, including a perforated stone hammer head, are in the Archaeological Society's Museum at Guildford, and in the Charterhouse Museum. On Broad Street Common a Roman villa was excavated in 1829. A piece of pavement of some interest was removed to Clandon Park by the Earl of Onslow, lord of the manor. Tiles and pottery, and some doubtful pieces of metal, but no decipherable coins were found.[2] Romano-British interments, with pottery, have been found at Burpham. Some of the pottery is in the Archaeological Society's Museum at Guildford ; but it is chiefly kept in private hands.

Close by Worplesdon Church, on the top of the hill, a tower used to stand with a semaphore, forming part of the communications between Portsmouth and London.

Two rather notable names occur among the rectors : Thomas Comber, 1615–42, Master of Trinity Colledge, Cambridge, and John Burton, 1766–71. The latter was author of a curious work, *Iter Surriense et Sussexiense*, published 1752, which contains two different accounts in Latin and Greek of a journey

99 *Bracton's Note Bk.* 769 ; also *Wykeham's Reg.* (Hants Rec. Soc.), i, 61, 156, &c.

100 Pat. 5 & 6 Phil. and Mary, pt. iv.
101 Ibid. 33 Eliz. pt. xx.
102 Ibid. 7 Jan. I, pt. xxii.

108 Winton Epis. Reg. Curle, fol. 42a.
1 *Hist. of Surr.* iii, 326.
2 Brayley, *Hist. of Surr.* ii, 44.

from Oxford through Henley, Windsor, Kingston, Epsom, Dorking, Horsham, Lewes, Brighton, Shoreham, Chichester. He also wrote a defence of the study of Greek. His Greek journey is peculiarly interesting from its notices of the country. He is said to have made at his own expense the causeway on which the road to Guildford runs, near Woodbridge, in order that he might ride to Guildford in flood time.

The Inclosure Act for Worplesdon dealt mainly with the Wyke portion in 1803.[m]

Burying Place Farm has its name from a Friends' burial-ground, presented by Stephen Smith of Worplesdon, one of the early Friends, a friend of Fox, who died in 1678. The meeting was amalgamated with that of Guildford in 1739. The burying-ground was sold in 1852.[2] There was a General Baptist Meeting

date, and on the west side of the green a red brick house of the same period with slight ornament in the form of brick labels to the windows. At the southwest is a pretty group of half-timbered cottages with brick filling and projecting bays with rounded pediments in brick over the lower windows. East of the green the ground rises to its highest point, on which the church is built. Though surrounded by trees a very fine and typical view of the county, particularly to the eastward, is obtained from the tower. William Cole the antiquary, who visited the parish in 1774, has left a description from which it appears that he had to drive up the hill to the church, although it is difficult to see by what route he approached.

Worplesdon Place is the residence of Sir J. L. Walker, C.I.E.; Rickford, of Lt.-Col. Montgomery; Rydes Hill, of Mr. F. Williams ; Stoke Hill, of Mrs. Paynter.

HALF-TIMBER COTTAGES AT WORPLESDON

at Worplesdon, removed to Meadrow, Godalming, after 1805.[4]

There is a Congregational chapel built in 1822, and a Congregational mission hall at Rydeshill. There is also a Primitive Methodist chapel at Burpham. On Whitmoor Common is a Joint Isolation Hospital, built in 1899 under the control of a Joint Guildford, Godalming, and Woking Hospital Board.

Schools (provided) were built at Perry Hill in 1861, and at Wood Street.

The village stands on high wooded ground, and is partly grouped round an oblong green and partly along the main road which runs north and south, with descents at both extremities of the village. There are several half-timber houses of 17th-century

The present rectory lies at the foot of a steep grassy slope south-west of the churchyard, with which it is connected by a footpath.

WORPLESDON (Werpesdene, xiii and
MANOR   xiv cents. ; Worpisdene, xv cent.) was
       held by Earl Roger in chief at the time of Domesday. Turald held it of him,[5] and like the rest of the land of Earl Roger in Surrey it became part of the honour of Gloucester.[6] In the 13th century Gilbert de Basseville held a knight's fee in Worplesdon of the honour of Gloucester, and Gilbert de Holeye held a third part of a fee of the same.[7] The manor of Gilbert de Basseville in Worplesdon appears early in the 13th century in two moieties. In 1314 Roland de Wykford held half a knight's fee of the Earl of

---

[b] Private Act, 43 Geo. III, cap. 120.
[9] W. March, *Early Friends*, 52, and local information.

[4] Ch. Bks. Meadrow Chapel.
[5] *V.C.H. Surr.* i, 313.
[6] *Testa de Nevill* (Rec. Com.), 220 ;

Chan. Inq. p.m. 8 Edw. II, 68, m. 63.
[7] *Testa de Nevill* (Rec. Com.), 220.

Gloucester, and the other moiety was held by Mary de Wintershull.[8] In 1317 the Wintershull moiety of the manor was said to be held of Nicholas de Seymour,[9] while in 1328 Thomas de Seymour, son of Nicholas, was declared to be intermediate lord between the heir of the Wintershulls and the Earl of Gloucester.[10] Mary de Wintershull died seised of this moiety in 1317.[11]

She left, as heirs, her sister Paulina de Hegham and the two daughters of Nathania de Ralegh, another sister, Joan wife of Ralph de Ditton, and Margaret.[12] In the next year Ralph, Joan, and Margaret joined in conveying their portion to Paulina,[13] who thus became seised of the whole moiety. She died in 1328 leaving as her heir her son Roger de Hegham.[14] She held of Thomas de Seymour, who held of the Earl of Gloucester as of the honour of Camberwell. When Hugh Audley, Earl of Gloucester, died in 1347, both moieties of Worplesdon, the Wintershull and Wykford parts, were still held of him. But in 1372 when Ralph Stafford, husband of Audley's daughter, died, there is no mention of Worplesdon among his lands.[15] The Wykford portion was conveyed to the Crown in 1363,[16] and the other half was probably also acquired at some time by the Crown, for the king's steward held a court for the whole manor in 1366.[17]

In 1387 John Worship, yeoman of the king's cuphouse, had a grant of the manor,[18] but only for life.[19] In 1453 it was granted to Jasper, Earl of Pembroke, later Duke of Bedford.[20] He was attainted by Edward IV, and in 1474 it was granted to the Duke of Clarence 'for the better maintenance of his estate.'[21] The Duke of Bedford was restored by Henry VII, but died without heirs in 1495. It was granted for life to Antony Browne in 1523,[22] and in 1570 his son, the first Lord Montagu, was made steward of the manor by the queen.[23] In 1623 a lease was granted to John Murray, Lord Annandale, for three lives.[24] He probably sold his interest to Charles Harbord, who had a grant for three lives in 1631.[25] In 1653 a court was held by Sir Charles Harbord, in 1665 by William Harbord. In 1668 John Payne of Hurtmore granted a moiety of the manor of Worplesdon to Thomas Newton of Stoke next Guildford for £510, having already sold him the other half.[26] Thomas Newton held a court in 1670. In 1681 it was bought by Richard Onslow, in whose family it has remained.

The history of the other half previous to 1363 remains to be traced.[27] In 1296 Thomas de Wykford granted a moiety of Worplesdon Manor to Margery widow of John de Wykford, to hold for life.[28] Roland de Wykford, possibly son of Thomas, was holding in

1314.[29] In 1347 Roland de Wykford granted the annual rent of 10 marks from his lands in Worplesdon to·Robert de Wykford,[30] who in 1363 conveyed his manor of Worplesdon to the Crown.[31]

The family of Wykford had the rights of view of frankpledge and assize of bread and ale in Worplesdon.[32]

The manor of BURGHAM (Borham, xi cent.; Burpham, xvi cent.) in Worplesdon was at the time of the Survey held by Turald[33] of Earl Roger.

At the time of the *Testa de Nevill* Thurstan le Dispenser was holding a knight's fee in Burgham as of the honour of Gloucester,[34] and in 1276 Adam le Dispenser, presumably Thurstan's heir, released Burgham Manor to William de Wintershull and Beatrice his wife.[35] In 1314,

WINTERSHULL. *Or two bars gules.*

at the death of the Earl of Gloucester, John de Wintershull, son of William and Beatrice, was holding Burgham.[36] John perhaps died without issue,[37] for the manor passed to his cousin Thomas, who died seised of it in 1340.[38] Burgham was assigned as dower to Alice widow of Thomas Wintershull,[39] who, a few years after her husband's death, became the wife of Henry de Loxley.[40] At her death in 1385 the manor passed to her second son Thomas de Wintershull, her eldest son William having predeceased her, and he died seised of it in 1388, leaving a son and heir Thomas.[41] The younger Thomas died in 1400 and was succeeded by his son Thomas,[42] who, however, left no issue, and the manor passed at his death in 1420 to his sister Agnes wife of William Bassett. She was in possession of it in 1436,[43] when she conveyed Burgham to trustees, probably in favour of the male heir of the Wintershull family, for Thomas Wintershull died seised of it in 1477, leaving Robert his son and heir.[44] It returned, however, to the Bassetts, for Richard Bassett died seised in 1509, leaving a son and heir Thomas then twelve years old.[45] Apparently Thomas died without issue, for at the death of Juliana widow of Richard in 1533 her heir was found to be her daughter Joan wife of Richard Unwyn, then twenty-nine years old.[46] In 1548 a certain Sir Anthony Windsor and his wife Joan were seised of the manor in Joan's right;[47] so that probably Sir Anthony was Joan Bassett's second husband. In 1566 Anthony Windsor, son of Joan and Anthony, died seised of the manor, leaving a son and heir Edmund, who was about four years old at

8 Chan. Inq. p.m. 8 Edw. II, 68, m. 63.
9 Ibid. 10 Edw. II, no. 49.
10 Ibid. 2 Edw. III (1st nos.), no. 31; De Banco R. 286, m. 165 d.
11 Chan. Inq. p.m. 10 Edw. II, no. 49.
12 Ibid.
13 Feet of F. Surr. 11 Edw. II, no. 13.
14 Chan. Inq. p.m. 11 Edw. III (1st nos.), no. 31.
15 Chan. Inq. p.m. 46 Edw. III, no. 62.
16 *Vide infra.*
17 Mins. Accts. Gen. Ser. bdle. 1015, no. 13, &c.
18 *Cal. Pat.* 1385–9, p. 307; 1399–1401, p. 42.
19 Rentals and Surv. pt. 15, no. 31.
20 Pat. 31 Hen. VI, pt. ii, m. 26.
21 *Cal. Pat.* 1467–77, p. 457.

22 Pat. 14 Hen. VIII, pt. i.
23 Land Rev. Rec. Accts. (Ser. i), 124–8.
24 Pat. 20 Jas. I, pt. v, m. 11.
25 Ibid. 6 Chas. I, pt. x.
26 Close, 20 Chas. II, pt. xviii, no. 19.
27 It is possible that this moiety alone represents the later manor, and that the Wintershull moiety disappears.
28 Feet of F. Surr. 24 Edw. I, no. 8.
29 Chan. Inq. p.m. 8 Edw. II, no. 68, m. 63.
30 Close, 20 Edw. III, pt. i, m. 23.
31 Deeds at Westminster quoted by Manning and Bray, *Hist. of Surr.* iii, 91; also *Cat. of Anct. D.* iii, 17.
32 *Plac. de Quo Warr.* (Rec. Com.), 744.
33 *V.C.H. Surr.* i, 319b.
34 *Testa de Nevill*, 220a–221a.

35 *Cal. Close*, 1272–9, p. 431. See also for confirmation of this grant, Feet of F. Surr. 22 Edw. I, no. 17.
36 Chan. Inq. p.m. 8 Edw. II, no. 68.
37 Wrottesley, *Pedigrees from the Plea Rolls*, 261.
38 Chan. Inq. p.m. 14 Edw. III (1st nos.), no. 7.
39 *Cal. Close*, 1346–9, p. 33.
40 Ibid.
41 Chan. Inq. p.m. 11 Ric. II, no. 54.
42 Ibid. 5 Hen. V, no. 52.
43 Close, 14 Hen. VI, m. 6.
44 Chan. Inq. p.m. 17 Edw. IV, no. 45.
45 Ibid. (Ser. 2), xxiv, 35.
46 Ibid. (Ser. 2), liii, 27.
47 Feet of F. Surr. Trin. 2 Edw. VI; Chan. Inq. p.m. (Ser. 2), clxii, 162.

the time of his father's death.[48] In 1592 Edmund conveyed the manor to Sir John Wolley,[49] who died in 1595. In 1597 Lady Elizabeth, widow of Sir John Wolley, was holding the manor in trust for her son Francis.[50]

Francis Wolley died seised of the manor in 1609, and bequeathed it to his illegitimate daughter Mary.[51] Chancery proceedings followed, but Mary Wolley was still in possession in 1629[52] of half at least of the manor. But in the same year her cousin Sir Arthur Mainwaring parted with one-sixth of it, which he claimed, to Robert Bacon and Thomas Acton ;[53] and in the same year Mary Wolley gave a warranty to Thomas Bosser against herself and her heirs for part of the manor. Mary Wolley married Sir John Wyrley,[54] and a court was held in their names in 1645. In 1679 a court was held by Sir John Wyrley alone. It seems that Mary Wolley compounded with the heirs-at-law for part of the manor, but kept the lordship. After her husband's death this passed to her half-brother Robert Wroth. Mr. Wroth was M.P. for Guildford in 1704, 1707, and 1714. He died in 1720, and the manor was bought by Lord Onslow, in whose family it has since continued. Burpham Lodge is the seat of Mr. J. B. S. Boyle.

The so-called manor of FRENCHES in Worplesdon originated perhaps in the 2 hides and a virgate held separately by two knights in Domesday. It certainly is represented by the knight's fee held there by Richard le French in 1349.[55] In 1402 John French, presumably a descendant of Richard, released the manor of Frenches to Robert Oyldesborough, brewer, of London.[56] In 1465 Robert Wintershull, son of John, granted the manor of Frenches to trustees in use for himself and his heirs.[57] In 1477 Thomas Wintershull died seised of Frenches,[58] and it is mentioned among the lands of Robert Wintershull at his death in 1547.[59] John Wintershull his son died in 1549 seised of Frenches. In 1570 John Wintershull his son parted with Frenches to William Hamonde of Guildford,[60] probably for the purposes of a settlement, as William Wintershull his son appears in possession later. In 1598 William Wintershull conveyed to Robert Russell.[61] The subsequent history of Frenches is lost,[62] but it is probably represented by Russell Place Farm. Anthony Russell was living in Worplesdon when Symmes wrote, about 1676.[63]

There is mention in 1742 of the 'manor' of

MERRIST WOOD in Surrey, when George Grenville levied a fine against James Grenville.[64] This is Merrist Wood in Worplesdon, but it was only a reputed manor. In 1582 the queen, by charter, granted a lease to George More of Loseley of 'Merest Wood,' described as 82 acres of wood and wooded ground in the Forest of Windsor, in Worplesdon in Surrey, at £3 8s. per annum.[65] It may have been originally a residential property, for a John de Merehurst was suing in 1317 for land in Worplesdon.[66] A genealogy of Merehurst of Worplesdon is in the Visitation of 1623,[67] and a John Merest was vicar of Woking 1674–99. Merrist Wood Hall is the residence of Mr. S. Brotherhood.

The manor of WYKE (Wucha, xi cent.) in Worplesdon apparently originated in the hide in Burgham held by Godric of Earl Roger at the time of Domesday.[68]

The manor appears in the 13th century in the possession of a family which took its name from the place.[69] In 1279 William of Wyke was holding the manor of Wyke,[70] and in 1316 Richard de Wyke made a settlement of it on himself and his wife Joan.[71] He died before 1342.[72] His son Peter survived-him, for in the inquisition on Hugh le Despenser,[73] Peter held a third of a knight's fee in Wyke as of the honour of Gloucester.

Peter was dead when his mother Joan died in 1353,[74] leaving as heirs Katerina, Joan, and Christine, daughters of her son Peter. From that date the history of the manor becomes obscure. In 1376 Walter Wyke, amongst others,[75] was reported to hold a fee of the honour of Gloucester,[76] but this is probably a reminiscence of a former tenant. Of the three shares of the co-heiresses one passed to John Logge or to his son John Logge by conveyance in 1457 and 1475 respectively.[77] Geoffrey the great-grandson of the first John Logge of Ash afterwards held these.[78] He had two co-heiresses, Alice and Mary, who married respectively John Bond and George Osbaldeston.[79] In 1563 Alice and Richard Osbaldeston, son of George and Mary, conveyed to William Harding.[80]

The remaining third was conveyed by one Stephen Parker to Thomas Manory, to whom and to whose daughter Anne there are brasses in Ash Church. Thomas settled in 1500 on Anne on her marriage with Ralph Vyne. Their son Henry Vyne, owner in 1552,[81] settled it on his son Henry in 1553. Henry the younger died in 1571 leaving a son Stephen,[82] who conveyed to Robert White in 1580, probably by way of mortgage,[83] and in 1584 sold outright to William

[48] Chan. Inq. p.m. (Ser. 2), clxii, 162.
[49] Feet of F. Surr. 34 & 35 Eliz.
[50] Hist. MSS. Com. Rep. vii, App. 657b.
[51] Chan. Inq. p.m. (Ser.2), cccxxxiv, 60.
[52] Recov. R. Trin. 5 Chas. I, m. 29.
[53] Feet of F. Surr. Hil. 5 Chas. I.
[54] Ibid. Hil. 11 Chas. I; Trin. 17 Chas. I.
[55] Chan. Inq. p.m. 23 Edw. III, pt. ii, (1st nos.), no. 69; Manning and Bray, op. cit. iii, 96, refer to a grant by Will. le Praunces of Worplesdon in 1290, saving suit and reliefs to his heir and his rights to the lord of Burpham.
[56] Feet of F. Surr. Hil. 3 Hen. IV.
[57] Deed from Mr. Percy Woods, C.B.
[58] Inq. p.m. 17 Edw. IV, no. 48.
[59] Chan. Inq.p.m. (Ser.2), lxxxv, 53. For the history of this family see Wintershull Manor in Bramley, and Bramley Manor.
[60] Close, 13 Eliz. pt. xiii.
[61] Com. Pleas Fine Enr. East. 40 Eliz.

[62] The Drake family occur in fines and recoveries in connexion with a manor of Frenches, but this -is evidently Frenches in Reigate. In a survey of Reigate Manor in 1623 Edward Drake is mentioned as holding Frenches, a subordinate manor to Reigate.
[63] See Harl. MS. 1561, fol. 168b, 174, 174b, for the Russells of Worplesdon about 1623.
[64] Feet of F. Div. Co. Trin. 16 Geo. II.
[65] Harl. Chart. 43 F. 41.
[66] Feet of F. 11 Edw. II.
[67] Harl. MS. 1561, fol. 172.
[68] V.C.H. Surr. i, 319b.
[69] Plac. de Quo Warr. (Rec. Com.), 744.
[70] Ibid. See also Testa de Nevill (Rec. Com.), 226, where John de Wyke is reported to hold one-third of a knight's fee of the honour of Gloucester.
[71] Feet of F. Mich. 10 Edw. II, no. 8.
[72] Will proved in Court of Archdeacon of Surrey.

[73] Chan. Inq. p.m. 23 Edw. III, pt. ii, no. 169.
[74] Ibid. 24 Edw. III (1st nos.), no. 75.
[75] The others are: the Abbot of Waverley, Thomas Baus and John de Lycewyrne. Possibly the three co-heiresses may have become the wives of Walter, John, and Thomas.
[76] Chan. Inq. p.m. 49 Edw. III, pt. i (2nd nos.), no. 46.
[77] Mr. Woodroffe's deeds, quoted by Manning and Bray, op. cit. iii, 91.
[78] See Feet of F. Surr. East. 3 & 4 Phil. and Mary. [79] Ibid.
[80] Ibid. Hil. 5 Eliz. ; Trin. 5 Eliz.; Div. Co. East. 5 Eliz.
[81] Star. Chamb. Proc. temp. Edw. VI, ii, 67. Henry's wife was — Logge, but she was not an heiress.
[82] Chan. Inq. p.m. (Ser. 2), clix, 428.
[83] Mr. Woodroffe's deeds, Manning and Bray, op. cit. iii, 94. Compare Poyle Manor, V.C.H. Surr. ii, 618.

A HISTORY OF SURREY

Harding,⁸⁴ who thus acquired the whole. Henceforth it descended as Claygate in Ash (q.v.).

In 1290 William of Wyke was reported to have had without charter, from time immemorial, assize of bread and ale and view of frankpledge in the manor of Wyke.⁸⁵

The church of ST. MARY consists CHURCHES of a chancel 42 ft. 1 in. by 15 ft. 7 in., with a north chapel 28 ft. 5 in. by 14 ft., a modern north-east vestry and south chapel ; a nave 41 ft. 4 in. by 21 ft. 6 in. with north and south aisles 9 ft. 4 in. and 6 ft. 8 in. wide respectively ; a western tower 14 ft. by 16 ft. 9 in., and a south porch. The nave and tower are faced with Heath stone, the north and south chapels with flint, and the former has, like the chancel, some ironstone conglomerate in its walls. The whole church has been much over-restored, and in consequence it is now almost impossible to assign a date for the oldest part of the church. The chancel, however, is probably of fairly early 13th-century date, and the north chapel seems to be of about the same time. The nave arcades and aisles appear to date from the middle of the same century ; and about the middle of the 15th century the west tower was built and the clearstory added. The porch, though much restored, is more than a century later, the date 1591 being still faintly discernible. In the middle of the 17th century the whole church was re-roofed, and in modern times the north vestry and south chapel were added, a new chancel arch inserted, and the arcade between the north chapel and chancel built.

The east window of the chancel is of late 14th-century style with modern tracery of two cinquefoiled and one trefoiled light, with a two-centred head and flowing tracery. On the north is a modern arcade of three bays opening to the north chapel, and on the south, at the east, is a window of two cinquefoiled lights under a square head which, though much restored, is of 15th-century date. West of this are three modern sedilia and a modern doorway and an arcade of two bays.

The north chapel is lit on the east by a lancet of which a few quoin stones are old, high up in the wall, two modern north windows of 15th-century detail, and a 13th-century lancet on the west, partly blocked by the aisle roof. In the north wall are two ogee-headed tomb recesses, now empty, of mid-14th-century date. Between the chapel and the north aisle is a plain chamfered arch with a few old stones in its jambs.

The south chapel is entirely modern with a two-light window on the east and on the south two two-light windows and one single light.

The nave is of three bays and has arcades with round columns and half-round responds, moulded capitals and bases of curious profile, the mouldings having been much cut down, and two-centred arches of two chamfered orders. Like all internal work here they are of chalk ; the plaster edges towards the nave are finished in scallop pattern, after an early fashion, but are here modern.

The tower arch is of two hollow-chamfered orders with a moulded capital at the springing line and shafted and moulded jambs, very fine and massive work in chalk. On a stone set in the north side of its east face is an inscription in 15th-century letters :

richarde exford made
xiv fote of yis touer.

The clearstory has, on either side, a single trefoiled light between two two-light windows, all under square heads.

Both aisles have two two-light windows in the side walls, with square heads, perhaps 15th-century work renewed, and in the west wall of the north aisle is a modern lancet.

A sketch of the church made in 1774 by William Cole shows these windows as apparently of late 14th-century date. At the south-east of the aisle is a plain pointed piscina. Between the windows is the south door with a plain modern four-centred head.

The south porch is a plain open timber one, a good deal restored. On the tie-beam over the entrance are faintly visible the royal initials E.R., the date 1591, and also the initials H.T. The sides are filled with modern arcading of 14th-century style.

The tower is of three stages built in Heath stone with an embattled parapet, and is surmounted by a small open lantern of 18th-century date, said to have been brought there from the rectory stables, and absurdly out of proportion. The belfry windows are of two cinquefoiled lights under a four-centred head. The west window is of 15th-century date, much restored, of five lights with sub-mullions and smaller lights over and a wide hollow external reveal. The west door, of the same date, and also much restored, has moulded jambs and head in two orders, the inner being four-centred and the outer square. The tower has a turret staircase on the north-east and diagonal buttresses.

The fittings of the church are largely modern. The font is of marble and of 18th-century date with a very graceful outline. The 18th-century notes referred to above, however, contain a sketch of a square font on angle shafts with an arcade on the bowl of pointed arches, apparently of 13th-century date.

The roofs are all apparently of the same date, except those which are modern, and on the moulded wall-plate of the north chapel is carved ' R.R. I.C. C.W. 1650. R.K.' They are all open and quite plain. The seating is all modern, but there is an extremely fine pulpit of late 17th-century date with moulded and raised panels and acanthus enrichment. This is said to have come from Eton College.

In the windows of the church is a quantity of stained glass mainly of 15th-century date, but some earlier. In the windows of the north aisle are two small 14th-century figures under contemporary canopies, and a kneeling priest in a cassock, over which is a red cloak and a brown hood. This is of the 15th-century, but the head of a bishop here is a piece of 14th-century work. In the same window are two shields : Argent three gimel bars gules impaling azure a cross argent ; and Gules a fret or on a chief azure a lis or—probably three lis originally.

In the south aisle are the following : the arms of King Henry VIII impaling the augmented arms granted on her marriage to Anne Boleyn, which are : Quarterly of six ; 1. Lancaster ; 2. Angoulême ; 3. Guienne ; 4. Butler quartering Rochford ; 5. Brotherton ; 6. Warenne. Another shield is that of Robert Bennet, Bishop of Hereford 1602–17 : Argent a cross gules between four demi-lions gules quartered with paly or and vert. This last is dated 1633. England quartered with France also appears,

⁸⁴ Feet of F. Surr. Mich. 26 & 27 Eliz.   ⁸⁵ Plac. de Quo Warr. (Rec. Com.), 744.

394

RIPLEY CHURCH : THE CHANCEL

and the arms of Eton College. In the south-east window is the name W. Roberts, 1802.

There are six bells : the treble and third cast by Thomas Mears in 1827 ; the second, fourth, and fifth by R. Phelps in 1726 ; and the sixth by Thomas Mears in 1826.

The church plate consists of a cup of 1616 ; a flagon of 1598, the gift of Lady Margaret Savill ; a repoussé salver, the gift of John Lancing in 1612 ; and a much-repaired unmarked standing paten, probably of early 18th-century date.

The first book of the registers contains entries from 'the 30 year of Henry VIII' (1538) to 1718. A second book contains entries between 1776 and 1812, the intermediate entries from 1718 to 1776 having been contained in one now fallen to pieces.

St. Luke's Church, Burpham, was built in 1859 as a chapel of ease to Worplesdon. It is a plain stone building of a nave and chancel and western bell-turret.

ADVOWSON The early history of Worplesdon Church is somewhat obscure. There was a church in Worplesdon at the time of the Domesday Survey,[86] but the advowson does not seem to be mentioned before 1291, when Laderena Valoynes released it to Sir John de Cobham.[87] It remained in the direct line of the Cobham family [88]

until the death of John, Lord Cobham, in 1407, when it passed to his granddaughter Joan, daughter of Joan de Cobham by her marriage with Sir John De La Pole.[89] The younger Joan, Baroness de Cobham in her own right, died in 1434 ;[90] and by a settlement made in 1428[91] her fifth husband, Sir John Harpenden, was to retain possession of the advowson for life, with remainder at his death to Joan, wife of Sir Thomas Brooke, and daughter of joan de Cobham by her second marriage with Sir Reginald Braybrooke.[92]

The advowson continued in the possession of the Cobhams till it was forfeited with the other possessions of Henry, Lord Cobham, who was attainted in 1603.[93] Before that Henry, Lord Cobham, had granted the next presentation to Sir George More of Loseley, who presented Thomas Comber, afterwards Master of Trinity College, Cambridge, in 1615.[94] The Crown presented in 1660, 1670, and again in 1683.[95] The advowson was granted to Eton College in 1690.[96]

Smith's Charity is distributed as in other Surrey parishes.

CHARITIES

In 1605 Mr. Shaw left £4 a year for the poor, charged upon the 'Nag's Head' in Guildford and land in Stoke.

In 1726 the rector, the Rev. C. Moore, left £200 in Government stock for educating poor children under the direction of the rector.

[86] *V.C.H. Surr.* i, 313*b*.
[87] Feet of F. Surr. 19 Edw. I, 34.
[88] Harl. Chart. 45 C. 24 ; *Wykeham's Reg.* (Hants Rec. Soc.), i, 52, 161, 216.
[89] G.E.C. *Complete Peerage.*
[90] Chan. Inq. p.m. 12 Hen. VI, no. 37.
[91] Ibid.
[92] G.E.C. *Complete Peerage.*
[93] Ibid.
[94] Winton Epis. Reg. Bilson, fol. 43
[95] Inst. Bks. (P.R.O.).
[96] Add. MS. 5847, fol. 414.

THE HUNDRED OF GODLEY

The hundred or half-hundred of Godley is made up of lands which, with the exception of Pyrford and Horsell, formed part of the early grants to the monastery of Chertsey.[2] The town of Chertsey, which formed the nucleus of the hundred, has occasionally lent its name to the latter. Bisley, which was parcel of the manor of Byfleet, and Horsell, which was and is included in the manor of Pyrford, are apparently not mentioned as separate townships in the hundred until about the 16th century.[3] Otherwise the hundred seems to have remained unchanged from its earliest formation until the present day. A detailed and somewhat lengthy account of the boundaries of Godley Hundred in 1446 is found in a cartulary of Chertsey Abbey[4]; they appear to coincide very generally with those of the present time.

The hundred of Godley was granted to the Abbot and convent of Chertsey by Edward the Confessor, to be held free of all dues and exactions and with full jurisdiction, with privileges of soc, sac, tol, team, infangthef, &c.[5] Pyrford is the only manor in the hundred named in Domesday which was not held by Chertsey Abbey. The grant was confirmed by succeeding kings.[6] Later on however the abbot ceased to exercise jurisdiction throughout the entire hundred as the king had certain rights in his manor of Byfleet. A rental of 1319 states that before the manor of Byfleet came to the king, the lord of it did suit at the abbot's hundred court of Godley, and the free tenants of Byfleet, Bisley, &c., and fifteen customary tenants came to view of frank pledge at Godley.[7] The Abbot of Westminster had also full jurisdiction in his manor of Pyrford; and all his men, for the tenements which they held of the abbot and his cells, were declared to be 'free from all scot and geld and from all aids of the sheriffs and their ministers, &c., quit of shire and hundred courts, swainmotes, pleas and suits, assizes, views, &c.'[8]

The hundred of Godley was free from all interference by the sheriffs or other king's officers provided that the king's mandates when brought to the abbot were executed by the latter's bailiff.[9] In 1280–1 the privilege of return of writs having been refused an inquiry was held concerning the matter and resulted in the abbot's favour.[10]

---

[1] *Pop. Ret.* 1831. The chapelry of Frimley, which, although included in this hundred, was in the parish of Ash, Woking Hundred, until 1866 (when it was made a separate parish), is given under Ash, q.v.
[2] Birch, *Cart. Sax.* i, 55, 64.   [3] Lay Subs. R. Surr. 17 Hen. VIII, bdle. 184, no. 162.
[4] Exch. K. R. Misc. Bks. xxv, fol. 74.   [5] Cart. Antiq. D 7, 8 ; Cott. MS. Vitell. A. xiii, fol. 501.
[6] *V.C.H. Surr.* ii, 56 ; *Cal. Chart.* 1257–1300, p. 306 ; Cott. MS. Vitell. A. xiii, fol. 53–69.
[7] Rentals and Surv. (P.R.O.), bdle. 623.
[8] Cott. MS. Faust. A. iii, fol. 83 *et passim* ; *Plac. de Quo Warr.* (Rec. Com.), 745.
[9] *Cal. Chart.* 1257–1300, p. 306.   [10] Chan. Inq. p.m. 9 Edw. I, no. 40.

GODLEY HUNDRED

In 1325 a coroner was granted to Godley Hundred, owing to the difficulty which the abbot and convent had hitherto experienced in dealing with the prisoners at Chertsey gaol (q.v.).[11]

When the abbey was dissolved in 1537 the hundred passed to the Crown.[12] James I granted it in 1609 to George Salter and John Williams, who conveyed it in the same year to William Garweye.[13] Two years later it passed from Garweye to John Hammond,[14] to whom the site of the abbey (q.v.) had previously been granted. Profits of the hundred court and common fines within the hundred were included in the grant thus made. From John Hammond the hundred passed to his son Robert, who in 1620 conveyed it to Prince Charles.[16] Charles as king granted it to Queen Henrietta Maria, with reversion to the Crown, for ninety-nine years.[16] It was sold during the Commonwealth as the 'hundred alias the half-hundred of Godley,' to John Blackwell.[17]

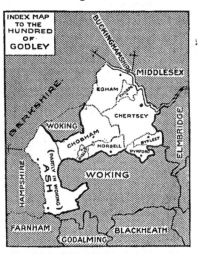

In 1672 the hundred, for the remainder of the term of ninety-nine years granted by Charles I, was granted to Queen Catherine, consort of Charles II, for her life, with reversion to the Crown.[18] The hundred was still in the Crown in the early 19th century,[19] but was probably sold together with all the land at Chertsey which belonged to the Crown, in 1827.[20] The hundred court of Godley was always held at Hardwick in Chertsey from the time of the Abbots of Chertsey until as late as 1827.[21] Manning states that in his time this hundred court was still held, as it always had been, on Whit-Tuesday at Hardwick; constables, tithing-men, and ale-tasters were chosen for the various parishes, the occasion giving rise to a gathering popularly known as Hardwick Fair. After 1827 and as late as 1841 this court leet was held at the Swan Inn at Chertsey.[22] It has not now been held for at least eighteen years.

[11] Cott. MS. Vitell. A. xiii, fol. 121.   [13] Feet of F. Div. Co. Trin. 29 Hen. VIII.
[12] Pat. 7 Jas. I, pt. xvi, m. 1 ; Close, 7 Jas. I, pt. xxix.   [14] Close, 9 Jas. I, pt. ii, m. 8.
[15] Com. Pleas D. Enr. Hil. 17 Jas. I, m. 32.
[16] Pat. 5 Chas. I, pt. xv ; Ct. R. (P.R.O.), bdle. 204, nos. 47, 53.
[17] Close, 1652, pt. xlvi, no. 12.   [18] Pat. 24 Chas. II, pt. ix, m. 1.
[19] Manning and Bray, Hist. of Surr. iii, 220.   [20] E. W. Brayley, Topog. Hist. of Surr. ii, 189.
[21] Manning and Bray, Hist. of Surr. iii, 220 (quoting from a Ct. R. of 1446 in possession of Le Neve) ;
Ct. R. (P.R.O.), bdle. 204, no. 53.
[22] E. W. Brayley, Topog. Hist. of Surr. ii, 189.

BISLEY

Busheley and Bussley (xiii cent.) ; Bisteleye (xvi cent.).

Bisley is one of the smallest parishes in Surrey, though now one of the most famous. It is 4 miles north-west from Woking. It is bounded on the north and west by Chobham, on the east by Horsell, on the south by Woking and Pirbright. It contains 922 acres, and measures barely a mile from east to west and a mile and a quarter from north to south. It lies on the Bagshot Sands (Bracklesham Beds) with some strips of alluvial soil by the little streams which run down from the peat bogs of Chobham Ridges. Bisley Common is a large open space adjoining the open ground of Chobham and Pirbright.

The place has become notable as the home, since 1890, of the National Rifle Association, which, with the War Office, owns most of the land. The establishment and ranges for the great rifle-shooting competitions[1] are in Bisley parish, and are connected by a short branch railway with the main London and South Western Railway line at Brookwood station. The ranges, however, and the ground utilized extend into Chobham and Pirbright.

The Inclosure Act, inclosing common fields, was passed in 1836, but the final award was not made till 6 August 1858.[2]

Near the church of St. John the Baptist is an ancient holy well, called St. John's Well, where according to tradition the children used to be baptized. It has recently been protected a little by a wooden cover. Bisley Farm School, in connexion with the National Refuges for Homeless and Destitute children, was opened by Lord Shaftesbury in 1868. In 1873 the Shaftesbury School in connexion with the same charity was opened, and in 1874 a chapel for their joint use. About 300 boys are accommodated. The schools (National) were built in 1847, enlarged in 1860, and taken over by a school board from 1893 to 1899. They are now again unprovided.

BISLEY was included within Chobham
MANOR in the charter of Chertsey ascribed to 673,[3] and is mentioned among the lands of the monastery in 967 when King Edgar confirmed their possessions to them.[3a] No mention of it occurs in the Domesday Survey,[3b] but in 1284 the hamlet of Bisley was held of the abbey of Chertsey by Geoffrey de Lucy, as parcel of the manor of Byfleet.[4] Geoffrey, son of Geoffrey de Lucy, conveyed Bisley with Byfleet to Henry de Leybourne in 1297.[5] Henry de Leybourne held Byfleet, and presumably Bisley, up to 1305.[6] Soon after it must have passed into the king's hands from Byfleet (q.v.), although some rent from land in Bisley remained due to the monastery, as the account of the possessions of Chertsey Abbey in the reign of Henry VIII includes the entry 'Waybragge and Bysteley 28 s.'[7]

In 1298 while Leybourne was still in possession,

he enfeoffed Hugh de Smerhulle of 54 acres of land, 2 acres of meadow, and 4 acres of wood in Bisley.[8] Hugh de Smerhulle in his turn enfeoffed Amice de Chabenham and Thomas her son of these lands in 1305, and in 1318 they granted them to John and Agnes Darderne, who in 1324 were ejected by the king's bailiff. At the instance, however, of Queen Isabella, to whom Bisley, as part of the manor of Byfleet, had been assigned in 1327, these lands were restored to John and Agnes Darderne in 1328.[9]

After Bisley, described as a hamlet and member or parcel of the manor of Byfleet, had passed with the latter into the possession of the Crown, it followed the history of this manor (q.v.) until the reign of James I. In 1620 a grant was made to Sir Edward Zouch of 'the customary tenements in Bisley, part of the manor of Byfleet,' and also of 'perquisites and profits of the courts of Bisley.'[10] This is the first reference which suggests that Bisley was recognized as an independent manor. Certainly as late as 1540 courts had been held at Byfleet for 'Byfleet with Bisley,'[11] but it is possible that the court baron of Bisley had really always been nominally distinct, and that on the occasion of the first independent grant of the manor its pleas and profits were separated from those of Byfleet in fact as well as in name. In its subsequent history, which is in no way connected with that of Byfleet, it is usually referred to as a manor and is held as such at present. The grant to Sir Edward Zouch included the manors of Woking, Chobham, and Bagshot. Henceforth the descent of Bisley is identical with that of these manors, and all are now in the possession of the Earl of Onslow.[12]

The church of ST. JOHN THE
CHURCH **BAPTIST** is a small building consisting of a chancel 20 ft. 10 in. by 13 ft. 8 in., vestry, nave 37 ft. 6 in. by 18 ft. 2 in., north aisle 6 ft. wide and a west porch of wood.

The nave is probably that of a 12th-century building, but no details of that or even of the two following centuries are left ; in the south wall is a 15th-century inserted window, which is almost the only old feature remaining. The present chancel is modern ; the former one was of brick and timber of 15th-century origin, but fell into a dilapidated state and the arch into it from the nave was closed up. In 1872 the present chancel was built and the church enlarged by the addition of the north aisle.

A tradition still remains in the village that the time for elevating the Host at High Mass was dependent upon the moment at which a sunbeam shining through a south window reached a particular spot on the north side of the nave.

The chancel is of brick and is lighted by three eastern lancets, nave 2 in the north wall. The chancel arch is modern of two orders of which the inner is carried by corbel shafts. The north arcade

---

[1] See *V.C.H. Surr.* ii, 149–50.
[2] *Blue Bk. Commons Ind. Awards.*
[3] Birch, *Cart. Sax.* iii, 470. See *Surr. Arch. Coll.* xxi, 206.
[3a] It was possibly then included in Chobham as King Edgar's charter (mentioned above) puts Chobham and Bisley together.

[4] Chan. Inq. p.m. 12 Edw. I, no. 16.
[5] Pat. 25 Edw. I, pt. ii, m. 10.
[6] Chan. Inq. p.m. 33 Edw. I, file 116, no. 214.
[7] *Valor Eccl.* (Rec. Com.), ii, 56.
[8] *Cal. Close,* 1327–30, p. 292. [9] Ibid.
[10] Pat. 18 Jas. I, pt. vi, m. 1 ; ibid. 23 Chas. II, pt. ix, no. 6, m. 22–8.

[11] Ct. R. (P.R.O.), bdle. 12, no. 19.
[12] Feet of F. Div. Co. Hil. 16 & 17 Geo. II ; Pat. 23 Chas. II, pt. ix, no. 6, m. 22–8 ; 22 Geo. II, pt. ii, m. 14 ; Feet of F. Surr. Trin. 25 & 26 Geo. II ; Close 26 Geo. II. pt. iii, m. 9 ; Recov. R. Hil. 49 Geo. III ; *vide* Woking, &c.

of the nave is of two bays, the middle pillar being circular with a moulded capital, and the pointed arches are of two chamfered orders. West of the arcade is a modern lancet window. Of the two south windows the first is a modern one of three lights and tracery under a pointed head ; the second is a 15th-century window of three trefoiled lights under a square head, the middle light being wider than the others ; it has modern mullions and sill. Between the windows a small trefoiled niche formerly a piscina, which was found at the restoration of the church beneath the ruins of the chancel. The west doorway is modern, of 13th-century style. The north aisle has a single-light window at each end and two two-light windows in the side wall.

The walling of the south wall of the nave is of conglomerate and of the west wall of roughly squared blocks of Heath stone. The roof of the nave is old, with plain collar beams which were formerly plastered. Over the west end is an old bell-turret covered with modern boarding, including the upper half of the west gable ; the vertical face of the turret is seen inside the nave with its old timbers ; it is capped by a modern wood spire covered with oak shingles.

The west porch probably dates from the 14th century ; its sides are open, with five square bays divided by hollow-chamfered mullions ; the entrance has a pointed arch formed by two solid pieces of wood with hollow-chamfered edges ; the barge-board of the gable over is foiled with rounded points, the middle foil being of ogee shape.

The altar table and font are modern ; but the pulpit is a 17th-century one with carved and moulded panels.

The church contains no ancient monuments.

There are three bells ; the oldest, which is the second, has this inscription in capitals on the shoulder : ' + Fraternitas fecit me in honore beate Mareie ' ; it is said to have been brought from the abbey of Chertsey, to which Bisley formerly belonged, and was probably cast early in the 14th century. The treble is by Thomas Swaine 1781 and the tenor by William Eldridge 1710.

The communion plate includes a silver cup of 1570 with a cover paten of 1569 ; the cup is a finely chased example, but somewhat misshapen ; there are also a plate of 1795 and a small paten of 1872.

The first book of the registers is a vellum copy beginning in 1561 and contains baptisms to 1672, burials to 1669, and marriages to 1670 ; also some briefs for 1661 and tithe rents of 1625 ; the second book has baptisms from 1673 to 1755, marriages 1673 to 1753, and burials from 1673 to 1757 ; the third contains burials from 1678 to 1812 ; the fourth has marriages from 1754 to 1807 ; the fifth, baptisms and burials 1760 to 1806, whence all three are continued in the later books; there are also a few loose sheets with accounts of 1673 and from 1682 to 1773.

The site of the church is about half a mile east of the village in an isolated position. The churchyard is small and surrounds the buildings ; there are several large trees on its boundaries, and near the porch is a yew-tree.

ADVOWSON The church of Bisley was in the possession of the abbey of Chertsey before 1284, as in that year Geoffrey de Lucy was patron and held it of the abbey.[13] Later the church came into the king's hands, probably at the same time as did the hamlet of Bisley. Presentations by the king or by the Prince of Wales date from the year 1346.[14] A pension of 3 lb. of wax and an annual rent of 18*d.* remained due to the monastery from the church of Bisley.[15]

In 1620 the grant to Sir Edward Zouch of the manor of Bisley included the advowson, rectory, and church, and, in addition, the 18*d.* rent to Chertsey Monastery,[16] which at the Dissolution had been surrendered to the Crown. The rectory and advowson remained in the hands of the lord of the manor until the latter half of the 18th century, since when the patronage appears to have changed hands. Henry Foster held it in 1800, the trustees of John Thornton in 1810,[17] and in 1889 the trustees of Mrs. P. Smith. It is at present in the gift of trustees.

CHARITIES Smith's Charity is distributed as in other Surrey parishes. In 1506 Isabella Campion of Bisley left Brachmead in Chobham for the repairs of Bisley Church.[18] In 1711 the Rev. Andrew Lamont, D.D., rector of Bisley, left £100 to be invested in land for the benefit of the poor of Bisley. The land is known as Queen Lane. The Dead Hill estate, producing about £16 a year for the poor, was left at an unknown time.[19]

BYFLEET

Biflet (xi cent.) ; Byflete (xiv cent.).

Byfleet is a village 5 miles south of Chertsey, 2 miles south-west of Weybridge Station. The parish, roughly triangular in form, is bounded on the north by Chertsey and Weybridge, on the east by Walton-on-Thames, on the south by Wisley and Pyrford. It measures 3 miles from east to west and a mile and a half from north to south at the eastern border, becoming narrower towards the west. It contains 2,045 acres of land and 30 of water. The soil is mainly the drift sand and gravel and alluvium of the

Wey valley, but on the east it abuts upon the rising ground of the Bagshot Sands which form St. George's Hill in Walton parish and Cobham Common. The natural River Wey and the artificial navigation both pass through the parish, and much of the ground is low and easily flooded by the former. The main line of the London and South Western Railway passes through the western part of the parish, and there is a station, Byfleet and Woodham. There are about 40 acres of common. Maps of the 17th century mark an iron mill on the old river where Byfleet corn mill

13 Chan. Inq. p.m. 12 Edw. I, no. 16 ; Exch. K.R. Misc. Bks. 25, fol. 49.
14 *Cal. Pat.* 1346-9, p. 1 ; Egerton MS. 2031.

15 Exch. K.R. Misc. Bks. 25, fol. 23 ; *Valor Eccl.* (Rec. Com.), ii, 56.
16 Pat. 18 Jas. I, pt. vi, m. 1.
17 Inst. Bks. (P.R.O.).

18 Tablet in church, contemporary.
19 Dr. Lamont left also £50 to be invested in land for the ministers of Bisley for ever (tablet in church).

stands. Manning says that it was 'lately an iron mill.'[1] It would be interesting to know whether it used ironstone from the Bagshot Sands or depended upon water carriage for ore from the weald. The present industries, apart from agriculture, are Mr. Newland's Rosewater and Essential Oil Distillery, and a brewery carried on by the Friary, Holroyds, and Healy's Breweries Company.

Neolithic flints occur on the slopes near St. George's Hill and Cobham Common.

Byfleet Park was one of the parks in the Surrey bailiwick of Windsor Forest which Norden surveyed for James I in 1607.[2]

A person once of some note was rector of Byfleet from 1752 to 1756—Stephen Duck, a Wiltshire labourer, who attracted the notice of Queen Caroline by his poems and was made by her a beefeater and keeper of her library at Richmond. He learned Latin and was ordained. His poems are of no great merit, but one of the earliest, 'The Thresher's Labour,' dealing with his real experiences, shows that he might have been as good as Blomfield and better than Clare if the fashion of the age had allowed him to continue to write naturally. He drowned himself in a fit of melancholy in the Thames.

An Inclosure Award was made in 1811[3] for 780 acres, including common fields of Byfleet Manor.

There are Wesleyan and Congregational chapels in the parish. The Village Hall was built in 1898 in commemoration of the Diamond Jubilee, and a public recreation ground was presented by Mr. H. F. Locke King on the same occasion.

Of the principal houses, Byfleet Manor belongs to Mrs. Rutson, St. George's Hill is the residence of Lady Louisa Egerton, Petersham Place of Mr. W. B. Owen. A number of small residential houses have lately been built in the parish. The present rectory was built by the Rev. Charles Sumner, rector, in 1834.

The School (national) was built in 1857 and enlarged in 1860 and in 1899. A school had been built in 1840, but was replaced by the present one.

MANORS *BYFLEET* is not in the original grant to Chertsey Abbey in the alleged foundation charter of 673, but is included and confirmed in the later charter of Frithwald, attributed to 727,[4] which, however, includes land granted at various times before the Norman Conquest, and must be looked upon merely as an assertion by the monks of their claims, perhaps preparatory to the Domesday Survey. (See Chertsey.) In 967 the grant was again confirmed by King Edgar as 'v mansas.'[5] At the time of the Domesday Survey Byfleet was held of the abbey as 2¼ hides by Ulwin, who had also held it in King Edward's time, when it was assessed for 8 hides.[6] It continued in the possession of the Abbot and convent of Chertsey,

and in the 13th century was held of them, as half a knight's fee, by Geoffrey de Lucy, who died in 1284 leaving as heir his son Geoffrey.[7] The latter enfeoffed Henry de Leybourne of the manor in 1297,[8] and Leybourne remained in possession until after 1305.[9] It is not clear how the manor became Crown property, but it was certainly in the king's hands in 1312.[10] The overlordship continued to be vested in the abbey for some time after the manor became the king's property. A rental of 1319 speaks of it as being held 'in chief of the Abbot of Chertsey' by the service of half a knight's fee and 15s. rent to the abbot for the vill of Weybridge and 13s. 4d. rent for the vill of Bisley; the surveyors add that before the abbot came to the king his lord did suit at the abbot's hundred court of Godley, and that all free tenants and fifteen customary tenants came to the view of frankpledge there.[11] A return of the feudal aids in the hundred of Godley in 1428 also refers to half a knight's fee in Byfleet which 'Edward, formerly Prince of Wales, used to hold of the Abbot of Chertsey.'[12] It is probable, however, that this overlordship, held by the abbey over the king or the Prince of Wales, soon became merely nominal. The courts of Byfleet were held by the king, and no further mention of Byfleet occurs in the records or court rolls of the abbey.[13]

Edward II appears to have stayed frequently at Byfleet, many of his ordinances being dated from here.[14] A grant to Piers Gaveston in 1308 of free warren in his demesne lands at Byfleet[15] suggests that he had been previously granted the manor also, probably as part of the lands belonging to the earldom of Cornwall. Edward III assigned Byfleet to his mother Isabella as part of her dower in 1327.[16] She surrendered it shortly afterwards,[17] and in 1330 the king granted it to his brother John of Eltham, Earl of Cornwall, to be held by knight's service; at his death it reverted to the Crown.[18] In 1337, when the king's eldest son received the title of Duke of Cornwall, the manor and park of Byfleet were among the lands granted to him,[19] to hold to him and his heirs, as parcel of the duchy of Cornwall.[20] The Black Prince held the manor until his death,[21] when it passed to his son.

DUCHY OF CORNWALL.
Azure fifteen bezants.

Richard II, as lord of the manor of Byfleet, granted it in 1389 to the Earl of Northumberland for two years,[22] and in 1391 to John, Bishop of Salisbury, for ten years 'for his easement and abode whenever he chooses to go thither.'[23] The bishop died in 1395, but two years before his death the manor was granted to William, Duke of Guelders, son of the Duke of Juliers,

[1] Manning and Bray, *Hist. of Surr.* iii, 181.
[2] The plan of it is in Harl. MSS. 3749.
[3] Under an Act of 40 Geo. III.
[4] Birch, *Cart. Sax.* i, 64.
[5] Ibid. iii, 469.
[6] *V.C.H. Surr.* i, 288, 310b.
[7] *Testa de Nevill* (Rec. Com.), 220b; Chan. Inq. p.m. 12 Edw. I, no. 16.
[8] Pat. 25 Edw. I, pt. ii, m. 20.
[9] Chan. Inq. p.m. 28 Edw. I, no. 148;
33 Edw. I, no. 14.

[10] *Cal. Pat.* 1307-13, p. 487.
[11] Rentals and Surv. (P.R.O.), bdle. 623.
[12] *Feud. Aids*, 1284-1431, vi, 123.
[13] Exch. K.R. Misc. Bks. 25; Cott. MS. Vitell. A. xiii; Lansd. MS. 434; Ct. R. (P.R.O.), bdle. 204, no. 10, 37, 38; 212, no. 19, &c.
[14] *Cal. Close,* 1307-13, pp. 48, 49; *Cal. Pat.* 1307-13; *Cal. Close,* 1313-18, &c.
[15] Chart. R. 1 Edw. II, m. 6, no. 7.
[16] *Cal. Pat.* 1327-30, p. 69.
[17] Ibid. 1330-4, p. 184.

[18] Chart. R. 4 Edw. III, m. 7, no. 2; *Cal. Pat.* 1330-4, p. 52. Gaveston had also been Earl of Cornwall; it looks as if the manor went with the earldom.
[19] Chart. R. 11 Edw. III, m. 28, no. 60.
[20] *Cal. Pat.* 1429-36, p. 443; 1436-41, p. 58.
[21] Ibid. 1338-40; 1340-3; 1343-5; ibid. 1377-81; *Cal. Close,* 1343-6.
[22] *Cal. Pat.* 1388-92, p. 90.
[23] Ibid. p. 467.

to hold for life without rent, he having 'become the king's vassal and done homage.'[24] The duke afterwards granted the manor and park to Roger Walden, Dean of York and Treasurer of England, and John Walden his brother, for their lives, on condition that he, the duke, might lodge there with his household whenever he should come there. Richard's grants were annulled by Parliament in 1399, and Byfleet was granted to Henry the son of the king.[25] Roger and John Walden surrendered their estate in the manor for £100 to Sir Francis Court, who was a trusted friend of Prince Henry, and Joan his wife. Both Walden and Court entered the premises without the king's licence, for which offence they were pardoned in 1401, Sir Francis and his wife receiving a confirmation of the grant to hold the manor for life, all fees, advowsons, wards, marriages, reliefs, escheats, franchises, liberties, warrens, reversions, &c., being included.[26] Sir Francis Court presented to the church during the time he held the manor.[27]

Byfleet continued to be granted by the Kings of England to their eldest sons until the time of Henry VIII.[28] The last-named king is said to have spent much of his boyhood at Byfleet.[29] As king, he granted the manor in 1533 to Katharine of Aragon, whom he had divorced in that year,[30] she being styled Princess Dowager of Wales. Sir Anthony Browne was at this time keeper of the manor.[31]

In 1537, when the monastery of Chertsey surrendered to the Crown,[32] the deed of surrender included among the manors belonging to the abbey that of Byfleet. This cannot refer to the manor, which was already in the king's hands. Certain rents, however, had remained due to the monastery when the manor passed to the Crown in the 14th century, since mention of 'assize rents in Byflete' occurs in the accounts of the surrendered abbey in 1538.[33] It was possibly those due from certain lands in Byfleet which were surrendered to the Crown as the manor of Byfleet in 1537, although there may have been some reminiscence of the overlordship which the abbey had undoubtedly held even when the manor was in royal hands.[34] It is also certain that several lands and tenements referred to in the abovementioned deed of surrender as 'manors' did not really occupy that standing.[35]

At the erection of the king's manor of Hampton Court into an honour in 1539 Byfleet was included in the possessions allotted to it.[36] Queen Elizabeth visited Byfleet in 1576.[37] James I granted the manor to Henry, Prince of Wales, and, after his son's death, to Anne of Denmark, his consort.[38] In 1617 the reversion of the manor, after her death, was granted to Sir Francis Bacon and others, for the term of ninety-nine years, in trust for Charles Prince of Wales.[39] During the Commonwealth the manor and park of

Byfleet were sold as Crown lands to Thomas Hammond.[40]

After the Restoration Byfleet, again in the Crown, seems to have been held by Queen Henrietta Maria until her death in 1669.[41]

In 1672 the lands were granted to Lord Hollis and others to hold in trust for Queen Catherine of Braganza for her life, and afterwards for Charles II and his heirs.[42] In 1694 Sir John Buckworth was accused, as lord of the manor of Byfleet, of neglect in repairing a bridge over the Wey within the said manor. It was found, however, that he was not responsible for such repair, as he was only a 'termer for years' in the manor under a 'lease made by the late queen mother's trustees.'[43] There is very little trace of the manor after this time. According to Manning, Byfleet was usually let to owners of Oatlands, and in 1804 Frederick, Duke of York, then owning Oatlands, purchased Byfleet with Walton and Weybridge, by Act of Parliament.[44]

The estate passed at the death of the Duke of York to E. Ball-Hughes, who in 1829 sold a considerable portion of the land to Lord King, whose younger son, the Hon. P. J. Locke King, inherited the land so purchased in 1833. Mr. Hughes, however, remained lord of the manor of Byfleet until after 1841.[45] At the present time Mr. H. F. Locke King is one of the principal landowners at Byfleet; Mrs. Rutson owns the Manor House, bought in 1891; and Messrs Paine & Brettell, solicitors, of Chertsey, are owners of the manor.

KING. *Sable three spearheads argent with drops of blood and a chief or with three battle-axes azure therein.*

The grant of the manor made to John of Eltham, Earl of Cornwall, in 1330 was supplemented by a further grant of all corn whether sown or for seed, livery of servants, plough-cattle and cart-horses, which had been in the manor when it was granted to him.[46] Free warren was granted with the manor to the Prince of Wales in 1337,[47] and was included in later grants to the king's eldest son.

In the Domesday Survey mention is made of a mill at Byfleet worth 5s., and of 1½ fisheries worth 325 eels.[48] Geoffrey de Lucy, who held under the abbey in 1284, owned both the mill and fisheries, as in an account of his property made in that year the site of the mill was valued at 18s., the miller's rent was 12d., and the value of the fisheries 3s.[49] Perquisites of the court were also his.[50] In 1279 he claimed assize of bread and ale in his manor,[51] and in 1284 he was in receipt of a toll of brewers called le Schench.[52] Mills known as the King's Mills at

[24] *Cal. Pat.* 1391-6, p. 315.
[25] Rymer, *Foedera*, viii, 93.
[26] *Cal. Pat.* 1401-5, p. 30.
[27] Egerton MS. 2033.
[28] *Parl. R.* (Rec. Com.), iii, 668; Close, 1 Hen. IV, pt. i, m. 27; *Parl. R.* (Rec. Com.), v, 357; vi, 13; Chan. Inq. p.m. (Ser. 2), xxii, 32.
[29] Aubrey, *Nat. Hist. and Antiq. of Surr.* iii.
[30] *Stat. of the Realm*, iii, 485.
[31] Mins. Accts. of Crown lands, Div. Co. 28-9 Hen. VIII, rot. 53, m. 1.

[32] Feet of F. Div. Co. Trin. 29 Hen. VIII.
[33] Mins. Accts. Surr. 29-30 Hen. VIII, rot. 115, m. 36.
[34] *Feud. Aids*, vi, 123; Rentals and Surv. (P.R.O.), bdle. 623.
[35] *Vide* Chertsey.
[36] *Stat.* 31 Hen. VIII, cap. 5.
[37] *Hist. MSS. Com. Rep.* vii, App. i, 629.
[38] Pat. 13 Jas. I, pt. xxix.
[39] Exch. L.T.R. Orig. R. 14 Jas. I, pt. iv, rot. 126.
[40] Close, 1653, pt. v, no. 2.

[41] *Cal. S.P. Dom.* 1694-5, p. 48.
[42] Pat. 24 Chas. II, pt. ix, m. 1.
[43] *Cal. S.P. Dom.* 1694-5, pp. 14, 48.
[44] Manning and Bray, *Hist. of Surr.* iii, 180.
[45] E. W. Brayley, *Topog. Hist. of Surr.* iii, 155.
[46] *Cal. Pat.* 1330-4, p. 184.
[47] Chart. R. 11 Edw. III, no. 28.
[48] *V.C.H. Surr.* i, 310.
[49] Inq. p.m. 12 Edw. I, no. 16.
[50] *Cal. Inq. p.m.* ii, 313, 314.
[51] *Plac. de Quo Warr.* (Rec. Com.), 743.
[52] See note 50.

Byfleet were used for paper-making in the 17th century.[53] Aubrey states that the Earl of St. Albans owned a mill here,[54] but this is probably a mistake.[55] Henry Jermyn, Earl of St. Albans, did, however, live in the manor-house here. John Evelyn records a visit to 'my lord St. Alban's house at Byflete, an old large building,' on 24 August 1678. He also visited the paper-mills at Byfleet on the same day, and gives a description of the process employed there for paper-making.[56] The present mill is a corn-mill.

The manor-house known as the King's House was built by Sir Anthony Browne, keeper of the park (*vide infra*). It was sold with other Crown lands during the Commonwealth, as 'Byfleete house, situated about the middle of Byfleete park, upon the river of Byfleete.'[56a]

According to Aubrey, Queen Anne of Denmark, when the manor was settled on her by James I, began to build 'a noble house of brick,'[57] afterwards completed by Sir James Fullerton, one of Prince Charles's trustees under the grant of 1617. It was built where the old manor-house had stood, and Evelyn in 1678 speaks of it as 'an old large building.'[58] The forecourt, garden-wall and gateway, and part of the existing manor-house are of early 17th-century date, but the house was rebuilt about 1724–34. A tile stamped with the former date and a halfpenny of the latter date, embedded in the mortar, bear out the evidence of the style. Part of it was pulled down early in the 19th century.

The first mention of the *PARK* of Byfleet occurs in 1337; it was probably not imparked before the manor came into the king's hands. In 1337 John de Chestre was granted the custody of the park and warren of Byfleet, with a robe worth a mark, or a mark, every year for his fee and 2d. daily for his wages.[59] Norden gives an interesting account of the park in 1607 when Sir Edward Howard was keeper. It was stated to lie partly within and partly without the bounds of the forest of Windsor, and was 3¼ miles in circuit. There were about 160 fallow deer, about 36 of antler, and 14 buck. He also adds that 'the Hooping birde, vulgarly held ominous, much frequenteth this park.'[60]

In 1337 the park of Byfleet was included in the grant of the manor to the Prince of Wales,[61] and was henceforth held, with the manor, by the Crown.[62] The grant of 1672 to Queen Catherine includes the park, but there appears to be no subsequent mention of it. Most of it had evidently been inclosed before the inclosure award of 1800, but a small part of it has always remained as open land round the manor-house.

Grants of the custody of the king's park were made at intervals from the 14th to the 17th century. Writs of aid to cut and sell underwood were occasionally issued.[63] In 1507 John Stoughton, late bailiff of the king's manor of Byfleet, was charged with committing waste of timber, having been ordered to cut down '50 great oaks worth 50s. in the king's wood at Byfleet.'[64] In 1513 John Wheler was appointed keeper of the park,[65] but he surrendered his patent, which in 1527 was transferred to Sir William Fitz William and Sir Anthony Browne.[66] Sir Anthony Browne apparently spent much of his time there,[67] and died at the manor-house in 1548.[68] In 1604 a grant of the park for life was made to Sir Edward Howard, the king's cup-bearer;[69] the reversion being granted to his brother, Sir Charles, in 1613.[70]

The church of *ST. MARY THE VIRGIN* consists of a chancel 19 ft. 6 in. by 12 ft. 7 in., south chapel and baptistery, south vestry, nave 42 ft. 10 in. by 17 ft. 2 in., north porch and south aisle 19 ft. 1 in. wide, all internal dimensions.

The chancel and nave seem to have been built early in the 14th century, and are of very plain detail. The dressings of the windows, &c. are all of chalk, and have a very sharp appearance suggesting that they have either been completely renewed in modern times or that the old material has been recut; the south aisle and the remainder of the building are quite modern, but the side windows of the aisle are those formerly in the south wall of the nave.

The east window of the chancel is of three lights with plain heads and intersecting tracery under a two-centred arch, and the two north windows are each of two plain lights under a two-centred arch; below the first is a plain square recess. On the south side are two modern arches opening to the organ chamber, the eastern arch containing two plain sedilia, which seem entirely modern, and a piscina with a cinquefoiled head partly restored and a sixfoiled drain in a projecting sill; at the back is a modern quatrefoil piercing, and the backs of the sedilia are also pierced. The chancel arch has chamfered jambs and a double chamfered pointed arch, the inner order being corbelled off at the springing line.

The three north windows of the nave are similar to those of the chancel, and the doorway between the second and third windows is of chalk in two chamfered orders and has a pointed head; outside is a modern porch of wood. The south arcade is of four bays having round pillars and responds with moulded bases and carved capitals, and pointed two-chamfered arches; the west window of the nave is also like the others—of two lights.

The south aisle is wider than the nave and opens by two arches into the south chapel and organ chamber. Its three side windows resemble those in the opposite wall, and it has a modern south doorway; the west window is of four plain lights with intersecting tracery. The organ chamber has a two-light east

[53] *Hist. MSS. Com. Rep.* xiii, App. v, 146.
[54] Aubrey, *Nat. Hist. and Antiq. of Surr.* iii, 194.
[55] *Hist. MSS. Com. Rep.* xiii, App. v, 436.
[56] *V.C.H. Surr.* ii, 418.
[56a] Close, 1653, pt. v, no. 2.
[57] Aubrey, *Nat. Hist. and Antiq. of Surr.* iii, 194; Dorney House, on the wharf, is said by Aubrey to have been the place where Henry VIII was nursed as an infant. It was not, however, according to the same authority, the same as the manor-house of Byfleet, referred to above, known as the King's House, which probably received its name from the kings who had dwelt there earlier (See *Surr. Arch. Coll.* iv, pp. xxiii–iv). An exhaustive account of Byfleet Manor House is contained in *Surr. Arch. Coll.* xx, 153–68.
[58] *Diary,* 24 Aug. 1678.
[59] *Cal. Pat.* 1334–8, p. 383.
[60] Harl. MS. 3749.
[61] Chart. R. 11 Edw. III, m. 28, no. 60.
[62] *Cal. Pat.* 1377–81, pp. 216, 236, 614; 1388–92, pp. 90, 183, 398, &c.; *Hist. MSS. Com. Rep.* vii, App. i, *vide* manor.
[62] *Cal. Pat.* 1377–81, p. 614.
[64] Chan. Inq. p.m. (Ser. 2), xxi, 45 (2).
[65] L. and P. Hen. VIII, i, 3675.
[66] Ibid. iv, g. 3324.
[67] Ibid. vii, 1198; xi, 461; xiii (1), p. 580; xvii, 976.
[68] Dict. Nat. Biog.
[69] Cal. S.P. Dom. 1603–10, p. 169.
[70] Ibid. 1580–1625, p. 535; 1611–18, pp. 202, 598.

BISLEY CHURCH : WEST PORCH

window and at the south-east a small baptistery or chapel serving as an approach to the vestry ; this baptistery has a modern single-light east window, and in its south wall an old chalk piscina has been re-set ; it has a sixfoiled drain and a plain pointed and chamfered arch.

The roof of the chancel is gabled and has a modern panelled ceiling. The nave roof has an apparently old truss with a king post from which struts branch four ways. Over the west end is a modern wood bell-turret partly supported by wood posts from the floor to the nave ; it has two pointed lights in each side and is hung with oak shingles. Over it is an octagonal spire also covered with shingles. The aisle and other roofs are modern.

The font dates from the 15th century and is octagonal in plan with quatrefoil panelled sides to the bowl; three of these panels contain heads of angels wearing diadems, and two others have plain shields, the other three inclosing paterae of foliage. The stem is panelled with two trefoiled sinkings on each face, and the base is moulded. The pulpit is six-sided and bears the initials and date RS 1616 RS ; each face has two rectangular panels, the lower and larger one inclosing a lesser formed by a moulded rib.

Set in the north jamb of the chancel arch is a brass figure of a priest above the following inscription :—

'Hic jacet Thoms Teylar rector ecclie pochialis de Biflete et unus canonicor' ecclesie cathedralis Lincoln qui quidm Thom's obiit . . . die mensis . . . A° dni millio cccc LXXX . . . cuius anime ppiciet' De'.' The exact date of the death has never been filled in. The figure is dressed in a fur almuce, alb, and cassock. The stone slab from which the brass was taken still remains in the chancel floor.

Over the north doorway are the remains of a mural painting, apparently that of a seated king under a canopy, and the wall is covered with a masonry pattern of double red lines with flowers in each compartment. This formerly covered the whole surface of the nave walls, and was revealed in 1853 ; the work is probably of early 14th-century date, and a little to the west of the doorway is also a painted consecration cross with expanded arms ; the masonry pattern seems to be painted over the cross, although probably nearly contemporary with it. Other instances

of the painting over of consecration crosses in this manner have been noticed.

The three bells are modern, dating from 1853, the old tenor having been a mediaeval bell, inscribed ' Protege Virgo pia quos convoco Sancta Maria.'

The oldest piece of the Communion plate is a cup of 1764 ; there are also two cups, two patens, and a flagon, all of silver, given in 1893.

In the register the baptisms begin in 1698, the marriages in 1755, and the burials in 1728.

There is a small iron mission church of St. John at Byfleet Corner.

ADVOWSON The church of Byfleet was among the possessions of the abbey of Chertsey at the time of the Domesday Survey,[71] and it so continued until after 1284, in which year Geoffrey de Lucy, who held Byfleet of the abbey, was patron of the church.[72] Shortly after this, however, the church passed into the king's hands with the manor (q.v.).[73] From that time until the present the patronage has remained in the gift of the Crown.[74] The living, a rectory, is now in the gift of the Lord Chancellor.

The chapel of Wisley was attached to Byfleet as early as 1535,[75] presentation to the chapel being included in that made to Byfleet until after 1646.[76] In 1648 George Bradshaw was appointed to Wisley alone.

The rectory of Byfleet was sequestered during the reign of Charles I. In June 1645 the wife of the rector, Hope Gifford, petitioned for aid towards the maintenance of herself and her children. A fifth part of all tithes due to the rector was ordered to be paid her by any person to whom the rectory might stand sequestered. Mr. Scuddamore, the person in question, refused, however, to do this, and in 1646 suffered sequestration himself on this account.[77] Nevertheless Calamy gives him among the ejected ministers of 1662.

CHARITIES The charities include Smith's, as in other Surrey parishes, also a sum of £11 10s. under the will of ' Lady Margaret Bruce,' probably Margaret daughter of the fourth Lord Balfour of Burleigh, who would have been Baroness Balfour of Burleigh but for the attainder in 1715 of her elder brother, whose heir she was. She died in 1769.

CHERTSEY

Cerotesege (earliest charters, ascribed to vii cent.) ; Certesia (in Latin of the same) ; Certesyg (xi cent.) ; Certeseye (xiii cent.) ; Certesay (xiv cent.).

Chertsey is a market town on the Thames 9 miles from Windsor and about the same from Kingston. The parish is bounded on the north-west by Egham and Thorpe, on the north-east by the Thames between it and Middlesex, on the south-east by Weybridge, Byfleet, and Pyrford, on the south-west by Horsell and Chobham. It measures about 4 miles each way, being roughly quadrilateral. The north-eastern and eastern parts are on the gravel, sand and alluvium of the Thames Valley and of the Wey Valley. The

old course of the Wey forms part of the eastern boundary, and the actual confluence of the Wey and the Thames is in Chertsey parish, not Weybridge. The Bourne Brook and the stream from Virginia Water which joins it flow through the parish to the Thames. The western and southern parts of the parish are on higher ground where the barren heaths of the Bagshot Sand begin, these stretching back to the commons of Woking and Chobham. Eminences of the Bagshot Sand stand out above the river valleys also, the most striking being St. Anne's Hill, west-by-north of the town. It is only 240 ft. above the sea, but from its situation in the middle of the valley it commands fine

71 V.C.H. Surr. i, 310b.
72 Chan. Inq. p.m. 12 Edw. I, no. 16.
73 See Cal. Pat. 1317-21, p. 102.
74 Ibid. 1381-5, pp. 306, 325, 411 ;

1385-9, p. 145 ; 1388-92, p. 121 ; 1399-1401, p. 543 ; 1422-9, pp. 5, 155, 388. Vide references to manor. Inst. Bks. (P.R.O.).

76 Valor Eccl. (Rec. Com.), ii, 31.
76 Inst. Bks. (P.R.O.) ; Lds. Journ. (1648), 588.
77 Surr. Arch. Coll. ix, 248-9.

views through gaps in the trees with which it is rather too thickly planted.

Chertsey still remains a pleasant country town. There are three chief streets, London Road and Windsor Street forming part of the road between those places, and Guildford Street at right angles to them. In the last is a Jacobean house, now the Queen's Head Inn, and the remains of the house where Cowley died in 1667, incorporated into a modern house. A room supported on posts, which projected over the road, was removed in 1786. The house is the residence of Mrs. Tulk. In 1791 the following description of it is given:—'A good old timber house, of a tolerable model. There is a large garden ; a brook arising at St. Anne's Hill runs by the side. They talk of a pretty summer house which he built, which was demolished not long since ; and of a seat under a sycamore tree by the brook which are mentioned in his poems. There are good fish-ponds of his making.'[1]

The parish was divided into tithings called Chertsey, Allesden, and Adisford (i.e. Addlestone), Lolewirth or Hardwitch in Hardwicke, Rokesbury in Lyne, Haim, Crockford or Crotchford, Woodham, and Botleys. The Hundred Court of Chertsey for Godley Hundred was held in Hardwicke. The parish is now an urban district under the Local Government Act of 1894,[2] and is divided into three wards, Chertsey, Addlestone, and Outer Ward.

Chertsey is served by the Weybridge and Chertsey branch of the London and South Western Railway, opened in 1848, with stations at Addlestone and Chertsey, and since continued to join the Wokingham branch at Virginia Water. The connexion with Woking was completed in 1885. The road from London to Windsor runs through the town, and a bridge connects the town, which lies nearly a mile from the actual banks of the river, with Shepperton in Middlesex.

There was no bridge at Chertsey in 1300,[3] when a ferry was the only means of conveyance. There was a bridge under Elizabeth, which was out of repair. This wooden bridge, kept up by the counties of Middlesex and Surrey, was badly out of repair in 1780, when the stone bridge was built. The bridges over the branches of the Water of Redwynde, as it was called, the stream which flows from Virginia Water, and over the water-course which left the Thames near Penton Hook and rejoined it near Chertsey, seem to have been originally built or repaired by the abbey. Abbot John Rutherwyk rebuilt the bridge at Steventon End, near the end of Guildford Street, in the time of Edward II,[4] but this bridge fell into disrepair and was rebuilt under Henry IV by the town with the king's licence, the king insisting that it should be called his bridge.[5]

A market was granted to the abbey in Chertsey by Henry I,[6] and was confirmed in 1249[7] and in 1281.[8] It was held on Mondays. Whether this market

lapsed at or before the Dissolution is unknown. But in 1599 Elizabeth granted by charter a market on Wednesdays, and a fair, over and above any existing fair, with a parcel of ground for the building of a market-house. The charter was to twenty-one persons, their heirs and assigns, but the profits of the tolls were to go to the poor of Chertsey.[9] A market-house of the usual type, supported on pillars, was accordingly built near the south-east angle of the churchyard. In 1809 it was demolished, and in 1810 a new market-house was built in Bridge Street.

Henry I also granted the abbot a three days' fair to be held at Chertsey every year at the festival of St. Peter in Chains.[10] A second grant for a three days' fair to be held annually on the vigil, feast, and morrow of the Exaltation of the Cross was made to the abbot in 1249.[11] This fair, now held on 25 September instead of the 14th, is called the Onion Fair.[12]

Yet another grant of a three days' fair, to be held at Ascension-tide, was made to the abbot and convent in 1281.[13] In 1440 they also received a grant for a fair to be held on St. Anne's Hill alias Mount Eldebury in Chertsey on St. Anne's Day,[14] 26 July. This is still continued in Chertsey on 6 August since the change of style.

Queen Elizabeth's charter (vide supra) established a fair on the first Monday and Tuesday in Lent, which still continues to be held on the Monday. Another fair on 14 May represents one held on 3 May, old style.[15]

In 1642 a petition was made by the gentry that a Mr. Boden might preach at Chertsey on market-days and on Sundays when the minister of the parish did not do so.[16] The business used to be considerable in agricultural produce and cattle. The modern industries of the parish are agriculture, much market gardening, and brick-making.

The Benedictine Abbey created Chertsey, which was a marshy island, inclosed by the Thames and the streams leaving and joining it, till the monks embanked the water. On higher ground in the outlying parts of the parish neolithic flints have been found, in the Charterhouse Museum is a fine polished celt, and on St. Anne's Hill a bronze celt has been found.[17] About three-quarters of a mile from Chertsey, on the right-hand side of the road to Staines, is a small square inclosure with very low but distinctly marked banks, and an area of under two acres. At Ham, close to the eastern border of Chertsey, is a large moated inclosure, nearly square. The house now inside it is not very old. In Addlestone, near New Haw Lock, on the Wey, is an old farm called Moated Farm, with a moat. This is also square ; it is not so large as Ham. There was an entrenchment on St. Anne's Hill. Manning[18] says ' there were visible traces of a camp.' There are certainly marks that the upper part of the hill has been artificially scarped and the earth thrown outwards, forming in places a counter-scarp. On the left-hand side of the

[1] Gent. Mag. 1791, p. 199.
[2] Loc. Govt. Bd. Order no. 31528.
[3] Wardrobe Accts. 28 Edw. I (Soc. Antiq.), p. 83.
[4] Lansd. MSS. 435, fol. 177b.
[5] Pat. 11 Hen. IV, pt. ii, m. 19.
[6] Harl. Chart. 58, H, 37.
[7] Ibid. 58, I, 8.
[8] Ibid. 58, I, 81.
[9] Charter in private hands. See Manning and Bray, Hist. of Surr. iii, 208 ; Pat. 41 Eliz. pt. x, m. 39.
[10] Cott. MS. Vitell. A. xiii, fol. 55.
[11] Ibid. fol. 64 ; Cal. Chart. 1226–57, p. 344.
[12] The tolls are now taken by the owner of the site of the abbey.
[13] Cal. Chart. 1257–1300, p. 260.
[14] Chart. R. 18 Hen. VI, no. 31.
[15] Aubrey (op. cit. iii, 172) says there was a fair on the Exaltation of the Cross, 3 May ; but this is the Invention of the Cross. The date of the Exaltation is 14 Sept., now represented by the fair on 25 September. Aubrey mentioned this as 'a fortnight before Michaelmas.'
[16] Hist. MSS. Com. Rep. App. v, p. 260.
[17] Arch. Journ. xxviii, 242.
[18] Manning and Bray, op. cit. iii, 226.

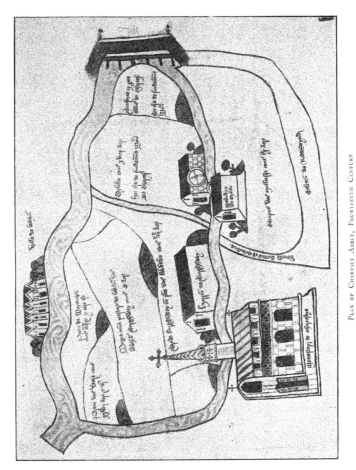

PLAN OF CHERTSEY ABBEY, FOURTEENTH CENTURY

public path leading down the north side of the hill it is obvious. The name, moreover, of the hill was Elde-bury Hill. Under this name a chapel of St. Anne was built upon it (*vide infra*).

The house St. Anne's Hill, whether built on the site of the chapel or not (*vide infra*), is famous as the home of Charles James Fox. It was copyhold of the manor of Chertsey Beomond. Almners Barns south of the hill and Monk's Grove east of it were both possessions of the abbey, the former the endowment of the Almoner. It is now the residence of Major-General Berkeley. St. Anne's is now the residence of the Hon. Stephen Powys, Monk's Grove of Mr. J. St. Foyne Fair. William Eldridge was a local bell-founder, and a house a few yards to the north of the church on the opposite side of the street is stated to have moulds in the cellars which he used for his foundry, and his family also lived there. Docket Point was the seat of the late Rt. Hon. Sir Charles W. Dilke, bart., M.P.

In 1800 an Act was passed for inclosing land in the manors of Walton-on-Thames and Walton Leigh, which included 565 acres of waste in the parish of Chertsey. Of this 60 acres were left for the use of the commoners. The award was dated 18 December 1804.[19] In 1808 another Act was passed for the inclosure of waste and common fields in the manor of Chertsey Beomond.[20] By statute 14 George III, cap. 114, there was an inclosure of common fields in the manor of Laleham lying in Chertsey in Surrey, but the meadow called Laleham Borough was not inclosed, and was specially excepted in the Act of 1808.

A church-room was built in 1897 as a memorial of the Diamond Jubilee. St. Anne's Mission Hall was presented by Mr. Tulk in 1890.

The cemetery is in Eastworth Road, with a mortuary chapel of St. Stephen, consecrated in 1851.

There is reason to believe that a Nonconformist congregation of Chertsey represents a Presbyterian congregation licensed under the Indulgence of 1672.[21] A chapel was built near the back of the Swan Inn in 1725, which was enlarged in 1823. A new chapel was built in 1876, and the body is now Congregational, not Presbyterian.[22] The Wesleyan chapel was built in 1863, and renovated in 1897. There are also Baptist and Primitive Methodist chapels.

The School of Handicrafts in Eastworth Road was built by Mr. T. Hawksley, M.D., in 1885, and endowed by him also at a total cost of £25,000 for the elementary and industrial training of boys. There are about 100 boys there.

Sir William Perkins by deed in 1725 founded a school for the education and clothing of twenty-five poor boys and twenty-five poor girls. The value of the property left having largely increased, a scheme was approved in Chancery in 1819 for rebuilding the school and making it available for the education in all of 250 boys and 150 girls, sixty-five of the former and thirty of the latter being clothed. Thorpe, Egham, and Staines children could be admitted by the trustees if Chertsey children were not excluded. An infants' school was built in 1845 and conveyed to the Perkins Trustees in 1890. The whole schools were rebuilt in 1889–92. They are Church of England schools,

and by the scheme of 1819 the head master was if possible to be a clerk in holy orders.

Longcross is a hamlet of Chertsey, 3¾ miles west of the town. It was made an ecclesiastical district in 1847. The school (Church) was founded in 1847 and enlarged in 1852. The Rev. W. Tringham, vicar, resides at Longcross and is the chief landowner.

Botleys and Lyne, a hamlet of Chertsey, is 2 miles south by west. The school was built in 1895. Botleys Park, the residence of Mr. Henry Gosling, Almners Barns, now called Almners, mentioned above, Foxhills, the seat of Sir Charles Rivers Wilson, and Fan Court, the seat of Sir Edward D. Stern, are in this district.

Ottershaw and Brox is an ecclesiastical district; the schools (Church) were built in 1870.

There are in the district three homes of the Ministering Children's League, for the rescue of destitute children, established by the Countess of Meath in 1888, 1890, and 1895 respectively. There is another home for children established in 1884 by Mrs. Goldingham of Anningsley Park, in memory of her husband. Messrs. Fletcher have extensive nursery grounds here.

Ottershaw Park is the seat of Mr. Lawrence James Baker, J.P.; the present house was built by Sir Thomas Sewell, Master of the Rolls. Anningsley Park is the seat of Mrs. Goldingham. It formerly belonged to Mr. Thomas Day, the once well-known author of *Sandford and Merton*. Ottermead is a seat of the Earl of Meath ; and Queenwood is the seat of Mr. R. H. Otter, J.P.

Addlestone, properly Atlesdon or Atlesford, is an ecclesiastical district which may be considered to have outstripped the original centre of the parish, Chertsey, in importance. This ward contains the largest number of people of the three wards into which the Chertsey Urban District is divided, and the number of new houses shows the growing character of the neighbourhood.

Ongar Hill is the seat of Mr. Henry Cobbett. It once belonged to Admiral Sir Hyde Parker the elder, who died in 1782. Sayes Court was an old house, the property of a family named Moore from the 17th to the end of the 18th century. It became in 1823 the property of Sir Charles Wetherell, Recorder of Bristol, who rebuilt it apparently, or altered it very much.

Another ecclesiastical district of Addlestone, called Woodham, was formed in 1902 on the boundaries of Chertsey and Horsell. A Baptist chapel was built in 1872, and a Wesleyan chapel in 1898. At Woburn Park is the Roman Catholic College of St. George, directed by Josephite Fathers, for the education of the upper and middle classes. There is a chapel, and a farm is attached to the college. It was removed from Croydon to Woburn Park in 1884.

The workhouse of the Chertsey Union is in Addlestone, and was built in 1836–8. The chapel was added in 1868. The Village Hall was built in 1887 by the Addlestone Village Hall Company. The Princess Mary Village Homes at Addlestone were established by the exertions of the late Duchess of Teck (Princess

---

[19] *Blue Bk. Incl. Awards.*
[20] Tithe Commutation Returns at Board of Agric.

[21] *V.C.H. Surr.* ii, 40.
[22] It was endowed by Mr. William White with land at Byfleet in 1752, and

by Mr. Thomas Willatts with £850 in 1837.

Mary of Cambridge) in 1871. They are certified industrial schools for female children of prisoners, or children otherwise in a destitute or dangerous position. They are conducted on the separate homes system, and are supported by voluntary contributions, with a Treasury allowance for children committed under the Industrial Schools Act. The village schools are St. Paul's (Church), built 1841, enlarged 1851 and 1885, for girls and infants. A boys' school was added in 1901. New Ham School was built in 1874. St. Augustine's School (Church) for infants was built in 1882, and Chapel Park (Church) in 1896.

CHERTSEY or *CHERTSEY BEO-MANORS MOND* was included in the original endowment made to the Abbey of St. Peter, Chertsey, by Frithwald, *subregulus* of Surrey, between the years 666 and 675.[33] The name appears in the charter as ' Cirotisege ' or ' Cerotesege '—that is, the island of Cirotis. The boundaries included the lands of Chertsey and Thorpe, and were as follows :—first from the mouth of the Wey along the Wey to Weybridge, thence within the old mill - stream midward of the stream to the old Herestraet (military way),

CHERTSEY ABBEY.
Party or and argent St. Paul's sword argent with its hilt or crossed with St. Peter's keys gules and azure.

along this to Woburn Bridge and along the stream to the great willow and to the pool above Crockford, from there to an alder tree, thence to the ' wertwallen,' to the Herestraet and along to the ' Curtenstapele,' from there along the street to the Horethorn, thence to the eccan trene (oak tree), to the three barrows, from the three barrows to 'sihtran,' to Merchebrook, to a torrent called Exlaepe, to the old maple tree, to the three other trees, along Depebrok straight to ' Wealegate.' Thence to Shirenpole, to Fullbrok, to the black willow and to ' Weales buthe ' along the Thames to the other side of the town called Mixtenham, thence by water between an island called Bury and Mixtenham by water to Nete Island, from there along the Thames round Oxlake, along the Thames to Buresburgh, and so along the Thames to the Isle of Hamme, along the river northward and midward along the Thames to the mouth of the Wey.[34] King Alfred, confirming this grant to the abbey, also set forth the boundaries of Chertsey, which differ slightly from those laid down by Frithwald, with separate boundaries for Egham and Chobham, and a reference to the heath of Geoffrey de Croix.[35]

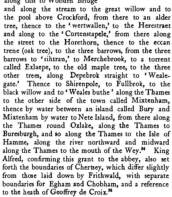

The charter of Frithwald also refers to eight islands, both large and small, which belonged to Chertsey and Thorpe, and to ' seven instruments, suitable for catching fish and keeping them, called weares,' all lying between Wealeshuthe and the mouth of the Wey.

Confirmation of this charter was made by Alfred, Edward the Confessor, and William the Conqueror,[36] and succeeding kings of England and popes confirmed this grant to the abbey.[37] At the time of the Domesday Survey Chertsey was held by the abbey as a manor and rated at 5 hides ; of these Richard Sturmid held 2½ under King William.[38] The abbey, however, claimed him as a tenant, and this claim was probably allowed, as he does not appear among the tenants in chief.[39]

The manor, known from about the 14th century by the name of ' Chertsey-Beomond '[30] as well as by the simpler form of ' Chertsey,' remained in the possession of the monastery until 1537,[31] when, upon the surrender of the latter, the abbot conveyed its lands to the king. The manor of Chertsey was leased in 1550 to Sir William FitzWilliam for thirty years.[32] He died before 1569, when the lease was extended for twenty-one years to his widow Joan.[33] Upon her death in 1574 the manor reverted to the Crown. James I granted it to his eldest son, Henry Prince of Wales,[34] after whose death Sir Francis Bacon and others held it in trust for Charles Prince of Wales for ninety-nine years, the term beginning in 1617.[35] Charles, when king, granted the manor to his queen, Henrietta Maria.[36] During the Commonwealth the manor of Chertsey was sold, as Crown land, to William Aspinall.[37] The sale included a wood called Birchwood, whereof 292 trees were reserved for the use of the navy. Returning to the Crown at the Restoration, it was granted by Charles II, for the remainder of the term of ninety-nine years fixed in 1617, to Denzil, Lord Holles, and others in trust for Queen Catherine of Braganza for life and afterwards in trust for the king and his successors.[38] In 1676, four years after this grant, the manor was granted, for forty-one years, to Sir Gilbert Talbot and Sir Peter Wicke.[39] The manor remained in the Crown throughout the 18th century. In 1779 a thirty-one years' lease was granted to the Duke of Bridgewater, who died in 1803.[40] According to Brayley, writing in 1841, the last tenant under the Crown was Frederick, Duke of York, who died in 1827, and in the following year the manor with other Crown lands was sold by the Crown for £3,330 to a Mr. Allison, who disposed of it to James Goren. The latter became bankrupt in 1834, and the manor was sold by auction to Mr. — Cutts of Essex.[41]

[33] Birch, *Cart. Sax.* i, 55–6.
[34] Ibid. ; Cott. MS. Vitell. A. xiii.
[35] Ibid. But Geoffrey de Croix was living at the time of the *Testa de Nevill* ; the reference to him therefore, the ascription of the date of 727 to a charter confirmed by Wulfhere of Mercia who died in 675, the witness by Humfrith, Bishop of Winchester, who became bishop in 744, of charters of 673 and 727, the reference in the boundaries to the Park Gate, and the Park Hedge of Windsor Park, make it impossible to accept the details of these early charters as worth much except for 13th-century matters. The Surrey Archaeological

Society have given a detailed account of these boundaries with various etymological explanations, coupled with local information concerning the places or landmarks in Chertsey which may coincide with those mentioned in the ancient charter. *Surr. Arch. Coll.* i, 80 et seq.
[36] Birch, *Cart. Sax.* ii, 203 ; *Cart. Antiq.* D. 9, 11.
[37] *Cart. Antiq.* D. 15, 17, 18, 23 ; Cott. MS. Vitell. A. xiii.
[30] *V.C.H. Surr.* i, 308.
[31] H. E. Malden, *Hist. of Surr.* 68.
[60] *Cal. Chart.* 1257–1300, p. 305, vide Beomond.
[61] *Pope Nich. Tax.* (Rec. Com.), 206 ;

Cal. Close, 1346–49, p. 134 ; *Valor Eccl.* (Rec. Com.), ii, 56 ; Lansd. MS. 434; Exch. K.R. Misc. Bks. 25 ; Feet of F. Div. Co. Trin.29 Hen. VIII ; Ct. of Aug. Surr. 54.
[32] *Acts of the P.C.* 1549–50, p. 415 ; Pat. 12 Eliz. pt. viii, m. 7. [30] Ibid.
[34] Pat. 8 Jas. I, pt. xli, no. 2.
[35] Exch. L.T.R. Orig. R. 14 Jas. I, pt. iv, no. 126.
[36] *Cal. S.P. Dom.* 1640–1, p. 552; Ct. R. (P.R.O.), bdle. 204, nos. 40, 52, 53.
[37] Close, 1650, pt. lvii, no. 24.
[38] Pat. 24 Chas. II, pt. ix, m. 1.
[39] Ibid. 28 Chas. II, pt. v, m. 11.
[40] Manning and Bray, op. cit. iii, 222.
[41] E. W. Brayley, *Hist. of Surr.* iii, 189.

Mr. H. E. Paine at present holds the manor, and the house is the seat of Mrs. Hawksley.

The Abbot and convent of Chertsey had full jurisdiction in Chertsey, as in all their lands.[42] William I, in confirming these privileges, also granted them 'freedom of court' in all their lands, the right of keeping dogs, taking foxes, hares, pheasants, &c., and of using their own woods for whatever purpose they chose, without hindrance from the royal foresters.[43] Henry I granted the abbot warren in all his lands, and forbade anyone to hunt there without the abbot's permission on pain of a fine of £10.[44]

The Domesday Survey records the existence of a forge at Chertsey which served the abbey, and also of a mill.[45] Gilbert Fitz Ralph held the latter of the abbey in 1197.[46] Water-mills known as the Oxlake or Okelake mills in Chertsey, appear to have been in existence at an early date. They belonged to the abbey and are marked in a chart of the abbey and its lands which is found in the ledger book of the monastery.[47] In 1535 these mills were valued at £10 13s. 4d.[48] Surrendered with the abbey, they were granted in 1550 to Sir William Fitz William,[49] together with the site of the abbey (q.v.), with which property they afterwards descended. This property also included the right of free fishery in water called the Bargewater at Chertsey, which had belonged to the monastery.[50]

A life-grant of the ferry of Redewynd or Chertsey ferry was made, in 1340, to William de Altecar, yeoman of the chamber.[51] A similar grant, including barge, boat, and ferry fees, was afterwards made to John Palmer, and in 1395 to Thomas Armner, both Gentlemen of the Chamber.[52]

Early rents and services due to the abbot and convent from tenants in Chertsey include a rent of 4s. 8d. due from two shops in Chertsey in 1271.[53]

Weirs, as instruments for catching fish, are alleged to have existed in the river at Chertsey as early as the 7th century.[54] In 1325 the abbot and convent were permitted to construct a weir there.[55]

There was a gaol, belonging to the abbey, at Chertsey in 1297.[56] In 1325 it was shown that, owing to the fact that there was no coroner in Godley Hundred, and that the two coroners of the county would not come as far as Chertsey to hear appeals and do the office of coroner, the prisoners of Chertsey gaol either died in gaol, or on their removal to Guildford gaol for trial were frequently rescued by their friends, wherefore many criminals escaped punishment. In consequence of this, a coroner was appointed for Godley Hundred.[57]

A survey of the manor of Chertsey made in 1627 mentions as common fields or pastures lands called Wheatworth, Wentworth, Adlesdon Moor, and Chertsey Mead.[58] The Parliamentary Survey of 1650 includes Marleheath, Childsey Common, and New Lodge Heath as common lands. Court rolls in the 17th century mention, as tithings of Chertsey, Addlesdon, Ham, Lolworth, and Rookbury.[59] The two latter were known by the alternate names of Hardwick and Lyne.[60]

The abbot and convent were responsible for the repair of Chertsey Bridge over the Thames.[61] In 1582, however, it was decided that the burden of repair could not fall on the queen, then lady of the manor.[62] In 1630 the inhabitants of Chertsey petitioned for the repair of Chertsey Bridge. It was deemed unfit to raise money by collection, and a warrant for sale of trees was applied for. The sum to be raised was £555, and it was suggested that £350 could be raised by sale of trees in Alice Holt, near Farnham, and of trees to be used for piles, &c., in parks near Chertsey.[63]

In the 17th century mention is made of timber wharves at Chertsey, owned in 1651 by Sir George Ayscue. Compensation for damage done to them was granted him in that year, at the petition of his wife, he himself being absent in command of the fleet which had sailed for the Barbados.[64] Other records refer to a rabbit-warren on St. Anne's Hill, otherwise Eldebury Hill, in Chertsey, which belonged to the monastery and was granted to Sir William Fitz William in 1550,[65] and sold during the Commonwealth to George Vincent.

The king's stables at Chertsey are mentioned in 1550, when certain meadows there were converted to the king's use 'for provisions of his stables for lack whereof he susteigneth an intolerable charge';[66] in 1617, 99 loads of hay and 68½ qrs. of oats were due from the tenant of the manor of Chertsey for the king's horses and for the deer in Windsor Park.[67] A letter written by Sir Philip Draycott in 1514 describes a royal hunt which took place in the 'meads under Chertsey.'[68]

After the surrender of the abbey in 1537 the site of the monastery remained in the Crown until 1553, when Edward VI granted it to Sir William Fitz William, his wife, and heirs, for ever.[69] The grantee conveyed it to his wife and daughter ; the latter held it at her death in 1564, after which date her mother Joan received all profits until she died in 1574.[70] In 1602 Matthew Browne, son and heir of the daughter Mabel who had married Thomas Browne,[71] conveyed the site of the abbey to John Hammond,[72] afterwards physician to James I ; a formal grant was made by the Crown in 1610.[73] Of this estate Hammond settled certain lands and 'a messuage next the gates of the late Abbey of Chertsey, in which Edward Carleton [74] then lived,' on his wife Mary for life, and afterwards

[42] See the charters quoted above.
[43] Cart. Antiq. O.O. 1 ; Cott. MS. Vitell. A. xiii, fol. 51b, 54.
[44] Cart. Antiq. O.O. 3, 4 ; Cott. MS. Vitell. A. xiii, fol. 56b.
[45] V.C.H. Surr. i, 308.
[46] Feet of F. Surr. East. 9 Ric. I.
[47] Exch. K.R. Misc. Bks. 25 ; Exch. Dep. 30 & 31 Eliz. Mich. 25.
[48] Valor Eccl. (Rec. Com.), ii, 56.
[49] Pat. 12 Eliz. pt. viii, m. 7.
[50] Ibid.
[51] Cal. Pat. 1338-40, p. 468.
[52] Ibid. 1391-6, p. 584 ; 1399-1401, p. 108.

[53] Feet. of F. Surr. Mich. 56 Hen. III.
[54] Birch, Cart. Sax. i, 64.
[55] Inq. a.q.d. file 183, m. 9.
[56] Cal. Pat. 1292-1301, p. 320 ; ibid. 1381-5, pp. 466, 532.
[57] Lansd. MS. 435, fol. 121.
[58] Rentals and Surv. (P.R.O.), R. 18, 3 Chas. I.
[59] Ct. R. (P.R.O.), bdle. 204, no. 53.
[60] Manning and Bray, op. cit. iii, 220.
[61] Vide supra.
[62] Hist. MSS. Com. Rep. vii, App. i, 637a.
[63] Cal. S.P. Dom. 1629-31, p. 454.

[64] Hist. MSS. Com. Rep. xiii, App. i, 574 ; Cal. S.P. Dom. 1639, p. 406.
[65] Pat. 12 Eliz. pt. viii, m. 7.
[66] Acts of the P.C. 1550-2, p. 56.
[67] Exch L.T.R. Orig. R. 14 Jas. I. pt. iv, rot. 126.
[68] L. and P. Hen. VIII, i, 873.
[69] Pat. 7 Edw. VI, pt. ii, m. 22.
[70] Chan. Inq. p.m. (Ser. 2), clxx, 5 ; Pat. 12 Eliz. pt. viii, m. 7.
[71] Chan. Inq. p.m. (Ser. 2), clxx, 5.
[72] Ibid. Misc. file 522, pt. xvii, no. 3.
[73] Pat. 7 Jas. I, pt. xix, m. 35.
[74] He died in 1663 and was buried at Chertsey.

for life on a younger son, Henry, later an eminent divine and scholar, who died in 1660.[74] The eldest son, Robert, died seised of the site of the abbey in 1623,[75] and it passed to his son John Hammond, who died in 1643 leaving a son Robert.[77]

In 1681 James Hayes and Griselda his wife conveyed the site of the monastery to Edward Read,[78] from whom it passed in 1685 to John Hussey.[79] At the close of the century the site appears to have been in the possession of Sir Nicholas Wayte, who built a house out of the abbey ruins called the Abbey House, a 'beautiful seat . . . adorned with pleasant gardens.'[80] His daughter, who married — Halsey, inherited the bulk of Sir Nicholas's property,[81] and was in possession of one-third of this estate in 1723.[82] She apparently sold it to Robert Hinde before 1734,[83] in which year he died and was buried at Chertsey. His son Robert Hinde inherited it. He mortgaged it and subsequently sold the property to William Barwell in 1751.[84] It was left by William Barwell's son to one Fuller, who sold the property in lots in 1809.[85] The site of the abbey was bought in 1861 by Mr. Bartrop, the secretary to the Surrey Archaeological Society. Among the appurtenances of the site of the abbey which descended with it were the watermills known as the Oxlake or Okelake mills and a small river or brook known as the Abbey River or the Bargewater.

Of the abbey[86] buildings only small fragments remain; a large barn or granary, the west end of which is intact, the rest much repaired, is probably part of the outbuildings. Opposite to it a wall contains early work and part of a blocked arch of the 12th or 13th century. The church and main part of the buildings had been pulled down before James I in 1610 granted the site to Dr. John Hammond. Sir Nicholas Wayte built a house out of the abbey ruins called the Abbey House, as mentioned above.[87]

The site of the church and other buildings has been partially excavated by the Surrey Archaeological Society and private enterprise,[87a] and a large number of flooring tiles of great merit have been removed, most of them to the Royal Architectural Museum, Tufton Street, Westminster, a few to the Surrey Archaeological Museum, Guildford.

Queen Elizabeth granted the site of the manor-house of Chertsey Beomond for twenty-one years to Thomas Holte some time before 1580, in which year an extension of thirty-one years was granted him, to begin at the expiration of the previous lease.[88] In 1606 John Hammond received a grant of the same for thirty-one years, dating from the termination of the leases on which Thomas Holte held it.[89] The last of these leases expired in 1631, when John son of Robert Hammond, and grandson of the original grantee, entered into

possession.[90] He married Margaret daughter of Sir Robert Rich, and died in 1643, leaving as heir his son Robert.[91] In the Parliamentary Survey of 1650, however Elizabeth, the mother of John Hammond was stated to be the tenant of the messuage and lands called Chertsey Beomond,[92] the lease having still twelve years to run. In this survey the manor-house is described as 'an old house part brick, part wood, covered with tiles and consisting of a hall, parlor, kitchen, buttery, brewhouse, milkhouse, and larder below staires and of 7 rooms above staires.' Among the stock 'as well alive as dead' which rightfully belonged to the tenant or farmer of the site of the manor were included '3 horses, 11 oxen, 3 heifers, 1 boore, 3 cows, 16 young hogs, 12 qrs. of wheat, 20 qrs. of barley, 10 qrs. of draggett, 40 qrs. of oats, 2 ploughs with all furniture, with 2 plough shares, 2 cutters, 3 harrows with front teeth, 1 cart with furniture for 3 horses and 3 leather head-stalls.' After the Restoration the site of the manor appears to have followed the descent of the manor, as no separate trace of it is found. The old manor-house has been evidently rebuilt.

The manor of Beomond had for a short time a separate history from Chertsey. In 1306 Walter of Gloucester and Hawisia his wife were holding the manor of Beomond or Bemond in Chertsey.[93] In 1311–12 Walter died seised of this land held of the abbey of Chertsey.[94] In 1320 Walter his son conveyed land in Chertsey to Master John Walewayn, in trust for the abbey, and Hawisia granted to John Rutherwyk, Abbot of Chertsey, tenements and lands 'formerly called Gloucester, now known as le Bemond,' which had previously been two holdings belonging to John de Chertsey and William Scot respectively.[95] In a cartulary of Chertsey Abbey, of the time of Edward III, mention is made of a holding called 'Gloucester,' apparently a sub-manor of Chertsey, and held with the latter. The name of Gloucester gave way to that of Bemond.[96] The manor of Bemond appears to have been united with that of Chertsey soon afterwards, the two being henceforth known as the manor of Chertsey or Chertsey-Beomond.

Before its alienation by Hawisia the tenement had been held of the abbot and convent at a rent of 28s. a year, a three-weekly suit at the abbot's hundred court, and for certain customary services.[97]

In 1319 John de Bottele of Chertsey, holding of the abbot and convent of Chertsey, made an exchange with them of lands in Chertsey,[98] and it is probable that the lands so held were those which became known later as BOTLEY'S Manor. According to Manning and Bray, John Manory owned the lands in the 15th century, and his son conveyed them in

---

74 Chan. Inq. p.m. (Ser. 2), cccxc, 145, 21 Jas. I; ibid. Misc. file 522, pt. xvii, no. 3.

76 Ibid. cccxcix, 143.

77 Ibid. Misc. loc. cit.

78 Feet of F. Surr. Trin. 33 Chas. II.

79 Ibid. Trin. 1 Jas. II.

80 Add. MS. 6167, fol. 38. Manning, perhaps misunderstanding Aubrey, says that in 1673 the site belonged to Sir Nicholas Carew, from whom it passed to the Orbys, and that Sir Charles Orby sold it to Sir Nicholas Wayte; of this account there appears to be no documentary evidence save that Sir Charles Orby held the

advowson; Aubrey (op. cit. iii, 174) says that 'the house is now (1673) in the possession of Sir Nicholas Carew.' Sir Nicholas Wayte was apparently in the East Indies, and Carew, Master of the Buckhounds, may have been in temporary possession of a house nearer Windsor than Beddington, his own seat.

81 Le Neve, Ped. of Knights, 467.

82 Feet of F. Surr. Hil. 9 Geo. I.

83 Close, 25 Geo. III, pt. iii, no. 15.

84 Ibid.

85 Manning and Bray, op. cit. iii, 219.

86 For the history of the abbey see V.C.H. Surr. ii, 55.

87 Add. MS. 6171, fol. 38.

87a Surr. Arch. Coll. i, 97.

88 Pat. 22 Eliz. pt. x, m. 31.

89 Cal. S.P. Dom. 1603–10, p. 281.

90 Parl. Surv. Surr. 1650, no. 9.

91 Chan. Inq. p.m. Misc. file 522, pt. xvii, no. 3.   92 See note 90.

93 Feet of F. Surr. 34 Edw. I, no. 129 Exch. K.R. Misc. Bks. 25, fol. 65b.

94 Chan. Inq. p.m. 5 Edw. II, no. 66.

95 Exch. K.R. Misc. Bks. 25, fol. 66, 1806; Pat. 17 Edw. II, pt. iv, no. 19.

96 Lansd. MS. 434.

97 Inq. a.q.d. file 165, no. 11.

98 Ibid. file 135, no. 6, 12 Edw. II.

1505 to Henry Wykes under the name of Botlese Park.[99] Sir Roger Chomeley was in possession of Botley's before 1541, in which year he granted the estate, then for the first time called a manor, to the king, in exchange for other lands.[100] Leases of the manor were made to Anne, Duchess of Somerset, in 1555[101] and to James Harden in 1599.[102] It was granted in 1610 to George Salter and John Williams,[103] who conveyed it in the same year to William Garwaie and his heirs.[104] The manor was sold by William Garwaie to John Hammond and his heirs for ever.[105] On the marriage of Robert Hammond son of John with Elizabeth Knollis the manor was settled on Robert,[106] whose son John Hammond died seised of it in 1643, leaving Robert his son as heir.[107] The manor afterwards passed to the Hall family. Samuel Hall 'of Botleys' died in 1707.[108] Later in the 18th century Mrs. Pleasance Hall held the estate for life, but in 1763, having purchased the reversion of her son, she sold it to Joseph Mawbey, afterwards Sir Joseph Mawbey, who built the present house.[109] His son succeeded him and died in 1817 leaving two daughters, one of whom had married John Ivett Briscoe and inherited the estate.[110] They sold it, however, in 1822 to David Hall, who conveyed it to John Beecles Hyndman, from whom it passed to Robert Gosling.[111] The estate known as Botley's Park is now the property of Mr. Hubert Gosling, J.P.

GOSLING. *Gules a cheveron between three crescents or and on the cheveron a pale ermine between two squirrels sitting back to back and cracking nuts with a like squirrel on the pale.*

Among the boundaries of Chertsey set forth in 673 is mentioned the isle of *HAM* or Hamenege,[112] which is later represented by Ham Moor and Ham Farm,[113] and which was known from the 12th to the 18th century as the manor of Ham. The manor was ancient demesne until the reign of Henry I,[114] who granted it to the Abbot of Chertsey. In 1197 Martin, Abbot of Chertsey, granted the manor to William de Hamme and his heirs,[115] and Robert de Hamme was lord of the manor in 1307.[116] Thomas de Saunterre, apparently acting as trustee for purposes of a settlement, enfeoffed John de Hamme and Alina of the 'manor of Hamme next Chertsey,' and land in Stanore.[117] John de Hamme died seised of the manor in 1319–20, leaving his brother Robert as heir.[118] Thomas de Hamme, probably a member of the same family, held the manor about 1323, when he

received licence to have divine service in his oratory at Ham.[119] He appears to have been still living in Chertsey in 1328.[120] It is not apparent how the manor passed from Thomas de Hamme to the Fitz Johns, but it was probably by marriage of heiresses. It is at least evident that in 1372 Robert Danhurst and Agnes his wife, possibly the widow of a son of Thomas de Hamme, conveyed all that they held in the manor of Hamme, their share being a life-interest held in the right of Agnes, to William Fitz John and Agnes his wife and the heirs of this second Agnes.[121] A further settlement of the manor on the Fitz Johns was made in 1381.[122] The manor descended to Nicholas[123] son and heir of William Fitz John, to Nicholas's son John and grandson Henry, about whose succession some difficulty arose, a claim to the manor being made in 1466 by John Goryng and John Sturnyn, who said they had been enfeoffed of it by John Fitz John, father of Henry.[124] The manor came soon afterwards into the possession of Sir Thomas Seyntleger, who in 1481 received licence to alienate it to the Dean and Canons of the free chapel of St. George's, Windsor,[125] for the support of a chantry, and it remained with the chapter when the chantry was dissolved.[126] Occasional leases of it were made during the 17th and 18th centuries, when it was known under various names—the manor of Ham or Ham Court or Ham Farm or Ham Haw Farm. It was leased in 1614 to Dr. Henry Hammond, the king's physician,[127] who held Chertsey (q.v.), and had also a life grant of the manor of Botleys. Later, Sir George Askew and Sir Ralph Clare held leases.[128]

DEAN AND CANONS OF ST. GEORGE'S, WINDSOR. *Argent a cross gules.*

In 1731 it was advertised for sale as held by the late Robert Douglas, on a lease from the Dean and Canons of Windsor, and was purchased by the second Earl of Portmore,[129] whose property in Weybridge it adjoined.[130] It is now held as a farm, on a lease from the dean and canons by Mr. H. F. Locke King, J.P.

The manor of *HARDWICK* was among the possessions of the abbey of Chertsey in this parish; the first reference to it occurs in 1430, when the manor, held by the abbey, was assigned to William Frowyk to farm.[131] From a later lease it would seem that this manor was usually demised to farm by the abbot, who reserved to himself the profits of leets and courts held

[99] Manning and Bray, op. cit. iii, 222; (quoting from information received).
[100] Pat. 32 Hen. VIII, pt. vii, m. 2.
[101] Ibid. 2 & 3 Phil. and Mary, pt. viii, m. 22.
[102] Ibid. 32 Eliz. pt. x, m. 16.
[103] Ibid. 7 Jas. I, pt. xvi, no. 1.
[104] Close, 7 Jas. I, pt. xxix.
[105] Ibid. 9 Jas. I, pt. ii, m. 8.
[106] Chan. Inq. p.m. Misc. 19 Chas. I, pt. xvii, no. 8; Feet of F. Surr. Mich. 14 Jas. I.
[107] Chan. Inq. p.m. Misc. 19 Chas. I, pt. xvii, no. 3.
[108] Add. MS. 6171, p. 65.
[109] Manning and Bray, op. cit. iii, p. 222; G.E.C. Complete Baronetage, v, 135.

[110] Ibid. v, 135; Brayley, op. cit. ii, 222; Recov. R. East. 3 Geo. IV, rot. 147.
[111] Ibid. 149; Brayley, op. cit. ii, 222.
[112] Birch. Cart. Sax. i, 56.
[113] V.C.H. Surr. i, 308 note.
[114] See, however, V.C.H. Surr. i, 308.
[115] Cott. MS. Vitell. A. xiii, fol. 55, 67 d.; Add. MS. 6167, fol. 96 b; Assize R. 877, m. 59; 878, m. 37.
[116] Exch. K.R. Misc. Bks. 25, fol. 64.
[117] Add. MS. 6167, fol. 96b; Assize R. 877, m. 59.
[118] Feet of F. Surr. Trin. 1 Edw. II.
[119] Chan. Inq. p.m. 13 Edw. II, no. 14.
[120] Egerton MS. 2032, fol. 23 d., 52 d.
[121] Cal. Pat. 1327–30, p. 336.
[122] Feet of F. Surr. 46 Edw. III, no. 89.

[123] Ibid. 5 Ric. II, no. 40.
[124] Wykeham's Reg. (Hants Rec. Soc.), ii, 556; Exch. K.R. Misc. Bks. 25, fol. 556.
[125] De Banco R. Hil. 6 Edw. IV, m. 116.
[126] Pat. 21 Edw. IV, pt. ii, m. 17; Exch. T.R. Misc. Bks. cxiii, fol. 34.
[127] It probably included Ham in Cobham, though separate court rolls for this exist in the hands of the Ecclesiastical Commissioners.
[128] Cal. S.P. Dom. 1611–18, p. 254.
[129] Ibid. 1660–1, p. 247.
[130] Manning and Bray, op. cit. iii, 229.
[131] See Weybridge parish.
[132] Exch. K.R. Misc. Bks. 25, fol. 105, 108.

there, and all other manorial rights, granting only to his tenant 'the other half of waifs and strays in the land of the manor.'[133] These courts would appear to be the courts-leet and views of frankpledge of the manor of Chertsey to which the half-hundred of Godley (q.v.) did suit. The manor of Hardwick has, throughout, followed the descent of the manor of Chertsey (q.v.). During the reign of Charles II the courts of Queen Henrietta Maria were held at Hardwick, as they had been before the Civil War.[134]

The site of the manor of Hardwick at the time of the Dissolution, or shortly after, was in the tenure of William Cooke.[135] It was leased with the manor to Sir William Fitz William in 1550 and afterwards to his widow Joan, who died in 1574.[136] It was again leased, in 1589, to Richard Lilley, this time without the manor,[137] and sold during the Commonwealth to Robert Boscoes or Bowes.[138] Later grants of the manor of Chertsey included both the site and manor of Hardwick.[139]

Land at WOODHAM was granted to Chertsey Abbey by Frithwald, the founder.[140] In 1402 tithes from the 'township' of Woodham were granted as augmentation of the vicarage of Chertsey.[141] Occasional references to lands in Woodham are found in the 14th century, but no one family appears to have held them for any length of time.[142] Symmes, in his collections for Surrey, made in the 17th century, states that Woodham was held as a manor in 1413 by John Erith, Robert Thurbane, and Richard Grene, and by John Brown and others in 1426. According to the same authority John Fagger was lord there in 1482. In 1526 Richard Covert and Robert Darknold, or Dorkenoll, were lords of the manor in the right of their wives, Elizabeth and Joan.[143] Richard Covert's wife was daughter of Richard Wasse.[143a] Robert Darknold relinquished his share in 1531, and Giles Covert, the son of Richard Covert, died seised of the manor in 1557, leaving his brother Richard as heir.[144] Richard Covert conveyed it to John Austin and Thomas Inwode in 1563,[145] possibly in trust for Walter Cresswell, as the latter, when he died in 1596,

COVERT. Gules a fesse ermine between three martlets or.

was seised of the 'manor or farm of Woodham,' which he held of the manor of Pyrford,[146] of which manor Woodham, though parochially in Chertsey, was a tithing. His heir, William Cresswell, by will dated August 1622, bequeathed two-thirds of the manor to his cousin Edward Cresswell, with remainder to the male heirs of another cousin, Richard.[147] The remaining third appears to have become the property of Richard's family immediately on William Cresswell's

death in January 1623, as Elizabeth Collins, daughter of Richard Cresswell, died seised of a third of the manor in 1627, leaving as her heir uncle, Christopher Cresswell.[146] He, as male heir of his brother Richard, had inherited the rest of the manor on Edward Cresswell's death in July 1623.[149] From Christopher the manor descended to his son Richard and to the latter's son Christopher, who possessed it at the beginning of the 18th century.[150] After his death the manor appears to have been split up among female heirs,[161] by whom it was eventually conveyed as a single property in 1714 to Sir John Jennings and his heirs.[162] In 1741 Sir John Jennings's estates were sold under a private Act,[163] and Woodham was ultimately acquired by Lord Onslow and is not now distinguished from the manor of Pyrford (q.v.). Ancient rentals of Woodham Manor were in the custody of Mr. Sibthorp, the steward of Woking and Pyrford Manors, in 1795.[164]

Land called 'Otreshagh,' OTTERSHAW, is mentioned in the charter of King Alfred to the monastery made about 890, in which he gives the boundaries of Chertsey and Thorpe.[165]

The Testa de Nevill states that the 'manor of Otterseye' had been given in alms to the abbey before the Conquest.[166] This is, however, perhaps not the same place as Ottershaw. Ottershaw in its subsequent history is referred to simply as a wood or lands. The possession of Ottershaw by the abbey is doubtful. It appears that in 1270 (vide infra) Nicholas de Croix was one of the holders, and the early charter of Chertsey, re-edited in the 13th century, seems to exclude the holding of Geoffrey de Croix, alive at the date of Testa de Nevill, from the lands granted to Chertsey. In the 14th century it appears to have been held of the king in chief.

Tithes from Ottershaw were due to the Abbot of Chertsey and formed the subject of a dispute in 1270 between the abbot and the rector of Walton, who claimed a portion.[167] The dispute, which was eventually terminated in favour of the abbot, was renewed in 1279, when Ottershaw was the property of the Earl of Hereford and Nicholas de Cruce.[168] In 1301 Walter de Langton, Bishop of Coventry and Lichfield, received licence to assart 300 acres of his wood of Ottershaw which he held for life by demise of Humphrey de Bohun, sometime Earl of Hereford and Essex.[169]

The latter conveyed part of Ottershaw, a messuage, 40 acres of land, &c., to Geoffrey de Parys, whose kinsman and heir, John Aylet, conveyed them to John de Tighele, from whom William Ingelard acquired them. From his heir Edward atte Brugg they passed to Robert Dachet and William his son, who were arraigned for entering into possession without licence from the king. Pardon and restitution of the estates were, however, granted them in 1337.[160]

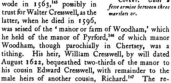

[133] Add. Chart. no. 23416, 21 Hen. VIII.
[134] Ct. R. (P.R.O.), bdle. 204, no. 52, 53.
[135] Pat. 12 Eliz. pt. viii, m. 7.
[136] Ibid. (Acts of the P.C. 1549-50, p. 415.
[137] Pat. 32 Eliz. pt. viii, m. 13.
[138] Close, 1650, pt. iv, no. 4.
[139] Pat. 24 Chas. II, pt. ix, m. 1; ibid. 28 Chas. II, pt. v, m. 11.
[140] Birch, Cart. Sax. i, 55, 56.
[141] Exch. K.R. Misc. Bks. 25, fol. 39 d.
[142] Feet of F. Surr. 21 Edw. III, no. 13; ibid. 34 Edw. III, no. 56; ibid. Div. Co. 10 Edw. II, no. 144.

[143] Add. MS. 6167, fol. 101 d.; Feet of F. Surr. East. 21 Hen. VIII.
[143a] Harl. MS. 1561, 356, 36.
[144] Chan. Inq. p.m. (Ser. 2), cxiv, 42.
[145] Feet of F. Surr. East. 5 Eliz.
[146] Chan. Inq. p.m. (Ser. 2), ccli, 148; Exch. T.R. Misc. Bks. 168, fol. 171 et seq.; vide Pyrford.
[147] Chan. Inq. p.m. (Ser. 2),cccxcvii, 93.
[148] Ibid. ccccxxxvi, 20.
[149] Ibid. cccxcvii, 93; Recov. R. Trin. 1 Chas. I.
[160] Add. MS. 6167, fol. 101 d.

[151] Feet of F. Surr. Hil. 9 Anne; East. 13 Anne.
[152] Ibid. Trin. Geo. I.
[153] 14 Geo. II, cap. 5.
[154] Manning and Bray, op. cit. i, 154, and private information from Lord Onslow.
[155] Vide Chertsey.
[156] Testa de Nevill (Rec. Com.), 215.
[157] Exch. K.R. Misc. Bks. 25, fol. 53b.
[158] Ibid. fol. 54.
[159] Inq. a.q.d. 29 Edw. I, file 34, no. 11; Cal. Pat. 1292-1301, p. 575.
[160] Cal. Pat. 1334-8, p. 432.

John Danaster was seised of Ottershaw in the early part of the 16th century, and at his death it passed to his widow Anne, with reversion to their daughter Anne, who married Owen Bray.[161] A complaint was lodged by Owen Bray and his wife against Sir Francis Dawtrey, second husband of Anne, his grandmother, on the ground that he had committed great spoil in their lands; in Ottershaw in particular he had cut down and sold 60 oaks of the value of 10s. each.[162]

The subsequent holders of Ottershaw are not always apparent. Manning, quoting from the title deeds of Edmund Boehm, who held Ottershaw in 1811, states that in the 17th century it belonged to the Roake family of Horsell, who in 1722 conveyed it to Lawrence Porter. He sold it to Thomas Woodford, who also held Stanners in Chobham. Woodford died in 1758, and the property passed from his son to Thomas Sewell, whose son sold it in 1796 to Edmund Boehm.[163] It afterwards became the property of Sir George Wood, and according to Brayley his son sold a portion of the estate, including the house, to Richard Crawshay.[164] Brox, mentioned by Aubrey as a tithing of Chertsey, is at present held with Ottershaw by Captain Sumner and Mr. R. Brettell. Mr. Lawrence J. Baker owns Ottershaw Park.

A tenement called SHRYMPLEMARSHE (Simple Marsh, or Simple Mere) was included among the abbey lands, being valued in the 16th century at 100s.[165] At the surrender of the monastery it was granted to John Prior; in 1550 it was leased to William Fitz William, after whose death it was granted in 1569 to his widow Joan for twenty-one years.[166] It was granted in 1613 to Francis Morrice and Francis Phillips.[167] In 1616 they conveyed it to Richard Tylney.[168] In 1739 John Tylney, afterwards Earl Tylney, whose grandmother was daughter of Mr. Frederick Tylney, sold it to Aaron Franks.[169] He sold it to Mr. Pembroke in 1807, and he to Mr. G. H. Sumner in 1810,[170] of whom Captain Sumner is grandson and heir.

In 1535 land called DEPENHAMS in Chertsey was valued among the possessions of the monastery at £6 13s. 4d.[171] It was conveyed to Henry VIII as a manor by the Abbot of Chertsey in 1537,[172] but no other reference to Depenhams as a manor occurs. It was granted in 1550 on a lease to Sir William Fitz William, being then, or having previously been, in the tenure of William Loksmyth.[173] The grant was extended in 1569 to Joan Fitz William, widow of Sir William, for twenty-one years.[174] In all these transactions Depenhams is referred to as a tenement only. It was granted as a messuage to William Holt and others in 1590,[175] and in the sale of Crown lands during the Commonwealth the 'brewhouse or farmhouse called Depenhams' became the property of Daniel Wyatt.[176] It was apparently included in the grants of Chertsey Manor made by Charles II.[177]

AMPNER'S BARN was also conveyed to the king by the abbot of Chertsey as a manor,[178] but there is no further evidence to show that it had any claim to be such. Tithes from it were due to the rectory of Chertsey.[179] After the surrender of Chertsey monastery it was in the tenure of William Stanlake or Robert Skyte, and was granted with other tenements in Chertsey to Sir William Fitz William, and on his death to Joan his widow in 1569 for twenty-one years.[180] At the sale of Crown land during the Commonwealth J. Bailly purchased Ampner's Barn, described as 'a farm.'[181] The tenement called Tyleholt or Tylecroft, probably identical with the tenement afterwards called le Tyle, was also referred to as a manor in the conveyance from the abbot to the king.[182] When granted to Sir William Fitz William it was in the tenure of Roger Fenne.[183]

A tenement called SAYES was granted to Edward Carleton in 1610, and was sold as Crown land to Samuel Oram during the Commonwealth. David More had a lease of it from the Crown in 1673.[184] Potter's Park, which still exists in Chertsey, is mentioned as early as the time of Henry VI among the boundaries of Godley Hundred.[185] During the reign of James I it was sold to the Crown by Richard Furbench. Charles I in 1634 demised the park to Sir Arthur Mainwaring for twenty-one years. His wife, Dame Gressell, was still in possession in 1650 when a survey was made of the property.[186] In 1661 John Lyne petitioned for a lease of the same park.[187]

The parish church of ST. PETER CHURCHES consists of chancel with north organ bay, a vestry, and south chamber with gallery stair, a nave with north and south aisles, the ends coterminous with the west tower and containing stairs to the galleries which surround three sides of the church.

The church was much rebuilt early in the 19th century, but the chancel and west tower have some 15th-century work remaining; the new work is faced with Heath stone. The east window of the chancel is modern of four lights in 15th-century style. On each side are shallow cinquefoiled image niches of 15th-century date. In the north and south walls are two bays of an arcade, now blocked up, showing pointed arches with a moulded order springing without capitals from square piers with rounded angles. On the two central piers are shallow cinquefoiled niches, like those on either side of the east window.

The chancel arch is contemporary with the side arcades and consists of two moulded orders, with small engaged shafts in the jambs having foliate capitals. The nave is of four bays with square piers carried up to the plaster vaulted ceilings of nave and aisles, and is entirely of modern date. The aisle windows have large dripstones to their labels, carved in a rather theatrical style, and under each are the carvers' names, Coade and Sealy of London, and the date 1806.

161 Chan. Proc.(Ser. 2), bdle. 22, no. 84.
162 Ibid.
163 Manning and Bray, op. cit. iii, 194, 223; Close, 36 Geo. III, pt. iii, m. 25, no. 13.
164 E. W. Brayley, op. cit. ii, 224.
165 Exch. K.R. Misc. Bks. 25; Valor Eccl. (Rec. Com.), ii, 56.
166 Pat. 12 Eliz. pt. viii, m. 7.
167 Ibid. 10 Jas. I, pt. xxii, no. 3.
168 Manning and Bray, op. cit. iii, 229.
169 Close, 12 Geo. II, p. 19, no. 9.

170 Manning and Bray, op. cit. iii, 221.
171 Valor Eccl. (Rec. Com.), ii, 56.
172 Feet of F. Div. Co. Trin. 29 Hen. VIII.
173 Pat. 12 Eliz. pt. viii, m. 7.
174 Ibid.   175 Ibid. 33 Eliz. pt. iv.
176 Particulars for sale of Crown lands, Commonwealth, Aug. Off. Z.z. 4 (3).
177 Pat. 24 Chas. II, pt. ix, m. 1; ibid. 28 Chas. II, pt. v, m. 11.
178 Feet of F. Div. Co. Trin. 29 Hen. VIII.

179 Pat. 3 Eliz. pt. ii.
180 Ibid. 12 Eliz. pt. viii, m. 7.
181 Sale of Crown lands during Commonwealth (Aug. Off.).
182 Feet of F. Div. Co. Trin. 29 Hen. VIII.
183 Pat. 12 Eliz. pt. viii, m. 7.
184 Cal. S.P. Dom. 1673–5, p. 122.
185 Exch. K.R. Misc. Bks. vol. 25, fol. 74.
186 Parl. Surv. no. 22.
187 Cal. of Treas. Bks. 1660–7, p. 41.

The tower arch is of two moulded orders, the inner resting on moulded half-octagonal capitals and shafts, the outer dying into the walls.

The tower is of flint and stone with patched diagonal buttresses. It has a west door, a two-light west window, belfry lights, and a brick parapet, all suggestive of 18th-century work, and appears to have been rebuilt, partly with the old materials.

The early monuments of interest are one brass to Edward Carleton, 1608, and a tablet of the same date to Lawrence Tomson.

The bells are eight in number, the treble, second, and tenor by G. Mears, 1859, the last being a bell of 1670 recast; the third by R. Phelps, 1730; the fourth by Lester and Pack, 1756; the fifth a 15th-century bell from the Wokingham foundry, inscribed, 'Ora Mente Pia Pro Nobis Virgo Maria.' The sixth is by William Eldridge, 1712, and the seventh by Robert Mot, 1588.

The present plate, consisting of two cups, two patens, a flagon, and an almsdish, was given in 1843 to replace a set which was stolen.

The registers date from 1610.

ALL SAINTS' Church, Eastworth Road, is of red brick with Bath-stone facings. It consists of a chancel, nave, and south aisle divided from the nave by an arcade with pointed arches.

CHRIST CHURCH, Longcross, was built c. 1847 by Mr. William Tringham, the principal landowner in Longcross. The church is of brick and stone, with a turret on the south side. The body was lengthened and a chancel added in 1878.

HOLY TRINITY Church, Botleys and Lyne, was built in 1849. It is a small cruciform church of stone, of 13th-century design, with a central tower. Lady Frances Hotham presented the site.

CHRIST CHURCH, Ottershaw and Brox, was built by the late Sir Gilbert Scott, in 14th-century style, of brick and stone, with a tower and spire. The whole cost was borne by Sir T. Edward Colebrooke, bart., who further gave £1,000 towards the endowment. A ring of bells was also given by Mr. William Edward Gibb of Sheerwater Court, in 1885, in memory of his father.

The church of *ST. PAUL*, Addlestone, built in 1838, is of brick with stone dressings, with a tower, the details of which are quite hidden with ivy. The windows are pointed. It was enlarged in 1857 and restored in 1883. The site was given by Mr. G. Holmes Sumner.

The iron church of *ST. AUGUSTINE*, Weybridge Road, was built in 1891.

ALL SAINTS', Woodham, is a picturesque stone church in the middle of the pine woods near the confines of Chertsey and Horsell, built in 1893.

ADVOWSONS A vicarage of Chertsey, with an endowment of £6 13s. 4d., is mentioned in the year 1291.[188] The church belonged to the abbot and convent, and remained in their hands until John Cordrey, the last abbot, gave up his possessions in 1537.[189] The vicarage was formally ordained in 1331;[190] the vicar and his successors were granted the house and certain lands belonging to the vicarage and oblations from the church. He was not required to pay any pension to the abbey, and was entitled to eat in the abbey at the abbey's expense on Rogation days and at Easter.[191] Augmentation of the vicarage was made in 1402, as the provision made for the vicar was found to be inadequate. He was henceforth to receive tithes of the 'townships' of Crockford and Woodham,[192] and, in addition, all tithes from the working artificers and merchandises of the parishioners; tithes of the fishing of the parishioners, unless done in the private waters of the abbey; tithes of milk, butter, cheese, cream, eggs, and pigeons; and half tithes of geese, honey, wax, hemp, apples, pears, onions, garlic, and all things titheable if they grew in the gardens of the parish. Various exceptions to the foregoing were made. The vicar was to pay all synodals, martinals, and tenths to the king for the portion of the vicarage.[193] The rectory and advowson of the vicarage became vested in the Crown in July 1537.[194] In December of the same year the king granted the rectory to the new foundation at Bisham,[195] which, however, was dissolved in six months. It remained in the Crown until 1551, when Edward VI granted it to John Poynet, Bishop of Winchester,[196] who was deprived of his see on the accession of Queen Mary, in whose reign Cardinal Pole appears to have had a grant of this rectory.[197] A lease of it had been held since 1535 by Henry Gyle, who held it under the Abbot of Chertsey and the Bishop of Winchester.[198] The lease, renewed by Mary and Elizabeth,[199] expired in 1587, when Elizabeth granted the rectory to Thomas Horsman for three successive leases of twenty-one years each.[200] Horsman presumably surrendered the leases, as in 1607 James I granted the rectory, including great and small tithes worth £14, to Richard Lydall and others,[201] and again in 1622 to Lawrence Whitaker.[202] The advowson of the vicarage was granted in 1558 to John White, Bishop of Winchester,[203] who was, however, deprived in 1559, when his lands were sequestered.[204] The advowson was in the possession of Peter Arpe before 1624.[205] It is probable that he acquired the rectory also, as his son held both rectory and advowson in 1644,[206] and both were henceforth held together. They remained in the possession of the family of Arpe or Orby until 1727,[207] when General Robert Hunter presented to the church.[208] He had married Elizabeth Orby, sister and heir of Sir Charles Orby.[209] Their children presented in 1737, and Thomas Orby Hunter, their son, in 1758.[210] Advowson and rectory were sold in 1764 to Sir Joseph Mawbey,[211] who presented in 1787,[212] his son Sir Joseph doing so in 1805.[213] The advow-

188 Pope Nich. Tax. (Rec. Com.), 206.
189 Cal. Pat. 1281–92, p. 493; V.C.H. Surr. ii, 9; Exch. K.R. Misc. Bks. vol. 25, fol. 39 et seq.; Valor Eccl. (Rec. Com.), ii, 56; Cott. MS. Vitell. A. xiii; Feet of F. Div. Co. Trin. 29 Hen. VIII.
190 Exch. K.R. Misc. Bks. vol. 25, fol. 39.
191 Add. MS. 2482, fol. 21.
192 Exch. K.R. Misc. Bks. vol. 25, fol. 39A.
193 Add. MS. 24827, fol. 21.

194 Feet of F. Div. Co. Trin. 29 Hen. VIII.
195 L. and P. Hen. VIII, xii (2), 469.
196 Pat. 5 Edw. VI, pt. vi, m. 26.
197 Ibid. 8 Eliz. pt. ii, m. 32.
198 Ibid. 1 Mary, pt. xi, m. 37.
199 Ibid. 8 Eliz. pt. ii, m. 32.
200 Ibid. 36 Eliz. pt. i, m. 7.
201 Ibid. 5 Jas. I, pt. xx, m. 1.
202 Ibid. 19 Jas. I, pt. x, m. 9.
203 Ibid. 5 & 6 Phil. and Mary, pt. iv, m. 6.

204 V.C.H. Hants, ii, 73.
205 Inst. Bks. (P.R.O.).
206 Cal. of Com. for Comp. 3054.
207 Inst. Bks. (P.R.O.); Feet of F. Surr. Hil. 32 & 33 Chas. II; ibid. Div. Co. East. 3 Will. and Mary.
208 Inst. Bks. (P.R.O.)
209 Manning and Bray, op. cit. iii, 230.
210 Inst. Bks. (P.R.O.)
211 Close, 4 Geo. III, pt. v.
212 Inst. Bks. (P.R.O.)
213 Ibid.

son was sold in 1819 to the Haberdashers' Company, as trustees to hold advowsons under the will of Lady Weld.[214] The presentation is now in the hands of the Company, but the Governors of Christ's Hospital nominate alternately with them.

THE HABERDASHERS.
Barry wavy argent and azure a bend gules and thereon a leopard of England.

CHRIST'S HOSPITAL.
Argent a cross gules with St. Paul's sword gules in the quarter and a chief azure with a Tudor rose between two fleurs de lis or therein.

Longcross was made an ecclesiastical district in 1847. The living is in the gift of the present vicar, the Rev. William Tringham.

The ecclesiastical district of Botleys and Lyne was formed in 1849. The Bishop of Winchester is patron.

Ottershaw and Brox was formed into an ecclesiastical district in 1865. The representatives of the late Rev. B. Hichens are patrons.

Addlestone was formed into an ecclesiastical district in 1838. The living is in the gift of the Bishop of Winchester.

Woodham was made into a separate ecclesiastical district in 1902.

A chapel on St. Anne's Hill, dedicated to St. Anne, existed in the 14th century. The augmentation of the vicarage of Chertsey, made in 1402, granted the vicar all oblations in Chertsey, with the exception of those coming from the chapel of St. Anne.[215] Licence to perform service in the newly-erected chapel had been granted in 1334.[216] There is an artificially lined well and a little stonework on the hill, perhaps the remains of the chapel. But Antony Wood says that the Chertsey tradition of his day was to the effect that Laurence Tomson, the Biblical scholar, who died in 1608 and is buried at Chertsey, built the house on St. Anne's Hill on the 'very place where that chapel stood.'[217] It is not known when the chapel perished. It does not appear among the suppressions of Edward VI of free chapels and chantries, neither does it appear among the possessions of Chertsey when surrendered.

Sir John Denham, in his poem on Coopers Hill, published in 1643, refers to

' . . . a neighbouring hill whose top of late
A chapel crowned, till in the common fate
Th' adjoyning abbey fell.'

CHARITIES Smith's Charity is distributed in Chertsey.

In 1721 Henry Sherwood left land for the clothing of three poor men and three poor women, but all trace of it has been long lost.

Miss Mary Giles, who died in 1841, gave in her lifetime £800, the interest to be devoted to bread for the poor on St. Thomas's Day, and £2 to the vicar and churchwardens for superintending it, and £1 towards keeping up the family monument. By will she left £2,700, clear of all duties, for the poor. From this two almshouses for widows were built and endowed.[218]

Mr. Edward Chapman, a draper of Chertsey, built two almshouses in 1668 for poor widows, in Windsor Street. In 1815 they were removed to Gogmore Lane. Mrs. Mary Hammond, widow, of the Abbey House, founded almshouses for four widows in 1645 ; Thomas Cowley for two widows in 1671. Richard Clark built new houses in place of these two in 1782, and Mr. Hammond's almshouses were rebuilt by the parish, all in Guildford Street.

In 1837 Mr. Thomas Willatts built two almshouses in Chapel Lane.

CHOBHAM

Cebeham (xi cent.) ; Chabbeham (in Chertsey Charter), and Chabham (xiii cent.).

Chobham is a village 3½ miles north-west of Woking Junction, 6 miles south-west of Chertsey. The parish is bounded on the north-east by Egham and Chertsey, on the south by Horsell, Bisley, and Pirbright, on the west by Ash, on the north-west by Windlesham. It measures about 6 miles from north-east to south-west, 4 miles from north-west to south-east at the north-eastern part, but 2 miles only further west. It contains 9,057 acres of land and 22 of water. It is traversed by the Bourne Brook and its tributaries which flow from the Chobham Ridges to the Thames near Weybridge, and the village and hamlets are chiefly on the gravel and alluvium of the stream beds, but the rest of the parish is on the Bagshot Sands, with extensive peat beds. There are very extensive open heaths with clumps of conifers.

Ironstone abounds, and there are several strong chalybeate springs. The Wokingham and Reading branch of the London and South Western Railway runs through the northern side of the parish, and Sunningdale Station is just beyond the border.

Neolithic flints are said to have been found, and there are several round barrows on the heaths ; three stand close together near Street's Heath, and the *Herestraet* or *Via Militaris* of the Chertsey Charters ran through Chobham parish. In 1772 silver coins of Gratian and Valentinian (? the first), and copper coins of Theodosius, Honorius, and Valentinian, a spear-head and a gold ring, were found near Chobham Park.[1]

Near Sunningdale Station is a very large inclosure of earthen banks on the heath. The old ordnance map marked it as 'old entrenchment,' but the later maps ignore it. It is artificial, and not round

[214] Deed enrolled in Chancery 19 June 1819.
[215] Exch. K.R. Misc. Bks. vol. 25, fol. 39.
[216] Winton Epis. Reg. Orleton, i, fol. 52.
[217] *Athenae Oxonienses* (ed. of 1721), i, 348.
[218] Monument to Miss Mary Giles in church.
[1] Manning and Bray, *Hist. of Surr.* iii, 195.

cultivated ground ; the greater part of the land within it is probably not susceptible of cultivation except at great cost, and bears no marks of having been cultivated. It forms a rough parallelogram with the corners towards the cardinal points ; the sides measure nearly 800 and 680 yards respectively, and it is not unlike the later form of Roman camp, but is not quite regular. One side has been cut into by cottages near the road.

A battery with embrasures for cannon, made in 1853, has been erroneously treated as an ancient fortification.

There are a few interesting old houses in the parish of Chobham. Unfortunately Chobham House is now only represented by a farm-house.

Brook Place, called Malt House on the old ordnance map, is a small, square, and picturesque 17th-century building, now a farm-house, situated about a mile to the west of Chobham village. It is built in red brick with tiled roofs, and two stories and an attic. The main front faces north towards the road, and has an ogee-shaped gable at its west portion, in which is a panel with the initials and date 'W B 1656.' A plain string divides the ground and first floors, and a moulded cornice and string the first and second. The windows are square with wood frames. On the south and east fronts are similar gables, but having no panels ; on the west a later timber-and-plaster wing has been added. From the front doorway (in the middle of the north front) is an original panelled screen with open turned balusters at the top, dividing the passage from the dairy east of it. The stairs are also old, having square newels with modern tops, and a plain moulded handrail, the space below the rails being filled with panelling. Two of the inside oak doors are good examples of the date. They have wide stiles or vertical boards joined by narrow V-shaped fillets. In one of the upper rooms is a fine cupboard of deal inlaid with oak panels, &c. Between the two rooms occupying the western half of the plan is a very thick piece of walling, more than sufficient to contain the flues to the fireplaces opening into it. In 1648 this house was the property of Edward Bray, a descendant of the Shiere family, who paid composition for his estate as a Royalist. It belonged to the manor of Aden, but was not the manor-house.

Chobham Place is, as it now appears, a fine Georgian house standing on rising ground north of the village. The hall was part of a house of much older date, and the woodwork of the dining-room is late 17th-century. It is said by Manning and Bray[2] to have been the seat of Mr. Antony Fenrother in Elizabeth's reign. His daughter Joan married Samuel Thomas, and their son Sir Anthony Thomas succeeded.[3] His grandson Gainsford Thomas died unmarried in 1721 and left it to his first cousin Mary, wife of Sir Anthony Abdy, bart.[4] It descended in that family till Sir William, seventh baronet, sold it in 1809. The purchaser, the Rev. Inigo William Jones, died very shortly afterwards, and it was sold to Sir Denis Le Marchant, bart. His son Sir Henry Denis Le Marchant is the present owner.

Broadford is the residence of Sir Charles George Walpole ; Highams, formerly occupied by Lord Bagot, is now the seat of Mrs. Leschallas.

The old vicarage house was the butcher's shop next the churchyard. The present vicarage was built in 1811 by the Rev. Charles Jerram, vicar 1810–34. Mr. Jerram was a noted tutor whose pupils included the late Lord Teignmouth, Horace Mann, and W. T. Grant, brother to Lord Glenelg. Lord Teignmouth's memoirs give a lively account of the secluded condition of Chobham in the early 19th century. He says that the small triangular plot between the churchyard and the White Hart Inn was the scene of a pig auction on Sunday mornings before service, the farmers adjourning to church.

Chobham Common was the scene of the first large military camp of exercise in England since the great French war. It was held in 1853, and was in fact the precursor of Aldershot. In 1901 a cross was erected in memory of Her Majesty Queen Victoria, on the spot where she had reviewed the troops on 21 June 1853.

An Inclosure Award was made in 1855,[6] but there are still several thousand acres of uninclosed land.

Chobham was divided into tithings, Stanners, Pentecost, and the Forest Tything, lying east, west, and north respectively, but the modern division is practically into hamlets. Of these, Valley End, to the west, is an ecclesiastical parish formed in 1868 from Chobham and Windlesham. West End, at the west side of Chobham village, is an ecclesiastical district formed in 1895. Lucas Green, Colony, and Fellow Green are in Chobham parish.

There are Wesleyan and Baptist chapels in the parish. Chobham Village Hall was built in 1887. The Gordon Boys' Home was built in 1885 as a memorial to Major-General Charles Gordon. The chapel was added in 1894 as a memorial of the late Duke of Clarence. The school maintains 240 boys, who are trained for civil, naval, or military life, according to their preference.

The schools (National) were built in 1814 and rebuilt in 1860 ; those at West End (National) were built in 1843, and the Valley End (National) schools by the Hon. Mrs. Bathurst in 1856.

CHOBHAM was granted to Chertsey
MANORS Monastery by Frithwald, *subregulus* of Surrey and founder of the abbey, before 675.[10] The grant was confirmed in 967 by King Edgar as ' v mansas apud Chabeham cum Busseleghe, cum Frensham et Fremeslye.'[1] At the Domesday Survey its assessment was 10 hides, as it had been in King Edward's time, and it was still held by the abbey of Chertsey. Of this land, Odmus held 4 hides of the abbey, and Corbelin held 2 hides of the land of the villeins. The monks' part was valued at £12 10s. and the homagers' part at 60s. In King Edward's time the whole manor had been worth £16.[7]

The manor of Chobham remained in the possession of the abbey until the surrender of the latter in 1537,[8] when John Cordrey the abbot granted it to the king.[9] The manor remained in the Crown for some time, during which the king kept it for his own use ;

[2] Op. cit. iii, 196.
[3] Inscriptions in the church.
[4] P.C.C. Will 118 Buckingham.
[5] *Blue Bk. Incl. Awards.*
[10] Birch, *Cart. Sax.* i, 55.

[6] Ibid. iii, 470. [9] Cott. MS. Vitell. A. xiii ; Cart. Antiq. D. 10, 13, 14, 16, 18 ; *Cal. of Chart. R.* 1257–1300, p. 305 ; Chan. Inq. p.m. 39 Hen. III, no. 26 ; *Pope Nich. Tax.*

[7] *V.C.H. Surr.* i, 310. (Rec. Com.), 206 ; *Cal. Pat.* 1324–7, p. 53 ; *Valor Eccl.* (Rec. Com.), ii, 56 ; Dugdale, *Mon.* i, 424 et seq.
[8] Feet of F. Div. Co. Trin. 29 Hen. VIII.

he was at Chobham in 1538 and again in 1542.[10] Sir Anthony Browne was made keeper of the manor in 1543.[11] Christopher Heneage appears to have had a grant of it during the reign of Elizabeth.[12] James I granted the manor to Sir George More in 1614 for the sum of £890 12s. 6d. to be held as of the manor of East Greenwich. Annual rent from the manor to the amount of £35 12s. 6d. was also granted him.[13] This rent was granted to Lawrence Whitaker and others in 1620.[14] The manor was granted in the same year to Sir Edward Zouch, including the rent previously reserved to Whitaker.[15] The grant included Bisley and the manors of Woking and Bagshot, and henceforth the manor of Chobham descended with these[16] and is at present held with them by the Earl of Onslow.

All rights and privileges pertaining to the manor of Chobham were enjoyed by the Abbot and convent of Chertsey, who appear to have exercised very complete power over their lands in Surrey.[17] John de Rutherwyk, who was abbot from 1307 to 1346 and who was noted for the many improvements which he carried out in his domain,[18] surrounded the manor-house of Chobham with running water in the first year of his rule as abbot.[19] In 1254 Geoffrey de Bagshot held Chobham under the abbot, and among the yearly dues of the abbot from that fee are included 10s. 4d. rent, 12 gallons of honey, valued at 6s., 2 sheep or 2s., 2 quarters of oats, 1 ploughshare, and a horse for carrying a monk to Winchester twice a year.[20]

The grant of Chobham to Sir George More and the later grants include land in Chobham called Langshott, Chabworth, Hill Grove, and Buttes, and a pond called Gratins Pond, also called Craches or Crathors Pond or the Greate Pond. A mill called Hurst Mill in Chobham was conveyed to the abbot by John de Hamme in the early 14th century.[21]

A court roll of the time of Charles II mentions 'Stanners' and 'Pentecost' as presenting tithingmen.[22] Sir Charles Walpole of Chobham has a note in his father's writing, 'I have a deed without date wherein is a Fine and Recovery by John de Pentecost of 5 acres in Chobham from John de Ardern and Agnes his wife.'[23] There is land near Chobham vicarage now called Penny Pot, which possibly means Pentecost. Ardern is the local pronunciation of Aden (q.v. infra).

The chief messuage of the CHOBHAM PARK manor of Chobham, called Chobham Park, was granted to the king by John Cordrey, Abbot of Chertsey, in 1535, two years before the surrender of the entire manor of Chobham.[24] The Manor Place, commonly called

Chobham Park, was sold in July 1558 by Queen Mary to Nicholas Heath her chancellor, Archbishop of York, for £3,000. The land was inclosed by a pale, whence it was called a park, and is marked as such in Norden and Speed's map of 1610. This grant was confirmed by Queen Elizabeth,[25] but as Heath had been deprived for refusing the oaths to the queen, the nominal possession was conveyed to his brother William in 1564.[26] The ex-archbishop continued, however, to reside, and died here or in London in 1578,[27] when his nephew Thomas is referred to by Lord Montagu as 'the nowe (or newe) owner.' Thomas forfeited his lands in 1588,[28] but was restored, and in 1606 conveyed them to Francis Leigh.[29] The next year he conveyed to Antony Cope,[30] who in 1614 sold to William Hale.[31] John Hale conveyed it to Henry Henn in 1654.[32] The same family held it in 1681.[33] The house was let, and before 1720 was the property of John Martin,[34] who conveyed it in that year to John Crawley.[35] Mr. Revel, M.P. 1734–52, is said to have owned it.[36] His daughter and heiress married Sir George Warren in 1758, and their daughter married Lord Bulkeley in 1777. The latter died in 1822, having left it to Sir Richard Bulkeley Williams, his nephew. From him it was bought by Sir Denis le Marchant, father of the present owner, Sir Henry le Marchant, in 1838.[37] The old house was pulled down and the park broken up in the 18th century. The farm called Chobham Park is on the old site, and parts of the double moat round the old house remain.

Le Marchant. *Azure a cheveron or between three owls argent.*

The manor of STANNARDS, STANYORS, or FORDS was held of the abbey of Chertsey with the manor of Ham next Chertsey by John de Hamme and Alina his wife from the feoffment of Thomas de Saunterre in 1307.[38] John de Hamme died seised of 'Stanhore' in 1319–20.[39] During the reigns of Edward II and Edward III it was held, under the de Hammes, by a family of the name of Ford,[40] whose name became attached to that of the manor, which in later times always appears under the name of the manor of Stanners and Fords. A dispute arose in 1343 concerning land in 'Stanore' which John de Totenhale claimed to have received from Alice de Ford and Ralph. It was adjudged that John de Totenhale, being illegitimate, could not inherit this land, which therefore became escheat to the abbey. It was afterwards claimed by Agnes, a daughter of Ralph and Alice.[41] The manor seems to

[10] L. and P. Hen. VIII, xiii (1), g. 519 (61); xvii, p. 482.
[11] Ibid. xviii (1), p. 546.
[12] Feet of F. Surr. Trin. 19 Eliz.
[13] Pat. 12 Jas. I, pt. xiv, m. 16.
[14] Ibid. 18 Jas. I, pt. ii, m. 8.
[15] Ibid. 18 Jas. I, pt. vi, m. 1.
[16] Vide Woking. Chan. Inq. p.m. (Ser. 2), dxxxviii, 136; Feet of F. Div. Co. Hil. 16 & 17 Chas. II; Pat. 23 Chas. II, pt. ix, no. 6, no. 22–8; Pat. 22 Geo. II, pt. ii, no. 14; Close, 26 Geo. II, pt. iii, no. 9; Feet of F. Surr. Trin. 25 & 26 Geo. II; Recov. R. Hil. 49 Geo. III.
[17] Vide supra.

[18] V.C.H. Surr. ii, 59; Dugdale, Mon. Angl. i, 424.
[19] Dugdale, Mon. Angl. i, 424; Exch. K.R. Misc. Bks. vol. 25, fol. 173.
[20] Cal. Inq. p.m. i, 88.
[21] Exch. K. R. Misc. Bks. vol. 25, fol. 250.
[22] Ct. R. P.R.O. bdle. 204, no. 53; Manning and Bray, op. cit. iii, 192.
[23] See Feet of F. 5 Edw. III, no. 68, in Surr. Arch. Soc.'s Volume of fines.
[24] Pat. 27 Hen. VIII, pt. ii, m. 28–9.
[25] Ibid. 7 Eliz. pt. ix, no. 9.   [26] Ibid.
[27] Not in 1579, as commonly stated; Loseley MSS. x, 71, 72. The letter seems to imply that he died at Chobham.

[28] Dep. Keeper's Rep. xxxiii, App. i.
[29] Feet of F. Surr. Hil. 3 Jas. I.
[30] Ibid. Trin. 5 Jas. I.
[31] Ibid. East. 12 Jas. I.
[32] Notes of F. Mich. 1654; Feet of F. Surr. Mich 1654.
[33] Feet of F. Surr. Mich. 11 Chas. II; Trin. 33 Chas. II.
[34] Ibid. Mich. 7 Geo. I.
[35] Ibid. Hil. 11 Geo. I.
[36] Manning and Bray, op. cit. iii, 195.
[37] Information of Sir Henry le Marchant.
[38] Feet of F. Surr. Trin. 1 Edw. II.
[39] Chan. Inq. p.m. 13 Edw. II, no. 14.
[40] Lansd. MS. 434, fol 168b, 187b, 200b, 201.   [41] Ibid.

haye remained united to that of Hamme for some time longer. It is at least probable that Nicholas Fitz John, who held the latter (q.v.) about 1400, also held land at Stanore.[42] After this date there appears to be no record of it until 1532, when the manor, then in possession of William Lambert, was leased for thirty-one years to John Rogers of Chobham at the rent of £7 2s. 8d.[43] William Lambert died before 1539, when his widow Alice and daughter Collubra, wife of Richard Warde, conveyed the manor to the king in exchange for other lands.[44] In 1554 the Crown extended the lease previously made to John Rogers to his son Henry for a term of twenty-one years.[45] The manor in 1559 was granted to Thomas Reve and George Evelyn and the latter's heirs, to hold by knight's service,[46] Reve being only a trustee. Evelyn died in 1603, and the manor of Stannards passed to his second son John Evelyn, a settlement having been made on the marriage of George eldest son of John Evelyn with Elizabeth Rivers.[47] In 1618 the moiety of the manor was conveyed by John Evelyn and his wife to Robert Hatton as a settlement on his younger son John Evelyn on the latter's marriage; George Evelyn released his right to his brother, and in 1621 the other moiety of the manor was conveyed to him.[48] John Evelyn the younger apparently re-sold the manor to his brother George and his son Sir John in 1624,[49] and the latter was in possession in 1636,[50] when he conveyed it to George Duncombe and Henry Baldwin in trust for James Linch, who died seised of the manor of Stannards and Fords in 1640, leaving as heiresses his granddaughters Eleanor, Susan, and Elizabeth Gauntlett.[51] It is probable that Eleanor and Susan married Robert Parham and Robert Hussey respectively and released their right in the manor in 1651.[52] In 1687 the manor was in possession of Francis Swanton,[53] son of William Swanton, who married Elizabeth his youngest granddaughter of James Linch.[54] Francis Swanton is said to have sold it to Nathaniel Cocke in 1694.[55] In 1721 his widow Anne Cocke was seised of it, with reversion to Zachariah Gibson,[56] to whom Joseph Paris and Sara, probably the daughter of Anne Cocke, had released their interest.[57] In the same year Anne Cocke and Zachariah Gibson conveyed 'the manor or lordship or reputed manor or lordship of Stannards and Fords' to John Martin, who in 1728 sold it to Thomas Woodford for £2,300,[58] the sale including two farms known as Forde Farm and Coxhill Farm, a common called Mynfield Green, and other lands. Thomas Woodford's son Thomas inherited the major part of his father's estate in 1758,[59] and in 1761 sold the manor of Stannards and Fords to Thomas Sewell, whose son and heir T. B. H. Sewell inherited it in 1784, selling in 1795 to Edmund Boehm, who owned it till 1819.[60] Mr. Boehm's property was sold in 1820 after his bankruptcy, and the manor was acquired by Mr. James Fladgate, corn merchant of

Chertsey. He died in 1857[60a] and left it to his son James Fladgate. The latter's son Henry sold the manor. The manor-house now belongs to Sir Henry Denis le Marchant, the land and manor to Mr. Otter, J.P., of Queenwood, and Miss Peele.[61] The manor-house, now tenanted by Mr. A. E. Greenwell, is in part an early 17th-century building with some good Jacobean woodwork. It was probably erected by one of the Evelyns, the old manor-house being a timbered house still standing on the other side of the road, or Stanner's Hill Farm belonging to Mr. Baker of Ottershaw Park. The former is a large, picturesque old cottage of whitewashed brick and half-timber with a tiled roof. It is on the plan of a T with gabled ends to the head and hipped roof at the foot ; and is in two stories. It is now divided into two cottages.

ADEN is a house and small estate in Chobham, sometimes called a manor in title-deeds. A John Ardern held land in Chobham in 1331.[62] John Danaster, baron of the Exchequer, died seised of the manor of Aden in 1540.[63] His daughter Anne, then aged two, afterwards married Owen Bray, second son of Sir Edward Bray of Shiere. Their son Edward had a son Owen,[64] whose daughter married a Mr. Sear, and their daughter married Mr. Johnson. The manor was sold to General Broome, and then to Mr. Jerram the vicar of Chobham in 1808. It passed through four more owners to Miss Perceval, the present owner. The house was rebuilt on another site, and is now called 'Chobham House.' The mill, which was part of the estate, was sold separately by Captain Sanders in the 19th century, and is now owned by Mr. F. W. Benham.

The church of *ST. LAWRENCE CHURCHES* consists of a chancel 28 ft. 1 in. by 15 ft. 11 in., a nave 72 ft. 6 in. by 18 ft., with a north aisle 11 ft. 3 in. wide and a south aisle and transept 6 ft. 10 in. wide. At the west end of the nave is a tower 11 ft. 1 in. square, with a wooden west porch, and at the east end of the north aisle is a small vestry.

The earlier church was a small building consisting of a chancel with a nave of about half the length of the present one, dating from the beginning of the 12th century or a little earlier. Parts of two of the early windows still remain high up in the south wall of the nave, cut into by the arcade which was built about 1180, when the south aisle was added. In the 13th century a transept chapel was added at the east end of the aisle, which with the nave was lengthened westwards by the addition of one more bay, the old west respond of the south arcade being replaced by a square pier. The history of the chancel during this time has been lost by its complete rebuilding, noted below. The tower was built about 1450, and thus the church remained until 1866, when the north aisle was added and the

42 Exch. K.R. Misc. Bks. vol. 25, fol. 55b.
43 Pat. 1 & 2 Phil. and Mary pt. xi, m. 5.
44 Ibid. 31 Hen. VIII, pt. iv, m. 27.
45 See note 43.
46 Pat. 2 Eliz. pt. iv, m. 27.
47 Chan. Inq. p.m. (Ser. 2), ccxc, 124.
48 Feet of F. Surr. Mich. 16 Jas. I ; Recov. R. Trin. 18 Jas. I ; Feet of F. Surr. Trin. 19 Jas. I.
49 Feet of F. Surr. Hil. 21 Jas. I ; Mich. 2 Chas. I.
50 Ibid. Hil. 12 Chas. I.

51 Chan. Inq. p.m. (Ser. 2), ccccxcii, 41.
52 Feet of F. Surr. Hil. 1651.
53 Feet of F. Surr. Mich. 3 Jas. II ; Recov. R. Mich. 3 Jas. II.
54 Manning and Bray, Hist. of Surr. iii, 194 ; Sir T. Phillips, Visit. Wilts. 1677, p. 17.
55 Manning and Bray, op. cit. iii, 196.
56 Close, 8 Geo. I, pt. ii, no. 1.
57 Feet of F. Surr. Hil. 8 Geo. I ; Manning and Bray, Hist. of Surr. iii, 194.
58 Close, 1 Geo. II, pt. v, m. 12 ; Feet of F. Surr. Hil. 1 Geo. II.

59 See P.C.C. 76 Arran (will of Thos. Woodford of Chertsey).
60 Manning and Bray, Hist. of Surr. iii, 194 (quoting from the title-deeds of Edmund Boehm, lord of the manor in 1811).
60a Will proved Dec. 1857.
61 Local information.
62 Feet of F. 5 Edw. III, 68, in Surr. Arch. Soc. Volumes of fines.
63 Chan. Inq. p.m. 32 Hen. VIII, pt. iii, no. 143.
64 Harl. MS. 1561, fol. 199.

galleries and high pews removed. In 1892 the west porch was reconstructed, a few old timbers being used. In 1898 the whole of the chancel and the chapel east of the south aisle were rebuilt.

In the east wall of the modern chancel is a triplet of lancets, and in the north wall is a single lancet, also modern. The old chancel had a second north window and a south doorway, but these were removed at the rebuilding. The chancel arch is two-centred and of one moulded order springing from scalloped corbels.

The south arcade of the nave is of five bays, the eastern bay, which opens to the south chapel, not being continuous with the rest. It has been lately rebuilt, and is a copy of the late 12th-century arcades, but without the half-round responds.

The next three bays have two large circular columns and a half-round east respond, all with moulded bases and scalloped capitals. The columns and arches are of chalk, the latter being two-centred and of a single order with chamfered edges and a splayed label towards the nave. The middle arch of the three is lower than the others, and the western half of the third arch seems to have been rebuilt, perhaps in the 13th century, at the lengthening of the church.

The second capital fits its column clumsily, and the arrangement of the scallops on the south side and the jointing suggest that it has been made up with the capital of the original west respond. The western bay is similar to the others as regards the arch, but has square piers with chamfered edges, and a respond to match. The abaci throughout are grooved and chamfered.

The two early windows already mentioned occur over the second bay from the east and the second circular column respectively. They can only be seen on the nave side, and appear as deeply splayed round-headed openings, with part of the stone head showing in the western one, all the rest being plastered.

The south chapel, which is practically a continuation of the south aisle, has a modern east window of two trefoiled lights with a pierced quatrefoil spandrel, and in the south wall are two modern lancets.

Below the sill of these lancets is inserted the head of a narrow round-headed recess of uncertain origin.

There is a modern two-centred arch with chamfered orders between the transept and the aisle.

There are two south windows in the south aisle, one of 15th-century date though much restored, and the other a modern copy of the same. They have each three cinquefoiled lights under a square head without a label, and their inner splays are old with stout wood lintels in the place of rear-arches. To the west of them is the south doorway, which is of late 15th-century date and has hollow-chamfered jambs and a four-centred head, with a wood lintel inside like the windows. The west window of the aisle is modern and has two trefoiled lights with a pierced circle in the spandrel.

The modern north arcade to the nave is of five bays with double shafts of a very meagre description with moulded bases and carved capitals, and the two-centred arches are of one order with moulded edges. The north-east window of the north aisle and that in the west wall are of 13th-century design, the remaining four being of 15th-century character, and in the east wall of this aisle is the doorway to the vestry.

The tower arch is of 15th-century date with two chamfered orders, and the west doorway, which has a moulded two-centred arch, is covered by an oak porch which is all new except its four-centred outer arch and parts of its panelled western uprights, which are 15th-century work. In the south wall of the tower is a small doorway leading to the stair-turret. The tower is faced with Heath stone, and is in two tall stages with an embattled parapet, a short octagonal leaded spire, and plain two-light belfry windows; the west window over the doorway is of three cinquefoiled

CHOBHAM CHURCH : NAVE, SHOWING EARLY WINDOWS

lights with tracery, and over it, partly hidden by a clock face, is a small single light.

The wall of the south aisle is built in a chequer pattern of Heath stone and ironstone conglomerate, and all the modern walling is entirely of this conglomerate. The roofs are tiled, that of the nave continuing without a break over the aisles, the eaves courses on the south side being of Horsham slates.

Near the south-east angle of the south chapel is an old dial-stone about 9 in. square, with two concentric circles within which are ten radiating lines unequally spaced.

The timbers of the nave roof are modern covered with modern boarding, but there are four massive old tie-beams still in position. The south aisle has an old roof with vertical posts on the north side standing clear of the wall and resting on wood brackets ; from these spring struts to the purlin, which is further strengthened by curved wind-braces. All the other roofs are modern.

The font is of 16th-century date, and is one of the very scarce instances of a font constructed of wood; it is octagonal, each side forming a heavily-moulded panel, and the basin is hemispherical and lined with lead. The stem and base are of modern stonework.

In the vestry at the east end of the north aisle is a fine old iron-bound chest of uncertain date; two of the iron bands have fleur de lis ends, and there are three locks; the lid is apparently of later date. The hinges of the south door also seem ancient, and in the nave hangs a fine brass chandelier for twelve candles, which bears the names of the vicar and churchwardens and the date 1737. In the chancel is a copy of this, made in 1899.

On the west jamb of the arch between the nave and the south transept is a brass inscription in two lines, the ends of the lines missing :—'Here lyeth buryed Willm̄ Heith of Chabhm̄ . . . Countye of Surray Esquire who died yͤ xix November in the yere of our Lorde God mcc. . . ' William Heath was brother of Nicholas Archbishop of York.

Eldridge, 1597. The sixth is by William Culverden of London, c. 1525, and bears in black-letter with crowned capitals 'Sancta Mergereta ora pro nobis,' with the founder's mark. The tenor is another of Robert Eldridge's bells, dated 1610.

The most interesting piece of the plate is a fine cup of 1562, the straight-sided bowl being alone of this date, while the fluted base and the stem with its knot appear to belong to a secular cup of c. 1540–50, but have no marks on them.

Beside this there is a paten of 1727, a flagon of 1755, and a large two-handled cup with a cover which was made in 1787. There is also a standing paten of 1840, another small paten of 1897, and a pewter almsdish inscribed 'Chobham Church in Surrey 1712.'

The church also possesses two small old collecting-boxes with handles and a circle of geometric ornament on the top.

There are five books of registers, the first two of which have been very carefully restored and bound. The first is of parchment, and contains all three entries

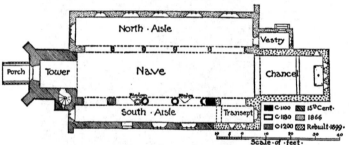

North · Aisle

Vestry

Porch Tower Nave Chancel

South · Aisle Transept

C·1100 15ᵗʰ Cent.
C·1180 1866
C·1200 Rebuilt 1899.

Scale · of · feet ·

PLAN OF CHOBHAM CHURCH

Below this is another brass to William Soker, undated, but of the 17th century, with a set of three elegiac couplets in Latin.

In the chancel is a floor-slab to Jane, widow of Samuel Thomas and daughter of Anthony Fenrother, 1638. The arms, as here shown, are :—A cheveron between three terrets with three ostriches on the cheveron, in a quarter a man on a tower holding a banner, the whole within an engrailed border.

Another slab is to Sir Anthony Thomas, 1641, and his wife Maria, 1658, and there are several other monuments to the same family.

There is also a copper tablet, fixed in the chancel in 1908, to Nicholas Heath, Bishop of Rochester 1539, of Worcester 1543, and Archbishop of York 1555. He lived at Chobham Park in 1571, 1573, and 1574, and died at Chobham or in London in 1578, and was buried in the chancel of this church. There are a number of late monuments to the Caldwell family.

In the belfry are eight bells, the treble and second being by Mears & Stainbank, 1892, and the third by the same firm, 1880. The fourth is by William Eldridge, 1684, and the fifth and seventh by Robert

from 1654 to 1730; the second has the same from 1730 to 1770, and is a paper book. The third contains baptisms and burials from 1770 to 1812; the fourth marriages from 1754 to 1783; and the fifth marriages from 1784 to 1812.

The church of ST. SAVIOUR, Valley End, is a small brick building, erected in 1867, and consisting of a chancel with a south vestry and organ-chamber and a nave with a north porch. Over the west gable is a wood bell-turret. The roofs are tiled and all the internal fittings are modern.

The parish church of HOLY TRINITY, West End, is a small building consisting of a chancel consecrated in 1890, nave consecrated in 1842, and a vestry built in 1906. The material is stone and the style is of the 13th century. Over the west end is a small bell-turret with a square spire. The entrance is at the west end.

There is also the iron mission chapel of St. Luke.

ADVOWSONS   The Domesday Survey records the existence of both a church and a chapel at Chobham, in the possession of the abbey of Chertsey.[65] The abbot caused the chapel to be repaired in 1318,[66] but after this there

⁶⁴ V.C.H. Surr. i, 310; cp. Surr. Arch. Coll. xxi, 206.   ⁶⁶ Exch. K.R. Misc. Bks. vol. 25, fol. 179.

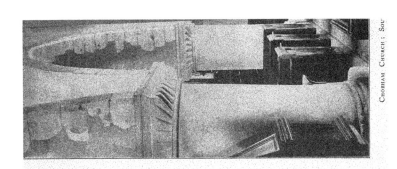

CHOBHAM CHURCH : SOU[TH]

CHOBHAM CHURCH : WEST PORCH

is no further mention of a chapel. As, however, it seems to have been dedicated in honour of St. Lawrence, it may probably be identified with the present church of St. Lawrence, in which case the church was presumably Bisley Church (q.v.).

The church of St. Lawrence remained in the hands of the monks until the surrender of the abbey in 1537.[67] A vicarage was ordained there in 1330 by Abbot John de Rutherwyk, and was augmented in 1427.[68] Among the pensions due to the abbot and convent was an annual one of 10*s.* and 6 lb. of wax, which was paid by Chobham vicarage.[69] This pension, previously amounting to 20*s.* and 6 lb. of wax, had been reduced in 1230.[70] In 1537 the church, with the rectory and advowson, were surrendered to the Crown by John Cordrey, Abbot of Chertsey.[71] Later in the same year a grant of the rectory was made to the new foundation at Bisham.[72] The grant must have included the advowson of the church, as in 1538 the abbot received licence to alienate both from the monastery to Sir Thomas Pope, treasurer of the Court of Augmentations. He, in his turn, alienated them to the Dean and Chapter of the cathedral church of St. Paul, London, who held them, by the service of one knight's fee, to the use of the chaplains of two chantries in the church of St. Paul.[73] At the suppression of the chantries the rectory and advowson returned to the Crown; an effort made by the Dean and Chapter of St. Paul's in 1587 to recover them proved ineffectual,[74] as they remained in the Crown until 1620. A grant of the rectory alone had been made to William James in 1551 for twenty-one years, reversion being granted in 1564 to William Haber and Richard Duffield,[75] from whom it passed immediately to Owen Bray of Aden in Chobham, who died

in 1568 possessed of it.[76] His grandson was Owen Bray, who conveyed it in 1638 to Sir Thomas White,[77] from whom it descended to the Woodroffes.[78] The latter conveyed it to Elizabeth and Philip Beauchamp in 1687.[79] After this date the rectorial tithes appear to have been divided. Sir Anthony Thomas Abdy of Chobham Place purchased a part of the great tithes of Anthony Beauchamp before 1774.[80] The present impropriators are Sir Neville Abdy and Sir Henry le Marchant, the owner of Chobham Place.

In 1620 the advowson was granted with the manor to Sir Edward Zouch,[81] and it remained in the possession of the lord of the manor until 1752,[82] when some of the Onslow property was sold, including the advowsons of Chobham and Bisley. They passed together for a time[83] (see Bisley), Henry Forster presenting in 1800, and the Thornton family in 1810 and 1833.[84] The vicarage is now in the gift of the Rev. W. Tringham.

Valley End was formed into an ecclesiastical parish separate from Chobham and Windlesham in 1868. The living is in the gift of the Bishop of Winchester.

West End became a parish in 1895. The vicarage is in the gift of Miss Tringham.

The older charities include Smith's, *CHARITIES* distributed as in other Surrey parishes.

In 1721 Gainsford Thomas of Chobham Place left by will a charge on land of £4 a year for the poor, and for teaching a child or children to read and write and keep accounts, and also three cottages for the poor. These do not, however, now exist.

In 1722 Mrs. Mary Hope left £5 a year for teaching girls, and 10 guineas a year charged on land for the poor.

EGHAM

Egeham (xi cent.).

Egham is a small town near the Thames, 5 miles from Windsor and 4 miles north-west of Chertsey. The parish is bounded on the north-east by the Thames, on the south-east by Thorpe and Chertsey, on the south-west by Chobham, on the north-west by Berkshire. It measures about 5 miles from southwest to north-east, and about 3 miles from north-west to south-east. It contains 7,624 acres of land and 162 of water. It is divided into four tithings, the Town Tithing in the northern part of the parish, Strode in the southern part, the Hythe in the north-eastern part along the Thames, Englefield, the western part. The soil is Bagshot sand with the gravel and alluvium of the Thames Valley. The Bagshot sand rises into considerable eminences, of which by far the most famous is Coopers Hill, remarkable not for its actual height but for its position above the Thames Valley, affording views from Windsor

to London, and celebrated by Sir John Denham, a native of Egham, in his well-known poem, which was written on the spot just before the Civil War and published in 1643.

The old south-western road from London came across Staines Bridge and through Egham parish, and the place was important for inns in coaching days; notorious also for the robberies committed on the road, so that according to Aubrey Egham had paid more in compensation for robberies than any other parish in England.

The Reading and Wokingham branch of the London and South Western Railway, opened in 1856, has stations at Egham and Virginia Water. The line from Woking to Egham was begun in 1881.

The Thames Valley and the less barren stream beds in the Bagshot sand were inhabited in early times. A polished stone celt has been found near Egham, and a bronze spear-head in the Thames

[67] Ibid. fol. 25; Cott. MS. Vitell. A. xiii; *Cal. of Papal Letters.* i, 6; *Valor Eccl.* (Rec. Com.), ii, 56.

[68] Exch. K.R. Misc. Bks. vol. 25, fol. 45, 46.

[69] Ibid. vol. 25, fol. 32, 44; *Pope Nich. Tax* (Rec. Com.), 208.

[70] Exch. K.R. Misc. Bks. vol. 25, fol. 44 *b*.

[71] Feet of F. Div. Co. Trin. 29 Hen. VIII.

[72] *L. and P. Hen. VIII,* xii (2), p. 469.

[73] Pat. 29 Hen. VIII, pt. v, m. 26; Feet of F. Surr. East. 30 Hen. VIII.

[74] *Hist. MSS. Com. Rep.* ix, App. i, 55 *b*.

[75] Pat. 7 Eliz. pt. ii, m. 15.

[76] Will proved Nov. 1568; Chan. Inq. p.m. (Ser. 2), cxlviii, 22.

[77] Feet of F. Surr. Mich. 13 Chas. I.

[78] Manning and Bray, *Hist. of Surr.* iii, 195.

[79] Recov. R. Mich. 3 Jas. II.

[80] P.C.C. 126 Alexander (will of Sir Ant. Abdy).

[81] Pat. 18 Jas. I, pt. vi, m. 1.

[82] Feet of F. Div. Co. Hil. 16 & 17 Chas. II; Inst. Bks. P.R.O.

[83] Pat. 33 Chas. II, pt. ix, no. 6, m. 22–3; Pat. 22 Geo. II, pt. iii, no. 14; Close, 26 Geo. II, pt. iii, m. 9.

[84] Inst. Bks. P.R.O.

near Runnimede.[1] The great Roman road from the Thames Valley to the south-west crossed the Thames near Staines and ran through Egham parish along the border of the counties of Surrey and Berkshire towards Easthampstead Plain in Berkshire, where it exists as the Devil's Highway. The line of the road was carefully explored about 1840 by Mr. Wyatt Edgell of Milton Place, Egham, and some officers of the Military College, Sandhurst. It ran through Virginia Water, an artificial lake of much later construction, past Englefield Green to the Thames. There is no doubt that the Roman station *Ad Pontes*, or *Pontibus*, was near Staines, and from its name appears to have been the passage of the Thames before other bridges were made. The road which comes out of Sussex through Somersbury and Ewhurst (q.v.) would lead here if continued in a nearly straight line. Nevertheless the Roman bridge has disappeared. The earliest record of a bridge at Staines seems to date from the reign of Henry III, 1229,[2] though the Danes crossed here in 1009,[3] uniting their forces, which had been on both sides of the river, without the aid of their ships, which were on the coast of Kent. It is not, of course, decisive evidence that the Roman bridge still stood, for they may have used ferry-boats. A new stone bridge was built in 1791–6, but almost at once gave way from insufficient foundations ; fortunately the old wooden bridge was still standing. An iron bridge was next built, and opened in 1803. This immediately cracked, and was closed. Another iron bridge was built in 1807, and the old wooden bridge pulled down. This failed in 1829, and the new stone bridge was built by Rennie and opened in 1832. Egham Causeway, leading from the town of Egham to the bridge of Staines, was constructed in the time of Henry III.[4] It was used both as a highway and also as a dyke, to prevent the inundation of the surrounding country by the River Thames. In 1350 a commission was appointed to find the persons responsible for the repair of the causeway damaged by flood.[5] As a result of the inquiry it was stated that the causeway had been constructed by a certain Thomas de Oxenford, at his own expense, in the reign of Henry III, for the easement of men crossing by the King's Way at Redewynd (v. Chertsey), which had formerly been the highway, and which had fallen into a bad condition. Thomas de Oxenford had not only built, but had also repaired his causeway, and the commission of 1350 therefore declared that no man was bound to repair the same except of his own free will.[6] In 1385 the causeway was found to be 'so destroyed and broken that the loss of all the adjacent country is to be feared,' whereupon the Sheriff of Surrey was ordered to make public proclamation 'that all persons, ecclesiastical as well as secular, shall each, according to the extent of his holding, cause the same to be repaired with all haste.'[7] Frequent attempts were made to shift the burden of this work on to the Abbot and convent of Chertsey, but it was decided that although they frequently undertook the repair 'out of charity, they were in no wise responsible.'[8] In 1392, however,

the abbot declared that, in spite of this decision, he was still charged with the 'procurance and malevolent instigation of his adversaries' with the repair, and prayed for remedy.[9] In the 15th century the repairs, both for the causeway and for Staines Bridge, were effected by Thomas Stanes, John Edmed, William Mulso and others, to whom grants of 'pontage' for terms of years were made, the proceeds of which were to be applied to this particular purpose.[10]

Reverting to the history of Egham, Englefield Green in this parish was not the scene of the battle with the Danes in 871 ; this was fought at Englefield near Reading. Runnimede, however, is in Egham, and one of the greatest events in English history was consummated on Surrey soil. The charter itself is the witness that it was given in Runnimede. Magna Charta Island, as the name of the island in the Thames, is a comparatively late name.

Egham lay in the confines of the forest of Windsor. The dispute about the boundaries of the forest finally left some of the parish and of the county of Surrey within it. The boundary perambulated in 1226 is for some distance the boundary of Berkshire and Surrey, but in its later course, where it runs from Thornhill to Harpesford, and then 'along the water to Inggfield' (Englefield) it followed the stream which runs into Virginia Water. The county boundary, now at all events, lies a little north-west of this. Harpesford Bridge must from the description have been on this stream, most likely where the Roman road crossed it, and would now therefore be covered by Virginia Water. Virginia Water was made by William, Duke of Cumberland, when he was ranger of Windsor Park (appointed 12 July 1746), between his return to England from the Netherlands, 1748, and his taking command in Germany, 1757. The dam confining the water broke down in 1768, and caused a disastrous flood. Thomas Sandby, an architect and surveyor whom the duke had employed in military surveying in Scotland and Flanders, was made by him deputy ranger of the Park, and was really responsible for laying out Virginia Water. He was the first Professor of Architecture at the Royal Academy.

Among the old houses in Egham parish the most notable is Fosters, or Great Fosters, or Foster House. It is said traditionally, and probably untruly, to have been a hunting-lodge of Queen Elizabeth.[11]

The Place, about a quarter of a mile north-east of Egham church, where Sir John Denham lived, was pulled down about forty years ago.

An Act of 1813–14 inclosed commons and common fields and pastures at Egham and on Runnimede.[12] The award is dated 12 June 1817. The common fields were at Egham and Hythefield, and are mentioned by Stevenson[13] as more highly rented than usual. The Act and award specially preserved rights of pasturage for certain people in the great common meadows, Runnimede, Long Mead, and Great Mead, provided always that inclosures should be thrown down to enable the horse-races held there to be continued as usual.

[1] *V.C.H. Surr.* i, 251–3.
[2] Pat. 12 Hen. III, m. 2.
[3] *Angl.-Sax. Chron. sub anno* 1009.
[4] Chan. Misc. Inq. file 164 (2nd nos.), no. 51.
[5] *Cal. of Pat.* 1348–50, p. 515.
[6] Chan. Misc. Inq. file 164 (2nd nos.), no. 51.

[7] *Cal. Pat.* 1381–5, p. 601.
[8] Ibid. 1391–6, p. 165.
[9] Ibid.
[10] Ibid. 1436–41, p. 78 ; 1461–7, p. 12. The statement in Manning and Bray, op. cit. iii, 256, and in Brayley, op. cit. ii, 275, that the Inq. p.m. 24 Edw. III, 51,

declares Thomas de Oxenford to have built Staines bridge as well as Egham Causeway is not the fact; it only states that he made the causeway.
[11] *Vide infra.*
[12] Stat. 54 Geo. III, cap. 153.
[13] *View of the Agric. of Surr.* 1809.

BYFLEET CHURCH FROM THE SOUTH-EAST

There are a large number of good houses in the neighbourhood. Potnall Park is the residence of the Rev. H. J. F. de Salis, Kenwolde Court of Mr. G. N. Stevens, Wentworth of the Countess de Morella, Markwood of Mr. J. S. Fletcher, Kingswood of Mrs. Eastwood, Alderhurst was the seat of the late Lord Thring.

Coopers Hill College was erected for the training of candidates for the Government service in India in the engineering, telegraphic, and forestry services. It was established in 1871, and was administered by a highly-distinguished staff of scientific men who gave a special character to the society of the neighbourhood. It was closed amid general regrets in October 1906, the Indian Government having adopted other means of supplying their services.

The Royal Holloway College for Women, Egham Hill, was founded by the late Mr. Thomas Holloway in 1879 and opened in 1886 by Her Majesty Queen Victoria. The founder gave £600,000 in the first instance, and by his will left £200,000 more for endowment in 1883. It was intended for the education of women by women. The building, consisting of two quadrangles, is in red-brick in the style of the French Renaissance. It in fact follows generally the model of the Château de Chambord in Touraine. There is a picture gallery 100 ft. long, 30 ft. wide, and 50 ft. high, containing a fine collection of paintings by Turner, Gainsborough, Constable, Crome, Morland, Copley Fielding, Landseer, Creswick, Millais (The Princes in the Tower), Long (The Babylonian Marriage Market), and other distinguished modern artists. The chapel is richly decorated and contains on the apsidal east end a high relief of the Creation of Eve and a ceiling designed and made by the late Signor Fucigno. The government of the college is in the hands of twelve governors, including the trustees of the property. It has not been found possible so far to dispense entirely with male teaching, and the undenominational services in the chapel have resolved themselves into alternate denominations, one Sunday service being usually conducted by a Canon of Windsor.

The same founder established the sanatorium at St. Anne's Heath for mentally afflicted persons of the upper and middle classes. It was opened in 1885. Mr. W. H. Crossland was architect of both buildings.

The Cottage Hospital, Englefield Green, was opened in 1880, and contains sixteen beds.

There are Wesleyan, Congregational, Baptist, and Primitive Methodist chapels in the parish.

The Schools are :—Station Road School, formerly Egham Parish School, built in 1870, taken over by the School Board in 1884, enlarged in 1895 ; Virginia Water School (National), built 1857 ; Englefield Green School (National), built in 1864, enlarged in 1885, 1896, and 1899 ; Hythe School, built in 1886, enlarged in 1890 and in 1900 ; Bishopsgate Infant School (Church of England), built in 1882 ; St. Anne's Heath School, built in 1896. The School Board was formed in 1884.

EGHAM was included in the original MANORS endowment of Chertsey Abbey in 666–75.[14] Confirmation of the grant was made in 727 and in 967, and in both cases the property at Egham is referred to as '20 mansac cum porcorum pascuis in þene wold.'[15] The Domesday Survey records that in the time of King Edward it was assessed for 40 hides, whereas in 1086 it was assessed for 15. Its value, previously £40, was then £30 10s. Of this land Gozelin held 3 hides which were of the abbey's demesne in King Edward's time.[16]

The manor was included in all subsequent confirmations of the abbey land, and was held with those of Chertsey, Thorpe, and Chobham (q.v.) until the surrender of the abbey in 1537,[17] since which time the manor of Egham has remained in the Crown. With the Chertsey manors Egham was leased to Sir William Fitz William in 1550 for thirty years,[18] and after his death the lease was renewed to his widow Joan,[19] who died in 1574.

The manor was included in the Crown grants to Prince Henry and Charles Prince of Wales in the reign of James I, and to Queen Henrietta Maria in the reign of Charles I.[20] During the Commonwealth the manor was sold to Thomas Richardson,[21] who in 1650 sold it to John Blackwele.[22] After the Restoration the manor was granted to Queen Catherine of Braganza.[23] A lease of the manor was granted to John Thynne, which expired about the year 1693.[24] The reversion was granted to Sir Richard Powle in 1673, but this grant was cancelled,[25] and in 1674 John Thynne was granted a further lease of forty years.[26] Aubrey says that this lease was acquired by Adrian Moore, attorney, of Egham.[27] In 1694, however, a lease of ninety-nine years, to date from the death of Queen Catherine, was granted by the Crown to William Blaythwayt.[28] The queen died in 1705, in which year, therefore, Blaythwayt's lease began. This lease also became the property of Adrian Moore, a relation of William Blaythwayt.[29] Adrian Moore held a lease of Milton Place also (q.v.). The lease from the Crown held by this family was finally surrendered about the year 1865,[30] Richard Wyatt, the heir of Adrian Moore (see under Milton), having in 1804 obtained a renewal of Blaythwayt's lease.[31]

Queen Elizabeth granted the site of the manor of Egham to William Grene in 1579 for a period of twenty-one years,[32] but in 1587 he sold all right, title, and interest in the premises to Thomas Stydolf, who then received a further grant of twenty-one years from the Crown.[33] This grant was extended in 1592 to Thomas Stydolf, Elizabeth his wife, and Francis his son, ' to have and to hold for the term of their natural life for the longest liver.'[34] In 1607 Thomas Merrye was granted the reversion of this site for a term of forty years,[35] but he in the same year assigned the capital messuage, site, and all his estate and term of years therein to Francis Stydolf.[36] The Parliamentary Survey of 1650 records that

14 Birch, *Cart. Sax.* i, 55–6.
15 Ibid. i, 64 ; iii, 469.
16 *V.C.H. Surr.* i, 309b.
17 Feet of F. Div. Co. Trin. 29 Hen. VIII.
18 *Acts of the P.C.* 1549–50, p. 415.
19 Pat. 12 Eliz. pt. viii, m. 7.
20 *Vide* Chertsey. Pat. 8 Jas. I, pt. xli, no. 2 ; Exch. L.T.R. Orig. R. 14 Jas. I, pt. iv, rot. 126 ; *Cal. S.P. Dom.* 1640–1, p.

552 ; Ct. R. (P.R.O.), bdle. 204, no. 47, 53.
21 Particulars for Sale of Crown Lands during Commonwealth, R. 1.
22 Feet of F. Surr. Mich. 1650.
23 Pat. 24 Chas. II, pt. ix, m. 1.
24 *Cal. S.P. Dom.* 1673, p. 385–6 ; ibid. 1673–75, p. 175.
25 Ibid. 1673–5, pp. 175, 185.
26 Ibid.

27 Aubrey, op. cit. iii, 150 (after 1673).
28 Pat. 6 Will. and Mary, pt. i, m. 13.
29 Information communicated by Mr. A. Wyatt-Edgell.   30 Ibid.
31 Manning and Bray, op. cit. iii, 150.
32 Pat. 22 Eliz. pt. iii, m. 21.
33 Ibid. 30 Eliz. pt. ix, m. 22.
34 Parl. Surv. 1650, no. 24.
35 Ibid. ; Pat. 4 Jas. I, pt. xxix, m. 1.
36 Parl. Surv. 1650, no. 24.

'the said Francis Stidolf, now Sir Francis Stidolf, is yet full of life and is 70 and lives at Mickelham,' and that he 'is therefore in possession now, and for his life and for 40 years after.' It also states that the manor-house and premises were in 'good tenantable repair and very fit to be continued as a farmhouse.' In 1672 the property was granted to Sir Richard Stidolf, bart., the son of Sir Francis,[37] for a period of seven years dating from 1695.[38] Sir Richard died in 1677, but in 1675 a forty-year lease, dating from 1702,

STIDOLF, baronet. *Argent a chief sable with two wolves' heads rased or therein.*

was made to Sir Richard Fowle. This lease was sold successively to William Cherry, Adam Bellamy, and Francis Bartholomew.[39] The lease of the manor of Egham, made to William Blaythwayt in 1694, mentions the site of the manor as among the premises to be leased. This is probably a mistake, the grant being made in general terms only.

The Survey of 1650 includes the meadow of Runnimede among the lands appurtenant to the site of the manor. When the lease of the manor was renewed in 1804, ninety-nine years after Catherine of Braganza's death, the manor-house was included and was apparently in Mr. Wyatt's possession.

The Parliamentary Survey of 1650 states that there was a court baron, belonging to the manor of Egham, usually kept at some known place within the same manor, at the will of the lord of the manor, and also a court leet, usually kept for the said manor at Hardwick in Chertsey. It also mentions, as common fields in Egham, Englefield, Hurst Heath, Southbrook Common, Wick Common, Deane Common, and Purche Heath.[40] At the courts of Queen Henrietta Maria, held both before and after the Commonwealth, tithingmen presented for the tithings of Englefield, Stroud, Lewith or Waryth, and Hicklie.[41]

In Egham, as in the other riverside lands belonging to the monastery, the abbot and convent had constructed weirs for catching fish. A 14th-century court roll has the following entry : ' To this court came Adam atte le Hale and surrendered into the hands of the abbot and convent a certain weir with a fisherman's house and small island adjacent with appurtenances at la Huche in Egham which he held of them as a tenant at will in villeinage, so that neither the said Adam nor his family nor anyone in his name should enter on the fore-mentioned weir, etc., nor yet sell or make any profit of them in the future. For which surrender the abbot and convent have granted the said Adam, for his whole life, 4 qrs. of corn, wheat and barley, to be received from the granary annually, etc. And if it should happen that the abbot and convent should neglect to furnish the above special corn for a year, then it shall be lawful for said Adam to re-enter said weir, etc., and to keep possession of them in perpetuity, on the same terms as he before

held them, without any obstruction from the abbot.'[42] In 1642 the inhabitants of Egham made a petition[43] in which they claimed the privilege, lately wrested from them, of depasturing their cattle in Windsor Great Park at very easy rates. The privilege had been granted in consideration of divers services performed by them, such as carrying in hay, sending ' treaders ' and the like, and also in respect that a great part of the park had been taken out of the commons belonging to the parish. The terms for which this depasturing was allowed were from 10 May till Lammas and from All Hallows tide until Christmas, and the weekly payment per animal had never exceeded 1½d. until recently. The petition stated, however, that, in view of the fact that ' the prices of land, as of all other commodities, are much increased,' the inhabitants were willing to pay 4d. weekly for a cow or a bullock, 6d. for a horse, mare, or colt. A representative of the inhabitants was ordered to attend the Attorney-General for settling the point.

Land at Pernehrs in Egham, described as ' half a hide of land and 5 acres, with appurtenances,' now known as *ANKERWICK PARNISH*, was confirmed to the priory of Ankerwick in Buckinghamshire by Henry III in 1252,[44] when it was stated to have been given to the priory by Hugh, Abbot of Chertsey. This Hugh must be the one to whom the charter of Stephen to Chertsey is addressed.[45] He is called Hugh the abbot, *nepos meus*, and if the charter is genuine must be Hugh de Puiset, Stephen's nephew, who became Bishop of Durham in 1153. The date of the grant to Ankerwick thus seems to be fixed as previous to that year.[46] The possessions of the priory in Egham included also 1 acre of land of the gift of Grunwin de Trottesworth, land which Almerus held of the gift of Godfrey de Middleton, 13 acres of land of the gift of Robert de Middleton, and a croft called Tutescroft of the gift of Henry son of Henry de Middleton.[47] Waste lands in Egham were granted to the prioress in 1280,[48] her possessions there in 1291 being taxed at 10s.[49] The prioress seems, by degrees, to have acquired all the land called Pernehrs or Parnish, giving the abbot in return other pieces of land which she possessed in Egham. In 1319 John, Abbot of Chertsey, confirmed to the prioress half an acre called Guldenhalfacre at Loderlake in Egham, in a certain field called Ermehrs between the land of Stephen de Purnehrs on the west and the land which had belonged to John de Walyngford on the east, in exchange for all that land which the prioress had in Egham in the field called Bokelnfrude.[50] Assart land called Patteshill next Pernehrs was also granted her in exchange for a croft called Litelcroft.[51] An annual rent of 28s. 6d. which the prioress paid the abbot was reduced in 1319 to 24s. 6d. At the survey of the priory's possessions in 1535 the manor of Parnish in Surrey was valued at £5 2s. 6d.[52] The estates of the priory, which were soon afterwards surrendered, were granted in 1537 to the monks of Chertsey in the new foundation at Bisham,[53] but reverted to the Crown at the final suppression of this monastery in 1538. Henry VIII

[37] Monument at Micklcham.
[38] That is forty years after the death of Sir Francis, 1655.
[39] Add. Chart. 6150.
[40] Parl. Surv. Surr. 1650, no. 25.
[41] Ct. R.
[42] Lansd. MS. 434, fol. 32.

[43] Cal. S.P. Dom. 1641–3, p. 318.
[44] Chart. R. 41 Hen. III, no. 3.
[45] Not Hugh, abbot from 1107.
[46] Cf. V.C.H. Bucks. i, 355.
[47] Chart. R. 41 Hen. III, no. 3.
[48] Inq. a.q.d. file 5, no. 19 ; Cal. Pat. 1281–92, p. 1.

[49] Pope Nich. Tax. (Rec. Com.), 206b.
[50] Exch. K.R. Misc. Bks. vol. 25, fol. 230.
[51] Ibid. fol. 230b.
[52] Valor Eccl. (Rec. Com.), iv, 222.
[53] L. and P. Hen. VIII, xii (2) g. 1311 (22).

granted the manor of Parnish to Andrew Lord Windsor in 1539 for life, with remainder to his sons William, Edmund, and Thomas.[54] William Lord Windsor sold this manor and others to the king for £1,000 in 1544.[55] Edward VI granted it in 1550 to Sir Thomas Smith,[56] a settlement on the latter's heirs being made in 1577.[57] The manor remained in this family until 1652, when it was sold by Thomas Smith, the nephew of the original grantee, to John Lee,[58] from whom it passed to his son John.[59] Elizabeth, daughter and heiress of this son, married Sir Philip Harcourt, she being his second wife. Their son was John Harcourt of Ankerwick, and the manor has remained in this family since that time.[60] The present lord of the manor in the fifth generation from John Harcourt is Mr. George S. C. Harcourt.

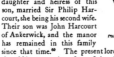

HARCOURT. Gules two bars or.

The first definite reference to the manor of MILTON does not occur until the middle of the 14th century, 1348, when Matilda Gatelyn, or Gacelyn, received licence from the bishop to celebrate divine service in the oratory of her manor of Middleton.[61] It is, however, possible to trace the history of land, which evidently formed the nucleus of this manor, to an earlier date, as in 1299 Henry de Middleton and Matilda his wife held a messuage, a mill, and lands in Egham and Thorpe.[62] After the death of Henry, Matilda presumably held the manor for her lifetime, marrying as her second husband John Gatelyn. A record occurs in 1319 showing that John Gatelyn and Matilda, together with Thomas son of Henry de Middleton, disseised the Abbot of Chertsey of various lands, of which, however, he afterwards regained possession.[63] After the death of Matilda the manor probably reverted to Thomas, her son by her first husband, as in the early 16th century the manor was still in possession of the Middletons.[64] Certain lands belonging to the manor were sold about this time by Henry de Middleton to Richard Fox, Bishop of Winchester and founder of the college of Corpus Christi, Oxford, and these lands, together with the manor of Middleton or Milton, were granted to the college in 1518, when

CORPUS CHRISTI COL-LEGE, OXFORD. Tierced in pale : (1) Azure a pelican or, for Bishop Fox ; (2) Argent with a scutcheon of the arms of the see of Winchester ; (3) Sable a cheveron or between three owls ar-gent and a chief or with three roses gules therein, for Bishop Oldham.

the Abbot and convent of Chertsey granted permission to William Frost and Ralph Lepton, then seised of the manor, to enfeoff John Cleymond, President, and the fellows of the college of Corpus Christi.[65] It is probable that Frost and Lepton were acting for the Middletons, as in 1522 John Middleton and Margaret made a confirmatory grant of the manor to John Cleymond and his successors, receiving in return the sum of £340.[66] The manor thus granted is still held by this college. The Valor of 1535 shows that the college paid a rent of £3 6s. to the Abbot of Chertsey.[67] It was demised in 1598 to Francis Morley, to hold for nineteen years.[68] In 1622 Mary More, widow, held the 'manor of Middleton or Mylton Place and other lands in Egham' of the college of Corpus Christi.[69] The manor appears to have been leased both before and after that date to the family of More, or Moore.[70] Adrian Moore, senior, who died in 1740, was of Milton, and his son Adrian Moore, who died in 1749, held the estate.[71] His sister's son was William Edgell, who succeeded to Adrian Moore's property, and his heiress and niece Priscilla married Richard Wyatt in 1766.[72] Edgell Wyatt their son inherited the estate in 1813, taking the additional surname of Edgell.[73] His son, Richard Wyatt-Edgell, succeeded him in 1853.[74] The

WYATT. Sable a fesse dancetty argent between three eagles or with a chief or.

EDGELL. Argent a cheveron sable between three cinqfoils gules with three bezants on the cheveron.

connexion between this family and the college was severed about 1870, when the unexpired portion of their lease was purchased by Baron de Worms.[75]

A water-mill known as Trumpes Mill was granted with the manor to the college of Corpus Christi.[76] Tithes from it to the value of 21s. 4d. remained due to the almoner of Chertsey Abbey until the Dissolution.[77] In a rental of 1622 Trumpes Mill, the property of Corpus Christi, and in the tenure of Mary More, is stated to be in Thorpe,[78] a mistake which is doubtless due to the fact that the mill is on a stream which divides the parishes of Egham and Thorpe.

In 1189–90 Nigel le Broc held land called TROTTESWORTH of the Abbot of Chertsey for the fourth part of a knight's fee,[79] and at some period during the latter half of the 12th century Maurice de Trotteswrth and others held land in

54 Pat. 31 Hen. VIII, pt. i, m. 18, 19.
55 Feet of F. Div. Co. Hil. 35 Hen. VIII.
56 Dugdale, Mon. Angl. iv, 230 ; Add. MS. 4705, fol. 145.
57 Pat. 20 Eliz. pt. v, m. 31.
58 Recov. R. Mich. 1651 ; Feet of F. Div. Co. Hil. 1652.
59 Feet of F. Div. Co. Trin. 31 Chas. II.
60 Com. Pleas D. Enr. Trin. 34 Geo. III, m. 4 ; Recov. R. East. 9 Geo. IV ; Burke, Landed Gentry ; E. W. Brayley, op. cit.

61 Winton Epis. Reg. Edendon, ii, fol. 13b.
62 Feet of F. Surr. Trin. 27 Edw. I.
63 Exch. K.R. Misc. Bks. vol. 25, fol. 228 d.
64 Ibid. fol. 245b.   65 Ibid.
66 Feet of F. Surr. Mich. 14 Hen. VIII.
67 Valor Eccl. (Rec. Com.), ii, 247.
68 Ct. of Req. lxxxvii, 54.
69 Rentals and Surv. (P.R.O.), Surr. R. 626.
70 Information received from Mr. A. Wyatt-Edgell ; Aubrey, op. cit. iii, 167.

71 Gent. Mag. 1749, p. 93.
72 Information received from Mr. A. Wyatt-Edgell ; Burke, Landed Gentry.
73 Burke, Landed Gentry.   74 Ibid.
75 Information received from Mr. A. Wyatt-Edgell.
76 Exch. K.R. Misc. Bks. vol. 25, fol. 245b.
77 Valor Eccl. (Rec. Com.), ii, 56.
78 Rentals and Surv. Surr. R. 626, 20 Jas. I.
79 Exch. K.R. Misc. Bks. vol. 25, fol. 64.

Surrey of the abbot for the same service.[80] During the 13th century Richard Russel held this ¼ knight's fee in Trotsworth or Troccesworth.[81] In 1252 a dispute arose between Richard Russel of Trottesworth and the Abbot of Chertsey concerning view of frankpledge in the hundred of Godley. It was finally agreed that Richard and his heirs should come to view of frankpledge at Godley Hill every year at the feast of the Epiphany. The abbot in return granted him a certain marsh called Losehall.[82] In 1428 John Tendale held in Egham ¼ part of a knight's fee which Margaret de Trottesworth formerly held of the Abbot of Chertsey.[83] The manor afterwards passed to the monastery of Abingdon in Berkshire, though the date of the conveyance is not apparent. At the suppression of this monastery in 1538 the manor of Trottesworth in Thorpe and Egham, with a tenement called le Strande, was valued at £5 3s. 4d.[84]

ABINGDON ABBEY. *Argent a cross paty between four martlets sable.*

In 1545 the manor was granted to John Broxholme, John Bellew and others in trust for Anthony Bond.[85] The next year Anthony Bond leased Trottesworth to William Knight for a term of eighty-one years, dating from 1552.[86] Bond sold the manor to the Crown shortly afterwards, and in 1555 Anne, Duchess of Somerset, received a life grant of it.[87] She died in 1587.[88] William Knight was still in possession of the lease in 1588, when the queen granted the reversion to James Bond for a period of twenty-one years.[89]

In 1599 the queen granted the manor 'lately in the tenure of James Bond' to George Austeyne and William Minterne and their heirs.[90] They were presumably trustees, as John Bond was in possession of the manor in 1609, in which year he sold it to John Worsopp.[91] The latter conveyed it in 1625 to John Machell and Deborah his wife,[92] and it remained in their family until 1750,[93] when Lancelot Machell sold it to Charles Simes and Samuel Meredith to the use of Charles Simes and his heirs.[94] The manor afterwards passed to John Forster, who conveyed it to his son George in 1802,[95] when the property included, besides the manor, a farm called Trottesworth Farm and closes called Hollymore Field, Knowle Field, Furzey Field, Blackshill Field, Reversfield, Packers Land, Lamsley Hill, Hams Mead, Horse Mead, One Brock, Holly Platt and the Slip.

Trottesworth seems to have ceased to be regarded as a manor about this period. The deed of 1802 refers to it as a 'manor or reputed manor.' Manning states that the property consisted of two farms, which were held in his time, about 1804, by Mr. Forster and Mr. Fournier.[96] The Countess de Morella held the estate in 1905.

BROOMHALL.—Among the possessions of the priory of Broomhall in Berkshire when it became escheat to the Crown in 1522 were certain tenements in Egham and Thorpe, including 32 acres of meadow in Egham, of which the priory had apparently been seised for some time.[97] The name Broomhall in Egham is as old as the perambulation of the forest boundaries in 1226.[98] In October 1522 the king granted the site and possessions of the late priory to the Master and Fellows of St. John's College, Cambridge. The deed included a 'manor' in Egham which was undoubtedly the land previously referred to.[99] In 1544 the college sold to the king a portion of their land in Egham, about 44 acres, called Knowle Grove.[100] A survey of Egham Manor in 1622 includes land called Broomhall Piece, property of St. John's, and in the tenure of William Minterne.[101] The college still holds the manor of Broomhall, in Egham.[102]

ST. JOHN'S COLLEGE, CAMBRIDGE. *France quartered with England in a border gobony argent and azure.*

IMWORTH.—A tenement and lands in Egham were in the possession of the family of Imworth in 1224, when John de Imworth brought a suit against Henry de Middleton concerning the land.[103] In 1298 John de Imworth conveyed the reversion of lands in Egham to Robert de Burghton and Sarah his wife, and to the heirs of Sarah, who was probably the daughter of John de Imworth. The latter was to hold it of Robert and Sarah for the remainder of his life for the annual rent of one rose and for the services due to the chief lords of the fee.[104]

In January 1339 Robert de Imworth received licence for the celebration of divine service in the oratory of his house in Egham.[105] In 1550 the manor of Inworths *alias* Fosters belonged to Sir William Warham,[106] and afterwards went to his heir, who held the manor in 1616.[107] Fosters apparently became a separate holding, for in 1622, when Sir John Doddridge was holding the messuage and lands called Fosters, Sir John Denham had the site of the manor of Imworth.[108] In 1638 Imworth passed to his son Sir John Denham the Royalist poet,[109] whose estates were sequestered, and in 1648 conveyed to John Thynne.[110] Thynne remained in possession, and his son was resident at Imworth in 1673.[111] Sir John Denham

80 Red Bk. of Exch. (Rolls Ser.), 158.
81 Testa de Nevill (Rec. Com.), 221b.
82 Exch. K.R. Misc. Bks. 25, fol. 241b.
83 Feud. Aids, v, 123.
84 Dugdale, Mon. Angl. i, 505.
85 Pat. 37 Hen. VIII, pt. ix, m. 26–36; Add. MS. 4705, fol. 28, 39.
86 Pat. 30 Eliz. pt. x, m. 6.
87 Ibid. 2 & 3 Phil. and Mary. pt. viii, m. 22.
88 Dict. Nat. Biog.
89 Pat. 30 Eliz. pt. x, m. 6.
90 Ibid. 42 Eliz. pt. xii, m. 1.
91 Feet of F. Surr. East. 6 Jas. I; Com. Pleas D. Enr. East. 6 Jas. I, m. 23.

92 Feet of F. Surr. Mich. 1 Chas. I.
93 Recov. R. East. 4 Chas. I, rot. 1; Mich. 34 Chas. II, rot. 208; Feet of F. Div. Co. Mich. 34 Chas. II; Recov. R. Mich. 3 Geo. I, rot. 146.
94 Com. Pleas D. Enr. East. 26 Geo. II, m. 60, 62.
95 Com. Pleas D. Enr. East. 42 Geo. III, m. 96; Recov. R. East. 42 Geo. III, rot. 17.
96 Manning and Bray, op. cit. iii, 255.
97 Exch. Inq. p.m. file 1075, no. 3 & 4, 13, 14 Hen. VIII.
98 V.C.H. Surr. i, 357.
99 Pat. 14 Hen. VIII, pt. ii, m. 5.
100 Information from St. John's College.

101 Rentals and Surv. (P.R.O.), R. 626.
102 Information from St. John's College.
103 Cal. Pat. 1216–25, p. 485.
104 Feet of F. Surr. East. 26 Edw. I.
105 Winton Epis. Reg. Orleton, i, fol. 70a. Compare Egerton MS.
106 Feet of F. Div. Co. Mich. 4 Edw. VI; Chan. Proc. (Ser. 2), bdle. 85, no. 22; Feet of F. Surr. East. 2 & 3 Phil. and Mary.
107 Chan. Inq. p.m. (Ser. 2), cccl, 57.
108 Rentals and Surv. (P.R.O.), R. 626.
109 Dict. Nat. Biog.
110 Cal. of Com. for Compounding, 1790.
111 Aubrey, op. cit. Ili, 164.

the elder had rebuilt the house. This is called the Place or Parsonage House by Aubrey, because Denham held the rectory. It has been incorrectly confused with the vicarage house. It is now pulled down.[113]

The other part of Imworth *alias* Fosters was perhaps separated at Sir William Warham's death. In 1568 Jasper Palmer and Rose his wife conveyed it to Thomas Burtell.[113] About this time Chancery proceedings are said to have been taken between Edward Owen and Thomas Burtell. Fosters passed from Owen to Sir Antony Manners, and from him to Sir John Doddridge.[114] Sir John died in 1628, and the name of Sir Robert Foster the judge, with which the name of the house has been erroneously connected. appears for the first time in connexion with it in 1639.[113]
Sir Robert was youngest son of Sir Thomas Foster, Justice of the Common Pleas 1607,[116] and was himself a Justice of Common Pleas, 1640–4, when he was removed. In 1660 he was restored and made Lord Chief Justice of the King's Bench. He died in 1663. His son Sir Thomas Foster succeeded to the property and died in 1685.[117] It changed hands several times, and early in the 19th century was a lunatic asylum. Fosters or Great Fosters is a good early 17th-century house.

Foster. *Argent a cheveron between three hunting horns sable.*

The messuage of RUSHAM or RUYSSHAMES in Egham appears to have been in the possession of a family of that name from very early times. Alice Rusham, who inherited the lands in the reign of Henry VI, and who married first Robert Ferly, and secondly John Wolley, was apparently the descendant of a line of Rushams,[118] and occasional references to Rushams of Egham, occurring as a witness or as owner of land, are found in the Ledger Book of Chertsey Abbey and elsewhere.[119] Agnes Ferly, granddaughter and heiress of Alice, is said to have married Thomas Day of Egham,[120] in whose family Rusham remained until 1679.[121] From the 16th century onwards Rusham is described as a manor, but there is no evidence to show that it was considered as such before that time. An account of the property in the reign of Henry VI describes it as 'a messuage, 160 acres of arable land, 12 acres of meadow, 80 acres of pasture and 20 acres of wood and 24*s.* rent in Egham in co. Surrey, called Ruysshames.'[122] A rental of Egham Manor taken in 1622 records that the sum of 20*s.* 4*d.* was paid by Richard Day for his manor of Rusham and for his fishing and greyhounds.[123] After 1679 all trace of the so-called manor is lost. Rusham Hall, formerly the seat of the family of Day, was destroyed before the 19th century,[124] but Rusham Green and a farm of the same name still exist in Egham.

The PARK OF POTENALL or PORTNALL belonged anciently to the Crown. It is not clear when it was imparked, but in 1485 the office of parker in the king's park of Potenall in the forest of Windsor was given to John Molle.[125] In 1528 Henry VIII granted the park to Sir William Fitz William and his heirs, 'for the service of one red rose annually.'[126] It was apparently disparked before 1607, for Norden's Survey of the parks in the forest of Windsor of that year does not include it.[127] The history of the property during the 17th century is not apparent.[128] During the latter half of the 18th century it is referred to as a manor held by families named Walker and Day.[129] The manor so called was conveyed in 1791 to Mr. Lowndes,[130] whose family owned property in Chertsey and Egham fifty years later. Part of the estate, however, was in the hands of Dr. Jebb, Dean of Londonderry. His son Mr. David Jebb exchanged it in 1804 for other land with the Rev. T. Bisse, whose son, Colonel Bisse Challoner, held it in 1840, and built the present house.[131] It is now the property of the Rev. H. J. A. Fane de Salis. A park was inclosed by Colonel Bisse Challoner. The site of the original park was probably not exactly where Portnall Park now is, but in Portnall Warren, where Norden's map marks Valley Wood.

De Salis. *Paly argent and gules a chief or with a willow tree torn up by the roots therein.*

In the 17th and 18th centuries occasional record is found of a reputed manor called WICK, or EGHAM WICK, in Egham. In 1618 Edward Anthony and William Willis sold the manor, which included two messuages or farms, to Francis Anthony and his heirs.[132] In 1768 it was the property of the Rev. William Robert Jones and Elizabeth his wife, and was apparently held in the right of Elizabeth.[133] They sold it as the 'manor or reputed manor of Egham' in 1782 to John Pitt and his heirs.[134]

CHURCHES

The church of ST. JOHN THE BAPTIST was built in 1817, and is of little architectural interest. It consists of a shallow chancel, a wide nave with galleries on three sides, and a west tower, and has three west doorways, the two side doors admitting to the gallery stairs. The building is in poor classical style, and built of brick with stone dressings. The chancel has north and south vestries, and on each side of the nave are six windows below the gallery, and six above it, some of them filled with stained glass from the chapel at Coopers Hill; the nave has a coved plaster ceiling.

[113] Information from Mr. F. Turner of Egham.

[113] Feet of F. Surr. Mich. 10 & 11 Eliz.

[114] Rentals and Surv. (P.R.O.), R. 626.

[115] Feet of F. Surr. Mich. 15 Chas. I.

[116] Monument in Egham Church.

[117] Monument in Thorpe Church.

[118] Harl. MS. 5830, fol. 250, 251 ; Chan. Proc. bdle. 54, no. 179.

[119] Exch. K.R. Misc. Bks. vol. 25, fol. 246*b*; *Cal. Close* 1821–5, p. 352.

[120] Harl. MS. 5830, fol. 250, 251.

[122] Feet of Surr. Mich. 44 & 45 Eliz.; Feet of F. Surr. Hil. 1650; Recov. R. Mich. 1653, rot. 48 ; Feet of F. Surr. Mich. 31 Chas. II.

[123] Early Chan. Proc. bdle. 54, no. 179.

[123] Rentals and Surv. (P.R.O.) R. 626.

[124] Manning and Bray, op. cit. iii, 253.

[125] *Cal. Pat.* 1476–85, p. 512.

[126] Pat. 19 Hen. VIII, pt. i, 12.

[127] Harl. MS. 3749.

[128] Manning had a privately communicated mention of deeds conveying 'Potter's Park' to Arthur Mainwaring and then to John Lyne in 1661. Manning and Bray, op. cit. iii, 255. But Potter's Park is another place in Chertsey.

[129] Recov. R. Trin. 17 Geo. III, rot. 132 ; Feet of Surr. Mich. 30 Geo. III.

[160] Feet of F. Surr. Hil. 31 Geo. III.

[131] E. W. Brayley, op. cit. ii, 297.

[132] Com. Pleas D. Enr. Trin. 15 Jas. I, m. 6.

[133] Recov. R. East. 8 Geo. III, rot. 276.

[134] Com. Pleas Recov. R. Trin. 22 Geo. III, m. 303.

There is a large modern wooden pulpit and a white marble font, the latter presented in 1902 by the parish clerk.

A print of the old church shows a large building with a central tower ; from it several monuments have been transferred to the present building when the other was taken down.

On the north wall is an alabaster and marble tablet to Richard Kellefet of Egham, 1595, son of George and Margaret Kellefet, and to his wife Cicely. He was 'a most faithful servant to Hir Majestie, chief groome in the removing garderobe of beddes, and yeoman also of her standing garderobe, of Richemount.' A shield over the tablet bears, Ermine, a chief azure, and a talbot passant thereon. On the east wall of the south aisle is a mural brass to Anthony Bond, 1576, his wife and two sons. He was a citizen and writer of the court letter of London. The arms above the monument are, Argent, two bends sable with a crosslet sable in the cantle. On the same wall is the very interesting inscription recording the building of the old church in 1327. + HEC : NOMUS : EFFICITUR : BAPTISTE : LAUDE : JOHANNIS : ‖ BISDECA : SEPTENIS TRECENTIS : MILLE : SUB : ANNIS : ‖ XPI : QUAM : STATUIT : ABBAS : EX : CUORDE : JOHANNS : ‖ DE : RUTHERWYKA : PER : TERRAS : DICTUS : ET : AMPNES.[134a]

Over the gallery stairs at the north-west angle of the nave is a monument to Lady Cicely Denham, and Eleanor Moor, first and second wives of Sir John Denham. Their half-figures are shown coloured and in high relief in a circular panel about which is a pilastered and pedimented feature of alabaster and marble. One of the women holds an infant in her arms, and the figure of a boy is shown half out of the frame. The design is very good and effective, but the execution is hardly equal to it. Above are the arms of Denham—Gules a fesse indented ermine, impaling Sable a fesse indented with three molets on the fesse. Over the other stairs to the south-west is a monument to Sir John Denham, without any memorial inscription, with a rather more elaborate architectural treatment and a most curious figure composition of very considerable merit. The plinth, on which is inscribed 'Ex ossibus armati,' has a frieze in high relief of skeletons emerging from their shrouds within a tomb whose sides are breaking up in all directions ; two of the figures, evidently meant for Sir John Denham and his wife, have reassumed their flesh.

Above this in complete relief is the nude and bearded figure of a man rising from his tomb, obviously a portrait of Sir John ; a shroud still partly covers his head and shoulders, and on his coffin is written ' Praeterita sperno.' Above is an entablature carried by Corinthian columns, on which are two angels blowing trumpets, with the words ' Surge a Somnis.' Another 17th-century monument, to Sir Robert Foster, is hidden by the organ. He was Chief Justice of the King's Bench, and died in 1663. His bust is in a circular frame, with shields of arms above and on either side. The upper shield has the arms of Foster—Argent a cheveron between three bugle-horns sable quartered with Argent a bend engrailed sable with three harts' heads cabossed or thereon. The other

shields bear (1) Quarterly gules and argent four scallops counterchanged, and (2) Quarterly or and gules a bend vair, which are the arms of Burton and Sackville respectively. In the chancel are several good modern monuments to the family of Gostling.

The tower contains six bells, cast in 1819 by T. Mears.

The church plate consists of a cup of 1618, inscribed in a dotted line as the gift of Adrian Moore and bearing the arms, a fesse, three pierced molets thereon ; a standing paten of the same date with similar inscription and heraldry but in an incised line ; a cup of 1793, and a very handsome flagon, in a curiously shaped leather case of 1749. There are also two standing patens or salvers of German or Flemish workmanship and 16th-century date, the bowls of which are elaborately engraved with figure subjects, one representing David harping, the other Christ in the house of Martha. The latter is signed H⧺B.

The first book of the registers contains marriages from 1560 to 1666, baptisms from 1560 to 1669, and burials from 1592 to 1651. The second book has all entries from 1653 to 1709 in the case of marriages, and to 1711 for the other entries. The fourth book has all entries from 1711, marriages running to 1751, baptisms and burials to 1771. Marriages are separately continued from 1754 to 1812, and a sixth book has baptisms and burials from 1771 to 1812.

CHRIST CHURCH, Virginia Water, consecrated in 1838, is cruciform, of brick with pointed arches, a tower and stone spire. The chapel of ease of St. Simon and St. Jude, Englefield Green, was built in 1859. It is of stone in 13th-century style, with a west tower. A cemetery adjoins it.

ADVOWSONS In 1291 the churches of Chertsey, Egham, and Chobham were together valued at £63 6s. 8d., and the vicarage of Egham at £9 6s. 8d.[135] This appears to be the first reference to the church, which must, however, have existed before this date. It was in the hands of the monks of Chertsey from its foundation until the dissolution of the abbey. The vicarage was formally ordained by the abbot in 1333 : the vicar, Robert de Wanynden, and his successors were to have a mansion well and honestly built, with the adjacent croft called Thorpeshull, containing 15 acres of arable land, a piece of land called Denacre, a small meadow called Thachmede, pasture called Wynclesworth Parva, and various other small parcels of land. Half the tithes coming from 20 acres of land towards Staines, formerly of Richard Barentin, were also granted to him.[136] Augmentation of the vicarage was made in 1421.[137] In the survey of the abbey's possessions, taken in 1535,[138] the rectory of Egham was valued at £17. Both rectory and advowson were surrendered to the king in 1537.[139] The rectory was granted to the new foundation at Bisham in the same year,[140] but reverted to the Crown once more on the final suppression of Bisham Monastery in July 1538. Edward VI granted the rectory of Egham to John Poynet, Bishop of Winchester, in 1551,[141] and John White, who was bishop in 1558, also received a grant of it, together with the advowson of the vicarage, from Queen Mary.[142]

[134a] Pictures show a Norman door to the old church, which was not therefore entirely built in 1327.
[134] *Pope Nich. Tax.* (Rec. Com.), 206b.
[135] Exch. K.R. Misc. Bks. vol. 25, fol. 40.
[136] Ibid. fol. 41.
[137] *Valor Eccl.* (Rec. Com.), ii, 56.
[138] Feet of F. Div. Co. Trin. 29 Hen. VIII.
[140] *L. and P. Hen. VIII*, xii (2), 469.
[141] Pat. 5 Edw. VI, pt. vi, m. 26.
[142] Ibid. 5 & 6 Phil. and Mary, pt. iv, m. 6.

The latter grant, however, was cancelled on the accession of Elizabeth. In 1611 James I granted both rectory and advowson to Francis Morrice and Francis Philipps,[142] probably trustees, as Maria Moore,[143] a widow, presented in 1620.[144] Sir John Dormer owned the rectory and advowson in 1624,[145] but Sir John Denham had acquired both before 1639.[147] In 1648 the estate of his son, Sir John Denham the poet, a delinquent, was conveyed to John Thynne, M.P., for a debt of £20.[148] The rectory and advowson were probably included in this conveyance, as John Thynne presented to the vicarage in 1662.[149] According to Manning, Thomas Sutton, son-in-law of John Thynne, sold the rectory to Adrian Moore, who sold it in his turn in 1734 to William Scawen,[150] whose family was certainly in possession in 1759.[151] It afterwards passed to John Dawe, whose son sold the rectory to George Gostling in 1788.[152] The advowson passed at the same time to Mrs. Challoner, who conveyed it to George Gostling in 1797.[153] He presented to the church in 1811.[154] The patronage remained in his family until 1879, when it passed to the Rev. W. Trevor Nicholson, who now holds it.[155]

Christ Church Virginia Water was formed into a parish in 1838. The living is in the gift of three trustees.

CHARITIES Of the older charities the most important is Henry Strode's, left by will in 1703. He left £6,000, of which the Cooper's Company became trustees, for almshouses and a school. Considerable litigation followed owing to alleged misappropriation of funds and to some ambiguity in the will, it being doubtful whether the almspeople need or need not be inhabitants of Egham. It was decided in 1749 that they must be chosen from the parish. The next question was about the schoolhouse, which Mr. Jeans, as master, wished to use as a first-grade school, relegating the teaching of poor children to other hands. This state of affairs is similar to that which occurred at Farnham.[156]

In 1812 the Court of Chancery decided that the school must be reserved for the poor children of Egham. In 1828 new almshouses were begun and in 1839 completed, on the north side of Egham Street (see inscription in almshouses). The school is now, however, discontinued, and the money formerly devoted to it has gone since 1870 to the Station Road School, formerly called Egham Parish School. There are twelve almshouses and a chapel. Before this, in 1624, Sir John Denham, baron of the Exchequer, father to the poet, founded almshouses for five poor women.

Ann Reid in 1838 founded five almshouses in memory of her husband.

In 1840 Mr. Stewart founded five almshouses.

In 1683 Mr. Richard Barker charged land with £2 10s. per annum, for the benefit of the poor.

In 1705 Mr. Edmund Lee left land producing then £60 per annum for the apprenticing of poor children.

In 1712 Mrs. Mary Barker left £5 per annum charged on land for the teaching of poor children.

Smith's Charity exists as in other Surrey parishes.

Egham parish has a nomination in rotation with thirty other parishes of one poor man to Lucas's Hospital at Wokingham in Berkshire, founded in 1663.

HORSELL

Horishull (xiii cent.) ; Horsehill (xvii cent.) ; Horshill (xviii cent.).

Horsell lies a mile north-west of Woking Junction. It is bounded on the north by Chobham, north and east by Chertsey, south by Woking, west by Bisley. It contains 2,913 acres. It measures about 3½ miles east to west, and from 1 to 1½ miles north to south. The soil is Bagshot sand. This lends itself to the chief industry of the place, nursery gardening. Messrs. Waterer, Messrs. Cobbett and others have nursery gardens of American plants and trees. There is also a brewery. Formerly there were extensive commons, of which Horsell Birch and part of Woodham Common are the largest remaining ; the Inclosure Act of 35 George III[1] affected part of the commons of Horsell, as being in Pyrford Manor. The Basingstoke Canal skirts the parish.

There are said to have been barrows upon the heath, but there is now no trace of their existence.[2]

The aspect of the eastern part of the parish has been quite transformed by the growth of the town about Woking Junction. When the railway was first opened the neighbourhood was so secluded that a spot in Horsell parish, near the Basingstoke Canal, was selected as a suitable place for a prize fight, as out of the observation of the police.[3] This is now covered with houses, a considerable number of which usually reckoned in Woking are really in Horsell. Gentlemen's houses are rising rapidly, and there are famous golf links in Horsell.

There is a Baptist chapel in the parish built in 1901.

The schools (National) were built in 1851 and enlarged in 1882. But a Church school and a Baptist school existed about 1845.[4]

MANORS HORSELL, though parochially a chapelry of Woking, appears to have been included in the manor and lordship of Pyrford (q.v.) from the time of its earliest records until the present day. No reference to it is found in the Domesday Survey, but that it was part of the land at the Pyrian Ford granted to Westminster in 956 is probable, as in 1278–9 the Abbot of West-

142 Pat 8 Jas. I, pt. xxxi, m. 1 ; 10 Jas. I, pt. ii, m. 1.

144 See manor of Milton. She was widow of Adrian Moore of London, merchant (Harl. MS. 1561, fol. 68). Her husband presented a chalice to the church.

145 Inst. Bks. (P.R.O.).

146 Feet of F. Surr. East. 22 Jas. I.

147 Recov. R. East. 15 Chas. I.

148 Cal. of Com. for Compounding, 1790.

149 Inst. Bks. (P.R.O.).

150 Manning and Bray, op. cit. iii ; Aubrey, op. cit. iii, 150.

151 Recov. R. Mich. 33 Geo. II.

152 Close, 29 Geo. III, pt. i, no. 17.

153 Manning and Bray, op. cit. iii.

154 Inst. Bks. (P.R.O.). 155 Clergy Lists.

156 V.C.H. Surr. ii, 189.

1 Award 29 Sept. 1815, Blue Bk. Incl. Awards.

2 Aubrey, op. cit. iii, 189, 193.

3 Information from Sir Denis Le Marchant of Chobham Place.

4 Brayley, Hist. of Surr. ii, 170.

minster claimed various privileges in his ' manors of Piriford and Horishill.' [4a] This is, apparently, the first reference to Horsell as a separate manor. Whether it was ever held as such is doubtful. Land at Sithwood, which was in the parish of Horsell,[5] was described as being part of the manor of Pyrford,[6] the two sub-manors in Horsell were held as of the manor of Pyrford,[7] and a survey of the manor of Pyrford, taken in 1547, includes Horsell, Sithwood, and Woodham as part of its demesne.[8] In 1678 it is again referred to as a manor,[9] being held at that time, as was Pyrford, by Denzil Onslow, from whom the property passed to the present lord, the Earl of Onslow, whose manor of Pyrford includes Horsell and Woodham.

In 1540 John Danaster of Chobham died seised of the manor or tenement called *HILL PLACE*,[9] which was held of the king as of his manor of Pyrford by fealty and rent of 21s. Danaster left the manor to his wife Anne for her life, with remainder to Robert, natural son of John and Anne, and his heirs, or in default to the right heirs of John.[10] His widow afterwards married Sir Francis Dawtrey, and they were in possession of the manor apparently about 1560.[11] It had passed, before 1571, to Christopher Hennage and Anne his wife,[12] daughter of John Danaster and formerly wife of Owen Bray, who had died in 1568.[13] They conveyed it in 1578 to Richard Hatton,[14] but it changed hands again and in 1599 Sir William and Sir George More, probably acting as trustees, conveyed it to Henry Weston,[15] from whom it passed in 1622 to Henry Collyer and Richard Simones.[16] The Collyer family continued to hold it, though it is not generally called a manor.[17] The Collyers of Hill Place were among the lay impropriators of the tithes (q.v.), mentioned about 1682 and in 1804. In 1841 the Collyer family sold Hill Place to Mr. G. Marshall of Godalming. In 1851 he settled it upon his daughter on her marriage with Mr. T. Shearburn. Her son Mr. R. W. Shearburn of the Hall, Scraith, Yorkshire, is the present owner. The house is let as a farm, and some of the land has been sold off, a small part having been bought by Mr. John Collyer of Horsell, a descendant of the former owners.[18]

In 1316 is found the first trace of the manor of *TWICHEN*, when Walter atte Rude settled on his son Walter the estate described as 1 messuage, 40 acres, half a mill, &c., with appurtenances in Chobham, Horsell, and Pyrford. William de Carleton and Alice his wife, and John atte Twichen and Alice his wife, also put in a claim to this land.[19] It is probable that it had previously belonged to John atte Twichen and his wife, as in 1326 he sought to replevy his and his wife's lands in Chobham, Horsell, and Pyrford, which had been taken into the king's hands for their default against Walter son of

Walter atte Rude.[20] In 1352 Roger Bernard and Katherine and William atte Twichen conveyed certain land in Horsell, Chobham, and Pyrford—a messuage, 80 acres of land, &c.—to Richard Doxeye and Alice his wife.[21] John atte Grenette in 1363 obtained from Richard Doxeye and Sabina his wife and the heirs of Sabina land in these parishes, consisting of two messuages, 100 acres of land, &c.[22] These different holdings seem to have become amalgamated before the middle of the 16th century. They were then known as the manor or capital tenement called Twichen, of which John Danaster died seised in 1540, and which he held of the king as of his manor of Pyrford by fealty and rent of 18s.[23] He left the manor to his wife Anne for her life, with reversion to their daughter Anne, who afterwards married Owen Bray.[24] Anne the mother married, as her second husband, Sir Francis Dawtrey, and they were apparently seised of the manor about the year 1560.[25] In 1572 this manor, together with that of Hill Place, was held by Christopher Hennage and Anne his wife.[26] The latter was the widow of Owen Bray, for the next reference to Twichen in 1607, records that the site of the manor was the property of Owen Bray ;[27] John Bray also held with Owen,[28] the two being grandsons of Owen and Anne Bray.[29] In 1607 the reversion of the site held for life by Susan,[30] wife of Richard Lumley, as of the inheritance of Owen Bray, was granted, on a forty-year lease, to Richard Bonsey.[31] In 1615 Owen and John Bray conveyed the site to John Bonsey and his heirs.[32] The term 'site of the manor' probably includes the manor, or reputed manor itself, of which John Bonsey was certainly possessed by 1621, and of which he was seised in fee at the time of his death, which occurred about 1638.[33] The manor passed to his son Richard, who held it in 1678, when he brought a suit against John Scotcher, whose father, William, was alleged to have held various lands in Horsell of the manor of Twichen for which the son refused to pay quit-rent or relief, declaring that 'he knew not whether there were any such manor of Twichen, nor knew the complainant's title thereto or to the demesne lands thereof, and he said he had no writings concerning the said estate, but he believed complainant might be seised of a certain messuage, farm and lands in Horsell, called Twichen. He had heard that some of the complainant's ancestors had seized oxen as heriots at the death of his grandfather, but his father maintained that no heriots were due.' [34] The case as regards the quit-rents was decided in favour of Bonsey, and Scotcher was ordered to pay the arrears. The manor was held in 1744 by another Richard Bonsey, who conveyed it in that year to Matthew Nicholls,[35] probably by way of mortgage, for in 1755 Richard Bonsey left it in

4a *Plac. de Quo Warr.* (Rec. Com.), 745 ; Assize R. Surr. 877, m. 59 and 878, m. 37.
5 Early Chan. Proc. bdle. 62, no. 459.
6 See Townesley Manor.
7 Chan. Inq. p.m. (Ser. 2), lxxxii, 143.
8 Exch. T.R. Misc. Bks. vol. 168, fol. 171 et seq.
9 Chan. Enr. Decrees, no. 1912, m. 6.
10 Chan Inq. p.m. (Ser. 2), lxxxii, 143.
11 Chan. Proc. (Ser. 2), bdle. 22, no. 84 ; Exch. T.R. Misc. Bks. vol. 168, fol. 188*b*.
12 Feet of F. Surr. East. 13 Eliz.
13 See below for references under 'Twichen.'

14 Feet of F. Surr. Hil. 20 Eliz.
15 Ibid. 41 Eliz.
16 Ibid. Hil. 19 Jas. I.
17 Ibid. Trin. 13 Geo. I'; East. 18 Geo. III.
18 Information from Mr. Collyer.
19 Feet of F. Surr. Mich. 10 Edw. II.
20 *Cal. Close*, 1323-7, p. 567.
21 Feet of F. Surr. 26 Edw. III, no. 76.
22 Ibid. 37 Edw. III, no. 92.
23 See under Hill Place.
24 Chan. Inq. p.m. (Ser. 2), lxxxii, 143 ; Chan. Proc. (Ser. 2), bdle. 22, no. 84.
25 Exch. T.R. Misc. Bks. vol. 168, fol. 188*b*.

26 Feet of F. Surr. Hil. 14 Eliz.
27 Ibid. Mich. 5 Jas. I.
28 Ibid. 13 Jas. I.
29 Harl. MS. 1561, fol. 199, where Danaster is miswritten 'Banester.'
30 Susan was the name of the mother of Owen and John Bray, who perhaps married again.
31 Feet of F. Surr. Mich. 5 Jas. I.
32 Ibid. 13 Jas. I.
33 Chan. Enr. Decrees, no. 1912, m. 6.
34 Ibid
35 Feet of F. Surr. Trin. 17 Geo. II.

his will to trustees for sale,[34] and in 1760 George Gilbourne and Anne, William Whitmore and Mary, Sarah Whitmore, widow, and John Armitage and Jane (evidently the heirs of Bonsey) conveyed the manor to Rowland Thomlinson.[37] After this date the manor changed hands frequently. According to Manning it was sold in 1774 to Sir Thomas Sewell, whose family sold it in 1795 to Edmund Boehm,[38] the owner of Ottershaw (q.v.) in Chertsey. He went bankrupt, and his estates were sold in 1820. At the present time the manor of Twichen is no longer in existence. Two farms, called Scotcher's and Bonsey's farms, lying in the north-east of Horsell and close to Chobham parish probably represent the lands formerly known as the manor of Twichen.

CHURCH
The church of OUR LADY consists of a chancel 29 ft. 8 in. by 18 ft. 7 in., with north vestries and a south organ-chamber, a nave continuous with the chancel 51 ft. 10 in. long, a south aisle 14 ft. 3 in. wide, and a west tower 10 ft. 3 in. square, all measurements being internal.

There is nothing of earlier date than c. 1320, and to this period belongs the north wall of the nave. The tower was added in the 15th century, and the south aisle early in the 16th century, while the rest of the building is quite modern. What the original chancel was like there is nothing left to show, but before 1890 it was of brick, and where the organ-chamber now stands there was a brick vestry. In 1890 the whole of the east portion of the building was rebuilt, and a bay added to the nave and aisle. The east wall of the aisle was originally close to the piscina still remaining in its south wall. The tower was entirely recased with the exception of the stair-turret about 1880, and when the east end of the church was rebuilt in 1890 the remainder of the church was restored.

There are several photographs in the vestry showing different parts of the church before the work of 1890 was carried out.

The chancel has a large five-light window in the east wall and a two-light one to the north, both being of 14th-century style with traceried heads. Opposite the north window are a modern piscina and sedilia of three bays, each with cinquefoiled ogee heads and pierced spandrels.

At the south-west is an archway leading to the organ-chamber, and a similar one in the north opens to the vestry.

There is no chancel arch, but the chancel and organ-chamber are separated from the nave and aisle by modern wood screens.

The four windows of the north wall of the nave are all of different date, the easternmost being a square-headed 15th-century window of two trefoiled lights, probably inserted to light an altar at the east end of the nave; while the next, c. 1320, has two trefoiled ogee-headed lights with a quatrefoil over in a two-centred arch. The third window is all modern, and has two lights with tracery over of flowing character, and the westernmost window is of 15th-century date much restored, and has three cinquefoiled lights with a square head and a moulded label. Only the lower part of the jambs and the sill are original. The head was once raised so as to light a gallery at the west end of the nave, which is now removed, and the window has been lowered again.

The south arcade of the nave is of four bays with hollow-sided octagonal columns and semi-octagonal responds. The three western bays are old, and the columns have octagonal moulded bases and capitals, and the two-centred arches are of two hollow-chamfered orders. The modern column and respond at the east have bases and capitals of different section. In the south wall of the aisle are three windows; the first modern, of three lights with intricate tracery in the two-centred head; the second window, to the west of this, has two trefoiled lights with a quatrefoil over, and is a modern copy of the 14th-century window in the north wall of the nave; while the third window is of 15th-century character, like that opposite to it in the north wall, and is of three trefoiled lights under a square head with a moulded label; a part of the double-chamfered jambs and the inside splays only are old. The west window of the aisle is modern and has three trefoiled lights with tracery over. Between the first and second of the south windows is an old piscina recess with a trefoiled ogee head. The basin, which was apparently large and shallow, has lost its projecting portion. The south doorway is between the second and third of the south windows, and has old plain-chamfered jambs and a two-centred head. The tower is not set centrally with the nave, but considerably to the south, the north face of its projecting north-east staircase-turret being set flush with the north wall of the nave. The stair is entered from the west end of the nave, and to the south of it a pointed doorway opens from the nave to the tower.

In the north and the south walls of the lower stage of the tower are modern windows of two trefoiled ogee-headed lights with a quatrefoil over, the inside jambs and rear-arches in each case being old. The west doorway of the tower is original, with the exception of a shallow outer order which belongs to the casing, and has heavy hollow-chamfered orders with a large roll between.

The tower is of three stages, embattled, and with belfry windows like those in the bottom stage; the nave has old timbers in the open timber roof with large tie-beams, and that to the aisle is similar, but has only one old tie-beam. This roof rests on stone corbels over the nave arcade.

There are two plain old chests in the tower; one on the floor above the ringing-chamber has three iron straps with staples and two curious padlocks, one having the initials I.B. and the other I.H. The covers to the keyholes cannot be opened without pressing aside similar covers on the opposite sides of the locks; one lock, however, has lost its covers.

The screen between the south aisle and the organ-chamber has old heads to six of its lights, of cinquefoiled ogee shape with foiled pierced spandrels.

The oak pulpit is of mid-17th-century date, and has a moulded cornice and panels carved with a diamond pattern. The double west doors of the nave appear to be mediaeval work, probably contemporary with the tower.

In the nave are several monuments and slabs. At the east end, on the floor near the screen, is a black-letter inscription in brass as follows : 'Hic jacet tumulatus Johñ Aleyn Capellan⁹ anime cuius ppiciet deus amen' Near this is a brass to Thomas Edmonds, 'citizen and mr. carpenter to the chamber and one of

---

[34] Manning and Bray, op. cit. iii, 198.   [37] Feet of F. (K.S.B.) Surr. Hil. 33 Geo. II.   [38] Manning and Bray, op. cit. iii, 198.

the four vewers of that Honorable City of London.' He married Ann Frognal, daughter of William Frognal, citizen and fishmonger of London, by whom he had five sons and two daughters and he died in 1619, ' she still surviving until . . .'; the date of her death is not filled in. He is represented above in a long robe and his wife in a full skirt and wearing a straw hat. Below are the children, the sons in one group and the daughters in another. Two of the sons, one of them a small boy, carry a skull each. Above are two shields, one containing the arms of London, and the second has a cheveron between three compasses, the Carpenters' arms. A stone slab near this records the death of John Collyer in 1689. On the north wall of the nave, fixed to a modern stone, is an inscription to 'Fayth Sutton,' the wife of John Sutton the younger, and daughter to 'Hwgh Fearclough of London, gentleman.' She died in 1603. Above on one plate are the figures of two sons and one daughter, but these are not in their right place and probably belong to John Sutton the elder, as this lady had two daughters only.

To the west of this is another modern stone on which is an inscription to John Sutton the elder, who lived a widower 24 years and died in 1603. He had two sons and one daughter. On the same stone is an inscription to Thomas, the elder of these two sons, who died in 1603. Above each inscription is a figure, the old man in a long robe and the son in a short cloak. Between the two figures are three shields, two having: quarterly (1) a cheveron between three cows, (2) a fesse between three ducks, (3) party cheveron-wise two voided molets in chief and one in base, (4) a fesse between two cheverons. On the centre point is a crescent for difference. The other shield has the quarterly coat impaling a lion between three fleurs de lis.

On the west wall of the nave is a small wall monument to John Greene, who died in 1651, and in the south aisle is a large white marble monument to James Fenn, 1793, who is shown in his robes as Sheriff of London, kneeling at a desk with his wife and daughter opposite him. The treatment is somewhat florid, but the survival of this Jacobean type of monument is very interesting and curious at the end of the 18th century.

There are five bells in the tower, originally all cást by R. Catlin in 1741, but the second and fifth have been recast in 1896 by Taylor & Son.

The plate comprises a silver cup of 1798, a chalice and paten of 1892, and a flagon of 1888. There is also a base metal paten dated 1818 and a flagon of the same material dated 1860 and an old pewter flagon dated 1713.

The registers are contained in five volumes the first having entries of baptisms from 1653 to 1770, marriages 1654 to 1754 and burials 1653 to 1765. The second contains marriages from 1754 to 1801. The third has baptisms from 1770, and burials from 1765, both up to 1798. The fourth continues the baptisms and burials from 1799 to 1812 and the fifth has marriages from 1801 to 1812.

ADVOWSON The chapel of Horsell originally belonged to the monastery of Westminster. The date of its foundation is not apparent, but in 1258 the Abbot of Westminster granted the advowson, with that of Pyrford, to the priory of Newark.[39] By 1262 both chapels had been annexed to the church of Woking, which was also among the possessions of Newark Priory.[40] In 1291 the chapels of Horsell and Pyrford were together valued at £10 annually,[41] and in 1428 were taxed at 15 marks.[42] In 1457, owing to the smallness of the receipts of the chapel of Horsell and its ruinous condition, Roger Hallye, a canon regular of Newark, received licence from the bishop to administer the sacraments to the parishioners for one year, more or less, dating from 2 April, during which time he would take all the profits.[43] Horsell remained attached to the rectory of Woking and was surrendered, with the priory's other possessions, in 1538, when the farm of the chapel of Horsell was valued at 2s.[44] After the Dissolution it appears that the benefice, a curacy, was rendered perpetual under a licence from the ordinary.[45] The great tithes of Horsell were granted, with those of Woking, to Francis Aungier, Baron Longford, being subsequently held by his son and by the latter's nephew, who was lay impropriator in 1679.[46] In the mean time, the king apparently presented perpetual curates, who both served and had an actual estate in the chapel at a rent of 2s.[47] In 1628, at the suggestion of the Earl of Anglesey, the chapel was granted to John Robinson, who served it.[48] The chapel, with the vicarage house and lands and the small tithes, was subsequently conveyed by the ministers themselves, or by their widows, to their various successors until about 1674, when Ann Alchorn, widow of the last curate, sold the property to Godfrey Lee, a layman, who appropriated the small tithes and closed the chapel while he himself occupied the house belonging to it.[49] In October 1679, however, the lay rector, Lord Aungier, came forward and brought a suit against Godfrey Lee,[50] maintaining that there could not be two lay fees in the tithes of one parish.[51] It was on the strength of this plea, apparently, that Lord Aungier had presented to Horsell earlier in the year, but doubts having arisen on that occasion as to his right to do so, the incumbent was again instituted a few weeks later by the Crown.[52] The dispute, however, was not immediately settled. Bishop Morley of Winchester, evidently wishing to arrange matters and to erect the curacy into a vicarage, bequeathed, by his will, proved 31 October 1684, £10 per annum for an augmentation to the 'vicarage' on the conditions that the 'vicarage' house and tithe should be restored to the church and that those who had bought the great tithe should settle £10 per annum more on the living for ever. The terms were not complied with however, and the benefaction became void.[53] Godfrey Lee about 1684[54] still held the chapel house and small tithes, but the property appears to have been handed to the lay rector soon after, as according to Manning both this and the great tithes were sold by Lord Aungier to Richard Lee and

[38] Feet of F. Surr. East. 42 Hen. III.
[39] V.C.H. Surr. ii, 103.
[40] Pope Nich. Tax (Rec. Com.), 208b.
[41] Feud. Aids, v, 117.
[42] Surr. Arch. Coll. vii, 167.
[43] Mins. Accts. 31-2 Hen. VIII, rot. 146, m. 32; 36-7 Hen. VIII. rot. 187, m. 31.

[44] Surr. Arch. Coll. vii, 167.
[45] Exch. Dep. Mich. 31 Chas. II, 5.
[46] See note 44. Rentals and Surv. P.R.O. bdle. 59, no. 39.
[47] Pat. 4 Chas. I, pt. xxv, no. 2.
[48] Close, 15 Chas. I, pt. v, no. 14 ; Exch. Dep. Mich. 31 Chas. II, 5.

[50] Exch. Dep. Mich. 31 Chas. II, 5.
[51] Surr. Arch. Coll. vii, 166.
[52] Inst. Bks. (P.R.O.) ; Surr. Arch. Coll. vii, 167.
[53] Surr. Arch. Coll. vii, 166.
[54] Feet of F. Surr. Mich. 36 Chas. II.

William Beauchamp in trust for Richard Bonsey, Richard Roake, John Collyer, and John Scotcher, each of whom was to enjoy a fourth share, and who, as lay impropriators, had the right to appoint the curate.[65] Manning gives the date of this conveyance as 1682 but it was probably a few years later, since, as has been shown, the small tithes at least were held by Godfrey Lee as late as 1684. In 1725 the advowson was in the hands of 'four lay impropriators.'[66] In 1804 Henry and Edward Roake, Richard Fladgate, and Henry Collyer were the lay impropriators, John

Collyer having purchased Bonsey's share and Richard Fladgate that of Scotcher.[67] As late as 1879 the south seats in the chancel were occupied by the Roake family and those on the north side by the Collyer and Fladgate families.[68] Throughout the 19th century the patronage remained in the hands of landowners at Horsell.[69] It is at present held by Mr. John Pares of Southsea. The curacy was styled a vicarage by the Act of 1868.[60]

CHARITY Smith's Charity is distributed as in other Surrey parishes.

PYRFORD

Pirianford (x cent.) ; Peliforde and Piriford (xi cent.) ; Purford (xvii cent.).

Pyrford is a small parish formerly a chapelry of Woking, on the Wey, 7 miles north-east of Guildford, and rather less from Chertsey. It is bounded on the north by Chertsey and Byfleet, on the east by Wisley and Ockham, on the south by Ripley, on the west by Woking. It contains 1,869 acres, and measures rather over 2 miles from east to west, rather less than 2 miles from north to south. It is traversed by the Wey navigation, by part of the natural river which helps to form its eastern boundary, and by the main line of the London and South Western Railway. The upper or western part of Pyrford is on the Bagshot Sand, the lower or eastern part is the alluvium, sand, and gravel of the Wey Valley. A few palaeolithic and neolithic flints have been found, but in no great quantity. Pyrford Stone is a Sarsen stone from the Bagshot beds standing not far from the Warren. It is put up on end artificially, but while it may very well be one of the few ancient standing stones in Surrey, nothing is known of the date of erection. The parish is well wooded, picturesque, and out of the world. Historically Pyrford is interesting as having been included in Windsor Forest, according to the charter of the Conqueror to Westminster ; while by the evidence of Domesday 3 hides here were in the forest. The subsequent attempts to extend Windsor Forest over all Surrey were met by the contention that no part of the county was anciently in the forest ; which is untrue in the case of Pyrford, and presumably therefore untrue in the case of places not named in Domesday lying between Pyrford and Windsor. In the Domesday Survey it is rated in Godley Hundred, the only place named in that hundred not held by Chertsey Abbey. Subsequently it seems sometimes, but wrongly, to have been considered as in Woking Hundred, probably because ecclesiastically it was in the parish of Woking.

The church stands upon the brow of a steep bank above the broad meadows and the River Wey. From whichever direction it is approached a hill has to be climbed, thus giving an unusually detached and isolated aspect to the tiny building. Tall elms and a thicket of silver birches and young saplings, through which a winding path ascends to the church, make a beautiful setting for the shingled spirelet, grey walls,

and long, low, red-tiled roofs, as viewed from the south-west ; and close to the little gate of the churchyard is a noble old oak. Near the church are some old red-brick houses with good chimney-stacks.

The Inclosure Award was made 29 September 1815, under an Act of the same year.[1] Certain waste land was put into the hands of trustees to provide fuel (peat) for the inhabitants.

The schools (provided) were taken over in 1891 and new buildings erected ; the first school had been built in 1847.

There was a duck decoy in the low ground near the old river when Manning and Bray wrote. It had been disused before their time and revived. Evelyn mentions in his *Diary*, 23 August 1681. It is now disused again.

Sherewater Pond, on the borders of Pyrford and of Chertsey parishes, was an extensive mere on the Bagshot Sand, and was drained and planted at the time of the inclosure. Aubrey[1a] and Brayley,[2] following him, have confused it with a pond by the Guildford road on Wisley Common, drained by Peter seventh Lord King at rather an earlier date. Sherewater Pond is marked on Rocque's map ; Sherewater Farm is close to it, just north of the London and South Western Railway line.

MANORS In 956 King Eadwig granted land in the Pyrian ford, described as *PYRFORD* or Pirford on the Wey in Surrey, to Eadric to hold free of all services save the *trinoda necessitas*.[3] Pirford was held under King Edward by Harold,[4] and was among the lands which the Conqueror reserved for himself at the time of the Conquest.[5] He, however, granted it to the monastery of St. Peter Westminster[6] certainly before 1070, for the charter is addressed to Stigand as archbishop. At the time of the Survey it was held by the abbey. Before Harold held it it had been assessed for 27 hides ; afterwards it was assessed for 16 at Harold's pleasure. There seems to have been some doubt as to whether it had been really fixed at so much, and in 1086 it paid geld for

WESTMINSTER ABBEY. *Gules St. Peter's crossed keys or.*

---

[65] Manning and Bray, op. cit. i, 162, 163 (quoting from inform. received from Rev. E. Emily ; see Woking).
[66] Bp. Willis, Visitation.
[67] Ibid.
[68] Surr. Arch. Coll. vii, 166.
[69] Clergy List.
[60] Act 31 & 32 Vict. cap. 117.
[1] Blue Bk. Incl. Awards.
[1a] Hist. and Antiq. of Surr. iii, 197.
[2] Hist. of Surr. ii, 147.
[3] Birch, Cart. Sax. iii, 136.
[4] V.C.H. Surr. i, 306.
[5] Ibid. 282.
[6] Ibid. ; Dugdale, Mon. Angl. i, 301, 307 ; Cott. MS. Faust A. iii, fol. 112b.

8 hides only. Its value had, however, increased from £12 to £18 since the time of King Edward. It was stated that 3 hides of the land belonged to the king, being in his forest of Windsor.[7] After 1086 William made a grant of eight hides in Pyrford to Westminster, these three and five more, unless the iii of Domesday be a mistake for viii.[8] The manor of Pyrford remained in the possession of the monastery of Westminster until the Dissolution,[9] being assigned to the portion of the abbot.[10] Between 1346 and 1366 licence was granted to the abbot[11] for his monks to celebrate mass in the oratory of his manor of Pyrford. In 1558 Queen Mary granted it to the new priory of Sheen which she had refounded in 1556–7.[12] Early in 1559, however, an Act was passed for the suppression of all the religious houses which had been refounded by Mary, and their estates were once more annexed to the Crown.[13] In 1561 Queen Elizabeth granted the site of the manor, lately in the possession of John Carleton and Joyce his wife, to George Revel for twenty-one years,[14] but in 1574 another grant of the same was made to Edward Clinton, Earl of Lincoln and Lord High Admiral of

England.[15] Queen Elizabeth granted the manor of Pyrford to Henry Weston, who in 1589 received licence to alienate to Sir John Wolley and his heirs for ever.[16] When Sir John died in 1596 he was seised both of the manor and of the site of the manor, which afterwards follow the same descent.[17] Nevertheless in 1609 James I made a special grant of the site of the manor, the park, and various lands to Sir Francis Wolley, which refers to the Earl of Lincoln as though he were the last tenant.[18] Sir John's widow Elizabeth, who afterwards married Sir Thomas Egerton, held the manor as dower for life, and at her death it passed to Francis Wolley, son of Sir John Wolley and Elizabeth.[19] Sir Francis Wolley (knighted in 1603) died in 1609,[20] when the manor apparently passed to Sir Arthur Mainwaring, his cousin,[21] who held it until 1628, when he sold it to Sir Robert Parkhurst.[22] Sir Robert held the manor jointly with his son Robert, a settlement having been made on the occasion of the latter's marriage with Elizabeth Baker.[23] Sir Robert the father died in 1636, and the manor passed to his son and grandson.[24] A fourth Robert Parkhurst, son of the latter, sold the

PYRFORD CHURCH FROM NORTH-EAST

[7] V.C.H. Surr. i, 306b.
[8] Cart. Antiq. C.C. (2).
[9] Mins. Accts. (Gen. Ser.) bdle. 1109, no. 4; Cott. MS. Faust. A. iii, fol. 4b; Cott. MS. Claud. A. viii, 54b; Valor Eccl. (Rec. Com.), i, 411; Mins. Accts. Rel. Houses, 31 & 32 Hen. VIII, rot. 113, m. 1.
[10] V.C.H. Lond. i, 450.
[11] Egerton MS. 2033, fol. 61.
[12] Pat. 5 & 6 Phil. and Mary, pt. iv, m. 9.

[13] Dugdale, Mon. Angl. vi, 30.
[14] Pat. 4 Eliz. pt. v, m. 5.
[15] Ibid. 16 Eliz. pt. xi, m. 5; Acts of the P.C. 1571–5, p. 396.
[16] Pat. 31 Eliz. pt. xv, m. 18; Feet of F. Surr. Trin. 31 Eliz.
[17] Chan. Inq. p.m. 39 Eliz. pt. i, no. 74.
[18] Pat. 7 Jas. I, pt. xxxvii, m. 24.
[19] Chan. Inq. p.m. 42 Eliz. pt. i, no. 133.

[20] Ibid. (Ser. 2), cccxxxiv, 60.
[21] Harl. Soc. Pub. xliii, 3; W. Brayley, op. cit. i, 359; Feet of F. Surr. Mich. 8 Jas. I.
[22] Feet of F. Surr. Hil. 4 Chas. I.
[23] Ibid. East. 4 Chas. I; Chan. Inq. p.m. (Ser. 2), ccclxxx, 21.
[24] Ibid.; Feet of F. Div. Co. East. 1657; Manning and Bray, op. cit. i, 157.

manor to Denzil Onslow in 1677, Sir Robert Gayer, Parkhurst's uncle, acting as trustee.[25] From Denzil Onslow the estate passed by will to his great-nephew, Thomas Lord Onslow,[26] and has descended to the present Earl of Onslow with the title and the rest of the Onslow estate.

John Evelyn, in his *Diary*, 23 August 1681, gives an account of a visit which he paid to Denzil Onslow ' at his seat at Purford, where there was much company and an extraordinary feast for any country gentleman's table.' He adds that ' what made it more remarkable was that there was not anything but what was afforded by his estate about it, as venison, rabbits, hares, pheasants, partridges, pigeons, quails, poultrie, all sorts of fowle in season from his own decoy near his house and all sorts of fresh fish. After dinner we went to see sport at the decoy. I never saw so many herons. The seat stands on a flat, the ground pasture rarely watered and exceedingly improved since Mr. Onslow bought it of Sir Robert Parkhurst, who spent a fair estate. The house is timber but commodious and with one ample dining room, the hall adorned with paintings of fowle & huntinges the work of Mr. Barlow who is excellent at this kind of thing for the life.'[27] The house was pulled down by Robert Lord Onslow, after the manor came into his possession in 1776. According to Camden and Aubrey it had been originally built by the Earl of Lincoln. Sir John Wolley on obtaining the estate at Pyrford had added to and improved the house,[28] where he received a visit from Queen Elizabeth.[29] Owing to the subsequent rebuilding, it cannot be determined how far he rebuilt or replaced the older one. The present farm-house occupies the site of the house pulled down by Lord Onslow. The gateway of the old house, still existing, used to bear the initials J. W. What is known as 'Queen Elizabeth's summer-house,' although probably a century later in date, is of some interest. It is square in plan and of two stories, the roof of the upper chamber showing slight traces of colour decoration. Parts of the terrace walks, and of the avenue of elms nearly half a mile long, remain. Here Dr. Donne was living when he made his clandestine marriage with the daughter of Sir George More of Loseley, niece to Lady Egerton wife of the Lord Keeper, in whose service Donne was secretary.[30]

There was a large deer-park which was disparked when the house was pulled down.

The earliest mention of *TOUNDESLEY* is found in a reputed cartulary of Westminster Monastery, which was in private hands in 1836, and of which a transcript was made.[31] In this document is found a

ONSLOW. *Argent a fesse gules between six Cornish choughs.*

charter of 1297–8 by which Adam de Toundesley granted the manor of Toundesley to his brother Simon and Agnes daughter of William Morrant of Kent and their heirs. The manor descended to Robert de Toundesley and afterwards to his son John, who in 1362 conveyed his manor of Toundesley to Richard Rook and John Pecche of Westminster.[32] The reversion of lands which Katharine widow of Robert de Toundesley held for life was also granted in 1363, when William, another son of Robert, also relinquished all his right in the manor. This last conveyance is enrolled on a Close Roll of 1363.[33] Richard Rook and John Pecche conveyed the manor to Nicholas, Abbot of Westminster, in 1366, receiving certain tenements in Westminster instead.[34] The cartulary also states that both Katharine and William de Toundesley received a pension from the Abbot of Westminster. After the manor passed out of the Toundesley family into the possession of Westminster there is no further record of it as a manor. It is henceforth referred to as 'Townesley lands' only. It was held, under this name, by the abbey of Westminster until the Dissolution, when the rent received from the farm of Townesley lands was stated to be £6 1s. 8d.[35] The land was afterwards leased to Sir Anthony Browne.[36] In 1548 it was granted to John Carleton and his wife Joyce, and in 1561 to George Revel for a term of twenty-one years.[37] In 1574 Queen Elizabeth granted the 'parcel of lands called Townesley lands, Blacke lands, Townsley Grove, Great and Little Barbrookes, Borrow Hill' and other lands to Edward Clinton, Earl of Lincoln, and his heirs.[38] All these lands afterwards passed to Sir John Wolley, lord of the manor of Pyrford, and henceforth descended with the manor.[39]

PYRFORD PARK.—The origin of the park is probably to be found in the 3 hides reserved by King William in his first charter in the forest, but presumably granted to the abbey by his second charter at the end of his reign. In 1278 the abbey claimed immunity from any interference by the officers of the forest, and free warren in their demesne lands at Pyrford.[40] The park does not seem to be specifically mentioned till after the Dissolution. The grant to John Carleton and Joyce in 1548 included the park of Pyrford, together with the capital messuage belonging to it. This, too, passed to George Revel and the Earl of Lincoln, and finally became the property of the lord of the manor (see above). Manning[41] states that Lord Onslow converted the land into farms about 1776.

The Domesday Survey records the existence of two mills at Pyrford, worth 10s., the property of the monastery.[42] They seem, however, to have fallen into disuse. The courts and view of frankpledge in Pyrford belonged, prior to the Dissolution, to the Abbot and convent of Westminster, who enjoyed extensive privileges in their lands of Pyrford and Horsell![43] At the beginning of the 19th century the manor still had courts leet and baron, at the

[25] Manning and Bray, op. cit. i, 157; Feet of F. Surr. Trin. 29 Chas. II; Close, 29 Chas. II, pt. vi, 3.
[26] Manning and Bray, *Hist. of Surr.* i, 153.
[27] Evelyn's *Diary* (ed. W. Bray).
[28] Aubrey, op. cit. iii, 197.
[29] *Dict. Nat. Biog.* [30] Ibid.
[31] *Abridgement of Cartul. of Westm. Abbey*

in possession of S. Bentley, 1836 (printed for private circulation by S. Bentley).
[32] Ibid.
[33] Close, 37 Edw. III, m. 34 d.
[34] See note on cartulary, Inq. a.q.d., file 358, no. 17.
[35] Dugdale, *Mon.* i, 328.
[36] Mins. Accts. Relig. Houses, 31 & 32 Hen. VIII, rot. 113, m. 1.

[37] Pat. 4 Eliz. pt. v, m. 5.
[38] Ibid. 16 Eliz. pt. xi, m. 5.
[39] Chan. Inq. p.m. 39 Eliz. pt. i, no. 74.
[40] Quo Warr. 7 Edw. I, rot. 28.
[41] Manning and Bray, op. cit. i, 153.
[42] *V.C.H. Surr.* i, 306.
[43] *Plac. de Quo Warr.* (Rec. Com.), 745.

former of which were appointed a constable and an ale-taster for each of the tithings of Pyrford, Horsell, Sithwood, and Woodham.[44]

The church of *ST. NICHOLAS CHURCH* remains very much as it was erected in about 1140–50, both as to general form and its principal features ; and the exceptionally sympathetic restoration which it underwent in 1869 at the hands of Mr. T. G. Jackson, R.A., has enhanced its archaeological interest, by bringing to light paintings and other things.

It is built of conglomerate, or pudding-stone, with sandstone rubble and heterogeneous materials, the walling being finished, as was commonly the case, with a rough daubing of sandy mortar which has worn off in places. The external dressings are mostly of clunch and firestone, with some Bargate stone in the later work, but internally it is a somewhat remarkable fact that the original dressings, such as in the doorways, the chancel arch and windows, are of Caen stone, presumably brought by water to London, and thence by the Thames and the Wey. The beautiful north porch (c. 1500) is of oak framework, the sides filled in with plaster. In Cracklow's view (c. 1824) some Horsham

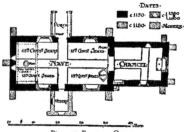

PLAN OF PYRFORD CHURCH

slabs are shown on the roof of the nave, and these no doubt formed the original covering, but the roofs are now tiled. The western bell-turret, with graceful spirelet, is covered with oak shingles.

In plan, save for the timber north porch, and the modern vestry that balances it on the south side of the nave, the church has preserved unaltered the proportions of the 12th-century building, having escaped the almost invariable addition of aisle, chapel, or tower. It consists of a nave 38 ft. by 16 ft. 7 in., and a chancel 19 ft. 8 in. by 13 ft., the south wall being 4 inches shorter than the north. The nave walls vary in thickness from 2 ft. 9 in. (S.) to 2 ft. 6 in., while those of the chancel are 2 ft. 3 in., except the east, which is 2 ft. 6 in. They are unusually low for an aisleless building—about 8 ft. from the nave floor level to the wall-plate—giving the building a long drawn-out appearance : and the roofs are of steep pitch, especially that of the nave.

The west wall retains its two original round-headed windows of firestone, and between them a large buttress has been added, probably about 1500. The north and south doorways also date from about 1150, the latter, quite plain and narrow, giving access to the modern vestry, while the north doorway, which

has always served as the principal entrance, is somewhat richly ornamented. It is of two orders, with a hood-moulding of chamfered section, having a border of little pellets between the chamfer and the square outer edge. The outer order is decorated with zigzag mouldings, and is carried upon nook-shafts, one with a scalloped capital, and the other a capital having broad angle-leaves, with a row of punched holes up the centre. The inner order is plain, with a narrow chamfer carried round the arch and jambs. The right-hand shaft has been cut away to allow the insertion of a holy-water stoup, probably when the porch was made ; the base of the shaft below this remains in a very perfect state. By a curious arrangement, the later timber porch is placed considerably to the west of the centre of this doorway, so that the eastern jamb is partly hidden by the post carrying the wall-plate.

The chancel arch is of two plain orders, the inner having only a narrow chamfer, with a pyramidal stop beneath the imposts, which are hollow-chamfered. The crown of the arch is somewhat depressed by a settlement of old date, so that it has assumed an elliptical shape, and the piers, from the same cause, are out of the upright. The hatched tool-marks on the Caen stone and firestone of this arch are remarkably sharp. In the east wall of the nave, on the north of the arch, is a rudely-formed pointed-headed niche, semicircular in plan, and evidently intended to hold a somewhat tall image. As this niche is not in wrought stone, but merely scooped out of the rubble wall and plastered, it is probably a century or so later in date than the arch, and indicates the existence of an altar at the rood-screen.

In the chancel two of the original windows remain—the only ones in the north and south walls—that in the north wall having a short and broad round-headed aperture, 10 in. by 2 ft. 6 in., chamfered externally, on which face clunch has been used, while on the inside the round arch and jambs of the splays are worked in Caen stone.

The opposite window in the south wall is similar, so far as the interior face is concerned, but about 1180 the external aperture was widened and changed to a depressed pointed shape, with a curious hood-moulding of acutely pointed form over it, leaving a large unpierced tympanum between the two arches. Neither piscina nor aumbry is now visible in the church. Fortunately, the external quoins of nave and chancel, in clunch, and in a somewhat crumbling state, were suffered to remain at the restoration, although the angles of nave and chancel were buttressed. A recess in the south wall of the chancel at its western end is of modern date, and apparently meant to give more room in a confined space.

At a period between about 1380 and the close of the 15th century the little chapel appears to have undergone a general restoration and re-fitting. The two-light east window, with cinquefoil heads and a quatrefoil over, suggests the earlier date, while the two-light windows of the nave, with square heads, devoid of arch or cusping, would seem to belong to the later date, to which also the porch, the roof panelling over the rood, and the nave seating may be referred, but in work of such plain character it is difficult to speak certainly. These square-headed windows are found in the low aisle walls of several Sussex churches, such as

[44] Manning and Bray, op. cit. i, 153.

Amberley, Bury, and Rogate, and in most cases an earlier date may be assigned to them than would at first sight appear probable. They were made to suit the exigencies of the situation, and, as in the case of these openings, oak lintels were employed, instead of arches, on the inside. Of the same period is a square-moulded corbel, for an image or light, on the nave wall, to the east of the south doorway.

The roofs of nave and chancel are ancient and of very massive timbers, with double wall-plates, hollowed and chamfered, similar to those of early date at West Clandon and Capel, Surrey. The tie-beams, which are of large scantling, have hollow mouldings, intersecting with the hollows on the wall-plates. These roofs may be coeval with the walls, but owing to their plain character it is equally possible that they belong to the period of restoration in the 15th century. The spaces between the rafters seem to have been plastered from the top of the wall-plate as far as to the end of the vertical part, above which the tiling was exposed. An interesting feature has survived in connexion with the nave roof, viz., a canted or wagon ceiling, a yard or more in width, covering the three end rafters at the east of the nave, and forming originally a sort of canopy over the rood and attendant figures. It is constructed with wide feather-edged oak boarding and simply moulded ribs, and at the bottom, on the vertical face over the struts of the rafters, is a battlemented moulding. The whole shows traces of decoration in colour, such as white stars and yellow flowers on a red ground. This panelled ceiling dates between 1450 and 1500.[44] The rood-loft was carried on a very massive beam over the chancel arch and on another to the west, the mortises of which remain in the wall-plates.

To about the same date belongs the picturesque porch — too much ivy-covered—which has plain sides of oak framework, filled with the original clay daubing, a flat four-centred arch to the front, and a barge-board of pierced intersecting archwork, having some shallow tracery spandrels cut in the solid timber at the apex. The design of the whole is unusual and pleasing.

The nave still retains its late 15th-century seating with square panelled ends and moulded cappings. Not less interesting is the fine pulpit with its sounding-board. It is almost unique in being partly constructed of red deal, mixed with oak and walnut or cedar, and bears the date 1628, with the initials N B on the front panel. The stiles and rails are carved, and there is some inlay work. The base is modern, replacing that which was destroyed, and before the restoration the whole pulpit was thickly coated with white paint, the removal of which disclosed the curious variety of woods used in the original construction.

At the restoration paintings of at least two dates in the mediaeval period were discovered beneath the

whitewash, the earlier representing the original scheme when the chapel was built, and the other principal one, which was a very loose and tender coat, corresponding to the 15th-century period, when so much was done to the building. Portions of the older scheme only were capable of preservation ; and among them are three consecration crosses (of the common form, a cross pattée, within a circle), one on either side of the chancel, and one on the west wall of the nave. Besides these, and also belonging to the 12th century, are some very curious fragments on the north and south walls of the nave. They are painted in little more than red outline. On the north wall, between

PYRFORD CHURCH : THE PORCH

the doorway and the eastern window, are depicted the sacraments of the Jews—the Giving of Manna and the Water out of the Rock. Below these are a band of conventional scroll-work and a flying angel. Opposite to this, on the south wall of the nave, is a still more singular subject, which appears to be Jezebel looking out through a lattice and 'tiring' herself. A wall with stone jointing, battlements, and windows with diamond-shaped lattice-work are shown, and at the top a disproportionately large head, perhaps intended to represent Jezebel. At the foot of the wall are six figures of soldiers marching past with spears in their hands, the last leading Jehu's horse, while Jehu

44 At Lapford, Devon, and Pulham St. Mary, Norfolk, are good examples of panelling on nave roofs in the space over the rood-loft.

himself stands in front, directing Jezebel to be thrown down.

To the eastward of this are the remains of another subject, also apparently of the latter part of the 12th century—the Scourging of Our Lord. The bound figure of Christ is discernible, and also a particularly vigorous drawing of the ' executioner,' whose pose and brutal expression, as he swings his whole body round to bring down the scourge with full force, is admirably rendered. His clothes are shown as spotted with the sacred blood.[46]

In the quatrefoil of the east window is preserved the only piece of ancient glass in the church. This, which is mentioned by Cracklow (though wrongly described as ' the Virgin holding a Crucifix '), depicts God the Father holding forth the Son upon the Cross. The date of this interesting fragment is the latter part of the 15th century. The lower lights are filled with stained glass.

A fitting of particular interest has unhappily disappeared quite lately. This was a wooden balance-lever, fixed to the wall-plate on the north side of the chancel. It projected about 16 in. from the face of the plate, and its underside was gently curved, the end being rounded off. Three holes were visible in the end as though for the purpose of suspending either the pyx or a lamp before the Sacrament.[47]

The font is modern, and there are no monuments of any importance or antiquity.

There are many small crosses scratched upon the stonework of windows and doors.

There are two bells in the small turret, one quite plain, and the other bearing a curious ' puzzle ' inscription which has defied all the efforts at interpretation of Mr. Stahlschmidt and other campanologists. It reads :—sᴠᴠs ʜᴄᴠᴠᴏ ᴠᴠᴢ ᴠɪᴀᴏɪʟ. The plain bell is probably mediaeval, and the other looks like the work of an 18th-century itinerant founder—perhaps the same who has left us the fourth bell at Woking, inscribed I.F. 1766.

Among the church plate is a most graceful cup of 1570, beautifully designed, a model of elegance. It bears the usual foliage strap-work band between plain fillets, which, interlacing, divide it three times : there is also a silver ' paten with a foot,' of the same date and of the usual shape, bearing a band of ' hyphens.' Both are in good preservation and have been well cared for. Besides there are a pewter paten and a tankard-shaped flagon, both dating from the latter part of the 17th century.

The register of burials dates from 1605, that of marriages from 1666, and of births from 1670.

ADVOWSON In 1258 the Abbot of Westminster conveyed the advowson of the chapel of Pyrford, with that of Horsell, to the Prior of Newark next Guildford. The grant included common of pasture for all animals in the common pasture in the vills belonging to the said churches except in ' Wathelisham ' and Townesley, in which they were not to have common of pasture for pigs. The prior paid 40 marks to the abbot in return.[48]

Before 1262 both chapels had been annexed to the church of Woking, which was in the hands of the same prior and convent,[49] and they remained so until the Dissolution.[50] During this time the duty of finding a chaplain devolved upon the vicar of Woking. In the 14th century it was found that the latter had omitted to provide a chaplain, and he was commanded to do so by reason of ' the composition made on that behalf to provide a chaplain to perform divine service in the chapel of Pyrford dependent on his church and to administer the sacraments to the parishioners in the said hamlet of Pyrford on pain of excommunication.'[51] It is probable that the chapel of Pyrford remained attached to the church of Woking for some time after the Dissolution, as no separate trace of it appears then. The date of the transference of the chapel from the benefice of Woking to that of Wisley, to which it has since been appendent, is not certain. The first evidence of it is in 1631, when the king presented, by lapse, to Wisley and the chapel of Pyrford,[52] and again in 1639.[53] In 1656 Sir Robert Parkhurst of Pyrford and Wisley, and the inhabitants of those parishes, petitioned against the intended union of the parishes of Wisley with Byfleet,[54] desiring the union of Wisley with Pyrford.[55] Despite this petition, however, the trustees for the maintenance of ministers issued an order in the following year for the union of Byfleet with Wisley, the church of Byfleet to serve for both parishes, no mention being made of Pyrford.[56] George Bradshaw, of the same name as the incumbent presented to Wisley and Pyrford in 1639, was appointed in 1648 to Wisley,[57] and died in possession of Wisley and Pyrford in 1668. The next presentation was to both places by Sir Robert Parkhurst, and the advowson passed with the manor to the Onslow family.

CHARITY Smith's Charity is distributed as in other Surrey parishes.

---

[46] These paintings bear a considerable resemblance to some of 12th-century date upon the west wall of East Clandon Church, one being the Last Supper.

[47] In Sussex a similar balance-lever, doubtless used for one or other of these purposes, still remains in the roof timbers of the chancel of West Grinstead Church, although stupidly concealed from view by a modern boarded ceiling. This is illustrated in a paper on the church by the late Mr. J. L. André, F.S.A., in *Suss. Arch. Coll.* xxxviii, 56. The same three holes in the end of the lever are shown in Mr. André's drawing.

[48] Feet of F. Surr. East. 42 Hen. III.
[49] *V.C.H. Surr.* ii, 103.
[50] *Valor Eccl.* (Rec. Com.), ii, 33.
[51] Egerton MS. 2033, fol. 151.
[52] Winton Epis. Reg. Neile, fol. 36a.

[48] Ibid. Curle, fol. 54a.
[54] A change projected by Wolsey (Reg. fol. 70b), which had not, however, apparently taken effect.
[55] *Cal. S.P. Dom.* 1656-7, p. 4 ; Misc. MS. Lambeth, dccccxci, 126, 135, 236.
[56] *Cal. S.P. Dom.* 1657-8, p. 82 ; Misc. MSS. Lambeth, dccccxc, 69 ; mxv, 21.
[57] *Lords' Journals*, x, 588.

THORPE

Torp (xi cent.).

Thorpe is a small parish on the banks of the Thames. The village is 2 miles north-west of Chertsey, and nearly 2 miles south-east of Egham. The soil is river gravel, sand, and alluvium. The Chertsey extension branch of the London and South Western Railway from Chertsey to Egham cuts the extremity of the parish on the south-west. It measures about 2 miles from north-east to south-west, about 2½ miles from north-west to south-east, and contains 1,545 acres of land and 15 of water.

The village is picturesque, and consists of a group of houses at the cross-roads, with others scattered along a winding road to the east. Several of these are of 17th-century date, of red brick with central chimneys. Close to the church on the north, one of these houses has two upper-floor rooms completely panelled with 17th-century oak panelling and a carved overmantel.

Of modern houses Thorpe Place, in a well-timbered park, is the seat of Mr. H. C. Leigh-Bennett. It is on the site of the old manor-house. Thorpe Lea is the residence of Lady Milford ; Thorpe House of Mr. W. C. Scott ; The Grange of Mr. E. H. Holden.

The church stands close against a background of trees. From it a path known as the 'Monk's walk' runs as far as Chertsey, traditionally to the abbey there.

There were lands called Redwynde in Thorpe which were granted for life to John the Parker in 1377 for keeping the king's deer.[1] The Water of Redwynde is the old name of the stream which skirts the parish and joins the Bourne Brook in Chertsey.

William Denham, citizen and goldsmith of London, father to Sir John Denham the judge, and grandfather to the poet, was buried at Thorpe in 1583,[2] and probably resided there. In the early 19th century Captain Hardy, Nelson's friend, resided in Thorpe.

Nearly half the parish lay formerly in common fields. The Inclosure Act[3] inclosed 700 acres of common fields, marked as 'Thorpe Field' on the 1-in. Ordnance map, to the north of the village.

The National Schools, built in 1848, were enlarged in 1901. An infants' school was built in 1873.

MANORS
Land at THORPE, '5 mansas in loco qui dicitur Thorp,' was given to the abbey of Chertsey by Frithwald before 675,[4] in which charter the boundaries of Thorpe are given. The manor of Thorpe is included with those of Chertsey, Egham, and Chobham in all subsequent confirmations of this grant made to the abbey. In 1086 it was held by the abbey as 7 hides, having been assessed in King Edward's time for 10, its value at both periods being £12.[5] It remained with the abbey until the Dissolution[6] ; in 1537 the abbot surrendered it with his other lands to the king.[7] A thirty-years' lease of the manor had been granted by the abbot to Richard Wykes in 1509, and in 1530 Maud Broke also received a grant for the same number of years, to date from the expiration of Richard Wykes's tenancy. She afterwards married Thomas Ford, and they entered into possession in 1539, when they sold their lease to

THORPE VILLAGE

[1] Pat. 1 Ric. II, pt. vi, m. 10.
[2] Brass plate in the church
[3] Stat. 47 Geo. III, cap. 63.

[4] Birch, Cart. Sax. i, 55.
[5] V.C.H. Surr. i, 309.

[6] See Chertsey, Egham, and Chobham for refs.
[7] Feet of F. Div.Co. Trin. 29 Hen.VIII.

John Balnet. A dispute concerning the stock, cattle, and stable implements, &c., which belonged to the manor, but which Wykes refused to hand over to the new tenants, terminated in favour of Wykes.[8] In 1550 the manor was leased for thirty years to William Fitz William,[9] who was afterwards knighted. In 1569 his widow Joan received a twenty-one years' lease of the lands.[10] She died in 1574.[11] In 1587 James Bond, described as queen's tenant of the manor of Thorpe, received an order to alter a dove-house there.[12] A grant of the site of the manor for thirty years had been made in 1571 to Henry Radecliffe, but in 1596 a further grant for twenty-one years was made to John Hibberd.[13] In 1610 William Minterne received a grant of it.[14] James I granted the manor itself to Henry, Prince of Wales, and after his death to Sir Francis Bacon and others, in trust for Prince Charles for a term of ninety-nire years.[15] In May 1627 the trustees granted the manor to William Minterne and his heirs for the remainder of the term, and in the following month the king granted the reversion of the manor to Minterne and his heirs for ever.[16] In 1628 the annual rent of £89 18s. 5¼d. due from the manor was apportioned to George Evelyn and others.[17] William Minterne died in 1627, shortly after the above grant had been made to him. He was also seised of the other manor in Thorpe, known as the manor of Hall Place (q.v.), and the two manors, thus united, became the property of Wolley Leigh, grandson and heir of William Minterne, by his daughter Elizabeth, who had married Sir Francis Leigh.[18] Both manors have remained in this family since that time.[19] The manor descended from father to son until 1737, when Sir John Leigh died, and his children having predeceased him, Mary and Anne, his cousins, became his heiresses. The estates were held by them jointly until the passing of an Act of Parliament, 7 Geo. III, cap. 7, when a partition was effected, and Thorpe and Hall Place went to the heirs of Mary, who had taken

A fishery in water called Le Flete in Thorpe, which had belonged to the abbey, was in the tenure of Henry Polsted after the Dissolution. It was granted with the manor to Sir William Fitz William and afterwards to his widow Joan.[21]

In 1303 the Abbot of Chertsey granted to Richard de Graveney of Thorpe and his heirs land in Thorpe described as 'a certain place in Lupinbrok lying between the land of Henry de Middleton called Renebrug and the pasture of Thomas de Sodyngton,' for which an annual rent of 2s. 8d. was to be paid to the monastery,[22] and in 1339 Alice wife of Richard de Graveney held land in Thorpe, including a mill, for her lifetime, with remainder to her children Reginald and Alice, and the heirs of Reginald.[23] This may have been the land which was later known as the manor of GRAVENEY, but further trace of this family in Thorpe does not appear, and the manor passed to the family of Thorpe, who were lords of Graveney during the 15th century. John Thorpe, son of John Thorpe, left the manor to his daughter Alice, who married Robert Osberne, from whom she was divorced. She afterwards married—Flemyng, probably between 1442 and 1456.[24] A lawsuit concerning various feoffments of the manor made by Alice Flemyng lasted for many years.[25] The heiresses of Alice Flemyng were her cousins Maud wife of William Revell, and Ela wife of Robert Blount. They were certainly living as late as 1471, and presumably held the manor after Alice's death.[26] It appears probable that the manor passed from these families, by marriage of female heirs, to the families of Wykes and Aughton, as in 1526–7 the manor, then referred to for the first time by the alternative name of HALL PLACE, was conveyed to John Chambers, clerk, and others, by Robert and Margaret Wykes; a quitclaim being made from Robert and Margaret and the heirs of Margaret, from Joan Aughton, a widow, and the heirs of Joan, and from Henry Wykes.[27] John Chambers appears to have purchased the claims of his co-grantees, as a settlement made on himself and his heirs was made in 1541.[28] This Dr. John Chambers, who was the king's physician, was also the Warden of Merton College, Oxford, and the Dean of St. Stephen's College, Westminster. In 1543 Sir Anthony Browne and Richard Millis received licence to alienate the manor to the Dean and College of St. Stephen's, Westminster.[29] The document giving the licence also states that Richard Millis held other lands in Surrey of the Warden and scholars of Merton College as of their manor of Malden. Probably Browne and Millis were acting merely as trustees. Chambers had originally bought the manor as his personal property ; the licence to alienate to him, as Dean of St. Stephen's, was apparently granted that he might endow the college, which he enriched in other ways

LEIGH. Or a cheveron sable with three lions argent thereon.

BENNETT. Gules a bezant between three demilions or.

the name of Leigh-Bennett, and who died in 1746. Her second son, the Rev. Wolley Leigh-Bennett, succeeded in 1772.[30] Mr. Henry Currie Leigh-Bennett is the present lord of the manor.

[8] Ct. of Aug. Proc. (Hen. VIII and Edw. VI), bdle. 12, no. 29.
[9] Acts of the P.C. 1549–50, p. 415.
[10] Pat 12 Eliz. pt. viii, m. 7.
[11] Chan. Inq. p.m. (Ser. 2), clxxv, 5.
[12] Dep. Keeper's Rep. xxxviii, App. 1 ; Exch. Spec. Com. 2252 (30 Eliz.).
[13] Pat. 38 Eliz. pt. iv, m. 14.
[14] Ibid. 7 Jas. I, pt. xxiv, no. 6.
[15] Exch. L.T.R. Orig. R 14 Jas. I, pt. iv, rot. 126.
[16] Pat. 3 Chas. I, pt. xx, m. 5.
[17] Ibid. 3 Chas. I, pt. xxxv, m. 4.
[18] Chan. Inq. p.m. (Ser. 2), ccccxxxviii,

[19] William Minterne was the son of a Margaret Wolley. Sir Francis Wolley, son of Sir John Wolley, by his will, proved in the Probate Court of Canterbury, Dec. 1609, left his estates in Thorpe, Egham, and Chertsey to his cousin William Minterne. Margaret Wolley was perhaps Sir John's sister.
Feet of F. Surr. Trin. 13 Chas. I ; Hist. MSS. Com. Rep. v, App. vii, 14 ; Chan. Inq. p.m. (Ser. 2), xxxvii, 10 ; Cal. of Com. for Compounding, 2884 ; Feet of F. Surr. Hil. 2 Anne ; Recov. R. Hil. 2 Anne ; Recov. R. Mich. 31 Geo. III.

[20] Surr. Arch. Coll. viii, 124 ; Manning and Bray, Hist. of Surr. iii, 242.
[21] Pat. 12 Eliz. pt. viii, m. 7.
[22] Exch. K.R. Misc. Bks. vol. 25, fol. 246.
[23] Feet of F. Surr. 12 Edw. III, no. 33.
[24] Early Chan. Proc. bdle. 15, no. 344.
[25] Ibid. bdle. 28, no. 511 ; bdle. 44, no. 70.
[26] Ibid.
[27] Recov. R. Mich. 18 Hen. VIII ; Feet of F. Surr. Hil. 18 Hen. VIII.
[28] Feet of F. Div. Co. East. 33 Hen. VIII.
[29] Chan. Inq. p.m. (Ser. 2), lxix, 98.

out of his private means, with this manor. The college was dissolved in 1547 and the manor became Crown property. In 1548 Hall Place, described as a capital messuage and tenement, and the land at High Graveney, was granted to Henry Folsted and William More and the heirs of Henry.[90] The latter died in 1555, leaving the manor as dower to his wife and after her death to his son Richard.[91] It was afterwards stated that Folsted had purchased the manor from John Avingdon for the sum of £17 14s. It is probable that Avingdon had merely acted as trustee for the purposes of a settlement.[92] Richard Polsted settled the manor on his wife Elizabeth, daughter of Sir William More, in 1569, and afterwards died there leaving no issue.[93] His widow married Sir John Wolley, and in 1584 Brian Annesley, Richard Polsted's rightful heir, remitted to them and their heirs all his claim in half the said manor. On the death of Elizabeth, who married, as her third husband, Sir Thomas Egerton, the manor was therefore divided, one half going to Brian Annesley, the other half, in which he had remitted his claim, to Francis Wolley, son and heir of Elizabeth by her second husband.[94] Sir Francis Wolley died in 1609, and left his share of the manor to William Minterne his cousin, with remainder to Elizabeth, daughter of William.[95] She married Sir Francis Leigh, and their son Wolley Leigh inherited the whole of the manor of Hall Place in 1627, his grandfather, William Minterne, having acquired to himself and his heirs the moiety of [?]manor left to Brian Annesley.[96] Wolley Leigh inherited also the principal manor of Thorpe (q.v.) from his grandfather. Hall Place was henceforth held with the manor of Thorpe; it apparently ceased to be regarded as a separate manor, and the whole was called Thorpe and Hall Place in the division of 1768.[97] Hall Place was the manor-house. It was pulled down by the Rev. John Leigh-Bennett, owner between 1806 and 1835, and the present house, called Thorpe Place, built.

The church of ST. MARY consists
CHURCH of a chancel 27 ft. by 17 ft. 6 in. with a small north vestry, a nave 35 ft. 4 in. by 21 ft. 3 in., north transept 11 ft. 2 in. deep, north aisle 8 ft. 3 in. wide, south transept 13 ft. 10 in. deep; south aisle 8 ft. 3 in. wide, and a west tower 11 ft. 8 in. by 11 ft. 3 in., all measurements being internal. The early history of the church has been greatly obscured by drastic restorations of a fairly recent date, and it is evident that at various late, though not modern, dates the fabric has been allowed to fall into disrepair and has then been clumsily restored. The chancel arch is in part of 12th-century date though much repaired. The aisles and transepts seem to have been added in the 13th century, and about the middle of the 14th century the chancel was rebuilt to its present dimensions. The tower is of 17th-century date, and the north vestry modern. The old walls are of chalk and flint, most of the new facings being in Heath stone.

The east window of the chancel is modern and of three lights with geometrical tracery of 14th-century design. On the north is a modern door to the vestry with a hood-mould formed by breaking over it a string-course which, passing round three sides of the chancel, is in part of 14th-century date. West of this is a much restored 14th-century two-light window with flowing tracery, containing in the head some original 14th-century glass, and following on this is a single cinquefoiled light of which the internal splay is old. The window itself is in two stages, both having cinquefoiled heads and the upper one simple cusped tracery. At the south-east are a trefoiled piscina and double sedilia of one design and mid-14th-century date. The piscina has a double basin and the sedilia are separated by a shaft with moulded capital and base, and their heads, of ogee form, are moulded. At the west, a modern niche has been placed in exact imitation of the piscina, but lacking the drain. The string-course noted above is broken square over the piscina and sedilia, and above it, over the sedilia, is an old moulded bracket. Slightly west of this, and partly broken into by the modern niche, is a window of the same date and detail as that opposite to it on the north. The westernmost window on this side also corresponds exactly to that on the north, and between this and the window last described is a small 14th-century door in which, externally, a badly fitting 15th-century head has been inserted. The chancel arch, of distorted semicircular form, is of two orders to the west and one to the east. The jambs are slightly chamfered and have hollow-chamfered abaci. On either side of it are two openings with segmental heads and sills at breast height, and on their eastern faces tracery of 15th-century date in two cinquefoiled lights under square heads; they have served the double purpose of squints and light for the nave altars. The nave is of three bays, being of similar detail with two-centred arches of two chamfered orders towards the nave and a single order towards the aisles. These look like scraped-down 13th-century work, the second column on the north being octagonal instead of round. All the windows in aisles and transepts have modern tracery of 14th-century style, but in the south transept is a 14th-century piscina. The nave roof is old, but hidden by plaster; at the east end it is panelled in two bays and has formed the ceiling over the rood.

The church has very good modern fittings, and at the west end of the nave is a pretty 17th-century gallery with twisted balusters.

The tower is built of red brick in old English bond, and has round-headed pairs of belfry windows in brick, with a modern Gothic west window and door on the ground stage. It is embattled and much overgrown with ivy.

On the south wall of the chancel is a brass to William Denham, his wife, five sons and ten daughters. He was a citizen and goldsmith of London, and died in 1583. Above are three shields; the first has the arms of Denham; the second, the arms of the Company of Goldsmiths: the third Denham impaling a cross paty with a bend over all and a ring for difference.

[90] Pat. 2 Edw. VI, pt. i, m. 32.
[91] P.C.C. 6 Ketchyn; Chan. Proc. (Ser. 2), cxxxix, 4; Chan. Inq. p.m.(Ser. 2), cvi, 56.
[92] Chan. Proc. (Ser. 2), cxxxix, 4. Or possibly Avingdon and Aughton are the

same name, and this conveyance was the surrender of claim by the Aughton family.
[93] Chan. Inq. p.m. (Ser. 2), cclx, 118.
[94] Ibid.
[95] Ibid. cccxxxiv, 60; ccccxxxviii, 125.

[96] Ibid. (Ser. 2), ccccxxxviii, 25.
[97] Feet of F. Surr. Hil. 14 Chas. I; Chan. Inq. p.m. (Ser. 2), dxxiv, 1; xxxii, 10; dxxxvii, 10; Feet of F.Surr. Hil. 2 Anne; Recov. R. Hil. 2 Anne; Mich. 31 Geo. III.

The font is modern and stands at the west end of the nave ; it is octagonal and of poor design.

The bells are three in number, the treble by T. Swain 1753, the second, by William Eldridge 1693, and the tenor by Richard Phelps, 1725.

The plate comprises a fine silver cup with the Copenhagen hall-marks for 1704, and the arms of Vernon impaling Buck ; a large silver flagon given in 1739 and made in the preceding year ; a paten which has lost its foot, has only the maker's mark ⊙ repeated four times, it is of late 17th-century date ; and two silver almsdishes of 1839 and 1869.

The first book of registers has an ornamented title-page and contains mixed entries 1653 to 1812, but marriages only to 1754 ; the second book contains banns and marriages 1754 to 1812.

ADVOWSON The church is not mentioned in the Taxation of Pope Nicholas, 1291, but was probably included with Egham, the vicar of Egham appointing a chaplain. This duty was neglected before 1401, as appears by a dispute between the abbey and vicar concerning the finding of a chaplain for the ' chapel of Thorpe in the parish of Egham.' [38] In 1428 a further dispute arose between the Abbot of Chertsey and the inhabitants of Thorpe concerning the finding and supporting of this chaplain. Finally the bishop arbitrated, and certain of the inhabitants were given the custody of the goods of the chapel, together with the duty of providing the chaplain. The rights of sepulchre were granted to Thorpe parish, an annual fixed payment of 6s. 8d., collected from the inhabitants, being allotted to the abbot as his portion of the burial dues. An annual rent of 4d. for the chaplain's house was to be paid to the abbot by the inhabitants. The abbot on his part was to induct the chaplain, to undertake the repair of the chancel, and to provide bread and wine for one mass daily, two candles for processions, and sufficient straw to strew the chapel twice a year. To the chaplain was allotted a cottage and garden, and some land, tithes of wool and lambs and other tithes in Thorpe, mortuaries, four loads of firewood annually and certain other rights.[39] This composition, by which the inhabitants were made responsible for the chaplain's stipend, appears to have held good, in theory at least, until the 17th century,

as in 1637 Henry Duncomb the chaplain petitioned the king stating that this ancient composition ' hath been for a long time concealed and the tithes, with the piece of land, unjustly detained by the parishioners, and only 20 marks paid yearly by them, to the great prejudice of the petitioner and the church.' [40]

The rectory and advowson were surrendered in 1537,[41] with the other possessions of the abbey of Chertsey, and the rectory was granted to Bisham monastery in the same year,[42] to return once more to the Crown in 1538. A twenty-one years' lease of the rectory was granted to Thomas Stydolf by the Abbot of Bisham in March 1538 ; the reversion for another term of twenty-one years was granted to Thomas Shelton in 1566, a further lease to Sir Francis Grey being made in 1581.[43] In 1590, however, the rectory of Thorpe was granted to Sir John Wolley and his heirs.[44] Francis Wolley, his son, inherited the property on his father's death in 1596.[45] He himself died in 1609, bequeathing the rectory of Thorpe to William Minterne, his cousin, whose grandson, Wolley Leigh, inherited this property, together with both the manors in Thorpe, in 1627,[46] and the rectory was held afterwards by the lord of the manor of Thorpe (q.v.).

The advowson—surrendered, as has been said, in 1537—remained in the Crown from that time until after 1860, the Lord Chancellor presenting during the last thirty years or so of this period.[47] It was bought by a Miss Fergusson, who presented Mr. Martin as vicar in 1874, and afterwards gave him the advowson, who sold it to his next successor, who also sold to the next incumbent, Mr. Morgan. Mrs. Morgan, his widow, afterwards presented. It was then sold to Mr. Freh-Bennett, father of the present patron, and the money invested for the benefit of the vicarage.[48]

CHARITIES The charities include Smith's Charity as in other Surrey parishes.

Giles Travers in 1706 left £6 a year for apprenticing poor children.

William Beddington in 1762 left £4 6s. 8d. a year for bread for the poor.

Isaac Townsend in 1765 left a house and land worth £6 a year for the poor. He was Admiral of the White and Governor of Greenwich Hospital. He is buried in the church.

[38] Winton Epis. Reg. Wykeham, ii (2), fol. 338a ; cf. Egerton MS. 2033, fol. 160.
[39] Exch. K.R. Misc. Bks. vol. 25, fol. 42.
[40] Cal. S.P. Dom. 1637-8, p. 318.
[41] Feet of F. Div. Co. Trin. 29 Hen. VIII.
[42] Pat. 29 Hen. VIII, pt. iv, m. 35.
[43] Ibid. 32 Eliz. pt. xvii, m. 1.
[44] Ibid.
[44] Chan. Inq. p.m. (Ser. 2) ccxlix, 74.
[45] Ibid. ccccxlviii, 125.
[47] Inst. Bks. (P.R.O.) ; Clergy Lists.
[48] Information from the Rev. E. W. Carpenter, late vicar of Thorpe.

THE HUNDRED OF ELMBRIDGE

(Or EMLEYBRIDGE)

CONTAINING THE PARISHES OF

COBHAM	STOKE D'ABERNON	WALTON UPON THAMES
ESHER	THAMES DITTON (MANORS OF	WEYBRIDGE
EAST AND WEST MOLESEY	IMBER COURT AND WESTON)	

The boundaries of this hundred have remained practically unchanged since 1086, when, however, Ember Court in Thames Ditton was part of the hundred of Kingston,[1] and the holding of Chertsey in Weybridge was attributed to Copthorne. It is not certain at what date the hundred passed into the hands of the men of Kingston, but it seems later to have been regarded as one of the liberties granted to them by King John in 1200, and was held at fee farm.[2] In 1280 it was said to be in the hands of their tenant Reginald de Imworth,[3] with whose manor of Imworth it descended until 1499, when Richard Ardern died seised of the manor of Imworth and half the hundred of Elmbridge, held of the men of Kingston.[4] Within the hundred there were several exempt jurisdictions. In 1253 John D'Abernon was successful in his claim to view of frankpledge in Stoke,[5] and Avelina, daughter of Geoffrey de Cruce and wife of Roger de Legh, also claimed the right in Walton.[6] At a later date Sir Thomas Henneage obtained a grant of Molesey Prior with view of frankpledge from Henry VIII,[7] and John Druell also had a view on his manor here.[8]

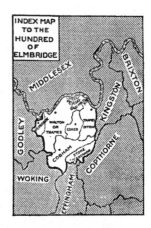

In a Subsidy Roll of about 1334 the hundred was valued at £24 0s. 6d.,[9] and it was assessed for ship-money at £346 in 1636.[10] The name by which it is known is derived from the bridge by which the road from London to Chertsey crosses the Mole or Emlyn on its way west, and here probably the hundred court was held.

[1] V.C.H. Surr. i, 305a.   [3] Assize R. 898, m. 5.   [4] Chan. Inq. p.m. 8 Edw. I, no. 23.
[4] Ibid. 15 Hen. VII (Ser. 2), xiv, 101.   [5] Plac. de Quo Warr. (Rec. Com.), 747.
[6] Ibid. 747.   [7] L. and P. Hen. VIII, ii, 1104.   [8] Chan. Inq. p.m. (Ser. 2), xi, 51.
[9] V.C.H. Surr. i, 443.   [10] S.P. Dom. Chas. I, cccxlviii, 82.

COBHAM

Covenham (xi cent.) ; Covenham and Coveham (xiii, xiv, and xv cents.) ; Coham (xvi cent.).

Cobham is a village about 4 miles south-east of Weybridge and the same distance south-west of Esher. The parish is bounded on the north by Walton, Esher, Thames Ditton, and a corner of Kingston ; on the south-east by Stoke D'Abernon ; on the south by Little Bookham, Effingham and East Horsley ; on the south-west by Ockham ; on the west by a corner of Wisley and by Walton—thus touching ten other parishes. It is about 5 miles from south-west to north-east, and rather under 3 miles from south-east to north-west, and contains 5,278 acres of land and 54 of water. The River Mole runs in a very circuitous course through the parish, and the soils are very various. The centre may be described as generally alluvium and gravel of the river valley ; to the north and on the west there is Bagshot sand, and the greater part of the east and south is on the London clay. There is open common and waste land with trees on it at Fairmile and Ockshot to the north-east and on Cobham Common, to the west, the Bagshot sand soil. Cobham Tilt is an open green near the Mole. Church Cobham was the original village, but Street Cobham is an equally large collection of houses north-west of the church, which has grown up near the Portsmouth road. Houses have grown up also about Cobham Tilt, east of Church Cobham, reaching to Church Cobham on one side, and now spreading towards the station on the other. The neighbourhood of Ockshot and Fairmile station is also becoming a village. There are brickfields in the parish.

The Portsmouth road runs through Street Cobham. The London and South Western Railway, Cobham and Guildford line, opened in 1885, runs through the east side of the parish, in which is Ockshot and Fairmile station. Cobham and Stoke D'Abernon station is in the latter parish.

In the autumn of 1906, during excavations for a new road at Leigh Hill, north of Cobham Tilt, circular rubbish-pits were found containing fragments of hand-made and wheel-made pottery, the latter Roman. There were also loom weights and pot-boilers, such as belong to a British settlement. The remains have been briefly noticed by Mr. Reginald Smith of the British Museum.[1]

There were two ancient bridges in Cobham. One was on the Portsmouth road across the Mole. It is stated[2] that a record formerly existing showed that the wooden bridge was made by Maud, queen of Henry I, for use in flood time only, as was the case at Godalming, the traffic at other times passing over by a ford. In 1782[3] a new brick bridge was built to be accessible at all times as a county bridge, the lords of the manors of Walton and Cobham, who had been

CHURCH STYLE HOUSE, COBHAM

[1] In *Surr. Arch. Coll.* xx   [2] Manning and Bray, op. cit. ii, 732   [3] Stat. 22 Geo. III, cap. 17.

responsible for the wooden bridge, contributing £400 to the first expense. There was a wooden bridge, subject to the same restrictions in use, on the road to Ockham and East Horsley, which was replaced by a brick bridge about the same date.

A fishery at Cobham Bridge was granted by Charles II to Thomas Wyndham, whose wife Elizabeth had assisted the king's escape after the battle of Worcester.[4] Down Mill is in the southern part of the parish, in Downeside (see below) ; Cobham Mill is close to Church Cobham. Both are on the Mole.

There was a fair on St. Andrew's Day, the patron saint of the church, changed to 11 December since new style came in, and another on 1 May. The Inclosure Act was among the first in the county ; the common fields were inclosed by an Act[5] procured by Mr. Thomas Page of Poynters in Cobham, who had just bought the manor. Again in 1793[6] the waste was inclosed, with the exception of 300 acres left for pasturage and turf-cutting, mostly about Fairmile.

On the high ground of Cobham Common was one of the semaphores in the line from London to Portsmouth.

St. John's Mission Church was built in 1899 by Miss Carrick Moore of Brook Farm, in memory of her father Mr. John Carrick Moore.

St. Matthew's, Hatchford, consisting of a chancel and nave in 14th-century style, was built in 1858.

There are Congregational, Wesleyan, and Baptist chapels in the parish.

The cemetery at Cobham Tilt was opened in 1883. The Public Hall was built in 1887.

The Old Church Style House was formerly used as a home of rest for ladies of slender means, and later as a home of rest for poor women of all classes. It is an old house, restored, by the churchyard gate. A modern inscription in the house says that it was built in 1432 and restored in 1635.

Cobham Park is the seat of Mr. Charles Combe, D.L., J.P. Close to it are the paddocks and stabling of the Cobham Stud Company. Cobham Park was formerly known as Downe Place, and that part of the parish was called Downeside, from a family of that name who are recorded in the Visitation of 1623. John Downe died in 1656 (see Charities). A Mr. John Bridges built a new house here, and sold it to the eminent soldier Sir John Ligonier in 1750.[7] Sir John was created, in 1757, Viscount Ligonier in the peerage of Ireland, in 1763 Baron Ligonier of Ripley in the peerage of the United Kingdom, and in 1766 Earl Ligonier. His property extended into Ripley. He died in 1770, aged 91, having served in the army since the reign of William III. His nephew and heir to his Irish peerage died in 1782, and Downe Place was then sold to the Earl of Carhampton, who in 1807 sold it to Mr. Harvey Christian Combe.[7a] The estate has since remained in his family. The present owner, Mr. Charles Combe, D.L., J.P., was born in 1836, and served in the 3rd Bombay Cavalry in Russia

and in the Mutiny. The house was rebuilt by him in 1874.

Cobham Court is on the site of the original manor-house. It was reserved out of the sale of the manor in 1708, and is now the seat of Mr. Philip Warren. Brook Farm was built on the land of a farm belonging to Mr. Porter by Colonel Edward Leatherland in 1800. In 1807 it was bought by Captain (afterwards Admiral Sir Graham) Moore, R.N., brother to Sir John Moore of Corunna, and son to Dr. Moore 'of Zelucco.' It was bought with the prize-money of the Spanish treasure ships, the capture of which by Captain Moore gave an excuse for war in 1804. It descended to his nephew Mr. John Moore, and is now the seat of that gentleman's daughter Miss Carrick Moore.

Hatchford, the property of Mrs. C. Stone, is on the site of an older house built by Mr. Lewis Smith in the 18th century. Miss Isabella Saltonstall, who endowed the living, died there in 1829. Lord Francis Egerton built a new house about 1842, which is now occupied by Sir Henry Samuelson, bart.

Fox Warren is the seat of Mrs. Buxton ; Sandroyd House, Fairmile, of Mr. C. P. Wilson ; Knowle Hill of Mr. John Early Cook ; Poynters of Mrs. Mount ; Brackenhurst was the seat of Mr. Edward Harbord Lushington, J.P.

Fairmile, which with Ockshot is becoming a residential neighbourhood reaching into Cobham, Esher, and Stoke D'Abernon parishes, appears from Bowen's map to have been originally the name of a straight stretch of the Portsmouth road north-east of Street Cobham.

MANORS. The manor of COBHAM for many centuries formed part of the possessions of the Abbot and convent of Chertsey. Frithwald, subregulus of Surrey, and Bishop Erkenwald are said to have granted to Chertsey Abbey in 675 'ten mansas at Coveham,'[8] and this grant was confirmed and augmented by Edward the Confessor in 1062.[9] At the time of the Domesday Survey the abbey held Cobham, including three mills.[10] Henry I gave the abbot a grant of free warren in the manor, with leave to keep dogs, and to inclose Cobham Park at his pleasure for hunting purposes.[11] This privilege was not however allowed him by the Quo Warranto Commissioners,[12] but in 1285 the king granted a new charter of free warren.[13] The monks from time to time obtained additions to their estate in the shape of small parcels of land acquired by gift or exchange.[14] In 1537 they handed over the manor to the king in return for £5,000.[15] It continued to belong to the Crown till 1553, when Queen Mary granted the reversion of the manor, then in the hands of lessees,

CHERTSEY ABBEY.
Party or and argent St. Paul's sword, its hilt or, crossed with St. Peter's keys gules and azure.

4 *Cal. S.P. Dom.* 1668–9, p. 323.
5 19 Geo. III, cap. 15.
6 33 Geo. III. cap. 69.
7 Manning and Bray, op. cit. ii, 735.
7a The Earl of Carhampton was not admitted to the copyhold of the manor, held by the second Lord Ligonier's daughters, or their assigns, till 1802. But Bray

was steward of the manor in 1782, and is therefore probably right in the date which he gives for the sale of Downe Place ; Cobham Ct. R.
8 Birch, *Cart. Sax.* i, no. 39.
9 Kemble, *Cod. Dipl.* iv, no. 812.
10 *V.C.H. Surr.* i, 307b.
11 Cart. Antiq. OO, 4.

12 *Plac. de Quo Warr.* (Rec. Com.), 744.
13 Chart. R. 13 Edw. I, pt. ii, no. 58.
14 Feet of F. Surr. Mich. 19 Hen. III, no. 12 ; Mich. 5 Edw. I, no. 34 ; Pat. 12 Edw. II, pt. ii, m. 18.
15 Feet of F. Div. Co. Trin. 29 Hen. VIII.

to George Bigley, gentleman, and Elizabeth his wife.[16] Early in the next reign it came into the hands of Robert Gavell,[17] through his marriage with Dorothy, one of the daughters and co-heiresses of Bigley. His immediate descendants held it under an entail [18] for upwards of a hundred and fifty years.[19] In 1708 Robert Gavell, senior, together with his son and heir-apparent, Robert Gavell, junior, conveyed the manor and several farms (reserving the manor-house, known as Cobham Court, and the farm attached to it, being demesne lands of the manor) to Frances, Viscountess Lanesborough,[20] and she in 1719 bequeathed it to her second grandson, James Fox, with remainder to other grandsons.[21] James Fox died without issue in 1753, and was succeeded by his brother, Sackville Fox, who died in 1760, and who left an only son James, in whom the estate ultimately became vested.[22] This gentleman in 1778 sold Cobham to Robert Mackreth, and he next year sold it to Thomas Page,[23] who then held a farm called Poynters in Cobham parish. Before his death in 1781 Mr. Page left his estates to trustees for sale, giving the option of purchase to his eldest son Thomas.[24] The latter bought the manor and farms belonging to it, and enlarged the house of Poynters for his own residence. He died in 1842 and left one daughter by his marriage with Catherine Brooksbank. Miss Page died in 1860, leaving the manor to her cousin Francis John Mount. On his death in 1903 his elder brother William George Mount succeeded under Miss Page's will, and made over the property in 1904 to his fourth son, Francis Mount, the present lord of the manor of Cobham.[25] Cobham Court, with its attached farm, descended from the Gavells to the Woods of Littleton, co. Middlesex. It continued in the family of Wood till the middle of the last century, and is now the seat of Mr. Philip Warren.

In 1535 the manor was valued at £37 9s. 8d. per annum.[26] In 1708 the appurtenances of the manor included two water grist-mills.[26a]

The lord had view of frankpledge. Constables and tithing-men were elected for the tithings of Street Cobham, Church Cobham, and Downeside, and one pinder and one ale-taster.[27]

Henry VIII visited Cobham on several occasions.[28] There appears to be no early history of the reputed manor of HEYWOOD in Cobham. A family named 'Heiwude' held land so called in 1206 [29] and two

GAVELL. *Sable an eagle argent and a chief or with three pheons sable therein.*

grants of land there occur in the 14th century [30] by William de Horwode, who was perhaps one of the same family.

A certain John Prudhomme held lands in Heywood in Cobham in 1317. In 1331 the Prior and convent of Newark by Guildford acquired from him lands in Cobham, amounting altogether to 80 acres of land and 20 acres of wood. These lands were held of Henry de Somerbury, who held of Henry atte Downe, who held of the abbey of Chertsey.[30a]

In 1594 James Sutton died seised of ' a messuage called Heywood' in Cobham, which he held of the Crown.[31] In 1711 Katherine Gyles, widow, and Thomas Machell quitclaimed to Robert Porter and his heirs, for £320, the manor of Heywood with its appurtenances, including a fishery in the River Mole.[32] The small property now called Heywood Park, near Fairmile Common, belonged to Lord Iveagh, and was recently sold by him to Mr. Hartmann.

It is almost equally difficult to trace the history of the manor of DOWNE. A certain Deodatus de Dunes held land at Cobham in the early part of the 13th century,[33] and it seems possible that the manor of Doneham (? = Downe) which is mentioned in 1280 [34] may have been this manor. The name of Thomas atte Downe occurs in 1340,[35] another Thomas Downe or Donne of Cobham is mentioned in the 15th century,[36] and a third in 1565. This last ' Thomas Adowne' held the mill on the River Mole called Downe Mill in Cobham.[37] But in 1395 the manor of Downe in Cobham was in the possession of Thomas Colney.[38] The name of Downe Common was familiar in Cobham in the 17th century,[39] and this part of the parish is called Downeside from this family. Their house, formerly called Downe Place, is now known as Cobham Park.[40]

DOWNE. *Azure three bulls' heads or cut off at the neck and having crowns argent.*

A piece of land called 'NORTHWOOD with Serichecroft and two acres of land in the field of Barett' was granted by Gilbert Walsh to the church of St. Swithun and William de Raleigh, Bishop of Winchester, in the 13th century.[41] This was probably the land held in 1086 by William de Wateville of the abbey of Chertsey, and considered part of the manor of Esher.[42] The bishop's successors held this land till 1538, when Bishop Gardiner was obliged to hand it over to the king along with the manor of Esher.[43] Northwood was restored to the see of Winchester by Queen Mary.[44] With Esher (q.v.) it was re-acquired by the Crown in 1582–3.

16 Pat. 1 Mary, pt. vi, m. 29.
17 Ibid. 7 Eliz. pt. vi, m. 6.
18 Chan. Inq. p.m. (Ser. 2), ccxlii, 33.
19 Harl. MS. 1561, fol. 42.
20 See Recov. R. East. 7 Anne, rot. 110.
21 Will, proved P.C.C. 9 June 1721.
22 Com. Pleas D. Enr. Mich. 18 Geo. III, m. 8.
23 Ibid. Mich. 20 Geo. III, m. 32. Page held his first court in 1779.
24 See Feet of F. Surr. Trin. 21 Geo. III.
25 Information kindly communicated by Mr. Mount.
26 Valor Eccl. (Rec. Com.), ii, 56.

26a Recov. R. East. 7 Anne, rot. 110.
27 Ct. R. of Cobham.
28 L. and P. Hen. VIII, i, 5383; xv, 633; Hist. MSS. Com. Rep. vii, App. 603b.
29 Feet of F. Surr. Mich 8 John, no. 25.
30 Ibid. Hil. 34 Edw. I, 5, 29; Harl. Chart. 58, B. 40.
30a Harl. Chart. 58, B. 40; Pat. 5 Edw. III, pt. ii, m. 24 ; Feet of F. Surr. Mich. 5 Edw. III ; Chan. Inq. p.m. 5 Edw. III (2nd nos.), no. 66.
31 Chan. Inq. p.m. (Ser. 2), ccxl, 36.
32 Feet of F. Surr. Hil. 10 Anne.

33 Feet of F. Surr. Mich. 8 John, no. 25 ; East. 5 Hen. III, no. 11.
34 Abbrev. Plac. (Rec. Com.), 199.
35 Feet of F. Div. Co. Hil. 14 Edw. III, no. 95.
36 Pat. 12 Hen. VI, pt. ii, m. 26; Anct. D. (P.R.O.) A. 9505.
37 Feet of F. Surr. East. 7 Eliz.
38 Ibid. Surr. Mich. 19 Ric. II, no. 32.
39 Chan. Inq. p.m. (Ser. 2), cccxvi, 59.
40 Brayley, Hist. of Surr. ii, 410.
41 Cal. Pat. 1313–17, p. 676.
42 V.C.H. Surr. i, 307, and note.
43 L. and P. Hen. VIII, xiii (1), 778.
44 Pat. 1 Mary, pt. ix, m. 18.

In the 14th and 15th centuries a messuage in Cobham known as Dodewikes or Dudwyke was held by a family of the name of Freke.[44]

The manor of *HAM* in Cobham, now in the hands of the Ecclesiastical Commissioners, and formerly part of the possessions of the Dean and Chapter of Windsor, may have been granted by Thomas St. Leger when he gave Ham in Chertsey to endow a chantry at Windsor (see Ham in Chertsey), and have been originally part of the same manor. It is now, however, a separate manor, the courts of which are still held. The court rolls exist only from 1704. The manor, which is very small, includes a house and land in Street Cobham, and land in Appleton, which seems to be the old name for the land south of Leigh Hill. There were holdings in the Cobham common fields and in Appleton fields. Heathfield and Bytham are described as in Appleton, and Tyrrel's Croft, 'next the gravel pits.' Emmet's Farm was also in Ham Manor.

CHURCH   The church of *ST. ANDREW* consists of a chancel 33 ft. 3 in. by 17 ft. 4 in., north chapel 25 ft. 1 in. by 13 ft. 2 in.,

north aisle at this time. This aisle is shown in Cracklow's plan of 1824, and Manning and Bray give its dimensions as 46 ft. long, or 12 ft. shorter than the nave, but since the middle of the 19th century the building has been considerably enlarged—both aisles with their arcades, the south chapel and organ-chamber, the chancel arch, the vestry, and the porch all being modern ; much restoration work has also been carried out ; and the 12th-century south doorway and the 15th-century windows were moved out with the south wall when the aisle was added. The dates of restoration and enlargement are 1853, 1872, 1886, and 1902.

The east window of the chancel is a modern one of three lights under a traceried head of 15th-century character. In the north wall are a square aumbry and a trefoiled recess, both apparently old, but with re-tooled stonework. The arcade opening to the north chapel is of two bays ; the responds are chamfered and stopped out square above the chamfered base and below the chamfered abacus ; the middle column is circular in plan with a moulded base and capital, and the arches are pointed and of one cham-

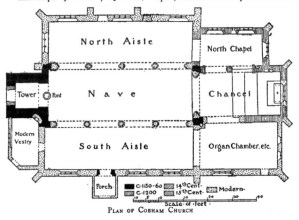

PLAN OF COBHAM CHURCH

south chapel and organ-chamber 31 ft. 10 in. by 16 ft. 3 in., nave 58 ft. 4 in. by 20 ft. 8 in., north aisle 16 ft. 7 in. and south aisle 16 ft. 8 in. wide, south porch, south-west vestry, and west tower 10 ft. 5 in. by 9 ft. 6 in.

About the middle of the 12th century the church seems to have consisted of chancel, nave, and west tower ; the chancel was probably lengthened early in the 13th century, and at the same time the north chapel was added with an arcade of two bays opening into the chancel ; part of one of the original small lancets remains in the north wall of the chapel, but the other windows are later insertions. A peculiar feature is the triangular-headed double piscina in the south wall.

If the arch in the west wall of the chapel is in its original position there must have been a

fered order. The arch towards the south chapel is modern ; it has hollow-chamfered jambs and a pointed arch of two hollow orders, the inner one springing from moulded corbels. The chancel arch is also modern with jambs of three clustered shafts and moulded arch.

The east window of the north chapel is of three lights under a traceried head of 14th-century style ; the inner jambs and hollow-chamfered rear-arch are old, but the tracery has been renewed.

The two north windows are each of three lights under a traceried square head ; both have modern mullions, but old stonework internally. Between these windows is a small blocked 13th-century lancet of which the west jamb and half the head can be seen outside ; it has rebated and chamfered jambs. In the south wall next the east respond of the arcade are

44 Anct. D. (P.R.O.) B. 1211, 1082 ; A. 8717, 5726, 5743, 5744, 8884, 5742, 8988.

two 13th-century piscina drains in a very plain triangular-headed recess ; their projecting faces have been cut away. A 13th-century archway opens into the north aisle ; its jambs are chamfered and have a moulded abacus, and the arch is pointed and of one chamfered order. The south chapel or organ-chamber is modern, but in its south wall is a re-used 15th-century window of three cinquefoiled lights under a four-centred head; the jambs are moulded and there is a moulded label outside ; a modern pointed archway opens to the south aisle.

Both arcades of the nave are modern and each of four bays ; that on the north side has piers of four clustered shafts with moulded bases and capitals of late 13th-century style and pointed arches of two orders ; the south arcade is of a later style with octagonal pillars and pointed arches. The north aisle has three north windows and one at the west, all of three lights, the former doorway was between the first and second windows, but this is now blocked and another doorway inserted farther west.

The south aisle has three re-used 15th-century windows on the south, all of similar detail to that in the chapel. A 12th-century round-arched doorway, a good deal repaired, has been reset in the south wall ; its jambs are of two orders, the inner with an edge-roll and the outer square with detached shafts in the angles, which have scalloped capitals with hollow-chamfered abaci ; the inner order of the arch has an edge-roll like the jambs, and the outer has a triple band of zigzag ; the label is double-chamfered with billet ornament on the inner splay. The porch is a modern one of wood.

A doorway in the west wall of the aisle opens into the modern vestry, which has an outer doorway to the south-west and a four-light window in the west wall.

The east arch of the tower dates from c. 1160 ; its jambs are square and have scalloped capitals with grooved and chamfered abaci, the scallops being small with vertical grooves cut in each, and the arch is round and of a single square order.

The west doorway of the tower is a 15th-century insertion with moulded jambs and a two-centred arch with a moulded label. Over it is a small round-headed window, modern externally, and above this the wall sets in slightly. The second story has a modernized round-headed light in its south wall. The bell chamber windows have been much modernized but are old inside ; each is of two round-headed lights within a round arched tympanum, and between the lights is a round shaft with a scalloped capital ; the material of the walling is of flint with stone dressings, but most of the quoin stones are modern ; above the tower rises an octagonal wooden spire covered with oak shingles. The east wall of the chancel has been coated with cement ; but the walling of the north chapel is exposed, and is built of flint and small pieces of ironstone conglomerate.

The only old roofs are those of the nave and north chapel ; the nave has old collar-trussed rafters with plaster filling between, and the north chapel has collar trusses and tie-beams. All the roofs are tiled except that of the north chapel, which is covered with Horsham slabs.

The fittings of the church generally, font, pulpit, &c., are modern.

In the north jamb of the archway between the south aisle and chapel is set a small palimpsest brass, the later figure is that of a bearded man in armour of the time of Elizabeth ; on the reverse is a 15th-century priest in mass vestments, holding a chalice and host ; on the chalice is inscribed in black letter ' ᴇꜱᴛᴏ ᴍ⁹ ᴊʜꜱ,' and on the host ' ᴊʜꜱ.' The second word on the chalice is perhaps ᴍᴇᴜꜱ or ᴍɪʜɪ. On the south wall of the chancel is a tiny brass representation of the Nativity c. 1500, and there was formerly in the church a plate with the figures of fifteen sons, part of a brass of about the same date. A small brass inscription in the north chapel over the arcade is to Aminadab Cooper, Citizen and Merchant Taylor of London, died 1618, 'he left behind Dorothy his wife and had issue God-helpe their only son.'

There are six bells ; the treble was cast in 1687 and recast in 1905 by Taylor & Co. ; the second is by Thomas Swaln, 1767 ; the third is like the treble ; the fourth by William Eldridge, 1687 ; the fifth by Pack & Chapman, 1773 ; and the tenor by John Taylor, 1902.

The communion plate is modern.

The registers date from 1562. There is a note in them that they were copied by the Rev. W. Tucker, vicar in 1700, from an old book. But the marriages and burials are lost from 1564 to 1610, and the baptisms from 1565 to 1610, and from 1628 to 1630 inclusive. From 1644 to 1656 the baptisms are imperfect, and from 1646 to 1656 there are no marriages or burials. Nor are there any burials from 1678 to 1684.

ADVOWSON   The advowson belonged with the manor to the abbey of Chertsey. Clement III (1187–91) granted leave to the abbey to appropriate the church on endowment of a vicarage. The bull was recited in 1292 [46] but the episcopal registers show the institution of rectors till 1465, when the monks of Chertsey received a licence for the appropriation to them of the church of St. Andrew, Cobham, which was of their own advowson and was held in chief, provided that they endowed a perpetual vicarage there, and distributed annually a certain sum of money among the poor of the parish. [47] At the Dissolution the rectory and advowson passed into the hands of the king, [48] who granted them to his new foundation at Bisham. [49] When the house at Bisham was dissolved the rectory and advowson reverted to the Crown. In 1549 it was leased to William Fountayn and Richard Moyn, [50] and in 1558 granted to William Hammond, [51] who presented in April, 1558. [52] He conveyed ultimately to James Sutton, [53] who died in 1594. [54] His son James presented in 1615. [55] According to Manning and Bray his son James settled the rectory on his marriage with Catherine Inwood in 1622. [56] Their only surviving child Catherine married first her cousin

[46] *Cal. Pat.* 1281–92, p. 493.
[47] Pat. 5 Edw. IV, pt. ii, m. 21.
[48] Feet of F. Div. Co. Trin. 29 Hen. VIII.
[49] L. and P. Hen. VIII, xii (2), g. 1311 (22). An inventory of the church goods

of Cobham Church in 1549 occurs in a MS. of W. M. Molyneux, *Hist. MSS. Com. Rep.* vii, App. 606a.
[50] Pat. 3 Edw. VI, pt. v
[51] Pat. 5 & 6 Phil. and Mary, pt. iv.
[52] Winton Epis. Reg. White, fol. 11a.

[53] Manning and Bray, op. cit. ii, 736.
[54] Chan. Inq. p.m. (Ser. 2), ccxl, 36.
[55] Winton Epis. Reg. Bilson, fol. 42b.
[56] She was patron when the Commonwealth Survey was made ; *Surr. Arch. Coll.* xvii, 210.

ESHER

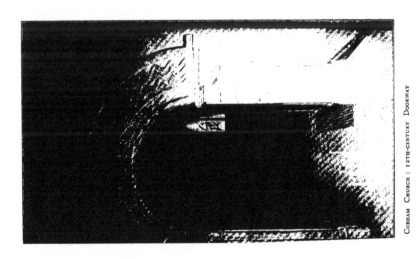

COBHAM CHURCH : 12TH-CENTURY DOORWAY

Sir William Inwood, and secondly the Rev. William Weston, on whom she settled the rectory, and died in 1692. Her only child Elizabeth married Mr. Skrine, and alienated part of the rectory, but on her death left the rest with the advowson to her first cousin Henry Weston of West Horsley. His son Henry Weston sold the tithes which he held in 1801 to the Rev. John Simpkinson, vicar of Cobham,[67] and the advowson after 1823 was conveyed to the son of the latter. The present patron is Mr. Charles Combe of Cobham Park.

CHARITIES Smith's charity is distributed as in other Surrey parishes.

In 1614 Mr. Rogers Bellow left £1 a year to the poor in bread on Good Friday.

In 1629 Mr. Edward Sutton left £2 a year to the poor.

In 1638 Mrs. Cecily Darnelly and Mrs. Sarah Cox, sisters, gave £80 to buy a house in Ripley, the rent to be applied in sums of 20s. to the vicar for a sermon on Good Friday, the remainder in bread to the poor after the service.

In 1641 Mr. Owen Peter left £1 a year to the poor, charged on his house in Claygate.

In 1656 Mr. John Downe of Downe Place left £2 to the vicar for sermons on Christmas Day and Ash Wednesday, and 20s. to the poor in bread on Ash Wednesday. As the celebration of these days was then contrary to the law Mr. Downe was evidently a churchman and a Royalist.

Mr. James Fox before 1724[68] endowed a charity school for forty children.

Mr. James Sutton (date unknown) left £2 to the vicar for a sermon, and £3 to the poor for bread on 5 November.[69]

In 1829 Miss Isabella Saltonstall left £25 a year to the vicar on consideration of his preaching every Sunday afternoon in the parish church.

In 1850 a school was built at Hatchford End.

In 1860 a school (National) was built at Cobham by Miss Coombe in memory of her brother.

In 1867 girls' and infants' schools were built at Downeside.

The Almshouse on Cobham Tilt was built in 1867.

ESHER

Aissela (xi cent.); Esere, Eshere, Esschere (xiii cent.); Eschere &c' Episcopi, Eschere &c' Watevil (xiii and xiv cents.); Asher (xvi cent.).

Esher is a village 4 miles south-west from Kingston. The parish is bounded on the north by East Molesey, on the east by Thames Ditton, on the south by Cobham, and on the west by Walton on Thames. It measures barely 3 miles from north to south, and scarcely 2 miles east to west. It contains 2,044 acres of land and 50 of water. The River Mole forms the greater part of the western boundary. The village itself and most of the parish lie upon the only considerable elevation of Bagshot sand which rises east of the Mole Valley, a situation which has at once rendered it picturesque, dry, and a favourite site for houses. The borders of the parish however touch the alluvium of the Mole Valley on the west and the London clay on the east, and in the north the sandy gravel of Ditton Marsh.

Esher is agricultural and residential. Esher Common is an extensive piece of open land now largely planted with conifers and birches, and adjoins other open land at Fairmile and Ockshot in Cobham parish. The London and Portsmouth road passes through the village. The main line of the London and South Western Railway has a station at Esher, and the Cobham line to Guildford skirts the eastern boundary of the parish.

Claremont, which was originally part of the manor of Esher Episcopi, was bought by Sir John Vanbrugh, who built a small house for himself, and began to ornament the grounds (Guest's poem 'Claremont' attributes the first improvements to Vanbrugh). The Earl of Clare (Duke of Newcastle 1715) bought the property in 1714 on coming of age, and called it after his own title 'Clare Mont.' On his death in 1768 the whole was bought by Lord Clive, who employed 'Capability' Brown to build the present house. It was unfinished at his death in 1774, and was sold to Viscount Galway. He

sold to the Earl of Tyrconnel, who in 1807 sold to Mr. Charles Rose Ellis. He in 1816 conveyed it to the Commissioners of Woods and Forests for the use of the Princess Charlotte on her marriage with Prince Leopold. After her death in 1817 Prince Leopold continued to reside here. When he became King of the Belgians it was occupied occasionally by Queen Victoria, to whom the king conveyed all his rights for life in the house. In 1848 it became the home of Louis Philippe, the exiled king of the French and of his family. He died here in 1850, and his queen Marie Amélie in 1866. It was granted to the late Duke of Albany on his marriage in 1882, and is now the seat of H.R.H. the Duchess of Albany. The house is of brick, with window-frames, portico and cornice of stone. The portico is supported by Corinthian columns, and the pediment bears Lord Clive's arms. Marble is extensively used in the internal decorations, and the rooms are very spacious and handsome.

Another phase of the associations of Esher is of a very different kind. At Sandon was a small hospital, founded in the 12th century.[1] In 1436, after an unfortunate history, during which in 1349 all its brethren had died of the plague, and later, great suffering had resulted from dishonest or incompetent masters, it was suppressed and its property granted to St. Thomas' Southwark. Sandon remained as the name of a farm only, till in 1875 the first meeting of the Sandown Park Racing Club revived public knowledge of it. The racecourse lies south of the line, close to Esher station, and is chiefly in Esher parish, but partly in Thames Ditton. The meetings stand at the head of the inclosed racecourse meetings in the kingdom.

Esher is an urban district with the Dittons, under a Local Government Board Order issued April 1895.[2]

There is an iron mission church at West End. The Baptist chapel was built in 1852, and the Wesleyan

[67] Manning and Bray, loc. cit.   [68] Willis Visitation.   [69] Ibid.   [1] V.C.H. Surr. ii, 118–19.   [2] No. 32638.

chapel in 1889, and there is a Quakers' meeting-house. The village hall was built in 1887. The drinking fountain was presented by Her Majesty Queen Victoria in 1877, in place of a public pump given by the late Comte de Paris, which had become unserviceable.

Besides Claremont and Esher Place (see under manor) there are several large houses in Esher : Esher Lodge, built late in the 18th century, is the seat of Mr. W. Seymour Eastwood ; Milburn of the Hon. Henry Lorton Burke ; Glenhurst of Lady Emma Talbot ; Moore Place of Mr. C. A. Moreing ; Littleworth, a modern house in a small park, of Mr. P. M. Martineau ; The Grove of Mr. Rhodes H. Cobb ; Hill House, in a small park, of Mr. G. B. Batchelor ; Hawksbill Place, in a park, of Mr. A. W. Drayson. Broom Hill was the residence of the late Sir Robert Hawthorn Collins, K.C.B.

The manor of *ESHER* (also called *MANORS ESHER EPISCOPI*) which Tovi had held of Edward the Confessor, was given to the Abbot and convent of Croix St. Leufroy in Normandy by William I,[3] on condition of finding two priests to say mass in the said manor for the souls of his predecessors.[4] In the reign of Henry III, before 1238, Peter des Roches, Bishop of Winchester, bought the manor from the monks of Croix St. Leufroy,[5] and gave it to the Abbot and convent of the Place of St. Edward at Netley in Hampshire.[6] In 1245 the Abbot and convent of Netley released the manor to William de Raleigh, Bishop of Winchester, and the church of Winchester,[7] and it remained among the possessions of the see till 1538, when Bishop Gardiner conveyed it to Henry VIII, who wished to annex it to the honour of Hampton Court.[8] In 1550 Edward VI granted the manor to John, Earl of Warwick, to hold of the king in chief by service of one knight's fee ;[9] but a few months later the earl reconveyed it to the king.[10] Queen Mary restored the estate to the see of Winchester in the first year of her reign.[11]

SEE OF WINCHESTER.
Gules St. Peter's keys crossed with St. Paul's sword.

In 1578 it appears that Charles Lord Howard of Effingham tried to prevail on Bishop Horne of Winchester to grant him a lease in perpetuity of the manor for £20 a year, and by the threat of compassing his end by other means if the bishop would not agree, and bribing him further by promising to support his scheme for reviving a school at Farnham,[12] induced him to comply.[13] Lord Howard was acting

in the affair for the queen on behalf of Richard Drake Her Majesty's equerry. In February 1582–3 the Crown bought up the lease[14] and granted the manor to Lord Howard, who evidently transferred the property to Richard Drake, for he died in possession in 1603.[15] His son Francis Drake held it in 1629, and died in 1634.[16] He had apparently sold the manor during his lifetime, for in 1635 Sir William Russell, bart., and his wife Dorothy conveyed it to George Price.[17] In 1659 George Price and Margaret his wife quitclaimed the manor to Walter Plomer and his sister Elizabeth,[18] who held a manorial court here in 1662,[19] and in 1663, in conjunction with John, son and heir of George Price, they conveyed it to Nicholas Colborne, citizen and vintner of London, in consideration of the sum of £9,104 14s. 6d. paid to Sir Walter and his sister, and a competent sum to John Price.[20] Colborne mortgaged the estate, which in 1677 was purchased by Philip Doughty.[21] He in 1679 sold Northwood, which, though in the parish of Cobham, was demesne land of the manor of Esher ; and it seems probable that he sold the manor also to Sir T. Lynch, who held it in 1680,[22] and whose daughter Philadelphia married Thomas Cotton. They held the manor jointly,[23] and sold it to John Latton,[24] from whom it was purchased in 1716–17 by Thomas Pelham, Duke of Newcastle.[25] After the duke's death in 1768 this manor, together with Esher Wateville and the mansion and estate of Claremont, was purchased by Lord Clive, who held the whole property till his death in 1774. It was then sold to Viscount Galway, from whom it was bought in 1807 by Charles Rose Ellis.[26] He in 1816 agreed to sell the entire property to the Commissioners of His Majesty's Woods and Forests for £66,000 for the use of Princess Charlotte, and the purchase was ratified by an Act of Parliament.[26a] Subsequently it reverted to the Crown, and the Duchess of Albany is now lady of the manor. Shortly after the time that the manor of Esher was sold to the Duke of Newcastle, the park and manor-house, which had been separated from the manor, were sold by John Latton to Peter Delaporte,[27] one of the directors of the South Sea Company. When in 1721 the South Sea crisis occurred, the estates of the principal directors were seized under the authority of an Act of Parliament, and sold for the benefit of those holders of South Sea stock who had lost their money. This estate was purchased by Dennis Bond in 1724,[28] and resold by him in 1729 to the Right Honourable Henry Pelham, the well-known statesman.[29] By a will dated 17 September 1748 Mr. Pelham devised the estate to Frances, his eldest surviving daughter, for her life.[30] She died unmarried in 1804, and this property passed to her

---

[3] *V.C.H. Surr.* i, 114.
[4] Pleas of the Crown, 7 Edw. I.
[5] He suppressed the chantry.
[6] Chart. R. 24 Hen. III, m. 2.
[7] *Cal. Pat.* 1313–17, p. 676.
[8] Close, 30 Hen. VIII, pt. i, m. 27 d. ; B.M. Arun. MS. 97, fol. 48*b*.
[9] Pat. 4 Edw. VI, pt. vii, m. 39.
[10] *Act of the P. C.* (new ser.) iii, 218.
[11] Pat. 1 Mary, pt. ix, m. 18.
[12] See *V.C.H. Surr.* ii, 188.
[13] Loseley MSS. ix, 26, 27, 28.
[14] Pat. 25 Eliz. pt. xiv, m. 25.
[15] *Surr. Arch. Coll.* viii, 203 ; monument in Esher Church.

[16] *Hist. MSS. Com. Rep.* iv, App. 22a.
[17] Feet of F. Surr. Trin. 11 Chas. I.
[18] Ibid. Hil. 1659.
[19] Brayley, *Hist. of Surr.* ii, 430.
[20] Recov. R. Trin. 15 Chas. II, rot. 32, (John Price is the vouchee) ; Close, 15 Chas. II, 20 Mar. 1663.
[21] Feet of F. Surr. East. 29 Chas. II.
[22] From the Ct. R. communicated to Manning and Bray, *Hist. of Surr.* ii, 747.
[23] Recov. R. East. 2 Anne, rot. 129.
[24] Feet of F. Surr. Trin. 6 Geo. I. John Latton died 1727 and was buried at Esher.
[25] He was residing at Claremont, and

bought the Esher manors under an Act of Parl. 3 Geo. I, cap. 10.
[26] Manning and Bray, *Hist. of Surr.* ii, 743.
[26a] 56 Geo. III, cap. 115.
[27] Feet of F. Surr. Trin. 6 Geo. I.
[28] In the deed of transfer it was described as consisting of ' a capital messuage, and lands, a wood, Esher farm, and the warren, late in the occupation of John Latton, esq. with the royalty of the River Mole within the extent of the premises, and some small rents issuing out of houses in Esher.' Brayley, *Hist. of Surr.* ii, 435.
[29] *Surr. Arch. Coll.* vii, 214.
[30] Brayley, *Hist. of Surr.* ii, 436.

nephew, Lewis Thomas, Lord Sondes,[31] who in 1805 sold the estate in parcels. The house and park at Esher were purchased by John Spicer,[32] whose son, J. W. Spicer, succeeded him in 1831.[33] The present owner is Sir Edgar Vincent, K.C.M.G.

There was a manor-house at Esher in early times, which was enlarged by John, Bishop of Winchester, in 1331.[34] Bishop Waynflete[35] built a stately brick mansion on the banks of the River Mole in Esher Park, the gate-house of which still remains and bears his name.[36] This house perhaps did not satisfy the gorgeous ideas of Cardinal Wolsey, to whom it was lent by Bishop Fox in 1519. The latter wrote on this occasion, ' Would God that the poor lodging of Esher did content your Grace as it reJoiceth me that it can please you to use it.' [37] When Wolsey in 1528 succeeded Fox as bishop he gave directions for the repair and partial rebuilding of this house ; and after his disgrace took up his residence there for some time.[38] In a survey of the manor taken in the reign of Edward VI it is stated that besides the 'sumptuously built' mansion-house there were an orchard and garden, with a park adjoining, 3 miles in circuit.[39] When restored to the see of Winchester by Queen Mary the manor comprised, besides the park, the rabbit-warren, about 185 acres of land, and the land called Northwood in Cobham.[40]

Henry Pelham, the statesman, employed Kent to rebuild wings to the gate-house.[41] The main part of the standing gate-house is of Waynflete's time. The porch is undoubtedly Kent's, and he probably altered the windows. How much of the original house was standing when he built in 1729 is unknown, but the view in Salmon seems to show the great hall on the side of a quadrangle opposite to the gate-house.

Mr. John Spicer pulled down Pelham's additions, leaving the original gate-house, and rebuilt on a new and higher site. The present house, of Palladian style, with Ionic porticoes, commands fine views, and the grounds are well planted and very picturesque.

ESHER WATEVILLE.—In 675 Frithwald, *subregulus* of Surrey, and Bishop Erkenwald are said to have granted to Chertsey Abbey 5 *mansas* at Esher.[41a] This grant was confirmed by King Edward in 1062,[42] "and during his reign an Englishman gave to the abbey 2 hides of land in Esher belonging to the manor of Esher.[43] At the time of the Domesday Survey the monks had 5½ hides of land in Esher, rated at only 5 virgates, which were held of them by William de Wateville.[44] The land apparently continued in the possession of the Wateville family till the reign of Henry III, when Robert de Wateville held under the Abbot of

Chertsey a fourth part of a knight's fee in Esher ; [45] and this constituted the manor of Esher Wateville. The manor descended to Matilda daughter of Robert de Wateville, probably son of the Robert mentioned above. She had three husbands, Reginald de Imworth,[46] Richard Russell,[47] and Nicholas de Wynton.[48] John de Imworth, son of Reginald and Matilda, conveyed the reversion of the manor to Margery and Joan, co-heiresses of Nicholas de Wynton and Matilda.[49] Margery married William de Milbourn, in whose family the manor remained.[50]

In August 1344 it was held by John de Milbourne,[51] and in 1360 it was settled on him and his wife Isabel, with remainder to William their son, and the heirs of his body, and in default to the right heirs of John.[52] John, then known as John Milbourne senior, was still living in 1383.[53] In 1533 the manor was in the hands of Cecilia Sympson, widow, daughter and heir of Sir Thomas Milbourne.[54] As late as 1539 Margaret York, widow, had a life interest in part of the manor ; [55] two years later Cecilia Sympson enfeoffed trustees of the manor to the use of herself for life, then to Margaret Hardwen for life, with remainder to the heirs of her cousin William Fawkner.[56] In 1567 William Fawkner was holding the manor,[57] and in 1572 he conveyed it to Thomas Brockholes.[58] The latter in the following year conveyed the manor with view of frankpledge to Richard Hatton.[59] In 1614 Richard Hatton and Robert Hatton levied a fine and made a settlement in jointure of this manor on Alice, wife of Robert Hatton.[60] Robert and Alice were holding in 1628,[61] but shortly after this the corporation of Kingston purchased the manor from Robert Hatton with the manor-house and about 45 acres of land, to be settled for charitable uses.[62] In 1716–17 the Duke of Newcastle, owner of Claremont, procured an Act of Parliament for vesting in himself this estate, subject to the payment of a perpetual fee-farm rent to Kingston of £95.[63] It was afterwards transferred with Esher Episcopi to other proprietors,[64] and so ultimately came into the hands of Leopold King of the Belgians,[65] and subsequently reverted to the Crown. The Duchess of Albany is now lady of the manor.

The house now known as Milbourne was presented by Princess Charlotte to Major-General Sir Robert William Gardiner, K.C.B.[66] It is now the seat of Mr. William Hartmann, J.P.

The manor of *SANDON* or *SANDOWN*, also called *SANDON CHAPEL* and occasionally *BURWOOD*, is said to have been the original endowment of the hospital of Sandon, in this parish, given by Robert de Wateville in the time of Henry II.[67] The

[31] Recov. R. Hil. 45 Geo. III.
[32] Surr. Arch. Coll. vii, 214.
[33] Brayley, Hist. of Surr. ii, 437.
[34] Cal. Pat. 1330–4, p. 99.
[35] Bishop from 1447 to 1486.
[36] Surr. Arch. Coll. vii, 203.
[37] L. and P. Hen. VIII, iii (1), 414.
[38] Ibid. iv (3), 6076, 6555 ; Stow, Chron. 921, 922.
[39] Brayley, Hist. of Surr. ii, 429.
[40] Pat. 1 Mary, pt. ix, m. 18.
[41] Walpole, Anecdotes of Painting, iii, 490. A plan by J. Rocque, 1739, was engraved, and there is a view in Salmon's Antiq. of Surr. 1736.
[41a] Birch, Cart. Sax. i, no. 39.
[42] Kemble, Cod. Dipl. iv, no. 812.
[43] V.C.H. Surr. i, 307b.

[44] Ibid. 307, 308.
[45] Testa de Nevill (Rec. Com.), 220b ; Cal. Close, 1227–31, p. 242.
[46] See Add. Chart. 5534.
[47] See Feet of F. Surr. 12 Edw. I, no. 13.
[48] Ibid. 18 Edw. I, no. 25.
[49] Deeds quoted by Manning and Bray, op. cit. ii, 744.
[50] Ibid. ; Year Book 17 & 18 Edw. III (Rolls Ser.), 414, 415.
[51] Cal. of Pat. 1343–5, p. 407.
[52] Manning and Bray, Hist. Surr. ii, 744.
[53] Feet of F. Surr. Trin. 7 Ric. II, no. 16.
[54] Ibid. Mich. 25 Hen. VIII.
[55] Recov. R. Mich. 30 Hen. VIII, rot. 435 ; East. 31 Hen. VIII, rot. 334.

[56] Manning and Bray, Hist. Surr. ii, 744.
[57] Feet of F. Div. Co. Hil. 9 Eliz.
[58] Recov. R. Mich. 14 & 15 Eliz. rot. 159 ; Feet of F. Mich. 14 & 15 Eliz.
[59] Ibid. Mich. 15 & 16 Eliz.
[60] Ibid. Mich. 11 Jas. I.
[61] Ibid. East. 4 Chas. I.
[62] Brayley, Hist. Surr. ii, 431.
[63] Manning and Bray, Hist. Surr. ii, 744, 745 ; Stat. 3 Geo. I, cap. 10.
[64] Feet of F. Surr. Mich. 59 Geo. III.
[65] See above under manor of Esher.
[66] Brayley, Hist. Surr. ii, 450.
[67] Manning and Bray, Hist. Surr. ii, 749 ; cf. V.C.H. Surr. ii, 118, 119.

hospital certainly existed in the reign of Henry III; but in the licence for its suppression in 1436 the foundation is attributed to an unknown Bishop of Winchester.[68] It is quite possible that the land had been part of the Wateville manor of Esher. It extended into Walton on Thames, Thames Ditton, and West Molesey.

In 1436 the hospital became so impoverished that it could no longer support itself, and was therefore united, with all its possessions, to the hospital of St. Thomas the Martyr, Southwark.[69] The rolls of the courts held by the master of St. Thomas's at Sandon in 1467–8 are extant.[70] In 1538 the master and brethren of the hospital conveyed the manor of Sandon and parsonage of Esher to the king in exchange for other parsonages, lately monastic property.[71] The manor remained in the hands of the Crown, and was leased by Queen Elizabeth to Elizabeth Nolte in 1577, under the name of the manor of Sandon Chapel.[72] In 1603 James I granted the manor to John Earl of Mar,[73] but five years later the king resumed it, granting the earl other lands in exchange.[74] Charles I in 1630 granted Sandon Manor to Dudley Carleton, Viscount Dorchester,[75] who died in 1632.[76] From him it descended to his nephew Sir Dudley Carleton, who with his wife Lucy and his elder brother Sir John Carleton, the heir-at-law of the viscount, conveyed the manor to William and Gerard Gore as the manor of Sandon and the manor of Sandon Chapel.[77] Courts were held by William and Gerard Gore till 1640, and by William Gore only till 1659. In 1665 and 1675 John Gore appears as lord, in 1768–9 courts were held by John and Gerard Gore, in 1684 and 1692 by John Gore only.[78] In 1694 Sir William Gore, Benjamin Dolphin and Tabitha his wife, daughter and heiress of Gerard Gore, conveyed to John Gore,[79] whose wife Joanna sold it in 1715 to Charles Earl of Halifax,[80] who had become Lord Lieutenant of Surrey in the previous December, but died in May 1715, about the time of the completion of the sale. He was succeeded by his nephew George, second Earl of Halifax, who entered into a contract for the sale of Sandon to George Tournay, then a resident at Esher. Tournay died before the purchase was completed, and after some litigation the estate was conveyed in 1740 to Marsh Dickenson and Henry Laremore in trust for the co-heirs of Tournay. A partition of the property was made, the manor falling to the share of Nathaniel Bateman, and the old buildings and Sandon Chapel to Mrs. Catherine Jenkin. In 1741 the manor was bought by Arthur Onslow, Speaker of the House of Commons, who died in 1768. In 1780 his son and heir George, Lord Onslow and Cranley, sold it to Sir John Frederick, bart., of Burwood Park, from whom it passed to his second son and successor, Sir Richard Frederick, who died without issue in 1873.[81]

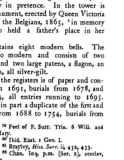

FREDERICK, baronet.
Or a chief azure with three doves argent therein.

Sandown House, the seat of Mr. J. P. Currie-Blyth, J.P., belonged in 1870 to Mr. Spicer of Esher Place. The Sandown Park Racecourse Company, which held its first meeting in 1875, has acquired some of the land.

The property is described as consisting, at the time of Lord Dorchester's death, of ' the manor of Sandon, and houses, chambers, &c., in the manor, belonging at the time of the Dissolution to the hospital of St. Thomas of Southwark, called 'le Master's lodgings,' to wit, a parlour and a chamber built above it, a small kitchen, and a garden, and the two chambers above the said chapel.'[82]

CHURCHES

CHRIST CHURCH is a completely modern structure, built in 1853–4, and consists of a chancel with north vestry and organ chamber and a south chapel or pew belonging to Esher Place; a large nave with north and south aisles and porches, and a west tower surmounted by a broach spire. The whole church is in 13th-century style, and contains no old work of any sort except one monument brought from the old church. This is on the wall of the south aisle and is to Richard Drake, who died in 1603, who was ' one of the Queries (i.e. Equerries) of Our late Soverane Elizabets Stable.' He married Ursula Stafford, and had one son, Francis. Above are three shields. In the centre a shield of seven quarters, arranged four and three; (1) Argent a dragon gules for Drake; (2) Argent on a chief gules three molets argent; (3) Gules on a fesse argent two molets gules; (4) Ermine on a fesse indented azure three crosslets argent; (5) Ermine three bars azure; (6) Azure six lions rampant or, three, two, and one; (7) Argent a cheveron azure. On the dexter side is a shield of six quarters; (1) and (6) Or a cheveron gules with a canton ermine; (2) Party festewise gules and azure a lion rampant or; (3) Azure, two bars or with three molets gules on each; (4) Azure a cross argent; (5) Or ermined sable a fesse azure. On the sinister is the first shield given above impaling the second. The crest over the first shield is a clenched hand. The monument itself is in the form of a small Corinthian order inclosing an arched recess in which is the kneeling effigy of a man in complete armour with ruffs at the neck and wrists. In the north aisle is a wall monument to Leopold Duke of Albany, died 1884, with his arms of England with the difference of a label of three points argent having three hearts gules thereon, and the arms of Saxony in pretence. In the tower is another modern monument, erected by Queen Victoria to Leopold King of the Belgians, 1865, 'in memory of the uncle who held a father's place in her affections.'

The tower contains eight modern bells. The church plate is also modern and consists of two chalices, two small and two large patens, a flagon, an almsdish and a spoon, all silver-gilt.

The first book of the registers is of paper and contains marriages from 1691, burials from 1678, and baptisms from 1684, all entries running to 1695. The second book is in part a duplicate of the first and contains marriages from 1688 to 1754, burials from

[68] Pat. 14 Hen. VI, pt. i, m. 4. [69] Ibid.
[70] Ct. R. Surrey, portf. 205, no. 4.
[71] Close, 30 Hen. VIII, pt. ii, no. 9.
[72] Pat. 20 Eliz. pt. i.
[73] Pat. 1 Jas. I, pt. xiii, m. 10.
[74] S.P. Dom. Jas. I, xxxiv, 31.

[75] Pat. 5 Chas. I, pt. v, m. 14.
[76] Chan. Inq. p.m. (Ser. 2), ccclxv, 89.
[77] Feet of F. Surr. East. 12 Chas. I; Close, 11 Chas. I, pt. xxi, no. 1.
[78] Ct. R. quoted by Manning and Bray, op. cit. ii, 749.

[79] Feet of F. Surr. Trin. 6 Will. and Mary.
[80] Ibid. East. 1 Geo. I.
[81] Brayley, Hist. Surr. ii, 432, 433.
[82] Chan. Inq. p.m. (Ser. 2), ccclxv, 89.

ESHER PLACE: EAST VIEW IN 1737

(From S. and N. Buck's drawing)

ESHER OLD CHURCH LOOKING EAST

1678 to 1812, and baptisms from 1682 to 1812, and there is a printed marriages and burials book from 1754 to 1812.

The church of *ST. GEORGE*, known locally as Sandy (i.e. Sandon) Chapel, consists of a chancel, nave, north aisle, projecting bay on the south with private pews above a vault, a south vestry, and a shingled bell-turret on the west gable.

The chancel and western part of the nave are built of stone ; the rest is in red brick. There is now no evidence of any work earlier than the 16th century, and the interior was till 1909 an interesting example of 18th-century fittings and arrangement.

The windows all have wooden frames, there being three in the chancel and north aisle ; in the south wall of the nave is a pointed window with stone jambs and above the west door is a square light.

Galleries extend round three sides of the church, and at the west end is a second at a higher level. A framed painting of our Lord hangs above the altar against a panelled reredos. There is no chancel arch or division between nave and chancel, and the north aisle is separated from the nave by wooden pillars carrying a beam. The opening to the bay on the south is filled by Corinthian columns and pilasters carrying a pediment cornice ; there are several pews in the bay, two of which have small fireplaces, and steps leading to an external door. There is a small marble font. The church was fitted throughout with box pews, but in 1909 the decay of the floor necessitated their removal, when the floor was relaid. The roof has collars and wind braces, but is partly plastered, and over the nave is pierced with a large skylight.

On a beam at the west end of the chancel are the arms of George II.

There are some late 17th-century and many 18th-century monuments to families of the neighbourhood, as well as several funeral hatchments.

The single bell which now remains is by John Warner & Son, 1799.

There is now no plate belonging to the church.

ADVOWSON The church of Esher is not mentioned in Domesday. There was a church there at the end of the 13th century, when the advowson belonged to the Bishop of Winchester,[82] and it seems probable that the advowson was purchased with the manor of Esher from the monks of Croix St. Leufroy by Peter, Bishop of Winchester.[84] It was included in the grant of the manor made by the Abbot of Netley to William, Bishop of Winchester, in 1245.[85] In 1284 the king quitclaimed to the bishop all right to the advowson of Esher.[86] Soon after this the advowson seems to have become separated from the manor and to have been in the hands of the hospital, for in 1535 the rectory of Esher formed part of the possession of the hospital of St. Thomas the Martyr, Southwark.[87] In 1538 the master and brethren conveyed it to the king in exchange for other parsonages, lately monastic property.[88] In 1620 it was granted by James I to Sir Henry Spiller, kt., and others.[89] George Price held the advowson with the manor in 1635,[90] and it descended with the manor till 1714,[91] when John Latton vested it in trustees for the benefit of Wadham College, Oxford, to the founder of which he was related,[92] and restored the impropriate tithes of the rectory. Under Latton's gift the patronage was vested in 1726 in Thomas Trevor,[93] and in 1744 in Henry Pye.[94] These trustees were bound to appoint a kinsman of the founder of Wadham College before any other person, if there were any such of that college and in Holy Orders at the time of the decease of the incumbent of Esher. The college is now patron.

Smith's Charity is distributed as in *CHARITIES* other Surrey parishes. Lady Lynch, widow of Sir Thomas Lynch, governor of Jamaica, who died in 1682,[95] gave £100, one third to the clergyman for a sermon annually, 5s. to the clerk, the rest to the poor people ; also 3½ acres of land for the repair of the church.[96]

In 1789 Mr. Nathaniel George Petree left £850 to the rector and churchwardens for the support of the Sunday school, also a library of religious books for the parish and £100, the interest to go to the schoolmaster for acting as librarian and to the poor in bread.

National Schools were fitted up by subscriptions in the disused workhouse in 1837 ; but in 1779 John Winkin left £6 yearly to educate three children, so presumably a school existed then. A new school (National) was built in 1858 and enlarged in 1891. West End Infants School (National) was built in 1879 by Mrs. Bailey of Stoney Hills in memory of her husband.

EAST AND WEST MOLESEY

Molesham (xi cent.) ; Mulesey (xiii cent.), Moleseye (xiv cent.).

The two Moleseys, East and West, are two small parishes, which consisted in 1086 of three manors, all called Molesham. Parochially they first appear as two chapelries, which later became parishes, and now form one urban district under the Act of 1894. West Molesey, 3¼ miles west of Kingston, is bounded on the north by the Thames, on the east and south by East Molesey, on the west and south by Walton-on-Thames, of which it was a chapelry. Its extreme measurements are a mile each way, and it contains 656 acres of land and 81 of water. The parish was agricultural till the recent building of suburban or country houses in the Thames Valley. The soil is the gravel and alluvium of the Thames and Mole valleys ; the latter partly bounds the parish. Dunstable Common is open ground south of the village,

[82] *Cal. Pat.* 1272–81, p. 378 ; 1281–92, p. 5.
[84] See above, under manor of Esher.
[85] *Cal. Pat.* 1313–17, p. 676.
[86] Chart. R. 12 Edw. I. m. 5.
[87] *Valor Eccl.* (Rec. Com.), ii, 60.
[88] Close, 30 Hen. VIII, pt. ii, no. 9.
[89] Pat. 18 Jas. I, pt. xxi, no. 5.

[90] Feet of F. Surr. Trin. 11 Chas. I. In the following year the rectory was leased to Michael Hudson for 31 years. Pat. 11 Chas. I, pt. i.
[91] For references see above, under manor of Esher, and Inst. Bks. P.R.O. 1689 and 1701.

[92] Manning and Bray, *Hist. of Surr.* ii, 752.
[93] Inst. Bks. P.R.O. 1726. Afterwards second Baron Trevor.
[94] Ibid. 1744.
[95] Monument in church.
[96] Willis's Visitation, 1724.

and Molesey Hurst is to the north of it on the banks of the Thames. This was a famous place for cricket-matches, prize-fights, and occasionally for duels. Hampton races used to be held upon it, Hampton being just across the Thames, over which is a ferry. The Hurst Park Racing Club was established on the ground in 1892. The Lambeth Waterworks have reservoirs partly in West Molesey.

There was an Inclosure Act in 1815 for East and West Molesey, though the award was not till 1 June 1821.[1] This inclosed commons and common fields.

In 1800, when Walton Commons were inclosed, the £6 13s. 4d. set apart from the Walton tithes for a curate of West Molesey was secured upon part of the inclosed land. The income has been raised to £150 by voluntary gifts.

East Molesey is a large scattered village 2 miles west of Kingston. It is bounded on the north-east by the Thames, on the east by Thames Ditton, on the south by Esher, on the west by Walton and West Molesey. It contains 743 acres of land and 38 of water. The Mole, which flows through the parish, divides to the south of the parish, the western branch forming part of the boundary between West and East Molesey, the eastern branch between East Molesey and Thames Ditton. They re-unite and fall into the Thames within the parish. Dun-stable Common and Molesey Hurst are partly in East and partly in West Molesey. The branch line from Surbiton to Hampton Court passes through part of the parish and terminates in it at Hampton Court station on the southern bank of the Thames. The soil is the gravel and alluvium of the river valleys.

Molesey was formerly a chapelry of Kingston parish, but was erected into a separate perpetual curacy by the Act 9 Geo. III, cap. 65. Previous to this date, however, it possessed parish officers of its own.

In 1856 Kent Town in East Molesey was made an ecclesiastical parish. A church (St. Paul's) was con-secrated that year, but was finally rebuilt in 1888. It is of 15th-century style, of stone, with a tower and spire. The Wesleyan Chapel was built in 1876 and the Baptist Chapel in 1885. The drinking fountain in Bridge Street was set up to commemorate the Jubilee of 1887. Hampton Court Bridge was built by James Clarke, who had a lease of the manor of Molesey Prior in 1750.[1a] It was of wood and soon fell into disrepair. It was rebuilt of wood in 1778, and remained till 1865, when it was replaced by an iron bridge.

The limit of the tide in the unlocked Thames was near Molesey. Drayton refers to it in the Polyolbion,[2] and Selden's note on the passage is 'Mole's fall into the Thames is near the utmost of the flood.' As usual, near the head of the tide, there was a ford. When there was a question of the route by which Monmouth was to be brought as a prisoner from Guildford to London, Lord Lumley wrote, 'I think the best way will be by way of Hampton, where there is a good ford (opposite Molesey), and I think is a much

better way than by Cobham and Kingston.'[3] How-ever, the ford was not used then.[4] But its existence, as well as fords at Coway Stakes and Halliford, all near the flood limits, make the identification of Cæsar's crossing-place impossible.

The Cottage Hospital was built by the Dowager Lady Barrow in 1890. There is a Roman Catholic convent in the parish, established in 1907.

At the time of the Domesday Survey **MANORS** there were two manors of 'Molesham' held of Richard de Tonbridge by John[5] and by Roger D'Abernon respectively. They were both probably parts of what was afterwards Mole-sey Prior. Aluric and Toco had been the respective holders under King Edward.[6] Unless the two were amalgamated under Richard in the hands of the D'Abernons or under-tenants, the former disappears altogether.

Between 1129 and 1135 Engelram D'Abernon granted to Merton Priory this manor, thenceforth frequently called MOLESEY PRIOR.[7] Much confusion has arisen from the fact that both this manor and the manor of Molesey Matham are spoken of as 'the manor of East Moulsey.'[7] Both seem to have in-cluded lands in both Moleseys and in Walton on Thames.

Early in the reign of Edward I the prior claimed rights of infangtheof, outfangtheof, &c., in Mole-sey. His claim was allowed.[8] In 1284 he com-plained that another of his rights there—pleas of theft —had been infringed. Amice of Ewell had been captured with stolen goods within his liberties at Molesey by two of his servants, and had been sub-sequently rescued.[9] The priory is stated in the Taxatio of Pope Nicholas to have held property at Molesey which was taxed at £3 6s.[10] At the time of the Valor of 1535 the possessions of Merton Priory in Molesey were valued at £25 12s. 2d., being rents of assize and other rents, farm of the mill, &c.[11]

In 1518 the prior and convent demised to Sir Thomas Heneage, kt., the manor of 'East Mole-sey, with all their land and all their tithes in the precinct of East Molesey and Thames Ditton, and their live stock there; for which he was to pay a rent, partly in money and partly in kind, amounting in all to £26 2s. 2d.' The lease was for a term of sixty-six years.[12]

Henry VIII, when engaged in making the Chase of Hampton, desired to obtain possession of the manor and estate of East Molesey, and gave in exchange for it to the priory of Merton certain lands, tenements, advowsons, &c., formerly belonging to the suppressed monastery of Calwich, co. Stafford.[13] Whereupon 'John, Prior of Merton, and the convent by inden-ture dated 1536 conveyed to the king all their tithes,

1 Blue Bk. Incl. Awards.
1a By Act 27 Geo. III, cap. 37.
2 Polyolbion, xvii, 71.
3 Lord Lumley to the Sec. of State, quoted by Fea, King Monmouth, 314.
4 Lond. Gaz. 16 July 1685.
5 This John is possibly John who held Woldingham and Walton on the Hill of

Richard, probably ancestor of the family of Dammartin; see V.C.H. Surr. i, 315, 316. The statement by Willis that Woldingham once belonged to Merton may originate in John's manor at Mole-sey having been granted to Merton with the D'Abernon land.
6 V.C.H. Surr. i, 318b.

7 Ibid.
8 Plac. de Quo Warr. (Rec. Com.), 748.
9 Cal. Pat. 1281–92, p. 199.
10 Pope Nick. Tax. (Rec. Com.), 206.
11 Valor Eccl. (Rec. Com.), ii, 48.
12 Brayley, Hist. of Surr., ii, 300.
13 L. and P. Hen. VIII, xi, 1411.

oblations, and profits in East Molesey, parcel of the parsonage of Kingston, and all their lands, &c., in East Molesey or elsewhere reputed parcel of the said manor.'[14]

Sir Thomas Heneage was Gentleman Usher to Wolsey and counsel to the Prior of Merton, and resided at East Molesey[15] in a stately house which he had himself built. The estate which he held on lease from Merton Priory becoming the property of the Crown, as shown above, he appears to have resigned his lease, and to have obtained from the king a new grant of Molesey Prior, with tithes in East Molesey of the annual value of £10, with court-leet and view of frankpledge. He died without issue in 1553; the renewed lease expired in 1584, but in 1571 Anthony Crane obtained from the queen a lease in reversion of the manor, which included a mansion-house, with 2 acres and 2 roods of land annexed, and 125 acres and 2 roods of other land, at the same rent at which it was held by Sir Thomas Heneage.[16] In 1594 the manor was granted to Richard Cox,[17] and in 1629 to Sir Nicholas Fortescue, kt., to hold for thirty-one years.[18]

After the Restoration Charles II, in January 1668-9, granted to James Clarke for a fine of £450 and a rent of £2 14s. 2d. 'the manor of East Molesey, parcel of the honour of Hampton Court, and formerly a possession of the late monastery of Merton ; except the advowsons of churches and chapels, and a mill and mines and quarries which were granted to Sir Nicholas Fortescue, kt., 19 October 1629, to hold for thirty-one years.'[19] This grant included the capital messuage called East Molesey Manor, the fishery of the River Mole from Cobham Bridge to the Thames, and Hampton Court ferry. In January 1675-6 James Clarke asked that the term for which he held the manor might be made up to ninety-nine years ;[20] and the grant was finally made out for the respective terms of seventy-eight, seventy-seven, and seventy-six years from Michaelmas 1697, 27 May 1698, and Lady Day 1699, at which times some intermediate leases that had been granted to other persons would terminate.[21]

In 1696 William III, in consideration of services done by Thomas, Duke of Leeds, granted the manor and fishing to Charles Bertie, brother-in-law to the duke, and others, to hold in trust for thirty-one years after the death of Catherine, queen dowager.[22] Brayley says :[23] 'Since the expiration of those terms (i. e. the terms of the grant to Clarke) in 1775, the lease of this manor has always been granted from the Crown to the proprietors of the manor of Molesey Matham, except in one instance when a grant in reversion was made to a stranger ; but before the estate came into his possession, his interest was purchased by the persons who held Molesey Matham.' The reversion is said by Manning and Bray[24] to

have been purchased by Mr. Sutton and Sir Beaumont Hotham,[25] afterwards second Baron Hotham. Captain Hotham, great-grandson of the latter, is now lord of the manor.

A second manor of *MOLESEY* is mentioned in Domesday as held by Odard the crossbowman. Tovi had held it of King Edward.[26] It appears that the descendants of Odard continued to hold the manor, and assumed a territorial designation. The name of Robert of Molesey occurs in 1164.[27] In 1176 Samson of Molesey was charged with 30 marks for an amercement in the forest.[28] In 1231 Samson of Molesey, whose name occurs in connexion with various lawsuits,[29] 'attornavit' Gilbert of Eye against Walter of the Wood[30] and Margaret his wife of customs &c. which Samson exacted (*exigit*) from them in East and West Molesey.[31]

Samson son of Samson held half Molesey by the service of supplying a crossbowman for the king's army.[32] His serjeanty descended to Walter of Molesey, probably his son.[33] This Walter had a daughter, by name Isabella, and in 1279 Roger Clifford held this land by the serjeanty of a crossbowman [*arcubalistarium*] as guardian to her.[34] It seems probable that Isabella married John de Matham, who in 1333 died seised of the manor of Molesey, held of the king in chief by finding one man for the army, and by paying by the hands of the men of Kingston 8s. and to them 3s. The manor included a capital messuage, a water-mill, three tenants holding three messuages and 24 acres of land, eighteen customars holding eighteen messuages and 5 virgates of land, &c.[35]

John de Matham left several sons, the eldest being Walter, who died a year after his father, and was succeeded by his brother Samson.[36] The latter in 1358 gave the manor to his son Hamelin in tail. The estate now comprised pastures at Walton and lands at Kingston, Esher, and Hersham (Hauerychisham).[37] In 1379 a licence was granted to Hamelin de Matham to settle the manor on his wife Cicely.[38] Hamelin died in 1382 seised of 1 acre of land in East Molesey[39] (possibly the manor was then in the hands of trustees), leaving two daughters co-heiresses of his property : Elizabeth wife of John Thorpe, and Margaret who married John Michell. Elizabeth died in 1421, and the whole manor became the property of her sister.[40] Margaret lived on for another thirty-four years, and died seised of the manor held of the king in chief by the service of one-twentieth part of a knight's fee.

The property was now divided into three parts. The first fell to the share of William Sydney, son and heir of Cecilia daughter of Margaret Michell ; the second to Margaret's second daughter, Elizabeth wife of John Wood ; and the last to her third daughter, Joan wife of William Druell.[41] In 1463

[14] *Stat. of the Realm* (Rec. Com.), iii, 623.
[15] Pat. 22 Hen. VIII, pt. ii, m. 22 ; L. and P. Hen. VIII, xiii (2), 1104.
[16] Pat. 13 Eliz. pt. i, m. 20.
[17] Pat. 36 Eliz. pt. xix, m. 1.
[18] Pat. 5 Chas. I, pt. vii, no. 2.
[19] Pat. 20 Chas. II, pt. vi, no. 14.
[20] *Hist. MSS. Com. Rep.* xiv, App. ix, 377.
[21] Brayley, *Hist. of Surr.* i, 301.
[22] Pat. 8 Will. III, pt. viii, no. 5.
[23] *Hist. of Surr.* i, 301.

[24] Manning and Bray, op. cit. i, 475, 475.[a]
[25] They were then holding the manor of Molesey Matham, see below.
[26] *V.C.H. Surr.* i, 327a.
[27] Pipe R. 11 Hen. II, m. 2 d.
[28] Manning and Bray, *Hist. of Surr.* ii, 782, from the Pipe R.
[29] *Cal. Pat.* 1216-25, p. 393 ; 1225-32, p. 297.
[30] Also called Walter atte Wode ; *Cal. Pat.* 1317-21, p. 98. He held land in Molesey.

[31] *Cal. Close*, 1227-31, p. 602.
[32] *Testa de Nevill* (Rec. Com.), 225, 417.
[33] Ibid. 228.
[34] B.M. Add. MS. 6167, fol. 309.
[35] Chan. Inq. p.m. 7 Edw. III (1st nos.), no. 27. [36] Ibid.
[37] Ibid. 32 Edw. III (2nd nos.), no. 92 ; *Abbrev. Rot. Orig.* (Rec. Com.), ii, 252 ; Feet of F. Surr. Mich. 32 Edw. III.
[38] *Cal. Pat.* 1377-81, p. 411.
[39] Inq. p.m. 5 Ric. II, no. 41.
[40] Ibid. 8 Hen. V, no. 23.
[41] Chan. Inq. p.m. 33 Hen. VI, no. 31.

John Wood, sen., and Elizabeth his wife settled their third of the manor on the heirs of Elizabeth.[43] In 1484 Sir John Wood, knighted in 1483,[43a] died seised of a third of the manor in right of his wife, but leaving no direct heirs. His sister-in-law, Joan widow of William Druell, therefore inherited this portion of the estate,[43] which she held together with her own share till her death in 1495. Upon this John Druell, son of her son William, without livery from the king, entered and intruded on the property as her 'cousin' and heir. He was not ejected, but only survived his grandmother by a few months, and was succeeded by his brother Richard Drueil, aged fourteen. This part of the manor is described as containing the site or house called 'le Manor Place,' 200 acres of land, 10 acres of meadow, 100 acres of pasture, a water mill, a free fishery in the Thames, 10s. rent due at Easter and Michaelmas yearly from divers free tenants, view of frankpledge, and court baron. It was valued at £4 clear yearly, and was held of the king in chief by one-fortieth of a knight's fee.[44] In 1511 Richard Druell and Grace his wife conveyed one-third of the manor, probably this same part subsequently known as the manor of MOLESEY MATHAM or EAST MOLESEY, to William Frost and others[45] in trust for Richard Fox, Bishop of Winchester, founder of Corpus Christi College, Oxford, who settled it on that foundation as part of its endowment by deed dated 17 December 1518.[46] Henry VIII, wishing to annex this manor to the Chase of Hampton Court, exchanged for it with the college the manor of West Henreth or Hendred, co. Berks., with certain church property in cos. Berks. and Oxford; and the college conveyed the estate to the king by indenture dated 4 March 1536. The transaction was ratified by an Act of Parliament.[47] From this date the manor remained vested in the Crown.

James I in 1624 granted to William Holt and others for thirty-one years a wood called Hurst Coppice, parcel of the manor of Molesey Matham;[48] and by letters patent dated a few months later granted the manor of Molesey Matham with a water-mill to John Littcott for a similar period.[49] In 1633 Sir John Littcott purchased[50] for £862 14s. 8d. the fee-simple of the manor of Ralph Freeman, alderman of London. To him, or rather to Basil Nicoll and others in trust for him, it had been granted in the previous year by Charles I by the description of the manor of Molesey Matham, a water-mill there, Hurst Coppice, &c., valued at £34 12s. 10d. per annum, to be held as of the manor of East Greenwich in socage.[51] In 1641 Sir John conveyed the manor and lands to trustees, to the use of himself for life, and after his decease to be sold for the benefit of his wife and family.[52] In April 1646 the trustees, the widow, and the eldest son of Sir John joined in a sale of the estate, with the rectory of East Molesey, for £4,000 to Henry Pickering of London;[53] who on 30 March following sold it for £4,050 to James Clarke.[54]

Mary[54] daughter and sole heiress of James Clarke conveyed the estate by marriage to Sir James Clarke, kt., of a different family from her own, by whom she had a son, James Clarke, who died in 1758. He married Ann, only daughter of Christopher Clarke, and Lydia Henrietta, their only daughter and heiress, became the wife of the Reverend Sir George Molesworth. In 1765 'the manor of Molesey Matham or East Molesey' with the rectory of East Molesey appears to have been held by Joseph Clarke and Frances his wife.[55] In 1816 Beaumont Lord Hotham held a moiety of the manor.[57] The other moiety belonged in 1809 to Sir Thomas Sutton, bart., by whose father it had been purchased.[58] Lucy co-heiress of Sir Thomas Sutton married General Sir G. H. F. Berkeley. Captain Hotham and the Earl of Berkeley are now lords of the manor.

The other third of the manor (after the division of 1455) was held by William Sydney at his death in 1462.[59] It was inherited by his two daughters, Elizabeth and Anne, between whom his share was divided.[60] Elizabeth, who was only six at the time of her father's death, subsequently married John

[43] Feet of F. Surr. Hil. 3 Edw. IV, no. 54.

[43a] He is evidently the John Wood, the Speaker of The House of Commons, knighted after Parliament was ended, 18 Feb. 1482–3; Shaw, *Knights of England*, ii, 21.

[43] Chan.Inq. p.m. Surr. 2 Ric. III, no.19.

[44] Ibid. (Ser. 2), xi, 51.

[45] Feet of F. Surr. Hil. 2 Hen. VIII; William Frost appears as agent in other transactions for the Bishop of Winchester.

[46] Brayley, *Hist. of Surr.* ii, 310; see *Valor Eccl.* (Rec. Com.), ii, 247.

[47] *Stat. of the Realm* (Rec. Com.), iii, 622.

[48] Pat. 22 Jas. I, pt. xii.

[49] Ibid. pt. xiv, no. 6. Brayley says

(op. cit. ii, 310) that Littcott obtained his lease of the manor as heir of Dorothy, wife of Sir Christopher Edmonds, to whom Queen Elizabeth granted the manor in 1585 on lease.

[50] Close, 8 Chas. I, pt. xxxv, no. 5.

[51] Pat. 7 Chas. I, pt. i, no. 6. There is in East Molesey Church a monument to Sir John Littcott, ob. 1641, on which he is called lord of the manor of Molesey.

[52] See Chan. Inq. p.m. 17 Chas. I, dxxii, 15.

[53] Feet of F. Surr. East. 22 Chas. II.

[54] Close, 23 Chas. I, pt. xix, no. 38; see Recov. R. Trin. 22 Will. III, rot. 105.

[54] The genealogy of the Clarkes, from

the monuments at East Molesey, is given at the bottom of this page.

[56] Recov. R. Hil. 5 Geo. III, rot. 253.

[57] Ibid. Hil. 56 Geo. III, rot. 293.

[58] Manning and Bray, *Hist. of Surr.* ii, 783.

[59] Escheat. Inq. (Ser. 1), file 1805. It was probably so called because most of the lands lay in West Molesey.

[60] There was an *inspeximus* of the inquisition in 1477 owing to a lawsuit. Elizabeth and Anne, returned as six and five, or more, in 1463, are there returned as nineteen and eighteen. The holding is called *medietas*, but it was really a third, and the half sold by Elizabeth was a sixth (See Loseley for Sydneys).

Sir James Clarke = Anne daughter
d. 1703   of James Clarke,
   d. 1712
   (Feet of F. Surr.
   Trin. 11 Will. III)

James Clarke, d. 1709 (lessee of Molesey Prior)

Sir James Clarke, d. 1728 = Mary, d. 1754
(Lord of the Manors of   (Feet of F. Surr.
Molesey)   Mich. 12 Geo.III)

James Clarke = Anne daughter of
d. 1758   Christopher Clarke

Lydia Henrietta = Rev. Sir George Molesworth

Hampden, and in 1511 Elizabeth wife of John Hampden held one-sixth of the manor.[61] In that year she with her husband conveyed it to William Frost,[62] so that probably this sixth also formed part of the lands granted by the Bishop of Winchester to Corpus Christi College. The other sixth seems to have been afterwards acquired by Sir Richard Page, who was living at Molesey in 1532.[63]

In 1538 the king ordered Page to leave Molesey, and gave him in exchange the nunnery of St. Giles in the wood, Flamstead, Herts, from which he ejected John Tregonwell to make room for Page, much to the former's indignation.[64] The king gave Sir Richard lands in exchange for West Molesey,[65] which he annexed to the honour of Hampton Court.

Edward VI in 1553 granted the manor to Sir Richard Cotton, kt., by the name of *WEST MOLESEY*,[66] and from him it passed to William Hammond early in Queen Mary's reign.[67] In 1570 Queen Elizabeth granted to William Hammond licence to alienate the lordship and manor of West Molesey, with a capital messuage, &c.,[68] to Thomas Brend, sen., and Thomas his son and heir. In September 1598 Thomas Brend, junr. died seised of the manor and farm in West Molesey late belonging to William Hammond, held of the Crown.[69] He was succeeded by his son Nicholas, whose will bears date 10 October 1601.[70] At the time of the death of Nicholas, his only son Matthew was not much over a year old.[71] Subsequently several conveyances took place between Matthew and his son Thomas and various members of the Smith family,[72] by whom it seems to have been ultimately acquired, for in 1767 the manor was in the possession of Sir Robert Smith, bart.[73] Before 1816 it seems to have become amalgamated with Molesey Matham, for Beaumont, Lord Hotham, then held a moiety of ' the manor of Molesey Matham, or West Molesey.'

In 1212 the Prior of Merton brought an action against Samson of Molesey, who had a mill in East Molesey called Upmilne, for having diverted the course of the water of Molesey to the injury of the free tenant of the priory there.[74] The grant to Sir Thomas Heneage by Henry VIII included a mill in East Molesey called Stert Mill, and two ferries leading from East and West Molesey to Hampton Court.[75] In 1585 Anthony Crane, tenant of the manor, having died, his widow had a grant of Stert Mill and the two ferries for forty-one years.[76] One ferry was granted to Lady Dorothy Edmonds in 1606 for forty years, together with Stert Mill.[77] In 1611 Stert Mill was granted to Felin Wilson and others ;[78] and in 1612 Martin Freeman received a grant of a rent of £7 reserved for the same mill.[79] ' Molesey-mill' is mentioned in 1536.[80]

Grants of free fishery at East Molesey occur from time to time.[81]

At Molesey Park was formerly an extensive powder-mill situated on the River Mole, which runs through the grounds. The powder manufacture has long been discontinued.[82]

CHURCHES   The church of *ST. MARY EAST MOLESEY* consists of chancel, north vestry, nave, north and south aisles, and a porch at the west end of the north aisle with a tower above it.

The church has been entirely rebuilt during modern times, and is in late 13th-century style. The east window of the chancel is of three traceried lights, and there is a single lancet in the north wall and three in the south. The nave has an arcade of four bays on the north and five on the south, with circular columns and foliate capitals, and the aisles are gabled to the north and south, the eastern bay of each aisle being larger than the rest, and marked by a wider arch in the nave arcades.

The west window of the nave is of three lights, and below it is a plain west door set in a slight projection.

The tower is in two stages with two-light belfry windows and a slated broach spire with a wooden spire-light on each face. On the east wall of the nave is a brass tablet to Anthony Standen, 1611, third son of Edmond Standen, ' which Antonie was cupbearer to ye king of Scotland sometyme Ld : Darnley father to King James now of England.' The tablet was put up by Elizabeth his widow.

Above is a shield charged with a single molet, and on a chief indented a lion passant. In the walls of the porch a fragmentary tablet records Francis Eedes, 1667, Richard Eedes his son, 1660, and Francis son of Richard, 1690. A separate fragment has a shield : two bars vair impaling three molets between two bends.

There are three bells, the treble, formerly of 1608, recast by Mears & Stainbank in 1871 ; the second by Lester & Pack, 1760, and the tenor by Bryan Eldridge, 1623.

The plate consists of a cup, paten, and flagon of 1873, and a spoon of 1880, with two silver topped glass cruets.

The registers date from 1668 only, previous entries having been either lost or destroyed.

The church of *WEST MOLESEY*, whose dedication is unknown, consists of chancel with north vestry, nave with north aisle, west tower, and south porch. With the exception of the tower the whole building is of yellow brick, having been rebuilt in modern times. The tower is of 16th-century date and is built of flint and stone. The tower arch is of straight-lined four-centred form with moulded capitals to the inner order. The west window of the ground stage has restored tracery of three trefoiled lights, and below it is a blocked four-centred doorway under a square head, with continuous mouldings and leaves in the spandrels.

The tower is in three stages, each slightly set back, with a square stair-turret at the south-east. Above the west window is carved a pelican in her piety. On the north and south faces of the second stage are single-

61 Feet of F. Surr. East. 2 Hen. VIII.

62 Ibid. (*vide supra*).

63 *L. and P. Hen. VIII*, v–xiv, *passim*.

64 Ibid. xiii (2), 74.

65 Ibid. xiv (2), 113, (16).

66 Pat. 7 Edw. VI, pt. ii.

67 Pat. 1 & 2 Phil. and Mary, pt. vii, m. 24.

68 Pat. 12 Eliz. pt. ix. The church of West Molesey contains a monument to

Thos. Breade, d. 1598. He is described as ' of West Molsey.'

69 Chan. Inq. p.m. (Ser. 2), cclvii, 68.

70 *Surr. Arch. Coll.* x, 302.

71 Chan. Inq. p.m. (Ser. 2), cclxxi, 151.

72 Feet of F. Surr. East. 22 Jas. I ; Div. Co. Mich. 1655.

73 Recov. R. Trin. 7 Geo. III, rot. 227.

74 *Abbrev. Plac.* (Rec. Com.), 86, 91 ; *V.C.H. Surr.* ii, 98.

75 Pat. 22 Hen. VIII, pt. ii, m. 22.

76 Brayley, *Hist. of Surr.* ii, 301.

77 Pat. 4 Jas. I, pt. xxi.

78 Pat. 10 Jas. I, pt. V.

79 Ibid. pt. xxV.

80 *L. and P. Hen. VIII*, x, p. 788.

81 Pat. 22 Chas. II, pt. iv ; Feet of F. Surr. Mich. 12 Geo. I.

82 Brayley, *Hist. of Surr.* ii, 307.

light windows in deep external reveals, and the belfry windows are square-headed with two uncusped lights. There is a plain brick parapet.

The church contains little of interest beyond a small altar table with 17th-century carving, and carved legs, partly gilt in modern times, and a good 17th-century pulpit with a fine hexagonal canopy which has a panelled soffit. The font is of 15th-century date and has an octagonal bowl with quatrefoiled panels inclosing flowers, an octagonal panelled stem and a moulded base. On the chancel floor is a brass tablet to Thomas Brend of West Molesey, 1598, the father of eighteen children, four sons and six daughters by Margery his first wife, ob. 1564, and four sons and four daughters by Mercy his second wife, ob. 1597.

Above are two shields, the first bearing a cheveron between three dexter hands, and the second the same impaling a cheveron with three rings thereon between three standing hinds.

There is also a slab without any date to 'Francesca Thorowgood.'

The bells are two in number, the treble by T. Mears, 1832, and the tenor by William Carter, 1614.

The plate comprises a cup of 1800, a paten without date-letter, but c. 1680, a flagon of 1782, and a pretty two-handled porringer of about the same date, a secular piece of plate given in 1686 by Francis Brend.

The registers date from 1720.

The church stands at cross-roads on the straggling street which forms West Molesey. It is about half a mile south of the river, this ground being occupied on the west and north-west by the reservoirs of the Lambeth Water Works. On the south are flat open fields with hedgerows.

ADVOWSON   East Molesey was formerly a chapelry to Kingston. Gilbert Norman, Sheriff of Surrey, is stated by Dugdale, on the authority of Leland, to have added to the endowment of Merton Priory, about the year 1130, the church of Kingston with the chapelry of East Molesey.[88] The church, which is in the deanery of Ewell, is not mentioned in the *Taxatio* of 1291. In 1387 the Bishop of Winchester commissioned the Dean of Ewell to cite the Prior and convent of Merton and the vicar of Kingston to appear and answer for dilapidations in the chancel of East Molesey.[84] The rectory was granted in 1613 to Francis Morrice and others, with tithes of hay, &c.[85] In 1619 an annual rent of £10 3s. 4d. reserved from the rectory was granted to Laurence Whitaker.[86]

Early in 1769 the living was constituted a perpetual curacy, independent of Kingston, and East Molesey became a distinct parish. The patrons and impropriators are the Provost and Fellows of King's College, Cambridge, who in 1786 purchased the advowson from George Harding. This purchase was subject to the deduction of the next presentation, which had been previously purchased by Mrs. Legh of Kingston, and afterwards sold by her to William Attwick, who presented in 1797.[87] The living is valued at £157.

There was a church on the Domesday holding of Odard at Molesey, the orgin of West Molesey Church ;

but the church is not mentioned in the *Taxatio* of 1291, and was a chapel of ease to Walton on Thames, the impropriators of which, St. Mary's Chantry, York, paid £6 13s. 4d. to a curate.[88]

Queen Elizabeth in 1583 granted the chapel of West Molesey to Theophilus Adams and Robert Adams and the heirs of Theophilus.[89]

It subsequently passed with Walton on Thames, the impropriator of which appointed. The endowment was increased in 1843, when the chancel was rebuilt and West Molesey was constituted a separate parish, with the advowson in the hands of the Rev. H. Binney. The patron was recently Lady Barrow, now Mrs. Forster.

CHARITIES IN EAST MOLESEY   Smith's Charity is distributed as in other Surrey parishes.

From 1710, but how much further back is unknown, the parish held 18 or 19 acres of land called Hale, Hale Platts, and the Platts, for the repairs of the church and the relief of the poor. In 1789 these were leased to Thomas Sutton, lessee of the manor, for ninety-nine years. In 1815, after the Inclosure Act (see West Molesey), the lessee claimed the fee simple as owner under the Inclosure Award of these lands as ancient waste of the manor. A Chancery suit ensued in 1818, decided in 1823 in favour of the parish.[90] In 1728 the will of William Hatton of East Molesey (made in 1703) became operative, by which he left premises in Mark Lane on trust to pay £20 a year to the minister of East Molesey, provided that he was established with the consent of the inhabitants, and for '6 ruggs' a year to the poor of East and West Molesey, Thames Ditton, and Kingston 'wanting bed-clothes.' He also left his house and another in East Molesey for the poor. In 1772 Mr. John Grindell left twenty loaves annually, and in 1780 Mr. Thomas Willett left money producing £3 10s. annually for the poor. In 1786 the churchwardens returned that £5 10s. was received annually for coals for the poor, out of the rent of a house in Horse Shoe Court, London, donor unknown ; and that there were three almshouses, donor unknown. In 1730 Mr. Thomas Kempe of Laleham left 10s. a year for the young men 'to ring the bells and make merry' on 6 August in memory of himself.

The schools (National) for boys were built in 1858 and enlarged in 1891 ; those for girls and infants, originally mixed, in 1855.

CHARITIES IN WEST MOLESEY   Smith's Charity is distributed here as elsewhere.

Mr. Joseph Palmer early in the 19th century built a gallery in the church, the two front pews in which were leased for the poor at £2 each. He also gave £500 3% consols for the poor in potatoes, coals, and bread, for coals for the church stove, and one guinea to the parish clerk.

In 1783 the parish provided six houses as almshouses, returned in 1786 to Parliament as an existing charity, but now not known.

The school was built in 1887 by a School Board elected in 1879.

[88] Dugdale, *Mon. Angl.* (ed. 1848), vi, 425 ; *V.C.H. Surr.* ii, 95.
[84] Winton Epis. Reg. Wykeham, ii, fol. 82 d.
[84] Pat. 11 Jas. I, pt. viii.
[85] Pat. 17 Jas. I, pt. iii.
[87] Brayley, *Hist. of Surr.* ii, 302.
[88] Chantry Cert.
[89] Pat. 25 Eliz. pt. iv.
[90] *Further Rep. of Com. for Inq. into Charities*, 618–19.

STOKE D'ABERNON[1]

Stocke (xi cent.), Estokes (xii cent.), Stokes D'Abernon (xiii cent.), Stokes Daberoun (xiv cent.), Stoke Dabernon, Dabernoun, Daubernoun (xiv and xv and xvi cent.), Stoke d'Alborne 1843.

Stoke D'Abernon is a small village 3 miles north-west of Letherhead and a mile and a half east of Church Cobham. The Mole separates the parish from the Bookhams, and also for a short distance from Cobham. The parish measures nearly 3½ miles north-east and south-west by 1¾ miles, and contains 2,022 acres. The north-east part is high ground on the London Clay, with patches of gravel. There is here an extensive common, Stoke Common, much overgrown with wood, and on it a medicinal spring called Jessopp's Well, containing Epsom salts, and very powerful. The lower part of the parish is in the alluvium of the Mole valley, and the village, church, and manor-house are on gravel near the river. The road from Letherhead to Cobham passes through it, and the Cobham and Guildford line of the London and South Western Railway has a station in the parish, Cobham and Stoke D'Abernon, opened in 1885.

The neighbourhood of the church was presumably occupied by some Roman building, many Roman tiles being employed in the original walls. In Letherhead parish close by the boundary there is a square entrenchment, and Roman tiles and coins have been found in a field close to this and next to the Letherhead and Cobham road.

Stoke D'Abernon is mentioned in the Metrical History of Guillaume le Marechal, as the scene of his honeymoon with the heiress of the Earl of Pembroke :—

Quant les noces bien faites furent,
Et richement, si comme els durent,
La dame emmena, ce savon,
Chies Sire Angeran d'Abernon,
A Estokes, en liu paisable,
E aesie e delitable.[2]

There was an Inclosure Act for the parish in 1821,[3] the award was made 30 july 1823.[4]

The bridge on the old road from Letherhead crossed the Mole near the manor-house. It was of wood, and, as elsewhere, used only in flood time, a ford supplying the ordinary means of crossing. The bridge was built by Sir Francis' Vincent, 1757–75. In 1805 it was replaced by a brick bridge higher up the river, the road being diverted. A line of oaks marks the old road leading to the ford, and some of the supports of the wooden bridge are still visible in both banks of the river.

Ockshot is a hamlet a mile and a half north-east of Stoke D'Abernon Church, where a number of houses have been built since the railway was opened. There is a National school in the hamlet which is used for services on Sunday. It was built in 1820, the Duchess of Kent laying the foundation stone, and was enlarged in 1897.

Woodlands Park, with a modern house, is the seat of Mr. J. W. Benson, and D'Abernon Chase is the residence of Sir William Vincent, bart. The Priory, in the north of the parish, was so called from its having belonged to Newark Priory. It has been incorporated with the Claremont estate.

The French Huguenot family of Vaillant owned the advowson of Stoke D'Abernon in the 19th century. François Vaillant fled from Saumur in 1685 and settled in London. His son Paul settled first at Battersea and then (1732) at West Horsley. He was born in France in 1672 and died at West Horsley in 1739. His son Paul, born in 1715, bought the advowson of Stoke D'Abernon and a house in the village in 1800, and died in 1802, having in 1801 presented his son Philip Vaillant to the living, which he held till 1846. The arms of the family are azure a herring argent, a chief or.[5]

Before the Norman Conquest STOKE MANOR [D'ABERNON] was held by Bricsi of King Edward.[6] William granted it to Richard de Tonbridge, lord of Clare,[7] and it remained part of the possessions of his family, a sub-tenant, however, being enfeoffed (probably) in the 12th century. In 1314 Gilbert de Clare, Earl of Gloucester and Hertford, was killed at the battle of Bannockburn. He left no issue and his estates were divided among his three sisters, while the earldoms of Gloucester and Hertford became extinct.[8] The manor of Stoke D'Abernon fell to the share of Eleanor, the eldest sister,[9] who married Hugh le Despenser the younger.

CLARE. Or three cheverons gules.

DESPENSER. Argent quartered with gules fretty or and a bend sable over all.

Their eldest son Hugh died childless, and was succeeded by his brother's son Edward, afterwards Baron Despenser,[10] who was overlord of the manor in 1375.[11] Edward's son and heir Thomas, created Earl of Gloucester in 1397 by Richard II, lost his earldom in 1399 through his faithful adherence to that king's cause.[12] In 1418 the manor was said to be held of the honour of Gloucester;[13] this came to the Crown through the marriage of Lady Anne Nevill with Richard III.[14]

The head of the family which held the manor of Stoke for centuries under the Earls of Gloucester, and gave its name to the place, seems to have been

[1] Aberon, as it is now spelt, is near Lisieux in Normandy.
[2] Lines 9545–50.
[3] 2 Geo. IV, cap. 19.
[4] Blue Bk. Incl. Awards.
[5] Inscription in church, and information from Rev. W. B. Vaillant.
[6] V.C.H. Surr. i, 279.
[7] Ibid. 318b.

[8] Burke, Dorm. and Ext. Peerages, 120.
[9] Chan. Inq. p.m. 1 Edw. III, no. 53.
[10] Burke, ut supra, 166.
[11] Chan. Inq. p.m. 49 Edw. III, pt. ii (1st nos.), no. 46.
[12] Burke, ut supra.
[13] Chan. Inq. p.m. 6 Hen. V, no. 30.
[14] See Chan. Inq. p.m. (Ser. 2), ccccxiii, 71.

It is noteworthy that it was not originally part of the honour of Gloucester, but of the honour of Clare, as being part of the original grant to Richard de Clare whose descendant Gilbert acquired the honour of Gloucester from his mother in 1225. It is correctly described as of the honour of Clare in Testa de Nevill (221).

Roger D'Abernon, who held in West Molesey of Richard in 1086.[15] The association of the name of the family with Stoke indicates an early and long connexion, but the first who can certainly be said to have been there was Ingelram D'Abernon in 1189,[16] when he lent his house there to William Marshal and the daughter of the Earl of Pembroke for their honeymoon.[17] In 1205 there were four brothers living, Ingelram, Walter, William, and Richard. Ingelram, son of Walter, died in 1235, without children, his heir being his kinsman Jordan.[18] Jordan ceded his claims to his uncle Gilbert,[19] which looks as if Ingelram and Jordan were grandsons, not sons, of two of the four brothers mentioned above. Gilbert was father to john,[20] who is commemorated by the larger brass in the church. john was apparently dead by 1278, when his son john was being pressed to take up knighthood as holder of a knight's fee.[21] John the younger died in 1327 leaving an heir john.[22] William, probably his son, died in 1359.[23] He had no son and the estate was inherited by his elder daughter Elizabeth, who married, first, Sir William Croyser, kt., and afterwards john de Grey of Ruthyn.[24] William Croyser, her son by her first husband, inherited the manor from her, and dying in 1415 left it to his widow, Edith Croyser.[25] On her death in 1418 it passed to their daughter Anne, who, though only thirteen years of age, was already married to Ingelram Bruyn, son of Sir Maurice Bruyn, kt.[26] Before the year 1436 Anne married her second husband, Sir Henry Norbury, kt., son of Sir john Norbury, Treasurer of England.[27] In 1439 the property was entailed on Sir Henry and his wife and their issue.[28] Their eldest son, Sir John Norbury, married Jane Gilbert.[29] The sole issue of this marriage was a daughter, Anne, who married Sir Richard Haleighwell.[30] From whom the estate descended to their daughter jane,[31] wife of Sir Edmund Bray, Lord Bray.[32] Lord Bray died in 1539. His son John, the second Lord Bray, who died in 1557, had a sister and co-heir, Frances, who married Thomas Lyfeld, and the manor having come into their hands in 1557, as Frances' share of her father's property,[33] they settled it[34] on their daughter and heir, Jane, and her husband, Thomas Vincent, for their lives, and then on jane's sons Francis and Bray Vincent, successively. A further settlement took place on the marriage of Francis Vincent with Sarah, daughter of Sir Amyas Paulet, in 1589.[35] Francis Vincent was made a

D'ABERNON. *Azure a cheveron or.*

baronet in 1620.[36] The manor descended in the Vincent family till the early part of the 19th century.[37] Before 1824 it was sold to Hugh Smith,[38] who died in 1831.[39] Almost immediately afterwards the manor-house was let to Mrs. Phillips a widow, who died there in 1842. Her son, the Rev. F. P. Phillips, hon. canon of Winchester and rector of Stoke D'Abernon from 1862 to 1898, bought the manor-house and manor. He died in 1904. His son Mr. F. A. Phillips died by an unhappy accident in 1908, leaving issue.[40]

VINCENT, baronet. *Azure three quatrefoils argent.*

The manor-house close by the church is no doubt on the site of that in which William Marshal stayed. In the wall of one of the bedrooms on the first floor are some very massive beams of 15th or 16th-century date. This was one of the ends of an E-shaped house (compare Slyfield, close by, in Great Bookham parish). There are also traces of a gallery, since cut up into smaller rooms. The house was practically rebuilt by Sir Francis Vincent, who succeeded in 1757, and who filled up the centre of the E with the present large hall. The stable walls are partly of a date about 1600, which perhaps indicates that the first Sir Thomas Vincent, who died in 1613, was the builder who designed the gallery. The earlier house might date to Sir John Norbury, who died in 1521. The house now contains a fine collection of Morland's pictures.

In 1253 john D'Abernon, then lord of the manor, received a grant of free warren from Henry III,[41] and when in the following reign his son john claimed that he and his ancestors time out of mind had held a view of frankpledge in Stoke, the claim was allowed.[42] In 1557 a free fishery in the River Mole was among the rights of the lord of the manor.[43] Free fishery in the waters of 'Emlyn' is mentioned in 1824.[44] Two mills were established in the manor at the time of the Domesday Survey, the profits of the one being worth 7s. and those of the other 6s. a year.[45]

There is in this parish a small manor within the district of *OCKSHOT* (anciently Occasate, Oggesethe, Hoggeset, &c.). Gilbert D'Abernon in the 13th century granted lands and pasture there to the monks of Waverley,[46] who seem to have retained them, or some part of them,[47] till the Dissolution, when they were granted to Sir William Fitz William, K.G.[48] There was a house in Ockshot called Ockshot Grange, perhaps part of the monks' holding, which was owned by

[14] *V.C.H. Surr.* i, 318b.
[16] Roger D'Abernon made a grant of land in Ockshot in the time of Hen. II. Add. MS. 5529.
[17] *L'histoire de Guillaume le Marechal*, lines 9545–50.
[18] Add. MS. 5562; *Excerpta e Rot. Fin.* (Rec. Com.), i, 270.
[19] Add. MS. 5541.
[20] *Excerpta e Rot. Fin.* i, 305.
[21] *Parl. Writs* (Rec. Com.), i, 214, 216, 218.
[22] Chan. Inq. p.m. 1 Edw. III, no. 53.
[23] Ibid. 32 Edw. III (1st. nos.), no. 23. There is an excellent paper on the D'Abernons by Dr. Spencer Perceval in *Surr. Arch. Coll.* v, 53, &c.
[24] Feet of F. Div. Co. Trin. 14 Ric. II, no. 205.
[25] Chan. Inq. p.m. 3 Hen. V, no. 37.
[26] Ibid. 6 Hen. V, no. 30.
[27] Brass in Stoke D'Abernon Church ; *Surr. Arch. Coll.* x, 284 ; Pat. 12 Hen. VI, pt. ii, m. 26.
[28] B.M. Add. Chart. 5618.
[29] *Surr. Arch. Coll.* x, 287.
[30] Ibid.
[31] Burke, *Dorm. and Ext. Peerages.*
[32] Chan. Proc. (Ser. 2), bdle. 158, no. 27.
[33] Feet of F. Surr. East. 3 & 4 Phil. and Mary.
[34] Ibid. Trin. 17 Eliz.
[35] Chan. Inq. p.m. Surr. (Ser. 2), ccxlvii, 99.
[36] *Cal. S.P. Dom.* 1619–23, p. 167.
[37] Recov. R. East. 50 Geo. III. rot. 231.
[38] Feet of F. Surr. Trin. 5 Geo. IV.
[39] Monument in church.
[40] Personal knowledge.
[41] *Cal. Chart.* R. 1226–7, p. 434.
[42] *Plac. de Quo Warr.* (Rec. Com.), 747.
[43] Feet of F. Surr. East. 3 & 4 Phil. and Mary.
[44] Feet of F. Surr. Trin. 5 Geo. IV.
[45] *V.C.H. Surr.* i, 318b.
[46] B.M. Add. Chart. 5528 to 5538.
[47] Pat. 15 Edw. III. pt. i, m. 45.
[48] Pat. 28 Hen. VIII, pt. ii, m. 9.

one of the Vincent family in the time of Charles I.[49] The priory of Newark by Guildford as early as the reign of Henry III had a small holding in Stoke D'Abernon granted by Hugh de Fetcham and confirmed by John D'Abernon,[50] taxed in 1291 at 12s. 6½d.[51] After the Dissolution john Carleton of Walton on Thames received a grant from the king of ' the messuage called Pryorne (i.e. the Priory) in Stoke D'Abernon which belonged to the late Priory of Newark, Surrey.'[52]

The church of *ST. MARY THE CHURCH VIRGIN* consists of a chancel 23 ft. 6 in. by 15 ft. 6 in.; a north chapel 21 ft. by 13 ft.; a nave 49 ft. by 21 ft. 3 in.; a north aisle and north transeptal organ-chamber; a north-west tower and a south porch. The earliest parts of the church are the chancel and the two eastern bays of the nave, which are, so far as the walls are concerned, of pre-Conquest date and represent a church consisting only of a chancel and nave, the latter being 35 ft. long. There was also very probably a south porch. In the closing years of the 12th century a north aisle of two bays was added, windows were inserted in both nave and chancel, and a new chancel arch was built. At the beginning of the 13th century the chancel was vaulted and buttresses and new windows were inserted in the south wall of the chancel, and probably in the north wall as well. A window was also inserted in the nave. In the middle of the 13th century a new south door was inserted and the early porch was destroyed. Probably at the same time a nave altar recess was constructed to the north of the chancel arch. This, however, no longer remains, but a water-colour sketch made before the modern restoration shows this feature very clearly.[53] Towards the end of the 15th century the north chapel was built and the rood stair inserted. In 1866 the whole church was enlarged and 'restored.' The nave and aisle were lengthened (the latter being completely rebuilt), the old chancel arch was destroyed with the nave altar recesses and the squints, and was replaced by a modern one. The old bell-cot over the west end of the nave was destroyed and replaced by the present tower at the north-west, and various new windows were inserted.

The east window of the chancel is a modern triplet of 18th-century design. On the north of the chancel is an arcade, of two dissimilar bays, to the chapel. The first of these has an obtuse four-centred head flanked by fluted pilasters, with moulded capitals and bases, which are carried up to an embattled cornice. The spandrels are filled in with plain moulded panels, and the soffit of the arch and the Jambs are panelled. Between this and the arch to the west is a short length of walling. The second arch has a more acute four-centred head, and is continuously moulded with a deep hollow between a double ogee and a hollow chamfer. There is no label or canopy. On the south are two windows of the same date as the vaulting, both single lancets with wide splays and pointed bowtel-moulded internal jambs and rear arch. The moulded external jambs, head and label, are completely restored in modern material. The chancel arch is entirely modern and of late 13th-century detail. It is two-centred and of two chamfered orders with a plain chamfered label The Jambs have circular

half shafts with plain moulded capitals and bases. The chancel is vaulted in two bays. The circular vaulting shafts are single in the angles and triple clustered on the north and south walls, where they are placed between the two arches and the two windows respectively. The capitals are circular, moulded, of varying design, and have plain bells. The bases have a water-mould of somewhat unusual angular profile, and are also circular. The vaulting ribs are moulded with undercut rolls and the cross ribs are enriched with dog-tooth. The vault is quadripartite with a filling of small stuff now stripped of its plaster. At the intersection of the diagonal ribs of the west bay is a small rosette boss. At the east is an elaborate modern marble reredos with stations of the cross in very high relief. On the north is a modern wall arcade of 13th-century design.

Above the chancel arch, and visible from the nave, is an opening to the space over the vaulting; and over and to the north of the north jamb is the rood loft door, a plain pointed one, of 15th-century date. The two western bays of the nave arcade have two-centred arches of one chamfered order, and a plain chamfered

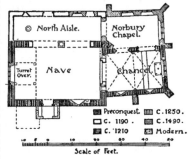

STOKE D'ABERNON CHURCH BEFORE 1866.

label. The respond is square with plain abaci, and is much restored. The column is circular with a circular roll-moulded base standing on a square plinth and having plain angle-spurs. The capital has a plain fairly shallow bell worked from the circular shaft to a square hollow-chamfered abacus. The third and fourth bays of the arcade are quite modern. At the south-east of the nave is a piscina of late 15th-century date. The head is segmental and with the Jambs continuously moulded with a double ogee. The western Jamb, however, has been mutilated to a different form. The back is curved and the basin circular with five channels, and the drain is masked by a small boss. Near this is a small modern door to the modern vestry, in the building of which a plain lancet window of the same date as those in the south of the chancel was blocked up. West of this again is the original south door, now blocked up. This is of mid-13th-century date and has a drop two-centred head. It is continuously moulded with a roll set in a hollow chamfer. In the east Jamb is a recess for a

49 Chan. Inq. p.m. (Ser. 2) ccccxlvii, 14.
50 B.M. Add. Chart. 5544.
51 Pope Nich. Tax. (Rec. Com.), 206.
52 Pat. 33 Hen. VIII, pt. ii, m. 22.
53 Surr. Arch. Coll. xx, 10.

holy-water stock, with a plain segmental head. Previous to 1865 this was covered by a plain brick porch of late date. Above the door is a small rough sundial, which projects from the face of the wall about 3 in. west of the door, and in the upper part of the wall is a blocked opening with plain quoined jambs and a flat stone lintel. This is possibly pre-Conquest, and may have opened to the first floor of an early porch covering the south door. Between this and the sundial a modern lancet window has been inserted. The present entrance is on this side, and is again further west and covered by a modern open timber porch. The west window of the nave is modern.

The north chapel is lit on the east by an original window of excellent design, of three trefoiled lights with sub-mullions and smaller lights over and an external label. The jambs, head, and mullions are moulded. In the south wall are a pair of windows of similar but less skilful design, and of only two lights. In these the jambs and mullions are plain. West of the second window is a blocked-up fireplace of the same date, with a flat four-centred moulded head. This is covered with scratchings. Amongst others the name 'Edmund de Bray, knight,' may be read, with a rough drawing of a bray. Near it, in square inclosing lines, are the names : 'Bastiano de Fan, Bern Macutto, Fran Latina,' all in roman capitals.

At the south-west is the door to and a part of the rood stair. At the west is a much restored and probably widened arch to the organ-chamber (originally to the aisle). It is of obtuse two-centred form, and is of two chamfered orders, the outer being continuous in the jambs. Above it is a much restored quatrefoil light.

The transeptal organ-chamber is quite modern and replaces part of the aisle, which was itself rebuilt and lengthened, and the tower, which fills the western bay, of the present aisle, is also modern. It is surmounted by a shingled spirelet. None of the old doors or windows of the aisle remain, all having been replaced by modern ones.

The font is placed under the tower, and is a plain octagonal one of late 15th-century date.

The pulpit is a handsome one of early 17th-century date. It is seven-sided in form and stands upon a central post with elaborately carved brackets. At the angles are fantastic Ionic pilasters surmounted by grotesques. The faces have carved and inlaid panels with enriched mouldings, and the crown mould and book-rest are elaborately ornamented.

At the back is a carved standard of similar detail with an oval shield charged with the Vincent arms and quarterings. This supports a large sounding-board with a carved central panel of grotesque design, angle pendants and a carved cornice, held up by a pair of elaborately scrolled wrought-iron stays, the whole being an unusually complete example of an early-17th-century church fitting. In the wall near it is a wrought-iron hour-glass stand of the same date. There is also a wooden eagle lectern of foreign design and workmanship. In the north aisle is a very fine chest of 13th-century date. It is of oak, and in size is 3 ft. 11 in. by 1 ft. 6½ in. by 2 ft. 2 in. high. It is raised from the floor about 7½ in. by end standards of board, the inner edges of which below the chest itself are roll-stop-chamfered. On the front of the chest are three roundels of geometrical incised

work. There are three lock plates, and two hasps remain. In the lid is a money slot. The altar table is also of early 17th-century date and has a movable top.

In the chancel floor is a large slab, some 8 ft. long, of blue-grey marble. The margin is inscribed in sunk Lombardic capitals : ' Sire Johan Daubernovn chivaler gist icy Dev de sa Alme eyt mercy.' Let into the slab is a life-size brass of a knight in armour, the earliest now known in England ; it dates from 1277. He is shown wearing a coif and camail of chain mail, the former strapped over the forehead. The hawberk reaches about two-thirds down the thigh, and the sleeves are corded at the wrists and terminate in mail mittens. The legs are encased in mail chaussés fastened to kneecops of cuir bouilli which are ornamented with rosettes and an engrailed border. The mail is then continued as a thigh covering. There are no visible traces of a gambeson, though some such garment would certainly be worn. The surcoat is very ample and open in front from a little below the waist. The edge of this opening and the skirts, which reach to the bottom of the calf, are fringed. At the waist is a narrow plaited girdle. The sword is large, about 4 ft. long. The hilt has a large circular flat pommel, a corded grip, and short heavy quillons curving slightly downwards. The scabbard is tipped with metal and brought up into an obtuse V clasping the guard on either side. The sword-belt is broad and fairly plain, being merely ornamented with a stitched border and punched work at the buckle-holes. The frog is elaborately arranged to cant the sword at a slight angle, and the whole belt passes diagonally round the hips.

The shield is small and heater-shaped and bears : azure a cheveron or, the field being enamelled. The cheveron is drawn very narrow and is carried up to the top of the shield. The shield, resting on the left arm, is slung over the right shoulder by a broad belt ornamented with a rose and swastica and having a broad buckle. In the crook of the right arm is a lance some 6 ft. long, without grip or vamplate, and with a small fringed pennon bearing a cheveron.

Plain prick spurs are worn with a rather thin strap. The hands are joined in prayer, and the feet rest upon a lion which bites the butt of the lance.

Near this is another slab with a brass representing Sir John D'Abernon the younger, 1327. The marginal inscription has unfortunately been lost except a few short lengths on which the words 'ici g . . . eit merci,' appear in Lombardic capitals. The figure is clad in armour, and wears first a gambeson, the longitudinally padded square skirts of which are visible and reach to just above the knee. Over this is a hawberk of banded mail worked at the skirts into a rounded point falling in front to a little below the gambeson, while at the sides it is slightly above it. The sleeves are wide and straight, the bands running lengthwise of the fore-arm and round the upper arm, and terminated without strapping at about the middle of the forearm. Beneath is visible some form of close-fitting arm defence, possibly of leather, and part of the gambeson. Over the hawberk is an aketoun of pourpoint with fringed skirts reaching to the middle of the thigh. Over this is worn a cyclas fitting the torso fairly closely and laced up the sides, but having fairly wide skirts of unequal

STOKE D'ABERNON CHURCH : NORBURY CHAPEL

STOKE D'ABERNON CHURCH : SOUTH DOOR, NOW BLOCKED UP, AND SUNDIAL

length. In front it reaches to a little below the fork, leaving visible two rows of the metal rosette studs of the aketoun. At the back, however, it falls to the bend of the leg, and the skirts are split at the side like a dalmatic. There is no girdle, but the sword-belt passing round the hips draws the cyclas together. The sword is of fair size with a long corded grip and an oval pommel and plain quillons with rounded ends. The belt is richly ornamented, but quite simply attached to the scabbard, which has an ornamental metal tip and is somewhat less diminished from haft to point than is the case in the earlier brass. On the head is a fluted oval bascinet reaching to below the ears and with a foiled point or socket at the top. The aventail of banded mail is riveted to the bascinet and covers the neck and shoulders, partly covering the circular pauldrons. Rerebraces of plate are worn strapped over the mail, which shows inside the arm. The elbow cops appear to be articulated on the rere-brace and are reinforced by circular plates tied on with points. No gauntlets are shown. The legs are clad in mail chausses, over which are strapped plate defences. The knee cops are large ridged and have engrailed borders. The thigh defences are not visible. The insteps are protected by articulated sollerets of five plates, and short prick spurs are worn with rosette bosses. A small heater-shaped shield of a rather acute form rests on the left arm, but has no belt. The hands are joined in prayer and the feet rest on a lion. Over the head is an ogee cinquefoiled canopy, each foil of which is subcusped to form a cinquefoil. This is slightly damaged. The shield is charged with a very broad cheveron.

In the chancel is also a plain marble slab with a small brass shield and the indents of three others and of an inscription in separate brass letters. The last is so worn as to be indecipherable. The one re-maining shield bears a cheveron with a label of four points. At the north-west of the chancel floor is a slab to 'Sir john Ackland, of Ackland, in the county of Devon, Barronett,' who died in 1647. Two brasses are fixed to the jambs of the east arch of the chancel arcade. That on the east jamb is of a lady wearing a long head veil, a pleated wimple, a full ungirt robe with moderate sleeves, and an ample cloak with loose cords to fasten it, which hangs down behind the hands, which are joined in prayer. At her feet and on her ample skirts are the figures to a smaller scale of her four sons and four daughters. At the foot is the following inscription : ' Hic jacet dña Anna Norbury nup' ux' Henrici Norbury milit' ‖ Ac filia Willi Croyser qu'dam dni hui' loci que obiit xii° die ‖ oc-tobr' anno dni m° cccc°Lx°iiii° cui' ai'e ppciet' deu' ame.' The second brass is of a 'chrysom' child. The swaddling clothes, which are brought over the head in a kind of hood, are bound with crossing bands, and over the forehead the clothes are marked with a cross. Below an inscription in black letter smalls with capitals : ' Pray for the soule of Elyn bray dowter of s' Edmond ‖ bray Knyght and jane hys wyfe whiche elyn dyed ye xvi ‖ day of Maij A° M V° xvi.' On the south side of the chapel is a brass to Frances (Bray), 1592, wife of Thomas Lyfield, with a long genealogical inscription. With this are the figures of Frances, her husband, and their daughter jane, the wife of Thomas Vincent.

On the south wall of the chancel is a brass plate with the following inscription : ' Hic jacet Johēs

Prowd Rector isti' ecclīē et quat' ‖ Rector ecclie de esthorsley qui obiit nono die Octobr' ‖ A° Dñi mccccLxxxvii° Cujus aīē ppciet' d' amen.

On the east wall of the chapel is a brass plate with the following inscription :

Thys Chauntrie foundyt by Syr John Norbury
The First Prest was Sir John Pinnoke truly :
Under thys stone lieth buryed His Body
Of whose soule Jesu have mercy.
He departed out of this world and from us he is
    gone
In the yeare of oure Lord fifteen twenty and one
The fyrst day of the Month of August
In the Marcie of J'hu Christ He puttys all his
    trust. Amen.

On the east wall is a small mural monument to Sir John Norbury put up in 1633, as the inscription explains, to replace ' the ould monument by injury of time demolisht.' He is represented in early 17th-century armour kneeling at a desk within a semi-circular arch which is surmounted by a broken pediment of classical design. Under the east window of the chapel is the monument of Sarah (Paulet), 1608, wife of Sir Francis Vincent. There is a life-size effigy lying on the left side with the cheek resting on the left hand. The costume consists of a tight fitting bodice with a pointed stomacher, and elabor-ately quilted sleeves, a heavily pleated skirt over a farthingale, a deep ruff, and a wide hood. On the plinth below are the kneeling figures of five sons and two daughters. The tomb has a high semicircular canopy the soffit of which is panelled. Above the effigy is an elaborate inscription on a slate slab. Three shields are shown, the first having the quatre-foils of Vincent, the second the three swords of Paulet, the third being Vincent impaling Paulet. Between the two windows on the north of the chapel is a second monument, of slightly later date, to Sir Thomas Vincent, 1613, and his wife, Lady Jane (Lyfield) 1619. Sir Thomas is wearing complete armour consisting of a globose breast-plate, a back-plate, a moderate gorget, articulated pauldrons, rerebraces and vambraces, large winged elbow cops, very wide articulated taces over stuffed trunks, articulated Jambs, knee cops, vamplate, and articulated sollerets. Over the gorget a fair sized ruff is worn, and the wrists are ruffed. He lies on his right side, and wears a pointed beard. His wife, placed a little below him, is in a recumbent attitude with the hands joined. She wears a close-fitting bodice with a pointed stomacher and moderate sleeves turned back at the cuff, a full skirt with a farthingale, a small hood, a moderate ruff and an ample cloak or mantle. The monument is very similar in design to the last described, but is ornamented with the scrollwork peculiar to the period. The Vincent arms appear on a shield crown-ing the arch. On the back of the tomb are the arms of Vincent and Lyfield, Or a cheveron thereon between three demi-lions gules with three trefoils or on the cheveron. In the churchyard are two ancient grave slabs. The first of these is of plain oblong form and mid-14th-century date with a mar-ginal inscription in square-sunk Lombardic capitals as follows :—' Johanna Femme de Sire Johan Dabernon chivaler gist icy dieu de sa alme eit merci.' The second is coffin-shaped and ornamented with a cross crosslet with rounded ends to the base and a long stem. It is marginally inscribed in Lombardic characters : ' Sire Richard Le Petit Iadis Persone de cest eiglise ici gist Receyve sa alme Isu christ.' It is of Sussex marble and is of mid-13th-century date.

On the south-east wall of the chancel are the remains of a painting of the same date as the vaulting. It is a portion of a representation of ' The adoration of the Lamb.' At the bottom is a crowned and cloaked figure playing a harp, probably one of the twenty-four elders ; above this is a tier of figures of the redeemed and then two tiers of angels, those in the lower tier playing musical instruments. In the last two cases and in the first only one figure remains, and only a few of the second-tier figures are left. On the one old pillar of the nave is painted a crucifix ; this is nearly obliterated. In the museum of the Surrey Archaeological Society at Guildford is preserved a sketch of a painting which was discovered in the nave altar recess which was destroyed in 1866. It consisted of the bearded figure of an archbishop in mass vestments, before whom a knight in armour was kneeling. Over the head of the figure was the partly obliterated name of ' S. T [H O M A S ' in Lombardic capitals.

In the window of the present tower are collected some fragments of old glass mainly of 15th-century date. Amongst others is the figure of an angel playing a fiddle, and also of St. Anne teaching the Virgin. There are also some old quarries painted with the ' bray ' or hemp-brake badge of the Brays in the modern screen between the chapel and the aisle. There are also some shields of arms, including those of the Dabernons ; Croyser impaling Daber-non; Norbury impaling Croyser ; Haleighwell impaling Norbury ; Bray impaling Haleighwell ; Lyfield impaling Bray ; Vincent impaling Lyfield ; Vincent ; Vincent impaling Paulet, &c. On an iron bracket in the chapel is a surcoat with a funeral helm.

There are three bells. The treble is by William Eldridge, 1687. The second was cast by Warner & Son in 1866. The third bears the initials I. S. and was probably cast by Joan Sturdy, c. 1450.

The church plate consists of a cup with cover, two patens, a flagon, and an alms basin, all electro plated.

The registers of baptisms and burials date from 1619, those of marriages from 1620.

ADVOWSON   There was a church on the manor at the time of the Domesday Survey.[54] The advowson of the rectory went always with the manor[55] till 1746, when it was included with certain lands in a term of 500 years created by the marriage settlement of Sir Francis Vincent for raising portions for younger children.[56] When sold under that authority about thirty years later it was purchased by Paul Vaillant, a gentleman of a Huguenot family, Sheriff of London.[57] He died in 1802, and in the following year it was sold by his executors, under the description of ' a neat house, thirty acres of glebe, and the great and small tithes of the parish,' to the Smith family,[58] one of whom held the manor. It was acquired, with the manor, by the Rev. F. P. Phillips. His son, Mr. F. A. Phillips, held it until his death in 1908.

CHARITIES   Smith's Charity is distributed as in other Surrey parishes. In 1786 land worth 3s. a year for the use of the poor, donor unknown, was returned.

THAMES DITTON

Ditone (xi cent.) ; Ditton-on-Thames (xv cent.).

Thames Ditton[1] is a village on the banks of the Thames, a mile and a half from Kingston, of which it was once a chapelry, separated by Act of Parliament in 1769. The parish measures 3 miles from north to south and about a mile and a half from east to west. It contains 2,964 acres of land and 17 of water. The greater part of the parish is on the gravel, sand, and alluvium of the Thames valley, the southern portion on the London clay. Ditton Marsh (that is *March* or boundary) is a common partly in the parish on the borders of Esher. The main line of the London and South Western Railway runs through the parish, and the branch line to Hampton Court separates from the main line in it. On this there is a Thames Ditton station.

Considerable finds of bronze implements have been made in the bed of the Thames and in the neighbourhood of the Dittons, but it was not recorded precisely whether they were in Thames Ditton or Long Ditton parish, or in the bed of the river exactly opposite Thames Ditton and Kingston parishes.[2] The river drift has yielded evidence of considerable population in prehistoric times. A primitive canoe was found in the river a few years ago, but efforts to obtain it for the Kingston Museum have so far failed. Thames Ditton is now, with Esher and Long Ditton, an urban district, formed in 1895.[3] There is an unusual amount of common land in the parish. The Inclosure Act of 1799[4] inclosing Walton and Walton Leigh (see Walton) included land in Ditton Marsh; that for Kingston[5] and Imber Court Manor inclosed waste and 50 acres of common fields in Thames Ditton.

At Weston Green, south of the village, is the chapel of ease of St. Nicholas, a plain red-brick building constructed in 1901, on a site given by Mr. S. Went. A Congregational chapel was built in 1804, and restored in 1887. Mr. H. Speer of the Manor House erected the drinking fountain in 1879 and the Village Hall in 1887.

Twenty years ago Thames Ditton was a picturesque small village, but the older houses are now rapidly disappearing to make room for small riverside villas and bungalows. There are, however, still some 16th- and 17th-century houses and cottages near the Manor House. The Swan Inn, next to the ferry, is well known to all lovers of the river and remains as it was in the days when the household of George II

[54] *V.C.H. Surr.* i, 318*b*.
[55] For references, see above under the descent of the manor, and Inst. Bks. P.R.O. 1620, 1665, 1690, 1732.
[56] Manning and Bray, *Surr.* ii, 726.
[57] Inst. Bks. P.R.O. 1801.
[58] Brayley, *Hist. Surr.* ii, 460.
[1] Called also Ember-and-Weston (S.P. Dom. 1644, p. 63),and Imber-Ditton (Recov. R. Trin. 8 Geo. III, rot. 310)
from the names of two of its manors.
[2] *V.C.H. Surr.* i, 251–3.
[3] Local Govt. Bd. Order no. 32638.
[4] 39–40 Geo. III, cap. 86.
[5] 48 Geo. III, cap. 134.

frequented it. Beyond the 'Swan' is the bronze foundry of Messrs. Hollinshed & Bruton, where the statue of the late Queen Victoria, designed by the Princess Louise and destined for Calcutta, was cast a few years ago, and where the process known as *cir perdu* was revived. On the opposite side of the ferry is Boyle Farm, formerly the property of Edward Sugden, Lord St. Leonards, a distinguished lawyer and Lord Chancellor of England, and famous for the 19th century law-suit concerning his will.[14] The estate is gradually being cut up, and the house, which belongs to Mr. H. Mainwaring Robertson, is now unoccupied. The Lodge, a picturesque old house with high surrounding walls by the side of the road leading from the village to the Green, is the property of Sir Guy Campbell, bart., and in the churchyard are the remains, brought from Paris, of his famous ancestress Pamela Fitzgerald. Thames Ditton House also faces the river, but its beautiful sweeping lawns once famous for their smoothness are now only a rough field. It was the property of the late Rt.-Hon. Hume Dick, M.P., who built a picture gallery for his art collection and otherwise altered the house. It afterwards passed to Mr. G. B. Tate. Ditton Lodge retains a small park with some very fine trees which can be seen from the railway. It is now the property of Lord Mexborough. The manor-house belongs to Mr. H. Speer, and is built on the sloping side of the hill which leads from the river to the station : the road branches at the station, one branch going to Imber Court and the other to Weston Green and Esher. Weston House, formerly the property of General Sir John Lambert, K.C.B., and of his son General John Lambert, has lately been pulled down, and the grounds are now the site of an almost entirely new village. Ruxley Lodge is the residence of Lord Foley, Gordon Lodge of Sir Richard D. Awdry, K.C.B. The Green is only divided by a few houses from Esher Common and Weston Green.

Claygate was formed as an ecclesiastical parish from Thames Ditton in 1841. As the name implies, it is upon the London Clay, here capped in places by sand in the southern part of the parish, and was probably traversed by an old road running from Kingston Hill to the ford of the Mole near the square entrenchment in Letherhead parish (q.v.). It is under the same urban council as Thames Ditton. The church, Holy Trinity, is of stone in 14th-century style, with a tower. It was built in 1840, enlarged in 1860, and restored in 1902. A vicarage house was built in 1843. The school was built in 1838 as a Church school, and enlarged in 1849. It was rebuilt by the School Board of Thames Ditton in 1885. There is a Baptist chapel, built in 1861.

Claygate has grown very much of late years since the opening of the Cobham line to Guildford ; Claygate station on this line was opened in 1885. There are brick and tile works near the station.

Claygate is in Kingston Hundred, in which the eastern part of Thames Ditton parish seems to have been always reckoned.

There appears to have been no manor MANORS in this parish known exclusively as the manor of Thames Ditton.[15] The name is applied to a manor in several deeds of the Evelyn family in the 17th century, but it was probably used as an *alias* for the manor of Claygate, q.v.

The manor of *CLAYGATE* was given to the Abbot and convent of Westminster by Tosti,[16] probably the son of Earl Godwin. The monks held it at the time of the Norman Conquest,[17] and until the dissolution of their house, when it fell into the hands of the king. In 1538 Cuthbert Blakeden obtained a lease of the manor from the Abbot of Westminster which was subsequently assigned to Juliana his widow, who married John Boothe.[18] In 1553 the reversion of the manor in fee was granted by Edward VI to john Child at a rent of £9 8s. 8d.[19] and not long after Child sold the estate to David Vincent, who died seised of it in 1565.[20] From him the manor passed to his son and heir Thomas Vincent,[21] and afterwards to Thomas's son Sir Francis Vincent. In 1603 George Evelyn died seised of the reversion of the manor after the death of Sir Francis.[22] Before 1613 the manor was in the hands of the Evelyn family, and in that year Thomas Evelyn, who then held it, settled it on his son Sir Thomas Evelyn and Anne his wife in tail male, with contingent remainders

EVELYN. *Azure a griffon passant and a chief or.*

successively to his younger sons George and William.[23] Thomas Evelyn the elder died in 1617, and was succeeded by his eldest son Sir Thomas.[24] From him the manor decended to his son Sir Edward Evelyn, kt. and bart., who held it in 1685.[25] He died in 1692,[26] and his son George Evelyn having died childless in 1685,[27] his estates passed to his daughter Sophia Evelyn. She must have conveyed the manor to her sister Lady Penelope Alston, for Sir Joseph Alston, husband of Penelope, held a court.[28] Joseph Alston their son settled it on his marriage in 1718, but died childless, and his brother Evelyn Alston sold it to Lord King before 1721.[29] Lord King was in possession of the tithes in 1727.[30] His lineal

14 *Dict. Nat. Biog.* 'The mysterious disappearance of his will, which he had made some years before his death, occasioned a lawsuit which established the admissibility of secondary evidence of the contents of such a document in the absence of a presumption that the testator had destroyed it *anima revocandi.*' He died in 1875.
15 The manor of Ditton, which Wadard held of the Bishop of Bayeux in 1086, has been identified in *V.C.H. Surrey*, i, 305a, as Thames Ditton. Further research shows that the Domesday manor was apparently one of the manors of Long Ditton in Kingston Hundred (q.v.).

16 Dugdale, *Mon. Angl.* (ed. 1846) i, 294.
17 *V.C.H. Surr.* i, 306.
18 *Surr. Arch. Coll.* vii, 226. There are monuments in Thames Ditton Church to Juliana and both her husbands.
19 Manning and Bray, op. cit. i, 460.
20 Chan. Inq. p.m. (Ser. 2), ccxlii, 131.
21 Recov. R. East. 9 Eliz. rot. 1003.
22 Chan. Inq. p.m. (Ser. 2), ccxc, 124. George Evelyn's mother was a daughter of David Vincent. Pedigree given to Aubrey by Sir John Evelyn before 1671.
23 Feet of F. Surr. Mich. 11 Jas. I.

24 Chan. Inq. p.m. (Ser. 2) ccclxxii, 161.
25 Recov. R. East. 1 Jas. II, rot. 8.
26 Ditton Registers.
27 Ibid.
28 Ct. R. in possession of William Bray. But in Manning and Bray, op. cit. ii, 461, there must be a misprint in the date 1691, unless the manor was conveyed before Sir Edward's death on the marriage of his daughter Penelope in 1690.
29 Deeds communicated to William Bray after the description of Claygate was written. See Manning and Bray, *Hist. of Surr.* iii, 15.
30 Feet of F. Surr. Hil. 13 Geo. I.

descendant, the Earl of Lovelace, is now lord of the manor.

The manor of *WESTON* in Thames Ditton was held by the abbey of Barking in 1086, and continued part of the property of that house till shortly before the Dissolution, when Henry VIII bought it to add to the honour of Hampton Court.[31] It was annexed to that honour by Act of Parliament in 1539,[32] and was leased in the following year to John Baker.[33] In later times it was

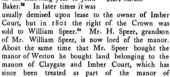

King, Earl of Lovelace. *Sable three spearheads argent with drops of blood and a chief or with three battle-axes azure therein.*

usually demised upon lease to the owner of Imber Court, but in 1801 the right of the Crown was sold to William Speer.[34] Mr. H. Speer, grandson of Mr. William Speer, is now lord of the manor. About the same time that Mr. Speer bought the manor of Weston he bought land belonging to the manors of Claygate and Imber Court, which has since been treated as part of the manor of Weston.[35]

A curious reminiscence of the ancient lordship of Weston is given by a notice board, which formerly stood on the common, headed 'Manor of Weston otherwise Barking.' The name of Barking Manor, for Weston, appears also in surveys of Imber Court.

At the time of the Domesday Survey Picot held of Richard of Tonbridge, lord of Clare, a piece of land called Limeurde, which Edwin and another homager had held in the time of King Edward.[36] This land has generally been identified with Imworth,[37] but the Limeurde of Domesday was situated in Kingston Hundred,[38] and also the holding afterwards known as the manor of *IMWORTH*, later *IMBER* or *IMBER COURT* must have been separate from any de Clare holding,[39] for it was held in socage of the king, by the service of paying £3 18s. 3d. yearly to the bailiff of Kingston,[40] and probably at Domesday formed part of Kingston.

Manning represents Imworth as having been generally held with Weston since 1539. It was certainly a distinct manor in the time of Henry III, for in 1223 Ralph de Imworth died seised of it, and of the hundred of Elmbridge.[41] Another Ralph de Imworth, probably a son of the preceding, appears in 1229 conducting a lawsuit against Samson de Molesey about a fishpond in Imworth.[42] This Ralph in 1252 received a grant of exemption from tallage for himself

and his tenants of this manor.[43] Not long afterwards the king granted to Robert de Bareville the wardship of Reginald, son and heir of Ralph de Imworth. Reginald died seised of the manor about 1280.[44] Later it came by sale or inheritance to john de Madham. He in 1332 granted the reversion of the manor after the death of his mother Eleanor, then wife of Roger de London, to Roger for life with remainder to Ralph, son of Roger, and Katherine his wife and their heirs.[45] Roger granted Imworth to Roger Salaman, who is said to have had the manor at his death in 1343, but presumably this can only have been Roger de London's life interest in it,[46] for later Ralph son of Roger de London conveyed the manor to Thomas de Braose and his wife Beatrice.[47] By a settlement made in 1361 Thomas and Beatrice granted the manor to john de Braose, brother of Thomas, and his wife Elizabeth and their heirs, failing such to revert to Thomas and his heirs.[48] Beatrice held the manor at her death in 1383 [49] (she having survived her husband, who died in 1361), and it then descended (in spite of the settlement) to her son Sir Thomas de Braose,[50] who died in 1395. At the time of his death he was seised of the manor of Imworth held of the king in socage, and of a certain park lying in the said manor, held of Thomas Earl of Kent, service unknown. He left two infant children, both of whom died within two months of their father's decease, and the manor passed to Elizabeth wife of Sir William Heron, kt., who was the next heir, being the daughter of Beatrice, sister of the said Thomas de Braose.[51] In 1405 William atte Welle and Joan his wife brought a suit against the feoffees of Thomas de Braose, asserting that the property belonged by right to joan as the daughter of Thomas, son of Isabel sister of Roger de London, jun. The suit was decided in favour of William and his wife.[52] In 1406, however, they quitclaimed their right to John Brymmesgrave, clerk, john Holyngbourne and another,[53] and in 1415 George Braose, son of the above John (brother of Thomas), also made a quitclaim to John Holyngbourne. The latter seems to have conveyed it to john Ardern, who was holding shortly afterwards.[54] In 1499 Richard Ardern died seised of the manor of Imworth and half the hundred of Elmbridge, held of the men of Kingston.[55] He left his estates to his half-brother John Holgrave, from whom it seems to have been acquired by John Dudley, afterwards Earl of Warwick and Duke of Northumberland.[56] In a survey of Imber Court, dated 1544, it is stated that Robert Smyth held a lease of Imber Court for thirty years, granted by Dudley

[31] *V.C.H. Surr.* i, 311b. It is not known by whom this manor was given to the nuns; possibly it formed part of the original endowment, but it is not mentioned by name in the charter of foundation; B.M. Cott. MS. Vesp. A. ix, fol. 142.

[32] 31 Hen. VIII, cap. 5.

[33] B.M. Add. Chart. 28236.

[34] Manning and Bray, *Hist. of Surr.* ii, 462. Mr. Speer presented to the living of Thames Ditton in 1835; Inst. Bks. P.R.O.

[35] Local information from Mr. A. J. Style, and Court Rolls of Imber Court in Surr. Arch. Society's Library.

[36] *V.C.H. Surr.* i, 317.

[37] Ibid. note.

[38] Ibid. i, 317.

[39] The De Clares had feet at Ditton, but these were their manor of Long Ditton.

[40] Chan. Inq. p.m. 19 Ric. II, no. 7.

[41] Fine R. 7 Hen. III, m. 3.

[42] Cal. Pat. 1225–32, p. 297.

[43] Ibid. 1247–58, p. 182; see also Feet of F. Surr. Hil. 25 Hen. III, no. 29.

[44] Chan. Inq. p.m. 8 Edw. I, no 23.

[45] Feet of F. Surr. Hil. 6 Edw. III.

[46] Chan. Inq. p.m. 17 Edw. III, no. 45. He held it of the men of Kingston for £3 18s. 3d. and suit of court.

[47] De Banco R. 577, m. 117. Manning and Bray's statement that Thomas Salaman had the manor in 1416 seems extremely doubtful. Unfortunately the rental they mention cannot now be consulted.

[48] Feet of F. Div. Co. 35 Edw. III, no. 75.

[49] She had received it by grant of Sir Peter de Braose, kt., and other feoffees in 1372.

[50] Chan. Inq. p.m. 7 Ric. II, no. 15.

[51] Ibid. 19 Ric. II, no. 7; see also Burke, *Dorm. and Ext. Peerages* (ed. 1883), 73.

[52] De Banco R. 576, m. 115; 577, m. 117. The transfers on Close, Hen. VI, pt. i, m. 224, 24 are by trustees.

[53] Feet of F. Surr. Mich. 7 Hen. IV.

[54] Manning and Bray, op. cit. i, 544.

[55] Chan. Inq. p.m. 15 Hen. VII, 14, 101.

[56] For a similar succession of the Dudleys to the Arderns, see Leigh Place in Leigh, Reigate Hundred.

in 1530, and this is repeated in a survey of 1608.[54] Dudley and Joan his wife still held in 1533, when they conveyed it to Lord Wentworth and others,[57] probably trustees for Thomas Duke of Norfolk. From him the king purchased it in order to annex it to the honour of Hampton Court.[58] During the reign of Elizabeth the manor was leased to various persons,[59] ultimately to Sir John Hill, who had a lease for forty years to expire in 1623.[60] After Hill's death his widow, Lady Hill, sold the remainder of her lease to Sir Dudley Carleton, created Baron Carleton of Imber Court in 1626 and Viscount Dorchester in 1628, to whom the king granted the manor in fee in 1630. He brought lime trees from the Hague to plant in the garden, and also improved the house, where he entertained the king and queen in 1630.[61] He died in 1632[62] and left the manor in his will to his nephew Sir Dudley Carleton.[63] The latter, who probably built the present house after designs furnished by Inigo Jones for his uncle, conveyed the estate to Edwin Knipe, merchant of London, who held it in 1669,[64] and conveyed it to Shem Bridges in 1672.[65] He died about 1711, leaving no issue, and was succeeded by his nephew Henry Bridges, who settled the manor with other estates on his niece Anne Bridges on her marriage with Arthur Onslow.[66] The latter, who resided at Imber Court, died in 1768, and in 1784 his son Lord Cranley sold the manor to George Porter. In 1791 Francis Ford purchased the estate,[67] and in 1793 conveyed it to Robert Taylor,[68] after whose decease in 1823 it passed to Sir Charles Sullivan, bart., in right of his wife, the only daughter of Mr. Taylor.[69] In 1861 the house and lands were sold to Charles Corbett,[69a] whose widow held them until her death in 1893. Her heirs and executors sold the house and park in 1899. The house is now again for sale ; the park is used for trotting races. Mr. Julian Corbett, son of the last lord, presented the manorial documents to the Surrey Archaeological Society.

In the reign of Edward III the manor was described as consisting of 'a capital messuage of no value, 120 acres of arable land, half of which may be sown every year, and is then worth £1 10s. ; the other half cannot be sown unless it is well tilled, and when left fallow is worth £1 for the pasturage ; 10 acres of meadow, valued at 10s. from the feast of Pentecost to the gule (that is, the first) of August, at other times of no value because it is in common ; rents of assize of free tenants, £3 14s. 0½d., 5 acres of wood valued· at £1 10s. for the underwood and 3s. 4d. for the pasturage.'[70] Early in the reign of Charles I a commission was issued for a survey of the manor of Imber. The annual value was rated at £18 6s. 8d., besides some small parcels of woodland worth £1 5s. 3d., and 3 acres not valued.[71] When

Lord Cranley sold the manor it included a capital mansion, other houses, and about 325 acres of land, all tithe-free.[72] A farm called Chapel Farm formed part of the Imber Court estate in 1632.[73] Imworth or Imber water-mill is mentioned in the different surveys of the manor.

In 1553 there were two tenants holding by copy of court roll who owed labour services.

Part of Ditton Common is known as Littleworth Common. The other parts are named after the other manors, Ditton and Weston, but no manor of Littleworth is known.

The church of ST. NICHOLAS con-
CHURCH sists of a chancel with north and south chapels and north vestry ; a nave with north and south aisles, a western tower, and a south porch.

The north wall of the chancel dates from the beginning of the 13th century, and part of a late-12th-century pillar piscina is evidence of earlier work. The north chapel was probably a 15th-century addition, and the north arcade of the nave is perhaps late 16th-century work. The broad and low tower is apparently of the 13th century, but all the rest of the church is modern, the nave having been widened on the south side.

The east window of the chancel is modern, of three trefoiled lights with geometrical tracery of late 13th-century design, and is set within the opening of an old window apparently of 14th-century date. On the north side of the chancel is a low four-centred arch of 15th-century date continuously moulded with two hollows, opening to the north chapel and designed to contain a tomb and perhaps to serve for the Easter sepulchre. Above this is a small lancet light, c. 1200, with a wide internal splay and semicircular rear arch and an external rebate. To the west is a two-centred arch of one slightly chamfered order, under which stands a fine but mutilated 15th-century monument. On the south are two bays of modern arcading opening to the south chapel. The chancel arch is of two chamfered orders, the outer continuous, the inner dying into flat responds ; it appears to be of no great age.

The north chapel has on the east a modern two-light window of similar design to the east window of the chancel, and like it set in an old opening. On the north is a modern door to the vestry and on the west the opening to the north aisle. The vestry is entirely modern and has two two-light windows, to east and north, and an external door on the north.

The south chapel is also quite modern and has a three-light window to the east, and two of two lights to the south, all of similar design to the chancel east window. On the west is a plain arch to the aisle.

[54] Surveys and Ct. R. in possession of Surr. Arch. Soc. The lands described in the surveys are in Long Ditton, Thames Ditton, and Molesey ; but *pertinentia* are generally mentioned in Godstone, Lingfield, Walkstead, Lagham, and Home. These outlying holdings in the Weald belong to a very ancient state of society (cf. Banstead and Ewell), but no mention of them is found before or after the grant to Robert Smyth.

[57] Feet of F. Div. Co. Mich. 25 Hen. VIII ; Recov. R. East. 25 Hen. VIII, rot. 357.

[58] Misc. Grants, 27 Hen. VIII.

[59] Feet of F. Surr. Mich. 10 & 11 Eliz. ; Pat. 10 Eliz. pt. iii ; Pat. 20 Eliz. pt. i.

[60] Land Rev. Misc. Bks. no. 198, fol. 96.

[61] Pat. 5 Chas. I, pt. v ; *Cal. S. P. Dom.* 1611–18, pp. 459, 596 ; *Hist. MSS. Com. Rep.* xii, App. pt. i, p. 414 ; information from Mr. Julian Corbett.

[62] Chan. Inq. p.m. (Ser. 2), ccclxv, 89.

[63] See S.P. Dom. Chas. I, ccclxiv, 15.

[64] Feet of F. Surr. Hil. 20 & 21 Chas. II.

[65] Ibid. Trin. 24 Chas. II.

[66] Ibid Hil. 10 Geo. I.

[67] Brayley, *Hist. of Surr.* ii, 415.

[68] Feet of F. Surr. East. 34 Geo. III.

[69] Brayley, *Hist. of Surr.* ii, 416.

[69a] The manorial rights were apparently sold to the owners of the manors of Weston and East Molesey. (Information from Mr. Julian Corbett.)

[70] Chan. Inq. p.m. 17 Edw. III, no. 45.

[71] Brayley, *Hist. of Surr.* ii, 415.

[72] Ibid. 416.

[73] Chan. Inq. p.m. (Ser. 2), ccclxv, 89.

3

59

The nave is of three bays. The arcade on the north, of 16th-century date, has no responds, the low three-centred arches of two chamfered orders dying into the surface of the east and west walls of the nave. The columns are octagonal with moulded capitals of slight projection and very plain bases. The south arcade is quite modern with octagonal columns, moulded capitals, and four-centred arches of two chamfered orders. The tower arch is plain 15th-century work of the full width of the tower, dying into the walls at the springing.

The north aisle is built of brick and has three large two-light stone-dressed untraceried windows to the north, with a similar one to the west. At the east is a door leading into a vestibule which has an external door and a staircase leading to a gallery running round two sides of the aisle.

The south aisle has two windows to the south, of three lights with tracery of late 13th-century detail, and the south door and the entrance of the south porch are designed in a style harmonizing with the windows, with shafted jambs and moulded two-centred heads. In the porch is a small door opening on to a stair, contained in a quarter-octagonal staircase, which leads to a gallery over the west of the aisle. In the west wall are two single trefoiled lights, above which, lighting the gallery, is a circular traceried window.

The tower is of three stages, the upper being of wood, weather boarded, on which is a small spire covered with lead. In the second and ground stages are small lights of 13th-century date with circular rear arches and wide internal splays. Externally the jambs and head have been replaced with brick, forming square-headed openings with wooden frames. The west door has been similarly treated.

The font is of early 12th-century date and is in the form of a modified cushion capital. The inverted lunettes of the faces are edged with a cable mould and have panels, in one of which occurs an Agnus Dei and in another a goat. The third has a star, and the fourth a cross with expanded arms and stem. At the angles are small projecting heads, two of which have been defaced. The circular stem has been recut and the base is modern. Under the two-centred arch between the chancel and the north chapel is a curious late 15th-century monument designed to contain two kneeling effigies. It is of two bays, with four-centred openings below a heavy panelled and embattled cornice, and has engaged shafts at the angles and middle of each side. At the north-east angle is the return of a panelled screen, or perhaps doorway, which formed part of the original design, but as the monument is clearly not in position nothing can be said of it. The carved details of leaves and flowers are good, but there is nothing to give a clue to the persons whom it commemorates.

There are a number of brasses. On the west wall of the north chapel is a plate with an arched head bearing the kneeling figures of a man in armour, his wife, six sons in civilian dress, and twelve daughters. The inscription begins : 'Here resten the bodyes of Erasm' fforde Esquyer sone and heyre of Walter fforde sometyme tresorer to Kynge Edward the iiijth in his warres at ye wynnyng of Barwyke' &c. The inscription gives the date of his death as 1533 and is also in memory of his wife 'Julyan' (Salford), who died in 1559. The arms are : Three lions rampant crowned ; quartering parted fessewise a lion rampant fretty.

A second shield shows the same coat impaling a fesse engrailed with three boars' heads thereon between three talbots, and beneath it 'Fforde and Salford,' and a third has the same impaling a cross engrailed within a border, and beneath it 'fforde and Legh.' On the north wall of the chancel is a brass to Robert Smyth, 1539, and Katherine (Blounte) his wife, 1549, who had four sons and three daughters. The arms are a fesse with three martlets thereon between three leopards' heads. Below is a brass to William Notte, 1576, and Elizabeth, his wife, daughter of the above Robert Smyth, 1587. The figures of the father, mother, and of fourteen sons and five daughters are shown. On the east wall of the nave is a brass to john Polsted, 1540, and his wife Anne Wheeler, who had four daughters, Anne, Jane, Elizabeth, and Julian, the last of whom erected the monument in 1582. The kneeling figures of the father, mother and children are shown, with two shields, one being Polsted, a bend between two molets with three trefoils on the bend and a chief with a pelican wounding itself between two trefoils ; and the second Polsted impaling a camel between three demi-catherine wheels, and on a chief a catherine wheel (for Wheeler). There is also a brass to the above Julian, 1586, and her two husbands, on the north wall of the north chapel ; the first was Cuthbert Blakeden, 1540, 'while he lyved Serjeant of the Confectionary to king Henry Theight,' by whom she had four daughters and two sons, the second, John Booth [ob. 1548], 'one of the ordynary gentleman ushers as well to the said King Henry theight ; as to his sonne Kyng Edward the vi,' by whom she had four daughters and one son. The figures are shown standing and the arms are : Ermine three lions rampant in a border engrailed (for Blakeden) ; and three boars' heads razed palewise (for Booth) ; also Polsted impaling Wheeler. Another brass on the east wall of the north aisle is to john Cheke, 1590, and his wife Isabel Seilearde, with the standing figures of the father, mother, and six sons. The arms are a cock, impaling (1) a chief ermine ; (2) a cross with a label of five points ; (3) three lions rampant ; (4) a lion rampant with a crescent for difference. There is also an inscription to Anne daughter of William Childe of East Sheen in the parish of Mortlake and county of Surrey, 1607 ; another (in Latin) is to Elizabeth (Hatton), 1608, wife of William Leygh. On the north wall of the north chapel is a marble monument and bust of Colonel Sidney Godolphin, Governor of Scilly and Auditor of Wales, 1732.

The tower contains six bells, all cast by Thomas Swain in 1753, except the fifth, which was cast in 1754.

The church plate consists of a chalice and cover paten of 1637, a paten of 1715 inscribed 'Ex dono Henrici Bridges, 1716,' a large flagon and almsdish made and dedicated to the church service in 1724, spoon strainer of 1807, and a modern almsdish.

The first book of registers contains mixed entries between 1663 and 1695, a second book has entries 1753 to 1778, a third appears to be a duplicate extending 1765 to 1773. There is a marriage book to 1781 and a printed marriage book, 1781 to 1812, also a book containing baptisms and burials 1781 to 1812.

THAMES DITTON CHURCH : THE FONT

ADVOWSON The date of the foundation of Thames Ditton Church is unknown. It was formerly one of the chapels belonging to Kingston parish, and was granted together with the advowson of Kingston to Merton Priory by Gilbert Norman, Sheriff of Surrey, founder of that house.[74] The canons retained the patronage till 1538.[75] After the Dissolution the advowson passed into private patronage till 1786, when it was bought by the Provost and Fellows of King's College, Cambridge, in whom it is still vested. William Speer, lord of the manor of Weston, presented in 1835.[76] Thames Ditton was separated from Kingston and made a perpetual curacy by Act of Parliament in 1769.[77]

The great tithes belonged to Kingston rectory; but were afterwards separated, for they were sold by Mr. Bridges to Mr. Onslow with Imber Court. Lord Onslow sold them in 1786. A part of them was ultimately bought by Mr. Taylor of Imber Court and passed with the manor.[78]

CHARITIES In 1720 Henry Bridges built ' six handsome brick houses ' and endowed them with £30 a year for poor old men and women.[78] Married couples are now allowed to occupy them. In 1670 Miss Elizabeth Hill left four others for widows or widowers, which were rebuilt in 1873 by subscriptions, and there are two others, founded by the Rt. Hon. W. W. F. Hume Dick and Helen his wife in 1873.

Smith's Charity is distributed as in other Surrey parishes. In 1703 William Hatton left a ' rugg ' every year for the poor wanting bedclothes (see Molesey), and in the same year he left £20 a year for the minister if approved by the inhabitants. In 1710 John Wicker left £2 a year for the poor in bread, and in 1735 Anne Whitfield left £3; in 1773 Mary Funge left £3, in 1776 Thomas Funge left £3, and in 1784 Josias Mitchener left £9 annually for the same object.

In 1724 ' a small close, the rent for the poor,' was returned to Bishop Willis. This seems to be lost.

A Church School was founded in 1860, taken over by a Board in 1881, and enlarged in 1890 and 1895.

An Infants' School founded as Church Schools in 1841 was taken over by the School Board in 1881 and enlarged in 1893.

WALTON ON THAMES

Waleton (xi cent.) ; Waletone and Walletone (xiii cent.) ; Waletone (xiv cent.) ; Waletone on Thames (xv cent.).

Walton on Thames is a village 5 miles south-west of Kingston, and the same distance south-east-by-east of Chertsey, on the Thames. It contains 6,701 acres of land and 158 of water, and measures nearly 6 miles from north to south and from 3 miles to 1 mile in breadth. The soil is river gravel and alluvium near the Thames and by the valley of the Mole, which river forms part of the eastern boundary of the parish while the Thames forms the northern boundary. Further south, where the ground rises to the higher level of St. George's Hill and the adjacent common, the soil is Bagshot sand. The scenery here is very picturesque. The hill is only 255 ft. above the sea, but it is of irregular form, singularly precipitous and broken in contour in places, and planted with a variety of fine conifers, rhododendrons, and other trees. The roads from London to Chertsey and from London to Guildford pass through the parish, which is intersected also by the main line of the London and South Western Railway. Walton Station is a mile from the body of the village.

Walton is now an Urban District under the Act of 1894, divided into the Hersham, Oatlands, and Walton Wards.

The neighbourhood of Walton on Thames is rich in ancient remains. Two cinerary urns have been found half a mile north of the station, and a neolithic flint knife or dagger.[1] Other neolithic flints have been found. An uninscribed gold British coin was found in the river,[2] and an Anglo-Saxon cinerary urn from Walton was exhibited at the Archaeological Institute in 1867.[3] At Oatlands was a large inclosure, variously described as a Roman or British camp, which was destroyed by the Earl of Lincoln in the 18th century when he was improving the park.[4] On St. George's Hill is a very considerable fortification. It covers 13½ acres on the highest part of the hill, and is the largest work of the kind in Surrey. The hill is now thickly planted, and covered with fern and brushwood, but the works are complete in circuit, though difficult to trace except in winter owing to the plantations.

The valleys of the Wey and the Mole approach each other closely on either side of the hill. Between the points where these two rivers fall into the Thames there was an ancient ford, Coway Stakes, opposite Halliford, and anyone approaching the ford from Surrey or coming across it from Middlesex would of necessity pass close under this fortification. Coway Stakes Ford has been often taken to be the place where Caesar crossed the Thames on his second invasion.[5]

On the other side of St. George's Hill, in the grounds of Silvermere, was a round barrow, removed when the house was built about 1830. In it were three cinerary hand-made urns, with bones and charcoal in them, about 18 in. high, 16 in. wide at the greatest diameter, and 13 in. at the lip. One of them was preserved at Silvermere.[6] Four or five British urns were found about 1900 in excavations on the Apps Court estate.

Near Walton Bridge, and removed when the bridge was rebuilt in 1750, were several barrows. ' Spear

[74] Leland, *Coll.* i, 67.
[75] *Surr. Arch. Coll.* vii, 222. It is not mentioned in the *Valor Ecclesiasticus*, and in the Ministers' Accounts of 1540, roll 32 Hen. VIII. Aug. Off. (Dugdale, *Mon.* vi, 248), the following entry occurs in the list of the possessions of the priory : ' Kingston rector. Non respond quia annex' honori de Hampton Court.'
[76] Inst. Bks. P.R.O. 1835.
[77] In 1650 Sir Dudley Carleton quitclaimed to Edward Knipe the chancel of the church of Thames Ditton ; Feet of F. Surr. East. 1650.
[78] Manning and Bray, op. cit. i, 462.
[79] Bishop Willis's Visit. 1724.
[1] *V.C.H. Surr.* i, 253.
[2] Ibid.
[3] Ibid. 268.
[4] Manning and Bray, op. cit. ii, 758.
[5] See *V.C.H. Surr.* iv, article on Roman Remains.
[6] Brayley, op. cit. ii, 368.

heads and earthen vessels' are said to have been found in them.[6a]

Mr. Samuel Dicker of Walton first built a wooden bridge, opened in 1750, at his own expense, obtaining an Act to enable him to do so and levy tolls.[7] In 1780 his nephew, Mr. Dicker Sanders, obtained another Act[8] to build a stone and brick bridge with additional tolls. The present iron bridge was opened in 1863, and is wholly in Shepperton parish. The story is that the river used to run (where it still runs in flood time) under the small arches on the Surrey side approach to the bridges. Probably the river has altered its course ; for, according to geologists, it used to run where the Broadwater in Oatlands Park is now.

In 1516 Henry VIII granted licence to Robert Nortriche and William Fleyter, constables, and the inhabitants of Walton on Thames, to hold a fair on

William Lilly the astrologer, famous in his day, lived in Walton parish at Hersham. On his death in 1681, he left his house to a son of Bulstrode White-locke, who had befriended him. john Bradshaw the regicide lived in Walton, in a house still partly pre-served. Admiral Sir George Rodney was born at Walton in 1718. His father Captain Rodney, and General Macartney, who killed the Duke of Hamilton, were both living in Walton in 1724.[9]

The Inclosure Act in 1800[18] inclosed 3,117 acres of land in the Walton manors, including parts of Chertsey, and 475 acres of arable common fields.

In the village is a Wesleyan chapel of red brick with stone dressings, with a tower and spire, built in 1887. The Baptist chapel was built in 1901.

The Public Hall, in High Street, was built by Mrs. Sassoon in 1879.

WALTON ON THAMES MANOR HOUSE

Tuesday and Wednesday in Easter week and another on 3 and 4 October in each year.[9] In 1601 a complaint was made of the increase in the number of vagrants in Surrey ; it was reported that at the Easter week fair at Walton no less than eighteen such vagabonds assem-bled together, and were heard engaging in treasonable talk about the death of the Earl of Essex,[10] who had been beheaded for high treason a few weeks earlier. .

The slopes of St. George's Hill were the scene of an interesting development of the Socialism of the 17th century, when a party of Levellers took possession of the ground in 1649 and began to cultivate it for roots and beans. They encroached upon the waste of the manor of Cobham, and the commoners rose against them and drove them away before the Commonwealth Government had had time to act, though Sir Thomas Fairfax as commander in chief had begun an interference which was as illegal as the acts of the Levellers themselves.[11]

The Metropolitan Convalescent Institution for patients from the London Hospitals was built on a site given by the Earl of Ellesmere in 1840 and enlarged in 1862 and 1868. It accommodates 300 patients, and is supported by voluntary contributions. There is a public cemetery at Walton.

The Metropolitan Water Board have reservoirs in the parish.

A School Board was formed in 1878. A pre-viously existing school was enlarged in 1881. The infant school was built in 1884.

Ashley Park is the seat of Mr. joseph Sassoon, J.P. The estate was one of those annexed to the honour of Hampton Court by Act of Parliament,[14] and the house was no doubt originally of about that date. It was of red brick, built in the form of an H. It was alienated by the Crown, and became the property of Christopher Villiers, Earl of Anglesey, brother to the first Villiers Duke of Buckingham. He died in 1624,

[6a] J. Douglas, *Naenia Brit.* 94.
[7] 20 Geo. II, cap. 22.
[8] 20 Geo. III, cap. 32.
[9] L. *and* P. *Hen. VIII*, ii (1), 2278.

[10] *Cecil MSS.* (Hist. MSS. Com.), xi, 170.
[11] See Whitelocke, *Memorials of English Affairs,* Apr. 1649, and *V.C.H. Surr.* i, 421–2.

[12] Bishop Willis's Visit. 1724.
[13] 39–40 Geo. III, cap. 86.
[14] 31 Hen. VIII, cap. 5.

WALTON-ON-THAMES BRIDGE

STOKE D'ABERNON CHURCH : NAVE LOOKING EAST

and his widow, who had remarried, died in 1662. The property then passed through several hands; Viscount Shannon bought it in 1718, and during his tenure the Rt. Hon. W. Pulteney (created Earl of Bath in 1742) lived there.[15] Lord Shannon died in 1740. He married Grace Senhouse, and their daughter Grace, Countess of Middlesex, died without issue and left Ashley Park to her cousins Colonel John Stephenson and his sisters in succession. The last of these died in 1786, when the property went to Sir Henry Fletcher, bart., another cousin. His son Sir Henry Fletcher, bart., very considerably altered the house.

Walton Grove, standing in a small park, is the seat of Mrs. Cababe; Holly Lodge of Mrs. Dyer.

At the northern end of the Manor Road is a red-brick house with brick pilasters forming a Tuscan order on two sides of the building. It is dated 1732.

Hersham (Heverisham) is an ecclesiastical parish formed in 1851 from the southern part of Walton-on Thames. It is, roughly, the part of the original parish south of the London and South Western Railway line. A chapel of ease (Holy Trinity) was built of yellow brick in Anglo-Norman style in 1839. The present church of St. Peter was built by Mr. J. L. Pearson, R.A., in 1887. It is of brick and stone in 13th-century style. It has a nave and aisles, of five arcades, chancel, transepts, and a western tower and spire. The site was given by Lieut.-Col. Terry of Burvale.

There is a Congregational church in the village built in 1839, restored in 1858, and enlarged in 1889.

An infant school was built when the first chapel of ease was opened in 1839. The present school was built in 1863 and enlarged in 1882.

The parish hall of Hersham was built by a company in 1885 and enlarged in 1892.

Pain's Hill is the residence of Mr. Alexander Cushney. It was celebrated as one of the earliest examples of natural landscape gardening on a large scale. It was laid out by the Hon. Charles Hamilton, youngest son of James sixth Earl of Abercorn, Receiver-General of Minorca 1743–58. The extensive grounds extend also into the parishes of Cobham and Wisley, and owe much to their natural position on the slopes of the high ground about St. George's Hill above the Mole Valley. The present house was built by the next owner Benjamin Bond Hopkins, who died in 1794. A later owner, 1804–21, was the Earl of Carhampton, who as Colonel Luttrell had opposed Wilkes in the Middlesex election.

Burwood Park, the seat of the Misses Askew, was rebuilt before 1809 by Sir John Frederick, bart., M.P. for Surrey, who owned it from 1783 to 1825. It had belonged to a family named Latton, the earliest of whom to come into Surrey was John Latton, steward of the manor of Richmond, 1694. He for a time held the manor of Esher and died 1727. His arms, Party argent and sable a saltire ermines and ermine counterchanged, used to be in a window taken from the old house. Burwood House is the seat of Mary Louisa Countess of Ellesmere; Silvermere of Mr. Archibald Seth-Smith; Burvale of Mr. J. B. Heath; Burhill Park is now used as a golf club.

Oatlands Park is an ecclesiastical parish formed in 1869 out of the north-western part of Walton on Thames. The church of St. Mary was built as a chapel of ease in 1861. It is of stone in 13th-century style, with a chancel, nave, aisles, south porch, and bell-turret. There are fourteen memorial windows, a marble pulpit, and a marble reredos set up as a memorial to the Rev. G. B. Watson, vicar 1885–7.

The Working Men's Club was built in 1884 on a site presented by Mr. F. B. Money-Coutts, J.P., and the parish room in 1887.

The school was built in 1882.

The old palace at Oatlands, acquired for the Crown by Henry VIII, was in Weybridge parish, and with the manor is described under Weybridge, but the greater part of the land was in Walton.

Henry Pelham Clinton, ninth Earl of Lincoln, extended the park and laid out the grounds in 1747 and the following years, when Woburn Park, Weybridge, Pain's Hill, and Oatlands were considered the finest collection of experiments in a romantic style of landscape gardening in England. The Duke of York, son of George III, resided here from 1791 to his death in 1827, and he and his duchess were extremely popular in the neighbourhood. She died here 6 August 1820 and is buried in Weybridge Church. A monument by Chantrey was placed there to her, and a column was erected to her memory on Weybridge Green by the inhabitants in 1822. The park was sold in lots for gentlemen's houses in the middle of the 19th century, and now forms a residential neighbourhood. The house is converted into the Oatlands Park Hotel. Foxholes is the seat of Miss Martineau; Templemere of Lt.-General Sir Arthur Lyttelton-Annesley.

In the time of Edward the Confessor **MANORS** Azor held *WALTON* Manor, with a mill, meadow land, woods, &c. William the Conqueror granted it to Edward of Salisbury, ancestor of the Earls of Salisbury. It passed as part of the dowry of his daughter Maud to Humphrey de Bohun, nicknamed 'Humphrey with the beard.'[16] Humphrey son of Humphrey and Maud married Margery eldest daughter of Miles Earl of Hereford. His grandson Henry was created Earl of Hereford in 1199, and this manor remained in the tenure of the Bohuns, Earls of Hereford,[17] until 1373, when Humphrey de Bohun, Earl of Hereford and Essex, died seised of it, leaving two daughters, Eleanor and Mary, his co-heirs.[18] Eleanor married Thomas of Woodstock, Duke of Gloucester. Mary became the wife of Henry of Bolingbroke, eldest son of John of Gaunt, who obtained the manor of Walton as part of her dower, and was created Duke of Hereford in 1397. Mary died in 1394.[19] After Richard II was deposed Bolingbroke ascended the throne by the title of Henry IV. The manor descended to his grandson, Henry VI, who in 1422 as-

Bohun, Earl of Hereford. *Azure a bend argent between two cotises and six lions or.*

15 Bp. Willis's Visit. 1724.
16 V.C.H. Surr. i, 324b.
17 See Feet of F. Div. Co. Hil. 54 Hen.

III, no. 39; Chan. Inq. p.m. 11 Edw. III (2nd nos.), no. 50; 37 Edw. III (1st nos.), no. 10.

18 Chan. Inq. p.m. 46 Edw. III (1st nos.), no. 10.
19 Doyle, English Baronage, ii, 166, 316.

signed it to Katherine his mother as part of her dower.[20]

Queen Katherine died at Bermondsey Abbey on 4 January 1437. In the same year the king, having formerly granted the lordship of Walton on Thames to john Penycok for a term of years at a yearly rent of £25, reduced that sum to £15, and extended the grant to the term of Penycok's life.[21] After Edward IV had obtained the crown Parliament bestowed upon him the personal estates of Henry VI, who died a prisoner in the Tower in 1471. Henry's only son Prince Edward being dead, and none of the other three sons of Henry IV by Mary Bohun having left issue, the inheritance of the Bohun estates legally devolved on Henry Stafford, Duke of Buckingham, who was descended from Eleanor the sister of Mary Bohun. King Edward, however, retained possession of the property.[22] On his death Buckingham espoused the cause of Richard Duke of Gloucester, and aided him so effectually that Richard, a few days after his accession, signed an order for the livery of the manor in question to Buckingham.[23] The duke's subsequent rebellion against the king, however, ended in his own

Circa 1500.
Later & Modern.
Scale of Feet.

PLAN OF MANOR HOUSE, WALTON ON THAMES

destruction, and neither he nor his family ever obtained Walton, which remained in the hands of the Crown,[24] and passed from Richard III to Henry VII.[25] The Tudor sovereigns granted leases of the manor of Walton to various tenants. In 1589 Queen Elizabeth granted to Katherine West, willow, wood, herbage, and pannage in Kingesridons Coppice, parcel of the manor,[26] and on 11 july 1593 John Woulde received a grant from the queen of the manor, together with the capital messuage known as Dorney House.[27] In 1612 Francis Drake of Esher had a lease for lives from James I.[28] Twenty years later Charles I granted the manor to Sir Henry Browne and John Cliffe (with the exception of such lands belonging to the manor as had been inclosed in Oatlands Park, certain rents anciently paid to the manor, and lands in Walton which had been annexed to the honour of Hampton Court), to hold in fee at a rent of £22 10s. 11¼d. In 1650 this rent was conveyed by Thomas Coke and others, trustees for the sale of the fee-farm and other

rents of the late king, to William Lilly of St. Clement Danes, gentleman, the famous astrologer.[29] In 1672 Francis Drake was lord of the manor,[30] but whether he held it under the lease above mentioned, or had purchased the fee-simple, is uncertain. In 1698 Sir Matthew Andrews and his wife Ann conveyed the manor to james justice and john Phillips, probably trustees,[31] for the same year William Robinson held his court there.[32] The manor descended to Sara wife of john Bonsey ; they jointly held their court at Walton in 1714.[33] Mr. Bonsey dying shortly afterwards, his widow married John Palmer,[34] who survived her and became owner of the estate,[35] which she settled on him. By his will, dated 1758, he gave this manor and that of Walton Leigh to Thomas and john, the sons of his brother Richard Palmer, and to Henry son of Henry Palmer. Henry's share descended to his daughter Frances, who married Thomas Hurst. His son, Palmer Hurst, sold it to the Duke of York previous to the passing of the Inclosure Act in 1800. The duke dying in 1827, his interest in the manor was sold to Edward H. B. Hughes, the purchaser of Oatlands. The two-thirds held by Thomas and john Palmer came into the possession of their nephew Richard Palmer, D.D., chaplain of the House of Commons from 1765 to 1769 ; and on his death passed to his son the Rev. john Palmer of Adisham, co. Kent. It was next held by Gillias Payne Palmer, but passed from him under a mortgage into the hands of William Clark, solicitor, of Chertsey,[36] and the present lord is Mr. Henry Edwards Paine of the firm of Paine, Brettell & Porter, solicitors, Chertsey.

The Manor Road, forming a loop from Walton village to the river, incloses the old Manor House, at the north end about 100 yards from the river, a fine specimen of 15th-century building, which has been called Bradshaw's house, but was never owned by him. It consists of a central hall running approximately north and south, with projecting wings at each end, built of timber framing originally filled in with brick and lath-and-plaster. The walls of the hall appear to have been thickened with modern brick in order to carry an inserted floor, and small additions of modern brick have also been made. This floor has in modern times been taken away, restoring the hall to its original design ; the wings have each an upper story which projects over the ground floor. The hall has a large brick chimney-breast in the west wall, and in the south wing is a larger stack which appears to have served the kitchen fireplace. In the north wing is a corresponding chimney-stack, and a modern one has been inserted in the northern room.

[20] Duchy of Lanc. Misc. Bks. vol. 18 (pt. 2), p. 49.
[21] Ibid. vol. 18, p. 96.
[22] Feet of F. Div. Co. Trin. 15 Edw. IV, no. 102.
[23] Dugdale, Baronage, 168, from the Stafford archives.
[24] Duchy of Lanc. Misc. Bks. vol. 20, p. 87d.
[25] Ibid. vol. 21, p. 184.
[26] Pat. 32 Eliz. pt. xii.
[27] Pat. 35 Eliz. pt. iv.
[28] Pat. 9 Jas. I, pt. xxviii. Drake by his will, dated 21 May 1603, left to his wife 'the Manor and demesne of Walton if the lease shall last so long,' with remainder to his son Francis Drake ; P.C.C. Harte, fol. 2.
[29] Manning and Bray, Hist. of Surr. ii, 763.
[30] Feet of F. Surr. Mich. 1672.
[31] Ibid. Hil. 9 Will. and Mary.
[32] Ct. R. quoted by Manning and Bray, Hist. of Surr. ii, 763.
[33] Ibid. ut supra.
[34] Feet of F. Div. Co. Hil. 3 Geo. I.
[35] Feet of F. Surr. Mich. 12 Geo. I.
[36] Brayley, Hist. of Surr. ii, 316 ; Recov. R. Hil. 1 & 2 Geo. IV, rot. 42.

The chief entrance is from the east by a wooden doorway at the north end of the hall, which has continuous mouldings, carved spandrels and a square head ; another door is opposite this one, but has been altered. From this a stair leads to the upper floor of the north wing. Each wall has a double tier of windows, with wood frames and mullions, but, as in the rest of the house, none appear to be original. A large tie-beam with a king-post spans the hall in the middle, and the roof is partly ceiled.

At the south end of the hall are the screens and gallery, the latter carried by four moulded posts probably originally filled in with panelling. Access to this was by a stair from the floor of the hall on the west side, where there is an opening in the framing which crosses the front of the gallery. From the gallery two doors open to the upper floor of the south wing. At both ends of the passage through the screens are the usual external doors, but these are only reproductions of old work.

From the passage two other doors open into the two ground floor rooms of the south wing, which occupy the normal position of the kitchen and buttery, the large fireplace on the south wall of the wing being partly blocked up, but the traces of decoration in these rooms, a large moulded post in the framing on each side of the east room and moulded joists in the ceiling, and some leaf carving on the frame of the window of the west room, seem to show that they were designed for living rooms and not domestic offices. It is evident, however, that the building has been considerably altered at various times.

The north wing is entered by a door at the northeast angle of the hall, with a moulded wood frame, and contains three rooms on the ground floor, and in the north wall a blocked window with hollow-chamfered wood mullions, which is possibly one of the original lights.

In 1086 Richard of Tonbridge, lord of Clare, held the manor of Walton, later known as *WALTON LEIGH*, which Erding had held of King Edward. There were on the manor a church, a mill, and a fishery.[37]

The overlordship continued with the Clares until 1314, when the last Gilbert de Clare died seised of it,[38] and it then seems to have been divided among his heiresses. In 1324 the manor was said to be held of Hugh Audley, husband of Margaret, one of the sisters of Gilbert.[39] In 1349 Hugh le Despenser, son of Eleanor, another of the heiresses, died seised of one-fourth of a knight's fee in Walton,[40] and this descended to Isabella Countess of Warwick, daughter of Thomas le Despenser, who held it at her death in 1439.[41] Her share probably escheated to the Crown after the attainder of her heir 'the King maker' in 1471. The descendants of Elizabeth, the third heiress, apparently also had a share, for in 1422 the manor was

said to be held of Edmund Earl of March, who was grandson of Edmund Mortimer, Earl of March, lord of Clare in right of his wife Philippa, daughter of Elizabeth, granddaughter of Elizabeth the heiress, as of his castle of Clare.[42] He died without issue in 1425, when his inheritance descended to his sister's son Richard, afterwards Duke of York, whose son became Edward IV, when this part of the overlordship came to the Crown.

Undertenants appear at the beginning of the 13th century, when half a knight's fee in Walton was held

MORTIMER. *Barry or and azure a chief or with two pales between two gyrons azure and a scutcheon argent over all.*

by Geoffrey de Cruce,[43-4] whose daughter Avelina, wife of Roger Leigh or de Legh, claimed view of frankpledge and assize of bread and ale within the manor.[47] She died seised of it in 1299, Joan described as widow of Nicholas de Cruce then being dowered in one-third of the manor.[48]. There were twenty-six free tenants, and the manor was valued at £10 12s. 7¾d. It descended to John Leigh, son of Avelina, who conveyed a moiety of this manor to Walter de Langton, Bishop of Coventry and Lichfield, the famous statesman, for his life ; the bishop obtained from Edward I a grant of free warren there.[49] He died in 1322,[50] and the lands reverted to John Leigh, who died seised of the whole manor in 1325.[51] In 1346 john Leigh is mentioned as holding the manor of the honour of Clare ;[52] but his mother Margaret, who after the death of his father had married Robert de Kendale, had possession of it for life ; she died in 1348.[53] In 1410 john Leigh of Shell or Shellegh (Shelley), co. Essex, is mentioned as holding the manor.[54] He was probably the john Leigh who in 1422 died seised of the manor of Leigh's Court, as it was then called. A court baron belonged to the manor.[55] From him it passed to his son Thomas, and so descended eventually to Giles Leigh, great-grandson of Thomas, who inherited it in 1509. It was then held by the service of half a knight's fee in fee-tail.[56] In 1537 Henry VIII purchased the manor of Leigh's Court from Giles Leigh, and annexed it to the honour of Hampton Court.[57] The manor remained vested in the Crown till late in the 18th century, and was granted on lease from time to time to different persons.[58] In the 18th century leases were generally granted to the owners of the manor of Walton on Thames, and thus the manor of Walton Leigh came into the possession of the Palmer family.[59] Mr. Palmer Hurst, who held one-third of the manor, sold his share in 1800 to the Duke of York. The other two-thirds belonged to the Rev. Richard Palmer,

[37] *V.C.H. Surr.* i, 317b.
[38] Chan. Inq. p.m. 8 Edw. II, no. 68.
[39] Ibid. 18 Edw. II, no. 71.
[40] Ibid. 23 Edw. III, pt. ii (1st nos.), no. 169.
[41] Ibid. 18 Hen. VI, no. 3. The holding was half a knight's fee in the *Testa de Nevill.*
[42] Ibid. 1 Hen. VI, no. 7.
[43-4] *Testa de Nevill* (Rec. Com.), 219, 221.

[47] *Plac. de Quo Warr.* (Rec. Com.), 744.
[48] Nicholas may here be an error for Geoffrey, otherwise there must have been a Nicholas holding previous to Geoffrey.
[49] Chart. R. 28 Edw. I, m. 10.
[50] Chan. Inq. p.m. 18 Edw. II, no. 71 ;
[51] Chan. Inq. p.m. 18 Edw. II, no. 71.
[52] Close, 20 Edw. III, pt. ii, m. 12.
[53] Chan. Inq. p.m. 21 Edw. III (1st nos.), no. 19.

[54] Close, 11 Hen. IV, m. 16.
[55] Chan. Inq. p.m. 1 Hen. IV, no. 7.
[56] Ibid. (Ser. 2), xxiv, 47.
[57] *Hist. MSS. Com. Rep.* viii, App. ii, 236 ; Pat 22 Jas. I, pt. ii, no. 3 ; Feet of F. Surr. East. 30 Hen. VIII ; Com. Pleas D. Enr. Hil. 29 Hen. VIII, m. 13 d.
[58] See *Cal. S.P. Dom.* 1623-5, p. 439 ; 1628-9, p. 223 ; 1661-2, pp. 419, 562 ; 1663-4, p. 41.
[59] See Feet of F. Div. Co. Hil. 3 Geo. I.

D.D., and descended to his son the Rev. John Palmer. On the sale of the Crown lands, which had been transferred to the Duke of York under an Act of 1804, the entire manor of Walton Leigh became vested in Edward H. B. Hughes.[60]

Early in the reign of Henry VIII a quarrel took place between certain fishermen of Walton and Giles Leigh, lord of the manor of Walton Leigh. The fishermen, Thomas Brewer, john Newman, and john and Richard Albroke, with others, claimed that they and their forefathers had been used to fish in the king's water of Thames beside Walton time out of mind. But Giles Leigh, ' by the sinister council of John Carleton, man of law and bailly there,' claimed a several water and fishing there of half a mile. Accompanied by certain persons armed with swords and bucklers he riotously came to Brewer's boats and took away his great salmon net. At other times he took from Brewer certain engines called ' clere weles ' for catching roach and dace ; and finally went to law with him and the two Albrokes for fishing in his water. Giles was non-suited, but he ' continued in his malicious mind,' and finally gave information which caused Robert Bawce, farmer of the king's moiety of Walton weir, to descend upon the luckless fishermen and ' uncharitably to vex them by privy seals and otherwise ' for infringing upon the royal rights, driving them at last to appeal for justice.[61]

APPS (Ebsa, xi cent.), which now forms part of the parish of Walton on Thames, was originally a separate vill. In 675 Frithwald of Surrey and Bishop Erkenwald are said to have granted five ' mansas ' there to Chertsey Abbey,[62] and this grant was renewed by Edward the Confessor when he restored its lost property to that monastery.[63] After the Conquest Richard de Tonbridge acquired some land in the manor,[64] or perhaps the whole manor, which was certainly afterwards held of his successors. The account of the matter given in Domesday is as follows :—' The same Richard has six hides in the manor of Ebsa which Abbot Wulfwold [of Chertsey] delivered to him in augmentation of Waleton, as Richard's homagers say. But the men of the hundred say that they have never seen the King's writ or livery officer who had given him seisin thereof. Nine thegns held this land [under Edward the Confessor] and they could seek for it and for themselves what lord they pleased.'[65]

A certain Picot held two separate half-hides of Richard de Tonbridge, and there was also half a hide held by a villein, for which he had previously paid rent to the homagers, but which he then held of the king.[66] This last half-hide appears in the *Testa de Nevill* as held of the king in free alms by Ralph Blundell, William son of Gunnild, William son of Gilbert, and Osbert Malherbe by the service of brewing and distributing beer for the benefit of the souls of Kings of England on All Souls' Day. In the escheats

in the same record the same tenure is in the hands of William le Fraunkeleyn, Osbert Malherbe, Osbert Blundus, and Matilda, a widow.[67] In 1318 this land belonged to Hawisia de Hautot, and was said to form part of the manor of Apps Court.[68]

The overlordship of the Clare lands descended after the death of Gilbert de Clare in 1314 to the Despensers,[69] and subsequently to Isabella Countess of Warwick, daughter of Thomas le Despenser. It probably escheated to the Crown after the attainder of Warwick ' the Kingmaker ' in 1471.[70]

Part of the Clare lands were held in mesne lord-ship in the early 13th century by the D'Abernons. Gilbert D'Abernon in or about 1235 granted to jane widow of Engelram D'Abernoun all his interest in half a knight's fee in Apps.[71] John D'Abernon appears as mesne lord of lands in the manor in 1318,[72] and in 1361 the manor was said to be held of Sir William Croyser,[73] husband of Elizabeth, daughter of William D'Abernon. It descended to his son William, after whose death it was held by his wife, Edith,[74] and the mesne lordship continued with the lords of Stoke D'Abernon until as late as 1546.[75] Other lands in the manor were held of various lords,[76] so that it appears to have been a consolidation of several holdings.

These various lands, forming the manor of Apps, were held as sub-tenant by Hawisia de Hautot, wife of Ralph le Hever, at her death in 1318. Thomas de Hever, her son and heir, succeeded her.[77] His daughter Margaret married Oliver de Brocas, who held the manor of Apps in his wife's right.[78] john Brocas, his son, succeeded him, and died without issue, leaving as heir Edward St. john, kt., lord of ' Wylde-brugge,' son of joan sister of Thomas Hever.[79] The manor was mortgaged under a statute staple for 1,000 marks to John Campden and others, who entered on possession. This probably accounts for a certain Bernard Brocas remitting all right in the manor in 1393 to John Nekelin and others.[80] Edward St. John therefore never seems to have been in possession. In 1418 the manor was held under the Croysers by John Pegays and William atte Field, probably feoffees.[81] In 1454 Ralph Agmondesham, whose family belonged to Row-barnes and East Horsley, and his wife Millicent[82] were tenants, and it continued in a branch of this family for some time.

In 1541 it was in the hands of john Agmondesham and Eleanor his wife,[83] and in 1546 John Agmondesham died seised of the manor, which he had settled on his wife, who survived him.[84] He was succeeded by Francis, his son and heir,

AGMONDESHAM. *Ar-gent a cheveron azure between three boars' heads sable with three cing-foils or on the cheveron.*

[60] Brayley, *Hist. of Surr.* ii, 318.
[61] Star Chamber Proc. Hen. VIII, bdle. 18, no. 79.
[62] B.M. Cott. MS. Vitell. A. xiii, fol. 22*b*.
[63] Ibid. fol. 50*b*.
[64] *Surr. Arch. Coll.* xv, 17 note.
[65] *V.C.H. Surr.* i, 317*b*.
[66] Ibid. 318*a*.
[67] *Testa de Nevill* (Rec. Com.), 225, 227.
[68] Chan. Inq. p.m. 12 Edw. II, no. 1.
[69] Ibid. 23 Edw. III, pt. ii (1st nos.),

no. 169 ; 49 Edw. III, pt. ii (1st nos.), no. 46.
[70] Ibid. 18 Hen. VI, no. 3.
[71] B.M. Add. Chart. 5562.
[72] Chan. Inq. p.m. 12 Edw. II, no. 17.
[73] Ibid. 17 Edw. III (1st nos.), no. 7.
[74] Ibid. 3 Hen. V, no. 17. See also Coram Rege R. Mich. 7 Hen. VII, m. 16 (Surr.).
[75] See Chan. Inq. p.m.(Ser. 2), lxxxv,65.
[76] Ibid. 1 Ric. II, no. 4.

[77] Ibid. 12 Edw. II, no. 17.
[78] Ibid. 17 Edw. III (1st nos.), no. 7.
[79] Chan. Inq. p.m. 1 Ric. II, no. 41 ; 2 Ric. II, no. 19.
[80] Close, 17 Ric. II, m. 31d.
[81] Chan. Inq. p.m. 6 Hen. V, no. 30. See also Feud. Aids for 1422.
[82] Feet of F. Surr. Hil. 38 Hen. VI.
[83] Ibid. Div. Co. East. 33 Hen. VIII.
[84] Chan. Inq. p.m. (Ser. ii), lxxxv, 65.

who in 1547 sold the manor to William Hamond, senior.[83] From him it passed to his son William, and he sold it in 1565 to Thomas Brend.[84] Thomas Brend and his son Nicholas in their turn sold the manor in 1584 to Robert Benne, citizen and iron-monger of London,[87] but it would appear that Benne had for ten years previously had some sort of hold over the property.[88] From him in 1592 it was bought by Cuthbert Blackden ;[89] and in 1602 Robert Blackden and his wife and Elizabeth Black-den conveyed the manor to Francis Leigh,[90] created a baronet by James I. He died in 1625,[91] and the estate descended to his son Francis, who subsequently became Baron Dunsmore and in 1644 Earl of Chichester. At his death in 1653 the property came into the hands of Thomas Wriothesley, Earl of Southampton, who had married Elizabeth daughter and co-heir of Francis. Thomas had by her four daughters, one of whom, Elizabeth, married Joceline, Earl of Northumberland, and after his death in 1670, Ralph, Earl, and later Duke, of Montagu.[92] He died in 1708–9, and was succeeded by his son John, Duke of Montagu, who died without surviving male issue in 1749.[93] In 1757 the manor was in the possession of Jeremiah Brown, whose daughter carried it in marriage to Jeremiah Hodges.[94] A descendant of his, Colonel Hodges, sold the manor in 1802 to Edmund Hill ;[95] he bequeathed it to John Hamborough, after whose death it was sold by the trustees of his will to Richard Sharpe.[96] Robert Gill bought it before 1867. Mrs. Gill occupied the house after her death. It was sold in 1898–9 to the Southwark and Vauxhall Water Company, who pulled down the house, and excavated the whole estate for a reservoir. A barrel of ale, and a quarter of corn made into bread, were still in the 19th century distributed annually to the poor by the owners of the property on All Souls' Day in respect of the customary tenure.[97] The Water Company tried to evade the tenure, but on petition of the inhabitants the Charity Commissioners sanctioned a scheme in 1903, by which the interest of £200 paid by the Water Board was vested in trustees for the use of the poor of Walton and Molesey.

In 1639 Francis Dunsmore received licence to inclose 150 acres of land, parcel of the manor of Apps Court, for a park.

The estate formerly called ASSHLEES, now known as ASHLEY PARK, was in 1433 in the hands of Joan widow of Robert Constable, who held it of the Crown. From her it descended to her son William Constable.[98] It consisted at that time of 12 acres of land, 4 acres of meadow, and half an acre of wood. Henry VIII bought out the tenant in order to annex it to the honour of Hampton Court.[100] In 1625 James I granted Ashley to Henry Gibb, together with the

manor of Walton Leigh and certain lands in Walton Mead.[101] The Countess of Anglesey, who married secondly Benjamin Weston, son of Lord Treasurer Weston, the first Earl of Portland, lived here and was buried in Walton Church in 1662.[102] In 1663 the estate was held by Henry, Lord Arundell of Wardour. Sir Richard Pine, Lord Chief Justice of Ireland, died here in 1710.[108] In 1718 it was bought by Richard Boyle, Viscount Shannon, who made considerable additions to the house and park. A fine monument to him is in the church. The Countess of Middlesex, his daughter by his second wife, Grace Senhouse, owned it, and died in 1763, leaving it to Colonel Stephen-son, son of Jane Senhouse, her mother's elder sister. After his death and that of his three sisters without issue, it came to Sir Henry Fletcher, bart., son of Isabel Senhouse, younger sister of Grace Senhouse. Sir Henry Fletcher was M.P. for Cumberland from 1768 until his death in 1807. He was succeeded by his son Sir Henry, who died in 1821, when the manor descended to Sir Henry, third baronet, who died in 1851. In the time of his son Sir Henry, fourth baronet, the property was sold.[104] It now belongs to Mr. J. S. Sassoon, J.P. Ashley Park is noted for the size and beauty of its trees. The house is believed to have been built in the reign of Henry VIII.

The estate known as BURWOOD, at one time in the possession of Corpus Christi College, Oxford, was demised by the president and fellows of that college to John Carleton. From him it was purchased by Henry VIII in 1540.[106] The family of Drake, who held the bishop's manor in Esher (q.v.), lived at Burwood,[107] and Mr. Latton, who sold the manor to the Duke of Newcastle, retained Burwood, where he died in 1777.[108] The arms of Latton used to be in the window of the house.[109] Later it came into the hands of the Frederick family, one of whom, late in the 18th century, built a large house there, and greatly increased the area of the park.[110] It is now the property of the Misses Askew.

Hersham contained a manor known as MORE-HALL alias SYLKESMORE alias SOUTHWOOD. There is a mention of a court held at Hersham in 1272 by Reginald de Imworth and Matilda his wife,[111] which may indicate that he was then lord of the manor. When Henry VIII built Nonsuch Palace as many as eighty loads of timber were obtained from Southwood, or the South Woods, for that purpose.[112] In 1540 Henry VIII purchased from John Carleton the manor of Morehall alias Sylkesmore in Hersham, together with lands and woods in Bur-wood and Hatch in Hersham.[113] The manor remained in the possession of the Crown, and was granted by Philip and Mary to David Vincent.[114] In 1579 Queen Elizabeth granted to Thomas Vincent

83 Feet of F. Surr. Hil. 1 Edw. VI.
84 Chan. Proc. (Ser. ii), bdle. 176, no. 2.
87 Com. Pleas Recov. R. Surr. East. 28 Eliz. no. 26.
88 Feet of F. Surr. Trin. 17 Eliz.; Trin. 19 Eliz.; Trin. 23 Eliz.; Trin. 24 Eliz.; Recov. R. Surr. Mich. 19 Eliz. rot. 142.
89 Ibid. Trin. 34 Eliz.
90 Ibid. Trin. 44 Eliz.
91 Chan. Inq. p.m. (Ser. ii), ccclxxii, 170.
92 Manning and Bray, Hist. of Surr. ii, 765–7.
93 Recov. R. East. 10 Anne, rot. 172.

94 See Com. Pleas Recov. R. Hil. 30 Geo. II, m. 28.; Mich. 31 Geo. II, m. 1; Hil. 32 Geo. II, m. 41; Recov. R. Mich. 30 Geo. III, rot. 51.
95 Com. Pleas Recov. R. Hil. 42 Geo. III, m. 139.
96 Brayley, Hist. of Surr. ii, 320.
97 Manning and Bray, Hist. of Surr. ii, 765.
98 Pat. 14 Chas. I, pt. x.
99 Chan. Inq. p.m. 13 Hen. VI, no. 7.
100 Brayley, Hist. of Surr. ii, 350 ; see Act 31 Hen. VIII, cap. 5.
101 Pat. 22 Jas. I, pt. ii, no. 3.
102 M.I. in Walton Church.

103 Manning and Bray, Hist. of Surr. ii, 767.
104 Burke, Peerage and Baronetage ; Landed Gentry ; and private information.
105 So at least it is stated in Chan. Proc. (Ser. ii), bdle. 90, no. 14.
106 L. and P. Hen. VIII, xv, 733 (48).
107 Wills dated there.
108 Par. Reg.
109 Manning and Bray, op. cit. ii, 767.
110 Brayley, Hist. of Surr. ii, 360–2.
111 Feet of F. Surr. Mich. 56 Hen. III.
112 L. and P. Hen. VIII, xiii (2), 342.
113 Ibid. xv, 773.
114 Pat. 3 & 4 Phil. and Mary, pt. iii.

the manor, site, and demesne lands of Morehall, and the wood called Sylkesmore coppice.[115] In the 18th century and until 1802 at least, the estate, then known as ' the manor of Southwood and Silksmore,' appears to have been held by the Frederick family.[116]

The Church of *ST. MARY* consists **CHURCH** of chancel with north vestry, nave with north and south aisles, west tower, and a south porch used as a vestry.

The earliest church for which evidence exists consisted of an aisleless nave, with a chancel of about the same size as at present. About 1160 a north aisle was added, and early in the 14th century a south aisle was built and the chancel remodelled or rebuilt. In the 15th century the present west tower was built. The tracery of the chancel windows is all modern ; the east window is of three lights with flowing net tracery, and the others are of 14th-century style, the jambs and rear arches so covered with colour wash and plaster that their age is difficult to determine. A north doorway leads to the vestry, which has a square sash window on the east, and in the south wall of the chancel is a 14th-century piscina with two drains and a restored cinquefoiled head, a single tall arched sedile, and close to it on the west a mutilated ogee-headed recess, probably a second sedile. All this work is old, but the south doorway close by has had its outer stonework renewed.

The chancel arch has two chamfered orders with half-octagonal responds and moulded capitals and bases, dating from c. 1330. The nave has arcades of four bays with pointed arches of two chamfered orders like those of the chancel arch and probably coeval, and the south arcade has octagonal pillars and moulded capitals of the same date, but in the north arcade the pillars are of 12th-century date, with circular scalloped capitals and moulded bases.

On the east respond of the south arcade is the well-known quatrain on the Holy Sacrament, in late 16th-century lettering renewed :

Christ was the worde and spake it
He took the bread and break it
And what the worde doth make it
That I believe and take it

The north aisle has a modern east window of two lights in 15th-century style. In the north wall are two late 15th-century square-headed windows, of three cinquefoiled lights with square labels and stops. A third between them is a modern copy in wood with red-brick jambs.

In the west wall is a small blocked single-light window, the head trefoiled and apparently of 14th-century date. The aisle wall has been heightened with brick when the gallery was set up. Three windows, each of three uncusped lights, have been inserted. The south aisle has a 15th-century east window with three cinquefoiled lights and tracery, and at the south-east is a like window, but with mullions and tracery removed, with another next to it on the west which retains its tracery. The south doorway is of 15th-century date with a pointed arch under a square head and quatrefoils with shields in the spandrels, each shield bearing a plain cross. There is a trefoiled piscina in this aisle.

The tower is in three stages with rough diagonal buttresses of brick. There is a modern west door, and above it a modern three-light window. The tower arch has three moulded orders with an engaged shaft to the inner order. On the north and south faces of the second stage are single lights, and the belfry windows are also single lights renewed. There is an 18th-century west gallery in the nave, carried by small pillars and a good moulded and carved beam, with a panelled front projecting on brackets ; galleries are also set up in both aisles, the organ being in the west gallery, blocking the tower arch. The chancel and nave are ceiled to the underside of the rafters, and have plain tracery and tie-beams which are probably of no great age. There is an octagonal panelled font, dated 1845, and all the rest of the fittings are modern.

On the chancel walls are several monuments, the most interesting being over the south doorway. It bears in an alabaster frame a set of verses ' in further memory of the said Thomas Fitts Gerald ' and Fraunces Randolph, dated 1619, and appears to be a pendant to a larger and now destroyed monument. In the north aisle is the large monument by Roubiliac to Richard Boyle Lord Shannon, Field-Marshal and commander in chief in Ireland, 1740, and close to it on the east a brass to john Selwyn, 1587, keeper of the park at Oatlands, with figures of himself, his wife, and eleven children. Above is a square plate with an engraving of a man riding a stag and plunging a sword into its neck ; this is repeated on the back of the same plate and probably refers to an exploit of the keeper's.

The bells are eight in number : the treble and second by john Warner & Sons, 1883 ; the third inscribed ' The gift of John Palmer, Esq., High Sheriff of this County 1726' ; the fourth by joseph Carter, 1608 ; the fifth by Richard Eldridge 1606, inscribed ' Our Hope is in the Lord, 1606 ' ; the sixth is by Warner, 1883 ; and the seventh by William Carter, 1610 ; while the tenor of 1651, by Bryan Eldridge, bears the names of the churchwardens, john Taylor and Thomas James. The sixth was formerly a 15th-century bell by a London founder, inscribed ' In Multis Annis Resonet Campana johannis.'

The plate consists of a cup of 1757, a cover paten without hall-marks, but c. 1728, a paten of 1713, two flagons of 1757, and a plated almsdish, dated 1829.

The registers date from 1636, but are imperfect. A scold's bridle is preserved in the church.

In 1086 there was a church on **ADVOWSON** the land of Richard de Tonbridge, afterwards called the manor of Walton Leigh, and the advowson belonged to the lords of this manor.[117] In 1382 Thomas Leigh conveyed the advowson to Geoffrey Michel.[118] He shortly afterwards enfeoffed john Gray and a number of others,[119] possibly trustees for Henry Bowett, afterwards Archbishop of York, who, in 1413 endowed his newly founded chantry in York Cathedral with 2 acres of land in Walton and the advowson of the church [120] for the support of two chantry priests, who had licence to appropriate the church. In 1542 Robert Gybbon and William Watson, the then chaplains of the

115 Pat. 21 Eliz. pt. xi.
116 Feet of F. Surr. Mich. 5 Geo. III ; Recov. R. Hil. 12 Geo. III, rot. 47 ; Com. Pleas Recov. R. Hil. 12 Geo. III,
m. 138 ; Feet of F. Surr. Hil. 12 Geo. III ; Trin. 42 Geo. III.
117 See references given under manor.
118 Feet of F. Surr. 6 Ric. II, no. 9.
119 De Banco R. 491, m. 2.
120 Pat. 1 Hen. V, pt. ii, m. 19.

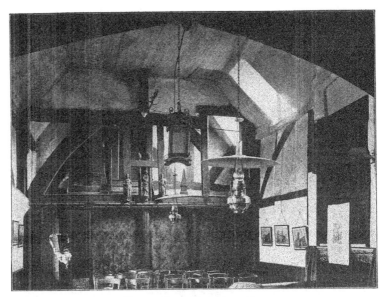

WALTON-ON-THAMES MANOR HOUSE : HALL.

WALTON-ON-THAMES CHURCH : NAVE LOOKING EAST

chantry, demised the rectory to John Carleton and Joyce his wife for forty-one years. Edward VI in 1552 granted a lease to Hugh Rogers at a reserved rent of £22 15s. 8d. After Rogers' death his wife Anne married George Sneyde, and they assigned their interest in the advowson to Richard Drake.[131] Philip and Mary granted the advowson and rectory in 1558 to john Bishop of Winchester.[132] In 1622 Thomas Watson died seised of it, or more probably of a lease of it,[133] for the Crown presented in 1623. In or about 1624 Richard Uridge, then vicar of Walton, asked for a reference to the Bishop of Winchester that the parson impropriate might be caused to increase the endowment of the vicarage.[134] The Crown presented to the living throughout the 17th and 18th centuries,[135] but the Rev. W. K. Bussell, the vicar, is now patron.

The rectory of Walton was granted in 1584 to Richard Drake and his son Francis Drake for their lives.[136] In 1594 a lease for thirty-one years was made to William Askewe, to begin after the expiration of the Drakes' lease.[137] It was granted in 1609 to Francis Morrice and Francis Phillips,[138] probably trustees, for in 1622 Thomas Watson died seised of the rectory.[139] It was ultimately re-acquired by the Drakes. Francis Drake (see the manor) by his will of 1698 left it to his son William. Adria, only daughter of William Drake, married Denton Boate, and died without issue in 1754. She left the rectory to Christopher D'Oyley of the Inner Temple, who was buried at Walton.[130] His widow received a share of the waste at the time of the inclosure in 1800 as lady of the Rectory Manor. In 1803 she sold most of the estate, and the tithes were bought by the various proprietors. The land inclosed from the waste was reserved for the payment to the vicarage appointed in 1413.

CHARITIES Smith's Charity is distributed as in other Surrey parishes.

In the church are records of the following bequests :—

By the will of Thomas Fennes, dated 8 February 1635-6, a tenement in Bishopsgate Street, now producing £500 a year (worth £10 a year when Feunes died in 1644), and land in this parish were left for the benefit of the poor.

In 1744, by will dated 1729, Mrs. Elizabeth Kirby left £200, which was increased to £336 by Jeremiah Brown of Apps Court, for ten poor widows, six nominated by the vicar and churchwardens, four by the owner of Apps Court. It was laid out in the purchase of land at Effingham, which in 1830 was exchanged for land in this parish.

The Apps Court Trust (see above) was settled in 1903.

Michael Kneebone, by will dated 1771, gave £350 3 per cent. consols for ten poor widows.

On the inclosure of 1800, land called Sandy Field containing 8 a. 1 r. 17 p. was given to the churchwardens and overseers for their expenses.

The overseers have also two small plots of land, on the south side of the road to Hersham and in Hersham respectively, the rents of which they may apply to their general expenses. The rent of a plot in West Molesey is applied by the churchwardens to the repairs of the church.

Over and above these, 189 acres were set apart for the poor at the inclosure of 1800. Part was sold to the railway, the rest is let as allotment ground and the rent distributed in coals.

William Sherwood, by will in 1822, left £716 19s. 6d. the interest of which is distributed to poor widows and other poor persons, and £1 to the vicar for a sermon.

In 1831 and 1862 Charles Smith and Miss Middleton left £150 for two poor widows and the sick poor.

In 1724 the vicar returned to Bishop Willis[131] that Baron Hilton, by an undated bequest, had left £16 yearly to the poor, secured upon lands in the bishopric of Durham. The Barons Hilton, so called by courtesy, but not peers of the realm, were owners of Hilton Castle. The last died in 1746. This benefaction appears to be lost.

WEYBRIDGE

Webrige and Webruge, 1086 ; Waybrugg (xii cent.); Weybrigge Juxta Byflet (xiv cent.).

The village of Weybridge is 8¾ miles south-west of Kingston. The parish is bounded on the north by the Thames. It measures 3 miles from north to south and 1 mile from east to west, and contains 1,330 acres of land and 41 of water. It is bounded on the west by the natural stream of the Wey, and for a short distance by the artificial navigation. The Wey Joins the Thames on the borders of the parish. The soil is Bagshot sand on the south, where St. George's Hill is partly in the parish. In the valleys of the Thames and Wey it is gravel and alluvium.

On the Wey are seed-crushing mills, and there are also extensive nurseries, but before the Inclosure Act of 1800 more than a third of the parish was waste, and a good deal of open land still remains, with 12¼ acres of allotments for the poor.

The road from London to Chertsey passes through Weybridge and crosses the river by a bridge which gave its name to the place.[1] The bridge dates back to very early times. In 1235 Henry III granted to William son of Daniel Pincerna, for his homage and service, two mills on the River Wey, one above the ' bridge of Wey,' and the other at Feyreford, at an annual rent of five silver marks.[2] In 1571 commissioners were appointed to report on the condition of the bridge. They stated that for some years it had been so decayed as to be unsafe for passengers, and that it was now ruinous. If the queen should be at her house at Oatlands and the waters should rise, ' as

131 Exch. Spec. Com. Surr. 26 Eliz. no. 2250.
132 Pat. 5 & 6 Phil. and Mary, pt. iv.
133 Chan. Inq. p.m. (Ser. ii), cccxcv, 119.
134 Hist. MSS. Com. Rep. xii, App. i, 171.
135 Inst. Bks. (P.R.O.), 1623, 1633, 1685, 1717, 1723, 1777.

136 Pat. 26 Eliz. pt. xvi, m. 21.
137 Pat. 36 Eliz. pt. xx, m. 12.
138 Pat. 7 Jas. I, pt. ii, m. 22.
139 Chan. Inq. p.m. (Ser. ii), cccxcv, 119.
130 Drake Wills in Manning and Bray, op. cit. ii, 771.

131 Visit. answers at Farnham Castle.
1 Emleybridge over the Mole, or Emlyn, which gives its name to the hundred, was on the same road.
2 Chart. R. 19 Hen. III, m. 2 ; Cart. Antiq. A. 29.

often they do,' she could not pass to her forest to hunt. It was accordingly ordered that a new bridge—a horse-bridge like the last—should be built, wood being used for its construction, as stonework would be too costly. The expense was to be borne by the queen, as the land on either side belonged to her.[2] The county rebuilt the bridge in 1809.[4]

Shadbury Eyot, an island in the Thames, is in Weybridge parish. A lawsuit took place in connexion with it in 1795.[5]

In 1641 it was proposed to make a canal from Arundel through Guildford to Weybridge. An Act for the purpose was read twice and committeed, but no further proceedings were taken.[6]

The main line of the London and South Western Railway passes through Weybridge, with a station which is the junction for the Chertsey line.

Weybridge was a place of very small importance, as appears from its 14th-century description as *juxta Byflet*, and was taxed under Edward III as half Thames Ditton and a third of Walton on Thames. In 1607 it is recorded to have protested against the burden of carriages for royal removals in Surrey, having only one cart in the parish ; [7] but it must have been increasing, probably on account of the proximity of the court at Oatlands, for in the ship-money assessment it stood at £24 to the £18 of Thames Ditton and the £38 of Walton on Thames.

In the reign of Charles II the Duke of Norfolk rebuilt a house at Weybridge near the confluence of the Wey and the Thames, which came to him from his second wife, Jane daughter of Robert Bickerton.[8] Evelyn says in his *Diary*, under 23 August 1678, ' I went to visit the Duke of Norfolk at his new palace at Weybridge, where he has laid out in building near £10,000 on a copyhold, and in a miserable barren sandy place by the street side ; never in my life had I seen such expense to so small purpose. . . . My lord [Thomas Howard] leading me about the house made no scruple of shewing me all the hiding-places for the popish priests, and where they said Mass.'[9] After the duke's death the duchess who had married again, sold the house to Catherine Sedley, Countess of Dorchester, former mistress of James II when Duke of York.[10] She married David Collyear, Earl of Portmore, and the house continued to be the seat of the Earls of Portmore until the title became extinct in 1835.[11] The house was shortly afterwards pulled down, but the grounds are still known as Portmore Park. A view of it is in Weybridge Museum.

The residence of Frederick Duke of York at Oatlands from the time of his marriage in 1791 made the neighbourhood, in which there were already many good houses, more fashionable, and Weybridge assumed its modern character of a great residential neighbourhood. There are a great many houses of a considerable size. Brooklands is the seat of Mr. H. F. Locke-King, Oakfield of Mr. J. A. Clutton-Brock, Noirmont of Mr. P. Riddell, Oatlands Lodge of Mr. justice Swinfen Eady. The last house contains a very fine oak mantelpiece, of the 16th century, bearing the arms of Elizabeth, brought from Winchester by a former owner. In 1907 Mr. Locke-King opened the motor racing track at Brooklands in Weybridge and Byfleet parishes. Waverley Cottage, Heath Road, is the residence of Mr. C. T. Churchill ; Bridge House, Heath Road, of Mr. H. Seymour Trower.

Weybridge is an urban district under the Act of 1894.

The Inclosure Act of 1800 [12] inclosed 422 acres, including common fields.

The church of St. Michael and All Angels, chapel of ease, was built in 1874, and is of red brick in 14th-century style, with nave, chancel, and side aisles.

St. Charles Borromeo Roman Catholic chapel was originally built by Mrs. Taylor in 1836 to take the place of a smaller chapel opened in 1834, and now used as a school. It was the temporary burying-place of Louis Philippe, king of the French, his queen, and many members of his family, whose bodies were removed to Dreux in 1876. In 1881 it was rebuilt and consecrated by Cardinal Manning. In 1894 the Comte de Paris was buried here.

The Congregational church, built in 1864, is cruciform, with a central tower and spire, in 14th-century style.

There is a meeting-house of Plymouth Brethren, built in 1873.

The village hall was built in 1883. There is a cottage hospital, and a cemetery with two mortuary chapels.

The schools (National) were built in 1849 and enlarged in 1895.

There is also a small British school, and a Roman Catholic school founded in 1876.

In 1822 a monument was erected in the centre of the village to the memory of the Duchess of York, who was much respected by the neighbourhood.

WEYBRIDGE is said to have been *MANORS* granted by Frithwald of Surrey to Chertsey Monastery before 675,[13] and in 933 this grant was confirmed by Athelstan.[14] At the time of the Domesday Survey the monastery held in demesne 2 hides in Weybridge, which Alured had held in King Edward's time ; and in the same vill an Englishman also held 2 hides of the same abbey.[15]

In 1239 Geoffrey de Lucy was holding the manor of the abbey and received a grant of a weekly market on Tuesday and of a yearly fair there on the vigil, feast, and morrow of the translation of St. Nicholas.[16] In 1284 he died seised of the hamlet of Weybridge held of the Abbot and convent of Chertsey in free socage, rendering to them 15s. yearly, to Richard le Grant for a meadow called Grant's-mead half a pound of pepper, and to Sir Hamo de Gatton one mark. The estate contained in demesne 20 acres of arable land, 16 acres of meadow, pasture called Contese and Gers'm, also rents of assize, a fishery, &c., and was valued at £6 13s. 10¾d. He left a son and heir Geoffrey, aged seventeen.[17]

It is not known when Weybridge became a royal manor. Byfleet, which often passed with it, and

[2] Exch. Spec. Com. 14. Eliz. Surr. no. 2237.
[4] Manning and Bray, op. cit. ii, App. 38.
[5] Com. Pleas Recov. R. Trin. 35 Geo. III, m. 31.
[6] Hist. MSS. Com. Rep. iv, App. 1, 52 ; Lords' Journ. iv, 167.

[7] Bray, op. cit. from *Records of Green Cloth*, vol i, p. lxvi.
[8] Surr. Arch. Coll. xvii, 52. Manning and Bray, op. cit. ii, 788, erroneously called it Ham House, but corrected the mistake in App. p. clxi.
[9] Evelyn's Diary (ed. W. Bray, 1850), ii, 120.
[10] Ibid. note.

[11] Brayley, Hist. of Surr. ii, 398.
[13] 39 & 40 Geo. III, cap. 87.
[12] Cott. MS. Vitell. A. xiii, fol. 19b.
[14] Ibid. fol. 37.
[15] V.C.H. Surr., i, 288, 308a. and notes.
[16] Chart. R. 23 Hen. III, m. 3 ; Plac. de Quo Warr. (Rec. Com.), 743.
[17] Chan. Inq. p.m. 12 Edw. I, no. 16.

which, like Weybridge, had been held of Chertsey and was annexed to the duchy of Cornwall, was in the king's hands in the reign of Edward I (see Byfleet). Weybridge was apparently annexed to the duchy of Cornwall before 1346, for in that year Reginald de Wodeham and others invaded the closes and houses of Edward the king's son, Duke of Cornwall, at Weybridge, mowed his hay, cut his trees, and hindered his servants in the collection of rents.[18] This seems to prove that there was some local feeling against the Justice of the royal acquisition.

DUCHY OF CORNWALL. *Sable fifteen bezants.*

In 1540 Henry VIII annexed it, together with Byfleet Manor, &c., to the honour of Hampton Court, assigning to the duchy in return the manor of Shippon, co. Berks.[19] From this time onwards the manor appears to have been held by the Crown and leased out to various persons, generally to the possessors of Oatlands. In 1578 Queen Elizabeth granted free warren in Weybridge Manor to Thomas Wilkins and others.[20] James I granted leases of the manor successively to Henry Prince of Wales,[21] to Queen Anne,[22] to Sir Francis Bacon,[23] and (in reversion) to Charles Prince of Wales.[24] Denzil Lord Holles held the manor under a lease from Charles II.[25] In 1749 Abel Walter received a grant of it in reversion after a lease for 1,000 years from George II.[26]

In 1804 an Act of Parliament[27] enabled the Duke of York to become owner of the leasehold under the Crown. His estates were broken up at his death in 1827 (see Oatlands). Mr. Henry Edwards Paine is now lord of the manor.

OATLANDS and the former manor of *HUN-DULSHAM,* or *HUNEWALDESHAM.* In 1086 Herfrey held Weybridge of Odo Bishop of Bayeux. Two sisters had held it in King Edward's time. When the bishop possessed himself of this land he had not the king's livery officer or writ therefor, as the hundred testified.[28] This cannot have been what was known as the manor of Weybridge, since that was held simultaneously by the Abbot and convent of Chertsey. It seems probable, therefore, that we have in this extract from Domesday the early history of the only other manor in the parish, that of Hunewaldesham or Hundulsham, afterwards included in the manor of Oatlands. Hunewaldesham was one of the alleged gifts of Frithwald to Chertsey,[29] so that this was another of the many usurpations of the bishop recorded in Domesday. There is, however, a gap of nearly two hundred years before any further mention of the estate occurs. In 1252–3 Richer Maunsell and his wife Cecilia conveyed land in Hunewaldesham to Sarra de Wodeham ; and Richer conveyed land in

Hunewaldesham to Joan widow of William de Hunewaldesham. In 1271–2 James de Wodeham made a grant in Hunewaldesham to John de Souwy.[30] In 1290 Robert atte Otlond and Sibill his wife granted to James son of James de Wodeham 2 acres of land in Weybridge at a yearly rent of one rose.[31] In 1324 the Wodehams held property in Weybridge consisting of a messuage, 64 acres of land, 10 acres of meadow, 5 acres of pasture, 6 acres of wood, and a rent of 6s.[32] Fifty years later John de Wodeham, son and heir of Reginald Wodeham,[33] granted to John Bouelythe lands in the parish of Weybridge called Hunewaldesham.[34] In 1383 Symon atte Otlond is mentioned as paying a rent to Byfleet Manor,[35] probably for 'Otlond,' which was held of Byfleet, and a Simon atte Weybridge appears in the Court Rolls in 1389 as holding ' Otlond.'

Late in the 15th century John de Wodeham died seised of Hundulsham Manor, which descended from him to his daughter and heiress, Margery Waker.[35] She was disturbed in her possession by the heirs of Sir Bartholomew Reed. In 1505 Sir Bartholomew Reed, kt., had died seised of land in Weybridge called ' Otland,'[35a] which he bequeathed to his wife Elizabeth, with remainder to his nephew William Reed.[37] After his death Dame Elizabeth and William Reed, the latter a goldsmith of London, took possession not only of these lands in Weybridge which Sir Bartholomew had undoubtedly held, but also of Hundulsham Manor. Thomas Waker, son and heir of Margery, appealed in the Court of Requests against the injustice of this proceeding, stating that he himself was a poor man with but few friends, while the Reeds were ' of great substance ' and had great friends in the county, he was not able to sue against them. The Reeds denied that there had ever been such a manor as Hundulsham,[38] but said that Sir Bartholomew had been seised of two messuages and various lands in Weybridge, and that his right to them had been admitted in 1499 by Joan Arnold, daughter of Elizabeth, daughter of John Wodeham, who had quitclaimed from her heirs to Sir Bartholomew and his heirs.[39] Rightly or wrongly, the Reeds won their case : the manor of Hundulsham is never mentioned again, and in September 1534 William Reed died seised of ' the manor called "Oteland" in Weybridge held of the ex-Queen Catherine,' and a number of tenements in Weybridge, under the will of his uncle Bartholomew.[40] His son John was still a minor, and was placed under the guardianship of Cromwell.[41] A letter from Thomas Stydolf to Cromwell is still in existence, arranging for

REED of Oatlands. *Or a griffin azure holding a sprig of green leaves in its beak.*

from the widow of Thomas Warner (who died in 1478). Feet of F. Surr. 9 Hen. VII, no. 18.
[37] Chan. Inq. p.m. (Ser. 2), xix, 53.
[38] Ct. of Req. bdle. 11, no. 98.
[39] This statement is borne out by Feet of F. Surr. Hil. 13 Hen. VII, but there is no mention of a manor, such as the Reeds claimed to hold later.
[40] Chan. Inq. p.m. (Ser. 2), lvii, 30.
[41] See L. and P. Hen. VIII, vii, 1246 ; ix, 1151.

[18] Pat. 20 Edw. III, pt. ii, m. 15 d. ; Close, 22 Edw. III, pt. ii, m. 15.
[19] Manning and Bray, Hist of Surr. ii, 785.
[20] Pat. 30 Eliz. pt. v.
[21] Pat. 8 Jas. I, pt. xli.
[22] Pat. 13 Jas. I, pt. xxix.
[23] Pat. 14 Jas. I, pt. xx.
[24] Pat. 14 Jas. I, pt. x.
[25] Pat. 24 Chas. II, pt. iv.
[26] Pat. 22 Geo. II, pt. ii.
[27] 44 Geo. III, cap. 25.

[28] V.C.H. Surr. i, 304b.
[29] Cott. MS. Vitell. A. xiii.
[30] Surr. Fines (Surr. Arch. Coll.), 48.
[31] Feet of F. Surr. East. 18 Edw. I, no. 26.
[32] Ibid. Trin. 18 Edw. II.
[33] See Weybridge descent.
[34] Anct. D. Surr. C. 628.
[35] Surr. Arch. Coll. xvii, 53.
[36] Ct. of Req. bdle. 3, no. 106.
[35a] Sir Bartholomew Reed had acquired 78 acres of land in Weybridge and Walton

477

John Reed to come to Weybridge to attend his father's month-mind. There was to be 'a great assembly of his kin,' and Isabel Reed, John's stepmother, thought it right for him to be present.[42] Mistress Isabel was a thorn in Cromwell's side; she continued to live at Oatlands for a time as his tenant, and made various efforts to get possession of her stepson's property.[43] However, in 1537 John Reed and his guardian conveyed the manor of Oatlands to Henry VIII, who wished to annex it to the honour of Hampton Court,[44] receiving in exchange the house, lands, &c., of the suppressed monastery of Tandridge.[45] In December 1537 the king spent a fortnight at Oatlands in the Reed's old house[46]; and he set on foot repairs there as well as at Hampton Court and Nonsuch.[46] The building of the new palace began in 1538. During the next few years he paid frequent short visits to his new palace, and was there married to Katherine Howard.[47] Queen Elizabeth visited Oatlands on several occasions,[48] for the last time in August, 1602, when she is said to have shot with a crossbow in the paddock.[49] James I, with the queen and prince, was at Oatlands for some time before his coronation.[50] In 1611 he granted the manor, house, and park to the queen for eighty years.[51]

Charles I stayed several times at Oatlands, partly for the sake of the stag-hunting,[52] though he found the accommodation insufficient for his retinue.[53] In 1640 his fourth son, Henry Duke of Gloucester, was born there.[54] The head-quarters of the royal army were there after the advance to London had been stopped at Turnham Green in 1642.[55] Charles himself was taken to Oatlands on his journey from Holdenby House in August, 1647,[56] and apparently spent some days there in the charge of the Commissioners, as Lord Montagu wrote from here to the Commons requesting more money for the king's privy purse, and that his clothes, table-linen, &c. might be sent there.[57]

Most of the buildings were destroyed and the land was disparked during the Interregnum, a quantity of timber being felled in the park for the use of the navy;[58] but after the Restoration the queen-dowager regained possession of Oatlands.[59] The estate was subsequently leased to Henry Jermyn, Earl of St. Albans (traditionally the second husband of Queen Henrietta Maria), who sold his interest in it to Sir Edward Herbert, who lived in the Reeds' old house.[60] Sir Edward was a faithful servant of James II, and was attainted in consequence of that king's invasion of Ireland; his estates were confiscated, and Oatlands reverted to the Crown. In 1696 Arthur Herbert, Earl of Torrington, his elder brother, obtained from William III a grant in fee-simple of Oatlands, which he bequeathed in 1716 to Henry Clinton, Earl of Lincoln. The latter formed the gardens at Oatlands about 1725, and rebuilt the house on the terrace, which was burnt down in 1793.[51] He died in 1728, and was succeeded by his son George, who only lived eighteen months after his father's death. The second son, Henry, came into the property, which he held for many years. He altered the garden, built the grotto, and made the Broad Water. He became Duke of Newcastle in 1768; and some time before his death in 1794 sold Oatlands to Frederick Duke of York.[52] The Duke of York died in 1827, and Oatlands was then sold to Mr. Edward Ball Hughes. The estate has since been broken up; much of it was bought by Lord Francis Egerton and the Hon. John Locke-King. The house of the Duke of York, rebuilt after the fire of 1793, has been mostly pulled down, but part is incorporated in the Oatlands Park Hotel. A great part of the park, in the two parishes of Weybridge and Walton on Thames, is covered with villa residences.

CLINTON. *Argent six crosslets fitchy sable and a chief azure with two molets or pierced gules therein.*

The site of the palace is in the grounds of Oatlands Lodge, Mr. Justice Swinfen Eady's estate. In the garden walls are two gateways, bricked up, surmounted by fine flat pointed arches of moulded brickwork, and the traces of two blocked windows. These belonged to the small building shown in views on the north-west side of the courtyard of the palace. There is much old brickwork in the garden walls. There also remains what is known as the Subterranean Passage, along the line of the west side of the main building. It is in places 10 ft. wide, but has been narrowed by party walls in others. It is covered by a pointed arch of brickwork, and a cellar opening from it has a good arched entrance of moulded brick. It apparently extended beyond the palace at both ends. It has been interrupted, and its length is not exactly known. Though rather puzzling from its length, it probably was a basement to keep the house dry. There is a well in it, still used to supply a pump in the gardens, and as the cellar opens from it, it was clearly not a sewer. Tradition says that it reached at the north-west to Dorney House, in Weybridge. In the grounds of the same estate is the well-known grotto, built of tufa, quartz, shells and spars, with winding passages, imitation stalactites, and a marble bath, now dry. It was made for the Duke of New-

[42] L. and P. Hen. VIII, vii, 1246.
[43] Ibid. vii, 1247; ix, 1151; x, 106.
[44] Manning and Bray, Hist. of Surr. ii, 786; see L. and P. Hen. VIII, xii (2), 1209.
[45] Ibid. xiii (1), 190 (2); Harl. MS. 4786.
[46] The old house was on the site of the Earl of Lincoln's later house. It was still standing in Walton parish when the Commonwealth Survey (q.v.) was made.
[46] L. and P. Hen. VIII, xiii (2), 1280; xiv (1), 904 (20); xiv (2), 236, &c.
[47] Ibid. xvi, 1470, &c.
[48] Egmont MSS. (Hist. MSS. Com.), i

(1), 21; Hist. MSS. Com. Rep. iv, App. i, 336.
[49] Hist. MSS. Com. Rep. xi, App. vii, 123; Manning and Bray, Hist. of Surr. ii, 786.
[50] Hist. MSS. Com. Rep. xiii, App. iv, 128.
[51] Pat. 9 Jas. I, pt. xxvii.
[52] Hist. MSS. Com. Rep. iv, App. i, 294.
[53] Ibid. xi, App. vii, 148.
[54] Weybridge Par. Reg. The duke was often called 'Henry of Oatlands.'
[55] Journ. of Prince Rupert's Marches, Engl. Hist. Rev. no. 52, p. 731.

[56] Lords' Journ. ix, 199; Com. Journ. v, 284.
[57] Hist. MSS. Com. Rep. xiii, App. i, 433.
[58] Ibid. App. i, xiii, 577.
[59] Land. MS. 252.
[60] Manning and Bray, Hist. of Surr. ii, 387; see Hist. MSS. Com. Rep. xiii, App. v, 241-6; Evelyn's Diary, 20 Dec. 1687, where Bray's editorial note is wrong.
[51] 'Probably,' Manning and Bray write. But a contemporary print fixes the date of the building before his death.
[52] Manning and Bray, ut supra; see Hist. MSS. Com. Rep. xv, App. vi, 546.

castle and was formerly much admired. The allied Sovereigns lunched in it in 1814. The skull of Eclipse, the race-horse, is kept in it.

The estate known as *BROOKLANDS* formed part of Oatlands Manor.[63] It was held by Isabel Reed in 1535, and was annexed by Henry VIII to the honour of Hampton Court.[64] In 1541 it was granted to Thomas Hungate.[65] In 1610 the king leased it to John Eldred and others.[66] The property was acquired by the Duke of York when he held Oatlands, and was sold to Mr. Ball Hughes. It was bought from him by the Hon. John Locke-King. The Duke of York pulled down the house built by George Payne, a friend of Warren Hastings.[67] A new house has now been built, the property of Mr. H. F. Locke-King, J.P. The Brooklands Automobile Club holds the ground covered by the motor racing track, which extends beyond Brooklands into Byfleet.

Dorney House also formed part of the Crown property in Weybridge. It was leased by Queen Elizabeth to John Woulde, yeoman,[68] who died in 1598.[69] In the reign of Charles I it was granted for twenty-five years to Humphrey Dethick, gentleman usher,[70] who died in 1642 and was buried in Weybridge Church. There is extant an address by the author of a history of the Netherlands to his two sons dated at Dorney House, 15 November 1621.[71]

In 1461 Edward IV granted to Thomas Warner, citizen and ironmonger of London, for life, two acres of land called Weybridge Hawe at a rent of 3s. 4d. per acre.[72] Two years later he licensed him to build a wharf or quay on this land, which bordered on the River Thames, and to load and unload vessels there, and take merchandise to and from the City of London and other places adjoining the river.[73] Henry VII granted the Hawe wharf to William Reed for 13s. 4d. yearly, and Reed leased it to Richard Allddere for £3 6s. 8d. over and above the king's rent. After Reed's death a dispute arose as to his tenure of the property, and Stydolf wrote to advise Cromwell to step in while the matter was yet undecided and take possession of it.[74] The name of Warner, wharfinger of Ham Hawe, occurs in 1636 ; he was summoned for sending his barges weekly to London in spite of the orders to the contrary which had been given in consequence of the prevalence of the plague.[75] But probably, though resident in Weybridge, his landing-stage was on the other side of the river, in Ham in Chertsey.

CHURCH — The church of *ST. JAMES* is a fair-sized modern structure designed by Pearson, and consists of a chancel with a north vestry and organ chamber, a nave with a north and two south aisles, one being a later addition, and a western tower with a stone broach spire. The whole church is in 13th-century style, and is of excellent design. The chancel is extremely ornate, and is completely lined with polished marbles and further decorated with glass mosaics. The colour scheme is so well conceived and the materials so well chosen that the general effect, while rich in the extreme, is quite free from gaudiness. The texture and degree of polish of the various marbles is also managed with considerable subtlety. It is worthy of note that the whole of this decorative treatment was at the cost of an anonymous benefactor. The old church stood in the present churchyard, a little to the north of the existing structure.

There are in the tower a number of brasses brought from the old church. On the south is one to John Woulde, esq., 1598, and his two wives ; the first—Adrye (formerly the wife of Thomas Street), 1596, by whom he had four daughters and four sons ; the second, Elizabeth (Notte, formerly the wife of Henry Standish), date of death left blank, by whom he had five sons and three daughters. There are three shields of arms. The first bears an owl standing in an orle. A second is Street, of six quarters : (1), three Catherine wheels ; (2), a cheveron ; (3) six griffons sergeant ; (4) three harts' heads razed ; (5) bendy ; (6) three roundels, between five croslets fitchy, impaling a bend with three martlets thereon between three leopards' heads, for Adrye. The third shield bears the coat given above impaling ermine three roundels and a cinqfoil. On the north side of the tower is a monument, with three skeletons, and the inscription :—

Three of ye children of	Sir John Trevor, Kt. and Dame Margaret	viz.	Francis Dorothy Thomas	buried	1596 1600 1605

Also an inscription plate to Humphrey Dethick, 1642, ' who was one of his Ma[ties] Gent[n] Vshers (Dayly waiter) ' ; with the arms (Argent) a fesse vairy (or and gules) between three water bougets (sable), for Dethick quartering Allestry and (?) Boshall. Another brass is to ' Thomas Inwood y[e] Elder, late of this towne, Yoman,' 1586, with the kneeling figures of himself and his three wives and their children.

There is a ring of eight modern bells.

The plate consists of a flat paten given in 1720, with the London date-letter for 1719, and a modern set of a chalice, a cover paten, a flat paten and flagons of 1844 and 1847.

The first book of registers contains mixed entries from 1625 to 1762, the burials to 1676 only. The second has burials from 1678 to 1775 ; the third, mixed entries from 1771 to 1797 ; the fourth, baptisms from 1797 to 1824 ; the fifth, marriages from 1797 to 1820. There is also a book of banns from 1754 to 1812.

A series of churchwardens' accounts and vestry books exist, beginning early in the 17th century.

ADVOWSON — The advowson of Weybridge Church belonged with the manor to Chertsey Abbey. In the early 13th century the monks transferred it to Newark Priory,[76] reserving a rent of 6s. 8d.[77] In 1262 the priory obtained licence for an appropriation, and from the Winchester Episcopal Registers it appears that vicars were instituted till 1414. The latter part of the Beaufort Register (1415–47) is lost, but in 1450 the church was presented to as a rectory by John Penycoke[78] (probably by grant from the priory), and the presentations have since continued under

63 L. and P. Hen. VIII, xvi, 1500.
64 Ibid. ix, 1151.
65 Ibid. xvi, 1500.
66 Pat. 8 Jas. I, pt. xlix.
67 Manning and Bray, op. cit. ii, 789.
68 Pat. 13 Eliz. pt. ix.

69 Surr. Arch. Coll. x, 300.
70 Surr. Arch. Coll. xvii, 46.
71 Hist. MSS. Com. Rep. iv, App. i, 252.
72 Pat. 1 Edw. IV, pt. i, m. 10.
73 Pat. 3 Edw. IV, pt. ii, m. 15.

74 L. and P. Hen. VIII, vii, 1247.
75 Surr. Arch. Coll. xvii, 45.
76 Harl. Chart. 51 C, 29.
77 V.C.H. Surr. ii, 58.
78 Called ' of Weybridge' Pat. 1 Ric. III, pt. i, m. 6.

[79] L. and P. Hen. VIII, xii (2) 1311. [80] *Book Ent. (P.R.O.)* ... ; [82] *Surr: Arch. Coll.* xvii, 48, &c.

THE HUNDRED OF KINGSTON

In the Domesday Survey Kingston, Petersham, Long Ditton, Thames Ditton, and Malden are entered under Kingston Hundred,[2] Richmond and Kew then forming part of Kingston. Southwark [3] and West Horsley [4] are also entered under it, evidently by an error. Chessington, which was a member of Malden, occurs under the hundreds of Kingston and Wallington [5] and was reckoned in Kingston Hundred in 1428 [6]; it was in Copthorne Hundred in 1610 [7] and afterwards. In a Subsidy Roll of 1333 the vills assessed in this hundred were Sheen, Ham and Petersham, Hartington and Combe, Malden and Talworth, Thames Ditton and Long Ditton.[8] Part of Thames Ditton is still in Kingston Hundred.

In 1199 the hundred of Kingston was said to pertain, and always to have pertained, to the lordship and vill of Kingston.[9] Probably a court of ancient demesne,[10] originally held for the manor of Kingston, had gradually extended its jurisdiction over the neighbouring vills.[11] The hundred court was held before the bailiffs on Saturday once every three weeks. In 1628 the manors of Richmond, Petersham, and Ham were removed from the jurisdiction of this court, and separate courts leet constituted for them. According to the Municipal Corporations Report of 1835 the hundred court had then fallen into disuse. A recovery had been suffered in it as late as 1609, and a fine levied in 1611.

---

[1] Population Ret. 1831.
[2] V.C.H. Surr. i, 297a, 305a, 306a, 308b, 317a, 319a, 323a.
[3] Ibid. 305a.   [4] Ibid. 323a, 325b.   [5] Ibid. 317b.
[6] Feudal Aids, v, 132.   [7] V.C.H. Surr. i, map facing p. 444.
[8] Subs. R. (6 Edw. III), bdle. 184, no. 4.
[9] Abbrev. Plac. (Rec. Com.), 25, see also 29.
[10] See Municipal Corp. Rep. 1835, p. 2900.
[11] The court was called in old court books 'curia cum hundredo.'

KEW

Kayhor (xiv cent.) ; Kayo (xv cent.) ; Keyowe, Kaiho, Kayhoo, Cewe (xvi cent.) ; Ceu (xvii cent.)

The parish of Kew lies on the Surrey bank of the Thames and is about 346¼ acres in extent, the greater part being occupied by Kew Gardens. Kew formerly lay in the parish of Kingston, from which it was not separated until 1769,[1] so that there are very few early references to it. At the begining of the 16th century it began to have a separate history, when the presence of the Court at Richmond caused courtiers to settle in the neighbourhood. Mary Tudor, in her father's reign, had an establishment there. In 1522 amongst her household expenses is entered the drive from Kew to Richmond.[2] Some years later Sir W. Paulet wrote to Cromwell that Mary's household was to be removed to Kew after the king had left Richmond,[3] and in 1537 a yeoman cook serving the Lady Mary was accused of robbery, and was said to be at Kew, ' where the Lady Mary lies.'[4] Sir John Dudley the son of Elizabeth, Baroness Lisle, lady of the manor of Kingston Lisle[5] in Berkshire, had an estate at Kew.[6] Henry Norris, Esquire to the Body, who was involved in the accusations against Anne Boleyn, also had a house there,[7] and after his execution in 1536 an inventory was taken of ' his wardrobe stuff,' including hangings, feather beds, &c., some of which came from Kew.[8] In Cromwell's remembrances, after a note to remind him ' that all Mr. Norris's patents be searched out,' there is another entry to the effect that he should call upon Sir Edward Seymour concerning ' the evidence of the house at Kew for my Lady Seymour.'[10] This was probably Norris's house, and the same that was then confirmed to Sir Edward Seymour,[11] who was in that year created Viscount Beauchamp of Hatch,[12] and who afterwards became Duke of Somerset.[13] In 1537, however, Cromwell informed Rowland Lee, Bishop of Coventry and Lichfield, that he was to give up his house in the Strand to Lord Beauchamp in exchange for the latter's house at Kew,[14] and in spite of Lee's protests the exchange was effected.[15] Another house there belonged to Charles Somerset, first Earl of Worcester, who was granted lands at Kew in 1517.[16] At his death in 1526 he left his estates at Kew and the tapestry in several rooms there to his third wife, Eleanor, with remainder to his son George.[17] Sir George Somerset sold the house to Thomas Cromwell in 1538 for £200,[18] and Cromwell conveyed it for the same sum to Charles Brandon, Duke of Suffolk,[19] who had probably already inhabited Kew during the life of his wife Mary, the daughter of Henry VII and widow of Louis XII.

According to Leland's 'Cygnea Cautio,' Kew was her dwelling-house for a time after her return to England.[20]

In Elizabeth's reign Sir John Pickering, Lord Keeper of the Great Seal, obtained certain lands in fee farm and had a house at Kew,[21] and on one occasion the queen dined with him there. The entertainment was described as ' great and exceeding costly.' The queen was met at different points ' after her first lighting ' and offered rare gifts, amongst them a fan set with diamonds ; while after dinner besides a pair of virginals, ' a gown and juppin ' were presented to her in her bedchamber.[22] A paper entitled ' Remembrances for furniture at Kew and elsewhere for entertainment,' is identified by Lysons as written by Sir John Pickering. It consists of notes of ' things to be remembered ' should the queen visit him, and deals chiefly with the accommodation for the queen and her ladies, their ' dyett,' and the rewards to be offered to her attendants.[23] Elizabeth, daughter of James I, was given an establishment at Kew in 1608,[24] and John, Lord Harrington, in whose charge she had been till then, was given the chief post in her household.[25] In the following year. he wrote from there to the Lord Treasurer that he could not personally bring the book of accounts, as ' the Prince' often called for Elizabeth to ride with him, and Harrington was consequently in constant attendance.[27] A number of other people of note have dwelt at Kew at various times, amongst them Sir John Hele, who was made serjeant-at-law to succeed Sir John Pickering,[28] Sir Roger Manley, cavalier, who died 1688,[29] Sir Peter Lely,[30] James Thomson, author of ' The Seasons,'[31] Thomas Gainsborough, who was buried in the church,[32] and Stephen Duck, the farm labourer who became a poet and rector of Byfleet. During the French Revolution, the English Court being then frequently at Kew, many refugees established themselves there.[33]

Three different buildings have at various times gone by the name of Kew Palace : the one that is now standing ; the house that was opposite to it until the beginning of the 19th century ; and a huge embattled castle which was planned by George III, and of which a large part was built after plans by Wyatt, but never completed.[34] The history of the other two palaces is difficult to trace with accuracy. The palace that was pulled down in 1802, and which was then a large house of plain exterior, was the more important of the two, and probably was on the site of the capital messuage

[1] Private Act, 9 Geo. III, cap. 65.
[2] L. and P. Hen. VIII, iii, 3375, p. 1407.
[3] Ibid. xi, 1291.
[4] Ibid. xii (1), 661.
[5] G.E.C. Peerage, under Lisle.
[6] Add. MS. 4075, fol. 114 ; L. and P. Hen. VIII, xiii (1), 696 ; xvii, 220 (50).
[7] Dict. Nat. Biog.
[8] L. and P. Hen. VIII, x, 878.
[9] Ibid. 794.   [10] Ibid. 871.
[11] Ibid. 1087 (9).
[12] G.E.C. Peerage.
[13] Ibid.
[14] L. and P. Hen. VIII. xii (1), 806, 821.
[15] Dict. Nat. Biog. s.v. Roland Lee or Legh.
[16] L. and P. Hen. VIII, ii, 3769.
[17] P.C.C. 13 Porch.
[18] L. and P. Hen. VIII, xiv (1), 336 ; Harl. Chart. 49, A 46.
[19] Ibid. ; L. and P. Hen. VIII, xiv (2), 782.
[20] Leland, Itin. ix, 12.
[21] Dict. Nat. Biog.
[22] Sidney State Papers (ed. Collins), i, 376.
[23] Harl. MS. 6850, fol. 91, 92.
[24] Dict. Nat. Biog.
[25] Ibid.
[26] Her brother, Prince Henry.
[27] Cal. S.P. Dom. 1603–10, p. 552.
[28] Ibid. 1601–3, p. 27 ; Dict. Nat. Biog.
[29] Dict. Nat. Biog.
[30] Ibid.
[31] Ibid.
[32] Ibid. See Phillips, A Morning Walk from London to Kew.
[33] Frederick Scheer, Kew and its Gardens, 18.
[34] Journ. of Kew Guild (1906), 297.

KEW PALACE

mentioned in ·16th and 17th-century documents, in which case the present palace was most likely that which was known as the Dairy House. These two buildings are often mentioned together, first in the 16th century, when there were belonging to them two gardens or orchards, a barn, and a stable that had been a chapel.[35] The capital messuage was probably the one held by Henry Courtenay,[36] Earl of Devon, afterwards Marquess of Exeter,[37] and then by his son Edward,[38] who apparently conveyed it to Sir Miles Partridge, a follower of the Duke of Somerset.[39] Partridge was involved with Somerset in the charge of conspiring against Northumberland, and was executed in February 1551–2.[40] In the same year the capital messuage and the house adjacent called the Dairy House passed into the possession of Sir Henry Gate.[41] Some six years later Elizabeth granted them to Lord Robert Dudley, afterwards Earl of Leicester,[42] who apparently sold them to Thomas Gardiner, a goldsmith of London, who inhabited the house.[43] Gardiner, who was one of four numerators of the receipt of the Exchequer, became heavily indebted to the Crown,[44] and in 1575 he released the property to the queen,[45] who then granted it to Thomas Handford and Kenard Delaber, the sureties for Thomas Gardiner.[46] At the beginning of the following century the houses were amongst the possessions of Sir Hugh Portman,[47] and passed at his death in 1604 to his brother and heir, John Portman.[48] Sir Henry Portman, son of John, died seised of them in 1621–2,[49] and was succeeded by his brother John, who, dying three years later under age, was succeeded by the third brother Hugh, then aged nineteen.[50] Hugh died in 1630; a funeral sermon on him is extant. His will was proved in 1632.[51] It was probably a few years after this that the capital messuage and the Dairy House became separate estates, the capital messuage being acquired by Richard Bennet, who was dwelling there in 1645, at which date he was presented to Parliament as a delinquent.[52] He was acquitted, however, and discharged from sequestration in November 1647.[53] In the following year he bought various lands in Kew from Robert Kerr, Earl of Ancram, who had purchased them from Sir William Portman in 1633.[54]

Richard Bennet's daughter, Dorothy, inherited the Kew estate which she brought in marriage to Henry, Lord Capell of Tewkesbury.[55] In 1683 John Evelyn came to visit his friend Sir Henry Capell

PORTMAN. Or a fleur de lis azure.

at Kew. At that time the house had been repaired; an artificial fountain played in a niche in the hall,

CAPELL. Gules a lion between three crosslets fitchy or.

BENNET. Gules a bezant between three demi-lions argent.

which was roofed with a kind of cupola. Nevertheless Evelyn describes the room as melancholy, and suggests that it would be improved if painted a fresca. Capell had also contrived a cupola in the garden between two elms. This was made of poles 'which being covered by plashing the trees to them is very pretty.'[56] Lord Capell died without children in 1696 and his wife survived him twenty-five years, dying at Kew in 1721. Her husband's great-niece Lady Elizabeth Capell was her heir. She had married in 1717 Samuel Molyneux, the astronomer, Secretary to George II, then Prince of Wales, M.P. and Privy Councillor, who arranged a private observatory in the house at Kew, from which he and James Bradley made the observations that led to the discovery by the latter of the aberration of light. The sundial in the garden marks the site of the palace, and commemorates the observations made there.[57]

Mr. Molyneux predeceased his wife by a couple of years in 1728. Shortly after her death Kew House was leased to Frederick, Prince of Wales. He also appears to have found the observatory a source of much interest, and during the winter of 1737–8 Dr. Desagulier read lectures on astronomy every day to the household. His observatory was then described as a large room at the top of the house, where he had all his mathematical and mechanical instruments at one end and a Planetarian at the other.[58] After the death of the Prince of Wales, the dowager Princess Augusta continued to spend much of her time here, bringing up her children in great seclusion. The palace, which was also called Kew House, had been flamboyantly decorated by William Kent, who was much in fashion at that period.[59] The drawing-room and ante-chamber of the common apartment on the ground floor were hung with tapestry; the cabinet was ornamented with 'panels of Japan,' designed by Kent, who was also responsible for a blue and gilt wainscot in the gallery. The state rooms were on ·the first floor, and here the gallery was

[35] Add. MS. 4705, fol. 114; Pat. 1 Eliz. pt. iv, no. 17.
[36] L. and P. Hen. VIII, ix, 479; xiii (2), 802.
[37] G.E.C. Peerage.
[38] Terrier of land in Surrey. Add. MS. 4705; Pat. 1 Eliz. pt. iv, no. 17.
[39] Dict. Nat. Biog.; Pat. 1 Eliz. pt. iv, no. 17.
[40] Ibid.
[41] Add. MSS. 4705, fol. 114.
[42] Pat. 1 Eliz. pt. iv, no. 17.
[43] Ibid. 17 Eliz. pt. vi, no. 31.
[44] Ibid.
[45] Feet of F. Surr. Mich. 17 & 18 Eliz.

[46] Pat. 17 Eliz. pt. vi, no. 31.
[47] Of Orchard Portman in Somerset, not 'a Dutch merchant' as Bradley says.
[48] Chan. Inq. p.m. (Ser. 2), cclxxxiii, 86.
[49] Ibid. ccccvi, 67.
[50] Ibid.
[51] G.E.C. Baronetage.
[52] Cal. Com. for Comp. i, 1011.
[53] Ibid.
[54] Egerton Chart. 306.
[55] G.E.C. Peerage.
[56] Evelyn, Diary (ed. Bray), 451. When Evelyn visited Capell on 28 Aug. 1678, he described the house as 'an old timber house.' It is difficult not to believe that

the 'repairs' must have meant considerable rebuilding. The hall, with the fountain and cupola, was not part of a timber house. The house when Frederick, Prince of Wales, lived there was apparently of brick and stone.
[57] Dict. Nat. Biog.
[58] Hist. MSS. Com.Rep. xv, App. vi, 190.
[59] It was probably rebuilt by him for the Prince of Wales. Sir William Chambers in Plans, Elevations, &c., at Kew, 1763, gives north and south elevations of the palace at Kew, designed and executed by the late Mr. Kent. They are ugly enough to carry conviction.

adorned by grotesque paintings of children in theatrical costumes by John Ellis, the piers between the windows being large painted looking-glasses from China. The state drawing-room was hung with green silk, and the ceiling painted with grotesque designs by Kent.[60] The Princess of Wales at this time held both the palaces, and about 1770 she gave up Kew House to George III, who purchased the freehold of it,[61] and moved over to the present Kew Palace, or the Dutch House, where she died in 1772.[62] George III, who had spent much of his boyhood at Kew,[63] began to use it again as a country residence when his family became too large to be accommodated in Richmond Lodge.[64]

The life led by the royal family at Kew was very domestic. According to a description written in the summer of 1775, the king and queen rose at six in the morning and enjoyed uninterrupted leisure until eight, when the elder children were brought from their several houses to breakfast with them. The younger ones were brought to the palace at nine. In the afternoons the queen worked and the king read to her, and once a week the whole family would make a tour of Richmond Gardens.[65] The house, according to Fanny Burney, who came here with the Court in 1786, was inconvenient and old-fashioned. Excepting the royal apartments the rooms were small and dark and there were staircases in every passage and passages to every closet. Miss Burney declares that on her first evening there she lost her way continually ' only in passing from my room to the queen's.'[66] When the king's madness finally declared itself at Windsor in the autumn of 1788, the doctors urged his removal to Kew, and this was only achieved by keeping him in ignorance of their purpose.[67] Queen Charlotte and the Court drove to Kew House on 29 November and awaited his arrival without unpacking their baggage lest they should fail to bring him, and Miss Burney relates how late that night she heard the carriage arrive and the sound of the king's voice talking incessantly and very fast.[68] Kew House was pulled down in 1802.[69]

The descent of the Dairy House cannot be traced with much certainty. It has been suggested that the date 1631 over the door is that of a sale to Samuel Fortrey after the death of Sir Hugh Portman.[70] On the other hand the initials S and C F (Samuel and Catherine Fortrey) and the date 1631 are in the usual place to indicate the date of building, and though the windows have no doubt been replaced and the house was generally retouched in the 18th century, its main features and design are not unlike the date 1631. Samuel Fortrey, to whom the building of it may therefore with some probability be ascribed, was a London merchant, the grandson of a Fleming of Lille, and himself married

to a Hainaulter,[71] whence the name the Dutch House, it being in a Flemish style. He had one son Samuel and two daughters,[72] the younger of whom, Mary, married first Sir Thomas Trevor and secondly Sir Francis Compton, son of Spencer, Earl of Northampton.[73] In the following century this palace was inhabited by the royal family, and it was no doubt here that the daughters of George II stayed in 1728, as they were said to be inhabiting a house at Kew 'over against where Mr. Molyneux lived.'[74] Some time before the Prince of Wales's death in 1751 the Princess Amelia was described as living opposite to his house, Kew Palace, in the house ' built by a Dutch Architect,' which Queen Caroline had bought or leased.[75] This was clearly the present palace or Dutch House. After the death of the Princess of Wales, this palace was used for the young princes, and was called the Princes' House or the Royal Nursery.[76] It was inhabited by George III and Queen Charlotte after the other palace had been pulled down in 1802, and it was here that the queen died a little more than a year before the death of her husband.[77] The palace was thrown open to the public in 1899.[78] It is a red brick building of three stories and attics ; the front entrance is in the middle of the south front and over it are the letters mentioned above, $_S{}^F_C$ united by a knot and the date 1631. The north front has projecting wings at either end and the south front has square bays. A distinctive decorative feature in these two fronts is formed by the pilasters which flank the middle windows, square on the first floor, round in the second and with moulded cornices. The windows generally have rusticated joints of brick. There are three shaped gable heads on the north and south fronts and two at each end, but those at the east are plain. The middle of the north front on the ground floor has been filled in flush between the projecting wings in modern times and has a balcony above. Almost all the internal fittings are of 18th-century or later insertion. Those with F upon them and the Prince of Wales's feathers were probably brought from the other palace. The main entrance opens on to a long passage through the building, at the north end of which are the main stairs of late 18th or early 19th-century date with carved ends to the heads. The first room on the left or west of the passage is the library ante-room, which is lined with some good 16th-century linen panelling which may be a relic of the old Dairy House. The library next to it is lined with 17th-century panelling. The two rooms to the east of the passage are the king's dining-room ' (south) and the ' king's breakfast room ' (north). The former is flagged with stone and lined with 18th-century panelling ; the latter has late 17th or early 18th-century panelling

[60] Chambers, *Plans of Gardens at Kew.*
[61] Manning and Bray, *Hist. of Surr.* i, 446.
[62] *Journ. of Mrs. Papendieck,* i, 43.
[63] *Dict. Nat. Biog.*
[64] *Journ. of Mrs. Papendieck,* i, 43.
[65] *Annual Reg.* 1775.
[66] Madame D'Arblay, *Memoirs* (ed. Austin Dobson), ii, 402.
[67] Ibid. iv, 187, et seq.
[68] Ibid.
[69] *Journ. of Kew Guild* (1906), 297.
[70] Ibid. Lysons dates the sale in 1636, and says that it was by a Sir John Portman, but there was no Sir John alive then.
[71] *Visit. of London,* 1634-5, p. 284.
[72] Ibid.
[73] *Genealogist,* iii, 297 ; Nichols, *Topog. and Gen.* iii, 32.
[74] *Hist. MSS. Com. Rep.* xv, App. vi, 54.
[75] *London and its Environs Described* (Anon. 1761), v, 260 ; iii, 274. The author says that the queen bought from Sir Thomas Abney. Lysons says that William Fortrey, grandson of Samuel, sold his house to Sir Richard Levett. Sir Richard Levett, who died in 1710,
had two houses in Kew (see his will at Somerset House). He and Abney served as Lord Mayor in consecutive years, and Abney may have bought part of his estate. In a map of 1771 the land between the Dutch House and the river is marked as belonging to Levett Blackburne, grandson of Sir Richard Levett. Probably Queen Caroline leased the property and Geo. III acquired the freehold.
[76] Madame D'Arblay, *Memoirs* (ed. Austin Dobson), iii, 195.
[77] *Dict. Nat. Biog.*
[78] *Journ. of Kew Guild* (1898), 6.

with bolection mouldings and fluted pilasters with the bases ornamented in low relief and Corinthian capitals. Over the doorway between the two (in the dining-room) is a carved head, probably of the 17th century. On the first floor is a similar long passage from north to south, communicating with the stairs at the north end. East of the latter in the north-east angle is the 'queen's boudoir' which has an 18th-century dado and a ribbed panelled ceiling with allegorical figures in low relief. To the south of this is the 'queen's drawing-room' which is lined with 18th-century panelling with bolection moulds, but has an earlier frieze with raised strap ornament; the fireplace has inlaid marble work and is flanked by grey marble pillars with alabaster capitals. The 'king's bedroom' and ante-chamber east of the passage at the south end and 'queen's bedroom' and ante-chamber at the north end have nothing worthy of mention. In one of the rooms on the second floor, east side, is a Tudor fireplace of stone with moulded jambs and a four-centred flat arch; the spandrels are carved with shields and foliage; the fireplace is at least a hundred years earlier than the present building, and may be a relic of the earlier building. Some others of the top rooms preserve the panelling and a door or two of the original house.

Kew Gardens originated in the private garden of Sir Henry Capell, the friend of John Evelyn, who is said to have brought fruits and rare trees from France.[79] He built two greenhouses for oranges and myrtles, which roused Evelyn's admiration, and he contrived palisades of reeds painted with oil to shade the oranges during the summer.[80] John Evelyn adds, however, that there were too many fir trees in the garden.[81] In the 18th century the grounds at Kew were laid out by the landscape gardener Lancelot Brown,[82] and between 1757 and 1762 Sir William Chambers the architect was employed by the Princess of Wales to adorn the gardens with buildings.[83] In an account of the palace and grounds, dedicated by Chambers to the Dowager Princess, he expatiated on the lack of all natural advantages.[84] According to him the soil was barren,[85] without wood and water, it was dead flat with no prospect, and he took credit for the contrivances that had transformed it from a waste into a garden. An orangery was built under his care in 1761. The Physic or Exoteric garden was begun in 1760; the centre of it was occupied by an immense bark house, 60 ft. long, 20 ft. wide, and 20 ft. high. The flower garden, divided by walks, led to the menagerie, a collection of pens and cages of rare birds surrounding a large basin of water. The pagoda was built by Chambers, as well as various semi-Roman and oriental buildings such as the Temples of the Sun, of Bellona, of god Pan, of Aeolus, a Moresque building, the theatre of Augusta, a Corinthian colonnade, and so on.[86] A good many of these erections were still standing in

1840.[87] The Pantheon or Temple of Military Fame was erected to commemorate Nelson's victory in Aboukir Bay.[88] In 1759 William Aiton, author of the *Hortus Kewensis*, was the manager of Kew Botanic Gardens, and in 1783 of the royal forcing and pleasure gardens of Kew and Richmond.[89] His son William Townsend Aiton succeeded him.[90] Queen Charlotte had her own flower-garden at Kew. Mrs. Papendieck relates how the queen's gardener, Mr. Green, was rearing orange trees with great care; but as the queen could not afford to rebuild the hot-houses, and the Board of Works would not, as it was the queen's private garden, the growth of the trees was stunted.[91] In 1854 George Bentham the botanist presented his collections and books to Kew, in return for which a room there was assigned to him, where he worked daily at descriptive botany.[92] Hanover House, where Ernest Duke of Cumberland, King of Hanover, dwelt from 1830 to 1831, is now the Herbarium,[93] and Cambridge Cottage, which used to be inhabited by Augustus Duke of Cambridge, is now the museum of British forest productions.[94] The Queen's Cottage in Kew Gardens was used by Queen Charlotte and the princesses as a sort of summer-house, or afternoon tea-room. When Kew Gardens were thrown open, at the beginning of Queen Victoria's reign, she kept this cottage and some 40 acres round it for her own use, whence its name. She appears, however, to have gone there very seldom, and in 1897 it was also thrown open to the public. The grounds were opened on 1 May 1899. The cottage, which is thatched, consists of three rooms only, one upstairs and a sitting-room and kitchen on the ground floor. Part of the lands round are covered with thick wood; the rest used to be laid out, but latterly has been allowed to grow wild.[95]

Until the middle of the 18th century there was no bridge across the Thames from Kew to Brentford. A ferry was granted by Henry VIII to John Hale,[96] servant to Henry Norris, but the inhabitants of Kew brought a suit against him, in which it was pleaded that 'for time out of mind' they had had the right of free passage across the Thames, and now, they said, John Hale 'would suffer no man to pass with any manner of boat, but only in his boat, exacting and requiring a certain sum for every passage over there.' In reply John Hale declared that the kings had always been accustomed to grant the ferry by their patents, enabling the holder of the ferry to charge for every man and horse one half penny and for every man, woman, and child one farthing,[97] There appears to be no record of the Judgement given, but the inhabitants evidently lost the suit. In 1631-2 Charles I granted the ferry late in the tenure of Walter Hickman to Basil Nicoll and John Sampson.[98] In 1691 William III granted protection against the pressgang to William Rose and Marmaduke Greenaway, as their services were essential

[79] Frederick Scheer, *Kew and its Gardens*, 13.
[80] John Evelyn, *Diary* (ed. Bray), 951, 514.
[81] Ibid. 451.
[82] *Dict. Nat. Biog.*
[83] Ibid.
[84] Sir W. Chambers, *Plans of Gardens and Buildings at Kew*.
[85] Sir Joseph Hooker has made exactly the same complaint.

[86] Sir W. Chambers, *Plans of Gardens and Buildings at Kew*.
[87] F. Scheer, *Kew and its Gardens*, 43.
[88] Ibid. 44.
[89] *Dict. Nat. Biog.* [90] Ibid.
[91] *Journ. of Mrs. Papendieck*, 51.
[92] *Dict. Nat. Biog.*
[93] *Journ. of Kew Guild* (1907), 359. The Church House was the earlier home of the Duke of Cumberland, and was revisited by the late blind king in 1853.

Hanover House belonged to a Mr. Theobald in 1771, according to a map still extant, and then to a Mr. Hunter, who died in 1812, and was called Hunter House. [94] Ibid.
[95] b.d. (1899), 6.
[96] L. and P. Hen. VIII, xi, 1417 (20).
[97] Star Chamber Proc. Hen. VIII, vol. 6, fol. 60-1.
[98] Pat. 7 Chas. I, pt. i, no. 6; *Cal. S.P. Dom.* 1603-10, p. 199.

for working the Kew ferry.[99] Thomas Tunstall acquired the ferry from William Churchman in 1732,[100] and in 1758–9 a wooden bridge was built by Robert Tunstall to take its place.[101] This bridge was replaced by a stone one which was begun in 1783–4[102] by Mr. Tunstall, whose descendant sold it to Mr. G. Robinson in 1819. A toll was charged on this bridge until 1873, when it was bought by the Corporation of London and the Metropolitan Board of Works for £75,000 and made free.[103] This bridge was closed to traffic in 1899, and a temporary one erected during the construction of the present bridge, which was opened 20 May 1903.[104]

Most of the houses in Kew are built round the Green and along the eastern side of the Richmond Road looking towards the gardens. The Green itself is a big triangular space. It is mentioned in a Parliamentary Survey of Richmond taken in 1649, and is there described as 'a piece of common or uninclosed ground called Kew Green, lying within the Township of Kew, conteyning about 20 acres.'[105] An 18th-century view, taken from a meadow to the east, shows the bridge on the right, a small irregular lake with an island to the left. A road led to the western point of the Green, where the palace was visible, a windmill behind it ; and trees, the trunks engirdled by seats, grew opposite the square-built church which stood isolated on the Green.[106] Some land at the end of the Green was inclosed by George IV, and a meadow east of the bridge was made common,[107] as part of a design, never carried out, of building a new palace at Kew in place of the Dutch House.[108] In the early 19th century Sir Richard Phillips described the Green as 'a triangular area of about 30 acres bounded by dwelling-houses,'[109] and another description of a slightly later date speaks of the 'well-built houses and noble trees' surrounding it.[110] In the last century the Green was the scene of village sports, such as climbing the pole, jumping in sacks, grinning through horse-collars, &c.[111]

The ecclesiastical parish of St. Luke, formed in 1890, includes a part of Kew. There are Roman Catholic (Our Lady of Loretto) and Wesleyan chapels in the parish.

St. Luke's Schools (National) were opened when the church was built. For the King's School, see Richmond, to which parish it properly belongs.

KEW formed part of the royal manor
MANOR of Richmond (q.v.). The name occurs in a Richmond Court Roll in 1348,[112] and Lysons quotes another of the time of Henry VII which also mentions Kew.[113] In 1484 the issues of the manor of Kew were granted to Henry Davy, keeper of the manor and park of Sheen, towards the maintenance of the deer in winter,[114] but this appears to be the only reference to it as a separate manor.

The church of *ST. ANNE* is a
CHURCH building of brick and stone in the Italian classic style consisting of a chancel, north organ-chamber and vestry, south chancel-aisle, nave, north and south aisles, and west porches and vestry. It stands at the south-east corner of Kew Green.

The building dates from 1714, but it has been much enlarged since that time, first by George III in 1770, and again by William IV in 1837. A plan dated 1805, in the church, shows a very small chancel and a nave with aisles of three bays, and the west porches as now. The present chancel was added in 1884 and the vestry in 1902 in memory of Queen Victoria.

The chancel has a small apsidal sanctuary, each of the three walls of which is pierced by a round-headed window of two lights with a circular piercing over. Between the windows inside are Corinthian columns forming shafts to the vaulted ceiling ; the entrance to the sanctuary is spanned by a round-headed archway. The chancel arch and each of the two side arches are segmental-headed and have red marble columns with quasi-Ionic capitals carved with winged cherubs' heads. Over the chancel rises an octagonal lantern lighted on its four main sides by circular windows and on the other four by half-round lights, and spanned by a domical roof covered with lead. Both chancel-aisles are lighted by round-headed east and side windows. The nave has a colonnade on either side of five bays with round plaster pillars having Doric capitals, above which are carved consoles ; the spaces between the columns are spanned by lintels, above which are elliptical-headed recesses forming cross groins with the elliptic barrel-vaulted ceiling of the nave. The aisles are lighted by round-headed windows and have flat ceilings. At the west end is a gallery extending right across the building and having an elliptical projecting front in the nave ; it contains the former royal pews with upholstered seats. At the west end is a porch having a vestry to the south of it, and a lobby with the stairs to the gallery on the north side. Outside is a portico about half the height of the building, with four shallow pilasters against the wall, and having four circular columns supporting a stone frieze enriched with triglyphs, and a moulded cornice above which is an open balustrade. The west wall proper, like the rest of the building, is of stock and red brick, and has a pediment head above which is a small clock-turret covered with cement and crowned by a copper dome ; in it hang eight tubular 'bells.' There were formerly three bells by T. Mears, 1838. The parapets of the side walls are plain. The roofs are covered with slates. The furniture generally is modern. The reredos is set with mosaics representing the Agnus Dei. Oak screens divide the chancel from its aisles, and it is fitted with oak seats. The font is of carved stone. To the east of the chancel is the burial vault, built of red brick and stone, of the Duke of Cambridge who died in 1850, and of the Duchess who died in 1889 ; the entrance to it is behind the altar. In the church there are many monuments to more or less celebrated people ; one in the south aisle is to Dorothy, Dowager Lady Capell, Baroness Tewkesbury, and another is to Thomas Gainsborough the painter, who was buried

[99] *Cal. S.P. Dom.* 1690–1, p. 345.
[100] Feet of F. Surr, Mich. 6 Jas. I.
[101] *Journ. of Kew Guild* (1903), 126.
[102] Ibid. ; Add. Chart. 16155.
[103] *Journ. of Kew Guild* (1903), 126 ; Stat. 31–2 Vict. cap. 17 ; 32–3 Vict. cap. 19 ; 37–8 Vict. cap. 21.

[104] Stat. 61–2 Vict. cap. 100, 155 ; *Journ. of Kew Guild* (1903), 126.
[105] *Vetusta Monum.* (Soc. of Antiq.), ii.
[106] *East view of Kew or Strand Green.*
[107] Local Act, 4 Geo. IV, cap. 75.
[108] *The Times,* 21 Dec. 1818 ; see above.

[109] R. Phillips, *A Morning Walk from London to Kew,* 1817.
[110] Frederick Scheer, *Kew and its Gardens,* 29.
[111] Ibid.
[112] Ct. Roll (gen. ser.), portf. 205, no. 5.
[113] Lysons, *Environs of London,* i, 202.
[114] *Cal. Pat.* 1476–85, p. 408.

in the churchyard in 1788; a third to Elizabeth Countess of Derby, daughter of Thomas Earl of Ossory and granddaughter of James Duke of Ormond, who died in 1717; and a fourth to Francis Bauer, F.R.S., &c., botanical painter to George III and resident draughtsman at Kew Gardens, who died in 1840.

The churchyard, which is at the south-east corner of Kew Green, surrounds the building and contains many graves.

The plate comprises a silver cup, paten, flagon, and almsdish of 1713, a cup and paten of 1892, and a cup of 1898. The only existing old register book is one containing baptisms and burials from 1714 to 1785 and marriages 1714 to 1781. The book following this to 1812 has been lost.

ADVOWSON In 1522 Fox, Bishop of Winchester, at the request of Thomas Byrkis and Anne his wife, granted licence to the inhabitants of Kew to have divine service in a chapel there during the lives of Thomas and Anne, reserving to the vicar of Kingston, in whose parish it lay, all customary rights, profits, &c.[115] This chapel was possibly the stable described as formerly a chapel and granted with the capital messuage in the 16th century. In the 18th century

Queen Anne gave a piece of land for a chapel of ease to Kingston (q.v.), and a church was built at the expense of the wealthier inhabitants and was consecrated in 1714 as St. Anne of Kew.[116] By Act of Parliament, 1769, the chapelry or curacy of Kew was separated from Kingston, and a vicarage was constituted there.[117] The right of presentation was reserved to the impropriator and patron of Kingston, then George Hardinge, who in 1786 sold it to King's College, Cambridge.[118]

The living was separated from Petersham in 1891, and is now a vicarage in the gift of the Crown.[119]

CHARITIES Elizabeth, Countess of Derby, who died at Kew in 1717, left £500, now represented by £763 consols, for the use of the poor.

There is an educational charity left by a Mr. Charles Jones, producing about £7 a year. Lady Capell, who died in 1721, left one-twelfth of her estate at Luddenham, Kent, for a charity school in Kew, or, failing that being established, to apprentice poor boys. She had also left one-twelfth to the Richmond Charity School, and £10 a year to the minister of Kew chapel so long as her family should be allowed two pews in the chapel and the family vault which she had built.

KINGSTON-UPON-THAMES

Cyningestun (xi cent.); Cyngestun (x cent.); Chingestun (xi cent.); Kingeston (xii cent.).

The town of Kingston is built on the river-bank; behind it is alluvium through which the Hogsmill river flows. On either bank are hills, those to the north-east carrying the ancient ridgeway to Wimbledon and along the slopes above the Thames valley, those to the south with roads to Mid-Surrey, Southampton, and the southern shires. All these converge at Kingston, for here in early times was one of the two great passages into Surrey from the north, at first by a ford near which the place probably first grew, then by the mediaeval bridge. Though the bridge now has fellows, and trade comes and goes by the branch line of the London and South Western Railway, completed in 1889, yet the river still influences the town, and brings the many pleasure-seekers who have made Kingston one of their favourite haunts by the river-side. Kingston is first mentioned in 836 or 838 as the meeting-place of the council at which King Egbert and the Archbishop Ceolnoth made their league.[1] This points to its being already a place of some importance, and the alliance here made between the West Saxon Crown and the Metropolitan See, which did so much to confirm their respective civil and ecclesiastical primacies in Britain, is the only reasonable explanation for the crowning here of the

West Saxon kings in the 10th century.[2] Edward the Elder was crowned here in 902.[3] Athelstan in 925,[4] Edmund and Edred in 940 and 946.[5] In 955 Edwig was elected at a gemot held here and crowned; at the coronation feast the young king left the hall and sought two ladies, Æthelgifu and her daughter Elfgifu, with the latter of whom he had formed an uncanonical marriage, and was dragged back to the feast by Dunstan and Bishop Cynesige.[6] In 958 Ethelred 'was very readily and with great joy' crowned here by Dunstan.[7] All these kings are said to have been crowned on the 'coronation stone' now preserved in the market-place.[8] This stone is not mentioned by Leland or Camden, but is traditionally said to have been preserved in the ancient chapel of St. Mary, which fell down in 1730.[9] It was then placed outside the town hall and used as a mounting-block until 1850, when the mayor, a local antiquary, placed it on its present pedestal and unveiled it with much ceremony on a public holiday.[10]

Kingston was a demesne manor of the West Saxon kings. Edward the Confessor let it out to farm and had a stud-farm in its neighbourhood.[11] It was its 'great bridge' over the Thames that gave it special importance, as in the 13th century, this was the most easterly of the bridges before London Bridge

[115] Manning and Bray, *Hist. of Surr.* i, 448; Egerton MSS. 2031-2034, iv.
[116] Manning and Bray, *Hist. of Surr.* i, 448; Aubrey, *Nat. Hist. and Antiq. of Surr.* v, 335; *Eccl. Topog.* no. 26.
[117] Private Act, 9 Geo. III, cap. 65.
[118] Manning and Bray, *Hist. of Surr.* i, 451; Inst. Bks.
[119] *Clergy List,* 1910.
[1] Kemble, *Cod. Dipl.* no. cccl, xiii.

[2] *V.C.H. Surr.* i, 338.
[3] Diceto, *Opera* (Rolls Ser.), i, 140.
[4] Diceto, op. cit. i, 44; *Anglo-Sax. Chron.* (Rolls Ser.), i, 139.
[5] Diceto, op. cit. i, 146; Kemble, *Cod. Dipl.* no. ccccxi.
[6] *Dict. Nat. Biog.* xvii, 140.
[7] *Anglo-Sax. Chron.* (Rolls Ser.), 238, 239; *Dict. Nat. Biog.* xviii, 27.

[8] Biden, *Hist. of Kingston,* 10.
[9] *N. and Q.* (Ser. 9), v, 392. In the rebus of the name of the town on the seal of the court of record, the last syllable is represented not by a stone but by the usual tun.
[10] Merryweather, *Half a Cent. of Kingston Hist.* 13.
[11] *V.C.H. Surr.* i, 297, 323.

was reached. In 1217 the peace between King John and Louis of France was first negotiated at Kingston though signed at Lambeth,[12] and Henry III came here in 1234, 1236,[13] and 1263.[14] In 1238 and 1261[15] assemblies of the barons were held here. Probably the castle captured by Henry III in 1264 on his march south to Rochester [16] was built to cover the bridge on land seized from the manor by Gilbert de Clare, who himself had no land nearer than Long Ditton (q.v.), for Kingston was held in demesne. Kingston, probably from its accessibility, was a favourite place for tournaments.[17]

In 1323 some rebels from the West Country made a disturbance here,[18] and for the next twenty years the country was in an unquiet state. In 1331 William Inge, Archdeacon of Surrey, complained that he had been attacked by no less than forty-six of the men, fishers, and others of Kingston, and imprisoned in the town,[19] and two years later Thomas Roscelyn applied for redress against several of the chief men of Kingston, who had taken away possessions of his worth £200.[20]

30 ft. of the bridge having b· removed before the insurgents' arrival.[21]

Until the 16th century the exter history of the town centred in the bridge, but with occupation of Hampton Court as a royal palace igston gained a new importance as a lodging-place those connected with the court, and accordin many orders were issued respecting infection from t plague, which attacked the town with great violenc 1625 and 1636.[22] During the Civil Wars the l'ortance of holding the bridge caused Kingston to b·arrisoned by Parliamentary troops, except for a brief ace on 14-19 November 1642, when it was held for the king, and in 1644 the City regiments were staned there.[23] In 1648 when the Earls of Holland and Peterborough and the Duke of Buckingham made a last effort in the royal cause they rose at Kingston, and after a march to Reigate retreated there again, when a skirmish took place near Surbiton Common, in which Lord Francis Villiers was killed, and the Cavaliers routed.[24] The Committees for Safety and

In 1346 commissioners were appointed to arrest the 'Roberdesmen, Wastries and Draghlaches,' who were harrying the neighbourhood [25] and who were perhaps responsible for the destruction of Hartington Coombe.[26] Kingston Bridge played a considerable part in the campaign of 1452, when the Duke of York, who had marched from the West Country and had been refused entry into London, was enabled to cross by it into Surrey and take up his position at Blackheath. Wyatt also used this passage in 1554 when, baulked of his intention to enter the city by way of London Bridge, he marched to Kingston. The extremely flimsy nature of the bridge stood the government in good stead, for considerable delay was caused by some

Sequestrations for Surrey both sat at Kingston, which from its proximity to London and accessibility has always been a centre for local administration. The 'general sessions' were held here in 1531,[27] and it was an Assize town until 1884 ;[28] it was also chosen as a centre by the Surrey County Council, whose fine offices stand in Penrhyn Road.

There is no evidence to determine at what date the great bridge over the Thames was built, but it was already endowed with lands for its maintenance in 1219,[29] when Master William de Coventry was master of the bridge. In 1223 Henry III passing through the town entrusted the work of the bridge to Henry de St. Albans and Matthew son of Geoffrey,[30]

[12] Flores Hist. (Rolls Ser. xcv), ii, 165.
[13] Cal. Pat. 1232–47, pp. 59, 140, 143.
[14] Cal. Chart, 1257–1300, p. 46.
[15] Cal. Pat. 1232–47, p. 204, Royal and Hist. Letters . . . of the Reign of Hen. III (Rolls Ser.), ii, 194.
[16] Hemingburgh, Chron. (Engl. Hist. Soc.), ii, 313.

[17] Lansd. MS. 225, fol. 10b.
[18] Cal. Pat. 1321–4, p. 385.
[19] Ibid. 1330–4, p. 205.
[20] Ibid. p. 503.
[21] Ibid. 1345–8, p. 180.
[22] See below.
[23] Stow, Annals (ed. 1615), 620.
[24] Cal. S.P. Dom. 1625–6, p.67 ; 1636–7, p. 138 ; 1637, p. 370.

[25] Ibid. 1642–56, passim; 1644, pp. 92, 102, 103, 107, 117.
[26] Ibid. 1648–9, p. 178; Dict. Nat. Biog. xxxviii, 403; The Hurly-Burly at Kingston.
[27] L. and P. Hen. VIII, v, 429.
[28] Lond. Gaz. 26 June 1884, p. 2781.
[29] Feet of F. Surr. 3 Hen. III, no. 22.
[30] Rot. Lit. Claus. (Rec. Com.) i, 558.

KINGSTON-UPON-THAMES : OLD BRIDGE, PULLED DOWN 1828

(From a water-colour drawing by T. Rowlandson)

KINGSTON-UPON-THAMES MARKET PLACE

(From a water-colour drawing by T. Rowlandson)

a local merchant, with seisin of the bridge, its charters, and the house pertaining to it.[31] This house was, it has been suggested, on a site in the horse market, where a curious crypt of shaped chalk stones was recently discovered.[33] The bridge probably underwent little modification from an early period until the 19th century. Sketches made in about 1800 show a long and flimsy wooden structure consisting of a narrow causeway railed on either side and resting on rows of piles disposed in groups of four or five banded together by wooden beams. At this time the ducking stool stood prominently at the east end of the bridge.[33] This lightness of build necessitated constant repairs; the bridge was in a dangerous condition in 1318, when pontage was granted to the bailiffs and good men for six years upon all wares for sale crossing and from each ship laden with wares for sale exceeding the value of 100s. passing beneath it.[34] The grant was renewed for five years in 1383,[35] and again in 1400 for three years, when the king's esquire, William Loveney, and two others were appointed surveyors.[36] A flood did much damage in 1435, and pontage was obtained for five years[37]; this developed into a regular system of toll,[38] which was so burdensome that Robert Hammond settled land valued at £40 for the support and redemption of the bridge, the gift being commemorated by the following inscription on a rail at about the middle of the bridge:

' 1565 Robert Hamon gentleman, Bayliff of Kingston heretofore,
He then made this bridge toll-free for evermore '

When these rails were replaced, a stone similarly inscribed was set in the brickwork of the north side of the western abutment.[39] The tolls had formed a considerable part of the revenue which the borough administered in support of the bridge through the bridgewardens, though there was also an estate appropriated to the purpose, and some benefit was derived from the lands of Clement Milan.[40]
In 1556 the decay of the bridge and the burdens sustained about its repair were the pretexts for the grant of the fair of St. Mary Magdalene's Day, and also of a fish weir[41] The bridgewardens' accounts begin at the close of the 14th century, but are not detailed until 1568; later they were rendered annually to the Court of Assembly and signed by the bailiffs.[42] The wardens kept a storehouse for necessary materials, their usual method being to buy timber and make the repairs by their own workmen; so in 1572 12d. was paid ' for making of the Plankes,' 5s. ' for two legges for the brydges,' and 2s. for ' stoping of holes '; gravel for the causeway was always a serious item.[43] In the same year 13s. was given to the poor on Easter Day, and probably the 18d. paid to the churchwardens in 1569 was also for alms.[44] The Court of Assembly made such by-laws as were

needful; so in 1680 and 1685 it was ' ordered that if upon any Saturday or other market or Faire day of the saide Towne two carts meere upon the Great Bridge of Kingston that then each carte shall forfeit the sume of 6d. which said Forfeiture shalbe paid by the owner of the said carte or partie driving the same to Thomas Styles keeper of the said Bridge to give an acct thereof to the Bayliffs and Freemen, and that everie emptie carte alwaies give way to the loaded.'[45] This order points to the narrowness of the bridge, which was only partly remedied when its Middlesex side was considerably widened in about 1791.[46] In 1812 the bridge was in such a state of decay as to be beyond repair, and the bridge estate was wholly inadequate to meet the cost of rebuilding. The corporation tried to shift the responsiblity on to the counties of Middlesex and Surrey, with the result that cross indictments were filed.[47] Judgement was finally given against the borough, and money was raised by the sale of lands. An Act of Parliament for rebuilding the bridge was obtained in 1825,[48] and the work was begun in that year, Lord Liverpool, the High Steward, laying the first stone.[49] The bridge, which rests on five arches of stone, was the design of Edward Lapidge, the architect of the Fitzwilliam Museum at Cambridge, and himself a local man.[50] It was built about 100 yards south of the old one and brought about a considerable change in the topography of this part of the town. Hitherto the way from London Street had been down Wood Street into the Horse Fair and then west from this down Old Bridge Street, at the corner of which probably stood the Bridge House. To approach the new bridge London Street was continued westward from the point at which Church Row touches it, sweeping away the row of houses abutting on the churchyard which now lay open to the view. The new street was called Clarence Street in honour of the Duchess of Clarence, wife of the prince afterwards William IV, who opened the bridge in grand procession in July 1828. The skeleton of the old bridge still stood, though with several bays broken to prevent its use. For some years tolls were charged and were let for £2,000 a year.[51] There was much rejoicing when the toll was abolished in 1870, and from this time the volume of traffic has continuously increased.
From the great bridge the way south into the town lay down Thames Street. The north end of this, the open Horse Fair, and the surrounding ' Back Laines,' as they were called in the 16th century,[52] were cleared of their ancient buildings and undesirable inhabitants in 1905, when the present houses were built. Farther south the 17th and 18th-century houses still remain: the street is divided from the river by shops with gardens behind; passages lead through darkness into alleys such as Fountain Court, where the houses stand round an enormous leaden

[31] *Rot. Lit. Claus.* (Rec. Com.), i, 558.
[33] Information kindly given by Mr. Benjamin Carter.
[33] Some interesting sketches of the bridge c. 1800, by Thomas Rowlandson, are exhibited in the Municipal Art Gallery and Museum.
[34] *Cal. Pat.* 1317–21, p. 113.
[35] Ibid. 1381–5, p. 219.
[36] Ibid. 1399–1401, pp. 389, 413.
[37] Ibid. 1429–36, p. 462.

[38] Manning and Bray, *Surr.* i, 346, where the tariff is given.
[39] Ibid. 347.
[40] Doc. of Corp. Accts. of the bridge-wardens, churchwardens, &c.
[41] Roots, *Charters*, 78.
[42] Doc. of Corp. Ct. of Assembly Bks. *passim.*
[43] Doc. of Corp. Bridgewardens' Accts. 1572.
[44] Ibid. 1569.

[45] Doc. of Corp. Ct. of Assembly Bk. 2 Dec. 1680 : 3 Apr. 1684.
[46] Manning and Bray, *Surr.* i, 347.
[47] Manning and Bray, *Surr.* iii, App. p. xxxvi.
[48] Local Act, 6 Geo. IV, cap. 125 ; 11 Geo. IV.–1 Will. IV, cap. 65.
[49] Brayley, *Hist. of Surr.* iii, 48.
[50] *Dict. Nat. Biog.* xxxii, 141.
[51] Brayley, *Hist. of Surr.* iii, 48.
[52] Roots, *Charters*, 105.

3

62

bowl. Near this is a passage preserving the name of the Bishop's Hall, once the property of the Bishops of Winchester. Probably it first came into their hands in 1202, when Bishop Godfrey paid 14s. to Osbert Horo for three messuages, retaining two and letting the other to Osbert.[52] The Bishop's Hall was soon deserted and was leased to tenants, certainly from 1392[53]; as Leland put it, 'now it is turned into a commune Dwelling House of a Tounisch man. Sum Bishop, wery of it, did neglect the House and began to build at Asher near the Tamise side 2 or 3 miles above Kingston.'[54] In the time of William of Wykeham it was described as between a lane leading to the Thames on the south, a tenement on the north, and the river on the west.[55] In 1533 the master of the chapel of St. Mary Magdalene leased a toft and garden abutting on 'le Byshoppe Hawe' on the north, the Thames on the west, and the tenement of Richard Benson on the east[56]; this last was described as situated between the highway and Bishop's Hall.[57] These descriptions prove that the hall faced the river and can have had no frontage to Thames Street. Sold to Henry VIII with other lands of the see, it was granted in 1544 as a garden and lands to Richard Borole, barber-surgeon, and John Howe, grocer, of London,[58] but in 1567 Mr. Starr paid 3s. 4d. to the bailiffs and freemen for 'Bisshopes Hall,'[59] and in 1670 Robert Viall paid 8s. for a tenement so called. By 1804 no traces of the building remained,[60] and the site is now occupied by stables and yards. Probably Thames Street has always been one of the chief shopping districts; in 1430-1 John Cheeseman was accused of making an encroachment on Thames Street by putting out there a porch and butt or movable counter.[61] At the south end of the street a turn brings the market-place into view. Standing here it is difficult to believe that the turmoil of London is but 12 miles away; only a few modern shop-fronts proclaim this present century, and even they do not hide the high-pitched roofs which show above the stucco of the walls and assert their age. A map ascribed to the 17th century suggests that the market-place originally extended to the Horse Fair as one open space with the church in the midst. Purprestures seem to have brought the town to its present state at an early period, for the houses round the market-place and churchyard were held in burgage. Probably here, as elsewhere, each trade had a particular pitch for its booths, which it retained when the stalls were replaced by houses, and hence the Butchery, Cook Row, in the market-place, and the Apple Market, an excellent example of the results of encroachment. Close to the town hall from at least the 17th to the 19th century stood a small octagonal building[62] of red brick with a high roof covered with tiles and supported on pillars, which thus formed an open space beneath. Its purpose is forgotten, but it may be suggested that it was to this that reference was made in 1685 when the toll of the Oat Market was leased at a rent of £4 a year 'to the use of the chamber and

of the Maior for the repairing, supporting, maintaining and amending the house over the said toll of the said Oate-Market called ye pillory-house.'[64] The Malt Market also is mentioned in 1670[65] and points to a trade very prosperous here in this and the following century; the Wool and Leather Markets paid rent to the bailiffs and freemen in 1417-18, and the Cheese Market is also mentioned.

One of the oldest houses in Kingston is a butcher's shop at the corner of the passage leading to the Apple Market. It is a house of three stories, the ground floor converted into the shop, the first floor overhanging and the top gabled; these are all cemented and have modern windows. On the side to the alley the upper stories also overhang and are cemented. In the wall are remains of a 15th-century wood window with a cinquefoiled ogee arch and a traceried head; the window head probably dates the whole building. An inn on the other side of the passage, in the Apple Market, may have been as old, but has been almost completely modernized. No. 5 Market Place, just opposite (now belonging to Messrs. Hide & Co. furniture dealers, etc.), formerly the Castle Inn mentioned in 1537,[67] retains an early 17th-century staircase from the ground to the second floor; the heavy square newels have carved and panelled sides and ball tops, the carriages or sloping strings are carved as laurel wreaths. The handrails are heavy, and the space between the strings and handrails is filled in with heavy foliage, roses, and other subjects; at the head of the first flight are three tuns, and on the first floor is a Bacchus seated on a tun and holding up a cup, and there are other human figures worked in with the foliage. Various initials, evidently original, are scattered over the work; on one newel head IORPGVP, on another newel CB EB SB AB; in a true lover's knot N B s; on a human face in a third newel FV and HB; on a fourth TS, TI, and another GD. The building has been modernized in front, but the back towards a courtyard is unaltered; it is of narrow bricks with moulded eaves, cornices, &c. Some of the bricks have initial letters in relief, like the stairs; among others SB and AB appear again, and the dates 1651 and 1656 (? 1636). The 18th-century outside gallery of the inn is also retained. In 1769 it paid 1s. 10d. quit-rent,[68] and remained in use as an inn until converted into dwelling-houses in the middle of the 19th century. Backing on to the south-east of the church is another row of three old houses converted into shops; they are of timber plastered over, and have overhanging second floors above which are four gabled heads.

The town hall was built in 1838-40; in 1837 the proposal that a new site should be chosen was fiercely opposed by the townsfolk,[69] who finally had their way. The old town hall, red brick and gabled, probably dated from the 16th century, and had beneath it an open market-stead extended on the south by a sort of shed; in 1670 Benjamin Woodfall paid £1 for his shop under the Court Hall,[70] or

[52] Feet of F. Surr. 4 John, no. 493; cf. Cott. MS. Clerp. C. vii, fol. 9b. 67.
[53] Manning and Bray, Surr. i, 345.
[54] Leland, Itin. vi, fol. 25.
[55] Manning and Bray, Surr. i, 345.
[56] Add. Chart. 23531.
[57] Chan. Inq. p.m. (Ser. 2), lxxxvii, 89.
[58] L. and P. Hen. VIII xix (1), g. 1035 (25).

[60] Doc. of Corp. Chamberlain's Accts. 1567, 1670.
[61] Manning and Bray, Surr. i, 345.
[62] Doc. of Corp. Ch. Bks.
[63] Shown in a sketch by Rowlandson in the Municipal Art Gallery and Museum.
[64] Doc. of Corp. Ct. of Assembly Bk. 28 Oct. 1685; cf. Chamberlain's Accts. 1670, 1679.

[64] Doc. of Corp. Chamberlain's Accts. 1670.
[65] Lansd. MS. 226, fol. 64-9b.
[67] Valor Eccl. (Rec. Com.), ii, 36.
[68] Doc. of Corp. Quit Rent Bk. 1769.
[69] Doc. of Corp. Ct. of Assembly Bk. 2 Mar. 1837.
[70] Doc. of Corp. Chamberlain's Accts. 1670.

Gildhall, for the terms were synonymous. In the upper rooms, then as now, were kept the records of the borough, for in july 1684 the Court of Assembly ordered that the bailiffs and nine others should meet to sort out their writings and leases.[71] The assizes were held here, and in the 17th century the hall was then decorated with hangings brought from Hampton Court.[72] In 1670 'Mr. Marriott' received £2 for their use.[73] In 1572 two watchmen were paid 6d. 'for watching under ye court hall at ye syes,' and in 1670 were in special charge of the hanging.[74] 'The arms' were painted in the Gildhall in 1572, and in 1660 the painted window still in the council-room was presented in honour of the Restoration; in 1670 John Baylis was paid 'for taking down the glasse in Guildhall att Session times.'[75] Several important trials took place here, perhaps the most sensational being that before Blackstone in which George Onslow

offices, and here the public library was housed until in 1904 it was moved to its present building in the Fair Field, given by Mr. Andrew Carnegie. Clattern House stands at the southern end of the market-place opposite the town hall on the bank of the Hogsmill, Malden River, or Lurteborne as it seems to have been called in 1439.[77] Clattern House preserves the name of Clattering Bridge, which though but 8 ft. wide in 1831[78] had at least one house on its western side, for which £1 rent was paid to the corporation in 1620 and 1670.[79] The bridge was widened in about 1882 and the present coping erected.[80] Across the road and next to the bridge is a row of gabled houses with plastered fronts, all more or less restored or altered for modern shops; near these must have stood 'The Crane,'[81] the most important inn in Kingston during the 16th and 17th centuries. It had belonged to the free

KINGSTON : HIGH STREET

brought an action for libel against John Horne Tooke the politician and philologist.[76] The poorness of the accommodation provided caused much grumbling among both Judges and counsel, and in 1808 the corporation obtained an Act of Parliament authorizing the sale of the common lands to raise funds for building a new court-house. In 1811 they purchased Clattern House for the judges' lodging and added on its eastern side a court-house which cost them about £10,000. When Kingston ceased to be an assize town Clattern House was made the municipal

chapel of St. Mary Magdalene, and was held in 1546 by John Agmondesham and inherited by his son, but in 1564 it formed part of the endowment of the grammar school.[82] It was much frequented by the Court, and in 1526 was the lodging-place of the Imperial Ambassadors.[83] When they passed through the town the Chamberlain's Accounts show items such as 'Payd at ye Crane for wyen and pypens geven to ye Byshops,' for a gallon of sack for my Lord Mayor at the Crane 5s. and 'to the goodman of the Crane for frewt 12d.'[84] During the Common-

[71] Ct. of Assembly Bk. 3 July 1684. The 17th-century transcriber who filled Land. MSS. 225, 226, had before him documents which have now disappeared, as have some of those mentioned by the Inspector in 1872 ; Hist. MSS. Com. Rep. iii, App. 331-3.

[72] Chamberlain's Accts. passim.
[73] Ibid. 1670.
[74] Ibid. 1572, 1670.   [75] Ibid.
[76] Dict. Nat. Biog. lvii, 40.
[77] Land. MS. 226, fol. 27.
[78] Merryweather, op. cit. 14 ; 17 B.M. King's Maps and Plans, xl, 15, z.

[79] Chamberlain's Accts. 1620, 1670.
[80] Merryweather, op. cit. 15.
[81] Chapman, Handbk. to Kingston, 16.
[82] Chan. Inq. p.m. (Ser. 2), lxxxv, 65 ; Surr. Arch. Coll. viii, 318.
[83] L. and P. Hen. VIII, iv, 2397.
[84] Hist. MSS. Com. Rep. iii, App. 332.

wealth the 'Crane' was the seat of the Committee for Safety for the county,[85] but it seems to have lost its reputation at the end of the century. Close by was the Debtors' Prison.[86]

Although West-by-Thames Street, as High Street was called until the 19th century, was one of the oldest parts of the town it was considered without the vill in 1253, when the bailiffs complained that the tenants of Merton Priory did not keep watch and perform other duties as did the king's men, and answer was made that they were never accustomed to keep watch beyond the water at the end of the market towards Guildford, which was without the vill ; but only *pro homine mortuo* did they as others, serve within the vill.[87] From the bridge the road slopes gradually towards the river ; picturesque old houses are on either hand, and open gates show glimpses of the river or green trees. One of the most interesting of the houses, that known as King John's Palace[88] or Dairy, stood at the corner of Kingston Hill Road, but was pulled down in 1805. Its name preserved the tradition that there was a palace in this part of the town in the early 13th century, with offices stretching into the Bittoms on the east. No record, however, of such a building has been found, though Richard II was certainly staying somewhere in Kingston at the time of the death of Edward III, when the citizens of London came here to greet their new lord.[89] A fruit shop at the northern end of the street shows signs of age ; it is an irregular building with a plastered front and gabled roofs, and close to it is a furniture shop calling itself 'Ye Olde Malt House' ; its front is modernized, but it has a round malting chimney. There are several other old half-timbered and gabled houses in the street. Among them is a low three storied house now called 'Ye Olde White House,' with plastered front and overhanging upper story, which probably dates from the 16th century. A row of three others are worth notice ; one, now a coal office, is weather-boarded and has an overhanging upper story and a tiled roof with the eaves to the road ; the second is cemented, and has an overhanging upper floor and eaves, it is now used as the works of a boat proprietor ; the third (a butcher's shop) is similar in front, but the side of the house towards a yard on the south is of half-timber filled in with lath and plaster and a little brick ; two of the rearmost windows in this side have four-centred heads and are unglazed. On the other side, in a narrow court, the walls are also of half-timber filled with lath and plaster towards the rear, but with more modern brick towards the front. The upper story overhangs on curved brackets and a moulded facia, the head is gabled and has a good cusped bargeboard. Some of the windows in this side retain their original wood frames. The

house is evidently work of the 16th century. Farther south the road touches the Thames, and here is a wharf alive with the trade of rivercraft.

North of the bridge the towing path is edged with small white houses. Here too are boat-houses, and the bank is covered with small craft. Across the river is a house with embanked garden, then come red wooden sheds, then orchards. Beyond the little houses, and protected from the towing path by a lawn set with sycamores, is Downhall, the property of Mrs. Nuthall, widow of the late Mr. G. W. Nuthall, a grey stuccoed house with jalousies and older kitchens behind. Downhall was held in the 13th century of the manor of Canbury (q.v.) by Lewin and Alan le Mariner, and was afterwards leased to Ralf Wakelin and Beatrice his wife.[90] In 1485–6 it was styled a 'capital messuage' or 'manor,' and was held of Merton by Robert Skerne, on whose death in that year it passed to Swithin his son.[91] It was conveyed in 1617 by Mildred Bond, widow, and Thomas Bond to Anthony Browne and Matilda his wife.[92] Downhill lies in Canbury ; not far away the ancient tithe-barn stood until sold in 1850 and pulled down. North of this is the railway bridge and station, the gasworks, a recreation ground, and, finally, Ham Common and Ham Fields.

Vicarage Lane takes its name from the old vicarage, which stood here until the modern house was built to replace that given by John Lovekyn to the vicar in 1366.[93]

In 1513 four Lollards were examined at Kingston, and one Thomas Denys was burned in the market-place on 5 March, the rest submitted.[94] There was a strong element of Puritanism in Kingston. Richard Taverner the controversialist lived at Norbiton, and was probably the Mr. Taverner who bought the roodscreen in 1561.[95] Before 1584 John Udall was lecturer or curate-in-charge, but was deprived of his licence to preach by the High Commission in 1588.[96] In the early 17th century Edmund Staunton was vicar for twenty years, but was suspended for a time before 1638,[97] probably for puritanical teaching ; he was known as 'the searching preacher,' and was diligent both in catechising and teaching from house to house.[98] In 1658 a strong Puritan, Richard Mayo, was presented to the living. He, though ejected in 1662, kept a separatist congregation together, which was licensed under the Indulgence of 1672.[99] In 1698 his more famous son Daniel Mayo[100] succeeded John Goffe as pastor of the Presbyterian congregation here. He died at Kingston in 1733 and was succeeded in the ministry there by George Wightwick of Lowestoft.[101] John Townsend, the founder of the London Asylum for Deaf Mutes, came here in 1781 as pastor.[102] The congregation, as was so often the case, became Independent. The chapel in Eden Street

---

[85] *Cal. S.P. Dom.* 1644, pp. 41, 165.
[86] Merryweather, op. cit. 23.
[87] *Abbrev. Plac.* (Rec. Com.), 136.
[88] A water-colour sketch of the house, and photographs of many other houses now pulled down in this part of Kingston may be seen at the Municipal Art Gallery and Museum. The oldest part of this house contained brick-work, perhaps of the 15th century, and was floored with beams of Spanish chestnut.
[89] Holinshed, *Chron.* iii, 415.
[90] Cott. MS. Cleop. C. vii, fol. 114.
[91] Chan. Inq. p.m. (Ser. 2), mlxv, 5. Ro-

bert Skerne was son of William Skerne, who founded the chantry in Kingston Church. William was nephew to Robert Skerne, who died in 1437, and has a brass in the church. Bray says (*Surr.* i, 375) that this Robert was also of Downhall, but this has not been proved.
[92] Feet of F. Surr. East. 15 Jas. I.
[93] *Surr. Arch. Coll.* viii, 143.
[94] Winton Epis. Reg. Fox, iii, fol. 69–76.
[95] *Surr. Arch. Coll.* viii, 93.
[96] *Dict. Nat. Biog.* is mistaken in calling him vicar. The vicar was Stephen Chat-

field, who became also rector of Charlwood in 1583 and lived there, but did not give up Kingston.
[97] *Cal. S.P. Dom.* 1637–8, p. 567.
[98] *Dict. Nat. Biog.* liv, 112.
[99] Photograph in the Kingston Municipal Library from the original document in the possession of Lady Tangye ; *Dict. Nat. Biog.* xxxvii, 174 ; *V.C.H. Surr.* ii, 39, 40.
[100] *Dict. Nat. Biog.* xxxvii, 171.
[101] Waddington, *Surr. Congregational Hist.* 234 (from the Church Bks.).
[102] *Dict. Nat. Biog.* lvii, 106.

KINGSTON-UPON-THAMES : ST. MARY MAGDALEN'S CHAPEL, FORMERLY USED AS THE GRAMMAR SCHOOL

KINGSTON-UPON-THAMES : ST. MARY MAGDALEN'S CHAPEL, USED AS THE SCHOOL GYMNASIUM

was built in 1856.[103] The Presbyterian Church of England chapel, built in Grove Crescent Road in 1883, has no connexion with this original Nonconformist body. Another early body of Nonconformists in Kingston was that of the Quakers. George Fox often preached here, the meetings being held in the house known as King John's Dairy. In 1769 they had a burial-place in Eden Street[104] and there they still have a meeting-house. The Wesleyans also have one chapel in Eden Street, another being at Kingston Hill. There are also four Baptist chapels : in Union Street, Queen Elizabeth Road, Cowleaze, and London Road. The first represents a secession from the Independents in the latter part of the 18th century. The Primitive Methodists have chapels in Victoria and Richmond Roads, while the Brethren meet in the Apple-market.

Heathen, now Eden Street, is said to have taken its name from being the Jews' quarter, and was so called when the earliest extant rentals were made. This and London Street are full of quaint houses, some timbered, some built of wood.

Next to the Grammar School chapel in the London Road are almshouses of red brick, six on either side of a projecting middle bay with a gabled head. The houses are of two stories with modern door and window frames and tiled roofs. In the middle bay a square-headed doorway with cemented rustic quoins opens into a small common room. On the first floor are three oval windows, and in the middle a tablet inscribed ' CHARITATI SACRUM Anno Salutis 1668 being the Gift of WILLIAM CLEAVE Alderman of London for Six Poor Men and Six Poor Women of this Town for whose Maintenance for Ever He hath given A Competent Revenue and also Caused these Buildings to be Erected at his own Expense for the Habitation and Convenience of the said People.' On a cartouche over are his arms : Argent on a fesse between three wolves' heads razed sable three molets or ; and crest, an eagle with a serpent in its beak. Above this is a sundial with the initials and date W C 1668.

The Technical Institute in Kingston Hill Road and the Polytechnic in Fife Road provide education in technical subjects, and secondary education is cared for by the Grammar and the Tiffin foundation schools, and there are several elementary schools.

Norbiton (Norbinton, xiii cent. ; Norbeton, xiv cent.), which lies towards the north end of London Street, is not mentioned in the Domesday Survey, but occurs early in the 13th century when William de Wicumb and Sailda his wife quitclaimed 6 acres of land there to Hamon son of Ralf and William son of Siward.[105] The hamlet was part of the manor of Kingston, and the common which lay to the north was under the control of the bailiffs and freemen,[106] who used the timber there for ' the mending, repairing and entreteyning of the wayes' as being appurtenant ' to the King's Royalty, the grant whereof they have in their fee farm.' [107] The right of felling the timber was upheld by an order in Council in 1543,[108] though violently opposed by the inhabitants

of Norbiton, and was of some value, for the Court of Assembly ordered, in 1680, ' that a book should be bought to enter ye accounts of ye wardens of Norbiton Common in, and that the same be left with the Town clerk to enter as other accounts.'[109]

In the East Field of Norbiton in the reign of Edward III lay Walepot, Adewellerthe, Kyondescroft, Crokkeres Forlang, and Wateryngcroft,[110] and the common of Norbiton is mentioned as the northern boundary of a road which had 'le Holefur' on the south.[111] The common lands were inclosed under an Act of Parliament obtained in 1808,[112] and from that date the population grew so rapidly that the new ecclesiastical district of St. Peter was formed in 1842, the parish of St. John the Baptist, Kingston Vale, in 1847, the consolidated chapelry of St. John the Evangelist in 1873, the parish of St. Paul, Kingston Hill, in 1881, and the parish of St. Luke, Gibbon Road, in 1890.[113] The population numbered 9,063 in 1901.[114] From the Kingston Road, Kingston Hill, and Park Road, innumerable streets have radiated, and nearly the whole space here between the Hogsmill river and Richmond Park is now occupied or about to be developed. Manor Gate Road takes its name from the 'Manyngate' mentioned with Tarendeslane in the reign of Richard III.[115] A road from Latchmere towards Manningate is mentioned in 1605,[116] Hog Lane Gate in 1683.[117]

Among the larger houses in Norbiton are Kenry House (Earl of Dunraven), Coombe Hurst (Mr. R. C. Vyner), Warren House (Gen. Sir A. H. F. Paget), Coombe End (Mr. B. Weguelan), Coombe Wood Farm (Lord Archibald Campbell), Coombe Warren (Mr. L. Currie), Coombe Court (Earl de Grey), and Latchmere House (Mr. P. Jackson).

The Elementary Schools are St. Peter's, Cambridge Road, 1852 ; St. Paul's School, 1871 ; and St. John the Evangelist's School, 1873 ; the Bonner Hill Road School was built in 1906, and schools in connexion with the churches of St. John the Evangelist, St. Luke, and the Roman Catholic Church of St. Agatha. In Church Road the Guild House School is for physically defective children.

Surbiton (Subertone, xiii cent. ; Subeton, xiv cent.) is not mentioned in Domesday Book, but was a hamlet in 1179 when the men of Surbiton, represented by John Hog and about twenty others, granted to the Prior and convent of Merton land in Grapelingham for twenty-one years, with a preference, under which a fresh lease was made in 1203.[118] The grange of Edith de la Stronde is mentioned in 1229,[119] and in 1296 Isabella widow of William le Haselye granted her curtilage to John le Poter with the hedge and ditch towards the field and with the wall towards the highway.[120] In 1417-18 seventeen tenements here paid £1 11s. 11¾d. quit-rent to the bailiffs and freemen of Kingston, the rate here as elsewhere being 2d. per acre.[121] Until the inclosure award made for Kingston in 1838 under authority of an Act of Parliament of 1808[122] about 190 acres remained commonable in Surbiton, and extended

[103] Waddington, Surr. Congregational Hist. 233 (from the Church Bks.).
[104] Doc. of Corp. Quit Rent Bk. 1769.
[105] Feet of F. Surr. 3 Hen. III, no. 17.
[106] Doc. of Corp. Ct. Bks.
[107] Acts of P.C. (new ser.), 1542-7, pp. 154-5.
[108] L. and P. Hen. VIII, xviii (1), 893.

[109] Doc. of Corp. Ct. of Assembly Bk. 7 July 1680.
[110] Rentals and Surv. (P.R.O.), R. 629.
[111] Ct. Bks.
[112] Local Act, 48 Geo. III, cap. 134.
[113] Lond. Gaz. 6 May 1873, p. 2249 ; 10 Jan. 1881, p. 120.
[114] Pop. Ret. 1901.

[115] Rentals and Surv. (P.R.O.), R. 629.
[116] Add. R. 26599.
[117] Corp. Ct. of Assembly Bk. 20 May 1683.
[118] Surr. Arch. Coll. viii, 14.
[119] Feet of F. Surr. 13 Hen. III, no. 22.
[120] Add Chart. 17273.
[121] Lansd. MS. 226, fol. 64.
[122] Local Act, 48 Geo. III, cap. 134.

from the Surbiton Hill Road, or a little below Villier's Path, on the north to the division of Surbiton from the parish of Long Ditton on the south, and from Clay Hill and King Charles's Road on the east to just beyond the houses on the near side of the Ewell Road on the west.

The only house in the district covered by the modern Surbiton marked on the maps of the 18th century was Berrylands Farm. It certainly existed in 1736,[132] and is probably much older, if it can be identified with Berowe, where William Skerne had licence to inclose land called the Fyfteen Acres in 1439,[134] and Berow or Barrow Hill held by Robert Skerne of Thomas Wyndsore in 1485–6.[135] Early in the 19th century building began in the valley towards Kingston with the original Waggon and Horses public-house, and the Elmers called Surbiton House until 1823 and pulled down before 1888. Maple Farm, afterwards called Maple Lodge, was built by Christopher Terry about 1815 as the Manor House. In 1808 Southborough Lodge, the first house on the hill, was built for Thomas Langley by John Nash, the architect of Buckingham Palace ; this with the three farms and a windmill was the only building here until 1811, when the White House, afterwards known as Hill House, was built [136] where the office of the Urban District Council now stands. Surbiton Hill House was next built in 1826 partly from material from the abandoned palace of Kew. Though still, as in the 13th century,[137] covered with furze and heath, the land was already considered of value as a building site.

The whole position of the neighbourhood was altered when in 1836 the main line of the London and South Western Railway was brought through Surbiton because, tradition says, the inhabitants opposed its original course through Kingston. A small cottage-like structure called Kingston Station was built in the deep railway cutting near the Ewell Road Bridge, and was used until 1840, when Thomas Pooley gave the present site to the company.[138] The 18th-century maps of the neighbourhood mark but one main road as passing through Surbiton. This, the Portsmouth Road, is a continuation of the Kingston High Street and follows the river, though separated from it for some distance by public gardens. There were of course minor roads : Leatherhead Mill Lane, Lower Marsh Lanes, and a road corresponding to the modern Clay Hill and King Charles's Road are mentioned;[139] a lane from the Ewell Road to Berrylands Farm is marked on a map of 1813, as is also the lane now called Villier's Path and Clay Hill.[130] The western side of Surbiton was the first to be developed. After the death of Christopher Terry in 1838 the Maple Farm lands were bought by Thomas Pooley, who began to lay out roads and build houses. Having insufficient capital he mortgaged heavily, principally to Coutts & Co., the bankers, who finally foreclosed. They managed the property well, and the Oakhill and Raphael estates followed, their streets of staid Victorian houses giving this quarter its essentially residential character. Lately, however, this has become

the shopping district of Surbiton, a feature emphasized since the opening of the United Tramways Company's electric service in 1905. In the extreme southern corner of this section lay the Seething Wells, yielding an abundant supply of water. The land inclosed under the Act of 1808 was purchased by the Lambeth Waterworks, and reservoirs opened in 1851 ; they were followed by the Chelsea Water Company, who, in 1852, built the works adjoining these on the north.

The Berrylands or eastern hill section was developed in 1851, the land making £500 per acre at public auction in 1853. In spite of the great change in the character of the neighbourhood, the roads, lighting, and drainage were still those of a hamlet. Under the Surbiton Improvement Act of 1855[131] the inhabitants secured local government by fifteen commissioners who, with some modifications in 1882,[132] retained their authority until Surbiton became an Urban District. The southern section was a little later in growth. In this district the land attains its highest point, being 120 ft. above ordnance datum on Oak Hill. The lowest point (20 ft. above sea-level) is by the river side. The soil on the lower levels is chiefly gravel on a subsoil of London Clay ; on Surbiton Hill it is clay, and there were brick-kilns near the Fish Ponds in 1838.[133]

Within the last five years an entirely new district has sprung up between the Surbiton Hill Road and Clay Hill, taking the estate of Crane's Park from the Cranes, the large house which stood here. The development of this estate has resulted in a continuation of King Charles's Road into Kingston, and has reduced Villier's Path, the traditional scene of the death of Lord Francis Villiers in 1648, to a mere footpath hemmed in with houses. The hillside east of this is now divided into building lots, and it is anticipated that Clay Lane will soon form the backbone of a further series of streets. On the island in the Thames opposite Surbiton, called Raven's Eyot, are the head quarters of the Kingston Rowing Club, founded in 1858. The population of the urban district in 1901 was 15,017.[134] The development of Surbiton was marked by the formation of the parish of St. Mark's, part of which was assigned in 1863 to Christ Church, Surbiton Hill ;[135] and in 1876 another part of St. Mark's parish was assigned to the consolidated chapelry of St. Matthew, which was partly formed from the parish of Long Ditton.[136] In 1854 the Congregationalists built a handsome church in Maple Road.[137] This becoming too small for the congregation a larger church was built in 1864 at the corner of Grove Road. The first Wesleyan services in 1861 were held in a hall and afterwards in an iron chapel ; the church in the Ewell Road was dedicated in 1882. In 1874 the Oaklands Baptist chapel in Oakhill Road was opened. The Baptist chapel in Balaclava Road was opened in 1905. In 1879 the Primitive Methodists built an iron church, now disused, in Arlington Road. The Roman Catholic church of St. Raphael was built by Charles Parker [138] for Mr. Alexander Raphael

---

[132] Rowley W. C. Richardson, *Surbiton, Thirty-two years of Local Self-government.* Southborough Farm was also probably standing at this date.
[134] Pat. 17 Hen. VI, pt. ii, m. 21.
[135] Chan. Inq. p.m. (Ser. 2), i, 22.
[136] Richardson, op. cit.

[137] Add. Chart. 17272.
[136] Richardson, op. cit. 12.
[139] Rocque, *London in 1741–5*
[130] Horner, *Map of the Town and Parish of Kingston-upon-Thames.*
[131] Local Act, 18 Vict. cap. 36.
[132] Ibid. 45 & 46 Vict. cap. 61.

[133] Richardson, *Surbiton*, 8.
[134] Pop. Ret. 1901.
[135] Clergy List, 1910.
[136] Lond. Gaz. 2 May 1876, p. 2719.
[137] Richardson, *Surbiton*, 82 et seq.
[138] Dict. Nat. Biog.

in 1846–7. It was here that many members of the
Orleans family were married. It was shut up for
some years, but was re-opened to the public in
1908.

New Malden and Coombe, 2 miles east of Kingston, is a newly created Urban District, formed by
the great growth of new houses in the neighbourhood
during the last forty years. It was constituted an
ecclesiastical parish, being separated from the new
ecclesiastical parish of St. Peter's, Norbiton, in 1867,
and in the same year a Local Board was formed. In
1895, under the Local Government Act of the previous year, it was constituted a civil parish under an
Urban District Council. It is divided into three
wards, Coombe, New Malden, Old Malden (q.v.).
The total area is 3,220 acres, and the population in
1901 was 6,233, of whom only 503 were in Old
Malden. There is a railway station on the main London
and South Western Railway, the Junction also for
the Kingston line. The Baptist chapel was opened
in 1862 ; the Congregational chapel in 1880.
There is also in the parish a Wesleyan chapel, a Free
Church of England chapel, and a Roman Catholic
chapel of St. Egbert, opened in 1908. The Lime
Grove (Church) School for girls and infants was
built in 1870 ; the Christchurch Elm Road Boys'
Schools in 1896, and the County Council (mixed)
School was opened in 1908.

Hook (Hoke, xiv cent.) is an ecclesiastical parish,
in the part of Kingston old parish which divides
Long Ditton into two parts. It was constituted an
ecclesiastical parish in 1839, the inhabitants then
being mostly cottagers in small houses on the road
from Kingston to Letherhead. A considerable
number of better houses have now been built. Part
of the ecclesiastical parish was made a civil parish in
1895 under the Act of the previous year, but the
northern part is in the Urban District of Surbiton.

There is an iron Wesleyan chapel in the parish.
The schools (National) were built in 1860.

The ecclesiastical parish of St. Andrew, Ham, was
formed in 1834 ; it had formerly been a chapelry to
Kew.

The earliest mention of organized
BOROUGH government in Kingston is in 1086,
when the royal manor was under
the control of bedels, or elected officers.[139]
They are not again mentioned, but the name was
preserved until the 15th century in the 'Bedelsford.'[140]
In or about 1195 the men of Kingston claimed to
have held their town at farm by a charter of King
Henry which had been burnt by misfortune, and
they gave 100s. for holding their vill until the coming
of the king, and offered 30 marks for a charter
under which they might pay the same farm as
before.[141] This farm appears to have been £28 10s.,[142]

the amount granted here in 1199 and 1200 to
Joscelin de Gant.[143] Accordingly, on paying a
further 60 marks in 1200,[144] the men received their
first extant charter which confirmed the previous
grant, and gave the vill to the freemen of Kingston,
at the rent of £12 beyond the farm owed and customary.[145] They continued to hold the town at this
farm until 1208 when King John granted it to them
at the fee farm[146] of £50 yearly. In 1222 this fee
farm had been granted to John de Atia for his
maintenance in the royal service,[147] and he drew it
until 1226.[148] In 1236 the town was assigned to
Queen Eleanor as part of her dower,[149] and in 1281
was said to be of the yearly value of £51 8s. 6d.[150]
In 1290 the manor of Kingston was extended at
£52 8s. 6d.[151] and was still in the hands of the queen-
mother. The extra sum above the amount of the
fee farm perhaps represents the money service from
Postei's land,[152] serjeanties, and purprestures which
are expressly mentioned with Kingston in 1299 when
the town was assigned in dower to Queen Margaret.[153]
In 1300 the custody of Kingston was granted to the
local merchant Edward Lovekin that he might
reimburse himself from the farm and other issues of
that town for £500 lent to the king.[154] The farm
was granted to Queen Isabel in 1327.[155] Under
Richard II in 1378 began a long series of grants[156] of
portions of the fee farm to various officers and persons
connected with the royal household. It is possible
that the freemen of Kingston at this time had made
considerable purprestures, for which they paid additional rent, as in 1381 the farm was said to be
£54 8s. 10d.,[157] and in aid of this the king granted
them, in 1392, a shop and 8 acres of land which were
escheats to the Crown.[158] Part of the farm was
assigned in the middle of the 15th century to the
expenses of the royal household,[159] and in 1507 the
manor of Kingston was farmed by Thomas Lovell,
who committed waste of timber in Walton-on-
Thames.[160] On the formation of the honour of
Hampton Court in 1540 the fee farm was annexed to
it,[161] and part remitted in consideration of the fact
that much of the land paying quit-rent towards the
farm was now inclosed in the royal parks.[162] The
abatement was questioned, but ratified in 1563.[163]
The farm of Kingston was assigned as part of the
dower of Queen Catherine in 1665–6,[164] but was
alienated in 1670,[165] and in 1794 was only about
£8.[166]

The greater part of mediaeval Kingston was held in
burgage in aid of the fee farm, a quit-rent of 2d.
being paid on the acre, and sums varying from 20s.
to a farthing on tenements.[167] Quit-rents were also
paid by lands throughout the manor, and were received
in the 16th century from the manors of Imworth,
Clay Gate, East Molesey, Molesey Matham, Berwell,

[139] V.C.H. Surr. i, 308b.
[140] Lansd. MS. 226, fol. 64.
[141] Abbrev. Plac. (Rec. Com.), 94 ;
Cur. Reg. R. (Rec. Com.), i, 15.
[142] Cart. Antiq. K. 18.
[143] Pipe R. 1 John, m. 5 ; 2 John, m.
15 d.
[144] Ibid. 2 John, m. 15 d.
[145] Chart. R. 1 John, m. 7 ; Cart. Antiq.
SS. 8.
[146] Cart. Antiq. K. 18.
[147] Rot. Lit. Claus. (Rec. Com.), i, 544,
634.

[148] Ibid. 610, 565 ; ii, 65, 109 ; Devon,
Issues of the Exch. 7.
[149] Cal. Chart. 1226–57, p. 218.
[150] Cal. Pat. 1272–81, p. 438.
[151] Ibid. 1281–92, p. 368.
[152] See below under Coombe.
[153] Cal. Pat. 1292–1301, p. 452 ;
1307–13, p. 216.
[154] Ibid. 1292–1301, p. 501.
[155] Ibid. 1327–30, p. 69 ; 1330–4, pp.
195, 530 ; 1343–5, p. 447.
[156] Cal. Pat. 1377–81, pp. 193, 150 ;
1381–5, pp. 391, 157 ; 1385–9, pp. 146,

521 ; 1388–92, p. 481 ; 1391–6, pp. 70,
258, 509, 619, 717, &c.
[157] Ibid. 1381–5, p. 6.
[158] Roots, Charters, 61.
[159] Parl. R. v, 174 ; vi, 802b, 500a.
[160] Chan. Inq. p.m. (Ser. 2), xxi, 4t.
[161] L. and P. Hen. VIII, xv, 498 (36).
[162] Roots, Charters, 61 et seq.
[163] Ibid. 97 et seq.
[164] Pat. 17 Chas. II, pt. ix, no. 1.
[165] Ibid. 22 Chas. II, pt. ii, 11 Nov.
[166] Lysons, Environs of Lond. i, 235.
[167] Lansd. MS. 226, fol. 79.

Canbury, Hatch, Hook, and Hampton Court, as well as from lands in Long Ditton and Sandon.[168] In 1287–8 Kingston paid £13 5s. 4d. tallage,[169] and 10 marks were exacted in 1197–8 and the following year.[170] In 1210 the Crown took 50s.,[171] and in 1214 30 marks.[172] This last sum was demanded in 1236–7, when Henry III pardoned 10 marks 'so that the poor and more oppressed feel themselves relieved'; the remaining 20 marks were to be levied according to the tenants' respective means.[173] The tallage assessed in 1234 was £18, but the excess above 20 marks (£13 6s. 8d.) was released,[174] and the tallage from the men of the almonry of Westminster remitted.[175]

Beside the charters of 1200 and 1208 the freemen obtained from Henry III three charters in 1256, dated 10, 12, and 13 September. By the last they obtained the right of 'having and holding their gild merchant as they have theretofore had and held it, and as the *probi homines* of Guildford hold it.'[176] Probably, as in Guildford, the gild merchant was closely connected with the government of the town; this seems to be the only time that it is referred to in words. These charters were confirmed in 1343, 1378, 1400, and 1413. In 1441 the town was formally incorporated with markets rights corresponding to Windsor and Wycombe, under two bailiffs and the freemen. This charter of incorporation was confirmed in 1481, 1494, 1510, 1547, 1556, 1559, and 1603. Additional privileges were obtained under the charter of 1481 and confirmed in 1559. Elizabeth exempted the freemen from toll in 1592 and gave or rather restored to them a grammar school in 1564. Further charters were obtained in 1603, 1628, and 1662. In January 1685 the charters were surrendered to Charles II. He died a month later, and the surrender was repeated to his successor James II, who granted a new charter in August 1685. This was in turn revoked, and the old charter re-confirmed in 1688.[177]

The earliest evidence for the constitution of the governing body of Kingston points to a state of things very similar to that still in existence in 1835. The various charters were, as has been said, granted to the freemen of the town, who in the early 19th century were chosen from the free tenants of the manor; these under the names of gownsmen, peers, and fifteens, with two bailiffs, a high steward, and recorder, in 1835 formed the Court of Assembly which exercised control over both the policy and property of the town until the corporation was reconstructed in that year.[178]

In the absence of any town records before the 15th century it is impossible to decide the origin of the Court of Assembly. In 1346 the bailiffs were ordered to appear with six lawful men before the king in council to answer certain allegations concerning the community of the town;[179] and in the 15th century leases were usually made by the bailiffs

of the liberty of the men of Kingston and by the whole community of the town,[180] or 'with the assent of the whole community'[181] or 'of the honest men and community.'[182] Such leases were enrolled in the roll of the view of frankpledge on Tuesday in Whitsun week, the law day. On the incorporation in 1441 the bailiffs and freemen were given power to meet at the Gildhall and to make laws for the government of the town, which they might enforce with penalties.[183] It is not evident at what date this gathering obtained the title of the Court of Assembly, but a 'Court of Common Council' is mentioned in 1655.[184] The 'Books of the Court of Assembly' date from 1680, and though reconstructed under the charter of James II the new body were entered in the minute book of its predecessor. There was also a separate and inferior Common Council of sixteen under this charter in place of the 'Fifteens' of the old charters, and it was ordered that 'the Common Councilmen should have their vote in all orders and bye-laws which should be made either for letting, selling, or passing away any lands, tenements, or hereditaments belonging to the corporation and all laws for the good government of the town made in the Court of Common Assembly.'[185] The Court of Assembly, which, besides its other functions had control of the school and bridge, consisted of fifty-seven members in 1835 when it was replaced by the present Town Council.[186]

The 'Fifteens,' so called from their number, are first mentioned in the 16th century, and were also headboroughs, the group being generally known in the 17th and 18th centuries as that of 'the fifteen headboroughs';[187] they took oath on election to be conformable to the customs of the town.[188] On the Sunday after Michaelmas in each year the Fifteens met at the Gildhall,[189] and by ballot voted out two of their number, henceforth known as Peers; their places were taken by two voted in from among the free tenants of the manor and these were immediately elected ale-tasters,[190] and took oath for that office as well as for the office of freemen and headboroughs.[191] They were liable to a fine of £15 for refusing office. Although two was the customary number of new freemen the power of election enjoyed by the court under the charter was unlimited.[192]

Gownsmen were those freemen who had filled the office of bailiff; they seem to have been generally called 'masters' until the 18th century,[193] and in 1638 [194] the three 'masters' received an order from the exchequer in the absence of the bailiff. A list of the officers of the corporation drawn up in 1555 shows them to have been two bailiffs, two constables, two chamberlains, two churchwardens, two bridgewardens and two ale-tasters.[195] The bailiffs were elected from four nominees chosen from the gownsmen and peers by ballot of the fifteen on the Sunday before Michaelmas.[196] In 1655 the gownsmen and peers chose two of the four proposed as bailiffs for the

168 Roots, *Charters*, 61.
169 Pipe R. 33 Hen. II, m. 15 d.
170 Ibid. 9 Ric. I, m. 15 d.; 10 Ric. I, m. 10 d.
171 Ibid. 12 John, m. 15.
172 Ibid. 16 John, m. 3 d.
173 *Rot. Lit. Claus.* (Rec. Com.), ii, 180.
174 *Cal. Close*, 1231–4, p. 413.
175 Ibid. p. 396.
176 Roots, *Charters*, 28. He misdated the first as 10 Dec. 1255.

177 Chart. R. 1–20 Hen. VI, no. 17, m. 31; Roots, *Charters, passim.*
178 *Munic. Corp. Com. Rep.* iv, 2892.
179 *Cal. Close*, 1346–9, p. 84.
180 Lansd. MS. 226, fol. 25*b.*
181 Ibid. fol. 41.
182 Ibid. fol. 26.
183 Chart. R. 19 Hen. VI, m. 31 Roots, op. cit. 122 et seq.
184 *Cal. S.P. Dom.* 1655, p. 149.
185 Ct. of Assembly Bk. 31 Oct. 1685.

186 Public Act, 5 & 6 Will. IV, cap. 76.
187 *Cal. S.P. Dom.* 1655, p. 149.
188 *Hist. MSS. Com. Rep.* iii, App. 333.
189 Roots, *Charters*, 162.
190 *Munic. Corp. Com. Rep.* iv, 2895.
191 Ct. of Assembly Bk. 22 Dec. 1681.
192 *Munic. Corp. Com. Rep.* iv, 2895.
193 *Cal. S.P. Dom.* 1655, p. 149.
194 Ibid. 1637–8, p. 498.
195 Ct. Bk. 37 Hen. VIII—11 Eliz.
196 *Munic. Corp. Com. Rep.* iv, 2895.

Kingston-upon-Thames, Clattering Bridge

Kingston-upon-Thames, King John's Dairy, demolished in 1884

ensuing year,[197] but in 1835 the method had changed and the gownsmen and peers elected one, while the bailiffs of the present year, with the recorder and high steward, chose a second.[198] The voting was by a species of ballot, the names of the fifteen being written out and placed aside in the council-room, the vote being recorded by scratching the chosen name with a pen.[199] The growth of the power of the bailiffs is one of the most interesting features of the borough history. Deriving their powers from the bailiffs of the royal manor, they are first mentioned in 1234–5 as holding a court at Kingston,[200] and in 1242 were impleaded for unjust exaction of tolls.[201] The bailiffs and freemen had been clerks of the market under the charter of 1441,[202] the bailiffs only in 1628.[203] The charter of 1603 rendering their presence necessary at every meeting of the Court of Assembly[204] probably only ratified an ancient practice and made abortive an attempt of a royalist minority to hold a court in 1655.[205] This charter further granted that the bailiffs should be *ex officio* justices of the peace. In 1626 the Commissioners recommended that the outgoing bailiffs should retain their commission of the peace for a year after holding office,[206] and this was embodied in the grant of 1628.[207] Their position may be gauged by the order confirmed by the Court of Assembly in 1680 that the bailiffs were not to take out of the chamber any sum above 20*s.* without the privity and consent of the whole corporation.[208] The bailiffs were empowered to appoint under-bailiffs and were to be preceded by two serjeants-at-mace.[209] The office of bailiff was suspended shortly after the Restoration, when Charles II forbade the election of bailiffs until the differences between members of the town had been settled,[210] and it was only restored after a petition in September 1661.[211] The bailiffs were abolished by the charter of James II in 1685 and a mayor elected by the magistrates substituted;[212] Mr. Agar the first mayor complained that one of the Common Councilmen had 'very much abused him,' and the offender was accordingly discorporated.[213] Restored on the resumption of the charter, the bailiffs retained their office until replaced by a mayor under the reconstruction of 1835.[214]

Of the constables little is known, their office being such that they are seldom mentioned. The chamberlains filled a more important office and acted as treasurers.[215] They were elected by the Fifteens from among their fellows on the charter day, and might hold office for several years in succession.[216] Being considered an integral part of the Court of Assembly they are not expressly mentioned among the officers detailed in 1628;[217] their accounts are preserved from the 15th century and are full of detail concerning the

life of the town. In 1835 it was said that in practice the senior chamberlain alone executed the office, 'the Junior only signing the accounts,'[218] and possibly this explains the election of a 'treasurer' in 1684.[219] In the 16th century two churchwardens were also officers of the corporate body, which seems to have retained its power over them for another hundred years. They were answerable to the bailiffs and yielded up their accounts at the Gildhall each St. Luke's-tide.[220] The reason for this term being chosen is obscure, as St. Luke was not patron of the church or its chantries, nor was it one of the recognized quarters;[221] it probably had some connexion with the borough year, which began on the Sunday after Michaelmas. A meeting corresponding to the vestry was first held in the church in 1535,[222] when the bailiffs are expressly mentioned as being present; the vestry minute books begin a century later.[223]

It is not known when bridgewardens were first appointed as custodians of the bridge and its property;[224] they were elected from among the freemen by the Court of Assembly, and submitted their accounts for signature by the bailiffs each Michaelmas.[225]

The ale-tasters have been already mentioned; it was part of their duty to give a dinner to the court, and so important was this considered in the 18th century that recalcitrant ale-tasters were threatened with a fine of £10 in 1706[226] and with discorporation in 1721.[227]

The high officials of the corporate body were the high steward, the steward of the court, and the recorder. The office of high steward probably originated in the 16th century, when it was advisable to have some prominent person at court directly interested in the town's welfare. Lord Howard of Effingham is the first named. The office was not purely nominal, for in 1684 the corporation immediately applied to their high steward, Lord Arlington, for advice as to the surrender of their charter.[228] James II under the new charter appointed Lord Ailesbury to the office, which still exists and has been held by Lord Liverpool and other distinguished persons.[229] The appointment was for life by patent of the Court of Assembly, the presentation being signalized by 'a handsome treate';[230] the annual present consisted of eighteen sugar-loaves, worth about £9 in 1835.[231] The steward of the Court or 'Learned Steward,' as he was more frequently called in the 17th century,[232] filled an office originally much more humble in character than it afterwards became. By the charter of 1628 the appointment was limited to the attorney-general,[233] who has always held the office since that date.

A recorder is first mentioned in the charter of 1603 when he and the bailiffs were empowered to hold a court of record and to be Justices of the peace.[234]

[197] *Cal. S.P. Dom.* 1655, p. 149.
[198] *Munic. Corp. Com. Rep.* iv, 2895.
[199] Ibid.
[200] Maitland, *Bracton's Note Bk.* no. 1122.
[201] *Abbrev. Plac.* (Rec. Com.), 119.
[202] Roots, *Charters,* 43.
[203] Ibid. 149.
[204] Ibid. 123.
[205] Merewether and Stephens, *Hist. of Boroughs* (ed. 1835), 1685–6.
[206] S.P. Dom. Chas. I, lxvii, 27.
[207] Roots, *Charters,* 179.
[208] Ct. of Assembly Bk. 8 Oct. 1680.
[209] Roots, *Charters,* 172.

[210] *Cal. S.P. Dom.* 1660–1, p. 455.
[211] Ibid. 1661–2, p. 95.
[212] Roots, *Charters,* 220.
[213] Lansd. MS. 226, fol. 56.
[214] Public Act, 5 & 6 Will. IV, cap. 76.
[215] Ct. of Assembly Bk. 1680–1724, fol. 1.
[216] *Munic. Corp. Com. Rep.* iv, 2897.
[217] Roots, *Charters,* 167.
[218] *Munic. Corp. Com. Rep.* iv, 2897.
[219] Ct. of Assembly Bk. 5 Nov. 1684.
[220] Doc. of Corp. Churchwardens' Bks. 1523, 1575, 1578.
[221] Healea, *Hist. of the Church of Kingston; Surr. Arch. Coll.* viii, 68.

[222] Doc. of Corp. Churchwardens' Accts. 1585.
[223] Healea, op. cit. 103.
[224] *Vide supra.*
[225] Doc. of Corp. Bridgewardens' Accts. extant from 1508.
[226] Lansd. MS. 226, fol. 56.
[227] Ibid. fol. 47.
[228] Ct. of Assembly Bk. 27 Nov. 1684.
[229] Manning and Bray, *Surr.* i, 341–2.
[230] Ct. of Assembly Bk. 7 Nov. 1683–4.
[231] *Munic. Corp. Com. Rep.* iv, 2896.
[232] Ct. of Assembly Bk. 1 May 1682; 4 Sept. 1684.
[233] Roots, *Charters,* 161.
[234] Ibid. 131, 134.

The appointment of ' one skilled in the laws of the realm ' as recorder was directed in 1628 and was made by the Court of Assembly for life, the salary being eighteen sugar-loaves and £26 5s. a year.[235] His duties in 1835 were to attend the election of the municipal officers on the charter day, to preside at the sessions and court of record, and to act as steward of the court leet and as legal adviser to the corporation.

There is no evidence to show at what date a town-clerk was first employed, but the trades companies in 1609 had a clerk who later invariably fulfilled both duties.[236] He is first mentioned in the charter of 1628 as ' a common clerk and clerk of the peace, who is called prothonotary of the court of the town.'[237] He was elected for life by the Court of Assembly and was himself generally a freeman.[238] It was a disputed election of this officer that led in 1655 to a tumultuous assembly at the Gildhall, when certain freemen sat as a court, censured the bailiffs for their choice of a clerk, and discharged them from bearing office.[239] The town-clerk in 1835 acted as senior coroner, clerk of the court baron and court leet and as clerk-solicitor and attorney of the corporation.[240]

There were other officials of less importance. After the restoration of the grammar school two school-wardens were chosen from among the freemen by the Court of Assembly, to which they were responsible for their expenditure.[241] Paving wardens are also mentioned in 1684.[242] Inferior to these in status were the two serjeants-at-mace authorized by the charter of 1481,[243] who, under the grant of 1556, could execute writs and be sent by the bailiffs on business before justices of the peace, coroners, and other royal officers.[244] Their numbers were increased to four in 1628,[245] but there is no evidence that more than two were ever appointed. Their duty was to execute the process of the court of record ; in 1835 one of the serjeants was gaoler, and probably the office of keeper of the toll-booth mentioned in 1683–4 was filled by his fellow.[246] In 1682 the Court of Assembly ordered that in the future the bailiffs at the first hall after their election should deliver 30s. apiece for gowns for the serjeants.[247] In 1835 there were also two mace-bearers to carry the maces before the mayor on occasions of ceremony,[248] as well as a hall-keeper or general attendant on the Court of Assembly.[249]

According to Stuart practice the charter of incorporation was expanded and defined in 1603, when a few additional rights were granted, but no very material difference made. Henceforth the bailiff, steward, and recorder were to be justices of the peace for the town, its liberties, and the hamlets of Surbiton, Ham, and Hatch, with power to make amerciaments and deliver malefactors to gaol.[250] A further charter in 1628 defined the constitution more closely by authorizing the ancient methods of election and by stipulating that the Attorney-General should be the steward of the borough-court.[251] With the exception of the period covered by the charter of James II this remained the governing charter until 1835.

Although not then a Parliamentary borough, Kingston was among the corporations which Charles II attempted to remodel. The first indication of the purpose of the Government appears to have been received in June 1682, when 10s. was paid for making a copy of the governing charter for the use of the recorder,[252] but nothing further was done until the autumn of 1684, when the recorder resigned, probably as a protest, Francis Brown being elected in his stead.[253] In September of that year the bailiff and all the gownsmen waited on the high and the learned steward to learn the royal pleasure concerning the surrender,[254] and two months later the Attorney-General gave formal notice that a writ of quo warranto would be brought against the charter.[255] The corporation was evidently severely frightened, and also puzzled as to their wisest course of action. Their high steward, Lord Arlington, was ill, but they secured the goodwill of his secretary by the gift of a guinea and obtained his promise to ' let them know if he heard anything against them at any time.'[256] The surrender was authorized,[257] sealed,[258] and delivered to the king on 20 January 1685.[259] Charles II died on 6 February, and the surrender not having been enrolled was rendered void.

A second quo warranto was brought against the corporation in May,[260] and the bailiffs now applied direct to Jeffreys, who ' was so kind to the corporation as to take the business upon him,'[261] and ' directed that the Attorney-General should prepare a new surrender which should contain an absolute surrender of every person in the corporation, their respective offices, and places therein.'[262] The corporation though unwilling and terrified,[263] made an absolute surrender in June of all liberties, charters, lands, and manors.[264] They were forced to borrow £40 from the bridgewardens and smaller sums from the trades companies towards the expenses of the new charter, which was granted in August 1685 and remodelled the constitution under a a mayor, twelve aldermen, a recorder, high steward, steward of the court, sixteen common councilmen, and fourteen headboroughs,[265] the minor offices remaining unchanged.[266] All officers were amovable by the king in council, and the right was exercised in 1688 against the recorder, Sir Francis Wythens, and the corporation required to choose Robert Power in his stead.[267] The new charter was recalled at Michaelmas 1688, and the old form of government resumed, Francis Brown, who had been removed in favour of Wythens in 1685, returning to the office of recorder.[268]

The constitution of the borough, though characterized by the commissioners of 1835 as ' harmless if not useful to the town,' was remodelled in the same year by an Act of Parliament.[269] The style of the

[235] Munic. Corp. Com. Rep. iv, 1896.
[236] Doc. of Corp. Bk. of Trades Companies.
[237] Roots, Charters, 167.
[238] Munic. Corp. Com. Rep. iv, 2897.
[239] Cal. S.P. Dom. 1655, p. 149 ; Merewether and Stephens, op cit. 1685–6.
[240] Munic. Corp. Com. Rep. iv, 2897.
[241] Ct. of Assembly Bks. passim.
[242] Ibid. 3 July 1684.
[243] Roots, Charters, 59.
[244] Ibid. 74.   [245] Ibid. 171.
[246] Ct. of Assembly Bk. 7 Feb. 1683–4.
[247] Ibid. 1680–1724, fol. 2b.
[248] Munic. Corp. Com. Rep. iv, 2897.
[249] Ibid. 2898.
[251] Ibid. 161.
[252] Ct. of Assembly Bk. 22 June 1682.
[253] Ibid. 5 Nov. 1684.
[254] Ibid. 4 Sept.
[255] Ibid. 27 Nov.
[256] Ibid. 27 Nov.   [257] Ibid.
[250] Roots, Charters, 139.
[258] Ibid. 10 Jan. 1684–5.
[259] Ibid. 29 Jan.
[260] Ibid. 4 May 1685.
[261] Ibid. 12 May.
[262] Ibid. 28 May.
[263] Ibid. 16 June, 18 June, 25 July.
[264] Doc. of Corp.
[265] Roots, Charters, 219.
[266] Ibid. i, 342. Wythens had been removed from the King's Bench in 1687.
[267] Doc. of Corp.
[268] Public Act, 5 & 6 Will. IV, cap. 76.

corporation from this time has been the Mayor, Aldermen, and Burgesses of the Borough of Kingston-upon-
Thames, and the town was divided into three wards
with six aldermen and eighteen councillors. In 1855,
by the Kingston-upon-Thames Improvement Act, a
fourth ward was added, and the corporation increased to
a mayor, eight aldermen, and twenty-four councillors,
the present governing body.

Kingston sent representatives to the Parliament of
1311, 1313, 1353, and 1373,[970] but no further writs
have been found. It is said that the townsmen begged
to be excused the responsibility and obtained their
wish.[971] At the same time they refused, in 1378, to
bear a part in contributions towards the expense of
knights of the shire, and succeeded in upholding their
exemption.[972] In 1591 they obtained a royal declaration of indemnity, as tenants in ancient demesne, from
this expense and from serving as jurors.

The first charter of King John, granted in 1200,
gave to the freemen, as has already been mentioned,
the town with all its appurtenances, and in 1208 this
was expanded by the clause ' with all the liberties and
free customs thereof.' [973] The prescriptive rights thus
obtained included not only the hundred court but
other liberties. One such right was that of amend-
ment of the assize of bread and ale ; this, though
recognized in 1292–3,[974] was disputed by the Crown
until 1441, when Henry VI granted that the clerk of
the market should not exercise his office within the
town, but that the freemen should have correction of
the assize of bread and ale in the town and liberty
and be clerks of the market there.[975] The office of
ale-taster owed its origin to the right under which the
body corporate had the custody of certain standard
measures. As tenants in ancient demesne the freemen
were quit of toll throughout the kingdom and of
service on juries outside the manor. These rights were
disputed in 1581 when 11s. were paid ' for writin a
copie or note owte of the Booke of Domesdeye ' [976] in
proof, and Queen Elizabeth confirmed these privileges
in 1592.[977]

It was in accordance with this prescriptive right
that the freemen claimed the purprestures. They
established their right by 1292–3,[978] though not
without conflict with the Crown, for in 1274 they
were accused of occupying and appropriating the
king's lands,[979] and at a date previous to 1312 the king
claimed 67s. 11d. yearly rent from a purpresture
which had been inundated by the Thames.[980] The
Court of Assembly asserted their right in 1680, when
they proposed proceeding against one Rymer whose
pales encroached on the highway.[981]

By the third charter granted to Kingston in 1256,
which gave the freemen that privilege from arrest
which was the aim of every trading town at this
period, no man of Kingston might be arrested for
debts for which he was not the surety or principal
debtor, unless the debtors were solvent or the men of

the town had failed to give the aggrieved persons
justice.[982]

This charter was followed three days later by one
of greater importance, by which the freemen realized
the ambition of all mediaeval towns and succeeded in
ousting the sheriff and other royal officers by getting into
their own hands the return of Exchequer and other
writs, unless by default.[983] The right to exclude the
sheriff was confirmed in 1628, but had fallen into abeyance fifty years later, for in 1682 the Court of Assembly
sought counsel's opinion ' whether an action did not
lie against the sheriffs who entered this liberty and
executed an execution without any warrant directed
to the bailiffs of the town ' ;[984] the answer being in the
affirmative. Six weeks later the suit had begun,[985]
and was only abandoned in November 1683 at ' the
request of Sir Edward Evelyn, Sir James Clarke, and
others of the neighbouring gentry.' [986] By 1835 the
right was no longer exercised.[987]

The charter of 1256, confirming the freemen in their
gild merchant, granted that they should not lose goods
which they could prove their own for the trespass or
forfeiture of the servants who might hold them, and
also freedom of inheritance.[988] The charter of 1441
granted to the freemen all kinds of escheats and forfeitures of land or chattels, with treasure trove, deo-
dands, goods and chattels of felons and suicides.[989] Yet
in spite of this the Privy Council in 1553 demanded
such plate—perhaps the property of the church or
gild—as they pretended to be theirs by way of escheat,[990]
and in 1635 process was discharged in the Crown
office against the bailiffs for a deodand.[991]

The jurisdiction of the borough courts was very
complicated, and was exercised within such varying
boundaries that in 1835 doubts as to both powers and
area were entertained.[992] At that date the courts held
were the hundred court, court of record, court leet or
law-day, court baron, petty sessions, and sessions of the
peace.[993] The hundred court of Kingston was a court
of ancient demesne, and in 1199–1200 was said to be
and always to have been appurtenant to the vill,
rendering to the king a farm of £28 10s., to which
the hundred of Emleybridge contributed 16s.[994] It
passed into the hands of the freemen as a prescriptive
right under the charter of 1208. Under their
prescriptive right of infangenthef the bailiffs would
hold such a court as that which in 1235 tried and
hanged Sarah wife of Stephen de Meudon, a villein,
who was arrested while cooking stolen grain.[995] The
men of Kingston did not however obtain the right of
choosing coroners until 1256,[996] the hundred being
amerced in 1224–5 because the bailiffs had permitted the burial of Henry de Heandon, who had died
from an accident, without view of the king's coroner.[997]
The right of choosing two coroners was confirmed by
James I in 1603,[998] and is still exercised. The
coroners were elected by the Court of Assembly from
its members, and in 1835 it was usual for the town-

[970] Ret. of Memb. of Parl.
[971] Prynne, Reg. Parl. Writs, pt. iv,
1176.
[972] Exch. Pleas, Mich. 2 Ric. II.
[973] Cart. Antiq. SS, 8.
[974] Assize R. 907, m. 5 ; 902, m. 3.
[975] Chart. R. 19 Hen. VI, m. 31.
[976] Hist. MSS. Com. Rep. iii, App. 332.
[977] Roots, Charters, 82.
[978] Assize R. 902, m. 3.
[979] Cal. Pat. 1272–81, p. 71.

[980] Cal. Close, 1307–13, p. 470.
[981] Ct. of Assembly Bk. 1680–1724,
fol. 2b.
[982] Roots, Charters, 23. [988] Ibid. 26.
[983] Ct. of Assembly Bk. 21 Dec. 1682.
[985] Ibid. 8 Feb. 1682–3.
[986] Ibid. 15 Nov. 1683.
[987] Munic. Corp. Com. Rep. iv, 1899.
[988] Roots, Charters.
[989] Chart. R. 1–20 Hen. VI, no. 17,
m. 31.

[990] Acts of P.C. (New Ser.), 1552–4,
p. 373.
[991] Doc. of Corp. Chamberlains' Accts.
1635.
[992] Munic. Corp. Com. Rep. iv, 1892 n.
[993] Ibid. 2899.
[994] Abbrev. Plac. (Rec. Com.), 4, 25.
[995] Maitland, Bracton's Note Bk. no.
1138. [996] Roots, op. cit. 27.
[997] Assize R. 863, m. 4, 8.
[998] Roots, Charters, 122 et seq.

clerk to be appointed senior and acting coroner, the junior bailiff being junior coroner, a sinecure post.

A court of record appears to have been held here as early as 1234–5, when Ralf de How questioned an essoin under a writ *de recto* ; [299] it was formally granted in 1481, and was to be held every Saturday before the bailiffs and steward of the town, with cognizance of all pleas of debt, covenant, trespass, and personal matters within the demesne of the town and the hundreds of Kingston and Emleybridge.[300] This privilege was extended in 1628 [301] to the hundreds of Copthorne and Effingham, and the court continued to be held until the end of the 18th century.[302] The court leet was part of the old manorial organization, and in the early 19th century was still held before the recorder on Tuesday in Whitsun week, when the Fifteens were the jury.[303] Its jurisdiction at one time extended throughout the hundred,[304] but the corporation surrendered their powers in Richmond, Petersham, Kew, Ham, and Effingham to Charles I in 1628.[305] The court baron, at which presentment of the death of free tenants and the alienation of free tenements was made, was held before the bailiffs on Tuesday in Whitsun week ; the gownsmen and peers formed the homage, and also signed the presentment of the leet jury.[306] In 1556 a court of pie-powder was granted with the fair, but does not appear ever to have been much exercised, and had fallen into disuse by 1835.[307] The petty and quarter sessions were, in 1835, held concurrently with the court leet, the bailiffs being *ex officio* Justices of the peace.

There were also Trades Companies, which were certainly established in the town by 1579, when certain constitutions were enacted which practically remained in force until the 19th century.[308] The freemen of the town divided into the four companies of mercers, woollen drapers, shoemakers or cordwainers, and butchers, later victuallers, whose ' arms ' may still be seen in the painted glass of the town hall. Each company was constituted in the same way, and consisted of a body of freemen governed by two wardens, with a clerk and a beadle.[309] The freemen of the companies were distinct from the freemen of the corporation, and were either ' apprentices bound to and serving a freeman in the town, or the eldest son living of a freeman upon the death of his father,' or freemen of the corporation, who could claim the freedom of one of the companies either on or after election.[310] In 1835 a member of either of these classes paid 6s. 8d. on admission to his freedom, but in 1635–7 the normal fee paid by apprentices was 3s. 4d.[311] The names of the freemen were entered in roll books,[312] now no longer extant ; the number of admissions yearly was considerable in the early 17th century, but diminished after the Restoration, the membership being sixty in 1835. The two wardens were elected every year by the freemen of the Company ; it was their duty to keep the accounts,

to act as treasurers generally, and to be present at the signing of indentures of apprenticeship in the trades under their control.[313] They had power to impose fines and distrain for breaches of their orders.[314] The town clerk acted as clerk of each company, receiving a fee of 5s.[315] Each company generally met but once a year by special summons, though sometimes as many as six meetings were held,[316] and an item would appear in the accounts such as ' expended at 2 several times in wyne at the Sarazen's Head.' [317] The greatest expense of the year was generally the money ' spent on the Company at the Dinner' on Easter Monday, the 'feast-day' on which the outgoing wardens presented the accounts of each company to the bailiff at the Gildhall before the newly-elected wardens and divers other freemen of the company.

None of the companies possessed property, and their revenues were derived solely from the fees paid by newly-elected freemen, from fines for breach of the orders, postponement of the swearing-in of apprentices, and from quarterages due from each freeman.[318] According to the by-law the quarterage of a householder was 8d., that of a journeyman 8d., but by 1835 8d. was paid by married and 4d. by single men ; [319] in 1609 the quarterage paid to the Mercers' Company was 13s. 4d. for the past year, while the woollen drapers received 20s. 8d. But though the expenses usually nearly balanced the receipts, as in the case of the woollen drapers, whose receipts in 1655 were £2 19s. and expenditure £2 17s. 7d., in 1688 the Court of Assembly was able to borrow £16 10s. from the victuallers, £17 of the mercers, and £26 10s. of the cordwainers, 20s. of which was repaid in ' brass money.' [320]

The companies were very dependent on the Court of Assembly, which kept their money stored in ' a chest with four boxes and six locks and keys for the four companies' bought in 1609–10.[321] The regulation of the trade of the town was really in the hands of the Court of Assembly, which in 1638 re-enacted orders of 1579 prohibiting any but freemen of the companies from exercising any trade, science or mystery, or keeping open shop or selling by retail within the town under penalty of 6s. 8d. for each offence and the like sum for every market-day he continued to transgress.[322] This seems to indicate that market-days were not like fair days, free, and in 1609 the Company of Mercers twice distrained Henry Woodfall for trading in the town contrary to orders, and spent 4d. in twice carrying his stall into the court-hall.[323] The Court of Assembly, moreover, reserved to itself the right of granting life-tolerations to those who were not freemen on payment of sums varying in 1835 between £5 and £30.[324] These tolerations became increasingly common after the Restoration, and brought the corporation into conflict more than once with the wardens of the companies, as in 1682, when the wardens of the Company of

299 Maitland, *Bracton's Note Bk.*, no. 1122.
300 Roots, *Charters*, 50.
301 Ibid. 174.
302 *Munic. Corp. Com. Rep.* iv, 2900. Information kindly given by the town-clerk, Mr. H. C. Winser.
303 *Munic. Corp. Com. Rep.* iv, 2900.
304 Doc. of Corp. Ch. Bks.
305 *Cal. S.P. Dom.* 1628–9, p. 406 ; Roots, *Charters*, 210.
306 *Munic. Corp. Com. Rep.* iv, 2900.

307 Roots, *Charters*, 77.
308 *Munic. Corp. Com. Rep.* iv, 2898.
309 Bk. of Trades Companies.
310 *Munic. Corp. Com. Rep.* iv, 2898.
311 Bk. of Trades Companies, Shoemakers, 1635–7.
312 Ibid. Woollen Drapers, 1640.
313 Ibid. Mercers, 1670.
314 Ibid. Woollen Drapers, 1609 ; Ct. of Assembly Bk. 6, 29 July 1682.
315 Bk. of Trades Companies, *passim.*
316 Ibid. Woollen Drapers, 1630–40.

317 Ibid. Mercers, 1631.
318 Bk. of Trades Companies, Woollen Drapers, 1611.
319 *Munic. Corp. Com. Rep.* iv, 2898.
320 Ct. of Assembly Bk. 28 Oct. 1685.
321 Bk. of Trade Companies, Shoemakers, 1610.
322 *Munic. Corp. Com. Rep.* iv, 2898.
323 Bk. of Trades Companies, Mercers, 1609.
324 *Munic. Corp. Com. Rep.* iv, 2898.

KINGSTON-UPON-THAMES MARKET PLACE (LATE 18TH CENTURY)

(From a water-colour drawing by J. Richards)

Shoemakers were ordered to cease disturbing Thomas Burchett, who had obtained a toleration in 1676.[315] The system opened a new source of revenue to the corporation, which in 1776 required the wardens to make a return of all persons following trades in the town who were not free or tolerated.[316] The search for 'foreigners' was active at this time, and even in 1835 tolerations were demanded of all but those keeping very small shops.[317] The trades companies were then still flourishing, though the Company of Woollen Drapers had already lapsed.

The market at Kingston was established in 1242, when the men of the Bishop of London came to it from Fulham.[318] It was included among the liberties granted by the charter of 1208 until 1603, when James I granted a market to be held every Saturday for all animals.[319] Grain was sold in the market in 1551,[320] and it was an important market for corn in 1623;[321] a few years later the justices of the peace told with pride how they had brought down the price of wheat from 9s. and 9s. 6d. to 7s. the bushel, while the poor were served with rye at 5s.[322] The corn market is now small and unimportant. The proximity of the royal household at Hampton Court evidently had a stimulating effect on trade at Kingston, and formed the pretext for a petition in 1662 for a second market,[323] which was granted for Wednesdays in the same year.[324] This second market has not, however, flourished so well as that on Saturday; it appears to have been abandoned at the close of the 18th century,[325] and though revived later was 'small and unimportant' in 1888.[326] The Saturday market on the other hand has always been considerable. Beneath the new town hall, as beneath the old town hall, is a covered space filled with stalls, which also stand in rows without, and are covered with fruit, flowers, fish, and miscellaneous articles. The whole space is alive with movement and colour, for the market is not only attended by the townsfolk but serves the whole neighbourhood, the fruit, flower, and fish markets being especially popular among the housekeepers of Norbiton and Surbiton. The fish market, which is perhaps the most important, was well established in 1619, when George Walker was paid various sums 'for whipping and cleaning the Fish Market.' There is also on Saturdays a busy cattle market, provided by the corporation in the middle of the 19th century at the request of the farmers in the neighbourhood.[327]

The fairs were likewise held in the market place; the first of these was granted to Kingston in 1256 for the morrow of the feast of All Souls and the seven following days.[328] A second fair was ordered to be proclaimed in 1351 for Thursday in Whitsun week

and the seven days after.[329] In 1555 the bailiffs petitioned for a third fair which, with a court of piepowder, stallage, picage and all amerciaments, was granted to them in the same year for the day and morrow of the feast of St. Mary Magdalene.[340] These three fairs were still held in 1792,[341] but under powers obtained in 1855 the November fair alone was continued, and at the same time this was shortened to three days and the cattle fair removed to the fair field. The pleasure fair remained in the streets of the town, but was abolished as a nuisance in 1889.[342]

MANORS The manor of KINGSTON-UPON-THAMES was ancient demesne of the Crown in 1086, and remained in royal hands until, in 1200, it passed to the freemen of the town under the charter of King John.[343-4]

The name of BERWELL (Berewell, xiii–xvi cent.) first occurs in 1252, when Henry III granted to the Prior of Merton free warren here and elsewhere.[345] In 1290–1 the priory received lands here and in other places from Richard de la Sterte, Reginald Rote, the Prior of St. Mary's, Southwark, and others,[346] and Berwell was called a 'vill' in 1336.[347] In 1537–8, when brought to the Crown by the Dissolution it was called a 'manor,' though there were no returns from the perquisites of court.[348] It was granted in 1579 with the manor of Coombe Nevill to Thomas Vincent and his heirs;[349] he sold it in 1595 to Edward Carleton,[350] whose son,[351] Matthew Carleton, with Margaret his wife conveyed it in 1645 to Sir Dudley Carleton.[352] He is said to have obtained unlimited right of common in Surbiton and Claygate from the corporation in 1636, and in 1651 sold the manor to Richard Glid, senior, Richard Glid, junior, and William Wright.[353] Richard Glid and Elizabeth his wife sold it in 1663 [354] to James Davidson, who devised it to his son-in-law, Richard Edes, in 1695.[355] The manor again changed hands in 1699 when Richard Edes and Mary his wife sold it to William Letheuillier;[356] his daughter married William Task,[357] who sold it in 1771 to Charles Terry.[358] From him it was purchased in the following year by Joseph Sales,[359] the sale being completed in 1774.[360] The new owner retained it until 1788,[361] when he sold it to John Richardson, who in the following year conveyed it to Marcus Dixon the lord in 1799.[362] His daughters were in possession in 1804 ; [363] one daughter Elizabeth-Morris, appears to have married Archibald Blair, and Maria a second was the wife of John Wales ; both conveyed fourth parts of the manor to Robert Blair, who may have been a trustee.[364] When Brayley wrote it had been 'for about twenty-five years,' that is, since about 1818, in the hands of John Sykes of Kensington.[365] It is now the property of Baron Foley.

[315] Ct. of Assembly Bk. 8 May 1682; cf. 6 July 1682.
[316] Ibid. 25 June 1776.
[317] Munic. Corp. Com. Rep. iv, 2898.
[318] Abbrev. Plac. (Rec. Com.), 120.
[319] Roots, Charters, 140.
[320] Acts of P.C. 1550–2, p. 324.
[321] Cal. S.P. Dom. 1619–23, p. 581.
[322] Ibid. 1629–31, p. 474.
[323] Ibid. 1661–2, p. 357.
[324] Ibid. pp. 358, 361 ; Roots, Charters, 215.
[325] Roots, Charters, 140 ; Royal Com. on Market Rights and Tolls, i. 207.
[326] Royal Com. on Market Rights and Tolls, iv, 131.
[327] Under Stat. 18 & 19 Vict. cap. 45.

[328] Roots, Charters, 25.
[329] Cal. Close, 1349–54, p. 365.
[330] Roots, Charters, 76–7.
[331] Royal Com. on Market Rights and Tolls, i. 207.
[332] Ibid. iv, 131.
[333-4] Vide supra.
[335] Plac. de Quo Warr. (Rec. Com.), 739.
[336] Inq. a.q.d. file 16, no. 3.
[337] Heales, Rec. of Merton, App. p. cxvi.
[338] Ibid., p. cxxvii.
[339] Pat. 21 Eliz. pt. xi, m. 5.
[340] Feet of F. Surr. East. 37 Eliz.
[341] Manning and Bray, Surr. i, 403, 669 ; ii, 806.

[342] Feet of F. Surr. Hil. 20 Chas. I ; Manning and Bray, Surr. i, 403.
[343] Feet of F. Surr. Hil. 1651.
[344] Ibid. Trin. 14 Chas. II.
[345] Lysons, Environs of Lond. i, 241.
[346] Feet of F. Surr. Hil. 10 & 11 Will. III.
[347] Lysons, op. cit. i, 241.
[348] Feet of F. Surr. Mich. 12 Geo. III.
[349] Lysons, op. cit. i, 241.
[350] Feet of F. Surr. Mich. 14 Geo. III ; Com. Pleas D. Enr. Hil. 14 Geo. III, m. 8.
[351] Feet of F. Surr. Trin. 28 Geo. III.
[352] Lysons, op. cit. i, 241.
[353] Manning and Bray, Surr. i, 403.
[354] Feet of F. Surr. Hil. 40 Geo. III ; East. 41 Geo. III.
[355] Brayley, Hist. of Surr. iii, 112.

COOMBE (Cumbe, xi cent. ; ·Cumbe Nevill, xiii cent.; Combe, xiv cent:).

Certain lands held here by Cola in the time of the Confessor had passed into the hands of Ansgot the Interpreter by 1086, when they were assessed at 1½ hides, half ·the previous computation.[366] In 1164–5 the sheriff rendered account of £7 from Coombe, already considered a member of Kingston,[367] and the payment was repeated in the following year, when an additional ·14*s*. was rendered from the pasture of the park there ;[368] these payments were still made in 1173–4.[369] Before 1167–8 the fee was held by Robert Belet, who in that year was dispossessed by Henry II,[370] but the lands were restored in 1190–1, when Robert Belet paid £80 to the Exchequer for restoration to his inheritance.[371] At the beginning of the 13th century it was held by Michael Belet, and with his manor of Sheen came into the hands of the Crown.[372] In 1215 King John gave Coombe to Hugh de Nevill,[373] and it was already known as Coombe Nevill in 1260.[374] In the following year John Nevill bought an acre of land in Kingston from Peter the Goldsmith.[375] At the beginning of the 14th century the manor was held by William de Nevill, who died without male issue, his lands being divided between his daughter Nicholaa, wife of John de Hadresham, and Henry son of the second daughter Alice, who had married Richard le Weyte.[376]

The moiety of the manor held by Nicholaa and John descended to John de Hadresham who was the tenant in 1341.[377] William de Hadresham was in possession at his death in 1361, when the manor passed to John his infant son.[378] During his minority the 'manorhouse' was accidentally burnt, and in 1368–9 the custody was granted to John de Hadresham who was charged with the reconstruction.[379] John de Hadresham died in 1417, his heirs being his cousins, Alice Virly and Joan wife of John Silverton, daughters of Christina sister of his father William, and his own child yet unborn.[380] In 1418 the manor was conveyed by Alice widow of Richard Virly, Elizabeth widow of Edward Herveys, and John Silverton and Joan his wife to trustees,[381] who in 1423 completed the transfer to Merton Priory.[382] The manor was still in the hands of the priory[383] at the Dissolution, when it came to the Crown, and in 1539–40 was leased for twenty-one years to John Jenyns of the household.[384] In 1547 it was granted to Edward Duke of Somerset,[385] but escheated to the Crown on his execution, and was re-granted in 1552 to William Cecil for twenty-one years.[386] On the accession of Queen Mary the reversion of the manor was granted to Anne widow of Edward Duke of Somerset for life, and in 1571 William Cecil, now Lord Burghley, obtained a further grant of the reversion,[387] and at the same time Anne, now the wife of Francis Newdigate, released the manor to him.[388] Burghley retained it until 1579,[389] when he quitclaimed to the queen, who forthwith granted it and the manor of Berwell to Thomas Vincent and his heirs.[390] In 1601 Thomas Vincent with Jane his wife and Francis his son conveyed his rights of free warren here to Edward Heron and another,[391] and in 1608 Sir Francis Vincent, kt., sold these ·rights and the manor itself to William Cockayne,[392] Lord Mayor of London, knighted in 1616.[393] Sir William was succeeded by his son Charles created Viscount Cullen in 1642.[394] He was a staunch Cavalier and raised a troop of horse for the king's service. He apparently refused to pay his church rate to the party in power in 1650, when an entry for 2*d*. occurs in the churchwardens' accounts as incurred 'in going to the Lord Cockayne for his rate money.'[395] He is said to have lost £50,000 by his loyalty, and was forced in 1651 to convey the manor of Coombe to Edward, Lord Montagu, and others,[396] apparently trustees for Elizabeth wife of Sir Daniel Harvey and daughter of Lord Montagu.[397] From Sir Daniel it descended to his son Sir Edward Harvey, who made various settlements of the manor in 1679.[398] His son Edward Harvey, jacobite M.P. for Clitheroe in 1714, resided here. Rent from the manor appears as the property of Edward Southwell, senior and junior, in 1729 and 1761,[399] but the manor is said to have passed to Michael, cousin of Edward Harvey, junior, and to have been sold in about 1753 to the trustees of John Spencer,[400] who was created Viscount Spencer in 1761 and Earl Spencer in 1765.[401] His son George John, Earl Spencer, succeeded his father as lord of the manor in 1783 and was still holding in 1804.[402] The manor is not mentioned after this date,·and· has now ceased to exist. Coombe House belonged to the Earl of Liverpool, the statesman ; and subsequently to the late Duke of Cambridge.

The most interesting fee in Kingston was perhaps that which was held in the time of the Confessor by Alured, who could seek what lord he pleased, and held land assessed at 3 hides. He was succeeded by a woman who, in the time of King William, placed herself and her land under the queen's protection. In 1086 the land was in the hands of Humfrey the Chamberlain ; he had in his charge one villein to collect the queen's wool, and took from him 20*s*. as a relief when his father died.[403] This land seems to have been granted by Henry II to one Postel.[404] In 1164–5 the sheriff rendered account of 9*s*. from one hide of land in Coombe which Postel held,[405] and in the following year this was increased

[366] *V.C.H. Surr.* i, 382.
[367] *Pipe R.* 11 *Hen. II* (Pipe R. Soc.), 111.
[368] Ibid. 12 *Hen. II*, 107.
[369] Ibid. 20 *Hen. II*, 3.
[370] Ibid. 14 *Hen. II*, 216.
[371] Pipe R. 2 Ric. I, m. 13.
[372] For descent see Sheen. In 1417 the tenants in demesne were said to hold in socage of the king as of his manor of Sheen.
[373] *Rot. Lit. Claus.* (Rec. Com.), 237.
[374] Feet of F. Surr. 44 Hen. III, no. 131.
[375] Ibid. 45 Hen. III, no. 32.
[376] Chan. Inq. p.m. 13 Edw. II no. 13ª ; *Cal. Close,* 1318–23, p. 315.

[377] Chan. Inq. p.m. 14 Edw. III (1st nos.), no. 7.
[378] Ibid. 35 Edw. III, pt. i, no. 93.
[379] *Abbrev. Rot. Orig.* (Rec. Com.), ii,247.
[380] Chan. Inq. p.m. 5 Hen. V, no. 45.
[381] ¹Feet of F. Surr. 6 Hen. V, no. 29.
[382] Close, 2 Hen. VI, m. 2, 5.
[383] Heales, *Rec. of Merton Priory*, App. p. cxxxiv.
[384] L. *and* P. *Hen.* VIII, xv, 565.
[385] Pat. 1 Edw. VI, pt. iv, m. 36.
[386] Ibid. 13 Eliz. pt. vii, m. 21.
[387] Ibid.
[388] Feet of F. Surr. Mich. 13 & 14 Eliz.
[389] Ibid. Trin. 21 Eliz.
[390] Pat. 21 Eliz. pt. xi.
[391] Feet of F. Surr. Trin. 43 Eliz.

[392] Ibid. Trin. 6 Jas. I.
[393] G.E.C. *Peerage,* ii, 435.
[394] Ibid.
[395] Churchwardens' Accts. 1650.
[396] Feet of F. Surr. Hil. 1561.
[397] Manning and Bray, *Surr.* i, 402.
[398] Recov. R. East. 31 Chas. II, rot. 8 ; Feet of F. Surr. East. 31 Chas. II.
[399] Feet of F. Surr. Trin. 2 & 3 Geo. II; Recov. R. East. 1 Geo. III, rot. 364.
[400] Manning and Bray, *Surr.* i, 402.
[401] G.E.C. *Peerage.*
[402] See Lysons' *Environs,* i, 235 ; Manning and Bray, *Surr.* i, 402.
[403] *V.C.H. Surr.* i, 297, 326.
[404] *Testa de Nevill* (Rec. Com.), 226.
[405] *Pipe R.* 11 *Hen. II* (Pipe R. Soc.), 111.

to 20*s.*[406] the normal rent,[407] being the money equivalent of the serjeanty.[408] Ralf Postel held this hide of the queen in 1203, in which year he granted it to Walkelin Rabus[409]; later it came into the hands of Peter son of Baldwin, who bought land in Kingston of Gunnora widow of Matthew son of Godfrey in 1238.[410] This perhaps was the Peter Baldwin who, though retaining 40 acres in his hands, alienated the remaining 50 acres of the fee for annual rents amounting to 33*s.* 4*d.* Peter made a fine of 20*s.* a year for himself and these tenants,[411] so that each of the tenants answered to him for a third of the worth of his tenement a year and Peter was responsible to the Exchequer for the whole of the fine.[412] Peter was dead in 1279, when his son of the same name was a minor and in the wardship of the queen; she gave the custody to Adam de Richmond, who in turn sold it to Walter Pewtarer.[413] In 1292–3 Peter Baldwin held the lands by the old tenure of collecting the queen's wool; the land on his death in or about 1299 consisted of 60 acres in Coombe, where he had tenants bound to find him three men in the autumn.[414] He also had a capital messuage and lands in Kingston held of the men of Kingston, and land at Talworth. He was succeeded by his son Peter, a boy of eleven.

Dower was assigned to Mabel widow of Peter Baldwin in 1302,[415] but no further mention of the family has been found. Part of the land came into possession of the chapel of St. Mary Magdalene, the warden paying 10*s.* for ' the serjeanty of Baldwin ' in the 15th century.[416]

In the 13th century land here was held by Robert Burnell and afterwards by John de la Linde,[417] from whom it passed to the family of Dymoke, and was attached as a member to their manor of Wallington. (q.v.).[418] John Dymoke paid 40*s.* to the priory of Merton for his manor of Coombe Nevill in 1536.[419]

In the early 13th century Hugh de Coombe held half a knight's fee here of the honour of Clare.[420] The mesne lordship of this fee was in the hands of Roger de Vilers in 1227, when he exchanged the homage and services of Wymund de Raleg', the tenant, for lands in Somerset and Dorset.[421]

HARTINGTON (Erdinton, xii cent.; Hertindon, Hartyngdon, xiii cent.) is first mentioned in 1173 and 1173–4, when 70*s.* were paid into the Exchequer from lands there.[422] In 1206 Adam de Dearhurst and Maud his wife claimed half a hide of land here against the Prior of Merton, but the Jurors declared that the prior had always held it, and that no ancestor of Maud had ever been tenant.[423] The prior was granted free warren here and elsewhere in 1252, and was returned as lord of the hamlet in 1374.[424] Merton retained the manor until the Dissolution, when it

passed to the Crown. Valued at 30*s.* in 1536,[425] in 1539 it was granted for life to Ralph Annesley, the ' king's servant,' with lands at Sheen and Kew.[426]

In 1544 the reversion was granted to Richard Taverner who, three years later, bought the manor of Norbiton (q.v.). He and Margaret his wife conveyed the manor to Edward, Earl of Hertford, in 1546,[427] probably in trust for their younger son Peter, who inherited it on his father's death in 1575.[428] Peter Taverner and Frances his wife conveyed the manor in 1585 to John Evelyn and Elizabeth his wife, who, with George Evelyn, re-sold it in 1605 to George Cole. In 1623 presentment was made at the hundred court that he had not entertained the minister, churchwardens, and parishioners on Monday in Rogation week at the farm called Hartleton Farm as heretofore.[429] George Cole died in 1624, and was succeeded by another of the same name who, with Jane his wife, sold the manor in 1637 to Charles I[430] to be added to Richmond Park.

In the 14th century land here, as at Kingston, Norbiton, and Coombe, was held by Thomas de Ludlow and descended to the family of Dymoke.[431] Hartington has been identified with Hartington Coombe,[432] and in 1372 the land held there by Sir John Dymoke is called ' Hartyndencombe.' [433] In 1339 the men of ' Hertindonescombe ' petitioned the king for a re-assessment of the fifteenth, as their vill had been lately burnt by certain malefactors, the goods and chattels there plundered and destroyed, and the inhabitants had for the most part withdrawn.[434] The ancient house known as Hertcomb or Hercomb Place stands ' at the right hand of the road at the entrance of Kingston from London,' [435] opposite the end of Coombe Lane. It is said to have once been in the hands of Archbishop Tillotson,[436] and in the middle of the 18th century was used as a boardingschool by Richard Woodeson, and later it became the workhouse for the parish till 1836. It now forms two houses. Kingston Lodge, opposite to it, was formerly occupied by Mr. George Meredith.

KINGSTON-CANBURY (Canonbury, xiv cent.) is not mentioned in 1086, but was held by Merton Priory at an early period. It probably represented the early endowment of the church, and followed the descent of the advowson (q.v.) until 1786, when George Harding sold the right of patronage, but retained the manor, which seems to have disappeared by the beginning of the 19th century. The name is preserved in the Canbury Gardens and Road.

KINGSTON-UPON-THAMES alias MILBORNE is a ' manor ' occasionally mentioned. It appears to have belonged to Sir Thomas Milborne, who at his death in 1492 was said to hold a toft, 100 acres of

406 *Pipe R.* 12 *Hen. II* (Pipe R. Soc.), 107.
407 Ibid. 13 *Hen. II*, 203; 14 *Hen. II*, 216.
408 *Red Bk. of Exch.* (Rolls Ser.), 456.
409 *Abbrev. Plac.* (Rec. Com.), 43, and see Feet of F. Surr. 6 John, no. 58. A Ralph Postel in 1292–3 was holding a certain serjeanty of Otho de Grandison (Assize R. 902, m. 2), and is last mentioned in 1299 as lord of an eyot held by Peter Baldwin; Chan. Inq. p.m. 27 Edw. I, no. 27.
410 Feet of F. Surr. 22 Hen III, no. 12.
411 *Testa de Nevill* (Rec. Com.), 228, where the name is printed Rabewin.
412 Ibid.
413 Assize R. 876, m. 50; 902, m. 2.

414 Chan. Inq. p.m. 27 Edw. I, no. 27.
415 *Cal. Close*, 1296–1302, p. 535.
416 Lansd. MS. 226, fol. 71*b.*
417 *Cal. Chart. R.* 1257–1300, p. 180.
418 Chan. Inq. p.m. (Ser. 2), xiv, 44.
419 *Valor Eccl.* (Rec. Com.) ii, 50.
420 *Testa de Nevill* (Rec. Com.), 219.
421 Feet of F. Div. Co. 11 Hen. III, no. 48.
422 *Pipe. R.* 19 *Hen. II* (Pipe R. Soc.), 95; 20 *Hen. II*, 5.
423 *Abbrev. Plac.* (Rec. Com), 52; Heales, *Rec. of Merton*, App. p. cxv.
424 Co. Plac. Surr. xxiii, no. 11.
425 *Valor Eccl.* (Rec. Com.), 48.
426 *L. and P. Hen. VIII*, xiv (1), 594.
427 Feet of F. Surr. Trin. 38 Eliz.

428 Chan. Inq. p.m. (Ser. 2), clxxv, 92.
429 Add. MS. 6167, fol. 51; Lysons, op. cit. i, 241.
430 Feet of F. Surr. Hil. 12 Chas. I.
431 *Abbrev. Rot. Orig.* (Rec. Com.), ii, 108; *Cal. Pat.* 1334–8, p. 308; 1391–6, p. 649. See Wallington, *V.C.H. Surr.* iv.
432 Manning and Bray, *Surr.* i, 404. There was a family of Hertcombes in Kingston in the 15th century, and a brass to John and Katherine Hertcombe may be seen in the church.
433 Inq. p.m. 46 Edw. III, no. 56.
434 *Cal. Close*, 1339–41, p. 202.
435 Manning and Bray, *Surr.* i, 404.
436 Merryweather, op. cit. 25, where the house is figured.

land, 20 acres of meadow, a weir, a water-mill, 10s. rent, and five gardens in Kingston of the king as of his borough there.[437] Sir Thomas left his lands here to his daughter Cecily until marriage, and in 1533 she, as Cecily Sympson, widow, conveyed rights of free fishing to Christopher More and others.[438] Henry Milborne was in possession of the weir in 1503, when he paid 6d. from it to the lamps of the church ; [439] he died without issue in 1519, leaving a widow Margaret, afterwards the wife of Roger Yorke, serjeant-at-law.[440] In 1538 she conveyed to Edward Marvyn and Robert Tederley two parts of this 'manor' and those of Esher-Watevill, and Hetchesham,[441] which she held apparently under settlement. Later the manor came into the hands of the corporation, who ordered a court baron to be held for it in 1583,[442] and must have exercised other manorial rights, for in 1684 'several tenants of the manor of Milborne complain that Richard Lee and john Gunner (being tenants of the manor) have since 25 March last cut ten loads of turf on the common of the manor, also two others have carried away three loads without licence of the lords of the manor.'[443]

NORBITON HALL was reputed a manor from the 16th century. It seems to have been granted by Maurice de Creon to Robert Burnell in 1271–2.[444] In 1503 Master Anthony Forde paid a rent of 4d. to the lamps of Kingston Church for a tenement in Norbiton which had belonged to William Long ; [445] the churchwarden received 2s. 4¾d., in 1504 'for wast of torches at ye derge and ij massys yt was made for ye beryeng of anthony forde.'[446] Erasmus Forde, probably his son, was well known in the town and signed the protest respecting mortuaries made in 1509.[447] He complained in 1532 that 'a taker of timber and board for Hampton Court "like an Hemprour enters into my ground bordered about with elms, the chief pleasure of all my house," and without his master's sanction "has dug up by the roots thirty-five of my purest and fairest elms." '[448] Erasmus was followed by Edmund Forde, who with Joan his wife in 1547 sold the 'manor' of Norbiton Hall to Richard Taverner,[449] the well-known editor of Taverner's Bible.[?] Richard Taverner died in 1575 ; by his will he bequeathed two-thirds of his lands equally to his sons Peter and Edmund,[451] but Norbiton Hall descended to his eldest son Richard, who, with Eleanor his wife, conveyed it to George Evelyn in 1584,[452] the sale being completed in 1588.[453] George Evelyn died seised of it in 1603. In 1605 John and George Evelyn and their wives resold it to Sir Anthony Benn ; [454] he died in 1618 in possession of a messuage with appurtenances called 'Popes' and land belonging, containing 20 acres at Norbiton, all held of the bailiffs of Kingston.[455] Probably the messuage called

'Popes' was not Norbiton Hall, for Sir Anthony's son and heir Charles Benn was but eight years old at his father's death, and Lady Benn had a house in Kingston, which in 1626 had been taken for the French Ambassador.[456] Norbiton Hall was certainly in the hands of Roger Wood on his death in 1623, when it was described as a 'manor, grange, and capital messuage.'[457] This Roger Wood, son of one Roger Wood late of Islington, was succeeded by Robert his son, an infant two years old.[458] Robert Wood was returned a knight of the shire for Surrey in 1654, but 'divers well-affected persons' alleged to the Council that he was illegally chosen, 'a derider of the people of God, a profane swearer, and of bad life, an enemy to his Highness and the army and had sided with the Cavaliers.' [459] A counter-petition declared that he had been one of the militia commissioners in 1651, had sent a man and horse to Worcester, and so far from opposing godly ministers 'improved his power to countenance them.'[460] His land was inherited by his daughter Ann, wife of Sir john Rous ; they were in possession in 1662, but it was in the hands of the Reeves family in the following year.[461] They retained it until 1744, when it was sold to one Greenly ; it was sold again in 1788 to a Mr. Twopenny, who disposed of it soon afterwards to William Farren the actor.[462] The house, which must have been rebuilt about this time,[463] remained in his hands until 1794, when he sold it to a Mr. Lintall ; he resold it in 1799 to General Gabriel Johnson.[464] Early in the 19th-century it appears to have come into the hands of Mrs. Dennis, who gave it to her daughter the wife of C. N. Pallmer, M.P. for Surrey in 1828, and a West Indian merchant.[465] Mr. Pallmer sold it in 1829 to the Dowager Countess of Liverpool, who resided here with Mr. R. H. Jenkinson, nephew of the first Earl of Liverpool.[466] It is now occupied by the White Rose Laundry. The handsome grounds set with cedars, and the arms of the Evelyns on the lodge still remain.

It is not always easy to disentangle the history of this house from that of another, equally called Norbiton Hall, though also, and more correctly, known as Norbiton Place. Both houses, Norbiton Hall and Norbiton Place, were comparatively modern. A house called Norbiton Place was sold by one Nichols to Sir John Phillips, who died in 1764.[467] His son Richard was raised to the peerage as Baron Milford in 1776 and sold the house to a Mr. Sherer, a London wine merchant.[468] He sold some of the property to Mrs. Dennis,[469] the owner of Norbiton Hall, who gave it to her son-in-law Hugh Ingoldsby Massey.[470] Mrs. Massey afterwards became the wife of Mr. Pallmer of Norbiton Hall, who built Norbiton Place, and they resided here. A great part of the house

[437] Surr. Arch. Coll. viii, 156b, 1.
[438] Feet of F. Surr. Mich. 25 Hen. VIII.
[439] Surr. Arch. Coll. viii, 72.
[440] Ibid. 156c.
[441] Recov. R. Mich. 30 Hen. VIII, rot. 435 ; East. 31 Hen. VIII, rot. 334.
[442] Ct. of Assembly Bk. 7 June 1683.
[443] Ibid. 5 June 1684.
[444] Chart. R. 56 Hen. III, m. 4.
[445] Surr. Arch. Coll. viii, 72.
[446] Ibid. 76.   [447] Ibid. 36.
[448] L. and P. Hen. VIII, v, 1728.
[449] Feet of F. Surr. East. 1 Edw. VI.
[450] Dict. Nat. Biog.

[451] Chan. Inq. p.m. (Ser. 2), clxxv, 92.
[452] Feet of F. Surr. Mich. 26 & 27 Eliz.
[453] Ibid. Mich. 30 & 31 Eliz.
[454] Ibid. Hil. 2 Jas. I.
[455] Chan. Inq. p.m. (Ser. 2), ccclxxx, 110. He was recorder of Kingston and, at his death, of London ; his monument is in Kingston Church.
[456] Cal. S.P. Dom. 1625–6, p. 568.
[457] Chan. Inq. p.m.(Ser. 2), cccclxxiii, 30.
[458] Ibid.
[459] Cal. S.P. Dom. 1654, p. 314.
[460] Ibid.
[461] Manning and Bray, Surr. i, 339.

[462] Ibid.
[463] Anderson, Hist. and Antiq. of Kingston-upon-Thames.
[464] Brayley, Surr. iii, 57 ; Manning and Bray, Surr. i, 349.
[465] Surr. Arch. Coll. vii, p. xliii.
[466] Brayley, Surr. iii, 57.
[467] Surr. Arch. Coll. vii, p. xliii.
[468] Ibid.
[469] But, according to Allen (Hist. of Surr. and Suss. ii, 354), continued to live in what had been Sir John Phillips' house after Mrs. Dennis had bought the house then called Norbiton Hall.
[470] Manning and Bray Surr. i, 349.

was pulled down after 1830. A Mr. A. S. Douglas resided in part of it in 1842,[471] and Commander Lambert, R.N., in 1852.

In the 12th century *HAM* (Hamma, xii cent.) was included in the royal demesne as a member of Kingston, and in 1168 contributed 43*s*. 4*d*. towards the aid for marrying the king's daughter Matilda.[472] In 1174 land to the value of £19 13*s*. 4*d*. in Ham was bestowed by Henry II upon Maurice de Creon,[473] a powerful baron of Anjou, whose English estates lay chiefly in Lincolnshire, by whom it appears to have been granted with his daughter to Guy de la Val.[474] The latter forfeited his estates for taking arms against the king,[475] and Ham next appears as an escheat of the Crown, part of which was granted to Godfrey de Lucy, Bishop of Winchester ; and is described in the *Testa de Nevill* as the vill of Ham, worth £6 per annum.[476] The bishop died in 1204,[477] and in the next year the king granted it to Roger de Mowbray, who already enjoyed a rent of £4 there in virtue of a previous grant[478] of the rest of the manor of Ham. Later it was granted in farm to the men of the manor who, in 1215 when the king decided to restore it to Peter son of Maurice de Creon, were ordered to render obedience to the latter as to their lord.[479]

Peter mortgaged the manor to William Joynier who, upon the death of the former in 1221, was confirmed in his tenure by Aumary, brother of Peter, who had inherited this estate.[480] Aumary appears to have died or forfeited before 1227, in which year this, with other of his estates in Surrey, was bestowed upon Ralph Nevill, Bishop of Chichester, to hold until the king should restore it to the heirs of Aumary, either of his free will, or by a peace.[481]

The bishop died in February 1244,[482] and three months later his lands in Ham and elsewhere were conceded for life to Imbert de Salinis to hold by the service of rendering yearly a bow of dogwood,[483] but in 1248 Imbert granted a five years' lease of the manor to Peter de Genevre,[484] which in 1252 was held by Geoffrey de Geynville who had married the widow of Peter.[485] About this time the manor appears to have been restored to the Creon family in the person of Maurice de Creon, who married Isabel half sister of Henry III, and died before 1251,[486] in the year after which his widow was granted the wardship of the manor.[487] Maurice de Creon, the son and heir,[488] described as a knight of the province

of Anjou, granted the manor to Sir Robert Burnell, afterwards Chancellor to Edward I and Bishop of Bath and Wells, who was confirmed in his title to it in 1272,[489] and, dying in 1292, was succeeded by his nephew Philip son of Hugh Burnell,[490] then aged twenty-five. Philip married Maud daughter of Richard Earl of Arundel, and died in 1294, leaving Edward his son and heir, then aged twelve years,[491] who in 1307 had livery of his father's lands.[492] Edward Lord Burnell married Aliva daughter of Hugh le Despenser, and died in 1315 without issue. He was succeeded in the manor by Maud his sister,[493] who in 1332 jointly with her husband, john de Handlo, paid 20 marks for licence to settle this estate upon themselves and their heirs.[494] Upon the death of John de Handlo in 1346, Nicholas his second[495] son by the said Maud, who afterwards assumed the name of Burnell, had livery of his lands in Ham,[496] and died seised of the same in 1383, leaving Sir Hugh Burnell his son and heir, then aged thirty-six.[497]

Sir Hugh Burnell[498] died in 1420 without male issue, and from this date the connexion of the Burnells with Ham is lost sight of ;[499] it appears to have escheated to the Crown shortly after, being included in 1466 in the dowry of Elizabeth Woodville, queen of Edward IV,[500] together with Sheen and Petersham ; and with those estates was bestowed by Henry VIII on Anne of Cleves in 1540 ;[501] by james I on Henry Prince of Wales,[502] and, upon the death of the latter, on Charles afterwards Charles I,[503] who in 1639 granted it to William Murray, whose descendants, the Earls of Dysart, hold it at the present day. (See Petersham.)

A rent of 50*s*. in this manor was bestowed by King John on the abbey of Clermund,[504] and an equal sum by Guy de la Val on the abbey of Savigny ;[505] both of these subsequently passed to the Abbot of Waverley,[506] who claimed in 1279 to hold them by a charter from Guy de la Val.[507]

Some idea of the early extent of the manor may be gathered from inquisitions taken at various times : in 1253 it comprised a capital messuage worth 20*s*. per annum ; 200 acres of arable land worth 4*d*. per acre ; 7½ acres of meadow at 3*s*. per acre ; common pasture for 200 sheep, but if the lord of the manor had no sheep he could take nothing from it ; a weir in the Thames worth 26*s*. 8*d*. per annum ; rents of assize £2 10*s*. 4½*d*. ; labour of customary tenants £1 10*s*. 4*d*. ; the total yearly value amounting

[471] Brayley, *Surr.* iii, 57.
[472] *Pipe R.* 14 *Hen. II* (Pipe R. Soc.), 210 ; Madox, *Hist. of the Exch.* i, 589.
[473] *Pipe R.* 20 *Hen. II* (Pipe R. Soc.), 3.
[474] Dugdale, *Baronage*, i, 625 ; Assize R. 876.
[475] Harl. MS. 5804.
[476] *Testa de Nevill* (Rec. Com.), 227.
[477] *Dict. Nat. Biog.*
[478] *Rot. Lit. Claus.* (Rec. Com.), i, 37, 40 ; *Testa de Nevill*, 226.
[479] *Rot. Lit. Pat.* (Rec. Com.), i, 142 ; *Rot. Lit. Claus.* (Rec. Com.), i, 222*b*.
[480] *Rot. Lit. Claus.* (Rec. Com.), i, 479, 482 ; *Excerpta e Rot. Fin.* (Rec. Com.), i, 64, 88.
[481] *Cal. Chart.* 1226–57, pp. 54, 86 ; *Testa de Nevill* (Rec. Com.), 227.
[482] *Dict. Nat. Biog.* ; Chan. Inq. p.m. 28 Hen. III, no. 20.
[483] *Cal. Chart. R.* 1226–57, p. 277.
[484] *Cal. Pat.* 1247–58, p. 15. A lease made the year before to the Abbot and

convent of Waverley (*Cal. Pat.* 1232–4, p. 519) was apparently revoked.
[485] *Cal. Pat.* 1247–58, p. 218.
[486] Ibid. p. 167.
[487] Ibid. pp. 218, 314.
[488] See *Cal. Chart. R.* 1257–1300, p. 181, where he is called the king's nephew.
[489] *Cal. Chart. R.* 1257–1300, p. 180.
[490] Chan. Inq. p.m. 21 Edw. II, no. 50. According to this inquisition the bishop had enfeoffed Otto de Grandison of the manor, who after holding it for two years had granted it back to Burnell on setting out for the Holy Land. See also Assize R. 902, m. 5.
[491] Dugdale, *Baronage*, i, 60.
[492] *Cal. Close*, 1307–13, p. 11.
[493] *Cal. Pat.* 1330–4, p. 75.
[494] *Abbrev. Rot. Orig.* (Rec. Com.), i, 60 ; *Cal. Pat.* 1330–4, p. 75 ; Feet of F. Div. Co. 5 Edw. III, no. 110.
[495] For settlement on Nicholas see *Cal.*

Pat. 1330–40, p. 302 and Feet of F. Div. Co. 14 Edw. III, no. 92.
[496] *Cal. Close*, 1346–9, p. 113 ; Chan. Inq. p.m. 20 Edw. III (1st nos.), no. 51.
[497] Chan. Inq. p.m. 6 Ric. II, no. 20.
[498] See Chan. Inq. p.m. 9 Ric. II, no. 70.
[499] It possibly passed to William, Lord Lovel, descended from Maud Burnell by her first husband. His son John Lord Lovel was a Lancastrian, and died in 1464, which would accord with the date of the grant to Elizabeth Woodville if his estate was confiscated after 1461.
[500] *Cal. Pat.* 1461–7, p. 525.
[501] L. and P. Hen. VIII, xvi, p. 717.
[502] Pat. 8 Jas. I, pt. xli, no. 2.
[503] Ibid. 14 Jas. I, pt. x.
[504] *Testa de Nevill* (Rec. Com.), 226.
[505] Dugdale, *Mon.* vi, 1102.
[506] Esch. Inq. 37 Hen. III, no. 54.
[507] Assize R. 876.

to £5 16s. 4½d.,[508] after deducting a £5 rent-charge to the abbey of Waverley. The survey taken on the death of Bishop Burnell in 1292 mentions 220 acres of arable land, a windmill, a dovecote and half of another weir besides that mentioned above.[509] In 1346 the manor was valued at £3 1s. 2d. yearly and included 60 acres of arable land worth, if well tilled, 4d. per acre; 40 acres of arable land worth 2d. per acre;[510] 5 acres of meadow and 5 acres of pasture at 1s. per acre; a weir on the Thames worth 5s.; and assized rents of free tenants worth 19s. 6d.[511] The weir and dovecote mentioned above were bestowed by Henry V on the convent of St. Saviour and St. Mary and St. Bridget, Syon, which he founded at Isleworth.[512]

In a survey taken in 1610 a barn called Court Barne is mentioned, and numerous closes; common of pasture in Ham Common; an island called Crowell Ait; rent of free tenants 64s. 2d.; assize rent of customary tenants 36s. 7d.; total yearly value £53 3s. 8d.[513] In 1650 the manor with its appurtenauces was valued at £117 3s. 1d. yearly, the trees on the estate being worth £64 5s.[514]

There was a hospital for lepers near Kingston in the 13th century, founded by the men of the vill on a site now unknown.[515] In 1227 the lepers received royal letters of protection,[516] but the house was abandoned by 1343–4, when it was ruined and escheat to the Crown.[517] In this year William de Veirdire, valet of the chamber of Queen Philippa, petitioned for a grant of the site called 'Ye old Hospital,'[518] and appears to have obtained it for life.[519] He died before 1366–7, when it was valued at 10s. a year and granted for life to Nicholas Gretton, sompter of the king's larder.[520] In 1392 he was dead, and the croft called 'Spitelland' was granted at a rent of 10s. a year to Robert Clay, yeoman of the spicery.[521] The grant was confirmed to Robert Spicer alias Clay in 1400;[522] and a croft, lands and tenements called Spittelland are again mentioned in 1534 as having belonged in the reign of Richard III to John Popyll.[523] In consequence of his murdering one John Byrde this and other land escheated to the Crown, which appears to have retained it until 1534, when it was granted to Richard Kynwelmershe, mercer, John Crymes, clothworker, and Richard Crymes, haberdasher of London.[524] No later mention of it has been found.

Rights of free fishery in the creek at Kingston were conveyed by William le Grys and Katharine his wife to John Celye in 1586;[525] he and William Barkworth sold them in 1612 [526] to William Ryder, whose heirs James Maxwell and Elizabeth his wife, Broome Whorwood and Jane his wife and Ann Ryder parted with them to Benjamin Agar in 1637–8.[527] They again changed hands in 1641, when they were bought by George Sheeres.[528] Similar rights were sold by John Evelyn to Anthony Benn in 1605,[529]

and by John Rowle and Elizabeth his wife to Edward Wilmot in 1778.[530]

The church of *ALL SAINTS* is a *CHURCHES* large building consisting of a chancel 43 ft. by 22 ft. 8 in., north chapel 25 ft. 2 in. by 17 ft. 9 in., now used as a vestry and organ chamber, north-east vestry, south chapel of the same length as the chancel and 20 ft. 4 in. wide with a shallow south transept at its west end 17 ft. 2 in. long by 11 ft. 3 in. deep, central tower 17 ft. square, north transept 27 ft. 4 in. by 18 ft. 11 in., south transept 29 ft. 11 in. by 18 ft. 9 in., nave 73 ft. 6 in. by 20 ft. 6 in., north aisle 18 ft. 11 in. wide, south aisle 21 ft. 3 in. wide, the latter with a small south transept at its east end in line with the transept wall and 10 ft. wide, and a north porch.

Apart from the destroyed chapel of St. Mary there appears to have been on the site of All Saints a 12th-century church, probably successor of the one mentioned in Domesday. A 11th-century doorway is said to have been discovered in the west wall of the nave when the modern restorations were begun about 1865; unfortunately it was only discovered to be again destroyed, but a photograph showing it was taken and is preserved in the vestry. This church must have been of considerable size and probably had a central tower, some of the stones of which may be still preserved in the piers and walling of the present one; it is said that when one of the piers was rebuilt in the restoration of 1877–8 it was found that the visible ashlar work was merely a casing about the older work with which it had no real bond. The south wall of the present nave and the present south arcade probably coincided in position, but the nave was evidently some 2 ft. narrower, the north wall being moved outwards subsequently. There were also probably transepts of a depth equal to the width of the present aisles, but all vestiges of them are destroyed, as also are those of the earlier chancel, excepting for a length of roll mould in the jamb of the arch opening into the north (Holy Trinity) chapel. This length of mould appears to be of 13th-century date and points to the enlargement of the 12th-century chancel by moving the north wall outwards, keeping the south wall in its old position. In fact the widening of both chancel and nave may very well have taken place in the 13th century. If the widening of the chancel took place in the 15th century (the date of the rest of the arch) it seems curious that this short length of mould should have been re-used in a rebuilding when the remainder was so thoroughly destroyed; but the fact that the mould was already *in situ* would assist in its preservation.

Before tracing the history of the present fabric, mention should be made of the chapel of St. Mary, which has now disappeared. It stood at the south-east of the church next to the south chapel of

[508] Add. MS. 6167, fol. 250.
[509] Chan. Inq. p.m. 21 Edw. I, no. 50.
[510] The decrease of arable acreage is remarkable. In 1383 there were 100 acres. Had 120 acres been enfranchised, or alienated?
[511] Chan. Inq. p.m. 21 Edw. I, no. 50.
[512] Cal. Pat. 1422–9, p. 205.
[513] Land Rev. Misc. Bks. vol. 198, fol. 101 d.

[514] Partics. for Sale of Comn. Land (Aug. Off.), R. 18.
[515] Chan. Inq. p.m. 17 Edw. III (Add.), no. 100.
[516] Cal. Pat. 1225–32, p. 116.
[517] Chan. Inq. p.m. 17 Edw. III (Add.), no. 100.
[518] Ibid.
[519] Abbrev. Rot. Orig.(Rec.Com.),ii,288.
[520] Ibid. In Cal. Pat. 1391–6, p. 53, the name is given as Birton.

[521] Cal. Pat. 1391–6, p. 58.
[522] Ibid. 1399–1401, p. 292.
[523] L. and P. Hen. VIII, vii, g. 1498 (36).
[524] Ibid.
[525] Feet of F. Surr. Hil. 28 Eliz.
[526] Ibid. East. 10 Jas. I.
[527] Ibid. East. 13 Chas. I.
[528] Ibid. Trin. 17 Chas. I.
[529] Ibid. Hil. 2 Jas.
[530] Ibid. Hil. 18 Geo. III.

St. James, and was pulled down in 1730 after a partial fall of the walling when the sexton was killed. There is nothing left to show its exact position, nor are any of its details remaining except perhaps the few stones which were discovered during the 19th-century restoration and which stand on the window-ledge east of the north chapel ; these include a piece of a 12th-century scalloped capital, a piece of stiff foliage of the same period, a 13th-century moulded base to a shaft, some grotesque corbel heads, probably of the 12th century, and a small corbel head with a wimple ; a fragment of stonework with some Saxon interlacing pattern carved upon it probably formed no part of the fabric. In a view shown by Manning and Bray [500a] from ' a draught taken in 1726 ' it appears that the lower parts of the walls were of 12th-century date, with a wide round-headed west doorway above which was a string running round the building and over two 13th-century lancet windows at the west end and five at the side ; the doorway and two end lancets were filled in when a large window was inserted in the 14th century ; this window had three lights under a net-traceried head. In the 15th century a large window was inserted in the east wall, an earlier bull's-eye gable-light being preserved but filled in. A south porch with an embattled parapet was added later in the century. Whether this chapel was connected with the earlier parish church is uncertain ; it is shown quite independent of the church in Manning and Bray's view, but obviously because they had no information on the point. The dimensions given by them are 60 ft. by 25 ft. outside, and 55 ft. by 20 ft. inside.

The earliest visible portion of the present structure is the lower half of the central tower, which dates from the 14th century. There is little detail to give its exact date, but it was rebuilt (or the older tower encased) probably early in the century. At the north-east corner it has a vice which has an early piscina in its north-west face ; this piscina, which served a transept chapel, is probably contemporary with the rebuilding or casing of the tower.

About 1400, aisles were added to the nave, their widths being governed by the depths of the pre-existing transepts, into which arches were made to open from the aisles. That into the south transept is of the same date as the arcades. The arch on the east side of the transept opening into the south chapel is some twenty years later, and it is probable that the chapel of St. James was then added, but less in length than the present south chapel. At the modern restoration it was discovered that this archway had another in line with and to the south of it, of which the springing stones still remain. Whether its original span of this second arch was as now restored is uncertain, but there is little doubt that it was inserted to open into the chapel of St. Mary. Presumably the transept was lengthened when the two arches were inserted ; and if the present end wall marks the limit of the lengthening, the modern inserted archway would appear to be of the correct span, just enough to make a comfortable opening into the earlier chapel, assuming that the west wall of St. Mary's Chapel was in a line with the two

arches, and the north wall of the same chapel formed the south wall of St. James's Chapel.

In February 1444–5 William of Worcester records that the church suffered from a fire (probably caused by a stroke of lightning) when a good part of the town was also destroyed. [531] The effects of this fire are not now evident, and it is uncertain whether it extended beyond the tower.

In 1459 licence was granted to William Skerne of Downhall to found a chantry in honour of the Blessed Virgin and the most Holy Body of Christ at the altar of St. James in Kingston. [532] From this it would appear that the altar of St. James was already in existence, and it is probable that the chapel was then lengthened to its present size with its east wall in line with that of the chancel, and that the arcade of three bays between the chancel and the chapel was then inserted. The archway in the south wall of this chapel at the west end also appears to be contemporary with the arcade, and was probably inserted then to enlarge the opening into the chapel of St. Mary. On 14 May 1477 Edward IV granted letters patent to Robert Bardsey for the foundation of a fraternity of the Holy Trinity in Kingston-on-Thames. The fraternity was to consist of two wardens and of clerks or laymen, both men and women. An annuity of £6 13s. 4d. was left by Bardsey to maintain a priest to sing mass in Trinity Chapel, this rent being collected from the tenants of Bardsey and his successors by the two wardens. After the Dissolution this rent was paid to the king. [533] Robert Bardsey was one of the feoffees of the property given for the endowment of the Skerne chantry ; it was therefore natural for him to copy as exactly as possible the detail of the south chancel arcade in the archway between the Trinity Chapel and the chancel. He retained the west jamb of the arch opening into the earlier chapel, of which his was an enlargement, but evidently widened the arch eastwards. There is some doubt as to the respective situations of the two chapels of the Holy Trinity and St. James, but we have adopted the late Major Heales' [534] suggestion that the former was on the north side and the latter on the south on the evidence of two wills. Clement Mylan in his will of 1496 directed his body to be buried in ' the trinitie chauncell on the north side of the church by the wall ' ; there are several sepulchral recesses in the north wall of the Trinity Chapel. William Skerne, the founder of the chantry in St. James's Chapel, by his will of 1463 directs his burial to be juxta ossa Roberti Skern his uncle. Manning and Bray [535] describe the brass of the latter as being at the east end of the south chapel. The vestry was probably added subsequently to the enlargement of the north chapel near the end of the 15th century. A porch was removed in 1530 according to the church-wardens' accounts. The tower seems to have fallen into a bad state by the beginning of the 16th century and needed considerable repair ; it was again much out of repair in 1699 when a levy of 6d. in the £1 was made to put it into order, but this did little good, as in 1708 its timbers were so rotten that it was in such great decay and danger that is was necessary to take it down, when the present brick superstructure

500a Op. cit. i, 370.
531 See Major Heales' article on the church in the Surr. Arch. Coll. viii.
532 Surr. Arch. Coll. viii, 57.
533 See Cal. Pat. 1471–85, p. 43 ; Cal. S.P. Dom. 1595–7, pp. 336, 337 ; Chant.
Cert. Surr. 48, no. 9 ; cf. Pat. 34 Eliz. pt. viii, m. 31.
534 Surr. Arch. Coll. viii, 48.
535 Hist. of Surr. i, 374.

was put up. Presumably the aisles also fell into decay as, according to Manning and Bray, they were rebuilt in 1729 of brick. The body of the church was 'beautified' in 1681.

Coming to the modern work: this was begun about the middle of the last century, but not a great deal had been done when the present vicar—the Rev. A. S. W. Young—was presented to the living; a new roof had been placed on the nave by Brandon, the west gallery had been removed, and the west wall was being rebuilt but was left unfinished, and some other work done to the windows, &c. Since his induction in 1878 a large sum of money has been spent in putting the building into substantial repair, including the following works: the restoration of the nave and aisles (the galleries being removed and the brickwork of 1729 being replaced with stonework and new traceried windows inserted in place of the former round-headed windows), new west windows and the finishing of the west wall, including the remodelling of the west doorway, new tracery in the chancel window, rebuilding and lengthening of the north transept and the heightening of both with the insertion of large windows; the addition of the west aisle to the south transept to match that on the east side, the heightening of the east and west arches of the tower and the addition of a stone vault in the tower, new roofs to the transepts and aisles, three heavy tie-beams to Brandon's nave roof which was thrusting out the nave walls, new seats in the chancel (just finished), and nave, a new organ, and much other work. During the heightening of the tower arches the south-east pier began to show signs of weakness and it had to be taken down and rebuilt; it was then found that the 14th-century outer skin of ashlar had no bond with the earlier core, which was made up of very loose material. Substantially the building is now in very good condition, the only exception being the north-east vestry, which has some much-decayed external stonework.

The chancel has an east window of five lights and tracery; the inner jambs are of the 15th century, but the rest is modern; the wall, which was probably of the original 13th-century thickness, has been thinned for the window. It has been cemented outside in imitation of stone; the buttresses on either side are veneered with thin stone slabs; the foundation of the walls is of brick. The north window is of three cinquefoiled lights under a traceried head; it dates from the 15th century. Below it is a modern tomb-recess. The doorway into the vestry is of the 15th century with moulded jambs and pointed arch. The archway opening into the north chapel has plain jambs, the eastern with slightly chamfered edges, the western with chamfered corners excepting on the south side where, to a height of 6 ft. 6 in. above the floor, it has an edge roll; the arch is two centred and has a wide hollow between smaller moulds which die on the jambs. The arcade of three bays dividing the chancel from the south chapel has arch moulds similar to the north arch; the piers are composed of four engaged round shafts with hollow-chamfered angles between; the shafts have moulded bases and bell capitals; the east respond resembles the piers but has also the outer order of the arch carried down; there is no west respond, the arch dying on the tower buttress; the arcade is built of chalk.

The tower has an arch in each of its four sides of two chamfered orders, the inner being carried down in the jambs, the other dying out. The north and south arches are of their original height, but the east and west have been heightened in modern times. A shallow buttress of ashlar serves to rebut the arches outside the wall line at each angle. The axial line of the tower is some 2 ft. to the south of that of the chancel and deflects to the north of it.

The north-east vestry is the least restored part of the church, its walls are of ashlar much weathered outside; it has a square-headed window in its east and north walls of two hollow-chamfered orders and with moulded labels all very much decayed; the lights are now boarded up. In the east wall is a modern doorway.

The north chapel has a modernized east window of four cinquefoiled lights, and in the north wall are two similar modern windows, each of three lights; the jambs of all three windows are similar in section to those of the east window of the chancel. Under the second window is a small modern doorway.

In the east wall below the window is a shallow recess 4 ft. 3 in. wide with moulded jambs and a four-centred arch in a square head. It dates from the 15th century and is part of a tomb, but whether it is in its original position is doubtful. It was probably moved from the north wall when the doorway was inserted. In the south wall next it are the remains of a piscina without its basin; it has a plain four-centred head. In the north wall is another tomb-recess of the same width and almost like that in the east wall, but of more elaborate detail; the inner parts of the splayed jambs are panelled, the arch is four centred (splayed and panelled as the jambs) and has traceried spandrels under a square head; the recess retains its base, which is panelled with quatrefoils, each containing a shield. To the east of this tomb-recess is a short length of a large mould of similar character to the side arches of the chancel; from its position it might almost be inferred that it is part of an archway which opened into a chapel or chamber, still farther north, and that it was abolished and filled in when the tomb-recess was inserted, but there are no other traces of such a chapel or chamber.

The walls of the chapel are cemented, excepting a small portion at the west end, where they are seen to be of flint with an admixture of stone. A modern archway through the west wall of the chapel opens into the north transept. South of the archway is the vice to the tower with semi-octagonal outer faces. In the north-west face is an old piscina with a pointed trefoiled head and a mutilated round basin; the piscina might be of either the 13th or the 14th century, but is more probably the latter; the vice is entered by a pointed chamfered doorway with broach stops. The transept has a modern north window of six lights and tracery, and, in the west wall, a modern archway replacing a smaller one of the 18th century.

The south chapel has an east window of five cinquefoiled lights and tracery below a two-centred head; the moulded jambs are similar to those of the chancel windows, and while the outer stonework and tracery are modern the inner jambs may be old. This also applies to the two south windows, which are each of three lights with tracery. The opening of

KINGSTON-UPON-THAMES CHURCH : NAVE LOOKING EAST

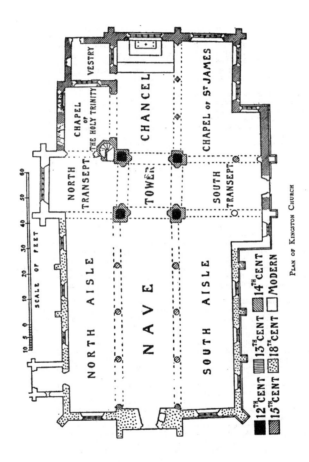

PLAN OF KINGSTON CHURCH

SCALE OF FEET

12TH CENT　13TH CENT　14TH CENT
15TH CENT　18TH CENT　MODERN

the shallow transept at the western end of the south wall is spanned by a four-centred arch of similar section to the arcade on the north side ; it rests on the pillar between the two west arches and has thrust this arcade out of the perpendicular. The east window of this shallow transept is of three trefoiled lights under a pointed head filled with net tracery ; the tracery and outer stonework are quite new, but the inner Jambs are old, and it is possible that they are the stones of the traceried west window of St. Mary's Chapel (mentioned above) re-used here after the fall of the chapel.

A large archway spans the west end of the chapel and a smaller one that of the shallow transept, both springing from a partly-restored octagonal pillar with a moulded base and capital (both old) ; the arches are of two moulded orders divided by a large three-quarter hollow and with moulded labels ; the larger arch is old, the springing stones of the smaller arch above the pillar are also old, but the rest of the arch is modern ; it is obvious from the old springing stones that there has been an arch here formerly, but it is not at all certain that the present one is an exact reproduction of the old. The two arches in the west wall of the transept are of like size to those opposite but are of much plainer detail. The pillar and smaller archway are entirely modern in conception and workmanship, but the larger arch, which is of two hollow-chamfered orders like the nave arches, is old. The large six-light traceried south window and the doorway beneath it are both modern.

The nave arcades each consist of four bays with octagonal pillars having simple bases and moulded bell capitals, the arches being two-centred and of two hollow-chamfered orders ; both arcades may be said to date from the beginning of the 15th century, but there are slight differences in detail which point to the work not having all been carried out at one time. The north pillars are more slender than those on the south side, whilst the easternmost pillar on the south side is of greater diameter than its fellows ; this pillar has no base (unless the base is buried), and it is not improbable that it may have formed part of some earlier arcade ; all the capitals, though generally similar, have slight differences in their depths and the sizes of their bells. Above the arcades is a clearstory lighted by four windows in either wall, each of three trefoiled lights and tracery under pointed segmental arches ; they are modern excepting the inner jamb stones and rear arches. The west doorway is a modern one set in a very thick wall under a gable head ; the wall thins again below the west window, which is also a modern one of four lights and tracery. All the aisle windows and the north doorway are modern as well as the north porch. At the east end of the south aisle is a small modern transept or aisle to the south transept containing a modern south window.

The upper part of the tower is of brick with a plain parapet and pine-apple corner-pinnacles ; the older walls, immediately above the roofs, are of flint with an admixture of freestone ; the ashlar angle buttresses are modernized. The windows to the bell-chamber are modern. In a panel on the south side is the date of the rebuilding of the tower—1708.

The roof of the chancel has a low arched barrel vault divided into panels by moulded ribs ; the transverse ribs spring from corbel-capitals in the moulded cornices, and the intersection of each alternate and larger rib with the ridge is covered by a foliage boss ; the work appears to date from late in the 15th century.

The south chapel roof has plain old rafters (formerly plastered) with collar-beam trusses, and three principal trusses supported on stone corbels carved as angels with shields, some of which may be old ; the roof is also of the 15th century. The north chapel has a flat plastered ceiling divided into panels by large moulded timbers, apparently old. The nave roof is modern with hammer-beam trusses and more recent tie-beams ; the north transept roof is also modern. The south transept roof is for the greater part modern, but the southernmost truss, at least, is old and has traceried spandrels and rests on carved corbel-heads which are also old. The aisles have modern roofs. The gable roofs are covered with slates. The altar table, oak quire seats, carved stone pulpit, carved stone and marble font, deal pews, and other furniture are all modern.

There are a large number of monuments in the church, of which the following are worthy of notice :— On a slab formerly in the south chapel, but now standing upright against the west jamb of the chapel arcade, is a brass figure of a man standing on a mound or hillock dressed in a fur-lined tunic reaching to the ankles and having loose sleeves with tighter wristlets and cuffs ; his waist is encircled by a belt with a pendant reaching to the knees ; his hands are in prayer ; on his right is the figure of his wife in a covered horn head-dress, a tight-fitting gown, over which is a loose cloak fastened across the breast by a cord ; the inscription faces towards them so that it is now reversed ; it is in black letter and reads :—'Roberti cista Skēni corpus tenet ista, Marmoree petre coniugis atq3 sue. Qui validus, fidus, discretus lege peritus, Nobilis ingenuus perfidiam rennit Constans sermone, vita sensu racione Committi cuiq3 iusticiam voluit, Regalis iuris vivens promovit honores, Fallere vel falli res odiosa sibi, Gaudeat in celis quia vixit in orbe fidelis Nonas Aprilis pridie qui morit9 Mille quadringintis dñi Trigintaq3 septemannis ipsius Rex miserere jesu.'

In the north transept is set a small gravestone with the brasses of a headless man in a long cloak girdled about the waist, and a lady in a tight-fitting dress and a butterfly head-dress ; both are kneeling ; over them are the indents of two shields and of a central figure, possibly a Trinity, to which their prayers are ascending ; the black letter inscription below reads :—'Hic jacent Joħes Hertcombe Geħosus et Katerina uxor ei9 qui quidm Joħes obiit xxii° die Julii Anno dñi millħo cccc°Lxxxviii° Et p'dicta Katerina obiit xij die Julii anno dñi millħo cccclxxxvii° quor9 aħab3 propicietur deus Amen.'

Below the first window on the south wall of the south chapel is an altar tomb in a recess to Anthony Benn, formerly Recorder of Kingston and afterwards Recorder of London, who died in 1618 ; it contains his recumbent effigy in his lawyer's robe and ruff collar and cuffs ; his hands which were in prayer are broken off. The arch of the recess is a coffered round one of alabaster ; the base is low and has shields, one of which is faded ; the other is charged quarterly 1 and 4 a griffon on a chief or (?) three molets sable ; 2 and 3 or (?) two bars sable between nine martlets sable, three, three and three ; the colours of the shield are indistinct. On the north wall of the chancel is a monument to Mark Snelling, alderman of the City of London and a benefactor of the church and parish, died 1633 (?) ; and two other monuments of about the same period. There are many 18th-century and later monuments.

On the pillar east of the south transept is an ancient painting (probably coeval with the chapel) of a bishop with his pastoral staff, mitre, &c., and holding what may be a comb, which would identify him with St. Blaize the patron of wool-combers.

In the tower is a fine ring of ten bells ; the treble is dated 1748 ; the second 1841, by T. Mears ; the third 1750, by Robert Catlin ; the fourth 1875, by Blews and Son, Birmingham ; fifth, sixth, and seventh 1826, by T. Mears ; the eighth is inscribed 'The 8 old bells recast and two new trebles added to make 10 by subscriptions, S. London, S. Belchier, Collectors, 1748' ; the ninth, 1879, was recast by Mears and Stainbank, and the tenor (which weighs 33 cwt.) by Mears, 1850.

The old communion plate, which was a large service dating from 1708 and 1716, has been stolen ; that in use is modern.

The registers date from 1542 and, up to 1812, they comprise twenty volumes as follows :— i. mixed baptisms, marriages and burials 1542 to 1556, a well-bound volume on the original paper ; ii. the same, 1560 to 1574 ; iii. mixed, 1574 to 1586, and marriages at the end also for 1574, 1575, and 1579 ; iv. 1586 to 1602 ; v. 1603 to 1609 ; vi. July 1620 to August 1621 ; vii. September 1622 to June 1636 ; viii. 1636 to 1653 (in this volume are many notices of banns published on market days and Lord's days) ; ix. 1653 to 1665, at the end a list of deaths from the plague 1665 ; the register has been lost or torn out from 1665 to 1668, this book is partly vellum and partly paper ; x. 1668 to 1693 (paper) ; xi. 1693 to 1713 (parchment) contains a list of the burials of Dissenters from 1696 to 1699 ; xii. 1712–13 to 1740, parchment with paper end sheets ; xiii. 1741 to 1749, parchment ; xiv. baptisms and burials 1749 to 1769 and marriages to 1757 ; xv. baptisms and burials 1770 to 1789 ; xvi. the same, 1789 to 1809 ; xvii. the same, 1810 to 1812 ; xviii. marriages 1754 to 1769 ; xix. the same, 1769 to 1807 ; and xx. the same, 1808 to 1812. The earlier books are of paper and are much torn and worn out, but have been carefully interleaved in recent years in paper volumes.

The churchwardens' accounts of Kingston are preserved from 1503 to 1538 and recommence 1561. A brief mention may be made here of some of the items affecting the fabric and fittings.[536] In 1504 and 1505 a mason was paid for building and repairing the steeple, which, from entries in 1508–9, had a weathercock and gilt cross. In 1523 the second bell was exchanged for a new one, and in 1529 the third bell was recast ; again in 1535 the second and third bells were recast at Reading. In 1553 there were five bells in the steeple, 'a sauns bell and a chyme for the belles.' In 1561 another bell was recast at Reading, while in 1566 the fourth bell, which weighed 6 cwt. 42 lb., was recast. The great bell was recast in 1574. There was a clock in 1508. A large payment was made for

lead in 1561, evidently for re-roofing. An order was made in 1585 for the removal of the pulpit from the place it 'nowe standeth unto the north-west piller,' and in the same year :—' It is ordered that the seats in the church shall be altered and the parishioners to be placed in order in their degrees and callings.'

The chapel of ST. MARY MAGDALENE, attached to the grammar school, and now used as a gymnasium, is a building of much interest. It was founded by the merchant, Edward Lovekyn, in 1309.[537] He apparently died childless, and his successor, Robert Lovekyn, was excommunicated for neglecting the endowment of the chapel.[538] Robert was succeeded by John, his son, who increased the endowment.[539] The chapel came into the hands of the Crown at the Dissolution,[540] but in 1560 was granted to the governors of the lately revived grammar school,[541] who have retained it until the present day. If the date of its erection—1351—were not known, it might have been ascribed to some twenty years later at least. It is a plain rectangular building, 38 ft. by 17 ft. 2 in., with octagonal vices at the eastern angles. The north vice retains many of its steps but has no outlet at the top ; the southern one now has no steps and has an outer doorway inserted in its south side ; both open off the east wall by a pointed doorway and both are of ashlar. The east window has three cinquefoiled pointed lights with two quatrefoils (rather after the 'Perpendicular' style) in the traceried two-centred arch ; the side windows are each of two cinquefoiled lights with a sexfoil over in the two-centred head ; only one (the easternmost) of the three in the north wall is now open, the second being filled in at the glass line, and the third (if a window ever existed in the bay) having lost all its tracery. On the south side two eastern windows remain, the existence of the westernmost being again doubtful ; the west window is similar to that at the opposite end. All the windows have widely-splayed inner jambs and arches, with the edges moulded as a double ogee-mould or, perhaps more properly, as the sides of two filleted rolls ; the mullions inside have two hollow chamfers ; the inner jambs and arches are original, but the external stonework of all the windows is modern excepting the north-east window, which is very much decayed. At the foot of the mullions of the east window were set two image brackets carved with the heads of Edward III and Queen Philippa, but the latter has now disappeared although it was existing in 1883,[542] its place being occupied by a modern foliated capital. In the south wall, east of the first window, is the piscina, rather tall for its width and rather shallow ; its sill contains an octofoil basin and is somewhat broken ; the upper shelf is also damaged ; the head has a cinquefoiled ogee arch.

Between the second and third bays in each side wall is a shallow recess 3 ft. 11 in. wide, the use of which is not apparent ; they are too shallow for sedilia but may, in connexion with the original woodwork, have formed the setting for the two most important and westernmost seats ; they have a transom moulded and embattled at the level of the window sills and, at about double the height, a foliated three-centred

536 Surr. Arch. Coll. viii, 68.
537 Ibid. 256.
538 Ibid. 258.

539 Add. Chart. 23524–7.
540 Surr. Arch. Coll. viii, 258.
541 Pat. 2 Eliz. pt. xi. See V.C.H. Surr. ii, 156 et seq. for the probability of a

school having been held in the chantry before its suppression.
542 See illustration to article by Major Heales in the Surr. Arch. Coll. viii, 296.

arch with plain sunk spandrels in a square head with a moulded and embattled cornice ; the jambs are moulded to match the piscina and windows. In the north wall are two modernized doorways, one between the first and second bays, and the other in the third bay and opening into a modern wing. The south doorway is in the third or westernmost bay ; it has an old two-centred arch and modern Jambs of two orders.

In the west wall south of the great window were two doorways one over the other, but they are now filled in. The walls were originally of flint, but the east wall and the first two bays of the south have been faced with modern ashlar ; in the west wall can be seen a worked stone with an edge roll, imbedded among the flints ; the turrets are also faced with ashlar and have rather perished surfaces. A general restoration of the building took place in 1886, before which time it was in a very dilapidated condition. Unfortunately Godstone stone was used for the dressings, with the consequence that some of the stones, particularly those in the head of the west window, are already beginning to show signs of decay ; modern buttresses strengthen the south wall. There was a porch with a chamber over it at the south doorway, but the dates of its erection and destruction do not now appear. A late or modern building still remains against the north wall. The roof is gabled, has two modern trusses, and a plastered cradle ceiling. The parapets are embattled.

The church of *ST. PETER, NORBITON*, London Road, is a building of white and stock brick with stone dressings, built in 1842 in the style of the 12th century and consisting of a chancel, north and south transepts, with a gallery on three sides, narrow gabled aisles, west porches and a north-west tower of four stages ; the roofs are covered with slates. The reredos and quire fittings are of oak and of later and better design than the fabric. The churchyard is chiefly on the north side towards the road, is planted with shrubs, &c., and fenced by an iron railing.

The church of *ST. JOHN THE EVANGELIST*, Grove Lane, is a building of Kentish rag with Bath stone dressings, erected in 1872 in the style of the latter half of the 13th century ; it has a chancel, nave, north and south transepts, aisles, north-east vestry, south porch, and the stump of a proposed south-east tower ; the roofs are tiled. The churchyard, sown with grass, surrounds the building, and has an iron railing on the west and south sides towards the roads.

ST. PAUL'S CHURCH, Queen's Road, Kingston Hill, is an unfinished building of stone dating from 1878 and in the style of the 13th century. It consists at present of a nave, with a clearstory, and north and south aisles, the chancel not being yet built.

ST. LUKE'S CHURCH, Gibbon Road, is a large building of red brick and stone in 13th-century style, erected in 1890. It has an apsidal chancel with a vaulted ceiling of wood, nave of five bays with stone pillars and brick arches and having a clearstory of lancets, north and south aisles, north organ-chamber, over which rises a tower with a tall octagonal brick spire, south chapel, vestry, porches, &c. The chancel and the chapel are closed by iron screens painted black and gold. The font is of alabaster and marble, the pulpit of carved oak. The roofs are covered with slates. The churchyard is small and planted with shrubs, &c.

ST. MARK'S CHURCH, Victoria Road, Surbiton, is a large building of stone in the 14th-century style, consecrated in 1845. It consists of a chancel, north and south transepts, north-east vestry, and south-east organ-chamber, nave with a clearstory, aisles, south porch and a north-west tower with a tall octagonal broach spire of stone. An arcade of five bays with grey stone pillars and plastered arches divides the nave from the south aisle, and a similar arcade with the addition of a smaller west bay from the north aisle. At the west end is a gallery. The pulpit and font are of stone and marble. The churchyard is triangular in plan ; it contains many graves, and is inclosed by a hedge and wood fence.

CHRIST CHURCH, King Charles Road, is a building of red and other coloured bricks with stone dressings of a late 12th or early 13th-century style, built in 1863. It has a chancel with gabled aisles, nave of five bays having stone pillars and brick arches, and a clearstory with small circular windows, low aisles, vestries, and south porch ; a small cote over the chancel arch contains one bell.

The church of *ST. ANDREW*, Maple Road, was built as a chapel of ease to St. Mark's in 1872. It is of various coloured bricks and stone in 13th-century style. It has a shallow chancel with deep transepts, nave, aisles, west baptistery, and a tall north tower with a gabled head. The nave has arcades of four bays, a clearstory of lancets, and a panelled vaulted ceiling ; the pulpit is of carved oak ; the font of stone with marble shafts ; the reredos is a tall one of stone.

ST. MATTHEW'S CHURCH, Ewell Road, is a large well-built structure of stock brick and stone in the style of the 13th century, erected in 1874. It has a vaulted apsidal chancel, north-east and south-east vestries, north and south transepts, nave, aisles, and a south-west porch-tower with a tall octagonal stone spire. The interior wall facing is of stock brick ; the nave arcades are of four bays with round pillars and pointed arches to the aisles and of a single large bay to each transept. The roofs are open-timbered and gabled. The churchyard, which is planted with shrubs and grass, is bounded by a stone wall to the roads on the south and east sides.

The church of *ST. ANDREW*, Ham, stands on Ham Common. It consists of a chancel erected in 1900, nave built in 1832, and south aisle added in 1860. The chancel with the vestry south of it are built of red brick with stone dressings. The nave is of stock brick and Bath stone, and has two small turrets at the west end. It is roofed by a flat gable. A stone arcade of four bays divides it from the aisle. Both nave and aisle are wide in proportion to their length. A gallery spans the west end.

A good oak lych-gate has been recently placed at the entrance to the churchyard, in which lie many naval and military officers and several members of the nobility.

ST. PAUL'S CHURCH, Hook, which has replaced an earlier church built in 1835, is a small building dating from 1883. It is of red brick and stone in the style of the 14th century, and consists of a chancel, north vestry and organ chamber, nave, north aisle, and south porch. There is an alabaster reredos with medallions of the Evangelists. The altar is of oak, cedar, and olive wood, the last brought from Palestine. The font, of Devonshire marble and mosaic with an oak cover, and the stained east window, were presented by Mr. Thomas Hare and Mrs. Hare of Gosbury Hill. The roofs are tiled.

The church of *ST. JOHN THE BAPTIST*, Kingston Vale, is a small building dating from 1861. It is built of stock and red brick with stone dressings, and consists of a chancel, nave, aisles, organ chamber, vestry, &c., and has a small bell-turret of wood over the east end of the nave.

CHRIST CHURCH, New Malden, is a stone building, begun in 1866 and finished in 1893. It is in the style of the 13th century, and consists of a chancel, vestries, nave, north and south aisles, and a west baptistery and porches ; arcades of six bays divide the nave from the aisles ; each bay of the north aisle has a transverse gabled roof, while the south aisle has a lean-to roof ; the end bay of the south aisle forms a sort of western transept.

ADVOWSONS The church of Kingston is said to have been part of the grant made by Gilbert Norman to his foundation of Merton Priory,[542] and in the early 13th century was reported to have been given a long time before that date.[543] The priory certainly had land here in 1177–86, and this may have been the manor of Kingston-Canbury (q.v.), which later was called a ' parcel of the rectory.' [544] In 1231–8 an allowance was made to the vicar, but this was given as a gratuity and not as his right ; [545] an endowment, however, was made in 1303, when among other grants was that of two quarters of wheat, one quarter of barley, and one quarter of oats from the prior's grange of Canbury.[546] The vicar's complaint that the allowance was insufficient reached the bishop, and the dispute was not finally settled until 1375.[547] In the middle of the 14th century the king claimed the patronage during the vacancy following the death of the prior,[548] and established his rights after some litigation.[549] The patronage for the next turn was granted by the prior in 1516 to Jasper Horsey and John and Richard Bowle, citizens of London,[550] and in 1536 an assignment was made to Sir Nicholas Carew and Sir Thomas Cheyney ; Sir Nicholas presented in 1536,[551] but after his attainder in 1538 the advowson, rectory, and Canbury Manor came into the hands of the Crown.[552] The rectory was the subject of various Crown leases,[553] and was bought for £4,000 by Sir John Ramsay in 1618.[554] He was created Baron of Kingston-upon-Thames and Earl of Holderness in 1620, and obtained a grant of the advowson in 1622 ; [555] he married Martha daughter of Sir William Cockayne and died without issue in 1626.[556] The rectory, manor, and advowson then passed, under a settlement,[557] to his

wife, who married as her second husband Montague, Lord Willoughby.[558] They assigned the advowson for a term to one Abraham Chamberlayne, merchant, who presented to the living in 1632.[559]

On the death of the Countess of Holderness without heirs in 1640,[560] the advowson, rectory, and manor came into the hands of the Crown and were granted to William Murray, created Earl of Dysart in 1643.[561] In the following year he assigned them to the Earl of Elgin in trust for his daughters,[562] who in 1656–7 made a settlement of them,[563] and in 1662 Lord Maynard, husband of one of these daughters, with others, presented to the living.[564] The family of Ramsay had rights in the manor of Canbury, the rectory, and advowson, which Patrick Ramsay and Elizabeth his wife conveyed to the Earl of Elgin in 1652 ; [565] John Ramsay and Alice his wife conveyed them to John Ramsay in 1664.[566] Four years later the right of patronage was in dispute between John Ramsay and Elizabeth, Countess of Dysart, daughter of William Murray.[567] Lady Dysart presented Thomas Willis, whose institution was hindered by a *caveat* entered by John Ramsay, with the result, as the bailiffs bitterly complained, that they had been ten months without a minister, and that the disaffected assembled at their meetings.[568] The dispute was settled in 1670, when the countess and the other heirs of William Murray quitclaimed their rights to John Ramsay.[569] He sold the manor, rectory, and advowson in 1671 to Nicholas Hardinge.[570] On the death of Dr. Willis in 1692 the right of presentation was again questioned, but Nicholas Hardinge established his claim,[571] and in 1692 presented his cousin Gideon Hardinge, father of Nicholas Hardinge the Latin scholar,[572] who, as clerk of the House of Commons, arranged the Commons' *Journals* in their present form.[573] This Nicholas inherited the estate from his kinsman of the same name, and lived at Canbury in the early 18th century. He was the father of George Hardinge (1743–1816) the author, the senior Justice of Brecon,[574] who had no children, and after making a settlement of the manor, rectory, and advowson in 1781,[575] sold them in 1786 to King's College, Cambridge,[576] the present patrons.

The chapelries of Kew, Sheen, Petersham, East Molesey, and Thames Ditton remained annexed to the church of Kingston until the 18th century ; they were separated by Act of Parliament obtained in 1769.[577]

A chapel of St. Augustine in the parish of Kingston is mentioned in 1422, but its site is not now known.[578]

The bishop of the diocese is the patron of St. Luke's Church, Gibbon Road. The advowson of St. Mark's, Surbiton, is vested in the donors, Messrs.

[542] Dugdale, *Mon.* vi, 247.
[543] Healea, ' Early Hist. of the Church of Kingston,' *Surr. Arch. Coll.* viii, 13 n.
[544] Pat. 11 Eliz. pt. ii, m. 10.
[545] *Surr. Arch. Coll.* viii, 16.
[546] Ibid. 20 ; *Valor Eccl.* (Rec. Com.), ii, 36.
[547] *Surr. Arch. Coll.* viii, 28–32.
[548] Ibid. 24.
[549] *Year Bk.* 20 *Edw. III* (Rolls Ser.), pt. i, 20–5 ; *Cal. Pat.* 1345–8, p. 350.
[550] *Surr. Arch. Coll.* viii, 37.
[551] Winton Epis. Reg. Gardiner, fol. 44 b.
[552] *Valor Eccl.* (Rec. Com.), ii, 36.
[553] *L. and P. Hen. VIII*, xviii (1), p. 557 ; Pat. 11 Eliz. pt. ii, m. 10.

[554] Harl. Chart. 79 G. 8.
[555] *Cal. S.P. Dom.* 1619–23, p. 374.
[556] Chan. Inq. p.m. (Ser. 2), cccxxxvi, 68.
[557] Duchy of Lanc. Misc. Bks. xxiv, 151.
[558] G.E.C. *Peerage*, iv, 238.
[559] Inst. Bks. (P.R.O.).
[560] G.E.C. *Peerage*, iv, 238.
[561] Duchy of Lanc. Misc. Bks. xxiv, 151.
[562] *Cal. Com. for Compounding*, 2553.
[563] Feet of F. Surr. Hil. 1656.
[564] Inst. Bks. (P.R.O.).
[565] Feet of F. Surr. East. 1652.
[566] Ibid. Hil. 1664.

[567] *Cal. S.P. Dom.* 1668–9, p. 96 ; G.E.C. *Peerage.*
[568] *Cal. S.P. Dom.* 1668–9, pp. 96, 98, 177, 184, 434.
[569] Feet of F. Surr. Mich. 22 Chas. II.
[570] Ibid. Trin. 23 Chas. II.
[571] Inst. Bks. (P.R.O.) ; *Cal. S.P. Dom.* 1691–2, p. 478.
[572] Manning and Bray, *Surr.* i, 383.
[573] *Dict. Nat. Biog.*
[574] Ibid.
[575] Recov. R. Hil. 21 Geo. III, rot. 316.
[576] Manning and Bray, *Surr.* i, 397.
[577] Private Act, 9 Geo. III, cap. 65.
[578] *Surr. Arch. Coll.* viii, 57.

Coutts & Co.,[580] that of Christ Church and St. Matthew's in trustees; St. Peter's, Norbiton, is in the gift of the vicar of Kingston, while St. john the Evangelist, Norbiton, and St. Paul, Kingston Hill, are in the gift of trustees.[581] The living of St. john the Baptist, Kingston Vale, is a vicarage in the gift of the Bishop of Southwark.

The advowson of St. Andrew's, Ham, belongs to King's College, Cambridge; of St. Paul's, Hook, to the bishop of the diocese; and of Christ Church, New Malden, to five trustees.

CHARITIES The Grammar School and the foundations of Thomas Tiffin and john Tiffin, and of other donors for charitable purposes, including the charities of Elizabeth Brown, Edward Belitha, john Dolling, King Charles I, Henry Smith, Nicholas Harding, john Hartop and Vandercomb are treated in the article on Surrey Schools.[582]

THE MUNICIPAL CHARITIES.

The charities formerly under the administration of the Corporation and now under a body of trustees appointed by the Charity Commissioners, comprise :—

1. The Almshouse and Pension Charity, regulated by a scheme, 9 December 1890, including the almshouse of William Cleave, founded by will, 11 May 1665, and the benefaction of John Pilsley, by will, date not stated. The trust property now consists of the old almshouses, erected by Mrs. Ranyard, the George Inn, let at £95 per annum, the Grange, Kingston Hill, and 2 a. 2 r. let at £180, several parcels of land, containing 27 a. 2 r. with messuages thereon producing £196 per annum, a sum of £406 17s. 6d. consols and a sum of £385 per annum, received by way of interest on a sum of £9,500 on loan to the Kingston Endowed Schools.

The scheme provides that the inmates should number twenty, of whom four should consist of two married couples, and the remainder single persons; the former to receive a stipend of not less than 12s. or more than 15s. weekly, and the latter 7s. 6d. up to 10s. weekly. There are also men and women pensioners, to whom the like amounts may be paid.

2. The Bridge Estate Charity, including the gifts of Clement Milam, by will, 11 November 1497; Richard Clark, by deed, temp. Henry VIII; Hugh Stephynson, by deed, 5 january 1520; Robert Hamonde, by will, 7 March 1556.

The trust estate consists of several parcels of land and tenements situate in Kingston producing £235 13s. per annum, and a sum of £4,618 18s. consols, producing £115 9s. 4d. yearly. The income is applied in lighting and in the general upkeep of the bridge.

3. Edward Buckland, by will, 1618, gave a wharf on the north side of Kingston Bridge, let at £80 per annum, and £50 15s. 8d. consols, applicable in the distribution of coal.

4. Mark Snelling, by will, 21 February 1533, gave trust property consisting of several parcels of land at Hersham, containing 28 a. or there-

abouts, producing £84 per annum, and £1,669 11s. 9d. consols, representing proceeds of sales of land, producing yearly £41 14s. 8d. The income is applicable in the distribution on the first Sunday in each month of a sixpenny loaf, and a sum of 6d. to twenty poor householders, and the residue in the distribution of coals.

5. Edward Hurst, by will, 28 April 1551, gave a yearly rent-charge of £6 out of land at Kingston, belonging to Hon. L. Powys-Keck, to be distributed to ten poor persons, each to receive 1s. on the first Sunday in the month, which is given to poor widows.

The following charities are under the administration of the vicar and churchwardens, namely, the charities of—

1. Sarah Madgwick, who died about 1806 and by her will bequeathed a sum of stock, now represented by £52 19s. 7d. consols, the annual income, £1 6s. 4d., being distributed in bread.

2. Mary, Countess of Dover (deed, 6 December 1644), consisting of an annuity of £5 4s. out of her land in Southwark, to be distributed in penny loaves to twenty-four poor persons every Sunday.

3. William Cobbett (will, 4 February 1820), trust fund, £270 consols, the annual income of £6 15s. to be applied in the distribution of bread on 1 January yearly.

4. The Right Hon. Robert Banks, Earl of Liverpool, by a codicil to his will, dated 4 january 1822. Trust fund, £833 6s. 8d. consols, the income, amounting to £20 16s. 8d. a year, to be distributed equally among five industrious poor, with a preference to such as have two or more children.

5. William Walton the elder, by will and codicil, proved in the P.C.C. 1847. Trust fund, £154 5s. 9d. consols, producing £3 17s. yearly, applicable in the distribution of coals equally amongst widows.

6. William Walton, Junior, by will, 19 April 1844. Trust fund, £55 14s. 11d. consols, producing £1 17s. 8d. yearly, which is distributed in bread to poor widows.

7. Mrs. Bythewood, by will, 18 August 1843, Trust fund (with accumulations), £246 15s. 1d. consols, the annual dividends of which, amounting to £6 3s. 4d., are applied in the distribution of 4-lb. loaves.

8. Mrs. Bythewood for Sunday School. Trust fund, £40 19s. 6d. consols, producing £1 0s. 4d. a year, applied towards the expense of the Sunday School.

9. Elizabeth Cumberpatch, by will, proved at London, 19 July 1854. Trust fund, £176 6s. 8d. consols, producing £4 8s. a year which is divided equally among six poor widows.

10. Richard Tollemache, by will, proved at London, 5 October 1865. Trust fund, £1,000 consols, the annual dividends of £25 are divided equally among five poor men and five poor women of the age of sixty years and upwards.

[580] Richardson, Surbiton, 14.   [581] Ibid. 78, 183–5.   [582] V.C.H. Surr. ii, 155–64.

The several sums of stock mentioned above are held by the official trustees.

In 1703 William Hatton, by will, directed that out of the rents of certain premises in Mark Lane, six rugs to the value of 15*s.* each should be provided for distribution among six poor housekeepers of either Thames Ditton, East Molesey, West Molesey, or Kingston.

In 1726 William Nicholl, by will, bequeathed £200, to be laid out in land, the rents thereof to be applied in the distribution of coal. The legacy with accumulations was laid out in the purchase of 12 a. or thereabouts, at Shenley, let at £12 a year; 16 a. in Malden, let at £35 a year; and a sum of £363 3*s.* 8*d.* consols is held by the official trustees in trust for this charity producing £9 1*s.* 4*d.* per annum.

In 1884 john Carn, by will, proved at London, 9 July, gave £1,000 consols, the income to be divided equally among three poor men and three poor widows of the age of sixty years or upwards not in receipt of parochial relief. The endowment is £1,010 4*s.* consols in the name of Bedford Marsh, esq., producing £25 5*s.* per annum.

Charities, founded by will, of Anne Elizabeth Savage proved in P.C.C. 6 January 1884 are :

1. For providing Nurses. Trust fund, £1,298 12*s.* 2*d.* consols, producing yearly £32 9*s.* 4*d.* regulated by scheme of 20 December 1892.
2. The General Charities Endowment £12,303 6*s.*3*d.* consols, annual dividends £307 11*s.* 8*d.*, applicable as follows, namely :—£13 19*s.* 1*d.* for Kingston Clothing Society; £5 11*s.* 7*d.* for inhabitants of poorhouse; £1 13*s.* 8*d.* for repair of husband's tomb; £67 10*s.* 2*d.* to Princess Charlotte Memorial; £63 2*s.* 11*d.* for twelve poor widows; £119 15*s.* 4*d.* for church services; £16 19*s.* 10*d.* for ringers and chimers, and £18 19*s.* 1*d.* for promoting psalmody in church.
3. Public School endowment, consisting of £558 4*s.* 3*d.* consols, producing £14 1*s.* 8*d.* a year, set aside by order of Charity Commissioners 1905. The income of £13 19*s.* is applied for educational purposes.
4. The Sunday School endowment, consisting of £563 11*s.* 9*d.* consols, producing £14 1*s.* 8*d.* a year, set aside by the same order, representing the gift of clothing for the girls of the Kingston Sunday School.

The several sums of stock belonging to these charities are held by the official trustees.

The official trustees also hold a sum of £92 16*s.* 7*d*. consols, producing £2 6*s.* 4*d.* yearly, purchased with £90, the trusts of which are unknown, which was paid to the credit of 'Princess Charlotte Memorial' on 2 June 1872. This fund is administered by the trustees of Mrs. Savage's Charities.

NONCONFORMIST CHARITIES.

In 1743 William Plomer, by will proved at London, 25 May of that year, gave £1,000 for the benefit of the minister of the Protestant Dissenting Meeting of Kingston-upon-Thames. Trust fund, £1,342 4*s.* 6*d.* consols, with the official trustees, producing £33 7*s.* per annum.

The Robert Dearle Charity (will of 1806) consists of a sum of £210 consols, producing £5 5*s.* yearly, and a piece of land at New Malden, unlet for several years. The income is applied for the benefit of the minister of the Baptist chapel in Union Street.

The Society of Friends' Charities in connexion with Kingston-upon-Thames Preparative Meeting and the Esher Preparative Meeting are regulated by a scheme of the Charity Commissioners of 13 September 1910. They comprise the charities of :—

1. Sarah Madgwick, will in 1806. Endowment £54 14*s.* 5*d.* consols.
2. The Old Burial Ground Estate, Declaration of Trust of 1677. The property consists of Nos. 74, 76, 78, 80, 82, and 84, London Road, Kingston-upon-Thames, with sites and appurtenances.
3. The Poor's Trust : Bequest of 1668 and augmentations. Endowment, £3,771 18*s.* 5*d.* consols and £7,248 5*s.* India 3 per cent. stock, with the official trustees, producing an income of £311 14*s.* 8*d.* a year.

The scheme directs that the 'income of the poor's estate shall be applied in the relief of poor members of the meetings.'

HAM AND HATCH.

The Almshouse and Pension Charities are regulated by scheme of the Charity Commissioners dated 9 june 1899, comprising :—

1. The Bread Charity, consisting of £289 15*s.* 5*d.* consols, with the official trustees, representing consideration for the release of parish rights in waste lands of the manor of Ham.
2. The almshouses of Thomas Hore and Mrs. Margaret Colyear-Dawkins, comprised in an indenture dated 28 February 1846.
3. The Kingston Road Gate House.

The almshouses consist of four houses in Ham Street and the Kingston Road Gate House ; and the income is applied in the upkeep of the almshouses and in the supply of coals to the inmates.

The income derived from the following properties is applied in aid of the poor's rate.

1. Common and waste lands, comprised in an indenture dated 14 December 17 Charles I, consisting of a house and 13 acres of land.
2. Poor's Land, comprised in an indenture dated 14 December 1641, consisting of several parcels of land containing 8 a. 1r. 8 p.
3. Poor's Acre, first noticed in indenture 20 January 1642, consisting of an acre of land in Flax Land.
4. Sudbrook Park rent, the origin of which is unknown, consisting of a rent-charge of £1 out of lands in Sudbrook Park.

HAMLET OF HAM.

In 1865 Richard Tollemache, by will proved at London 5 October, gave £200 consols to the minister and churchwardens, to be applied in aid of the parochial schools.

The same donor also gave £100 consols in aid of the school of St. john's, Robin Hood Gate, in Ham.

In 1892 the Hon. Algernon Gray Tollemache, by will and codicil, proved at London 12 February, gave £500 to the poor. This sum was augmented by gifts of £100 each from his widow the Hon. Frances Louisa Tollemache and the Earl of Dysart. The fund was in £704 9s. 9d. consols in the names of the Rt. Hon. Baron Sudeley and others, the trustees appointed under the will, who by indenture, dated 2 March 1894, directed that the income should be applied in or towards the support of a sick nurse.

The Hon. Frances Louisa Tollemache also founded six almshouses in memory of her late husband, by deed, 16 November 1892, for the accommodation of nine inmates, and endowed the same with £16,000, which is now invested in certain British and Colonial securities, producing an annual income of £490. Each of the single inmates receives 7s. 6d. a week, and each married couple (of whom there may be three) 13s. 6d. a week. The surplus income is applied in out pensions and in subscriptions to various local institutions. A scholarship of £10 a year is also granted to a boy or girl at the Ham National Schools.

HAMLET OF HOOK.

In 1859 Anne Greene, by a codicil to her will proved at London 8 September, directed that the interest on a sum of £200 should be applied in a dinner to the poor on Christmas Day, or in gifts of 5s. each at Christmas to poor widows, or in apprenticing poor boys and girls, as the incumbent and churchwardens should think fit. Owing to a deficiency of assets a sum of £101 17s. 2d. consols only was received in satisfaction of the legacy. The dividends, amounting to £2 11s. per annum, are distributed in sums of 5s. to ten poor widows.

In 1888 William Mercer, by deed, dated 25 April 1888, settled a sum of £81 13s. 10d. consols upon trust that the income should be applied in the repair and maintenance of the church of St. Paul, Hook, and for the services thereof.

The sums of stock are held by the official trustees.

LONG DITTON

Ditune (xi cent.).

Long Ditton is a village one and a half miles south-west of Kingston. It was at the time of the Domesday Survey in Kingston Hundred. There was a church there then, and it may have been already parochially distinct from Kingston. In the grant of Kingston and Long Ditton churches to Merton Priory, soon after the foundation in 1117,[1] Long Ditton was not included among the chapelries of Kingston which are enumerated. The parish is divided into two parts, Long Ditton proper and Talworth (q.v.), with a strip of Kingston parish, the hamlet of Hook, intervening. The western portion, which contains the village of Long Ditton, abuts on

LONG DITTON RECTORY FROM THE SOUTH-WEST

[1] Dugdale, Mon. Angl. vi, 425 ; Plac. Coram Rege, 7 Edw. I.

the Thames to the north. It is rather over 2 miles from north to south, less than a mile broad, and contains 896 acres of land. The parish is traversed by the road from Kingston to Guildford, and the main line of the London and South Western Railway runs through it. The soil is chiefly London clay, but to the north is Thames alluvial gravel and sand, and it contains two patches of Bagshot Sand in the southern part. Long Ditton gives one of the few examples in Surrey of an ancient church and village standing on the London Clay.

The parish is now agricultural and residential. A large number of small country houses and villas have been built in the parish during the last thirty years.

The only house of archaeological interest is the rectory, of which the greater part is half-timber, probably of the 16th century. The interior was re-arranged and refitted in the 18th century, and modern wings have been added. The original plan appears to have been of an L-shape, the main portion lying east and west, and the wing containing the kitchen, &c., being at the east end and projecting to the south. The main building had two rooms apparently, with large fireplaces as now; but an 18th-century stair has been inserted in the one, and the other has an 18th-century passage on its south side from the present stair hall to a doorway or to a wing now displaced by the modern drawing-room wing at the west end. The kitchen and another room filled the east wing, but the rooms there are now all more or less re-arranged, and a modern dining-room wing projects to the north at the same end. The south front of the main house has plain vertical uprights and curved brackets brought out in support of the overhanging first floor, which projects 2 ft. beyond the lower part. The window frames generally are of 18th-century insertion. The western third of this front has been modernized, a main post having been inserted before an 18th-century passage window, now blocked. The porch in the angle of the two wings appears to be as old as the rest, but has an 18th-century doorway; the front over the porch also projects 2 ft. beyond the ground story. The front of the east wing is of one plane throughout; the two ground-floor windows are ancient retaining their iron frames and old fasteners, but the upper windows have sash frames like the others. The back of the house (north front) is also all in one plane, and some of the old heavy posts reach from the floor to the eaves. There is an 18th-century moulded cornice of wood. The roofs are tiled. In one of the south windows of the first floor is some old stained and heraldic glass of several dates. There are also a man in the dress of the time of Charles I and four large diamond quarries with square flowers. In the garden to the north is a summer-house constructed of some Elizabethan or early 17th-century woodwork. On the south side stands an ancient yew tree probably as old as the house.

The Manor House, Ditton Hill, is the residence of Baron O. E. von Ernsthausen; Woodstock, Ditton Hill, of Mr. C. L. L. Smith.

A few industries are carried on in Long Ditton. Messrs. Barr & Sons' nurseries are partly included in

it; some barge building is carried on upon the Thames, and the Lambeth Water Works reservoirs are also partly in the parish.

A Primitive Methodist chapel was built in 1875, and in 1889 a mission hall for revival services. A workmen's club was established in 1883. The schools, National, were founded in 1840. The present schools were built in 1874.

Talworth is the eastern portion of Long Ditton parish, separated from the rest by Hook in Kingston. It is on the London Clay, and has an area of 1,193 acres. On the eastern borders is the Hogsmill Stream, which early in the 19th-century here worked the Gunpowder Mills, commonly called Malden Mills, of Mr. Taylor. The original powder mills of the Evelyns may have been on the same site.[2] According to Manning and Bray[3] Talworth always elected separate parochial officers. It is now ecclesiastically in Surbiton, to which it was annexed in 1876; it was made a civil parish in 1895,[4] but is included in the Surbiton Urban District. Since the sale of the Earl of Egmont's property it has been covered with small houses.

There was an inclosure act for Talworth in 1818, the award being made on 2 February 1820.[5] The manors had originally been all open fields.[6]

St. Matthew's National Schools were opened in 1880.

MANORS The manor of *LONG DITTON*, which under King Edward the Confessor was held by Almar, in 1086 formed part of the possessions of Richard de Tonbridge, of whom it was held by Picot. The extent then included a mill, and a rent of 500 herrings payable from a house in Southwark.[7]

The overlordship passed through Eleanor, sister and co-heir of Gilbert de Clare, who died in 1314,[8] to the Despensers.[9] Isabel, daughter of Thomas le Despenser, married Richard Beauchamp, Earl of Warwick,[10] and was the mother of Anne, wife of Sir Richard Nevill, the Kingmaker. In 1474 the estates

CLARE. *Or three cheverons gules.*

DESPENSER. *Argent quartered with gules fretty or a bend sable over all.*

BEAUCHAMP. *Gules a fesse between six crosslets or.*

NEVILL. *Gules a saltire argent and a label gobony argent and azure.*

2 *V.C.H. Surr.* ii, 312, 327.
3 *Hist. of Surr.* iii, 15.
4 Local Govt. Bd. Order 32638.
5 *Blue Bk. Incl. Awards.*

6 Chan. Inq. Misc. file 103, no. 18.
7 *V.C.H. Surr.* i, 317.
8 See Chan. Inq. p.m. 8 Edw. II, no. 68 (m. 65).

9 Ibid. 23 Edw. III, pt. ii (1st nos.), no. 169; 49 Edw. III, pt. ii (1st nos.), no. 46.
10 See Chan. Inq. p.m. 18 Hen. VI, no. 3.

of Anne, the latter's widow, were settled on her daughters Isabel, the wife of George Duke of Clarence, and Anne, the wife of Richard Duke of Gloucester, afterwards Richard III.[11] Both their husbands were attainted, and they both died before the Dowager Countess Anne. Another Act of Parliament early in the reign of Henry VII restored the estates to the countess, who immediately conveyed them to the king,[12] who thus became overlord of Long Ditton.

At the beginning of the 13th century the manor was held under the de Clares by Geoffrey de Mandeville, Earl of Essex,[13] and seems to have been granted by his brother and heir William de Mandeville to the priory of St. Mary Spital without Bishopsgate.[14] In 1314 the manor was returned as held by the Prior of Bishopsgate for the fourth part of a knight's fee.[15]

St. Mary Spital. *Party argent and sable a mill-rind cross counter-coloured with a martlet gules in the quarter.*

The farm of Long Ditton in 1535 was valued at £5, other lands and tenements at £5 1s. 8d., and the perquisites of court, &c., at 2s.[16] After the Dissolution woods belonging to the manor were sold by the king to Sir Thomas Heneage,[17] and in 1552 Edward VI granted the manor in exchange for lands in Richmond[18] to David Vincent, a groom of the Privy Chamber, who died in 1565 leaving the property to his son Thomas,[19] who sold it almost immediately to George Evelyn, the great maker of gunpowder,[20] whose mother was daughter of another David Vincent. At his death in 1603[21] he left a son Thomas, who, dying in October 1617, left also a son Thomas,[22] who had been knighted in the July of that year.[23] Concerning the conduct of Sir Thomas Evelyn and his family towards himself, Richard Hinde, minister of Long Ditton, made complaint to Archbishop Laud. He complained that he had suffered much indignity from Sir Thomas and his lady, which he had borne in silence, until Dame Ann Evelyn, immediately after divine service, while yet in the church, before all the people thus addressed him : 'You are a base man, and a base unworthy priest ; you have abused me basely, and your base carriage and usage of me shall

Evelyn of Wotton, baronet. *Azure a griffon passant and a chief or.*

not any longer be endured,' and yet more vilifying speeches. Sir Thomas complained that the minister had abused his lady. The archbishop appointed a time for a private hearing of these disagreements.[24] In 1657 Sir Thomas was again in trouble with the parson. According to the petition of Richard Byfield, officiating as minister in Long Ditton, money that had been collected in 1641 and 1642 for the rebuilding of the church had remained in Sir Thomas Evelyn's hands, while meantime the church fell down.[25] Another complaint was that Sir Thomas entertained a prelatical household chaplain who used the words of the book of Common Prayer, and gathered a concourse of people of like views and invaded the parson's right, with regard to which Sir Thomas was warned to remove his chaplain.[26] He died in 1659. His son Sir Edward Evelyn, knighted in 1676 and created a baronet in 1682–3, held this manor,[27] which, when he died without leaving male issue in 1692, descended to his daughter and co-heiress Penelope and her husband, Sir Joseph Alston, third baronet, the manor having been settled on the occasion of Penelope's marriage on himself (Sir Edward Evelyn) for life, with remainder to Penelope and her husband.[28] joseph, their eldest son, succeeded to the manor,[29] and he dying without issue, it passed to his brother, Sir Evelyn Alston, bart., who in 1720–1 sold it to Sir Peter King of Ockham, co. Surrey,[30] who was made Lord High Chancellor in 1725, and was created Lord King, Baron of Ockham, in the same year.[31] His successor and heir male, William King, was, in 1838,

King, Earl of Lovelace. *Sable three spearheads argent with drops of blood and a chief or with three battle-axes azure therein.*

created Viscount Ockham and Earl of Lovelace. Lionel Fortescue King, third Earl of Lovelace, is the present lord of the manor.

Another manor of DITTON is entered in Domesday as held by Wadard of Odo, Bishop of Bayeux, Wadard being the successor of Leuegar, who had held under King Harold.[32] The Arsics succeeded here as elsewhere to the lands of Wadard, and this manor appears at the beginning of the 13th century as a knight's fee in Ditton belonging to the barony of Arsie, which was one of the baronies charged with castle ward to Dover.[33] The overlordship descended with the barony of Arsie, which appears to have escheated to the Crown after the succession of female heirs to the lands of Robert de Arsie, who died in

[11] *Parl. R.* vi, 100 ; *Pat.* 14 Edw. IV, pt. i, m. 7.

[12] Feet of F. Div. Co. Hil. 3 Hen. VII.

[13] Manning and Bray, *Hist. of Surr.* iii, 12. The reference for the Close R. which they quote does not seem to be correct.

[14] Assize R. 876, m. 1.

[15] Chan. Inq. p.m. 8 Edw. II, no. 68 (m. 65).

[16] *Valor Eccl.* (Rec. Com.), i, 400.

[17] Chan. Proc. (Ser. 2), bdle. 83, no. 12.

[18] *Acts. of P.* C. 1552–4, p. 57 ; Pat. 6 Edw. VI, pt. iv, m. 45.

[19] Chan. Inq. p.m. (Ser. 2), cxlii, 131.

[20] Pat. 9 Eliz. pt. ix, m. 7 ; Recov. R. East. 1567, rot. 1003.

[21] Inq. p.m. (Ser. 2), ccxc, 124.

[22] Ibid. ccclxxii, 161.

[23] Shaw, *Knights of Engl.* ii, 164.

[24] *Cal. S.P. Dom.* 1637, pp. 342, 354.

[25] Ibid. 1657–8, p. 139. They were reconciled through Cromwell's intervention. *Dict. Nat. Biog.*

[26] *Cal. S.P. Dom.* 1657–8, p. 159.

[27] Recov. R. East. 1 Jas. II, rot. 8, &c.

[28] Manning and Bray, *Hist. of Surr.* iii, 15. *See* Feet of F. Surr. Hil. 1 Anne ; Trin. 9 Anne.

[29] Manning and Bray, loc. cit ; Recov. R. Hil. 3 Geo. I, rot. 118.

[30] Com. Pleas D. Enr. Hil. 7 Geo. I, m. 4 ; Feet of F. Surr. Hil. 7 Geo. I ; Com. Pleas D. Enr. Trin. 8 Geo. I, m.

[31] Feet of F. Surr. Trin. 8 Geo. I. In these last two conveyances Sophia Glynne, another of Evelyn's co-heiresses, with her husband Sir Stephen Glynne, bart., and Edward Hill, representing Anne the third co-heiress, joined with Sir Edward Alston. In his will Sir Edward Evelyn had left his estates between his daughters. (Will at Somerset House proved 1692.)

[32] G.E.C. *Peerage.*

[33] This manor is identified in *V.C.H. Surr.* i, 305a, as Thames Ditton, but from the subsequent descent of Long Ditton it seems more probable that the latter was the Domesday manor.

[34] *Red Bk. of Exch.* (Rolls Ser.), ii, 617, 709, 720.

1244–5. In the 16th and 17th centuries the manor was said to be held of the Crown as of the castle of Dover or as of the barony of Arsie.[34]

In 1257 this fee was in the tenure of john de Guglesham, who conveyed it under the name of a carucate of land, with a mill in Kingston and Ditton, to William de Brademere.[35] From an inquisition taken in 1290, it appears that William de Brademere held it of Robert le Tut, husband of Alice daughter of Robert Arsie, by a rent of 25s.[36] Robert le Tut held of the king in chief for rent of 10s. to Dover Castle every twenty-four weeks, which payment he ceased to render after his wife's death, so that William de Brademere, Richard his son, and William Richard's son, were distrained for the money.[37] Alice wife of Richard de Brademere, who died in 1288, and Bartholomew de Morle, her second husband, claimed the custody of the land in Long Ditton during the minority of William son of Richard.[38] William de Brademere was apparently still holding in 1310.[39] Nothing more appears concerning the manor until 1398, when Walter Pembroke and Margery his wife quitclaimed Long Ditton to john Gravesende and Isabel his wife,[40] and about 1418 Henry Haweles and Margaret his wife were holding it with successive remainder to john Haweles son of Henry, and Elizabeth, daughter of Margaret, and her issue.[41] Elizabeth wife of William Stowe, who in 1505 quitclaimed the manor of Long Ditton to Robert Fenrother, may have been a descendant of Henry and Margaret Haweles, as the manor was warranted against her and her heirs. It was also warranted against john, Abbot of St. Peter's Westminster.[42] In 1560 the manor was in the possession of Thomas Rede,[43] and he conveyed it in 1566 to William Notte,[44] who proved before the Exchequer Court that there were two manors called Long Ditton, one held, at the time, by David Vincent, the other by himself. The manor that he held had, he said, been owned by Thomas Rede, who held it of the queen as of Dover Castle by rent of 21s. 8¾d.,[45] and had been granted to himself by Rede. He maintained that there was no reason why it should be taken into the hands of the Crown for alienation by fine without licence, as it was not held of the queen in chief. William Notte died in 1576, leaving an heir, his son Anthony,[46] who died in 1586 holding this manor.[47] He also held a wharf named Jeffereyes Wharf (which had formerly belonged to the hospital of St. Mary without Bishopsgate) and other land in Long Ditton.[48] He left a son Thomas. In 1621–2 Thomas Notte sold the manor to Anne Goulde or Gold, widow.[49] She, in 1623, mortgaged it to Mark Snelling of Kingston,[50] but died in seisin of it

in 1629.[51] Her heir was her daughter Anne, wife of Sir Thomas Evelyn,[52] by whom both the manors of Long Ditton became vested in the same family.

There is one reference to a third manor of Long Ditton. In 1386 Sir Miles de Windsor died possessed of this manor, which was held of him by Geoffrey de Metham,[53] but there seems to be no further trace of it.

The overlordship of the manor of *TALWORTH*, or *TALWORTH COURT*, was from 1086, when Talworth formed part of the possessions of Richard de Tonbridge, vested in the family of Clare, passing thence to the Despensers, Beauchamps, and Nevills.[54] (See manor of Long Ditton.)

In 1086 Picot held under Richard de Tonbridge the land that had formerly been held by Alwin in Talworth, while Ralph held that land in Talworth which Edmer had formerly held.[55] The first of these holdings was probably Talworth Court. Early in the 13th century, William Picot appears as witness to a charter of Peter de Talworth, by whom 12 acres in this place were granted to the hospital of St. Thomas of Southwark,[56] and the Picots were still holding land there in 1291, when Henry Picot (Pycoch) granted 8 acres in Talworth to the Prior of the Hospital of St. John of Jerusalem.[57] But the manor of Talworth was probably held by the above-mentioned Peter de Talworth (who granted the advowson to Merton), and later by a family named Planaz. Among the fees of the *Testa de Nevill* was half a fee in Ditton and Talworth, held of the honour of Clare by john de Planaz,[58] and in 1255 Ralph de Planaz, brother of john, demanded suit at his court of Talworth and foreign service from the Prior of Merton, who held of him the eighth part of a knight's fee there.[59] In 1314 Herbert de Borhunte held the manor of Talworth of Gilbert de Clare, by service of the third part of a knight's fee, this property being the hereditament of his wife,[60] who may be that Joan widow of Henry de Saye who in 1316 held the vill of Talworth.[61] She possibly afterwards married Thomas Corbett, who with joan his wife in 1320 granted the manor of Talworth to Hugh le Despenser, junior (the overlord in right of his wife),[62] who had also acquired the manor of Turberville, henceforth reckoned a member of Talworth. Turberville, which was held of the manor of Sheen, was about 1312 in the tenure of john de Berewyk, whose heir at his death was Roger son of John de Husee, aged five years.[63] Directly after the death of John de Berewyk, Hubert de Swynesford his 'groom' entered into the manor, and afterwards granted it to Walter de Waldeshelf. Hugh le Despenser, junior, coveting the manor, then contrived to obtain a grant of it from Waldeshelf.[64] From this

[34] Memo. R. (L.T.R.) Trin. 8 Eliz. rot. 61 ; Chan. Inq. p.m. (Ser. 2), clxxix, 93 ; ccxii, 16 ; dxxi, 105.
[35] Feet of F. Surr. 42 Hen. III, no. 18.
[36] Chan. Inq. p.m. 18 Edw. I, file 56, no. 20.
[37] Ibid.
[38] *Abbrev. Rot. Orig.* (Rec. Com.), i, 67.
[39] Inq. a.q.d. file 78, no. 25 (3 Edw. II).
[40] Feet of F. Surr. Hil. 22 Ric. II.
[41] Ibid. Trin. 6 Hen. V, no. 28.
[42] Ibid. Mich. 21 Hen. VII, no. 31.
[43] Ibid. Hil. 2 Eliz.
[44] Ibid. Hil. 8 Eliz.
[45] Memo. R. (L.T.R.) Trin. 8 Eliz. rot. 61.
[46] Chan. Inq. p.m. (Ser. 2), clxxix, 93.

[47] Ibid. ccxii, 16.
[48] Ibid. cclxiii, 78 ; ccli, 153.
[49] Feet of F. Surr. Trin. 19 Jas. I ; Hil. 19 Jas. I ; Close, 19 Jas. I, pt. xxi, no. 25. According to Manning and Bray she was daughter and heir of Hugh Gold by Anne heir of Thomas Notte. Sir Edward Evelyn's settlement on his daughter confirms that she was his own grandmother, and calls the manor her inheritance, and later the inheritance of Thomas Notte.
[50] Com. Pleas D. Enr. Trin. 21 Jas. I, m. 5.
[51] Chan. Inq. p.m. (Ser. 2), dxxi, 105.
[52] Ibid.
[53] Ibid. 10 Ric. II, no. 46.
[54] *Testa de Nevill* (Rec. Com.), 221 ;

Chan. Inq. p.m. 8 Edw. II, no. 68 (m. 65) ; 23 Edw. III, pt. ii (1st nos.), no. 169 ; 35 Edw. III, pt. i, no. 104 ; ibid. 49 Edw. III, pt. ii (1st nos.), no. 46 ; 18 Hen. VI, no. 3, m. 44 ; Exch. Inq. p.m., file 1059, no. 9.
[55] *V.C.H. Surr.* i, 317.
[56] Add. Chart. 23666.
[57] Inq. a.q.d. file 15, no. 25.
[58] *Testa de Nevill* (Rec. Com.), 221.
[59] Assize R. Surr. Trin. 39 Hen. III, rot. 12d.
[60] Inq. p.m. 8 Edw. II, no. 68 (m. 65).
[61] *Feud. Aids*, v, 110.
[62] Feet of F. Surr. 14 Edw. II, no. 13.
[63] Chan. Inq. p.m. 6 Edw. II, no. 43.
[64] *Parl. R.* ii, 48b.

date Turberville was annexed to the manor of Talworth, which had also another member called Wyke. After the death and forfeiture of Hugh le Despenser an extent of the manor of Talworth with its members Wyke and Turberville was taken in 1327,[63] whereby it appears that at Talworth there was a moated mansion-house with a gateway and drawbridge, which contained two halls (aule), six chambers, kitchen and scullery, bake-house and brew-house and a chapel. Beyond the moat were the lands pertaining, and two granges, two ox-houses with stable and pig-sty, a garden and a water-mill. Suit was rendered to this manor by tenants holding thirty-two and a half knights' fees, and the quarter of a fee.[64] At Wyke there was a messuage, various lands and tenants. To the messuage at Turberville a chapel was attached. The mill which was known as 'Brayest Mulne' was held of the lord of Long Ditton. In the same year Talworth was granted to Edmund Earl of Kent,[65] who in 1330 was sentenced to death on a charge of being engaged in a plot to assist his brother the king, Edward II, who was said to have escaped from Berkeley, but in reality because he opposed the rule of Mortimer and the queen-mother. He died seised of the manor of Talworth with its members Wyke and Turberville, held of the honour of Gloucester by service of the fourth part of a knight's fee.[66] In 1330 Roger Husee petitioned the king for the manor of Turberville, as the heir of John de Berewyk,[67] but this petition had apparently no effect. In 1330 Bartholomew de Burghersh was granted Talworth for life ;[68] but this grant must have been revoked when the young Earl of Kent was restored in his blood and honours in the year following the overthrow of Mortimer. The king then granted to Margaret wife of the late Earl of Kent the custody of the manor, to hold for John the younger son of Edmund,[69] although Edmund the elder son did not die until 1333. William de Arderne in 1332 sued the countess,[70] apparently without success, for the manor of Wyke, which was still held by her as a member of Talworth in 1347,[71] and John Earl of Kent died in 1352 seised of the manor and its members.[72] His sister Joan, the Fair Maid of Kent, was his heir. This Joan and her husband, Thomas de Holand, granted the manor of Talworth for life to Sir Otho de Holand, his younger brother, who died in 1359,[73] when the manor reverted to Sir Thomas de Holand, who died in

Holand. *England in a border argent.*

1360, leaving his son Thomas as heir.[74] The last-named Thomas died in 1397 seised of the manor of Talworth held of Lord le Despenser, and also seised of a toft, two carucates of land and a water-mill in the parish of Kingston, called 'Turbelvyle,' held of the king for 18s. rent at his manor of Sheen.[75] He left a son Thomas through whom once more Talworth became an escheat. This last Thomas de Holand was created Duke of Surrey in 1397, and was in favour with Richard II, but after that king's deposition his title of duke was annulled, and grants were rescinded that had been made to him since the meeting of the preceding Parliament. Joining in a conspiracy against Henry IV he was taken at Cirencester and executed by the inhabitants there in January 1399–1400.[76] He was attainted and his estates were confiscated.[77] Alice, his father's widow, was holding the manor at her death in 1416, and as his brother Edmund, who was apparently allowed to succeed to Thomas's estates, died without issue in 1408, the manor passed eventually to Sir John de Nevill, kt., son of Ralph first Earl of Westmorland, who had married Elizabeth, one of the sisters of this last-named Thomas de Holand.[80] She died in January 1422–3, and Ralph de Nevill the second Earl of Westmorland was her son and heir.[81] He granted the manor for the rent of a rose to his son John, who married Anne daughter of John Holand, Duke of Exeter, and died in March 1450–1 without issue.[82] Anne being left a widow married her late husband's heir, who was his uncle Sir John de Nevill, kt.[83] At her death in 1486 she was holding the manor, her son and heir being Ralph third Earl of Westmorland.[84] He settled the manor on his son Ralph and his son's wife Edith, but Ralph dying before him in 1498, the manor reverted to him and passed at his death to his grandson Ralph then aged four years,[85] subject, however, to the life-interest of Edith, who married Thomas, Lord Darcy.[86] Queen Elizabeth by her letters patent confirmed the manor to Ralph's son Henry fifth Earl of Westmorland in 1559,[87] and he in the same year granted it to Sir Ambrose Cave under the name of Talworth *alias* Talworth Court.[88] Sir Ambrose in 1564 conveyed the manor to George Evelyn.[89] The manor remained with the Evelyn family[90] until the death of Sir Edward Evelyn, bart., in 1692, who left three heirs ; Edward Hill son of his daughter Anne, Mary wife of Sir William Glynne,

Nevill, Earl of Westmorland. *Gules a saltire argent.*

[63] Chan. Inq. p.m. Misc. file 103, no. 18. Herein described as acquired by the king from Thomas Corbett, and by him granted to Le Despenser. The inquisition was taken when Le Despenser was adjudged a traitor and while being was a prisoner.

[64] These may be the tenants of the honours of Gloucester and Clare in Surrey.

[67] Chart. R. 1 Edw. III, m. 43, no. 82.

[68] Inq. p.m. 4 Edw. III (1st nos.), no. 38.

[69] Parl. R. ii, 48b.

[70] Cal. Pat. 1327–30, p. 516.

[71] Abbrev. Rot. Orig. (Rec. Com.), ii, 55 ; De Banco R. 291, m. 225 d.

[72] De Banco R. 291, m. 225 d.

[73] Cal. Close, 1346–9, p. 280.

[74] Chan. Inq. p.m. 26 Edw. III (1st nos.), no. 54. The extent of Talworth gives a capital messuage, moated, an old mill, land and rents ; and at Turberville was a water-mill, a messuage, garden and land held of the king as of the manor of Sheen.

[75] Chan. Inq. p.m. 34 Edw. III, no. 37.

[76] Ibid. 35 Edw. III, pt. i, no. 104.

[76] Inq. p.m. 20 Ric. II, no. 30.

[76] G.E.C. Peerage.

[78] Fine R. 1 Hen. IV, m. 18.

[80] Inq. p.m. 4 Hen. V, no. 51. He had five sisters, Eleanor, Countess of March, Joan, Duchess of York, Margaret, Duchess of Clarence, Eleanor, Countess of Salisbury, and Elizabeth, who were heirs on the death of their brother. Margaret the Duchess of Clarence, held half a fee in Talworth in 1428 (Feud. Aids, v, 122).

[81] Chan. Inq. p.m. 1 Hen. VI, no. 45.

[82] Ibid. 29 Hen. VI, no. 13.

[83] Manning and Bray, Surr. iii. 19.

[84] Exch. Inq. p.m. file 1059, no. 9.

[85] Inq. p.m. (Ser. 2), xiv, 98.

[86] L. and P. Hen. VIII, i, 721 ; Feet of F. Div. Co. Trin. 16 Hen. VII.

[87] Feet 1 Eliz. pt. ix, m. 1.

[88] Feet of F. Surr. Mich. 1 & 2 Eliz.

[89] Pat. 3 Eliz. pt. iv, m. 22 ; Feet of F. Surr. Hil. 6 Eliz.

[90] Vide Long Ditton supra.

bart., and Penelope wife of Sir Joseph Alston.[91] By his will he devised this manor as Talworth or Talworth Court to Dame Mary Glynne. Both Mary and her son William predeceased Sir William Glynne, who devised the manor of Talworth or Talworth Court to his brother Sir Stephen Glynne.[92] He conveyed it in 1724 to Hugh Viscount Falmouth and others, trustees of the will of Sir William Scawen, in trust for Thomas Scawen.[93] From Thomas it descended to James Scawen his son, who in 1777 mortgaged the manor to Robert Waters of Whitehaven,[94] and it was sold by his trustees in 1781 to Nathaniel Polhill, tobacconist, M.P. for Southwark.[95] He died in 1782, and Nathaniel his son and heir died in the following November, leaving an infant son. This son dying just before he would have come of age in April 1802, the estate came to his uncle john Polhill, owner in 1810.[96] Before 1835 the manor was bought by the fourth Earl of Egmont. The land was sold before the death of the seventh earl in 1897, and a number of small houses were built upon it by a building company. Talworth Court was burnt down in April 1911.

The manor of NORTH TALWORTH may be identified with the land which previous to the Conquest had been held by Edmer, and in 1086 was held by Ralph of Richard de Tonbridge. Afterwards it seems to have been held under the Clares by the Dammartins [97] and in 1314 appears among the fees held of Gilbert de Clare by Thomas de Warblington, who held the manors of Tandridge, North Talworth, and Ockley by service of three and a half knights' fees.[98] John de Warblington held the same of Hugh le Despenser in 1349,[99] and the three manors were in 1376 held by Alice the widow of John de Warblington.[100] In 1440 they formed part of the fees of Isabel, Countess of Warwick, daughter of Thomas le Despenser, grandson of Hugh, being described as those which Thomas de Warblington formerly held.[101] There seems to be no further trace of this manor, the overlordship of which was in the same hands as that of Long Ditton, with which perhaps it was united, unless it be the property in Talworth of which john Danaster, baron of the Exchequer, died seised in 1540,[102] which he settled on his daughter Anne, afterwards the wife of Owen Bray of Chobham. Manning and Bray [103] say that Danaster's land was held in 1571 by Margaret Lambard (Lambert), whose heir was Christopher Muschamp. Christopher married a daughter of a Margaret Lambert,[104] who was also apparently his cousin. He died in 1587. His will was dated from his capital messuage of Talworth, and he held lands in Carshalton, Beddington, Sutton, and Wallington 'eidem capitali messuagio spectantes.' His widow Dorothy, who had been

apparently his second wife, had a life interest with reversion to his son Henry.[105]

The priory of Merton held a manor in Talworth, called by Manning and Bray SOUTH TALWORTH, which was also part of the Clare fee.

At an early date Huelmus le Fleming acquired a virgate of land in Talworth from Robert, Prior of Merton, which the prior had before received from Hugh son of Isold.[106] In 1255 the Prior of Merton held the eighth part of a knight's fee in Talworth of Ralph de Planaz, for which he denied that he owed suit of court at the manor of Talworth,[107] and in 1314 among the fees of Gilbert de Clare was a manor of Talworth held by the Prior of Merton by the service of a quarter of a knight's fee, value

100s.[108] In 1349,[109] 1376,[110] and 1440,[111] the inquisitions on the Clares and their descendants mention the same fee.

At its dissolution the priory held rents of assize in Kingston, Ditton, Talworth, Chessington, Hook, and elsewhere amounting to £1 16s. 1¾d.[112] These were annexed to the honour of Hampton Court.[113]

The Knights of St. John in the reign of Henry III held a knight's fee in Talworth of which they had been enfeoffed by Henry Kyrrel. Their prior in that reign was fined for withdrawing his men of Talworth so that they did not render suit at the king's court at Kingston, nor pay tallage when due.[114] In 1294 Henry Pycot granted 8 acres in Talworth to the prior of this order.[115]

CHURCH   The church of ST. MARY is a building of Godalming stone in the style of the 13th century, consisting of a chancel, chamber, vestry, nave, transepts, aisles, and south porch. It was erected in 1878–80 some distance to the north of a former building on a neighbouring site; the foundations of this are still visible, and some portions of its chancel walls still stand. It was of a small Greek-cross plan and built of brick in the place of the ancient building, which dated partly from the 12th century and which had fallen into a bad state of decay. Nothing remains to show the size and appearance of the ancient church, but from the disposition of the churchyard it must have been very small, no larger than the 18th-century building.

Some of the floor slabs and mural monuments have been left in their original places in the 18th-century remains. The earliest is a slab to Thomas Evelyn, 1659, and there are others to Sir Edward Evelyn, bart., 1692,

[91] G.E.C. Baronetage, iv, 131.
[92] Manning and Bray, Hist. of Surr. iii, 19.
[93] Ibid.; Feet of F. Surr. Mich. 11 Geo. I; Recov. R. Mich. 33 Geo. II, rot. 328.
[94] Com. Pleas D. Enr. Hil. 17 Geo. III, m. 18c.
[95] Manning and Bray, Hist. of Surr. iii, 19; Recov. R. East. 1 Will. IV, rot. 36.
[96] Manning and Bray, Surr. iii, 20.
[97] The Dammartins held Ockley, which also belonged to Ralph in 1086, and afterwards to the Warblingtons, and William de Dammartin appears as witness in the grant of land in Talworth to the hospital

of St. Thomas, Southwark, mentioned above. See also Tandridge.
[98] Inq. p.m. 8 Edw. II, no. 68, m. 65.
[99] Inq. p.m. 23 Edw. III, pt. ii (1st nos.), no. 169.
[100] Chan. Inq. p.m. 49 Edw. III, pt. ii (1st nos.), no. 46.
[101] Fees of Edward le Despenser, Inq. p.m. 18 Hen. VI, file 96, no. 3, m. 44.
[102] Chan. Inq. p.m. (Ser. 2), lxxxii, 143. See also manor of Aden in Chobham.
[103] Surr. iii, 19. But see note 105 below.
[104] Visit. of Surr. (Harl. Soc.), 82, 94, 95.
[105] Chan. Inq. p.m. (Ser. 2), ccxiv, 214. John Danaster, however, had no lands

in these other parishes; so that possibly his holding was not the same as Muschamp's.
[106] Cott. MS. Cleop. C vii.
[107] Assize R. 872, m. 12 d.
[108] Chan. Inq. p.m. 8 Edw. II, no. 68.
[109] Chan. Inq. p.m. 23 Edw. III, pt. ii (1st nos.), no. 169.
[110] Ibid. 49 Edw. III, pt. ii (1st nos.), no. 46.
[111] Ibid. 18 Hen. VI, no. 3, m. 44.
[112] Dugdale, Mon. vi, 245.
[113] Mins. Accts. Surr. 33–4 Hen. VIII, no. 169.
[114] Assize R. Surr. 873, m. 7 d.
[115] Cal. of Pat. 1292–1301, p. 101.

Lady Mary Evelyn, 1696, Lady Anne Evelyn, 1669, and to other members of the same family, also to Anthony Balam, February 1691–2, Mary infant daughter of Sir William Glynne, bart., 1692, and other later slabs, besides some modern mural tablets. Several ancient brasses were removed to the new building and are now affixed to the walls. One at the east end of the north aisle has the figures of a man in a long fur gown and his wife, both with their hands in prayer. The inscription below reads :—' Hic jacent Robtus Castelton armig⁹ unⓠ justic' dñi Regis ad pacem in Cõm Surr ac Clïcus pⓣitor' in Sⓔcio eiusdⓔ dñi R apud Westⓜ et Elizabeth ux⁹ eius qui quidem Robtus obiit XXIII die Decⓔbr an° dñi millⓜo Vᵉ XXVII cujus anime propicietur Deus Amen.'

Below are the small figures of their six daughters; but the indent only remains of the sons. There is also a shield with their arms, on a bend three roundels (? buckles).

By the side of this brass is another of a knight and lady of the Elizabethan period, but it has no inscription.

On the south wall of the chancel is a brass inscription which reads :—

' Here lieth Maist' John Haymer M. of Arts and late pson of this chirche of whose goods was dispende an C Mck. among pore people and upon highways nere unto this town and w'in the same on whose soule Jhesu have mercy.'

john Haymer was rector of the church from 1492 to 1535. These are the only antiquities preserved in the church, which is a well-built structure, one of the last designs of the late George Edmund Street, and contains some good stained glass. The pulpit is of stone, the font of green and white marble. Two bells hang in a cote above the chancel arch.

The churchyard is fairly large, having evidently been augmented when the new church was erected ; it contains many graves, and there are some large trees around it, especially the older part at the south end. A new lych-gate stands at the entrance to the north, by the road.

The communion plate consists of a silver cup dated 1659 but without a hall-mark, a stand paten with the hall-mark of 1770, ' The gift of a worthy person to the parish of Long Ditton,' a large silver flagon of 1715, a smaller cup and stand paten of 1894, and a salver of 1856. The first book of the registers is a parchment volume containing baptisms, marriages and burials 1564 to 1655, the second is a large paper book with baptisms 1659 to 1812, marriages 1659 to 1752, and burials 1658 to 1812 ; the third is a paper copy of part of the second book, from 1695 to 1710 ; the fourth has marriages from 1754 to 1793, and the fifth continues them to 1812.

There is also a book of churchwardens' accounts and vestry minutes dating from 1663, but it gives little information as to the repairs or state of the fabric ; there were many repairs carried out in 1675, and mention of three new bell-ropes and mending of the wheels in 1676. In 1680 is an entry giving a list of the communion plate as follows:—' (1) 2 flaggons

of pewter, (2) 1 chalice of silver with a cover to it of silver, (3) 2 pattons of pewter, (4) a faire surplice, (5) a table Cloath of Holland.' The list is continued with later items :—' (6) a large coffin the gift of Mr. Ro. Pocock, rector, (7) a large carpet of green cloath for the Communion table, (8) a faire green velvet cushion for the pulpit, the gift of Mrs. Sarah Pocock, the wife of Mr. Ro. Pocock a.d. 1690, (9) a faire piece of plate to put the Communion bread on in the fashion of a patten or Pattison, being the gift of Mrs. Sarah Pocock, the wife of Mr. Robert Pocock the present rector, April 1696, (10) a Common Prayer Book, the gift of Madame Sophia Glynne wife of Stephen Glynne, esq., given in August 1696, (11) a velvet cushion with a cloath round the pulpit a rich fringe about it of crimson colour lined with fine silk, 1699.' It would be interesting to know whether in the sixth item the word ' coffin ' represents a coffer or chest, or whether it is really a late example of the common coffin used for the burial service of poor persons who were interred simply in their grave clothes.

In 1716 George London, gent., gave a large Common Prayer Book for the Communion Table ; in 1720 John Willis, Virginia merchant and citizen of London, gave a rich green velvet furniture for the pulpit laced with a broad gold lace, and a cushion of the same, for which the parishioners erected a new pulpit.

In 1715 is a note of the anonymous gift of a silver flagon. In 1778 the vestry decided to pull down and rebuild the church, but no information is given as to the progress and cost of the work, except that in 1779 the rector complained that the work was still unfinished and money unobtainable.

ADVOWSON   A church existed at Long Ditton at the time of the Domesday Survey.[116]

The advowson was claimed by the Prior of Merton at the end of the 13th century against the lord of the manor of Long Ditton as having been granted by Peter de Talworth to the Priory of Merton and confirmed by King Henry the elder.[117] The Priors of Merton presented until the Dissolution, but did not appropriate the church.[118] Edward VI granted the advowson of the rectory to David Vincent [119] and the advowson then followed the descent of the manor of Long Ditton. Anne Evelyn, widow, presented in 1662 and 1665.[120] Sir Evelyn Alston sold the advowson to Sir James Clarke in 1700.[121] An Act of Parliament was passed in 1753 for the sale of the advowson after the death of the Rev. Joseph Clarke,[122] and it was then sold, according to Manning and Bray, to Mrs. Pennicott, George Elers, as a trustee for Mrs. Pennicott, presented in 1750,[123] but he with Mary his wife sold the advowson in 1767 to New College, Oxford,[124] to which it still belongs.

CHARITIES   Smith's Charity, which amounts to about £30 a year, is distributed usually in clothing. Bishop Willis's Visitation in 1725 mentions land called Kingswood leased for relief of the poor. This is not the estate upon which Smith's Charity is now charged.

116 *V.C.H. Surr.* i, 317.
117 Assize R. Surr. 876, m. 1 (7 Edw. I).
118 Egerton MSS. 2031–3.
119 Pat. 6 Edw. VI, pt. iv, m. 45.
120 Inst. Bks. (P.R.O.).

121 Feet of F. Surr. Trin. 5 Geo. I. According to Manning and Bray it was sold in 1719 to Dr. Joseph Clarke, the rector. In 1714 Robert Coleman presented ; Inst. Bks. (P.R.O.).

122 Manning and Bray, *Surr.* iii, 20.
123 Inst. Bks. (P.R.O.).
124 Feet of F. Surr. Hil. 7 Geo. III ; Inst. Bks. (P.R.O.).

MALDEN

Meldone (xi cent.), Maldone, Melden, Malden, &c. *passim*.

Malden is a small village nearly 3 miles southeast of Kingston. The Hogsmill Stream divides it from Talworth in Long Ditton. It stands upon the London Clay, being one of the few ancient villages in Surrey which stand on this soil. An outlying part of the parish, separated from the rest of it by Talworth and Chessington and adjacent to Ashtead and Letherhead commons, 3 miles or more away from the main portion, was amalgamated with Chessington in 1884. Ecclesiastically the latter parish has always been a chapelry of Malden.

The London and South Western Railway line to Epsom runs through Malden, and Worcester Park station is in the parish. Worcester Park represents the 120 acres which Henry VIII took from the manor of Merton College in Malden to add to Nonsuch Great Park, but most of the residential neighbourhood now known as Worcester Park is in Cuddington.

The present parish measures rather more than a mile in each direction, and contains 842 acres. It is a rural parish not very thickly inhabited. It must be distinguished from New Malden, a new district in Kingston parish; especially as the parish of Malden is under the New Malden Urban District Council.

The history of Malden is involved with that of Merton College, Oxford. Walter de Merton, chancellor of England and Bishop of Rochester, whose foundation of Merton College, Oxford, afforded the example and pattern of statutes which were followed by all subsequent collegiate foundations in Oxford and Cambridge, is commonly said to have founded a college first at Malden. Walter was called de Merton, probably from education or residence there. His parents, it appears from his will, were buried at Basingstoke. But he was very possibly of the family of the Watevilles who held Malden and much other land under the Clares. His arms, as recorded at Merton College, were differentiated from those of Wateville, and he probably acquired Malden Manor from his own relatives (see account of manor). His charter of 1264[1] implies that the manor was for the benefit of scholars in the schools of Oxford, and that the only 'college' at Malden consisted of a warden and priests who looked after the property. It is only the modern perversion of the word 'college,' to mean a sort of school, which has led to the confusion. The grant of Malden Church by the priory of Merton to Walter for the same end bears out the same explanation. The revenues of the church were for the support—'Scolarium in Scolis

degentium, et ministrorum altaris Christi in ipsa domo (sc. the manor house of Malden) commorantium'. The scholars were in schools (the plural term possibly showing that the reference is not to the foundation at Malden). The 'college' of three or four priests was in the house at Malden. The latter migrated to Oxford after the foundation there was complete. A John de Malden was Provost of Oriel College in 1394–1401.

The national schools were founded in 1869, and enlarged in 1878 and in 1881.

At the time of the Domesday Survey *MANOR MALDEN* formed part of the large fiefs of Chertsey Abbey and of Richard de Tonbridge. It was chiefly included in the land of the latter, whose holding in Malden was four hides with a chapel and a mill. The land of Chertsey was assessed at one hide less a virgate.[2] Chertsey must have lost at an early date her lands in Malden, for there is no further mention of the abbey in connexion with this parish, and the only overlords mentioned in later times are the descendants of Richard de Tonbridge. The overlordship passed through Eleanor sister and co-heiress of Gilbert de Clare to the Despensers, and descended to Isabel, Countess of Warwick.[3] It probably came to the Crown, as Long Ditton (q.v.) came, by the settlement of the Countess of Warwick's estates upon her daughters in 1474, the subsequent attainder of their respective husbands, the Duke of Clarence and Richard III, the restoration of the estates to the widowed Countess of Warwick, and her immediate settlement of them on Henry VII.

In 1086 Robert de Wateville was tenant of Malden under Richard de Tonbridge, and William de Wateville held of Chertsey.[4] In 1225 the Watevilles' holding in Malden was three knights' fees, and at this date Richard de Vabadun impleaded Hamo de Wateville concerning these fees.[5]

Before 1216, however, the Watevilles seem to have subinfeudated a part at least of their holdings to a family with the local name. Eudo de Malden son of William held land here in the reign of Henry II.[6] A Brian son of Ralph and his wife Gunnora, possibly Eudo's daughter, held land in Malden in the early 13th century,[7] and in 1205 they disputed the possession of the advowson with the Prior of Merton (see advowson). Brian was succeeded by his son Eudo de Malden, who held two knights' fees in Malden.[8] In 1249 Eudo's cousin and heir Peter de Cuddington *alias* de Malden with the consent of William de Wateville granted the manor of Malden to Walter de Merton,[9] to whom a further conveyance

[1] Harl. Chart. 53 H. 12 (copy) and at Merton Coll. Oxford.
[2] *V.C.H. Surr.* i, 317.
[3] Chan. Inq. p.m. 8 Edw. II, no. 68 ; Inq. a.q.d. file 286, no. 9 ; Chan. Inq. p.m. 49 Edw. III, pt. ii, no. 46 ; 18 Hen. VI, no. 3.
[4] *V.C.H. Surr.* i, 317.
[5] Maitland, *Bracton's Note Book*, no. 1077.
[6] They evidently retained some land in

Malden, to Judge by a grant from William de Wateville to Ascer de la Dune in 1235. Feet of F. Surr. 19 Hen. III, no. 189.
[7] Cur. Reg. R. 42 (7–8 John), m. 3 d.
[8] Close, 17 John, pt. ii, m. 16.
[9] See Feet of F. Surr. 31 Hen. III, no. 306.
[10] Kilner, *Accts. of Pythagoras School*, 60. To Judge from his arms Walter de

Merton may himself have been descended from the Watevilles, as the Maldens may have been ; Merton, Malden, Cuddington being strictly names from locality, applied to branches of the same family. Farley (q.v.), which Walter de Merton also acquired, was held by Robert de Wateville in 1086, and it appears from the descent there that William de Wateville was heir to Peter de Malden or Cuddington when the latter conveyed it to Walter.

of the manor with the reversion of a third part of two knights' fees which Cecily widow of Eudo Fitz Brian held in dower was made in 1247 by Simon son of Richard,[11] apparently an attorney of Peter de Malden.[12] A grant of free warren in the demesne lands of Malden, Chessington, and Farley was made to Walter de Merton in 1249.[13]

At Malden Walter de Merton, Chancellor of England, founded the house of the Scholars of Merton, which he endowed in 1264 with his manors of Malden, Chessington, and Farley.[14] It seems clear that the scholars did not reside at Malden, for in his charter Walter de Merton states that he founded the house at Malden for the support of twenty scholars residing in the schools at Oxford or elsewhere and of two or three priests residing in the house itself, which seems as though the intention of the founder was that the warden and priests of a religious house at Malden should be 'a college' to manage the revenues of certain estates to be applied for the maintenance of themselves and certain scholars at one of the universities. In 1274, on the founding of Merton College in Oxford, the warden and priests were removed there.[15]

The manor has ever since belonged to Merton College, the Watevilles retaining their overlordship as late as 1287; [16] subsequently Malden was held directly of the successors of the Clares.[17] In the reign of Elizabeth an attempt was made by the Crown to obtain the manors of Malden and Chessington from the college, in order to bestow them on the Earl of Arundel in exchange for Nonsuch. The college was prevailed upon to make a lease, inclusive of the advowson and appropriation, for 5,000 years under a yearly rent of £40. The queen at once passed on the lease to the earl, who made a grant to Joan mother of John Goode. The college, being dissatisfied with these alienations, applied for ejectment against the possessor.[18] A compromise was effected by which the lease was assigned to trustees for the benefit of the then holder for eighty years, after which it was to revert to the college, who were to have the advowson immediately. In 1633 the college obtained a confirmation from Charles I, who reserved the 120 acres which Henry VIII had seized.[19] The eighty years' lease expired in 1707, and the manor was surrendered to the college by Dame Penelope, widow of Sir Thomas Morley, heir of Goode. The demesne lands were afterwards granted to Richard Willis, Dean of Lincoln, later Bishop of Winchester, whose descendants continued to hold the same on lease.[20] The Manor House is now the residence of Mr. E. B. Hansen.

MERTON COLLEGE, OXFORD. Or three chevrons party and counter-coloured azure and gules.

The church of ST. JOHN THE BAPTIST consists of a chancel, nave, south chapel, south aisle, and south-west tower. The nave and chancel were erected in 1875, before which year the present south chapel was the chancel and the aisle the nave. It is recorded that the nave and tower were built in 1610, but it is probable that the chancel, which leans to the north, was erected at least a century earlier.

The modern chancel and nave are built of red brick with stone dressings; a modern archway opens from the chancel to the chapel, and an arcade of two bays separates the nave and south aisle.

The south chapel or old chancel measures 17 ft. 3 in. by 18 ft. 1 in.; it has an east window of three lights with plain pointed heads. In the south wall is a small square piscina with old jambs and mutilated basin and a modern lintel. The south window of the chapel is an old one of two four-centred lights, repaired outside with cement. Across the entrance to the chapel is a modern wood arch. The aisle and former nave is 29 ft. 6 in. by 20 ft. 9 in., and has two south windows each of two lights with four-centred heads. The tower is built of red brick and consists of three stages; the ground stage is 12 ft. square inside, has a modern west doorway; the second has old windows with four-centred arches in square heads; the third has a two-light window in each wall with four-centred arches in a square head; the mullions have been removed. The parapet is plain brick.

All the fittings are modern; the font has a marble bowl on a stone stem. In the south chapel window is a panel of glass dated 1611 containing a shield of the arms of Mynors :—Quarterly (1) Azure an eagle or and a chief argent; (2) Sable a fesse argent; (3) Argent a bend between six martlets gules with a crescent or on the bend; (4) Argent a sun gules. On a mantled helm over is the crest of a man's arm grasping a black lion's paw in the hand. Two wall monuments in the chapel are to Sir Thomas Morley, who died in 1693, and John Goode, 1627. In the tower are gravestones to John Hammett, who died in 1643, and others of later date. There are six modern bells in the tower. The plate consists of a silver cup and cover of 1622, and a set of 1768.

The registers begin in 1676, the first volume containing baptisms from 1677 to 1806, marriages 1676 to 1754, and burials 1678 to 1807. The second has baptisms from 1806 to 1812, and burials 1807 to 1812; the third contains marriages from 1759 to 1812.

ADVOWSON A chapel or church existed in Malden at the time of the Domesday Survey,[21] and was then included in the property of Robert de Watevile. It was granted by Eudo de Malden before 1189 to the priory of Merton.[22] In 1245 the Prior of Merton unsuccessfully sued for a writ ordering Brian Fitz Ralph and Gunnora his wife to restore to him the advowson of the church of Malden.[23] Brian then contested the

11 Feet of F. Surr. Trin. 31 Hen. III, no. 306.
12 See Feet of F. Div. Co. 39 Hen. III, no. 123.
13 *Cal. Chart. R.* 1226-57, p. 345.
14 Harl. Chart. 53 H. 12; Feet of F. Div. Co. 55 Hen. III, no. 482. Licence from Richard de Clare for the assignment of Malden was granted in 1262. Hey-

wood, *Foundation Charters of Merton College, Oxford,* 3.
15 Manning and Bray, *Hist. of Surr.* iii, 4.
16 De Banco R. East. 15 Edw. I, m. 53.
17 Chan. Inq. p.m. 8 Edw. II, no. 68; Inq. a.q.d. file 286, no. 9.
18 Manning and Bray, *Hist. of Surr.* iii, 3; *Cal. S.P. Dom.* 1603-25, p. 593.

19 Pat. 9 Chas. I, pt. v.
20 Manning and Bray, *Hist. of Surr.* iii, 3.
21 *V.C.H. Surr.* i, 317.
22 Cur. Reg. R. 42 (7 & 8 John), m. 3d.; Cott. MS. Cleop. C vii, 61-2.
23 *Rot. de Oblatis et Fin.* (Rec. Com.), 329. See note above and *Abbrev. Plac.* (Rec. Com.), 50.

MALDEN CHURCH FROM THE SOUTH-EAST IN 1809

claim,[34] but seven years later he and Gunnora granted the advowson in frankalmoign to Walter, Prior of Merton,[35] who gave it back to them in exchange for some land in Malden.[36]

The priory, in 1264, at the request of Walter de Merton, released any claim which they had in the advowson to his house of the scholars of Merton.[37] The fine by which Simon Fitz Richard granted the manor of Malden to Walter de Merton had included a grant of the advowson,[38] but as the advowson is not included in Walter de Merton's endowment of his college, and as the right to the advowson had been in dispute earlier, it seems that Walter had preferred to wait for a formal and conclusive settlement with

the priory. The college has ever since held the advowson.[39]

The chapel of Chessington in the same patronage is annexed to this church, though Chessington has a separate parochial existence. In 1291 at the taxation of Pope Nicholas the church of Malden was assessed at 12s.[40] The vicarage was endowed in 1279.[41] At the beginning of the 18th century the tithes of the demesne lands were demised by the college to the vicar, Dr. Bernard, together with a few acres of land near the vicarage house,[42] and this lease was continued to his successors.

CHARITIES   Smith's Charity is distributed as in other Surrey parishes.

PETERSHAM

The modern parish of Petersham is included in the borough of Richmond, and the village, which comprises a large number of good old-fashioned houses, is in fact a pleasant suburb of Richmond. It is between the Thames and the higher part of Richmond Park, which shelters it from the east.

By the 'Richmond, Petersham, and Ham Open Spaces Act, 1902,'[1] Petersham Common and certain meadows and manorial rights in the same were vested in the Richmond Corporation for purposes of public enjoyment. The Lammas lands on the manor were also, by the same Act, taken from the commoners who had enjoyed rights of pasture, and, with Petersham Common, were placed under a Board of Conservators. The river-side, from Petersham to Kingston, has also been put under the Richmond Corporation and the Surrey County Council, in two sections, for enjoyment by the public for ever.

The chief interest of Petersham lies in its old houses, some of which are historically famous.

HAM HOUSE, the seat of the Earls of Dysart, was built by Sir Thomas Vavasour, Knight-Marshal to James I, traditionally for Henry Prince of Wales. The date 1610, the words *Vivat Rex*, and the initials T. V. over the door, probably relate to its completion. Owing possibly to the death of the prince it was conveyed to the Earl of Holderness, from whom it seems to have passed to the Murray family. It is mentioned in the Court Rolls of the manor of Petersham in 1634 as a house lately built on customary land by Sir Thomas Vavasour, and surrendered by Robert Lewis (probably a trustee), who was then holding it, to the use of Katherine Murray

TOLLEMACHE, Earl of Dysart. *Argent a fret sable.*

wife of William Murray.[1] This was by way of a marriage settlement on the marriage of Elizabeth daughter of William and Katherine with Sir Lionel Tollemache. The heir-general of the Ramsay family, Earls of Holderness, afterwards surrendered all claim in the court baron.[2] Ham House then followed the descent of the manor of Petersham (q.v.). After the Earl (later Duke) of Lauderdale had married Elizabeth, Countess of Dysart, meetings of the Cabal ministry are said to have been held in the room still called the Cabal Room.[3] Another name for it is the Queen's room, owing to a tradition that it was fitted up for Catherine of Braganza. In 1688 when William of Orange wished James II to remove from Whitehall he suggested Ham House as his abode; James objected to it as 'a very ill winter house, damp and unfurnished,' and preferred to stay at Rochester, whence he escaped to France.[4]

During the life of the Duchess of Lauderdale the place was considered one of the finest near London. Evelyn wrote of it as 'inferior to few of the best villas of Italy itself; the house furnished like a great prince's; the parterres, flower gardens, orangeries, groves, avenues, courts, statues, perspectives, fountains, aviaries, and all this at the banks of the sweetest river in the world, must needs be admirable.'[5] After the death of the duchess in 1698 the place was neglected. The excuse of James II that it was in 1688 'unfurnished' was scarcely true, for much of the furniture now is of the reign of Charles II, and peculiarly magnificent. But the surroundings of the house were possibly then neglected. When Horace Walpole's niece Charlotte was married to the fifth earl, her uncle wrote, 'I went yesterday to see my niece in her new principality of Ham. It delighted me, and made me peevish. Close to the Thames, in the centre of all rich and verdant beauty, it is so blocked up and barricaded with walls, vast trees, and gates, that you think yourself an hundred

[34] On the grounds that, first, Eudo was not seised; secondly, that he executed the charter making his grant after he had entered the house as a canon; Cur. Reg. R. ut sup.
[35] Feet of F. Surr. 1 John, no. 43, 44.
[36] Ibid. no. 92, 93.
[37] Cott. MS. Cleop. C vii, no. 21, fol. 142 (Cart. fol. cxlii, no. 329), and a copy at Merton College. The words of the release, 'Quidquid iuris habere potuimus

seu nos habere dicebamus,' must refer to Merton's former ownership. In a return of the possessions of Merton, about 1242, the church of Malden does not appear; Cart. fol. cxxv, no. 281.
[38] Feet of F. Surr. 31 Hen. III, no. 306.
[39] Egerton MS. 2031-4; Inst. Bks. P.R.O.
[40] *Pope Nich. Tax.* (Rec. Com.), 206.
[41] Winton Epis. Reg. Orleton, i, fol. 110a; Waynflete, i, fol. 21a.

[42] Manning and Bray, *Hist. of Surr.* iii, 3.
[1] Brayley, *Hist. of Surr.* iii, 117; Ct. R. portf. 205, no. 1.
[2] Ibid.; *Cal. Com. for Compounding,* 2553.
[3] When Aubrey says of Ham House, 'where the court for the king is met' he is referring to the courts leet of Richmond and Ham. *Vide infra.*
[4] *Hist. MSS. Com. Rep.* vii, 227b.
[5] Evelyn, *Diary,* 27 Aug. 1678.

miles off, and an hundred years back. The old furniture is so magnificently ancient, dreary, and decayed, that at every step one's spirits sink, and all my passion for antiquity could not keep them up. Every minute I expected to see ghosts sweeping by, ghosts I would not give sixpence to see, Lauderdales, Tollemaches, Maitlands.' Horace Walpole clearly preferred the sham antiquity of Strawberry Hill to the genuine antique. The situation of the house is low-lying ; the house stands some way back from the river bank, from which it is screened by a row of elms and other trees.

The original building, erected by Sir Thomas Vavasour in 1610, was of an H-shaped plan, the main portion being about 65 ft. long by 21 ft. broad, and each wing about 74 ft. by 17 ft. The house remained practically unchanged until it came into the possession

The bays on the north ends of the two old wings are obviously of a later date, apparently 18th-century work. The building underwent a complete restoration in 1887 ; the arches to the porticoes in the two inner angles on the north side have been completely renewed.

The building is of three stories with basement and attics, and is built of red brick throughout with stone or cement dressings. The oldest portion has narrow bricks laid in English bond (alternate courses of headers and stretchers), and so also has the large stair-hall, which is built with unusually thin walls ; in these parts the dressings and string-courses are of stone. The windows on the ground floor (north face) have moulded jambs, mullions, and transoms, and are of two lights with rectangular lead glazing ; the first-floor windows were like them, but have lost their

HAM HOUSE : NORTH FRONT

of the Countess of Dysart and Duchess of Lauderdale, who enlarged it considerably and re-arranged the rooms. The first addition appears to have been the erection of the projecting stair-hall in the east wing with the insertion of the carved staircase. The windows in this stair-hall, and the whole outward appearance of it (excepting the rusticated stone quoins at the angles), tally with the style of the original building. After this a great increase was made by the filling in of the space between the wings on the south side, and by the erection of smaller wings against the east and west ends with a frontage to the south. The length of the east face of the south-east wing was ruled by the pre-existing stair-hall, but the south-west wing was made larger to include a secondary stair-hall. The date of this work is uncertain, but it was probably finished by 1680.

mullions below the transom ; the second-floor windows are for the most part perfect, like those in the ground story. The main entrance is in the middle of this face ; it is flanked by grey marble pillars on square pedestals relieved with oval bosses in strap-work panels, and with Tuscan capitals enriched with egg-and-dart ornament, supporting an entablature with a frieze of triglyphs and lozenges, and a moulded cornice. The doorway proper has a round arch decorated with rosettes alternating with a nail-head ornament ; in the crown of the arch is a keystone and ogee-shaped bracket. The spandrels are filled in with ornament in low relief inclosing shields, that in the east spandrel has the Tollemache crest of a winged demi-horse, the other has the arms of Tollemache quartering Murray ; the spandrels are surrounded by a band with rose and nail-head ornament. The wood

PETERSHAM: HAM HOUSE, DOOR OF NORTH FRONT

door has a carved and fluted head, below which is the inscription '1610 VIVAT REX.' The porticoes in the angles formed by the north front with the wings have single arches to the north, and two facing inwards, and their back walls are plastered and painted with landscapes. All around the three sides of this front towards the court are oval niches with busts of Roman emperors, &c., and two in the west wing are of Charles I and Charles II. The 18th-century bays in the ends of the wings have plain brick windows with wood sashes, and the bays are not relieved with string-courses like the main house. The walls of the older portion are finished with a moulded cornice with plain modillions running right round the front and either wing until it meets the later work on the east and west. The windows of the projecting stair-hall are similar to those on the north front, while those of the small added wing are like those on the south front. In the old wings are bay windows, which appear to be as old as the wings themselves, but are modernized in the lower part ; the windows in them have plain Portland stone jambs and wooden sashes. The bays stop at the level of the second floor with a balustraded parapet, the second-floor windows overlooking them having round-headed middle lights and square side lights under a pediment ; they are evidently later than the walls in which they are set. The eaves cornice of all the later work is much more elaborate than the other, being enriched by egg-and-dart ornament and rosettes on the soffit.

The west face agrees with the south face in its southern half ; at the north end of the south-west wing is a doorway admitting to the library staircase. The older wing on the north half of this front has a very large chimney-stack, which serves the kitchen fireplace and those over it. The roofs of the house are covered with slates. The main entrance in the middle of the north front opens directly into the north-west corner of the 'Marble Hall,' a fine room 42 ft. by 21 ft. with a black and white marble floor and a slightly raised platform at the east end, which is of wood parquetry. It is lighted by three north windows and has a fireplace of black marble with gilded swags in the lintel, and a white marble shelf on ogee brackets. The walls are panelled in wood painted green and gold, and there are doorways on the south to the dining-room and the passage next to the ' green drawing room,' and on the west to the long passage traversing the west half of the house, while an archway in the east wall gives access to the main staircase. The hall, originally of one story, was opened in the 18th century to the second floor, with a gallery running all round at the old first-floor level. The newels of the staircase are square with carved panels in their sides, and heads carved as wicker baskets filled with fruit and flowers, and the balustrades and wall panels are divided into bays filled with trophies of arms. The stair ascends from the ground to the second floor, the doorways opening on to it having classical busts set in broken pediments over them.

The ground-floor room of the east wing is occupied by the chapel, which is fitted with 18th-century wood panelling and seats, and has an altar table at the north end in the recess formed by the bay ; the lights of the bay are, however, closed by the oak panelling, as are the lower halves of the side windows. The ceiling is plastered and has a wood cornice. The

space west of the marble hall and north of the passage to the west door is now occupied by offices, and the north end of the west wing contains two apartments lined with oak panelling which were formerly the still-room and the housekeeper's room. The dining-room is entered from the south-west corner of the marble hall, the doorway being in the middle of its north wall and fitted with a two-leaved door ; on either side of it in the same wall are recesses matching the doorway ; all with carved architraves. This wall is very thick, consisting of a later wall built against an earlier one. The room is lighted through the south wall by two windows and a middle doorway opening out on to the south terrace ; the fireplace in the east wall is a square opening with moulded blue-veined white marble jambs and lintel. The ceiling is plain and has a moulded cornice with a laurel-leaf frieze. The Red Room is a smaller apartment east of the dining-room, from which it is entered. The fireplace in its north wall is of a red marble. The ceiling is plain with the laurel-leaf cornice. A door in the north wall opens into a small stair-hall, formerly called the Volary Room, between this room and the marble hall. The Green Room is next, east of the Red Room, and occupies the south end of the original east wing. It is lighted by a bay window and has a marble fireplace with an old fireback in its east walls and is lined with white and gold raised panelling over which are hung tapestries representing the Flight of Pyrrhus and other subjects ; the ceiling is plain. To the north of the room is a narrow passage with a stair at its end. The later south-east small wing is divided into two rooms ; the 'card room' is entered from the Green Room ; it has a corner fireplace of marble and is panelled in white and gold ; the ceiling is coved and painted by Verrio. The other room, north of the card room, is the china closet, filled with valuable old china ; this also has a corner fireplace and a painted ceiling. Next to it is a very small staircase to the first floor, approached from the china closet and from the narrow passage next the Green Room which communicates with the marble hall, &c. Lord Dysart's study is west of the dining-room, and to the north of it is a small staircase. Lord Dysart's bedroom (formerly the Duchess of Lauderdale's) lies west of the study and occupies the south end of the old west wing ; it is lighted by a bay window, has a square fireplace of black white-veined marble in its west wall, and on the north side an alcove, the ceiling of which is painted with allegorical figures, flowers, and festoons in an oval panel in which also are the initials E.D.L. The room is lined with brown and gold bolection moulded panelling. Beyond is the Duchess of Lauderdale's dressing-room. The later small west wing contains the valet's room, lavatory, &c. The staircase in the north end of this wing has a moulded oak handrail and turned balusters. A doorway on the first floor opens from this stair-hall into the library (over the valet's room, &c.), which has an ornamental plastered ceiling. It contains many valuable MSS. and books, including no less than fourteen Caxtons. In the same wing to the south is a smaller room through which entrance may be gained into the long gallery which fills the whole of the old west wing and is some 73 ft. 6 in. long with a bay window at each end. The walls are panelled and divided into bays by fluted pilasters with Ionic capitals ; the cornice with the laurel frieze is painted brown and gold ; the ceiling is plain.

A doorway in the middle of the gallery gives access to the north drawing-room, which is lighted by two windows in the north side and has a white marble fireplace in the south wall ; the walls are panelled in white and gold, over which are Mortlake tapestries representing scenes of husbandry, &c. ; the ceiling is panelled, the main ribs being enriched with festoons, &c. Next, east of this, is the round gallery or upper part of the marble hall ; the gallery, which is octagonal in plan, runs all round the hall, being narrow at the sides and wider at the ends ; the ceiling is an enriched one with a large oval centre-piece with fruit and flowers. Also opening out of the north drawing-room is the Miniature Room over

east wing (east of the bedroom) has an earlier stone fireplace with a four-centred Tudor arch with shields in the spandrels and a carved lintel. The room is lined with painted oak panelling with bolection moulds, and has a plain cornice and ceiling. The small room next to it, over the china closet, has similar brown panelling and a red marble fireplace.

The yellow satin room opens into the small stair-case west of it, from which admittance is gained to a small room (with the laurel-frieze cornice), whence is entered the Queen's audience closet. Adjoining it is another small room, richly decorated and with an arched recess at its end containing a tapestry with the arms of the Duke of Lauderdale and having a painted ceiling representing the Rape of Ganymede ; the fireplace of this room is of scagliola work,

HAM HOUSE : SOUTH FRONT

the north-west portico ; this room has a painted ceiling by Verrio.

The room over the other portico is a dressing-room communicating with the 'Feathers' or 'Prince of Wales's' bedroom in the north end of the west wing, so called because it formerly had the Prince of Wales's feathers above the fireplace and over the bed. The dressing-room has a stone fireplace with a carved lintel and a shield in the middle. The bedroom has a large plain dark grey marble fireplace, and is lighted by a bay window. The round gallery and the 'feathers' bedroom can both be entered from the grand stair-hall. South of the stair-hall is the 'Yel-low satin bedroom,' which, as its name implies, is hung with yellow satin brocade ; the fireplace is of yellow-veined grey marble and has a white marble keystone ; the cornice has a deep carved jacobean frieze, original with the first building ; the room is lighted by a bay window. The dressing-room in the later small

forming a foliage design in the lintel and twisted pillars in the jambs and with the initials E.D.L. ; the floor is of inlaid parquetry like the Cabal Room, the window ledge is inlaid marble like the fireplace ; opposite the fireplace is a tapestry similar to that in the recess. The Cabal Room, next west, is a large room hung with Mortlake tapestries of the four seasons ; the floor is of oak parquetry of plain basket pattern for the greater part, but for a space of 9 ft. 6 in. across the east end of a much more elaborate design in which the monogram E.D.L. again occurs ; the dado is of white and gold with egg-and-tongue enrichment. The fireplace is of red marble, and the picture frame over it has gilded festoons about it ; the plaster ceiling is ornamented in high relief, the main ribs and the cornice having a laurel-leaf en-richment. The 'Blue and Silver Room' lies between the Cabal Room and the long gallery, and is lined with blue and silver striped tapestry ; it has a green and

PETERSHAM : HAM HOUSE, CABAL ROOM

PETERSHAM : HAM HOUSE, DRAWING-ROOM

white marble fireplace and an enriched ceiling. The floor is of the basket pattern parquetry. The upper floors of the house are occupied by the bedchambers, &c. The kitchen, servants' rooms, and offices are for the greater part in the basement. An adequate description of the wonderful collection of furniture, china, &c., of which the house is literally full, would far exceed the limits of space here available.

The gardens and terraces are well laid out. In the forecourt inclosed by the north wings are two terrace walks, one above the other, with flights of stone steps leading up to the main doorway. The drive before these terraces is inclosed by walls brought out with a curved sweep from the wings; in these walls are niches containing busts of Roman emperors, &c., like those in the front of the house. In the middle of the courtyard is a recumbent statue of a river deity representing the Thames. The front of the courtyard (towards the river) is closed by an iron railing with large iron gates. On the south side is a long gravel terrace raised some feet above the large grass lawn; on the other side of the lawn are some ancient Scotch fir-trees said to be the first planted in England, and beyond them an entrance with large iron gates of the late 17th century, now never opened. The ilex-oak walk west of the lawn leads through into another inclosed garden and contains a marble statue of the dancing Bacchus. The kitchen gardens lie to the south and west of this court. North of it are the former orangery buildings, now used as a laundry. The kitchen court is on the west side of the building, having various outbuildings about it, and leading from it; farther west past the laundry is the drive from the road through the stables, which were rebuilt at the end of the 18th century with some of the old material.

In a document dated 1266 mention is made of an ancient hamlet called *SUDBROOK*.[6] Later in 1550 there is record of a suit as to the ownership of half a tenement called 'Underhylle' and half a tenement called 'Sudbrooke.' These premises, which were copyhold in the manor of Petersham, included a house and 30 acres of land, meadow, and pasture in Petersham.[7] At a court held in 1637 a customary cottage in Sudbrook, with a parcel of pasture and part of a close, was surrendered by Thomas Cole and John Yeates to the use of John Hewson and William Bell in payment of certain sums to the poor of Petersham, Ham, and West Sheen.[8]

The present house, known as Sudbrook Lodge, with its surrounding park, was the residence of John, Duke of Argyll and Greenwich, who died there in 1743.[9] His mother was Elizabeth, elder daughter of Sir Lionel Tollemache and the Countess of Dysart, and he was born at Ham House. From him it passed to his eldest daughter and co-heir Caroline, created in 1767 Baroness of Greenwich, who married first Francis Scott, Earl of Dalkeith, eldest son and heir apparent of Francis, second Duke of Buccleuch. Lord Dalkeith died in April 1750, before his father, and at his wife's death in 1794 Sudbrook descended to

their son Henry, third Duke of Buccleuch. He sold the property to Sir Robert Horton, who sold it to the Crown. The house is now occupied by the Richmond Golf Club. It was erected early in the 18th century, and consists of two square wings connected by a large central hall, on either side of which was a portico with Corinthian columns and balustraded parapet. The south portico was closed in later with brick walls built between the columns, and now serves as a smoking-room. The hall (now the dining-room) extends the height of two stories; it has a marble fireplace with a bevelled mirror, over which are the Duke of Argyll's arms. The walls are divided into panels by fluted Corinthian pilasters with a rich cornice, over which is a cove with circular lights and panels. The doorheads in the hall are carved with trophies of arms. The doorways in the later hall to the north of the large hall also have carved architraves and heads. There are stairs at both ends of the building with twisted balusters, &c. A double flight of stone steps leads up to both main entrances. A later wing, connected to the main house by a long narrow passage, extends to the northwards, east of it.

Another once-famous mansion in Petersham was that known as *PETERSHAM LODGE*, which was purchased by Charles I of Gregory Cole.[10] In 1660 Charles II granted the office of keeper of the house or lodge and the walk at Petersham, within the Great Park near Richmond, to Ludowick and John Carlisle,[11] who in 1662–3 surrendered their right in the same to Thomas Panton and Bernard Grenville;[12] and in 1671 the same keepership, with an annual pension of £50, was granted for life to Lord St. John and his son Charles Paulet.[13] In 1686 the mansion-house called Petersham Lodge, with all out-houses, brewhouses, and dove-houses belonging, and the green before the house in the north-west corner of the New Park, containing 15 acres and bounded on the east by the thick covert under the mount called King Henry's Mount, was granted by James II to his nephew Viscount Cornbury.[14] This mansion in 1721, being then the property of the Earl of Rochester, was entirely destroyed by fire, the damage being computed at between £40,000 and £50,000, and including the destruction of the library of the famous Earl of Clarendon,[15] grandfather of the Earl of Rochester. It was rebuilt by William, Earl of Harrington,[16] created in 1742 Viscount Petersham, after a design of the Earl of Burlington; and is alluded to in the lines of the poet Thomson:

'The pendent woods that nodding hang o'er Harrington's retreat.'

In 1783 an Act of Parliament was passed to enable George III to grant the inheritance of the capital messuage or mansion-house called Petersham Lodge to Thomas Pitt, first Baron Camelford, who had purchased it from Charles, Earl of Harrington,[17] and by whom it was sold in 1790 to the Duke of Clarence, afterwards. William IV, who occasionally

[6] Manning and Bray, *Hist. of Surr.* i, 439.
[7] Star Chamb. Proc. Hen. VIII, bdle. 22, no. 224, 218.
[8] Manning and Bray, *Hist. of Surr.* i, 440.
[9] *A news letter of 1714* (see *Hist. MSS.*

Com. Rep. iii, 460) says that the Duke of Argyll had lately purchased Ham House of the Earl of Dysart. This is probably a confusion with Sudbrook.
[10] Orig. R. pt. ii, 2 Jas. II, rot. 44; Cl. R. (P.R.O.), portf. 205, no. 1.
[11] *Cal. S.P. Dom.* 1660–1, p. 282.

[12] Ibid. 1663–4, pp. 75, 95.
[13] Ibid. 1671, p. 590.
[14] Pat. 2 Jas. II, pt. viii, no. 16.
[15] Lyons, *Environs of London,* i, 399, Supp. 57.
[16] Ibid.
[17] Private Act, 23 Geo. III, cap. 13.

lived there. He sold it to Lord Huntingtower, heir apparent of the Earl of Dysart, who predeceased his father in 1833. In 1834 it was sold by the executors of Lord Huntingtower to the Commissioners of Woods and Forests, by whom it was entirely destroyed and its grounds incorporated with the park. The site of the house was close to some cedars on the slope of the hill.

The present Petersham Lodge, a handsome Georgian mansion, has no relation to the original house ; it is situated close by the river bank and was purchased in 1902 by Sir Max Waechter to preserve the view from Richmond Hill, and presented to the Richmond Corporation, who leased it at a nominal rent to Queen Mary for a governesses' home.

PETERSHAM HOUSE, next to the church, is a brick structure dating from about 1680, but with later fittings. The entrance, hall was decorated by Verrio, but the painting has been badly restored. The house contains some good marble fireplaces by the Adams, one with marble inlay, and some good white marble reliefs by Flaxman. In the grounds is a curious narrow bridge of brick.

There are several good 18th-century houses in the village, such as Douglas House, once the residence of Lady Caroline Gilt the novelist, who died here in 1857, and Rutland House. Elm Lodge was a favourite summer retreat of Charles Dickens, who there wrote the greater part of *Nicholas Nickleby*.

At Bute House lived the Earl of Bute, minister of George III. The estate was bought by the late Mrs. Warde of Petersham House as a memorial to her father, in order to preserve the foreground of the view from Richmond Hill. The house has been demolished, the foundations alone being left to show its size and position. There are also several cottages of an early date, as the Farm Lodge with its shaped gables.

The Petersham Institute and Church Room, and the New Church, have been built on the Bute House Estate.

The Petersham Schools (British) were built by Lord John Russell in 1842, when he was living at Pembroke Lodge in Richmond Park.

The first mention of *PETERSHAM MANOR* occurs in the alleged grant from Frithwold *subregulus* of Surrey and Bishop Erkenwald to Chertsey Abbey,[18] which included ten *mansae* at Petersham. This was confirmed by Athelstan in 933,[19] by Edgar in 967,[20] and by Edward the Confessor in 1062.[21] At the time of the Domesday Survey the Abbot of Chertsey held it in demesne for four hides, though in the time of Edward the Confessor it had been assessed for ten hides. There was a church and a fishery of 1,000 eels and 1,000 lampreys.[22] In 1324 the abbot was granted protection in his manor in Petersham.[23] In 1415 the Abbot of Chertsey surrendered this manor to the Crown,

together with the advowson of Ewell,[24] and the lordship of Petersham, annexed to the manor of Sheen (now Richmond), formed part of the manor of Elizabeth Woodville, queen of Edward IV, in 1466.[25] In 1479–80 the manor was held at farm by Robert Radclyff,[26] and in 1483–4 by Henry Dain.[27] In 1518 the custody of the manor, together with Ham and Sheen, was leased by the Crown to Richard Brampton to hold for twenty years at a rental of £23 6s. 4d.,[28] and this grant having been cancelled in 1522, the same manors were in that year leased for thirty years to Massi Villiarde, serjeant of the king's pleasure water, and Thomas Brampton,[29] the grant being subsequently renewed for forty years in the name of Sir Nicholas Carew.[30] In 1541 Henry VIII, on the occasion of his divorce from Anne of Cleves, granted to the latter the manors of Sheen, Petersham, and Ham with the Island of Crowell and Richmond Park to hold for life.[31] In 1546 Anne granted a lease of these estates at farm to David Vincent, steward of the king in his privy chamber, who in the reign of Edward VI made over the remainder of his interest in the same to Gregory Lovell, who was holding them in 1564.[32] In 1607 [33] the same estates were granted at farm to Sir Thomas Gorges, who in 1608 transferred the lease to George Cole.[34] In 1610 the manor was granted by James I to Henry Prince of Wales,[35] and after his death to trustees for Prince Charles,[36] through whom it returned to the Crown. George Cole, the lessee, died at Petersham in 1624,[37] and in 1629 the name of his widow, Frances Cole, appears on the court rolls as lady of the manor.[38] In 1635 the court baron and view of frankpledge were held in the name of Gregory Cole, son of the above, who married jane daughter of William Blighe of Botathan, co. Cornwall,[39] and in this year conceded to his brother Thomas Cole of the parish of St. Dunstan in the West, London, gentleman, all his capital messuage in Petersham with dovecotes and all tenements held by copy of court roll of the manor of Petersham.[40] In the next year, however, the court baron was held in the name of William Murray, who had received a lease from Queen Henrietta Maria, to whom Charles I had granted the manor, and to this court came the above-mentioned Gregory, jane, and Thomas, and having been examined alone and secretly by the steward, surrendered up their tenancy of the above premises in Petersham.[41]

William Murray had been the whipping-boy of Charles I while Prince of Wales, and continued his friend and favourite in his faithful supporter in his later adversities. In 1639, in consideration of the

COLE. *Argent a bull passant sable in a border sable bezanty.*

[18] Birch, *Cart. Sax.* i, 64 ; Kemble, *Cod. Dipl.* 988.
[19] Kemble, *Cod. Dipl.* 363.
[20] Ibid. 802 ; Birch, *Cart. Sax.* iii, 469.
[21] Kemble, *Cod. Dipl.* 812.
[22] *V.C.H. Surr.* i, 308.
[23] *Cal. Pat.* 1324–7, p. 53.
[24] Close, 3 Hen. V, m. 31 d.
[25] *Cal. Pat.* 1461–7, p. 525 ; 1467–77, p. 64.

[26] Mins. Accts. (Gen. Ser.), bdle. 1904, no. 5.
[27] Mins. Accts. Duchy of Lanc. bdle. 41, no. 799.
[28] Pat. 14 Hen. VIII, pt. i, m. 5.
[29] *L. and P. Hen. VIII*, iii (2), p. 1134 ; Pat. 14 Hen. VIII, pt. i, m. 5.
[30] Add. Chart. 22631.
[31] *L. and P. Hen. VIII*, xvi, p. 717.
[32] Memo. R. Mich. 6 Eliz. rot. 96.
[33] Pat. 5 Jas. i, pt. xxvi, m. 20.

[34] Parl. Surv. Surr. no. 31.
[35] Pat. 8 Jas. I, pt. xli, m. 2.
[36] Pat. 14 Jas. I, pt. xx, m. 2.
[37] Mon. Inscr. Petersham Church ; Chan. Inq. p.m. (Ser. 2), ccccvi, 56.
[38] Manning and Bray, *Hist. of Surr.* i, 439.
[39] Chan. Inq. p.m. (Ser. 2), ccccvi, 56.
[40] Ct. R. portf. 205, no. 1.
[41] Ibid.

PETERSHAM : HAM HOUSE, STAIRCASE

RICHMOND : THE TERRACE

losses sustained by the inclosure of the New Park, he petitioned that the lease of the manor of Petersham, which had been made out for twenty-seven years, might be exchanged for a grant in perpetuity of the manor.[42] This request was acceded to, and in 1643 Murray was created Earl of Dysart. In the troubles which followed, however, these estates were sequestered,[43] and in 1651 Sir Lionel Tollemache and Elizabeth his wife—who, with Katherine, Anne, and Margaret Murray, was one of the four daughters and co-heirs of William and Katherine Murray—begged allowance of their title to Ham and Petersham Manors.[44] After the Restoration the same ladies were again pleading for a renewal of the grant of these estates at the same rental of £16 9s. at which they had been held by their father, and they pleaded that none had suffered more in the late times than they, having been twice plundered, sequestered, and forced to purchase their lands at an unreasonable rate.[45] After many renewals of the same petition, 75 acres of land in the manors were granted to them in 1665 at a rent of 4d. per acre,[46] and in 1666 a lease of the demesne lands, consisting of 289 acres 27 perches, was bestowed for a term of sixty-one years upon Sir Robert Murray,[47] one of the founders of the Royal Society, extolled by Burnet as 'the worthiest man of the age,'[48] to hold on behalf of the same persons. Sir Lionel Tollemache died in 1668, and his widow married John, Earl of Lauderdale, who in 1672 obtained a grant of the manors of Petersham and Ham in right of his wife for the same rent of £16 9s., exception being made, however, of the portion granted as above to Sir Lionel Tollemache.[49] The countess was succeeded by her eldest son Lionel, third Earl of Dysart, and from this date Petersham remained with the Earls of Dysart. Lionel, fifth earl, suffered a recovery of all his estates in Ham and Petersham in 1773,[50] and, dying without issue in 1799, was succeeded by his brother Wilbraham Tollemache, sixth earl.[51] On the death of the latter without issue the estate was divided, in accordance with a settlement made by the previous earl, between his sisters, Lady Louisa Manners,[52] Lady Frances Tollemache, and Lady Jane Halliday.[53] The manors have been held since 1878 by William John Manners, ninth earl, descendant of Lady Louisa Manners, who was herself Countess of Dysart.

A charter dated 1464 enumerates certain customs as pertaining to the lordships of West Sheen, Petersham, and Ham. These include the holding of an annual court, fines of a minimum of 2d. being imposed on such as failed to attend. On the death of a tenant the inheritance passed by the custom of the manor to his youngest son, or failing such youngest son to his youngest daughter. The quit-rent of the land at Petersham was 4d. per acre and 6d. the houses, and the fine one year's quit-rent. The charter is attested by five tenants : John Hart, William Ballet, John Howe, John Brewtell, and William Thorne.[54] A survey of the manor taken in 1649 gives a list of customs granted to the tenants

of Petersham in 1481 by Edward IV and confirmed by divers monarchs ; namely, that the lord of the manor might 'sell all wood and waste lands to any man by copy, paying a fine to the lord and a yearly quit-rent to the king.' A court baron for the manor was kept at the will of the lord, and a court leet once a year. The youngest son and youngest daughter inherited as above. There was a little common belonging to the manor called Petersham Common on the west side of Richmond Hill. In a survey taken in 1609 this common is said to contain 200 acres, the tenants having common of pasture there for their cattle, and common of estover.[55]

In the charter granted by James I to Kingston in 1603 it was enacted that the court leet and view of frankpledge should no longer extend into Petersham, and in 1609 the king is said to hold a court leet for Petersham twice yearly, after Easter and Michaelmas.[56] Kingston appears subsequently to have claimed court leet in Petersham, however, for in 1628 the bailiffs and freemen of Kingston were confirmed in their former liberties on condition of relinquishing their court leet in Richmond, Petersham, Ham, and Effingham,[57] and in that year the king appointed Sir Robert Douglas steward of the court leet for the manor of Richmond, at which the tenants of Petersham were to make attendance, the same court to be held twice a year.[58] In the survey taken in 1649 the courts baron and the courts leet were valued at £35 yearly.[59]

CHURCH   The church of ST. PETER is of unusual plan, having a chancel 15 ft. 6 in. by 15 ft., nave 28 ft. 2 in. east to west by 62 ft. north to south, and west tower 7 ft. square, with a porch to the west of it and a vestry to the north.

The church is said to have been built in 1505, but a blocked 13th-century lancet window in the north wall of the chancel shows that part at least is of much older date. Originally, as it seems, a plain rectangle 15 ft. 6 in. by 43 ft., it was enlarged early in the 17th century by the addition of a south transept and a west tower of red brick. In 1790 a north transept was added, more than half as long as the church and of a depth nearly as great as its width ; the west porch was then added and the upper half of the tower rebuilt. In 1840 the former south transept gave way to a very much larger one, the east wall of which lines with that of the north transept, while its west wall overlaps the tower. Galleries were inserted, various alterations being made in the north transept, which was heightened and had some of its windows blocked up, and an inclosed staircase was built against the west wall. The vestry north of the tower probably dates from 1790.

The chancel is plastered and has diagonal eastern buttresses ; the small blocked lancet in the north wall is rebated and chamfered, and the east and the south windows are each of two lights with wood frames. All the nave windows are round-headed except on the north, where they have been blocked by the

42 Cal. S.P. Dom. 1630–9, p. 609.
43 Cal. of Com. for Compounding, 2552.
44 Ibid. 2553.
45 Cal. S.P. Dom. 1661–2, p. 34.
46 Ibid. 1664–5, p. 492 ; 1665–6, pp. 10, 315.
47 Pat. 17 Chas. II, pt. iii, no. 5 ; Cal. S.P. Dom. 1665–6, p. 315.

48 Burnet, Hist. of His Own Time, ii, 20.
49 Pat. 23 Chas. II, pt. x ; Cal. S.P. Dom. 1671–2, pp. 225, 312.
50 Recov. R. Mich. 11 Geo. III, rot. 35.
51 See Recov. R. Hil. 40 Geo. III, rot. 229.
52 See Feet of F. Trin. 51 Geo. III.
53 Will P.C.C. 348 Howe.

54 Petersham Parish Notes (1886).
55 Parl. Surv. Surr. no. 45.
56 Land Rev. Misc. Bks. vol. 197, fol. 99a.
57 Cal. S.P. Dom. 1628–9, pp. 325, 350, 399.
58 Ibid. 329, 350.
59 Parl. Surv. no. 45.

gallery and replaced with smaller segmental-headed lights; there was formerly a north doorway in the middle of the wall. The outer arch of the west porch is round, but the doorways through the tower are square-headed. The ceilings are flat and plastered.

The altar-table and font are modern; and a modern screen spans the entrance to the chancel, within which are two large box-pews. The nave is also filled with box-pews, and there are north, west and south galleries. In the chancel on the north side is a large monument erected by Gregory Cole in 1624 to his father and his son, both named George. It formerly stood in the old south transept, which was probably built to contain it. The elder George married Frances Preston and had eight sons and five daughters, and Gregory married Jane Blighe and had three sons, George, buried in this tomb, Thomas, and Robert. The effigies of George and Frances Cole lie under a round arch flanked by Corinthian columns, and in a small niche in the base is the figure of their grandson. Above are the arms of Cole quartering Argent three bends in a border engrailed gules. In the east spandrel of the arch are the arms of Preston: Argent two bars gules and a quarter gules with a cinquefoil or thereon; and in the west spandrel Preston impaled by Cole. On the frieze are two other shields, one with the quartered coat of Cole and the other: Argent a fesse between two roundels sable in the chief and a martlet in the foot sable, a molet gules for difference impaling Cole, which records the marriage of Henry Lee of London with Elizabeth daughter of George and Frances Cole. On the south wall is a monument to Sir Thomas Jenner, kt., Justice of the Common Pleas, 1706–7; and to Elizabeth, Countess of Dysart and Duchess of Lauderdale, 1697. There is one bell, by Brian Eldridge, 1620.

The communion plate comprises a silver-gilt cup of 1562, and silver cup and cover paten of 1570, two silver-gilt patens of 1663 and 1696, a silver paten of 1760, and a silver flagon 1740.

The registers begin in 1570, the first book (without its first leaf, which only survives as a copy) containing entries from 1574 to 1681, the second continuing to 1716; the third is a copy of the other two made in 1698 and continued to 1786 for baptisms and burials, and 1756 for marriages. In the third book are entries that the church was built on the 'south side of the abbey' (i.e. probably a house belonging to Chertsey) in 1505, and that the 'chapell' was 'new repaired and whitened and glazed in 1668.' The fourth book has marriages from 1756 to 1786, and the fifth marriages 1807 to 1812, the register of marriages between 1786 and 1807 appearing to be lost; the sixth has baptisms from 1786 to 1812, and the seventh burials for the same period.

In the vestry is a photograph of a certificate, dated 30 July 1664, by Henry Bignell, minister, of the marriage of Prince Rupert to Lady Francesca Bard; but the register contains no entry of such marriage. The church stands to the north of the road below Richmond Hill, and is approached by a narrow passage.

On a site in the grounds of the former Bute House is the new church of *ALL SAINTS*, completed in 1909. It is a red brick and terra-cotta building of a Romanesque style, consisting of an apsidal chancel, nave with aisles, octagonal north baptistery, and a tall south-west tower with a pyramidal roof crowned by a figure of Christ. The altar is raised to a considerable height above the floor of the nave, and has a tall reredos and rood, and the baptistery has a tank for total immersion.

ADVOWSON A church existed at Petersham at the time of the Domesday Survey, and in 1266 was appropriated to Merton Priory as a chapelry of Kingston. In this year an assignment was made for the endowment of a chaplain to celebrate divine service three times a week in the said chapel, namely, on Sunday, Wednesday, and Friday, and freely dispense there the sacrament of baptism, the prior and convent allowing him two quarters of white wheat, one quarter of barley, and one of oats, to be paid on the feast of All Saints, and saving the rights of the mother-church of Kingston; whilst the parishioners of Petersham conceded, for the sustentation of the same chaplain, one bushel of wheat for every 10 acres, the whole amounting to 25½ bushels from 255 acres.[60]

In 1553 David Vincent, a groom of the privy chamber (see manor), had a grant of land and tithes, including the site of the chapel of Petersham, with 13 quarters of wheat pertaining thereto.[61] The appointment of the curate was found in 1658 to be in the hands of the vicar of Kingston;[62] but from a note in the parish registers it appears that when the Rev. Henry Walker intimated his appointment by the vicar to the Countess of Dysart in 1667, she claimed it as her right. She was, however, content to approve of Mr. Walker as curate.

The commissioners of 1658 recommended the union of Petersham with Ham and Hatch as a separate parish, but it was not done. Bishop Willis's Visitation Returns, 1725,[63] say that Petersham chapel had been 'partly endowed' by a Mr. Hatton and his family, probably the Mr. William Hatton of East Molesey who left an endowment to Thames Ditton (q.v.) in 1703. A Robert Hatton had also been Recorder of Kingston in 1638.

In 1769 Petersham was separated from Kingston by Act of Parliament and joined to Kew (q.v.),[64] to which it remained attached until 1891, when, in accordance with the Kew and Petersham Vicarage Acts, it was separated therefrom. It is now a vicarage in the gift of the Crown. The rectorial tithe is held by the Earl of Dysart.

CHARITIES Almshouses for six persons were built in 1867 by Madame Tildesley de Bosset, who endowed them by will. George Cole in 1624 gave a small benefaction charged on land in Sudbrook Park for the poor, which was returned in 1894 as not paid since 1859.

Dr. Triplet's benefaction of 1668 for apprenticing children is partly shared by Petersham. The Poor's land or the Poor's Half-acre, a house, and some cottages, the rent of which is applied for general purposes of poor relief, were also given by him at the same date.

Smith's Charity is distributed as in other Surrey parishes. The whole are under one management by a scheme of the Charity Commissioners.[65]

[60] Cott. MSS. Cleop. C. vii.
[61] *Acts of P.C.* 1552–4, p. 288.
[62] Lambeth MS. Certificate, fol. N. 6. (vol. 21).
[63] Farnham MSS.
[64] Stat. 9 Geo. III, cap. 65.
[65] *Ret. to Surr. Co. Council* (1894).

RICHMOND ANCIENTLY SHEEN

Richemount, Rychemonde (xvi cent.). Syenes, Shenes, Scenes, Senes (xiii cent.) ; Shene, Shine, and West Sheen,[1] later.

The parish of Richmond, with its church of St. Mary Magdalene, lies on the right bank of the River Thames, which forms its western boundary, 16 miles above London Bridge. The acreage of the civil parish of Richmond is 1256, of which 557 belong to the Crown and include 67 acres in Richmond Park, 353 in the Old Deer Park, and 137 in Kew Gardens.[1a] The greater part of the parish lies low, being about 50 ft. above the ordnance datum, but the ground rises to 100 ft. on the summit of Richmond Hill, the upward slope being from north to south. The top of the hill, however, where the 'Star and Garter' stands, is in Petersham parish. The top soil is gravel, sand, or clay, on a subsoil of London Clay.

The original hamlet of Richmond, or Sheen as it was called before the reign of Henry VII, lay in a hollow on the north-east side of the royal palace which stood between the river and the green. There is nothing to show when a palace was erected here. In 1292 there was a capital messuage appurtenant to the manor.[2] Edward I was at Sheen on 5 August 1299,[3] and resided there during part of September and October 1305.[4] In the latter year he gave audience at this place to the commissioners sent from Scotland to arrange the Scottish civil government.[5] It is probable that Edward III, who frequently stayed at Sheen,[6] either built or enlarged an already existing manor-house,[7] where he ultimately died. Richard II was there immediately afterwards, if not at the time.[8] The palace was one of his favourite resorts, and his queen, Anne of Bohemia, dated several instruments here. She held the manor of Isleworth on the other side of the Thames.[9] The queen died here in 1394, and Richard's distress was so great that he ordered the royal house to be destroyed.[9a] It remained in partial ruins until it was rebuilt, according to Stow, by Henry V about the same time as he founded the Carthusian monastery near it, soon after his accession.[10] The rebuilding, however, probably more truly belongs to Henry VI,[11] who carried it on in order that the palace might be worthy of the reception of his queen, Margaret of Anjou.[12] Edward IV granted it to his queen for life.[13] Henry VII frequently made it his residence, and in 1492 he held a grand tournament there which is described by

Stow : ' In the moneth of May following, was holden a great and valiant justing within the kinges manor of Shine, nowe called Richmond, in Southerie, the which endured by the space of a moneth, sometime within the saide place, and sometime without, uppon the greene without the gate of the said mannor. In the which space a combate was holden and done betwixt Sir James Parkar, knight, and Hugh Vaughan, gentleman usher, uppon controversie for the armes that Gartar gave to the sayde Hugh Vaughan ; but hee was there allowed by the king to beare them, and Sir James Parkar was slaine at the first course.' [14] In December 1497,[15] while the royal family were staying at Sheen, the palace was almost entirely destroyed by fire, but was rebuilt by Henry with great splendour and completed in 1501. It was at this time that the name of the manor was changed by command of the king from Sheen to Richmond, after his earldom of Richmond in Yorkshire.[16] A second fire broke out in 1507, but the palace was again repaired in the same year.[17] Henry VII was at Richmond when he died.[18] Henry VIII spent the Christmas after his accession at the palace with his queen, Katharine of Aragon. The king and queen resided constantly at Richmond, which was the scene of great festivities during such times. Their son, christened Henry, was born there on New Year's Day, 1511, but died on 22 February.[19] In 1515 peace between England and France was sworn at Richmond.[20] Some years after this the king received a present of Hampton Court (q.v.) from Wolsey, and as a return the cardinal received permission to reside at the royal manor of Richmond,[21] where he kept up so much state as to increase the growing ill-feeling against him.[22] Among other occasions Wolsey retired to Richmond in 1525 on account of the plague which was then raging in London.[23] When he fell into disfavour he took up his residence at the Lodge in the 'great' park, and subsequently moved to the Priory,[24] where, shortly before his death, he is known to have conferred with Thomas Cromwell in the gallery.[25] The palace was used as a residence by Anne of Cleves from 1540 until the accession of Edward VI, who seems to have been much attached to it, although it was not considered to suit his health.[26] Mary occasionally held her court at Richmond,[27] and spent part of her honeymoon here in 1554.[28] In that year her sister Elizabeth was taken to Richmond as a prisoner on her way to Woodstock,[29] but the

[1] West Sheen was a separate hamlet (so marked on Norden's map), which was pulled down in 1769.
[1a] Burt, Richmond Vestry, 13.
[2] Chan. Inq. p.m. 21 Edw. I, no. 50.
[3] Cal. Pat. 1292–1301, pp. 430, 472.
[4] Ibid. 1301–7, pp. 378–82, 384, 403–4.
[5] Folkestone Williams, Domestic Memoirs of the Royal Family, i, 20.
[6] Cal. Pat. 1327–54, passim.
[7] Abbrev. Rot. Orig. (Rec. Com.), ii, 294.
[8] Walsingham, Gesta Abbatum S. Albani (Rolls Ser.) i, 326, 330.
[9] Pat. 17 Ric. II, pt. ii, m. 5 bis ; 18 Ric. II, pt. i, m. 19, &c.
[9a] V.C.H. Surr. i, 363 ; Stow, Chron. (ed. 1), 307.

[10] Mem. of Hen. V (Rolls Ser.), 102.
[11] Pat. 20 Hen. VI, pt. iii, m. 33 ; 23 Hen. VI, pt. ii, m. 5, 25, &c.
[12] See Patent Roll cited above, date of 8 May 1445, for stone, brick, tiles, lead, iron, glass, timber, nails, &c., taken to Sheen for repairs of the king's house.
[13] Pat. 6 Edw. IV, pt. i, m. 4.
[14] Stow, Annales (ed. Howes), 475.
[15] The date is given by other authorities as 1498 or 1499 ; Vetusta Monumenta (Soc. of Antiq.), ii ; Manning and Bray, Surr. i, 410 ; Lysons, Environs of London, i, 438.
[16] Stow, op. cit. 483 ; Folkestone Williams, op. cit. i, 319 ; Cat. Anct. D. A. 8422.

[17] Stow, op. cit. 483.
[18] L. and P. Hen. VIII, iv (3), 5774 (5, v).
[19] Folkestone Williams, op. cit. ii, 1–3; L. and P. Hen. VIII. i, 1491, 1495.
[20] Ibid. ii (1), 307.
[21] Stow, op. cit. 526.
[22] Folkestone Williams, op. cit. ii, 13.
[23] L. and P. Hen. VIII, iv (1), 1525.
[24] Stow, op. cit. 553.
[25] L. and P. Hen. VIII, iv (3), 6530.
[26] See manor ; Folkestone Williams, op. cit. ii, 69.
[27] Acts of P.C. 1552–6, passim.
[28] Stow, op. cit. 625.
[29] Ibid. 624.

memory of this did not diminish the attraction of the place for her. She was constantly here when she became queen, and it was during her reign that Richmond perhaps reached the height of its brilliance and gaiety.[80] The queen at length died at the palace, having contracted a cold and removed to Richmond, which she regarded as the 'warm winter-box to shelter her old age.'[81]

On the accession of the Stuarts Richmond became less frequently the abode of the sovereigns. James I used the palace very little, although the courts of Exchequer, Wards, Liveries and Duchy of Lancaster were temporarily moved to the manor of Richmond in October 1603[82] in consequence of the plague.[83] The palace, however, still continued to have a royal resident in the person of the young Prince Henry, who spent a large sum of money on improvements and passed most of his time here from 1604 until his death in 1612.[84] His brother also lived here as Prince of Wales,[85] and a few months after his accession to the throne as Charles I the Exchequer and the records belonging to it were again moved to Richmond, owing to the plague,[86] which, however, attacked the village itself in the summer of 1625.[87] The king gave the palace with the manor (q.v.) to Queen Henrietta Maria, probably in 1626, and it became the home of the royal children.[88] Richmond was again visited by the plague in 1640,[89] and in 1641 a member of the prince's household died of it, the prince himself having joined the queen at Oatlands.[40] When, in 1647, the Parliament was anxious to take the king out of the hands of the army, they voted that he should be removed to Richmond,[41] but the impeachment of the eleven members by the army caused the idea to be abandoned.[42] After the execution of Charles a very interesting and detailed survey of the palace was taken.[43] It is stated in the course of it that the capital messuage, palace, or court-house consisted of 'one large and fair structure of free stone, of two stories high covered with lead'; and that the higher story contained 'one fayt and large room, 100 feet in length and 40 in breadth, called the great hall.' This, no doubt, was of the height of two stories; for the 'Privy lodgings' were three stories high, and the whole appears to have been of one height, except the towers. In the chapel building the 'third storie conteyns one fayt and large room 96 feet long and 30 feet broad, used for a chapel. This room is very well fitted with all things useful for a chapel; as fair lights, handsome cathedral scates and pewes, a removeable pulpit, and a fayr case of carved work for a payr of organs.' Richmond Green 'conteyns twenty acres, more or less, excellent land, to be depastured only with sheep; is well turfed, level, and a special ornament to the palace. One hundred and thirteen elm trees, forty-eight whereof stand all together on the west side, and include in them a very handsome walk.'

The palace was sold in 1650 to Thomas Rookesby, William Goodrick, and Adam Baynes,[44] on behalf of themselves and other creditors, and subsequently to Sir Gregory Norton, but it was restored with the manor (q.v.) to Queen Henrietta Maria in 1660,[45] although in a dismantled condition, having suffered much dilapidation during the interregnum. A certain Elizabeth wife of Andrew Mollett gave evidence that Henry Carter of Richmond was the first puller-down of the king's house there, sold stones to the value of £1,000, and raised forces within the previous three months to oppose the Restoration.[46] The ruined palace was never rebuilt. The 'capital messuage' was included in the grant of the manor (q.v.) to James, Duke of York, in 1664, but in 1703 the remains of it were broken up into several houses and tenements.

Now but little is left to confirm the fact that there was a palace upon the site built as late as the time of Henry VII and standing in the 17th century. The most conspicuous of the remains are those in the house occupied by Mr. John Lyell Middleton (facing Richmond Green) and the gateway to Wardrobe Court, with its upper chamber forming part of the house. The gateway is of red brick, and has a large four-centred archway of stone over which is a perished stone panel bearing the arms of Henry VII, on the east side towards the green. North of the large archway is a doorway with a Tudor head towards the green and a square-headed doorway towards the court. Over the panel of arms on the east side is an 18th-century oriel window, and on the other side three blocked windows above a stone string-course with a moulded top member and a bead at the bottom. The building is cut short north of the gateway, but evidence of its continuation in that direction is given by the arched recesses on the ground floor and the blocked doorway in the upper story, besides the marks showing the position of the first floor and the flat roof on that face which now overlooks the gardens of the Old Court House, an 18th-century building occupied by Mrs. B. Crowther. Some of the lower walls of Mr. Middleton's house no doubt retain the original brickwork, and the three projecting bays on the east front—a semi-octagonal one between two five-sided bays—are evidently on the old foundations, but there is little in the house to call attention to its age excepting a fireplace on the first floor with a Tudor arch and a 17th-century chimney-stack on the west side.

Running back from this house and forming the present south-east boundary of the Wardrobe Court is the house occupied by Mr. George Cave, K.C., M.P.; it seems very doubtful whether the walls of this house are on the Tudor foundations. Wynyardes' view of the east front, taken in 1562, shows the gateway to be almost in the middle of the courtyard instead of very

[80] Cal. S.P. Dom. and Acts of P.C. for reign of Eliz.; also Hist. MSS. Com. Rep. xii and xiii, passim.

[81] Hist. MSS. Com. Rep. ix, App. ii, 423; Strickland, Lives of the Queens of Engl. iv, 771, 783.

[82] Stow, op. cit. 828.

[83] Manning and Bray, Surr. i, 411.

[84] Ibid.; Folkestone Williams, op. cit. ii, 199; iii, 23; Hist. MSS. Com. Rep. xii, App. iv, 396.

[85] Folkestone Williams, op. cit. iii, 43.

[86] Cal. S.P. Dom. 1625-6, p. 73.

[87] Hist. MSS. Com. Rep. xi, App. i, 29. See the Richmond Parish Registers.

[88] Folkestone Williams, op. cit. iii, 129; Cal. S.P. Dom. 1640, p. 167; Hist. MSS. Com. Rep. xiii, App. ii, 132.

[89] Cal. S.P. Dom. 1640-1, p. 333. Richmond Parish Registers show an unusual number of burials from June to the end of August.

[40] Ibid. 1641-3, p. 134.

[41] Commons' Journ. v, 210.

[42] Whitelocke, Mem. of Engl. Affairs, June 1647.

[43] The survey of 1649 is printed in the Vetusta Monumenta (Soc. of Antiq.), ii, and is also transcribed by Mr. Chancellor in his Hist. of Richmond, Kew, Petersham, and Ham, App. B. See also Surr. Arch. Coll. v, 75-103.

[44] Lysons, Environs of London, i, 442.

[45] Commons' Journ. viii, 73. Sir Gregory was a regicide.

[46] Cal. S.P. Dom. 1660-1, p. 71.

RICHMOND PALACE IN 1611

(From Speed's 'Theatre of the Empire of Great Britain')

RICHMOND PALACE : THE GATEWAY

much to the south of the centre line as now. A straight joint in the wall between the two houses in question appears to mark the original depth of the building east of the court ; the other building running east and west has an 18th-century brick face on its south side, but the wall towards the court has bricks of the previous century at least ; it is not improbable that when this house was erected the large number of old bricks about the site were utilized for the north wall, or it is possible that the court was reduced in size by James II when he repaired the palace, and this wall built then ; the interior of the house has fittings of the 18th century and later.

The house to the west of the court, sometimes called the Trumpeting House, and occupied by the Rev. Arthur Welsh Owen, is also an 18th-century building, said to have been erected by Richard Hill, brother to Queen Anne's favourite, Mrs. Masham, who had it on lease in 1703.[47] It has a fine ceiling in the drawing-room. The 'Trumpeters' are two half-size stone figures of men or boys in the dress of the time of Henry VII—flat caps, long hair, long cloaks, and tight hosen—with their arms (formerly) in such a posture as to suggest they were blowing trumpets ; their arms are now broken off.[48]

Asgill House occupies the site of the north-west corner of the palace ; it is a stone building in the form of a Greek cross, built by Sir Robert Taylor for Sir Charles Asgill, Lord Mayor 1757-8, in the middle of the 18th century ; the rooms in the west wing are octagonal, and there is very little doubt that this wing stands on one of the octagonal turrets in the north-west corner of the palace and that the plan was influenced somewhat by the pre-existing foundations. This has also occurred in the new house, called Garrick House, built on the site of the north-east corner of the palace, after the old theatre was demolished and the road widened. When the excavations were made for the foundations of the house the foundations of an octagonal turret were opened out, and these being very hard to destroy, the architect accepted the situation and used the old foundations for an octagonal chamber in his new structure. The 'Tea House' is a summer-house in the gardens of the Trumpeting House, and seems to be another small relic of the palace buildings ; it possesses no very distinctive architectural features, but is evidently of some age, and the position it occupies seems to coincide almost exactly with the small square wing at the south-west corner, as shown by Hollar's view of the west side made in 1638. It is cemented externally, but it would be interesting to know if the cement conceals the round-arched doorway shown by Hollar.

Beyond the above-mentioned relics there is little else above ground to confirm the old views as to the size and character of the palace. Various garden walls

with straight joints here and there, a small rectangular ' peep hole ' or loop light, and other slight evidences, all point to their having had some connexion with the buildings ; but without some further aid from other sources, such as excavations, &c., may afford, their exact relation to the whole can only remain a matter for surmise.[49]

Henry VII is said to have formed a library at Richmond Palace,[50] and to have appointed Quentin Paulet to the librarianship.[51] In 1516 Giles Duwes was granted the office of keeper of the king's library in the manor of Richmond or elsewhere with an annual rent of £10 out of the customs of the port of Bristol ; the reversion of this office and rent were granted to William Tyldesley in 1534.[52] The library existed in 1607,[53] but no mention of it occurs in the survey of 1649, and it has been suggested that before this date it may have been incorporated with the library at Whitehall.[54] From the reign of Edward IV until that of Charles II there are successive grants of the keepership of the wardrobe to various persons, frequently the grantees of the custody of the manor.[55] Philip I, King of Castile, was entertained at the palace by Henry VII in 1506,[56] and the Emperor Charles V by Henry VIII in 1522.[57] The story that Eric of Sweden visited Elizabeth at Richmond[58] is probably incorrect, for it was the prince's brother John who came over in 1559 to ask her hand for Eric, and another suitor, the Duke d'Alençon,[59] was one of the queen's guests there.[60]

The park which was attached to the palace is now known as the Old Deer Park. The palace stood south of it, facing the river. A warren is mentioned as appurtenant to the manor in 1292,[61] and in 1455 begins the mention of the 'New Park,' probably in contradistinction to an older or smaller park. There are said to have been two parks in the reign of Henry VIII called the 'Great Park' and the 'Little Park,' and it has been presumed that these two were laid together between 1617 and 1649.[62] At the latter date the entire park contained a little over 349 acres, and was then called Richmond Little Park[63] (as afterwards Old Park) to distinguish it, from the much larger park, now called Richmond Park, which had been inclosed by Charles I. In 1455 the custody of the 'New Park' was in the hands of Thomas Barton, who had received a grant of it for life from Henry VI with wages of 2d. a day and 7 acres of meadow lying near Chertsey Bridge for the sustenance of the deer of the park in wintertime.[64] The same grant, together with a mansion standing between the house of the Clerk of the Works and the palace, was made to Edmund Glase for life in 1461, and again in 1463.[65] The park was granted with the manor (q.v.) to Queen Elizabeth Woodville for life in 1466, and she granted the custody of it, during her life, to Robert Ratcliffe in 1471.[66]

[47] Land Rev. Misc. Bks. ccxxvi, 166-82.
[48] They now stand in the garden exposed to the weather, which may account for the breakage of their arms, shown to be whole in earlier sketches of them.
[49] Dr. Garnett, in Richmond-on-Thames, quotes a MS. description of the palace in 1503, and also the parliamentary survey, mentioned above. See also E. Beresford Chancellor, Hist. and Antiq. of Richmond.
[50] Manning and Bray, op. cit. i, 412.
[51] Chancellor, op. cit. 16.

[52] L. and P. Hen. VIII, vii, 419 (11).
[53] MSS. of Lord Montagu of Beaulieu, (Hist. MSS. Com.), 74.
[54] Chancellor, op. cit. 17.
[55] Mins. Accts. bdle. 1094, no. 5 (20 Edw. IV) ; L. and P. Hen. VIII, iv, 6083 (29) ; xii, 539 (12) ; Acts of P.C. 1552-4, p. 245 ; Cal. S.P. Dom. 1595-7, p. 490 ; 1660-1, p. 140.
[56] Holinshed, Chron. (ed. Hooker), 793.
[57] Hall, Chron. 641.
[58] Brayley, Surr. iii, 63.

[59] Dict. Nat. Biog. vii, 215.
[60] Hist. MSS. Com. Rep. xv, App. ii, 35.
[61] Chan. Inq. p.m. 21 Edw. I, m. 50.
[62] Manning and Bray, op. cit. i, 413 ; Stow, op. cit. 553 ; Land Rev. Misc. Bks. cxc, fol. 100-2.
[63] Survey of Richmond Manor, 1649.
[64] Parl. R. (Rec. Com.), v, 313.
[65] Cal. Pat. 1461-7, pp. 124, 274.
[66] Mins. Accts. bdle. 1094, no. 5 (20 Edw. IV).

Subsequent grants of the custody of the manor (q.v.) included that of the park until the Commonwealth, when. the latter was valued at £220 5s. and sold by order. of the Parliament to William ; Brome of London.[67] Shortly afterwards it seems to have come into the hands of Sir John Trevor.[68] On the Restoration the custody of the park, here still called the New Park, was granted to Edward Villiers, and the park itself in 1664 to james, Duke of York.[69] In 1675 Edward. Villiers, then custodian, obtained licence to keep a pack of beagles to hunt within the manor.[70] At this time the royal palace was fast falling into decay, and the lodge in the Little Park, situated to the east of the present Kew Observatory,[71] became the chief residence in Richmond. Originally the keeper's lodge,[72] it had been distinguished by the presence of Wolsey in the time of Henry VIII. It seems to have been occupied by a Mr. Webb before the Civil War and to have been then appropriated by Sir Thomas Jarvis.[73] In 1694 the lodge was leased for thirty-one years to john Latton,[74] who sold his interest, soon after the accession of Queen Anne, to the Duke of Ormonde.[75] The latter petitioned that the lease might be renewed to him for ninety-nine years or three lives, and this suit was granted in 1704.[76] The duke, who was also ranger or keeper of the park, rebuilt the lodge and lived there until his forfeiture in 1715.[77] It was granted by George I to George, Prince of Wales, for ninety-nine years, or for his life and those of his wife and his daughter Anne, in 1722.[78] In that year it was thus described by Macky : 'His (the Duke of Ormonde's) 'lodge a perfect Trianon ; but since his forfeiture it hath been sold[79] to the Prince of Wales, who makes his summer residence here. It does not appear with the grandeur of a Royal Palace, but is very neat and pretty. There is a fine avenue which runs from the front of the house to the town of Richmond, at half a mile's distance, one way, and from the other front to the river-side, both inclosed with balustrades of iron. The gardens are very spacious and well kept. There is a fine terrace towards the river. But, above all, the wood cut out into walks, with the plenty of birds singing in it, makes it a most delicious habitation.'[80] On his accession George II settled the lodge on his queen, Caroline,[81] and it continued to be one of their favourite resorts. The queen had a dairy and menagerie here,[82] and among the additions to the gardens made by her were a hermitage and a grotto called Merlin's Cave.[83] George III made the lodge a frequent place of residence during the first few years of his reign, and, as his grandfather had done, settled it on his wife in 1761.[84] Queen Charlotte pulled down the lodge about 1770, intending to build a new palace on its site, but

although the foundations were laid the design was never completed.[85] In the course of these alterations in 1769 eighteen houses, the remains of the hamlet of West Sheen, were pulled down and the site added to the royal grounds. An Act of Parliament of 1785 enabled the king to unite Richmond Gardens with Kew Gardens by closing a footpath of over a mile in length called Love Lane.[86] The park is still Crown land, but ninety-seven acres are held on lease by the corporation and are open to the public ; part of this is used as a golf-course ; another part, acquired on lease by some of the leading tradesmen,[88] is reserved as an athletic ground, and here also the far-famed Richmond Horse Show takes place every year.

The other park, at first called the 'New Park' and now Richmond Park, was inclosed by Charles I from lands extending into the parishes of Richmond, Petersham, Ham, Kingston, Wimbledon, Mortlake, and Putney, partly owned by the Crown and partly by private persons. In 1634 the king declared his intention of making a new park for deer, and issued a special commission to Francis Lord Cottington and others to compound with owners in the parishes for the purchase of the necessary property.[89] An account is given by Lord Clarendon[90] of the refusal of some of the proprietors to meet the wishes of the king, who determined nevertheless to proceed with his resolution. He did in fact begin building the surrounding wall before he had obtained the consent of his subjects, and thereby caused a great deal of bitterness. The park, which was stocked with red and fallow deer,[91] was completed in 1637, and the first rangership granted for life in that year to Jerome Weston, Earl of Portland, with a fee of 12d. a day, pasture for four horses, and the use of the brushwood.[92] Owing to the many objections made against the formation of the park, gates were placed at intervals in the wall, and permission was given to the public to use the roads, the poor of the various parishes being also allowed to take away firewood as they had formerly been accustomed to do.[93] After the execution of Charles I the park was settled by the House of Commons on the mayor, commonalty, and citizens of London and their successors, with the expressed desire that it should be preserved as an ornament to the city.[94] On the Restoration it was returned by the corporation to Charles II,[95] who appointed Sir Lionel Tollemache, bart., and his wife Elizabeth, Countess of Dysart, to the rangership in 1660,[96] shortly afterwards granting the reversion of it to Sir Daniel Harvey.[97] In 1664 a warrant was issued forbidding any person to bring a dog within ten miles of Richmond during hay and corn harvest in order that the game might be preserved,[98] but two years later Lord Crofts was authorized

[67] Lysons, op. cit. i, 446.
[68] Mystery of the Good Old Cause, printed in Corbett's Parl. Hist. iii.
[69] See Manor.
[70] Cal. S.P. Dom. 1675-6, p. 73.
[71] The observatory was built in 1768-9, (Manning and Bray, op. cit. i, 414).
[72] N. and Q. (Ser. 6), viii, 518.
[73] Mystery of the Good Old Cause.
[74] Pat. 6 Will. and Mary, pt. ix, no. 11.
[75] Land Rev. Misc. Bks. ccxxvi, fol. 166-82.
[76] Pat. 3 Anne, pt. iii, no. 4.
[77] N. and Q. (Ser. 6), viii, 518.
[78] Pat. 8 Geo. I, pt. vi, no. 10.

[79] Presumably by the Earl of Arran, who was empowered to re-purchase his brother's estates in 1721 (G.E.C. Peerage, vi, 152).
[80] N. and Q. (Ser. 6), viii, 518.
[81] Pat. 1 Geo. II, pt. i, no. 9.
[82] Lysons, op. cit. i, 446-7.
[83] Folkestone Williams, op. cit. iii, 296-7.
[84] Manning and Bray, op. cit. i, 414 ; Statutes at Large, xxv, 4.
[85] N. and Q. (Ser. 6), viii, 518 ; Camden, Brit. (Gough's additions), i, 177.
[86] Statutes at Large, xxxv, 130 ; Brayley, op. cit. iii, 66.

[87] Information kindly supplied by Mr. H. Sagar, town clerk.
[88] Gascoyne, Recollections of Richmond, 144.
[89] Rymer, Foed. xix, 515.
[90] Hist. of the Rebellion (ed. Macray), i, 132-5. See also Cal. S.P. Dom. 1635, p. 25 ; 1636-7, p. 388.
[91] Ibid. 1636-7, p. 457.
[92] Ibid. 1644, p. 234.
[93] Manning and Bray, op. cit. i, 415.
[94] Commons Journ. vi, 246, 365.
[95] Manning and Bray, op. cit. i, 416.
[96] Cal. S.P. Dom. 1660-1, p. 142.
[97] Ibid. 1660-1, p. 210.
[98] Ibid. 1663-4, pp. 654, 659.

RICHMOND IN 1710

RICHMOND GREEN : EAST VIEW OF KING HENRY VII PALACE IN 1737

(From S. and N. Buck's Drawing)

to hunt round Richmond Palace, notwithstanding the king's prohibition.[99] The Duke of Lauderdale obtained the office of rangership of the park for life in 1673,[100] and Laurence Earl of Rochester in 1683,[101] but his son, afterwards Lord Clarendon, sold the remainder of the term to the Crown in 1727, and the rangership was given by George II to Robert Walpole, son of the celebrated prime minister Sir Robert Walpole. The latter was created Earl of Orford in 1742,[102] and spent much of his leisure at Richmond, frequently hunting in the park.[103] The prime minister, although he effected improvements and spent much money on the park, made several encroachments on the rights of the public by shutting up gates and taking away step-ladders on the walls ; and after his death in 1745, and that of his son, the ranger, in 1751, these encroachments were continued by the Princess Amelia, who was the next holder of the rangership. Several complaints were made by the neighbourhood,[104] and in 1754 a special Jury gave a verdict for the princess,[105] but in 1758 a decision was given in favour of the public, and the step-ladders and gates were restored. The princess resigned her office of rangership in 1761,[106] and in the same year it was granted to the Earl of Bute, who held it until his death in 1792.[107] About 1814 the Prince Regent, afterwards George IV, appointed as ranger his sister Princess Elizabeth,[108] who held the office until 1825, when it passed to the Landgravine of Hesse.[109] She was succeeded in the office by Adolphus, Duke of Cambridge, who held it from 1835 till his death in 1850,[110] after which the Duchess of Gloucester held it until her death in 1857.[111] George, Duke of Cambridge, was then made ranger,[112] and after his death in 1904 the preservation of game and the private shooting in the park were abolished.

As well as several picturesque keepers' lodges, Richmond Park contains some important houses which may be mentioned here, although situated outside the parish boundary.

Pembroke Lodge, formerly known as Hill Lodge and the Molecatcher's, stands a short distance from Richmond Gate, just beyond the Terrace Walk,[113] and commands a splendid view of the Thames valley. The Countess of Pembroke died here in 1831 at the age of ninety-three,[114] after which it was occupied by the Earl of Errol, subsequently by Earl Russell, and since the death of his widow by Georgina Countess of Dudley.[115] Within the grounds is a board on which is inscribed a poem on James Thomson, ' the poet of Nature,' alluding to the beautiful prospect which he loved. In the grounds also is a barrow, traditionally said to have been the spot where Henry VIII stood to see the rocket which gave him intimation of the execution of the sentence on Anne Boleyn.

White Lodge is situated between Sheen and Robin Hood Gates. The central part was built by George II,

and originally called Stone Lodge, the two wings being added later by the Princess Amelia. In the reign of George III it was occupied by Lord Bute, and later by Lord Sidmouth, who was here visited by William Pitt and Lord Nelson. It was the home of the Duchess of Gloucester when ranger. Queen Victoria spent a short time here after her mother's death, and King Edward, when Prince of Wales, also lived here at one time. It afterwards became the home of the Duke and Duchess of Teck, whose grandson Edward the present Prince of Wales was born here in 1894.[116]

Sheen Lodge, near Sheen Gate, once a keeper's lodge called the Dog-Kennel, is distinguished as having been the home of the great physiologist Sir Richard Owen, K.C.B., who here entertained Dickens, Millais, Mr. Gladstone, and other noted guests. It is now occupied by Mrs. Owen.

Thatched Cottage, which stands near Ham Gate, was also a keeper's lodge in former days. It was occupied during part of the 19th century by Sir Edward Bowater, General Meadows, and Sir Charles Stuart ;[117] and has recently been lent to Sir Frederick Treves, bart., G.C.V.O., C.B., LL.D., F.R.C.S.

Four religious bodies have had houses at Richmond. From 1315 to 1318 twenty-four Carmelite friars stayed by command of Edward II at the manor-house of Sheen and celebrated divine service there, but in the latter year they moved to a place which the king granted them outside the walls by the North Gate of Oxford. These friars were endowed with a grant of 120 marks out of the Exchequer.[118] A house of Friars Observant[119] was founded by Henry VII in 1499 and suppressed in 1534. The site was granted in 1572 to Percival Gunstan and his heirs,[120] and the survey of 1649[121] represents the remaining rooms to have been then used as a chandler's shop. The approximate position of the convent is indicated by a lane called Friar's Lane which leads from the Green past Queensberry House to the river ; and is described in the 1649 survey as having been on this side of the palace. Henry V established two religious houses in Sheen in 1414, one of which, a house of Celestines,[122] was, however, abolished shortly afterwards.[123] The Carthusian Priory of Jesus of Bethlehem founded by him, of which an account has already been given in this history,[124] was situated in the Old Deer Park where Kew Observatory now stands. This monastery is one of the two chantries referred to in Shakespeare's *Henry V*, where the king says on the eve of the battle of Agincourt—[125]

' I have built
Two chantries where the sad and solemn priests
Sing still for Richard's soul.'

The house was granted in 1540 to Edward Seymour, afterwards Duke of Somerset. He conveyed it

[99] *Cal. S.P. Dom.* 1666–7, p. 202.
[100] Ibid. 1673, p. 223.
[101] Pat. 35 Chas. II, pt. ii, no. 8.
[102] G.E.C. *Peerage*, ii, 278 ; vi, 128.
[103] *Hist. MSS. Com. Rep.* xv, App. vi, 165 ; xiv, App. ix, 241.
[104] H. Walpole, *Mem. of Reign of Geo. II* (ed. Lord Holland), i, 401–2 ; G.E.C. *Peerage*, vi, 130.
[105] *Hist. MSS. Com. Rep.* x, App. vi, 257 ; xv, App. vi, 204.
[106] Manning and Bray, op. cit. i, 416.
[107] G.E.C. *Peerage*, ii, 91.

[108] *A. H. W. Guide to Richmond New Park*, 16.
[109] Mrs. A. G. Bell, *Royal Manor of Richmond*, 112.
[110] G.E.C. *Peerage*, ii, 122.
[111] Ibid. iv, 47.
[112] Ibid. ii, 123.
[113] Made in 1832 (Chancellor, op. cit. 231).
[114] G.E.C. *Peerage*, vi, 224.
[115] Bell, op. cit. 115.
[116] Ibid. 113–14.
[117] Ibid.

[118] *Cal. Pat.* 1313–17, p. 377 ; 1317–21, p. 103.
[119] For an account of it see *V.C.H. Surr.* ii, 116.
[120] Pat. 14 Eliz. pt. i, m. 13.
[121] See above.
[122] Walsingham, *Ypodigma Neustriae* (Rolls Ser.), 450. The third house referred to by Walsingham was the Abbey of Syon in Middlesex.
[123] Chancellor, op. cit. 74.
[124] *V.C.H. Surr.* ii, 89.
[125] Act. iv, sc. i.

3

68

back to the Crown in 1547.[126] Later it was granted to the Duke of Suffolk, but was again resumed by the Crown after his attainder in 1554. The monastery was refounded for the remnant of English Carthusians, to be finally dissolved by Elizabeth. It was thus the latest founded and the last dissolved of the greater English monasteries. The site was granted by the queen to Sir Thomas Gorges and his wife, the Marchioness of Northampton, in 1584.[127] James, Duke of Lennox, obtained a grant of it in 1638.[128] At the time of the Commonwealth a detailed survey was taken of the buildings, and the site, valued at £92, was sold as Crown land to Alexander Easton.[129] In 1660 Charles II granted a lease of it for sixty years to Viscount Lisle,[130] who made it his residence for a time and transferred it to Lord Belasise about two years later, the latter obtaining a new lease of it in 1662 for sixty years.[131] In 1675 a lease of the priory was granted to certain persons in trust for Henry (afterwards Viscount) Brouncker and Sir William Temple.[132] Sir William had made the house which occupied the site of the priory his home since 1663,[133] and constantly averred his delight in his sequestered abode,[134] which, however, he eventually gave to his son.[135] In 1696 another grant of the site of the monastery was made to Charles Bertie and others for thirty-one years, apparently in trust for the Duke of Leeds.[136] Two leases dated 1750 and 1760 conveyed separate parts of the estate to John Jefferys and Charles Buckworth for a term of years.[137] No remains of the priory are now in existence, the gateway which was the last survival having been taken down in 1769.[138]

The present town of Richmond has grown up for the most part on the other side of the site of the royal palace. During the 18th century the growth of the parish, judged by the number of its inhabitants, was considerable.[139] A place of entertainment called Richmond Wells, which had been opened in 1696 near a medicinal spring then existed in the grounds of Cardigan House on the hill, attracted a great many people during the early part of the century, but it had lost its reputation when about 1755 the property was bought and the wells closed by the Misses Houblon, then living in a house nearly opposite, now Ellerker College.[140] In 1792 the number of houses, exclusive of the new workmanship built by George III about 1785, and the almshouses, was 815.[141] Apart from the few relics of the Tudor Palace, and one or two other structures, old Richmond is essentially a Queen Anne and Georgian town. Among these exceptions is a bicycle-maker's shop at the corner of Duke Street on the Green which contains some early 17th-century oak panelling, whilst it is said that a large Elizabethan fireplace was found when the present shop-front was put in. A shop next to the police station in the main road also has an old fireplace with moulded jambs and lintel of grey marble with a black marble keystone; it is not unlike the fireplaces in Ham House of the time of Charles II, and is probably contemporary. Of the later period many examples could be enumerated.

A large house with two projecting wings in the Sheen Road, now divided into three houses, has an 18th-century brick front, but the side walls are evidently of an earlier date. Streatham Lodge, as the north wing is called, has mostly 18th-century or modern fittings, but the staircase is evidently the work of the beginning of the 17th century; the three upper flights are of exceptionally heavy woodwork, the moulded hand-rail being 7 in. wide by 6 in. deep, and the turned balusters 4 in. square; the newels are plain (7 in. square) with ball tops, and the stair carriage or sloping string is also plain; the lower flights are early 19th-century. The staircase is also the principal feature of Beverley Lodge, which occupies the south wing of the house; this is a very fine example of early 18th-century workmanship; the treads have moulded soffits and carved ends, the balusters are square with fluted sides, the newels are fluted Corinthian columns, and the hand-rail is moulded; it is in four flights, and may have replaced one like that in Streatham Lodge, than which it is much wider, lighter, and more elegant.

No. 5 Hill Street is a late 17th or early 18th-century house with a staircase and fittings of the period; the stair has twisted balusters. A carved over-door with fruit, flowers, &c., off the stair hall, is reminiscent of the work of Grinling Gibbons, as is also a carved picture-frame with a broken pediment fixed in the wall in the upper part of the stair hall.

'Queen Anne' House (or No 11 The Green) is a building, as its name implies, of the beginning of the 18th century, with some good ironwork in front. In the front hall or passage is an oak carved and pierced screen which appears to be earlier than the house and brought from elsewhere. In the basement is a good lead cistern dated 1715.

There are several other old lead cisterns remaining in the neighbourhood; at 'Abbotsdene' on the Green is one dated 1709 with ornamental work in relief and the initials A B M; in Palace Place adjacent another dated 1718, another at the back of Mr. Cockburn's shop inscribed 1735 G W I, and a fourth in Gloucester Road, Kew, dated 1768, with the letters T A A and with crests of stags in relief upon it.

Many of the doorways in Richmond are good examples of 18th-century workmanship and carving. Some in the Sheen Road are of similar character to the carved over-door in No. 5 Hill Street; in Church Terrace are others worthy of notice; and three in Michels Terrace are striking with their winged cherubs; these all appear to be work of the first half of the century. A very good example of the ironwork of the period remains in the gateway to Marshgate House, Sheen Road. On the other side of the same road are the almshouses founded by Rebecca and Susannah Houblon in 1757; the entrance to the front quadrangle has some fairly good iron gates bearing that date. Perhaps two other relics of older Richmond are a gabled cottage in the passage east of the church, of timber cemented over, and three cottages in Vine Row of timber construction filled in

[126] Pat. 1 Edw. VI, pt. vi, m. 20.
[127] Ibid. 26 Eliz. pt. iii, m. 15.
[128] Ibid. 14 Chas. I, pt. xliii, no. 23, m. 10.
[129] Dugdale, Mon. vi, 30.
[130] Cal. S.P. Dom. 1660–1, p. 208.
[131] Pat. 14 Chas. II, pt. ii, no. 5.

[132] Dugdale, Mon. vi, 30.
[133] Dict. Nat. Biog. lvi, 43.
[134] Lysons, op. cit. i, 452.
[135] Dict. Nat. Biog. lvi, 48.
[136] Pat. 8 Will. III, pt. viii, no. 5.
[137] Dugdale, Mon. vi, 30.

[138] Lysons, op. cit. i, 453.
[139] Ibid. i, 462.
[140] Chancellor, op. cit. 121; Bell, op. cit. 79.
[141] Lysons, op. cit. i, 462; Burt, Richmond Vestry, 16.

RICHMOND : GENERAL VIEW FROM TWICKENHAM PARK IN 1755

RICHMOND : WEST VIEW FROM THE STAR AND GARTER

(From an old Print)

with some solid material, apparently flint, and all coated with cement. A later but very interesting house is that in which Mrs. Fitzherbert lived, No. 3 The Terrace, on the hill above the Terrace Gardens and commanding a beautiful view across the Surrey hills. It was built by one of the brothers Adam in the time of George III, and is one of the finest examples of their work. The staircase has wrought-iron balustrading and a black-wood hand-rail; the ceilings of the two rooms on the ground floor and the drawing-room and front bed-room on the first floor are all richly decorated; the fireplaces are of marble, that of the drawing-room being a fine one of white marble with some carved figures in low relief. The iron grill to the front doorway and the iron railing in front of the house are also of good design. The house is now occupied by Mrs. Aldin.

By the side of the Trumpeting House, referred to above, is Queensberry House, a modern mansion built in the grounds of an older one called Cholmondeley House, which was erected at the beginning of the 18th century by George, third Earl of Cholmondeley. It afterwards came into the possession of the Earl of Warwick and subsequently passed to Sir Richard Lyttelton, from whom John Earl Spencer purchased it for his mother the Countess Cowper. After her death in 1780[143] it was bought by the Duke of Queensberry, during whose ownership it was the scene of great gaiety. At a later date it was occupied by the Marquess of Hertford; but in 1830, after some years of neglect, it was pulled down with the exception of a few arches which still remain. The present house, which was built in 1831, is the residence of Mr. Geoffrey de Trafford. The next two houses higher up the river are called Cholmondeley Lodge and Cholmondeley Cottage. These look down upon the picturesque embankment called Cholmondeley Walk. Above it another walk called Waterside is overlooked by the modern St. Helena Terrace, and higher up are the gardens of Heron, once Herring, Court, which now occupy the site of the old Royal Hotel. One of these houses is the residence of Gen. Sir Harry Prendergast, K.C.B., V.C., R.E. There are some interesting houses near and above the bridge. One of them, originally Camborne House, but now called Northumberland House after Eleanor Dowager Duchess of Northumberland, who lived here in recent years, is let to the Richmond Club. Bridge House was built by Sir Robert Taylor about the same time as Asgill House. Ivy Hall was a residence of William IV when Duke of Clarence, and Gothic House was occupied for a short time by Madame de Staël. Bingham Villa, named after Lady Anne Bingham, who lived there, stands on the site of a small inn called the 'Blue Anchor.' Higher up the river is the charmingly situated Buccleuch House, once called Montagu Villa, which was built for George Duke of Montagu, and passed on his death in 1790 to his son-in-law the Duke of Buccleuch.[144] A magnificent fête was given here by the fifth duke in 1842 in honour of Queen Victoria and the Prince Consort. A museum belonging to the house, which stands on the other side of Petersham Road, is connected with it by a subterranean passage. Buccleuch House and grounds and the grounds of Lansdowne House,[144] which stood on the hill above

the river, were afterwards united and the estate sold to the Richmond Vestry in 1886. The greater part of the gardens are beautifully laid out as a pleasure ground called the Terrace Gardens, which were opened to the public by the late Duchess of Teck, representing Queen Victoria, the lady of the manor, in 1887. Buccleuch House itself and part of the grounds were sold by the vestry to Sir Whittaker Ellis, to whom they still belong. Beyond this house stands Devonshire Lodge, formerly the Wilderness Club, which was built after the demolition of Devonshire Cottage, so named after the celebrated beauty Georgiana Duchess of Devonshire who lived there. Above the river, on the slope which reaches to the Terrace, is the Mansion Hotel, which occupies the site of Nightingale Hall, formerly the abode of the Ladies Ashburnham. On the Terrace itself are two houses, one called The Wick, on the site of the old Bull's Head Tavern, and the other Wick House, built for Sir Joshua Reynolds, who here entertained many royal and aristocratic sitters as well as numerous literary friends. Among the houses opposite the Terrace are Downs House, once the residence of Richard Brinsley Sheridan, and the other of the twenty-fifth Earl of Crawford, author of the *Lives of the Lindsays*. A large house which afterwards became the Queen's Hotel was at one time occupied by the Countess of Mansfield, who died in 1843.[146] Doughty House is the residence of Sir Frederick Cook, bart., and the one next to it was occupied by Rhoda Broughton. Terrace House is owned by Sir Max Waechter, D.L., J.P. Next to the park gates is Ancaster House, named after the Duke of Ancaster, who sold it to Sir Lionel Darell, a favourite of George III. Opposite to this, overlooking the river, is the famous Star and Garter Hotel, which will always be associated with Richmond, although nearly the whole of it is actually in the parish of Petersham. Originally built in 1738, it acquired its great reputation during the 19th century, when it was a favourite resort of the fashionable world. In the centre of the cross-roads at the top of the hill there is a drinking fountain that was erected a few years ago by the Society for the Prevention of Cruelty to Animals. Many other noteworthy houses in different parts of the parish might be enumerated if space permitted. Among them are four of red brick facing the Green, known as Maids of Honour Row, which were built in the reign of George I. In one of these the late Sir Richard Burton lived when a boy. Lichfield House in Sheen Road, so called after the bishop who once resided there, is now occupied by Mrs. Maxwell (Miss Braddon) and her son Mr. W. B. Maxwell. Spring Grove in the lower part of Queen's Road is the residence of Sir Charles Rugge-Price, bart., D.L., J.P. It was built by the Marquess of Lothian in the early part of the 18th century and was purchased by the grandfather of the present owner in 1797. At No. 8 Parkshot, near the station, now the offices of the Richmond Board of Guardians, 'George Eliot' lived from 1855 to 1859 in lodgings that have since been pulled down. Here she wrote *Scenes of Clerical Life* and part of *Adam Bede*, and here also she and George Lewes were visited by Herbert Spencer and other friends. Abercorn House is now used as a residence by H.M. the King of Portugal.

143 G.E.C. *Peerage*, ii, 395.
143 Ibid. v, 344–5.

144 Lansdowne House belonged to the Marquess of Lansdowne, but was pulled down about 1865.

146 G.E.C. *Peerage*, v, 215.

Of the few old shops that remain in the town the most noted is the Original Maid of Honour Shop which existed in the 18th century, where the cheese-cakes supposed to have been introduced by one of the maids of honour are still sold. In 1823 it was acquired by a Mr. Bilton, who sold the goodwill, lease, and famous recipe to Mr. J. T. Billett (grandfather of the present owner) for £1,000. Richmond was formerly celebrated for its inns, but the greater number of the original houses have disappeared. In 1634, out of twenty-five ale-houses licensed within the hundreds of Kingston and Emley Bridge, ten were allowed in Richmond alone 'by reason of the Prince's Court often residing there and being a place of much resort and recreation for divers gentlemen and citizens.'[146] Shops in George Street now occupy the sites of the 'Queen's Arms' and the 'Black Boy,' and also of the old Castle Inn, the licence of which was removed in 1761 to the later Castle Hotel in Hill Street, and of the original 'Red Lion,' whose licence is supposed to have been transferred to the present hotel about 1755. Of the once-famous Feathers Inn at the junction of King Street[147] and Walter Lane, only the staircase and assembly room now remain ; and there is no vestige of the 'Rose and Crown.' The 'King's Head' stands at the corner of Bridge Street on the site of the old Ferry Inn ; opposite to it was another in Hill Street, which was superseded by the Talbot Hotel, now Talbot House. Tickets for the Old Theatre were sold at the 'Three Compasses.' The 'Greyhound,' still existing in George Street, although much altered, was the meeting-place appointed for putting the first Act relating to the government of the parish (see below) into execution.[148] The present 'Lass of Richmond Hill' has been rebuilt more than once ; it deserves notice on account of its name, which is sometimes thought to commemorate the heroine of a ballad and a tale about whom much controversy has arisen. It seems, however, that the true home of this young lady was Richmond in Yorkshire, although the tradition that she belonged to Richmond in Surrey still persists.[149]

The increase of the population at the end of the 18th century occasioned an application for the building of Richmond Bridge. Previous to this time communication with the opposite bank had been by a ferry, which was held on lease from the Crown.[150] An Act was passed in 1773 by which the commissioners were enabled to purchase the ferry from the then lessee, and after building the bridge to exact tolls until the money borrowed and the interest on it was repaid and £5,000 vested in the funds for the support of the bridge, after which the tolls were to cease.[151] The bridge, consisting of five stone arches, was begun in 1774 and finished in 1777, and in 1841 was said to be almost free, the only toll taken being a halfpenny on Sundays for foot passengers passing from the Surrey side, and a much reduced toll

for carriages.[152] The money for building the bridge had been raised on the tontine system, and after the death of the last shareholder in 1859 the bridge became free.[153] The embankment was continued from Kew to Cholmondeley Walk also in 1774.[154]

In the middle of the 19th century Richmond was still called a village, although it was then said to resemble a town in all respects. The railway to London was opened in 1846,[155] and since that time the development of the town, possessing as it does the attractions of a beautiful situation combined with proximity to London and facility of conveyance by land and water, has been exceedingly rapid. The population has increased from 9,255 in 1851[156] to 22,684 in 1891 and 25,577 in 1901.[157]

The government of the town was in the hands of a vestry, constituted under George III in 1785,[158] until 1890, when Richmond was incorporated by royal charter.[159] In 1892 the municipal borough was extended to include the civil parishes of Kew, Petersham, and that part of Mortlake which was created the civil parish of North Sheen in 1894.[160] It is divided into six wards, and is governed by a mayor, ten aldermen, and thirty councillors. It has a separate commission of the peace, but no separate court of quarter sessions.[161]

Richmond, from its entrance on the north, extends for about a mile to the crest of the hill. The road from Kew, leaving the Old Deer Park on the right, passes between shops and above the combined stations of the London and South-Western Railway (over which the North London Railway has running powers) and the Metropolitan and District Railways, to the beginning of George Street,[162] where it is joined by the road from Sheen,[163] which, running parallel with the railway, leads from the lower end of Queen's Road. The fire-engine station is situated at the angle formed by the junction of Kew and Sheen roads. George Street has its continuation in Hill Street, which bears round to the left and divides a short distance above the turning of the bridge, the lower road running parallel with the river towards Petersham, and Hill Street itself becoming Hill Rise and ascending towards Richmond Park, from the gates of which Queen's Road slopes downwards in a north-easterly direction to meet the road from Sheen. These roads outline the thickly populated part of the parish, a network of smaller roads covering the ground between.

To one approaching Richmond Park from the town, the Terrace Gardens are on the right, and on reaching them there first breaks upon the view, through a few openings in the intervening trees, the lovely scene that has been immortalized by painters and poets ;[165] while from the Terrace itself, just beyond the gardens, there is an uninterrupted view of the landscape. Far below is the winding river with its willow-covered islets, forming with the surrounding woods and meadows a beautiful foreground which fades away into a blue or hazy distance. In clear weather, however,

[146] *Cal. S.P. Dom.* 1634-5, p. 19.
[147] Formerly Furbelow Street (Burt, op. cit. 11).
[148] Burt, op. cit. 8.
[149] Much of the above information is derived from Lysons, Brayley, Chancellor, and Bell, op. cit.
[150] *Cal. of Pat.* 1476-85, p. 171 ; *L. and P. Hen. VIII,* x, 226 (18) ; *Cal. S.P. Dom.* 1591-4, p. 459, &c.

[151] Local Act, 13 Geo. III, cap. 83.
[152] Brayley, op. cit. iii, 98.
[153] Chancellor, op. cit. 153.
[154] Bell, op. cit. 52.
[155] Lewis, *Topog. Dict.* iii.
[156] Burt, op. cit. 13.
[157] *Pop. Ret.* 1901, pp. 6, 16.
[158] The Act 25 Geo. III, cap. 41, is sometimes referred to as the Richmond Local Act, 1784 ; Burt, op. cit. 12.

[159] *London Gazette,* 1890, iii, 2681. For a copy of the charter see Burt, op. cit.
[160] *Pop. Ret.* 1901, p. 12 and note.
[161] Ibid.
[162] Called High Street until 1769 ; Burt, op. cit. 11.
[163] Formerly called Marshgate Road.
[165] Reynolds, Turner, Pope, Collins, and Thomson are among many who have painted or described this prospect.

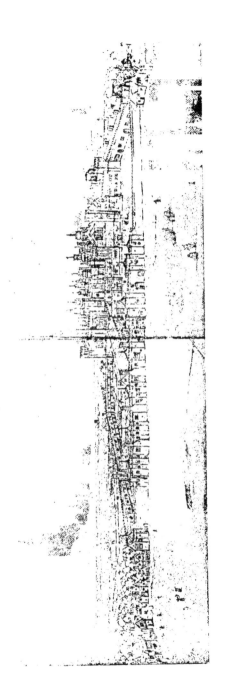

RICHMOND PALACE FROM THE RIVER IN 1562

(From a drawing by Antonius van den Wyngaerde)

Windsor Castle is distinctly visible. This view was frequently threatened, until it was permanently secured to the town by an agreement between the corporation and the trustees of the Earl of Dysart in 1896, by the purchase of the Marble Hill Estate, Twickenham, by the London County Council in 1902,[166] and by Sir Max Waechter's recent gift of the Petersham Ait, or Glover's Islet, to the corporation.

A theatre is said to have existed in Richmond as early as 1715.[167] Another one called the Old Theatre was built on the slope of the hill in 1719 on the site of an old stable for donkeys ; its licence was forfeited in 1756, and ten years later a new theatre was opened on the Green where Garrick House now stands, the prologue for the occasion being written by David Garrick. Edmund Kean acted here in 1817 and took a great fancy to Richmond ; he became the lessee of the theatre in 1831, and took up his residence in the house connected with it. He died and was buried at Richmond in 1833.[168] This theatre was pulled down in 1886, and another one built in 1889, but it was not found to pay. A new theatre of varieties has been lately erected on the little green adjacent to the large Green. Other means of popular entertainment are found in the Terrace Field,[169] the athletic grounds, swimming baths, the free library,[170] and boating. The common called Pesthouse Common, owing to a pest-house existing here, once extended from the bottom of Queen's Road to the park gates ; but it was granted to the vestry by the Act of 1785, and inclosed for a workhouse and burial ground, except for a small portion that adjoins the lower part of Queen's Road. The pest-house itself was pulled down in 1787.[171]

The Royal Hospital, on the outskirts of the Old Deer Park, was opened in 1868 and has been several times enlarged. Part of it was formerly the home of the poet Thomson. The town hall, built between Hill Street and the river on the site of the old Castle Hotel which was given by Sir Whittaker Ellis, bt., then M.P. for the division, was completed in 1893. A footbridge and lock were opened in 1894.

The ecclesiastical parish of St. John the Divine was constituted in 1838, the church having been built in 1826–9, and that of Holy Trinity in 1870 out of the parish of Richmond. The parish of St. Luke was formed in 1890, and that of Christ Church in 1894, out of Richmond and Mortlake. There is a Roman Catholic church dedicated in honour of St. Elizabeth in a branch road from Hill Rise called the Vineyard, first opened in 1824. At the lower end of Queen's Road is a Roman Catholic Marist convent. A Presbyterian church of England erected in 1885 is situated on the little green ; there are also Congregational, Primitive Methodist, and Wesleyan places of worship (the first built in 1830), and a Free Church.

The Wesleyan Theological Institution was founded in 1844. It is a large and well-appointed building in Bath stone of 16th-century style.

In 1725 there was a charity school at Richmond for 50 boys and 50 girls, founded in 1713 by Margaret Lady Vandeput, wife of Sir Peter Vandeput, kt.[172] In 1786 the minister and churchwardens returned that Lady Capell had left in 1721 £11 a year charged on land for the charity school, where in 1786 24 boys and 34 girls were educated. Other benefactions and subscriptions brought the total income up to £218 6s.[173] This was the general school for Richmond, in which, when Brayley wrote, about 1844, 400 children were educated at fees of 1d. a week, and the charity children also clothed as well as educated free. It is now represented by the King's School in Kew (Public Elementary), entirely rebuilt in 1887.

St. Mary's (Parochial) School was built in 1853, the Vineyard (British) School in 1866, Holy Trinity (National) Infants' Schools in 1866, Kew Road (Wesleyan) School in 1867, Holy Trinity (National) Girls' School in 1867, St. Elizabeth's (Roman Catholic) School in 1870, St. john's (National) School in 1873, Holy Trinity, Prince's Road, (National) Girls' and Infants' School in 1875, rebuilt in 1898, Holy Trinity, Mortlake, (National) Boys' School in 1885, and Darrell Road (Council) School was opened in 1906.

Among the place-names that have been found in connexion with the parish are 'blacke Henry,' 'Kingslease,' 'the Pray,' 'Cranes Croft,' 'Barbadoes Close,' 'Rachells Peece,' 'Lyttle Praise,' 'Greate Prayse,' 'Robinhoodes Walke.'

MANOR   There is no mention of *SHEEN*, now known as *RICHMOND*, in the Domesday Survey, as it was at that time included in the neighbouring manor of Kingston (q.v.), which was held by the king. By the reign of Henry I, however, the manor had acquired a separate existence under the name of Sheen, and was granted by the king to the family of Belet, who held it by the serjeanty of butlery.[174] In 1206 Master Michael Belet paid the sum of £100 for the office of butlership.[175] He seems to have forfeited his lands, and those in Sheen were granted to Hugh de Nevill in 1215.[176] Michael was evidently restored shortly afterwards, as he granted a virgate and a half of land in the manor of Sheen to Walkelin de Canetone early in the reign of Henry III.[177] At his death the custody of his daughter and heir, with her inheritance in Sheen, was acquired by Wimund de Ralegh.[178] This daughter appears to have been the Maud Belet who died in or before 1229, when her lands devolved on her kinsman John Belet, who paid ten marks for relief in that year.[179] He died in 1231,[180] leaving two daughters, Emma Oliver, and Alice who married John de Vautort a tenant on the manor,[181] and thus the manor of Sheen became divided. In 1253–4 Emma Oliver, or Emma Belet as she is here called, was party to a fine with John de Vautort and Alice his wife as to lands in Sheen and other places which were said to have been the right of John Belet the father of Emma.[182] By 1258 Emma Oliver had become the wife of

166 *London Statutes* (prepared under the direction of the Parl. Committee of the L.C.C.), ii, 493-4.
167 Brayley, op. cit. 101.
168 Bell, op. cit. 71-9.
69 Granted to the vestry in 1786 ; Bell, op. cit. 85.
170 Opened in 1881 ; Burt, op. cit. 49.
171 Ibid. 7, 15.

172 Willis's Visitation MS. at Farnham. She was daughter of Sir John Buckworth of West Sheen. Sir Peter Vandeput was a merchant of Flemish descent, father of Sir Peter Vandeput, bart.
173 *Parl. Return*, 1786.
174 *Testa de Nevill* (Rec. Com.), 226.
175 *Rot. de Oblatis et Fin.*(Rec.Com.), 358.
176 *Rot. Lit. Claus.* (Rec. Com.), i, 237.

177 Harl. Chart. 45 H 45.
178 *Testa de Nevill* (Rec. Com.), 227. The text gives 'the daughter and heir of Nicholas Belet.'
179 *Excerpta e Rot. Fin.* (Rec. Com.), i, 190.
180 Ibid. 218.
181 *Testa de Nevill* (Rec. Com.), 228.
182 Feet of F. Div. Co. 38 Hen. III, no. 90.

Robert de Meleburn, and in that year they confirmed a lease of the manor of Sheen (as Emma's moiety was always called) to john Maunsel, treasurer of York and reeve of Beverley, for fourteen years.[168] In 1264 Emma conveyed all her lands held in chief in Sheen to the king, for him to grant to Gilbert de Clare, Earl of Gloucester and Hertford, which was accordingly done.[164] A few years later the manor of Sheen came into the possession of Hugh de Windsor, who granted it in 1272 to Robert Burnell, Bishop of Bath and Wells,[165] the gift being confirmed by Henry III. The bishop then enfeoffed Otto de Grandison of the manor in tail-male, with reversion to himself in case of Otto's death without issue, but Edward I took it into his own hand, because he was given to understand that Hugh de Windsor had enfeoffed the bishop while he was of unsound mind. Afterwards, however, the king inspected the confirmation of Henry III, and on reflection that no right in the manor could accrue to him he restored it to Otto de Grandison,[186] who was a specially trusted servant and friend of the king's, and granted him free warren in his demesne lands there in 1279.[187] On setting out for his second expedition to Palestine, before the fall of Acre (1291), Grandison appears to have delivered the manor to the custody of Burnell, who died holding it in 1292.[188] Otto de Grandison survived the bishop, and in 1299 the king gave a curious order that no person, with the sole exception of the king's son, should enter, stay, or lodge in Otto's manor of Sheen, or put his baggage or goods there, against his will or the will of the keeper of the manor, as it appeared that great damage had been done by people lodging in the houses there.[189] Otto seems to have conveyed the manor to the king, probably about 1305, for Letters Patent, &c., are dated there from that year onwards, and in 1316 Sheen is called the king's manor.[190]

The other property in Sheen, which descended to john Belet's daughter Alice, was held by her husband john de Vautort by the grand serjeanty of being one of the king's cup-bearers. He died seised of the vill

GRANDISON. *Paly argent and azure a bend gules with three eagles or thereon.*

THE KING OF ENG-LAND. *Gules three leopards or.*

of Sheen about 1301, and was succeeded by a son john,[191] who appears as John de Vautort of Sheen in 1313.[192] This john was deprived of his lands there by Hugh le Despenser the elder, who granted them to Edward II ; and the petition to Edward III for their restoration by Richard de Vautort, brother and heir of john, in 1329, was apparently without avail.[193] They were evidently added to the Crown manor, which has remained in royal hands from about 1305 until the present day, although granted out at various times by successive kings. In 1315 it was described as the king's manor of Sheen, and Edward II made it an occasional place of residence, as his father had done towards the close of his reign.[194] Edward III granted the manor in 1331 to his mother, the dowager Queen Isabella, for her life.[195] She died in 1358,[196] and in 1359 William of Wykeham, at that time an influential favourite with the king,[197] was given the custody of the manor.[198] Two years later Ralph Thurbarn was made keeper. In 1377 John de Swanton, who had previously been granted the custody of the warren of Sheen, was appointed to the keepership of the manor for life. He held the office during the greater part of the reign o. Richard II, but gave it up to his son Thomas in 1390.[199] Edward IV, soon after his accession, made William Norburgh custodian of the manor of Sheen for life.[200] In 1466 the king granted the manor for life to his queen Elizabeth Woodville, together with the park, warren, and all appurtenances,[201] and she conceded the office of custodian to William Norburgh in 1468, allowing him to hold it himself or by deputy.[202] A few months after the accession of Richard III, however, Henry Davy obtained from the king a grant of the keepership of the manor for life. This grant included the custody of the garden, warren, and park belonging to the palace, and it is interesting to notice that the several offices were worth 6d. a day for the manor, 4d. a day for the garden, 3d. a day for the warren, and 2d. a day for the park, with another 2d. for the maintenance of the palings of the park.[203] The custody of the manor was again transferred on the accession of Henry VII, who granted it for life to Robert Skerne in 1485.[204] The manor itself was still the right of Queen Elizabeth, the widow of Edward IV, but in 1487 Henry VII held a council at Sheen, and declared that she had forfeited her property by deserting his cause before he became king. After that time she retired into the

ELIZABETH WOOD-VILLE. *Argent a fesse and a quarter gules.*

[163] Cal. Pat. 1247-58, p. 615 ; Feet of F. Surr. 42 Hen. III, no. 18.
[164] Cal. Chart. R. 1257-1300, p. 50.
[165] Feet of F. Mich. 56 Hen. III, no. 23. In 1279 a quitclaim was made to the bishop by Ralph de Berners and his wife Christine (Feet of F. Surr. 7 Edw. I, no. 35), the latter being probably the daughter of Hugh de Windsor ; see descent of West Horsley.
[166] Cal. Close, 1272-9, p. 520 ; Cal. Pat. 1272-81, p. 357.
[187] Cal. Chart. R. 1257-1300, p. 221.
[188] Chan. Inq. p.m. 21 Edw. I, no. 50.

[189] Cal. Pat. 1292-1301, p. 418.
[190] Ibid. 1313-17, p. 514. Otto was lord of Grandison (hodie Granson) in Neuchâtel. He withdrew there in his later life, and was not in England after 1307, though he lived till April 1328. He seems to have surrendered English lands into the custody at least of his old master and friend Edward I ; C. L. Kingsford in Trans. Roy. Hist. Soc. 1909.
[191] Chan. Inq. p.m. 29 Edw. I, no 35.
[192] Cal. Pat. 1313-17, p. 4.
[193] Ibid. 1327-30, p. 433.
[194] Ibid. temp. Edw. I and Edw. II, passim.

[195] Ibid. 1330-4, p. 195.
[196] Strickland, Lives of the Queens of England, i, 539.
[197] Dict. Nat. Biog. lxiii, 226.
[198] Abbrev. Rot. Orig. (Rec. Com.), ii, 225.
[199] Cal. Pat. 1377-81, p. 236.
[200] Ibid. 1461-7, pp. 53, 186.
[201] Ibid. p. 525.
[202] Mins. Accts. bdle. 1094, no. 5 (20 Edw. VI).
[203] Ibid. Duchy of Lanc. bdle. 41, no. 799.
[204] Pat. 1 Hen. VII, pt. i, m. 34.

abbey of Bermondsey, where she died in 1492.[205] Henry, having appropriated the manor of Sheen, held it throughout his reign, and changed its name to Richmond.[206] In 1522 Henry VIII granted a lease of the lordship of Richmond for thirty years to Massi Villiarde, serjeant of the king's pleasure-water, and Thomas Brampton, with the exception of the palace and the park, of which they were only granted the custody.[207] In 1540 the king bestowed the manor, palace, and park upon Anne of Cleves as part of the provision made for her after her divorce.[208] She granted a lease for eighty years to David Vincent, which was confirmed to him by Edward VI in 1547, a reservation being made of the palace and park, or one of the parks, belonging to it.[209] Later Vincent transferred his lease to

ANNE OF CLEVES. Gules a sharbocle or growing out of a scutcheon argent.

Gregory Lovel.[210] Sir Thomas Gorges received a grant of the keepership of the house, park, and garden, with the wardrobe, vessels, and victuals, in 1597.[211] This grant was repeated to himself and his wife, the Marchioness of Northampton, for their lives, about 1603,[212] and in 1607 Sir Thomas Gorges obtained a grant of the manor for forty years, with the exception of the palace, park, and ferry.[213] Sir Thomas died in 1610,[214] and in the same year the king granted the manor, palace, and park to Henry Prince of Wales and his heirs.[215] In January 1617, a few years after the death of Prince Henry, they were assigned to Sir Francis Bacon and others in trust for Prince Charles,[216] who received a direct grant of the manor, palace, and park for himself and his heirs in February of the same year.[217] As Charles I he is said to have settled them on his queen, Henrietta Maria, in 1626.[218] A court leet, to be held twice a year, was appointed for the manor of Richmond in 1628, and the king ordered that the tenants of the manors of Richmond, Petersham, and Ham should attend it instead of the court leet at Kingston, as had been the custom. Sir Robert

HENRIETTA MARIA. Azure three fleurs de lis or.

Douglas was made steward of the court for life.[219] In 1638 he, as Viscount Belhaven, was the keeper of the palace and park, as well as steward of the court leet and court baron ; but he surrendered these offices in that year,[220] and the king granted the custody of the palace and park to James Stuart, Duke of Lennox.[221] In 1639 William Murray, afterwards Earl of Dysart,[222] was the lessee of Richmond Manor under the queen, and on her determination to surrender it to the king, Murray petitioned for a grant of the manor in fee-farm together with the court leet and view of frankpledge. An order to this effect was accordingly given,[223] but was evidently not carried out, as the manor remained part of the queen's Jointure. It became the property of Sir Gregory Norton, bart., and later of his son Sir Henry Norton [224] during the Commonwealth, but was restored to Queen Henrietta Maria in 1660.[225] In July of that year the custody of the manor, palace, and park was consigned to Edward Villiers, who petitioned that the grant might extend during the lives of his two sons.[226] Queen Henrietta Maria did not die until 1669,[227] but perhaps exchanged the manor with the king, as in 1664 it was granted with the 'capital messuage' and the park to James, Duke of York, afterwards James II, and his heirs.[228] On his accession he settled the manor on his queen, Mary Beatrice, as part of her jointure.[229] It must have been appropriated with the rest of her Jointure by William and Mary, as in 1690 her trustees desired that no grant of the manor might be made until they were first heard on her behalf.[230] The manor does not appear to have been granted out again until 1733, when it was conferred by George II upon George, Earl of Cholmondeley, to hold during the life of Queen Caroline,[231] who died in 1737.[232] In 1770 it was granted, exclusive of the site of the palace, to Queen Charlotte for her life, by George III.[233] This is the last grant of the manor that has been found, and it is now in the possession of His Majesty King George V.

One or more fisheries were appurtenant to the manor from very early times. The first mention of a free fishery occurs in an extent of the manor in 1292.[234]

Among the customs claimed by the tenants of Richmond Manor by grant of 1481 which still survive is that of Borough English, or the succession of the youngest son to all copyhold lands ; if there are no sons the youngest daughter inherits.[235]

The church of ST. MARY MAGDALENE consists of a chancel, north organ-chamber and vestry, south chancel aisle,

CHURCH

205 Dict. Nat. Biog. xvii, 199.
206 See above.
207 L. and P. Hen. VIII, iii (2), 2694.
208 Ibid. xv, 899. In 1541 there was a grant of the manor and advowson for life to Thomas, Earl of Wiltshire (L. and P. Hen. VIII, xvi, 1500, p. 717), but this date must be erroneous, as he died without male heirs in 1539 (Exch. Inq. p.m. [Ser. 2], file 639, no. 4).
209 Land Rev. Misc. Bks. cxc, fol. 100–2.
210 Memo. R. Mich. 6 Eliz. rot. 95.
211 Cal. S.P. Dom. 1595–7, p. 490.
212 Ibid. 1603–10, p. 63 ; G.E.C. Peerage, vi, 70.
213 Pat. 5 Jas. I, pt. xxvi, m. 20. There is a grant of the palace to William Risbrooke dated 1605 in which Sir Thomas Gorges is said to be deceased (Cal. S.P.

Dom. 1580–1625, Addenda p. 471), but apparently there is some error. A grant of the reversion of the custody of the palace and park was made to Sir Edward Gorges, after Sir Thomas Gorges and his wife, in 1608 (Cal. S.P. Dom. 1603–10, p. 395).
214 G.E.C. Peerage, vi, 70.
215 Pat. 8 Jas. I, pt. xli, no. 2.
216 Ibid. 14 Jas. I, pt. xx, no. 2 ; Exch. Orig. R. L.T.R. 14 Jas. I, pt. iv, m. 126.
217 Pat. 14 Jas. I, pt. x, no. 3.
218 Manning and Bray, op. cit. i, 411. No mention of the manor and palace can be found in the documents quoted by Manning, but they evidently became part of the queen's Jointure. See Cal. S.P. Dom. 1628–9, p. 609.
219 Cal. S.P. Dom. 1628–9, pp. 329, 350, 399.

220 Ibid. 1637–8, p. 274.
221 Pat. 14 Chas. I, pt. xliii, no. 23, m. 10.
222 G.E.C. Peerage, iii, 228.
223 Cal. S.P. Dom. 1638–9, p. 609.
224 Notes of Pines, Surr. Hil. 1659.
225 Commons' Journ. viii, 73.
226 Cal. S.P. Dom. 1660–1, pp. 140, 141.
227 Dict. Nat. Biog. xxv, 436.
228 Pat. 16 Chas. II, pt. viii, no. 5.
229 Ibid. 1 Jas. II, pt. xii, m. 1.
230 Cal. S.P. Dom. 1690–1, p. 28.
231 Pat. 10 Geo. III, pt. v, no. 7.
232 Dict. Nat. Biog. ix, 144.
233 Pat. 10 Geo. III, pt. v, no. 7.
234 Chan. Inq. p.m. 21 Edw. I, no. 50 ; Feet of F. Surr. Hil. 3 Jas. I.
235 Surr. Arch. Coll. (Surr. Arch. Soc.), v, 97 ; Land Rev. Misc. Bks. ccxxvi, fol. 166–82.

and to the south of that a chapel, nave, north and south aisles with west porches and a west tower.

A chapel at Richmond is mentioned in the reign of Henry I when Gilbert the Norman founded Merton Abbey, giving it the advowson of Kingston and the four chapels of Petersham, Sheen (now Richmond), East Molesey, and Thames Ditton. It is mentioned again in 1339, and several wills in Somerset House prove the use of the church in 1487. In a manuscript of the expenses of Henry VII is the entry : 'Item given to ye Parish Clerke of Richmond towards ye building of his new church £5.'

In 1614 the first vestry was held, and the minutes of the meetings are still extant. The steeple was found to be in a ruinous state in 1624, and it was rebuilt, the contract with the mason being :—'First, That he is to make the Tower tables a plaine plenth and to make the upper Table plaine with such stone as he shall find there in the churchyard and to make the rest of the battlement a plaine cooping answerable to the thickness of the wall. To make the windows according to the Plote with a champfare on the outside and a Rabbatt on the inside or near thereabouts and to bring up the Buttresses answerable to the work and to make a Table over the heads of the windows with such stone as shall be found there and to make it plaine and strong And the masons work to be done according to this order—the church finding the materials and scaffolding stuff and tacklings for raysings and to make ready the scaffolds.' An estimate of £30 was accepted from a Henry Walden, the parish finding the materials, and £32 was paid to William Halsey for lead for the steeple. £40 4s. 10d. was the sum paid to one George Charley for a bell. The tower then erected is still standing, being the oldest part of the church, but it has been greatly restored. Six years later (in 1630) the churchwardens were requested to take a view of the steeple and report on the same at the next meeting, and also take a view for the hanging of five bells. In 1624 a gallery was made ; in 1673 rose the question of repairing the south aisle ; and in 1683 a south gallery was taken into consideration. In 1671 the communion table was ordered to be 'inclosed with rails and balusters 12 ft. in length by 7 ft. in width, with panels of wainscot and settles on both sides, and also a 'false flower (floor) under the said Table.'

In 1699, partly by the munificence of William III, who gave £200 towards the enlargement, the accommodation was improved and the pulpit ordered to be removed to the 'south-east pillar between the church and chancel.' In 1701 the roof of the tower and the steeple were defective and the bell frames rotten, and these parts were restored. The building suffered some damage from the Great Storm in 1703. The church was enlarged in 1750, and the nave and aisles then erected are those still standing, and an organ was placed there by George III and Queen Charlotte in 1770. The church was thoroughly repaired in 1822, when a new burial-ground was also added to the churchyard ; and it was again renovated in 1866 and newly reseated, whilst the organ was removed and a new one placed on the north side of the chancel. The chancel and its aisles were rebuilt and considerably enlarged in 1904.

In the Free Public Library is preserved the carved oak head of a monument or a doorhead which is said to have been on the north wall of the church in 1669 and was transferred to the west door in 1702 and removed from the church in 1864, being finally presented to the library in 1907 ; the carving is allegorical of Death and the Resurrection; on one side cherubim are represented as winds blowing upon human bones, and on the other a cherub with a trumpet, bones below, and a sun with rays ; in the middle is a winged skull, cross-bones, &c. There is also a fragment of 17th-century panelling carved with a vertical wreath of foliage and fruit, and having enriched mouldings ; this is probably a piece of the 1671 panels of wainscot set about the altar.

The chancel has an east window of seven lights and tracery and a three-light window in either side wall. In the north wall a doorway opens into the vestry and an archway west of it into the organ-chamber. An arcade of two bays divides the chancel from its south aisle and a similar arcade divides the aisle from the south chapel. The aisle is lighted by a traceried east window of five lights, and the chapel by one of four lights, and two south windows, each of three lights, whilst it has an outer doorway in its west wall. Moulded arches open into the chancel and its aisles from the nave and aisles.

The nave is divided from either aisle by an arcade of five bays with plain Doric columns and spanned by wood lintels with moulded cornices. Above is a clearstory lighted by wide segmental-headed windows with wood frames. The north aisle is lighted by five round-headed windows of red brick with keystones, and plain stone strings at the springing level. The wall is of stock brick and has a moulded brick cornice.

A doorway at the west end of the aisle opens into a semi-octagonal porch lighted by round-headed windows and with a round-headed doorway in its north-west wall. The south aisle is lighted by five similar windows, but the three middle lights are included in a slightly projecting portion above which is a pediment to the wall, and on either side of it a plain parapet with a stone coping. At the west end is a square porch with a round doorway in its south side.

The tower is of three stages ; the archway opening into it, which is of three chamfered orders, is old, but the rest of its stonework as well as the outside facing of flint is all modern. A stair turret is carried up in its south-east corner, and its two western angles are strengthened by diagonal buttresses. The west doorway has a four-centred arch in a square head with shields in the spandrels and with a moulded label. The second stage is lighted by a plain rectangular window in its north, west, and south walls, and on the north is a clock. The bell-chamber has two similar lights in each of its north, east, and west sides, and one to the south ; the parapet is embattled. The gabled roofs of the new work (chancel, &c.) are covered with tiles ; the nave and aisle roofs are slated. An oak screen spans the chancel arch. The font is modern.

The church contains a large number of monuments mostly of the 18th and 19th centuries, but a few of Elizabethan date. One at the east end of the north aisle is a brass set in a grey marble panel ; on it are the figures of a man and woman kneeling. Behind him are four sons, and behind her four daughters; Over the sons is a shield with the arms—A cheveron between three skeins of cotton. The inscription below is in Roman capitals, and reads :—' Here lyeth buried the bodie of Mr. Robert Cotton gentlemā sometime an officer of the remooving Wardroppe of Bedds of Queen Marie whoe by her Matie speciall choise was taken from the Wardroppe to serve her Matie as a Groome in her Privie Chamber al her lyfe time and after her decease againe he became an officer of the Wardroppe wher he served her Matie that now is Quene Elizabeth many yeres and died Yeomā of the same office (the date omitted). He maryed one Grace Cawsen, of whom he had issue 4 sonnes and 4 daughters.'

On the north wall are two 17th-century monuments. One to Lady Margaret Chudleigh (daughter of Sir William Courtney), first the wife of Sir Warwick Hele, kt., and afterwards of Sir john Chudleigh, kt., who died in 1628, has two round-headed recesses in which are the kneeling effigies of a man and woman. The other has a round-headed recess flanked by Corinthian columns supporting an entablature with roses on the soffit. In the recess is the kneeling figure of Walter Hickman of Kew, who died in 1617.

On the south wall is a small brass inscription as follows :—' To the memory of Margarite ye vertuous wife of Thomas jay, late of Midds. Esq : in these unhappy warrs his Maties Comissary Generall for Pvisions for all his Armye^s of Horse who had by her Thomas Jay Capt. of Horse whos^e short life was beautefyed with many Graces of nature and Rare Pieces of Arte and his end exprest his Loyalty and Courage ; Dame Francis wife to Sir Thomas Jervoyse of ye coūū. of South : and Elizā : Ex̄p : ult Sept. 1646.' Over the inscription is a shield with the arms—On a bend engrailed three roses impaling quarterly (1 and 4) two bars between three towers, (2 and 3) in a border engrailed two cheverons. On the dexter side of the shield is a wolf statant and on the sinister a lion's paw holding a key.

Also on the wall is a mural monument with the kneeling figures of a man and woman, and underneath their three sons and four daughters. The inscription is to Lady Dorothie wife of Sir George Wright, kt., who died in 1631; in some lines which follow she is described as being by birth a Farnam. There is also a floor slab to Sir George, who died in 1623.

On the west wall above the gallery is a mural monument of black marble to Lady Sophia Chaworth, relict of Sir Richard Chaworth, kt., and daughter of Robert, Earl of Lindsay, Lord Great Chamberlain of England ; she died in 1689. Another monument on the same wall is to Henry, Viscount Brouncker, Cofferer to Charles II, who died in 1687; and a third is to John Bentley, who died in 1660, Elenor his wife, who died in 1657, and Elenor their daughter, who died in 1656, with three portrait busts. Among the late monuments is one on the west wall to Edmund Kean the actor, who died in 1833; it was formerly outside the church.

There are eight bells ; the first three by Robert Catlin are dated 1740, the fourth is inscribed ' Lambert made me weake not fit to ring, But Bartlett among the rest hath made me sing 1680 ' ; the fifth by Catlin bears the date 1742; the sixth by James Bartlett 1680 ; the seventh by the same founder, 1681 ; and the tenor by Lester and Pack, 1760.

The communion plate comprises silver-gilt cups of 1630, 1663, 1825, and two of 1871; a silver-gilt paten of 1700 and two of 1871; a silver-gilt

basin of 1660 ; a silver salver of 1711 and a plated copy of it ; a silver salver of 1818 and three more of white metal ; two silver-gilt flagons of 1660 ; and a silver spoon of 1805. The registers are contained in six books, and begin in 1583. They have been printed by Mr. Challoner-Smith for the Surrey Parish Register Society.

The church of *ST. JOHN THE DIVINE*, Kew Road, consists of a chancel, north organ-chamber and vestry, south chapel, and a wide nave with west porches. The nave, which is built of white bricks and stone, dates from 1829, and is in a mixed Gothic style ; the chancel, &c. were rebuilt and enlarged in 1905 of stock brick and stone. An archway opens into an organ-chamber from the chancel, and an arcade of two bays divides the latter from the chapel, while both chapel and organ-chamber open into the nave. The high altar has a tall triptych of oak with beautifully painted panels, standing on a marble base ; the walls and roof of the chancel are also being treated with a good scheme of colour decoration which is not yet finished. The ceiling of the chancel is a pointed barrel-vault of wood ; a low stone screen crosses the chancel arch. The chapel altar is of oak with a marble top and marble reredos. The nave has a gallery across the west end and half-way along either side ; the ceiling is a flat one of plaster between the cross ties. Below the window-ledge level on the side walls is an excellently painted set of panels of the stations of the Cross. The pulpit is of green oak with decorated panels. The churchyard surrounds the building and has an iron railing on the west side towards the road ; it is planted with trees and shrubs.

The church of *ST. MATTHIAS* stands at the corner of Mount Ararat Road in the King's Road. It is a large building dating from 1858 in the style of the 13th century, and consists of an apsidal chancel, with organ-chamber, south chancel-aisle, nave of five bays with a clearstory, north and south aisles and porches, and a lofty north-west tower with a tall stone broach spire. The walls are of squared rubble with Bath stone dressings ; the roofs are covered with slates. An oak rood-screen spans the chancel arch.

The church of *HOLY TRINITY* is a stone building of middle 13th-century style erected in 1870, and consisting of a chancel, transepts, north-cast vestry, nave with a clearstory, low aisles, south porch-tower, and west porch, the last approached by an asphalt walk from Sheen Park. The roofs are covered with slates. The walls are of square rubble with ashlar dressings.

CHRIST CHURCH, Kew Road, is a similar stone building dating from 1893 and also of the style of the 13th century. It has a chancel with vestries, &c., nave with a clearstory of lancets, low aisles, south-east and west porches, and the stump of a future north-west tower. The roofs are tiled. The churchyard is narrow, and paved with asphalt except where shrubs are planted ; it has an iron fence with stone gate-posts on the west side towards the road.

ST. LUKE'S church, in The Avenue, was built in 1890 of stone in the style of the 13th century, and consists of a chancel, south chapel, nave of five bays, north and south aisles, and a west narthex ; provision is made for a future south-west tower. It has good oak furniture and a rich marble font with a tall oak cover.

ADVOWSONS
A chapel at Sheen was one of four annexed to the church of Kingston when the latter was granted to the priory of Merton,[236] and continued to be dependent on Kingston (q.v.) until 1769, although in 1658 the commissioners appointed to inquire into the state of ecclesiastical benefices had recommended that it should be separated from the mother church.[237] By an Act passed in 1769,[238] Kingston parish was divided, and Kingston with Richmond and the hamlets of Ham and Hook were consolidated into one vicarage called 'The Vicarage of Kingston-upon-Thames with Shene, otherwise Richmond.' The patronage has from that time descended with that of Kingston. The Provost and Fellows of King's College, Cambridge, acquired it in 1781, and their successors still hold it. Richmond was severed from Kingston and constituted a distinct vicarage in 1849.[239]

The living of St. John the Divine, now called a vicarage under the Act of 1868,[240] was in the gift of the vicar of Kingston until 1849, when it was transferred to the vicar of Richmond.[241]

The patronage of Holy Trinity and Christ Church is in the hands of trustees, and that of St. Luke belongs to the bishop.[242]

The incumbency of St. Matthias is held with that of the parish church, to which it serves as a chapel of ease.[243]

CHARITIES
There are six sets of almshouses in Richmond. Sir George Wright, who died in 1623, founded the almshouses commonly called Queen Elizabeth's Almshouses. The foundation was completed by his executors in 1636.[244] They were benefited by John Michel in 1739, by will of Charles Selwyn in 1747, and by Whichcote Turner in 1770. The last removed them in 1767 from the Lower Road, next Camborne House, to the present site in the Vineyard. They are for eight almswomen. Bishop Duppa's Almshouses were founded in 1661 for ten unmarried women, and endowed from an estate at Shepperton. The old red brick building, near the Terrace, is not unpicturesque. In 1695 Humphrey

Michel founded almshouses for ten poor men. He died the next year, and his purpose was carried out by his nephew John Michel. In 1722 William Smith conveyed property for their further support. In 1810 they were rebuilt, and in 1858 six additional almshouses were built. Part of Michel's original foundation was a house which was taken into the old Adelphi Theatre. William Hickey in 1727 left property to provide pensions for the inmates of Duppa's Almshouses, and for other poor people, men and women, over fifty-five years of age. In 1834 the trustees built almshouses for the pensioners, six men and ten women. The houses form three sides of a square, with a chapel in the centre of the building. There is also a house for the chaplain. Houblon's Almshouses were founded in 1757 and 1758 by Rebecca and Susannah Houblon respectively, daughters of Sir John Houblon, first Governor of the Bank of England. They are for nine poor women. The Church Lands Almshouses were built in 1843. They are supported by part of the income of the Church or Parish Charity Lands. These lands are supposed to have been given by Thomas Denys in 1558 for the use of the poor and repairing and sustaining the church. The funds were misappropriated, and it was not till 1626 that they were delivered into the hands of the churchwardens. In 1650 the churchwardens conveyed them to trustees, apparently illegally, with new trusts substituted for the original. They were applied 'for the necessary use of the parish church, the maintenance of the minister, and no other purposes whatsoever.'[245] The cost of rebuilding the church in 1823 was defrayed from these funds. In 1828 the original trust was restored by a private Act of Parliament of 9 George IV. Part was allotted for the maintenance of two churches in Richmond, part for the almshouses, built in 1843 as above mentioned, the rest in pensions for the poor. The charity now provides an income of about £1,000 a year, which is applied in aid of the rates.[246] Smith's Charity is distributed as in other Surrey parishes, and there are other numerous small charities for bread, clothing, apprenticing, &c.

[236] Dugdale, *Mon.* vi, 247; *Commons' Journ.* xxxii, 155.
[237] *Commons' Journ.* xxxii, 155; *Surr. Arch. Coll.* (Surr. Arch. Soc.), xvii, 104, quoting Parl. Surv.
[238] Private Act of 9 Geo. III, cap. 65.
[239] Local Act, 12 & 13 Vict. cap. 42.

[240] Public Act, 31 & 32 Vict. cap. 117.
[241] See above.
[242] *Clergy List*, 1908.
[243] Ibid.
[244] Lysons and Manning and Bray say 1606. The *Parl. Ret.* of 1786 says 1636. Sir George's death is in the parish register in 1623.

[245] *Parl. Ret.* 1786.
[246] Brayley, *Hist. of Surr.* iii, 93; *Rep. of End. Charities in Co. Surr. for Surr. Co. Council*, from *Parl. Ret.* 411 (14), 15 July 1868, and 103, 17 Feb. 1891.

THE BOROUGH OF GUILDFORD

Guldeford (x cent.) ; Geldeford (xi cent.) ; Geldefort, Geldesfort, Gildeforda, Gildeforde (xii cent.) ; Geldeford, Guldeford (xiii and xiv cents.) ; Gylford and Guldeford (xv and xvi cents.) ; Guildeford, Gildford, Gilford, and Gillford (xvi and xviii cents.).

Guildford is the old county town of Surrey, 30 miles from London, lying on the banks of the Wey, where the river breaks through the line of chalk hills. On the west side the ridge of the Hog's Back is called Guildown (Geldesdone by Geoffrey Gaimar, 12th century ; Geldedone in the Pipe Roll of 1192–3). On the east the hill is known as Pewley Hill, from the manor of Poyle or Puille.

The town consisted formerly of a steep street, the High Street, running west and east, from the bridge, by the side of which there existed a ford, up to the hill above Abbot's Hospital, with a parallel street to the north, latterly known as North Street, before that as Lower Back Side, earlier still the North Ditch. A curving street, Chertsey Street, connects North Street and High Street at the east end. A similar parallel road, South Street, runs on the other side of High Street, formerly known as Upper Back Side and the South Ditch. This communicated with the Castle Ditch, now Castle Street, on the south-west of the High Street. Quarry Street runs from the High Street, through what was the outer ward of the castle, southwards ; and Friary Street connects the High Street, northwards, with the old liberty of the Friars. The lanes running north and south from High Street were known as Gates. On the west side of the river a small group of houses clustered round the foot of the Mount, the ascent to Guildown, and on the Little Mount the ascent to the Portsmouth road ran south-westward past St. Nicholas's Church and up by the present Wiclyffe Buildings. On this side of the river lay the Town Fields, Bury Fields as they were called.[1] The continuation of High Street, outside the old town limits, was called Spital Street, from St. Thomas's Hospital at the junction of the London and Epsom roads. The part of the street from Trinity Church to the grammar school and beyond was called in the 18th century Duke Street, from a house of the Duke of Somerset's on the south side, which is still standing, but converted into two houses.

The old defensible town ditch ran, as the names indicate, from the Dominican Friary near the river along North Street (the North Ditch) and round to South Street (the South Ditch). It has been traced at the corner of Chertsey Street and right across Trinity Churchyard between these two lines. When Trinity

Church was enlarged in 1888, and graves were removed in consequence, the ditch was traced, with much mediaeval pottery in it.

It is possible that the oldest town was walled, and of yet smaller dimensions. A very thick ancient clunch wall, with a well on the south side of it, showing that to be the inside, ran about 30 yds. south of the High Street, nearly parallel to it. It has been laid bare under the late Mr. Mason's ironmongery shop in High Street, and elsewhere. It would have included St. Mary's Church and a small town, clustered under the castle mound. If this was so the High Street itself was originally a suburban extension, later included by the ditch.

The town has been extended by residential building along the London and Epsom roads to the east and north-east, along the Portsmouth road and on Guildown to the south-west beyond the river, on South Hill to the south, and northwards and north-westwards by business streets and small houses near the Guildford junction and London Road railway stations. A great part of these latter extensions, and those on the Epsom and London roads, are in Stoke parish.

The railway is now the chief industrial feature of Guildford, though breweries, an iron foundry, printing works, and motor works also exist, besides minor industries, including the sale of old furniture. The London and South Western Railway came to Guildford in 1845, and the extension to Godalming was sanctioned by Parliament the same year. In 1849 the South Eastern Railway came to Guildford, and in 1865 the London, Brighton, and South Coast Railway's Guildford to Horsham line was opened. In 1884 London Road station and the Guildford, Cobham, and Letherhead lines were opened.

Guildford probably began its history as a centre of traffic. The great way across the south of England by the chalk downs passed through it, and across the ford of the Wey. It is possible that a Roman road from the Sussex coast to Staines, traced farther south in Ewhurst, passed through the gap in the downs, and also a road from the Portsmouth direction. Some recent sewage works have revealed an ancient flint pavement in St. Catherine's on this line. The London and Portsmouth road of later times ran through it. The east and west road appears in many deeds as *Via regia*, and in the Pipe Roll of 1192–3[2] as *Strata regia de Geldedone*.

There is no certain trace of Roman occupation of Guildford, though some of the tiles built into the castle may be Roman, and a Roman villa has been

---

[1] The theory that the town originally stood on this side of the river is without foundation, and is contradicted by the name Bury Fields, by old maps marking the fields, and by the size of St. Nicholas's parish, a country not a town parish. Part of this parish, including the church of St. Nicholas, lies in Guildford, but that portion of it which is outside the old borough is in Godalming Hundred, and the general description of the parish has been treated there.

[2] Pipe R. 4 Ric. I, m. 8 d. This is the so-called Pilgrim's Way ; though there is no historical ground for applying the name in West Surrey. The road from village to village south of the downs was probably only a local road, not used for through traffic, and has even less right to the name.

found on Broad Street Common in the neighbourhood. It was a royal possession under Alfred, and is named in his will. It was the scene in 1036 of the arrest of the Etheling Alfred by Earl Godwine. Alfred had sailed from Wissant to the coast of Kent, and was travelling to Winchester to join his mother, Emma. His way was evidently the great east and west road on the chalk down s, and if Geoffrey Gaimar is correct he had passed through Guildford and was stopped on Guildown, and brought back into Guildford, where apparently the decimation of his followers was made. The castle is not mentioned in connexion with the story, as is erroneously asserted by many writers. The only building in Guildford which might possibly be contemporaneous with the event is the lower part of the tower of St. Mary's Church, which is Anglo-Saxon, but more likely of the reign of Edward the Confessor. Guildford was the seat of a mint under the Anglo-Saxon kings. Coins struck at Guildford of the kings Ethelred the Unready, Cnut, Hardicnut, Edward the Confessor, Harold, and William I, have been found.

The greater part of St. Nicholas was an extensive country parish on the outskirts of Guildford and was in Godalming Hundred (q.v.). The part outside the borough is called Artington as early as 1664.[8] The immediate vicinity of the west end of the bridge was, however, in Guildford borough from an unknown date, and may be the holding in Guildford of the church of Salisbury mentioned in the charter of Henry II.[4]

The village of Stoke has become a northern suburb of Guildford, and little remains to show what it was once like. West of the church is a small plain half-timber building with red brick filling, probably of 17th-century date. Except for this and one or two buildings of an even plainer nature the old buildings have been replaced by modern. The church is situated on the road to Woking, which forms the principal axis of the place, and is within the boundaries of Stoke Park. On the south, the road running north and south, Stoke merges imperceptibly into the streets of Guildford. The appearance of the village in the bottom of the valley of the Wey has a degree of picturesqueness unusual in so new a place, on account of the fine timber, and Stoke Park is also well wooded.

Except the castle, which will be noticed later, perhaps the most important building in Guildford from the archaeological point of view is *TRINITY HOSPITAL*, otherwise known as *ABBOT'S HOSPITAL*. It stands at the top of the High Street on the north side, on the site of an old inn, 'the White Horse.' It was founded by Archbishop Abbot, a native of Guildford, for decayed townsfolk. The hospital consists of four sides built about a courtyard and placed approximately to the four points of the compass. It is constructed of red brick with some rubbed and moulded work, and with dressings originally of chalk but now almost entirely replaced in stone. Accommodation is provided

ABBOT. *Gules a chevron between three pears or.*

for twelve brethren, ten sisters, the master, and a nurse, and there is a chapel, common rooms, offices, &c. The whole building is of early 17th-century date, and there have been no important structural alterations. The first stone was laid in 1619, and the hospital was incorporated as the Master and Brethren of the Hospital of the Blessed Trinity in Guildford in 1622. The statutes were completed in 1629. They are closely modelled on those of Whitgift's Hospital at Croydon. Whitgift had been brought up as a child in a monastery before the Dissolution,[6] and the foundation represents the post-Reformation evolution of the monastic ideal, at a time when only the old and infirm needed the shelter of an asylum. The foundation was for twelve brethren and eight sisters, over sixty years of age, unmarried, natives of Guildford or resident for twenty years. There was a master, also a native of Guildford or resident for twenty years, except in the case of a rector of Holy Trinity, who might be master without these qualifications. In the case of a vacancy an unmarried rector might take the office, otherwise the mastership was filled up by election by governors and the two elder brethren. If they failed to elect it lapsed to the archbishop, on his failure it went to the Bishop of Winchester, to the heirs of Sir George More of Loseley, and to the original electors successively. The endowment was increased by Mr. Thomas Jackman of Guildford in 1785. The original scheme of the archbishop included a further endowment for reviving manufactures in the town, and his brethren and sisters were to wear gowns of blue Guildford cloth. But the decaying cloth manufacture was not revived by the encouragement. By a decree in Chancery, 3 July 1656, the money was ordered to be distributed among poor tradesmen of the town. As this naturally had a bad result, the poor tradesmen in receipt of the outdoor relief living idly, another decree was obtained after Mr. Jackman's benefaction had been made, on 14 December 1785, whereby half only was to be used in this way, and the other half added to Mr. Jackman's gift to support four more poor sisters. The moiety still devoted to pauperizing was diverted in 1855 and added to the endowment of Thomas Baker's Blue Coat School, founded by him in 1579, which had been suspended for many years. The school was called Archbishop Abbot's School. It was formerly carried on in the tower of Holy Trinity Church, now in buildings in North Street. The corporate life of the hospital has much decayed. The inmates meet now only in chapel, but live in their own rooms. The common rooms are used for parish and other meetings. There are some pictures of no great merit ; a portrait of Archbishop Abbot is the most valuable, but there is also a curious view of Wotton House as it was in John Evelyn's lifetime, and of Leith Hill behind it with a semaphore upon it. The archbishop is said to have been the son of a poor clothier, and to have been born in a house near the bridge in St. Nicholas's parish.[6] His brother Robert became Bishop of Salisbury, his brother Maurice a knight and Lord Mayor. They were all educated at Guildford School. It is questionable, however, whether his father was in such a humble condition as is usually said. The archbishop's mother, Alice March, was daughter of a gentleman of coat-armour, and his

[8] In the first extant county rate.
[4] *Reg. of St. Osmund* (Rolls Ser.), i, 203.
[5] *Dict. Nat. Biog.*
[6] Parish registers of St. Nicholas contain his baptism.

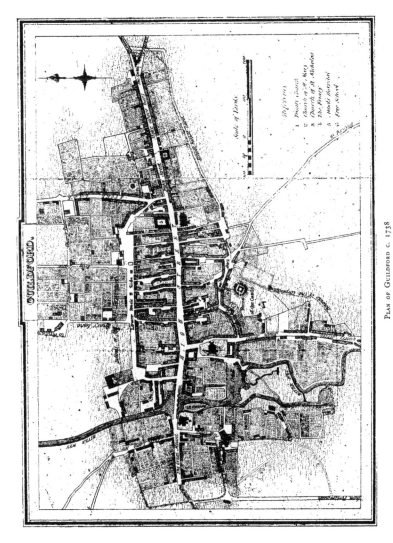

PLAN OF GUILDFORD C. 1738

(From Richardson's Survey)

GUILDFORD: ABBOT'S HOSPITAL, FRONT VIEW

two elder brothers, Richard and Antony, otherwise unknown to fame, married ladies of the same rank[7] before their younger brothers had become very eminent men. The main entrance wing of the hospital faces on to the High Street (south), and consists in elevation of a main wing with a central tower, set back from the street, flanked by two wings projecting to the street line. From the angles of the latter is carried a stone balustrade of 18th-century date, with an opening in the middle opposite the archway to the court

four small octagonal turrets, of which that to the north-west contains a stair to the upper floors and roof, while all are finished with lead-covered cupolas, and rise a stage above the tower. In the first floor is the large window of the board-room, of five mullioned and transomed lights, and above this the close-barred window of the treasury, of four rounded lights. The elevation of the tower to the courtyard is of a similar nature, but the arch is simpler in detail. The archway has a coved plaster ceiling, and large contemporary

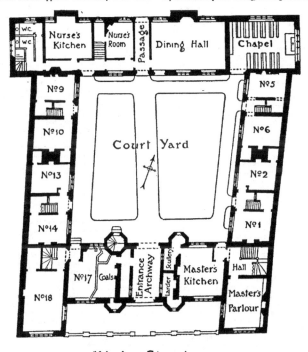

High Street

Scale of Feet

PLAN OF ABBOT'S HOSPITAL, GUILDFORD

which pierces the central tower. This archway is set in a complete pedestalled Doric order with fantastically rusticated pilasters and arch, and is apparently a complete restoration. Above this is a quartered shield of the royal arms of James I. On it is the inscription : 'These arms erected by S. Robinson, master 18(25).' At the angles of the tower are

doors elaborately panelled and with pierced heads. In the main and projecting wings are mullioned and transomed windows symmetrically placed in two stories, and in the curvilinear gables of the projecting wings are smaller untransomed windows to the attics with square-headed labels. The other windows are tied by string-courses. The board-room over the archway is panelled to the ceiling in early 17th-century oak, with fluted Doric pilasters on pedestals, two on each wall, and a modillioned moulded cornice. The fireplace is of chalk with a moulded straight-sided four-centred head, and has an elaborate mantel with carved figures and panel of 'strapwork' ranging with the panelling. A small door in the north-west corner of the room, opening on to the turret stairs, retains its original latch, lock, bolt, and hinges, while the main entrance door on the east is elaborately panelled, has a carved lunette, and retains its heavy strap-hinges and wood-cased lock. There is some very fine furniture in this room. The table, of early 17th-century date, has carved bulging baluster legs and an extension top. There are also a smaller circular gate-legged table of slightly later date, and two sets, each of eight, of Chippendale chairs, one with honeycomb-pattern backs. There are also some fine 17th-century chairs. In this room the Duke of Monmouth was confined on his way to London after Sedgemoor. West of the arch are lodgings and offices, while east of the arch are the master's apartments on two floors. The east and west wings contain the main provision for lodgings, the brethren being on the west, the sisters on the east. These two wings are of two stories with attic space in the roof lit from the north and south gables, and from gables in the centre of each wing on the courtyard side. The lodgings consist of single rooms with a small cupboard or pantry, and there is a simple closed staircase to each pair, reached from a door on to the courtyard, which also serves the ground-floor lodgings. These door-ways have solid oak frames moulded with a chamfer and an ogee. They are square-headed, and the mouldings are stopped with a moulded half-octagonal stop on a broad chamfer. There is no arch in the brickwork, the top of the frame forming a lintel. The doors themselves are of late 18th-century date and in two leaves, the staircases also belonging to this time. The internal doors to the individual lodgings, however, are original, and are made up of tongued and moulded battens. The windows are all stone-dressed and of three square-headed lights without labels, but in both floors tied by moulded strings. The gable windows are of two lights with a square-headed label. The walls are finished with tile copings and parapets. The north wing contains, on the east, the chapel, which is carried up two stories. Internally the chapel has been a good deal modernized, but retains its original open-oak seating, and an almsbox on a turned post. There are two windows, one to the east of five cinquefoiled lights with tracery over of pseudo-Gothic design, the other to the north of four cinquefoiled lights with a three-centred head. What at once strikes an observer is the disproportionate size of these windows for the small chapel. The east window cuts through an outer string-course, showing pretty clearly that windows of this size were an afterthought. They are filled with painted glass of two, and perhaps three, dates. In the upper parts of both is glass of Abbot's time, showing his arms and those of the sees which he held, of James I, Queen Anne of Denmark, and the Elector Palatine their son-in-law. In the lower part a portion only of the story of Jacob and Esau appears. Dr. Ducarel, writing more than a century after the time, says that Abbot got the windows from the Dominican Friary in Guildford. As some of this glass is apparently

Flemish glass of *circa* 1490–1500, it is possible that this is true, and that the remainder was made up as nearly as possible in the same style. The windows are evidently an afterthought, the subject is incomplete, the glass composite, and the verses under it not such as would be composed in England in the 17th century, when the old Latin hymn metres were quite disused. About the time that the chapel was being built the friary buildings were being finally demolished to build the Earl of Annandale's house. The door in the north-east corner of the court has raised and mitred panels with a fluted lunette, while in the corner of the square-headed moulded frame are carved spandrels, and there is a heavy moulded keyblock. West of the chapel is the former common dining-room, now used as a reading-room. It is completely panelled in early 17th-century panelling with butted mouldings and a dentilled and carved cornice. The top range of panels is carved in flat arabesques and the mantel is an enriched continuation of the panelling. The fireplace, a wide one, is of chalk, with a moulded straight-sided four-centred head and a raised brick hearth projecting in an oval. The crane and fire-dogs remain, and there are fire-irons, plate warmers, &c., of 17th and early 18th-century date. A fixed bench runs round the walls with a moulded nosing, baluster legs, and a foot rail. There is some good 17th-century furniture in the room, including a table with baluster legs and four-way feet and a carved panelled settle with a high back. There is an entrance from the court, and also a door from a passage which runs through the north wing from the court to the garden at the back of the hospital. Both of these doors are of similar detail to the chapel door. This passage has an archway at each end, of two orders of moulded rubbed brickwork, the inner semicircular, the outer square-headed. Opposite the door from the dining-hall is a similar one entering a passage leading to the kitchen, which is at the west end of the north wing, and a serving hatch. This passage is also entered from the north-west corner of the court, and gives on to a broad staircase of early 18th-century date with a heavy moulded hand-rail, turned balusters, and plain newels. This stair leads to a hall over the dining-hall somewhat similarly fitted, with a plain barrel-vaulted plaster ceiling, to the spring of which oak panelling is carried. The fireplace is of chalk and has an elaborate mantel, carved figures, enriched panels, &c. The entrance door from the landing is elaborately ornamented with small corbel columns and a moulded cornice. The north wing has a range of cellars under it, and shows to the north a picturesque gabled elevation with wide projecting chimney-breasts. The passage from the court leads to a wide double flight of steps to the garden, which is at a much lower level than the court, and runs down to North Street. In the garden at the south-east is a square brick summer-house with open round-headed arches on three sides. It has a hipped tiled roof and a heavy wooden cornice, and is of early 18th-century date. In the middle of the north side of the court is a stepped gable in which is a clock dated 1619, but apparently modern, and above and on each side of this are three terra-cotta panels with the arms of Canterbury, the initials G.A., and Archbishop Abbot's own coat. The chimney-stacks are good. They are of two designs, the simpler having square flues with

GUILDFORD : ABBOT'S HOSPITAL COURTYARD

chamfered angles and moulded heads. The more elaborate have octagonal flues, are richly moulded, and have angle spurs. On the street elevation are a couple of very fine rain-water heads of lead. Both have the arms of the see of Canterbury impaling those of Abbot and the initials G.C., and are ornamented with pierced cresting, while one bears the date 1627. This date and the same heraldry appears upon some of the rain-water heads in the court, where are also several plainer moulded heads.

The *TOWN HALL* stands on the north side of High Street and was erected by subscription in 1683, taking the place of an earlier building, which, as appears from the town books, was in existence in 1587-8, when it was enlarged and the garden behind it inclosed. When the new town hall was built, an old market-house in the street opposite to it was pulled down. The street front is of two stories, the ground floor being partly open to the road and being divided into three bays by wood posts with gates between. From each post spring two supporting brackets carved with grotesque human figures and foliage. The first floor projects over the pavement and has a balcony with ornamental iron railings. The front of this floor consists of three large windows and two side lights, all with square-leaded glass and ornamental iron fittings to the casements and separated by wooden Ionic pilasters. Above the windows are small moulded pediments· over which is a moulded cornice with carved modillions and egg-and-tongue ornament. This cornice also continues round the gable, which is cut short to form a base for an octagonal open-work turret with a balustrade. A large projecting clock dial attached to a long arm is a feature of the front of the building. It was made by John Aylward, who settled in Guildford at this time. The dial has a segmental pediment, and it is enriched with gilded carving. At the base is the date of the erection of the building. Additional support is given by five elaborate tie-rods. The striking bell is in the turret over the gable; the minute hand was added in 1828. The only room on the ground floor of any importance is the Court Room, which has its original open-timber roof. The walls have 18th-century panelling up to about 14 ft. The north window contains three panels of 17th-century glass, including royal coats and the ancient and modern arms of Guildford. In this room are hung full-length portraits of Charles II, James II, William III, and Mary II. The Council Chamber on the first floor is a large rectangular room, panelled from floor to ceiling. In one corner is a fireplace which was brought from Stoughton House in the neighbouring parish of Stoke. The iron grate has a cast ornament of vine and other foliage, around which is a stone mantel with figures of a man and a woman in scroll-work blocking, their feet appearing below the scroll-work. The frieze is carved to represent the four human temperaments, respectively labelled, *Sanguineus, Cholericus, Phlegmaticus,* and *Melancholicus.* The wood jambs beyond the stonework have tapering Ionic pilasters, and the overmantel has Corinthian pilasters and is divided into two panels. In the first is the quartered shield of Howard, Duke of Norfolk : (1) Howard, with the augmentation for Flodden ; (2) Thomas of Brotherton ; (3) Warenne ; (4) Fitz Alan. The second panel contains the Abbot arms. Near the top of the overmantel is a painting

of the arms of James II dated 1686, and the old and new arms of Guildford. In the room are hung portraits of James I (full length) and the Rt. Hon. Arthur Onslow. There is also a painting of 'Vice-Admiral Sir Richard Onslow receiving the Dutch flag after the Victory 1797' by J. Russell, R.A., which was presented in 1798. The corporation plate is interesting. The mayor's staff is dated 1563. The standard measures (gallon, bushel, quart, and pint) are of bronze, dated 1602. By Statute 11 Henry VII, cap. 4, Guildford is named as one of the county towns where standard measures are to be kept. The small silver mace dates probably from the same reign, though additions have been made to it. The great mace was presented by Henry Howard, afterwards Duke of Norfolk, in 1663; the mayor's gold chain by Arthur Onslow, high steward, in 1673.

The *GRAMMAR SCHOOL* is situated on the south side of the High Street. It is quadrangular in plan, having an inclosed court 36 ft. by 29 ft. 3 in., and dates from a little after the middle of the 16th century. The earliest portion is the south wing, two stories in height, which is largely built of brick, and as originally planned consisted of two long rooms each filling the whole of one floor and about 65 ft. long by 22 ft. wide. The three other wings were all added in the latter half of the 17th century, first the west wing containing the master's house, then the east wing with the usher's house, and finally the north wing with the completion of the present street front. The latter, however, before taking its present form, had consisted of a wooden bridge upon posts forming a means of communication between the master's and the usher's houses, and was built about the same time or a little after the latter. Finally, towards the end of the century, in order to form a library, this gallery was inclosed, a stone front was built connecting the ends of the east and west wings, which are also of stone, and an attic story was added. The ground floor of the south wing has been altered in modern times by the insertion of a partition at the west end to provide a drawing-room for the master's house. The remaining and greater portion of the ground floor is occupied by a classroom which largely retains its school fittings of the 18th century with the head master's and usher's desks. The class-room on the upper floor has an open roof with queen-post trusses, the tie-beams of which are moulded with a quarter roll. During the 18th century an attic story was inserted in the roof, the floor being carried on the tie-beams and dormers being inserted in the roof. This was used as a dormitory. This room has two chalk mantelpieces with moulded straight-sided four-centred arched openings with moulded stops at the jambs. Over this is a frieze of flutes alternating with circular plaques and a moulded cornice of semi-renaissance detail. The windows are all mullioned, with rounded heads, and of stone, while the walls are of brick. On the first floor is a small door with a four-centred head opening into the class-room from the usher's wing, with which it is contemporary. The main entrance to the class-room is from the court, where there is a small porch with a four-centred entrance and door. Rough arches have been cut in the flanking walls, and the whole porch is a good deal modernized. The head master's house retains little of interest except some plain chalk mantelpieces with straight-sided four-centred heads and some good late 16th-century panelling of a plain kind. The usher's wing retains its old beams, moulded with a quarter roll and an ogee. In this wing is a chained library, containing a considerable number of volumes, but the fittings are all new. The two wings last described are of three stories, the ground floor being somewhat lower than that of the south wing. The library wing is a rough-cast half-timber structure with a stone front, and the back wall is carried upon two heavy chamfered posts. The

windows. In the middle of the wall is a doorway to the court with a four-centred head and its original door of oak in small panels with a fluted lunette. Over the door is a carved stone panel with the royal arms and the inscription : ' Schola Regia Grammaticalis Edwardi Sexti.' Over this is the library window of six mullioned and transomed lights with a square label. The two side wings have had similar windows, but not transomed, and of four lights, on four stories. There are also two-light attic windows in the three gables. The gables have brick-coped parapets and small terra-cotta balls upon iron spikes as finials.

Besides the important buildings in the High Street just described there are many others of early 17th-century date, and even earlier. Several houses, however, were re-fronted about 1700. No. 25 is an interesting example of domestic architecture of the early part of the 17th century, remodelled at the end of the century, only the staircase and some panelling being left of the original work. The street front belonging to the later date has been much damaged by the insertion of a comparatively modern shop window, but above this is compiete. The two upper stories are treated with a single order of Doric pilasters set upon pedestals mainly in plaster, and with wood-framed mullioned and transomed windows. At the first-floor level is a simple iron balcony. The rear elevation is hung with tiles made in imitation of brickwork and set in mortar, after a fashion not uncommon in the south of England in this period. On the ground floor is a projecting bay, with rounded corners,[a] decorated with plaster-work. The front room of the ground floor is completely modernized and is occupied by a shop. This opens at the back into the staircase, and beyond this is a back room which is panelled

HIGH STREET, GUILDFORD

ground floor of this wing, originally intended to be open to the court, is now inclosed to form cloak-rooms, &c. On the court side of the library are two windows with ogee moulded jambs, heads, and wooden mullions which were discovered under the rough-cast during some recent repairs. The main front on the street consists of the gabled ends of the east and west wings and the wall connecting them, which is gabled in the centre and is of Bargate stone. The two side wings are buttressed and string-courses are run across the elevation and serve as labels to the

with oak in small butted panels of the earlier work. The ceiling is cut up by moulded and enriched ribs of late 17th-century date. The mantelpiece has been removed. The bay has wooden frames and iron casements with leaded glass in square panes. The staircase is of deal ; it is set in a square well and is divided into three short flights with two half landings between each floor. The newels are square, surmounted by enriched urns, and have carved pendants. The handrail is heavy, simply moulded, and is without ramps. In place of balusters there

Guildford Town Hall

Guildford Grammar School

are square and raked panels of elaborately carved and pierced acanthus scrolls. At the first-floor landing an entrance hall is arranged to the room over the shop. This ante-room is a part of the later work and is treated with arcading against the wall on one side and on to the stair well on another, where is also a range of turned and twisted balusters. The partition wall between this and the room is treated with large bolection-moulded panels. The fourth side retains the original window and iron casements. The furniture of these is extremely ingenious and is beautifully designed. It consists of a combination of a latch and a twisting bolt, the latter engaging with two pins in the sill and transom and drawing the casements tight.[9] The front room is entirely of the later date. It is beautifully panelled with large bolection-moulded panels. The ceiling is of richly modelled plaster and the mantelpiece is a simple continuation of the panelling. The windows are fitted with large double iron casements in wood frames with wood transoms and have leaded glass in large panes. Here again are similar but simpler bolt fasteners.

No. 140 has a good plastered front of late 17th-century date with two overhanging gabled bays. There are sash and casement windows, all in wood, and a good wooden cornice. No. 136 is of about the same date. It has a square projecting bay and a plaster coved cornice. The angles are quoined in plaster. No. 133 retains, in the main, its old front. It has three gables on the street front which overhang the first floor and have moulded barge-boards. No. 129 shows a very narrow elevation to the street, and is treated on its projecting and overhanging bay with a somewhat elaborate arrangement of plain superimposed orders inclosing the sash windows of the first and second floors. The front is in wood and plaster and is of late 17th-century date. Nos. 127 and 128 are perhaps a little later in date. The whole front is plastered with rustications, architraves, pediments, &c., of a purely classical type, and all in plaster. The cornice is fairly heavy and deeply coved. Nos. 40 and 41 are similar in style, but somewhat more elaborately rusticated. No. 125 and No. 121 both belong to the middle of the 17th century, but have been a good deal restored. The former has a large gable with deep modillioned eaves, and overhangs at the first and second floors. The front is plastered and the windows are casements. No. 121 has an overhanging bay with a wall ornament of square balustradings, all in wood and plaster. The old post office, No. 56, has a very picturesque front of two gables. At the first floor are two square projecting bays with hipped tile roofs, and between them, but on the second floor, is a circular projecting bay which ties the whole design together in a singularly happy manner. At the bottom of the hill is a house of mid-18th-century date. It is built of red and yellow brick and has flush sashes and a good modillioned cornice with a tiled roof set back from the crown mould.

On the road to the station and in Mount Street are a number of simple but picturesque cottages in half-timber, plastered and in some cases weather-boarded. There are also several others which have been refronted. In Bury Fields is a row of cottages

all a good deal restored, but retaining, in the majority of cases, their old iron casements and casement furniture. Adjoining these is a house with the remains of an elaborate early 17th-century doorway with small pilasters, lozenged rustications, fantastic capitals, and a moulded cornice.

In Quarry Street are a number of houses dating from the 17th century. Near St. Mary's Church is one of early 17th-century date, a good deal disfigured with stucco, with an overhanging gabled first floor on carved brackets of crude renaissance design. Farther south on the west side of the street is No. 6, dating from the end of the 17th century, with a panelled plaster front and some casement windows and a wood modillioned cornice. No. 5, a red brick building a little later in date than the last, has a good modillioned wood cornice. No. 19 and Millbrook House, opposite the castle arch, are much restored examples of 17th-century work with overhanging gables, &c.

Under a part of the Angel Hotel is a sub-vault, possibly of the 13th century, consisting of three double bays of plain pointed rib vaulting with circular columns with plain bases, no capitals, and chamfered ribs. It is about 32 ft. by 22 ft., and is entered from the north by a door with a pointed chamfered head. The archway from the street to the yard of the hotel retains some work of early 17th-century date. The beams over the archway are old but plain, and there is an elaborate door with fantastically rusticated Ionic pilasters in the half-timber walling. Almost exactly opposite, on the south side of the street, is a somewhat similar vault about 19 ft. 6 in. by 32 ft. 6 in. ; but having hollow-chamfered wall ribs, plain moulded bases of rather deep profile, and moulded bell capitals. Mr. Simon[10] has collected notices of the storage of wine in Guildford for the kings, Henry III in particular, who were frequently resident in the castle, and who received large dues of wine from Gascony ; and it is, on the whole, probable that the crypts were from the first, as now, wine cellars.

On the site of one of the lodges to the Royal Park, north of the station, at the end of Walnut Tree Close, is an old house of red brick, now divided into two cottages. It probably dates from the 17th century, and runs north and south, with a gabled wing crossing it in the middle of its length. The end gables have been refaced with modern brick and tiles. There is a small amount of old half-timber work on the east front and a modern projecting wing. The roofs are tiled.

The new gaol has now been removed from Guildford. The keep of the castle was the county gaol for Surrey and Sussex[11] from 1202, when 4s. were paid for the repair of the gaol in the castle, as late as December 1508,[12] when a deed records the agreement for the maintenance of prisoners, but apparently was not the county gaol under Elizabeth, as the Loseley papers make no reference to it as such, prisoners being then sent to the 'White Lion' and the Marshalsea in Southwark. In 1604 a new gaol was built in Quarry Street. It was rebuilt in 1765, and pulled down and rebuilt on a higher site on South Hill in 1822. The new prison was abolished in 1851, the prisoners being removed in April of that year to the newly built House of Correction at Wandsworth.

---

[9] See *V.C.H. Surr.* ii, 479.
[10] *Hist. of the Wine Trade in England.*

[11] The county gaol for Sussex was established in Lewes in 1487-8.

[12] *Surr. Arch. Coll.* xv, 157.

Kingston gaol was abolished at the same time.[13] Debtors used to be confined under the town hall, and in the building across the street where the Judges sat in circuit. An old print is extant of a man being hanged on a scaffold in the street there ; but the more usual place of execution was at Henley Grove on the slope of the Hog's Back, opposite the present hospital. The judges sat in this house or in a hall which had been part of the old Red Lion Inn in Market Street, bought and altered for this purpose by Lord Onslow and Lord Grantley in 1789.[14] On the site of part of the same old inn was the Cock Pit, and the theatre was close by. A bill of sale of 1744 records that the Cock Pit was let for 15 guineas for the race week. Opposite the town hall now is the Tuscan façade of the old Corn Market erected in 1818. It is not now used as the market (*vide infra*). Next to this is the old Three Tuns Inn, a fine house with three gables. Among modern buildings is the Royal Surrey County Hospital on the west side of the river. It was built in 1866 as a memorial to the late Prince Consort. Adjoining the hospital are Hilliers' Almshouses, originally founded in 1800 by Elizabeth Hillier in Shoreditch for seven women, and enlarged by Nathaniel Hillier of Stoke Park, Guildford, in 1812, for eight women. The almshouses were removed from Curtain Road, Shoreditch, to Guildford in 1879. The Isolation Hospital between the South Eastern and South Western Railway lines, in Woodbridge, was founded in 1886. The County and Borough Hall in North Street, where the Assizes are held, was built in 1845. The public baths in Castle Street were opened in 1889.

The cemetery, on the end of the Hog's Back, was consecrated in 1856. Close by it is Booker's Tower ; a tower built for the view from the top of it by one Charles Booker. It is the property of the corporation.

The old bridge, of five arches, was of stone and very narrow. A ford crossed the river by the south side of it. It was repaired with brickwork, and the central arch was rebuilt to admit the passage of barges on the making of the Godalming Navigation in 1760. In 1825 the bridge was widened by iron arches and balustrades, which probably weakened the original structure from which they projected. In 1900 a great flood washed large quantities of timber out of Messrs. Moons' timber yard above the bridge. This blocked the narrow arches and the bridge collapsed entirely. A new iron bridge was built about two years later. Fortunately in 1882 an iron bridge had been built lower down near the railway station. The foot-bridge at the foot of Quarry Hill, built by subscription, was opened 25 August 1909.

The King's Mills must from their description as ' in the parishes of St. Mary and St. Nicholas ' have stood across the river very near the present mills. Before 1256-7 they were removed to a place below the bridge, next Guildford Park, to the great injury of the joint-holders of the manor of Artington, and of Richard Testard who had mills near St. Nicholas's Church and in St. Mary's parish opposite, respectively. The result of the complaints made was that ulti-mately the mills were removed back to their previous site.[15] The Artington Mill has disappeared, leaving its name in Mill Mead. The other mills were employed for fulling besides grinding corn, and the fulling mill was in St. Mary's parish, as appears from the parish registers. In 1701 waterworks were set up in the fulling mill for the supply of the town from the river.[16] The waterworks are still employed to pump the water of the Guildford Waterworks. The mills were rebuilt in 1766.

Among buildings which have disappeared from Guildford was the Spital, or St. Thomas's Hospital. It stood in the angle between the Epsom and London roads, and a small ancient building was in existence when Manning wrote, but a sketch by John Russell, R.A., in 1791, exhibits no architectural features. A prior or master appears in the Court Rolls of Stoke Manor, to the lord of which he paid 6d. a year, but in 1491 it belonged to the manor of Poyle (q.v.). It does not appear to have been suppressed under Edward VI. A single cripple, dignified by the title of prior, was nominated to it by the magistrates up to the 18th century.[17]

The Dominican Friary has been treated under the section of Religious Houses. It has left its name in Friary Street and in Friary Ward. The precincts of the Friars are still strictly extra-parochial. The house of the Friars, after being leased by the Crown to various holders, was partly pulled down in 1606 by Sir George More, who carried away the materials by leave of George Austen, to whom he had sold his rights.[18] This was possibly to build the wing which Sir George added to Loseley. The site was granted in fee-simple to the Earl of Annandale in 1630.[19] He had a new house built by Inigo Jones. After various alterations this was changed into barracks in 1794 and pulled down in 1818.

The Trinity and St. Mary's National Schools were founded in 1814 and enlarged at various dates down to 1905. The St. Nicholas Boys' and Girls' Schools (National) in the Portsmouth Road were built in 1851, the Infants' School in 1860, and the Ludlow Road School (mixed) in 1890.

The Congregational and the Wesleyan Methodist chapels are in North Street, and there is an old Baptist chapel in Castle Street. The Friends' Meeting House and Unitarian chapel are in Ward Street on the borders of Guildford and the parish of Stoke. Land was bought for a Friends' Meeting House as far back as 1673. The Nonconformists were strong in Guildford from 1662, and there is a well-attested tradition[20] of Bunyan preaching just outside the borough. An Independent chapel was built of wood in Black Horse Lane soon after the Toleration Act of 1689, but had no settled minister till 1704.[21] The old Baptist chapel was called Charcoal Barn Chapel, for it was on the site of a town storehouse of charcoal where the congregation formerly met.

THE CASTLE Guildford Castle is of the mount and bailey type of castle, belonging perhaps to the era of the Conquest. The whole area covered by the castle works is about

[13] Information from the son of the last gaoler.

[14] Manning and Bray, *Hist. of Surr.* i, 32.

[15] Inq. p.m. 7 Edw. I, no. 73.

[16] Manning and Bray, op. cit. i, 33.

[17] Speed's mention of Crutched Friars at Guildford, sometimes connected with this hospital, is not supported by other evidence.

[18] Loseley MSS. iii, fol. 4a.

[19] Pat. 6 Chas. I pt. viii, m. 2.

[20] In the family of Mr. Williamson, an old Nonconformist family, a member of which was arrested under the Conventicle Act in 1683. The late Mr. David Williamson kindly supplied the editor with most of the information upon the Nonconformist bodies, and other valuable facts.

[21] Church Bks.

GUILDFORD : OLD HOUSE IN

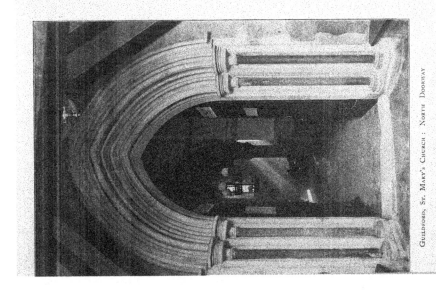

GUILDFORD, ST. MARY'S CHURCH : NORTH DOORWAY

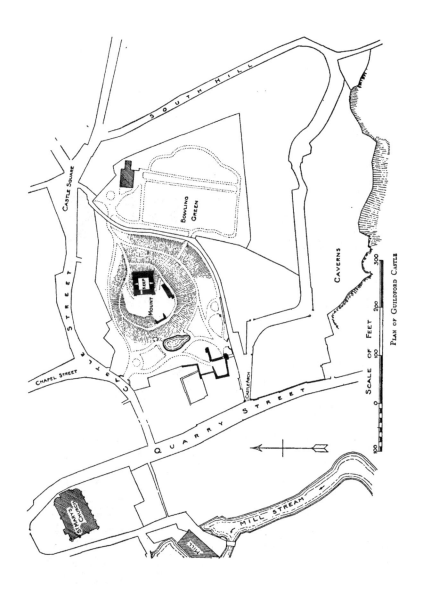

PLAN OF GUILDFORD CASTLE

SCALE OF FEET

SOUTH HILL

CASTLE SQUARE

CASTLE STREET

CHAPEL STREET

CASTLE

BOWLING GREEN

MOUNT

CAVERNS

CASTLE ARCH

QUARRY STREET

ST MARY'S CHURCH

MILL

MILL STREAM

6 acres. The mound is about 90 ft. across at the top and about 200 ft. across the base, while its height is about 30 ft. from the ditch to the east, as it now is, or about 40 ft. from the lower ground to the west. It was made by cutting a ditch through a spur of the chalk hill and piling the débris upon the west end of the spur.

The outworks of the castle reached to what is now called Quarry Hill House in Quarry Street. Close to this are the remains of a sally port. The outer walls continued round by the south and south-east and east, inclosing the present bowling-green. The limits are marked by the boundary of the extra-parochial precincts. The curving line of Castle Street marks the outer walls to the north. On the west it· is probable that an outer ward included Quarry Street, abutting upon the steep declivity above the river. By the steps which lead up here from the river to Quarry Street is the jamb of an ancient stone doorway. At the south-west angle, by Quarry Hill House, it is obvious that the castle ditch, now occupied by a greenhouse, has been abruptly broken off by the street crossing it. It ran across the street, no doubt, so that this way into Guildford came through the outer ward of the castle.

The principal building now on the castle site is a square keep of early 12th-century date, near which are a few remains of a shell keep of earlier date,[22] an artificial mound on which these stand, and fragments of the outer buildings, some of which are possibly a part of the hall, and are, so far as they can be dated, of about the same period as the keep. The entrance from Quarry Street is through a mediaeval gateway known as the Castle Arch, adjoining which on the north side is a building also in part of mediaeval date, but much altered in the 17th century, and now used as the head quarters of the Surrey Archaeological Society. On the higher ground to the east of it are considerable remains of 12th and 13th-century building, unfortunately too fragmentary to be identified, but doubtless representing the palace of which so many details are preserved in the documents quoted.

The keep consists of an approximately square structure about 42 ft. each way, and is set a little west of north, and at the east of the top of the mound. It is built of Bargate stone rubble in thin slabs with some flint rubble as a core, and externally irregularly placed bands of herring-bone work in Bargate stone, some bands of scappled flints, and a certain amount of ashlar mainly in Bargate stone but with a little chalk. The lower part of the east wall has been repaired in modern times.

Externally the four faces are broken by broad angle and central pilaster buttresses running the whole height of the keep. The angle buttresses appear to have been carried slightly higher than the rest of the wall, while over the north-west angle was a turret over the vice. The doors and windows were all originally quoined with dressed Bargate stone, which in some cases has been replaced by brickwork, apparently in the 17th century. On the north and east of the tower the ground falls away rather rapidly, and the pilaster ˙buttresses spring from a battered plinth faced in part with ashlar. The original access to the mound was under the north side of the keep, and on the face of the latter the remains of the spring of an arch which spanned the entrance are

visible. The tower was originally divided into four stories, but the lowest one has been filled in nearly up to the level of the floor, the beam-holes of which remain. This, with the present ground floor, formed a basement, the main entrance being on the first floor. The foundations of the east wall of the keep are on the natural ground at the foot of the mound ; those of the other three walls, which terminate with an interior set-off, are in the artificial mound.

The ground floor is entered by a rough opening made at a recent date in the west wall. There are two windows, one in the north and one in the south walls, both of which have round heads with internal splays and semicircular rear arches which are sloped up from inside to outside. The walls are of rough rubble in flint and Bargate stone with a carefully laid inside facing of thin stones which in places has been hacked away. Portions of the plaster

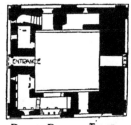

PLAN OF PRINCIPAL FLOOR

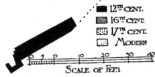

■ 12ᵀᴴ CENT.
▤ 16ᵀᴴ CENT.
▨ 17ᵀᴴ CENT.
▢ MODERN

SCALE OF FEET

PLAN OF GUILDFORD CASTLE KEEP

adhere to the south wall. In the north wall is. cut a rough fireplace, a flue for which has been contrived in the thickness of the wall.

The entrance, on the west, has a very slightly pointed door of two orders, the outer of which is flush with the face of the pilaster buttress on this side. The door leads into a passage with parallel sides through the thickness of the wall, and is faced with wide jointed ashlar which shows diagonal tooling. It has a rough pointed barrel-vault. South of this is the door to a wall chamber, all the worked stones of which have been picked out. North of it is a small round-headed door to a chamber in the thickness of the wall. The north and south walls are offset at this level for the wood floor which once existed. In the middle of the north wall is an opening with a segmental head, the jambs of which are much cut about, which opens into a long narrow barrel-vaulted chamber or passage in the

²² 'Shell Keep of Guildford Castle,' Surr. Arch. Coll. xvi.

GUILDFORD CASTLE

GUILDFORD CASTLE : KEEP, EXTERIOR

thickness of the wall, lit by a single loophole. West of this is a round-headed opening with dressed jambs and head slightly chamfered. This forms the rear arch to a window of two round-headed lights set in a round-headed outer order. The mullion, presumably a column, is missing. The splay is carried to the floor level, and forms a vestibule to a vice in the north-west angle of the keep, the door to which is in the west internal jamb of the window. This door is very much defaced and the steps of the vice are gone. The wall internally retains in patches a facing of diagonally-tooled ashlar in square blocks. In the middle of the east wall on this floor is a deep window splay retaining a few ashlar quoins, but externally restored in brickwork, apparently of 17th-century date. This wall contains no chambers, as it forms part of the line of defence. In the south wall, but to the east of the centre, is a similar window which retains most of its ashlar work and is unrestored. The dividing column, however, is gone. In the west part of the wall is a segmental-headed opening to a small wall-chamber, probably the chapel, which is entered through an ante-chamber, probably the ante-chapel, in the thickness of the west wall. The round-headed door of the ante-chamber, of two orders, retains little more than its rough opening. The ante-chamber is 14 ft. 2 in. long and 5 ft. wide, and has on the west a wall arcade of four bays with rounded engaged columns with scalloped and palmette capitals and moulded base approximating to the Attic type and semicircular arches of one slightly chamfered order. In the northernmost bay is a small round-headed original window. The ante-chapel is vaulted with an obtuse pointed barrel-vault of rubble which has been plastered and has at its spring a chamfered string. The angles of the room are ashlared, and the whole arcade with its wall spaces is of carefully wrought chalk masonry, while the end wall and the east wall are of rubble and have been plastered.

The chapel, which is in the thickness of the south wall, is really an extension at right angles to the other chamber, and had, originally, a continuation of the arcade carried along its south or exterior wall; but of this little remains except one column and capital imbedded in a later partition wall at the west end of the chapel, while west of this are traces of two more bays. From these it would appear that the arcade was originally of six bays. Two capitals of similar detail to those in the ante-chapel remain. At the east end of the chapel is a block of rubble, the remains of a stone bench, and at the south-east is a small square recess partly blocked. There are two windows on the south, that to the east is of three mullioned lights with square heads and is a 17th-century insertion and responsible for the destruction of part of the arcade; the wide opening opposite to it is of the same date, and meant to transmit the light to the interior of the keep. The defaced window to the west appears to have been original and similar to that in the ante-chapel. The chapel is vaulted in the same way as the ante-chapel, the two vaults intersecting, but at the east end is a half-vault at right angles to the main ceiling and very clumsily connected up with it. On the arcade of the ante-chapel are a

number of scratched designs, mainly of mediaeval date. Amongst other subjects are representations of St. Christopher, the Crucifixion, and a seated king and queen.

The top floor of the keep originally contained four two-light windows, one in each wall, of which little remains now but the splays, the windows themselves having been replaced in stone. There is also on the north a segmental-headed recess which, turning at right angles, leads to the vice, and east of this are traces of a brick-backed fireplace, probably part of the 17th-century domestic repairs,[22a] while at the south-east is a round-headed opening to a small garderobe in the thickness of the wall with a double corbelled shoot.

South and west of the keep and below the crest of the mound are two fragments of walling, apparently part of the earlier polygonal shell keep. The former of these is very fragmentary, but the latter is still some height above ground, and has at the west the remains of two garderobe shoots, one above the other. The other end appears to have been connected up with the east side of the square keep, into which it has been incorporated. Both these fragments are of chalk. Buck's view, dated 1737, shows these walls as remaining to a height of at least two stories, while at the north-west of the mound is a suggestion of further remains of which only foundations now remain.

No documentary evidence exists regarding the history of the castle till the 12th century. It was one of the many castles set in order at the time of the 'young king's' rebellion in 1173-4, some £26 being then expended upon it.[33] In 1202 it is mentioned as a prison, but nothing is known of the building until 1246, when a hall and chamber for the use of the Sheriffs of Surrey were built on the mound[34] (mota). Four years later, in 1250, orders were given to repair the wall of the castle with columus and underpinning, to whitewash it and the keep (turris), and to repair the lead on the keep.[35] Further whitewashing and repairs were done to the keep and the walls of the bailey in 1256,[36] and next year a kitchen was built and the gaol repaired,[37] while in 1268 a further £20 was spent on the keep.[38] In 1293 the kitchen was repaired, the gaol cleaned out and 36 pairs of fetters (firgii) provided; one of the gates was rebuilt, tables were fixed in the hall and repairs done to a solar and the castle bridge.[39] Almost the only other reference to be noted occurs in 1360, when a large stone was set under the door of the chapel in the keep, and a small window in the chapel was strengthened with iron bars for the safer custody of prisoners.[30]

South-east of the keep and sheltered by the outer wall of the castle was the royal palace, of whose buildings more traces remain in records than in ruins. During the latter half of the reign of Henry III references to its fabric are numerous. In 1243 a door was made at the end of the hall, between the pantry and buttery, leading to the kitchen, and the windows on the west of the royal dais were glazed; a fireplace was also put into the larder so that the building could be used as the queen's garderobe

22a The 17th-century repairs were due, no doubt, to Mr. Carter when he received the castle from James I and lived in it (see below).

33 Pipe R. 20 Hen. II.
34 Liberate R. (Chan.), 31 Hen. III.
35 Ibid. 35 Hen. III.
36 Ibid. 41 Hen. III.

37 Ibid. 42 Hen. III.
38 Ibid. 53 Hen. III.
39 Exch. K. R. Accts. bdle. 492, no. 10.
30 Ibid. bdle. 493, no. 6.

when she came there.[31] In 1245 the sheriff was ordered to build a room for the use of Edward, the king's son, to be 50 ft. long and 26 ft. broad, stretching along the wall towards the field to the corner of the wall towards the kitchen, and in breadth from the wall towards the field towards the almonry ; the upper part of the building to be for the king's son and the lower for the pages-in-waiting (*vadiettorum nobilium*), with barred windows, a fireplace, and a privy chamber in each room. Also, under the east wall opposite the east part of the king's hall a pentice with fireplace and privy chamber was to be made for the queen's garderobe. In the queen's chamber the existing window was to be replaced by one as much broader as could be set between the two walls and as high as reasonably possible, with two marble columns, between which were to be glass windows with a panel that could be opened, the upper part of the window boarded, and the whole provided with wooden shutters ; at the same time the upper window at the west end of the hall by the dais was glazed with white glass with the image of a king seated on one side and a queen on the other.[32] A porch was built in front of the door of the hall in 1247,[33] and in 1250 the pillars (*postes*) of the hall were restored and underpinned with Reigate stone ; at the same time the roofs of the steward's room (*dispensatoria*) and buttery were mended and a new window made in each, the roof-ridge (*cumulum*) of the royal chamber was raised 5 ft. and the walls also raised to allow of the insertion of three windows like the new window in the same chamber. The passage between the hall and the chamber was to be boarded and given a plaster ceiling (*desuper terrari*) and the wainscoted bedrooms were to be painted green. The low garderobe (*bassa warderoba*) of my lord Edward's bedroom was to be wainscoted and a stone vault (*vouta*) made in it ' in which our chests and relics can be placed ' ; the wall between that bedroom and the almonry was to be coped (*crestetur*), and the wall outside the king's bedchamber was to be thrown down and rebuilt 15 ft. away from the same chamber, the space between being used for a garden (*herbarium*). A window was to be made in the small garderobe near the gate, and the high window in the queen's garderobe was to be glazed. A new lattice (*laticium*) was to be made in front of the chapel of St. Stephen, and in the chapel of St. Katherine the figure of the saint and scenes from her life were to be painted behind the altar ' suitably, without gold or blue ' (*honeste absque auro et azuro*) and the wall round the chapel to be rebuilt.[34]

Not long after this there was evidently a fire at the palace, as in 1253 orders were given to mend the gutters of the burnt hall that the walls might not be injured, and to support the part of the hall roof which had not been burnt, so that it should not be dangerous. The burnt portion of the hall was to be pulled down.[35] Rebuilding seems to have proceeded slowly, as in November 1255 the king stated that he

would be at Guildford for the Feast of the Circumcision (1 January), and as the buildings were not yet ready he ordered greater dispatch to be made with them.[36] In January 1256,[37] accordingly, King Henry being at Guildford gave instructions as to the royal chapel, the queen's chapel, and certain chambers newly built, and ordered the porch of the hall to be built of stone, the story of Dives and Lazarus to be painted in the hall opposite his seat, and ' a certain image with beasts ' to be made on the said seat ; the chamber of the chaplains was also to be lengthened.[38] Later in the year the sheriff was told to have the hall whitewashed inside and out, the pillars and arches marbled (*marbrari*), the two gables pointed, the great chamber whitewashed and marked out in squares (*quarellari*) and its ceiling painted green, spangled (*extencellari*) with gold and silver. A porch (*oriolum*) was to be made in front of the door of the hall and a cloister with marble columns in the garden.[39] Next year a stone gateway was to be made and over it a solar 32 ft. ' within the walls ' and 18 ft. broad, with a garderobe. In the chancellor's chamber the fireplace was to be moved further north, the screen (*halder*) of the chamber was also to be moved and put elsewhere, and the chamber whitewashed and boarded behind the chancellor's bed. Four glass windows were to be put into the gable of the hall and a pentice to be made between the chaplain's chamber and the kitchen.[40] The latter was again ordered next year, as well as another pentice from the king's son's chamber to the kitchen and a small building for warming up (*calefaciendum*) the queen's food. A stable was to be built between the hall and the kitchen, also a saucery (*saltaria*) and larder under one roof, and a wood-lodge. The queen's chapel and her chamber were to be paved and the outer and inner doors of the chamber under the oriel to be blocked and a new door made from that chamber into the king's garderobe.[41] In 1260 orders were given to pave the cloister and make two doors and a bench therein, and also to put two glass windows in the pentice near the queen's lawn (*pratellum*).[42] Next year, in january, when the king was again at Guildford, he ordered the great window of the hall over against the royal seat to be glazed, a wooden sperre (*espurrum*) to be made at the head of the table in the hall towards the entrance into the royal chamber, and figures of St. Edward and of St. John, holding the ring in his hand, to be painted there. The same figures were also to be painted on the wall by the king's seat in his chapel, and an image of the Blessed Mary was to be made and placed in the queen's chapel.[43] In 1267 several rooms were built ; one chamber with a settle (*stadium*), fireplace, garderobe, and vestibule, and a chapel at the end of the same chambers with glass windows, for the use of Eleanor wife of Edward the king's son, and another chamber with settle, fireplace, garderobe, and vestibule, for the use of the knights of Queen Eleanor.[44] At the same time the queen's garden (*herbarium*) was set in order under the direction of William Florentyn, the king's painter, who

[31] Liberate R. (Chan.), 28 Hen. III, m. 2.
[32] Ibid. 30 Hen. III, m. 17.
[33] Ibid. 32 Hen. III, m. 8.
[34] Ibid. 35 Hen. III, m. 3.
[35] Ibid. 38 Hen. III, m. 3.
[36] Ibid. 40 Hen. III, m. 7.

[37] Ibid. m. 16.
[38] The wages, 50s. yearly, of the two chaplains (of St. Katherine and St. Stephen) at the castle and of a third at the leper hospital of St. Thomas outside the town occur regularly about this time : e.g. ibid. 33 Hen. III, m. 2.

[39] Ibid. 40 Hen. III, m. 10.
[40] Ibid. 41 Hen. III, m. 12.
[41] Ibid. 42 Hen. III, m. 4.
[42] Ibid. 44 Hen. III, m. 3.
[43] Ibid. 45 Hen. III, m. 14, 13.
[44] Ibid. 52 Hen. III, m. 11.

BOROUGH OF GUILDFORD

was at this time in charge of the works at Guildford, where he had been employed some eight years earlier in touching up the paintings in the hall and chapel.[45]

After the death of Henry III Guildford seems to have been rather neglected, and by 1333 the buildings of the palace were in a very bad state, every room, apparently, requiring some repairs.[46] A survey made in that year, giving an estimate of the cost of repairs, mentions the following buildings as needing repairs: the 'Frereschaumbre,' with garderobe ; the wall between the same chamber and the great chapel ; one aisle of the great chapel ; the king's hall ; a chamber between the great chapel and the king's great chamber ; the king's chamber, with garderobe ; the foundations of the garderobe of the same great chamber adjoining the castle ; the queen's chamber ; the chamber of the damsels (*puellarum*), which 'below the lead' required a new fireplace and 'above the lead' a rail with posts and laths; the chapel of St. Katherine ; the chamber of the Earl of Chester (afterwards the Black Prince), with garderobe and the nursery (*camera Noricerye*) ; a cloister ; a party wall from the king's great chamber to the small gate by the Earl of Chester's garderobe and the garden by the cloister; a room over the great gate, with garderobe ; the queen's garderobe by the great gate ; the 'Aumerye' with garderobe and another chamber adjoining ; the Earl of Cornwall's chamber with cellar and garderobe ; the treasurer's chamber, called Queen's Hall, with cellar, containing a fireplace with a double vent (*cum dupplici tuello*) ; the king's great garderobe by the water pit ; the larder ; the royal kitchen ; a wall between the king's kitchen and the 'Frereschaumbre.' This evidently completes the circuit of the buildings ; then are mentioned the palings between the garden and the castle ; a piece of the mantle wall round the chapel 52 ft. in length, 20 ft. high, and about 10 ft. thick at the base ; the rest of the mantle wall round the castle, which lacked buttresses and was weak at the foundation ; the palings upon the king's ditch between the castle (*sic*), and gutters, lead, &c., with two louvres (*fumerelli*) over the hall. Edward I, his son ai. .d grandson, and Edward IV and Richard III were all at Guildford in the course of their reigns, either in the castle or in the manor-house in the park, probably the former. In 1337 Robert of Artois was to be lodged in the king's house in the castle,[47] and to be allowed to hunt in the park.

In 1611 the castle was granted to Francis Carter.[48] The initials of his grandson, John Carter, 1699, used to stand above the arch of the entrance.

The stone is now in the Archaeological Society's museum. The place was not regarded as a fortress during the Civil Wars, and Manning and Bray[49] preserve a tradition that the keep had been dismantled and the roof taken away about 1630.[49a] A parliamentary survey was taken in 1650 as of the late king's lands, Mr. John Carter's title being doubted. From it we find that the dismantled keep had been used as a cock-pit. The only habitable house, containing a handsome hall, a large parlour, kitchen, buttery and cellar, with three chambers and two garrets above stairs, was that now used for the Surrey Archaeological Society's museum and library, with the caretaker's cottage and its adjacent cottage. The hall

GUILDFORD CASTLE FROM THE SOUTH-WEST

is now cut up into rooms in the middle of the house. The parlour and the upper chamber over it contain good Jacobean fire-places. John, son of the John Carter of 1650, put up additional buildings at the back of these. His initials and those of Elizabeth his wife, and the date 1672 or 1675, are upon them. The site remained in the possession of the descendants of Francis Carter in the female line till 1813, when Mr. Thomas Matchwick sold it to the Duke of Norfolk. His successor sold it to Lord Grantley c. 1842, from whose successor it was bought by the corporation in 1886 and laid out as at present, in gardens.

[45] Liberate R. (Chan.), 44 Hen. III, m. 11.

[46] Exch. K. R. Accts. bdle. 492, no. 23.

[47] Pat. 11 Edw. III, pt. i, m. 9.

[48] Pat. 9 Jas. I, pt. iii, m. 5.

[49] Hist. of Surr. i, 13.

[49a] See Cal. S. P. Dom. 1625–6, p. 474. It seems that the keep must have been dismantled by that year.

Underneath the castle and in the hill south of it are very extensive galleries in the chalk, known as the Caverns. A large cave of about 45 ft. by 20 ft. and 9 ft. high leads to these passages, which run as far as 120 ft. in different directions horizontally. They are quarries, whence the street is named, from which the harder strata of chalk were excavated for the castle and other early buildings. A perpendicular shaft has been sunk into them at one place which, by the discolouring of the chalk, seems to have been a cess-pit,[50] probably in connexion with the gaol above.

The origin of the borough of BOROUGH Guildford is somewhat obscure. There is little in the Domesday[51] account to suggest that it had attained the status of a borough at that time ; but the fact of its containing ' seventy-five closes wherein dwelt one hundred and seventy-five homagers' is sufficient to show that it was already a place of considerable importance. The town also possessed the characteristic often found in mediaeval boroughs of including houses which, for purposes of jurisdiction and the like, formed part of manors outside the walls.[52] The word ' burgum' was not used by the Commissioners in their description of Guildford, although it is found in other parts of the Survey ; and instead of being above the king's land, where the boroughs of the county were usually placed,[53] it merely forms the first item in that section. In the Burghal Hidage attributed to the 10th century a borough seems to be placed at Eashing, ' Mid-Eschingum' (compare Alfred's will, ' at Æscengum'),[54] and its importance may have passed to Guildford, unless this clearly tribal name be taken to have then covered the country as far as Guildford.

Before 1130, however, Guildford had asserted its right to the name of borough, for in that year the sheriff made account for 100s. ' de auxilio burgi de Geldeford.'[55] This sum continued fairly constant throughout the reign of Henry II,[56] rising in 1165 to 160s. odd,[57] and occasionally to 10 marks.[58] In the reign of John it was tallaged once for 30 marks,[59] and on another occasion for 35 marks.[60] It is a sign of the growth of the town that there were Jews here in 1187.[61]

The first recorded charter to Guildford occurs in 1257, when Henry III granted to the 'good men of Guildford' that they and their goods ' should be free from arrest for debt' with certain conditions.[62] In the same year they also gained the privilege of having

the county court always held in Guildford.[63] The probi homines of Guildford evidently already existed as a corporate body, for the charter to Kingston of 1256 grants to that town a gild merchant ' to be held as the Probi Homines of Guildford hold it.'[64] In 1340 Edward III inspected their charter[65] and made them further concessions ;[66] they also obtained a second charter from him in 1346.[67]

The year 1367 marked a distinct epoch in the history of the town, for at that time the burgesses were granted the right of holding their town at fee farm.[68] In the year before they had petitioned for an inquiry into the profits received by John Brocas, who had formerly farmed the town as the king's deputy.[69] At the same time the king confirmed the gild merchant according to the ancient custom and according to the custom of Winchester.[70] Henry VI in 1423 inspected and confirmed the charters of his predecessors, including one of Richard II.[71] Probably the latter refers to Richard's renewal of the Guildford charters[72] which had been burnt at the time of Wat Tyler's rising.[73] A charter of incorporation was granted by Henry VII in 1488, the style being the ' mayor and good men of Guildford.'[74] The charters were confirmed at the same time ; and they were again confirmed by Elizabeth in 1580, including one granted by Henry VIII and one by Edward VI.[75]

In 1603 the corporation petitioned the king to the effect that the late queen had agreed that the mayor, the late mayor for one year, and two others of the corporation, and a fifth person skilled in the law, should be Justices for the borough, but died before her intention could be fulfilled. The petition was granted in consideration of the importance of the road through the town leading to Portsmouth and Chichester.[76] By another petition, in 1626, the mayor and burgesses requested a renewal of their charters, and also that the demolished Castle and the districts of Stoke-above-Bars and Stoke Lanes might be included in the borough.[77] Those districts were apparently the resort of bad characters,[78] who made use of separate justice to the prejudice of the king's town of Guildford.[79] In the next year Charles I confirmed the former charters and granted the extension of jurisdiction,[80] which, however, seems never to have taken effect.[81] In 1686 the mayor and good men of the town surrendered their former charters to James II, and received a new one,[82] which was annulled by the proclamation of 1688. From this date until the

[50] Major-Gen. E. R. James, The Guildford Caverns (Guildford, 1871).
[51] V.C.H. Surr. i, 295a.
[52] Ibid. See also Maitland, Domesday Bk. and Beyond, 179 et seq. ; Engl. Hist. Rev. Jan. 1896, p. 17.
[53] Maitland, Domesday Bk. and Beyond, 179 et seq.
[54] Ibid. 188, 503. N.B.—On p. 188 Prof. Maitland overlooked a misprint of Eastling for Eashing.
[55] Mag. Rot. Scac. 31 Hen. I (Rec. Com.) 52. See also a writ of c. 1130 directed to the burgesses of Guildford (Add. Chart. 19572).
[56] Gt. Roll of the Pipe, 2–4 Hen. II (Rec. Com.), 12, 94 ; Pipe R. Soc. Publ. v, 47 ; xiii, 168; xv, 163; xvi, 145; xviii, 142, &c.
[57] Ibid. viii, 111.
[58] Ibid. i, 156 ; xix, 95.
[59] Pipe R. 12 John, m. 15.

[60] Ibid. 16 John, m. 3 d.
[61] Ibid. 33 Hen. II, m. 3 d.
[62] Cal. Chart. R. 1226–57, p. 456.
[63] Ibid. It was no doubt already usually held there, in spite of the complaint (Assize Roll, 873, 43 Hen. III) that Letherhead was the old place. A charter of Hen. II to the Bishop of Salisbury (Registers of St. Osmund [Rolls Ser.], i, 238) refers to the county court at Guildford.
[64] Confirmed Pat. 17 Edw. IV, pt. i, m. 42. For the connexion between gild merchant and corporation, see Pollock and Maitland, Hist. Engl. Law, i, 669 et seq.
[65] Chart. R. 14 Edw. III, m. 1.
[66] A fair. See below.
[67] Chart. R. 20 Edw. III, m. 3, no. 7.
[68] Ibid. 39–40 Edw. III, no. 157; also Orig. R. 41 Edw. III, m. 31.
[69] Chan. Inq. p.m. 40 Edw. III (1st nos.), no. 59.

[70] Chart. R. 39–40 Edw. III, m. 2, no. 2 ; Orig. R. 41 Edw. III, m. 1.
[71] Cal. Pat. 1422–9, p. 158.
[72] Parl. R. iii, 646.
[73] Ibid.
[74] Conf. R. 4 Hen. VII, pt. ii, no. 16.
[75] Ibid. 19–33 Eliz. pt. i, no. 7.
[76] The Letters Patent are copied in the Town Books, and are countersigned "Ellesmere," who was Lord Chancellor 24 July 1603.
[77] Cal. S.P. Dom. 1625–6, p. 474.
[78] Unless ' malefactores' be used merely in its original sense ; ' ubi malefactores lacetant et confugiunt ' (Pat. 3 Chas. I, pt. xxxvii, no. 3).
[79] Pat. 3 Chas. I, pt. xxxvii, no. 3.
[80] Ibid.
[81] Parl. Papers, Rep. on Munic. Corp. 1835, p. 2871 et seq.
[82] Pat. 2 Jas. II, pt. vi.

Municipal Corporation Act of 1835 the borough was governed under the charter of Charles I.[83]

The borough is now divided into six wards. The corporation, since 1904; has consisted of the mayor, six aldermen, and eighteen councillors. The Earl of Onslow is high steward, and there is a recorder. The boundaries of the borough were enlarged in 1835, and again in 1904, on the latter occasion the aldermen were increased from four to six, and the councillors from twelve to eighteen.

A book containing the minutes of the gild meetings has fortunately been preserved; and the entries in it offer abundant proof touching the importance of this institution. The Close Rolls of 1324[84] and 1352[85] contain writs directing in one case the bailiffs and in the other the mayor and bailiffs to furnish the members of Parliament with their expenses. The payment in 1361 was voted at a meeting of the gild merchant.[86] Probably the absorption of civic functions by the gild tended to produce two courts, with separate meetings, but identical functions.[87] The regular meetings of the *Gilda mercatoria* were on the Mondays after Hilary and Michaelmas, respectively. The 'Great Law Day' or borough court was on Monday after Hoke Tide, but the former meetings are also called law days. The business was certainly of the same kind. Thus in 1537 the meeting of the gild enacted certain sanitary regulations [88] with regard to the kennels of the inhabitants, which may be compared to another entry made at the meeting of the law day in 1529: 'The mayor commandeth in the King's name that victuals brought into the market be good and lawful and wholesome. That no common poulterer buy any victuals in the market before eleven of the clock. That no baker buy any corn before eleven of the clock. That every man sell by lawful weights and measures, and that they be assized by the King's standard. That butchers bring the skins of their beasts and sheep to the market and shew the same openly during all the market. That the bakers bake good bread and according to assize. That the brewers make good and wholesome ale, and that they sell none till it be tasted by the ale-taster. That

they sell a gallon of the best ale for 1½d., and of stale ale for 2d. That the tipplers sell by lawful measure and set out their ale signs.[89]

The social aspect of gild life seems to have been accorded somewhat undue prominence at Guildford. Members were elected on the Monday after Hilary to provide a bull for baiting on the Monday after St. Martin, subject to a penalty of 20s. each in default.[90] The expenditure for some of the feasts is given. In 1364 the brethren paid for bread 5d., ale 13s. 6d., meat 3s. 11d., wine 8d., spices 3s. 6d., wafers 3s., garlic 2d.[91]

HOUSE OPPOSITE ST. NICHOLAS'S CHURCH, GUILDFORD

The local record of the courts breaks off in 1738, and is resumed in 1761.

In 1661 the corporation feasted Charles II, and presented him with a piece of plate at the cost of £140, of which £100 was borrowed. On the other hand the Puritan régime in corporations manifested

[83] *Parl. Papers* (1835), xxvi, 2, 71 et seq.

[84] *Cal. Close*, 1323–7, p. 160

[85] Ibid. 1349–54, p. 469

[86] Printed in Gross, *Gild Merchant*, ii, 94. It is remarkable that the members'

expenses were reduced from 20d. to 12d. *per diem* in the course of one decade.

[87] Mr. Gross says, with reference to the later history: 'It is difficult to detect any difference between the two courts, the

same kind of business being apparently transacted at both.' Op. cit. p. 106.

[88] Add. MSS. 6177, fol. 201 d. [89] Ibid.

[90] Law Day, Monday after Hilary, 6 Hen. VIII; Add. MS. 6167, fol. 199 d.

[91] Gross, *Gild Merchant*, ii, 96.

itself in Guildford by the expulsion of Thomas Smalpece from the corporation for his 'contempt and disordered behaviour' (Court Monday after Michaelmas, 3 Jas. I). His offence, we learn from a letter at Loseley, was 'going about to set up' a maypole. The corporation was severe against foreigners trading in the town ; in 1521 they were excluded altogether from the markets, except victuallers, graziers, and sellers of oats at the discretion of the mayor. At the same time clothiers were forbidden to send any wool to be spun into yarn within 8 miles of Guildford unless under a bond that it should be brought back to be woven in Guildford. The number of 'approved freemen' subsequently dwindled, and in 1654 was only 159, but others were admitted to trade in the markets on payment. The token coinage in Guildford is of the dates 1652 to 1669 and 1765 to 1797. The latter issue often has a wool-pack on it, though the wool trade of Guildford was long dead.[91a]

There seems to be no definite mention of town officials before the 14th century. In 1368 the election is noted of a seneschal, two farthing men, a clerk, two butlers (*pincernae*), who superintended the arrangements for the feast, and two hall wardens.[92] The earlier charters (q.v.) are directed to the good men of the town. The style of incorporation in 1488 was the 'mayor and good men,'[93] but the name mayor had probably superseded that of seneschal long before. The government of the unreformed corporation was entrusted to a steward, mayor, recorder, two Justices, bailiff, four coroners, town clerk, hall warden, two serjeants-at-mace, and a beadle.[94] The property of the corporation in 1834 consisted of the old town hall with a dwelling-place attached, a new market house or court house with a small garden and stable, tolls and fines, sundry small quit-rents and other payments, with the appointment of the master of the grammar school.[95]

A court of pie-powder was held at Guildford in the Middle Ages at the time of the fair.[96] A court of record was held every third Monday, but was much fallen into disuse in 1835.[97]

The borough was represented by two members in the Parliament of 1295.[98] There is no record of members for 1299, but with one or two other exceptions it was constantly represented by two members. In 1654 and 1656, in the reformed Parliaments elected under the Instrument of Government, Guildford had one member. The franchise till 1832 was in the freemen and the freeholders paying scot and lot, if resident. These did not number more than 150 in the 19th century. In 1867, by the Redistribution Act of that year, the number of its representatives was reduced to one.[99] By the Act of 1885 the borough became for the first time part of the county for electoral purposes.

A fair in Guildford was granted by Edward III in 1340 to be held during five days, beginning on the eve of Trinity.[100] Some seven years later the date was changed to Whitsuntide, owing to the fact that the men of Guildford did not derive so much profit as they ought, because so many neighbouring fairs were held at Trinity.[101] This fair is now held on 4 May, and is for cattle ; another, also for cattle, is held on 22 November, both formerly in North Street, but now in the new market.

The markets[102] used to be held in the High Street, and the parts to be occupied by various dealers are clearly defined in the corporation orders of Elizabeth's time. Thence they were removed to North Street, except the corn market, which was held in a building in the High Street, built in 1818.[103] A new cattle market was built in 1896 off the Woodbridge Road. The cattle market is on Tuesdays, the vegetable market, in the same place, on Saturdays. The corn market, also held on Tuesdays, was removed to the same neighbourhood in 1902. One-third of the tolls of Guildford, according to the custom of English boroughs, was the right of the Earls of Surrey and continuously passed to them.[104] The other two-thirds belonged first to the Crown and then to the borough, but many people, including the Bishop of Salisbury,[105] and the Archbishop of Canterbury and the Prior of Christchurch,[106] claimed to be free of them. In 1835 the mayor farmed the tolls of the town for the annual payment of £150.[107] They were declared to produce from £170 to £200.[108]

The manor of GUILDFORD was Crown property at the time of the Conquest[109] and throughout the Middle Ages.[110] It was assigned as dower to Eleanor mother of Edward I,[111] and also to his second wife Margaret.[112] The grant of the vill at fee farm to the

ELEANOR of Provence.
Or four pales gules.

MARGARET of France.
Azure powdered with
fleurs de lis or.

'probi homines' in 1369 evidently included the manor. The park was however reserved and is treated under Artington (q.v.).

The manor of POYLE in Guildford is said to have originated in a grant of land made by William the Conqueror to Robert Testard.[112a] Robert Testard's

[91a] Boyne, *Tokens* ; Williamson's Coll. ; see also *Surr. Arch. Coll.* iii ; R. Whitbourne, *Surrey Mints* ; and G. C. Williamson, *Trade Tokens of Surrey*, x.
[92] Gross, *Gild Merchant*, ii, 97. The seneschal was the custodian of the town charters ; ibid. 101.
[93] Conf. R. 19–23 Eliz. pt. i, no. 7.
[94] *Parl. Papers* (1835), xxvi. See under Guildford. [95] Ibid.
[96] Chan. Inq. p.m. 40 Edw. III (1st nos.), no. 59.
[97] *Parl. Papers* (1835), xxvi, Guildford.
[98] Ibid. (1878), lxii.
[99] 30 & 31 Vict. cap. 102.
[100] Chart. R. 14 Edw. III, no. 1.
[101] Ibid. 20 Edw. III, no. 7.
[102] A market is mentioned in 1276. See Chan. Inq. p.m. 4 Edw. I, no. 90.
[103] The corn market was under the old market house, which stood across the street. This was pulled down in 1683, and the market was held under the present town hall till 1818.
[104] See Dorking and Reigate, which were part of the earl's possessions.
[105] *Plac. de Quo Warr.* (Rec. Com.), 741.
[106] Chan. Inq. p.m. 4 Edw. I, no. 90.
[107] *Parl. Papers, Rep. on Munic. Corp.* (1835), xxvi, 2871 et seq. [108] Ibid.
[109] *V.C.H. Surr.* i, 295.
[110] *Cal. Pat.* 1272–81, p. 71 ; 1292–1301, p. 342, &c.
[111] Ibid. 1292–1301, p. 452.
[112] Pat. 27 Edw. I, m. 4.
[112a] *Testa de Nevill* (Rec. Com.), 225 ; and see *V.C.H. Surr.* i, 295 for houses in Guildford held separately from the body of the place.

heir was entrusted to the custody of Ralph de Broc by King Henry III.[113]   Richard Testard was holding at the time of the *Testa de Nevill*.[114]   A list of tenants holding land of him is given.   In 1254 Thomas de la Puille held a serjeancy in Guildford by grant from Richard Testard[115]; this had formerly been held by the service of looking after the washerwomen of the king's court, but at this date was held by annual rent of 25s., and was valued at 100s.[116]   In 1299 Walter de la Poyle died seized of what was then definitely styled the manor of Poyle.[117]   The inquisition taken

POYLE. *Gules a saltire argent in a border argent with roundels azure thereon.*

GAYNESFORD. *Argent a chevron gules between three running greyhounds sable with golden collars.*

at his death seems to justify the identification of this manor with the entire holding of the Testard family, for several of the families given here are represented in the earlier list of tenants.[118]

From this date the manor followed the descent of Poyle in Tongham for some years.   In 1410 John de la Poyle conveyed the reversion after his death to Robert Warner, John Gaynesford, and others.[119]   John de la Poyle died in 1423.[120]   In 1437–8 Richard Wakeryng, clerk, conveyed Poyle in Guildford, &c. (not Tongham), to Robert Warner and his heirs, John Gaynesford and John his son.[121]   Robert Warner died seised of it in 1439.   There were then two corn-mills and two fulling-mills under one roof in the manor, view of frankpledge and court baron.[122]   John Gaynesford was heir of Robert Warner.   The Gaynesford family held it 1491, when Richard Battenor, clerk, acquired it by common recovery from John Gaynesford and Alice his wife.[123]   The lands were then as before in Guildford, Stoke, Chiddingfold, and Slyfield, and the patronage of the hospital of St. Thomas at Guildford was included.   Thereafter there is a long gap.   In 1595 John Eversfield died in possession.[124] In 1624 the widow of his son Sir Thomas, and Sir Thomas her son, conveyed it to Harry Smith, and he in 1627 settled it on trustees for his well-known charitable foundation.[125]

In the time of Symmes (*circa* 1670) the court leet and court baron were still held.[126]

CHURCHES   The church of *ST. MARY* consists of a chancel, central tower, north chapel and south chapel with apsidal ends flanking the tower and half the chancel, nave, north and south aisles, and north porch.[127]

The tower alone survives from the church of the 11th century, which probably consisted only of chancel and western tower.   There is no trace of an early nave, but one may have existed.   The north and south transepts were added about 1120.   About twenty years later the chancel was rebuilt on a larger scale and, forty to fifty years later still, narrow aisles were added, and the nave was added or rebuilt if already existing, and the two chapels added, their width being governed by the earlier transepts.

Early in the 13th century the passages between the chapels and the sanctuary may have been cut.   The stair-turret between the chancel and the south chapel was probably built at the same time.   About the same date the vaulting of the chancel was made, the unequal width of the east and west bays being governed by the earlier side arches.

About 1260 the side walls of the aisles were brought out to the line of the chapel walls, and wider arches were inserted between the aisles and the chapels.

In the 14th century a large number of windows were inserted; and possibly at the same time the floor line of the church was altered from an east-to-west slope to an easier slope, with flights of steps leading to the chapels and chancel.

The 15th-century alterations include some of the windows and the re-roofing of the church throughout. Modern restoration is responsible for the refacing of the whole church, except the tower and the east end, and the replacing of almost all the exterior stonework of the windows.

The chancel has a 15th-century east window of five cinquefoiled lights with tracery over, in a four-centred head.   Below the window on the interior is a scroll-moulded string.   On the north and south are to be seen the eastern jambs and part of the heads of two early 12th-century lights, blocked by the building of the chapel apses.   The openings of the skew passages from the chapels are between these and the east wall.   That on the north has a pointed arch at the north end and is roughly rounded at the chancel end.   The proximity of the vice narrows the southern skew passage, which is pointed throughout.   The north chapel opens to the chancel by an arch with responds which have been flattened to receive a wooden screen.   The capitals are scalloped, and the abaci grooved and chamfered.   The pointed arch is of a simple square order with a grooved and chamfered label on each face.   The corresponding arch on the south has square jambs with small engaged half-round shafts, having moulded bases and moulded bell capitals with grooved and hollow-chamfered abaci The arch is two-centred. A small round-headed squint from the western half of the south chapel pierces the west jamb and part of the shaft.

The chancel vault is of two bays, the eastern being about 2 ft. narrower than the western; the transverse arch is of a single order, with edge rolls spring-

113 *Testa de Nevill* (Rec. Com.), 225.
114 Ibid. 228.
115 Richard Testard granted lands in Guildford to Thomas de la Poyle in 1252 (Feet of F. Surr. 37 Hen. III, no. 37).
116 Assize R. 872, m. 24 d.
117 Chan. Inq. p.m. 27 Edw. I, no. 44.
118 e.g. Fairchild, Gomme, Gerard, Gilbert Marshall in the *Testa* and John Fitz

Gilbert Marshall in the *Inquisitio*. The state of the inquisition makes it difficult to identify a large number of names.
119 Close, 2 Hen. VI, m. 10.
120 Chan. Inq. p.m. 2 Hen. VI, no. 26; *Cal. Pat.* 1422–9, p. 164.
121 Feet of F. Surr. 16 Hen. VI, no. 215.
122 Chan. Inq. p.m. 17 Hen. VI, no. 12.
123 De Banco R. East. 6 Hen. VII, m. 152.

124 Manning and Bray, *Surr.* i, 17.
125 Smith's Char. D.
126 Add. MS. 6167, fol. 189.
127 Dimensions : Chancel, 23 ft. 5 in. by 16 ft. 6 in.; tower, 12 ft. 10 in. by 14 ft. 4 in.; north chapel, 26 ft. 8 in. by 15 ft. 9 in.; south chapel, 26 ft. 8 in. by 17 ft. 11 in.; nave, 46 ft. 4 in. by 17 ft. 4 in.; north aisle, 14 ft. 9 in. wide; south aisle 17 ft. 10 in. wide.

ing from attached wall shafts which rise from the floor of the chancel. These are formed of three shafts, the middle one keeled, with moulded bases and plain bell capitals with moulded abaci. The main rib against the east wall is carried on pairs of shafts of a similar type with two shafts supported on pointed corbels. The ribs at the western end are also carried on corbels. The diagonals have a hollow chamfer between two rolls, the hollow in those of the western bay being filled with dog-tooth ornament. The chancel arch is pointed. The north and south tower arches are round, with chamfered labels on the sides toward the chapels. Each of these arches cuts into a double-splayed 11th-century window above, that on the north side being almost in the middle of the wall, and that on the south, east of the middle. On the outer face of either wall are four pilaster strips of flint masonry, the middle pair of each being interrupted by the archways. The western archway is

string-course runs round the apse below the windows, broken by the first three-light window and dropped below the other.

The apse of the south chapel, St. Mary's Chapel, is lighted by two lancet windows—restored outside—the east lancet is original, and the south shows a 13th-century heightening. The head of a third appears above the round-headed doorway to the vice in the angle of the apse with the chancel. The vaulting of this apse is of similar detail to the other, but the three bays are equal in size. On the south side of the apse is a small 14th-century piscina, now much damaged; it has an ogee trefoiled head, a projecting half-round basin, and an intermediate shelf; below the windows is a half-round string-course, continuing along the south wall to the west arch of the chapel.

The two south windows of the chapel are modernized outside, but were probably inserted in the 14th century. Each is of three trefoiled lights under a square head. Below the first window is a modern doorway.

The nave has an arcade of four bays on either side; the pillars are circular. The responds are half-round, as are also the jambs of the archway from the nave to the tower. All the capitals, including those to the tower arch — but excepting the middle one of the north arcade — are square, and carved with scallop ornament enriched in various manners, some having spirals at the angles and others nail-head or tooth ornament; the abaci are grooved and hollow chamfered. The middle capital on the north side has been mutilated by being cut back in order, it is said, to enable an occupant of the former west gallery in the north aisle to see

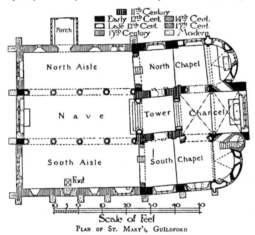

Scale of Feet

PLAN OF ST. MARY'S, GUILDFORD

contemporary with the arcades of the nave, and will be described with them.

The apse of the north chapel has three windows. That to the south is an original lancet; the middle one is of three lights, and the northern of two lights; both are of 14th-century date. The arch at the entrance of the apse is pointed, of a single order, with roll edges. The south jamb has been cut away, and the arch springs on that side from a plain corbel supporting a grooved and hollow-chamfered abacus similar to that of the north jamb, which runs to the ground.

The early 14th-century north window next to the apse is of three ogee lights, cinquefoiled and having quatrefoils over, in a square head. Opposite the east face of the tower the wall thickens from 2 ft. 8 in. to 3 ft. 2 in., giving evidence of the earlier transept. In this wall is a mid-14th-century window similar to that just described. The tracery is restored. Both these windows have wooden lintels. A half-round

the pulpit from his seat; it is now moulded and of round plan; the corners of the arches have been chamfered off also to find a seating. The arches are all pointed and of a single order with a small keeled edge roll towards the nave and a small hollow chamfer on the other side; the label on the east side of the tower arch is chamfered; that on the west side, and those on either side of each arcade, are grooved and hollow chamfered. Over the north jamb of the tower arch is a late 15th-century doorway to the rood-loft from the tower; it was evidently approached by a wood stair or ladder in the tower.

The west doorway, which is restored throughout, has jambs of two chamfered orders and a two-centred arch; the rear arch has a double-ogee mould, which is old. The window over is all modern excepting the inner stones of the jambs and arch; it is of five uncusped lights under a traceried head; the jambs are moulded inside and out with a wide hollow.

The archway from the north aisle to the chapel

GUILDFORD : ANGEL HOTEL CRYPT

GUILDFORD, ST. MARY'S CHURCH : NORTH CHAPEL

has semi-octagonal jambs with modern bases and moulded bell capitals ; the detail of the north capital is earlier than that of the south capital ; the arch is pointed and of two chamfered orders. In the gable above the arch is a lancet window (with its rear arch to the east) which formerly helped to light the chapel before the aisle was widened. The easternmost window of the aisle is a 14th-century insertion, but wholly restored outside ; it has three trefoiled lights with quatrefoils above in a two-centred arch ; below it is a square aumbry rebated all round. The second window is a wide lancet with widely splayed inner jambs ; this also is restored outside. The north doorway is a fine one of the 13th century ; the jambs are of three orders with Sussex marble shafts in the angles ; the shafts have double roll bases and moulded bell capitals ; the arch is moulded with a series of rolls and hollows ; of the two principal rolls one is triple filleted and the other keeled, and the label is also moulded ; in the jambs inside are two small sinkings for draw-bars. The wood porch protecting the doorway is modern. The third light in the north wall resembles the second. Below the windows is a round string-course, which is interrupted by the three-light window, but continues over the doorway. The west window is old inside and restored outside ; it is of three trefoiled lights with tracery. Below it a small plain square window, now all modernized, the use of which is said to have been to hold a light to guide travellers across the ford of the River Wey, from which it is little more than 200 yds. distant. It is not, however, opposite the ford. The archway between the south aisle and chapel differs from the corresponding arch on the other side ; it has half-round jambs with modern bases and moulded capitals ; the arch is of two chamfered orders. Over it is a lancet window which lighted the chapel. North of the arch in the east respond of the arcade is a small mutilated piscina with a square basin in a square recess ; probably it dates from the 13th century and may have been set here when the 14th-century piscina in the south wall was inserted. The latter piscina is now much mutilated, but was originally a fine example ; it is semi-hexagonal in plan and vaulted; it was formerly moulded and crocketed on the face, but this is now all cut away. The first south window, above this piscina, is modern outside like the rest in this wall, but has old quoins and moulded rear arch ; it was probably a late 14th-century insertion of three trefoiled lights under a square head. The other three windows are wide lancets with old inner jambstones and splayed rear arches. Below the third window is a blocked doorway of which only the segmental rear arch and inner jambs are visible. An early 18th-century plan shows a porch outside it. The west window of the aisle is of four ogee trefoiled lights under a head filled with net tracery ; the inside jambstones and arch are the only old ones remaining. Below, and to the south of this window outside, is a curious niche with a cinquefoiled head ; its jambs are skewed to the north.

The whole of the exterior of the walling (excepting that of the tower and the east wall, which is of chalk) has been encased with flint, and all the buttresses are modern except one ; the south wall has been strengthened by seven buttresses and the west by four ; the north wall has a buttress at the west end and one rebutting the cross arch, both modernized ; against the entrance to the chapel apse is a small original

buttress in which is a stone carved with a panel having a feathered trefoiled head ; probably it formed the back of a lamp niche and had a bracket.

The tower, built of rough flint, can be seen above the roofs on all four sides ; the shallow 11th-century pilasters, two on the west face but four on each of the others, are all of rough flints ; a few tiles have been mixed with the flint-work. The chamber immediately above the church is lighted only by a small modern window on the north side and is approached through the space above the chancel vaulting from the east vice. The bell-chamber is lighted by six windows ; of the two in the north wall the east and lower has a trefoiled and square modern head and partly restored jambs, the west and higher is a lancet, modernized outside ; on the east side is a large modern lancet, on the west side is an old lancet, and on the south a long narrow lancet and a trefoiled light. The former has an older half-round rear arch evidently belonging to a former and much wider window. At a line roughly about 5 ft. below the parapet string-course the walling is later and composed of flint and stone ; the string is modern, as also is the embattled parapet.

Above the chancel vaulting is a gabled wood roof covered with tiles. The two chapels have open-timbered gabled roofs which appear to be old ; the rafters lean over considerably to the west. The nave roof is also open-timbered with collar-beam trusses. The space below the tower has a modern flat wood ceiling. The aisle roofs are both gabled and open-timbered ; they have moulded tie-beams with traceried spandrels to the struts below them. These trusses are supported on curiously carved stone corbels, all of late 15th-century date; one (in the north-east corner) shows a grotesque beast gnawing a bone. The corbel over the re-cut north capital is plain and apparently modern. All the roofs are tiled.

The altar table is a light one of polished mahogany with square fluted legs and fluted rails.

The font is entirely modern ; it has a square bowl of clunch with scalloped under-edge, resting on a chamfered square stem and four small stone shafts with scalloped capitals and moulded bases.

The pulpit is a modern one of stone and marble ; it replaced a 19th-century stone pulpit, the successor of one of 17th-century date, abolished because of its extreme decay.

Forming a part of the organ-case, in the south chapel, are the remains of a late 15th-century screen, part of which formerly closed off the apse of the south chapel and formed the backing to an altar ; there are eight bays, of which two have plain depressed three-centred arches and another a four-centred arch with trefoiled spandrels ; these three evidently formed doorways on either side of the altar and to the stair. The other five heads are cinquefoiled ogees and have plain tracery over. The posts between are double hollow-chamfered and have buttresses with moulded offsets ; the cornice is also moulded.

On the vault of the apse of the north chapel are a series of 12th-century paintings. The upper portion of the series contains a version of the favourite mediaeval subject, the 'Doom' or 'Last judgement.' In the centre is a 'Majesty' or figure of Christ seated in Judgement within a vesica-shaped aureole ; on the right hand of Christ is St. Michael with outstretched wings, holding the balance, one scale of which a winged demon is endeavouring to depress, while a figure between the two scales, representing the soul whose merits and offences are being weighed, turns towards St. Michael for help. On the left stands an angel who has driven out the condemned souls, which are being carried off by a demon to the fires of hell, seen below. The great interest of this series, however, lies in its lower portion, which consists of six round medallions.[198] These may be divided into two sets, three to the right of the 'Majesty' (the north) and three to the left (the south). The three on the right relate to the history of St. John the Evangelist, in whose honour this chapel was probably dedicated.[199] Reading from the centre outwards, the first of these shows a man of hideous aspect with a pitchfork holding the saint down in a large tub, evidently the vessel of boiling oil into which he was cast by command of Domitian. Only the head and shoulders of the saint are visible, and his joined hands pointing towards a seated figure of Christ, who extends His right hand in benediction. On the knees of the seated Christ, resting his head against His shoulders, is the sleeping figure of St. John as 'the disciple who leaned upon jesus' breast' at the Last Supper.[200] The second medallion of this series shows St. John at Ephesus. In the centre the apostle is shown raising to his lips the cup of poison, which he drank unharmed, while in front of him are the bodies of two men who died from the effects of the same poison and were afterwards raised to life by the apostle's cloak being cast upon them. On the left of the picture is a seated, cross-legged figure holding a staff of office, either the proconsul or the priest of Diana, both of whom were concerned in the trial and converted as a result of the miracle. On the right of the picture is a figure seated on a chair before a lectern on which is a book in which he is writing, holding in his left hand the knife used by the scribes for erasing purposes; this is evidently St. john as evangelist. The third medallion, again, contains two subjects. On the right the apostle extends his hands in benediction over three rods and a number of stones. Mr. Waller identified this as part of the miracle of St. John and 'Crato the philosopher.' In this legend certain young men having been persuaded by St. John to sell their jewels and other possessions and give the price to the poor, repented having so done; the apostle then took certain rods and stones and converted them into gold and gems of miraculous purity, bidding the young men choose between these and heavenly riches. The remaining portion of the medallion is taken up with another miracle. The saint is shown standing beside a square altar, upon which is a cup or chalice; his right hand is extended in benediction over a figure lying in front of the altar with joined hands; over the saint is the Hand of God, in benediction, issuing from clouds. This, Mr. Waller suggests, represents the raising of Drusiana, a lady of Ephesus, who, ardently desiring to see St. john, died just before his arrival in the city and was by him restored to life.

Of the second or left-hand series of medallions, the middle one shows a king with crown and sceptre, seated cross-legged upon a throne, pronouncing sentence upon a bearded prisoner, who is led by a rope round his neck by a hideous gaoler; on the right a still more hideous executioner is shown striking off the same prisoner's head. This is no doubt, as Mr. Waller suggests, St. John the Baptist and King Herod. In the next medallion Christ is seen standing with right hand stretched in benediction over a font, from which issue the head, shoulders, and joined hands of a man with a pronouncedly jewish nose; on the right the same man is shown committing a parchment with two seals to the flames (shown as alternate wavy streaks of red and white).[201] This shows, no doubt, the conversion of a usurer. In the last medallion we again see Christ standing; at His feet kneels an adoring figure, over whose head are two demons of unintentionally humorous aspect; behind these is a figure with its hands tied behind its back, being pulled forward by two more demons by a rope round its neck; a man with a sword, evidently in charge of the bound figure, appears to be accusing his prisoner to Christ, whose left hand is raised in admonition. The most probable explanation seems to be that the prisoner is the 'woman taken in adultery,' while the kneeling figure may possibly be Mary Magdalene, 'out of whom He had cast seven devils.'

The explanation of the whole series seems to be that, instead of the usual representation of the blessed souls of the righteous on the right hand of the 'Majesty' and the tormented souls of the wicked on the left hand, the artist portrayed on the right three scenes from the life of St. john, the patron of the chapel, as typical of good works, and on the left three scenes relating to the vices of Anger, Usury or Greed, and Lust.

The church contains no ancient monuments, but standing in the nave is a stone slab on which are the small brass figures of a man and woman in early 16th-century dress; this is said to have been dug up in the roadway east of the church, and no doubt had been previously removed therefrom. The man has long hair and wears a long cloak with fur collar and loose sleeves, and from his belt is suspended a purse; the lady has a tight bodice, loose skirt, long belt, and long head-dress. The only other stone of note is a slab lying in the south chapel, near the organ, to one Zelotes Parson, son of Nicholas Parson, who died in 1673 aged ninety-four years and two months. There are six bells, all cast by Lester and Pack in 1754.

The communion plate comprises a silver flagon and a large paten, both of 1829, a small chalice and stand paten of 1881, and a small thin circular concave plate without a date-letter, but stamped with the head of George III. There are also four pewter plates.

The registers begin in 1540; the second book contains baptisms, marriages, and burials arranged in columns from 1653 to 1699. On loose sheets at the end is a list of those not baptized; the third contains baptisms, marriages, and burials from 1689 to 1753, and the baptisms and burials to 1812; the fourth has marriages from 1754 to 1812.

The churchyard falls from east to west and surrounds the building, but lies chiefly to the north and south, at the east and west being mere passage-ways.

[198] Drawn and described by Mr. J. G. Waller, F.S.A., *Archaeologia*, xlix, 199–212.
[199] *A* chapel of St. John occurs in a will of 1547; Manning and Bray, *Hist. of Surr.*
[200] Mr. Waller's suggestion that 'the reclining figure must symbolize St. John at Patmos' is unsatisfactory.
[201] Mr. Waller takes the red and white as symbolic of blood and water, and bases thereon his interpretation.

BOROUGH OF GUILDFORD

An iron fence now divides it from Quarry Street along its east boundary, and from the other surrounding south and west roads ; entrance gates are at the south-east corner and to the north-east. The church-yard formerly extended farther east, Quarry Street being a mere bridle-way till 1755, when the roadway was widened. In 1825, the road being still very narrow, the east end of the chancel was taken down and rebuilt 12 ft. shorter with the original stones. Before this an old plan shows windows on the north and south of the chancel close to the east end. The church rate was doubled for the year, and there was a voluntary subscription besides.

The original church of *HOLY TRINITY*, to judge from imperfect pictures and a plan of Guildford, had a square-ended chancel and apsidal side chapels like St. Mary's, and a tower with a spire on the south side. The south side chapel was called the Lady chapel, and its vaulting survived the fall of the tower. The old church fell down in 1740 owing to the arches under the tower having been taken away to improve its acoustic properties when the church was repaired in the previous year. The present building, which was erected on the old site (i.e. on the extreme edge of the ancient town) in 1749–63, consists of an apsidal chancel with north and south chapels and a wide aisleless nave with a west end and porches at the west end and a south-west vestry. It is partly modelled upon St. Katherine Coleman, Fenchurch Street. In 1869 the galleries were removed, and the windows altered from two rows to one. The church was enlarged by the addition of the chancel and chapels in 1888. What is now the vestry was formerly a chapel which belonged to Sir Richard Weston (who received a grant of Sutton Place in 1521) and his descendants. It has restored walls of flint and stone set in a chequer pattern, and its two south windows have late 15th-century moulded jambs, four-centred heads and labels. The last of Sir Richard Weston's family who was buried in the chapel was Mrs. Melior Mary Weston, who died in 1782.

The tower is of three stages with an embattled parapet and contains a ring of eight bells, seven being cast by Lester and Pack in 1769, and the eighth, cast in 1748, was recast by Pack and Chapman in 1779. Mr. Peter Flutter, Mayor of Guildford, paid for recasting the bells, one of which bears the inscription ' Peter Flutter gave me.' There is an hexagonal oak pulpit with sounding-board and inlaid soffits.

The chancel and apse walls are covered with paintings, and are separated from the chapels by arcades with Corinthian columns. The north chapel, known as the 'Queen's Chapel,' contains memorials connected with the Queen's Royal West Surrey Regiment. A feature of the nave is the very wide span of the roof. The timbers are hidden by a panelled plaster ceiling, but the extremely ingenious way in which the roof is hung from the rafters can be seen by going above the ceiling.

The fragments in the porch under the tower include 12th-century scalloped capitals and mouldings of 13th and 14th-century dates. There is also a part of a stone coffin lid, on which is carved a foliate cross, probably of 14th-century date.

The church contains a number of monuments which belonged to the old building. The most important is a large Renaissance tomb, in the south-east chapel, to George Abbot, Archbishop of Canterbury, who was born in 1562 and died in 1633. It is of grey, white, and black marble. The sides have plain marble panels, and the end is carved with a grating, inside which are represented skulls and human bones. On the top of the base is a recumbent effigy of the archbishop in cap, rochet, &c., and holding a book in his right hand. From projecting pedestals around the base rise six classic columns which support a large canopy having scrollwork gables on each side. In the end gable is an inscription. Round the canopy are shields bearing Canterbury and others impaling Gules a cheveron or between three pears or a molet for difference. The back of the tomb stands against the east wall and is divided into three panels, the centre one containing an inscription ; the north one a figure of the sun over which are the words ' Hine lumen ' and the south one another female figure holding a chalice, over which is ' Hine gratia.' The tomb was erected by Sir Maurice Abbot, Lord Mayor of London, the brother of the archbishop, in 1640, and was placed in the Lady chapel of the old church, the roof of which withstood the fall of the tower in 1740. It was removed into Abbot's Hospital during the rebuilding, and was again removed to its present place, east of the place where the arch-bishop is buried, in 1888.

On the north side of the porch under the tower is another large monument to Sir Robert Parkhurst, a Guildford man, sometime Lord Mayor of London, who died in 1637, and to Lady Parkhurst his wife, who died two years later, and to the wife of his son who put up the monument. The third figure is now missing. The front of the base is divided into three panels, the centre one containing an inscription recording the erection of the monument by his son, Sir Robert Parkhurst, who died in 1651, and its decoration by Elizabeth, eldest daughter of Sir Robert, in 1681. The other two panels contain brass shields which clearly do not belong to it. On the top of the base is the reclining figure of a man in plate armour, over which he wears a cloak and ruff and his chain of office. Near his feet is the headless figure of a kneeling woman. The back of the tomb is flanked by classic columns and contains the original inscription, 1636–8. Above it is a stone shield with mantled shield and crest. The arms are almost defaced. This tomb stood in the north side of the chancel of the old church, and after the ruin was piled with other fragments under the western gallery.

On the opposite side of the porch is another box tomb which has no inscription, but it is almost cer-tainly that of Anne, Lady Weston, afterwards Lady Knyvett, who died in 1582, and gave directions that she should be buried near her first father-in-law, Sir Richard Weston, in Trinity Church. The tomb is said to have been once in the Weston chantry. The front of the base is carved to represent human bones behind two grates. On the top is a painted recumbent figure of a woman in an ornamented fur-trimmed dress and a ruff. But in this case too the base may not belong to the figure, as the monuments were all confused during the ruin and rebuilding.

On the north wall of the nave is a small brass with the following black-letter inscription : ' An° M¹ Vᶜ | LVII | Lett no man wonder | thoghe here lyt under | the servant of God I truste | Baldwin Smythe by name | of London in good **fame** | **departyd in his best lust** | the XIIIth daye of **Julye** | on whose soule god have m̄cy | and send hym **life Eternall** | amongst godę true Elect | to have his prospect | in the place celestyall | .'

Near the east end of the north wall is a large marble cenotaph to 'Speaker' Onslow, who died in 1768 and was buried at Merrow. On the top is the reclining figure of a man in Roman costume.

On the south wall of the nave is a brass to Maurice Abbot and Alice his wife, parents of the archbishop. She died on 15 September 1606 and he died ten days later. Above they are both represented in outline together with their six sons, all kneeling. Near this is a large marble monument to James Smythe, who married Elizabeth the eldest daughter of Sir Robert Parkhurst of Pyrford. He died in 1711 and his wife in 1705.

In 1486 a chantry called Norbrigge's and Kyngeston's Chantry was endowed in the Lady chapel. From the inscription to Henry Norbrigge, formerly Mayor of Guildford, who died in 1512, it appears that he was the chief founder. He was buried in the Lady chapel. Another chantry was founded for the term of twenty years by Sir Richard Weston of Sutton Place in 1540.

The iron screen across the entrance of the southeast chapel was erected in memory of Canon Valpy, formerly rector, who died in 1909. The colours of the 'Queen's' Royal West Surrey Regiment are laid up in the north-east chapel. In 1910 the north-west porch was converted into a baptistery, and an alabaster font has been erected in it. The iron railings between the church and the street, dated 1712, are a fine piece of Wealden ironwork.

The communion plate includes a cup and paten, both made at Norwich about 1570, but having no hall mark. Round the cup is engraved 'HALB WESSEN,' the old name of a village near St. Neots, Hunts. It was sent from there to London to be melted up into a new cup, but the silversmith kept the old one intact and made the new one entirely fresh metal. After passing through various hands the old one was bought for use at Guildford. The next oldest piece of plate is a silver alms-basin of 1675'; there is also a silver-gilt paten of 1691; a cup and cover paten of 1730; a silver-gilt fiagon of 1757; a cup of 1873; and two silver-gilt cups and patens of 1888. Besides these there are six pewter plates.

There are two small wooden collecting boxes with handles measuring over all 9¼ in. by 2¾ in. On the tops is a circle of geometric incised ornament. Similar ones are to be found at Chobham.

There are five books of registers; the first contains baptisms, marriages, and burials from 1558 to 1693; the second contains the same from 1693 to 1783, but the marriages stop at 1739. The marriages between the years 1739 and 1754 and from 1758 to 1763 were entered in the St. Mary's register owing to the rebuilding of this church; the third book contains marriages from 1754 to 1812; the fourth has baptisms from 1784 to 1794 and burials from 1784 to 1795; and the fifth continues the baptisms from 1794 to 1812 and burials from 1795 to 1812.

The church of *ST. NICHOLAS* is a large building comprising a chancel with an apsidal end, a tower, north organ chamber, south chapel or extension of the south aisle, vestry, nave, north and south aisles, south-west porch, and a private chapel (called the Loseley chapel) to the south of the chancel aisle and west of the vestry. Excepting the Loseley chapel, the church was rebuilt in 1870–2.[138] The original building was on a lower level, and was often damaged by floods. It had been much repaired, but was entirely rebuilt in 1836–7 in churchwardens' Gothic. This church was higher than the original, but was still liable to floods. The present is raised still more. The Loseley chapel, which is of the 15th century, is closed off from the church by a glazed stone screen, and its floor level (doubtless that of the earlier church) is much below the floor level of the present church. There are two prints hanging in the vestry portraying the two former churches. The earlier, dated 1834, is a north-west view showing two gabled ends, probably of two aisles with a west tower of three stages between them. The second print shows the church after the first rebuilding, with chancel, nave, and aisles and a west tower; this building was however rendered unsafe by floods from the river and was replaced by the present church in 1872.

In the churchyard is a 13th-century capital of a pillar, much perished, from the first church. The Loseley chapel has a modernized south window under a traceried head of 15th-century style and a west doorway with a four-centred arch in a square head. It contains many monuments of the More and More-Molyneux family. In the south wall is an altar tomb to Arnold Brocas which has been removed from the north wall of the former chancel. On it lies the effigy of a priest, with feet to the west, in a red cope, or possibly the gown of a bachelor of laws, above his other vestments, which appear to consist of an alb, rochet, and stole. A part only of the original brass inscription remains along the top edge of the base, and reads :—'Hic jacet Arnald(us) Brocas baculari' ut'usq̄ iuris canonic' lincol̄n & wel̄n & q̄dm̄ Rector isti' loci qui obiit vigiliȷ (assū̄pcōis be Marie Anno Domini Millesimo ccc nonagesimo quinto)' : the words in brackets are a modern restoration, in paint, of the text. The front of the base has five bays with quatrefoil panelling, each inclosing a shield; the first or easternmost is charged with a leopard rampant, for Brocas, with the difference of a border engrailed; the second is Brocas quartering Roches, with a label over all for difference; the third, in a border a lion; the fourth as the first; and the fifth the undifferenced coat of Brocas. The recess over the tomb has panelled sides and a vaulted soffit divided into three bays by cinquefoiled arches terminating in the two middle ones with carved bosses; in the two inner angles the vaulting springs from shafts with moulded capitals and the two intermediate main ribs from carved corbels, one representing an angel's head with hair bound by a circlet, from which riset a small cross in front, and the other a bearded man's head also with a circlet, enriched by small flowers; at the intersections of the vaulting ribs are carved bosses, some as flowers and others as lions' faces with protruding tongues; the

---

[138] In 1797 the old church was largely reconstructed, having been damaged by floods. The interior arcades were apparently replaced by cast-iron pillars.

BOROUGH OF GUILDFORD

cornice, partly restored, is moulded and enriched with square flowers.

Against the east wall is the large altar tomb of alabaster to Sir William More, kt., son and heir of Sir Christopher More, who died at Loseley in 1600, and Dame Margaret his wife, the daughter of Ralph Daniel, who left issue George More, &c. It is divided into bays by pilasters containing marble panels. On it lie the alabaster effigies of Sir William and Lady Margaret ; the former in full-plate armour. The lady wears a tight bodice and full farthingale, and both are very well preserved. The inscription is on a black marble panel in the back above the figures. At the sides are brackets on which are seated cherubs ; on either side of the middle panel are dark coloured marble shafts with gilded Corinthian capitals, and over the cornice above are three shields with coats of arms ; the middle one is quarterly 1 and 4, Azure a cross argent with five martlets sable thereon, for More ; 2 and 3, Argent a cheveron between three cockatrices gules, for Mudge ; the north shield has More impaling Dingley, Argent a fesse with a molet between two roundels sable in the chief, the south shield has More and Mudge quartered impaling a coat of seven quarters.

Extensions or wings were thrown out on either side for other members of the family ; the north wing forms a monument to Sir George More and his wife Anne, but the inscription in the panel behind is to the lady only ; she was one of the daughters and co-heirs of Sir Adryan Poynings, kt., second brother to Thomas last Lord Poynings (who died without issue) and of Mary wife to Sir Adryan, daughter and sole heir to Sir Owen West, kt., brother and heir to Thomas, Lord De La Warr ; she died in 1590 leaving issue Robert More and others. On the base are the kneeling figures face to face of Sir George and Lady Anne. The south wing has the kneeling figures of two ladies, the first of whom is described in the inscription as Elizabeth daughter of Sir William More ; she was married three times, first to Richard Polsted of Albury, secondly to Sir John Woolley, one of the secretaries for the Latin tongue to Queen Elizabeth, and thirdly to Thomas, Lord Ellesmere, Lord Chancellor of England. She had no issue by the first and third husbands, by the second she had Sir Francis Woolley, kt. The second lady is Anne daughter of Sir William More, married to Sir George Manwaring of Ightfield, Shropshire, and had issue Sir Arthur, Sir Henry, and Sir Thomas, kts., and George Manwaring and two daughters. Over these four last-mentioned figures are their respective coats of arms.

The monument to Sir Christopher is a much smaller one, affixed to the east wall north of the large tomb ; it is a black marble tablet in a stone setting of Renaissance design with a shield of arms over a large swag of fruit and flowers. He was one of the king's remembrancers of the Exchequer and was twice married ; first to Margaret daughter and heir of William Mudge, by whom he had issue Sir William and five other sons and seven daughters ; the second wife was Constance the daughter of Richard Sackville and widow of William Heneage ; he died in 1549, but the monument is of much later date, c. 1660. On the south wall is a monument, which is an almost exact replica of the last, to Sir Robert More, one of the Honourable Band of Pensioners to King

James and King Charles, son and heir of Sir George More, kt. He married Frances (daughter of Sampson Lennard and his wife Margaret, Baroness Dacre daughter of Thomas Fiennes, Lord Dacre, and sister and heir of Gregory Fiennes, last of that name), by whom he had issue Sir Poynings and others ; he died at Loseley in 1625 ; over the monument is a shield of forty-five quarters. A third similar monument is that on the west wall to Sir Poynings More, created baronet in 1642 ; he married Elizabeth daughter of William Fytche of Woodham Walter (Essex) and had issue Sir William and other children ; he died at Loseley in 1649, and Elizabeth in 1666. There are other monuments to later members and descendants of the family. Mr. William More-Molyneux was the last to be buried there in 1907. It is now closed for interments. The chapel has a modern plaster panelled and vaulted ceiling with corbel heads on the walls to the main ribs ; these are also of plaster and are repetitions of the heads of a king and a lady. In the window are twelve modern shields of arms of the More family.

There was an ancient monumental brass in the former church, but it has now disappeared excepting a scroll in two pieces with the inscription ' Mater Dei memento mei.' The original is mentioned in Aubrey's *History of Surrey* (1719) as the figure of a priest in vestments with a scroll issuing from his mouth and the inscription below :—' Hic jacet Dñs Thomas Calcott presbyter parochialis istius ecclesiae qui obiit xx die Mensis Julii anno domini MCCCCLxxxxvii cujus anime propicietur deus Amen.'

In the porch among other monuments is a mural brass inscription to Caleb the son of Philip Lovejoy, who died in 1676 aged seventy-four ; the epitaph in verse was composed by himself. He left a house in Southwark for the benefit of the parish.

Of the ten bells which hang in the tower, eight were cast by Taylor & Co. in 1879, and the other two by Warner & Sons, 1894.

The communion plate comprises a silver cup of 1601, standing paten of 1791, a large flagon of 1749, two plates of 1835, and a silver spoon probably of Norwegian make ; there is also an electro-plated cup, probably of the 18th century. Besides these there are two cups, two patens, and an alms-basin, all of silver-gilt, dating from 1872.

The registers begin in 1562 ; the first book contains baptisms, marriages, and burials from that year to 1681 ; the second has all three, arranged in columns, from 1682 to 1736 ; the third, the same from 1737, the marriages finishing in 1754, and the others in 1812 ; the fourth continues the marriages from 1754 to 1812. The register contains the baptism of Archbishop Abbot in 1562, and of a son of Robert Devereux, second Earl of Essex, born at Loseley, 5 November 1636, who is not mentioned in any peerage.

The iron church of *ST. LUKE* in Addison Road is a chapel-of-ease to Holy Trinity.

The church of the *ASCENSION* is an iron chapel-of-ease to St. Nicholas's in the district called Guildford Park, near the railway station.

ADVOWSONS The advowsons of Holy Trinity and St. Mary are commonly stated to have been granted by William Testard to the Prior and convent of Merton in the 13th century.[130] This, however, is apparently not correct. In the episcopate of Richard of Ilchester, 1173-88, it appears that Merton had rights, confirmed to them then by the bishop, of payments from the rector of the church of Guildford (St. Mary's), and from the rector of the church of the Holy Trinity at Guildford, on institution and at other times, and that Merton had received these payments in past times.[134] It certainly raises the presumption that the convent already possessed the advowson in the 12th century.

The right of presentation remained with the convent until the Dissolution,[135] when it passed to the Crown.[136]

Bishop Morley planned the union of the benefices of Holy Trinity and St. Mary, the incomes being small, and left £1,000 in his will of 1684 for the object of increasing their value. This was supplemented by £200 from Sir Richard Onslow, and the union was completed by Act of Parliament in 1699, and became effective in 1715, when Holy Trinity became vacant and the rector of St. Mary's was instituted to both churches.

Most of the parish of St. Nicholas on the west side of the Wey was always in Godalming Hundred ; but part of it, including the church, was in the borough of Guildford from time immemorial. The advowson of the church, however, belonged to the church of Salisbury, probably from the date when the church or bishop, for the two are not clearly separated, acquired Godalming (q.v.) under Henry I.[137] On 1 February 1324 Edward II, who refused to acknowledge John Stratford, newly-appointed Bishop of Winchester by Papal provision, and ignoring Raymond de la Goth, Dean of Salisbury, also a Papal nominee, whose admission as dean was stoutly resisted at Salisbury, tried to present by Letters Patent ; but his nominee was never instituted, and on the following 4 May 1324 the dean's nominee, Bernard Brocas, a fellow-Gascon, was instituted. The advowson remained with the church of Salisbury, by which it was usually leased, till about 1847, when it was transferred to the bishop of the diocese together with Godalming. The Bishop of Winchester first presented in 1856.

CHARITIES The following charities relate to the town in general :—

The Poyle Charity, founded by Henry Smith in 1627, is administered under a scheme of the Charity Commissioners of 1880, and is chiefly devoted to small pensions for persons over fifty-five. (See manor of Poyle.)

In 1579 Thomas Baker founded the Blue Coat School for teaching poor boys till they were apprenticed or passed on to the Grammar School. It is now amalgamated with Archbishop Abbot's foundation (q.v.).

In 1582 Joan Austen left by will 13s. 4d. a year for the poor, charged on a house in St. Mary's parish.

Thomas Jackman, by deed in 1785, gave £600 to augment the endowment of Abbot's Hospital.

In 1653 Henry Baldwin gave 6s. 8d. a year, similarly secured.

In 1674 john Howe left £400, the interest of which was to be cast lots for by two poor serving-maids who had lived for two years with credit in the same family. The competitors are nominated by the mayor and magistrates.

In 1702 John Parsons gave the annual produce of £600 for the setting up in business of a young man who has served seven years' apprenticeship in Guildford, or failing such a young man, a young woman who has lived three years in one situation (not at an inn). If the magistrates fail to appoint to this charity, the charity lapses from Guildford to Chichester.

Jasper Yardley, second master of Abbot's Hospital, left in 1639 twenty nobles apiece to the three parishes of Guildford for apparelling and placing poor children thence.

The following charities relate to the parish of Holy Trinity :—

John Austen of Guildford, by will 1612, left £8 charged upon the rectory of Shalford for the poor of Guildford. It was applied to ten widows of this parish.

Olive Duncombe, 1705, left about £500, the income of which was applied to apprenticing poor boys of this parish.

The following charities apply to the parish of St. Mary :—

The bequest of John Austen, above mentioned, was partly applied to sixteen widows of this parish.

John Howe, by will 1674, gave a house for the use of the poor, directing that two poor men and their wives should inhabit it. The churchwardens' books in the tower of St. Mary's have references to this house, but it has apparently been sold and the price misapplied.

Benefactions by William Shaw of 16s. 8d., by Matthew Wise of 5s., and by Thomas Peters of 2s. 6d., all annual, seem also to have disappeared.

The following relate to the parish of St. Nicholas :—

Caleb Lovejoy in 1676 left a house in Southwark for the education of children, apprenticing boys, and for almshouses, for a sermon also at St. Nicholas's yearly in commemoration of himself. The funds were insufficient for more than the schooling of twenty boys till the 19th century, when land was acquired in Bury Street and almshouses for four women built in 1840. By a curious coincidence the almshouses are nearly on the site of Lovejoy's father's house which was next the old rectory, the latter being removed from here to the Portsmouth Road (when the church was rebuilt in 1836-7). The evidence for this is an agreement copied out in the registers, concluding a violent quarrel between Lovejoy and the rector upon their respective garden boundaries.

George Benbrick, by will 1682, left land at Alton and in Shalford for eight poor freemen of the town, or their widows, being Protestants, residing in St. Nicholas's. The income is now £60 a year.

[130] Dugdale, *Mon. Angl.* vi, 247.
[134] Cott. MS. Cleopatra, C. vii.
[135] Egerton MSS. 2031, fol. 14 d. 77 ;
2032, fol. 56 d. ; 2033, fol. 19 d. 87 d. 88; 2034, fol. 55, 78. *Wykham's Reg.* (Hants Rec. Soc.), i, 83, 184, 206, 246 (Holy
Trinity) ; ibid. 23, 59, 78, 180 (St. Mary).
[136] Inst. Bks. P.R.O. Crockford.
[137] *Reg. of St. Osmund* (Rolls Ser.), i, 203.

ND - #0071 - 100723 - C0 - 229/152/41 [43] - CB - 9780656240876 - Gloss Lamination